T0397557

Hercules

Hercules

Seneca

*Edited with Introduction, Translation,
and Commentary by*
A. J. BOYLE

OXFORD
UNIVERSITY PRESS

OXFORD
UNIVERSITY PRESS

Great Clarendon Street, Oxford, OX2 6DP,
United Kingdom

Oxford University Press is a department of the University of Oxford.
It furthers the University's objective of excellence in research, scholarship,
and education by publishing worldwide. Oxford is a registered trade mark of
Oxford University Press in the UK and in certain other countries

Published in the United States of America by Oxford University Press
198 Madison Avenue, New York, NY 10016, United States of America

British Library Cataloguing in Publication Data
Data available

Library of Congress Control Number: 2022944326

ISBN 978-0-19-885694-8

Printed and bound in the UK by
Clays Ltd, Elcograf S.p.A.

For Athena,
Helen,
and James

Let Hercules himself do what he may,
The cat will mew, and dog will have his day.
Shakespeare, *Hamlet* V.i.286–7

Preface

The painting featured on the front cover of this book, 'Hercules as Heroic Virtue Overcoming Discord' (c.1632–3: MFA, Boston, Accession No. 47.1543), is a study for a panel on the Rubens ceiling of the Banqueting House, Whitehall, London, the only part of the Whitehall Palace inhabited by the Stuart monarchs that still survives today. The panel was one of nine paintings celebrating the reign of James I, commissioned from Rubens in 1629 by Charles I two decades before the latter's execution. To twenty-first-century viewers of the panel and presumably to some members of the Carolingian court the question posed by the panel is or was 'What is heroic virtue?' That question is at the heart of Seneca's *Hercules*, and Rubens's presentation of that question through the image of violence inflicted on the body of a woman by Hercules' club will be matched in the action of Seneca's play. There was also an ironic match in history. Several Roman political figures, including Sulla, Pompey, Antony, Caligula, Domitian, Commodus, and Maximian, associated themselves with Hercules for the purpose of political self-fashioning; so, too, the Florentine Medici and a plethora of early modern European rulers. The English monarch, Charles I, through this panel associated the Herculean myth with himself—only to meet, like most of the named Roman predecessors, with premature death. To unite Charles's death with Seneca's play, the great English poet of the mid seventeenth century, John Milton, cited Hercules' sentiment at *Herc.* 922–4 to describe the king's beheading (see Comm. *ad* 918–24). A similarly bloody end was to befall Seneca's pupil and imperial master, Nero, who, as fate would have it, sang in the last years of his reign many tragic roles, including that of 'Hercules the Mad'. The play edited, translated, and commented upon in this book was subject to an unusual degree of imbrication with both literature and history.

Seneca's *Hercules* (entitled thus in the 'Codex Etruscus', but *Hercules Furens* in several branches of the *A* MS tradition), has been dated plausibly to c.53–4 CE, at the intersection of the Claudian and Neronian principates. It appears almost certainly to have been written between *Agamemnon* and *Thyestes*. Foreshadowed perhaps by the final choral ode of *Agamemnon* on Hercules' birth and 'labours', the play prefigures—through its dramatization of the sacrificial slaying of children—the more elaborate description of this horror in *Thyestes*. *Hercules* is a complex and important drama, examining a complex and important cultural figure, the legendary founder of one of Rome's earliest religious monuments (the *Ara Maxima*), occupier of several of the city's shrines, and a major Roman paradigm of human achievement: monster-slayer, pacifier, and civilizer, for whom divinity was part reward, part birth-right, and who was explicitly associated with imminently 'divine' Roman emperors from Augustus onwards (Virg. *Aen.* 6.791–803, Hor. *Carm.* 3.3.9–12, 4.5.33–6). But Hercules was a model, too (Hor. *Carm.* 1.3.36), of hybristic ambition, a murderous thug and violent transgressor of boundaries, whether provided by gods, nature, or humankind. Celebrated and castigated in ancient myth, religion, literature, history, and art, Heracles/Hercules was also a significant figure in philosophy from the fifth century BCE onwards (Prodicus), becoming prominent in Cynicism and Stoicism, where his violence was sometimes taken as a force for good. Seneca himself exploits the paradoxical status of Hercules. In his philosophical works he proclaims him 'unvanquished by adversity, a despiser of pleasure and conqueror of every terror' (*De Constantia Sapientis* 2.1) and 'an enemy of the wicked, defender of the good, and bringer of peace to land and sea' (*De Beneficiis* 1.13.3); yet he focuses in his tragedy, *Hercules*, on the hero's bloody killing not only of a violent enemy but of his own innocent children and wife.

That focus generates a tragedy of great theatrical, literary, social, and cultural value. Among the major issues explored: violence and its psychological, familial, and social consequences; the imperatives of family and of self; sanity and madness, identity and place; the possibility of moral redemption; the human longing for immortality; the empire of death. The presentation of Hercules' mind is at the heart of the play. For some scholars partial illumination may be found in modern discussions of PTSD, 'combat trauma', and 'family annihilators'. One central issue, of which both dramatic action and dramatic script constitute a prolonged examination, is the one mentioned at the start of this preface: the nature of 'heroic virtue', indeed the nature of *uirtus*, 'virtue', *simpliciter*, the (ideal) property or properties of being a *uir*, a 'man'—a core value of Roman Stoicism and of Roman elite male identity. *Hercules* is very much a Roman play, perhaps the most Roman of the Senecan 'eight'.

Hercules is also potent drama. Seneca presumably learned from Euripides the thematic and dramatic power of casting the same actor as the violent, tyrannical Lycus and as his conqueror Hercules. *Hercules* is a play with strong theatrical qualities throughout, in which the choral lyrics are not only among the most moving and intellectually engaging in Senecan tragedy (even Eliot praised the fourth ode's final lines), but are always dramatically functional. The tragedy features a fiery, monumental god-prologue (the only one in Senecan tragedy), impassioned prayers and speeches, meditative entrance soliloquies/monologues, trenchant dialogue (with some quick-fire *stichomythia* and *antilabe*), a failed wooing scene with an impressive after-life in Tudor drama, an innovative quasi-messenger episode, involving a lengthy ecphrastic dialogue on the world of death and a climactic narrative of Hercules' abduction of the hell-hound, Cerberus. It features, too, a spectacular 'madness scene', in which wife and children are slaughtered, and an emotionally turbulent, non-violent finale, a *spectaculum* perhaps 'worthy of a god' (*De Prouidentia* 2.8), in which the instinct for self-punitive suicide is thwarted by the claims of kinship and the acceptance of intolerable suffering—suffering juxtaposed with an apparent offer of moral cleansing and redemption. The play had a substantial influence on early modern European literature and drama and beyond. Apparent debtors include: Garnier, La Taille, Legge, *Rare Triumphs of Love and Fortune*, Kyd, Hughes, Marlowe, Greene, Shakespeare, *Locrine*, Marston, Fulke Greville, Chapman, Jonson, Prévost, Rotrou, L'Héritier de Nouvelon, Milton, Racine, Lee, Young, Voltaire, Glover. Eliot's twentieth-century *The Waste Land* and *Marina* seem also to manifest a debt, as do several twentieth- and twenty-first-century works on the Heracles/Hercules theme (see Introd. §VIII).

But despite all this—and notwithstanding earlier, distinguished editions of the play (see below)—Seneca's *Hercules* has been relatively understudied in modern criticism and scholarship, and has been performed rarely even in translation or adaptation. There is but one 'recent' performance reported on the website of the Archive of Performances of Greek and Roman Drama (APGRD): at the Théâtre de Gérard Philipe de Saint-Denis in Paris 1996. The same website does not, however, record a vigorous, PTSD-oriented adaptation of Seneca's *Hercules Furens* in Los Angeles in 2011 and 2013.

The present edition of Seneca's *Hercules* offers a substantial introduction, a new Latin text (with over eighty different readings and many other changes from the Zwierlein Oxford text of 1986: see pp. 262–5 below), an English verse translation designed for both performance and serious study, and a detailed commentary on the play which is exegetic, analytic, and interpretative. The format is identical to that which I adopted in my editions of *Octavia* (Oxford, 2008), *Oedipus* (Oxford, 2011), *Medea* (Oxford, 2014), *Thyestes* (Oxford, 2017), and *Agamemnon* (Oxford, 2019). The aim again has been to elucidate the text dramatically as well as philologically, and to locate the play firmly in its contemporary historical and cultural context and in the ensuing literary and theatrical tradition. I am aware of the interpretative nature of all aspects, including the philological, of any modern reconstruction of an ancient text, and have endeavoured to provide the grounds for my textual, literary, and cultural judgements. It is hoped that the resulting edition may prove useful to drama students, to Latin students at every stage of the language, to professional scholars of Classics, Theatre, and Comparative Literature—and to anyone interested in the cultural dynamics of literary reception and the interplay of theatre and history. The aim has been to encourage a greater and more intense engagement with Seneca's play at the scholarly, critical, and theatrical levels.

There are many debts to acknowledge. Like all new editions of classical texts the present one owes much to previous scholarship. There are several editions and translations of Seneca's *Hercules* to which I am indebted, as will be clear from the Commentary, but I want specifically to name the distinguished, large-scale editions of Fitch (1987*a*) and Billerbeck (1999*a*), to the fine scholarship of which I have constantly turned in moments of aporia. My debts to them go beyond the many passages in the Introduction and Commentary where their names may be found. Of much older works I have found the early fourteenth-century commentary of Nicholas Trevet and the early seventeenth-century edition of Thomas Farnaby interesting and helpful. Most of this book was written and reviewed in the long years of the Covid 19 pandemic, during which much of the professoriat 'languished'. I am deeply appreciative of the unsuppressed energy and commitment exhibited by my readers, friends, colleagues, and students in their unstinting efforts to help me produce a better book. I owe a special debt to five friends and colleagues who read earlier drafts of this book and offered advice: Joseph Smith (San Diego State University) commented critically (often acerbically) and in detail on a preliminary draft of the whole book and saved me from both omissions and errors; Hannah Čulík-Baird (University of California, Los Angeles), John Henderson (King's College, Cambridge), Stefano Rebeggiani (University of Southern California), and Christopher Trinacty (Oberlin College) commented on later versions with enviable insight and acuity. I thank them most sincerely. My principal research assistants on the project, Melina McClure and Madeline Thayer (both USC), performed text, translation, and commentary proofing and other duties with admirable expertise and acumen. Thanks are also due to several other friends and colleagues who helped in diverse ways, including Peter Davis (Universities of Tasmania and Adelaide), Lucas Herchenroeder (USC), Sara Lindheim (University of California, Santa Barbara), Gesine Manuwald (University College London), Robert Morstein-Marx (UCSB), Emma Stafford (Leeds

University), and Ryan Prijic, the USC Classics Department's administrator, who was unfailing in response to my research and printing needs. Erica Bexley (Durham University) kindly sent me the proofs of her 2022 book on Senecan drama in advance of publication. Finally two graduate seminars at USC (Spring 2020, Fall 2021) provided a fertile, critical context in which to explore Seneca's *Hercules* and its rich semiotics. I thank the students in those classes for two pleasurable and intellectually illuminating semesters, which shone the more brightly because of the dark clouds of Covid encompassing them.

I should again like to record my gratitude to the Classics editorial staff at the Oxford University Press, who have been a pleasure to work with on this and earlier commentaries. Responsibility for mistakes of fact and judgement stays firmly with me. I should also like to thank Routledge for permission to include rewritten material from my *Tragic Seneca* (London, 1997) and *Roman Tragedy* (London, 2006) and Francis Cairns Publications for permission to include material from my *Seneca's Troades* (Leeds, 1994) in various parts of the Introduction. I have not hesitated to make use, where appropriate (especially in the Introduction and Commentary), of material from my previous OUP Senecan editions. Sections I–IV, IX, and X of the Introduction are updated and recalibrated versions of the similarly numbered sections in earlier Introductions. Finally profound gratitude is due to the University of Southern California, whose many years of institutional and collegial support have assisted immeasurably. The book is dedicated to three people without whom it could not have been written.

A.J.B.

USC, Los Angeles
Nones of March 2022

Contents

INTRODUCTION

I. Seneca and Rome

Quasi in tutte le sue tragedie, egli avanzò (per quanto a me ne
paia) nella prudenza, nella gravità, nel decoro, nella maiestà,
nelle sentenze, tutti i Greci che scrissero mai.

In almost all his tragedies he surpassed (in my opinion) in prudence, in gravity, in decorum, in majesty, in epigrams, all the
Greeks who ever wrote.

Giraldi Cintio *Discorsi* (1543)

Life and Works

Lucius Annaeus Seneca was born in 1 BCE or shortly before in Corduba
(modern Córdoba or Cordova) in southern Spain, the second of three sons
to Helvia, the *mater optima* ('best of mothers') of Seneca's 'Consolation' from
exile, and the cultivated equestrian, Annaeus Seneca (*c.*55 BCE to
*c.*40 CE—*praenomen* probably also Lucius), author of a lost history of Rome
and surviving but badly mutilated works on Roman declamation,
Controuersiae and *Suasoriae*. The youngest son, Mela, became the father of
the epic poet Lucan. Brought to Rome as a young child and given the standard 'elite' education in language, poetry and rhetoric, Seneca had become by
the early years of Tiberius' principate (14–37 CE), while still in adolescence,
a passionate devotee of philosophy. He studied Stoicism with the philosopher Attalus, but was drawn also to Sextianism, a local, ascetic form of
Stoic-Pythagoreanism with a strong commitment to vegetarianism, taught
by the philosophers Papirius Fabianus and Sotion. Before long he had been
dissuaded from Sextian practices by his father (*Ep. Mor.* 108.17–22). During
his youth and throughout his life Seneca suffered from a tubercular condition, and was impelled on one occasion to contemplate suicide when he
despaired of recovery. He records that only the thought of the suffering he
would have caused his father prevented his death (*Ep. Mor.* 78.1–2).

Ill health presumably delayed the start of his political career, as did a
substantial period of convalescence in Egypt during the twenties under the
care of his maternal aunt. He returned to Rome from Egypt in 31 CE (surviving a shipwreck in which his uncle died), and entered the senate via the

quaestorship shortly afterwards, as did his elder brother, Gallio. By the beginning of Claudius' principate (41 CE) he had also held the aedileship and the office of tribune of the people (*tribunus plebis*). During the thirties, too, he married (although whether it was to his wife of later years who survived him, Pompeia Paulina, is uncertain), and he achieved such fame as a public speaker as to arouse the attention and jealousy of the emperor Gaius, better known as Caligula (Suet. *Gai.* 53.2, Dio 59.19.7–8). By the late thirties Seneca was clearly moving in the circle of princes, among 'that tiny group of men on which there bore down, night and day, the concentric pressure of a monstrous weight, the post-Augustan empire'.[1] His presence in high places was initially short-lived. He survived Caligula's brief principate (37–41 CE) only to be exiled to Corsica in the first year of Claudius' reign (41 CE). The charge was adultery with Caligula's sister, Julia Livilla, brought (according to Dio: 60.8.5) by the new empress, Claudius' young wife, Messalina.

Seneca's exile came at a time of great personal distress (both his father and his son had recently died: *Helu.* 2.4–5), and, despite pleas for imperial clemency (see esp. *Pol.* 13.2ff.), lasted eight tedious years. During those years Rome's dominion expanded. The emperor's power depended upon his control of Rome's army and, during Seneca's exile, that army was put to work, acquiring five new provinces for the empire (two Mauretanias, Lycia, Britain, and Thrace) in a period of rapid imperial expansion. In 48 CE Messalina was executed after her treasonous 'wedding' to the consul-elect, Gaius Silius. In the following year Seneca was recalled to Rome by Claudius' new wife, Agrippina (great-granddaughter of Augustus, another of Caligula's sisters and Claudius' niece—Seneca was later accused of having been her lover: Tac. *Ann.* 13.42.5, Dio 61.10.1), and was designated praetor for 50 CE. His literary and philosophical reputation was now well established (Tac. *Ann.* 12.8.3), and, towards the end of 49 (Tac. *Ann.* 53.2) or in 50 CE (following Claudius' adoption of Nero: Suet. *Nero* 7.1), he was appointed Nero's tutor. This appointment not only placed Seneca again at the centre of the Roman world, but brought him immense power and influence when Agrippina (allegedly) poisoned her emperor-husband and Nero acceded to the throne (54 CE).

Throughout the early part of Nero's principate Seneca (suffect consul probably in 56 CE)[2] and Afranius Burrus, the commander of the praetorian guard, acted as the chief ministers of the young emperor, whose speeches Seneca initially wrote, but whom they were increasingly unable to control.

---

[1] Herington (1966: 429). For the Cinthio citation in the epigraph, see e.g. Crocetti (1973: 184).
[2] On the date of Seneca's suffect consulship, see Griffin (1976: 73–4).

During this period Seneca became extremely wealthy. Nero's matricide, however, in 59 CE, to which it seems likely that neither Seneca nor Burrus were initially privy,[3] but for which Seneca wrote a *post factum* justification (Tac. *Ann.* 14.11), signalled a weakening of the ministers' power. When Burrus died (perhaps poisoned) in 62 CE, Seneca, although his requests to quit public life were officially rejected by Nero (Tac. *Ann.* 14.53–6, 15.45.3), went into semi-retirement.[4] In 65 CE he was accused of involvement in the Pisonian conspiracy against Nero and was ordered to kill himself. This he did, leaving to his friends 'his one remaining possession and his best— the pattern of his life (*imaginem uitae suae*)' (Tac. *Ann.* 15.62.1).

Apart from a body of epigrams (many of which are certainly spurious) and a prose-verse Menippean satire on Claudius' deification, *Apocolocyntosis* (the 'Pumpkinification'), Seneca's extant writings can conveniently be divided into the prose works and the tragedies. The prose works comprise *Naturales Quaestiones* ('Natural Questions'), the *Dialogi* (twelve books of so-called 'Dialogues', which include the three books of De Ira, 'On Anger'), *De Clementia* ('On Clemency'—addressed to Nero on his accession), *De Beneficiis* ('On Benefits'), and *Epistulae Morales* ('Moral Epistles'—addressed to his friend Lucilius). Lost works include a biography of Seneca the Elder, speeches, ethnographical and geographical treatises on India and Egypt, treatises on physics, and several philosophical works (among them *De Amicitia*, 'On Friendship', *De Matrimonio*, 'On Marriage', and *De Immatura Morte*, 'On Premature Death'). The prose works focus on practical ethics and the progress to virtue. They are infused to a greater or lesser extent with Stoic ideas concerning fate, god, virtue, wisdom, reason, endurance, self-sufficiency and true friendship, and are filled with condemnation of the world of wealth and power (to which Seneca belonged) and contempt for the fear of death. Central to their conception of the world is the Stoic belief in divine reason/*ratio* as 'the governing principle of the rational, living and providentially ordained universe', in which 'only the Stoic sage (*sapiens*)...can achieve virtue...and live the truly happy life'.[5] Seneca's philosophical writings cover a considerable period of time—from the thirties CE to their author's death. Among the earliest to be written was *Consolatio ad Marciam*, composed under Caligula (37–41 CE); among the last were *Naturales Quaestiones* and *Epistulae Morales*, written during the years of Seneca's 'retirement' (62–5 CE).

---

[3] See Barrett (1996: 189).
[4] Tac. *Ann.* 14.52: *mors Burri infregit Senecae potentiam*, 'Burrus' death shattered Seneca's power'.
[5] Williams (2003: 4).

Ten extant plays have come down under Seneca's name, eight of which are agreed to have been written by him: *Hercules, Troades, Phoenissae, Medea, Phaedra, Oedipus, Agamemnon*, and *Thyestes*. Such are their titles in the *E* branch of the MS tradition. In the *A* branch *Hercules, Troades, Phoenissae*, and *Phaedra* are respectively entitled *Hercules Furens* (still in general use), *Tros, Thebais*, and *Hippolytus*. Of the eight only *Phoenissae*, which lacks choral odes, is (probably) incomplete. The remaining two plays are a tragedy, *Hercules Oetaeus*, and the tragic *fabula praetexta, Octavia*. The former is almost twice as long as the average Senecan play and seems to many—on stylistic, linguistic, thematic, and dramaturgical grounds— non-Senecan.[6] The latter, in which Seneca appears as a character and which seems to refer to events which took place after Seneca's death, is missing from *E* and is certainly not by Seneca.[7] Each of the eight tragedies is marked by dramatic features which were to influence Renaissance drama: vivid and powerful declamatory and lyric verse, psychological insight, highly effective staging, an intellectually demanding verbal and conceptual framework, and a precocious preoccupation with theatricality and theatricalization.

Composed presumably in the second half of Seneca's life, the plays cannot be dated with certainty. Many commentators accept a *terminus ante quem* of late 54 CE for *Hercules* on the grounds that *Apocolocyntosis* (probably dated to November/December 54 CE)[8] seems to parody it. And, though the parody theory is clearly not certain, I have adopted a working hypothesis of a date of *c*.53–4 CE for this play. The earliest unambiguous reference to any of Seneca's plays is the *Agamemnon* graffito from Pompeii, of uncertain date but obviously before the catastrophe of 79 CE.[9] The next is a citation from *Medea* by Quintilian, writing a generation after Seneca's death (*Inst.* 9.2.8; see also *Inst.* 8.3.31). Seneca, although he refers to tragedy and the theatre in his prose works, makes no mention there of his own plays. Some commentators assign them to the period of exile on Corsica (41–9 CE) during the principate of Claudius; others regard it as more likely that their composition, like that of the prose works, was spread over a considerable period of time. The important stylometric study of Fitch not only supports the latter position but attempts to break the plays into three chronologically consecutive groups: (i) *Agamemnon, Phaedra, Oedipus*; (ii) *Hercules, Troades*,

---

[6] See Boyle (2006: 221–3).
[7] It is most plausibly dated to the early Flavian period: see Boyle (2008: xiii–xvi).
[8] Griffin (1976: 129).
[9] *CIL* iv. Suppl. 2.6698: *idai cernu nemura*, 'I see the groves of Ida' = *Ag*. 730.

Medea; (iii) *Thyestes, Phoenissae*.[10] The groupings and implied chronology are by no means agreed, but most modern scholars would probably accept that on stylometric, dramatic, and other grounds *Thyestes* and *Phoenissae* are Seneca's final extant tragedies. The present editor also accepts that these final tragedies are probably Neronian.[11]

The relationship between the tragedies and the prose works continues to be debated. Although the tragedies are not referred to in the prose works, they are still sometimes regarded as the product of Stoic convictions and the dramatization of a Stoic world-view. Certainly they abound in Stoic language and moral ideas (many of them evident in the prose works), and their preoccupation with fate, with human emotion, psychology, and action, and the destructive consequences of passion, especially anger, is deeply indebted to the Stoic tradition.[12] But this Stoicism is no ideological clothing but part of the dramatic and critical texture of the plays.[13] And to many, including the present editor, the world-view of most of the plays is decidedly unStoic, even an inversion of Stoicism, cardinal principles of which are critically exhibited within a different, more disturbing vision.[14]

Julio-Claudian Rome

Although Seneca was born only a few years after Horace's death he inhabited a different world. Horace (65–8 BCE) lived through Rome's bloody transformation from republic to empire; he fought with Brutus and Cassius at

---

[10] Fitch (1981).

[11] A Tiberian or Caligulan date for Seneca's plays, though theoretically possible, is most unlikely, given Tiberius' hostility to the theatre and reported execution of at least two tragic dramatists and the 'volatile and dangerous atmosphere' of Caligulan Rome. Several Senecan tragedies are perhaps to be assigned to the Claudian principate. Under Claudius imperial support for the dramatic festivals came without the oppressive control of a Caligula. The consular tragedian, Pomponius Secundus, with whom Seneca debated tragic language, was active in Claudian Rome. The stylistic differences, however, noted by Fitch, suggest a considerable gap between the earlier plays and *Thyestes* and *Phoenissae* (perhaps even late Neronian: see Boyle 2017: xix n. 11).

[12] See e.g. *De Ira* (for an analysis, see Boyle 2019: lvii–lxiv). For Stoic language and ideas in *Hercules*, see Comm. *ad* 162–3.

[13] Cf. Trinacty (2015: 38): 'Stoicism is not the key by which one can unlock the single meaning of Seneca's tragedies but rather one of many keys that help us to uncover the myriad associations that these works suggest.'

[14] The question of the relationship between Seneca the philosopher and Seneca the tragedian has tended to privilege the former. But what is clear is that Seneca's philosophical mode is itself essentially theatrical. His letters and 'dialogues' are filled with scripted voices (of others and himself) and his prime philosophical position is that of spectator/audience—spectator of others and of himself. Senecan philosophy 'stages ethics' (cf. Gunderson 2015: 105).

Philippi (42 BCE). Seneca never knew the republic. Born under Augustus and committing suicide three years before Nero's similar fate, he lived through and was encompassed by the Julio-Claudian principate. Throughout Seneca's lifetime—despite the preservation of Rome's political, legal, moral, social, and religious forms—power resided essentially in one man, the *princeps* or emperor, sometimes (as in the case of Caligula) a vicious psychopath. Political and personal freedom were nullities. Material prosperity increased (for all Romans, not simply for the upper classes), but for the social elite the loss of political power brought with it a crisis of collective and individual identity. In Rome and particularly at the court itself, on which the pressure of empire bore, nothing and no one seemed secure, the Roman world's controlling forms used, abused, and nullified by the *princeps'* power. Servility, hypocrisy, corrupting power indexed this Julio-Claudian world.

Or so at least the ancient historians would have us believe, most notably Tacitus, whose *Annales*, written in the first decades of the second century CE, documents the hatreds, fears, lusts, cowardice, self-interest, self-abasement, abnormal cruelty, extravagant vice, violent death, the inversion and perversion of Rome's efforming values and institutions—and, more rarely, the nobility and heroism—which to his mind constituted the early imperial court. Tacitus' indictment of the Julio-Claudian principate is as clear as it is persuasive. In the case of Nero, for example, the emperor's debauchery (*Ann.* 15.37), fratricide (*Ann.* 13.16–18), matricide (*Ann.* 14.8–10), uxoricide/sororicide (*Ann.* 14.60–4) are melodramatically portrayed. Witness the murder of Octavia, sister, step-sister, and ex-wife in 62 CE (*Ann.* 14.64):

> ac puella uicesimo aetatis anno inter centuriones et milites, praesagio malorum iam uitae exempta, nondum tamen morte adquiescebat. paucis dehinc interiectis diebus mori iubetur, cum iam uiduam se et tantum sororem testaretur communisque Germanicos et postremo Agrippinae nomen cieret, qua incolumi infelix quidem matrimonium sed sine exitio pertulisset. restringitur uinclis uenaeque eius per omnis artus exsoluuntur. et quia pressus pauore sanguis tardius labebatur praeferuidi balnei uapore enecatur. additurque atrocior saeuitia, quod caput amputatum latumque in urbem Poppaea uidit.

> So the girl, in her twentieth year, in the midst of centurions and soldiers, already cut off from life by the foreknowledge of suffering, still lacked the

quietude of death. After a few days' interval she is ordered to die, although she pleaded that she was now an ex-wife and only a sister and evoked the shared lineage of the Germanici and lastly the name of Agrippina, under whom, while she survived, she had endured an unhappy but non-fatal marriage. She is bound, and her veins are opened in every limb; then, because her blood flowed too slowly, checked by fear, she is suffocated with the steam of a boiling bath. There is an additional, more savage cruelty: her head was cut off and taken to Rome, where it was viewed by Poppaea.

And the corollary of imperial vice and power: the black farce of Roman servility. Witness the city's 'joy' in the aftermath of the failed conspiracy of Piso in 65 CE (*Ann.* 15.71):

sed compleri interim urbs funeribus, Capitolium uictimis. alius filio, fratre alius aut propinquo aut amico interfectis, agere grates deis, ornare lauru domum, genua ipsius aduolui et dextram osculis fatigare.

Meanwhile funerals abounded in the city, thank-offerings on the Capitol. Men who had lost a son or brother or relative or friend gave thanks to the gods, bedecked their houses with laurel, fell at the feet of Nero and kissed his hand incessantly.

Indeed the 'farce' of Roman aristocratic behaviour, its theatricality, is a major focus of Tacitus' vision of the Julio-Claudian principate.[15] Roman political life had always been theatrical.[16] To the author of *Annales*, however, imperial Rome was the unacceptable apogee of earlier political theatre, a profoundly histrionic culture, in which role-playing had become the dominant behavioural mode and acting the emblematic metaphor. In his account of the principates of Augustus, Tiberius, Caligula, Claudius, and Nero the distinction between play and public reality disappears. Nero's initial 'mimicries of sorrow' (*tristia imitamenta*, *Ann.* 13.4), for example, at the funeral of his adoptive father, Claudius, led into insistent attention not only to the emperor's appearances on the stage but to the political and social

[15] Tacitus is not alone. For self-dramatization and theatricality at the Caligulan court, for example, see Philo *Leg.* 79, 93–7, 111, Suet. *Gaius* 11, 15.1, 31, 36.1, 54.1, 55.1, Dio 59.5.5, 26.6–8, 29.6. On the theatricality of early imperial Rome, see Rudich (1993: xvii–xxxiv), Bartsch (1994: *passim*), Boyle (2006: 160–88).

[16] See Boyle (2006: 3–23). On theatricality in the late republic, note Cicero's analysis of the individual in terms of four *personae*: *Off.* 1.107–15.

imperatives of role-playing in the theatricalized world of imperial Rome, where citizens mourn what they welcome (*Ann.* 16.7), applaud what they grieve (*Ann.* 14.15), offer thanksgivings for monstrous murder (*Ann.* 14.59, 64), and celebrate triumphs for national humiliation or horrendous and impious sin (*Ann.* 15.18, 14.12–13). In the narrative of Nero's notorious matricide there is a focus not only on role-play and sets, but props, dialogue, stage directions, and tragic structure (*Ann.* 14.1–13). The theatrics are overt and highly allusive. Agrippina's 'final words' even draw Seneca's Jocasta into the text, as Nero's mother reveals herself as the theatrical, incestuous figure she had always been.[17]

Nor does Nero's death end the political theatre. The description in Tacitus' *Historiae* of the people's reaction to Otho's conspiracy in 69 CE or to the bloody fighting between the Vitellian and Flavian armies at the end of the same year parades the theatricality of their behaviour (*Hist.* 1.32 and 3.83):

> uniuersa iam plebs Palatium implebat mixtis seruitiis et dissono clamore caedem Othonis et coniuratorum exitium poscentium ut si circo aut theatro ludicrum aliquod postularent. neque illis iudicium aut ueritas, quippe eodem die diuersa pari certamine postulaturis, sed tradito more quemcumque principem adulandi licentia adclamationum et studiis inanibus.

> The whole populace together with slaves now filled the palace, demanding with raucous cries the death of Otho and the destruction of the conspirators as if they were calling for some show in the circus or theatre. They had neither sense nor sincerity (for on the same day they would clamour for the opposite with equal passion), but followed the convention of flattering whoever was emperor with unlimited applause and empty enthusiasm.

> aderat pugnantibus spectator populus utque in ludicro certamine hos rursus illos clamore et plausu fouebat.

> The people attended the fighting as the audience for a show, and, as with a stage battle, supported now this side, now that with shouts and applause.

Seneca's prose works provide contemporary testimony of this theatricalized world.[18] Nature herself is said to have created us as 'spectators for the great

---

[17] See Boyle (2011: lxxxi–lxxxii).
[18] For the many allusions in Seneca's prose works to 'le théâtre et les spectacles', see Aygon (2016: 13–140).

spectacle of reality' (*spectatores nos tantis rerum spectaculis, Ot.* 5.3), Cato is paraded as a moral 'spectacle' (*spectaculum, Prou.* 2.9ff.), Lucilius is exhorted to do everything 'as if before a spectator' (*tamquam spectet aliquis, Ep. Mor.* 25.5; cf. *Ep. Mor.* 11.8ff.), 'human life' is declared 'a mime-drama, which assigns parts for us to play badly' (*hic humanae uitae mimus, qui nobis partes quas male agamus adsignat, Ep. Mor.* 80.7). Though the Stoic goal is the single part, 'we continually change our mask (*personam*) and put on one the very opposite of that we have discarded' (*Ep. Mor.* 120.22). Indeed Seneca's addressees are sometimes specifically instructed to 'change masks' (*muta personam, Marc.* 6.1), or to stop performing: for 'ambition, decadence, dissipation require a stage' (*ambitio et luxuria et impotentia scaenam desiderant, Ep. Mor.* 94.71). In life, as in a play (*quomodo fabula, sic uita*), what matters is not the length of the acting but its quality (*Ep. Mor.* 77.20). Stoicism as a philosophy abounds in theatrical tropes, as both Greek Stoic writings and Seneca's own *Epistulae Morales* testify,[19] demanding from its heroes a capacity for dramatic display and exemplary performance. And Stoicism was a philosophy of regular choice for the Roman imperial elite.

It was not primarily Stoicism, however, which turned Rome's male elite into actors. Few educated Romans would have found either theatrical self-display or a multiplicity of *personae* difficult. On the contrary, rhetorical training in declamation (*declamatio*), including mastery of the 'persuasion-speech' or *suasoria*, which required diverse and sustained role-playing, gave to contemporary Romans not only the ability to enter into the psychic structure of another, i.e. 'psychic mobility' or 'empathy',[20] but the improvizational skills required to create a *persona* at will.[21] As works such as Petronius' *Satyricon* exhibit, the cultural and educative system had generated a world of actors. So, too, the political system. The younger Pliny's depiction of Nero as 'stage-emperor', *scaenicus imperator* (*Pan.* 46.4), catches only one aspect of the theatricality of the times. Nero's public appearances onstage late in his principate seem to have been designed in part to parade his familial crimes as acts of theatre. Among the tragic roles which he is reported by Suetonius (*Nero* 21.2–3) as singing, sometimes 'wearing the tragic mask' (*personatus*), were 'Niobe', 'Canace in Labour' (*Canace Parturiens*), 'Orestes the Matricide'

---

[19] See e.g. *Ep. Mor.* 74.7, 76.31, 115.14ff.; also *Marc.* 10.1. On Stoicism and self-dramatization, see Rosenmeyer (1989: 47ff.).

[20] Terms used by the sociologist Lerner, quoted by Greenblatt (1980: 224ff.), in his detailed discussion of the Renaissance capacity for 'improvisation'.

[21] For this 'rhetorical fashioning of the self and others' in Roman education, see Bloomer (1997: 59) and also §III, 33–8 below.

(*Orestes Matricida*), 'Oedipus Blinded' (*Oedipus Excaecatus*), and 'Mad Hercules' (*Hercules Insanus*). Juvenal (8.228–9) adds the roles of Thyestes, Antigone, and Melannipe, and Dio (62.9.4, 22.6) those of Thyestes and Alcmaeon.[22] That some of the masks he wore were made to resemble either his own features and those of women with whom he was in love (Suet. *Nero* 21.3, Dio 62.9.5) further confounded the distinction between illusion and reality, between Rome's theatre and Rome's world. But Nero's stage performances made not only himself but the audience an actor and object of spectatorial attention.[23] Degrees of enthusiasm, adverse responses, indifference, and absence were noted in the audience by Nero's claques and military staff (Tac. *Ann.* 16.5).

Upper-class Romans seated in the theatre were well fitted for the required role of approving, adoring *spectator*, as for many others. Even private iconospheres—at least so the evidence from Herculaneum and Pompeii and from Nero's own Domus Aurea suggests—were theatrical. The walls of the houses not only of the elite seemed regularly to have been adorned with theatrical paintings, pre-eminently of subjects drawn from tragic myth. It is arguable that in early imperial Rome's confounding culture the distinction between *persona* and person began to collapse. Certainly the distinction between 'reality' and 'theatre' dissolves conspicuously within the theatre/amphitheatre itself, where buildings burn, actors bleed, spectators are thrust into the arena, human and animal bodies dismembered, and pain, suffering, death become objects of the theatrical gaze and of theatrical pleasure.[24] In the year after Nero's death the emperor Vitellius sought popular support by joining 'the audience at the theatre, supporters at the circus' (*in theatro ut spectator, in circo ut fautor*, Tac. *Hist.* 2.91) only to become later the spectacle itself.

Tacitus' account of imperial Rome's distemper is prejudicial, in part myopic. The author of *Annales* had experienced at first hand the human degradation at the centre of the early principate, the paralysing nightmare of a tyrant's court (in his case that of Domitian). As had Seneca. And, as in Tacitus, it shows. Indeed for Seneca late Julio-Claudian Rome was not simply a theatricalized, but a self-consciously dying, world. A world in which death was a source of aesthetic pleasure (*NQ* 3.18) and the death-wish (*libido moriendi*, *Ep. Mor.* 24.25) a paradigmatic emotion, as individuals

---

[22] Philostratus *Vit. Apoll.* 5.8 mentions the role of Creon. Suetonius also records that Nero towards the end of his life intended to 'dance Virgil's Turnus' (*saltaturumque Vergili Turnum*, *Nero* 54).

[23] See Bartsch (1994: 2ff.).

[24] Strabo 6.2.6, Suet. *Gaius* 35.2, *Nero* 11.2, 12.2, Mart. *Spec.* 7, 8, *Epig.* 8.30, Dio 59.10.3.

sought the empowerment they lacked in life through the controlled artistry of death. A world which felt the onset of its own dissolution (*Thy.* 875–81):

> nos e tanto uisi populo
> digni, premeret quos euerso
>   cardine mundus?
> in nos aetas ultima uenit?
> o nos dura sorte creatos,
> seu perdidimus solem miseri,
>   siue expulimus.

> Did we of all mankind seem
> Worthy to be crushed by
>   A world disjoined?
> On us has the final age come?
> O we are creatures of bitter fate,
> Whether we wretches destroyed the sun,
>   Or banished it.

The themes of Seneca's tragedies—vengeance, madness, power-lust, passion, irrational hatred, self-contempt, murder, incest, hideous death, fortune's vicissitudes and savagery, a theatricalized and dying world—were the stuff of his life. Critics who think them merely rhetorical or literary commonplaces have not stared into the face of a Caligula (see *Ira* 3.18–19.5).

II. Roman Theatre

> etenim tribus locis significari maxime de re publica populi Romani iudicium ac uolutas potest: contione, comitiis, ludorum gladiato-rumque consessu.

> The judgement and will of the Roman people in public affairs can be made most manifest in three places: at a political meeting, in the assemblies, at a gathering for plays or gladiators.

Cic. Sest. 106

Republican Theatre

Product of the Hellenization of Rome in the third and second centuries BCE, Roman drama from its first attestation in 240 BCE until its gradual decline after the first century CE was a vital and formative cultural force.[25] Its forms were complex and many. The main ones: tragedy, comedy, history plays, satyr plays, Atellan plays, and mime (the last two being, initially, unscripted vaudeville farces).[26] Both tragedy (*fabula*—more precisely, to use the term of the grammarians, *fabula crepidata*—or *tragoedia*) and early comedy (*fabula palliata*) were creative, 'Romanizing' adaptations of Greek dramatic forms, fifth-century Attic tragedy in the case of *fabula*, Hellenistic Greek New Comedy in the case of *fabula palliata*. Two kinds of scripted drama, however, focused on Roman or Italian subject matter: the history play known as the *fabula praetexta*, which Romans allied to tragedy, and the *fabula togata*, which arose in the second century and transferred the comic situations of the bourgeois *palliata* to the lower-class citizens of the country towns of Italy. From the end of the third century BCE to the beginning of the first, eight dramatists stand out: in tragedy and the *praetexta*, Naevius,

---

[25] For a more detailed and fully annotated account of the history of the Roman (esp. tragic) theatre, see my *Roman Tragedy* (2006); for the republican theatre, see also Manuwald (2011). Eliot's infamous comment on Roman theatre bears citation here because of the totality of its error and the survival of that error in many minds today (1951c: 70): 'The theatre is a gift which has not been vouchsafed to every race, even of the highest culture. It has been given to the Hindus, the Japanese, the Greeks, the English, the French, and the Spanish, at moments; in less measure to the Teutons and Scandinavians. It was not given to the Romans, or generously to their successors the Italians.'

[26] Both became scripted and 'literary' in the first century BCE. They seem also often to have functioned as *exodia*, 'closural pieces', at the end of a sequence of plays: Csapo and Slater (1995: 371).

Ennius, Pacuvius, and Accius; in the *palliata*, Plautus, Caecilius, and Terence; in the *togata*, Afranius. But complete dramatic texts have survived only from Plautus and Terence.

Like that of Athens, Roman drama was constituent of a political, social, and religious context. During the late third and the second centuries BCE *ludi scaenici*, 'theatrical shows', including drama, music, and dancing, were incorporated into the annual festivals held in Rome in honour of Magna Mater, Ceres, Flora, Apollo, and Jupiter. At the same time the practice arose of performing plays at the triumphs or funerals of distinguished members of Rome's elite and at the consecration of temples. Occasionally also there were 'great votive shows', *ludi magni uotiui*, in honour of Jupiter, vowed by a Roman military commander in battle or by the consuls instructed by the senate. The *ludi scaenici* were organized by Roman magistrates, who used them to impress their peers, clients, and the citizen body as a whole, and (especially where the *praetexta* was concerned) for specific political goals. And that citizen body came increasingly to regard the provision of extravagant spectacles and *ludi* as its due, an appropriate tribute to its own civic standing, its *dignitas* (Cic. *Leg. Agr.* 2.71).

Initially the bulk of the credit or odium for a performance went to the magistrate who commissioned the plays, contracted their staging, and arranged for the *ludi*. The earliest playwrights themselves were of low social status, essentially paid employees of the commissioning magistrate. The situation began to change during the second century BCE (especially after the formation of the *Collegium Poetarum*, 'Guild of Poets'), and by the first century the early Roman dramatists were being regarded as the fathers of an important indigenous literature. They were sometimes thought to excel their Greek counterparts (Cic. *Tusc.* 2.49).

Tragic and comic actors, however, were from the beginning socially stigmatized and, at least from the late republic, legally marginalized (Just. *Dig.* 3.2.1, 3.2.2.5, Cic. *Rep.* 4.10). Many actors were either slaves or non-citizens. But even those who were Roman citizens were legally classified as *infames*, 'disgraceful', 'without reputation',[27] banned apparently from the army and disenfranchised, removed from the higher social orders of which (in exceptional cases) they were members, liable in the late republic to be flogged by

---

[27] The latter is the translation of Edwards (1994: 84). See Cornelius Nepos' description of late republican Roman attitudes to competing in athletic contests and acting on the stage: *quae omnia apud nos partim infamia, partim humilia atque ab honestate remota ponuntur*, 'With us [as opposed to the Greeks] all such things are classified either as disgraceful or as base and far removed from respectable conduct' (*Pref.* 5).

Roman magistrates anywhere, unable (by Augustan times) to marry free-born citizens, and subject along with prostitutes and gladiators to a large range of other restrictions. Like prostitutes and gladiators they displayed their bodies for the pleasure of others. There were distinguished actors who managed to escape the various bans, including the great comic actor of the first century BCE, Roscius, raised to equestrian status by the dictator Sulla and regarded by Cicero as a friend (Macrob. *Sat.* 3.14.11ff.). Evidently, too, participants in the Atellan farce seem to have been exempt from legal restrictions, if Livy is to be believed (7.2.12). But, on the whole, actors (*histriones*), like gladiators, were Rome's celebrities and its dregs, a social contradiction, penalized by Roman law and adored by Rome's citizens, who 'loved those they punished' (*amant quos multant*, Tertullian *Spec.* 22.2). Their employment by Rome's elite in something so prestigious as a great statesman's funeral procession changed nothing (Diod. Sic. 31.25.2). The guilds in which actors and other theatricals organized themselves, unlike their Greek Dionysiac counterparts, seem to have had no political clout.

As to how early Roman drama was staged, much remains obscure. It is clear, however, that in Rome until 55 BCE all plays were staged on temporary wooden structures, erected for the duration of the *ludi scaenici*. Both the stage (*pulpitum*) and the stage-building (*scaena*) with its three doorways, roofing, and painted scenery-panels were constructed of wood. The wealthier Greek cities of southern Italy and Sicily had stone theatres dating from the fifth century (the theatre of Syracuse was dedicated *c.*460 BCE) and by the end of the second century several Italian towns had acquired their own permanent stone theatres (the large theatre of Pompeii with seating for 5,000 dates from *c.*200 BCE). Not so Rome itself, which (despite several attempts to construct a stone theatre in the first half of the second century BCE)[28] had to wait for its first permanent theatre until the dying days of the republic. Theatres were places where, as the epigraph to this section notes, 'the judgement and will of the Roman people in public matters' (Cic. *Sest.* 106) could be, and often were, directly expressed. The objections to a stone theatre in Rome were often 'officially' moral (see Livy *Per.* 48). The real reasons had to do with power. A stone theatre arrived late in Rome precisely because it took control of the theatre out of the hands of the Roman senate and provided a permanent site for irregular, popular political display.

---

[28] See Boyle (2006: 22), Tan (2016).

Senatorial resistance to a permanent theatre in Rome had ample grounds. The Roman theatre of the mid to late republic was intensely political.[29] The *fabula praetexta* and even tragedy often served expressly partisan purposes, promoting the causes of particular members of Rome's elite (such as the Marcelli with Naevius' *Clastidium*, or Fulvius Nobilior with Ennius' *Ambracia*) or attacking populist revolutionaries (such as Tiberius Gracchus with Accius' *Atreus*). Evidence from the late republic shows that tragedies were revived and re-performed for new political purposes (Accius' *Clytae-mestra* to present Pompey as the new Agamemnon in 55 BCE, Pacuvius' *Armorum Iudicium*, 'Judgment of Arms', in 44 BCE to elicit pity for the assassinated Julius Caesar, Accius' *Tereus* later in 44 to attack the tyranny of the same man). Lines were often used or new lines interpolated to eulogize contemporary political figures or to attack members of the elite in the audience itself.[30]

The membership of that audience—far more so than that of Athens[31]— came from all sections of the community: patrician, plebeian, aristocratic, base, freeborn, slave, male, female. From 194 BCE, when special seating was set aside for senators (Livy 34.44.5, 54.3–8), the theatre became a mirror of the city's social hierarchy. Laws were passed at different times restricting various sections of the theatre to discrete social groups, the most famous being the Roscian Theatre Law of 67 BCE assigning the first fourteen rows in the theatre to members of the equestrian class.[32] Augustan legislation took this further. The theatre was where Rome's structures of power were visibly and vulnerably displayed. Hence the legal restrictions placed upon actors. Hence the successful baulking by self-protective politicians of all attempts to provide the capital with a permanent stone theatre—until the construction of the Theatre of Pompey in 55–52 BCE.

The wait was perhaps worthwhile. A revolutionary concrete, tufa, and marble structure, in which stage-building, semi-circular orchestra, and tiered concave auditorium were united in a closed, holistic space, the

[29] For an unpersuasive attempt to play down the political nature of republican tragedy, see Gildenhard (2010).

[30] For further details on the plays cited here and on the 'politics' of Roman tragedy, see Boyle (2006).

[31] The composition of the Athenian theatre audience in the fifth and fourth centuries BCE is still debated. Some literary texts indicate the presence in the audience of women and male children (with slave-tutors). But the audience, if not exclusively adult male citizens, were still 'notionally' so, as the direct addresses to them by comic dramatists suggest. For texts, see Csapo and Slater (1995: 286–93).

[32] The Athenian theatre did not assign seats according to social class but according to the residential district inhabited by the spectators.

Theatre of Pompey became instantly Rome's most dazzling recreational monument and the model for the theatres of the capital and the empire to come. Even in the fourth century CE it was still heralded as one of the outstanding architectural complexes of Rome (Amm. Marc. 16.10.14). The auditorium or *cauea* had seating, according to the Regionary Catalogues, for some 11,000 or so *spectatores*—a fourth-century CE figure, perhaps reflective of the Theatre's contemporary (reduced) capacity. Its exterior, which was 150–60 metres in diameter, consisted of three arcaded tiers of peperino, possibly with engaged columns of red granite (although these may have been added in a later restoration), rising from forty-four giant vaulted arches at ground level. Bronze and marble statuary abounded (Plin. *HN* 7.34). The *spectatores* seem from the beginning to have been sheltered from the sun by massive linen awnings (*uela*), stretching over the auditorium, and cooled by water flowing down the aisles (Val. Max. 2.4.6). To increase their sensuous delight, Cilician saffron was frequently sprinkled on the stage (Lucr. 2.416–17, Prop. 4.1.16, Ov. *Ars* 1.104, Plin. *HN* 21.33). Much of that sensuous delight, however, came simply from being seen. The smartest women, as Ovid quipped (*cultissima femina*, *Ars* 1.99), came to the theatre to be the spectacle itself.

They had much to compete with. The *scaenae frons* of Pompey's Theatre, initially perhaps of wood, probably soared to the height of the triple-storeyed *cauea* opposite it. Decorated with sculpture and fantastic paintings (Plin. *HN* 7.34), it contained three (probably columniated) doorways which opened onto a high and extremely wide stage (probably about 1.5 metres in height, about 95 metres in width). Perspective, architectural painting—of the kind common in second-style wall-painting—may well have adorned the façade. The stage may also have featured revolving painted scenery stands (*periactoi*) and (movable) sets, mentioned by Vitruvius (5.6.8–9), and various other theatrical devices including trapdoors, the stage machine for revealing interior scenes (the *exostra*: Cic. *Prou. Cons.* 14), and special curtains (*siparia*) for concealing part of the *scaenae frons*. The main stage curtain (*aulaeum*) would have been of the late republican kind (see below) and lavishly decorated.[33]

The spectacular space of Pompey's Theatre suited the spectacular productions of Roman drama, which were both more visually elaborate and more operatic than their Greek predecessors. Lyric sections, which are prominent in Plautine comedy and take up a far greater proportion of the

---

[33] On the Theatre of Pompey, see Richardson (1992: 383–5), Sear (2006: 57–61).

surviving lines of Roman republican tragedy than of extant Attic tragedy, were accompanied by the music of a piper, *tibicen*, whose importance to the production is indicated by the practice (unknown in the Greek tradition) of recording his name in the play-notices. Both comedy and tragedy featured three distinct kinds of verbal performance, corresponding to different metres: simple dialogue (in iambic senarii/trimeters), unaccompanied by music; recitatives (in trochaic septenarii/tetrameters, iambic octonarii, and related systems), accompanied by music; and *cantica*, arias sung to music in complex lyric metres.[34] Unsurprisingly, given that Roman playwrights, unlike those of Greece, frequently wrote both tragedy and comedy, the sharp metrical distinctions that existed between Greek tragedy and Greek comedy were not manifested in Roman drama. One generic distinction, however, in Roman drama was that tragedy—but not comedy—featured passages of choral lyric, sung by a dramatic chorus. Although some ancient scores for the plays of the Greek tragedians existed in the second century BCE, the music composed for the double-piped reed instrument of the Roman *tibicen* was surely not only original, but quite different from that written for the Athenian *aulos*.[35]

By at least the first century BCE actors were wearing the tragic and comic mask (Cic. *De Orat.* 2.193, 3.221), and generically appropriate footwear: the raised boot (*cothurnus* or *coturnus*) for tragedy, the slipper (*soccus*) for comedy. Some have suggested that masks were worn from the beginning of Roman drama.[36] From 56 BCE there is evidence of a stage-curtain (*aulaeum*), which was rolled down at the beginning of a performance and raised to conceal the stage at the end.[37] This was presumably the kind used in Pompey's Theatre. An acting company (*grex*, literally 'flock') seems to have included a *choragus*, responsible for the costumes (and possibly also the props).[38] Elaborate costuming was normal in tragedy; the *fabula praetexta*

---

[34] Recitatives, frequent in comedy and the fragments of early tragedy, are used sparingly in Senecan tragedy. Moore (2012: 102–3) argues for no 'hard and fast' distinction between the dramatic verse-forms accompanied by music, preferring to apply the term *cantica* to all of them. On the emotive force of tragic *cantica* as cited and described by Cicero, see Čulík-Baird (2022: 178–96).

[35] See Jocelyn (1967: 46–7). The pipes, *tibiae*, played by the *tibicen*, often classified as of equal (*pares*) or of unequal (*impares*) length or as *Sarranae* ('Phoenician'), actually 'came in innumerable varieties': Moore (2012: 56), who concludes that the instrument, 'capable both of great stridency and of gentle, soft, sweet playing' was 'an exceptionally fine tool for the accompaniment of theatrical performances' (p. 63).

[36] e.g. Beacham (1992: 184–5). If Beacham is right, then they seem to have disappeared in the late second century BCE to be reintroduced in the first.

[37] Cic. *Cael.* 65. This difficult question is discussed by Beare (1964: 267–74).

[38] P. G. McC. Brown (2002: 229).

featured characters wearing the purple-bordered toga of a Roman magistrate. All actors in tragedy, comedy, *praetextae*, and the Atellan farce seem to have been male. Although actors frequently specialized in tragic or comic drama (e.g. Aesopus in the former, Roscius in the latter), they regularly performed in both (Cic. *Orat.* 109).[39] As has already been observed, these dramatic forms were never the separate institutions they had been in Athens.

Acting itself seems to have been a virtuoso performance in a self-consciously 'grand' or 'comic' style, involving highly expressive gesture, stance, and movement, as well as power and nuance of voice (see e.g. Cic. *De Orat.* 3.102, 217, *Sest.* 121). Like the dramatists themselves, actors played for the favourable judgement of an audience, who were quite explicitly represented by the comic writers as 'judges' (*iudices*) of the performance (e.g. Ter. *Ad.* 4). Claques (*fautores*) supporting particular actors are known from Plautus' day (*Amph.* 65–85), and audience response was often noisy and disruptive. The Latin word for that 'audience', *spectatores*, defines it as a body of 'viewers' not 'listeners'. And what those Roman *spectatores* necessarily wanted and received in increasing quantity and splendour—at the theatre, amphitheatre, and triumphal or funeral procession—was spectacle. Thus Horace:

> si foret in terris, rideret Democritus, seu
> diuersum confusa genus panthera camelo
> siue elephans albus uulgi conuerteret ora;
> spectaret populum ludis attentius ipsis
> ut sibi praebentem nimio spectacula plura;
> scriptores autem narrare putaret asello
> fabellam surdo. nam quae peruincere uoces
> eualuere sonum referunt quem nostra theatra?
> Garganum mugire putes nemus aut mare Tuscum,
> tanto cum strepitu ludi spectantur et artes
> diuitiaeque peregrinae, quibus oblitus actor
> cum stetit in scaena concurrit dextera laeuae.
> 'dixit adhuc aliquid?' 'nil sane.' 'quid placet ergo?'
> 'laena Tarentino uiolas imitata ueneno.'

> Were he on earth, Democritus would laugh, whether
> Some mongrel breed of camel-crossed-with-panther
> Or a white elephant enticed the crowd's eye;

---

[39]   Manuwald (2011: 88).

He'd watch the people more keenly than the shows
As providing far the greater spectacle;
He'd think the playwrights were telling their tale
To a deaf ass. For what voices have prevailed
To drown the din echoing from our theatres?
You'd think the Garganus forest or Tuscan sea roared,
So great is the noise when they view the shows, art-works
And foreign finery, plastered with which the actor
Steps on stage to the crashing of right hand with left.
'Has he said something yet?' 'Nothing.' 'Why the applause?'
'It's that violet cloak dyed in Tarentum.'

(*Ep.* 2.1.194–207: trans. Boyle 1997)

Cicero reported to his friend Marcus Marius that, at the opening of Pompey's Theatre, the entrance of Agamemnon in Accius' *Clytaemestra* was accompanied by 600 mules, and in *Equos Troianus*, 'Trojan Horse' (by Naevius?), 3,000 wine-bowls were used (*Fam.* 7.1.2). The audience, if not Cicero, loved it. A generation later Livy wrote of the theatre's 'madness (*insania*) scarcely able to be supported by opulent kingdoms' (7.2.13).

Imperial Theatre

One of the changes in the late republic observed above was the increasing social status of the Roman dramatist, especially the tragedian, and in the first century BCE we find for the first time tragedies written by members of the Roman social elite. Both Julius Caesar Strabo at the beginning of the century and later Asinius Pollio wrote tragedies that were admired; and even Julius Caesar and Augustus were credited (respectively) with an *Oedipus* and an *Ajax* (Suet. *Iul.* 56.7, *Aug.* 85.2). The latter, though clearly *divertissements*, testify to the social status of the form, to which several distinguished poets of the early empire aspired. Varius Rufus, for example, wrote a *Thyestes*, commissioned for the Actian Games of 29 BCE, and Ovid wrote a *Medea*. Both plays were held in high esteem by the Flavian writer, Quintilian (*Inst.* 10.1.98).[40]

But the main development in Roman drama, in tragedy especially, under the empire had little to do with the tragedian's social status. It was bound up

---

[40] Also Tac. *Dial.* 12.5. For Varius' *Thyestes*, see Boyle (2017: lxxvi–lxxvii); for Ovid's *Medea*, see Curley (2013: 19–58).

with momentous political change. As Rome's political structure changed from a senatorial oligarchy (the republic) to an autocracy (the empire), its theatre became less political, or at least less politically overt. The number of public venues was increased (from one to three permanent stone theatres in the city) and the theatrical repertoire was diversified, but accompanying this expansion was a trivializing, spectacularizing, and depoliticizing of the repertoire itself. During the Augustan period the traditional, 'low culture' dramatic forms of mime and Atellan farce continued to flourish—accompanied by a new Augustan form, the pantomime. Mime, despite its name, was not mute, but a lively, maskless farce or vaudeville, featuring women 'actresses' (*mimae*) in the female roles and uninhibited in its staging of sexual activity. It was generally obscene, often parodic and/or sententious.[41]

Pantomime was little like its modern namesake. Introduced in Rome *c.*20 BCE, this highly expressive 'ballet' featured a masked, silent performer who, accompanied by instrumental music and/or a choir, narrator, or solo singer, interpreted through dance and gesture a theme (generally from Greek mythology) in a comic or tragic mode, dancing all the roles in the story, changing his mask for each one. The leading dancers of the early Augustan period, Pylades and Bathyllus,[42] were closely associated with, and possibly freedmen of, respectively Augustus and Maecenas. Pantomime was a demanding art form, in which the dancer had to represent character, feeling, and plot through bodily movement and a complex code of gestures, in which the hands had great importance.[43] It became hugely popular and received imperial support, projecting its main practitioners to 'stardom'; in the process, although it may have used excerpts from the dramatic repertoire as libretti for the accompanying singers,[44] it marginalized the more discursive (and potentially political) forms of drama. Pantomime's popularity led to occasional outbreaks of violence between the dancers' rival supporters. But that this scenic entertainment had a politically quietist function was, according to Dio, recognized by the dancers themselves.[45] The evidence

[41] On mime, see Fantham (1989) and Panayotakis (2005: 139–46). Wiseman (2002: 84) suggests that mime also included 'scenarios that claimed to be historical'. Clearly some mimes had more developed, 'literary' scripts than others. The distinction, however, between 'literary' and 'popular' mime, adopted by modern commentators, is not ancient.

[42] Tac. *Ann.* 1.54.2, Athen. *Deipn.* 1.20d–e, Dio 54.17.5, Macrob. *Sat.* 2.7.12–19. Pylades also wrote a treatise on dancing.

[43] On this, see Lucian *De Salt.* 67–9 and *passim*. See also Sen. *Ep. Mor.* 121.6. On pantomime, see Hall and Wyles (2008).

[44] It certainly deployed the poetry of Virgil (Suet. *Nero* 54, Macrob. *Sat.* 5.17.5) and Ovid (*Tr.* 2.519–20, 5.7.25) for this purpose.

[45] See Pylades' remark to Augustus reported by Dio (54.17.5): συμφέρει σοι, Καῖσαρ, περὶ ἡμᾶς τὸν δῆμον ἀποδιατρίβεσθαι, 'It profits you, Caesar, that the people waste their time with us.'

suggests that mime, too, which in the republic was also used politically, was actively depoliticized.[46]

But the Roman tradition of politicized theatre was too ingrained to kill. And it is clear that, despite the emphatic popularity of these other theatrical forms, both tragedy and comedy continued to be written and publicly performed (even if far less often) into the second century CE itself.[47] There is evidence too of 'political' tragedy during this period. Mamercus Aemilius Scaurus, for example, wrote a tragedy, *Atreus*, which angered Tiberius (Dio 58.24, Tac. *Ann.* 6.29), and in Tacitus' *Dialogus* (2.1, 3.4) Curiatius Maternus is credited with a tragic *praetexta*, *Cato*, which may have offended the emperor Vespasian, and with a political 'mythical' tragedy, *Thyestes*. We have no knowledge of whether *Octavia* similarly offended, but the play is deeply political and perhaps to be ascribed to Vespasian's reign.[48]

Maternus, whose literary output also included a *Medea* (Tac. *Dial.* 3.4), is described as reciting his tragedies in public (Tac. *Dial.* 2, 3, 11.2), but he seems also to have been involved with the theatre (Tac. *Dial.* 10.5). And that tragedies were still being written for, as well as performed on, the stage in the middle of the first century CE is clear from the example of Seneca's contemporary Pomponius Secundus, a distinguished dramatist (Tac. *Dial.* 13.7), who, according to Quintilian, excelled in 'learning', *eruditio*, and 'brilliance', *nitor* (*Inst.* 10.1.98), and who definitely wrote for the Claudian stage (*is carmina scaenae dabat*, Tac. *Ann.* 11.13).[49] Pomponius Secundus figured in a celebrated argument with Seneca on tragic diction observed by Quintilian (*Inst. Or.* 8.3.31).[50] Seneca's own tragic output was considerable: eight extant tragedies, of which several are masterworks. As observed above,[51] no certainty has been reached concerning the dates of Seneca's plays, but it seems probable that some were written during the artistic renaissance of Neronian Rome (54–68 CE), when extraordinary resources were lavished on the theatre. As for comedy, it was still not only being performed but also being written in the early empire. Some forty years after Seneca's death the younger Pliny compared the comedies written by his friend Vergilius Romanus with those of Plautus and Terence (*Ep.* 6.21.4).

[46] Suet. *Aug.* 53.1. Boyle (2006: 266 n. 37).
[47] See e.g. Manil. 5.459–85, Sen. *Ep. Mor.* 76.31, 80.7–8, 108.6, Quint. *Inst.* 11.3.73–4, 112, 178ff., Juv. *Sat.* 6.67–75, Suet. *Nero* 11, *HA: Hadrian* 19.6, 26.4. See also Bieber (1961: 227ff.), Jocelyn (1967: 47ff.).
[48] See n. 7 above.   [49] See also Plin. *Ep.* 7.17.11.
[50] The date of this debate is uncertain, but perhaps around 51 CE.
[51] See §I, 6–7.

Although the century after Nero witnessed the gradual death of serious drama in Rome,[52] under the Flavians (69–96 CE) the theatrical scene was vibrant. Mime and pantomime remained primary forms, but tragedies and *fabulae praetextae* continued to be written.[53] Vespasian revitalized Rome's theatrical venues, even if Domitian later attempted to curb the theatre and restrict performances to private houses (Suet. *Dom.* 7.1). The major known figure of this period was Curiatius Maternus; the major unknown figures, of course, were the playwrights of *Octavia* and *Hercules Oetaeus*, if either (as perhaps both did) wrote in the Flavian period. Both anonymous playwrights show through their very emulation of Seneca's plays that Senecan tragedy was known, 'culturally alive', and a medium for serious thinking in the period after his death.[54] Other Flavian tragedians are named in the pages of the unsympathetic Martial: Varro, Bassus (*Epig.* 5.30, 5.53), and Scaevus Memor, whom Martial proclaims the *Romani fama cothurni*, 'glory of Roman tragedy' (*Epig.* 11.9.1).

All forms of serious theatre, however, had eventually to compete with— and eventually conceded to—the theatrics of the arena. From the building's inaugural games in 80 CE onwards, the 'murder-shows' of the Colosseum dominated Roman theatrical life. In 69 CE the theatre still served as a public space for the display of citizen grievances (Tac. *Hist.* 1.72 and Suet. *Galba* 13), but the arena eventually took over most of the theatre's unofficial political function, providing at the heart of the city and the empire a permanent site for civic confrontation, exhibition, negotiation, and control. The arena took over some of the theatre's narratives, too. Its pragmatics of spectacle and death often cruelly mimicked the subjects of tragedy and the *praetexta* through 'fatal charades',[55] in which scenes from tragedy, mime, or Roman history were parodically and lethally enacted before an engrossed audience of some 50,000 *spectatores*.

Not that Roman audiences were deprived of spectacle before the opening of the Colosseum. The theatres of late Julio-Claudian and early Flavian Rome were technological marvels. Although temporary wooden stages were still erected for occasional theatrical performances, throughout Italy and the empire stone theatres abounded. The three in Rome itself—the Theatre of Pompey, of Balbus (dedicated 13 BCE), and of Marcellus (dedicated 13 or 11 BCE)—provided, according to one estimate,[56] over 35,000

---

[52] 'Gradual' is important, and, although Roman tragedy/*praetexta* as 'creative writing or fully staged/recited performance died', Greek tragedy flourished into (perhaps beyond) the third century CE: Boyle (2006: 237–8).
[53] See Boyle (2006: 229–35).   [54] See Goldberg (2003: 31–2).
[55] Coleman (1990).   [56] Sear (2006: 62, 66).

seats. Their concrete structures, marble revetments, socially stratified seating (beneath a great linen awning), holistic design, deep stages, richly decorated stage curtains, revolving scenery-stands, massive flying devices and collapsible sets, their baroque stage-buildings adorned with statues, scene-paintings, masks, and garlands—all constituted spectacle informing spectacle. Seneca himself (*Ep. Mor.* 88.22) draws attention to the Roman theatre's penchant for the spectacular, when he comments on Posidonius' second category of 'arts', *artes ludicrae*, 'the arts of entertainment/of the theatre':[57]

> his adnumeres licet machinatores qui pegmata per se surgentia excogitant et tabulata tacite in sublime crescentia et alias ex inopinato uarietates, aut dehiscentibus quae cohaerebant aut his quae distabant sua sponte coeuntibus aut his quae eminebant paulatim in se residentibus.

> To this category are to be assigned the 'stage technicians', who devise scaffolding which rises by itself and platforms which soar silently aloft and other diverse surprises, as when things joined fall apart or things not connected come together automatically or things standing erect collapse into themselves little by little.

Reference was made above to such devices of the republican stage as *siparia* and the *exostra*. Other features of the late Julio-Claudian *ludicrae artes* include perhaps the more developed stage curtain, raised at the beginning of a performance and lowered at the end,[58] and probably such devices, evident in Greek theatre from the fifth century BCE, as the *eccyclema* (a movable platform which could be wheeled out to reveal an interior scene) and the *mechane* (a crane used to transport dramatic figures in mid-air and similar in some of its functions to the *pegma* or *pegmata* mentioned by Seneca).[59] Although there is no clear evidence to this effect, it is possible that the *eccyclema* and *mechane* were devices of the republican theatre, too.[60] An increasingly sophisticated use of scene-painting may be inferred, perhaps with semi-circular tableaux (*hemicyclia*) positioned 'by the orchestra' and paintings known as 'reveals' (*stropheia*) indicating the aftermath of

[57] See also Strabo 6.2.6, Phaedr. 5.7.   [58] See Beare (1964: 271–4).

[59] The earliest explicit testimony to the *eccyclema* and *mechane* is the second-century CE Pollux (4.127–32), but for the use of the *pegma*, see Phaedr. *Fab.* 5.7.7; Juv. 4.122. The *eccyclema* could have found a use in Act III of *Hercules*, the final acts of *Agamemnon* and *Thyestes*, Act IV of Seneca's *Medea*, Act IV of *Phaedra* (assuming that it is a six-act play), and the first act of *Octavia* (although the *exostra* may have been used instead in each case), the *mechane* in the last scene of Seneca's *Medea*. For *Hercules*, see Comm. before 592–617.

[60] For possible allusions to the *mechane*, see Sall. *Hist.* 2.59, Cic. *Harusp.* 62.

an event (e.g. an apotheosis).[61] Probably, too, the tragic mask with its tower-ing *onkos* or 'peak' had reached the canonic imperial form represented in Pompeian wall-paintings and the tragic boot its full height. Other items of the tragic actor's costuming, such as the full-length, belted tunic, padded round the chest and stomach (see Lucian *De Salt.* 27), continued the trend towards the elaborate and spectacular evident in Horace's observations cited above—and accorded with the emotional focus and gestural force of tragic (and other) acting (Sen. *Ep. Mor.* 11.7).

Public theatrical performance, however, was by no means the only way in which Roman imperial dramatic texts were experienced. Tragedies were also published/circulated and therefore read. They seem also to have been performed in the imperial palace (perhaps from Augustus' time), and in private houses (*intra domum*: a phenomenon even in Marius' day: Sall. *BI* 85.13). Comedies and tragedies were also 'recited' (by a single speaker). The recitation took place in a private house or recitation-hall, *auditorium*, both for its own sake and as a preliminary to theatrical performance and/or pub-lication (see Plin. *Ep.* 1.15.2, 3.1.9, 7.17.11). It was perhaps such 'readings' (complete with 'prefaces') prior to performance or publication that Quintilian witnessed. Recitations whether of dramatic or other texts were, like theatrical performances themselves, often lively occasions in which speakers were interrupted with cries of approval or heckling (Hor. *AP* 428–30, Pers. *Sat.* 1). Sometimes the dramatic recitation took place in the theatre itself as a virtuoso recital of a tragic speech or episode or the singing of a tragic aria (*tragoedia cantata*), the latter perhaps in theatrical counterpoint to the popular *tragoedia saltata* ('danced tragedy') of the pantomime. The virtuoso recital or aria might be accompanied (by other speaking actors, or a chorus) or performed solo. The *tragoedia saltata* was itself often accom-panied by choral or solo singing (sometimes perhaps of excerpts from an existing tragedy on the appropriate subject). To the category of *tragoedia cantata* belong Nero's own 'singing of the tragedies of heroes and gods wear-ing the tragic mask (*cantauit personatus*)' (Suet. *Nero* 21.3).[62]

Unfortunately, while an intricate but clear picture emerges of the evolv-ing technologies of the Roman theatre and the developing complexity of Roman drama as both social institution and literary form, little is known of its dramaturgical practices and conventions—from the republican theatre to that of Flavian Rome. This applies notably to the dramaturgy of tragedy.

---

[61] See Beacham (1992: 181–2) for a discussion of the Pollux testimony.
[62] For the titles of some of these tragedies, see §I, 11–12 above.

Contemporary witnesses of republican tragedy mention such matters as the presence of the *tibicen* or piper, the wearing of tragic masks, and the predominance of spectacle, but provide little detailed information. The Augustan picture is a little clearer. Vitruvius' comments in *De Architectura* 5.6, although confined essentially to theatre design and construction, include important remarks on stage-scenery and the different functions of the two stage-exits; and Horace in *Ars Poetica* (189–92) draws attention to the five-act rule, the three-actor rule (neither of which are adhered to strictly by Seneca), and the *deus ex machina*. The evidence, however, remains largely internal. What the fragments of the early Roman tragedians suggest is that already in the republic there had been a pervasive fusion of classical and Hellenistic techniques.[63]

Certainly the Senecan tragic *corpus*, while it reveals and exploits an obvious counterpoint with the plays of Aeschylus, Sophocles, and Euripides, displays dramaturgical features foreign to fifth-century Attic tragedy: the five-act structure (*Oedipus, Octavia,* and, possibly, *Phaedra* are exceptions here), the use of extended asides, including entrance monologue-asides,[64] choral exit and re-entry, and various items of stage-business (withdrawing to plot future action, as at *Ag.* 308–9, or surveying the stage for eavesdroppers, as at *Pha.* 599–601). These practices are derived in the main from the conventions of Hellenistic drama, particularly New Comedy of the fourth and third centuries BCE. Even the probably reduced size of the regular Senecan tragic chorus (estimated by some to consist of between three and seven members) has Hellenistic precedent,[65] although the delivery of the choral odes from the stage itself, to which the chorus was confined at least by Vitruvius' day (*De Arch.* 5.6.2), seems decidedly Roman.[66] Some of these non-Attic features can be found in Roman tragedy of the late republic. It is not unreasonable to suppose that by the Augustan period, when Hellenistic influence on Roman poetry was at its height, most (if not all) were standard

[63] Cf. Tarrant (1978: 256–7).

[64] Extended asides: e.g. *Tro.* 607ff., *Pha.* 424ff., 592ff., *Thy.* 903ff.; entrance monologue-asides: e.g. *Ag.* 226ff., *Herc.* 332ff., *Tro.* 861ff., *Med.* 177ff., 431ff., *Thy.* 404ff., 491ff.

[65] Gomme and Sandbach (1973: 12 n. 1). Calder (1975: 32ff.) argues for a Senecan tragic chorus of between three and seven members, as against the twelve or fifteen member choruses of the fifth-century Attic tragedians. A smaller chorus allowed for greater flexibility in the matter of choral entrances and exits and in the number of choruses. A large chorus could, of course, be used on occasion for spectacular impact—as in the 'Processional Ode' of *Medea* (56–115: see Boyle *ad loc.*) or the 'Trojan Ode' of *Agamemnon* (589–658). Seneca writes about large theatrical choruses in *Epistle* 84, in which, though the chorus consists of 'the voices of many' (*multorum uocibus*), a unity results (*Ep. Mor.* 84.9–10).

[66] See Comm. *ad* 125–204 (introd.).

Roman practice. Seneca was certainly indebted to Augustan tragedians for their refinement of the crude iambic dialogue line (the *senarius* or 'sixer') of the earlier playwrights (Hor. *AP* 251ff.),[67] and probably also for aspects of their tragic language. It seems likely that the debt extended to Augustan dramaturgy too.

The Performance Debate

Not all have agreed. Some scholars have believed that most writers of imperial tragedy and/or *praetextae* (including Seneca) were not much interested either in dramaturgy or in theatrical spectacle since (it has been argued) they wrote drama not for performance in the great theatres of Rome or in a private house or villa, but rather to be read (privately) or recited.[68] The theatrical situation and practice of Seneca's day, as described above, were complex; and plays admitted differing forms of realization. We have no way of knowing the performability of the plays of authors such as Curiatius Maternus. But to assign Senecan tragedy (or indeed *Octavia*) to the category of recitation drama or closet drama seems misdirected. It is not known and may never be known whether Seneca's plays were performed onstage or otherwise during their author's life.[69] But it is certainly the case that they were and are performable: they have been and are performed.[70] The

---

[67] Horace's own (non-dramatic) iambics would also have had an influence on Seneca, just as his lyric compositions did.

[68] Senecan drama: for 'reading', see Fantham (1982: 34–49); for 'recitation', see Zwierlein (1966); for 'dramatic realizability/stage performance', see Herington (1966: 444), Walker (1969), Calder (1983: 184), Sutton (1986), Dupont (1995), most contributors to Harrison (2000), and more recently Aygon (2016).

[69] However, the piece of epigraphic evidence mentioned at n. 9 above is suggestive: the opening words of Sen. *Ag.* 730 (from the theatrically powerful clairvoyant speech of Cassandra) inscribed (*CIL* iv. Suppl. 2.6698) on a wall in Pompeii (perhaps together with a few words from *Ag.* 693: Lebek 1985). This only 'proves' that Seneca's *Agamemnon* was known, not that it had been performed. But Pompeii had an active theatrical culture, and it is far more plausible to assume that a performance of some kind influenced the writing of the graffito.

[70] It is customary to cite performances of Senecan tragedy in Renaissance Europe and Tudor England. More interesting is the fact that Seneca has been and is regularly performed in modern Italy, France, Spain, and Switzerland. The Teatro Antico of Segesta, Sicily, featured productions of five Senecan plays and *Octavia* in the last two decades of the twentieth century: *Troades* (1981), *Phaedra* (1983), *Medea* (1989), *Thyestes* (1991), *Agamemnon* (1995), *Octavia* (2000). In the English-speaking world some late twentieth- and early twenty-first-century performances of Senecan tragedy may also be mentioned: Seneca's *Oedipus* at the Old Vic Theatre, London, March 1968, the Almeida Theatre, London, August 1988, and The Wharf, Sydney, July 2000; *Phaedra* at the Sydney Opera House, July 1987, and the Almeida Theatre, London, March 1997; *Troades* at the Alexander Theatre, Melbourne, September 1988; *Thyestes* at the Green Room, Manchester/ Royal Court Theatre, London, May/June 1994, the Court Theatre, Chicago, October 2007, the

contemporary practice of *recitatio* clearly affected the form of Seneca's plays, which, appropriately edited, could have been used for selective theatrical recital or for a public 'reading' by the author prior to performance. The latter seems to have been Pomponius Secundus' practice, as it was later the (occasional) practice of the French tragedian, Corneille.[71] Extracts from the tragedies could also have served as libretti for *tragoediae cantatae* or (like Virgil's *Aeneid* and Ovid's *poemata*)[72] for the sung accompaniments to *tragoediae saltatae*, the pantomimic dance. Indeed aspects of Seneca's own dramaturgy—especially descriptions by the chorus or another actor of the movements and emotions of impassioned women or other characters[73]— may have been influenced by pantomime itself. Seneca's nephew, Lucan, is said to have written numerous libretti for pantomime (*salticae fabulae*).[74] It has been suggested, too, that some of Seneca's choral odes may have featured a pantomime realizing the themes of the odes in dance.[75]

But, just as the purpose of the tragedies was clearly not to serve as a collection of arias or pantomimic adjuncts linked by iambic dialogue, so there is little possibility that either recitation or (even less) private reading was their intended primary mode of realization. Not only do the 'reading' and the 'recitation' hypotheses generate more problems than those they seek to address,[76] but they are vitiated by the theatricality of these plays, their concern with dramatic structure and effect and with the *minutiae* of stagecraft. Analysis of Seneca's stage techniques has revealed theatrical mastery in the shaping of dramatic action, the structural unfolding of dramatic language and imagery, the blocking of scenes and acts, the disposition of roles, the handling of actors and of the chorus, the interrelationship between the choral odes and acts, the use of ghosts, messengers, mutes, the dramatic and thematic use of stage-setting and props, the employment of implicit stage

Latham Theatre, New York, April 2013 (performance in Latin with English surtitles), and La Sala Rossa, Montreal, Canada, February 2015; *Hercules* at the Théâtre Gerard Philipe de Saint-Denis, Paris, January 1996, the Getty Villa, Malibu, May 2011, and Miles Memorial Playhouse, Santa Monica, June 2013; *Medea* at the Citizens' Theatre, Glasgow, October 1998 and the Oxford Playhouse, Oxford, February 2011; *Agamemnon* at the Scoundrel and Scamp Theatre, Tucson, University of Arizona, April 2018. Worth noting, too, are two twenty-first-century performances of *Octavia*: at the Experimental Theatre, San Diego State University, April 2006, and the Todd Theatre, University of Rochester, New York, November to December 2017.
[71] On Corneille, see Boyle (2006: 269 n. 10).   [72] See n. 44 above.
[73] See e.g. *Herc.* 991–1031, *Oed.* 1004–9, *Ag.* 710–19, *Med.* 382–90, *Pha.* 583–6, *Tro.* 945–8. For pantomime and Senecan tragedy, see Zimmermann (2008), Zanobi (2014). Zanobi argues also for possible pantomimic influence on Seneca's self-analytical monologues and descriptive/narrative set-pieces.
[74] The *Vita* attributed to Vacca attributes fourteen *salticae fabulae* to Lucan.
[75] Slaney (2013*b*). See also Comm. *ad* 569–89 (introd.).
[76] For details, see Boyle (2006: 269 n. 11).

directions in the text itself (particularly entrance and exit cues, random but more substantial than often noted, identification cues, and implicit directions for stage business)[77]—and in Senecan tragedy's manipulation of pace, time, movement, space, violence, spectacle, and closure.[78]

Indeed the 'recitation' hypothesis is not only contradicted by the evidence of the plays; it self-destructs. If Seneca's tragedies were written for recitation *in toto*, they were written for a number of voices playing separate parts or for a single actor 'playing' the separate parts with changing voice and gesture, that is to say, for 'dramatic' performance[79]—whether the performance envisaged was in the theatre or in a private house to a coterie audience (or both). Indeed it was partly on the grounds of representational power (*rappresentazione*), i.e. theatrical effectiveness, that Giraldi Cinthio, a practical dramatist who 'never for a moment imagined that Seneca did not write for a stage performance', preferred Seneca to the Greeks.[80] The Elizabethan translators would have concurred. Even Eliot, whose pronouncements on Seneca have been as injurious as any, thought that the plays might be regarded as 'practical models for…broadcasted drama'.[81] Senecan tragedy belongs to the category of Roman performance theatre.

---

[77] On implicit stage directions and the 'implied visuality' of ancient dramatic scripts (and their relationship to reading practices), see Kragelund (2016: 149–50).

[78] On Senecan stagecraft, see e.g. Seidensticker (1969: 145), Sutton (1986: 28ff., 43ff.), Segal (1986: 152–3), Boyle (1997: *passim*), Harrison (2000), and Schmidt (2014: 539–41), who argues persuasively for Seneca's semantic use of dramatic space.

[79] Herington (1966: 444–5), Bexley (2015).

[80] Cinthio, *Scritti critici* (Crocetti 1973), 184. The English quotation is from Charlton (1946: lxxx n. 6).

[81] Eliot (1951c: 70).

III. The Declamatory Style

oratio certam regulam non habet; consuetudo illam ciuitatis,
quae numquam in eodem diu stetit, uersat.

Style has no fixed rules; the usage of society changes it, which
has never stayed still for long.

Sen. *Ep.* 114.13

But, if the performance values of Senecan tragedy have often been inappropriately criticized, so, too, has Seneca's rhetoricity. *Hercules*, like all Seneca's
plays, not only flaunts its rhetoricity, but uses it to structure the action and
to articulate some of the drama's theatrically most powerful, affective
moments: the fiery hatred, frustration, and relentless determination of Juno
(1–124); the pain, devotion, and despair of Megara (279–308); the clash of
values and entire worlds in the exchanges of Lycus, Megara, and Amphitryon
(359–494); the prayerful entrances of Hercules in Acts III (592–604) and IV
(898–908, 926–39); the descent into hell (658–827); the agony and despair
which frame the final act (1138–86, 1321–41), the cosmic *Schreirede* (1202–18)
instantiating Juno's initial script (116–17). Similarly the quick-fire exchange
between Medea and her Nurse (*Med.* 150–67), Andromache's turbulent
entrance speech in *Troades* (409–25), Oedipus' *Schreirede* after the revelation of his birth (*Oed.* 868–81), Theseus' declamation of agony in *Phaedra*
(1201–12), Cassandra's brilliant, rapier-like verbal duel with her conqueror
and master in *Agamemnon* (791–9) and final, ironic triumphalism (*Ag.*
1004–11), Thyestes' joy and terror before the Tantalid palace, his vigorous
moral sermon to his sons, his climactic display of ineffable pain in *Thyestes*
(404–20, 446–70, 1006–21, 1035–51, 1068–96)—all use verbal and declamatory power not simply to overwhelm, entertain, or impress an audience but
to drive home the theatrical moment.[82] Balanced cadences and clauses, allit-
erated consonants, metrical stringency,[83] sonal and syntactic repetitions,
violent imagery, portentous, 'poetic' diction,[84] crescendo structure, 'steady
rhythmic punch',[85] hyperbole, paradox, epigram, far from being indices of a

---

[82] See Boyle (2006: 193–6).
[83] For Seneca's view of how metre and *carminis arta necessitas* ('the stringent constraints of
poetry'—he is citing Cleanthes) clarify meaning and empower thought, see *Ep. Mor.* 108.10 and
Trinacty and Sampson (2017*b*).
[84] For analysis of 'poetic' words used in Senecan tragedy but absent from his prose works,
see Albrecht (2014: 705–6).
[85] The phrase is taken from Herington (1966: 423).

self-referential, indulgent, even decadent style, are essential, quickening ingredients of Senecan dramatic language and of Senecan dramatic technique.

It is a dramatic language which empowers the plays and satisfies generic expectation,[86] creating mood, atmosphere, meaning, and dramatic authority, as the Commentary displays. It is a language too—it should be noted—which enhanced the tragedies' contemporary accessibility. Seneca's declamatory style accorded with a contemporary passion for rhetoric and a contemporary fullness of response to rhetoric, to declamation, dialectic, verbal brilliance, and ingenuity. Late Julio-Claudian Rome was a highly rhetorical age, in which public declamations by rival professors and declamatory 'debates' between them, epideictic competitions and the quasi-theatrical recitations of verse were a social institution and a regular form of public and imperial entertainment, to which audiences responded noisily with heckling and acclaim.[87] Even the iconosphere itself, its architecture, sculpture, and painting, moved towards the rhetorical and the baroque.[88]

But not only were the members of Rome's elite adept at responding to the employment of declamatory techniques and rhetorical role-play by other speakers, they were themselves, as was observed above,[89] trained in those techniques. The *Controuersiae* and *Suasoriae* of Seneca's father, which were probably written in the thirties CE and must have had a profound impact on Seneca himself, document the kind of training Rome's schools of rhetoric provided. There were essentially two kinds of speech in which students were practised: deliberative (*suasoriae*) and disputatious (*controuersiae*). In the former students purported to 'advise' mythological or historical figures at critical points in their lives ('Agamemnon deliberates whether to sacrifice Iphigenia', *Suas.* 3; 'Cicero deliberates whether to beg Antony's pardon', *Suas.* 6); in the latter they played the role of litigants or advocates in imaginary lawsuits, debating intricate and generally far-fetched moral and legal issues. An armoury of rhetorical techniques was the progeny of such training. Students were taught the declamatory employment of antitheses and

---

[86]   Generic expectation derived both from the Greek tradition and from the Romanization of that tradition. For the Greek tradition, see Goldhill (1997) 127: 'in the classical polis "the tragic" has become synonymous with a certain grandeur of expression, high-flown periphrasis and even heroic posturing.…There is a style and vocabulary proper to the genre.' See further Trinacty (2014: 128), who cites the Goldhill passage. Ancient Greek and Roman audiences, readers, and critics (see e.g. Aristotle's *Rhetoric* or Demetrius' *On Style*) seem to have revelled in the rhetoricity of poetry and drama. For play with generic expectation, see the prologue to Plautus' *Amphitryo*.
[87]   See Sen. Rhet. *Con.* 2.3.19, 3 Pref. 16, 9 Pref. 2, Quint. *Inst.* 2.2.9–12.
[88]   See Boyle (1997: 23–9); also §I above.   [89]   See p. 11 above.

conceits, of descriptive set-pieces (*descriptiones/ekphraseis*) and historical *exempla*, of moralizing commonplaces (*loci communes*) and rhetorical flourishes. They learned the use of apostrophe, alliteration, assonance, tricolon, anaphora, asyndeton, homeoteleuton, polyptoton, *figura etymologica*, *commutatio*; the use of synonyms, antonyms, oxymora, paradox, innuendo (*suspicio*), epigram, point. They studied *ethopoeia, prosopopeia, dubitatio*, and declamatory structure. The watchwords of the new rhetoric, as proclaimed by Marcus Aper at Tacitus *Dialogus* 20ff., give the essence of the instruction: *nitor*, 'brilliance', *cultus*, 'elegance', *altitudo*, 'elevation', *color*, 'colour', *laetitia*, 'luxuriance', *aliquid inlustre*, 'splendour', *dignum memoria*, 'memorability', *sententia*, 'maxim/aphorism/epigram'.

The rhetorical schools were later much criticized—for the unreality of the declamatory themes and the unsuitability of the education they provided for the rigours of lawcourt life.[90] But their popularity was considerable, as was that of the virtuoso public declamations of the *rhetores* themselves. And, whatever the new rhetoric's success in preparing pupils for public careers (and Seneca's own life indicated that not all students failed), it taught verbal strategy, psychic mobility, and public role-play, and played a substantial part in forming the mental sets of the Roman reader and audience and their ability to respond with intellectual sophistication and emotional depth to imperial tragedy. Seneca's alliterative, asyndetic, pointed, even mannerist, declamatory style would have had substantial contemporary appeal. A similarly 'declamatory age', Elizabethan England, found Senecan rhetoric exemplary.

Elizabethan England is cited advisedly. As with the rhetoric of Kyd, Marlowe, and Shakespeare, so too with that of Seneca, it is important to recognize the complexity of its function and its effects. The latter range from cosmic or global annexation (geographical and astronomic catalogues), through the creation and nuancing of dramatic mood and tonality, to, ubiquitously, the exhibition of speaker psychology. Senecan bombast, paradox, word-play, and epigram are regularly used to display states of mind and to create tragic character. Lycus' entrance-monologue (*Herc.* 332–57) reveals beneath the self-assurance, pride, and power a profound, social insecurity, which will drive him to attempt an 'elevating' marriage with the daughter of his slain enemy. Similarly Clytemnestra's amalgam of shame and grief over the sacrificial death of her daughter (*Ag.* 162–70) exhibits a mind about to be driven to mariticide, whatever the consequences; Thyestes' castigation of

[90] Sen. Rhet. *Con.* 3 Pref., 9 Pref.; Petr. *Sat.* 1ff.; Quint. *Inst.* 2.10.4ff.; Tac. *Dial.* 35.

the false world of power at *Thyestes* 446–70 displays a mind which will suc-cumb to that world almost immediately; the asexual idealization of the wild by Hippolytus at *Phaedra* 483ff. parades before the audience the self-delusion and psychological pathology which will prove motor to tragic dis-aster. The opening speeches of Hercules (*Herc.* 592–617), Cassandra (*Ag.* 659–3, 695–709), Oedipus (*Oed.* 1–81), Phaedra (*Pha.* 85–128), Theseus (*Pha.* 835–53), Hecuba (*Tro.* 1–66), Helen (*Tro.* 861–71), Medea (*Med.* 1–55), and Jason (*Med.* 431–44) similarly dramatize minds about to shape the dramatic action.

Indeed Seneca's declamatory style is as much an instrument of self-dramatization as it is of theatrical shock. Hence the frequent focus in Senecan speeches on the 'I' of the speaker and the positioning of that 'I' at the centre of a moral and physical cosmos which is being tested and is even sometimes expected to respond. So *Oedipus* begins with a declamatory soliloquy presenting its protagonist as agent and victim within a cosmic scheme as problematic as it is vast (*Oed.* 1–36). So in Hippolytus' linguistic assault on the universe and transcendent crescendo of moral rage caused by his stepmother's revelation of lust (*Pha.* 671–9) a rhetoric of cosmic and psychic violence is used for self-construction and self-dramatization. So Medea in her speech prior to the entrance of Jason (*Med.* 397–414) purloins the universe for the construction of herself and unleashes that self and its passion in a rhetorical avalanche of turbulence and 'psychic aggression'.[91] So Hercules in his 'Golden Age speech' (*Herc.* 926–39) presents his fantasy of the entire cosmos at peace as product of Jupiter and himself before toppling into madness. So Clytemnestra creates with potent, declamatory, analytic language, which fuses passion, memory, and pain (*Ag.* 131–44, 162–73), a strong sense of her tortured self as subject and object of raging, conflicting emotions—emotions which seem to have their own coercive agency arising from and within a morally problematic world.

Sometimes the self-constructing rhetoric arises from a kind of existential nihilism, an empowerment which comes from total loss, in which Senecan language again is pointer to a mind. Thus Cassandra at *Agamemnon* 695–709:

> uicere nostra iam metus omnes mala.
> equidem nec ulla caelites placo prece
> nec, si uelint saeuire, quo noceant habent.
> Fortuna uires ipsa consumpsit suas.

---

[91] The phrase is that of Braden (1985: 62).

quae patria restat, quis pater, quae iam soror?
bibere tumuli sanguinem atque arae meum.
quid illa felix turba fraterni gregis?
exhausta nempe. regia miseri senes
uacua relicti totque per thalamos uident
praeter Lacaenam ceteras uiduas nurus.
tot illa regum mater et regimen Phrygum,
fecunda in ignes Hecuba fatorum nouas
experta leges induit uultus feros.
circa ruinas rabida latrauit suas,
Troiae superstes, Hectori, Priamo, sibi.

Our sufferings now have conquered every fear.
Indeed, no prayer of mine placates the gods.
Should they wish to rage, they cannot harm me.
Even Fortune has consumed her powers.
What fatherland, what father, what sister remain?
Burial mounds and altars have drunk my blood.
What of that happy, thronging band of brothers?
All gone, of course. In the empty palace
Sad old men are left to view many rooms
Filled with widows except for Sparta's woman.
That mother of many kings, Phrygia's helm,
Flame-fecund Hecuba, suffered new laws
Of fate and adopted bestial looks.
Rabid, she barked around her own ruins,
Surviving Troy, Hector, Priam—and herself.

Sometimes the rhetoric arises from self-annihilating guilt and a rejection of the possibility of redemption. Thus Hercules (*Herc.* 1323–9):

quis Tanais aut quis Nilus aut quis Persica
uiolentus unda Tigris aut Rhenus ferox
Tagusue Hibera turbidus gaza fluens
abluere dextram poterit? Arctoum licet
Maeotis in me gelida transfundat mare
et tota Tethys per meas currat manus,
haerebit altum facinus.

What Tanais, what Nile or what violent
Tigris with Persian flood or frenzied Rhine

Or turbid Tagus, awash with Spain's gold,
Can cleanse this hand? Though icy Maeotis
Pour its Arctic sea on me, and Tethys
Stream across my hands with all her waters,
The crime will stick deep.

At other times the cosmic rhetoric is used like a knife to slice through the soul and annihilate the self. Hercules again, at 1202–18:

nunc parte ab omni, genitor, iratus tona.
oblite nostri, uindica sera manu
saltem nepotes. stelliger mundus sonet
flammasque et hic et ille iaculetur polus.
rupes ligatum Caspiae corpus trahant
atque ales auida. cur Promethei uacant
scopuli? paretur uertice immenso feras
uolucresque pascens Caucasi abruptum latus
nudumque siluis. illa quae Pontum Scythen
Symplegas artat hinc et hinc uinctas manus
distendat alto, cumque reuocata uice
in se coibunt saxaque in caelum expriment
actis utrimque rupibus medium mare,
ego inquieta montium iaceam mora.
quin structum aceruans nemore congesto aggerem
cruore corpus impio sparsum cremo?
sic, sic agendum est. inferis reddam Herculem.

Now, father, from every zone rage and thunder.
Thou didst forget me—with thy late hand at least
Avenge thy grandsons. Let the starry firmament
Roar, flames shoot from pole to pole. Let Caspian
Crags and ravening bird tear apart my
Fettered flesh. Why are the Promethean
Rocks empty? Get the Caucasus' sheer cliff
Ready, bare of trees, feeding beasts and birds
On its measureless peak. Let the Symplegades
Throttling the Scythian Pontus stretch both
My hands, bound to each side, across the deep,
And, when the rocks clash in turn and spurt sea
Skywards, imprisoned by the moving cliffs,

> Let *me* lie and block the mountains without rest.
> Why don't I pile up a forest, build a pyre,
> Burn my body drenched with impious blood?
> Thus, thus I must act. I'll return Hercules to hell.

Psychological observations can be made about declamatory 'set-pieces' elsewhere in the tragedies: Hecuba's discourse on the fragility of power (*Tro.* 1ff.), for example, or Creon's defence of his banishment of Medea (*Med.* 252ff.), or, as noted above, Hippolytus' denunciation of urban life (*Pha.* 483ff.). It should be observed that *sententiae* (maxims) in such speeches are not only used for rhetorical punctuation and closure (as e.g. at *Herc.* 329, 340–1, 353, 368–9), but serve also a larger dramatic purpose, viz. to display—even in a sense create—a mind, as it grapples with itself and its moral and existential context, often grasping at *sententiae* as purported grounds for action. Some of Clytemnestra's most powerful *sententiae* in Act II of *Agamemnon* are precisely of the latter kind (115, 202, 243, 267, 307), as indeed are those of Lycus in his opening soliloquy in *Hercules* (332–53). Sometimes the intellectual grappling and the *sententiae* occur in lyric. The opening choral ode of *Hercules*, especially in its second half, uses a whole series of *sententiae* (178, 185, 188, 191, 198, 201) to build its moral world.[92]

In non-declamatory iambic mode, too, the use of *sententiae* is rarely simply rhetorically or theatrically clever. Oedipus' sententious exchanges with Creon (210–46, 509–29, 669–708) or with Phorbas (843–67), Theseus' with Phaedra (*Pha.* 872–81), Medea's with her Nurse (*Med.* 150–67), Agamemnon's with Pyrrhus (*Tro.* 325–52), Lycus' with Megara (*Herc.* 422–38), Atreus' with his *satelles* (*Thy.* 204–19), Jocasta's with Eteocles (*Pho.* 653–64) are directed not only to providing the kind of verbal and conceptual duel which Roman audiences enjoyed, but to generating a context in which latent aspects of tragic character are exhibited, even (and not only in the case of Medea: *Med.* 166–7) a redefinition of the protagonist's self. In Clytemnestra's rapid exchange with her Nurse (*Ag.* 145–61)—rhetorical, sententious, stichomythic—the contest of commonplaces and epigrams generates a detailed *ratio ulciscendi*, based on Clytemnestra's earlier tragic suffering (159–70), enabling a 'new' Clytemnestra to emerge, a quintessentially 'Senecan' figure ready to kill her husband at the cost of her own life (199–202) and certainly ready to manipulate her lover.[93] Megara in *Hercules* moves

---

[92] See further Comm. *ad* 125–204 (introd.).

[93] For similar dramatic point, see the exchanges at *Pha.* 872–81, *Tro.* 327–36. On *sententiae*, see Comm. *ad* 125–204 (introd.); on *stichomythia*, see Comm. *ad* 422–38.

from a despairing, if devoted, wife of Hercules in her opening speech into a powerful, energic figure during her long verbal exchange with Lycus (359–438)—an exchange rhetorical, sententious, and climactically stichomythic—but that transformation through rhetoric leads not to a controlling dramatic figure as in *Agamemnon*, but to one whose head, removed from her 'truncated body', 'is nowhere' (*nec usquam est, Herc.* 1026). What Senecan dramatic rhetoric achieves in the case of Megara is the construction of a powerful figure, whose devotion is ignored by a vengeance-seeking husband and whose body is annulled by manic Herculean force. The audience are left to make of it what sense they may.

A fusion of rhetorical power, psychological expressivity and dramatic point may be found in certain aspects of Seneca's tragic verse such as the dramatist's notable fondness for a 'noun' as opposed to a 'verbal' style,[94] or his characters' linguistic proclivities for combining the abstract with the concrete, the figurative with the literal, the grandiose with the mundane, for juxtaposing periodic or clausular plenitude with epigrammatic pith, the poetic or ornate with the distilled and the simple.[95] Seneca's dramatic style, including its declamatory modes and multiplicity of stylistic registers, rather than indexing the superficiality of his tragedies, their surface rhetoric and linguistic glint, is a major instrument of profound interiority, enabling the Roman dramatist to achieve a non-Greek focus on the psychologies behind and informing the masks[96]—even as the verbal violence and imagistic power of the declamatory speeches themselves quicken the tragedies' theatrical force for a violent, rhetorical, imperial age.

---

[94] See Comm. *ad* 11–18.

[95] On these stylistic proclivities, see Tarrant (1985: 25–7), who finds Seneca's 'intense, restless and discordant style' a 'natural medium of expression' for Seneca's 'troubled characters'. It is also a culturally potent 'medium of expression' for Rome's declamatory world.

[96] What Segal (2008: 141) refers to as the 'enclosed inner space of pathos, suffering, vehemence of feeling'. Similarly Regenbogen (1927–8: 207) refers to Seneca's 'psychoplastic portrait of emotional affect' (Segal 2008: 140). On theatrical masks and their ability to suggest the psychologies behind and indexed by them, see Bexley (2022: 194): 'ancient masks were not immobile but supple, expressive objects capable of imparting a range of emotions according to the angle at which they were positioned.' Her probing analyses of Seneca's characters confirm the propositions advanced above.

IV. Seneca's Theatre of Violence

Der Mensch nicht ein sanftes, liebebedürftiges Wesen ist...ist ihm der Nächste nicht nur möglicher Helfer und Sexualobjekt, sondern auch eine Versuchung, seine Aggression an ihm zu befriedigen, seine Arbeitskraft ohne Entschädigung auszunützen, ihn ohne seine Einwilligung sexuell zu gebrauchen, sich in den Besitz seiner Habe zu setzen, ihn zu demütigen, ihm Schmerzen zu bereiten, ihn zu martern und zu töten. *Homo homini lupus.*

Man is not a gentle creature requiring love...his neighbour is to him not only a possible helper and sexual object, but also a temptation, to satisfy his aggression upon him, to exploit his labour without compensation, to use him sexually without his consent, to take possession of his property, to humiliate him, to cause him pain, to torture and to kill him. *Homo homini lupus.*

Sigmund Freud, *Das Unbehagen in der Kultur*[97] (1930)

Horace's prescriptions about the staging of tragic violence and fantasy are well known (*AP* 179–88):

> aut agitur res in scaenis aut acta refertur.
> segnius irritant animos demissa per aurem,
> quam quae sunt oculis subiecta fidelibus et quae
> ipse sibi tradit spectator. non tamen intus
> digna geri promes in scaenam, multaque tolles
> ex oculis quae mox narret facundia praesens.
> ne pueros coram populo Medea trucidet,
> aut humana palam coquat exta nefarius Atreus,
> aut in auem Procne uertatur, Cadmus in anguem.
> quodcumque ostendis mihi sic, incredulus odi.

> An event is either staged or reported.
> The mind is stirred less vividly through the ear
> Than by what is cast before trusted eyes and which
> The audience see for themselves. But don't produce on stage
> What should be performed inside, and keep from sight
> Much which may be eloquently told to us later.

---

[97] = *Civilization and its Discontents*. The German citation may be found conveniently in the Severus edition of 2013, p. 72.

> Don't let Medea butcher her boys before an audience,
> Nor monstrous Atreus cook human flesh in full view.
> Nor Procne turn into a bird and Cadmus a snake.
> All such displays I loathe in disbelief.

Senecan tragedy breaks these prescriptions. In a direct rejection of Horace, Seneca has 'Medea butcher her boys in full view' of the audience,[98] and stages not only the filicide but the shedding of Medea's blood during the 'black mass' of Act IV. *Thyestes* is also in breach of Horace's mandate, for, although the Messenger narrates the bloody killing of the children, their dismemberment and the cooking of their flesh, the children's severed heads, hands, and feet are displayed in the final act. Neither *Oedipus* nor *Phaedra* would have met with Horace's approval, since Jocasta commits suicide onstage at the end of the former, as does Phaedra at the end of the latter, where the final act is conspicuously bloody as Theseus attempts to assemble Hippolytus' corpse. The (probably) incomplete *Phoenissae* may well have ended in a scene of sexual suicide.[99] *Agamemnon* seems similarly to close in unHoratian bloodletting, as Clytemnestra plunges Aegisthus' sword into Cassandra's body.[100] *Hercules* also at least partially exhibits violent death on stage, since Hercules is clearly on the stage when he slays the first child at *Hercules* 991–5, even if the slain child is not,[101] and the bloody corpses of the dead sons and sparse remains of Megara are displayed in the final act. Only *Troades* would definitely pass the Horatian test. Such violence and bloodshed could have been 'vividly' represented, where needed, through the use of animal blood and artificial blood-bags, the latter attested for the Roman stage from the time of Caligula.[102]

Much violence, too, is narrated in Senecan tragedy in accordance with Hellenic modes and what seems to have been standard Roman republican practice. The narrated violence is generally graphic and extensive. The bloody deaths of Agamemnon, Megara, Hercules' children, Astyanax, Polyxena, Thyestes' children and Hippolytus, and the self-blinding of Oedipus are conveyed to the audience aurally (*per aurem*, Hor. *AP* 180) in emotively potent detail by messengers or eye-witnesses (in *Agamemnon* a clairvoyant one). The audience paradoxically see with their ears. In these

---

[98] Others have echoed Horace's condemnation. See e.g. August von Schlegel (1846: 211). For Schlegel's repudiation of Senecan tragedy, see §VIII, 138–9 below.
[99] See Boyle (1997: 104–5).   [100] See Boyle *ad Ag.* 1012.
[101] See Comm. *ad loc.*
[102] Suet. *Gaius* 57.4, Josephus *IA* 19.4. See also Sutton (1986: 63–7).

narrations there is a focus on the body, its inner and outer parts, their penetration and/or dismemberment entirely in accord, it seems, with Roman
tragic practice and with Roman non-dramatic poetic practice since Ovid.
Accius'descriptive gore' was famous;[103] so, too, that of Ovid himself (see e.g.
the flaying of Marsyas at *Met.* 6.387–91), whose poetic practice overtly
repudiates Horace's theory of decorum, and who in his opening poem of
Amores 3 parades a personified *Tragoedia* as paradigmatically *uiolenta* (*Am.*
3.1.11). Indeed defiance of Horatian decorum is sometimes presented as a
defining feature of 'later Augustan and post-Augustan' verse.[104] The 'gore' of
Lucan (see e.g. the torture and death of Marius Gratidianus at *BC* 2.174ff.) is
physical, plentiful, and pervasive; less pervasive but equally physical are the
sanguineous moments in Statius (see e.g. Tydeus' cephalophagy at *Theb.*
8.751–66). Relevant (especially to Seneca) is Stoicism's preoccupation with
the body. Stoic physics, which regarded the entire universe as material, made
the body and the language of the body a defining constituent of its
discourse.[105]

The violence of Senecan tragedy should be neither underestimated nor
exaggerated. Its purposes and effects are not easy to describe. The attractions of violent entertainment—modern and ancient—are not obscure.[106]
And much has been made of the relationship of Seneca's tragic violence to
the spectatorial cruelty of the era, the 'murderous games' and bloodshed of
the arena,[107] where the public killing of gladiators and condemned criminals was frequently conducted on a massive scale for the pleasure and occasional (alleged) edification of Roman *spectatores*. But the construction of
this relationship as an attempt by Senecan tragedy to cater to contemporary
Blutdurst misconstrues. It not only overplays Senecan violence, and ignores
what may be inferred from the tragedies themselves (see e.g. *Troades* Act
V), but takes little cognizance of Seneca's own epistolary testimony on the
degrading effect of the arena's butchery on spectators (*Ep. Mor.* 7.2–5):

---

[103] See Beacham (1992: 124).
[104] See D. F. Kennedy (2018: 237–8). One should, however, observe that scenes of gore and
bodily disfigurement are the staple of ancient epic from Homer onwards and are found in
Virgil—not only in military narrative (e.g. *Aen.* 9.329–34) but even on the shield of Roman
history (*Aen.* 8.642–5).
[105] See Rosenmeyer (1989: 118ff.). On the 'Neronian obsession with the dismemberment of
the human body', see Most (1992).
[106] For a range of perspectives on such attractions, see Goldstein (1998). For ancient Rome
specifically, see Coleman (1990), Gale and Scourfield (2018*b*).
[107] 'Murderous games' is the phrase of Hopkins (1983: 1), whose opening chapter (1–30)
contains an informative discussion of this issue.

nihil uero tam damnosum bonis moribus quam in aliquo spectaculo desi-
dere. tunc enim per uoluptatem facilius uitia subrepunt. quid me existimas
dicere? auarior redeo, ambitiosior, luxuriosior? immo uero crudelior et
inhumanior, quia inter homines fui…mane leonibus et ursis homines,
meridie spectatoribus suis obiciuntur. interfectores interfecturis iubent
obici et uictorem in aliam detinent caedem; exitus pugnantium mors est.
ferro et igne res geritur. haec fiunt dum uacat arena. 'sed latrocinium fecit
aliquis, occidit hominem.' quid ergo? quia occidit, ille meruit ut hoc
pateretur; tu quid meruisti miser ut hoc spectes?

Nothing is so injurious to morals as sitting at the games. Then vices more
easily steal upon one through the medium of pleasure. What do you think
I mean? I return from the games more greedy, more ambitious, more
self-indulgent? Yes, and far more cruel and inhuman—for being among
humans.…In the morning they hurl men to lions and bears, at noon to the
spectators. They demand that killers be killed in turn and reserve the victor for another slaughter. The outcome for the fighters is death. Sword and fire
keep the show going. It goes on while the arena is empty. 'But he committed
robbery; he committed murder.' So what? Because he's a murderer, he deserved
to suffer this. But what have you done, wretch, to deserve to watch it?

In his *History of the Decline and Fall of the Roman Empire* Edward Gibbon
commented on *Epistle* 7 that 'Seneca shews the feelings of a man'.[108] They
were the feelings of a remarkable man, one who expresses similar sentiments elsewhere (*Breu. Vit.* 13.6–7). They are sentiments not normally displayed by members of the Roman aristocracy. Of course, there is regularly
little concinnity between the prose works and the tragedies. But the tragedies themselves suggest that Seneca's theatrical violence is in no sense an
attempt to cater to what he depicts in the prose works as a decadent appe-
tite, as if theatricalized death were competing with the blood of the arena.
Rather, by controlling the representation of violent death on the stage, the
tragedies are able to shape the perception and evaluation of it in a way that
the arena could not. Every spectator at the games saw dehumanized, even
demonized individuals and groups dying bloodily on the sand, as they provided what Seneca describes as a *spectaculum* from the death of a sacral
object, man himself (*Ep. Mor.* 95.33).[109] Senecan tragedy humanizes the

---

[108]   Gibbon (1776–89: Vol. 2, ch. xxx, n. 59).
[109]   *Homo sacra res homini iam per lusus ac iocum occiditur…satisque spectaculi ex homine
mors est* ('Man, that sacred object to man, is now killed in sport and play…and man become
death is spectacle enough').

sufferers and the suffering, controls in the theatre what the audience see and how they see it, and furnishes them with a conceptual framework with which to judge it. In some of Seneca's 'violent' plays, such as *Phaedra*, *Medea*, and *Thyestes*, that framework includes the determinism of family and of history and, in the case of *Thyestes*, the contra-rational, appetitive, even (in Freud's sense) 'lupine' nature of man, the violence of which finds visible representation in theatricalized death and suffering. Such theatricalized suffering evokes responses different from—generally more complex and occasionally more powerful than—those generated by human suffering itself.[110] Sometimes, as, for example, in the 'Trojan Ode' and Acts IV and V of *Agamemnon*, or in the 'Lamentation Ode' and Acts IV and V of *Hercules* the responses to cruel death and suffering are themselves dramatized and their complexities and ambivalencies displayed. If such dramatization generates an increased understanding of the violence acted out before the audience, then Senecan tragedy performs precisely that 'patient, critical analysis' of violence that modern cultural theorists advocate.[111]

Theatricalized violence, death, and suffering are thus cardinal elements of Senecan drama's reflection of and on late Julio-Claudian Rome, on 'the very age and body of the time'.[112] Some critics see Senecan violence as 'dramatizing a deep-seated sense of alienation, or an unease in regard to personal autonomy and identity',[113] typical of the literature of this period. Certainly, but its historical reach and cultural semiotics seem to go further. Theatricalized death is a trope Seneca shares with Rome's historians. Livy's self-stabbing and self-consciously exemplifying Lucretia (1.58–9) is well known. So, too, is the violent death of Tacitus' Agrippina, who plays Jocasta in her final moments (*Ann.* 14.5.4).[114] His Lucan suicides quoting self-referentially from his own poetry (*Ann.* 15.70). Similarly theatrical is Suetonius' actor-emperor Nero, who cites Homer's *Iliad* in Greek before the knife is plunged through his throat (*Nero* 49). For the death of Seneca,[115] constrained to commit suicide by Nero, Tacitus creates one of his most

---

[110] At *Pelopidas* 29 Plutarch recounts how the tyrant Alexander of Pherae (fourth century BCE) murdered without pity many of his citizens but wept at a performance of Euripides' *Troades* to see the sufferings of Hecuba and Andromache. The story is used by Sidney in his *Apologie* to defend the moral value of 'the sweet violence of a Tragedie': G. G. Smith (1904: 1.178).

[111] See e.g. Žižek (2008: 7).

[112] Shakespeare, *Hamlet* III.ii.21ff.: '[The] end, both at the first and now, was and is, to hold, as 'twere, the mirror up to nature; to show virtue her own feature, scorn her own image, and the very age and body of the time his form and pressure.'

[113] Gale and Scourfield (2018*b*: 20).

[114] See also *Oct.* 368–72 and Boyle (1997: 101–2).

[115] On which, see Ker (2009*b*), Gloyn (2017: 101–4).

extensive, theatricalized narratives, which climaxes as follows (*Ann.* 15.64.3–4):

> Seneca interim durante tractu et lentitudine mortis Statium Annaeum diu sibi amicitiae fide et arte medicinae probatum orat prouisum pridem uenenum, quo damnati publico Atheniensium iudicio extinguerentur, promeret. adlatumque hausit frustra, frigidus iam artus et cluso corpore aduersum uim ueneni. postremo stagnum calidae aquae introiit, respergens proximos seruorum addita uoce libare se liquorem illum Ioui Liberatori. exim balneo inlatus et uapore eius exanimatus, sine ullo funeris sollemni crematur. ita codicillis praescripserat, cum etiam tum praediues et praepotens supremis suis consuleret.

> Seneca, meanwhile, as death's protracted slowness lingered, begged Statius Annaeus, long valued for his loyal friendship and medical skill, to produce the poison he had long prepared, which was used to execute those condemned by the public tribunal of Athens. It was brought, he drank—to no purpose. His limbs were already cold and his body closed to the poison's power. Finally he entered a pool of heated water, and, sprinkling some on the slaves nearby, he remarked that he poured the liquid as libation to Jove the Liberator. He was then lifted into the bath, suffocated by its vapour, and cremated without death-rites. He had given these instructions in his will, written when he was at the height of his wealth and power and taking thought for his end.

As the Stoic philosopher, tragedian, and Nero's ex-minister plays Socrates in his own constructed theatre of death, Tacitus' moving and ironic account leaves little doubt that the *imago uitae*, 'image of his life' (Tac. *Ann.* 15.62), which Seneca leaves to friends and posterity, is in part an *imago mortis*, 'image of his death'. To the imperial historian and the imperial tragedian theatricalized death was emblem and 'mirror' of Rome's histrionic, 'lupine', and self-destructive culture—even, in Seneca's case, of the 'tragic self-mutilation at the very root of civilisation'.[116] The attraction of Senecan violence to Elizabethan and Jacobean dramatists seems index in no small way of profound social and cultural affinities between the ancient and early modern worlds.[117]

---

[116] Eagleton (2002: 208).   [117] See Boyle (1997: 185–6, 201–12).

V. Seneca and Suicide

namque nec sibi potest (Deus) mortem consciscere, si uelit, quod homini dedit optimum in tantis uitae poenis.

For He (God) is not able, if He wishes, to commit suicide—which is the supreme gift He has given to humanity amid the great toils of life.

Plin. *HN* 2.27

The elder Pliny's *Natural History* was 'published' just over a decade after Seneca's death, but he may well have had Seneca's end in mind when he wrote the above eulogy of suicide. He would not, however, have read Tacitus' moving account (cited above)[118] of the final part of the fatal event. That event took place in 65 CE, in the aftermath of the failed conspiracy to overthrow Nero, some fifty years or so before the Tacitean narrative (*Ann.* 15.64.3–4) was written. Seneca's theatrical 'suicide' (*uoluntaria mors*, *Ann.* 15.61.2),[119] including its overtly Socratic mode (the drinking of hemlock),[120] must have impressed Tacitus' readers. The curt account of Cassius Dio (62.25) a century later would have impressed no one. The libation to Iuppiter Liberator in Tacitus' account almost transforms the deed into the military self-sacrifice of *deuotio*, lending it an aura of triumph before the forces of oppression and making it an act for the common good. The suicide received approbation from later ages. In the thirteenth century Jacobus de Voragine (*Golden Legend* 89.3, 'St. Peter the Apostle') even claimed that 'suicide' was built into Seneca's name, which he saw as derived from *se necare*, 'to kill oneself'.

There are ample grounds for such a false, if imaginative, etymology. Suicide is a permeating theme of Seneca's tragedies and prose works.[121] The

---

[118] See §IV, 43–4.

[119] 'Voluntary death', *mors uoluntaria*, is Tacitus' term. It occurs also at *Ann.* 2.31.3, 11.2.2, *Hist.* 3.54.3, 4.67.1 (cf. *uoluntarius finis*, 'voluntary end', *Ann.* 4.19.5), and is used, too, by Seneca (*Breu. Vit.* 6.2) and Suetonius (*Tib.* 54.2). The modern Latin word, *suicidium*, did not exist in classical Latin. Even the English term 'suicide' is attested only from the mid seventeenth century, as Griffin (1986*a*: 68), observes. Throughout this section I am much indebted to the work of Griffin (1976, 1986*a*, and 1986*b*), Rist (1969, 1978), and Inwood (2005).

[120] The Socratic mode would not have surprised readers of Seneca, who in his writings regularly praised the Athenian philosopher's death, perhaps most tersely at *Ep. Mor.*13.14: *cicuta magnum Socratem fecit*, 'Hemlock made Socrates great'. See also e.g. *Prou.* 3.4, *Tranq.* 16.1–4, *Ep. Mor.* 24.4, 67.7, 70.9, 98.12. Indeed from the younger Cato through Seneca and Thrasea Paetus to Epictetus (e.g. 4.1.159–69) Socrates became something of a Stoic saint, his death a martyrdom to truth.

[121] So much so that scholars sometimes talk of an obsession with suicide (T. Hill 2004: 146), and speculate on its physical, psychological, or social causes: see Griffin (1976: 368). Scholars

latter mention and/or describe such famous suicides as those of Socrates, Zeno, Cato, Cremutius Cordus, and Seneca's friend, Tullius Marcellinus. His plays dramatize suicide, presenting onstage the fatal self-stabbings of Jocasta and Phaedra and the suicide threats of Hercules, Amphitryon, Aegisthus, Phaedra, Thyestes, Oedipus (in *Phoenissae*), and Antigone. They also present via a messenger's report the suicide of Astyanax and the suicide threat of Oedipus (in *Oedipus*). Dramatized, too, in Senecan drama is the psychological motor of suicide: the death-wish, which is displayed by most of Seneca's major tragic figures. Witness in *Hercules*: Hercules (1202–26, 1338–40), Megara (419–21), Amphitryon (509–10, 1027–31, 1302–13); in *Phaedra*: Phaedra (250–66, 710–12, 880, 1159–63, 1181–90), Hippolytus (671–84), Theseus (1201–42); in *Agamemnon*: Clytemnestra (199–202), Aegisthus (233), Electra (971–94), Cassandra (1004–11); in *Oedipus*: Oedipus (71–7, 868–81, 925–34), Jocasta (1024–39); in *Troades*: Andromache (418–23, 577), Helen (938–44), Polyxena (945–8), Hecuba (1171–7); in *Medea*: Medea (170, 531–7); in *Thyestes*: Atreus (190–1), Thyestes (1006–21, 1077–96); in *Phoenissae*: Oedipus (1–319 *passim*).[122]

In two of the plays the morality of suicide is extensively examined. In *Hercules*, in which two suicides are threatened but none committed, the discussion is part of the moral focus of its final act. That focus is commented upon below.[123] In *Phoenissae*, perhaps Seneca's final drama, suicide is the theme of the long opening section or act, and is not resolved until line 319. Oedipus enters the play racked by the desire for death, exacerbated by the self-inflicted paradox of being seen without having the power of sight (1–10). He is unable to act because he is bound by the 'pestilential love' (*pestifero…amore, Pho.* 38–9) of his daughter. Antigone's protestations of love include the resolve to follow her father in death, should he decide to die, and is accompanied by the contention that suicide is cowardice and a confession of defeat (51–79). Oedipus maintains his desire for death even to the point of a resolve to plunge his hands into his brain once more, only to have Antigone produce a series of arguments against this resolve (182–215). The most important of these is her first (a variation of

---

also debate the matter of what constitutes suicide. Here is the much-criticized definition of Durkheim (1897: 5), which I use as a general guide: 'tout cas de mort qui résulte directement ou indirectement d'un acte positif ou négatif, accompli par la victime elle-même et qu'elle savait devoir produire ce résultat.' The killing of oneself when under the sentence of death (as happens with Seneca, Thrasea Paetus, and Astyanax) thus qualifies as 'suicide' in the Durkheimian sense.

[122] The death-wish was not avoided by the dramatists who followed: see Octavia at *Oct.* 107–8, 135–6, 961–8, and Deianira and Hercules at *HO* 841–1024, 1711–12.

[123] See pp. 98–107 below and Comm. *ad* 1295–1321.

'suicide is a mark of the coward'), which places the emphasis on a central moral concept of Seneca's *Hercules*, *uirtus* (190–2):

> non est, ut putas, uirtus, pater,
> timere uitam, sed malis ingentibus
> obstare nec se uertere ac retro dare.

> It's not, as you think, father,
> Virtue to fear life, but to confront great
> Evil and not to turn away and retreat.

Oedipus maintains both his sense of pollution and desire for death until Antigone forsakes argument, falling in supplication and tears at her father's feet (306–7), and Oedipus responds with (he is speaking of himself in the third person): *iubente te uel uiuet*, 'on your orders he will even live' (*Pho.* 319). As happens at the end of *Hercules*, suicide is averted not by argument but by *pietas*, by the bonds and love between child and father.

There are extensive treatments of suicide in Seneca's prose works, in which Seneca stresses the importance of suicide as a Stoic response to life. To the Stoic 'To die well is to escape the peril of living badly' (*bene autem mori est effugere male uiuendi periculum*, *Ep. Mor.* 70.6; cf. *Tranq.* 11.4); 'You are allowed to return whence you came' (*licet eo reuerti unde uenisti*, *Ep. Mor.* 70.15). A 'Stoic friend' of Seneca and Lucilius is quoted at *Epistle* 77.6:

> non est res magna uiuere. omnes serui tui uiuunt, omnia animalia. magnum est honeste mori, prudenter, fortiter. cogita quamdiu iam idem facias. cibus, somnus, libido: per hunc circulum curritur. mori uelle non tantum prudens aut fortis aut miser, etiam fastidiosus potest.

> It's no great thing to live. All your slaves live, all your animals. It's a great thing to die honourably, wisely, bravely. Consider how long you have been doing the same thing. Food, sleep, lust: such is the daily round. The death-wish may be felt not only by the wise or the brave or the wretched, but even by the fastidious.

Seneca could be citing himself. Cf. *Epistle* 70, which devotes itself entirely to suicide (1.4–5):

> non enim uiuere bonum est, sed bene uiuere. itaque sapiens uiuet quantum debet, non quantum potest. uidebit ubi uicturus sit, cum quibus, quomodo,

quid acturus. cogitat semper qualis uita, non quanta sit. si multa occurrunt molesta et tranquillitatem turbantia, emittit se. nec hoc tantum in necessitate ultima facit, sed, cum primum illi coepit suspecta esse fortuna, diligenter circumspicit numquid illic desinendum sit.

For living is not a good, but living well. And so the sage will live as long as he ought, not as long as he can. He will see in what place he is to live, with whom, how, in respect of what he is to act. He always meditates on the quality, not the quantity of his life. If many troublesome things happen which disturb his tranquillity, he releases himself. He does not do this only at the final crisis, but, as soon as fortune has begun to seem hostile to him, he looks around diligently to see whether he should end it there.

The Stoics classified suicide as an 'appropriate act' (καθῆκον: Chrysippus, Plut. *Stoic. Repug.* 1042d), if committed with good reason (Cic. *Tusc.* 1.74), i.e. to escape unacceptable conditions of life. Such unacceptable conditions needed recognition. The early Stoics restricted the ability to recognize the appropriate circumstances for suicide to a 'sage' (σοφός/*sapiens*).[124] Roman Stoics, including Seneca (see e.g. *Ira* 3.15.3–4),[125] seem more catholic in their list of moral agents. Here is Marcus Cato, a spokesman for Stoicism in Cicero's *De Finibus* (3.60–1):

> in quo enim plura sunt quae secundum naturam sunt, huius officium est in uita manere. in quo autem aut sunt plura contraria aut fore uidentur, huius officium est de uita excedere. ex quo apparet et sapientis esse aliquando officium excedere e uita, cum beatus sit, et stulti manere in uita, cum sit miser....itaque et manendi in uita et migrandi ratio omnis iis rebus quae supra dixi metienda.

The man in whom there is a preponderance of things according to nature may 'appropriately' remain in life. When there are or evidently will be a preponderance of the contrary things, it is 'appropriate' for him to exit from life. From this it is clear that it is sometimes 'appropriate' for the sage to exit from life, though he is happy, and for the fool to remain in life, though he is miserable....Therefore the reason both for remaining in life and for leaving it is entirely to be measured by those things which I mentioned above.

---

[124] See Arnim *SVF* iii.x.11: *De rationali e uita excessu*. It is worth noting that the first two heads of the Stoic school, Zeno and Cleanthes, killed themselves when health declined (in Cleanthes' case) or (in Zeno's case) was about to decline: see Griffin (1976: 375–6). Both presumably were 'sages'.

[125] See Inwood (2005: 113 n. 49).

The focus on *ratio* is important. This departure from life had to be a 'rational exit' (εὔλογος ἐξαγωγή), based on reason (*ratio*), not anger (*ira*), rage (*furor*) or passion (*affectus*).[126] But the acceptable conditions were wide-ranging. They went beyond the divine 'necessity' (ἀνάγκη) argued by Socrates in the *Phaedo* (62c), and included injury (actual or foreseen) to one's personal and social identity (*dignitas, libertas*) and/or moral integrity (*fides, pudicitia, mens bona*), and physical decline or extreme pain (*Ben.* 1.11.4, *Ep. Mor.* 14.2, 30.2).[127] Even the later Plato seems to have allowed great pain as justification for suicide (*Laws* 9.873c–d), though Aristotle did not (*NE* 3.1116a10–15). Diogenes Laertius in his *Zeno* (7.130) summarizes the Stoic position thus:

> They say that the sage will make a rational exit from life (εὐλόγως ... ἐξάξειν ἑαυτόν τοῦ βίου) either for the sake of his homeland or his friends, or if he suffers unbearable pain or mutilation or incurable disease.

Seneca himself asks (*Ep. Mor.* 58.34):

> at si inutile ministeriis corpus est, quidni oporteat educere animum laborantem?

> But if the body is useless for service, why should one not release the labouring soul?

And contends (*Ep. Mor.* 120.14):

> nec domum esse hoc corpus sed hospitium (et quidem breue hospitium), quod relinquendum est ubi te grauem esse hospiti uideas.

> The body is not a home but an inn (and a short-stay inn at that), which must be left when you see that you are a burden to the host.

All of this follows from the orthodox Stoic proposition that life itself is among the 'indifferents' (*indifferentia*, ἀδιάφορα). As cited above: 'Life itself is not a good', *non enim uiuere bonum est* (*Ep. Mor.* 70.4).

Acceptance of suicide as a morally appropriate exit from intolerable conditions of life was not limited to Stoicism. Though generally viewed

---

[126] See e.g. Sen. *Vit. Beat.* 20.5, *Ira* 2.36.5, *Ep. Mor.* 4.4, 14.2, 24.24–6, 30.12–15.

[127] Seneca seems especially concerned to point to suicide as a way to avoid the service of an evil ruler (*Ira.* 3.15.3–4, *Ep.* 70.6–7). Cicero's 'Cato' in *De Finibus*, written in 45 BCE (the year after Cato's death), is notably silent about 'politically motivated suicide' on the part of the Stoics. There were reasons for this: see A. G. Long (2019: 198–9).

negatively by Epicureanism (see *Vit. Beat.* 19.1),[128] it was prominent in Cynicism (DL 4.3, 6.18, 6.86),[129] and is to be found in Greek literature from Homer onwards (see e.g. *Il.* 18.88ff., *Od.* 10.49ff.). It was also distinctly Roman. At Rome by Seneca's day 'suicide to escape disgrace, conviction, or punishment, had long been accepted'.[130] By Seneca's day it was also distinctly fashionable. No data exist on the frequency of suicide in Rome in the early imperial period. But the suicide of the younger Cato after the Battle of Thapsus (46 BCE), praised by Cicero as soon as he received word of it (*Fam.* 9.18.2) and accorded an emotional eulogy by Seneca (*Prou.* 2.9–12), set a model for Stoic martyrdom, followed evidently by Seneca and Thrasea Paetus (Tac. *Ann.* 15.64, 16.35),[131] and seemed precursor to a whole host of non-Stoic suicides, including the consul of 65 CE, Vestinus; Seneca's nephew the poet Lucan (*Ann.* 15.69–70); and eventually Nero himself (Suet. *Nero* 49). Even servile suicides sometimes received lavish commendation from upper-class writers (see that of the freedwoman, Epicharis: Tac. *Ann.* 15.57.2). Permeating them all, too, were the historico-literary suicidal paradigms of Livy's and Ovid's Lucretia and Virgil's Dido, which themselves influenced the Senecan suicides of Phaedra and Jocasta. Such suicides, whether in Roman epic, drama, or in Roman life, were often overtly theatrical—so much so that the jurist Ulpian labelled as one of the motives for actual suicide, *iactatio*, 'self-display' (*Dig.* 28.3.6.7), a defining property of what has been called *Romana mors*, 'death possessing implications for the social standing of the deceased'.[132]

This *iactatio* was much criticized. Thus Martial *Epigrams* 1.8:

> quod magni Thraseae consummatique Catonis
>   dogmata sic sequeris saluus ut esse uelis,
> pectore nec nudo strictos incurris in ensis,
>   quod fecisse uelim te, Deciane, facis.
> nolo uirum facili redemit qui sanguine famam,
>   hunc uolo laudari qui sine morte potest.

[128] The Epicurean attitude to suicide, though generally negative (Epicur. *Menoec.* 125–6), was ambivalent: suicide was reluctantly allowed 'under the extreme circumstances of inevitable and insupportable pains' (Warren 2004: 209): see Cic. *Fin.* 1.49.

[129] Hence the Cynic saying: 'Reason or Rope' (λόγος ἢ βρόχος, DL 6.24). For the Cynics and suicide, see Rist (1969: 237–8).

[130] Griffin (1976: 386).

[131] Tacitus even has Thrasea Paetus make the same toast to Iuppiter Liberator (*Ann.* 16.35.2) as Seneca makes (*Ann.* 15.64.4). One aspect of Cato's suicide which is reproduced in the account by Tacitus of Seneca's and Thrasea's deaths is their Socratic nature. Cato is said by Plutarch (*Cato Minor* 68.2, 70.1) to have read Plato's *Phaedo* just before he died. Hence a Socratic suicide = a Catonian suicide.

[132] T. Hill (2004: 11).

That you follow the tenets of great Thrasea
  And perfect Cato with safety in mind
And plunge no naked breast on drawn swords,
  You act, Decianus, as I would want.
I give the man who buys his fame with cheap blood
  No praise, but one who earns it without dying.

Cato, as we can see from the Preface to *Epigrams* 1, was not Martial's favourite Roman. His suicide is criticized again in *Epigrams* 1.78 and 6.32—poems which praise the suicides of a diseased friend and of the emperor Otho, the latter because it was committed to save others. Martial clearly had little problem praising suicide when he thought it appropriate (*Epig.* 1.13):

casta suo gladium cum traderet Arria Paeto,
  quem de uisceribus strinxerat ipsa suis,
'si qua fides, uulnus quod feci non dolet,' inquit,
  'sed tu quod facies, hoc mihi, Paete, dolet.'

When chaste Arria was handing to her Paetus
  The sword she had drawn from her guts,
She said, 'By my faith, the wound I dealt does not hurt,
  But the one you'll make, Paetus, *that* hurts me.'

A cardinal feature of Seneca's treatment of suicide is its association with *libertas*, 'freedom'. In *De Ira* 3 (15.4) he lets the rhetoric run on this topic. Justifiably perhaps, for he has just been describing the intolerable experience of someone witnessing the slaying and dissection of his own son or even of participating in ignorant paedophagy:

uides illum praecipitem locum? illac ad libertatem descenditur. uides illud mare, illud flumen, illum puteum? libertas illic in imo sedet. uides illam arborem breuem retorridam infelicem? pendet inde libertas. uides iugulum tuum, guttur tuum, cor tuum? effugia seruitutis sunt. nimis tibi operosos exitus monstro et multum animi ac roboris exigentes? quaeris quod sit ad libertatem iter? quaelibet in corpore tuo uena.

Do you see that precipice? From there is the descent to freedom. Do you see that sea, that river, that well? At their bottom sits freedom. Do you see that tree, small, blighted, barren? From it hangs freedom. Do you see your neck, your throat, your heart? They are exit points from slavery. Are the exits I am showing you too laborious and in need of much courage and strength? Do you ask what is the road to freedom? Any vein in your body.

At *Ep. Mor.* 26.10 he is more simple:

'meditare mortem'; qui hoc dicit meditari libertatem iubet.

'Think on death'; who says this bids us to think on freedom.

Seneca seems to be the first author in whom we encounter the connection between suicide and freedom in its fullest personal and political sense.[133] Plato's Socrates had discoursed on the soul's release from the body at death (*Phaed.* 61cff.), and that release figures in epic poetry and accounts of the underworld from Homer onwards. But for a linkage between suicide and freedom in the largest sense, *libertas*, we have to wait until Seneca, where we encounter it frequently.

The 'freedom of death', *libera mors*, is a core notion of Seneca's thinking in both the philosophical and the dramatic works: see e.g. *Prou.* 2.10, *Ira* 3.15, *Marc.* 20.3, *Ep. Mor.* 12.10, 26.10, 70.14, 91.21, *Ag.* 589–610, 796–7, *Tro.* 49, 145–6, 574, 791, 1171–7, *Pha.* 139, *Oed.* 934.[134] It is used as an argument against those who would condemn suicide as immoral and thereby 'close off the path to freedom' (*libertatis uiam cludere, Ep. Mor.* 70.14). It pervades the plangent opening of one of his most spectacular choral odes (*Ag.* 589–92):

> heu, quam dulce malum mortalibus additum
> uitae dirus amor, cum pateat malis
> effugium et miseros libera mors uocet,
>   portus aeterna placidus quiete.

---

[133] Rist (1978: 204–6). For *libertas* and Stoicism, see Bobzien (1998); for *libertas* and Seneca, see Inwood (2005: 302–21). Bobzien's argument is that *libertas* was originally a political concept which was applied by philosophers to such 'freedoms' as freedom from passion and desire. In Seneca's concept of *libertas* (see e.g. the Trojan ode of *Agamemnon*) it is clear that the political, psychological, moral, and existential fuse: freedom from slavery, from passion, from evil, from harm. Commitment to *libera mors* brings to the living a secondary freedom, something perhaps akin to the concept of freedom in the 1960s protest movement in the USA: 'Freedom's just another word for nothing left to lose' (Janis Joplin/Kris Kristofferson's 'Me and Bobby McGee'). Witness, for example, the behaviour of Electra and Cassandra in the final act of *Agamemnon*.

[134] Seneca bequeathed the idea to others: see e.g. Luc. 7.818, Stat. *Theb.* 3.216–17, *HO* 107–10. Inwood (2005: 320–1), cites Josephus' account of Eleazar's speech at Masada (7.344), in which the association of death and 'freedom' is powerfully made. It became a commonplace of European drama: so Cleopatra at Shakespeare, *AC* V.ii.236: 'he brings me liberty'.

> O, how sweet a vice planted in mortals
> Dire lust for life, though refuge from pain
> Opens and death's freedom beckons wretches—
> A calm port of eternal peace!

The death-wish, as noted above, is repeatedly articulated in Senecan tragedy, where it is frequently conjoined, as here, with the concept of *libera mors*.

But *libera mors* connotes not only 'death's freedom', but also 'death freely chosen' (Tarrant *ad Ag.* 591, citing Marc. Aur. 10.8). One of Seneca's core concerns is individual human agency, and, when presenting death's freedom in the prose works and the dramas, he emphasizes that agency and its concomitant moral choices. Observe Amphitryon's position at *Herc.* 1027–8: *habes mortem paratam*, 'Death stands by', i.e. death is ready and waiting to free him and to be chosen freely and gladly by him. At *Thy.* 367–8 the 'true king' meets his death 'gladly' (*libens*); at *Tro.* 49 Priam 'gladly' (*libens*) receives Pyrrhus' sword-thrust; at *Prou.* 3.13 Socrates 'joyfully and gladly' (*laetus et libens*) drinks the hemlock; at *Ep. Mor.* 61.2 'dying well is dying gladly' (*bene autem mori est libenter mori*). See also *Tro.* 1102–3 (Astyanax), 1151–9 (Polyxena), and *Ag.* 607–8. Castigation of 'ignorance of how to die' (*nescire mori*) is plentiful: see e.g. *Herc.* 426, *Ag.* 610; as is praise of the appropriate knowledge: see *Breu. Vit.* 7.3, *Ep. Mor.* 26.9, *NQ* 6.32.[135] The issue was debated in the rhetorical schools, where Cato was paraded as *maximum uiuendi moriendique exemplum*, 'the greatest paradigm of how to live and die' (Sen. Rhet. *Suas.* 6.2). To Epicurus, who is reported to have experienced a slow, painful death (DL 10.15), living well and dying well were the product of the same training (*Menoec.* 125–6). So also to Seneca, who is almost obsessively interested in how human mortality allows control of living and dying. Death empowers (*Ep. Mor.* 26.10):

> qui mori didicit seruire dedidicit. supra omnem potentiam est, certe extra omnem.

> Who has learnt to die has unlearnt slavery. He is superior to all power, indeed beyond all power.

Moral qualifications arise. The most important is that the decision to commit suicide needs to be based on *ratio*, 'reason', primarily that of the

---

[135] His nephew continued the motif. Note the brilliant *sententia* at Luc. 9.211: *scire mori sors prima uiris, sed proxima cogi*, 'Man's best lot is to know how to die, but the next best is to be forced to'.

decision-maker him/herself. Even in the case of the fool who takes the right decision (see Cic. *Fin.* 3 above), the decision would have been the same, had *ratio* been applied. What Seneca condemns is a decision based on 'passion', on *affectus*, on what he calls not a death-wish (*mori uelle*), but a 'lust for dying', *libido moriendi.*[136] Thus *Ep. Mor.* 24.24–5:

> etiam cum ratio suadet finire se, non temere nec cum procursu capiendus est impetus. uir fortis ac sapiens non fugere debet e uita sed exire; et ante omnia ille quoque uitetur affectus qui multos occupauit, libido moriendi. est enim, mi Lucili, ut ad alia, sic etiam ad moriendum inconsulta animi inclinatio, quae saepe generosos atque acerrimae indolis uiros corripit, saepe ignauos iacentesque. illi contemnunt uitam, hi grauantur.

> Even when reason persuades us to end oneself, the impulse is not to be acted upon rashly or in a rush. A brave and sage person ought not to flee from life but exit; and also above all he should avoid the passion which has possessed many, the lust for dying. For, my dear Lucilius, just as there is an unconsidered tendency of the mind toward other things, so there is one towards dying, which often seizes high-born men and those of the fiercest character, often cowards and the lowly. The former have contempt for life, the latter find it irksome.

A further qualification is one most pertinent to Act V of *Hercules*. Suicide as *libertas* applies only to the suicide him/herself. But there is also the issue of its effect on others. Thus in *Ep. Mor.* 104 (3–4) an ill Seneca, responsive to the loving concerns of his wife Paulina, advocates that, even when one's own personal circumstances may seem to make suicide an appropriate act, its predictable effect on others may cancel that appropriateness:

> et interdum, etiam si premunt causae, spiritus in honorem suorum uel cum tormento reuocandus et in ipso ore retinendus est, cum bono uiro uiuendum sit non quamdiu iuuat sed quamdiu oportet. ille qui non uxorem, non amicum tanti putat ut diutius in uita commoretur, qui per-seuerabit mori, delicatus est. hoc quoque imperet sibi animus, ubi utilitas suorum exigit, nec tantum si uult mori, sed si coepit: intermittat et se suis commodet. ingentis animi est aliena causa ad uitam reuerti, quod magni uiri saepe fecerunt.

---

[136] Cf. Epict. 1.9.12–17. With Seneca's *libido moriendi*, cf. the *odium uitae*, 'hatred of life', which the Epicureans regarded as an inadequate reason for suicide: Lucr. 3.79–82; see also DL 10.125–6.

And sometimes, though there are pressing reasons, one's breath should be recalled and retained on the lips for the sake of loved ones, even at the cost of pain, since the good man should live not as long as it delights him but as long as he ought. He who does not value his wife or his friend sufficiently to remain longer in life, who will insist on dying, is self-indulgent. The mind should also issue the following command to itself, when the needs of loved ones demand it, and not only if it wishes to die, but if it has begun to: pause and oblige one's loved ones. It is the mark of a mighty mind to return to life for the sake of another, which men of greatness have often done.

The history of European thought is filled with philosophers who failed to practise what they taught, and Seneca has often been judged as one such hypocrite. But he leaves behind testimony that, at least in this instance (viz. resisting the impulse towards suicide for the sake of a loved one), he himself was a prime example. Like Hercules in Act V below,[137] he pulled back from suicide for the sake of his father (*Ep. Mor.* 78.1–2):

poterat adhuc adulescentia iniurias ferre et se aduersus morbos contu-maciter gerere. deinde succubui et eo perductus sum ut ipse destillarem, ad summam maciem deductus. saepe impetum cepi abrumpendae uitae. patris me indulgentissimi senectus retinuit. cogitaui enim non quam forti-ter ego mori possem, sed quam ille fortiter desiderare non posset. itaque imperaui mihi ut uiuerem. aliquando enim et uiuere fortiter facere est.

My youth was still able to endure injury and to display a brave face to dis-ease. Finally I succumbed and was reduced to such a state that I just dripped fluids, shrunken to extreme thinness. I often developed the impulse of ending my life. The old age of the kindest father checked me. I thought not of how bravely I would be able to die, but how he would not be able bravely to bear my loss. And so I ordered myself to live. For some-times even to live is to act bravely.

Of course, this could be fiction,[138] but I doubt it. Seneca's *Epistulae Morales*, an acknowledged landmark in the history of introspection, are to a marked

---

[137] See also T. Hill (2004: 151).

[138] Several scholars are sceptical about the psychological truth-value of Seneca's epistles: see e.g. Griffin (1976: 5): 'we must admit that Seneca's picture of his personality in the Letters lacks plausibility and consistency.' There are, of course, across the 124 letters 'fissures and slippages in the picture of the authorial self' (Edwards 1997: 33) and a concern on Seneca's part to play

degree an exploration of 'the notion of the self'.[139] The focus here on a central constituent of that self, the author's own moral agency, sits well with Seneca's emphasis on agency throughout his philosophical works, his dramas, and in the final act of *Hercules*. This extraordinarily difficult moment in the early life of Seneca described by the philosopher-dramatist towards the end of that life seems less self-fashioning and self-glorifying fiction, more perhaps the Rylean 'ghost in the machine' impelling the morally complex conclusion of this great play.[140]

different roles, sometimes 'the Stoic sage', sometimes 'the Stoic aspirant', sometimes 'the senator', etc., but they do not necessitate the reader's rejection of their introspective analyses, which Foucault saw as cardinal in the history of the self and which two millennia of readers have found helpful in their struggle to transform. Their introspective analyses help with other things, too, as my comments above try to show.

[139] Edwards (1997: 25); see also Foucault (1986).

[140] For the 'ghost in the machine', see Ryle (1949).

VI. The Myth before Seneca

ὁ κλεινὸς Ἡρακλῆς ποῦ κεῖνος ὤν;

Where is that famous Heracles?

Eur. *Herc.* 1414 (MS *L*)

salue, uera Iouis proles, decus addite diuis,
et nos et tua dexter adi pede sacra secondo.

Hail, true seed of Jove, the gods' augmenting glory,
Approach us and thy rites with favour and support.

Virg. *Aen.* 8.301–2

Hercules was a Roman mythic, religious, and cultural figure. Though in origin both an Etruscan (Hercle) and an ancient Greek hero (Heracles, sometimes spelt 'Herakles'), whose exploits date from Homer's *Iliad* (5.392–7, 18.117–19) and *Odyssey* (11.601–26, 21.25–30), and whose image appeared in Etruscan art from the sixth century BCE and on the coinage of Alexander the Great two centuries later,[141] Hercules was also profoundly Roman, and on every Roman citizen's lips when uttering the expletive, *mehercule* ('By Hercules!'). He pervaded Roman domestic spaces, a ubiquitous figure in the wall-paintings of Pompeii and Herculaneum (he was the legendary founder of the latter: DH 1.44.1). In lists of Roman deities he was often grouped with such figures as Castor and Pollux, Bacchus, Liber, Quirinus/Romulus (and occasionally Augustus) as a benefactor of mankind: see e.g. Cic. *ND* 2.62, *Tusc.* 1.28, Hor. *Odes* 1.12.25, 3.3.9–36, 4.8.28–34, *Ep. Mor.* 2.1.5–17, Philo *Emb.* 92; cf. Cic. *Off.* 3.25. The Augustan historian Livy (5.13.5–6) informs us that he was invoked in communal sacrifice and ritual in the first *lectisternium* in Rome in 399 BCE along with Apollo, Latona, Diana, Mercury, and Neptune.

Like other Roman deities, Hercules became embroiled in Roman politics. In late republican Rome he was associated with (*inter alios*) Mummius, Sulla, Crassus, Pompey, Julius Caesar, Marc Antony, and Octavian. Mummius dedicated a temple to Hercules Victor, following his Achaean triumph; Sulla dedicated the Temple of Hercules Magnus Custos in the Circus Flaminius (Ov. *Fas.* 6.209–12) and put the head of Hercules on his coinage; Pompey built/restored a temple to Hercules by the Circus Maximus (Vitr. 3.3.5, Plin.

---

[141] Stafford (2012: 145, fig. 5.2). I am indebted to Stafford's wide-ranging, informative account of Heracles throughout this section of the Introduction.

HN 34.57) and affixed his name to it; Marc Antony had coins minted with his image on one side and that of Anton, a legendary son of Hercules from whom he claimed descent, on the other;[142] Octavian entered Rome to celebrate his triple triumph in 29 BCE on the day (August 13) following the annual festival of Hercules Invictus (see below). In Virgil Hercules is made to function as a model both for Augustus (*Aen.* 6.791–805) and for his distant ancestor, Aeneas (*Aen.* 8.362–5);[143] his trans-global labours (*Aen.* 6.801) are used by the poet as *comparanda* to Augustan imperial expansion. Ovid, in a satiric denunciation of overreaching human ambition, conjoins Romulus, Bacchus, Hercules, and the deified Julius Caesar (*Am.* 3.8.51–2), but also pointedly proclaims the apotheosized Hercules an 'august' figure (*Met.* 9.270; cf. Livy 1.7.9). For Horace, although Hercules is introduced into the *Odes* (1.3.36) as a transgressor of divinely ordained boundaries, the apotheosized Hercules is the model and the mould for the new *princeps* (*Odes.* 3.3.9–12, 3.14.1–4), and the hero's labours (*Ep.* 2.1.10–12) are presented as analogue to Augustus' achievements. In Roman religious practice the cult of Hercules at Tibur seems to have been 'linked to Augustus'.[144] Horace, too (*Odes* 4.5.29–36), connects the worship of Hercules with that of the *princeps*.

Augustus was not the only early emperor associated with Hercules. Caligula sometimes appeared in public, dressed as Hercules 'with lion skin and club' (Philo *Emb.* 78, Dio 59.26.5ff.); Claudius is represented in Seneca's *Apocolocyntosis* as conducting law courts before the temple of Hercules in July and August (*Apoc.* 7.4). In the last years of his reign Nero associated himself with Hercules in several ways, including performing the part of *Hercules Insanus* onstage and being hailed as 'Nero Hercules' on his return from Greece (Suet. *Nero* 21.3, Dio 63.9.4, 20.5).[145] Nero's infancy was marked—so Tacitus (*Ann.* 11.11.3) and Suetonius (*Nero* 6.4) report—by the appearance of a serpent in his cot. But his prime 'Herculean' behaviours and his commissioning of coins *Herculi Augusto* postdate Seneca's *Hercules*.[146]

Even apart from this play Hercules was a presence in Senecan tragedy, sometimes as a minor figure in choral odes (*Pha.* 317–29, 807, *Med.* 634–42) or an exemplary one in an aria (*Tro.* 718–31), or a major and prophetic

---

[142] See Zanker (1988: 45–6), who also provides evidence of statues of Antony as Heracles/Hercules.

[143] Aeneas is associated with Hercules often in the *Aeneid*; see Rebegianni (2018: 133).

[144] Galinsky (1972: 139–40).

[145] The Neronian epigrammatist Lucillius (*Anth. Gr.* 11.184) also reports on 'fatal charades' modelled on Hercules' fiery death. For Nero and Hercules, see Champlin (2003: 135–8).

[146] For further associations between Nero and Hercules, see Fitch (1987a: 40), and Rebeggiani (2018: 130).

paradigm (*Ag.* 808–66, where a whole choral ode is devoted to him). He would be a presence, too—a recurring one—in Roman mosaics and in the sculptural reliefs of sarcophagi. He was a major cult figure in Rome. He was associated not only with the early removal of local monsters (Cacus: Virg. *Aen.* 8.190–267, Prop. 4.9, Ov. *Fas.* 1.543–80) but with ancient rituals (e.g. that of the Argei: Ov. *Fas.* 5.621–62). Women were excluded from his cult. Richardson (1992) lists in the city of Rome more than a dozen temples, shrines, or monuments to the hero, none more important than the Ara Maxima (*Ara Maxima Herculis Inuicti*). This most ancient and venerable place of Herculean worship, referenced by Virgil in *Aeneid* 8 (271–2), by Propertius in Book 4 (9.67–70), and by Ovid in *Fasti* 1 (581–2), was the venue for an annual sacrifice to Hercules Invictus on August 12 presided over (from 312 BCE) by the urban praetor, who acknowledged the Greek origins of the deity by performing the sacrifice in accordance with 'Greek rites' (*ritu Graeco*, Macr. 3.6.17). The Ara Maxima was situated within the *pomerium* of the original city in the Forum Boarium, where also (from the second century BCE) stood one of the three temples in Rome to Hercules Victor, underscoring Hercules as divine protector of that ancient market-place. Indeed according to Dionysius of Halicarnassus (1.40.6), writing in the latter part of the first century BCE, Hercules was worshipped throughout the whole of Italy. His rescue of Hesione from the sea-monster is even found in the early imperial white stucco reliefs decorating the walls and ceiling of the so-called 'Neo-Pythagorean Basilica' beneath the Porta Maggiore in Rome (perhaps mid first century CE). His conquest of death made him a fit subject for funerary reliefs.

Hercules' status in Seneca's play as a paradigm of local and trans-global achievement meriting divinity and of the conquest of death is thus a Roman moral and religious paradigm. It is also an imperial paradigm. At the time of this play's composition Augustus had already been deified, Caligulan deifications had been annulled, and the apotheosis of Claudius had either taken place or, if the play is Claudian rather than early Neronian, been foreshadowed (see e.g. *Pol.* 12.3–5). It is a paradigm which brings the disturbing narrative arc of this play—global, trans-world, and local victory followed by the killing of kin—home to Rome.[147]

A profoundly Roman figure, Hercules was also an aetiologically and semiotically complex one. As already noted, his origin was twofold.[148] He

---

[147] For Roman referentiality in this play, see Comm. *ad* 46–52.

[148] The view that Heracles/Hercules had his origin in the Phoenician god Melqart, who becomes identified with Heracles in the fifth century BCE, is not generally accepted: see Stafford (2012: 195).

came from: i. Etruria, where he was Hercle, son of the gods Tinia and Uni, a strong, heavily muscled figure often depicted in Etruscan art (sculpture, gems, vase-painting, mirror-cases) with lion skin and/or club, whose deeds earned him immortality; ii. Greece (Magna Graecia and the Greek mainland—the primary source, whence the Etruscan Hercle was derived), where he was Heracles, son of Alcmene and Zeus, a muscular figure equipped with lion skin and/or club, bow, arrows, sword, who eventually became a god himself with a goddess wife, Hebe ('Youth'). Alcmene was the granddaughter of Perseus and Andromeda and the daughter of Electryon, king of the Argolid (Tiryns/Mycenae/Argos), who was accidentally killed by Alcmene's husband, the general Amphitryon. Husband and wife fled to Thebes for purification, where Alcmene refused to consummate the marriage until Amphitryon had avenged the deaths of her brothers by destroying the Taphians and Teleboans. This he did, but just before his return Zeus, disguised as Amphitryon, impregnated Alcmene with a child, the demi-god Heracles. On the same night Amphitryon, having returned, impregnated his wife with the mortal Iphicles.[149] Myths of Heracles circulated in a variety of forms, but two important early events of Heracles' life which gained wide currency were the strangling of a pair of snakes sent by Hera to kill him when he was an infant,[150] and, when he was approaching adulthood, the choice of Virtue over Vice, who visited him in the guise of young women (Xen. *Mem.* 2.1.21–33).

Heracles' heroic career embraced many exploits of strength, courage, violence (just and unjust), and aetiological significance. The most popular accounts included physical encounters with evil or perjured kings (Busiris, Eryx, Emathion, Laomedon), centaurs (Nessus, centaurs of Mt. Pholoe), giants (Antaeus, Alcyoneus), gods (Nereus or Triton, Dis/Pluto, Hera, Achelous, Thanatos, Geras), and sons of gods (Cycnus, possibly the Moliones); participation in the Gigantomachy and the Argonautic expedition; rescue of distressed females (Alcestis and Hesione), heroes (Theseus), and Titans (Prometheus); enslavement to others (Queen Omphale of Lydia, King Eurystheus of the Argolid); the slaying of innocents (music teacher Linus, host Iphitus, heralds of Erginus); the founding or sack of cities (the many Heracleias, Troy, Elis, Pylos, Oechalia, Herculaneum); the creation of massive changes of landscape and seascape (the separation of Mt Ossa and Mt Olympus, the formation of the Strait of Gibraltar); the provision of

---

[149] See Gantz (1993: 1.374–8).   [150] See *Herc.* 213–22 and Comm. *ad loc.*

cosmic support (in place of Atlas); the institution of the Olympic Games.[151]
One should add to the above list Heracles' multitudinous sexual 'conquests'
(most remarkably, the bedding of the fifty daughters of Thespius)[152] and the
multitudinous children (primarily sons) generated. There were boyfriends,
too, most famously Hylas, whom he loses on the Argonauatic expedition
(Theoc. 13), but also including, at least according to Plutarch (*Erot.* 17,
Pelop. 18), his nephew Iolaus. The motivations behind the hero's diverse
exploits were inevitably also diverse; but vaingloriousness, vengefulness,
anger, lust, as well as the defeat of evil (a cult title was Ἀλεξίκακος, 'Deliverer
from Evil', another was Καλλίνικος, 'Fair Victor') and the taming or civilizing of the world seem frequently to have been part of the myths.

Homer signals from the start of the Greek tradition the moral ambivalence of Heracles, drawing attention to his assaults upon the gods and his
murder of innocents (*Il.* 5.392–404, *Od.* 21.22–30). He also emphasizes in
the *Nekuia* of the *Odyssey* (11.617–26) Heracles' performance of 'hard contests' (χαλεποὺς ἀέθλους, *Od.* 11.622), setting up Heracles' strength in
endurance as one of his defining features. He was indeed most celebrated
for his completion of the so-called 'labours' (μόχθοι/πόνοι/ἆθλοι), which
became the canonic 'twelve' in the aftermath of their depiction on the
metopes of the Olympian Temple of Zeus (*c.*460 BCE).[153] These were completed (some with the aid of his nephew) during the period of enslavement
to his cousin Eurystheus,[154] who had succeeded to the Argolid throne by
being born before Heracles—an event engineered by Hera/Juno.[155] The
order of the twelve labours varies.[156] Here is the sequence in Apollodorus
(2.5): 1. The Slaying of the Nemean Lion; 2. The Slaying of the Lernaean
Hydra; 3. The Capture of the Cerynitian/Arcadian Hind; 4. The Capture of
the Erymanthian Boar; 5. The Cleaning of the Stables of Augeas, king of
Elis; 6. The Shooting of the Stymphalian Birds; 7. The Capture of the Cretan
Bull; 8. The Capture of the Mares of Diomedes, king of the Bistones; 9. The

[151] See Comm. *ad* 68–74, 226–30, 235–40, 283–95, 465–71, 477–80, 480–9, 558–68, 838–49, 976–86, 1138–42, 1202–18.
[152] Apollod. 2.4.10. Some accounts reduce this to forty-nine: Paus. 9.27.6. More famous sexual conquests were Omphale, to whom Hercules was enslaved, and the Oechalian princess, Iole.
[153] See Comm. *ad* 213–48.
[154] The reason for Hercules' enslavement to Eurystheus varies. Euripides' Amphitryon con-tends that it was the price of his being able to return to Argos (*Herac.* 13–25). In Diodorus (4.10.7) and Apollodorus (2.4.12) the labours were dictated by the Delphic oracle as a path to apotheosis. In Apollodorus the enslavement, which follows Hercules' murder of his children, seems also to be a penalty for it.
[155] See *Herc.* 830 and Comm. *ad loc.*
[156] See Comm. *ad* 222–48, 222–5, 226–30, 231–4, 235–40, 241–8.

Taking of the War Belt of Hippolyte, queen of the Amazons; 10. The Capture of the Cattle of Geryon, a monster of triple form; 11. The Taking of the Golden Apples of the Hesperides; 12. The Capture of Cerberus, the three-headed hound of hell. The Capture of Cerberus, described at *Herc.* 782–827, is generally presented as the final labour; it features as twelfth in Hyginus (*Fab.* 30), Apollodorus (2.5.12), and Quintus of Smyrna (6.260–8), though it is number eleven in Diodorus Siculus (4.25.1–26.1). Bow and arrows are the weapons associated with Heracles in Homer (*Il.* 5.392–404, *Od.* 8.224–5, 11.601–8), but the club appears most frequently on the Olympian metopes and seems to be the weapon most tied to his identity.[157]

The Capture of Cerberus, which receives detailed narrative attention from Theseus in Act III of *Hercules*, is one of the most famous of the hero's labours; it is referred to from Homer onwards (*Il.* 8.367–8, *Od.* 11.623–6) and is often depicted on Greek vases. Indeed Heracles is a common subject of Greek vase-painting and temple sculpture, and one of the most frequent figures in Greek literature from Homer through archaic Greek epic,[158] Hesiod (*Theogony*), *The Shield of Heracles* and *The Catalogue of Women*, lyric (Archilochus, Stesichorus, Bacchylides, Pindar), elegy, tragedy (from Phrynichus onwards),[159] comedy, mythography, and history to Calli-machean hymn, Theocritean pastoral, and beyond. The apotheosis of Heracles is alluded to in Homer (*Od.* 11.602–4) and Hesiod (*Theog.* 950–5), where we learn also of his divine wife, Hebe, and forms the conclusion of Pindar's first *Nemean Ode* (69–72; cf. *Nem.* 10.17–18, *Isthm.* 4.55–60). The apotheosized hero even appears as a character in Sophocles' late fifth-century tragedy, *Philoctetes*, and indirectly (via a messenger's speech) in Euripides' *Heraclidae*. Sophocles' *Trachiniae*, which offers a brutal presenta-tion of Heracles, dramatizes the hero's unintended death at the hands of his last wife, Deianira, and his burning on Mt Oeta in Thessaly, both of which lurk in the background of Seneca's play. Heracles' madness and killing of his family are found early in the Greek tradition. The seventh/sixth-century lyric poet Stesichorus (Paus. 9.11.2) seems to testify to Heracles' murder of

---

[157] See *Herc.* 625 and Comm. *ad loc.*

[158] Among the authors of a *Heraclea*: Pisander of Rhodes (perhaps seventh century BCE), Panyassis of Halicarnassus (active in the first half of the fifth century BCE). For the edited frag-ments of the latter's poem, see Matthews (1974). Another Heraclean epic, *The Capture of Oechalia*, is attributed to the legendary Creophylus of Samos, alleged contemporary of Homer, but thought by some to be 'the fictitious eponym of a Samian rhapsodes' guild' (West 2003*a*: 21).

[159] Phrynichus' plays on Heracles were of such importance to the modern playwright, Tony Harrison, that he begins *The Labourers of Herakles* (1995) with a surviving fragment from Phrynichus' *Alcestis*, sung in turn by Labourers 1, 3, and 2, and then echoed by a voice from a silo.

his children and the sixth century *Cypria* mentions τὴν Ἡρακλέους μανίαν ('the madness of Heracles', *Argumentum* 4 West 2003*a*). In the early fifth century, Panyassis (Paus. 9.11.2) and Pherecydes (*FGrH* 3.F.14) seem to attest the familicide. Panyassis (frag. 2 West 2003*a*, Paus. 10.8.9) also refers to a visit by Heracles to Delphi, perhaps (West suggests *ad loc.*) 'to seek purification' after the familicide. Aeschylus, who alone of the three great Attic tragedians seems to have written no play on Heracles, did have the great hero rescue Prometheus in *Prometheus Unbound* (if that play is Aeschylean).

Our first detailed, extant testimony of Heracles' madness and killing of his children and wife is Euripides' *Heracles* (*c.*416 BCE), in which the positioning of the killings after the completion of the labours may be the dramatist's innovation, as most certainly is Euripides' introduction of the usurper Lycus and of Theseus, and the latter's offer of refuge and honours in Athens.[160] Bacchylides *Epin.* 5 seems to place the labours after the death of Megara, and some later accounts (Diodorus 4.10–11, Nicolaus of Damascus *FGrH* 90.F.13, Apollodorus 2.4.11–12) are clear in placing the madness and familicide before the labours. In Apollodorus the labours are prescribed by the Pythia at Delphi, which Heracles visits after the familicide (see Panyassis above). The Euripidean Theseus, of course, does not enter with Heracles, as in Seneca's play, but arrives much later to bring help. Euripides' major themes— humanity's relationship to the gods, madness and violence, 'virtue' (ἀρετή) and valour, glory, guilt, shame and suicide, family, friendship and trust—will be major themes of Seneca's play, where they will be Romanized, expanded, and given a different intellectual treatment and restructured dramatic form.

Heracles was a *dramatis persona* also in Euripides' *Alcestis*, *Auge*, and (if it is by him) *Pirithous*, and he figured in three known Hellenistic plays, entitled *Heracles*, and one entitled *Heracles Perikaiomenos*,[161] the contents of which, however, are unknown. The mad, filicidal Heracles appears on a

---

[160] Theseus' offer of honours and a home in Athens reflects the strong presence of Heracles in fifth-century Athens and Attica. In addition to cults, shrines, and altars in Attica, an annual festival (Heracleia) in Athens, and the sanctuary at Cynosarges (with gymnasium, temple, and grove), there were prominent sculptures in the city, including those of Heracles' labours (along-side the deeds of Theseus) on the Hephaesteum (*c.*450–440 BCE) facing the Agora. In part to underscore the association with Athens Euripides refers explicitly to the tradition that Heracles had been initiated into the Eleusinian Mysteries (see *Herac.* 613; see Comm. *ad* 299–302) before his descent into the underworld. In Euripides' earlier play, *Heracleidae* (*c.*430 BCE), the children of Heracles find refuge in Athens. For Euripides' innovative positioning of the famili-cide in *Heracles*, see e.g. Jebb (1892) and Bond (1981).

[161] The authors of these plays were Diogenes, Lycophron, Timasitheus, and Spintharos. A scholiast on Homer's *Odyssey* also ascribes a play involving Lycus and Heracles and the latter's filicide to Asclepiades of Tragilus. See further Fitch (1987*a*: 47).

well-known calyx-krater from Paestum (dated *c*.350), accompanied by Megara, Alcmene, Iolaus, and Mania (Madness), in a scene with significant differences from the Euripidean account,[162] though Euripides' *Heracles* was itself reperformed on the Hellenistic stage.[163]

But Heracles was not just a Greek tragic or epic figure. He was also (and frequently) a figure in Greek comic drama (old and middle), where his treatment was generally that of burlesque. From the early comic dramatist Epicharmus onwards Heracles was portrayed as gluttonous and/or lustful and/or prone to drunkenness—so regularly that Aristophanes praises himself in the parabasis of *Peace* (741–3) for driving from the stage the kind of stock Heracles in which Epicharmus and his successors seem to have revelled.[164] Nor was the drunken, gluttonous Heracles confined to comedy. He makes a celebrated appearance in *Alcestis*, cited above, one of Euripides' most famous plays. Satyr-drama, too, regularly featured Heracles in less than dignified mode. Sophocles, who wrote a tragedy *Heracles* and one entitled *Amphitryon* as well as *Trachiniae*, is also credited with having written a satyr-drama *Heracles*. Only *Trachiniae* has survived. The fifth-century dramatists Ion of Chios and Achaeus of Eretria both wrote satyr-dramas on Heracles entitled *Omphale*. His satyric and comic persona was to continue in the 'phlyax plays' of southern Italy and Sicily. One of its major writers, Rhinthon of Tarentum (*c*.300 BCE), is credited with both a *Heracles* and an *Amphitryon*.

There was another Heracles, too—one destined to have a substantial influence on Seneca—Heracles the philosophical paradigm. This other Heracles could be seen most overtly in Xenophon's *Memorabilia* (2.1.21–33), where the sophist Prodicus' story of the 'Choice of Heracles' is first told, viz. how Heracles, approached by Virtue (Ἀρετή) and Vice (Κακία) in the form of two young women, is persuaded by the former to pursue the part of Virtue.[165] From that point on Heracles was used by philosophers, especially Stoics and Cynics, as a paradigm of endurance, self-control, and the pursuit of virtue. Already Pindar had presented Heracles as *exemplum* of 'virtue'

---

[162] See Taplin (2007: 143–5), who suggests that the vase may combine elements of Euripides' treatment with features of some pre-Euripidean accounts.

[163] Billerbeck (1999*a*: 1), citing Sifakis (1967: 80 and 84), and Xanthakis-Karamanos (1980: 30).

[164] Aristophanes did, however, bring Heracles onstage in two of his extant comedies, *The Birds* and *The Frogs*. In the latter, too, there seems to be an allusion to Heracles' madness (564–8).

[165] American readers may be interested to know that the 'Choice of Hercules' was suggested by John Adams as a possible candidate for incorporation into the design of the Great Seal of the United States.

(ἀρετή), piety, and justice and a benefactor of humankind (*Nem.* 1.33–4, 66–72, *Isth.* 4.57). Euripides, too, began his *Heracles* with praise of him as civilizer of the world (*Herac.* 20), and the Theban chorus laud him for producing a 'calm life' (ἄκυμον...βίοτον, *Herac.* 698–9) for mortals through his slaying of fearsome beasts. Socrates' follower Antisthenes, who advocated the life of 'virtue', devoted three or four books to Heracles. The fourth century intellectualized Heracles further. Isocrates presented the hero in the Xenophontine mode as a paradigm of 'virtue' (ἀρετή) and of wisdom, honour, and justice (*Dem.* 8, 50, *Phil.* 110); the Cynic philosopher Diogenes of Sinope and his follower Crates saw him as a Cynic hero, an *exemplum* of freedom and of resistance to pleasure, avarice, lust, and hardship (DL 6.71, Dio Chrys. *Diog.* 8.27–35, Apul. *Flor.* 22.3–4). Heracles seems to have remained a Cynic hero into the Roman empire, since Epictetus names him first in a list of such heroes at *Discourse* 3.22.57. In the Hellenistic period Heracles' filicide, which receives extensive description in the anonymous *Megara* (17–28), does not seem to tarnish the hero's role as a model for the θεῖος ἀνήρ, the man who through his own deeds earns apotheosis; hence Theocritus (17.13–33) pictures Alexander the Great with Heracles. Theocritus is also picking up on the politicization of Heracles, with whom, as the coinage attests,[166] the Macedonian royal house and several Hellenistic kings claimed association, even that of descent. One of those kings, Eumenes II of Pergamum, commissioned *c.*170 BCE the baroque Altar of Zeus, on which is depicted Heracles fighting on the side of the Olympian gods in the Gigantomachy, even as his son Telephus receives an entire frieze in the Altar's courtyard narrating his birth to Heracles and Auge, his subsequent heroic life and the founding of Pergamum itself.

Heraclean pedigrees were not limited to Greeks. Several Romans, too, boasted a genealogical connection to (now) Hercules, including the entire Roman *gens* of the Fabii (Ov. *Fas.* 2.237). Each of the members of the first triumvirate developed strong associations with Hercules. Crassus held a great sacrifice and feast to celebrate Hercules' festival (Plut. *Crass.* 2.2); Pompey, as observed above, built a temple. Even Julius Caesar, who boasted a genealogical connection to Venus, created a relationship to Hercules by writing a poem in praise of him (Suet. *Iul.* 56.7). Marc Antony, his surviving co-consul of 44 BCE, went further by claiming descent from Hercules himself.[167] But in Hellenistic and late republican Rome no drama is attested on the hero-god. One of the tragedies of Naevius (*Aesiona*) featured Hercules

---

[166] See Stafford (2012: 145–50).   [167] See p. 58 above.

as a character, as did some plays of Accius (*Alcestis*, *Phinidae*, possibly *Philocteta*); but there is no evidence of a *Hercules*. Perhaps the nearest any of the republican dramatists seem to have come to such are the two plays entitled *Amphitruo*, one by the comic playwright Plautus, the other by Accius.[168] Only the former has survived.

There is, of course, the possibility that Hercules was the prime subject of a republican tragedy now lost.[169] He is clearly an important figure in pre-Augustan and Augustan authors, some of whom are referenced above. Cicero repeats Xenophon's account of Prodicus' tale of Hercules' 'Choice' (*Off.* 1.118), and later in the same work promotes Hercules as a civilization hero for undergoing 'the greatest toil and tribulation in order to save or help the whole world' (*pro omnibus gentibus...conseruandis aut iuuandis maximos labores molestiasque, Off.* 3.25). Perhaps a decade or so earlier, Lucretius, in a sustained attack on the insignificance of Hercules' labours, had dismissed Hercules' achievements as of little value in comparison with those of the divine Epicurus (5.22–54). Virgil follows Cicero in exalting the hero (in company with Liber) as conqueror and pacifier (*Aen.* 6. 801–3), and remover of monsters from the land (*Aen.* 8.184–275), but creates in him an ambivalent paradigm for both Augustus and the latter's putative ancestor, Aeneas.[170] Ovid makes much of Hercules, returning the Roman reader to Sophocles by penning a fictive letter from Deianira to her husband (*Heroides* 9)[171] and leaving the hero's apotheosis fittingly to his great poem of transformation (*Met.* 9.134–272). Ovid's poet-friend Carus wrote a *Hercules* (*Pont.* 4.16.7). In Ovid's Rome, however, the madness of Hercules seems to have been left to pantomime. *Hercules Furens* was danced by the pantomime 'star' Pylades both in the theatres and in Augustus' dining-hall, enlivened disconcertingly by the occasional shooting of arrows into the audience (Macr. *Sat.* 2.7.16–17).

Roman Stoics, too, embraced Hercules, including Seneca himself, who remarks on how Stoicism regarded Hercules and Ulysses as *sapientes* or 'sages', 'because they were unconquered by toils, despisers of pleasure and victors over all fears' (*inuictos laboribus et contemptores uoluptatis et uictores omnium terrorum, Const.* 2.1). Seneca expresses reservations about Hercules

---

[168] For arguments against the fragments of Accius' *Amphitruo* having any relevance for the subject-matter of Seneca's *Hercules*, see Fitch (1987a: 48). The contention of Tarrant (1978: 261), that an Augustan tragedy, inspired by Accius' *Amphitruo*, influenced Seneca in the composition of *Hercules* lacks both plausibility and any evidentiary base.

[169] See Fitch (1987a: 48–9).

[170] On the ambivalence of Hercules in *Aen.* 8, see Boyle (1999: 155).

[171] The letter is supposedly written as Hercules is dying from his wife's poisoned gift.

in the same treatise (*Const.* 2.1), and even uses him as a comic figure in his Menippean satire, *Apocolocyntosis*, where Hercules' role is that of 'the much travelled, monster-slaying Greekling, shockable, gullible, blustering, cowardly and ridiculously prone to believe in his own tragic image'.[172] But neither the reservations in *De Constantia Sapientis* nor the comic usage in his satire prevent Seneca from two of his strongest philosophical statements concerning the hero in *De Beneficiis*:

i. Hercules was a selfless protector of the good (*Ben.* 1.13.3):

> Hercules nihil sibi uicit. orbem terrarum transiuit non concupiscendo sed iudicando quid uinceret, malorum hostis, bonorum uindex, terrarum marisque pacator.

> Hercules conquered nothing for himself. He crossed the world not from lust for what he might conquer but from judgement thereto, foe of the wicked, protector of the good, pacifier of land and sea.

ii. Hercules is an image of the Stoic 'God', *Deus* (*Ben.* 4.8.1):

> hunc (Deum) et Liberum patrem et Herculem ac Mercurium nostri putant:...Herculem, quia uis eius inuicta sit quandoque lassata fuerit operibus editis in ignem recessura.

> Our school think of Him (i.e. God) as Father Liber and Hercules and Mercury:...as Hercules, because his power is invincible and, when it is exhausted from the performance of his works, will pass into the fire.

Seneca's *Apocolocyntosis* seems to have been written shortly after his *Hercules*; the *De Beneficiis* belongs to the closing years of Seneca's life. The disparate representations of Hercules contained in these two works, separated perhaps by close to a decade, index something of the cultural and religious complexity of the familicidal figure dramatized by Seneca in this tragedy.

---

[172] Eden (1984: 84). Eden adds: 'He has much in common with the Herakles of Aristophanes' *Ranae*.'

VII. The Play

> nunc hoc age, anime. non in occulto tibi est
> perdenda uirtus. approba populo manum.

> Now do your work, soul. Don't hide and squander
> Virtue. Have the people applaud your deeds.

Sen. Med. 976–7

It is a truism to say that *Hercules* is one of Seneca's intellectually most exacting and rewarding plays. It is Seneca's most focused dramatic investigation of a core value of his philosophical thinking and of Roman elite culture, namely *uirtus*, the ideal constituents of a *uir*, a 'man'.[173] That investigation joins with other areas of focus, some familiar from other plays, some not. Among the issues examined: violence, aggression, boundary violation, political power; megalomania, mental derangement, guilt, obsession, hate; divinity, heroism, ancestry, social identity, the longing for apotheosis, the imperatives of family and of self; the problematics of suicide, the semiotics of place, the bridge between sanity and madness, the repetition of history, the empire of death. Much of the distinctness of Seneca's examination of these issues arises from the play's palimpsestic nature.[174] Beneath the Senecan text lies the *Heracles* of Euripides, whose dramatization of the great hero's triumphant return from the underworld, slaughter of the usurping tyrant Lycus, descent into madness, and familicide informs Seneca's treatment.[175] Seneca's tragic output reveals profound knowledge of fifth-century Attic tragedy and this play is no exception.[176] Some Hellenistic and Augustan treatments may also have influenced Seneca.[177] But the play is neither Euripidean nor Greek. Seneca's *Hercules* is a Roman play, pervaded with Roman imagery and motifs, and explicitly modelled for a Roman audience and a Roman world.[178] Unsurprisingly: as the preceding section of this

---

[173] *Virtus* is translated throughout the play as 'virtue'. For a discussion of the semiotics of *uirtus*, see Comm. *ad* 35–40.

[174] As will become clear, by 'palimpsestic' I mean something different from, and more specific than, the 'ghostliness' or 'haunted' nature of theatrical production, the sense that it has all been seen before, which is often observed (see e.g. Carlson 2003: 1).

[175] Seneca knew Euripides well. He quotes from Euripides' tragedies several times in the prose works, including on one occasion (*Ep. Mor.* 115.14) in a Latin verse translation.

[176] So, too, Braden (1993: 246): 'there is no escaping Seneca's obvious reliance on Euripides' unforgettable but enigmatic play as his direct source.'

[177] See §VI above, pp. 65–6, and Fitch (1987a: 44–50). Dramas dealing with Hercules' madness seem to have been comparatively rare.

[178] For Roman referentiality in *Hercules*, see Comm. *ad* 46–52.

introduction has observed, the play's eponymous hero was a constitutive feature of Roman religious, political, and social life.

Act I: Juno, *Furor*, and Place

The play begins with a Roman deity, Juno, the goddess who begins the defining epic of Roman *imperium*, Virgil's *Aeneid*. And as might have been expected from the opening lines of Virgil's poem, where her wrath is posited as 'unforgetting' (*memorem*, *Aen.* 1.4), she is consumed with anger and hate (27–9):

> non sic abibunt odia. uiuaces aget
> uiolentus iras animus et saeuus dolor
> aeterna bella pace sublata geret.

> My hate will not just stop. My violent mind
> Will enact undying wrath, and savage pain
> Will banish peace and wage eternal wars.

The language is Virgilian.[179] The Roman audience know this goddess and her pathological *odium* and *ira* well. And enacting wrath, as readers of Seneca's *De Ira* would know, means exacting revenge (*Ira* 2.3.5). Her complaints, which occupy over half of her speech (1–74), would thus not have surprised. They are motivated, as they were in the *Aeneid* and in Ovid's *Metamorphoses*, by the pain, *dolor*, of personal injury, and are (at the macro level) about the disruption of cosmic order and (at the micro level) about place, *locus* (4). No longer 'both sister and wife of Jove' (*Iouis...et soror et coniunx*, *Aen.* 1.46–7), as she was in Virgil's great epic and elsewhere,[180] she is but *soror* only (the opening word of the play), and has lost her place in the skies and heaven to Jupiter's whores; hence her dramatic presence in Thebes (1–30). One of the offspring of the Theban whores, Hercules, is himself an agent of cosmic disorder, transgressing the boundaries of place, triumphing in the underworld and on earth, opening hell, making the sun shrink, and aiming at the conquest of heaven (30–74).[181] With self-conscious

---

[179] See Comm. *ad loc.*

[180] See Comm. *ad* 1–5. Note especially Ovid's echo at *Met.* 3.265–6 of Virgil's canonic self-description by Juno (*Aen.* 1.46–7) with the sarcastic supplement, *certe soror*, 'at least sister', to which Seneca seems to allude.

[181] The view of Shelton (1978: 21), that the final part of this section (63–74) presents the 'progressive stages in the development of Hercules' pride, ambition and madness' has little to commend it. For a refutation of the view, see Riley (2008: 67–8).

etymological irony Juno even criticizes herself for creating Hercules' 'glory' (36).[182] Her language becomes more turbulent and the emotionality increases in the second part of the speech (75–122), as the goddess plots her revenge and punishment, assailing the audience with an avalanche of imperatives, questions, jussive subjunctives, clipped indicatives, and assertive futures. Her aim is to use Hercules himself as the instrument of her vengeance, and, summoning the Furies to make both Hercules and herself mad, she predicts and prescripts the filicide to come and the role of Hercules' *uirtus* in the slaughter. The maddened Juno notes the dawn and lets the play begin. It is her play; for the script which she has written will be performed. Her exit with the Furies into the royal palace (so I interpret) signals where the *locus* of the slaughter will be.[183]

Dramatically the prologue is 124 lines of rhetorical and visual energy, moving from the raging queen of heaven alone onstage beneath the still darkened night sky, which she hates, to (if one accepts this edition's dramaturgy) a spectacular finale in which a troop of Furies enters, perhaps through trapdoors, and dominates the stage, hair flaming and bristling with snakes. They brandish snake-whips and blazing torches, and infuriate Juno herself. The oratorical pace of Juno's whole speech is rapid and forceful. Each new section opens with a potent phrase or question (19, 30, 46, 63, 75, 86, 100, 112, 123), and often the sections themselves close trenchantly with rhetorical and dramatic 'point' (46, 63, 74, 85, 99, 112). This linguistic energy is like that of parturition, designed clearly to give birth to the play itself, even as the prologue not only prescripts the action to follow but, through its focus on Juno's hatred of Hercules, displays one of the structural principles of the whole tragedy. For all the speaking characters who enter this play will be defined by their relationship to its titular character:[184] from divine enemy (Juno), foster-father (Amphitryon), and wife (Megara) to human enemy (Lycus) and companion and friend (Theseus). Together with Hercules they will constitute six *dramatis personae*,[185] who will probe the relationship between identity and place.[186]

---

[182] See Comm. *ad loc.*

[183] On the first act of *Hercules*, see Sampson (2017: 18–23), who emphasizes the theme of cosmic and domestic disorder.

[184] For the view that identity in Senecan tragedy is a relational phenomenon, see Calabrese (2017).

[185] Astutely termed 'six characters in search of a *locus*': J. A. Smith (1997: 34). Smith's comment, of course, alludes to Luigi Pirandello's *Six Characters in Search of an Author* (1921), a seminal, modernist play concerned with such 'Senecan' issues as theatre, self, and identity.

[186] Much bruited in the ancient world from Homer's *Odyssey* (*Od.* 9.504–5) to Cicero's *Academica*, in which it is claimed that Varro's writings taught Romans 'to recognize who and where we were' (*qui et ubi essemus agnoscere*, 1.9). Notably Virgil signs off the *Georgics* with

Juno will not appear as a character again, though the actor playing her undoubtedly will (he probably also takes the roles of Lycus and Hercules).[187] That is to say, she is a protatic character. Euripides' *Heracles* does not begin with a protatic figure; it begins with Amphitryon, who will have an important role in the action of the drama and who provides in his prologue essential background information for the comprehension of the play and establishes the stage-setting as Thebes. Juno also provides background information and establishes the stage-set (20), but she is not limited to that role. Her protatic status has the effect of separating the prologue from the rest of the drama, giving it a more pronounced metatheatrical function than that served by Euripides' prologue. Part of that function may be seen in her introduction of a pattern of language, imagery, and motifs, which will be repeated and echoed later in the play.[188] Part may be seen in her inauguration of a tone, even an atmosphere, of high emotionality and passion, which will dominate the succeeding acts of the drama. This soaring tone may even extend into the articulation of a poetics of sublimity,[189] as Juno's cosmic allusions and her descriptions of heaven, earth, and hell both signal and create the highest of aesthetic registers. This sublimity foreshadows and seems to characterize the great speeches of Hercules, a transgressor of boundaries like sublimity itself.

There is another signal issue. Seneca has protatic characters opening plays elsewhere in his *corpus*: viz. the Ghost of Thyestes in *Agamemnon*, and the Ghost of Tantalus (together with a Fury) in *Thyestes*. And in each of them, as here, one main effect is a pronounced metatheatricality, seen especially in their providing in advance the script for the play, while being driven by passion—clearly, in the cases of the Ghost of Tantalus and Juno, by *furor*. *Furor*, 'rage/madness', was both a destructive and creative force, one commonly regarded in the ancient world not only as the motor for

reference to his 'place' (*Geo.* 4.563–4), as do Propertius with the *Monobiblos* (1.22.9–10) and Horace with his first three books of odes (*Odes* 3.30.10–12). To Cicero in *Pro Archia* (20) Ennius was *Rudinus homo*, 'the man from Rudiae'.

[187] See Comm., 'Disposition of Roles', p. 273.

[188] Among these motifs, those of 'place' (*locus*), 'impiety' (*impietas*), 'hate' (*odium*), 'violence' (*uiolentia*), 'anger' (*ira*), 'pain' (*dolor*), 'glory' (*gloria*), 'virtue' (*uirtus*), 'divinity' (*deus*), 'the monstrous' (*monstrum*), 'covenant' (*foedus*), 'death' (*mors*), 'pride' (*superbia*), 'hand' (*manus*), 'power' (*regnum*), 'delusion' (*error*), 'madness/rage' (*furor*), 'victory', 'conquest', 'vengeance', and 'war' (*uincere, uictor, poena, bellum*). Imagery introduced includes (but is not restricted to) military, Roman, and legal imagery, See Comm *ad* 1–5, 19–29, 35–40, 40–6, 46–52, 52–6, 57–63, 63–8, 77–83, 92–9, 109–12, 112–18, 118–22, 123–4.

[189] See Littlewood (2017: 154–8).

wide-spread devastation but as the affective base of poetic composition. So Cicero testifies (*Diu.* 1.80):[190]

negat enim sine furore Democritus quemquam poetam magnum esse posse, quod idem dicit Plato.

For Democritus says that no one can be a great poet without *furor*, and Plato says the same.

Seneca concurs at *De Tranquillitate Animi* 17.10–11. Juno is not simply a 'fate-figure', speaking what will happen, *fatum*, playing a dark version of the Virgilian or Stoic Jupiter. The fury in the goddess seems in part the creative *furor* of the poet-dramatist,[191] driving the created play into existence and anticipating, even as it prescripts, the dramatic action itself. Juno even invokes the Furies like a poet invoking the Muses (*incipite, famulae Ditis,* 'Begin, handmaids of Dis' 100), while making it clear through *famulae,* 'handmaids', that she is their superior.[192] Immediately after her dramatized infuriation by them (100–12) she announces the plot of her and Seneca's play (113–23):

> natos reuersus uideat incolumes precor
> manuque fortis redeat. inueni diem,
> inuisa quo nos Herculis uirtus iuuet.
> me uicit? et se uincat et cupiat mori
> ab inferis reuersus. hic prosit mihi
> Ioue esse genitum. stabo et, ut certo exeant
> emissa neruo tela, librabo manu,
> regam furentis arma, pugnanti Herculi
> tandem fauebo. scelere perfecto licet
> admittat illas genitor in caelum manus.
>   Mouenda iam sunt bella.

> I pray he return to see sons unharmed
> And come back strong of hand. I've found the day
> When Hercules' hated virtue may delight me.
> Did he conquer me? Let him conquer himself
> And want death on return from hell. Let it help me

---

[190] See e.g. Plato *Ion passim, Apol.* 22a–c, *Men.* 99c–e. Cicero also makes it clear that such *furor* was of the praiseworthy kind. He conceives of it as a 'divine power' (*uis diuina, Diu.* 1.80). See also Stat. *Theb.* 12.808.

[191] See further pp. 124–6 below.   [192] See Frangoulidis (2020: 147).

Now that he's born from Jove. I'll stand and aim
With my hand, so shafts fly sure from his bow.
I'll guide the mad man's weapons. At last I'll side
With Hercules in the fight. When the crime's done,
His father may admit those hands to heaven.
      Let war now begin.

Mouenda iam sunt bella, 'Let war now begin'. The echo of Virgil's commencement of the 'Iliadic *Aeneid*' (*Aen.* 7.45) underscores the metapoetics
of Juno's and Seneca's phrase.[193] In a sense what Juno is doing in the prologue, as she 'performs' her anger (*aget...iras*, 27–8),[194] hatred, and rage is
what Seneca will later do in *Epistulae Morales* 94 (59–69): she is analysing
the career of a so-called 'Great Man', one of the *magni felicesque*. Seneca in
Ep. Mor. 94 focuses on Alexander, Pompey, Caesar, and Marius, Juno here
on Hercules; both see their respective objects of analysis not as conquering
but as conquered, conquered by desire and ambition to become violators of
boundaries. They see them as men who commit violence upon nature.[195]
Juno's action at the conclusion of the analysis is to punish Hercules by
bringing into existence a series of events in which he will turn his violence
upon himself. These events are a play by Seneca, exemplifying what she has
said and dramatizing what she has prescribed.[196] As in other Senecan tragedies, most notably in *Agamemnon*, *Medea*, and *Thyestes*, *furor* begets the
drama.[197]

Ode I and Act II: Dawn to Imminent Execution

Seneca pays particular attention to choral ode and act interrelations, often
using the final words of an act to drive the succeeding ode into existence.
Thus the opening word of Ode 1, *iam*, 'now', picks up Juno's *iam* of 123, as if
the Chorus were taking dramatic direction from Juno herself. Military
imagery follows, developing Juno's programmatic *bella* (123). As their references to Theban topography and history display, the Chorus is a group of
Thebans, and, unlike their counterparts in Euripides' *Heracles*, they show no

---

[193] Cf. Trinacty (2014: 135–6).   [194] See Comm. *ad loc.*
[195] *Ipsi Naturae uim parat*, 'He threatens violence against Nature herself', Seneca writes of
Alexander (*Ep. Mor.* 94.63).
[196] For Juno as tragedian, see Littlewood (2004: 120); for Juno as author, see Schiesaro
(2003: 186).
[197] See further below, pp. 124–6.

indication of being elderly or frail. Their entrance song with its soft, anapaestic rhythms is calm and reflective,[198] even quietly joyous as it delineates
the breaking of dawn and the accompanying rural activity; its lyric simplicity effects a clear tonal contrast with the turbulent passions, high emotionality, and poetic grandeur of the encompassing acts. Juno's final subject, the
light of dawn (*clarescit dies… Titan lucidus*, 'The day starts to glow; | Bright
Titan', 123–4), opens the ode, which bursts into an imagistic description of
the stars withdrawing like military troops before the rising sun (125–36),
followed by a sharp focus on the rural world, on man, animal, bird, awake
and filled with life in their engagement with 'nature' (137–58). But beneath
the lyrical beauty, the cosmic order and cyclicity lurk the tragic tales of
Phaethon, Pentheus, and Philomela and the burning of Hercules on Mount
Oeta,[199] all pointers to a bloody calamity to come.

The Chorus' tone becomes moral and critical as they move into a sharply
satiric mode,[200] and a contrast is made between the 'carefree peace' of the
rural world, Virgil's Epicurean ideal of *secura quies* (175 and *Geo.* 2.467),
and the anxieties and vices (hope, fear, ambition, greed, self-delusion,
corruption) generated by urban life (159–77). Overt didacticism ensues:
the fixity and inevitability of death generate imperatives: live joyously in the
present (*dum fata sinunt, uiuite laeti*, 178), unobserved, humbly and secure,
for 'spirited virtue', *uirtus animosa*, falls (178–201). Notable in the ode is
the progression from the natural to the human world, from the order of the
firmament to the order of human rural activities, which are then contrasted
with urban activities driven by hope, fear, and false values, and patently
transgressive of the rhythms and order of the cosmos. A sense of urgency
develops towards the end of the choral song, when the Chorus focus on
time, an existential integral to nature itself and underlying the ode from
its starting point in the most particular, present time of dawn (*iam…
iam…iam*).

The ode merits the audience's intellectual attention. In Euripides' *Heracles*
the Chorus of frail old men sympathize in the parodos with the desperate
plight of Heracles' family and offer strong resistance to Lycus in their
encounter with him. Seneca's Chorus present a position of political quietism

---

[198]   For the semiotics of the anapaestic metre here, see Comm. *ad* 125–204 (introd.).

[199]   See Comm. *ad* 125–31, 132–6, 146–51. There may also lurk the bloody killings of Virgil's
ninth *Aeneid* (see Comm. *ad* 125–31).

[200]   For Senecan tragedy's appropriation here of 'the satiric mode', see Cowan (2017: 106–9).
Cowan describes *Herc.* 159–73 as 'a satiric cityscape as hectic as Lucilius frag. 1228–34 Marx,
Horace *Satires* 2.6.23–31 or Juvenal 3, peopled with Horatian misers and downtrodden clients
straight out of Martial and Juvenal.'

in their opening lyric and a view of the world antithetic to the values of Hercules, who is addressed at 186 and clearly referred to in the criticism of *uirtus animosa* (201). Hercules is also criticized through one of the ode's principal subtexts, viz. the parodos of Euripides' *Phaethon*, a 'dawn ode', which ironically celebrates the prospective marriage of Phaethon, the paradigm of overreaching ambition, on the eve of his fatal celestial ride.[201] Like Phaethon, Hercules will attempt but fail to replace his heavenly father (*Herc.* 963–73). The entrance of the Chorus in *Hercules* has clear 'dramatic' motivation (the heralding of dawn announced by Juno at 123–4), but its primary function, like that of all Senecan opening choral odes, seems thematic. It provides the audience with a critical frame for the prologue's presentation of Hercules' *uirtus* by linking Hercules' ambition and values to the vices of the city, and by setting up as a preferable mode of life a quasi-Epicurean ideal of withdrawal, peace, and isolation more in accord with the natural rhythms of the cosmos. To many members of Seneca's original audience much of what the Chorus advocate would have smacked of Virgil's denunciation of urban life at the end of *Georgics* 2 (458–540) and of Horace, whose opening priamel, *Odes* 1.1, seems imitated in the second half of this ode and whose overt rejection of his contemporaries' pursuit of athletic, political, or military glory lies beneath the surface of this choral song.[202]

Especially subtle is Seneca's use of imagery, as the Chorus transfer the permeating military imagery of the prologue (29–33, 44–54, 75–85, 116–23), which underscored the theme of cosmic disruption, to the natural movements of the heavens (125–36), and relocate Juno's focus on law and its breach (49) to one on the existential, unbreachable laws governing human life (189–91). Juno's concluding reference to Titan (124) is picked up (133) to show a different, more ordered world than that filling Juno's mind. The 'whores' of this world are not erotic rivals translated to heaven (5) but nightingales nurturing their young (149). *Virtus* is not something to be worshipped (39) or hated (115), but, at least in its 'spirited' form (*uirtus animosa*), to be shunned as lethal (201). The focus on *uirtus* will lead to the discussion of Hercules' *uirtus* and *uirtus* itself in the following act (252, 325, 340, 433–5, 476). But what would perhaps have impressed a Roman

---

[201] See Comm. *ad* 125–204 (introd.).

[202] See Comm. *ad* 159–61, 162–74, 164–74, 178–82, 192–6, 197–201. One might note here Seneca's remark on the process of 'imitation' (*Ep. Mor.* 79.6): *praeterea condicio optima est ultimi; uerba parata inuenit quae aliter instructa nouam faciem habent*, 'Moreover the position of last (being the last writer) is the best; he finds words prepared which, arranged differently, have a new look.'

audience most powerfully is the strong personal note at the end of the ode (197–201),[203] which, though not without its own ambiguities, seems designed both to signal the Chorus' commitment to the stated ideals and to impress the audience with the importance of those ideals for an evaluation of the dramatic action. Indeed even metrically this ode proves harbinger of what is to come. The anapaestic metre, in which the Chorus sing, will return in the final ode of the play, where what began as the metre of a choral parodos becomes the metre of collective lamentation. As always in Senecan tragedy, the interrelationship of act and choral ode is essential to dramatic meaning.

The Chorus announce (in vivid and semiotically resonant language: 202–4)[204] the entry of five new dramatic figures, Amphitryon, Megara, and the latter's three sons, to set in motion the second act, which will comprise two scenes. The two scenes take the audience directly to Euripides, rewriting the dialogue and action of the prologue and first two episodes of his *Heracles*. Scene i (205–331) starts with consecutive appeals for Hercules' return and passionate, allusive statements of political, moral, and/or personal malaise from Amphitryon and Megara (205–308). The sudden move to Euripides' *Heracles* (it has been absent so far) has a strong metadramatic effect, making the audience aware of the specific tradition which the play inherits and rewrites.[205] Part of the function of the initial scene is clearly expositional, almost prologic: viz. to lay out the current situation in Thebes, completely unnoted in Juno's actual prologue. The local political upheaval is described (249–78), not immediately but rather late in Amphitryon's speech, as in Euripides (*Herac.* 26–42), but in greater (and occasionally more gory) detail than in the Euripidean play and with increased rhetoric and moral outrage.

And there is the issue of Amphitryon's opening catalogue of Hercules' labours (231–48), a list of deeds of glory which Euripides assigns to a choral ode (*Herac.* 359–435). The labours seem to be given strong emphasis here partly perhaps to give dramatic body to the *uirtus animosa* just referenced by the Chorus (201). Many of the labours consist in the slaying of monstrous beasts quite other than the animals and birds described in the Chorus' pastoral idyll. For some, the inversion of the gentle creatures of the 'Dawn Ode' may have contained the suggestion that the pastoral idyll itself

---

[203] See Comm. *ad loc.*

[204] See Comm. *ad loc.*

[205] See J. A. Smith (1997: 62). The metadramatic effect is underscored, too, by the use of metadramatic language: see Comm. *ad* 202–4.

was made possible by Hercules' removal of *monstra* from the world. But perhaps for most, what Amphitryon's catalogue does is create a tower of achievement momentarily to be admired but ultimately to be questioned, even perhaps brought to nothing, by Hercules' subsequent slaughter of kin.[206] In the Greek tragedy it is Heracles himself who questions the value of his labours, ironically arguing for their worthlessness if they come at the cost of the death of his children (*Herac.* 574–82). Seneca lays the ground for the audience's interrogation of the labours by having Amphitryon follow his catalogue with a simple, biting question (249): *quid ista prosunt?* ('What good is served by this?).

The question is attended by a highly emotional statement of the crime, injustice, murder, and revolutionary mayhem stemming from Hercules' absence from Thebes. The audience have already been told (in a passage echoing the language of the preceding choral ode: *secura…requies*, 208/212; cf. *secura quies*, 175) that the one thing which Hercules has *not* generated through his labours is 'carefree peace/rest'. Indeed Amphitryon will remain a staunch advocate in the play for *quies*, the first ode's central value.[207] But here he is concerned with more than the absence of rest; he is describing massive moral and social turmoil. Climaxing his speech with a direct address to the fallen Theban people, perhaps to the Chorus themselves (*Cadmea proles…*, 'Seed of Cadmus…', 268), he concludes with a desperate prayer that Hercules return as 'Saviour' (*Sospes*, 277).[208] His desperation and hope are continued by Megara (279–308), who immediately joins in what is becoming a ritualistic evocation of the 'dead' hero, inheriting Amphitryon's language and transforming it. But her intensely emotional speech, which dwells upon the celebrations awaiting her husband's return, ends in apparent despair.[209]

One constituent of Amphitryon's self-presentation in Euripides' play is absent from the Senecan treatment: the longing of his son and himself for Argos, Amphitryon's native city (13–20). The only city Seneca's Amphitryon mentions is Thebes. Noteworthy, too, is that Seneca begins his opening Amphitryon-Megara scene, as Euripides does not, with prayers—prayers by Hercules' family for the hero's return, which certainly occur in Euripides' play but much later and in a different order (see on 205–78). Prayer will

---

[206] See below.
[207] See Comm. *ad* 924–6, 1048–53.   [208] See Comm. *ad loc.*
[209] See Comm. *ad loc.*

have a major structural role in this play.[210] The rest of the scene (309–28) falls into the common Senecan category of a 'Passion-Restraint' scene (cf. Acts II of *Phaedra, Agamemnon, Troades, Medea, Thyestes*, also Act III of *Troades*), in which Amphitryon attempts to restrain the intense and turbulent emotions of Megara, who is a more passionate figure than in Euripides and who seems to display a profound despair not evident in the Greek tragedy.[211] In the other Passion-Restraint scenes in Senecan tragedy the dialogue involves characters of different social status, which is not the case here: an aristocratic 'father-in-law' attempts to restrain his son's aristocratic, formerly royal wife, whose intense passion matches that of Juno in the prologue, maintaining the high emotional register of the play.

As in Act II of *Medea* and Act III of *Troades*, the Passion-Restraint scene leads to confrontation with a 'tyrant', here the new ruler of Thebes, a self-proclaimed anti-Hercules figure who appears onstage as if in ironic fulfilment of Megara's invocation of her husband. Scene ii (332–523), the main body of the act, is the well-known 'Lycus Scene', which is prefaced by a description of the usurper's entrance (329–31). The whole scene is brilliantly constructed and much more varied in its dramatic tone and techniques than the opening scene of the act. An entrance-monologue/closed soliloquy (332–57) by Lycus, 'Mr. Wolf',[212] begins the scene with a fascinating revelation of the tyrant's values, fears, and inner self. It is followed by a double *agon*, two carefully constructed, interactive dialogues between Lycus and Megara (358–438) and Lycus and Amphitryon (439–94), involving stichomythic exchanges, *antilabe*, short speeches, 'Stichworttechnik' (see on 422–38) and 'trigger-words', in which the new king attempts, as he does not in Euripides, to win Megara as wife. In the process, as happens in all such scenes in Senecan tragedy involving monarchs, Lycus displays his character, values, and attitude to power. He displays, too, a Roman obsession with a lack of social pedigree (*nouitas*) and with his own individual 'virtue' (*uirtus*) or 'manliness'. In Euripides, Lycus from his entry at *Herac.* 140 onwards is only interested in killing off Heracles' family. For Seneca's Lycus that is a fall-back plan (350–1). He is much more concerned to shore up his social status and civic authority through marriage to the surviving princess (344–8), from whom he might get royal offspring (494).

The Megara who confronts him, however, has dropped the earlier pessimism concerning her husband (308). Parading an optimistic loyalty to

---

[210] Prayer opens Acts II, III, and IV and closes Act II. Prayer also opens the great ecphrastic narrative of Theseus in Act III (658–61).

[211] See Comm. *ad* 305–8.   [212] See Comm. *ad* 329–31.

Hercules, she successfully resists the 'tyrant',[213] drawing attention not only to Lycus' bloody killing of her kin but to Thebes' impious and self-destructive history (384–96), which will recycle itself in Lycus;[214] she even threatens the tyrant with death at her hands (495–500). When she embraces the altar, Lycus, driven to his fall-back plan by Megara's potentially lethal aggression, resolves to destroy the whole family by burning Megara, Amphitryon, and the children in the temple behind them. He seeks to reduce the cosmic achievements of Hercules to the death of his family in a single place (*unus...locus*, 508).[215] Rejecting Amphitryon's offer to be the first to die, he exits to sacrifice to Neptune (501–15). The scene and act, however, conclude not with Lycus' exit but with Amphitryon's second prayer to Jupiter and an invocation of Hercules, followed by ominous sounds, perhaps heralding an epiphany (516–23). One salient aspect of Amphitryon's short speech is his cynicism about the gods as guardians of justice: 'Why invoke the gods in vain?' (*Quid deos frustra precor?* 519), he asks. The question could have been asked in any of Seneca's tragedies.[216]

Both scenes of Act II continue and develop the play's exploration of social, moral, genealogical, and geographical 'place'. They are also dramatized in relation to, and have a strong bearing on, the play's evaluation of the nature and identity of Hercules, whose heroism is both celebrated and problematized in the act's opening scene and debated along with his *uirtus* and divine paternity in the ensuing exchanges between Lycus, Megara, and Amphitryon. Indeed Lycus, who seems to have been played by the actor later playing Hercules,[217] provides what an ancient audience may have viewed (at least initially) as a negative version of Hercules, an *exemplum* of false *uirtus*, physical force wrongly and tyrannically used. The play, however, will show a continuity between the figures of Lycus and Hercules rather than a disjunction. Even Lycus' murderous impiety (503–8) will be repeated in Hercules' dramatized behaviour (920–4, 1036–8).[218]

---

[213] For this motif in Senecan tragedy, see Comm. *ad* 414–21.

[214] The *semper idem* theme (the repetition of the past), common in Senecan tragedy, is raised here in respect of Lycus' forthcoming fate, but obviously predicts ironically the familicide of Hercules. The theme, however, seems more muted in this play than in the other tragedies.

[215] The 'place' includes the temple behind him and the theatre in which the tragedy is being performed. See Comm. *ad loc.*

[216] See Comm. *ad loc.*

[217] See Comm., 'Disposition of Roles'. The same actor may also have played Juno.

[218] For the many parallels between Lycus and Hercules, see A. Rose (1979–80: 137–8), and Bexley (2022: 176–8).

The theatrical energy of the two scenes is evident. Both scenes pick up
and expand the dynamic impetus of the prologue, transforming Hercules'
absence from Thebes and Juno's ominous threats into a different kind of
danger for the hero's family, incineration in their temple of refuge, left as the
climactic problem to be resolved by a Hercules. The act's final sounds signal
the imminence of the problem's resolution. It is noticeable how the act
begins and ends with Amphitryon, who is being 'groomed' to play a much
more important role in this play than in Euripides and whose second invocation of Jupiter *rector* (516–19) rounds off the whole act with a plangent
echo of his initial, more optimistic prayer (205–7), but one which the audience know will immediately be fulfilled. The 'fire' threatened by Lycus (*igne
subiecto*, 508) will be extinguished by Hercules as surely as the 'stray fires'
(*uagos…ignes*, 126–7) of the night sky were extinguished by dawn.

Ode II and Act III: Hercules and Hell

The second choral ode, the 'Hercules Ode', like the final ode at 1054–1137
and several others in Senecan tragedy,[219] commences with apostrophe. The
apostrophe is to Fortune. The Chorus have been onstage throughout the
long second act and, far from interrupting the action at an 'inopportune
moment',[220] they respond to the ambiguous signs described by Amphitryon
at the end of Act II and sing a song of protest, laudation, and exhortation in
respect of Hercules. Their tone is one of utter seriousness, as the apostrophe
to Fortune is immediately transformed into a proclamation of Hercules'
unjust treatment (524–5) and a protest against the burdens imposed upon
him, in which they nominate several of his 'labours', including the most
recent, his *catabasis*, the descent into hell (526–57). The Chorus' criticism of
Hercules evident in the opening ode has not disappeared entirely, since they
question the purpose of his *catabasis* (547–9). The protest gradually merges
into exhortation, as the Chorus narrate Hercules' past defeat of the death-
god and plead for the hero's return to the upper world (558–68). A moral
exemplum follows (569–91), the case of Orpheus, who successfully overcame death through the power of his song and serves as precedent for the
conquest of death through *uires*, i.e. through the manifestation of *uirtus* in
victorious physical force (590–1):

---

[219] See Comm. *ad* 524–91 (introd.).   [220] As Eliot (1951c: 69) notoriously contended.

quae uinci potuit regia cantibus,
haec uinci poterit regia uiribus.

The palace one could conquer with song,
That palace one can conquer with force.

The analogy between song/poetry and physical force may have struck a discordant note with some members of Seneca's audience,[221] but these triumphalist final lines are not opaque. They provide a formal, ritualistic
ending to a formal, ritualistic ode, which is in part prayer—a prayer and an
exhortation for Hercules' safe return from hell. The use of the Orphic paradigm, of course, both reflects what the Chorus themselves are attempting to
do (draw Hercules back from the dead) and augurs ill for what will ensue.
Orpheus himself returned from the land of the dead but lost his loved one
in the process. And any recollection of what followed the 'Hercules Ode'
(808–66) of *Agamemnon* (if, as seems likely, that play predated this one)
would have further underscored this ode as pointer to the disaster to come.
But the triumphalist tone remains. The semiotics of Seneca's adopted metre
are relevant here. The lesser asclepiad, famously used by Horace in *Odes*
3.30 as the metre of the poet's conquest of death,[222] underscores the triumph
over the underworld for which the Chorus pray and which Hercules' entry,
as the final lines are being sung, spectacularly displays.

'Spectacularly' is used advisedly. The audience's first sight of Hercules is a
scene of literally and emblematically 'monstrous' visual power. The stage
directions in this edition's translation are as follows:

AMPHITRYON, MEGARA, *and her* SONS *stand by the temple doors under
the watchful eyes of* LYCUS' GUARDS. *Also present are the* CHORUS. *Enter
from stage right (outside Thebes)* HERCULES, bearded, wearing a lion skin
draped over his left shoulder, and equipped with bow, quiver, arrows, club,
and sword. He is accompanied by THESEUS. They drag a movable platform onto the stage behind them. On it is a representation of the hell-
hound CERBERUS in chains.

The supra-human nature of the spectacle is a theatrical index of the supra-
human figure presented to the audience, who, almost as if in response to the
Chorus' final words, enters in victorious and triumphant mode with the

---

[221] Especially those who had recently read Virgil's *Eclogues* (see *Ecl.* 9.11–13).
[222] See Comm. *ad* 524–91 (introd.). Cf. the use of the lesser asclepiad in the 'Processional
Ode' of *Medea* (56–74, 93–109) and in the 'Hippolytus Ode' of *Phaedra* (753–60, 764–82,
785–823), where the celebratory semiotics of the metre are also followed by catastrophe.

captured Cerberus and with Theseus. This is the first climax of the play, awaited and anticipated from Juno's prologue onwards. It manifests itself visually not only in the grand spectacle of Cerberus in chains but in the costume of Hercules himself, which, though not unexpected, seems index of the hero's unique status on the boundary between animal, human, and divine.[223] It manifests itself verbally in the deliverance of a prayer to Phoebus, 'lord of light',[224] to Jupiter and to Neptune, in which Hercules begs forgiveness for his bringing hell to earth (592–604). He raises his hands high to heaven, realizing in powerful fashion the soaring verticality of the Roman theatrical space. His next entrance, too, will feature prayer (900–8) and again a dramatic employment of vertical space. This is a hero conscious of his relationship to gods (and an actor conscious of the semiotics of space). He tells the audience about himself, moving into soliloquy, as he broods on his obsession with Juno, his conquest of the underworld—*morte contempta redi*, 'I spat on death and returned' (612)—and his preparedness for any further trials; he even boasts to himself that he 'could have reigned' (*regnare potui*, 610),[225] supplanting Dis, i.e. 'dire Jove' himself. He sees Lycus' soldiers by the temple, who rapidly disappear (616–17), is greeted and embraced by Amphitryon, learns from him of recent events in Thebes, briefly addresses him and Megara, and exits (with Cerberus and probably the Chorus in tow)[226] to slay Lycus (618–40).

Seneca, who clearly likes to keep his audience waiting, is prone to delay the entrance of major figures: Theseus in *Phaedra*, Agamemnon in *Agamemnon*, Andromache in *Troades*, Jason in *Medea*, Thyestes in *Thyestes*—and here Hercules. But Hercules is onstage for less than fifty lines. The audience's hunger for their hero, who has been the subject of every character's discourse from Juno to Lycus, is deliberately left unsatisfied. The comparable scene in Euripides' *Heracles* occupies more than 120 lines of the second Episode (*Herac.* 514–636); there is an initial greeting of hearth, home, and family, strong physical contact between Heracles and his sons, and the leading interlocutor of Heracles is Megara. Seneca's Megara is silent throughout her husband's appearance, the desire for his embrace, which she expressed earlier (297), pointedly unrealized (639). When her husband, Cerberus and (probably) the Chorus depart, Theseus and Amphitryon, whose loving address to his son was met with almost a scolding response (622–8), are left

---

[223] See Comm. before 592–617.
[224] For possible Phaethonic allusions in the prayer to Phoebus, see Comm. *ad* 592–7.
[225] See Comm. *ad loc.*   [226] See Comm. after 590–1 and before 640–57.

onstage to console her—perhaps also to console the audience. They go through the usual preliminaries of a messenger scene (640–57) before the long narrative of Theseus, during which (so I propose)[227] Megara and her sons perhaps sit by the altar as Theseus reports on hell and Hercules.

Theseus' narrative occupies most of Act III. It serves the dramatic function of occupying the time required for Hercules to kill Lycus and return, contrasting notably with the visual shocks and movements of the brief opening scene of the act. Long, detailed, slow-moving, and verbal, it is also structurally and thematically the keystone of the play. It takes the form of a discontinuous messenger speech such as that delivered in Act IV of the later *Thyestes*, and has a distinctly dramatic structure, comprising six segments or narrative 'acts', which follow a formal invocation (658–61) and are separated by five 'choral interventions' by Amphitryon (697, 707–8, 727–30, 747–9, 760–1). Theseus' ecphrastic discourse moves from hell's entrance and riverscape, through its wasteland and the palace of Dis, its system of justice and of punishment, to the climactic, extensive narrative of Hercules' victorious descent into the underworld and his capture and removal of Cerberus.[228] The level of evocative detail in Theseus' narrative is compelling. Like Virgil before him and Dante after him, Seneca is clearly obsessed with, even (from a poetic point of view) in love with, hell, to which he turns with similarly affective gusto in *Agamemnon*, *Oedipus*, *Phaedra*, *Medea*, and *Thyestes*. Theseus combines the eye of a landscape artist with the soul of an existential nihilist (*Herc.* 701–6):

> sterilis profundi uastitas squalet soli
> et foeda tellus torpet aeterno situ—
> rerumque maestus finis et mundi ultima.
> immotus aer haeret et pigro sedet
> nox atra mundo. cuncta maerore horrida
> ipsaque morte peior est mortis locus.

> A barren vastness encrusts the lower soil,
> The foul earth stiffens with eternal mould—
> The grim cessation of things, the world's end.
> The air clings motionless and black night sits
> On a languid world. All things bristle with grief:
> The place of death is worse than death itself.

---

[227] See stage directions after 644 and Comm. *ad loc.*
[228] For further analysis, see Comm. *ad* 658–827.

The whole ecphrastic narrative is one of the great 'pause al mezzo' of Senecan tragedy, and in that respect bears comparison with Eurybates' account of the Greek shipwreck in *Agamemnon* (421–578), the *extispicium* scene and Creon's necromancy speech in *Oedipus* (299–383, 530–658), the Messenger's discontinuous narrative of the hellish Tantalid grove and the sacrificial slaughter and cooking of the children in *Thyestes* (641–788), and Medea's Black Mass in *Medea* (670–842). Such pauses necessarily halt the dramatic action, and create space not only for extensive *descriptio loci* but for the narrative and rhetorical pyrotechnics, including δείνωσις ('speech adding force', *addens uim oratio*: Quint. *Inst. Or.* 6.2.24), often associated with public declamation. Ecphrastic narratives expand the audience's field of vision beyond the confines of the stage-set, but they do so without being 'undramatic'; rather, they instantiate a different kind of drama—in the case of *Hercules, Agamemnon, Thyestes*, and the third act of *Oedipus*, a narrative/ recitation/epic/ecphrastic drama—which they use to intensify the audience's intellectual and emotional engagement, even as they develop and explore central issues of the respective play. Especially prominent, for example, in Theseus' long discourse are the investigations of such prominent themes of *Hercules* as those of death, life, punishment, justice, victory, defeat, and place. In addition, the climax of the account (762–827) offers the audience a narrative critique of the psychology and moral character of the play's eponymous hero, as Hercules implements the axiom articulated at the end of the previous choral ode (591) and uses his physical strength to board Charon's ferry, master the hound of hell and bring it and Theseus out of the underworld. The audience would remember that this is Theseus' response to Amphitryon's request for a detailed account of Hercules' 'virtues' in action (*uirtutum ordinem*, 647), and thus his narrative contributes greatly to the play's exploration of *uirtus*. But the long discourse also provides, as is common in Senecan messenger speeches (see e.g. those of *Agamemnon, Troades*, and *Thyestes*), revelation, even development, of the character of the speaker, here Theseus, whose loyalty to Hercules and courage under pressure seem affirmed, his passion for justice openly declared (see below), and his aesthetic sense and moral and existential values pervasively displayed.[229] And Seneca achieves this, while at the same time according Theseus the omniscient narrator role common in messenger-speeches.[230]

---

[229] For a contrary view, see Henry and Walker (1965: 61), who contend that the character of Theseus is 'resolutely undeveloped'—a position recently endorsed by Baertschi (2015: 180).

[230] The convention ensures that the audience suspend their concern with how, for example, Theseus could have known the details of Hercules' encounter with Charon from his imprisoned

Evident in Theseus' narrative, as in all accounts of the underworld, and underscored here by Amphitryon's questions, are an implicit comparison and contrast between the world of the dead and that of the living. Virgil's Aeneas made this comparison at *Aen.* 6.719–21, where, reversing the perspective of Homer's Achilles (*Od.* 11.487–91), he deemed the underworld preferable to the world above. Almost immediately after the completion of Theseus' account of hell and Hercules' glorious final labour therein, Hercules will perform his most inglorious deed and turn the world of the living into that of the dead. This transformation was prescripted by Juno in Act I (116–19), and Hercules will observe the transformation at the start of Act V (1143–6). Thus Theseus here is presenting a recitation drama within the body of an acted drama which not only refracts and reflects upon the main drama itself, but which provides an opaque mirror—and an idealizing mirror (for the underworld has a clear moral structure)—of the world of Thebes.[231]

Nor only of the world of Thebes. In the middle of his narrative Theseus overtly breaks the 'fourth wall'. He is no longer addressing Amphitryon; he is addressing Rome—the theatre's audience and Rome's masters (735–47):

> quod quisque fecit, patitur. auctorem scelus
> repetit suoque premitur exemplo nocens.
> uidi cruentos carcere includi duces
> et impotentis terga plebeia manu
> scindi tyranni. quisquis est placide potens
> dominusque uitae seruat innocuas manus
> et incruentum mitis imperium regit
> animaeque parcit, longa permensus diu
> felicis aeui spatia uel caelum petit
> uel laeta felix nemoris Elysii loca,
> iudex futurus. sanguine humano abstine

position in hell. For Allendorf (2013), 133, 'the long *ekphrasis*…feels like an epic narration, but without giving us the comforting guidance of an omniscient, full-scale epic narrator'. But the dramatic convention is that the messenger narrates what actually happened offstage. In this case Theseus, a prisoner in the underworld himself, is clearly an authoritative guide (as is Eurybates in *Agamemnon*), and his account of the underworld may have an 'epic feel', but is 'dramatic' nonetheless. Seneca's audience, who would have experienced messenger speeches in the tragedies of Seneca and others, would have been expecting an ecphrastic/recitation drama within the body of the play being performed. That is precisely what they get.

[231] Shakespeare tries for an analogous effect (the world of the play = the world of hell) in a minaturized and comic way through his 'Porter's Scene' in *Macbeth* (II.iii). For Roman referentiality in *Hercules*, see Comm. *ad* 46–52.

quicumque regnas. scelera taxantur modo
maiore uestra.

All suffer their own deeds. Crime seeks its author;
The guilty are crushed by their own example.
I saw blood-drenched leaders locked in a jail
And the backs of raving tyrants scourged
By plebeian hands. The gentle monarch
And life's master, who keeps his hands guiltless
And rules an empire mildly without blood,
Sparing life—he measures for years long tracts
Of a happy age and heads for heaven
Or the Elysian grove's joyous places happy,
A judge-to-be. Abstain from human blood,
All you who rule. Greater punishments await
Your crimes.

The protreptic contrast between Theseus' bloodless imperative and Hercules' recently displayed lust for blood (636) is clearly designed to reflect not only on the son of Jupiter. But when he re-enters the play at the end of the third choral ode, covered in Lycus' blood, Hercules will present a dramatic paradigm of the *cruentus dux* (737).[232]

Ode III and Act IV: Death, Triumph, and Madness

The Theban Chorus return in festive mode as the advanced party of Hercules' triumphal procession, which is celebrating the hero's bloody victory over the tyrannical usurper, Lycus. They sing a kletic and in part political ode (initially) in sapphics[233]—with the pre-announced theme of 'Hercules' merited praises' (*meritas Herculis laudes*, 829). The ode is bookended with this theme (830–7, 875–92), but the bulk of the ode attends to a different matter, one which arises directly from the long narrative of Theseus in the preceding act (which the Chorus did not hear): death. The contrast with the stasimon sung after the killing of Lycus in Euripides' *Heracles*, in which the laudations of Heracles are sustained (*Herac.*

---

[232] See Comm. *ad* 735–9, 739–45, 745–7.
[233] For the complex question of the semiotics of the sapphic verse form here, see Comm. ad 830–94 (introd.).

763–814), is marked. Here the opening laudation (of Hercules for his conquest of hell) is quickly suspended for a sombre reflection on the more urgent imperative of death. Members of the audience are drawn not to the triumphs of Hercules but to the number and diversity of the dead and the darkness, lethargy, and silence of death itself (838–63). For the Chorus the world of death is formless, dark, foul, sickly, torpid, silent, empty, though packed (861–3); their presentation of death is a continuation and intensification of the attitude both of Theseus, as displayed in Act III, and of the Chorus themselves, as manifested in their previous odes (see esp. 183–8, 550–7). Their meditation gives way to the Chorus' personal assessment of their own existential position (870–4):

> tibi crescit omne
> et quod occasus uidet et quod ortus:
> parce uenturis. tibi, Mors, paramur.
> sis licet segnis, properamus ipsi.
> prima quae uitam dedit hora carpit.

> For thee grows all that
> The sun sees, set and rising: spare
> The doomed. For thee, Death, we are groomed.
> Though thou be slow, ourselves we rush.
> Life's first hour begins its end.

The language is congruent with the Chorus' earlier pronouncements (183–91) and unites Hercules, the Chorus, Orpheus, and humankind (187, 589, 867, 873).

The lyric ends, however, as it began, with praises of Hercules, whose defeat of Lycus is celebrated in universal terms as the creation of global peace, the *Pax Herculea*. In Euripides Heracles' achievement is simply the liberation of Thebes (*Herac.* 763–814). And, as if to indicate overtly that their ode went off-track, the Chorus initiate a metrical change, singing now in glyconics to make their celebratory purpose clear.[234] At last the 'merited praises of Hercules' are sung in full joyous voice, as the Chorus bring their ode to a climax on what will prove to be Hercules' most ironic accomplishment, banishment of the human fear of death: *iam nullus superest timor*, 'Now no fear is left' (891). This opponent of the Epicurean ideal articulated

---

[234] See Comm. *ad* 875–92.

in the play's opening choral ode is here credited with Epicurus' prime accomplishment.[235] The tragedy is hurtling towards *peripeteia*.

The double change of tone in the ode merits comment. The third ode of *Thyestes* features a prominent change of choral tone at its centre (596), as the Chorus move from communal joy about the apparent reconciliation of the two brothers to pronounced apprehension about the future. The third ode of *Hercules* offers the audience a double move: from a tone of laudatory celebration (830–7) to a grim meditation on death (838–74), back to a tone of laudatory celebration (875–92). One may label the closural laudatory tone as contextually 'ironic', and Senecan tragedy features several ironic celebratory odes.[236] But what is effected here in *Hercules* includes but also transcends irony. It is the creation in the audience of profound intellectual and emotional ambiguity. The figure of Hercules is celebrated by the advanced party of Hercules' triumphal procession. But the conquest of death which begins and ends the ode is problematized by the Chorus' own recognition that death cannot be conquered: the triumphalism associated with Hercules (and with the *Pax Romana* which he emblematizes)[237] is inherently ungrounded.

The audience are then presented with the second climax of the play: Hercules' triumphant return. Again an act opens with Herculean spectacle. The triumphant hero enters to the praises of an adoring crowd of Thebans, viz. the Chorus, who append to their lyric specific instructions for the ritual to come (893–4). Hercules is surrounded by slaves and attendants, who lead animals (or carry sculpted heads of the same) in preparation for the intended thanksgiving sacrifice and bring with them all that will be needed. Onstage, too, are Theseus, Amphitryon, Megara, and Hercules' sons. This opening scene is the apex of the play, dramatizing Hercules at the moment of his great victory just before he topples into madness. He has saved his family from the murderous tyrant, but will shortly collapse into delusion and familicidal violence. His initial speech seems appropriately 'pious', focusing not simply on just vengeance and victory (the 'tyrant' is dead) but on the necessary sacrifice of thanksgiving to the gods (895–9):

> ultrice dextra fusus aduerso Lycus
> terram cecidit ore. tum quisquis comes

---

[235] See Littlewood (2017: 162). Lucretius, of course, compared Hercules unfavourably with Epicurus: 5.22–54.

[236] See Comm. *ad* 830–94 (introd.).

[237] See Comm. *ad* 882–8.

fuerat tyranni iacuit et poenae comes.
nunc sacra patri uictor et superis feram
caesisque meritas uictimis aras colam.

My avenging hand made Lycus sprawl;
He crashed and bit the earth. Then each comrade
Of the tyrant fell, comrade, too, in death.
Now victor, I'll sacrifice to father and gods
Honouring due altars with slain victims.

Important opening lines, incorporating the motifs of vengeance, violence, conquest, and sacrifice. 'Sacrifice' will become the master image of Act IV, as Hercules conflates it with murder. Euripides' Heracles is similarly beginning a sacrifice after the death of Lycus (*Herac.* 922–7), when madness strikes him, but that sacrifice is one of purification (*Herac.* 922–3). Here the sacrifice is one of thanksgiving. But even at this stage the well-known Senecan ambiguity of 'victim' (*uictimis*) might give the audience pause.

Imagery of sacrifice has pervaded the play,[238] and reaches full fruition in this act, in which thoughts of a perverted sacrifice of Lycus (920–4), modelled on his treatment of the monstrous Busiris,[239] will lead to Hercules' actual, though deranged, perverted sacrifice of his family to Juno (1035–8). Seneca likes to play with the motif of perverted sacrifice in his tragedies (see esp. *Phaedra, Agamemnon, Troades, Medea, Thyestes*). Sacrifice was a ritual in the ancient world which sustained the ordered ontological distinctions of life: god, human, beast.[240] The perversion of it confounded those distinctions. The result: moral and ontological chaos. The production of that chaos by a raging, insane man of violence (*uiolento…iuueni*, 43–4), a liminal figure, whose appearance, behaviour, and nature themselves confound the categories concerned,[241] is dramatized in Act IV of *Hercules*.

The act has three parts: celebration (895–939), hallucination (939–86), familicide (987–1053). The celebrations, which began at the end of Act III and received particular focus in the final lines of the preceding choral ode, dominate the opening. After Hercules' victory speech, dialogue with Amphitryon and instructions for sacrifice to attendants and to Theseus, a dramatic high

---

[238] See Comm. *ad* 918–24.

[239] In which he treated Busiris as 'monstrously' as Busiris had treated others. See Comm. *ad* 918–24.

[240] The view, for example, of Marcel Detienne (1972: 71–113). Cf. also Segal (1977: 104): 'Sacrifice creates a series of mediations between god and beast and god and man and thereby asserts an orderly distinction of these planes of existence in the biological and alimentary codes.'

[241] See Comm. before 592–617.

point is reached in the proclamation of a 'Golden Age' brought to pass by
Hercules himself (926–39):

> ipse concipiam preces
> Ioue meque dignas. stet suo caelum loco
> tellusque et aequor. astra inoffensos agant
> aeterna cursus, alta pax gentes alat,
> ferrum omne teneat ruris innocui labor
> ensesque lateant. nulla tempestas fretum
> uiolenta turbet, nullus irato Ioue
> exiliat ignis, nullus hiberna niue
> nutritus agros amnis euersos trahat.
> uenena cessent, nulla nocituro grauis
> suco tumescat herba; non saeui ac truces
> regnent tyranni. si quod etiamnum est scelus
> latura tellus, properet, et, si quod parat
> monstrum, meum sit.

> I'll form prayers worthy
> Of Jove and myself. Let sky, earth, and sea
> Stand in their place. Let eternal stars drive
> Unhindered orbits, deep peace nourish nations,
> All iron belong to toil of guiltless land
> And swords lie hid. Let no violent tempest
> Flay the sea, no flame burst from angry Jove,
> No river nursed by the snows of winter
> Ravage the fields and drag them with it.
> Let poisons cease, no plant swell heavy
> With noxious juice, no cruel and brutal
> Tyrants rule. If earth even now will bear
> Some evil, let her rush, and, if she grooms
> A monster, let it be mine.

Few members of Seneca's audience would have failed to discern the irony of
this articulation of a world of quietude and peace by the most violent of
ancient heroes and its ending in a request for a monster which will, as many
have observed,[242] immediately prove to be 'mine' in the strongest ontological
sense, viz. Hercules himself. To underscore the irony, Seneca prefaces the

---

[242] See e.g. Shelton (1978: 65), Fitch *ad loc.* See further Comm. *ad 935–9.*

megalomaniac vision with the speaker's hybristic concatenation of himself with Jupiter (927), which, like the blood still staining Hercules' hands, pollutes the ensuing prayer and joins with the very impossibility of the world described to signal the beginning of the insanity.[243] Madness and chaotic hallucinations immediately envelop Hercules, ranging from darkness at midday to fiery threats in the heavens, 'quasi-parricidal' assaults by himself upon his father Jupiter and the Olympians, joining the Titans in such battles, thence to a Gigantomachy and to Furies with whips, torches, and snakes.[244] The last, longest, and most bloody part of the act is the slaughter of family which ensues. The family has been onstage since the beginning of Act II,[245] but the slaughter is realized mostly offstage, described gruesomely by a powerless Amphitryon, who has failed to restrain his foster-son's *furor* (973-5).[246] Sometimes darkly ironic in his account,[247] Amphitryon offers himself as Hercules' final victim, even as the great killer collapses before him. Some have likened the Euripidean Heracles' madness and some recent adaptations to 'the berserk state', the blind and intense frenzy of the warrior who is bent solely on destruction, killing friend and foe alike.[248] Seneca's Hercules is close to this, but is not blind. He possesses cognition, but 'sees' wrongly. His megalomania and desensitized propensity to violence have made him (temporarily) mad.

Act IV of *Hercules* rivals two very different fourth acts, those of *Agamemnon* (659-807) and *Medea* (670-848), in terms of spectacle. But in terms of its focus on blood, slaughter, and perverted sacrifice, it is close to the fourth act of *Thyestes* (623-788), with its messenger's vigorous description of the gruesome, sacrificial rites of Atreus. But Seneca eschews the distancing mechanism of a messenger speech employed in the later play and favoured by Euripides, who has Heracles' madness and slaughter of family reported after the fact

---

[243] On 'the sheer impossibility of what he prays for', see Fitch (1987a: 27). For the Roman semiotics of what Hercules prays for, see pp. 118-22 below. See further Comm. *ad* 926-39.

[244] Fitch (1987a: 29-30), comments well on the 'associative' connections between the hallucinations, which he analyses as resulting from 'anxieties and conflicts present, whether at a conscious or subconscious level, in his "sane" mind.' Hercules' obsession with violence and his celestial ambitions feature strongly in the hallucinations.

[245] In order (among other things) to underscore and make personal to the audience the horror of the familicide. Megara and the children are onstage for the whole of Acts II and III, most of Act IV and probably (so I interpret) the intervening choral odes (*Herc.* 202-1020). Children appear in other Senecan plays, but never for such a duration. Even Astyanax in *Troades* is onstage only for one act, the long Act III (*Tro.* 409-812).

[246] Amphitryon at 973-5 acts like one of the restraining figures in a standard Senecan 'Passion-Restraint' scene, but, of course, to no avail.

[247] See Comm *ad* 1022-31.

[248] See Riley (2008: 330-5), discussing Simon Armitage's *Mister Heracles* (2000) and Euripides' *Heracles*.

(*Herac.* 922–1015). Seneca seems to have developed a technique from pantomime,[249] which enables him to present the horror as it takes place, while allowing for further horror to come when the bloody and fragmented bodies are brought onto the stage. This is a violent, 'impious' scene. More than the play of his Greek predecessor, Seneca's *Hercules* here becomes a kind of perverted *Odyssey*, in which Hercules has returned home and killed the harassing, usurping suitor, but then—against all the ideological logic of the 'homecoming'—goes on to kill the family whom his actions initially saved.[250] And his 'impiety' is not restricted to the horror of familicide. Hercules kills his family not, as in Euripides, simply thinking that he is killing the children of his mortal enemy, but thinking, too, that he is attacking his divine enemy, Juno (1018–20), and his divine father, Jupiter (963–73).

The killing of children is at the heart of several Senecan tragedies: *Phaedra, Troades, Medea, Thyestes, Hercules*.[251] But only in *Medea* and *Hercules* does the Roman tragedian have the bloody violence performed in real stage time, *coram populo* (Hor. *AP* 185), before the audience—even if, in the case of *Hercules*, its bloodiest ingredients are kept offstage. In Euripides' account (*Herac.* 1000) the final living son and his mother are killed together. In Seneca the horrific climax of the slaughter is the mother, Megara, by herself, whom Seneca had built up in Act II as a major tragic figure, a model of devotion, intelligence, courage, and passionate, independent spirit, an *animosa coniunx* (1150) to a man of *uirtus animosa* (201)—her head now consigned by the violence of the latter to 'nowhere' (*nec usquam est*, 1026). Seneca also famously avoids Euripides' 'divine agency' scene (*Herac.* 815–73), in which Iris and Lyssa/Madness, daughter of Night, arrive onstage before the eyes of the Chorus and the audience, and enter the royal palace to cause the madness of Heracles and his slaughter of kin. Seneca's audience receive no such scene but, after the bloody action is over, are left to contemplate the relationship of Hercules' actions to Hercules himself and to the external figures of Juno and the Furies introduced in the prologue. Seneca similarly removes overt divine agency from the ending of the madness, excising any role for the Greek tragedian's Athena (*Herac.* 1002–8). Seneca certainly had one eye on Euripides' account, since his treatment of the killings themselves seems clearly derived from it, even as it

---

[249] See §VI, 66.

[250] See Rehm (2002: 110–13). The plot of the *Odyssey* is more evident in Seneca's play because of Lycus' role as a suitor.

[251] One might add here the attempted/intended killing of children in *Oedipus* and *Agamemnon*.

reveals telling differences.[252] One major difference is in the presentation of Amphitryon, who takes a strong role in the final stages of the Senecan action by offering himself as Hercules' climactic victim and providing a foretaste of the part he will play in the final act of the play.

Ode IV and Act V: Hercules, *Furor*, and Place

But before Act V the audience are presented with one of the most moving choral odes of Senecan tragedy, the 'Lamentation Ode' of *Hercules*, possibly the closest of all Senecan choral odes to the Horatian ideal of chorus as actor.[253] Perhaps its main rivals in this are the dirge for the fall of Troy and the deaths of Hector and Priam, which opens Seneca's *Troades* (67–163), and the lamentation for the fall of Troy by the Trojan Chorus of *Agamemnon* (589–658). All three are lyric drama of astonishing, emotive power. The present ode is a dirge (*nenia*, κομμός, θρῆνος) for the victims of Hercules' insane and violent rampage. Much of its power and energy come from its ritualistic form and a pervasive use of apostrophe, which moves from the firmament and the gods to Sleep, Hercules, the fatal arrow, and the dead sons, whose bodies (and remains of Megara) are brought onto the stage during the ode. The short stasimon following the Messenger's speech in Euripides' play mentions the possibility of a 'groan or lamentation or song for the dead' (στεναγμὸν ἢ γόον ἢ φθιτῶν ᾠδάν, *Herac.* 1025–6). Seneca's ode realizes that possibility (1054–60), even as it indexes the truth of the Chorus' opening ode,[254] by utilizing its anapaestic rhythms and by beginning again with allusion to the all-seeing Sun-god, Titan (cf. 133):

> lugeat aether magnusque parens
> aetheris alti tellusque ferax
> et uaga ponti mobilis unda,
> tuque ante omnes, qui per terras
> tractusque maris fundis radios
> noctemque fugas ore decoro,
>   feruide Titan.

> Let sky weep and the soaring sky's
> Great father, and fertile earth,
> And the shifting sea's vagrant waves,

---

[252] See Comm. *ad* 987–1026.   [253] See Comm. *ad* 1054–1137.
[254] See Comm. *ad* 1054–1137.

> And thou above all, who dost pour
> Light across lands and ocean's tracts
> And banish night with beauteous face,
> > Blazing Titan.

There is alliteration and repetition throughout the ode typical of a dirge, and formal, even grandiose phrasing,[255] in keeping with the ritualistic mode and solemn tone and atmosphere of a *nenia*. Especially appropriate is the global reach of the Chorus' referents (1054–62•, 1100–14), reflective of the global status of the main subject of the ode, Hercules, and the cosmic nature of the tragedy being witnessed.[256] What the cosmic outcry of the Chorus implies (naively, some members of Seneca's audience may have thought and several Senecan tragedies imply) is an interconnection between the cosmos and human suffering allied to the Stoic concept of cosmic 'sympathy', in which the universe is itself a moral being prone to respond sympathetically to human tragedy and pain.[257]

At the heart of the ode is the famous apostrophe to Sleep, who is asked to soothe Hercules and restore him to sanity (1066–81). Though the ode's focus shifts considerably, the continuous anapaestic rhythms sustain a plangent, elegiac tone, even as they contrast sharply with their quite different use in the play's opening lyrics (125–204).[258] The beginning and end of the ode are strongly threnetic. Its final lines underscore the lost potential of the slain sons, whom the Chorus send on their way to the harbours of the dead (1131–7):

> ite ad Stygios, umbrae, portus,
> > ite, innocuae,
> quas in primo limine uitae
> scelus oppressit patriusque furor.
> ite, infaustum genus, o pueri,

---

[255] Much of the language is taken from the great Augustans, Virgil, Horace, Ovid: see Comm. *ad* 1154–37.

[256] Such referents (sky, earth, ocean, hell), rather than providing an 'escape' from the horrific events of Act IV, as Fitch suggests *ad* 1054–62 (for, while the Chorus sing, the bodies of the slain family are brought onto the stage), lift the moral significance of what Hercules has done to the level of the cosmic. It may seem otiose to point out that such cosmic referents would have allowed the Chorus in their gestures to make potent use of the verticality of the Roman theatrical space (for which see Comm. *ad* 1–124 introd.) and thereby augment the dramatic power of their singing.

[257] See Comm. *ad* 1054–62•.

[258] For the semiotics of the anapaestic metre here, see Comm. *ad* 1054–1137 (introd.).

> noti per iter triste laboris;
> ite, iratos uisite reges.

> Go to Stygian harbours, go,
>   Innocent shades,
> Whom on life's first threshold
> Crime has crushed and father's fury.
> Go, boys, O curséd brood,
> Along that famed labour's grim path;
> Go, meet the angry monarchs.

Seneca has crafted these verses not only to attend to such issues as undeserved death and irreparable loss but, through the emphasis on *scelus*, 'crime', and *furor*, 'fury/rage', to recall the Juno-summoned entities of the prologue (96–8) and to anticipate the moral discussion to come,[259] in which the Chorus seem to have already staked a position. The last line touches on the anger of Dis, who, as the audience know, always receives a compensatory death or deaths to make up for the loss of the heroes who return from hell. The Chorus will sing no more. Their completed dirge will resonate throughout the rest of the play. Unlike the professional mourners at a Roman aristocrat's funeral, they are politically, socially, and emotionally invested in the tragedy which they have so movingly described and mourned.[260] They will remain onstage as a dramatic audience, a mirror of the audience before them, silent *spectatores* of the moral and emotional action of the play's concluding act, upon which the fate of their city hangs.

Act V of *Hercules* is the second longest and perhaps the most meditative final act of Seneca's act-divided plays.[261] The contrast with the preceding act could not be more severe. Slow-moving, morally and psychologically focused, the act is one long, continuous scene, in which (after the entrance of Theseus as Hercules awakes) no new speaking characters enter and no existing speaking character exits. The only movement off and onto the stage is by slaves returning Hercules' weapons at 1295. The act proceeds from Hercules' awakening and recognition, through his horror, lamentation, and resolution to commit suicide, Amphitryon's and Theseus' resistance, and Amphitryon's own threat of suicide, to Hercules' decision to live, his final speech of dislocation, pain, and despair, and Theseus' offer of purification in Athens. The whole act is a study of Hercules' mind at the hero's moment of

---

[259] See Comm. *ad loc.*   [260] See Comm. *ad* 1100–14.
[261] See Comm. *ad* 1138–1344 (introd.).

greatest vulnerability, and, like the final act of the (probably) later *Thyestes*, achieves some of its dramatic power from the contrast with the more distant perspective of the protatic divine figure of the prologue (in *Thyestes* the Fury; in *Hercules* Juno). Hercules does not end the play which bears his name. That role is performed by Theseus, who lives up to the etymology of his name in attempting to 'place' Hercules in Athens.[262] Only one Senecan tragedy ends with a line from its titular character: *Oedipus*.

But, as in *Oedipus* and also in *Medea*, the titular character dominates the act's discourse. Though there are three speaking characters, Hercules speaks over 75 per cent of the lines of the act and has several long speeches,[263] which not only display the hero's pain but reflect and reflect upon the grief, anger, rage, guilt, shame, self-disgust, and despair present in Hercules' mind. No member of a Roman audience, even those ignorant of Euripides' *Heracles*, would have been surprised by Hercules' potent presence in this final act. Hercules had dominated the dialogue and choral odes of the play before he even entered the stage: Acts I and II and their attendant choral lyrics were in part meditations on what it was to be Hercules. Hercules entered the play in Act III, but, even after he left the act at 640, his deeds (viz. the final labour in the underworld) became the focus of the speech of others. His actions and speech dominated Act IV. The Chorus focused their third ode on Hercules in its initial and concluding lines and devoted the entirety of their final ode to Hercules and his dead sons. Hercules' climactic dominance of this tragedy is product of the play's ontology, its permeating construction out of multiple and diverse verbal allusions to him.

Seneca uses this climactic dominance well. Immediately worthy of attention in Act V is a costuming difference from Acts III and IV: viz. the semi-nakedness of Hercules. His lion skin (= weapon, clothing, and bed) was taken offstage by slaves at the end of the fourth act. Hercules' upper body is uncovered. He himself proclaims this at 1172—*en nudus asto*, 'Look, I stand naked', 1172—drawing attention to his lack of clothing and of weapons. The lion skin (with its semiotics of liminality) and Hercules' regular stage-costume and props (club, bow, quiver, arrows, sword), central to the hero's stage-identity, seem to have been deliberately removed by Seneca not simply to make a metatheatrical point,[264] but to focus on Hercules' humanity, using

---

[262] See Comm. *ad* 1341–4.
[263] He speaks more lines in Act V than in the rest of the play.
[264] See Comm. *ad* 1149–55.

nudity in a manner anticipatory of its use in Shakespeare's *King Lear*.[265] For this is an act in which, as in Shakespeare's tragedy, core human values will be examined and displayed.

Also interesting to observe is the solitary nature of the recognition part of this act. In Euripides Heracles discovers his responsibility for the killings through dialogue with Amphitryon, who informs him bluntly of his role (*Herac.* 1131–9). Seneca's Hercules works out his guilt onstage.[266] Though he himself cannot weep (see later at 1228–9), he notes the tears of Amphitryon and Theseus, their 'shame', their shunning of his gaze (1173–80) and of his hands, and finally, triggered by observation of his supplicating hands, he sees the material evidence of the blood spattered upon them, and then notes the blood on his own poisoned arrow, marking his father's and Theseus' silence (1192–1200):

> miserere, genitor, supplices tendo manus.
> quid hoc? manus refugit. hic errat scelus.
>   unde hic cruor? quid illa puerili madens
> harundo leto? tincta Lernaea nece—
> iam tela uideo nostra. non quaero manum.
> quis potuit arcum flectere aut quae dextera
> sinuare neruum uix recedentem mihi?
>   ad uos reuertor. genitor, hoc nostrum est scelus?
> tacuere. nostrum est.

> Have pity, father, I stretch suppliant hands.

> AMPHITRYON *moves back.*

> (*Aside*) What's this? He shuns my hands. Crime hovers here.

> HERCULES *sees the blood on his hands and the arrow which killed one of his* SONS.

>   Where is this blood from? What of that arrow
>   Wet with a boy's death? Stained with Lerna's poison—

---

[265] I allude to the use of the nudity of Edgar, qua Poor Tom, in *King Lear*, which draws from Lear the famous response: 'Is man no more than this?…thou art the thing itself' (*KL* III. iv.101–4). Quite different is Seneca's deployment of nudity in the opening choral ode of *Troades*, where the Chorus' nudity indexes the collapse of a world in which shame and moral values had a defining role: see Boyle (1994: 20).

[266] Seneca likes to present characters 'thinking' and 'working things out' onstage. See Comm. *ad* 1194–1200.

> Now I see my shaft. The hand I do not seek.
> Who had strength to bend the bow? Or what hand
> Could have drawn the string which scarce yields to me?
> (*To* AMPH. *and* THES.) I turn to you again. Father, is this crime mine?
> (*Aside*) They're silent. It's mine.

Hercules has reached this recognition by himself. He will remain a solitary figure to the play's close.

Notable in this final act is the interplay of reason and moral emotion, especially the interplay of reason, *pietas*, and shame, *pudor*, which, akin to the αἰδώς displayed by Heracles in Euripides' play (*Herac.* 1160, 1199), drives Hercules' words (1147, 1173–80, 1240–1) and behaviour at crucial parts of the action. Critics have remarked on the similarity of the act's structure to the 'Passion-Restraint' scenes of Senecan tragedy,[267] which regularly appear in the earlier part of a play (e.g. in the second acts of *Phaedra*, *Agamemnon*, *Troades*, *Medea*, and *Thyestes*), and can be found in a somewhat abbreviated version in Act II of *Hercules* itself.[268] But the scale of the interplay in this act is quite different, as are its consequences and the values addressed. Hercules allows his drive to suicide to dominate the action of the latter part of the act (1240–1317) and gives it the nomenclature of *uirtus* (1315), providing the model for a whole dramatic tradition of heroic, 'virtuous' suicides from Jean de La Taille and Robert Garnier to Shakespeare and beyond. But Hercules in this play, unlike La Taille's Saul or Shakespeare's Antony or Othello, does not kill himself. He has his *uirtus* and *pudor* yield not to the dictates of reason but to the pull of *pietas*, his filial bond to Amphitryon;[269] he saves his 'father' by preserving his own life.

This thematic core of the act, absent from Euripides' *Heracles* (from which Seneca's finale differs markedly),[270] is underscored by Seneca's divergences in plot, dramaturgy, and thematic focus. In Euripides it is Theseus who takes the major role in the closural dialogue with Heracles and who persuades Heracles to live, offering him worldly goods in Athens (*Herac.* 1313–57).[271] In Seneca's finale the dramatist has Theseus play a minor role, reducing the latter's offer and making it late, and has Amphitryon become Hercules' major interlocutor (and perhaps realize the etymology of his

---

[267] See e.g. Fitch *ad* 1138–1344 (introd.).   [268] See Comm. *ad* 205–523 (introd.).

[269] Compare the later *Phoenissae* (306–19), where Oedipus yields to 'the pull of *pietas*', as he abandons his suicide resolution in response to his daughter's supplication and tears. See §V, 47 above.

[270] Contrary to what Billerbeck (1999a: 561) seems to suggest.

[271] See Comm. *ad* 1341–4 below.

name),[272] thrusting the father-son issue to the fore,[273] and making the value of *pietas* and Hercules' status as *impius* central to the dramatic action (see 1217, 1241, 1280, 1329).

Seneca emphasizes this dramaturgically with other changes from Euripides: the return of Hercules' *arma* and the creation of two on-the-point-of-suicide scenes, both revolving around highly charged stage props: the poisoned arrow which killed Hercules' son, and the recently returned Herculean sword. These two material props join with the plethora of bodies on the stage to underscore the materiality of suffering and emotional union, as the two separate bodies of 'father' and 'son' eventually touch in a spectacle of reconciliation, structured through a final and pointed use of *genitor*, *pater*, and *parens* and a quasi-Catullan cry of *uiuamus*, 'Let us live'. It is the third climax of the play (1314–21), and perhaps the most Shakespearean of Senecan tragedy:[274]

HERCVLES   iam parce, genitor, parce, iam reuoca manum.
                succumbe, uirtus; perfer imperium patris.
                eat ad labores hic quoque Herculeos labor:
                uiuamus.
                      artus alleua afflictos solo,
                Theseu, parentis. dextra contactus pios
                scelerata refugit.

AMPHITRYON   hanc manum amplector libens,
                hac nisus ibo. pectori hanc aegro admouens
                pellam dolores.

HERCVLES   Now spare, father, spare yourself; now—pull back
                Your hand. Yield, virtue; bear a father's rule.
                To Hercules' labours add this labour, too:
                Let us live.

                        AMPHITRYON *collapses.*

[272] See Comm. *ad* 1302–13.

[273] Words for 'father'—*genitor, pater, patrius, parens*—occur over twenty times in Act V, used in reference to both Amphitryon and Jupiter, making the issue of 'what is it to be a father?' permeate the dialogue and action of this act. The play's answer to this question seems to lie in the fact that the final uses of *genitor* (1269, 1295, 1314), *pater* (1245, 1256, 1310, 1315) and *parens* (1248, 1263, 1318) refer only to Amphitryon. Note how at 1184–5 Seneca has Hercules himself elevate Amphitryon's status as *genitor* almost to that of Jupiter.

[274] Gray (2016: 215): 'What Shakespeare admires is not brutal dominance, but…the voluntary surrender or delegation of individual agency…in the interests of a greater good: compassion.' See also Gray (2016: 226–7).

Lift my father's crushed body,
Theseus, from the ground. My criminal hand
Shuns contact with the good.

AMPHITRYON *grabs* HERCULES' *hand, as he is lifted up by* THESEUS.

AMPHITRYON   I gladly clasp this hand.
It'll be my prop. I'll hold it to my ailing breast
To banish pain.

Euripides' Heracles is deterred from suicide in substantial part because it
would have been the act of a coward (*Herac.* 1347–50). Seneca's hero has his
guilt, pain, *pudor*, yield to the imperatives of *pietas*.

Seneca's finale manifests another major difference from the ending of
Euripides' *Heracles*; it lies in the area of cosmic scale. Seneca is famous for
his creation of figures who annex the universe in the articulation of their
pain. Hercules does this to perfection, as Euripides' Heracles does not, and
the ramifications of the former's great speeches in the final act can be seen
from Shakespeare to T. S. Eliot.[275] But this cosmic scale and the grand spectacle of two threatened but aborted suicides, though dramatizing most
powerfully the triumph of *pietas* and *uirtus* and (for the role of Theseus is
not without thematic function) of *fides* and *amicitia*, dissolve into moral
and existential ambiguity. To view Hercules at the end of the play simply as
a 'protagonist who triumphs over uncontrollable passion and suffering'[276]
misses much. Hercules is self-critical throughout the act, including its end,
viewing himself as a *monstrum* (1279–81) haunting his own life, destroying
every place he visits, even *place* itself (1321–31):

quem locum profugus petam?
ubi me recondam quaue tellure obruar?
quis Tanais aut quis Nilus aut quis Persica
uiolentus unda Tigris aut Rhenus ferox
Tagusue Hibera turbidus gaza fluens
abluere dextram poterit? Arctoum licet
Maeotis in me gelida transfundat mare
et tota Tethys per meas currat manus,
haerebit altum facinus.

in quas impius

---

[275] See Comm. *ad* 1138–42, 1321–41.   [276] Miola (1992: 125).

terras recedes? ortum an occasum petes?
ubique notus perdidi exilio locum.

> What place of exile shall I seek?
> Where shall I hide, in what land be erased?
> What Tanais, what Nile or what violent
> Tigris with Persian flood or frenzied Rhine
> Or turbid Tagus, awash with Spain's gold,
> Can cleanse this hand? Though icy Maeotis
> Pour its Arctic sea on me, and Tethys
> Stream over my hands with all her waters,
> The crime will stick deep.
> To what lands will you
> Run, impious man? Will you head east or west?
> Known everywhere, I've destroyed a place for exile.

Seneca's dramatization of Hercules' yielding to the imperatives of *pietas* may be modelled on the playwright's own life (*Ep. Mor.* 78.2),[277] but the protagonist's final speech is one of dislocation and despair.[278] He is fuelled by *furor* in the final act as Juno was (and Seneca was) in the prologue, and is similarly preoccupied with *locus*, with 'place'.[279] Hercules, i.e. 'Hera's/Juno's Glory', mirrors in part prologue-Juno herself,[280] even as his displayed *uirtus* and *pietas* mark a profound difference from his stepmother. This play's *spectaculum* of a 'brave man matched with ill fortune' (*uir fortis cum fortuna mala compositus*, *Prou.* 2.9), which Seneca thought in Cato's case worthy of the divine and human gaze, seems unlikely to have been intended as an unqualified, moral paradigm, certainly not of the Stoic *sapiens*. Shakespeare was perhaps inspired by this act to create the great scene of reconciliation and forgiveness between Lear and Cordelia (*KL* IV.vii),[281] but such is not what Seneca's audience are left with. At the end of a play structured and permeated by prayer,[282] Hercules utters a despairing final plea. It is a plea to his mortal friend, Theseus (1338–41).

---

[277] See further p. 3 above and pp. 105–6 below.   [278] See further Comm. *ad* 1321–41.

[279] *Locus* begins and ends the speech (1321, 1340) and punctuates its centre (1331). It is not only the last noun to be uttered by Hercules in Act V, but also the first (1138).

[280] The play's cyclical dramatic structure was ordained by its prologue, and is evident in language, theme, and motif. It is also quintessentially Senecan. A conspicuous feature of the two other Senecan plays with protatic characters, *Agamemnon* and *Thyestes* (see Boyle 2019: ciii–vi; 2017: ciii–v), it is also a defining aspect of *Phaedra*, *Troades*, and *Medea* (see Boyle 1987: 24; 1994: 25–6; 2014: lxxix).

[281] See Miola (1992: 165–8), Braden (1993: 260).   [282] See pp. 77–8 above and n. 210.

> redde me infernis, precor,
> umbris reductum, meque subiectum tuis
> restitue uinclis. ille me abscondet locus—
> sed et ille nouit.

> Recall, return me,
> I beg, to the shades of hell; restore me
> Fettered with your chains. That place will hide me—
> But it, too, knows me.

The plea is ignored. Theseus' abbreviated Euripidean offer follows (1341–4). If Hercules is to live on, he will do so—despite the closural offer of purification and refuge from the man whom he rescued from hell[283]—in a universe in which he manifestly has no place.

Performing Virtue

'Rise, virtue' (*exurge, uirtus*), exclaims Hercules, as he lifts himself up in the final act (1157). He later talks of 'virtue's violated glory' (*uiolatum decus uirtutis*, 1270–1), and, at the climax of the act, he addresses 'virtue' once more, and, reaching back to his past in order to act in the present,[284] he expresses his resolution to live (1315–17):

> succumbe, uirtus; perfer imperium patris.
> eat ad labores hic quoque Herculeos labor:
> uiuamus.

> Yield, virtue; bear a father's rule.
> To Hercules' labours add this labour, too:
> Let us live.

'Virtue', *uirtus*, literally 'manliness', the defining properties of manhood, of an ideal *uir*, 'man', is a prominent motif of this play from the prologue onwards. The word itself occurs some seventeen times; in the rest of Senecan tragedy it is found on only thirteen occasions. The whole dramatic action is

---

[283] For discussion of the complexities and ironies of the play's last four lines, see Comm. *ad loc.*
[284] See Comm. *ad* 1314–17.

structured around this value.[285] Act I draws attention to Hercules' *uirtus*, *indomita* ('untamed', 39) and *inuisa* ('hated' (115)), which, as Juno prescripts and the dawn ode foretells (201), will prove the hero's undoing. Act II offers a varied discourse on *uirtus* in the dialogue of Amphitryon, Megara, and Lycus, only to be followed by Act III's presentation of 'virtue in action', both on earth (the mission to kill Lycus) and in hell (the capture of Cerberus), the latter narrated in response to an explicit request for an account of Hercules' *uirtutes* (647). Act IV opens with the celebration of virtue's action, the bloody slaying of Lycus, only to have virtue's action transformed into insane familicide, performed before the audience. Act V reflects on *uirtus* and witnesses its final transformation into something which responds to the human-bonding values of *pietas*, *fides*, and *amicitia*.

But what is this *uirtus*, 'virtue', naked or transformed? *Virtus* was a traditional Roman aristocratic ideal, which 'consisted in the winning of *gloria* by the commission of exemplary deeds according to a proper standard of conduct in the service of the state'.[286] Cicero and Sallust had attempted to democratize *uirtus*, the latter by defining it as 'the functioning of *ingenium*, a man's innate talent, to achieve exemplary deeds',[287] and making it applicable not only to non-aristocratic Romans but to a wide range of human activities.[288] The Stoics restricted *uirtus* to the *sapiens*, 'sage', and divided it into the 'sub-virtues' of self-control, fortitude, prudence, and justice (*temperantia*, *fortitudo*, *prudentia*, *iustitia*, *Ep. Mor.* 120.11), aligning it with reason (*ratio*). This play dramatizes *uirtus* pervasively as 'manliness' or 'valour' in its crudest and most popular sense, namely physical courage, physical prowess, physical power. Even Lycus, the poor man's Hercules, claims *clara uirtus*

---

[285] See Comm. *ad* 35–40. *Virtus* is inherited as a prominent dramatic motif by the author of *Hercules Oetaeus*, where the word occurs fourteen times, perhaps most notably in the final lines of the play (*HO* 1971, 1983) and Hercules' climactic claim (*HO* 1942–3):

> iam uirtus mihi
> in astra et ipsos fecit ad superos iter.

> My virtue has made
> A path for me to the stars and very gods.

Cf. the role of 'virtue' in Marlowe's *Tamburlaine*, a play much influenced by Seneca's *Hercules*: 'virtue is the fount whence honour springs' (*1 Tam.* IV.iv.125); 'virtue solely is the sum of glory' (*1 Tam.* V.ii.126).

[286] Earl (1967: 52). For Cicero's and Sallust's concepts of *uirtus*, see *Id.* 47–58. See further Comm. *ad* 35–40.

[287] Ibid.

[288] See Sallust *Cat.* 2. Sallust's view that political failure and a failure in *uirtus* were interconnected has relevance to all the Senecan tragedies.

('renowned virtue', 340). It is at the centre of his dialogue with Megara (434–5):

LYCUS   obici feris monstrisque uirtutem putas?
MEGARA   uirtutis est domare quae cuncti pauent.

LYCUS   Think it 'virtue' being thrown to beasts and monsters?
MEGARA   It is 'virtue' to tame what all men dread.

Hercules' wife is soon to feel the effect of that 'virtue as valour' gone mad. Indeed for Hercules, who, as noted above, even addresses his own *uirtus* (1157, 1315), *uirtus* is intimately bound up with physical force, to what his 'hands' can do. The words *manus*, 'hand', and *dextra*, 'right hand', dominate the linguistic texture of this play as of no other, and pervade most especially Hercules' own dialogue and the descriptions by others of Hercules' power.[289] The Chorus, who provide ambivalent, at times critical presentation of Hercules' *uirtus animosa* ('spirited virtue', 201) throughout the play, voice the most ringing endorsement of this power at the moment of Hercules' triumphant return from the killing of the tyrant (882–8):

> pax est Herculea manu
> Auroram inter et Hesperum,
> et qua Sol medium tenens
> umbras corporibus negat.
> quodcumque alluitur solum
> longo Tethyos ambitu,
> Alcidae domuit labor.

> Peace from Hercules' hand
> Reigns from Dawn to Hesperus,
> And where the midday Sun
> Gives bodies no shadows.
> Whatever tract is lapped
> By Tethys' long circuit
> Alcides' toil has tamed.

However, the 'hand', which brought peace, is also the instrument of anger, violent aggression and narcissistic, megalomanical ambition, viz. the instrument of an amalgam of passions or *affectus* which move easily into madness

---

[289] See Comm. *ad* 118–22.

and familicide. The Euripidean gods, Iris and Lyssa (*Herac.* 822ff.), are not required to make Hercules mad; this play dramatizes a seamless transition from the sane to the insane mind.[290]

Contemporary modes of thought pervade the drama, including Stoic ones. In the Greek and Roman literary traditions Hercules was an ambivalent figure: a wielder of just force and civilizer on the one hand, a hybristic, brutish thug on the other, the latter sometimes burlesqued in comedy.[291] Stoic moral theory focused on the former image, and cast him regularly as a model of the Stoic *sapiens* or 'sage' and of the *uirtus* which defined him, a paradigm especially of the sage's ability to endure adversity. He was also paraded by the Stoics as a benefactor of mankind, a 'pacifier of land and sea', *terrarum marisque pacator*, as Seneca calls him in *De Beneficiis* (1.13.3). The latter 'title' was a constituent of the Roman imperial image.[292] And while Hercules exhibits the gap between this image (*pacis auctorem*, 250; cf. 441ff., 882–92), even self-image (926ff.), and the reality of manic violence which problematizes the whole concept of *uirtus*, this tragedy comes closer than any of the surviving plays to exhibiting a Stoic moral position.

One of Seneca's most extraordinary innovations in this play is its ending, which not only secures the connection to the contemporary intellectual and political world but is quite unlike anything else in Senecan drama.[293] In Euripides, Heracles' suicidal state of mind is changed perhaps rather easily by Theseus' offer of refuge in Athens (*Herac.* 1311ff.). In Seneca, Hercules' decision not to kill himself requires a lengthy, arresting scene, in which Amphitryon threatens suicide, while making it clear that such a suicide will be Hercules' responsibility and 'sane' crime: *aut uiuis aut occidis* ('Your choice is life or murder', 1308). Hercules responds to this attempt and to Amphitryon by commanding his 'virtue' to yield (1315–17, cited above). 'It

---

[290] Fitch (1987*a*: 30) writes of the 'continuity between the sane and insane mind'. See also Shelton (1978: 63–6), Braden (1993: 249–52), Harrison (2014: 623), and Fitch's excellent discussion (24ff.) of Hercules' 'obsessive' psychology and its proximity to madness. This focus on 'the *psychological* causation of madness' Fitch sees as absent from Euripides and 'original to Seneca' (p. 31). See further below pp. 111–12.

[291] Heracles/Hercules as civilizer: Pindar *Isthm.* 4.57, Virg. *Aen.* 6.802–3; as thug, Hom. *Il.* 5.403, *Od.* 21.28, Soph. *Trach.* Virgil's treatment of Hercules in *Aeneid* 8 epitomizes the ambivalence: see Boyle (1999). See further (and for Heracles in Greek comedy) §VI above.

[292] Aug. *RG* 13; Sen. *Clem.* 1.2; Calp. Sic. 1.42ff.

[293] Fitch (1987*a*: 35–8), who sees no transformed *uirtus* in this final act and paints a negative picture of Hercules throughout the play, aligns the ending closely with that of other Senecan tragedies. There are certainly similarities, especially in the way the play suddenly stops, but there are also important differences, as I try to outline. Self-transformation is, of course, a recurring goal of the later *Epistulae Morales*, applicable to both the author of the epistles and their addressee: see Edwards (1997). Bexley (2022: 161–3, 338) follows Fitch in seeing Hercules as solely concerned with *fama*.

is the mark of a mighty mind to remain alive for another's sake', wrote Seneca in *Epistulae Morales* (*ingentis animi est aliena causa ad uitam reuerti*, 104.4). Hercules complies. Gone is the Lucretia paradigm: 'If I live, I did the crimes—dead, I suffered them', *si uiuo, feci scelera; si morior, tuli* (1278). Gone is the Aeneas paradigm and its conflation of *uirtus* and *arma*. Victim of Juno's *furor*, Hercules yet resists the impulse to violence which marks the end of Rome's great epic. Gone, too, perhaps most importantly, are the claims of divine paternity and status (1157ff., 1202ff.). Indifferent earlier to the emotional suffering of his family (the Euripidean Heracles' speech of affection for wife and children at *Herac.* 621–36 is omitted by Seneca), Hercules responds with recognition of his all too obvious humanity and of the importance of the ties of kin. The *pietas uirtusque* for which the Chorus prayed (1093–4) return to Hercules in an unexpected and (in part) Stoic form. *Pietas* is dramatized as a human virtue displayed in the behaviour of men to men, *uirtus* as (among other things) *temperantia*,[294] self-control, even self-abnegation, the ability to resist violence and to submit one's will to another, even if intolerable suffering ensues. The values perverted by contemporary Roman culture, especially the Julio-Claudian court, are affirmed as the basis of human relations. This is self-conquest, not in the sense intended by Juno in the prologue (*se uincat*, 116), but in an almost transcendent form, self-mastery, even self-imperialism. The *Epistulae Morales* again (113.31):

> imperare sibi maximum imperium est.

> The greatest command is to command oneself.

And/or: The greatest empire is the empire of the self.

Importantly self-imperialism sometimes involves yielding to another's *imperium*, here (1315) the *imperium* of the father, as Seneca himself had done. Hercules gives himself an order which not only emanates from and confirms the empire of his self, but one which cuts into the world and life of the man who created this scene and authored this play.

But despite Hercules' self-conquest, despite his climactic performance of *pietas* and *uirtus* transformed, the agony, the isolation, the *furor* remain (1323–9):

---

[294] One of the four sub-divisions (*partes*) of Stoic *uirtus* listed at *Ep. Mor.* 120.11 (cited p. 103 above). *Fortitudo*, another of the *partes* listed, is also clearly evident in Hercules' decision to live.

quis Tanais aut quis Nilus aut quis Persica
uiolentus unda Tigris aut Rhenus ferox
Tagusue Hibera turbidus gaza fluens
abluere dextram poterit? Arctoum licet
Maeotis in me gelida transfundat mare
et tota Tethys per meas currat manus,
haerebit altum facinus.

What Tanais, what Nile or what violent
Tigris with Persian flood or frenzied Rhine
Or turbid Tagus, awash with Spain's gold,
Can cleanse this hand? Though icy Maeotis
Pour its Arctic sea on me, and Tethys
Stream over my hands with all her waters,
The crime will stick deep.

The hand which murdered his children (1192–3) and was to murder the impious monstrosity (*monstrum impium*, 1280) he had become, and which (so Hercules asserts) cannot be cleansed, is also the hand which his earthly father has clasped (1319). His loyal comrade Theseus, tolerant towards the 'guilty' (*nocentes*, 1337), concludes the play by offering a place of purification. In Euripides' drama Heracles responds to Theseus' offer; Seneca's Hercules does not. He has destroyed all place for himself. The play, like several other Senecan tragedies, does not end, but stops. A tableau of bloody corpses still dominates the stage. The possibilities of redemption expressed in Theseus' short speech seem but sounds upon the air.

The Heroic Self

The presentation of Hercules' mind is in the forefront of the play from Juno's prologue to the protagonist's final speech of despair. That mind is viewed from a plethora of perspectives: those of Juno, the Theban Chorus, Amphitryon, Megara, Lycus, and Theseus—and is viewed most crucially from the words and actions of Hercules himself. Juno's extensive psychological portrait of the hero frames the play, which she prescripts and begins. Her focus is on his joy in her wrath (34), his untamed virtue (39) and love of her commands (42), his propensity for violence (42–4), his bursting of boundaries (46–56), his savagery and pride (57–8), and his overweening celestial ambitions (64–74, 89–90). It is a biased portrait of a violent, unbalanced, megalomanical personality. The Chorus moderate Juno's assessment but yet sustain it, by concluding their initial ode with a more modulated criticism of Hercules' breaking of boundaries (186–91) and the flawed nature of his 'spirited virtue' (*uirtus animosa*, 201).

Hercules has not yet entered the drama but by the end of the first choral ode the audience already have two distinct perspectives from which to view him. Four more are added in Act II. To Amphitryon Hercules seems a heroic juggernaut, moving from labour to labour with 'no rest, no idle time' (212–13), and a true son of Jupiter (439–89); to Lycus Hercules is trapped in hell, and neither a true son of Jupiter nor even heroic (430–80). Megara offers a double perspective. Longing for her husband and exhorting him to 'burst…the bounds of things' (*erumpe rerum terminos*, 290), she yet despairs of his return from hell in the dialogue with Amphitryon (308), but switches, when conversing with Lycus, to a belief in his certain return and future deification (422–38). The choral ode which follows is non-psychological. Just before the hero's first appearance in the play it focuses on Hercules' deeds and, using the problematic example of Orpheus, calls for him to 'conquer the laws of wild Styx' (*euincas…iura ferae Stygis*, 558), utilizing not Orphic song but physical force (*uiribus*, 591).

The audience are then presented with Hercules' triumphant return and a twenty-six-line speech filled with pointers to the hero's mind (592–617). Character, as Aristotle observed,[295] is a function of practice, actions taken and deeds performed, not of the second-hand accounts of others. At last the audience get to compare the preceding, prejudicially narrated examples of Hercules' actions with those of the hero himself. An opening prayer for forgiveness from Phoebus, Jupiter, and Neptune quickly turns into a display (through closed soliloquy) of Hercules' obsession with Juno and with his own supreme self (604–13), even as he gives hybristic voice to the claim of power over death, expressed ominously as victory over 'dire Jove' (*diro…Ioui*, 608). This is a man/god, a person between worlds, a cosmically liminal figure,[296] not only obsessed with himself, but restless for more achievement, complaining about the 'idleness' (*cessare*) of his hands (614–15). Only the sudden sight of hostile soldiers draws him away from his own self-imaging (616–17). Not for one second in his opening speech does Hercules mention

---

[295] *NE* 2.1.1, where he presents ἦθος, 'character', as derived from ἔθος, 'habit': see Bexley (2022: 23).

[296] Hercules' costuming seems itself to reflect his liminal nature: see Comm. before 592–617.

'home', 'family', or any of its members.[297] Euripides' Heracles could not be more different. He mentions every member of his family (children, wife, father), together with his 'house, doors and hearth' (μέλαθρον πρόπυλά θ' ἑστίας ἐμῆς), in his much shorter speech when entering the play (*Herac.* 523–30). Seneca seems concerned to lay out—in a way in which Euripides is not—the psychological foundation for the madness to come.

In the short scene between Hercules and his family (618–40) Amphitryon movingly initiates an embrace from his son, who, after noticing the squalor of the dress of his family and learning of Lycus' capture of the city and fatal designs on his kin, criticizes the 'ungrateful land' (*ingrata tellus*, 631) of Thebes for failing to help 'the house of Hercules' (*Herculeae domus*, 631), and moves immediately to thoughts of bloody slaughter, asking his foster-father and wife to 'defer embraces' (*differ amplexus... differ*, 638–9). Acting like the heroic automaton described at the beginning of Act II (212–13), Hercules exits to slay Lycus, leaving his wife in a desolate state. It is Theseus not Hercules who consoles Megara (640–4). But Megara is not the only one left wanting more of Hercules; so, too, as remarked above, is each member of Seneca's audience, who are made to feel what Amphitryon and Megara have felt, though that feeling will in part be assuaged by a long narrative of Hercules' *catabasis* and his capture of Cerberus by one who has also returned from hell.

Theseus' narrative reveals much about Hercules, especially (and unsurprisingly) his use of violence to resolve all problems, even such a simple matter as the boarding of Charon's ferry. The contrast with the more diplomatic embarcation of Aeneas is readily apparent in Seneca's Virgilian handling of the event. The successful use of violence (*uiribus*, 591) to conquer the kingdom of the dead was what the preceding choral ode had exhorted. Hercules' whole mentality, as recorded in Theseus' narrative, is focused entirely on that goal. But there is also a proleptic dimension to the story of hell not apparent at the time of Theseus' telling: its role as semiotic precursor of the hell of Hercules' mind about to be displayed and the world of death he is about to create, which, when brought onto the stage after the killings of Act IV, will turn that stage into a terrestrial inferno.[298] Theseus' warning to 'abstain from human blood' (*sanguine humano abstine*, 745) will be patently unrealized in the actions of this play's hero.

---

[297] Even such flawed figures as Agamemnon (*Ag.* 782–3) and Thyestes (*Thy.* 404–10) greet their 'home' on their return.

[298] See 1143–6.

The positive side of Hercules' violence is emphasized in the next choral ode, where his role as pacifier of both earth and hell is lauded (881–92) just before his victorious entry at the opening of Act IV. In the conversation with Amphitryon as the blood-stained hero prepares to sacrifice (918–24), Hercules reveals an indifference to the imperatives of religious ritual (the requirement to self-purify) and a perverted concept of sacrifice (the confla- tion of human and animal victim), which cast an ominous shadow over his whole triumphant behaviour. The 'Golden Age' speech follows, and it begins in a way which develops the narcissistic tendencies of his opening speech (592–617) and confirms Hercules' grandiose, even hybristic, celestial ambi- tions (926–39):

> ipse concipiam preces
> Ioue meque dignas. stet suo caelum loco
> tellusque et aequor. astra inoffensos agant
> aeterna cursus, alta pax gentes alat,
> ferrum omne teneat ruris innocui labor
> ensesque lateant. nulla tempestas fretum
> uiolenta turbet, nullus irato Ioue
> exiliat ignis, nullus hiberna niue
> nutritus agros amnis euersos trahat.
> uenena cessent, nulla nocituro grauis
> suco tumescat herba; non saeui ac truces
> regnent tyranni. si quod etiamnum est scelus
> latura tellus, properet, et, si quod parat
> monstrum, meum sit.

> I'll form prayers worthy
> Of Jove and myself. Let sky, earth, and sea
> Stand in their place. Let eternal stars drive
> Unhindered orbits, deep peace nourish nations,
> All iron belong to toil of guiltless land
> And swords lie hid. Let no violent tempest
> Flay the sea, no flame burst from angry Jove,
> No river nursed by the snows of winter
> Ravage the fields and drag them with it.
> Let poisons cease, no plant swell heavy
> With noxious juice, no cruel and brutal
> Tyrants rule. If earth even now will bear

> Some evil, let her rush, and, if she grooms
> A monster, let it be mine.

The pairing of himself and Jupiter and the projected cosmic reach of their power are followed by the fantasy of a golden world ordered by the hero himself. Psychologically what is presented is a hero both 'illusionary and unstable',[299] whose articulation of this ideal world climaxes disruptively in the image of a monstrosity which will indeed belong to Hercules, because it will be himself.

The 'madness scene' which ensues commences in a patently realistic way—*sed quid hoc?* 'But what's this? (939)—to underscore the psychological continuities involved. Seneca seems to be showing how this self-obsessed man of violence can become so intoxicated with his bloody victories and the supremacy of his physical might and of himself as to topple into madness. There is no divine figure such as Euripides' Lyssa to enter the stage to make Hercules mad,[300] nor any Euripidean messenger to tell the audience that Hercules 'was no longer himself' (Eur. *Herac.* 931). Hercules becomes mad *because he is Hercules*. He is a victim of his own ambitious, overreaching, narcissistic, isolated, and violent self.[301] Juno, of course, has a role, since she summoned the Furies and prescripted the play (discussed below). But here in Act IV Seneca wants the audience to observe the psychological consequences of a life of constant and unrelieved violence— for that is how Amphitryon described his foster-son's existence in the opening words of Act II (205–13). A modern audience are likely to find partial illumination in recent discussions of PTSD, 'combat trauma' and 'family annihilators'.[302] Whatever one's terminology, Seneca has deliberately left out the gods from this cardinal moment in the play to underscore the human nature of what is being dramatized. It's as if he took inspiration from the question Euripides' Amphitryon puts to Heracles (*Herac.* 966–7):

---

[299] Motto and Clark (1994: 270).

[300] A problem for Wilamowitz's thesis of Euripides' Heracles: see next n.

[301] A similar view was propounded of Euripides' Heracles by Wilamowitz in his 1895 edition of the Greek tragedy (1.150): 'die tat aber ist eine folge der herakleischen eignen natur geworden.' As Riley (2008: 212) observes, Wilamowitz's interpretation 'better applies to Seneca's *Hercules Furens*'.

[302] See e.g. N. Bernstein (2017: 112): 'Hercules' unexpected outburst of violence against his family, followed by an equally abrupt collapse into a stupor, fits a pattern that modern readers are tempted to associate with the domestic violence perpetrated by veterans of the Iraq and Afghanistan conflicts.'

οὐ τί που φόνος σ᾽ ἐβάκχευσεν νεκρῶν,
οὓς ἄρτι καίνεις;

Surely the slaughter of men you just killed
Didn't make you mad?

Hercules' hallucinations follow: the darkening of the midday sky, Leo's cosmic threat, an imminent Titanomachy, a witnessed Gigantomachy, an
encounter with the Furies. The madness inflicted on Euripides' Heracles has
a coherent narrative structure (*Herac.* 931–1008): a journey to Mycenae,
where he slays the children of Eurystheus and aims to kill Eurystheus himself. The shifting hallucinations of Seneca's Hercules are united not as conjoined narratives but as mutually corroborating indices of psychological
instability and megalomania.[303] Madness is realized onstage in a way which
confirms the megalomaniacal proclivities of Hercules' earlier speeches
before the bloody climax of the act is realized, the slaughter of children
and wife.

Little is said psychologically about Hercules in the play's final choral ode,
as the hero turns and twists in his sleep. But Act V is profoundly psychological,
and presents onstage and in depth the operations of Hercules' mind.
Hercules' opening speech begins grandly, even grandiosely, and continues
with the focus sharply on Hercules' obsession with self. But the audience are
about to witness Hercules' 'war with himself' in a manner neither prescripted nor foreseen by Juno, when she laid down the plot of the play (*Herc.*
85). This psychological dramatization moves through five stages: i. the
gradual recognition of the familicide; ii. the acceptance of responsibility and
guilt for it; iii. the resolution to commit suicide; iv. the decision to live for
the sake of Amphitryon; v. the agony and despair of existential dislocation.

Stage ii merits particular analysis. Amphitryon, aware of Juno's hostility
and acting metatheatrically as if he had witnessed the play's prologue, tries
to put the blame on Juno (1199–1201):

HERCVLES   genitor, hoc nostrum est scelus?
                      tacuere. nostrum est.

AMPHITRYON   luctus est istic tuus,
                   crimen nouercae. casus hic culpa caret.

---

[303] Fitch (1987a: 29): 'it is the relevance of the visions to Hercules' individual psychology
that is of primary importance in the play.' For an excellent discussion of the madness scene in
Hercules, see Riley (2008: 76–84).

HERCULES   Father, is this crime mine?
(*Aside*) They're silent. It's mine.

AMPHITRYON   The grief is yours, the crime
Your stepmother's. What happened leaves you blameless.

And at 1297:

> hoc Iuno telum manibus emisit tuis.
>
> Juno fired this arrow with your hands.

At 1237 he excuses the action as involuntary, a 'mistake':

> quis nomen usquam sceleris errori addidit?
>
> Who ever gave error the name of crime?[304]

But Hercules will have none of it. He accepts full responsibility for the familicide (1216–18):

> quin structum aceruans nemore congesto aggerem
> cruore corpus impio sparsum cremo?
> sic, sic agendum est. inferis reddam Herculem.
>
> Why don't I pile up a forest, build a pyre,
> Burn my body drenched with impious blood?
> Thus, thus I must act. I'll return Hercules to hell.

Rather than blame Juno or the Furies, he addresses the latter simply as denizens of hell. The self-recrimination and self-assault are specific. In a speech which completely upends the weeping and words of Euripides' hero (*Herac.* 1353–7, 1377–85, 1394),[305] Hercules poignantly acknowledges his own emotional deficiencies and then fiercely attacks the constituents of himself responsible both for the triumphs of his labours, that tower of achievement promoted by Amphitryon at the start of Act II, and for the destruction of his family (1226–36):

> pectus o nimium ferum!
> quis uos per omnem, liberi, sparsos domum
> deflere digne poterit? hic durus malis

---

[304] For metatheatrical aspects of Amphitryon's question, see Comm. *ad loc.*
[305] See Comm. *ad* 1226–30, 1231–6.

> lacrimare uultus nescit. huc ensem date,
> date huc sagittas, stipitem huc uastum date.
> 　tibi tela frangam nostra, tibi nostros, puer,
> rumpemus arcus. at tuis stipes grauis
> ardebit umbris. ipsa Lernaeis frequens
> pharetra telis in tuos ibit rogos.
> dent arma poenas. uos quoque infaustas meis
> cremabo telis, o nouercales manus.

> 　　　O too brutal heart!
> Who can shed fitting tears for you, children,
> Spattered through all the palace. This face, hard
> With suffering, cannot weep. Bring here my sword,
> Bring here my arrows; my great club—bring it here.

> 　　*Addresses the bodies of his* SONS *and* MEGARA.

> For you I'll break my arrows, for you, child,
> I'll smash my bow. But the heavy club I'll burn
> For *your* spirit. The quiver itself, packed
> With Lernaean shafts, will join your pyre.
> Let these weapons pay. You, too, I shall burn—
> Curse of my weapons—O stepmother hands.

Like Shakespeare's Prospero offering to 'break' his staff and 'drown' his book,[306] Hercules seeks to destroy the constituents of his own identity. But note that, though he castigates his hands as 'stepmother hands' (1236), he is filled not with anger at Juno but with shame (*pudor*, 1240).

Amphitryon even concedes that Hercules' lethal actions might have been a crime, but argues for their singularity (*unius…criminis*, 'the one crime', 1266). Hercules protests (1267–8):

> ueniam dabit sibi ipse, qui nulli dedit?
> laudanda feci iussus; hoc unum meum est.

> Will he pardon himself, who pardoned none?
> My lauded deeds were ordered; this one's mine.

What Seneca is doing here is what he does at the end of *Oedipus*, namely, combining two distinct theories of causation: the theory that human action

---

[306] See Comm. *ad* 1231–6.

is caused by outside forces ('fate', 'Juno', 'the Furies') and the theory that it is caused by human agency.[307] This play has presented the thesis that it is caused by both, but in the crucial fourth act, where Hercules descends into madness, the playwright has emphasized the psychological basis of the event.[308] Whereas in Euripides' play Heracles blames Hera (*Herac.* 1303–10, 1392–3) and it is Amphitryon who assigns primary responsibility for the act to his foster-son (*Herac.* 1135, 1139, 1184);[309] in Seneca's play the roles are reversed. Whatever the causal role of Juno or fate (or the dictates of the mythological and literary tradition and the play's prologic script)—and it is clear that they all have a significant role—actions and their consequences, whatever the intention of the agent, are what matter in this play.[310] An 'unknowing' familicide, like an unknowing, incestuous parricide, is exempt neither from the moral and social impurity entailed by what has been done nor from the guilt of the deed's performance. Hercules is guilty and a *monstrum*; and he accepts this (1279–81):[311]

> iamdudum mihi
> monstrum impium saeuumque et immite ac ferum
> oberrat.

> For a long time
> A monster, impious, savage, pitiless,
> Brutal ranges before me.

[307] Virgil similarly combines the theories; hence the 'double causation' often found in the *Aeneid* (see e.g. the final lines of Jupiter's speech at *Aen* 10.111–13). The psychological explanation of madness appealed to Cicero, who preferred it as an explanation of the insanity which follows parricide (which is, of course, *not* Hercules' madness) to the notion of its causation by avenging Furies (*Rosc. Am.* 67).

[308] Lawall (1983) in his fine essay on the play ignores the psychological focus in Act IV, and misdescribes when he assigns full responsibility for Hercules' familicide to 'the goddess who maliciously plunges him into a disaster for which none of the human characters in the play blame him' (6). One of the human characters explicitly blames Hercules, namely Hercules himself. And the final line of the play (1344), spoken by Theseus, implies that Hercules is 'guilty', *nocens*. Lawall's ascription of full responsibility to Juno/Hera (see also Billerbeck and Guex 2002: 26–8) applies to Euripides' *Heracles*, not to the *Hercules* of Seneca. Similarly, those who advance the psychological thesis only (Owen 1968, Shelton 1978, Fitch 1987a, Riley 2008, etc.) dismiss too easily the dramatic and thematic force of Juno's prologue (recalled by the hallucinated Furies of 982–6), Amphitryon's ascription of blame to Juno (1200–1, 1297), and the causal role of Juno's *ira* emphasized in the Roman literary tradition. See also Billerbeck (2014: 430).

[309] Simon Armitage's Amphitryon in *Mister Heracles* (2000) is blunter than Euripides': 'Heracles, you killed them, nobody else' (p. 44).

[310] Stoicism taught a version of 'character and motive' ethics, evaluating the morality of an action by the intention of the agent. This play, like *Oedipus*, profers rather a form of 'act and consequence' ethics, examining an act in terms of its results.

[311] For discussion of these lines, see Comm. *ad loc.*

But what is he to do? The second half of Act V devotes itself to a more nuanced view of the heroic self, one in which its apparently inflexible view of 'guilt', 'shame', 'honour', and 'self-image' (*scelus, pudor, decus, fama*), and the accompanying loss of 'all things of value' (*cuncta... bona*, 1279), yield to the claims of *pietas* and the softer values of *fides* and *amicitia*.[312] Hercules' *uiuamus* ('let us live') resolution signals the triumph of *uirtus* transformed, even as it leads to pain, increased isolation, and despair. Though suicide has been renounced, Hercules' longing for death and punishment seems undiminished at the play's end (1338–40). One might argue that Theseus' traditional offer of sanctuary in Athens provides a way forward out of this pain and self-loathing, and offers the possibility of moral reparation. Many, perhaps most, have thought so. But Seneca deliberately leaves the matter ambiguous. No response is forthcoming from Hercules. The audience are left to reflect upon the augmented agony of a transformed heroic mind, indeed a transformed heroic self, and perhaps the impossibility of redemption. The jussive *uiuamus* augurs the continuance, not the end of suffering. There seems to be no final labour.[313]

Rome, Death, and the End of Place

The audience are also left to contemplate the value of Hercules' storied conquest of death, the immediate and ironic consequences of which have been the deaths of Hercules' sons and wife. Like Seneca's great drama of collective suffering, *Troades*, this play is preoccupied with death. But unlike that drama,[314] this play, despite an occasional use of the motif, offers no sustained view of death as liberation. The view of death's dominion provided by the Chorus and Theseus was discussed above. What this play particularly underscores—and this is most palpably dramatized in the final choral ode and act—is not only death's dominion, but (and this is precisely the opposite of a Stoic position and is to be found also in *Troades* and *Phaedra*) death as irreparable human loss. Thus the Chorus' final lyric lines (1131–7):

---

[312] The view of Riley (2008: 125), that Hercules' 'understanding and manifestation of virtue remains unchanged' seems precisely the opposite of what Seneca's ending shows. She dismisses Hercules' Catullan *uiuamus* 'as, at best, an act of delayed and grudging *pietas*' (89). The Seneca of *Ep. Mor.* 78.2—*imperaui mihi ut uiuerem*, 'I ordered myself to live'—is unlikely to have agreed with her.

[313] See Gunderson (2015: 131). Contrast Euripides' Heracles, who describes his filicide as the 'final labour' (λοίσθιον...πόνον, *Herac.* 1279).

[314] And others: see e.g. *Agamemnon*. For Seneca's view of death as liberation in the prose works, see esp. *Ep. Mor.* 26.

> ite ad Stygios, umbrae, portus,
>   ite, innocuae,
> quas in primo limine uitae
> scelus oppressit patriusque furor.
> ite, infaustum genus, o pueri,
> noti per iter triste laboris;
> ite, iratos uisite reges.

> Go to Stygian harbours, go,
>   Innocent shades,
> Whom on life's first threshold
> Crime has crushed and father's fury.
> Go, boys, O cursèd brood,
> Along that famed labour's grim path;
> Go, meet the angry monarchs.

And yet, of course, Rome was an empire founded on death, the death of enemies, peoples, realms. Indeed Rome's entwinement with death seems to be a powerful subtext at particular moments in the play. Hercules was very much a Roman deity; and *Hercules* is very much a Roman play, whose titular figure was associated with several Julio-Claudian emperors, and whose action and linguistic structure have been modelled for a Roman world. As noted above and throughout the Commentary, the whole drama is saturated with Roman imagery, conceptions, practices, and motifs.

Euripides begins his *Heracles* with dialogue between Amphitryon and Megara (Act II in Seneca): Seneca recasts Virgil's and Ovid's Juno to provide from the start a Roman frame,[315] and confirms that frame not only through continuing Virgilian and Ovidian allusion, but through triumphal, military, legal, and other Roman imagery permeating both prologue (see esp. 46ff., 57ff.) and play (military and legal motifs compete for dominance in Act V), and through motifs and language of religion, sacrifice (see esp. 634ff., 895–939), theatre and amphitheatre (esp. 838–9, 939ff.), especially potent to a Roman audience.[316] Particularly pervasive throughout the play is the language of metatheatre,[317] which, in underscoring the theatricality of the

---

[315] For details, see Lawall (1983: 6ff.).
[316] See further Comm. *ad* 19–29 (Roman military imagery), 46–52 (Roman referentiality), 57–63 (triumphal imagery), 731–4 (legal language/imagery), 918–24 (imagery of sacrifice). Hadas (1939) discusses the amphitheatrical modelling of the scene at *Herc.* 939ff., where Hercules kills his wife and children.
[317] See Comm. *ad* 109–12.

play's action, underscores, too, the theatricality of the Rome which that action reflects.

Striking in its appeal to Roman structures is a scene such as the moment of Hercules' return from his slaughter of Lycus, when the motifs of death, triumph, and sacrifice fuse (895–9):

> ultrice dextra fusus aduerso Lycus
> terram cecidit ore. tum quisquis comes
> fuerat tyranni iacuit et poenae comes.
> nunc sacra patri uictor et superis feram
> caesisque meritas uictimis aras colam.

> My avenging hand made Lycus sprawl;
> He hit the earth face-down. Then each comrade
> Of the tyrant fell, comrade, too, in death.
> Now victor, I'll sacrifice to father and gods,
> Honouring due altars with slain victims.

Or when a metatheatrical opening is followed by the ceremonial language of sacrifice to describe insane murder (1035–8):

> bene habet. pudendi regis excisa est domus.
> tibi hunc dicatum, maximi coniunx Iouis,
> gregem cecidi. uota persolui libens
> te digna, et Argos uictimas alias dabit.

> All is well. The shameful king's house is razed.
> For thee, wife of greatest Jove, I have slain
> This consecrated flock. I've gladly paid vows
> Worthy of thee. Argos will give other victims.

So the deranged Hercules on the murder of his children. Interesting is the phrase *te digna* ('worthy of thee', 1038). *Dignus* with the ablative is used elsewhere in this play, sometimes in heavily ironic contexts. At 926–7 Hercules forms 'prayers worthy Of Jove and myself' (*preces Ioue meque dignas*)—just before the onset of madness. When madness descends, he desires to assault the heavens, 'labour worthy of Alcides', *dignus Alcide labor* (957). Suetonius claims to quote an imperial rescript of Nero, during his infamous tour of Greece in 66–7 CE, suggesting that the advice from Rome should be that he 'return worthy of Nero' (*ut Nerone dignus reuertar*, *Nero*

23.1). Such an incident postdates this play. But there may have been some-thing imperial in this mannerism, which Seneca wishes to embed in Hercules' words.

Similarly Hercules' competition with Jove may have reminded the audi-ence of Caligula's insane attempt to replace Jupiter (Suet. *Gaius* 22). What is clear is that from the late republic onwards politicians and emperors had associated themselves with Hercules,[318] and, like Seneca's Hercules (926ff.), some (Augustus and Nero) claimed to inaugurate a new Golden Age.[319] The criticism in Juno's prologue of Hercules being 'storied a god' (*deus narratur*, 39–40) by the whole world and of his own desire for Olympus (74) rewrites Euripides' underplaying of Heracles' destined divinity to frame the drama with contemporary imperial practice. By the time Nero succeeded to the throne Julius Caesar, Augustus, and Claudius had been 'storied a god', and this is not to mention Caligula's deification of his sister. Even Ovid took issue with contemporary apotheoses, including Hercules among the precedents, in this address to humanity (*Am.* 3.8.51–2):

> qua licet adfectas caelum quoque. templa Quirinus,
> > Liber et Alcides et modo Caesar habent.

> Where it's allowed, you aim for heaven, too. Quirinus, Liber
> > And Alcides have temples and now Caesar.

Most pertinent of all, perhaps, is Theseus' exclusive focus on princes in his non-Euripidean and non-Virgilian account of the judgement of the dead,[320] which can only have pointed in the direction of the imperial court (735–47):

> quod quisque fecit, patitur. auctorem scelus
> repetit suoque premitur exemplo nocens.
> uidi cruentos carcere includi duces
> et impotentis terga plebeia manu
> scindi tyranni. quisquis est placide potens

---

[318] See §VI above 57–8.   [319] See Virg. *Aen.* 6.791ff. Calp. Sic. 1.33ff., 4.5ff.

[320] Despite the plethora of Virgilian allusions throughout Theseus' description of hell: see Comm. The Virgilian Sibyl's description of the judgment of the dead at *Aen.* 6.60ff., differs markedly from that of Theseus. The Sibyl lists a large variety of contemporary crimes but devotes less than a single line to tyranny (*Aen.* 6.621).

dominusque uitae seruat innocuas manus
et incruentum mitis imperium regit
animaeque parcit, longa permensus diu
felicis aeui spatia uel caelum petit
uel laeta felix nemoris Elysii loca,
iudex futurus. sanguine humano abstine
quicumque regnas. scelera taxantur modo
maiore uestra.

All suffer their own deeds. Crime seeks its author;
The guilty are crushed by their own example.
I saw blood-drenched leaders locked in a jail
And the backs of raving tyrants scourged
By plebeian hands. The gentle monarch
And life's master, who keeps his hands guiltless
And rules an empire mildly without blood,
Sparing life—he measures for years long tracts
Of a happy age and heads for heaven
Or the Elysian grove's joyous places happy,
A judge-to-be. Abstain from human blood,
All you who rule. Greater punishments await
Your crimes.

The Roman socio-political term *plebeia*, 'plebeian' (738), and politico-military term *imperium*, 'empire' (741), intensify the contemporary force of this description. So, too, does Theseus' concluding address (745–7), as dramatically arresting as it is inappropriate. It is as if the character has stepped from the play and is haranguing the audience (or certain members of it). Seneca breaks the 'fourth wall' to make his meaning non-opaque.

The fourth act and its preceding choral ode have strong political semiotics. The Chorus describe Hercules' 'civilizing' of the world in the cosmic and global imagery of the *Pax Romana* (882–8):

pax est Herculea manu
Auroram inter et Hesperum,
et qua Sol medium tenens
umbras corporibus negat.
quodcumque alluitur solum
longo Tethyos ambitu
Alcidae domuit labor.

> Peace from Hercules' hand
> Reigns from Dawn to Hesperus,
> And where the midday Sun
> Gives bodies no shadows.
> Whatever tract is lapped
> By Tethys' long circuit
> Alcides' toil has tamed.

The laudation for Heracles at the comparable point in Euripides' play (*Herac.* 763–814) is for his slaying of the tyrant and the deliverance of Thebes. Seneca has universalized and Romanized the laudation to reflect contemporary political concerns. He has also problematized it. For the area covered by the *Pax Herculea*, 'from Dawn to Hesperus' (*Auroram inter et Hesperum*, 883), has been pronounced as part of the dominion of death (870–1). The Romanization is continued by Hercules himself in his proclamation of the 'Golden Age' state of the world (926–39, cited above), in which the allusions to the Roman Golden Age of Virgil's fourth *Eclogue* make the political semiotics overt.[321] But then Hercules topples into madness. That this concept of a Golden Age world, the *Pax Herculea*, and the madness which follows are intricately connected is shown by their concurrence at 955–7.

> perdomita tellus, tumida cesserunt freta,
> inferna nostros regna sensere impetus.
> immune caelum est, dignus Alcide labor.

> Earth is tamed, the swelling seas have yielded,
> The infernal realm has felt our onslaught.
> Heaven escapes—labour worthy of Alcides.

Golden Age language is repeated in the midst of the madness to reveal the interconnection of such aspirations and the bursting of moral and religious boundaries. It is as if Hercules' striving for this Golden Age has indexed a megalomania,[322] which now collapses upon itself, and the result is a kind of Oedipal state, a failure to recognize both self and kin.[323] There may even be

---

[321] For the allusions, see Comm. *ad loc.*

[322] One aspect of this megalomania is Hercules' fondness for self-naming, revealed in 957 above and in nine other instances in this and the final act: see Comm. *ad* 957. On self-naming in Senecan tragedy, see Comm. *ad* 109–12, and Fitch and McElduff (2008: 163–6).

[323] See Braden (1993: 249).

an allusion to Phaethon, the subtextual figure of the 'Dawn Ode', as over-weening pride leads to disaster.[324]

The Oedipal analogy seems both sharper and more pressing in its ramifications for the Roman world. Rome's primal and defining sin, *scelus nostrum* ('our sin', Virg. *Ecl.* 4.13), lay precisely in the failure to recognize self and kin, i.e. in civil war, whether mythologized in the fratricidal act of the city's foundation or realized in the civil wars of the late republic and (beyond this play) in the post-Julio-Claudian struggle for imperial power. What the audience witness in Act IV is the perversion of one of Rome's defining institutions, the religious sacrifice, as the Golden Age image implodes into monstrosity and madness and into a theatrical slaughter of kin, which predates on the stage the bloody internecine killings of 68–9 CE. This dramatization of the global conqueror turning his own violence upon kin is a Janus-like image, perhaps Seneca's clearest and most potent, of Rome itself.[325]

As well as the perversion of a religious institution and a political ideal, Act IV also presents, as noted above,[326] the perversion and inversion of a literary *topos*, the hero's homecoming. Hercules returns like Odysseus and kills the enemies of his family but he kills his family as well. The killing of family was a feature of earlier Roman, 'Herculean' emperors (Augustus, Tiberius, Caligula, Claudius) and will be a conspicuous feature, too, of Seneca's pupil, as the dramatist of *Octavia* will display. The overreaching Julio-Claudian monarchy is one of the institutions examined in Seneca's play.

Act V opens with a thoroughly Roman Hercules, imitating the great ancestor of the Roman race, Aeneas (1138):[327]

> quis hic locus, quae regio, quae mundi plaga?

> What place is this, what region, what stretch of world?

The Roman nature of this grandiose opening is important. For this act will scrutinize the central Roman value of *uirtus* and the relationship between Rome and place. Hercules' transformation of his 'virtue' and how this

---

[324] As Littlewood (2004: 112) suggests.

[325] 'Global conqueror' is important here. In a sense Hercules is fulfilling in advance Lucan's advice to Rome (*BC* 1.22–3): *totum sub Latias leges cum miseris orbem,* | *in te uerte manus,* 'When you have subdued the whole world, | Then turn your hands upon yourself.' 'Self-killing Rome' is a *topos* of late first-century BCE literature: see e.g. Hor. *Epod.* 16.2, Livy 1. Pref. 4.

[326] See p. 92.

[327] See Comm. *ad loc.* The line may also have reminded some members of Seneca's audience of the Homeric Odysseus' words when awaking on Ithaca (*Od.* 13.200), underlining Hercules' inversion of Odysseus' return in the *Odyssey*.

accorded with Seneca's life have been discussed.[328] What was not observed
was how this constituted a rejection of the central Stoic paradigm of a
rational and moral suicide, that of Cato the younger in Utica. What was also
not observed was the relationship between Act V's focus on place and the
play's bearing on Rome. Echoing Juno's opening complaint that her place,
locus (4), has been usurped, Hercules, 'Hera's Glory' ('Ηρακλῆς), has not
only lost his place in Thebes, but laments that no place remains even for
exile, no place in which he may hide (1331):

> ubique notus perdidi exilio locum.

> Known everywhere, I've destroyed a place for exile.

Place, *locus*, to the ancients (nor only to the ancients) was a core constituent
of identity.[329] This great transgressor of bounded spaces, slayer of kin and precursor of Rome believes that he has destroyed all places, even place itself.
Theseus, either echoing or anticipating the ironic thesis of Seneca's Medea
that 'There can never be no place for *uirtus*' (*numquam potest non esse uirtuti
locus, Med.* 161), suggests that he is wrong: that for Hercules, as for his great
descendant, Shakespeare's Coriolanus, 'There is a world elsewhere' (*Cor.* III.
iii.135). Another place 'awaits' (*manet*, 1341), Athens, a place however not for
revenge, but for purification, one which can make even gods innocent (1344).
To Euripides' Athenian audience the transference of Heracles from Thebes to
Athens was a fact of civic history and ideology. But this is a play created in late
Julio-Claudian Rome and Theseus' invitation has literary echoes of death
(1341).[330] The irony for the imperial city, whose boundaries were coextensive
with the civilized world, was that at the time of this play's creation there was
no place to go. As Ovid had trumpeted in his exile poetry (*Tr.* 1.69–70) and in
his most political work, the *Fasti* (1.85–6, 2.684), Rome was place:

> sed quae de septem totum circumspicit orbem
> montibus, imperii Roma deumque locus.

> But she who surveys the whole world from seven hills,
> Rome, the place of empire and gods.

---

[328] See pp. 105–6.   [329] See n. 186 above.
[330] See Comm. *ad loc.* Fitch (1987*a*: 38) misdescribes Theseus' final speech 'as essentially an
epilogue'. No Senecan tragedy ends in an epilogue. Several, including *Hercules*, stop abruptly.

> Iuppiter arce sua totum cum spectet in orbem,
> nil nisi Romanum quod tueatur habet.

> Jupiter viewing the whole world from his tower
> Has nothing unRoman to gaze upon.

> Romanae spatium est urbis et orbis idem.

> Rome's city and the world are the same space.

The purification of Mars, Rome's god (1342–3), bruited by Theseus, predated the existence of Rome. For Ovid, as for Seneca, there was no *locus* beyond Rome. No alternate world now awaited where the *impius* could be cleansed. In Euripides' play Heracles accepted the offer of Theseus, the great 'placer'.[331] Seneca's play ends with no response from its protagonist, unlocated and isolated in worlds he cannot inhabit.[332]

Theatre of Rage

But there is an alternate world already in existence, a *locus* for Hercules, his *uirtus*, *pietas*, and grief: the world of the play, a world dominated by the emotion he has primarily projected in the final two acts and indeed, given the metatheatrical nature of this play's prologue, a world constructed out of that emotion. The emotion is 'Rage'.

Furor, 'Rage', sometimes (in an extreme form) 'Madness', is a quintessentially Roman concept, one which pervades the entire work of the city's and empire's defining poet, Virgil. Virgil's *oeuvre* can be seen as a poetic wrestling with *furor*, whether it is the erotic *furor* of Gallus in the *Eclogues*, Orpheus in the *Georgics*, and Dido in the *Aeneid*, or the bloody rage for slaughter, which despite the promise of its control in the ideological sermon of Book 1 (293–6), manifests itself throughout the *Aeneid*, most notoriously in the 'founding' act of its final lines (*Aen.* 12. 946–52):

---

[331] See Comm. *ad* 1341–4.

[332] Anne Carson in her generically rich *H of H Playbook* (2021), a remodelling of Euripides' *Heracles*, seems somewhat Senecanesque when she has her Heracles figure proclaim his unlocatedness in a voiceover monologue before he even sets foot onstage:

> So I get done with the Labours, I come home, I look in the mirror
> and the mirror is *uninhabited*. No one there.

See further Comm. *ad* 1329–34.

furiis accensus et ira
terribilis: 'tu ne hinc spoliis indute meorum
eripiare mihi? Pallas te hoc uulnere, Pallas
immolat et poenam scelerato ex sanguine sumit.'
hoc dicens ferrum aduerso sub pectore condit
feruidus. ast illi soluuntur frigore membra
uitaque cum gemitu fugit indignata sub umbras.

Inflamed with rage and terrible
In his anger: 'Are you, decked with spoils of my comrades
To be snatched from me? Pallas, Pallas with this wound
Sacrifices you and draws payment from guilty blood.'
Speaking, he sinks the sword in the upturned breast
On fire. The other's limbs go limp with cold;
With a groan life protesting flees beneath shadows.

There is an abundance of rage, *furor*, in Seneca's tragedies. Eliot crudely
misdescribed when he wrote that Seneca's 'characters all speak with the
same voice, and at the top of it,'[333] but there is an observation behind the
error. Rage, *furor*, is commonly displayed on Seneca's stage. Whether it be
the rage of Hippolytus, Theseus, Oedipus, Clytemnestra, Andromache,
Hecuba, Medea, Atreus, or Thyestes, *furor* is never absent from Senecan
tragedy. His drama can be termed a 'theatre of rage', with *Hercules* as one of
its paradigmatic plays. Juno, Megara, Hercules, are all generators of rage.
The play moves from the prologue rage of Juno (1–122) and that of Megara
in Act II (279–308, 372–96, 495–500) to the rage of Hercules in Acts IV and V
(*passim*). By commencing the play with *Iuno furens*, Virgil's divine embodi-
ment of *furor*, Seneca is marking his position—a position soon to be chal-
lenged by his nephew—as Virgil's imperial successor.

As *exemplum* of Seneca's theatre of rage, *Hercules* is rivalled by *Medea*
and *Thyestes*. But Medea's rage, like that of Atreus, controls both plot and
play. Hercules' rage does not. Indeed, though it causes the disaster of Act IV
and is moving to increase that disaster in Act V, it has to be suspended to
allow the play to reach its conclusion. But even when *pietas* triumphs, that
victory is followed by another outburst of Herculean rage, the final state of
the play's hero. *Medea* ends with the titular character's fulfilment and
apotheotic ascension; *Thyestes* ends with the fulfilment and triumph of Atreus.

---

[333] Eliot (1951c: 68).

The plot of *Hercules* ends in a manner less satisfactory to its protagonist. That plot has been controlled, indeed generated, not by the *furor* of Hercules but by that of Juno and of Seneca, who leaves it ambiguous whether Hercules' rage is ended by Theseus' final lines and the dramatic tradition to which they refer (*solet*, 1344).[334]

Other Senecan plays begin from rage. *Agamemnon*, which, like *Hercules* and *Thyestes*, has a protatic character, *Troades* and the late *Phoenissae* are also generated by rage. Seneca in *De Tranquillitate Animi* (17.10–11), following a tradition which leads back to Democritus and Plato,[335] specifies 'madness' as an essential prerequisite for 'sublime' (*grande, sublime*) poetry. And certainly several of the speeches of Hercules in Seneca's play reach the highest registers of the sublime. But Senecan *furor* is about more than poetic register. It is not accidental that Seneca locates *Furor* and the Furies in hell (86–8, 98),[336] or that in one of the central choral odes of *Hercules* (838–9) he figures hell itself as a theatre to which humanity inevitably proceeds. But it is, perhaps, into more than an imaginative hell that Seneca's poetic mind must descend to generate his dramatic fury—a fury which, like the characters of this drama, is in search of a *locus*. Juno tries to find a *locus* on earth, Amphitryon, Megara, and Lycus in Thebes, Theseus in Athens, Hercules in Thebes, in heaven and in hell. They—and Seneca's poetic *furor*—all find it in Seneca's play and in the *theatrum* where it might be performed. Seneca places the *noui ludi theatri*, 'a new theatre's shows' (839), as a *locus* of desire at the heart of this drama as well as a figure for another realm of being. If Rome and the world are coextensive, so, too, are the *dramatis personae* of this play, the play itself, the creative *furor* of its composition and the venue of its performance. But they reflect, and reflect upon, something beyond themselves. They provide a mirror of a Roman world made theatrical by the performance culture of its citizens and made narrow by the restricting bonds of place, and they illumine that world by underscoring within it things which matter.

---

[334] For the metatheatrical force of *solet*, see Comm. *ad loc.*

[335] See pp. 71–2 above.

[336] Seneca is the first author attested to have located *Furor* in hell. See Comm. *ad* 92–9.

VIII. Reception of Seneca's *Hercules*

When on the stage to the admiring court
We strove to represent Alcides' fury
In all that raging heat and pomp of madness
With which the stately Seneca adorned him;
So lively drawn and painted with such horror
That we were forc'd to give it o'er, so loud
The virgins shrieked, so fast they dy'd away.

Lee, *Theodosius or The Force of Love* (1680), I.i.257–63

Antiquity

As with several Senecan tragedies, the reception of *Hercules* begins with
Seneca himself. Hercules does not feature as a character in any of the later
tragedies, but he does in the early Neronian *Apocolocyntosis*, probably 'published' in late 54 CE not long after the composition of this play. There
Hercules and the emperor Claudius are lampooned, with Hercules himself
playing the self-conscious role of a tragic figure (*tragicus*, *Apoc.* 7.1) not in
possession of his own mind (*mentis suae non est*, *Apoc.* 7.3), delivering a
speech in iambic senarii to the dead emperor. The satire also features a
mock *nenia* or dirge for Claudius (*Apoc.* 12.3), in the same anapaestic metre
as, and imitative of, the 'Lamentation Ode' of Seneca's *Hercules*. A work
composed shortly after *Apocolocyntosis*, Seneca's *De Clementia*, also seems
to point back to his *Hercules*, especially to the 'political' section of Theseus'
great *ekphrasis* of Act III.[337] If the beginning of Nero's reign began with
Hercules, so, too, did its end, since one of the stage roles reported by
Suetonius (*Nero* 21.2–3) and Dio (62.9.4) as being 'sung' by Nero in the last
years of his principate, when he associated himself ubiquitously with
Hercules,[338] was that of *Hercules insanus*. Perhaps post-Neronian but certainly before 79 CE is the fresco in the Casa del Centenaro Pompeii, depicting Hercules, Amphitryon, Megara, and (seated) Lycus in the performance
of a play,[339] and that in the Casa di Casca, depicting the same scene without

---

[337] See Comm. *ad* 735–9, 739–45, 745–7.   [338] See Champlin (2003: 135–8).
[339] Bieber (1961: 229, fig. 766).

Hercules.[340] Though Hercules and Lycus do not appear onstage together in either Seneca's *Hercules* or Euripides' *Heracles* (in each case Hercules/ Heracles and Lycus would almost certainly have been played by the same actor),[341] given the licence allowed to representational artists, this *may* have been modelled on a performance of Seneca's tragedy.

Seneca's *Hercules* seems to have had a clear impact on the epic of his nephew Lucan, who reproduces some of the Senecan hero's moral ambiguity in his fragmenting poem,[342] and on the post-Senecan plays, *Octavia* and *Hercules Oetaeus*, as can be seen from the Commentary which follows.[343] Its influence on *Hercules Oetaeus* is especially strong. The anonymous dramatist seems to have fastened onto certain features of the earlier play (the narcissism of Hercules, the monologues, the dramatization of pain) and enlarged them, while augmenting the importance of several key terms.[344]

The Flavian epicists make many references to Hercules. In Valerius' *Argonautica* he features as a character, and there are several moments in which the influence of Seneca's tragedy and even the 'mad Hercules' motif are evident.[345] In Silius' *Punica* Hercules serves as a *uirtutis imago*, 'an icon of virtue' (*Pun.* 3.45), against which Hannibal, who self-consciously models his *uirtus* on that of Hercules (*Pun.* 1.510–12), and Scipio (*Pun.* 17.649–50) are measured.[346] Silius seems also indebted to Seneca's *Hercules* for his description of the underworld (*Pun.* 13.523–612). But it is in Statius' *Thebaid*, perhaps, that Seneca's *Hercules* makes itself most felt in Flavian epic. Hercules is referenced nominally some twenty times in the *Thebaid*.[347] Indeed Statius seems to construct the characters and lives of two of the 'Seven', Tydeus and Capaneus, on the paradigm of Seneca's hero.[348] Capaneus' 'boundary-violating virtue', *uirtus egressa modum*, seems an

---

[340] Ibid.: fig. 767, Ling (1991: 161, fig. 172).

[341] See Comm: 'Disposition of Roles'.   [342] See Zientek (2018: 132–4).

[343] The Nero of *Octavia* seems in part modelled on Seneca's Lycus as well as on his Atreus: see Comm. *ad* 258–67.

[344] See Slaney (2016: 23).

[345] See Buckley (2014: 311), who sees the prologue of Seneca's *Hercules* as adumbrating 'the socio-political and narratological conditions which set the *Argonautica* in motion' and argues (p. 321) that the Hylas episode of *Argonautica* 3 (esp. the *furor* of Hercules at *Arg.* 3.572–97) is much influenced by Seneca's play. There is also a reference to Hercules' madness at *Arg.* 3.676. One should also note that, as in Seneca's *Hercules* but not in Apollonius' *Argonautica*, Hercules has already completed his 'labours'. The role of Juno in Valerius Flaccus seems clearly a Senecan inheritance: see Manuwald (2021: 101–7). See further Comm. *ad* 1–24 (introd.), 40–6, 86–122, 791–802.

[346] See Galinsky (1972: 160–2).

[347] Under four names: Alcides, Amphitryoniades, Hercules, Tirynthius.

[348] See Rebegianni (2018: 138–47), who argues that Tydeus' 'transition from near-god to monster follows the pattern of Seneca's *Hercules Furens*' (p. 142) and that 'Capaneus' attack on

overt descendant of Hercules' *uirtus animosa* (*Herc.* 201).[349] Verbal emulation abounds. The description of Dis and the underworld in the opening lines of *Thebaid* 8 seems clearly influenced by Theseus' ecphrasis in *Hercules* Act III, and the speech of Dis himself (*Theb.* 8.65–79) echoes that of Juno in Seneca's prologue and replays its metaliterary function.[350]

Notably the Flavian epicists seem silent on the issue of the familicide. The 'Mad Hercules' motif, though not absent, seems not to have been a prominent motif in post-Senecan Greek and Latin literature.[351] The boisterous epigrammatist Martial—in a poem comparing Hercules and Domitian to the favour of the latter (*Epig.* 9.101)—makes sure to omit any suggestion of the killing of kin or even insanity, but both he and his satirical successor Juvenal seem cognizant of Seneca's play.[352] In the third century CE, however, Philostratus has no difficulty describing at length a painting of 'Heracles Mad' (*Imag.* 2.23), which depicted in detail the bodies of the first two slain children amid a crowded scene, involving Megara and the third child, servants, animals, and sacrificial paraphernalia. Though Philostratus pads his account with memories of a performance of Euripides' play, the death of the second child corresponds to the account of neither Euripides nor Seneca, and the overall sacrificial scene better suits the context of Seneca's play.

Other major ancient reception points for Seneca's *Hercules* include Claudian's *De Raptu Proserpinae*, another work on hell. Claudian clearly knew Seneca's play, since he practises standard *imitatio* in respect of it. Theseus' description of Dis at *Herc.* 720–7 strongly influenced Claudian's own account (*Rapt.* 1.79–84):

> ipse rudi fultus solio nigraque uerendus
> maiestate sedet. squalent immania foedo
> sceptra situ; sublime caput maestissima nubes
> asperat et dirae riget inclementia formae.
> terrorem dolor augebat. tunc talia celso
> ore tonat.

heaven develops the delirious projects of Seneca's mad Hercules' (p. 143). Rebegianni also sees Statius' Theseus as indebted to Seneca's *Hercules*.

[349] See Comm. *ad loc.*

[350] See further Comm. *ad* 86–8, 112–22, 197–201, 384–96, 697–706, 720–7, 1138–42. For resonances of Seneca's *Hercules* in *Thebaid* 2, see Gervais (2021).

[351] Domitian's own association with Hercules, to whom he dedicated a new temple on the Latin way (Mart. *Epig.* 9.64, 9.101), featuring a statue of Hercules in the likeness of the emperor, may have been a partial reason for at least the Flavian silence on the familicide. Martial even terms Domitian 'the greater Alcides' (*Alcides maior, Epig.* 9.101.11).

[352] See e.g. Comm. *ad* 30–5, 86–8, 164–74, 697–706.

> The master sits propped on a primitive throne,
> Fearsome in his dark majesty. Foul dust encrusts
> His massive sceptre; melancholy clouds gloom
> His towering head, a dire shape's cruelty stiffens.
> Pain increased his terror. Then he thunders this
> With soaring voice.

Allusion seems to be made to Hercules' slaughter of his family at Claud. *Ruf.* 1.79–80, but in Orpheus' song of the 'deeds of Hercules' (*actus...Herculis*) in the Preface to *Rapt.* 2 silence on the bloody event is once more maintained. Similarly silent on Hercules' familicide is the late fifth-century poet Dracontius, who, however, in his description of the infant Hercules' killing of the snakes in *Romul.* 4 seems to have been influenced by Seneca's play.[353] His older contemporary Sidonius seems also to reference Seneca's *Hercules.*[354] In the next century Boethius put Hercules' labours to verse (*Cons. Phil.* 4, Metrum 7.17–36) and was steeped in Seneca's tragedies. He clearly knew *Hercules* well, since he bases his speech of Pluto to Orpheus in *Consolatio Philosophiae* (Book 3, Metrum 12.40–6) on Seneca's account of the speech in the second choral ode of *Hercules* and on the choral verses of *Hercules Oetaeus* at *HO* 1061–1101.[355]

Renaissance to 1800

Seneca's *Hercules* is certainly not absent from the medieval literary and intellectual tradition—a tradition which combined the denigration of the hero by the church fathers with occasionally positive allegorization of Hercules as exemplary virtue and laudation of him as benefactor of mankind.[356] Hercules' brutal killing of Cacus and his 'ten labours' (*sic*) even appear in Theodulf of Orléans' poem *Contra Iudices* (*c.*799 CE), where they are described (sometimes in bloody detail) as scenes engraved on a vase. Seneca's *Hercules* is mentioned in the mid eleventh-century Lexicon of Papias and later in that century the 'Codex Etruscus' of Seneca's tragedies was created. In the twelfth century it seems that 'Seneca's tragedies were clearly read in schools',[357] but little knowledge may be gleaned about the

---

[353] See Comm. *ad* 213–22   [354] See Comm. *ad* 68–74.
[355] For an analysis of Boethius' debts to Seneca, see Fitch *ad Herc.* 569–89.
[356] See Galinsky (1972: 188–91).   [357] Schubert (2014: 74).

reception of Seneca's play. The late thirteenth, fourteenth, and fifteenth centuries, however, witness both an emphatic, especially allegorizing interest in the figure of Hercules (as paradigm of heroic *uirtus* or even analogue to Christ) and a large-scale resurgence of Seneca's tragedies. The former is marked by several works, including Chrétien le Gouays's *Ovide Moralisé* (1340), Petrarch's unfinished biography of Hercules (mid fourteenth century), Boccaccio's *Genealogie deorum gentilium* (1360–74), Colucio Salutati's *De Laboribus Herculis* (1406), Pietro Andrea di Bassi's *Le fatiche d'Ercole* (1431), and William Caxton's *Recuyell of the Historyes of Troye* (1473: a translation of Raoul Lefèvre's work of nine years earlier).[358] The resurgence of Seneca *tragicus* is initially marked by, and in part is the result of, the discovery of a new manuscript of the tragedies by Lovato de Lovati (1241–1309), a detailed commentary on the plays by Nicholas Trevet (1311–17),

---

[358] In *Ovide Moralisé* Hercules functions as a symbol of/analogue to Christ, as in several other works including Dante's *Inferno* (1320: see Stafford 2012: 204–5) and the much later Pierre de Ronsard's *L'Hymne de l'Hercule chrestien* (1555) and Francis Bacon's *The Wisdom of the Ancients* (1609). In the latter Hercules becomes 'the word of God' (ch. 26). Petrarch's biography, *De Viris Illustribus* 2, praises the hero for being a 'famous philosopher' (*famosior philosophus*) as well as a 'man incomparable in war and of more than human strength' (*uir bello incomparabilis et plus quam humanarum uirium*). In Caxton's translation of Lefèvre, the first book to be printed in English, Hercules is presented as a chivalric medieval knight. Notably Caxton and Lefèvre do not omit Hercules' madness, but transform it into a cuckold's vengeance, in which Lincus (= Seneca's Lycus) falsely claims that he has taken his 'fleshly desires' with Megera (*sic*) and Hercules kills them both (p. 346). Since Megera was 'with chylde', Hercules' act is filicidal. Salutati's *De Laboribus Herculis* is especially important, being in part a direct response to Seneca's *Hercules*. Salutati, inheriting the idea of Hercules as *uir perfectus*, allegorizes Hercules' descent into hell and justifies his familicide by representing his three sons and wife as symbols of moral vices. Cf. Enrique de Villena's similarly allegorizing *Los doze trabajos de Hercules* (1417). To be noted, too, is the proliferation of emblematic images of Hercules in fourteenth- and fifteenth-century Florence (which had Hercules on its seal), climaxing in the paintings and sculptures of the Pollaiuolo brothers. Indeed throughout Italy and Europe (e.g. Florence, Venice, Ferrara, Dresden, Paris, Seville, Copenhagen, London), especially from the sixteenth century onwards, paintings, tapestries, and sculptures of Hercules' exploits abound (see Stafford 2012: 209ff.). Hercules, the exemplary figure of *uirtus*, the Prodican hero who chose virtue over vice/pleasure and whose labours display the conquest of evil, dominates both Renaissance thinking and artistic production. Giraldi's *Ercole* (1557) and Spenser's *Faerie Queene* (1590) present their authors succumbing to a European cultural orthodoxy which was to last well beyond the Renaissance, as the Rubens painting on the cover of this book and his representation of Hercules elsewhere illustrate. Indeed in both England and France of the sixteenth and seventeenth centuries the political appropriation of Hercules by monarchs and ministers (witness the commissions of Henri IV of France and of Cardinal Richelieu: see Blanshard 2005: 85–8) was in full display. Paintings of the madness were, of course, rare; for an example, see Alessandro Turchi, 'The Raging Hercules' (*c*.1620), 'imitated' by Johann Peter Pichler (1797). The Senecan Hercules' madness, however, found a strong place in Renaissance culture through a regular term for epilepsy: *morbus Herculeus* or *morbus Herculanus*, 'Hercules' disease' (see Comm. *ad* 895–1053). It found an even stronger place through the transformation of Seneca's protagonist into new dramatic creations, as noted below.

and the most important fourteenth-century text for the illustration of Senecan *dramatic* influence, *Ecerinis*.

Albertino Mussato's *irata tragoedia*, *Ecerinis*, was written in Padua in 1315 and is the first known Renaissance tragedy. This five-act drama models itself in theme, language, structure, style, metre, and dramaturgy on the Senecan tragic *corpus*, on which Mussato himself wrote a commentary.[359] In the next century (1426–7) Correr's *Progne*, which opens with a ghost-scene replete with Senecanesque diction and closes with a gruesome feast, was similarly to display overt debts to Seneca, as the *argumentum* of the play acknowledges. The neo-Latin tragic tradition which Mussato founded and Correr developed continued until the seventeenth century,[360] and, though it was soon to be marginalized by a complex, evolving vernacular drama, from Mussato onwards Seneca encodes Renaissance tragic theatre.

Texts of Seneca's dramatic *corpus*, which had been circulating slowly as early as the twelfth century, abounded in the centuries which followed.[361] From the late fifteenth century his plays were performed regularly in European theatres, in universities, schools, and Inns of Court.[362] In non-Latin

---

[359] For the commentary, see Megas (1969) and MacGregor (1980). *Ecerinis* was sufficiently Senecan to entice Salutati to include it in his MS of Seneca's tragedies: Berrigan (1975: 6). For some possible debts of *Ecerinis* to Seneca's *Hercules*, see Comm. *ad* 720–7, 955–63.

[360] Apart from *Progne*, *Ecerinis*' successors include Loschi's *Achilles* (*c.*1390), Satorres' *Delphinus* (1543), Muret's *Iulius Caesar* (1544, publ. 1553), Buchanan's *Baptistes* (publ. 1576) and *Jephthes* (publ. 1554), Thomas Legge's *Richardus Tertius* (performed in Cambridge 1573, 1579, 1582), William Gager's *Meleager*, *Dido* and *Ulysses Redux* (written and performed in Oxford in 1580s and 1590s), William Alabaster's *Roxana* (performed in Cambridge *c.*1592), Matthew Gwinne's *Nero* (1603), Hugo Grotius' *Christus Patiens* (1608), and Nicolas de Vernulz's *Henricus Octavus* (1624). On *Ecerinis* and its aftermath, see Braden (1985: 99ff.). Texts of *Ecerinis*, *Achilles* and *Progne* may be found in Grund (2011).

[361] The first printed edition of Seneca's tragedies was published in Ferrara in 1478 by Andreas Bellfortis/Andrea Beaufort (for the date, see Petrini 1999: 127 n. 1). By the end of the sixteenth century approximately thirty editions of the collected plays had been published in five countries alone: Italy, Germany, France, Holland, and England. Erasmus himself was involved in both the Ascensius Paris edition of 1514 and the Avantius Aldine edition (Venice) of 1517. By 1600, too, translations were available of the tragedies in Catalan, Spanish, French, Italian, English, Polish, and (of *Troades*) in Dutch.

[362] Boas (1914: 389). Noted productions of Seneca's tragedies were those of *Phaedra* by Pomponius Laetus in Rome in the mid 1480s and in England by Alexander Nowell at Westminster School in the mid 1540s. In 1551–2 *Troades* was produced at Trinity College, Cambridge, and at the same college in 1559–61 *Oedipus*, *Medea*, and (probably twice) *Troades* again; at Queen's College, Cambridge, in 1563 *Medea* again. *Octavia* (considered today non-Senecan) was performed at Christ Church, Oxford, in 1588. For other performances in England, see Charlton (1946: cxliii), Binns (1974: 206). Two lost plays (*I Hercules*, *II Hercules*) were performed by the Admiral's Men in 1595 (Miola 1992: 124), but their relationship to the Senecan tragic *corpus* is not known. The APGRD database also lists a production of Seneca's *Hercules* by Uppsala University in Sweden in 1648 and a possible production of *Hercules Furens* (though it might have been *Amphitruo*) by an Italian Travelling Troupe in Nuremberg, Bavaria, Germany, a century earlier in 1549.

tragedy Seneca's informing paradigm was acknowledged by dramatist and critic alike: Giraldi's *Orbecche* (1541) and *Discorsi* (1543), Jodelle's *Cléopâtre Captive* (1552), La Péruse's *Médée* (1553), Norton and Sackville's *Gorboduc* (1561–2), Garnier's *Hippolyte* (1573), *La Troade* (1579), *Antigone* (1580), *Les Juifves* (1583), and Sidney's *Apologie* (1595) underscore the position of Seneca within contemporary theatrical thinking.[363] The Newton translations of 1581, which appeared shortly after the opening of the public theatres in London and which reprinted translations published separately between 1559 and 1567 (with one exception),[364] were both index and product of a theatrical ideology in which Seneca had a primary position. The Shakespearean Polonius' famous instruction to *Hamlet*'s Players—'Seneca cannot be too heavy, nor Plautus too light' (*Ham.* II.ii 396f.)—despite its baldness and boldness embodied a cultural truth.[365]

Recent studies of Renaissance drama—its Senecanesque devices, strategies, conventions, and themes; its use of quotation and allusion; its rewriting of Senecan texts; its concept of tragic experience and the tragic self; its metatheatrical focus; its exhibition of theatre as self-reflective and as cultural mirror—have displayed the profundity and complexity of the Senecan reception. Although it is not always possible to isolate the influence of individual Senecan plays, the following is a selective list of authors, composers, and their works between 1500 and 1800 who or which may be claimed to show the influence, direct or indirect, of Seneca's *Hercules*:[366] Ariosto, *Orlando Furioso* (1532); Muret, *Iulius Caesar* (1544);[367] Garnier, *Porcie* (*c.*1564), *Marc Antoine* (1578); La Taille, *Saül Le Furieux* (1572);[368] Thomas

---

[363] For Giraldi, see §I, 3, §II, 30 above; for Sidney, see his praise of *Gorboduc* in *An Apologie for Poetrie* (published 1595) as 'clyming to the height of *Seneca* his stile, and as full of notable moralitie, which it doth most delightfully teach, and so obtayne the very end of Poesie' (quoted from G. G. Smith [1904]: 1.197). For Sidney and *Oedipus*, see Boyle (2011), *ad* 705–6. For further testimony, see Cunliffe (1893: 9–12). For the 'Senecanism' of early modern English tragic theatre, see Slaney (2016).

[364] The exception was *Thebais* (= *Phoenissae*), translated for the collection by Newton himself. Jasper Heywood's translation of *Hercules Furens* in the Newton collection was first published in 1561.

[365] Seneca, of course, was not the only determinant of the evolution of Renaissance tragedy. Among other important influences were Renaissance chronicles, the medieval and Christian traditions (esp. *De Casibus* narratives, biblical 'cycles', and morality plays), the Italian *novella*—as well as non-Senecan ancient authors and genres. On Seneca and English Renaissance drama, esp. that of Shakespeare, see Burrow (2013: 162–201).

[366] The dates appended to the works are those of performance or publication (or both). A different date in the Select Bibliography may reflect a difference in the dates of publication and performance. For the dates of several of the works listed here and in later sections of this chapter, I am indebted to the APGRD database online. For references in the Commentary to the works listed throughout this section of the Introduction, see General Index under the author's name.

[367] See Comm. *ad* 955–63.   [368] See Comm. *ad* 939–44, 1138–42, 1194–1200.

Legge, *Richardus Tertius* (1579);[369] Anon., *The Rare Triumphs of Love and Fortune* (1582);[370] Kyd, *The Spanish Tragedy* (1587, publ. 1592);[371] Marlowe, *Tamburlaine Parts I and II* (c.1587–8, publ. 1590);[372] Hughes, *The Misfortunes of Arthur* (1588);[373] Torelli, *Merope* (1589);[374] Greene, *Orlando Furioso* (c.1590), *Groats-worth of Wit* (1592);[375] Spenser, *The Fairie Queene* (1590/1596); Peele/Greene (?), *Locrine* (c.1591);[376] Shakespeare, *Richard III* (c.1591), *King John* (c.1594–6), *A Midsummer Night's Dream* (c.1596), *Hamlet* (1601), *Othello* (1603), *King Lear* (1603–6), *Macbeth* (1606), *Antony and Cleopatra* (1606–7), *Coriolanus* (c.1607–8), *Cymbeline* (1610), *The Tempest* (1610–11), *The Winter's Tale* (c.1611);[377] Marston, *Antonio and Mellida* (1599), *Jack Drum's Entertainment* (1599–1600), *Antonio's Revenge* (1600), *The Malcontent* (1602–3), *The Insatiate Countess* (c.1610);[378] Fulke Greville, *Alaham* (c.1600);[379] Jonson, *Sejanus His Fall* (1603), *Catiline His Conspiracy* (1611);[380] Tomkis (?), *Lingua* (1607); Chapman, *Byron's Tragedy* (1608);[381] Beaumont and Fletcher, *Philaster* (1609); Prévost, *Hercule* (1613); Heywood, *The Silver Age* (1613), *The Brazen Age* (1613);[382] Mainfray, *Les Forces incomparables et amours du grand Hercules* (1616); Massinger, *The Duke of Milan* (c.1621); Shirley, *Love Tricks* (1625); Groto, *La Hadriana* (1626);[383] Tristan L'Hermite, *Marianne* (1636);[384] Rotrou, *Les Sosies* (1638);[385] L'Héritier de Nouvelon, *Hercule Furieux* (1639); Francisco López de Zárate, *Tragedia de Hércules Furente y Oeta* (1651); de' Dottori, *Aristodemo*

---

[369] See Comm. *ad* 1138–42.   [370] See Comm. *ad* 1042–53.
[371] See Comm. *ad* 569–89, 762–827.
[372] See Comm. *ad* 955–63, 963–73, 1035–8, 1283–94. Slaney (2016: 83) describes Tamburlaine as a 'Herculean hero operating at the limits of human capacity'. It is clear, too, that Marlowe consciously models his Tamburlaine on Hercules (*1 Tam.* I.ii.157–61):

> His looks do menace heaven and dare the gods,
> His fiery eyes are fixed upon the earth
> As if he now devised some strategem,
> Or meant to pierce Avernus' darksome vaults
> To pull the triple-headed dog from hell.

See also §VII, 105, n. 285 above.
[373] See Comm. *ad* 325–8, 341–8, 359–69, 495–500, 864–74, 1219–21, 1237–9, 1258–62.
[374] See Comm. *ad* 372–83.   [375] See Comm. *ad* 213–48, 1042–53.
[376] See Comm. *ad* 332–523.
[377] See Comm. *ad* 118–22, 332–523, 341–8, 495–500, 735–9, 991–5, 1092–9, 1138–1344 (introd.), 1202–18, 1231–6, 1258–62, 1278–82, 1321–41.
[378] See Comm. *ad* 1042–53, 1138–42, 1202–18, 1321–41.
[379] See Comm. *ad* 1138–42, 1258–62.
[380] See Comm. *ad* 249–58, 313–16, 348–53, 640–4, 1138–42.
[381] See Comm. *ad* 1258–62.   [382] See Comm. *ad* 40–6, 213–48.
[383] See Comm. *ad* 426–9, 495–500.   [384] See Comm. *ad* 1321–41.
[385] See Comm. *ad* 84–5.

(1657);[386] Anon., *Hercule Perseguitato* (1657); Jacopo Melani, *Ercole in Tebe* (librettist Moniglia, 1661); Racine, *Phèdre* (1677);[387] Lee, *Theodosius or The Force of Love* (1680);[388] Saunders, *Tamerlane the Great* (1681); Rowe, *Tamerlane* (1702); Vivaldi, *Ercole su'l Termodonte* (librettist Bussani, 1723); Young, *Night-Thoughts* (1742–5);[389] Voltaire, *Mérope* (1743);[390] Handel, *Hercules* (English librettist Broughton, 1745);[391] Glover, *Medea* (1761);[392] Silva (librettist Martinelli), *Megara Tebana* (1788). This period closed with David's colossal statue of Hercules for the Festival of the Unity and Indivisibility of the Republic in revolutionary Paris of 1793 and with the 1799 painting, 'Ercole saetta i figli' (Museo Civico, Bassano), by Antonio Canova.[393] What it did not close with was the figure of Hercules on the Great Seal of the newly liberated United States, a suggestion of John Adams.

The indebtedness of many of the above authors, composers, and artists to Seneca merits further analysis, especially that of Shakespeare, whose relationship to the Roman dramatist has received attention from several scholars.[394] The 'wooing scene' of Act II of *Hercules* was influential in early modern drama and finds imitations in Garnier, Legge, *Locrine*, and Marston,[395] but most famously in Shakespeare's *Richard III* (I.ii). Gloucester's wooing of Anne 'has no basis in the chronicles',[396] and is clearly a descendant of Seneca's innovative, brilliant execution of a dramatic paradox, viz. 'the mourner sought in marriage by the slayer of those she is mourning for'.[397] Several critics have observed the detailed parallels between Seneca's scene and that of Shakespeare:[398] the lamentation for the victims of the tyrant-figure prior to the latter's entrance (*Herc.* 254–8, 303–5, *RIII* I.ii.1–32); the brutish entrance of the tyrant-figure (*Herc.* 329–31, *RIII* I.ii.33–42); the spirited response of the wooed (*Herc.* 372ff., *RIII*, I.ii.34ff.), dressed in mourning clothes (*Herc.* 202–3, 355–6, *RIII* SD I.ii); the wish for the wooer's death (*Herc.* 384–96, *RIII* I.ii.62–7, 83–4, 154, 188); the justification for the

---

[386] See Comm. *ad* 205–9.

[387] See Comm. *ad* 226–30, 1321–41. [388] See epigraph to §VIII.

[389] See Comm. *ad* 864–74. [390] See Comm. *ad* 341–8.

[391] The Deianira mad scene seems to echo aspects of Seneca's presentation of Hercules; see also the entrance of Hercules in Act I, Sc. iv, cited in Comm. *ad* 592–617.

[392] See Comm. *ad* 1138–1344 (introd.), 1202–18, 1321–41.

[393] Canova's painting was followed in 1803–4 by a plaster relief of the same subject by him (Museo Gipsoteca Antonio Canova, Possagno). For pertinent (and witty) discussion of the Hercules statue by David, see Blanshard (2005: xi–xvi), who also comments on the plaster relief (pp. 41–6).

[394] See esp. Miola (1992) and Riley (2008), to whom I am much indebted.

[395] See Comm. *ad* 332–523. [396] Miola (1992: 82).

[397] H. F. Brooks (1980: 728).

[398] e.g. H. F. Brooks (1980: 728–33), Miola (1992: 82–4).

killings and appeal for a softer response from the wooed (*Herc.* 397–408, *RIII* I.ii.118–34); a focus by the wooer on the bloody savagery of war (*Herc.* 402–5, *RIII* I.ii.160–7); the wooer's confidence in his suit (*Herc.* 348–9, *RIII* I.ii.116). The motives of both wooers are, of course, the same: political self-advantage (*Herc.* 345–8; *RIII* I.i.155–9). And to mark the Senecan nature of his scene Shakespeare includes a generous amount of Senecanesque *stichomythia/antilabe* in the dialogue between Anne and Gloucester (*RIII* I.ii.196–206). Of course, Gloucester, i.e. Richard, will have much in common with Hercules: both will reveal themselves as child-slayers. And though the climax of the scene in which Richard offers his breast to his sword in Anne's hand is not derived from *Hercules*, it does seem to be a remodelling of analogous scenes in Seneca's *Agamemnon* and *Phaedra*. Shakespeare clearly wanted an accolade for his Senecanism (*RIII* I.ii.232–3):

> Was ever woman in this humour woo'd?
> Was ever woman in this humour won?

Thus Gloucester brags. But beneath Gloucester's self-congratulations lurk Shakespeare's own, as he admires his own virtuosity in remodelling Seneca's scene, outshining Seneca, just as Gloucester, whose suit is successful unlike that of Lycus, outshines the Theban tyrant.[399]

What Gloucester displays, too, is what one critic has called an 'unappeasably ambitious selfhood',[400] evident in such figures as Seneca's Hercules and found also in Shakespeare's Macbeth and Coriolanus,[401] and in Marlowe's Tamburlaine. Othello does not have this 'flaw', but, like Hercules driven by *furor*, i.e. by transforming madness and rage, this global traveller and warrior wages war with himself and, consumed by his 'bloody passion' (*Oth.* V.ii.44), as his eyes 'roll' (*Oth.* V.ii.38), slays his own wife, even as the villainous Iago plays Juno to his Hercules, prescripting his demise.[402] When Othello recognizes the horror he has enacted, like Hercules (*Herc.* 1202, 1221–6, 1338–40) he calls for thunder and prays for hell (*Oth.* V. ii. 232–3, 275–8).[403] As he commits suicide, he sees himself as his traditional enemy,

---

[399] H. F. Brooks (1980: 728).   [400] Braden (1993: 257).
[401] Coriolanus is compared explicitly to Hercules by Menenius (*Cor.* IV.vi.100–1). Like Seneca's Hercules, Coriolanus, whose solitariness is even more emphatic than that of Seneca's hero, submits to the imperatives of kin. See also p. 123 above, and Comm. *ad* 1173–7.
[402] Iago's reference to Othello's 'epilepsy' (i.e. 'Hercules disease': *Oth.* IV.i.50) further aligns Shakespeare's protagonist with the Senecan hero.
[403] Cited Comm. *ad* 1202–18, 1334–41.

'a malignant and a turbanned Turke' (*Oth.* V.ii.351), just as Hercules sees himself as *monstrum impium* (*Herc.* 1280), one of the monstrous beasts he has opposed and removed from the earth. Like Hercules, too, he exploits the metatheatrical and self-dramatizing power of his name; and like Hercules, his final problem is one of place: 'Where should Othello go?' (*Oth.* V.ii.269).

Other Shakespearean characters have Hercules within: the raging Antony, for example (*AC* I.iii.84–6):[404]

> Look, prithee, Charmian
> How this Herculean Roman does become
> The carriage of his chafe.

—or even the aged Lear. Witness the scene where, like Hercules, Lear wakes from his madness, uttering a line (*KL* IV.vii.52)—

> Where have I been? Where am I? Fair daylight?

—which descends from Hercules' *Quis hic locus* speech (*Herc.* 1138ff.) via closer versions or direct citations in La Taille, Legge, Marston, and Fulke Greville.[405] Leontes, too, may be cited. His 'repentance for his crimes against his own family' in *The Winter's Tale* seems an appropriation of Hercules' behaviour in Act V.[406]

And then there is Shakespeare's most notorious child-slayer Macbeth, who finds Herculean rhetoric (*Herc.* 1323–6) cascading from his mouth (*Mac.* II.ii.59–62):

> Will all great Neptune's ocean wash this blood
> Clean from my hand? No, this my hand will rather
> The multitudinous seas incarnadine,
> Making the green one red.

Marston was to remodel even more closely the cited Senecan lines.[407] Shakespeare's *Macbeth* also echoes—indeed promotes to the status of a prominent theme[408]—the attention in *Hercules* to ambition or 'hope', *spes*, which the 'Dawn Ode' cites as a driving force of human distress (*Herc.* 162–3)

---

[404] See also Comm. *ad* 112–18.
[405] See Comm. *ad* 1138–42. For other connections to *King Lear*, see also Comm. *ad* 1092–9, 1138–1344 (introd.), 1202–18.
[406] See Gray (2016: 226–7).   [407] See Comm. *ad* 1321–41.
[408] For details, see Miola (1992: 110–11).

and which the play's action presents as motivating both the play's villain and its 'hero'. Similar, too, is the focus in both plays on 'hands'. The *manus* motif of *Hercules* is noted frequently in the Commentary; Shakespeare's *Macbeth* is almost itself a commentary on that motif, which it employs pervasively in the play,[409] most strikingly in its concern with sanguineous hands (cf. e.g. II.ii.58–62, *Herc.* 1193–6). Then there is Shakespeare's creative 'imitation' in *Macbeth* of one of the most plangent statements of Seneca's Hercules (*Herc.* 1259–61):

> cuncta iam amisi bona:
> mentem arma famam coniugem natos manus—
> etiam furorem.

> I have now lost all things
> Of value: mind, weapons, glory, wife, sons,
> Hands—even rage.

Thus Macbeth, echoing after a millennium and a half the world-weariness of Hercules' words (*Mac.* V.iii.22–6):

> I have liv'd long enough: my way of life
> Is fall'n into the sere, the yellow leaf;
> And that which should accompany old age,
> As honour, love, obedience, troops of friends,
> I must not look to have.

Shakespeare took much from Seneca's play. It gave him language, imagery, dramatic techniques, structure, and ideas, just as it inspired, indeed nourished, other early modern dramatists.

After 1800

In the Vienna of 1808 August von Schlegel delivered his celebrated *Lectures on Dramatic Art and Literature*, which contained a ferocious attack on Senecan tragedy as 'bombastic and frigid, unnatural both in character and action, revolting from their violation of propriety, and so destitute of

---

[409] See Miola (1992: 114–17), and Comm. *ad* 1066–81, 1186–93, 1231–6. For Macbeth and Hercules, see also Comm. *ad* 1226–30, 1321–41.

theatrical effect, that I believe they were never meant to leave the rhetorical schools for the stage'.[410] Schlegel's lectures heralded a decline in Seneca's reputation at least in academic circles, from which it did not start to recover until the second half of the twentieth century. Outside academia, however, in opera and drama, for example, Seneca's influence continued, even if at a less heady pace than in the preceding centuries.[411] The early part of the new century produced Kleist's *Penthesilea* (1808), Shelley's *The Cenci* (1819), and Grillparzer's *Medea* (1821)—all heavily indebted to Seneca, primarily to *Phaedra*, *Thyestes*, and *Medea* respectively.[412] But Seneca's *Hercules*, too, was not forgotten. Hercules/Heracles was important in the poetry of Schiller (died 1805) and Hölderlin (died 1843), as in that of Leconte de Lisle, Sully Prudhomme, Robert Browning, José Maria de Heredia, some of whom seem to show Senecan touches.[413] Even Byron makes a couple of references to *Hercules Furens* (*Don Juan*, Cantos 11 and 17).[414] Hercules features, too, in the *Bible d'Humanité* (1864) of the French historian Jules Michelet. And paintings and sculptures of Hercules abound in the nineteenth century, including the famous paintings of Delacroix, Moreau, and Leighton.[415]

Dramatic works featuring Hercules, however, seem rare at best.[416] The APGRD database records a single performance of a Euripidean *Heracles* in the nineteenth century (directed by Antonis Varveris at an unknown venue in Greece in 1879) and none of a Senecan *Hercules* or *Hercules Furens* or adaptation thereof. Things changed in the twentieth century, which began

[410] Schlegel (1846: 211) (Black's translation). For the 'high reputation' of Schlegel's lectures, see the 'Preface of the Translator', 1–3 of the 1846 edition.

[411] For details in respect of Seneca's *Oedipus* and *Medea*, see Boyle (2011: xcvi, cix–cx), (2014: cxxviii–cxxxviii).

[412] On the 'Senecanism' of Kleist's *Penthesilea*, see Slaney (2013a: 227–32), (2015: 318–22), (2016: 209–17); on Shelley's *The Cenci*, see Boyle (2017: cxxxi–cxxxiii); on Grillparzer's *Medea*, see Boyle (2014: cxxxii–cxxxiv).

[413] Browning translates the whole of Euripides' *Heracles* in *Aristophanes' Apology* (1875). For Leconte ('L'Enfance d' Hèraklès' 1856), see Comm. *ad* 309–13, 618–21.

[414] Note especially the witty reference in Canto 11 to 'That prodigy, Miss Araminta Smith | Who at sixteen translated "Hercules Furens" | Into as furious English.'

[415] Eugène Delacroix, Hercules-Lunettes for the Salon de la Paix in the Hôtel de Ville, Paris (1849–52), 'Hercules and Alcestis' (1862); Frederic Leighton, 'Hercules Wrestling with Death for the Body of Alcestis' (c.1870); Gustave Moreau, 'Hercules and the Lernaean Hydra' (1875–6), 'Hercules at Lake Symphalos' (1875–80).

[416] On Hercules' relative rarity in the nineteenth century Blanshard (2005: 135) writes: 'Romanticism is partly to blame. Hercules was perceived as lacking human flaws and the introspection they generated. He was too robust to be a Romantic hero'. However, one should not forget the nineteenth-century writers mentioned above nor Hercules' presence in the visual arts, from Canova's relief of 1803–4 (n. 393 above) through to the works listed in the previous note. The brutal American civil war witnessed the use of Hercules in cartoons and, in its aftermath, even the text of Seneca's play in the pamphlets of the Ku Klux Klan (for which, see Comm. *ad* 463–4).

with a stage performance of Wilamowitz's translation of Euripides' *Heracles* in Vienna at the Theater in der Josefstadt (1902), followed by Yeats's play, *On Baile's Strand* (1904), staged at the Abbey Theatre in Dublin, in which Yeats's Irish folk hero Cuchuclain is a Herculean figure who kills his son and is overcome by madness, and by George Cabot Lodge's unperformed dramatic poem, *Herakles* (1908), which treats directly of Heracles' madness and fili-cide (they occur, however, *before* the labours). Lodge's 'play', like that of Yeats,[417] displays Senecan touches, emphasizing, among other things, the hero's isolation and search for self-perfection.[418] Described by one scholar as 'a colossal failure',[419] Lodge's excessively long work yet contains some powerful writing (*Herakles*, sc. xi):

> They are dead—my sons!—and he,
> My Herakles, my love—he is not dead!
> He lives and lurks within the empty house,
> A mouthing idiot, crouching like a beast,
> Sullen and fierce and frenzied in his lair!

The end of the new century's first decade saw the publication of Émile Verhaeren's *Les Rhythmes souverains*, with its long poem, 'Hercule', which has much in common with Seneca's dramatization.[420] Like Seneca, Verhaeren underscores the hero's solitariness and his wish to rival heaven, focuses on his rage and senseless violence and presents him as a conqueror of death. Like Euripides and Seneca, Verhaeren catalogues and questions the value of Hercules' labours, and exploits the hero's paradoxical nature, epi-grammatizing it in this brilliant self-description:

> Je suis heureux, sauvage, immense et rayonnant.

Hercules' violence, too, is at the heart of Frank Wedekind's First World War play, *Herakles, Dramatisches Gedicht in drei Acten* (1917), in which, as in the Roman drama, Hercules/Herakles' madness is at least in part product of his own violent past. Other aspects of Seneca's *Hercules* realized in Wedekind's play include the hero's isolation and the liberty of death. Thirteen years after Wedekind's *Dramatisches Gedicht* (1930) T. S. Eliot famously epigraphed his poem *Marina* with a citation in Latin of the first line (1138) of Act V of Seneca's

---

[417] See Comm. *ad* 1194–1200.
[418] See Comm. *ad* 125–204 (introd.), 1035–8, 1321–41. [419] Galinsky (1972: 218).
[420] See the analysis of the poem by Galinsky (1972: 276–9).

tragedy.[421] Seneca's *Hercules*, the allusion seemed to imply (even if Eliot did not intend this), was integral to modernist culture. Certainly in 1920s and 1930s Italy Hercules (Senecan or not) was an important cultural emblem because of Mussolini's adoption of the mythic hero as a prime icon of himself.[422]

The middle of the twentieth century saw a flurry of poetic, dramatic, and even comic book activity centred on the figure of Hercules/Heracles. In 1940 the short-lived Blue Ribbon comic book series on 'Hercules, Modern Champion of Justice' made its appearance together with the longer-lived Hit Comics series, centring on Hercules and others. The 1950s witnessed Theodore Morrison's *The Dream of Alcestis* (1950), Friedrich Dürrenmatt's *Herkules und der Stall des Augias* (1954), and Ezra Pound's *Women of Trachis* (1954). In the early part of the decade, too, there was also a ballet, *Héraklès*, perfomed by Ballets de France in Paris (1953).

The 1960s were fertile years for Senecan tragedy, partly because of the influence of Antonin Artaud, self-professed admirer of Seneca,[423] whose notion of a 'theatre of cruelty' deeply impressed many theatrical practitioners. 1960 itself saw a revival of the 1953 Gassman production of Seneca's *Thyestes* in Italy, and later in the decade (1967) Jean Vauthier's translation of Seneca's *Medea* was produced in Paris at the Odéon, directed by the Argentinian Jorge Lavelli. A year later Peter Brook's celebrated production of Ted Hughes's adaptation of *Seneca's Oedipus* took place at the National Theatre in London. Brooks's *Oedipus* was perhaps the most commercially successful production of a Senecan tragedy in the modern era and became landmark.[424] Seneca's *Thyestes* was also the focus of theatrical attention in the 1960s by Hugo Claus, the Belgian dramatist, poet, film-maker, and admirer of Artaud,[425] whose adaptation was performed at the Stadsschouwburg in Leuven, Belgium, in May 1966. A film version of the play was produced by Belgian and Dutch television later that year, and (shortly after this) a French translation of Claus's play entered the repertoire of the Odéon in Paris. Claus later adapted Seneca's *Oedipus* (1971) and *Phaedra* (1980).

---

[421] See Comm. *ad* 1138–42.

[422] See e.g. Mussolini as Hercules on the Littorali Medal 1932 and other Fascist badges. Mussolini's head is depicted covered with the head of the Nemean lion.

[423] In 1932 Artaud had written: 'On ne peut mieux trouver d'exemple écrit de ce qu'on peut entendre par cruauté au théâtre que toutes les Tragédies de Sénèque': Letter to Jean Paulhan 16 December 1932 in Artaud (1961), III.303–4.

[424] The Brook production is discussed at Boyle (2011: cxiv–cxvi).

[425] Indeed there is some evidence that Claus's *Thyestes* was an attempt to realize Artaud's uncompleted project on the myth: see Van Zyl Smit (2015: 332).

The 1960s did not bypass Hercules/Heracles. He began to feature as a regular character in DC and Marvel comics and in such innovative dramas as Archibald MacLeish's *Herakles* (1964, first performed 1965, revised 1967), Heiner Müller's *Herakles 5* (1966, first performed 1974), and Hartmut Lange's Brechtian *Herakles* (1968). MacLeish's play, which deals with the filicide, uses the power of Hercules, who removes both monsters and his own sons from the earth, as a metaphor for the political, military, and scientific power of the USA and its enemies at the height of the cold war.[426] Archibald MacLeish was himself a Senecan figure: statesman, teacher, poet, dramatist. It is unsurprising that, despite the 'Greek' title and a reference to Euripides in the 'Author's Note', his play shows distinctly Senecan qualities. Particularly Senecan is the strong doubt cast on the value of Herakles' journey to hell, the concern with individual agency and the self-glorification of the hero. When MacLeish's Herakles enters the play in Act II, he combines the entrance-appeal to Apollo of Seneca's Hercules (*Herc.* 592–6) with the braggadocio of his re-entrance at the opening of Act IV (*Herc.* 895–7):

> Apollo! ...
> Apollo! Lord god Apollo! ...
> Look!
> I'm back. I'm home. Enemies defeated,
> deeds done, bloody, mucking
> world made over like a summer's day;
> where's the welcome for it?

Importantly what MacLeish and Seneca dramatize is the continuity of the violence, the inevitable movement from the violence of the labours to that of the filicide, and, as a warning to the USA or Rome, the dangers of men playing God.[427]

The 1950s and 1960s, of course, saw the rise of the Hercules film industry, which developed considerable momentum in the wake of the Italian-made 1958 OSCAR Galatea Film *Hercules*, directed by Pietro Francisci, starring Steve Reeves and Silvia Koscina. There followed sixty-plus years of an almost uncountable series of films and television productions, reinterpreting, or inventing episodes in the hero's life. Productions were generally

---

[426] The first version of MacLeish's play, consisting of Act II of the later edition, was published in 1964 in the aftermath of the Cuban missile crisis of late 1962 and the assassination of President Kennedy in late 1963.

[427] On MacLeish and Seneca, see further Comm. *ad* 864–74, 926–39.

sanitized, wiped clean especially of any familicide,[428] but some more recent versions of the Hercules story at least include the killing of Hercules' family, even if they rewrite it.[429] This rewriting took place despite the excellent editions both of Seneca's *Hercules* and of Euripides' *Heracles* created in the late twentieth century.[430] One film stands out, Werner Herzog's nine-minute *Herakles* (1962),[431] a sharp visual satire amid an ocean of cinematic refuse.

The last decade of the twentieth century testified to a great upsurge in performances of translations of Euripides' *Heracles*,[432] and a rekindled fascination with the visual possibilities of the Hercules/Heracles narrative (see John Kindness, 'The Savage God: Scenes from the Life of Herakles', 1999). The decade witnessed, too, a growing interest in the Hercules/Heracles myth from the point of view of the issue of male violence, including, but not restricted to, familial violence resulting from PTSD. Tony Harrison's *The Labourers of Herakles* (1995), produced in the context of, and topographically proximate to, the killing fields of the Bosnian civil war (it was performed in Delphi, Greece), uses Herakles' destructive madness as a powerful metaphor for genocide, ethnic cleansing, child slaughter, and, more generally, for the role of male violence in the generation of women's grief. The following year saw a production of Seneca's *Hercules* in Florence Dupont's translation at the Théâtre de Gérard Philipe de Saint-Denis in Paris, directed by Jean-Claude Fall.

Four years later (2000) the new millennium greeted the publication of Simon Armitage's *Mister Heracles*, which was performed the following year in the UK at the West Yorkshire Playhouse, Leeds, directed by Natasha Betteridge and Simon Godwin. Though proclaiming itself a modern

---

[428] The sanitization can go beyond mere omission. In Disney's 1997 animated feature, *Hercules*, in a flagrant inversion of the mythological tradition, Hercules is made to say to 'Meg' (= Megara), 'I would never ever hurt you', to be echoed later by Meg herself: 'He would never do anything to hurt me.' The film actually starts with a question central to the dramatizations of Euripides and Seneca (voiced by the 'authoritative' Charlton Heston): 'What is the measure of a true hero?' Similarly Simon Armitage introduces his *Mister Heracles* (2000) with the question: 'What do we mean by hero?' (p. vii).

[429] In *Hercules* (2014), for example, directed by Brett Ratner and starring Dwayne Johnson, the slaughter of Hercules' family is a permeating motif, which is resolved in the end by the revelation that Hercules did not kill his wife and children but that the murder was committed by Eurystheus who drugged Hercules and used wolves to slay Hercules' family. Hercules as *uir perfectus* is thus maintained. For discussion of 'Hercules the Movie Star', see Stafford (2012: 232–9).

[430] For Seneca's *Hercules*, see esp. the editions of Fitch (1987a) and Billerbeck (1999a); for Euripides' *Heracles*, see esp. those of Bond (1981) and Barlow (1996).

[431] Available on YouTube.

[432] Discussed in Riley (2008: 280). The performances took place worldwide and included: New York, USA; London, England; Barcelona, Spain; Vicenza, Italy; Amsterdam, the Netherlands; Ludwigshafen, Germany; Schaan, Liechtenstein; Istanbul, Turkey; Epidauros, Greece; Zagreb, Croatia.

adaptation of Euripides, Armitage's play has much in common with Seneca in the analysis of heroism, the focus on the isolation of the hero, the devaluation of the labours, the underscoring of the violence (pp. 32–3):

> but poor Heracles—a born killer through and through—
> there's no telling what a man like that might do.

—and (most tellingly) the thesis that Heracles' madness comes from within (p. 54):[433]

> I remember one thing—feeling alive.
> That's how far I've come: only butchery
> of those I love most provokes life in me…
> Oh, my children and my wife, that your death
> were in me all the time, waiting to hatch.

As in Seneca, Heracles recognizes his guilt and culpability.[434] There are other Senecan touches.[435] But one especially Senecan aspect is Armitage's treatment of the chorus, who are not the elderly male chorus of Euripides but one of 'mixed gender, age and ethnicity'.[436] They take over the Senecan Amphitryon's role in telling the twelve labours.[437] And when Heracles enters Armitage's play, he does so like Seneca's Hercules, bellowing 'The conqueror returns!' (*Mister Heracles*, p. 19). Armitage's chorus sum up one of the central observations of Euripides' and Seneca's play and one of the central truths of military service (p. 23):

> Hard to be a hero out in the world
> and the same hero back in your own home.

The Hercules of Seneca and the Heracles of Euripides are not leaving our intellectual landscape soon. Their presence goes beyond the performances of translations of Euripides' *Heracles*, which are now not uncommon. In the same year as the publication of Armitage's play (2000) appeared Jay Scheib's

---

[433] See Kathleen Riley's online review of a performance of the play (2001): 'Both Amphitryon and Heracles recognize the violence as the product of a life of trained violence.'

[434] The question of individual responsibility for one's actions is raised early in Armitage's play: see Comm. *ad* 1200–1. In Seneca's *Hercules*, as in his *Oedipus*, it is raised late.

[435] See e.g. Comm. *ad* 402–8.

[436] See Riley's review (n. 433 above). The composition of the chorus is not apparent in Armitage's printed text.

[437] In Armitage's play they are of course modern labours: see Comm. *ad* 213–48.

Herakles (after texts by Euripides, Heiner Müller, Pindar), only to be followed by Martin Crimp's *Cruel and Tender* (2004: after Sophocles' *Trachiniae*, performed at the Young Vic, London, UK, directed by Luc Bondy),[438] Mary Fulham's *Hercules in High Suburbia* (2004: performed by Watson Arts at La MaMa ETC, New York City, USA, directed by Mary Fulham), Opéra National de Paris' production of Handel's 1745 opera *Hercules* (2004: performed at the Palais Garnier, Paris, France, conducted by William Christie and directed for the stage by Luc Bondy), the world première of MacLeish's revised two-act version of *Herakles* (2005: performed by Natural Theatricals at the George Washington Masonic National Memorial, Alexandria, Virginia, USA, directed by Rip Claassen),[439] Jeanette Winterson's novella, *Weight: The Myth of Atlas and Heracles* (2006), Daniel Algie's *Home Front* (2006: performed at La MaMa ETC, New York City, USA, directed by E. Randall Hoey), Vivaldi's recently recovered opera, *Ercole sul Termodonte* (2006: performed at the Spoleto Festival, Italy, conducted by Alan Curtis and directed by John Pascoe), Marian Maguire's exhibition of lithographs and etchings, 'The Labours of Herakles' (first exhibited 2008: Blenheim, New Zealand), a reissue of Fitch's 1987 commentary on Seneca's *Hercules* (2009) and of Wilamowitz's 1895 commentary on Euripides' *Heracles* (2010), Helen Eastman's play, *Hercules* (2010: written for a family audience, performed at the Grosvenor Park Open Air Theatre Chester, UK), and Peter Sellars's production of Handel's *Hercules* (performed at the Lyric Opera of Chicago, USA, 2011, and in Toronto, Canada, 2014, at the Four Seasons Theatre, conducted in each case by Harry Bicket).

The Sellars production of Handel's opera, like that by the Opera National de Paris in 2004, was in modern dress, including military dress, but this time with strong visual references to the Iraq and Afghanistan wars. Though dealing with the subject matter of Sophocles' *Trachiniae* and *Hercules Oetaeus* rather than of Seneca's *Hercules*, Sellars emphatically underscored the thesis, common in recent Hercules productions, that the great hero's behaviour was the product of PTSD. Combat trauma was also emphasized in the adaptation of Seneca's *Hercules* by the Not Man Apart Physical Theatre Ensemble, performed at the Getty Villa, Pacific Palisades, California in 2011. Directed by John Farmanesh-Bocca, a revised version

---

[438] See Comm. *ad* 926–39.
[439] It is testimony to the neglect of MacLeish's play that Natural Theatricals seem to have been unaware that it was a world-première: Riley (2008: 304).

was world-premiered in 2013 at the Miles Memorial Playhouse, Santa Monica, California. Nor has the politicization of Hercules, his utility as a figure for political self-presentation, been abandoned. Recalling Mussolini's use of Hercules almost a century earlier, an art exhibition (2014) in Moscow, Russia, was devoted to the '12 Labours of President Putin', in which the current Russian president is pictured riding the Cretan Bull of Crimea or fighting the Hydra of the EU, USA, Canada, and Japan.[440]

Perhaps the most salient feature of the Hercules productions of the new millennium is that, despite their frequent claim to be adaptations of Greek tragedy and myth, they have an essentially Senecan nature, especially in their focus on Hercules' familicidal violence as the product of the Herculean self and the past violence which created that self.[441] These productions are world-wide. As Seneca dramatized, there is nowhere for Hercules to hide. The modern film, television, and book industries—and, one should add, the political world—are unlikely to accept any Herculean erasure;[442] so, too, live theatre, music, opera, and the visual arts, as they respond to the urgent problems of contemporary violence: domestic, social, political, military. Ironically the constant reproduction of Hercules' many stories recreates a cardinal Senecan paradox: Hercules is known everywhere, because he destroyed place itself.

---

[440] The 2022 invasion of Ukraine reveals, as I send this book to the press, that the 'labours' are not over.

[441] I am not alone in this judgement. Cf. Riley (2008: 357): 'In our attempt to create a Herakles for our times, Seneca has provided us with a powerful medium through which to anatomize "the heart of contemporary darkness"'. It should be observed, however, that Seneca's dramatic analysis of Hercules' violence is more complex than that of modern play-wrights: though his *Hercules* focuses on the hero's psychology and his history of, and proclivity to, violence, it also devotes its prologue to other agents, viz. Juno and the Furies. See §VII, 114–16 above.

[442] Disney are at present (2022) in pre-production of a live-action version of their 1997 animated feature, perhaps to be released in 2023. Even the James Bond movie released in 2021, *No Time to Die* (MGM and Eon Productions), could not exclude Hercules. It features a bio-weapon of mass destruction named 'Project Heracles'. Seneca's Amphitryon would have found the name appropriate, although he would obviously have preferred the Latin nomenclature. In 2021, too, appeared Anne Carson's *H of H Playbook*, a version of Euripides' *Heracles*, using both drawings and language, described by Casey Cep in the *New Yorker* (21 November 2021) as 'a performance of thought, one that speaks not only to the heroic past but to the tragic present'. Carson's text is not without its Senecan touches: see p. 124 n. 332.

IX. Metre

From an ancient point of view, if we deny the metrical dimension of a
poetic artefact its full significance, we are discounting what identifies it
as a poem.

Llewelyn Morgan, *Musa Pedestris* (2010)[443]

Dialogue

Iambic Trimeters

The standard metre of *Hercules*' dialogue lines is the iambic trimeter or (less
accurately) the *senarius*. This is a six-foot line based on the iambus ($\smile -$), for
which several equivalents are allowed: the spondee ($--$), tribrach ($\smile \smile \smile$),
dactyl ($- \smile \smile$), anapaest ($\smile \smile -$), and proceleusmatic ($\smile \smile \smile \smile$). Aristotle pronounced it the metre most suitable to ordinary speech ($\mu \acute{a} \lambda \iota \sigma \tau a \ \lambda \epsilon \kappa \tau \iota \kappa \acute{o} \nu$,
Poetics 1449a 24–5; see also Cic. *Orat.* 184). All 'dialogue' lines in *Hercules*
are in this metre. Its six-foot schema is as follows:

1	2	3	4	5	6
$\smile -$	$\smile -$	$\smile -$	$\smile -$	$(\smile -)$	$\smile \underline{\smile}$
$--$		$--$		$--$	
$\smile \smile \smile$	$\smile \smile \smile$	$\smile \smile \smile$	$\smile \smile \smile$		
$- \smile \smile$		$- \smile \smile$		$(- \smile \smile)$	
$\smile \smile -$		$(\smile \smile -)$		$\smile \smile -$	
$(\smile \smile \smile \smile)$					

Bracketed feet occur rarely. Caesuras (word-divisions within feet) occur
regularly after the first syllable of the third foot and the first syllable of the
fourth foot. Diaeresis (word-division between feet) after the second or
fourth foot may replace either caesura but not both. It seems clear that
Seneca thought of his iambic line as consisting of three pairs (dipodies or
metra) of iambi rather than six independent feet, and thus that it is more
accurate to call it an iambic trimeter rather than a *senarius* ('sixer'). The line
is much closer to the iambic dialogue lines of the Greek tragedians than to
the *senarii* of the Roman republican tragedians, who allowed spondees, for

---

[443] Morgan (2010: 384).

example, in every foot. It should also be noted that in over 85 per cent of Seneca's iambic trimeters a dissyllabic word forms the final foot.

Choral Odes

Seneca has been described as 'the most important Latin lyric poet after Horace and until Boethius' *metra* in the *Consolatio*'.[444] His drama, though more restrictive metrically than Attic tragedy, employs a variety of lyric metres in its choral odes and *cantica* (anapaestic, asclepiadic, sapphic, alcaic, glyconic, pherecratean, dactylic, iambic, trochaic, aristophanean, ithyphallic). Senecan choral odes are sometimes comprised of sections in different metres (see e.g. the first, second, and fourth odes of *Phaedra*, the first odes of *Oedipus* and *Medea*, and the third choral ode of *Hercules*). *Agamemnon* and *Oedipus* are unusual in Senecan tragedy for containing 'polymetric' odes (or sections of odes), where the metre generally changes from line to line and innovative metrical combinations are regularly used in the lines themselves. 'Such metrical virtuosity indicates Seneca's interest in exploring the possibilities of lyric verse,'[445] but it also reveals his concern with the semiotics of metrical form and the latter's bearing on dramatic meaning.[446] His main lyric model was, of course, Horace. There are no polymetric choral odes in *Hercules*. The absence of strophic responsion in *Hercules'* choral odes accords with Senecan practice and is in marked contrast to the strophic patterning of the Greek tragedians. It seems to have been typical of Roman tragedy from the beginning.

The following schemata cover the different lyric metres used in *Hercules*.

Anapaests

Anapaestic dimeters and monometers occur in the first and fourth choral odes (125–203, 1054–1137). These are lines based upon the anapaest ($\smile\smile-$), but which allow the spondee ($--$) or dactyl ($-\smile\smile$) as equivalents. A run of four short syllables (dactyl followed by anapaest) occurs only once in Seneca: *Herc.* 1064 (it occurs twice in *Oct.*, four times in *HO*). A completely spondaic line is avoided by Seneca and the author of *HO* (but is found three times in *Oct.*). The schema for the dimeter (four feet) is as follows:

---

[444] Mazzoli (2014: 366).   [445] Trinacty (2014: 146).
[446] See p. 151 below.

	1	2	3	4
	⌣⌣–	⌣⌣–	⌣⌣–	⌣⌣–
	– –	– –	– –	– –
	–⌣⌣	(–⌣⌣)	–⌣⌣	(–⌣⌣)

Anapaestic monometers (two feet) also occur. The anapaestic dimeter was Seneca's favourite lyric line. Often used in Greek tragedy for the entrance and exit odes of the chorus, it was regularly employed by the early republican dramatists in choral odes anywhere in the play and in individual monodies (Tarrant 1985: 32). For Senecan anapaestic colometry (i.e. the distribution of dimeters and monometers, reported inconsistently in the manuscripts), see below.

Asclepiads

A dodecasyllabic lyric line, the so-called 'minor asclepiad' (cf. Hor. *Odes* 1.1 and 3.30), is used throughout the second choral ode (524–91).

$$– \; – \; – \; – \; ⌣⌣ \; – \; – \; ⌣⌣ \; – \; ⌣ \; \underline{⌣}$$

Sapphics

The so-called 'minor sapphic' hendecasyllabic line (Hor. *Odes* 1.2.1–3, etc.) is frequently used by Seneca on a large scale in tragic choral odes and is regularly accompanied by adonii (–⌣⌣–⌣̲). In *Hercules* sapphics are restricted to the earlier sections of the third choral ode (830–74) and appear without adonii.

$$– \; ⌣ \; – \; – \; – \; ⌣⌣ \; – \; ⌣ \; – \; \underline{⌣}$$

Glyconics

The glyconic is an octosyllabic (or heptasyllabic) lyric line, which in Senecan tragedy may have a spondaic or trochaic 'base' (the initial two syllables).

$$– \; \underline{⌣} \; – \; \underline{⌣⌣} \; – \; ⌣ \; \underline{⌣}$$

It occurs in the final section of the third choral ode (875–94), where the form used has a spondaic 'base'.

Anapaestic Colometry

There is no consensus on the colometry of the anapaestic lyrics of the Senecan *corpus*. One aspect of the difficulty is the self-contained nature of imperial anapaestic monometers. I have used the following principles in the arrangement of the anapaestic lines of *Hercules*.

1. I have allowed no anapaestic trimeters. The reports of anapaestic trimeters in the Senecan *corpus* are inconsistent (e.g. trimeters may be found at *Herc.* 1135b–1136 in *A*, but not in *E*, at *Herc.* 1136b–37 in *E*, but not in *A*, at *Ag.* 665–5•, 667–8, 676–8•, 681–2, 685–5• in *A* but not in *E*, and at *Thy.* 829–30, 930b–33a in *E* but not in *A*), and their presence often obscures conspicuous metrical and verbal patterning. The trimeters in the MSS are best explained as due to scribal economy.

2. I have used the dimeter as the basic metrical unit, variegated and enlivened by occasional monometers.

3. I have ensured in a majority of lines a correspondence between metrical and sense/syntax unit, a recurrent, if not universal, feature of the anapaestic colometry of the Senecan *corpus* in the MSS. (This criterion, which derives from the observations of Richter 1899: 32–47, should not be elevated to the status of an inflexible principle, overriding all other factors, in the manner of Fitch 1987*b*, 2002*a*, 2004*a*, 2018, whose approach is rightly criticized by M. Wilson 1990.)

4. I have allowed some enjambement for variety and poetic effect in accordance with the playwright's practice in iambic dialogue.

5. I have avoided such metrical anomalies as hiatus and *syllaba breuis in longo* at the diaeresis or synaloephe (elision) across the diaeresis, but have allowed both hiatus and *syllaba breuis in longo* at the verse-end. Contrary to the assertion of Raven (1965: 117), the anapaests of Senecan tragedy do not observe synaphea (metrical continuity between lines): see Fantham (1982: 113).

6. In choosing dimetric and monometric units I have had regard not only to sense but to verbal and grammatical patterning of the kind noted by W. Marx (1932: 28–35), and to considerations of dramatic and poetic effect. Fitch (2004*b*: 264–5) rightly shows that the clausulating function of monometers is a myth. Monometers are 'no more common at the ends of odes or sections of odes than elsewhere'.

Much of the above I share with (and in part have derived from) other modern editions of the Senecan tragic *corpus* and of *Hercules*, including those of Zwierlein (1986*a*), and Fitch (1987*a*, 2002*a*, 2018). Fitch, however, seems to me too radical in his use of monometers (esp. of monometric combinations), and too rigid in his adherence to a total correspondence of sense and metrical units. His view (2004*b*: 271–4) that the authors of the Senecan *corpus* were interested solely in the aural effect of their verse and had little or no interest in the visual impact of its written form is unpersuasive. My colometry thus diverges from that of Fitch and is closer to, but not identical with, that of Zwierlein (for differences from Zwierlein see p. 265).

Line Numbering

Throughout this edition the traditional line numbering (derived from Gronovius) has been preserved with additional lines resulting from colometric arrangement indicated by •.

Semiotics of Seneca's Lyric Metres

Discussion of this complex and controversial subject (on which little agreement is evident: see Mazzoli 2014: 566–7) may be found, where appropriate, in the Commentary: see Comm. *ad* 125–204, 524–91, 830–94, 1054–1137.

X. The Translation

Traduttore traditore.

Italian adage

Any translator of the plays of the Senecan *corpus* is indebted to predecessors. I have consulted, and learned from, several earlier translations, principally those of Heywood (in Newton 1581), F. J. Miller (1917), Shelton (1990), Fitch (2002, 2018), E. Wilson (2010), Scott Smith (2011), and Konstan (2017). Identity of word or phrase does not, however, necessarily index indebtedness. The translation which follows adopts the principles outlined in my earlier English versions of Seneca's *Phaedra* (Liverpool, 1987, repr. Leeds, 1992), *Troades* (Leeds, 1994), *Oedipus* (Oxford, 2011), *Medea* (Oxford, 2014), *Thyestes* (Oxford, 2017), and *Agamemnon* (Oxford, 2019), and the non-Senecan *Octavia* (Oxford, 2008). Its diction is that of contemporary English (except for occasional, 'religious' archaisms in hymns, prayers, or other divine address), and aims to convey to the Latinless reader as much as it is possible to convey in English and without violation of English idiom about the form and meaning of the Latin play. It is with few exceptions line by line, and employs as its standard dialogue verse-form the ten-syllable iambic line of English blank verse. For the translation of plays from the Senecan *corpus*, whose iambic trimeter had such a formative impact on the development of English blank verse,[447] there is no real alternative. I have, however, not hesitated to use an eleven-syllable (or more rarely longer) line—allowing myself metrical substitutions and feminine endings—where appropriate. The result, I hope, is a dramatic dialogue line which reproduces something of the tautness of Seneca's verse.

For the lyric sections (the choral odes) I have again used lines of fixed syllabic length where Seneca's line is similarly fixed and lines of variable syllabic length where Seneca's line is also variable. For Seneca's anapaests (theoretically eight to twelve syllables) a line of six to nine syllables with a corresponding shorter line for the occasional monometers; for his lesser asclepiads (twelve syllables) I have used a line of nine syllables, for his sapphics (eleven syllables) a line of eight syllables, for his glyconics (eight

---

[447] See Eliot (1951c: 85), who argues (concerning early modern English playwrights) that 'the establishment of blank verse as the vehicle for drama…received considerable support from its being obviously the nearest equivalent to the solemnity and weight of the Senecan iambic'.

syllables) a line of six syllables. Occasionally I have allowed diphthongs to function as dissyllabic. The goal has been to produce lines whose syllabic relationship to my dialogue lines is similar to that of *Hercules'* lyric lines to the play's iambic trimeters.

Few modern translators of ancient texts are unaware of the Italian pun cited above and its tendentious equation of change (which is what translation is) with treason. The reader should note that the following translation is intended to reveal, not to betray. Any *tradimento* apparent in the English version is a consequence of the difficulties of the task and this translator's lack of ability to resolve them.

TEXT AND TRANSLATION

Hercules

Personae

Iuno

Furiae (mutae)

Amphitryon

Megara

Nati Herculis (muti)

Lycus

Hercules

Theseus

Milites, Famuli (muti)

Chorus Thebanorum

Scaena Thebis

Hercules

Characters

Juno, Queen of the Gods, Wife and Sister of Jupiter

Furies (silent), Fiends of the Underworld

Amphitryon, Foster-father of Hercules and Husband of Alcmena

Megara, Daughter of the former Theban King, Creon, and Wife of Hercules

Sons of Hercules (silent)

Lycus, Present Tyrant-King of Thebes

Hercules (also called 'Alcides'), Famed Hero, Son of Jupiter and Alcmena

Theseus, King of Athens

Guards, Attendants, Slaves (silent)

Chorus of Thebans

Scene

Thebes: before the royal palace and a temple.

Time

The action begins just before dawn and takes place during a single day.

Actus Primus

Iuno—Furiae tacitae

IUNO   Soror Tonantis—hoc enim solum mihi
        nomen relictum est—semper alienum Iouem
        ac templa summi uidua deserui aetheris
        locumque caelo pulsa paelicibus dedi.
        tellus colenda est, paelices caelum tenent.   5
        Hinc Arctos alta parte glacialis poli
        sublime classes sidus Argolicas agit;
        hinc, qua recenti uere laxatur dies,
        Tyriae per undas uector Europae nitet.
        illinc timendum ratibus ac ponto gregem   10
        passim uagantes exerunt Atlantides.
        ferro minax hinc terret Orion deos
        suasque Perseus aureus stellas habet.
        hinc clara gemini signa Tyndaridae micant
        quibusque natis mobilis tellus stetit.   15
        nec ipse tantum Bacchus aut Bacchi parens
        adiere superos. ne qua pars probro uacet,
        mundus puellae serta Cnosiacae gerit.
        Sed sero querimur. una me dira ac fera
        Thebana tellus matribus sparsa impiis   20
        quotiens nouercam fecit! escendat licet
        meumque uictrix teneat Alcmene locum
        pariterque natus astra promissa occupet,
        in cuius ortus mundus impendit diem
        tardusque Eoo Phoebus effulsit mari   25
        retinere mersum iussus Oceano iubar,
        non sic abibunt odia. uiuaces aget
        uiolentus iras animus et saeuus dolor

Act I

The scene is Thebes: a public space before two buildings in the background, the royal palace and (stage left) a temple. In front of the temple is an altar (perhaps together with statues of JUPITER and CERES). The time is just before dawn; the night-stars are still visible. JUNO is alone onstage.

Juno—Furies silent

JUNO   Sister of the Thunder-god—for that's my
        Sole name now—husbandless, I've left ever
        Alien Jove and high heaven's precincts,
        Yielding place to whores—exiled from heaven.
        Earth must be my home; whores hold the sky.   5
  (*Points skyward*) Look, here Arctos soars by the icy pole,
        Guiding the Argive ships as their lodestar;
        Here, where day unbinds in the early spring,
        Tyrian Europa's sea-ferry shines.
        There the far-strayed daughters of Atlas flock,   10
        Creators of fear for ships and ocean.
        Here menacing Orion's sword frightens gods,
        And golden Perseus owns his constellation.
        Here glitter the twin Tyndarids' bright stars
        And those whose birth halted the drifting land.   15
        Bacchus and Bacchus' mother were not alone
        In reaching the gods. So no part lack disgrace,
        The world wears the crown of the Cnossian girl.
          But my complaints come late. How often this one,
        Dire, savage land of Thebes, strewn with impious   20
        Mothers, made me stepdame! Though Alcmene
        Ascend and take my place triumphant
        And her son, too, gain his promised stars—
        For whose rising the world disbursed a day
        And Phoebus shone late from the Eastern sea   25
        Ordered to keep his light sunk in Ocean—
        My hate will not just stop. My violent mind
        Will enact undying wrath, and savage pain

aeterna bella pace sublata geret.
   Quae bella? quidquid horridum tellus creat   30
inimica, quidquid pontus aut aer tulit
terribile dirum pestilens atrox ferum,
fractum atque domitum est. superat et crescit malis
iraque nostra fruitur: in laudes suas
mea uertit odia. dum nimis saeua impero,   35
patrem probaui, gloriae feci locum.
qua Sol reducens quaque deponens diem
binos propinqua tinguit Aethiopas face,
indomita uirtus colitur et toto deus
narratur orbe. monstra iam desunt mihi   40
minorque labor est Herculi iussa exequi,
quam mihi iubere. laetus imperia excipit.
quae fera tyranni iussa uiolento queant
nocere iuueni? nempe pro telis gerit
quae timuit et quae fudit. armatus uenit   45
leone et hydra.
              Nec satis terrae patent.
effregit ecce limen inferni Iouis
et opima uicti regis ad superos refert.
parum est reuerti: foedus umbrarum perit.
uidi ipsa, uidi nocte discussa inferum   50
et Dite domito spolia iactantem patri
fraterna. cur non uinctum et oppressum trahit
ipsum catenis paria sortitum Ioui
Ereboque capto potitur et retegit Styga?
patefacta ab imis manibus retro uia est   55
et sacra dirae mortis in aperto iacent.
at ille, rupto carcere umbrarum ferox,
de me triumphat et superbifica manu
atrum per urbes ducit Argolicas canem.
uiso labantem Cerbero uidi diem   60
pauidumque Solem. me quoque inuasit tremor,
et terna monstri colla deuicti intuens
timui imperasse.
             Leuia sed nimium queror.
caelo timendum est, regna ne summa occupet
qui uicit ima. sceptra praeripiet patri.   65

Will banish peace and wage eternal wars.
   What wars? Every terror the hostile earth   30
Creates, every dread, dire, fierce, ferocious,
Pestilential thing sea and air produced,
Is crushed and tamed. He triumphs, grows by suffering,
And delights in our wrath: he transforms my hate
Into his praise. Such cruel commands from me   35
Have confirmed his father, placed his glory.
Where the Sun restores and where he sets the day,
Tinting both Ethiopians with close torch,
His untamed virtue's worshipped; the whole world
Stories him a god. I've no monsters left,   40
And it's less labour for Hercules to follow
Orders than for me to give them. He loves commands.
What tyrant's cruel orders could damage
That violent man? Indeed he bears as weapons
What he feared and felled. He comes armed with   45
Lion and Hydra.
                The wide earth does not suffice.
See, he smashed infernal Jove's gate, and lugs
To those above the conquered king's prime loot.
Returning's not enough: hell's covenant is dead.
I saw, myself saw the night below shattered,   50
Dis tamed, and *him* flaunting to his father
Fraternal spoils. Why not drag Jove's equal,
Bound and crushed with chains, and become lord
Of captured Erebus and unroof the Styx?
A way back from the deep shades has opened   55
And dire death's mysteries lie exposed.
But he, savage from bursting death's prison,
Triumphs over me and with haughteous hand
Leads the black hound through Argive cities.
At sight of Cerberus I saw the day wilt   60
And the Sun fear. Trembling blasted me, too.
Viewing the conquered monster's triple neck
I feared my commands.
                But I complain too lightly.
Heaven is at risk: this victor of depths may seize
The highest realms. He'll snatch his father's sceptre.   65

nec in astra lenta ueniet ut Bacchus uia.
iter ruina quaeret et uacuo uolet
regnare mundo. robore experto tumet,
et posse caelum uiribus uinci suis
didicit ferendo. subdidit mundo caput   70
nec flexit umeros molis immensae labor;
meliusque collo sedit Herculeo polus.
immota ceruix sidera et caelum tulit
et me prementem. quaerit ad superos uiam.
    Perge, ira, perge et magna meditantem opprime,   75
congredere, manibus ipsa dilacera tuis,
quid tanta mandas odia? discedant ferae,
ipse imperando fessus Eurystheus uacet.
Titanas ausos rumpere imperium Iouis
emitte, Siculi uerticis laxa specum.   80
tellus Gigante Doris excusso tremens
supposita monstri colla terrifici leuet.
sublimis alias Luna concipiat feras—
sed uicit ista. quaeris Alcidae parem?
nemo est nisi ipse. bella iam secum gerat.   85
    Adsint ab imo Tartari fundo excitae
Eumenides, ignem flammeae spargant comae,
uiperea saeuae uerbera incutiant manus.

    I nunc, superbe, caelitum sedes pete,
humana temne. iam Styga et manes, ferox,   90
fugisse credis? hic tibi ostendam inferos.
reuocabo in alta conditam caligine,
ultra nocentum exilia, discordem deam
quam munit ingens montis oppositi specus.
educam et imo Ditis e regno extraham   95
quidquid relictum est. ueniet inuisum Scelus
suumque lambens sanguinem Impietas ferox
Errorque et in se semper armatus Furor—
hoc, hoc ministro noster utatur dolor.
    Incipite, famulae Ditis, ardentem incitae   100

He'll not reach the stars by Bacchus' slow path.
He'll seek a route through ruin and want to reign
In a vacant sky. He swells with tested might.
By bearing the heavens he learnt his strength
Can conquer them. His head upheld the sky.   70
The vast bulk's task did not bow his shoulders
But the world sat better on Hercules' neck.
That neck, unmoved, bore stars and sky—and me,
Pressing down. He seeks a path to those above.
    Go, wrath, go, and grind this glory seeker.   75
Fight, tear him apart yourself with your hands.
Why delegate such hate? Let beasts be gone,
Let Eurystheus rest, tired from his mandates.
Release the Titans who dared to rupture
Jove's rule, open the cave of Sicily's peak.   80
Let Doric land convulse as its Giant shakes
And free the fierce monster's buried neck.
Let the soaring moon conceive still other beasts—
But he's conquered their like. You seek Alcides' match?
There's none but he. Now he must war with himself.   85
    Let the Eumenides come, stirred from Tartarus'
Deepest pit, let their flaming hair spread fire,
Their savage hands snap viperous whips.

Enter a troop of FURIES, *perhaps through trapdoors, accompanied by
smoke and fire. Their hair flames, bristling with snakes. They brandish
snake-whips and blazing torches.*

    Go now, proud man, seek a home in the sky,
Scorn humanity. Do you now think, savage,   90
You've left Styx and the dead? Here I'll show you hell.
I shall call, concealed in caverns of mist
Beyond banished sinners, divine Discord,
Whom a mountain barrier's vast cave immures.
I'll lead and drag from the deepest realm   95
Of Dis all that remains. Hateful Crime will come,
And savage Impiety licking its own blood,
Delusion, and, ever armed against itself, Rage—
This last, this last must be servant to my pain.
(*To* FURIES) Begin, handmaids of Dis, violently   100

concutite pinum et agmen horrendum anguibus
Megaera ducat atque luctifica manu
uastam rogo flagrante corripiat trabem.
hoc agite, poenas petite uiolatae Stygis.
concutite pectus, acrior mentem excoquat   105
quam qui caminis ignis Aetnaeis furit.
ut possit animum captus Alcides agi,
magno furore percitus, uobis prius
insaniendum est. Iuno cur nondum furit?
me, me, sorores, mente deiectam mea   110
uersate primam, facere si quicquam apparo
dignum nouerca.
                        Vota mutentur mea.
natos reuersus uideat incolumes precor
manuque fortis redeat. inueni diem,
inuisa quo nos Herculis uirtus iuuet.   115
me uicit? et se uincat et cupiat mori
ab inferis reuersus. hic prosit mihi
Ioue esse genitum. stabo et, ut certo exeant
emissa neruo tela, librabo manu,
regam furentis arma, pugnanti Herculi   120
tandem fauebo. scelere perfecto licet
admittat illas genitor in caelum manus.
    Mouenda iam sunt bella. clarescit dies
ortuque Titan lucidus croceo subit.

CHORVS   Iam rara micant sidera prono   125
          languida mundo, nox uicta uagos
          contrahit ignes luce renata,
          cogit nitidum Phosphoros agmen.
          signum celsi glaciale poli
          septem stellis Arcados Vrsae   130
          lucem uerso temone uocat.
          iam caeruleis euectus equis
          Titan summa prospicit Oeta.
          iam Cadmeis inclita Bacchis

Brandish blazing pine, let Megaera lead
The snake-bristling troop and with baleful hand
Snatch massive beam from a burning pyre.
Do your work, avenge the violated Styx.
Hammer your breasts, scorch your minds with fire   105
More fierce than rages in Etna's forge.
To capture Alcides' mind, to propel
Him spurred to great rage, you must first be mad
Yourselves. Why is Juno not raging yet?
Me, me, sisters, unhinge, and hurl me first   110
From my mind, if I plot some action
Worthy of a stepmother.   Change my prayers.
I pray he return to see sons unharmed
And come back strong of hand. I've found the day
When Hercules' hated virtue may delight me.   115
Did he conquer me? Let him conquer himself
And want death on return from hell. Let it help me
Now that he's born from Jove. I'll stand and aim
With my hand (*mimes the action*), so shafts fly sure from his bow.
I'll guide the mad man's weapons. At last I'll side   120
With Hercules in the fight. When the crime's done,
His father may admit those hands to heaven.
    Let war now begin. The day starts to glow;
Bright Titan rises from the saffron east.

                              Exeunt ALL *into the palace.*

The time and scene are the same. Enter CHORUS OF THEBANS *from stage
left* (*the city*). *They sing, accompanied by the double-piped* tibia.

CHORUS   Now scattered stars faint-glitter   125
                In the setting world, vanquished night
                Rallies stray fires as light's reborn,
                Phosphoros marshals gleaming troops.
                The high pole's icy sign, the Bear
                Of Arcas with its seven stars,   130
                Has turned its wain and summons light.
                Now Titan drawn by cerulean
                Horses peers from Oeta's summit.
                Now thickets famed for Cadmean

aspersa die dumeta rubent   135
Phoebique fugit reditura soror.

Labor exoritur durus et omnes
agitat curas aperitque domos.
pastor gelida cana pruina
grege dimisso pabula carpit.   140
ludit prato liber aperto
nondum rupta fronte iuuencus;
uacuae reparant ubera matres.
errat cursu leuis incerto
molli petulans haedus in herba.   145
pendet summo stridula ramo
pinnasque nouo tradere soli
gestit querulos inter nidos
          Thracia paelex,
turbaque circa confusa sonat   150
murmure mixto testata diem.
carbasa uentis credit dubius
          nauita uitae
laxos aura complente sinus.
hic exesis pendens scopulis   155
aut deceptos instruit hamos
aut suspensus spectat pressa
          praemia dextra.   •
sentit tremulum linea piscem.

Haec, innocuae quibus est uitae
          tranquilla quies   160
et laeta suo paruoque domus.
spes iam magnis urbibus errant
          trepidique metus.
ille superbos aditus regum
durasque fores expers somni   165
colit. hic nullo fine beatas
componit opes gazis inhians
et congesto pauper in auro.
illum populi fauor attonitum
fluctuque magis mobile uulgus   170

Bacchantes blush with splashing day.   135
Phoebus' sister flees and will return.

Hard toil rises. It quickens all
Anxiety and opens homes.
The shepherd unpens his flock,
Plucks pasture cold-grey with frost.   140
A calf plays free in the open
Fields, its brow still unhorned;
Idling dams refill their udders.
A nimble, unsteady kid gambols
Friskily in the tender grass.   145
Perched upon the highest bough,
The shrill whore of Thrace longs
Amid plaintive nests to spread wings
　　　To the new sun.
All around a mingled choir   150
Witness day with diverse sound.
The sailor risks life trusting
　　　Sails to winds,
As a breeze fills billowing folds.
A man perched on battered rocks   155
Baits cheated hooks, or tightens
His grip and anxiously gazes
　　　At the prize.   •
His line feels the quivering fish.

So live those with the tranquil peace
　　　Of guiltless life   160
And homes joyous in their own and little.
Now in the great cities roam hopes
　　　And trembling fears.
One man haunts the proud doorways
And hard thresholds of the great,   165
Sleepless. One gathers blessed riches
Without end and gawps at his treasure—
A pauper amid heaps of gold.
The people's favour stuns another;
A mob more fickle than the waves   170

aura tumidum tollit inani.
hic clamosi rabiosa fori
        iurgia uendens
improbus iras et uerba locat.
nouit paucos secura quies,   175
qui uelocis memores aeui
tempora numquam reditura tenent.

Dum fata sinunt, uiuite laeti.
properat cursu uita citato
uolucrique die rota praecipitis   180
        uertitur anni.   •
durae peragunt pensa sorores
nec sua retro fila reuoluunt.
at gens hominum fertur rapidis
obuia fatis incerta sui;
Stygias ultro quaerimus undas.   185
nimium, Alcide, pectore forti
properas maestos uisere manes.
certo ueniunt ordine Parcae.
nulli iusso cessare licet,
nulli scriptum proferre diem.   190
recipit populos urna citatos.

Alium multis Gloria terris
tradat et omnes Fama per urbes
garrula laudet caeloque parem
        tollat et astris.   195
alius curru sublimis eat.
me mea tellus lare secreto
        tutoque tegat.   •
uenit ad pigros cana senectus,
humilique loco sed certa sedet
sordida paruae fortuna domus.   200
alte uirtus animosa cadit.

Lifts and swells him with empty air.
Another sells the raucous forum's
        Rabid strife,
Wantonly trading wrath and words.
Carefree peace knows but few,   175
Who, mindful of the speeding years,
Embrace unreturning time.

While fate allows, live joyously.
Life rushes with rapid steps,
The headlong year turns its wheel   180
        As days fly by.   •
The brutal sisters spin the wool
And their thread is not rewound.
But the self-unsure race of men
Is swept to meet the grasping fates;
We seek Stygian waves ourselves.   185
Too strong your heart, Alcides,
Rushing to meet the grim ghosts.
In fixed order the Parcae come.
None may delay when bidden,
None defer the day inscribed.   190
The urn admits its summoned throngs.

Let Glory transport one man to
Many lands, prattling Fame praise him
Through all cities and lift him equal
        To heaven and stars.   195
Let another soar in his chariot.
Me—let my own land conceal in safe,
        Secluded home.   •
Grey old age comes to the inert.
The foul fortune of a little home
Sits secure in its lowly place.   200
Spirited virtue falls from the heights.

Sed maesta uenit crine soluto
Megara paruum comitata gregem,
tardusque senio graditur Alcidae parens.

Enter MEGARA *(dressed in mourning garb, wearing a hooded shawl or* ricinium, *with the hood down) and* AMPHITRYON *(squalidly dressed) perhaps from the temple. With them (also squalidly dressed) are the three small* SONS *(personae mutae) of* HERCULES *and* MEGARA.

> But Megara comes in mourning,
> Hair unbound, tending her small flock,
> And—steps slowed by age—Alcides' father.

The CHORUS *remain onstage throughout the second act.*

Actus Secundus

Amphitryon—Megara—Lycus—<Nati Herculis taciti>

AMPHITRYON   O magne Olympi rector et mundi arbiter,   205
iam statue tandem grauibus aerumnis modum
finemque cladi. nulla lux umquam mihi
secura fulsit. finis alterius mali
gradus est futuri. protinus reduci nouus
paratur hostis. antequam laetam domum   210
contingat, aliud iussus ad bellum meat.
nec ulla requies tempus aut ullum uacat—
nisi dum iubetur.
                    Sequitur a primo statim
infesta Iuno. numquid immunis fuit
infantis aetas? monstra superauit prius   215
quam nosse posset. gemina cristati caput
angues ferebant ora, quos contra obuius
reptabat infans igneos serpentium
oculos remisso lumine ac placido intuens.
artos serenis uultibus nodos tulit,   220
et tumida tenera guttura elidens manu
prolusit hydrae. Maenali pernix fera,
multo decorum praeferens auro caput,
deprensa cursu. maximus Nemeae timor
pressus lacertis gemuit Herculeis leo.   225
quid stabula memorem dira Bistonii gregis
suisque regem pabulum armentis datum,
solitumque densis hispidum Erymanthi iugis
Arcadia quatere nemora Maenalium suem,
taurumque centum non leuem populis metum?   230
   Inter remotos gentis Hesperiae greges
pastor triformis litoris Tartesii

Act II

The time is early to mid-morning; the scene is the same. AMPHITYRON, MEGARA, *and her three* SONS *gather around the altar (perhaps before statues of* JUPITER *and* CERES*).*

Amphitryon—Megara—Lycus—<Sons of Hercules silent>

AMPHITRYON   O great lord of Olympus and world-judge,   205
                        Now fix at last a limit to the grave toils
                        And end our calamity. No carefree dawn
                        Ever shone for me. The end of one evil
                        Is step to the next. Straight on his return
                        A new foe's ready. Before touching this house   210
                        Of joy, he goes ordered to another war.
                        There is no rest, no idle time—except
                        While he's being ordered.
                                       Right from the first,
                        Hostile Juno hunts him. Was his infancy
                        Even immune? He overpowered monsters   215
                        Before he could know them. Crested serpents
                        Offered him twin mouths. The infant crawled
                        To meet them, gazing at the snakes' fiery
                        Eyes with a relaxed and tranquil look.
                        He bore tightening coils with face serene,   220
                        And, squeezing swollen throats with tender hands,
                        Practised for the Hydra. Maenalus' swift beast,
                        Flaunting a fair head well decked with gold,
                        Was run down and caught. Nemea's greatest fear,
                        The Lion, groaned in Hercules' strangling arms.   225
                        Why recall the Bistonian herd's dire stables
                        And the king served as pasture for his horses,
                        Or the bristly Maenalian Boar which shook
                        Arcadian groves on Erymanthus' wooded heights,
                        Or the Bull—no slight scare to one hundred towns?   230
                         Among the far herds of Hesperia's folk
                        The triformed drover of the Tartesian shore

peremptus. acta est praeda ab occasu ultimo;
notum Cithaeron pauit Oceano pecus.
penetrare iussus solis aestiui plagas   235
et adusta medius regna quae torret dies
utrimque montes soluit ac rupto obice
latam ruenti fecit Oceano uiam.
post haec adortus nemoris opulenti domos
aurifera uigilis spolia serpentis tulit.   240
    Quid? saeua Lernae monstra, numerosum malum,
non igne demum uicit et docuit mori,
solitasque pinnis condere obductis diem
petit ab ipsis nubibus Stymphalidas?
non uicit illum caelibis semper tori   245
regina gentis uidua Thermodontiae,
nec ad omne clarum facinus audaces manus
stabuli fugauit turpis Augei labor.
    Quid ista prosunt? orbe defenso caret.
sensere terrae pacis auctorem suae   250
abesse terris. prosperum ac felix scelus
uirtus uocatur. sontibus parent boni,
ius est in armis, opprimit leges timor.
ante ora uidi nostra truculenta manu
natos paterni cadere regni uindices   255
ipsumque, Cadmi nobilis stirpem ultimam,
occidere. uidi regium capiti decus
cum capite raptum.
             Quis satis Thebas fleat?
ferax deorum terra quem dominum tremit!
e cuius aruis eque fecundo sinu   260
stricto iuuentus orta cum ferro stetit
cuiusque muros natus Amphion Ioue
struxit canoro saxa modulatu trahens,
in cuius urbem non semel diuum parens
caelo relicto uenit, haec, quae caelites   265
recepit et quae fecit et—fas sit loqui—
fortasse faciet, sordido premitur iugo.
    Cadmea proles atque Ophionium genus,
quo reccidistis! tremitis ignarum exulem,
suis carentem finibus, nostris grauem.   270

Was killed. Booty was brought from the far west;
Cithaeron fed cattle known to Ocean.
Ordered to invade zones of the summer sun   235
And the fiery realms scorched by midday,
He split mountains apart and, with the barrier
Burst, made a broad path for Ocean's rush.
Next he invaded the rich grove's domain
And took the wakeful serpent's golden spoils.   240
    What? Lerna's fierce monster, a numerous pest—
Did he not finally defeat it with fire,
Train it in death, and from the very clouds shoot
Stymphalids, whose shroud of feathers buried day?
The manless queen of the Thermodon race   245
And ever virgin bed did not defeat him,
Nor did the Augean stables' foul toil
Repel hands bold for all deeds of glory.
    What good is served by this? He lacks the world
He saved. Earth felt the author of its peace   250
Absent from earth. Successful crime thrives—
It's called 'virtue'. The good serve the guilty,
Justice lies in arms, terror stifles law.
Before my eyes I saw sons fall to savage
Hands, in defence of their father's kingdom,   255
And the king himself fall, last of noble
Cadmus' line. I saw his head's royal crown
Removed—with the head.
                              Who could mourn Thebes enough?
What a master this god-fruitful land fears!
The land from whose fields and fecund lap   260
Arose warriors standing with drawn swords,
Whose walls were built by Amphion, son of Jove,
Hauling the stones with songful harmonies,
Whose city the father of gods not just once
Left heaven to enter, which welcomed gods,   265
Which has made and perhaps—be it right to say—
Will make gods, this land is pressed by a foul yoke.
    Seed of Cadmus and Ophion's race,
How far you've fallen! You fear an obscure exile
Lacking his own land, a weight upon ours.   270

qui scelera terra quique persequitur mari
ac saeua iusta sceptra confringit manu
nunc seruit absens fertque quae fieri uetat,
tenetque Thebas exul Herculeas Lycus.
sed non tenebit. aderit et poenas petet   275
subitusque ad astra emerget. inueniet uiam
aut faciet. adsis Sospes et remees precor
tandemque uenias uictor ad uictam domum.

MEGARA   Emerge, coniunx, atque dispulsas manu
abrumpe tenebras; nulla si retro uia   280
iterque clusum est, orbe diducto redi
et quidquid atra nocte possessum latet
emitte tecum. dirutis qualis iugis
praeceps citato flumini quaerens iter
quondam stetisti, scissa cum uasto impetu   285
patuere Tempe—pectore impulsus tuo
huc mons et illuc cecidit, et rupto aggere
noua cucurrit Thessalus torrens uia—
talis, parentes liberos patriam petens,
erumpe rerum terminos tecum efferens,   290
et quidquid auida tot per annorum gradus
abscondit aetas redde et oblitos sui
lucisque pauidos ante te populos age.
indigna te sunt spolia, si tantum refers
quantum imperatum est.
                              Magna sed nimium loquor   295
ignara nostrae sortis. unde illum mihi
quo te tuamque dexteram amplectar diem
reditusque lentos nec mei memores querar?
tibi, o deorum ductor, indomiti ferent
centena tauri colla. tibi, frugum potens,   300
secreta reddam sacra; tibi muta fide
longas Eleusin tacita iactabit faces.
tum restitutas fratribus rebor meis
animas et ipsum regna moderantem sua
florere patrem. si qua te maior tenet   305
clausum potestas, sequimur. aut omnes tuo
defende reditu, Sospes, aut omnes trahe.
trahes nec ullus eriget fractos deus.

The man who hunts crime by land and by sea
And crushes cruel sceptres with his just hand,
Now a slave and gone, suffers what he forbids,
And the exile Lycus holds Herculean Thebes—
But shall not hold it. *He'll* come and seek revenge,   275
Rise sudden to the stars. He'll find or make
A path. I pray you come, Saviour, return,
And appear at last—victor to a vanquished house.

MEGARA   Rise, husband, dispel and burst the darkness
With your hand. If there is no way back   280
And the path is barred, rip the world apart,
Then return, and what inky night conceals
Release with yourself. As you once stood,
Shattering cliffs to find a plunging path
For the river's rush, when Tempe split open   285
Before your vast power—struck by your chest
Mountains fell asunder, the mound burst
And Thessaly's torrent ran its new course—
So too, to find parents, children, homeland,
Burst and bear with you the bounds of things   290
And bring back all that lusty time concealed
For many passing years, drive before you
The self-forgetting throngs fearful of the light.
Spoils are not fit for you, if you bring only
What was ordered.

But I speak too mightily,   295
Ignorant of my fate. How will that day come
On which I shall clasp you and your right hand
And scold your slow return, forgetting me?
For thee, O Leader of Gods, untamed bulls
Will give a hundred necks. For thee, Queen of Crops,   300
I'll enact mystic rites; for thee by mute pact
Silent Eleusis will wave the long torches.
Then I shall think my brothers' lives restored
And that father himself governs his realm
And thrives. If a mightier power holds you   305
Imprisoned, we follow. Either return,
Saviour, and protect all, or drag all down. (*Pauses slightly*)
You'll drag all down. No god will lift the broken.

AMPHITRYON   O socia nostri sanguinis, casta fide
               seruans torum natosque magnanimi Herculis,   310
               meliora mente concipe atque animum excita.
               aderit profecto, qualis ex omni solet
               labore, maior.

MEGARA   Quod nimis miseri uolunt,
               hoc facile credunt.

AMPHITRYON   Immo quod metuunt nimis
               numquam moueri posse nec tolli putant.   315
               prona est timoris semper in peius fides.

MEGARA   Demersus ac defossus et toto insuper
               oppressus orbe quam uiam ad superos habet?

AMPHITRYON   Quam tunc habebat, cum per arentem plagam
               et fluctuantes more turbati maris   320
               abit harenas bisque discedens fretum
               et bis recurrens, cumque deserta rate
               deprensus haesit Syrtium breuibus uadis
               et puppe fixa maria superauit pedes.

MEGARA   Iniqua raro maximis uirtutibus   325
               Fortuna parcit. nemo se tuto diu
               periculis offerre tam crebris potest.
               quem saepe transit casus, aliquando inuenit.

               Sed ecce saeuus ac minas uultu gerens
               et, qualis animo est, talis incessu uenit   330
               aliena dextra sceptra concutiens Lycus.

LYCVS   Vrbis regens opulenta Thebanae loca
               et omne quidquid uberi cingit solo
               obliqua Phocis, quidquid Ismenos rigat,
               quidquid Cithaeron uertice excelso uidet   335

AMPHITRYON	O partner in our blood, loyal, chaste custodian
	Of great-souled Hercules' marriage and sons, 310
	Be of better thoughts and uplift your mind.
	He will surely come, and, as after every
	Toil, greater.

| MEGARA | What the wretched want too much |
| | They readily believe. |

AMPHITRYON	No, what they fear too much
	They think can never be changed or lifted. 315
	Fear's conviction ever veers to the worse.

| MEGARA | He is sunk, buried, crushed by the whole world. |
| | What path does he have to those above? |

AMPHITRYON	The same as when he crossed the arid zone,
	Those sand dunes undulating like a sea 320
	In riot, and the twice ebbing and twice
	Returning waters—when, leaving his ship
	And caught stuck in Syrtes' shoals with vessel
	Grounded, he overcame the seas on foot.

MEGARA	Hostile Fortune rarely spares the greatest 325
	Virtues. No one can safely hurl himself
	At such frequent perils for very long.
	Whom chance often misses, someday it finds.

Enter LYCUS *from the palace, accompanied by* GUARDS *and* SLAVES. *He is dressed as a king and 'brandishes' the sceptre of Thebes.*

But look, the savage comes, face marked by threats,
Gait matching his spirit, and the right hand 330
Brandishing another's sceptre: Lycus.
Pulls hood of the ricinium *over her head.*

LYCUS	(*Aside*) I rule the rich places of Thebes' city
	And all that sloping Phocis girdles
	With fertile soil, all that Ismenos waters,
	All that's viewed by high-peaked Cithaeron 335

et bina findens Isthmos exilis freta,
non uetera patriae iura possideo domus
ignauus heres. nobiles non sunt mihi
aui nec altis inclitum titulis genus,
sed clara uirtus. qui genus iactat suum   340
aliena laudat.
     Rapta sed trepida manu
sceptra obtinentur. omnis in ferro est salus.
quod ciuibus tenere te inuitis scias
strictus tuetur ensis. alieno in loco
haut stabile regnum est. una sed nostras potest   345
fundare uires iuncta regali face
thalamisque Megara. ducet e genere inclito
nouitas colorem nostra. non equidem reor
fore ut recuset ac meos spernat toros.
quod si impotenti pertinax animo abnuet,   350
stat tollere omnem penitus Herculeam domum.
inuidia factum ac sermo popularis premet?
ars prima regni est posse et inuidiam pati.
  Temptemus igitur. Fors dedit nobis locum.
namque ipsa, tristi uestis obtentu caput   355
uelata, iuxta praesides adstat deos
laterique adhaeret uerus Alcidae sator.

MEGARA Quidnam iste, nostri generis exitium ac lues,
    noui parat? quid temptat?

LYCVS   O clarum trahens
    a stirpe nomen regia, facilis mea   360
    parumper aure uerba patienti excipe.
    si aeterna semper odia mortales gerant
    nec coeptus umquam cedat ex animis furor,
    sed arma felix teneat, infelix paret,
    nihil relinquent bella. tum uastis ager   365
    squalebit aruis, subdita tectis face
    altus sepultas obruet gentes cinis.
    pacem reduci uelle uictori expedit,
    uicto necesse est.

And slender Isthmos, splitting the two straits.
Yet I'm no idle heir with ancient rights
To ancestral home. I have no noble
Forebears, no family famed for lofty titles;
I have renowned virtue. Flaunting one's birth   340
Lauds others.
                              But stolen sceptres are held
With trembling hand. All safety lies in steel.
What you know you hold against the city's will
The drawn sword protects. In an alien place
Power is unstable. But one woman   345
Can secure my might, joined through royal torch
And chamber: Megara. My 'newness' will draw
Colour from her famed family. Indeed I don't think
It'll be that she refuse and spurn my bed.
But if her wild will stubbornly denies me,   350
I'm resolved to raze all Hercules' house.
Will hatred and the people's voice check the deed?
Kingship's prime art is the power to cope with hate.
    So, let's try. Chance has granted us a place.
She herself stands next to her guardian gods,   355
Her head covered with the cloth of mourning.
By her side clings Alcides' true begetter.

                LYCUS *walks to the altar, where* MEGARA *stands.*

MEGARA   What's he plotting now, this holocaust and plague
           On our family? What's he after?

LYCUS   O heir
           To a renowned name received from royal stock,   360
           Briefly lend a ready, patient ear to my words.
           If mortals ever bear eternal hate
           And rage once begun never leaves the mind,
           But winners stay armed and losers conspire,
           War will leave nothing. Fields will then lie waste, 365
           Farmland decay, and, after homes are torched,
           Deep ash will mantle the buried nations.
           To want peace restored is good for the victor,
           For the vanquished a necessity.

Particeps regno ueni;
sociemur animis. pignus hoc fidei cape.   370
continge dextram.

Quid truci uultu siles?

MEGARA   Egone ut parentis sanguine aspersam manum
fratrumque gemina caede contingam? prius
extinguet ortus, referet occasus diem,
pax ante fida niuibus et flammis erit   375
et Scylla Siculum iunget Ausonio latus,
priusque multo uicibus alternis fugax
Euripus unda stabit Euboica piger.
patrem abstulisti regna germanos larem
patriam—quid ultra est? una res superest mihi   380
fratre ac parente carior, regno ac lare:
odium tui, quod esse cum populo mihi
commune doleo. pars quota ex isto mea est!
    Dominare tumidus, spiritus altos gere;
sequitur superbos ultor a tergo deus.   385
Thebana noui regna. quid matres loquar
passas et ausas scelera? quid geminum nefas
mixtumque nomen coniugis nati patris?
quid bina fratrum castra? quid totidem rogos?
riget superba Tantalis luctu parens   390
maestusque Phrygio manat in Sipylo lapis.
quin ipse toruum subrigens crista caput
Illyrica Cadmus regna permensus fuga
longas reliquit corporis tracti notas.
haec te manent exempla. dominare ut libet—   395
dum solita regni fata te nostri uocent.

LYCVS   Agedum efferatas rabida uoces amoue
et disce regum imperia ab Alcide pati.
ego rapta quamuis sceptra uictrici geram
dextra regamque cuncta sine legum metu   400
quas arma uincunt, pauca pro causa loquar
nostra. cruento cecidit in bello pater?

                        Come, share my rule;
Let's join our hearts. Accept this pledge of faith.   370
Clasp my hand.

                                        Offers his right hand.

                Why the silence and savage look?

MEGARA   Would *I* clasp a hand splashed with father's blood
          And twin slaughter of my brothers? Sooner
          Will the East quench day, the West restore it,
          Sooner will snow and fire make trusted peace   375
          And Scylla join Sicily's flank to Ausonia,
          Far sooner will swift Euripus' shifting tides
          Stand motionless in Euboea's waters.
          You took my father, kingdom, brothers, home,
          Fatherland—what else remains? One thing's left   380
          Dearer than brother, father, kingdom, and home:
          Hatred of you, which—to my pain—I share
          With the people. What small part of it is mine!
             Play the swollen despot, adopt high airs;
          A vengeance-god follows behind the proud.   385
          I know Thebes' realm. Why mention mothers
          Who suffered and dared crimes? Why the twin sin
          And the name of husband, son, father fused?
          Why the brothers' two camps? Why the two pyres?
          Mother Tantalis stiffens proud in grief,   390
          And drips—sad stone on Phrygia's Sipylus.
          Even Cadmus raised a savage, crested head,
          As he crossed Illyria's realm in flight
          And left long marks from his slithering body.
          These examples await. Play despot as you please—   395
          Until called by our kingdom's common fate.

LYCUS   Come, my rabid one, drop these frenzied words;
          Learn from Alcides to cope with kings' commands.
          Though my triumphant hand bears a stolen
          Sceptre and I rule all, unafraid of laws   400
          Vanquished by my arms, I'll briefly defend
          My case. Your father fell in bloody war?

cecidere fratres? arma non seruant modum.
nec temperari facile nec reprimi potest
stricti ensis ira, bella delectat cruor.   405
sed ille regno pro suo, nos improba
cupidine acti? quaeritur belli exitus,
non causa.
         Sed nunc pereat omnis memoria.
cum uictor arma posuit, et uictum decet
deponere odia. non ut inflexo genu   410
regnantem adores petimus. hoc ipsum placet
animo ruinas quod capis magno tuas.
es rege coniunx digna; sociemus toros.

MEGARA   Gelidus per artus uadit exangues tremor.
quod facinus aures pepulit? haut equidem horrui, 415
cum pace rupta bellicus muros fragor
circumsonaret. pertuli intrepide omnia.
thalamos tremesco; capta nunc uideor mihi.
    Grauent catenae corpus et longa fame
mors protrahatur lenta. non uincet fidem   420
uis ulla nostram. moriar, Alcide, tua.

LYCVS   Animosne mersus inferis coniunx facit?

MEGARA   Inferna tetigit, posset ut supera assequi.

LYCVS   Telluris illum pondus immensae premit.

MEGARA   Nullo premetur onere, qui caelum tulit.   425

LYCVS   Cogere.

MEGARA   Cogi qui potest nescit mori.

LYCVS   Effare thalamis quod nouis potius parem
regale munus.

MEGARA   Aut tuam mortem aut meam.

Your brothers fell? Arms observe no bounds.
The wrath of drawn swords cannot easily
Be tempered or checked: war's pleasure is blood.   405
But did *he* not act to save his kingdom,
I from base lust? War's outcome, not its cause,
Is the issue.
                But let all memory now fade.
When victors lay down arms, the vanquished, too,
Rightly lay down their hate. We don't ask you   410
To beg your ruler on bent knee. I like
That you embrace your ruin with great spirit.
You're a wife fit for a king; let's join our beds.

MEGARA   (*Aside*) A chill tremor runs through my bloodless limbs.
           What crime struck my ears? Yet I didn't shiver   415
           When the peace shattered and the din of war
           Roared round our walls. I endured all, fearless.
           I tremble at wedlock; now I seem enslaved.
(*To* LYCUS)   Let chains shackle my body and long starvation
           Stretch a lingering death. No force will conquer   420
           My fidelity. I'll die, Alcides, yours.

LYCUS   Such spirit with a husband sunk in hell?

MEGARA   He has touched hell to reach the higher realm.

LYCUS   The weight of the vast earth crushes him.

MEGARA   No weight will crush the bearer of the sky.   425

LYCUS   You'll be forced.

MEGARA   The 'forced' don't know how to die.

LYCUS   State, rather, what royal gift I should provide
           For our new marriage.

MEGARA   Your death or mine.

LYCVS   Moriere demens.

MEGARA   Coniugi occurram meo.

LYCVS   Sceptroque nostro potior est famulus tibi?   430

MEGARA   Quot iste famulus tradidit reges neci!

LYCVS   Cur ergo regi seruit et patitur iugum?

MEGARA   Imperia dura tolle: quid uirtus erit?

LYCVS   Obici feris monstrisque uirtutem putas?

MEGARA   Virtutis est domare quae cuncti pauent.   435

LYCVS   Tenebrae loquentem magna Tartareae premunt.

MEGARA   Non est ad astra mollis e terris uia.

LYCVS   Quo patre genitus caelitum sperat domos?

AMPHITRYON   Miseranda coniunx Herculis magni, sile.
                     partes meae sunt reddere Alcidae patrem   440
                     genusque uerum. post tot ingentis uiri
                     memoranda facta postque pacatum manu
                     quodcumque Titan ortus et labens uidet,
                     post monstra tot perdomita, post Phlegram impio
                     sparsam cruore postque defensos deos   445
                     nondum liquet de patre? mentimur Iouem?
                     Iunonis odio crede.

LYCVS   Quid uiolas Iouem?
                     mortale caelo non potest iungi genus.

AMPHITRYON   Communis ista pluribus causa est deis.

LYCVS   Famuline fuerant ante quam fierent dei?   450

LYCUS	You'll die, mad woman.
MEGARA	I'll meet my husband.
LYCUS	So you prefer a slave over my sceptre? 430
MEGARA	How many kings that slave has sent to death!
LYCUS	Why then does he serve a king and bear a yoke?
MEGARA	Remove harsh commands: what will virtue be?
LYCUS	Think it 'virtue' being thrown to beasts and monsters?
MEGARA	It is 'virtue' to tame what all men dread. 435
LYCUS	Dark Tartarus overwhelms the braggart.
MEGARA	The path from earth to stars is not gentle.
LYCUS	Who's his father that he hopes to live with gods?

AMPHITRYON *intervenes.*

AMPHITRYON Hapless wife of great Hercules, silence.
It's my role to restore to Alcides his father   440
And true descent. After the mighty hero's
Many famous deeds, after his hand pacified
All that Titan views, risen and setting,
After many monsters tamed, after spattering
Phlegra with impious blood, after defending gods,   445
His father's still unproven? Jove a hoax?
Trust Juno's hate.

LYCUS   Why blaspheme Jupiter?
The mortal race cannot be joined to heaven.

AMPHITRYON That's the origin shared by several gods.

LYCUS But were they slaves before becoming gods?   450

AMPHITRYON   Pastor Pheraeos Delius pauit greges.

LYCVS   Sed non per omnes exul errauit plagas.

AMPHITRYON   Quem profuga terra mater errante edidit.

LYCVS   Num monstra saeuas Phoebus aut timuit feras?

AMPHITRYON   Primus sagittas imbuit Phoebi draco.   455

LYCVS   Quam grauia paruus tulerit ignoras mala?

AMPHITRYON   E matris utero fulmine eiectus puer
mox fulminanti proximus patri stetit.
quid? qui gubernat astra, qui nubes quatit,
non latuit infans rupis exesae specu?   460
sollicita tanti pretia natales habent
semperque magno constitit nasci deum.

LYCVS   Quemcumque miserum uideris, hominem scias.

AMPHITRYON   Quemcumque fortem uideris, miserum neges.

LYCVS   Fortem uocemus cuius ex umeris leo,   465
donum puellae factus, et claua excidit
fulsitque pictum ueste Sidonia latus?
fortem uocemus cuius horrentes comae
maduere nardo, laude qui notas manus
ad non uirilem tympani mouit sonum,   470
mitra ferocem barbara frontem premens?

AMPHITRYON   Non erubescit Bacchus effusos tener
sparsisse crines nec manu molli leuem
uibrare thyrsum, cum parum forti gradu
auro decorum syrma barbarico trahit.   475
post multa uirtus opera laxari solet.

LYCVS   Hoc Euryti fatetur euersi domus
pecorumque ritu uirginum oppressi greges.

AMPHITRYON	The Delian shepherd grazed flocks by Pherae.
LYCUS	But didn't wander exiled through all the world.
AMPHITRYON	A fugitive mother bore him on wandering land.
LYCUS	Did Phoebus fear monsters or savage beasts?
AMPHITRYON	First to stain Phoebus' arrows was a snake. 455
LYCUS	You don't know the grave tests he faced when small?
AMPHITRYON	The boy cast by lightning from his mother's Womb soon stood next to his lightning father. What? Didn't he who directs stars, who shakes clouds, Hide—as a child—in a cave on a crumbling cliff? 460 Anxiety is the price of high birth. It's always costly to be born a god.
LYCUS	See someone wretched, know he is human.
AMPHITRYON	See someone heroic, know he's not wretched.
LYCUS	Call him heroic, from whose shoulders fell 465 The Lion and club to be a girl's gift, Whose gaudy flank shimmered in Sidon dress? Call him heroic, whose bristling hair dripped With nard, who moved those praised and noted hands To the unmanly sound of a timbrel, 470 His savage brow bound with foreign turban?
AMPHITRYON	Tender Bacchus never blushes to toss His streaming hair or shake the light thyrsus With soft hands, when with dainty step he trails A tragic gown crusted with foreign gold. 475 After much work virtue often relaxes.
LYCUS	As witnessed by ruined Eurytus' house And the flocks of virgins harried like sheep.

hoc nulla Iuno, nullus Eurystheus iubet.
ipsius haec sunt opera.

AMPHITRYON   Non nosti omnia.   480
ipsius opus est caestibus fractus suis
Eryx et Eryci iunctus Antaeus Libys,
et qui hospitali caede manantes foci
bibere iustum sanguinem Busiridis.
ipsius opus est uulneri et ferro inuius   485
mortem coactus integer Cycnus pati,
nec unus una Geryon uictus manu.
eris inter istos—qui tamen nullo stupro
laesere thalamos.

LYCVS   Quod Ioui hoc regi licet.
Ioui dedisti coniugem, regi dabis,   490
et te magistro non nouum hoc discet nurus:
etiam uiro probante meliorem sequi.
sin copulari pertinax taedis negat,
uel ex coacta nobilem partum feram.

MEGARA   Vmbrae Creontis et penates Labdaci   495
et nuptiales impii Oedipodae faces,
nunc solita nostro fata coniugio date.
nunc, nunc, cruentae regis Aegypti nurus,
adeste multo sanguine infectae manus.
dest una numero Danais? explebo nefas.   500

LYCVS   Coniugia quoniam peruicax nostra abnuis
regemque terres, sceptra quid possint scies.

Complectere aras. nullus eripiet deus
te mihi, nec orbe si remolito queat
ad supera uictor numina Alcides uehi.   505
    Congerite siluas. templa supplicibus suis
iniecta flagrent, coniugem et totum gregem
consumat unus igne subiecto locus.

No Juno, no Eurystheus ordered that.
They are his work.

AMPHITRYON   You do not know it all.   480
His work is Eryx, smashed by his own gloves,
And, with Eryx, Libyan Antaeus,
And the hearths which dripped with the gore of guests
And then drank the just blood of Busiris.
His work is Cycnus, impervious to wound   485
And steel, compelled to suffer death intact,
And un-single Geryon vanquished by one hand.
You will join them—yet they never debauched
His bed.

LYCUS   What Jove may do, a king may do.
You gave Jove a wife, you'll give one to the king,   490
And teach your daughter a lesson un-new:
To take the better man with husband's consent.
But if she's stubborn and refuses to wed,
I'll get my noble offspring—even by force.

                                MEGARA *responds furiously.*

MEGARA   Ghost of Creon and gods of Labdacus   495
And nuptial brands of impious Oedipus,
Now grant our marriage the common fate.
Now, now, gory wives of King Aegyptus' sons,
Come to me, hands drenched with copious blood.
One Danaid's missing? I'll complete the horror.   500

LYCUS   Since you staunchly reject our marriage
And threaten the king, you'll know a sceptre's power.

                        MEGARA *puts her hands on the altar.*

Embrace the altar. No god will snatch you from me,
Not if Alcides could upheave the world
And ride triumphant to the gods above.   505
(*To* GUARDS *and* SLAVES) Pile up wood. Let the temple fall blazing
On its suppliants and rising fire consume
Wife and her whole flock in a single place.

AMPHITRYON   Hoc munus a te genitor Alcidae peto,
             rogare quod me deceat, ut primus cadam.   510

LYCVS   Qui morte cunctos luere supplicium iubet
             nescit tyrannus esse. diuersa inroga:
             miserum ueta perire, felicem iube.
             ego, dum cremandis trabibus accrescit rogus,
             sacro regentem maria uotiuo colam.   515

AMPHITRYON   Pro numinum uis summa, pro caelestium
             rector parensque, cuius excussis tremunt
             humana telis, impiam regis feri
             compesce dextram!
                              Quid deos frustra precor?
             ubicumque es, audi, nate.

                              Cur subito labant   520
             agitata motu templa? cur mugit solum?
             infernus imo sonuit e fundo fragor.
             audimur? est—est sonitus Herculei gradus?

CHORVS   O Fortuna uiris inuida fortibus,
             quam non aequa bonis praemia diuidis!   525
             Eurystheus facili regnet in otio,
             Alcmena genitus bella per omnia
             monstris exagitet caeliferam manum,
             serpentis resecet colla feracia,
             deceptis referat mala sororibus,   530

SLAVES, *commanded by* GUARDS, *begin to bring in wood and place it before the temple.*

AMPHITRYON   As Alcides' father, I beg this of you—
Which it is right I ask—that I die first.   510

LYCUS   One who orders death for all does not know
Tyranny. Vary the sentence: keep death
From the wretched, order it for the happy.
While this pyre grows with logs for burning,
I'll worship the sea-lord with votive rites.   515

Exit stage left (to the city), attended by some GUARDS.

Other GUARDS *and* SLAVES *remain. The latter continue to bring in wood.*
AMPHITRYON *prays (perhaps turning to* JUPITER'S *statue).*

AMPHITRYON   O divine force supreme, O lord and father
Of the celestial gods, whose hurled shafts
Make mankind tremble, check the impious hand
Of this brutal king!
                                    Why invoke the gods in vain?
Wherever you are, hear me, son.

Sounds are heard by AMPHITRYON.

                                    Why does   520
The temple suddenly rock? The ground rumble?
The roar of hell rises from the lowest depths.
We're heard? Is—is it the sound of Hercules' tread?

AMPHITRYON *is led under guard to the doors of the temple together with*
MEGARA *and her* SONS. ALL *remain onstage.*

The CHORUS *sing.*

CHORUS   O Fortune, envious of heroes,
How unjust thy rewards to the good!   525
Should Eurystheus reign in ease and peace,
But Alcmena's son wage all those wars,
Thrust sky-bearing hands at monsters,
Re-slice a serpent's fertile necks,
Retrieve the apples from duped sisters,   530

cum somno dederit peruigiles genas
pomis diuitibus praepositus draco?

Intrauit Scythiae multiuagas domos
et gentes patriis sedibus hospitas,
calcauitque freti terga rigentia   535
et mutis tacitum litoribus mare.
illic dura carent aequora fluctibus,
et qua plena rates carbasa tenderant,
intonsis teritur semita Sarmatis.
stat pontus, uicibus mobilis annuis,   540
nauem nunc facilis, nunc equitem pati.
illic quae uiduis gentibus imperat,
aurato religans ilia balteo,
detraxit spolium nobile corpori
et peltam et niuei uincula pectoris,   545
uictorem posito suspiciens genu.

Qua spe praecipites actus ad inferos,
audax ire uias irremeabiles,
uidisti Siculae regna Proserpinae?
illic nulla Noto nulla Fauonio   550
consurgunt tumidis fluctibus aequora.
non illic geminum Tyndaridae genus
succurrunt timidis sidera nauibus.
stat nigro pelagus gurgite languidum,
et cum Mors auidis pallida dentibus   555
gentes innumeras manibus intulit,
uno tot populi remige transeunt.

Euincas utinam iura ferae Stygis
Parcarumque colos non reuocabiles.
hic qui rex populis pluribus imperat,   560
bello cum peteres Nestoream Pylon,
tecum conseruit pestiferas manus
telum tergemina cuspide praeferens.
effugit tenui uulnere saucius
et mortis dominus pertimuit mori.   565
fatum rumpe manu. tristibus inferis

When a dragon-guard of precious fruit
Has ceded vigilant eyes to sleep?

He trekked to Scythia's nomad homes
And tribes estranged in their fatherland,
And trod on the water's stiffened back,   535
The muted main with its silent shores.
There the hardened sea-plains have no waves;
And where ships had spread billowing sails
The long-haired Sarmatians tread paths.
The sea stands, shifting with yearly change,   540
Ready to bear now ships, now horsemen.
There the queen-general of manless tribes,
Groin bound with a gilded baldric,
Stripped her body of the noble spoil
And shield and bands of her snowy breast,   545
And knelt gazing up at the victor.

What hope drove you to hell's pit, to walk
Bold the paths of no return, and see
Sicilian Proserpina's empire?
There no waters rise with swelling waves   550
Caused by Notus or Favonius.
There no twin Tyndarids with their stars
Bring succour to the terrified ships.
The sea stands motionless, its pool black,
And, when pale Death with its lusty teeth   555
Has brought unnumbered tribes to the dead,
One oarsman transports the multitudes.

May you conquer the laws of wild Styx,
The Parcae's irrevocable distaff.
This king who rules the most nations,   560
When you sought war with Nestor's Pylos,
Battled you with pestilential hands,
Brandishing his spear of triple point.
He fled injured with a paltry wound;
The lord of death was afraid to die.   565
Break fate with your hand. Let the grim dead

prospectus pateat lucis et inuius
limes det faciles ad superos uias.

Immites potuit flectere cantibus
umbrarum dominos et prece supplici   570
Orpheus, Eurydicen dum repetit suam.
quae siluas et aues saxaque traxerat
ars, quae praebuerat fluminibus moras,
ad cuius sonitum constiterant ferae,
mulcet non solitis uocibus inferos   575
et surdis resonat clarius in locis.
deflent Eumenides Threiciam nurum,
deflent et lacrimis difficiles dei,
et qui fronte nimis crimina tetrica
quaerunt ac ueteres excutiunt reos   580
flentes Eurydicen iuridici sedent.
tandem Mortis ait 'uincimur' arbiter,
'euade ad superos, lege tamen data:
tu post terga tui perge uiri comes,
tu non ante tuam respice coniugem,   585
quam cum clara deos obtulerit dies
Spartanique aderit ianua Taenari.'
odit uerus amor nec patitur moras.
munus dum properat cernere, perdidit.

Quae uinci potuit regia cantibus,   590
haec uinci poterit regia uiribus.

See the light and the pathless border
Grant easy paths to the world above.

Orpheus could sway the shades' pitiless
Lords with songs and suppliant prayer,   570
When he claimed his dear Eurydice.
The art which had moved forests and birds
And rocks, which had made rivers delay
And arrested wild beasts with its sound,
Soothes the dead with unfamiliar notes   575
And rings more clear in that noiseless place.
The Eumenides weep for Thracian
Bride; gods also weep, not prone to tears.
Even judges who examine crimes
With sternest brow and review ancient   580
Guilt sit weeping for Eurydice.
At length Death's arbiter says, 'We're conquered.
Go to those above, but on these terms:
You escort your husband from behind;
You don't look back at your wife before   585
Clear daylight has disclosed the gods
And Spartan Taenarus' gate is reached.'
True love hates delay, nor suffers it.
Rushing to see his gift, he lost her.

The palace one could conquer with song,   590
That palace one can conquer with force.

                              The CHORUS *remain onstage.*

Actus Tertius

Hercules—Amphitryon—Megara tacita—Theseus—<Nati Herculis taciti>

HERCVLES O lucis almae rector et caeli decus,
      qui alterna curru spatia flammifero ambiens
      inlustre laetis exeris terris caput,
      da, Phoebe, ueniam, si quid inlicitum tui   595
      uidere uultus. iussus in lucem extuli
      arcana mundi. tuque, caelestum arbiter
      parensque, uisus fulmine opposito tege;
      et tu, secundo maria qui sceptro regis,
      imas pete undas. quisquis ex alto aspicit   600
      terrena, facie pollui metuens noua,
      aciem reflectat oraque in caelum erigat
      portenta fugiens. hoc nefas cernant duo:
      qui aduexit et quae iussit.
             In poenas meas
      atque in labores non satis terrae patent   605
      Iunonis odio. uidi inaccessa omnibus,
      ignota Phoebo quaeque deterior polus
      obscura diro spatia concessit Ioui.
      et, si placerent tertiae sortis loca,
      regnare potui. noctis aeternae chaos   610
      et nocte quiddam grauius et tristes deos
      et fata uici. morte contempta redi.
      quid restat aliud? uidi et ostendi inferos.
      da, si quid ultra est; iam diu pateris manus
      cessare nostras, Iuno. quae uinci iubes?   615

Act III

The time and scene are the same. AMPHITRYON, MEGARA, *and her* SONS *stand by the temple doors under the watchful eyes of* LYCUS' GUARDS. *Also present are the* CHORUS. *Enter from stage right* (*outside Thebes*) HERCULES, *bearded, wearing a lion skin draped over his left shoulder, and equipped with bow, quiver, arrows, club, and sword. He is accompanied by* THESEUS. *They drag a movable platform onto the stage behind them. On it is a representation of the hell-hound* CERBERUS *in chains.*

Hercules—Amphitryon—Megara silent—Theseus—<Sons of Hercules silent>

HERCULES O lord of gentle light and heaven's glory,
Whose chariot of fire rounds both spheres
And lifts thy shining head above joyous lands,
Grant pardon, Phoebus, if thine eyes have seen   595
Things forbidden. On orders I brought to light
The world's secrets. Thou, too, judge and father
Of gods, shield thy sight with a thunderbolt,
And thou, whose second sceptre rules the seas,
Seek waves most deep. All who view earth from above   600
And fear pollution from this novel sight
Should turn their eyes and lift their face to heaven,
Shunning the monster. Two should see this evil:
He who fetched it, she who ordered it.
                                      (*Aside*) For my pains
And labours the wide earth does not suffice,   605
Given the hate of Juno. I saw things banned
To all, unknown to Phoebus—those murky
Spaces which the baser pole gave dire Jove.
And, if the places of the third lot had pleased me,
I could have reigned. I vanquished eternal night's chaos 610
And something heavier than night, and the grim
Gods and fates. I spat on death and returned.
What else is left? I saw and exposed hell.
If there's more, give it, Juno; you've let my hands
Now idle long. What conquest do you command?   615

                        Looks toward the temple doors.

Sed templa quare miles infestus tenet
limenque sacrum terror armorum obsidet?

AMPHITRYON   Vtrumne uisus uota decipiunt meos,
an ille domitor orbis et Graium decus
tristi silentem nubilo liquit domum?   620
estne ille natus? membra laetitia stupent.

O nate, certa at sera Thebarum salus,
teneone in auras editum an uana fruor
deceptus umbra? tune es? agnosco toros
umerosque et alto nobilem trunco manum.   625

HERCVLES   Vnde iste, genitor, squalor et lugubribus
amicta coniunx? unde tam foedo obsiti
paedore nati? quae domum clades grauat?

AMPHITRYON   Socer est peremptus. regna possedit Lycus.
natos parentem coniugem leto petit.   630

HERCVLES   Ingrata tellus, nemo ad Herculeae domus
auxilia uenit? uidit hoc tantum nefas
defensus orbis?
                         Cur diem questu tero?
mactetur hostis, hanc ferat uirtus notam
fiatque summus hostis Alcidae Lycus.   635
ad hauriendum sanguinem inimicum feror.
Theseu, resiste, ne qua uis subita ingruat.
me bella poscunt.

                         Differ amplexus, parens,
coniunxque differ. nuntiet Diti Lycus
me iam redisse.

(*Aloud*) Why do hostile soldiers guard the temple
And armed terror besiege the sacred doors?

Moves toward temple doors.

Exeunt GUARDS (*alarmed*) *stage left* (*to the city*).

AMPHITRYON   Do prayers trick my eyes, or has the tamer
Of the world and the glory of Greece quit
The silent house and its melancholy gloom?   620
Is that my son? My limbs are numb with joy.

Embraces HERCULES

O son, sure, if late, salvation for Thebes,
Do I hold a breathing man or take false joy
In an empty shade? Is it you? I recognize
Muscles, shoulders, hand, known for its tall club.   625

HERCULES   Why this squalor, father, and my wife dressed
For mourning? Why are my sons so foully
Smothered in filth? What tragedy loads the house?

AMPHITRYON   Her father is dead. Lycus has the realm.
He intends to kill your sons, father, wife.   630

HERCULES   Ungrateful land, did no one come to help
The house of Hercules? Did the world I saved
Watch such evil?
                          Why waste the day whining?
An enemy must be slaughtered, virtue marked,
And Alcides' last foe must be Lycus.   635
I am driven to drink his hated blood.
   Theseus, stay, lest sudden violence erupt.
I'm called to war.

AMPHITRYON *moves to embrace him again, as does* MEGARA

Defer embraces, father;
Wife, defer. Let Lycus take Dis a message:
I have now returned.

Exit stage left (*to the city*).

THESEVS   Flebilem ex oculis fuga,   640
                 regina, uultum, tuque nato sospite
                 lacrimas cadentes reprime. si noui Herculem,
                 Lycus Creonti debitas poenas dabit.
                 lentum est 'dabit': dat. hoc quoque est lentum: dedit.

AMPHITRYON   Votum secundet qui potest nostrum deus   645
                 rebusque lassis adsit. O magni comes
                 magnanime nati, pande uirtutum ordinem,
                 quam longa maestos ducat ad manes uia,
                 ut uincla tulerit dura Tartareus canis.

THESEVS   Memorare cogis acta securae quoque   650
                 horrenda menti. uix adhuc certa est fides
                 uitalis aurae, torpet acies luminum
                 hebetesque uisus uix diem insuetum ferunt.

AMPHITRYON   Peruince, Theseu, quidquid alto in pectore
                 remanet pauoris neue te fructu optimo   655
                 frauda laborum. quae fuit durum pati
                 meminisse dulce est. fare casus horridos.

THESEVS   Fas omne mundi teque dominantem precor
                 regno capaci teque quam tota inrita
                 quaesiuit Aetna mater, ut iura abdita   660
                 et operta terris liceat impune eloqui.
                     Spartana tellus nobile attollit iugum,
                 densis ubi aequor Taenarus siluis premit.
                 hic ora soluit Ditis inuisi domus
                 hiatque rupes alta et immenso specu   665
                 ingens uorago faucibus uastis patet
                 latumque pandit omnibus populis iter.
                 non caeca tenebris incipit primo uia.
                 tenuis relictae lucis a tergo nitor
                 fulgorque dubius solis afflicti cadit   670

The platform on which the representation of CERBERUS *stands is wheeled offstage behind* HERCULES, *surrounded and/or followed by the* CHORUS.

THESEUS   Banish from your eyes,   640
                     Queen, that doleful look, and you—your son safe—
                     Check falling tears. If I know Hercules,
                     Lycus will pay the price owed to Creon.
                     'Will pay' is slow: he pays. Also slow: he paid.

Consoles MEGARA, *who sits down with her* SONS *by the altar.*

AMPHITRYON   May divine power support our prayer   645
                     And aid troubled times. O great-souled comrade
                     Of great son, disclose his virtues in order,
                     The length of the path leading to grim ghosts,
                     How the Tartarus-hound bore the harsh chains.

THESEUS   You compel me to recount deeds dreadful   650
                     Even to the mind of one now safe. I scarce
                     Yet trust the vital air; my eyesight's dazed,
                     My dull vision scarce endures the strange daylight.

AMPHITRYON   Conquer, Theseus, whatever fear remains
                     Deep in your breast. Don't be robbed of labour's   655
                     Greatest joy. What was hard to bear is sweet
                     To remember. Tell the fearful story.

THESEUS   I pray to the world's whole Sanctity and thee,
                     Lord of endless realm, and thee whom thy mother
                     Sought vainly round all Etna: let me safely   660
                     Tell of laws hidden and buried in the earth.
                          The Spartan land rises to a famous ridge,
                     Where Taenarus presses the sea with dense woods.
                     Here the house of hated Dis opens its mouth,
                     A high cliff gapes wide and the huge abyss   665
                     Of an immense cave yawns with its vast throat
                     And reveals a broad highway for all nations.
                     At first the path is not obscured by darkness.
                     The abandoned light glows dimly behind,
                     And the feeble sun's dubious glimmer   670

et ludit aciem. nocte sic mixta solet
praebere lumen primus aut serus dies.
hinc ampla uacuis spatia laxantur locis,
in quae omne mersum pergat humanum genus.
nec ire labor est; ipsa deducit uia.   675
ut saepe puppes aestus inuitas rapit,
sic pronus aer urguet atque auidum chaos,
gradumque retro flectere haut umquam sinunt
umbrae tenaces.
        Intus immenso sinu
placido quieta labitur Lethe uado   680
demitque curas, neue remeandi amplius
pateat facultas, flexibus multis grauem
inuoluit amnem—qualis incerta uagus
Maeander unda ludit et cedit sibi
instatque dubius litus an fontem petat.   685
palus inertis foeda Cocyti iacet.
hinc uultur, illinc luctifer bubo gemit
omenque triste resonat infaustae strigis.
horrent opaca fronde nigrantes comae
taxo imminente, quam tenet segnis Sopor,   690
Famesque maesta tabido rictu iacet
Pudorque serus conscios uultus tegit.
Metus Pauorque, Funus et frendens Dolor
aterque Luctus sequitur et Morbus tremens
et cincta ferro Bella. in extremo abdita   695
iners Senectus adiuuat baculo gradum.

AMPHITRYON   Estne aliqua tellus Cereris aut Bacchi ferax?

THESEVS   Non prata uiridi laeta facie germinant
nec adulta leni fluctuat Zephyro seges,
non ulla ramos silua pomiferos habet.   700
sterilis profundi uastitas squalet soli
et foeda tellus torpet aeterno situ—
rerumque maestus finis et mundi ultima.
immotus aer haeret et pigro sedet
nox atra mundo. cuncta maerore horrida   705
ipsaque morte peior est mortis locus.

Fades and tricks the eye—just as the day's start
And end provide light mingled with darkness.
Here large zones open up with empty places,
Into which plunge the whole human race.
To go is no labour. The path itself leads down.   675
As currents often seize unwilling ships,
So the down-draught and lusty chaos urge
On, and the grasping ghosts never let you
Retrace your steps.
                                   Within, in a vast chasm,
Silent Lethe glides with its placid stream   680
And removes care. To decrease the chances
Of returning, it twists its sluggish stream
In many loops—just as wandering Maeander
Plays with shifting waters, self-yields and flows on,
Undecided to head for shore or source.   685
The foul marsh of listless Cocytus sprawls.
Here a vulture wails, there a baneful owl;
A curséd screech-owl's grim omen echoes.
Black foliage bristles with shady leaves
On overhanging yew, home to dull Sleep.   690
Morose Hunger lies there with rotting jaws
And tardy Shame veils its guilty face.
Then Fear and Panic, Death and grinding Pain
Follow and black Grief and trembling Disease
And War, iron-girt. Hidden at the end,   695
Listless Old Age helps its step with a stick.

AMPHITRYON   Is there land rich in Ceres or Bacchus?

THESEUS   No verdant, revelling meadows flower,
             No grown crops ripple with gentle Zephyr,
             No forest has branches laden with fruit.   700
             A barren vastness encrusts the lower soil,
             The foul earth stiffens with eternal mould—
             The grim cessation of things, the world's end.
             The air clings motionless and black night sits
             On a languid world. All things bristle with grief: 705
             The place of death is worse than death itself.

AMPHITRYON   Quid ille opaca qui regit sceptro loca?
             qua sede positus temperat populos leues?

THESEVS   Est in recessu Tartari obscuro locus,
             quem grauibus umbris spissa caligo alligat.   710
             a fonte discors manat hinc uno latex,
             alter quieto similis (hunc iurant dei)
             tacente sacram deuehens fluuio Styga;
             at hic tumultu rapitur ingenti ferox
             et saxa fluctu uoluit Acheron inuius   715
             renauigari. cingitur duplici uado
             aduersa Ditis regia, atque ingens domus
             umbrante luco tegitur. hic uasto specu
             pendent tyranni limina. hoc umbris iter,
             haec porta regni. campus hanc circa iacet,   720
             in quo superbo digerit uultu sedens
             animas recentes. dira maiestas deo,
             frons torua, fratrum quae tamen specimen gerat
             gentisque tantae. uultus est illi Iouis—
             sed fulminantis. magna pars regni trucis   725
             est ipse dominus, cuius aspectus timet
             quidquid timetur.

AMPHITRYON   Verane est fama inferis
             iam sera reddi iura et oblitos sui
             sceleris nocentes debitas poenas dare?
             quis iste ueri rector atque aequi arbiter?   730

THESEVS   Non unus alta sede quaesitor sedens
             iudicia trepidis sera sortitur reis.
             aditur illo Cnosius Minos foro,
             Rhadamanthus illo, Thetidis hoc audit socer.
             quod quisque fecit, patitur. auctorem scelus   735
             repetit suoque premitur exemplo nocens.
             uidi cruentos carcere includi duces
             et impotentis terga plebeia manu
             scindi tyranni. quisquis est placide potens
             dominusque uitae seruat innocuas manus   740
             et incruentum mitis imperium regit

AMPHITRYON   What about the dark places' sceptered king?
Where does he sit to rule the weightless throngs?

THESEUS   There is a place, in a gloomy recess
Of Tartarus, wrapped by dense mist and deep shadows.   710
From a single source pour discordant streams.
One, like a thing at rest (gods swear by it),
Carries the sacred Styx with silent flow.
The other, ferocious Acheron, sweeps along
With massive roar, rolling rocks in a course   715
None may recross. Ringed by this double moat
The palace of Dis looms; a shady grove
Shrouds the great house. Here in a vast cave
Hang the tyrant's doors. This is the way for shades,
This the kingdom's gate. Round it lies a field   720
In which he sits with prideful mien and sorts
The new souls. Fearsome the god's majesty,
Fierce his brow, yet bearing signs of both brothers
And his great race. His face is that of Jove—
But of Jove when he thunders. A large part   725
Of the realm's grimness is the lord himself,
Whose look the feared fear.

AMPHITRYON   Is the rumour true
The dead now get justice late and the guilty
Pay due penalty for crimes they forgot?
Who is the lord of truth and judge of justice?   730

THESEUS   No one magistrate sitting aloft allots
Trembling prisoners their tardy judgements.
Cnossian Minos controls one court, Rhadamanthus
Another, Thetis' in-law presides in a third.
All suffer their own deeds. Crime seeks its author;   735
The guilty are crushed by their own example.
I saw blood-drenched leaders locked in a jail
And the backs of raving tyrants scourged
By plebeian hands. The gentle monarch
And life's master, who keeps his hands guiltless   740
And rules an empire mildly without blood,

animaeque parcit, longa permensus diu
felicis aeui spatia uel caelum petit
uel laeta felix nemoris Elysii loca,
iudex futurus. sanguine humano abstine   745
quicumque regnas. scelera taxantur modo
maiore uestra.

AMPHITRYON   Certus inclusos tenet
locus nocentes? utque fert fama, impios
supplicia uinclis saeua perpetuis domant?

THESEVS   Rapitur uolucri tortus Ixion rota;   750
ceruice saxum grande Sisyphia sedet.
in amne medio faucibus siccis senex
sectatur undas, alluit mentum latex,
fidemque cum iam saepe decepto dedit
perit unda in ore. poma destituunt famem.   755
praebet uolucri Tityos aeternas dapes
urnasque frustra Danaides plenas gerunt.
errant furentes impiae Cadmeides
terretque mensas auida Phineas auis.

AMPHITRYON   Nunc ede nati nobilem pugnam mei.   760
patrui uolentis munus an spolium refert?

THESEVS   Ferale tardis imminet saxum uadis,
stupente ubi unda segne torpescit fretum.
hunc seruat amnem cultu et aspectu horridus
pauidosque manes squalidus gestat senex.   765
impexa pendet barba, deformem sinum
nodus coercet, concauae lucent genae.
regit ipse longo portitor conto ratem.
    Hic onere uacuam litori puppem applicans
repetebat umbras. poscit Alcides uiam   770
cedente turba. dirus exclamat Charon:
'quo pergis, audax? siste properantem gradum.'
non passus ullas natus Alcmena moras
ipso coactum nauitam conto domat
scanditque puppem. cumba populorum capax   775

Sparing life—he measures for years long tracts
Of a happy age and heads for heaven
Or the Elysian grove's joyous places happy,
A judge-to-be. Abstain from human blood,   745
All you who rule. Greater punishments await
Your crimes.

AMPHITRYON   Does a fixed place imprison
The guilty? And, as rumour says, does savage
Torture tame the godless in eternal chains?

THESEUS   Ixion is racked and spun on speeding wheel;   750
A huge boulder sits on Sisyphus' neck.
Amid a stream with dry throat an old man
Chases waves, the water splashes his chin;
The waves gain trust from one so often tricked
And die on his lips. Fruit mocks his hunger.   755
Tityos feeds the bird an eternal feast
And Danaids vainly carry full urns.
Impious Cadmeids wander in rage,
A ravening bird frightens Phineus' table.

AMPHITRYON   Now present my son's heroic fight. Is he   760
Here with a willing uncle's gift—or spoils?

THESEUS   A deathly crag overhangs sluggish waters—
The waves are numb, the torpid strait stagnates.
A foul old man, vile in his dress and looks,
Guards the stream and ferries the frightened ghosts.   765
A tangled beard hangs from him, a knot constricts
An ugly cloak, his sunken eyes blaze.
The ferryman directs his boat with a long pole.
     He brought the barque to shore without its load,
Looking for shades. Alcides demands passage   770
As the crowd give way. Dread Charon exclaims:
'Where do you go, bold one? Check that rash step.'
Alcmena's son brooks no delay, but forces
And subdues the boatman with his own pole,
And boards the vessel. The skiff with room for nations   775

succubuit uni; sedit et grauior ratis
utrimque Lethen latere titubanti bibit.
tum uicta trepidant monstra, Centauri truces
Lapithaeque multo in bella succensi mero.
Stygiae paludis ultimos quaerens sinus   780
fecunda mergit capita Lernaeus labor.
    Post haec auari Ditis apparet domus.
hic saeuus umbras territat Stygius canis,
qui trina uasto capita concutiens sono
regnum tuetur. sordidum tabo caput   785
lambunt colubrae, uiperis horrent iubae
longusque torta sibilat cauda draco.
par ira formae. sensit ut motus pedum,
attollit hirtas angue uibrato comas
missumque captat aure subrecta sonum,   790
sentire et umbras solitus. ut propior stetit
Ioue natus antro, sedit incertus canis
et uterque timuit. ecce latratu graui
loca muta terret; sibilat totos minax
serpens per armos. uocis horrendae fragor   795
per ora missus terna felices quoque
exterret umbras. soluit a laeua feros
tunc ipse rictus et Cleonaeum caput
opponit ac se tegmine ingenti tegit,
uictrice magnum dextera robur gerens.   800
huc nunc et illuc uerbere assiduo rotat;
ingeminat ictus. domitus infregit minas
et cuncta lassus capita summisit canis
antroque toto cessit. extimuit sedens
uterque solio dominus et duci iubet;   805
me quoque petenti munus Alcidae dedit.
    Tum grauia monstri colla permulcens manu
adamante texto uincit. oblitus sui
custos opaci peruigil regni canis
componit aures timidus et patiens trahi   810
erumque fassus, ore summisso obsequens,
utrumque cauda pulsat anguifera latus.
postquam est ad oras Taenari uentum et nitor
percussit oculos lucis ignotae nouus,

Sank beneath one man. The boat sat heavier;
As it rocks, it gulps Lethe on both sides.
Then conquered monsters cower, brutal Centaurs
And Lapiths, made hot for war by much wine.
The labour of Lerna seeks the Stygian   780
Swamp's furthest coves and sinks its fecund heads.
   Next, the palace of greedy Dis appears.
Here a savage hell-hound terrifies shades.
Shaking its triple heads with mighty roar,
It guards the kingdom. Serpents lick its heads   785
Foul with gore, the manes bristle with vipers
And a long snake hisses in the twisted tail.
Its anger matches its looks. On hearing steps,
It lifts the shaggy manes of quivering snakes
And pricks its ears to catch emitted sounds,   790
Good at hearing even shades. When Jove's son
Stood nearer the cave, the hound crouched unsure,
And both felt fear. Look! With deep bark it scares
The silent places; menacing snakes hiss
Along its shoulders. A monstrous voice roars,   795
Dispatched through a triple mouth, and panics
Even happy shades. *He* frees the fierce jaws
Then from his left side, thrusts out the Cleonaean
Head and shields himself with its huge shielding,
Wielding the great club in triumphant hand.   800
Here and there he whirls it now with constant blows;
He doubles the strikes. The dog, mastered, broke off
Its threats, wearily lowered all its heads
And left the entire cave. Both rulers quaked
On their thrones and ordered it led away.   805
At Alcides' petition they gifted me, too.
   Then, stroking by hand the monster's heavy necks,
He binds them with adamant chains. Forgetting
Itself, the dark realm's unsleeping guard-dog
Timidly droops its ears, suffers being led,   810
Accepts its master, lowers its muzzle,
Docile, thumping each flank with its snake-tail.
When we arrived at the rim of Taenarus
And the strange light's novel glow struck its eyes,

resumit animos uictus et uastas furens   815
quassat catenas. paene uictorem abstulit
pronumque retro uexit et mouit gradu.
tunc et meas respexit Alcides manus.
geminis uterque uiribus tractum canem
ira furentem et bella temptantem inrita   820
intulimus orbi. uidit ut clarum diem
et pura nitidi spatia conspexit poli,
oborta nox est. lumina in terram dedit,
compressit oculos et diem inuisum expulit
aciemque retro flexit atque omni petit   825
ceruice terram. tum sub Herculeas caput
abscondit umbras.

              Densa sed laeto uenit
clamore turba frontibus laurum gerens
magnique meritas Herculis laudes canit.

CHORVS   Natus Eurystheus properante partu   830
iusserat mundi penetrare fundum.
derat hoc solum numero laborum:
tertiae regem spoliare sortis.
ausus es caecos aditus inire,
ducit ad manes uia qua remotos   835
tristis et nigra metuenda silua,
sed frequens magna comitante turba.

Quantus incedit populus per urbes
ad noui ludos auidus theatri;
quantus Eleum ruit ad Tonantem,   840
quinta cum sacrum reuocauit aestas;
quanta, cum longae redit hora nocti
crescere et somnos cupiens quietos

It gains strength from defeat and shakes the huge   815
Chains in rage. It almost bore off the victor,
Hauled him back face-down, pulled him from his post.
Alcides even looked to my hands.
With twice the strength both of us dragged the dog
Raging with anger and fighting in vain,   820
And lugged it into the world. When it saw
Clear day and viewed bright heaven's lucent spaces,
Darkness arose. It stared down at the ground,
Closed its eyes tight, expelled the hated day,
Turned away its gaze, and lowered every   825
Neck to the ground. Then it hid its heads
In Hercules' shade.

Enter CHORUS OF THEBANS *from stage left* (*the city*), *their heads wreathed with laurel.* MEGARA *and her* SONS *rise from their seated position at the altar.*

But a dense throng come
With cheers of joy and brows wreathed with laurel;
They sing great Hercules' merited praises.

ALL *remain onstage.*

The CHORUS *sing.*

CHORUS   Eurystheus, born with quickened birth,   830
Bade you probe the world's foundation.
Number of labours lacked but this:
Taking spoils from the third realm's king.
You dared enter blind approaches,
Where a path leads to distant ghosts,   835
Grim and dismal with its dark woods,
But packed with great, attending throng.

As great a crowd move through cities
Avid for a new theatre's shows;
As great rush to Elis' Thunderer,   840
When five summers revive the rite;
As great a mass pack mystic Ceres,
When hours return and night grows long,

Libra Phoebeos tenet aequa currus,
turba secretam Cererem frequentat   845
et citi tectis properant relictis
Attici noctem celebrare mystae:
tanta per campos agitur silentes
turba. pars tarda graditur senecta,
tristis et longa satiata uita;   850
pars adhuc currit melioris aeui—
uirgines nondum thalamis iugatae
et comis nondum positis ephebi
matris et nomen modo doctus infans.
his datum solis, minus ut timerent,   855
igne praelato releuare noctem;
ceteri uadunt per opaca tristes.
qualis est uobis animus, remota
luce cum maestus sibi quisque sensit
obrutum tota caput esse terra?   860
stat chaos densum tenebraeque turpes
et color noctis malus ac silentis
otium mundi uacuaeque nubes.

Sera nos illo referat senectus.
nemo ad id sero uenit, unde numquam   865
cum semel uenit potuit reuerti.
quid iuuat durum properare fatum?
omnis haec magnis uaga turba terris
ibit ad manes facietque inerti
uela Cocyto. tibi crescit omne,   870
et quod occasus uidet et quod ortus:
parce uenturis. tibi, Mors, paramur.
sis licet segnis, properamus ipsi.
prima quae uitam dedit hora carpit.

Thebis laeta dies adest.   875
aras tangite supplices,
pingues caedite uictimas;
permixtae maribus nurus
sollemnes agitent choros.
cessent deposito iugo   880
arui fertilis incolae.

And fair Libra, wanting calm sleep,
Holds Phoebus' chariot, and Attic   845
Initiates quick-leave their homes
And rush to celebrate the night:
So great a mass is herded through
Mute fields. Some walk in slow old age,
Grim and surfeited with long life;   850
Others of better years still run—
Virgins not yet joined in wedlock,
Ephebes with tresses not yet shorn,
Infants just taught their mother's name.
These alone, to lessen fear,   855
May ease the dark with carried flame;
The rest go grimly through the gloom.
How do you feel now light is lost
And each in their sadness senses
The whole earth crushing their head?   860
Dense chaos yawns and foul darkness
And night's sickly shade and a mute
World's lethargy and empty clouds.

May old age carry us there late.
No one arrives too late from where,   865
Once come, he can never return.
What joy lies in rushing harsh fate?
This whole crowd roaming the great earth
Will reach the dead and sail listless
Cocytus. For thee grows all that   870
The sun sees, set and rising: spare
The doomed. For thee, Death, we are groomed.
Though thou be slow, ourselves we rush.
Life's first hour begins its end.

Thebes' joyous day is here.   875
Touch altars in prayer,
Slay the fattest victims;
Let young women join with
Husbands in solemn dance.
Let tillers of rich fields   880
Put down their yoke and rest.

Pax est Herculea manu
Auroram inter et Hesperum,
et qua Sol medium tenens
umbras corporibus negat.   885
quodcumque alluitur solum
longo Tethyos ambitu,
Alcidae domuit labor.
transuectus uada Tartari
pacatis redit inferis.   890
iam nullus superest timor:
nil ultra iacet inferos.

Stantes sacrificus comas
dilecta tege populo.

Peace from Hercules' hand
Reigns from Dawn to Hesperus,
And where the midday Sun
Gives bodies no shadows.   885
Whatever tract is lapped
By Tethys' long circuit
Alcides' toil has tamed.
He crossed Tartarus' streams,
Pacified hell and came   890
Back. Now no fear is left:
Nothing lies beyond hell.

Enter HERCULES *from stage left (the city), dressed as before but drenched with blood. He is accompanied by* SLAVES *and* ATTENDANTS *leading animals (or carrying sculpted heads of the same) for the planned sacrifice.*

(*To* HERCULES) For sacrifice, crown rough
          Hair with cherished poplar.

                                        ALL *remain.*

Actus Quartus

Hercules—Theseus—Amphitryon—Megara—<Nati Herculis taciti>—Chorus

HERCVLES   Vltrice dextra fusus aduerso Lycus   895
terram cecidit ore. tum quisquis comes
fuerat tyranni iacuit et poenae comes.
nunc sacra patri uictor et superis feram
caesisque meritas uictimis aras colam.
     Te, te, laborum socia et adiutrix, precor,   900
belligera Pallas, cuius in laeua ciet
aegis feroces ore saxifico minas.
adsit Lycurgi domitor et Rubri Maris,
tectam uirenti cuspidem thyrso gerens,
geminumque numen Phoebus et Phoebi soror   905
(soror sagittis aptior, Phoebus lyrae),
fraterque quisquis incolit caelum meus—
non ex nouerca frater.
             Huc appellite
greges opimos. quidquid Indorum est seges
Arabesque odoris quidquid arboribus legunt   910
conferte in aras: pinguis exundet uapor.
populea nostras arbor exornet comas.

     Te ramus oleae fronde gentili tegat,
Theseu. Tonantem nostra adorabit manus;
tu conditores urbis et siluestria   915
trucis antra Zethi, nobilis Dircen aquae
laremque regis aduenae Tyrium coles.

     Date tura flammis.

Act IV

The time is now midday; the scene is the same. HERCULES *stands at the altar.*

Hercules—Theseus—Amphitryon—Megara—<Sons of Hercules silent>—Chorus

HERCULES	My avenging hand made Lycus sprawl;	895
	He crashed and bit the earth. Then each comrade	
	Of the tyrant fell, comrade, too, in death.	
	Now victor, I'll sacrifice to father and gods,	
	Honouring due altars with slain victims.	
	To thee, thee I pray, partner, helpmate of my toils,	900
	Soldier Pallas, on whose left arm the fierce	
	Aegis threatens with petrifying face.	
	Come, tamer of Lycurgus and the Red Sea,	
	Bearing green thyrsus with hidden spear-point,	
	And Phoebus and Phoebus' sister, twin gods	905
	(Sister skilled in arrows, Phoebus in the lyre),	
	And all my brothers in heaven—not brothers	
	From my stepmother.	

(*To* ATTENDANTS *and* SLAVES) Drive here the prime flocks.
Whatever crop the Indians yield,
Whatever Arabs pluck from perfumed trees,   910
Pile on the altar: let the rich smoke billow.
The poplar tree should ornament my hair.

Puts poplar wreath, handed to him by an ATTENDANT, *on his head.*

(*Turns to* THESEUS) You should wear an olive bough's native leaves,
Theseus. My hand will worship the Thunder-god;
You'll revere the city founders, the woodland   915
Cave of wild Zethus, Dirce's famous spring
And the immigrant king's Tyrian god.

Preparations for the sacrifice begin. THESEUS *dons an olive wreath handed to him, and exits stage left* (*to the city*).

(*To* ATTENDANTS/SLAVES) Put incense on the flames.

AMPHITRYON   Nate, manantes prius
manus cruenta caede et hostili expia.

HERCVLES   Vtinam cruorem capitis inuisi deis   920
libare possem. gratior nullus liquor
tinxisset aras. uictima haut ulla amplior
potest magisque opima mactari Ioui
quam rex iniquus.

AMPHITRYON   Finiat genitor tuus
opta labores, detur aliquando otium   925
quiesque fessis.

HERCVLES   Ipse concipiam preces
Ioue meque dignas. stet suo caelum loco
tellusque et aequor. astra inoffensos agant
aeterna cursus, alta pax gentes alat,
ferrum omne teneat ruris innocui labor   930
ensesque lateant. nulla tempestas fretum
uiolenta turbet, nullus irato Ioue
exiliat ignis, nullus hiberna niue
nutritus agros amnis euersos trahat.
uenena cessent, nulla nocituro grauis   935
suco tumescat herba; non saeui ac truces
regnent tyranni. si quod etiamnum est scelus
latura tellus, properet, et, si quod parat
monstrum, meum sit.

                               Sed quid hoc? medium diem
cinxere tenebrae. Phoebus obscuro meat   940
sine nube uultu. quis diem retro fugat
agitque in ortus? unde nox atrum caput
ignota profert? unde tot stellae polum
implent diurnae?
                        Primus en noster labor
caeli refulget parte non minima Leo   945
iraque totus feruet et morsus parat.
iam rapiet aliquod sidus. ingenti minax

AMPHITRYON Son, first expiate
Your hands, dripping with a foe's bloody slaughter.

HERCULES Would I could pour blood from his hated head
As libation to the gods. No liquid more pleasing
Would have stained the altar. No choicer victim
Or more prime can be slaughtered for Jove
Than an unjust king.

AMPHITRYON Pray that your father
End these labours, that the weary be granted
At last peace and rest.

HERCULES I'll form prayers worthy
Of Jove and myself. Let sky, earth, and sea
Stand in their place. Let eternal stars drive
Unhindered orbits, deep peace nourish nations,
All iron belong to toil of guiltless land
And swords lie hid. Let no violent tempest
Flay the sea, no flame burst from angry Jove,
No river nursed by the snows of winter
Ravage the fields and drag them with it.
Let poisons cease, no plant swell heavy
With noxious juice, no cruel and brutal
Tyrants rule. If earth even now will bear
Some evil, let her rush, and, if she grooms
A monster, let it be mine.

Begins to hallucinate.

But what's this?
Darkness has besieged midday. Cloudless Phoebus
Moves with shrouded face. Who makes day flee back
And drives it to its dawn? Why does strange night
Rear its black head? Why do so many stars
Fill the sky in daytime?
(*Points to the sky*) Look, my first labour,
Leo, shines in no small part of heaven,
Burns hot, consumed with wrath, ready to bite.
Now it'll seize some star. It stands threatening

stat ore et ignes efflat et rutilat, iubam
ceruice iactans. quidquid autumnus grauis
hiemsque gelido frigida spatio refert   950
uno impetu transiliet et uerni petet
frangetque Tauri colla.

AMPHITRYON   Quod subitum hoc malum est?
quo, nate, uultus huc et huc acres refers
acieque falsum turbida caelum uides?

HERCVLES   Perdomita tellus, tumida cesserunt freta,   955
inferna nostros regna sensere impetus.
immune caelum est, dignus Alcide labor.
in alta mundi spatia sublimis ferar,
petatur aether: astra promittit pater.
quid si negaret? non capit terra Herculem   960
tandemque superis reddit. en ultro uocat
omnis deorum coetus et laxat fores—
una uetante.
                         Recipis et reseras polum?
an contumacis ianuam mundi traho?
dubitatur etiam? uincla Saturno exuam   965
contraque patris impii regnum impotens
auum resoluam. bella Titanes parent,
me duce furentes. saxa cum siluis feram
rapiamque dextra plena Centauris iuga.
iam monte gemino limitem ad superos agam.   970
uideat sub Ossa Pelion Chiron suum.
in caelum Olympus tertio positus gradu
perueniet—aut mittetur.

AMPHITRYON   Infandos procul
auerte sensus. pectoris sani parum,
magni tamen, compesce dementem impetum.   975

HERCVLES   Quid hoc? Gigantes arma pestiferi mouent.
profugit umbras Tityos ac lacerum gerens
et inane pectus quam prope a caelo stetit.

With massive jaws, vomits fire and glows red,
Tossing mane on neck. All that sick autumn
And chill winter bring round in its frozen zone   950
It will leap in one bound, and strike and crush
The neck of springtime Taurus.

AMPHITRYON   What's this sudden ill?
Son, why turn your gaze fiercely this way and that,
And see a false sky with turbulent eyes?

HERCULES   Earth is tamed, the swelling seas have yielded,   955
The infernal realm has felt our onslaught.
Heaven escapes—labour worthy of Alcides.
I must soar to the high regions of the world,
Aim for the aether: stars are father's promise.
If he renege? Earth cannot contain Hercules,   960
But restores him at last on high. Look, the whole mass
Of gods itself calls and opens the gates—
With one veto.
(*To* JUPITER, *perhaps turning to his statue*) Do you unlock the sky in welcome?
Or do I tear down proud heaven's doorway?
Hesitation—still? I'll strip Saturn of his chains,   965
And set my grandsire against this impious
Father's unbridled rule. Let Titans prepare war;
I'll lead their rage. I'll hoist rocks and forests,
Rip up by hand ridges thronged by Centaurs.
Now with twin peaks I'll drive a path to gods.   970
Let Chiron view his Pelion beneath Ossa.
Olympus will reach heaven as the third step—
Or else be hurled there.

AMPHITRYO   Banish far away
Such monstrous thoughts. Restrain the demented
Impulse of a heart barely sane, if great.   975

HERCULES   What's this? Death-bearing Giants brandish arms.
Tityos has fled hell. How near he stands
To the heavens with torn and gaping chest.

labat Cithaeron, alta Pallene tremit
marcentque Tempe. rapuit hic Pindi iuga,   980
hic rapuit Oeten; saeuit horrendum Mimans.
    Flammifera Erinys uerbere excusso sonat
rogisque adustas propius ac propius sudes
in ora tendit. saeua Tisiphone, caput
serpentibus uallata, post raptum canem   985
portam uacantem clausit opposita face.

    Sed ecce proles regis inimici latet,
Lyci nefandum semen. inuiso patri
haec dextra iam uos reddet. excutiat leues
neruus sagittas. tela sic mitti decet   990
Herculea.

AMPHITRYON   Quo se caecus impegit furor?
uastum coactis flexit arcum cornibus
pharetramque soluit. stridet emissa impetu
harundo. medio spiculum collo fugit
uulnere relicto.

HERCVLES   Ceteram prolem eruam   995
omnesque latebras. quid moror? maius mihi
bellum Mycenis restat, ut Cyclopia
euersa manibus saxa nostris concidant.

Huc eat et illuc claua disiecto obice
rumpatque postes. columen impulsum labet.   1000
perlucet omnis regia. hic uideo abditum
natum scelesti patris.

AMPHITRYON   En blandas manus
ad genua tendens uoce miseranda rogat.

Cithaeron totters, high Pallene trembles,
Tempe withers. One Giant seized Pindus' ridge,   980
One seized Oeta; Mimans rages terror.
    A flaming Erinys has cracked her whip,
Thrusts a pyre-charred stake closer and closer
To my face. Fierce Tisiphone, head fenced
With serpents, has stretched out her torch to block   985
The gate, unguarded since the dog was snatched.

Looks at his SONS.

    But look, skulking here, the enemy-king's spawn,
Lycus' vile seed. This hand will now return you
To your hated father. Let my bowstring spew
Its light shafts. Such targets befit the weapons   990
Of Hercules.

MEGARA *and the* SONS *rush into the palace. As* AMPHITRYON *speaks,*
HERCULES *strings his bow and fires into the palace through its open door.*

AMPHITRYON   Where has blind madness struck?
His huge bow is bent, tips drawn together;
The quiver is opened. An arrow hisses
Sent with force. The point passes through mid-neck
And leaves the wound.

The palace door is shut and barred.

HERCULES   I'll root out the other spawn   995
And all their hideouts. Why delay? Greater war
Awaits in Mycenae, to rip up and topple
The Cyclopian rocks with my own hands.

He attacks the door of the palace with his club.

Let my club fly all about, smash the bolt,
Burst the posts. Let the battered roof collapse.   1000
The whole palace lights up. Here I see hid
An evil father's son.

Exit into the palace.

AMPHITRYON   (*Looking into the palace*) Look, the boy begs
Piteously, lifts pleading hands to knees.

scelus nefandum, triste et aspectu horridum!
dextra precantem rapuit et circa furens   1005
bis ter rotatum misit. ast illi caput
sonuit. cerebro tecta disperso madent.

At misera, paruum protegens natum sinu,
Megara furenti similis e latebris fugit.

HERCVLES   Licet Tonantis profuga condaris sinu,   1010
               petet undecumque temet haec dextra et feret.

AMPHITRYON   Quo misera pergis? quam fugam aut latebram petis?
               nullus salutis Hercule infesto est locus.
               amplectere ipsum potius et blanda prece
               lenire tempta.

MEGARA   Parce iam, coniunx, precor,   1015
               agnosce Megaram. natus hic uultus tuos
               habitusque reddit. cernis ut tendat manus?

HERCVLES   Teneo nouercam. sequere, da poenas mihi
               iugoque pressum libera turpi Iouem
               sed ante matrem paruulum hoc monstrum occidat. 1020

MEGARA   Quo tendis amens? sanguinem fundes tuum?

AMPHITRYON   Pauefactus infans igneo uultu patris
               perit ante uulnus; spiritum eripuit timor.
               in coniugem nunc claua libratur grauis.
               perfregit ossa. corpori trunco caput   1025
               abest nec usquam est. cernere hoc audes, nimis
               uiuax senectus? si piget luctus, habes
               mortem paratam.
                              Pectori tela indue

Evil crime, grim, a horror to behold!
He seized the suppliant; he whirled him round   1005
In rage—twice, three times—and he let him go.
Then his head cracked. The house drips spattered brains.

MEGARA *rushes from the palace holding her youngest* SON, *followed by*
HERCULES.

But poor Megara runs like a mad woman
From hiding; she shields her small son in her breast.

HERCULES   Though you take refuge in the Thunderer's bosom,   1010
This hand will seek and grab you anywhere.

AMPHITRYON   Run where, poor wretch? What refuge or hideout seek?
No place is safe from Hercules' assault.
Embrace him instead; try to soften him
With gentle prayer.

MEGARA   Now spare me, husband, I beg;   1015
Recognize Megara. Your son here mirrors
Your looks and bearing. See how he extends his hands?

HERCULES *grabs* MEGARA *and looks into her face.*

HERCULES   I hold my stepmother. Come with me and pay;
Liberate Jove from a foul, oppressive yoke.
But let this tiny monster die before its mother.   1020

Takes MEGARA *and their* SON *into the palace, as she responds.*

MEGARA   Where with this madness? Will you spill your own blood?

AMPHITRYON   (*Looking into the palace*) The infant, scared by his father's
        fiery gaze,
Dies from no wound; terror snatched his soul.
The heavy club's now levelled against his wife.
He has smashed her bones. Her truncated body   1025
Lacks a head—it's nowhere. Can you view this,
Life-clinging age? If your grief is too much,
Death stands by.
(*To* HERCULES *in the palace*) In my breast sink your arrows

uel stipitem istum caede monstrorum inlitum
conuerte. falsum ac nomini turpem tuo   1030
remoue parentem, ne tuae laudi obstrepat.

CHORVS   Quo te ipse, senior, obuium morti ingeris?
quo pergis amens? profuge et obtectus late
unumque manibus aufer Herculeis scelus.

HERCVLES   Bene habet. pudendi regis excisa est domus.   1035
tibi hunc dicatum, maximi coniunx Iouis,
gregem cecidi. uota persolui libens
te digna, et Argos uictimas alias dabit.

AMPHITRYON   Nondum litasti, nate. consumma sacrum.

Stat ecce ad aras hostia, expectat manum   1040
ceruice prona. praebeo occurro insequor.
macta!

Quid hoc est? errat acies luminum
uisusque maeror hebetat? an uideo Herculis
manus trementes? uultus in somnum cadit
et fessa ceruix capite summisso labat.   1045
flexo genu iam totus ad terram ruit,
ut caesa siluis ornus aut portum mari
datura moles.
              Viuis an leto dedit
idem tuos qui misit ad mortem furor?
sopor est. reciprocos spiritus motus agit.   1050
detur quieti tempus, ut somno graui
uis uicta morbi pectus oppressum leuet.

Remouete, famuli, tela, ne repetat furens.

Or turn on me that club smeared with the blood
Of monsters. Get rid of the false father   1030
Staining your name, lest he drown your glory.

CHORUS   Why hurl yourself towards death, old man?
                What is this madness? Run, conceal, lie hid,
                And remove one crime from Hercules' hands.

                                    HERCULES *enters from the palace.*

HERCULES   All is well. The shameful king's house is razed.   1035
                For thee, wife of greatest Jove, I have slain
                This consecrated flock. I've gladly paid vows
                Worthy of thee. Argos will give other victims.

AMPHITRYON   The sacrifice isn't done, my son. Finish it.

                                              Walks to the altar.

        Look, a victim stands at the altar, neck bowed,   1040
        Waiting for your hand. I offer, present, insist.
        Strike!

                    HERCULES *begins to tremble and collapses.*

                What's this? Does my eyesight fail? Does grief
        Dull my vision? Or do I see Hercules'
        Hands trembling? His face falls into a sleep,
        The head sinks, his weary neck collapses.   1045
        Knees bend, the whole body now crashes to earth,
        Like an ash felled in the woods or harbour
        Stone dropped in the sea.
                        (To HERCULES) Are you alive, or did
        The same rage kill you which killed your loved ones?
        It is sleep. His breathing is regular.   1050
        Give him time to rest, so heavy sleep may conquer
        The disease's force and lighten his vexed heart.

                                    (*To* SLAVES) Slaves,

        Move the weapons, lest he want them again—in rage.

CHORVS   Lugeat aether magnusque parens
         aetheris alti tellusque ferax   1055
         et uaga ponti mobilis unda,
         tuque ante omnes, qui per terras
         tractusque maris fundis radios
         noctemque fugas ore decoro,
                 feruide Titan.   1060
         obitus pariter tecum Alcides
         uidit et ortus nouitque tuas
                 utrasque domos.   •

         Soluite tantis animum monstris,
                 soluite, superi,
         rectam in melius flectite mentem.   1065

         Tuque, o domitor Somne malorum,
                 requies animi,   •
         pars humanae melior uitae,
         uolucre o matris genus astraeae,
         frater durae languide Mortis,
         ueris miscens falsa, futuri   1070
         certus et idem pessimus auctor,
         pater o rerum, portus uitae,
         lucis requies noctisque comes,
         qui par regi famuloque uenis,
         pauidum leti genus humanum   1075
         cogis longam discere noctem:
         placidus fessum lenisque foue,
         preme deuinctum torpore graui.
         sopor indomitos alliget artus

SLAVES *take the weapons (including the lion skin) into the palace.* ATTENDANTS *take the sacrificial paraphernalia and animals (or sculpted heads) offstage left.* ALL *others remain.*

The CHORUS *sing. During the ode the bodies of* HERCULES' SONS *and the remains of* MEGARA *(and the arrow which killed the first* SON*) are brought from the palace (on stretchers borne by* SLAVES *or on a movable platform) and placed (probably) centre-stage.*

CHORUS	Let sky weep and the soaring sky's	
	Great father, and fertile earth,	1055
	And the shifting sea's vagrant waves,	
	And thou above all, who dost pour	
	Light across lands and ocean's tracts	
	And banish night with beauteous face,	
	Blazing Titan.	1060
	Like thee, Alcides has viewed	
	The west and the east, and known	
	Thy two abodes.	•

Free his mind from these great monsters,
    Free him, high gods,
Restore his straightened wits.   1065

And thou, O Sleep, tamer of woes,
    The mind's peace,   •
Better part of human life,
O winged child of starry mother,
Languid brother of brutal Death,
Mixing false with true, the future's   1070
Sure author and its worst,
O father of the world, port of life,
Day's rest and night's companion,
Who dost visit king and slave
Alike and force death-phobic   1075
Humankind to learn the long night:
Calm and gentle, soothe his weariness,
Hold him fast in heavy torpor.
Let sleep chain those untamed limbs

nec torua prius pectora linquat,   1080
quam mens repetat pristina cursum.

En fusus humi saeua feroci
corde uolutat somnia (nondum est
tanti pestis superata mali)
      clauaeque graui   •
lassum solitus mandare caput   1085
quaerit uacua pondera dextra,
motu iactans bracchia uano.
nec adhuc omnes expulit aestus,
sed ut ingenti uexata Noto
seruat longos unda tumultus   1090
et iam uento cessante tumet.

Pelle insanos fluctus animi.
redeat pietas uirtusque uiro—
      uel sit potius
mens uesano concita motu,   1095
error caecus qua coepit eat.
solus te iam praestare potest
      furor insontem.   •
proxima puris sors est manibus
      nescire nefas.

Nunc Herculeis percussa sonent   1100
      pectora palmis,
mundum solitos ferre lacertos
uerbera pulsent uictrice manu.
gemitus uastos audiat aether,
audiat atri regina poli   1105
      uastisque ferox   •
qui colla gerit uincta catenis
imo latitans Cerberus antro.
resonet maesto clamore chaos
latique patens unda profundi
et qui melius tua tela tamen   1110

And not leave the savage breast   1080
Till his former mind regain its path.

> HERCULES *turns and twists in his sleep.*

Look how he sprawls on the ground,
Whirling wild dreams in savage heart.
Not yet is the evil scourge crushed.
    With empty hand   •
He feels for the weight of heavy club,   1085
Tired head's accustomed pillow—
Flinging arms in vain motion.
He has yet not expelled all the storm,
As a wave roiled by mighty
Notus prolongs its turmoil   1090
And, though the wind drops, still swells.

> *The* CHORUS *address the sleeping* HERCULES.

Expel the mad billows of your mind.
Let piety and virile virtue
    Return, or, better,
Your mind seethe with madness,   1095
Blind error surge as it began.
Rage alone now can make
    You innocent.   •
The next-best fate to pure hands:
    Ignorance of sin.

Now let Hercules' breast resound   1100
    With pounding fists,
Let blows from your triumphant hand
Strike arms, often props of the world.
Let heaven hear your mighty groans,
The queen of the dark pole hear them   1105
    And fierce Cerberus,   •
Necks bound by mighty chains,
Cringing in the lowest cave.
Let chaos echo the grievous cries
And the vast deep's open waters
And air, which had felt your weapons   1110

senserat aer.
pectora tantis obsessa malis
non sunt ictu ferienda leui.
uno planctu tria regna sonent.

Et tu, collo decus ac telum   1115
suspensa diu, fortis harundo,
        pharetraeque graues,
date saeua fero uerbera tergo.
caedant umeros robora fortes
        stipesque potens   •
duris oneret pectora nodis.   1120
plangant tantos arma dolores.

Non uos patriae laudis comites
ulti saeuos uulnere reges,
non Argiua membra palaestra
flectere docti fortes caestu   1125
fortesque manu, iam tamen ausi
telum Scythicis leue corytis
missum certa librare manu
tutosque fuga figere ceruos
nondumque ferae terga iubatae.   1130

Ite ad Stygios, umbrae, portus,
        ite, innocuae,
quas in primo limine uitae
scelus oppressit patriusque furor.
ite, infaustum genus, o pueri,   1135
noti per iter triste laboris;
ite, iratos uisite reges.

More happily.
The breast besieged by massive ills
Should bear the brunt of no light blows.
Three realms should sound one dirge.

The CHORUS *turn to the dead bodies now displayed onstage, and address
the arrow used to kill one of* HERCULES' SONS, *which lies beside them.*

You too, strong arrow, glory   1115
And shaft long hung from his neck,
  And the grave quiver,
Rain fierce blows on brutal back.
Let oakwood pummel strong shoulders,
  The potent club   •
Tax his breast with hardened knots.   1120
His weapons should mourn such griefs.

    The CHORUS *address* HERCULES' *dead* SONS.

You were not comrades of your father's
Fame, striking down savage kings.
You did not train in schools
Of Argos for strength with gloves,   1125
Strength with hands. Yet you dared
Fire light shaft from Scythian
Quivers with a sure hand
And pierce stags in safe flight
And backs of beasts yet unmaned.   1130

Go to Stygian harbours, go,
  Innocent shades,
Whom on life's first threshold
Crime has crushed and father's rage.
Go, boys, O curséd brood,   1135
Along that famed labour's grim path;
Go, meet the angry monarchs.

        ALL *remain.*

Actus Quintus

Hercules—Amphitryon—Theseus

HERCVLES   Quis hic locus, quae regio, quae mundi plaga?
ubi sum? sub ortu solis, an sub cardine
glacialis Vrsae? numquid Hesperii maris   1140
extrema tellus hunc dat Oceano modum?
quas trahimus auras? quod solum fesso subest?

Certe redimus—unde prostrata domo
uideo cruenta corpora? an nondum exuit
simulacra mens inferna? post reditus quoque   1145
oberrat oculis turba feralis meis?
pudet fateri: paueo. nescioquod mihi,
nescioquod animus grande praesagit malum.
ubi est parens? ubi illa natorum grege
animosa coniunx? cur latus laeuum uacat   1150
spolio leonis? quonam abit tegimen meum
idemque somno mollis Herculeo torus?
ubi tela? ubi arcus? arma quis uiuo mihi
detrahere potuit? spolia quis tanta abstulit
ipsumque quis non Herculis somnum horruit?   1155
libet meum uidere uictorem, libet.
exurge, uirtus! quem nouum caelo pater
genuit relicto? cuius in fetus stetit
nox longior quam nostra?

Quod cerno nefas?
nati cruenta caede confecti iacent,   1160

Act V

The time and scene are the same. Enter THESEUS, *wearing an olive wreath, stage left (from the city), as* HERCULES, *asleep throughout the previous choral ode and now semi-naked (i.e. without his lion skin, removed at the end of Act IV), awakes.*

Hercules—Amphitryon—Theseus

HERCULES What place is this, what region, what stretch of world?
Where am I? Beneath rising sun or pole
Of icy Bear? Is this the Hesperian   1140
Sea's furthest land, curbing Oceanus?
What air do I breathe? What earth bears me weary?

    Sees but does not recognize the bodies of his family onstage.

I'm back, surely—why do I see bloody
Corpses, a palace in ruin? Or has my mind
Not yet stripped its images of hell? A horde   1145
Of ghosts meets my eyes, even when I'm back?
I'm ashamed to say it: I fear. There's something,
Some consummate evil my mind forebodes.
Where's my father? Where's my spirited wife
With her flock of sons? Why's my left side bare   1150
Of the lion spoils? Where is it—my shield
And its soft bedding for Hercules' sleep?
Where are my arrows? Where's my bow? Who could
Have torn weapons from me alive? Who stole
Such spoils—who did not fear Hercules' sleep?   1155
I want, I want to view my conqueror.
Rise, virtue! (*Stands up*) What new son has my father sired
Away from heaven? For whose conception did night
Halt longer than for us?

    Views and recognizes the corpses.

       What horror do I see?
My sons lie murdered in bloody slaughter,   1160

perempta coniunx. quis Lycus regnum obtinet?
quis tanta Thebis scelera moliri ausus est
Hercule reuerso? quisquis Ismeni loca,
Actaea quisquis arua, qui gemino mari
pulsata Pelopis regna Dardanii colis,   1165
succurre: saeuae cladis auctorem indica.
ruat ira in omnes. hostis est quisquis mihi
non monstrat hostem.
                                  Victor Alcidae, lates?
procede, seu tu uindicas currus truces
Thracis cruenti siue Geryonae pecus   1170
Libyaeue dominos: nulla pugnandi mora est.
en nudus asto. uel meis armis licet
petas inermem.

                         Cur meos Theseus fugit
paterque uultus? ora cur condunt sua?
         Differte fletus. quis meos dederit neci   1175
omnes simul, profare. quid, genitor, siles?
at tu ede, Theseu—sed tua, Theseu, fide!
         Vterque tacitus ora pudibunda obtegit
furtimque lacrimas fundit. in tantis malis
quid est pudendum?

                         Numquid Argiuae impotens   1180
dominator urbis, numquid infestum Lyci
pereuntis agmen clade nos tanta obruit?
per te meorum facinorum laudem precor,
genitor, tuique nominis semper mihi
numen secundum, fare. quis fudit domum?   1185
cui praeda iacui?

AMPHITRYON   Tacita sic abeant mala.

HERCVLES   Vt inultus ego sim?

AMPHITRYON   Saepe uindicta obfuit.

HERCVLES   Quisquamne segnis tanta tolerauit mala?

My wife slain. What Lycus holds the realm?
Who dared to create such crimes in Thebes
Now Hercules has returned? All who dwell
By Ismenos, in Attic fields or realms
Of Dardan Pelops lashed by twin seas, help me: 1165
Reveal the author of this cruel carnage.
Let my wrath fall on all. Foes to me are all
Who do not show my foe.
                                        Alcides' conqueror,
Do you hide? Come forth, whether you avenge
The bloody Thracian's brutal chariot, Geryon's   1170
Herd or Libya's lords: I won't delay the fight.
Look, I stand naked. With my arms attack
Me unarmed.

THESEUS *and* AMPHITRYON *turn away, hiding their faces in their robes.*

                    (*Aside*) Why does Theseus shun my gaze—
And my father? Why do they hide their faces?
(*To* AMPH. *and* THES.) Defer your tears. Say who killed my   1175
                    whole family
With one stroke. Why are you silent, father?
Then *you*, Theseus, deliver—but, Theseus, by your faith!
        (*Aside*) Both mutely veil faces filled with shame
And shed secret tears. What need for shame
Amid such evil?
(*To* AMPH. *and* THES.)   Has the raving master   1180
Of Argos city or dying Lycus'
Violent troops buried us in such ruin?
I beseech you by the fame of my deeds,
Father, and the ever propitious divinity
Of your name, speak. Who made our house sprawl?   1185
Who made me fallen prey?

AMPHITRYON   Let these ills pass in silence.

HERCULES   Would *I* be unrevenged?

AMPHITRYON   Vengeance often harms.

HERCULES   Has anyone borne such ills without action?

AMPHITRYON   Maiora quisquis timuit.

HERCVLES   His etiam, pater,
              quicquam timeri maius aut grauius potest?   1190

AMPHITRYON   Cladis tuae pars ista quam nosti quota est.

HERCVLES   Miserere, genitor, supplices tendo manus.

              Quid hoc? manus refugit. hic errat scelus.

              Vnde hic cruor? quid illa puerili madens
              harundo leto? tincta Lernaea nece—   1195
              iam tela uideo nostra. non quaero manum.
              quis potuit arcum flectere aut quae dextera
              sinuare neruum uix recedentem mihi?
                  Ad uos reuertor. genitor, hoc nostrum est scelus?
              tacuere. nostrum est.

AMPHITRYON   Luctus est istic tuus,   1200
              crimen nouercae. casus hic culpa caret.

HERCVLES   Nunc parte ab omni, genitor, iratus tona.
              oblite nostri, uindica sera manu
              saltem nepotes. stelliger mundus sonet
              flammasque et hic et ille iaculetur polus.   1205
              rupes ligatum Caspiae corpus trahant
              atque ales auida. cur Promethei uacant
              scopuli? paretur uertice immenso feras
              uolucresque pascens Caucasi abruptum latus
              nudumque siluis. illa quae Pontum Scythen   1210
              Symplegas artat hinc et hinc uinctas manus
              distendat alto, cumque reuocata uice
              in se coibunt saxaque in caelum expriment
              actis utrimque rupibus medium mare,
              ego inquieta montium iaceam mora.   1215

AMPHITRYON   Whoever has feared worse.

HERCULES   Really, father,
Can something be feared worse or graver than this?   1190

AMPHITRYON   How small a part of your tragedy you know.

HERCULES   Have pity, father, I stretch suppliant hands.

AMPHITRYON *moves back.*

(*Aside*) What's this? He shuns my hands. Crime hovers here.

HERCULES *sees the blood on his hands and the arrow which killed one of his* SONS.

Where is this blood from? What of that arrow
Wet with a boy's death? Stained with Lerna's poison—   1195
Now I see my shafts. The hand I do not seek.
Who had strength to bend the bow? Or what hand
Could have drawn the string which scarce yields to me?
(*To* AMPH. *and* THES.) I turn to you again. Father, is this crime mine?
(*Aside*) They're silent. It's mine.

AMPHITRYON   The grief is yours, the crime 1200
Your stepmother's. What happened leaves you blameless.

HERCULES   Now, father, from every zone rage and thunder.
Thou didst forget me—let thy late hand avenge
At least thy grandsons. Let the starry firmament
Roar, flames shoot from pole to pole. Let Caspian   1205
Crags and ravening bird tear apart my
Fettered flesh. Why are the Promethean
Rocks empty? Get the Caucasus' sheer cliff
Ready, bare of trees, feeding beasts and birds
On its measureless peak. Let the Symplegades   1210
Throttling the Scythian Pontus stretch both
My hands, bound to each side, across the deep,
And, when the rocks clash in turn and spurt sea
Skywards, imprisoned by the moving cliffs,
Let *me* lie and block the mountains without rest.   1215

> quin structum aceruans nemore congesto aggerem
> cruore corpus impio sparsum cremo?
> sic, sic agendum est. inferis reddam Herculem.

AMPHITRYON   Nondum tumultu pectus attonito carens
mutauit iras, quodque habet proprium furor,   1220
in se ipse saeuit.

HERCVLES   Dira Furiarum loca
et inferorum carcer et sonti plaga
decreta turbae—si quod exilium latet
ulterius Erebo, Cerbero ignotum et mihi,
hoc me abde, Tellus. Tartari ad finem ultimum   1225
mansurus ibo.

                          Pectus o nimium ferum!
quis uos per omnem, liberi, sparsos domum
deflere digne poterit? hic durus malis
lacrimare uultus nescit. huc ensem date,
date huc sagittas, stipitem huc uastum date.   1230

                          Tibi tela frangam nostra, tibi nostros, puer,
rumpemus arcus. at tuis stipes grauis
ardebit umbris. ipsa Lernaeis frequens
pharetra telis in tuos ibit rogos.
dent arma poenas. uos quoque infaustas meis   1235
cremabo telis, o nouercales manus.

AMPHITRYON   Quis nomen usquam sceleris errori addidit?

HERCVLES   Saepe error ingens sceleris obtinuit locum.

AMPHITRYON   Nunc Hercule opus est. perfer hanc molem mali.

HERCVLES   Non sic furore cessit extinctus pudor   1240
populos ut omnes impio aspectu fugem.
arma, arma, Theseu, flagito propere mihi

Why don't I pile up a forest, build a pyre,
Burn my body drenched with impious blood?
Thus, thus I must act. I'll return Hercules to hell.

AMPHITRYON   His heart's not yet free of frenzied turmoil;
The anger shifts. As is the nature of rage,   1220
It savages itself.

HERCULES   Dire haunts of Furies,
The dungeon of hell, the district decreed
For the guilty throng—if some exile hides
Beyond Erebus, unknown to Cerberus and me,
Hide me there, Earth. I'll go to Tartarus' furthest   1225
End—there to remain.

Turns to his dead SONS.

O too brutal heart!
Who can shed fitting tears for you, children,
Spattered through all the palace. This face, hard
With suffering, cannot weep. Bring here my sword,
Bring here my arrows; my great club—bring it here. 1230

Addresses the bodies of his SONS *and* MEGARA.

For you I'll break my arrows, for you, child,
I'll smash my bow. But the heavy club I'll burn
For *your* spirit. The quiver itself, packed
With Lernaean shafts, will join your pyre.
Let these weapons pay. You, too, I shall burn—   1235
Curse of my weapons—O stepmother hands.

AMPHITRYON   Who ever gave error the name of crime?

HERCULES   Great error is often the site of crime.

AMPHITRYON   Now there's need of Hercules. Bear this weight of woe.

HERCULES   Shame is not gone, nor so quenched by rage   1240
That all nations flee my impious face.
Arms, arms, Theseus, stolen from me—I demand

subtracta reddi. sana si mens est mihi,
referte manibus tela; si remanet furor,
pater, recede. mortis inueniam uiam.   1245

AMPHITRYON   Per sancta generis sacra, per ius nominis
utrumque nostri, siue me altorem uocas
seu tu parentem, perque uenerandos piis
canos, senectae parce desertae, precor,
annisque fessis. unicum lapsae domus   1250
firmamen, unum lumen afflicto malis,
temet reserua. nullus ex te contigit
fructus laborum. semper aut dubium mare
aut monstra timui. quisquis in toto furit
rex saeuus orbe, manibus aut aris nocens,   1255
a me timetur. semper absentis pater
fructum tui tactumque et aspectum peto.

HERCVLES   Cur animam in ista luce detineam amplius
morerque nihil est. cuncta iam amisi bona:
mentem arma famam coniugem natos manus—   1260
etiam furorem. nemo polluto queat
animo mederi. morte sanandum est scelus.

AMPHITRYON   Perimes parentem?

HERCVLES   Facere ne possim, occidam.

AMPHITRYON   Genitore coram?

HERCVLES   Cernere hunc docui nefas.

AMPHITRYON   Memoranda potius omnibus facta intuens   1265
unius a te criminis ueniam pete.

HERCVLES   Veniam dabit sibi ipse, qui nulli dedit?
laudanda feci iussus; hoc unum meum est.
    Succurre, genitor. siue te pietas mouet
seu triste fatum siue uiolatum decus   1270
uirtutis, effer arma. uincatur mea
Fortuna dextra.

Their quick return. If I am sound of mind,
Restore weapons to my hands; if rage remains,
Father, stand back. I'll find the path of death.   1245

AMPHITRYON   By the sacred laws of family, by the rights
                      Of either name, whether you call me 'guardian'
                      Or 'father', by my white hair, respected
                      By the good, spare my lone old age, I beg,
                      And weary years. Sole pillar of a fallen   1250
                      House, the one light in this calamity,
                      Keep yourself alive. I have got no joy
                      From your labours. Always I feared fickle seas
                      Or monsters. Every cruel king in the world
                      Who rages with guilty hands or altars   1255
                      Makes me fear. I seek a father's joy of one
                      Ever absent: the touch and sight of you.

HERCULES   There's no cause for me to live and linger
                      Still in this light. I have now lost all things
                      Of value: mind, weapons, glory, wife, sons,   1260
                      Hands—even rage. There is no one able
                      To heal a mind diseased. Death must cure the crime.

AMPHITRYON   Will you kill your father?

HERCULES   I'll die so I can't.

AMPHITRYON   Before your father?

HERCULES   I've trained him to watch evil.

AMPHITRYON   Gaze rather at your deeds, famous to all;   1265
                      Try to pardon yourself for the one crime.

HERCULES   Will he pardon himself, who pardoned none?
                      My lauded deeds were ordered; this one deed's mine.
                      (Kneels) Help me, father. Whether moved by pious love,
                      Grim fate or my virtue's violated   1270
                      Glory, bring out my weapons. Let my hand
                      Conquer Fortune.

THESEVS   Sunt quidem patriae preces
                  satis efficaces, sed tamen nostro quoque
                  mouere fletu. surge et aduersa impetu
                  perfringe solito. nunc tuum nulli imparem   1275
                  animum malo resume, nunc magna tibi
                  uirtute agendum est. Herculem irasci ueta.

HERCVLES   Si uiuo, feci scelera; si morior, tuli.
                  purgare terras propero. iamdudum mihi
                  monstrum impium saeuumque et immite ac ferum   1280
                  oberrat. agedum, dextra, conare aggredi
                  ingens opus, labore bis seno amplius.
                     Ignaue, cessas, fortis in pueros modo
                  pauidasque matres?
                                    Arma nisi dantur mihi,
                  aut omne Pindi Thracis excidam nemus   1285
                  Bacchique lucos et Cithaeronis iuga
                  mecum cremabo, aut tota cum domibus suis
                  dominisque tecta, cum deis templa omnibus
                  Thebana supra corpus excipiam meum
                  atque urbe uersa condar—et, si fortibus   1290
                  leue pondus umeris moenia immissa incident
                  septemque opertus non satis portis premar,
                  onus omne media parte quod mundi sedet
                  dirimitque superos in meum uertam caput.

AMPHITRYON   Reddo arma.

HERCVLES   Vox est digna genitore Herculis.   1295
                  Hoc en peremptus spiculo cecidit puer.

AMPHITRYON   Hoc Iuno telum manibus emisit tuis.

HERCVLES   Hoc nunc ego utar.

THESEUS   A father's prayers indeed
                Suffice, but yet be moved, too, by our tears.
                Rise up and break through this adversity
                With customary force. Now recover   1275
                Your spirit, uncowed by evil; now you
                Must act with great virtue. Stop Hercules' wrath.

                                        HERCULES *rises.*

HERCULES   If I live, I did the crimes—dead, I suffered them.
                I rush to cleanse the earth. For a long time
                A monster, impious, savage, pitiless,   1280
                Brutal ranges before me. Come, hand, try
                A mighty task, grander than twelve labours.
            (*Aside*) Do you cringe, coward, brave only with boys
                And frightened mothers?
                            (*Aloud*) If I'm not given arms,
                I'll either fell Thracian Pindus' entire forest   1285
                And burn Bacchus' groves and Cithaeron's ridge
                Along with myself, or pile on my body
                The whole city with its homes and masters,
                Theban temples with all their gods, and be buried
                By the ruined town—and if the fallen walls   1290
                Weigh too lightly on these strong shoulders
                And seven gates are not enough to crush me,
                I'll draw on my head the mid-firmament's
                Entire mass, the boundary of gods.

AMPHITRYON   I return the arms.

HERCULES   Words worthy of Hercules'   1295
                Father.

HERCULES' *weapons* (*club, sword, bow, lion skin, quiver, arrows*) *are
brought onstage by* SLAVES. *They are placed near the arrow which killed
one of his sons.* HERCULES *picks up the fatal arrow.*

                This shaft, look, felled and killed my boy.

AMPHITRYON   Juno fired this arrow with your hands.

HERCULES   Now *I* will use it.

AMPHITRYON   Ecce quam miserum metu
                    cor palpitat pectusque sollicitum ferit.

HERCVLES   Aptata harundo est.

AMPHITRYON   Ecce iam facies scelus   1300
                    uolens sciensque.

HERCVLES   Pande, quid fieri iubes?

AMPHITRYON   Nihil rogamus. noster in tuto est dolor.
                    natum potes seruare tu solus mihi,
                    eripere nec tu. maximum euasi metum.
                    miserum haut potes me facere, felicem potes.   1305
                    sic statue, quidquid statuis, ut causam tuam
                    famamque in arto stare et ancipiti scias:
                    aut uiuis aut occidis. hanc animam leuem
                    fessamque senio nec minus fessam malis
                    in ore primo teneo.
                                          Tam tarde patri   1310
                    uitam dat aliquis? non feram ulterius moram.
                    letale ferrum pectori impresso induam.
                    hic, hic iacebit Herculis sani scelus.

HERCVLES   Iam parce, genitor, parce, iam reuoca manum.
                    succumbe, uirtus; perfer imperium patris.   1315
                    eat ad labores hic quoque Herculeos labor:
                    uiuamus.

                              Artus alleua afflictos solo,
                    Theseu, parentis. dextra contactus pios
                    scelerata refugit.

AMPHITRYON   Look how my poor heart
                    Quivers with fear and thumps my anxious breast.

HERCULES *places the poisoned arrow close to his body (perhaps his breast or neck).*

HERCULES   The arrow is poised.

AMPHITRYON *takes* HERCULES' *sword from the pile of weapons and points it at himself.*

AMPHITRYON   Look! Now your crime will be   1300
                    Willing and knowing.

HERCULES   Speak, what do you order done?

AMPHITRYON   We ask nothing. My pain has found safety.
                    You alone can save my son for me; you
                    Can't take him. I've escaped my greatest fear.
                    You can't give me pain, you can give me joy.   1305
                    Whatever you decide, decide knowing
                    Your case and fame are in perilous straits:
                    Your choice is life or murder. My very lips
                    Hold back this frail breath wearied by old age,
                    Wearied no less by woe.
                                            Can one so slowly   1310
                    Grant his father life? I'll delay no more.
                    I'll sink this deadly steel in my pierced breast.
                    Here, here shall lie the crime of Hercules sane.

HERCULES   Now spare, father, spare yourself; now—pull back
                    Your hand. Yield, virtue; bear a father's rule.   1315
                    To Hercules' labours add this labour, too:
                    Let us live.

                                            AMPHITRYON *collapses.*

                    Lift my father's crushed body,
                    Theseus, from the ground. My criminal hand
                    Shuns contact with the good.

AMPHITRYON *grabs* HERCULES' *hand, as* THESEUS *lifts him up.*

AMPHITRYON   Hanc manum amplector libens,
hac nisus ibo. pectori hanc aegro admouens   1320
pellam dolores.

HERCVLES   Quem locum profugus petam?
ubi me recondam quaue tellure obruar?
quis Tanais aut quis Nilus aut quis Persica
uiolentus unda Tigris aut Rhenus ferox
Tagusue Hibera turbidus gaza fluens   1325
abluere dextram poterit? Arctoum licet
Maeotis in me gelida transfundat mare
et tota Tethys per meas currat manus,
haerebit altum facinus.
                     In quas impius
terras recedes? ortum an occasum petes?   1330
ubique notus perdidi exilio locum.
me refugit orbis. astra transuersos agunt
obliqua cursus; ipse Titan Cerberum
meliore uultu uidit.
                     O fidum caput,
Theseu, latebram quaere longinquam, abditam;   1335
quoniamque semper sceleris alieni arbiter
amas nocentes, gratiam meritis refer
uicemque nostris. redde me infernis, precor,
umbris reductum, meque subiectum tuis
restitue uinclis. ille me abscondet locus—   1340
sed et ille nouit.

THESEVS   Nostra te tellus manet.
illic solutam caede Gradiuus manum
restituit armis. illa te, Alcide, uocat,
facere innocentes terra quae superos solet.

AMPHITRYON   I gladly clasp this hand.
It'll be my prop. I'll hold it to my ailing breast   1320
To banish pain.

HERCULES   What place of exile shall I seek?
Where shall I hide, in what land be erased?
What Tanais, what Nile or what violent
Tigris with Persian flood or frenzied Rhine
Or turbid Tagus, awash with Spain's gold,   1325
Can cleanse this hand? Though icy Maeotis
Pour its Arctic sea on me, and Tethys
Stream over my hands with all her waters,
The crime will stick deep.
                        To what lands will you
Run, impious man? Will you head east or west?   1330
Known everywhere, I've destroyed a place for exile.
The world shuns me. Slanting stars run transverse
Courses; Titan himself viewed Cerberus
With more friendly gaze.
                        O faithful friend,
Theseus, seek a distant, secret hideaway;   1335
And, since whenever you judge another's crime
You love the guilty, thank and repay me
For my services. Recall, return me,
I beg, to the shades of hell; restore me
Fettered with your chains. That place will hide me—   1340
But it, too, knows me.

THESEUS   Our land awaits you.
There Gradivus cleansed his hands of murder
And restored them to battle. This land, Alcides,
Calls you. It often makes innocents of gods.

                                        Curtain.

Selective Critical Apparatus

The text of the plays attributed to Seneca is preserved in two distinct branches, *E* and *A*, dating perhaps from recensions made in or about the fifth century CE. Though the *A* branch seems more prone than *E* to interpolation, neither branch is to be preferred in respect of authority. The main MS of the *E* branch is the eleventh-century 'Codex Etruscus' (*E*), housed in the Laurentian Library in Florence, from which all succeeding members of the *E* branch (most notably the fourteenth-century MSS *F*, *M*, and *N*) are derived. The *A* branch exists in two subdivisions: δ and β. Its main MSS are: (δ) *P* (early thirteenth century) and *T* (early fifteenth century—reappraised by MacGregor 1978), both to be found in the Bibliothèque Nationale in Paris; (β) *C* (early thirteenth century), now in the library of Corpus Christi College, Cambridge, *S* (late thirteenth century), now in the Biblioteca Real, Escorial, and *V* (late thirteenth century), now in the Vatican Library. The text of *Hercules* in this edition is based primarily on the 'codex Etruscus' and the MSS of the *A* branch listed above. In my reportage of textual variants and the conjectures of scholars I have benefited from the *apparatus critici* of Viansino (1965), Zwierlein (1986), Fitch (1987*a*), Chaumartin (1999), Billerbeck (1999*a*), and Giardina (1966 and 2007), and the discussions of Fitch (2004*b*). For a historical catalogue of conjectures and emendations pertinent to Seneca's *Hercules*, the reader is directed to Billerbeck and Somazzi (2009), 35–56. The following selective apparatus primarily lists the important *EA* disagreements. It cites scholarly conjectures and other MSS occasionally—especially when the readings of the main MSS have been rejected in their favour. Some lacunae, deletions, and line transpositions posited by previous editors, as well as the scene-headings recorded in the MSS, are also noted. A list of departures from Zwierlein's Oxford text of 1986 (and subsequent revisions) may be found on pp. 262–5.

SIGLA

E Florence, Biblioteca Medicea-Laurenziana. Plut. Lat. 37.13 ('Codex Etruscus'). Late eleventh century.

P Paris, Bibliothèque Nationale. Lat. 8260. Thirteenth century (first half).

T Paris, Bibliothèque Nationale. Lat. 8031. Early fifteenth century.

C Cambridge, Corpus Christi College 406. Early thirteenth century.

S Escorial, Biblioteca Real. 108 T III 11. Late thirteenth century.

V Rome (Vatican City), Biblioteca Apostolica Vaticana. Lat. 2829. Late thirteenth century.

A Consensus of *PTCSV*.

F Paris, Bibliothèque Nationale. Lat. 11855. Fourteenth century (first half).

M Milan, Biblioteca Ambrosiana D 276 inf. Fourteenth century.

N Rome (Vatican City), Biblioteca Apostolica Vaticana. Lat. 1769. Fourteenth century.

K Cambrai, Bibliothèque Municipale 555. Early to middle fourteenth century.

Q Monte Cassino. Biblioteca dell' Abazia 392 P. Middle fourteenth century.

Ox. Oxford, Bodleian Library Canon. Class. Lat. 93. Fourteenth century.

e Eton, College Library 110. Middle fourteenth century.

O Naples, Biblioteca Gerolamini. XI.38 ('Codex Oratorianus'). 1400.

recc. More recent MSS.

τ Codex (now lost) used by Nicholas Trevet in his early fourteenth century commentary on Seneca's tragedies.

Where conjectures are given, the name of the scholar believed to be the first to have made the conjecture follows. E^{ac} indicates the MS before correction; E^{pc} indicates the MS after correction.

Before 1 scene title added IVNO *ET*: omitted *PCSV* 6 glacialis $E^{pc}A$: glaciales E^{ac} 8 recenti $E^{ac}FMN$: tepenti $E^{pc}A$. 12 ferro minax hinc terret E^{ac}: fera coma hinc exterret $E^{pc}A$ 13 aureus *E*: aureas *A* 18 puelle serta gnosiace gerit $E^{pc}TCSV$: puellas fert. anobis lac egent (or egerit) *E* 19 sero *Leo*: uetera sero *EA* Between 19a and 19b lacuna posited *Richter* 19b–21a omitted *A* 20 matribus *Axelson*: nuribus *EA* 21 escendat E^{ac}:

254   SELECTIVE CRITICAL APPARATUS

ascendat $E^{pc}A$ **34** fruitur $E^{pc}A$: fruimur $E^{ac}FM$ **36** probaui $E^{ac}FM$: probauit $E^{pc}A$ glorie feci locum *FMN*: inde qua lucem premit $E^{pc}A$ **37** qua sol reducens quaque reponens (deponens *FM*) diem *E*: aperitque thetis qua ferens titan *A*   **38** ethiopas *TSV*: ethyopas *PC*: ethyopes E^{pc} **43** quae ET^{pc}: quo *A*   iussa $E^{pc}A$: iura $F^{ac}M$ **49** transposed after 54 *Leo*   perit $EP^{pc}T^{pc}CSV$: petit $P^{ac}T^{ac}$ **52** uinctum *E*: uictum *A*   **54** et *EA*: en *Baden*   **56** dire $E^{pc}A$: dur(a)e $E^{ac}FMN$ **62** terna *FMN*: t(h)etra $E^{pc}A$ deuicti $E^{pc}A$ F^{pc}: deuicta $E^{ac}F^{ac}MN$ **63** nimium $E^{pc}A$: minimum E^{ac} **66** lenta $E^{pc}TCSV$: lentus $E^{ac}P$ **67** iter *A*: inter E^{ac} **68** experto *E*: expenso *A*   **71** transposed after 72 *Peiper*   **72** meliusque $E^{ac}FMN$: mediusque $E^{pc}A$ **76** dilacera *E*: iam lacera *A*   After 82 line 123 placed *A*   **83–9** omitted *A*   **83** deleted *Leo*   **90** placed after 91 E^{ac}, corrected E^{pc} ferox $E^{pc}A$: feros $E^{ac}FMN$ **92** conditam *E*: conditum *A*   **94** quam $E^{pc}A$: qua E^{ac} **96** ueniet *E*: ueniet et *T*: ueniet et in *P*: uel ueniet utinam et *CSV*   **100** incit(a)e $E^{pc}A$: cite E^{ac} **102** luctifica $ET^{pc}CSV$: ludifica $T^{ac}P$.   **103** flagrante $E^{pc}A$: flagrantem E^{ac} **104** uiolate *A*: uiciatae *E*   **107** animum *A*: animo *E*   **108** uobis *EPCSV*: nobis *T* τ *recc.*   **109** furit *A*: furis *E*   **110** deiectam $E^{pc}A$: delectat $E^{ac}FM$ **112** uota *FMN*: iam odia $E^{pc}A$ **113** precor *EA*: pater *Zwierlein*   **116** uicit *FN*: pariter $E^{pc}A$ **119** manu *E*: manum *A*   **123** placed after 82 *A*   **124–61** omitted *A*   Before **125** CHORVS METRVM ANAPESTICVM *E*   **125–203** dimeters (apart from 151b monometer) *E*   **127** renata E^{pc} **128** phosforos E^{pc}: bosforos E^{ac} **130** deleted *Leo.*   **131** uocat *recc.*: uocant *E*   **132** equis *E*: aquis *recc.*   **134** in clita E^{pc}: in cluta E^{ac} **146–51** transposed after 136 *Zwierlein*   **162–203** dimeters (apart from 195, 197• monometers) *A*   **162** spes iam magnis *E*: chorus turbine magno spes sollicitae *A* E^{pc} *marg.* (without chorus): spes immanes *Schmidt*   **164** regum $ET^{pc}CSV$: regno *P*   **166** hic *Ascensius*: ac *EA* beatas $ET^{pc}CSV$: beatus $PT^{ac}V$ **171** tollit $EPTC^{pc}$: uoluit $C^{ac}SV$ **181** dur(a)e $EPT^{ac}CV$: dura $T^{pc}S$ **183** fertur $E^{pc}A$: flatur MN^{ac} **184** sui $E^{pc}A$: suis E^{ac} **188** ordine $E^{pc}A$: tempore *FMNe*   **190** proferre $EPT^{pc}C$: preferre $T^{ac}S$ **193** after 194 E^{ac}, order restored E^{pc} **204** one verse *E*: two verses (t.s.g.| a.p.) *A*   Before **205** AMPHITRYON MAEGERA LYCVS *E*: megera amphitrion licus *PTCS*: omitted *V*   **205** AMP. *E*: omitted *A*   **210** paratur $ET^{pc}CSV$: paratus PT^{ac} **211** meat *E*: exeat *A*   **212** uacat *EP*: datur *TCSV*   **213** aprimo $E^{ac}FMN$: aprime E^{pc}: apprime T^{pc}: a prima *PCS*   **216** posset $E^{pc}A$: possit E^{ac} **218** reptabat *E*: reptauit $PT^{pc}CSV$: raptauit T^{ac} **219** lumine $E^{ac}FMN$: pectore *A*: uultu E^{pc} **224** cursu *E*: cursu est *A*   **225** pressus lacertis gemuit *E*: gemuit lacertis pressus *A*   **236** qu(a)e $E^{pc}A$: qua E^{ac} **237** soluit $ET^{pc}C^{pc}SV$: solum PC^{ac} ac rupto *Gronouius*: abrupto

EA 238 latam *E*: etiam *A* 241 lerne *A*: lerinae (with i expunged) *E* 244
petit *E*: petiit (peciit) *A*. 248 stabuli $E^{pc}A$: stabilis E^{ac} augei *A*: angaei
E^{pc} 257 capiti E^{ac}: capitis $E^{pc}A$ 258 quis *A*: qui *E* thebas *EP*: thebis
TCS 259 tremit $E^{pc}A$: tremet E^{ac} 268 Ophionium genus *Bentley*: ophionius cinis *EPCSV*: ophionius ciuis *T* 269 quo recidistis $E^{pc}A$: quor excidis-
tis E^{ac} ignarum $EPT^{ac}CSV$: ignauum T^{pc} τ 271 mari $E^{pc}A$: mare E^{ac} 272
confringit *EP*: confregit *TCSV* 274 herculeas *EV*: herculeus *PT*: herculis
CS 277 assis sospes *FMN*: adsiso sospes *E*: assis hospes *A* precor *E*: tuis
A 279 mark for Megara *E*: omitted *A* emerge *ET*: emergere *PCSV* dispulsas *E*: depulsas *A* 280 retro *E*: uento $PT^{ac}V^{ac}$: uetito $T^{pc}CS$: uenturo
V^{pc} 281 diducto $EPP^{pc}TCP^{cs}SV$: deducto $P^{ac}C^{ac}$ 284 flumini *TCSV*: flu-
minis *P*: fulmini *E* 285 stetisti *ETCV*: fetisti *P*: fecisti *S* 295 imperatum
$E^{ac}A$: impertitum E^{pc} 301 muta *E*: multa *A* 302 eleusin tacita *A*: eleus
tacita E^{pc}: eleus intacita E^{ac} iactabit *E*: iactabo *A* 306 omnes *A*: omnis
E 313 quod $E^{pc}A$: quid E^{ac} 315 moueri *E*: amoueri *A* 316 assigned to
Amphitryon *E*: to Megara *A* timoris $E^{ac}FMN$: timori $E^{pc}A$ 318 uiam $E^{pc}A$:
uim E^{ac} 321 abiit $E^{pc}A$: adit E^{ac}: adiit *FMN* 324 superauit $E^{pc}A$: super
habuit *N* 326 tuto $E^{pc}A$: pute E^{ac} 330 animo *ETCV*: in animo *PS* 332
mark for Lycus *E*: omitted *A* urbis $E^{pc}PTV^{pc}$: urbes E^{ac}: urbi CSV^{ac} 333
uberi *A*: ubere *E*: uberis *Heinsius* solo *EA*: soli *Heinsius* 335–6 deleted
Peiper 335 placed after 336 *E*, corrected E^{pc} 336 deleted *Leo* 337 no
mark *E*: mark for Lycus *A* 342 obtinentur *A*: optinentur *Ee* 343 tenere te
$E^{ac}FMNe$: tenetur $E^{pc}A$ 347 thalamisque *A*: thalamis *E* e *recc.*: et *EA* 352
factum E^{ac}: fastum $E^{pc}A$ 353 et inuidiam *Grotius*: ad inuidiam *A*: inuidiam
E: in inuidia *Richter* 354 fors *EPSV*: sors *TC* nobis locum $E^{pc}A$: locum
nobis E^{ac} 356 omitted E^{ac}. added in margin E^{pc} 362 gerant *E*: agent
A 368 reduci $E^{pc}A$: reduce *F*: reducere *MN* 370 sociemur E^{ac}: sociemus
$E^{pc}A$ animis *E*: animos *A* 377 uicibus $E^{pc}A$ 380 patriam *EA*: patrium *Ed.*
Patau. 381 carior $E^{pc}AN^{pc}$: careo *FM* 383 ex isto *PT*: existo $E^{pc}F^{pc}$: ex
ista *CSV*: exicio E^{ac} 385 ultor *recc.*: uictor *EA* 392 quin $E^{pc}A$ 397 efferatas *TCSVFN*: effratas *P*: effrenatas E^{pc} 400 regamque *E*: geramque
A 403 modum ET^{pc}: domum *PCSV* 408 pereat ET^{pc}: pergat *PCSV* 414
exangues *A*: exanguis *E* 418 tremesco E^{ac}: tremisco $E^{pc}A$ 423 supera
$E^{ac}PT^{ac}$: superna $E^{pc}T^{pc}CSV$ 425 premetur $E^{pc}AFMN$: premeretur
E^{ac} 430 sceptroque $E^{ac}A$: sceptro quoque $E^{pc}V$: sceptrone *recc.* famulus
est potior *E*: potior est famulus *A* 433 quid $E^{pc}A$: quod E^{ac} 436
loquentem *EA*: sequentem *Bentley* 438 sperat *E*: penetrat *A* 440 meae *E*:
mee hee *PTSV*: mee he *C* 449 pluribus causa est $EP^{pc}T^{pc}C^{pc}SV$: pluribus
est causa T^{ac}: pluribus est P^{ac}: est causa C^{ac} 453 terra mater *E*: terre mater

T^{pc}: mater mater $PT^{ac}CSV$ errante edidit E: errantem dedit A 454 num E: nunc PT^{ac}: non $T^{pc}CSV$ seuas A: saeua E 456 assigned to LYCUS *Gruter*, to AMPHITRYON *EA*   paruus *EA*: partus *Housman*   460 exese A: ideae E 461 tanti pretia A: precia tanti E 462 constitit $ETCSV$: conscit P 475 barbarico E: barbaricum A 477 mark for Lycus $E^{pc}A$: no mark E^{ac} euriti E: euritis CS: eurytis PT: herutis V 479 erased mark for Lycus E^{ac}: no mark A 483 hospitali cede manantes A: hospitalem caedem minantes E 485 uulneri $EPT^{pc}C$: uultum $T^{ac}SV^{ac}$: inultum V^{pc} inuius *Heinsius*: obuius *EA*   486 integer cycnus E: ante geriones A 490 dabis *EA*: dabit *Leo*   497 nostro $T^{pc}\tau QM$: uestro $EPT^{ac}CS$ 500 dest *edd.*: deest *EA*   504 remolito A: demolito E 508 locus *EA*: rogus *Auantius*   512 inroga Q: irroga A: in loca E 513 ueta EPT^{pc}: uita CSV 515 colam E: rogem A 516 pro…pro E: proh…proh T: proth…proth P: pro…oro CS numinum $ET^{pc}CSV$: nimium PT^{ac} 521 agitata $ETC^{pc}SV$: agita PC^{ac} 522 sonuit e $E^{pc}CSV$: sonu ite E^{ac}: sonuit est PT^{ac} 523 est est EPT: e est CS Before 524 METRVM ASCLEPIADEVM. CHORVS. E 526 euristeus A: auristeus E 529 feracia *recc.*: ferocia *EA*   536 mutis $K\tau$: multis *EA*   538 tenderant TCV: tenderent E: tendeant S: tendantur P 539 semita $ET^{pc}CSV$: semitas PT^{ac} 543 omitted A 546 suspiciens *recc.*: suscipiens *EA*   548 irremeabiles $PTCV$: inremeabiles S: inremediabiles E 559 colos E: colus A 561 bello $EPTS^{pc}$: bella $CS^{ac}V\tau$ peteres *recc.*: peteret *EA*   566 tristibus E: tristis et A 571 repetit E: recipit A 575–6 omitted A 577 placed after 580 A Eumenides Threiciam nurum *Schmidt*: eurydicen (-em E) t(h)reici(a)e nurus *EA*   583 euade ET^{pc}: et uade A 590 uinci $EPSV\tau$: uincit C cantibus A: carmine E 591 poterit $ECSV$: potuit P Before 592 scene title moved from before 618 with changes *Boyle*   Hercules A: Metrum iambicum. archiloycum. HERCVLES E 594 l(a)etis A: latis E 597 archana E: secreta A c(a)elestum $T^{pc}CV$: c(a)elestium $EPT^{ac}S$ 598 tege $ETCV$: rege PS 601 pollui metuens ET: pollui timens P: metuens pollui CSV 604 iussit E: uexit A 606 inaccessa E: in accessa CV: inactessa T: in accensa P: inacensa S 607 qu(a)eque A: quaque E 612 redi E: redii A 614 iam diu E: tam diu $PCSV$: tandiu T 615 quae E: quid A Before 618 AMPHITRION. HERCVLES. MEGERA. THESEVS E Amphitrion. hercules. theseus. A (see before 592)   622 at *Gruter*: et *EA*   623 teneone in auras editum an uana fruor E: uerumne cerno corpus an fallor uidens PT: uerumne cerno corpus an fallor uel tua uidens CSV 625 nobilem trunco manum *EA*: nobile in trunco caput *Axelson*   629 regna EPT: regnaque CSV 632 uidit EPC^{ac}: uidet $T^{pc}C^{pc}SV$: uide T^{ac} 634b–636 assigned to Hercules E: to Theseus A 637 no mark E: mark for Hercules A 644 est

lentum *EPT*: lentum *CSV*   651 certa E^{pc} 654 peruince *A*: peruincet *E*   in
E: omitted *A*   659 tota *EA*: toto *Schmidt*   660 ethna *EA*: orbe
Schmidt   661 eloqui *A*: loqui *E*   664 inuisi *E*: inuicti *PTCV*: inuiti *S*   665
hiatque $E^{pc}A$: hitque (?) E^{ac} immenso $ET^{pc}CSV$: uniuerso PT^{ac} 667 pan-
dit E^{pc} 671 nocte sic mixta *E*: tale non dubie *A*   674 mersum *PTC*: men-
sum *S*: uersum *E*   pergat *Peiper*: pereat *EA*   678 umquam $ETCS^{pc}$:
numquam PS^{ac} 679 immenso sinu *A*: immensi sinus *E*   680
lethe $E^{pc}FMN$: lethes *A*: lethos E^{ac} 683 incerta *A*: incertis E^{pc}: incertus
E^{ac} 684 meander ET^{pc}: leander *A*   unda *A*: undis *E*   ludit $T^{pc}PCSV$:
errat ludit *E*   687 hinc *Kenney*: hic *EA*   illinc *Kenney*: illic $EPTC^{pc}V$: hic
S   luctifer $ET^{pc}CV$: lucifer $PT^{ac}S$ 688 omenque *ETCV*: omneque *PS*   691
iacet *Withof*: iacens *EA*   693 metus *A*: metusque *E*   697 cerereris E^{ac}, corrected E^{pc} ferax *E*: tenax *A*   703 deleted *Wakefield*   709 recessu *E*:
secessu *A*   717 aduersa *ET*: auersa *PCSV*   722 deo *A*: dei *E*   728 iam
Ageno: tam *EA*   reddi *A*: reddit *E*   733 aditur *E*: auditor *A*   Cnosius *Leo*:
Gnosius *EA*   734 hoc *A*: hos *E*   738 plebeia $ET^{pc}CSV$: plebia PT^{ac} 739
tyranni $ET^{pc}CSV$: tyrannum PT^{ac} 741 regit $E^{pc}A$: regis E^{ac} 742 anim(a)
eque *EPCSV*: animoque T^{pc}_τ 753 alluit $E^{ac}T^{ac}$: aluit *P*: abluit
$E^{pc}T^{pc}CSV$ 757 gerunt *E*: ferunt *A*   759 terretque mensas auida phineas
(phy-) auis *A*: terrentque mensas auidae fineas aues *E*   763 stupente...unda
A: stupent...undae *E*   766 impexa $ET^{pc}CSV$: impensa PT^{ac} 767 lucent
TSCV: luent *P*: squalent *E*   768 longo portitor conto *E*: conto portitor
(potior *V*) longo $PTCS^{pc}V$ 769 uacuam *E*: uacuus *A*   puppem *E*: puppim
A   770 umbras *E*: undas *A*   776 succubuit *EPTSV*: succumbit *C*   sedit *EA*:
sidit *Gronouius*   777 titubanti *E*: titubato *A*   778 tum *E*: tunc *A*   uicta *E*:
uasta *A*   779 deleted *Fitch*, who places lacuna between 778 and 780   in *E*:
omitted *A*   784 trina $EPT^{ac}CS$: terna $T^{pc}V$ 788 par *A*: per *E*   790 subrecta
E: subiecta *A*   791 propior $ET^{pc}CSV$: prior PT^{ac} 793 et uterque *EA*: leuiterque *Madvig*   797 feros *recc.*: ferox *EA*   799 tegit *E*: clepit $PTC^{pc}SV$ 807
tum *ET*: tunc *PCSV*   814 nouus *Bücheler*: nouos *Rutgers*: bono *EA*   815
uictus *E*: uinctus *A*   821 diem *E*: ethera *A*   822 nitidi $ET^{pc}CSV$: mundi
PT^{ac} 823 deleted *Bothe*   824 compressit *A*: comspexit *E*   826 tum EPT^{pc}:
cum $T^{ac}CSV$ 826–7 Herculeas...umbras *E*: Herculea...umbra *A*   Before
830 METRVM SAPHICVM. CONSTAT TROCHEO. SPONDEO. DACTILO.
ET DVOBVS TROCHEIS. CHORVS. *E*   832 derat *edd.*: deerat *EA*   834 es
E: est *A*   836 nigra metuenda silua *E*: silua metuenda nigra *A*   840 quantus
recc.: qualis *EA*   ruit *EP*: currit $T^{pc}CSV$: coit T^{pc} 841 reuocauit *ETCSV*:
renouauit *P*   842 nocti *E*: noctis *A*   844 phebeos *A*: thebeos *E*   849
graditur *E*: gradiens *A*   855 his *ECS*: hiis *PTV*   858 uobis $EPT^{ac}SV$: nobis

$T^{pc}C$ **868** haec $ET^{pc}CSV$: hoc PT^{ac} **870** crescit A: crescet E **873** properamus $EPTC$: properamur SV **874** single verse ET: two verses (p. q. u.| d. h. c.) $PCSV$ carpit E: carpsit A Before **875** metrum hoc gliconicum · constat spondeo · choriambo · et iambo · uel pyrrichio · CHORVS E **875–94** single verses A: pairs of verses conjoined with initial letters distinguished (apart from the initial and last verse which remain separate) E **878** maribus A: matribus E **883** auroram A: aurora E **893** sacrificus $ECSV$: sacrificiis PT **894** tege ET: rege $PCSV$ Before **895** HERCVLES. AMPHYTRION. MEGERA. CHORVS E: Hercules. theseus. amphitrion. megera A **895** ultrice $PP^{c}T^{pc}CSV$: altrice $P^{ac}T^{ac}$: uictrice E aduerso E: aduersam A **896** tum A: tunc E **899** aras colam $E^{pc}A$: sacra scolam E^{ac} **904** uirenti A: uirente E **909** Indorum est seges *Düring*: Indorum seges EA After **909** lacuna posited *Leo*   **911** conferte $ET^{pc}CSV$: conferre PT^{ac} exundet $EPTCV$: extundet S **915** no mark E: mark for Theseus A tu E: dii A **916** zethi E: theti $TCSV$ nobilis $EPT^{ac}SV$: nobiles $T^{pc}C$ dircenaque E: dirces aquas A **917** coles E: colis A **918a** no mark E: mark for Hercules A **920** cruorem A: cruore E **922** haut $CS^{pc}V^{pc}$: aut $EPS^{ac}V^{ac}$: haud T **924** iniquus $EPTSV$: iniquis C **928** aequor *Heinsius*: (a)ether EA **934** amnis $ECSV$: annis PT **937** etiam num est ECV: eciam nunc est (eciam est nunc) T^{pc}: etiam ñ est P: etiam non est S **947** rapiet $PTC^{pc}SV$: rapiat EC^{ac} **948** rutilat $E^{ac}A$: rutilam E^{pc} **951** uerni $EPSV$: uerum C^{ac}: iterum $T^{pc}C^{pc}$ **953** huc et huc EPT^{ac}: huc et illuc CSV **957** dignus $E^{pc}TCSV$: dignum $E^{ac}P$ **959** promittit $ETCSV$: promisit P **963** recipis et A: recipi. sed E **967** parent $ETCSV$: parant P **971** ossa $ET^{pc}C$: osse $T^{ac}SV$: orse P **973** mittetur ET^{pc}: mutetur $PT^{ac}CSV$ **974** single verse E: auerte sensus attached to 973 A **976** pestiferi EP: pestifera $TCSV$ **979** pallene A: pellene E **980** marcentque A: macetumque E **981** horrendum $EPTC$: horrende SV Mimas *Auantius*: minans EA **989** leues A: leuis E **991** impegit E: inuergit A **993** stridet E: stridit A **994** medio A: medium E **995** eruam EPT: eruat CSV **996** omnes A: omnis E -que E: omitted A **997** cyclopea EA **999** et A: omitted E claua *Withof*: aula EA disiecto $TCSV$: deiecto E: obiecto P **1000** columen $TCSV$: columem P: culmen E **1001** perlucet E: procumbat A **1005** dextra E: dextram A precantem A: precante E **1006** ast EPT: at CSV **1009–10** omitted P **1009** e $ET^{pc}C$: est T^{ac}: ē SV **1010** mark for Hercules ET^{pc}: no mark $PT^{ac}CSV$ **1012** mark for Amphitryon ET^{pc}: no mark $PT^{ac}CSV$ latebram E: latebras $PT^{pc}CSV$ **1017** tendat A: tendam E **1020** occidat E: auferam A **1021** mark for Megara A: mark for Hercules E: mark for Amphitryon MN fundes $EPT^{ac}V$: fundens $T^{pc}CS$ **1022** mark for

Amphitryon A: no mark E: no mark MN infans igneo A: igneo infans E 1023 eripuit E: rapuit A timor E: puer $PCSV$: pauor $T^{pc}\tau$ *recc.* 1024 coniugem A: coniuge E 1028 pectori tela *Axelson*: pectus in tela EA indue $ECSV$: moue PT 1029 istum EA: istum huc *Axelson* 1032 mark for Chorus M: mark for Theseus EA senior E: genitor A 1033 late A: latet E 1038 dabit ET^{pc}: dabis $PT^{ac}CSV$ 1041 prebeo A: praebe E 1043 meror A: maemor E 1047 portum mari E: portus manet A 1050 motus A: in ortus E 1051 graui E: grauis A 1054–1137 dimeters apart from one monometer (1111) and one trimeter (1135b–36) A, dimeters apart from one monometer (1114b) and one trimeter (1136b–37) E 1054 (a)ether: $ET^{pc}CSV$: et hoc PT^{ac} 1057 omnes A: omnis E 1064 superi A: o superi E 1068 uolucre o *Leo*: uolucre $T\tau$: uolucer $EPCV$ 1070 futuri $T^{pc}CSV$: futuris EPT^{ac} 1072 pater EA: pax *Wilamowitz* 1074 famuloque $ET^{pc}CSV$: famulosque PT^{ac} 1076 noctem *Dousa*: mortem EA 1077 placed before 1075 A foue EA: fouens *Scaliger* 1078 deuinctum CSV: deuictum EPT torpore $PTC^{pc}SV$: corpore EC^{ac} 1080 torua EPT^{pc}: tortua T^{ac}: tot tua CSV 1082 en fusus A: infusus E 1083 uolutat A: uoluat E 1085 lassum $ET^{pc}CSV$: lassim PT^{ac} caput $ECSV$: capit P 1088 omnes A: omnis E After 1091 lacuna posited *Withof* 1103 uictrice EA: ultrice M 1105 regina A: regia E 1105• uastisque A: uastusque E 1109 unda $ETCSV$: ora P 1110 melius A: medius E 1111 aer EPT: ether CSV 1117 graues E: leues A 1118 saeua E: sera A 1123 ulti seuos $KQOx.$: uilisceuos E: ulti seuo A 1124 non argiua $ET^{pc}CSV$: nargiua PT^{ac} 1125 docti E: forti A 1127 scithycis…corytis E: scythici (variously written)…goryti or coriti (both variously written) A 1135–6 transposed after 1121 *Leo* 1136 per iter E: pariter A Before 1138 Hercules. Amphitryon (Amphitrio PT). Theseus EA 1138 mark for Hercules ESV: no mark C PTC 1140 glacialis A: glatiali E 1143 domo EA: ad domum *Schmidt* 1146 oberrat A: oborrat E oculis…meis E: oculos…meos A 1149 est A: es E 1150 cur A: cur en E uacat $E^{pc}CSV$: uagat PT: uocat E^{ac} 1151 abit E: abiit $PTC^{pc}SV$: ad huc C^{ac} 1155 quis A: qui E somnum ECS^{pc}: somnium (sompnium) PTS^{ac} 1157 uirtus E: uictor A 1158 in fetus *Fitch*: in foetu E: incestu $PT^{pc}CSV$: incessu T^{ac} 1162 deleted *Leo* 1166 seue $TCSV$: saeue E: siue P 1167 ruat ira $PTC^{pc}V$: ruit ira C^{ac}: ritat ira S: ruatur E omnes A: omnis E 1169 currus $ET^{pc}CV$: curru PT^{ac}: curris S 1170 siue gerione PCS: siue gerionis $T^{pc}\tau$: siuergeryone E 1171 lybiaeue (libieue) $ET^{pc}CSV$: lybi(a)ene PT^{ac} 1175 differte fletus TC: differre fletus PS: defer tellus E 1176 omnes A: omnis E 1177 at tu ede A: aut tuae de E 1180 impotens E: potens A 1181 lyci ET^{pc}: mihi A

1185 fudit domum *EPT*: domum fudit *CSV*   **1188** tolerauit *A*: tolerabit *E*   **1191** tu(a)e *ET*^{pc}: me *PT*^{ac}: ne *CSV*   **1195** lernea *A*: lernae *E*   **1198** sinuare *ET*^{pc}*C*^{pc}*SV*: sinuate *C*^{ac}: sumare *P*   neruum *A*: neruom *Baehrens*: neruos *E*:   **1206** ligatum *ET*^{pc}*CSV*: ligaui *PT*^{ac} **1208** paretur *T*^{pc}*CS*: parent *PT*^{ac}: uagetur *E*   **1209** abruptum *EPT*^{pc}: abrutum *CS*: obtutum *V*   **1210** siluis *ET*^{pc}*CSV*: illius *PT*^{ac} **1213** coibunt *ECV*: cohibunt *T*^{pc}*S*: cohibent *PT*^{ac} saxaque *EA*: saxa et *Bentley*   **1215** iaceam *ETCSV*: taceam *P*   **1216** structum *ET*^{pc}*CSV*: struetur *PT*^{ac} congesto *ET*^{pc}*S*: coniesto *C*: agesto *PT*^{ac} **1218** omitted *A*   **1219** attonito carens *E*: attonitum caret *A*   **1220** mutauit *ET*^{pc}*CSV*: mutant *PT*^{ac} **1223** si *E*: et si *A*   latet *EA*: patet *Zwierlein*   **1225** hoc *E*: huc *A*   **1227** uos *ET*^{pc}*C*: nos *PT*^{ac}*SV*   **1228** deflere *ECSV*: desse *PT*   **1229** ensem *EA*: arcum *Bentley*   **1230** omitted *E*   **1232** tuis *ETCV*: tuus *PS*   **1235** uos *ET*^{pc}*CSV*: nos *PT*^{ac} infaustas *EPT*: infausta *CSV*   **1237** mark for Amphitryon *E*: mark for Theseus *A*   usquam *E*: umquam *PT*: numquam *CSV*   **1238** sepe error *A*: semper furor *E*   **1239** mark for Amphitryon *E*: mark for Theseus *A*   **1240** furore cessit *A*: furor recessit *E*   **1244** referte *ET*^{pc}: reuerte *PCSV*   **1247** altorem *recc.*: auctorem *EA*   **1250** laps(a)e *EPCSV*: lass(a)e *T*   **1251** afflicto *A*: afflictis *E*   **1252** contigit *ETCSV*^{pc}*V*: contingit *PS*^{ac} **1263a, 1264a, 1265–6** mark for Amphitryon *E*: mark for Theseus *A*   **1266** pete *EPT*^{ac}: peto *T*^{pc}*CSV*   **1269** siue *ET*^{pc}*CSV*: si non *PT*^{ac} **1270** fatum *A*: factum *E*   uiolatum *E*: uiolate *A*   **1272** fortuna *E*^{pc}*T*^{pc}*CSV*: fortu *E*^{ac}: forma *PT*^{ac} quidem *EPC*^{pc}*SV*: quidam *T*^{pc}*C*^{ac} **1280** et *TCSV*: omitted *EP*   immite *TCSV*: immitte *EP*   **1281** age dum *ETV*: agendum *PCS*   **1284** pauidasque matres *A*: pauidamque matrem *E*   dantur *E*: dentur *A*   **1285** aut *EA*: altum *Axelson*   excidam *ETSV*: excindam *PC*   **1287** aut *τ recc.*: omitted *EA*   **1290** uersa *A*: euersa *E*   **1291** moenia *EPT*: media *CSV*   incident *ECSV*: incidunt *PT*^{ac}: incidant *T*^{pc} **1293** quod mundi *E*: quo mundus *A*   **1295a** mark for Amphitryon *E*: no mark *A*   reddo *E*: redde *A*   **1295b** mark for Hercules *E*: mark for Amphitryon *A*   digna genitore *A*: dignatore *E*   **1297** mark for Amphitryon *E*: no mark *A*   emisit *A*: immisit *E*   **1299** pectusque *Gronouius*: corpusque *EA*   **1300a** mark for Hercules *E*: no mark *A*   **1300b** mark for Amphitryon *E*: no mark *A*   **1301b** assigned to Hercules *O Rutgers*: to Amphitryon *EA*   **1304** eripere nec tu *E*: theseu ipse necdum *A*   **1305** potes me *TCSV*: me potes me *P*: potes *E*   **1309** fessam malis *E*: quassam malis *A*   **1312** ferrum pectori *recc., Delrius*: ferro pectus *EA*   impresso *E*: impressum *A*   induam *ECSV*: uiduam *PT*   **1315** perfer *ET*^{pc}: profer *PT*^{ac}*CSV*   **1316** herculeos *A*: herculeus *E*   **1317** afflictos *EA*: afflicti *recc.*   **1319** hanc *E*: hanc ego *A*   **1320** pectori *A*: pectore *E*

SELECTIVE CRITICAL APPARATUS 261

(a)egro *EP*: ego *TCSV*   **1322** obruar *E*: obruam *A*   **1324** renus *A*: thenus *E*   **1325** tagusue (thagusne *T*) hi(y)bera turbidus *A*: padusue hiberatur bibus *E*   **1330** recedes *A*: recides *E*   **1336** quoniamque *E*: cum iamque *PT*[ac]: quique *CSV*: quicunque *T*[pc]   **1342** illic *E*: illuc *A*   cede *A*: crede *E*   gradiuus *ET*[pc]*CSV*: gradimus *PT*[ac]

Differences from the 1986 Oxford Classical Text

	Boyle	Zwierlein
19	sero *Leo*	uetera sero *EA*
54	et *EA*	en *Baden*
72	meliusque *E*^{ac}*FMN*	mediusque *E*^{pc}*A*
100	incitae *E*^{pc}*A*	citae *E*^{ac}
108	uobis *EPCSV*	nobis *T* τ *recc*
109	furit *A*	furis *E*
113	precor *EA*	pater *Zwierlein*
132	equis *E*	aquis *recc.*
134	inclita *E*^{pc}	incluta *E*^{ac}
137	omnes *e recc.*	omnis *E*
162	iam magnis *E*	immanes *Schmidt*
188	ordine *E*^{pc}*A*	tempore *FMNe*
218	reptabat *E*	reptauit *PT*^{pc}*CSV*
219	lumine *E*^{ac}*FMN*	pectore *A*
269	ignarum *EPT*^{ac}*CSV*	ignauum *T*^{pc}τ
272	confringit *EP*	confregit *TCSV*
277	precor *E*	tuis *A*
299	tibi o *EA*	tum tibi *Bothe*
306	omnes *A*	omnis *E*
321	abit *E*^{pc}*A* (abiit)	adit *E*^{ac}
333	uberi *A*	uberis *Heinsius*
333	solo *EA*	soli *Heinsius*
342	obtinentur *A*	optinentur *Ee*
353	et inuidiam *Grotius*	in inuidia *Richter*
380	patriam *EA*	patrium *Ed. Patauina*

390	superba *EA*	superbo *Ascensius*
414	exangues *A*	exanguis *E*
430	sceptroque *E*ac*A*	sceptrone *recc.*
430	potior est famulus *A*	famulus est potior *E*
436	loquentem *EA*	sequentem *Bentley*
454	saeuas *A*	saeua *E*
456	paruus *EA*	partus *Housman*
485	inuius *Heinsius*	obuius *EA*
490	dabis *EA*	dabit *Leo*
505	numina *EA*	lumina *Heinsius*
508	locus *EA*	rogus *Auantius*
538	tenderant *TCV*	tenderent *E*
548	irremeabiles *PTCV*	inremeabiles *S*
590	cantibus *A*	carmine *E*
625	nobilem trunco manum *EA*	nobile in trunco caput *Axelson*
659–60	tota…Aetna *EA* (ethna)	toto…orbe *Schmidt*
683–4	incerta…unda *A*	incertis *E*…undis *E*pc
687	hinc…illinc *Kenney*	hic…illic *EA*
728	iam *Ageno*	tam *EA*
733	Cnosius *Leo*	Gnosius *EA*
742	animaeque *EA*	animoque *recc.*
769	uacuam *E*	uacuus *A*
776	sedit *EA*	sidit *Gronouius*
778	tum *E*	tunc *A*
793	et uterque *EA*	leuiterque *Madvig*
799	tegit *E*	clepit *A*
814	nouus *Bücheler*	nouos *Rutgers*
866	potuit *EA*	poterit *Bentley*
904	uirenti *A*	uirente *E*
909	Indorum est seges *Düring*	Indorum seges *EA*
920	cruorem *A*	cruore *E*

928	aequor *Heinsius*	aether *EA*
948	rutilat *E*^{ac}*A*	rutilam *E*^{pc}
980	marcentque *A*	Macetumque *E*
989	leues *A*	leuis *E*
996	omnesque *A*	omnisque *E*
1012	latebram *E*	latebras *A*
1023	timor *E*	pauor *T*^{pc}*τ recc.*
1028	pectori tela *Axelson*	pectus en telo *M. Müller*
1029	istum *EA*	istum huc *Axelson*
1051	graui *E*	grauis *A*
1057	omnes *A*	omnis *E*
1068	astraeae *EA*	asteriae *Bentley* (Asteriae)
1072	pater *EA*	pax *Wilamowitz*
1077	foue *EA*	fouens *Scaliger*
1088	omnes *A*	omnis *E*
1103	uictrice *EA*	ultrice *M*
1110	melius *A*	medius *E*
1143	domo *EA*	ad domum *Schmidt*
1158	in fetus *Fitch*	in fetu *E* (in foetu)
1167	omnes *A*	omnis *E*
1176	omnes *A*	omnis *E*
1198	neruum *A*	neruom *Baehrens*
1213	saxaque *EA*	saxa et *Bentley*
1223	latet *EA*	patet *Zwierlein*
1229	ensem *EA*	arcum *Bentley*
1270	fatum *A*	factum *E*
1285	aut *EA*	altum *Axelson*
1287	aut *τ recc.*	omitted *EA*
1312	letale *EA*	senile *Withof*
1312	ferrum pectori *recc., Delrius*	ferro pectus *EA*
1317	afflictos *EA*	afflicti *recc.*

Lacunae: Zwierlein indicates a lacuna between 19a and 19b (following Richter), 909 and 910 (following Leo), and 1091 and 1092 (following Withof). No lacunae are postulated in this edition.

Deletions: lines 703, deleted by Wakefield, and 823, deleted by Bothe, are marked for deletion by Zwierlein but are retained in this edition.

Transpositions: Zwierlein transposes 71 to follow 72 (following Peiper), 146–51 to follow 136, and (following Leo) 1135–6 to follow 1121. This edition leaves them in their consensus manuscript position. Zwierlein follows *A* in placing 1077 before 1075; this edition follows *E*.

Colometry: differences in anapaestic colometry may be found at 1062–2•, 1084•–5, 1094–5, 1097•–9, 1105•–6, 1119•–20, 1126–7.

Miscellaneous: this edition differs substantially in matters of punctuation, capitalization, and paragraphing. Major cases are signalled in the Commentary.

Orthography: some of the textual differences listed above are orthographic. Minor differences in orthography are not always noted (e.g. *gnatus* of the MSS is always written *natus*): on orthographic questions see Tarrant, *Seneca Agamemnon* (1976), 363–8, to which I am indebted.

Changes in the OCT: in later editions Zwierlein reads:

94 *oppositu* (*Zwierlein*), rather than *oppositi* (*EA*), printed in this edition.

505 *numina* (*EA*), as printed in this edition, rather than *lumina* (*Heinsius*).

553 *sidere* (*Housman*), rather than *sidera* (*EA*), printed in this edition.

814 *nouus* (*Buecheler*), as printed in this edition, rather than *nouos* (*Rutgers*).

866 *potuit* (*EA*), as printed in this edition, rather than *poterit* (*Bentley*).

874 *carpsit* (*A*), rather than *carpit* (*E*), printed in this edition.

928 *aequor* (*Heinsius*), as printed in this edition, rather than *aether* (*EA*).

1223 *latet* (*EA*), as printed in this edition, rather than *patet* (*Zwierlein*).

COMMENTARY

Commentary

The following commentary is exegetic, analytic, and interpretative. It aims to provide the reader with literary, mythological, political, cultural, linguistic, and textual information relevant to an understanding of the play and its received form. It also aims to elucidate the text dramatically as well as philologically, cross-referencing, where appropriate, dramatic/literary analysis and interpretation with the Introduction. To highlight the playwright's particular dramatization of the Hercules myth, attention has been given to treatments of the material by earlier dramatists and to the play's position within the Senecan tragic *corpus* and the Greek and Roman dramatic and literary tradition. Intertextual allusions are given especial prominence, not least because Seneca advocated the creative *imitatio* of predecessors (*Ep. Mor.* 79.6). Attention has also been given to the play's influence on the works of Seneca's successors from antiquity to the present. I have assumed in the Commentary that *Hercules* is likely to have belonged to the middle group of Seneca's plays (which perhaps included also *Troades* and *Medea*) and would certainly have predated both *Thyestes* and *Phoenissae* (see Introd. §I, 6–7). The grammatical and syntactical notes have been written with Latin students of every level in mind, who are referred on most occasions to relevant sections in Woodcock 1959 (repr. 1985). Lemmata in bold are from the translation, in bold italics from the Latin text. Lemmata concerned with stage directions are also in bold italics. Throughout the Commentary 'Senecan tragedy' refers to the eight genuine Senecan plays, the 'Senecan tragic *corpus*' to the ten plays attributed to him. References to the names of scholars other than Woodcock without the year of publication are to their editions of the relevant classical text, most often to their editions of *Hercules* or (more likely) *Hercules Furens* (for the title, see below), sometimes within an edition of the Senecan tragic *corpus*. References to the works of non-ancient dramatists are to the editions listed in the Select Bibliography. Unless otherwise indicated, all English translations in the Commentary are my own.

Title

The play is entitled *Hercules* in the 'Codex Etruscus', but *Hercules Furens* in the manuscripts of the *A* tradition, presumably changed to distinguish it from another play (which is not by Seneca), also entitled *Hercules* in the *E* tradition, but *Hercules Oetaeus* in *A*. The *E* title, *Hercules*, adopted also by Zwierlein in his OCT (1986), by Fitch in his Loeb editions (2002 and 2018), and by Giardina in his second edition (2007), seems not only more probable (*Furens* was more likely added than removed), but puts it in line with the other plays of the Senecan 'eight', all of which have single word titles, and displays more openly the play's relationship to its Euripidean predecessor. When a play takes its title from one of its characters (rather than, say, from its chorus), there is a working assumption that the character concerned constitutes the play's leading dramatic figure (as in *Phaedra*, *Oedipus*, and *Medea*). This working assumption is sometimes negated by the drama itself, as in the cases of Seneca's *Agamemnon* and *Thyestes*, but is here confirmed, although not in a straightforward way. Hercules dominates the action and language of the opening of Act III and the whole of Acts IV and V. He is absent from Acts I and II, but dominates those acts, too, together with their attendant choral odes, in that both the Chorus and the *dramatis personae* make him the focus of their discourse. See further Introd. §VII, 96.

Dramatis Personae

Juno: queen of the gods, wife and sister of Jupiter. Her persecution of Hercules as supreme index of Jupiter's infidelity resulted in Juno's arranging for Hercules' cousin Eurystheus, a great-grandson of Jupiter, to receive the Argolid throne and for Hercules to be assigned the twelve 'labours' by him.

Furies (silent): fiends/avenging spirits of the underworld, also called Erinyes or Eumenides. They avenged bloodshed, inflicted terror, and carried out curses, even sometimes = the curses themselves. Often described as the daughters of Night (see, esp., Virg. *Aen.* 12.845–52), they were also regularly conceived of as three in number: Megaera (named at 102 and *Medea* 963), Tisiphone (named at 984, *HO* 1012), and Allecto. A Fury appears onstage in the (probably) later *Thyestes* and Furies either appear or are imagined as appearing onstage in *Medea* (Boyle *ad Med.* 958–71). See further on 86–8.

Amphitryon: foster-father of Hercules and son of Alcaeus, king of Tiryns, and husband of Alcmena, a princess of Argos/Mycenae, whose father, Electryon, he accidentally slew. The couple fled to Thebes, where Amphitryon became a leading general and Hercules was born. He is now an old man.

Megara: daughter of the former Theban king, Creon, wife of Hercules and mother of his sons.

Sons of Hercules (silent): three in number, ranging in age, the youngest being an infant.

Lycus: present tyrant-king of Thebes, who lacks aristocratic pedigree and a wife, and has captured the throne of Thebes by military force.

Hercules (also called 'Alcides'): famed hero, son of Jupiter and Alcmena, whom Jupiter impregnated on a famous 'long night', while Amphitryon was absent on campaign. Praised as a civilizer of the world, bringer of peace, slayer of monsters, and enemy of the wicked (*Ben.* 1.13.3), and especially for his 'twelve labours' or impossible tasks (described at *Herc.* 222–48: see nn. *ad loc*), the last of which, the bringing of the hell-hound Cerberus from the underworld, has just been completed when the play begins. See further Introd. §VI.

Theseus: king of Athens and another of the great mythic, monster-slaying heroes. Imprisoned in the underworld, where he had gone to assist his friend Pirithous in the latter's attempt to rape Proserpina, he was recently rescued by Hercules and brought to the upper world with Cerberus. He is a major character in the (probably earlier) Senecan tragedy, *Phaedra*.

Guards, Attendants, Slaves (silent)

Chorus of Thebans: the age or gender of these Thebans is not determined. The only description of them is at the start of Hercules' triumphal procession (827–8): a 'dense throng…brows wreathed with laurel' (*densa…turba frontibus laurum gerens*).

Scene

The action takes place in Thebes before two buildings in the background, the royal palace and (stage left) a temple. In front of the temple is an altar (possibly together with statues of Jupiter and Ceres). As regularly on the imperial Roman stage, entrance to and from the palace seems to have been via the large, central double door of the *scaenae frons*, the *ualuae regiae* (Vitr. 5.6.8, Suet. *Aug.* 31.5), or *porte royale*. Entrance from/exit to the city was via stage left; entrance from/exit to the country/abroad/exile/the harbour etc. was via stage right (see Beare 1964: 248–55).

Time

The play begins just before dawn (see 123–36) and takes place during a single day. By Act IV it is midday (939). The action of four other Senecan dramas commences at dawn (*Pha.*, *Ag.*, *Oed.*, *Thy.*), as does *Octavia.*

Act Division

I have divided *Hercules* into the conventional five acts favoured by Seneca, whose choral odes seem clearly to have had an 'act-dividing' function. Of the other seven Senecan tragedies, *Ag.*, *Tro.*, *Med.*, and *Thy.* have a five-act structure. *Oed.* has six acts, and *Pha.*, too, may be considered a six-act play (see my edition p. 134). *Pho.* lacks choral odes and is either unfinished (as most scholars believe) or boldly experimental. Of the two non-Senecan plays in the *corpus*, *HO* has five acts and *Oct.* six. The five-act division is foreign to fifth-century BCE Attic tragedy and seems to have entered Roman tragedy from Hellenistic drama. Its profound influence on Renaissance tragedy clearly derives from the Senecan tragic *corpus*. Notably the Elizabethan translators of 1581 divide all the plays of the *corpus* into five acts except for *Octavia* and the (probably) incomplete *Thebais* (= *Phoenissae*), which are allocated four acts.

Stage Directions

The Latin MSS of the tragedies attributed to Seneca contain no stage directions as such, but do contain scene headings (apparently not original) indicating the speakers in a particular scene, which are reproduced in this edition. It is, however, generally Seneca's practice (and the practice of ancient dramatists as a whole) to make stage directions implicit in both the dialogue and lyric sections of a play (such implicit directions being useful not only to producers and actors of ancient plays but also to readers, who were thus able to visualize the script as dramatic performance: see Kragelund 2016: 149–50). Accordingly minimal stage directions have been added to the translation where appropriate. They are mainly concerned with the dramatic time and setting, the entry and exit of characters, costuming, props, asides, and changes of addressee, and are discussed in the Commentary when this seems required.

Disposition of Roles

The three-actor rule of Greek tragedy, regarded as prescriptive by Horace (*AP* 192), was clearly not universally adhered to in Roman tragedy, as the ancient commentators note (see Brink 1971: 253–4). Seneca's *Oedipus* and *Agamemnon* require four speaking actors (in Act II and IV of the former, in Act V of the latter). Even where a play seems designed for three speaking actors, it is not clear that only three such actors were used. *Hercules* may seem designed for four speaking actors (plus choral singers and *personae mutae*), since Hercules, Amphitryon, Megara, and Theseus are on stage together in Acts III–IV. If four speaking actors were involved, a plausible assignment of roles (giving each of the actors time to change costume) would have been: Actor 1: Juno, Lycus, Hercules; Actor 2: Amphitryon; Actor 3: Theseus; Actor 4: Megara. Theoretically, Juno could have been played by any of the speaking actors. It makes dramatic sense not to have Juno played by the Amphitryon or Megara actors, and adds nothing if played by the Theseus actor. It is dramatically and thematically best played by the protagonist, who through his voice would unite the figures of Juno, Lycus, and Hercules, underscoring the psychological and moral connections between them. Euripides has his protagonist play both Lycus and Hercules; Seneca astutely seems to take this a step further by having the relationship between Juno, *furor*, and those two *personae* embodied in the disposition of roles. Almost the same disposition of roles could have been realized with *Hercules* as a three-actor play: Actor 1: Juno, Lycus, Hercules; Actor 2: Amphitryon; Actor 3: Megara and Theseus. Note that, for the same actor to have played Megara and Theseus, a non-speaking supernumerary would have been required to replace Megara in Act III and the early part of Act IV, in which she does not speak (the switch occurring during the second choral ode and the switch back after Megara flees into the palace in Act IV): see Sutton (1986: 29). This would explain why Megara, Hercules' *animosa coniunx* (1150), whose voice is so strong in Act II, does not speak in Act III or in Act IV prior to her exit from the palace. Other dispositions are possible. But the disposition presented by Kohn (2013: 95), who has the same actor playing Megara and Hercules, is both impossible and dramatically absurd.

Masks

The dispositions of roles suggested above were facilitated on the ancient Roman stage by the use of masks. All tragic and comic drama at least from the late republic onwards was performed by actors wearing appropriate dramatic masks. For tragedy these became highly ornate and stylized with a towering *onkos* or peak. The testimony of Suetonius (*Nero* 21.3) and Dio (63.9.5) indicates also the existence of veristic masks on the Neronian stage based on the features of historical persons, viz. Nero and Poppaea. Masks are likely to have been used in any staged performance of Seneca's *Hercules* in imperial Rome, and could have been used to indicate the family resemblance of Hercules and his sons. Masks of the children modelled on the mask of Hercules (not Amphitryon) would have underlined that Hercules was killing parts of himself when he killed them, and would have increased the dramatic impact of the scene when he recognizes the corpses of his sons. They would also have signalled that Hercules and his sons were not descended from Amphitryon.

Audience

It is clear from the texts themselves that Seneca's plays were designed for performance (see Introd. §II). It is equally clear from our knowledge of Roman theatrical audiences that any audience for Seneca's *Hercules*, if it was performed in one of the great stone theatres of Rome, would have been socially, culturally, and intellectually diverse. Its members would have varied in degrees of theatrical and literary competence, in their ability to recognize and respond to literary and theatrical allusion, the utilization of theatrical space, metatheatrical language, verbal patterning and generic markers, and the evolving dramatization of moral and existential themes. When the term 'audience' is used in this commentary, there is no assumption of identical response from a monolithic body of viewers, only a working hypothesis that some members of Seneca's audience may have responded in the ways suggested.

Act I (1–124)

The form of the opening acts of Seneca's tragedies varies. The iambic monologue is favoured in *Agamemnon, Hercules, Troades, Medea*; in *Oedipus* and *Thyestes* an iambic monologue leads to iambic dialogue; in *Phoenissae* iambic dialogue is employed throughout. *Phaedra* (like the non-Senecan *Octavia*) opens with an anapaestic monody. The opening speech/song is delivered by a major human character in *Phaedra, Oedipus, Troades, Medea*, and *Phoenissae*; by a ghost in *Agamemnon* and *Thyestes*; by a deity in *Hercules*. In *Oedipus, Thyestes*, and *Hercules* a character or characters enter during (or at the start of) the monologue and are addressed; but in *Hercules* the new *dramatis personae* (Furies) do not speak. Note, too, that, as in *Agamemnon* and *Thyestes*, in *Hercules* the opening monologue is delivered by a protatic character who does not appear in the play after the first act—a device common in ancient drama (both tragedy and comedy).

Like the prologues of several Senecan tragedies (e.g. *Oed., Tro., Ag., Med.*) that of *Hercules* is partly expository in function and outlines in some detail the play's background (Jupiter's infidelities, bastards, and cosmic mistresses, Juno's anger with Thebes and hatred of Hercules, the latter's successful 'labours'), present situation (Hercules' triumphant conquest of the underworld, return to the upper world, and celestial ambitions) and future action (Hercules' madness and 'conquest of himself'). Although Euripidean prologues sometimes predict some of the play's action (e.g. the prologue of Euripides' *Hecuba*, delivered by the Ghost of Polydorus), that of Euripides' *Heracles* does not. In it (*Herac.* 1–59) the focus is on Theban history, Amphitryon's past, Hercules' labours and underworld expedition, and on the political and domestic situation in Thebes, including Amphitryon's and Megara's desperate straits. The Senecan Juno's more universal concept of time, embracing past, present, and future, anticipates the action of the second half of the play, providing structural unity to its bipartite plot. It frames the whole action of the play, including its second half, as permeated with Juno. For the question of how this relates to the issue of personal agency and responsibility, see Introd. §VII, 114–15.

Some aspects of this prologue need particular attention. Juno is the only divine being apart from the Furies to appear in Senecan tragedy (it is to be noted that Hera does not appear onstage in any extant Greek tragedy: see Fitch: 44, n. 57). Her wrath gives the prologue an unusual mythic and literary authority. It not only realizes onstage the legendary hostility between herself and one of Jupiter's most famous 'illegitimate' sons, but it also reminds Seneca's audience of the role she played in the great epics of Rome, the *Aeneid* of Virgil and *Metamorphoses* of Ovid. Her literary status is important; for this post-Virgilian/Ovidian figure has a clear metaliterary and metatheatrical function; she will shape and prescript the play in the manner in which Seneca's protatic characters do in other tragedies: the Ghost of Thyestes in *Agamemnon*, the Fury in *Thyestes*. And she will employ appropriate language as she does so. But, unlike either of those prologue-*personae*, she is a figure of Roman religious authority and awe, who is in Rome not only *not* displaced, as she is in *Hercules*, but occupies a position at the summit of the city's religious hierarchy with a revered 'place' in the temple of Iuppiter Optimus Maximus, the oldest and most important temple in Rome. Simultaneously Roman, Greek, religious and literary, this displaced Juno expands the territory of the play. While the *locus* of *Hercules* is technically the city of Thebes, the cosmic allusions in Juno's speech make the real *locus* the *mundus* itself: heaven, earth, hell. Hercules has been to hell, returned to earth, aims at heaven. This prologue frames the issues of this play as cosmic: the boundaries and structures of existence.

Noteworthy too, as in other Senecan prologues, is the sustained focus on the psychology of the prologue-speaker, whose narrative of events is intensely subjective, shaped and coloured by her emotions. Until line 86 or thereabouts, when (so I interpret see n. *ad loc.*) the Furies enter, the monologue is a closed soliloquy, delivered by a protatic character (cf. the ghosts of *Agamemnon* and *Thyestes*), who embodies the dark desires and feelings, especially the *ira* and *furor*, to be laid out and played out in the dramatic action itself. Her psychologically intense speech not only exhibits a train of emotion and thinking from which she creates and allusively prescripts the main plot of the play but sets the mood for that play, introduces some of its major themes, and anticipates through image and motif the dramatic events to come (especially the murderous *furor* of Hercules and the latter's destruction of 'place'): see Introd. §VII, 70–3. Because a 'raging Juno', *Iuno furens* (see on 109–12), would inevitably conjure up memories of Virgil's *Aeneid* (of which there are several linguistic and situational echoes: see on 1–5, 19–29, 35–40, 46–52, 52–6, 86–99, 92–9, 100–3, 104–9, 123–4), this prologue-speaker 'Romanizes' the play from its very inception, arriving onstage not only from heaven but from the pages of Virgil's epic, making of her intended victim a 'pre-formulation of Aeneas' (Smith 1997: 38), as Virgil himself had done in *Aeneid* 8 (362–9: a passage admired by Seneca at *Ep. Mor.* 18.12, 31.11). Juno's complaints also resonate throughout Ovid's *Metamorphoses* (Seneca is especially indebted in the prologue's opening lines to the Callisto episode of *Met.* 2.2.508–17; see also *Met.* 3.259ff., 4.447–511, where, as at *Aen.* 7.286–340, Juno employs a Fury as infernal assistant). But only in the *Aeneid* does Juno, as here, utter the work's first speech and initiate its entire action (*Aen.* 1.34–49). *Hercules'* prologue clearly impressed Valerius Flaccus, who imitates it in the representation of his own Juno (*Arg.* 1.111–19, 3.510–20). For the prologue's 'pronounced metatheatrical function', in which Juno 'embodies the creative power of the author' (Schiesaro 2003: 186), see on 109–12, 118–22, and Introd. §VII, 72.

The prologue is bipartite in structure with a closural couplet. Part I (1–74: Juno's Complaints) moves through five stages: (i) (1–18) Juno exiled from heaven: Jupiter's whores hold the sky (with catalogue of examples 6–18); (ii) (19–29) Eternal war pledged with Thebes, esp. Hercules; (iii) (30–46) All attempts at war with Hercules failed: his *uirtus* and labours brought him glory; (iv) (46–63) His latest labour in the underworld was a mighty triumph; (v) (63–74) His next step: the conquest of heaven. Part II (75–122: Juno's Revenge) moves through four stages: (i) (75–85) Old and new monsters pointless: Hercules must war with himself; (ii) (86–99) Juno summons Furies and will summon other fiends from hell; (iii) (100–12) The Furies are commanded to make Hercules and Juno mad; (iv) (112–22) Juno (infuriated) prays for/predicts Hercules' slaughter of his sons by means of his *uirtus* and with Juno's help. Close (123–4): Let the war (and play) begin; dawn rises. Part I of the speech indexes in an emotional but relatively analytic manner the many markers of Juno's distress. The primary mood of the verbs is indicative. In the second part of the speech (75ff.), in which Juno articulates her vengeance, the emotionality increases and the language and its modality become more turbulent.

Notice, too, as in many of Seneca's prologues, a dramatic use of the vertical structure of the Roman stone theatre. If the play had been performed in one of Rome's permanent theatres, the movement from the contemplation of, and reference to, the heavens in the opening lines (1–29), to earth, sky, and the underworld (30–63), the heavens (63–74), the underworld, the Furies, and finally heaven again (75–124), accompanied by appropriate gestures from the actor, would have made immediate, dramatic use of the verticality of the theatrical space. (The *cauea* of the Theatre of Marcellus, for example, rose to a height of *c.*32 metres: Sear 2006, 135.) Cf. the similar use of the verticality of the cosmos in the speeches of Hercules, esp. at 592–615, 926–39, 1202–18, 1321–41, which incorporate into the dramatic action the whole theatrical space ('sympathetic space', E. A. Schmidt 2014: 539). See further on 1054–1137 (introd.).

For further discussion of Act I and its dramatic and thematic function in the play, see Introd. §VII.

Metre: iambic trimeters. See Introd. §IX.

The scene is Thebes: a public space before two buildings in the background, the royal palace and (stage left) a temple: the palace/royal house (210, 1001,

1007, 1035, 1143, 1228) and the temple (506, 521, 616–17) are explicitly mentioned during the course of the play and figure in the dramatic action. For the position of the temple as stage left, see on 616–17.

In front of the temple is an altar (perhaps with statues of Jupiter and Ceres): an altar features prominently in the play: in the Lycus scene (503), in Hercules' sacrifice scene (899ff.) and at the end of Act IV, where Amphitryon offers himself as sacrifice (1040–1). Amphitryon and Megara presumably pray at the altar in Act II. In Euripides' *Heracles* there is an altar to Zeus the Saviour (48). Statues of Jupiter and Ceres are perhaps indicated by the opening prayers in Act II to these deities by Amphitryon and Megara and by Lycus' remark that Megara and Amphitryon are standing next to their *praesides deos*, 'guardian gods' (356: see n. *ad loc.*). There are also later addresses to Jupiter (516–19, 963–5), which would be rendered more powerful if addressed to a statue of the deity onstage. One effect of a statue of Ceres on stage would be to remind the audience of the Eleusinian Mysteries and their bridge between life and death. For references to the Eleusinian Mysteries in the play see 300–2, 842–7, and nn. *ad locc.*

The time is just before dawn: see 123–4.

JUNO *is alone onstage*: as are the prologue-speakers of *Agamemnon*, *Medea*, *Troades*, and (probably) *Oedipus*.

1–18 Juno's displacement

1–5 Juno announces herself and her exile from heaven.

Soror Tonantis/Sister of the Thunder-god: a forceful opening, the earliest of the Senecan tragedies in which the prologue-speaker identifies her-/himself in the initial words of the play. Cf. the opening of *Phoenissae* in which Oedipus identifies himself with a telling opening phrase: *caeci parentis*, 'blind father' (*Pho.* 1). See also *Agamemnon* and *Thyestes*, in which again a protatic supernatural prologue-speaker self-identifies early in the opening speech (*Ag.* 4, *Thy.* 3). In *Oedipus*, *Medea*, and *Troades*, the non-protatic opening speakers identify themselves less immediately (*Oed.* 12, *Med.* 8, *Tro.* 36); in *Phaedra* the prologue is a monody, whose singer never actually identifies himself (nor does he need to). The divine prologue is quite common in Euripides, where, however, deities regularly self-name in the initial lines (Hermes, *Ion* 4; Poseidon, *Tro.* 2; Kypris/ Aphrodite, *Hipp.* 2; Dionysus, *Bacch.* 2). In *Alcestis* the divine prologue-speaker (Apollo) does not self-name in his opening speech but makes allusive self-identificatory references, as here. Seneca's Juno does eventually self-name at 109. Note that the prologue-speaker of Euripides'

Heracles, Amphitryon, identifies himself (by self-naming) in the play's second line.

Identifying oneself on stage through proclaiming a family relationship is a standard mode of character identification in the tragedies: see e.g. Clytemnestra at *Ag.* 110–11, Electra at *Ag.* 910, Oedipus at *Oed.* 12, Jocasta at *Oed.* 81, Phaedra at *Pha.* 91–2, Andromache at *Tro.* 415–18. Other modes include (most obviously) self-naming, which is found at *Ag.* 4 (Thyestes), *Ag.* 233 (Aegisthus), *Ag.* 918 (Strophius), *Med.* 8 (Medea), *Tro.* 36 (Hecuba), *Tro.* 863 (Helen), *Thy.* 3 (Tantalus), *Thy.* 180 (Atreus). Juno, as observed above, will self-name at 109 (see further *ad loc.*), but the device is never used for character identification in this play. Sometimes a Senecan character will identify her/himself by indicating a relationship to a character on stage (e.g. Nurse at *Med.* 157, Jason at *Med.* 435, Jocasta at *Oed.* 81, Tantalus at *Thy.* 421–2), or by using other language which identifies her/himself immediately (e.g. Hercules at 592–615, the Old Corinthian at *Oed.* 784–5, Thyestes at *Thy.* 404–10). A new character may also be identified simply by being addressed (e.g. Calchas at *Tro.* 352–9, Nurse at *Pha.* 177–9). Often, too, a character or chorus onstage will identify a new, entering character: see e.g. *Oed.* 202–5 (Creon), 288–90 (Tiresias and Manto), 911–14 (Messenger); *Tro.* 518 (Ulysses); *Med.* 177–8 (Creon); *Pha.* 829–34 (Theseus), 989–90 (Messenger); *Ag.* 388–91 (Eurybates), 778–81 (Agamemnon); and on 202–4, 329–31 below. Costumes, masks and props would also play an important role in character identification.

Note the bitterness of Juno's self-identification, which is underscored through evident allusion to her former and more powerful Virgilian self, where she was 'queen and both sister and wife of Jupiter' (*regina Iouisque et soror et coniunx*: Virg. *Aen.* 1.46–7). Indeed *soror et coniunx*, 'sister and wife' was a regular title for Juno (and Hera, Hom. *Il.* 16.432, 18.356): see e.g. *Ag.* 340, Cic. *ND* 2.66, Hor. *Odes* 3.3.64, Ov. *Met.* 13.574, Aug. *CD* 4.10; see also *magni…consors sceptri*, 'consort of the great sceptre' (*Ag.* 340–1). Also relevant is the Ovidian Juno's self-description (*soror et coniunx—certe soror*, 'Sister and wife—at least sister', *Met.* 3.266), uttered in the context of Semele's impregnation by Jupiter and which here seems intentionally echoed. The Senecan Juno's words themselves seem echoed in Octavia's self-description in the (probably) Flavian *fabula praetexta*, *Octavia*: *soror Augusti, non uxor ero*, 'I'll be Augustus' sister, not wife', *Oct.* 658 (cf. Octavia's *tantum sororem*, 'only a sister', at Tac. *Ann.* 14.64.2)—see also the Valerian Juno's proclamation: *en ego nunc regum soror*, 'Look, I, now sister of kings' (*Arg.* 3.514). Note Deianira's address to Juno as *coniunx Tonantis* at *HO*

257—an address in which she reenacts Juno's *ira* towards Hercules. Matthew Gwinne was to continue this echoic tradition, when he began Act V of his *Nero* (1603) with the Ghost of Octavia declaring somewhat playfully: *Soror Neronis, nec tamen uere soror,* | *nedum uxor,* 'Sister of Nero, yet not truly sister, | Still less wife'. One problem for a late Julio-Claudian audience of Seneca's *Hercules* was that the relational paradoxes of Olympus (*soror et coniunx*) had become the norm at the imperial court: Agrippina was niece and wife of Claudius and rumoured lover of her son Nero; Octavia was stepsister and wife of Nero.

The description of Jupiter here as *Tonans*, 'Thunder-god' or 'Thunderer', a title used by Seneca most often in this play (840, 914, 1010; elsewhere in the tragedies only at *Ag.* 356, 595, and *Med.* 59), seems itself to reflect the separated state of the divine couple. In Rome Juno, together with Jupiter's daughter, Minerva/Pallas, shared with the supreme god the great temple of Iuppiter Optimus Maximus on the Capitol. She did not share the nearby separate and splendid temple of Iuppiter Tonans, dedicated by Augustus in 22 BCE.

hoc enim solum...nomen/for that's my Sole name: echoes again of Virgil's *Aeneid*, viz. the abandoned Dido's complaint that Aeneas' 'sole name' (*solum nomen*) now was 'guest', *hospes* (*Aen.* 4.324). *Nomen*, one's 'name', was a core concept in Roman culture, whose elite members were much obsessed with perpetuating their 'names' through family and inscribed monuments. Those at the very top of the social pyramid were also concerned with enhancing personal nomenclature with additional names derived (especially) from foreign conquest. They sought through the consulship (at least in the republic) to impose their name on time itself. The 'eternal name', *aeternum nomen*, i.e. everlasting fame, was perhaps the central pursuit of elite Rome, as Virgil explored in his *Aeneid*. False names and nominal confusion are thus culturally important issues in the tragedies: see e.g. Oedipus' and Jocasta's concern with the morality and falseness of names (*nostri nominis fas ac nefas*, 'sanctity and sin of our names', *Oed.* 1023, *nomine haud uero*, 'by an untrue name', *Oed.* 1035), Oedipus' whole 'fusion of names' (*mixtum nomen*, 388 below), Thyestes' diatribe against the 'false names' (*falsis...nominibus*, *Thy.* 446) given to 'great things', Phaedra's desire to take on a 'more lowly name' (*humilius nomen*, *Pha.* 610), as she erotically pursues Hippolytus. Note also Seneca's focus on *falsa nomina* in the prose works, see e.g. *Ben.* 1.5.5, *Ep. Mor.* 110.8, 119.12. What Juno claims here is that *coniunx* is for her a false name, as it will be for Hercules by the end of the play: see further on 19–29 (*nouerca*). For earlier preoccupation with this issue, see Cic. *Cluent.* 199, Ov. *Met.* 10.346–8. Mark Seneca's rare use of *enim*, its unique appearance in the play. It occurs only four times elsewhere in Senecan drama.

*alienum Iouem/*Alien Jove: *alienus* is a difficult epithet to translate; it seems here primarily to mean, as Fitch notes *ad loc.*, 'belonging to another' (see *OLD* 1b), though the sense of 'alien/hostile' (*OLD* 7) seems also present. It is found regularly in erotic contexts (see e.g. Ter. *Hec.* 158, Ov. *Rem.* 681), where it is sometimes translated as 'estranged'. The English word 'alien' is perhaps as close as one can get without a paraphrase. For *semper* qualifying an epithet in *Hercules*, see 98, 1256.

*templa summi... aetheris/*high heaven's precincts: a remodelling of the Ennian (*Ann.* frags 48, 54–5 Skutsch) and Lucretian (e.g. 1.1064, 2.1001, 6.1228) phrase *caeli templa* to embrace *templa* in the sense of both 'regions' (*OLD* 4) and 'sacred precincts' (*OLD* 2c). Behind the Latin phrases lies Aeschylus' τέμενος αἰθέρος, *Pers.* 365.

*uidua/*husbandless: *uiduus* is a common word in Senecan tragedy, meaning not 'widowed' but 'lacking a male protector or owner'; it is even used of *uirgines* (*Ag.* 195). Seneca applies it to the Amazons: see below 246, 542, *Tro.* 13, *Med.* 215. See also *HO* 334 (Deianira). There is also a secondary syntax and meaning here: *uidua* can also be taken as modifying *templa*, which are here 'widowed', 'bereft' of Juno. Cf. Seneca's use of *uiduus* of the lands of Thebes 'bereft/widowed of their tillers' at *Oed.* 111–12 (*uiduas colonis... terras*).

*locum/*place: the first occurrence of this seminal word, which occurs twenty-six times in the play, viz. lines 4, 22, 36, 199, 332, 344, 354, 503, 576, 609, 673, 706, 707, 708, 744, 748, 794, 927, 1013, 1138, 1163, 1221, 1238, 1321, 1331, 1340. The grand climax of the word's use occurs in Hercules' statement of the destruction of *locus* (1331). Juno will not be the only figure in this play to be displaced. See further Introd. §VII, 123–4.

*pulsa/*exiled: Ovid's Juno also talks about her 'banishment' (*pulsa... Iunone*, *Met.* 2.525).

*paelicibus/*whores: *paelex* is a married man's mistress. The word occurs regularly in Senecan tragedy, *Octavia* and *Hercules Oetaeus*, where it is used not only by married women or goddesses of their rivals (see *Ag.* 185, 253, 258, 1002; *Med.* 462, 495). Its application to Juno's rivals is found as early as Plautus (see e.g. *Merc.* 690, where it is applied to Hercules' mother); it is common in Ovid. For a similar concern with a husband's *paelex*, cf. Seneca's Clytemnestra, whose rage against her husband's Trojan paramour (*Ag.* 185: *paelice... barbara*; 1002: *regii paelex tori*) may be one of the models for Juno's wrath here. In the Senecan tragic *corpus* the more prosaic term, *adultera*, is notably avoided, but not *adulter* or *adulteri*: see *Ag.* 884, 955; *Pha.* 988; *Med.* 456.

tellus colenda est/Earth must be my home: *colo* is used regularly of inhabiting a place, and especially of deities taking up residence to protect a place and be worshipped in it (*OLD* 2). Notably Virgil uses the verb of Juno's relationship to Carthage (*Aen.* 1.16). Here the inhabitation is less willing.

paelices caelum tenent/whores hold the sky: an echo of the Ovidian Juno's complaint about Callisto (called *paelex* at *Met.* 2.508): *pro me tenet altera caelum,* 'another holds the sky in my place' (*Met.* 2.513). Fitch *ad loc.* notes the chiastic alliterative pattern in line 5 (*t-l-c-c-l-t*), which produces a neat, structured, epigrammatic line on the model of a *sententia* (for which see on 125–204 introd.). For similarly epigrammatic climaxes to a play's opening lines, cf. *Oed.* 5, *Ag.* 4.

6–18 Juno's statement of line 5 is not left uncorroborated. A catalogue of Jupiter's mistresses and bastards (and their associated enshrinements in the sky) follows: Callisto/Great Bear, Taurus and Europa, the Pleiads and Orion, Perseus, the Gemini/Tyndarids, Apollo and Diana, Bacchus and Semele, Ariadne and her Crown. Such catalogues (whether of places, persons, deities, sinners, constellations, etc.) are a well-known aspect of Seneca's style and regularly feature, as here, in the early part of the prologues of his plays: *Pha.* 1–30, *Ag.* 12–21, *Med.* 1–12, *Tro.* 8–13, *Thy.* 6–12, *Pho.* 12–26. For catalogues later in this play, see on 213–48, 332–6, 480–9, 524–91 (introd.), 750–9, 1163–8, 1321–41. Lists of Jupiter's mistresses/rapes are common in Latin poetry: see e.g. *Pha.* 301–8, *Oct.* 203–12, *HO* 551–3, [Virg.] *Aetna* 89–90, Stat. *Silu.* 1.2.134–6. The *locus classicus* of Jupiter as serial rapist is Arachne's searing indictment at Ov. *Met.* 6.103–14. Worth observing is that the order of Jupiter's bastards in lines 14–23 (Pollux and Castor, Bacchus, and then Hercules) is followed by Seneca's dramatic successor at *Oct.* 208–12.

6–11 *Hinc... hinc... illinc... hinc... hinc*/here... Here... There... Here... Here: deictic words indexing Juno's gestures as she points to various parts of the night-sky; hence the stage-direction at line 6. For this gestural use of demonstratives in a Senecan prologue, cf. *Ag.* 7–11. For their use to enhance narrative immediacy, see *Ag.* 902–7 (the murder of Agamemnon).

Arctos: the northern constellation of the 'Great Bear' (Ursa Maior), 'Plough', or (USA) 'Big Dipper', known as *Helice* to the Greeks, formed, according to legend, by the apotheosis of the Arcadian nymph, Callisto (for whose rape by Jupiter, see Ov. *Met.* 2.409–530, *Fas.* 2.153–92): hence it is referred to at *Oed.* 477 as 'Arcady's star', *sidus Arcadium*. This seven-star constellation (130 below) was also known as the 'Wain', *plaustrum*. The constellation is mentioned later by both the Chorus (129–31) and Hercules (1140). See further on 125–31.

alta parte glacialis poli/soars by the icy pole: lit. 'in the high region of the icy pole'. The northern pole ('id est septemtrionalis', Trevet *ad loc.*) and the constellations of the Bears are regularly associated with ice or cold: see 129, 1140, *Pha.* 288, Virg. *Aen.* 6.16, Ov. *Met.* 2.173, Stat. *Silu.* 3.5.19. The 'soaring' (*alta parte*, lit. 'in the high part') perhaps alludes to another property of the Great Bear: as a circumpolar constellation it never sank beneath the horizon in the northern hemisphere (Virg. *Geo.* 1.245–6, Ov. *Met.* 2.530, *Fas.* 2.191–2), a phenomenon to which Seneca draws attention in several of the tragedies: *Oed.* 507, *Ag.* 69–70, *Med.* 404–5, *Thy.* 476–7. Juno's words are echoed by the Chorus at 129.

sublime classes sidus Argolicas agit/Guiding the Argive ships as their lodestar: the Great Bear was used by Greek sailors to find north. The 'Little Bear' (Ursa Minor), used by the Phoenicians, served this purpose better: Arat. *Phaen.* 36–44, Germ. *Arat.* 39–47. See also *Med.* 695–7, Cic. *ND* 2.105–6, Ov. *Her.* 18.149, *Tr.* 4.3.1–2, *Fas.* 3.107–8. Note the interlocking of pairs of adjectives and nouns in a parallel pattern aBAb (where capital letters signal nouns and lower-case letters their modifiers). Such an interlocking, parallel arrangement (sometimes in other forms: abAB, AbaB, ABab) was a neoteric poetic practice (see e.g. Catullus 64) and is common in Senecan tragedy: see e.g. below 14, 38, 60, 62, 81, 82, 83, 88, 221, 223, 236, 240, 246, 248, 274, etc.; *Ag.* 54, 194, 231, 408, 424, 425, 436, 451, 479, 505, 506, 551; *Pha.* 85, 318; *Tro.* 240; *Pho.* 95. For such verbal interlocking on a chiastic pattern, see on 11–18 below. *Argolicus*, 'Argive', like *Argiuus*, is sometimes used metonymically (= 'Greek'), as here and *Tro.* 813, but sometimes not (= 'Argive'), as at *Ag.* 806. Sometimes it may intimate both: see 59 and n. *ad loc.* For Argos, see on 1035–8.

recenti uere/in the early spring: Taurus was traversed by the sun from April to May, and was thus associated with 'early spring'. The ablative is a locatival ablative of time (Woodcock §54).

laxatur dies/day unbinds: i.e. 'extends'; for *laxare* similarly used of time, cf. *Med.* 420.

Tyriae per undas uector Europae/Tyrian Europa's sea-ferry: the constellation of Taurus, 'the Bull', had its mythological origins in the catasterism of the bull (alias Jupiter) which raped Europa, daughter of the Phoenician king, Agenor (or sometimes in the catasterism of the cow into which Io was transformed): Ov. *Fas.* 5.603–20, Hyg. *Astr.* 2.21, Amp. 2.2, [Eratosth.]

Catast. 14. For the rape of Europa, see also *Pha.* 303–8; Ov. *Met.* 2.836ff., 6.103–7; *HO* 552–3; *Oct.* 206, 766–7.

timendum ratibus ac ponto gregem...exerunt/flock, Creators of fear for ships and ocean: the *Pleiades* (see next n.) were particularly associated with storms: Ov. *Ars* 1.409, Stat. *Silu.* 1.3.95. Lucan applies the epithet *imbrifera*, 'rain-bringing' (8.852). The association seems derived from the morning setting of the constellation in November: Hes. *WD* 618–23; Arat. *Phaen.* 1065–6, 1084–5; VF 2.357ff. The rhetorical paradox that 'ocean' should be afraid of its own storms is rendered persuasive by its conjunction with 'ships', *ratibus*. *Gregem...exerunt* is a singular collocation; the standard objects of *exerere*, applied to heavenly bodies, are, as Fitch notes *ad loc.*, *caput* or *uultus* or *sim.* For *grex*, 'flock', of the *Atlantides/Pleiades*, see *Med.* 96: *Pleiadum greges*, 'flocks of Pleiads'.

passim uagantes...Atlantides/far-strayed daughters of Atlas: the *Pleiades* or Pleiads, the famous cluster of seven stars found in the constellation of Taurus. The standard legend was that they were originally the seven daughters of Atlas and Pleione, who were pursued by the great hunter, Orion. Three of the daughters (Maia, Electra, Taygete) bore children to Jupiter: viz. Mercury, Dardanus, Lacedaemon. A unique version of the myth in Callimachus (frag. 693 Pfeiffer) has them as daughters of the Amazon queen. Note the line-ending in a polysyllabic Greek name, as at 244, 246, 484, 758. For the 'wandering' nature of stars, see 126 below, *Pha.* 962, *Thy.* 834, *Oct.* 1, 389, Lucr. 2.1031, Virg. *Aen.* 9.21.

11–18 *ferro...terret Orion deos*/Orion's sword frightens gods: lit. 'Orion frightens gods with his sword'. Orion is included in this catalogue of Jupiter's bastards, although he was the product not of Jupiter's semen but his (and Neptune's and Mercury's) urine, with no *paelex* involved: see Ov. *Fas.* 5.531–6. Orion was generally thought to be (amorously) pursuing the Pleiads (Hes. *WD* 619–21, Quint. Smyrn. 5.367–9), but not by Statius (see below). Seneca reapplies the language to Atreus: *ultro deos terret*, 'even frightens gods' (*Thy.* 704–5). *Deos*, 'gods', here may be general or specific (with reference to the stars, as at Stat. *Silu.* 1.1.44–5, *quanto mucrone minatur...et sidera terret Orion*, 'with so great a blade Orion threatens...and frightens stars') or both. This is Orion's only appearance in Seneca. The initial *o* is here long.

suasque Perseus aureus stellas/And golden Perseus...his constellation: the hero Perseus was the bastard son of Jupiter by the Argive princess, Danae, whom the god visited as a shower of gold (Ov. *Met.* 4.611). Hence 'golden Perseus' has a double sense: both 'golden', as stars are sometimes said to be (see e.g. Virg. *Aen.* 2.488, Ov. *Fas.* 3.516, Manil. 5.539, 5.723) and 'golden' because of his mother's 'golden' impregnation (he is termed *aurige-nae*, 'gold-born', by Ovid at *Met.* 5.250). See Fitch and Billerbeck *ad loc.* As a renowned slayer of monsters, he obviously functions as a precursor of Hercules, whose mother Alcmena was Perseus' granddaughter. Among his heroic triumphs were the decapitation of the Gorgon Medusa and the rescuing of Andromeda from the sea-monster, Cetus. The constellation of Perseus (Manil. 5.22) is situated in the northern sky near that of his beloved Andromeda. Note the chiastic verbal patterning (adjective/noun or noun/ adjective in agreement encompassing another adjective/noun or noun/ adjective in agreement: also, like the parallel pattern noted on 6–11 above, a neoteric practice), not uncommon in the tragedies: see e.g. 59, 94, 103, 124, 220, 225, 231, 238, 367, 508, 1034, 1146, etc. below; *Ag.* 127, 136, 745, 1006; *Pha.* 156; *Oed.* 1, 46; *Tro.* 217, 456; *Med.* 4, 216; *Thy.* 175, 647, 1039; *Pho.* 80, 157, 162. Here the arrangement is aBbA, as at 59, 231, 508.

clara gemini signa Tyndaridae/**twin Tyndarids' bright stars**: the Tyndarids are the Spartan heroes, Castor and Pollux, twin sons of Leda and either Jupiter or Tyndareus (or both—their paternity was controversial), and brothers of Helen of Troy. From Homer (*Il.* 3.237) onwards Pollux was famed as a boxer, Castor as a horseman; both joined Jason in the Argonautic expedition (their role as Argonauts dates from Pindar: *Pyth.* 4.171–2). They were paradigms of *pietas*, 'piety/brotherly love', renowned for their mutual affection (Ov. *Tr.* 4.5.30) and for sharing the immortality granted to one of them (Hyg. *Fab.* 80, Apollod. 3.137). Known as the Dioscuri or 'Heavenly Twins', they were identified with the constellation Gemini (referred to at *Thy.* 853), and were often thought of as the patrons of sailors. Some commentators point to an anachronism on the grounds that at the mythic time of the play's action the brothers seem not yet to have been catasterized. There was a temple to Castor and Pollux in the south-east corner of the Roman Forum, dating from the early fifth century BCE and restored by Tiberius in 6 CE. Note the interlocking appositional phrasing: see on 550–7 below. For the rape of Leda by Jupiter, see *Pha.* 301–2, *Oct.* 764–5, Ov. *Met.* 6.109. With *clara…signa*, 'bright stars', cf. Horace's nearly synonymous expression, *lucida sidera*, 'shining stars', used of the Gemini at *Odes* 1.3.2.

quibusque natis/**And those whose birth**: the reference is to Apollo/the Sun and Diana/the Moon. The traditional myth held that the island Delos drifted freely in the Aegean, unfixed to any position in the sea, until Latona/ Leto gave birth on the island to Apollo and Diana/Artemis: see Callim. *Hymn* 4.23–54. The story is also referenced at 453, *Ag.* 369–74, *Thy.* 595, and is found frequently in Roman verse: e.g. Virg. *Aen.* 3.75–6; Prop.

4.6.27-8; Ov. *Met.* 6.190-1, 333-4, 15.336-7; Stat. *Theb.* 8.197-8; Claud. *Rap.* 2.2.34-5; Dracont. *Rom.* 10.594-5. Cf. Horace's description: *natalem ...Delon Apollinis,* 'Apollo's natal Delos' (*Odes* 1.21.10). Fitch *ad loc.* argues for a problem here, since the sun has not yet taken its place in the sky. But the actor playing Juno can point to the moon in the (imagined) dark sky and gesture to the east, from where the sun is beginning to rise.

Bacchus aut Bacchi parens/Bacchus and Bacchus' mother: Bacchus (Greek Dionysus) was the child of Jupiter and the Theban princess, Semele, daughter of King Cadmus. Jupiter killed the pregnant Semele when he appeared to her as a thunderbolt (as a result of Juno's trickery of the hated Semele), and Bacchus was taken from Semele's womb and sewn in Jupiter's thigh until the time of his birth. See Ov. *Met.* 3.259-315, and *Med.* 84, where he is called 'the child of pitiless lightning', *proles fulminis improbi.* Bacchus was the god of vegetation, vines, wine, intoxication, and ecstasy, of poets, drama, and poetic inspiration. Berkoff's description (2000: 168), 'god of bursting life', captures him well. His cult, thought in antiquity to have come from the east (see *Oed.* 114-23, Eur. *Bacch.* 13-22), where in some versions he was born (*Hom. Hym.* 1.7-10), involved wild, ecstatic behaviour; its practitioners were usually women (Maenads, Bacchantes). In the Roman tradition he is sometimes linked with Hercules as a paradigm of heroic conquest (see e.g. Virg. *Aen.* 6.801-5) and as a model for Alexander the Great (*Ben.* 1.13.2, 7.3.1; *Ep. Mor.* 94.63). His divinity was not accepted immediately, and he had to impose his cult violently on Thebes, of which he became the patron deity. For the divinity of his mother, see Pindar *Ol.* 2.25-6, Philostrat. *Imag.* 1.14, Nonnus 8.408ff. One version claimed that it was through the agency of Bacchus that his mother became a goddess (Diod. Sic. 4.25.4, Apollod. 3.5.3). For Bacchus' fear of Juno, his 'angry stepmother' (*irata nouerca*), see *Oed.* 418. With the polyptoton Billerbeck compares Ov. *Am.* 2.18.24: *Hippolytique parens Hippolytusque.* Polyptoton is not always noted in the Commentary; but for other instances in *Hercules* (including verbal and adjectival polyptoton), see e.g. 41-2, 60, 116, 266-7, 274-5, 307-8, 487, 590-1, 644, 706, 726-7, 1167-8. For verbal polyptoton, see on 112-18.

superos/gods: for the ambiguity of this term, see on 46-52.

ne qua pars probro uacet/So no part lack disgrace: ironic purpose clauses, not uncommon in Latin literature (see e.g. Sall. *Cat.* 16.3; Virg. *Aen.* 8.205-6; Ov. *Her.* 4.61, *Ars* 2.359, *Met.* 1.151, 10.468, 13.496, 15.760; Luc. 8.603-4; Juv. 5.120), are a regular feature of Senecan tragic dialogue: cf. e.g. *Ag.* 32, 184-5; *Tro.* 431; *Thy.* 689-90, 717, 891; *Pha.* 1250-1; *Pho.* 121, 271, 513-14. Note here, too, an example of tragic Seneca's so-called *dictio nominis*, 'noun style' (Smereka 1936), i.e. the favouring of nouns and periphrases involving nouns rather than verbs or adverbs and verbs to articulate meaning. It is noticeable that the tragedies attest a much higher proportion of nouns to verbs than do the prose works (where a *dictio uerbi*, 'verb style' may be found). Seneca's *dictio nominis* is evident in the prologue (see e.g. 26–9, 36, 49, 61, 71) and throughout the play (where it will only occasionally be noted). For *uacare* in the sense of 'empty of/free from' *probrum/flagitium* or the like, see *Med.* 279, *Ag.* 279, *Thy.* 321, and Cic. *Fam.* 7.3.4.

puellae serta Cnosiacae/crown of the Cnossian girl: the garland worn by Ariadne, daughter of King Minos, whose palace was at Cnossos in Crete. She assisted Theseus in his escapade with the Minotaur, was abandoned by him on the island of Naxos, but was subsequently married to the god Bacchus, who turned her (via her garland) into a goddess (*utque perenni | sidere clara foret sumptam de fronte coronam | immisit caelo* ('and that she might shine | As a perennial star he took the crown from her brow | And sent it to the heavens', Ov. *Met.* 8.177–9). The resulting constellation was the Corona Borealis. Ariadne's catasterism, which was taken from the Greek tradition (see e.g. Aratus 71–3, Ap. Rhod. 3.1002–4), was popular with Roman poets: Cat. 66.59–61, Virg. *Geo.* 1.222, Hor. *Odes* 2.19.13–14, Prop. 3.17.7–8, Ov. *Ars* 1.555–8, *Fas.* 3.459–516. Note Juno's dismissive term for Ariadne, viz. *puella*, the standard term for a Roman elegist's mistress. According to Watson (1985: 43–4), the word (which substantially replaced *puera*) 'retained the emotional associations of a diminutive', perhaps apparent in Juno's contemptuous use. It is used also by Manilius (1.323) in his description of the Corona: *Cnosia desertae...monumenta puellae*, 'Cnossian monument of the deserted girl'—a description to which Seneca may be indebted. *Puella* is found only four times in Senecan tragedy (*Herc.* 18, 466, *Oed.* 479, *Ag.* 349), where the standard word for 'girl' is *uirgo*. Ariadne, of course, was Bacchus' wife when the catasterism occurred. For allusions elsewhere to Ariadne in Seneca's tragedies, see *Pha.* 245, 662–6, 760; *Oed.* 488–502. See esp. *Pha.* 663–6, where Ariadne, qua the constellation, is addressed by her sister, Phaedra.

19–29 Juno proclaims undying hatred for Alcmena and Hercules, and pledges eternal war. Hera's/Juno's angry pursuit of Heracles/Hercules, one of the firmest constituents of the Hercules myth, dates from Homer (*Il.* 14.249–56, 15.24–8, 18.117–19).

Sed sero querimur/But my complaints come late: cf. Medea, who similarly early in her prologue complains about her complaints, although Medea's criticism is of their vanity: *querelas uerbaque in cassum sero*, 'Are my complaints and words sown in vain?' (*Med.* 26). Cf. also 63, where Juno

again uses the complaint motif to effect a transition in her speech. For the
motif of 'lateness', see also 622, 692, 728, 732, 864–5, 1203, and e.g. *Ag.* 242,
Tro. 208, *Thy.* 487, 778, 964, and *Breu. Vit.* 6.2, *Ben.* 1.1.1, where *sero querimur* occurs again. Line 19 cannot stand as it is in *EA*, which read *sed
uetera sero querimur*. Like Fitch (1987*a* and 2018), I have omitted the *uetera*
of the MSS, preferring to avoid a lacuna after *querimur*, postulated by
Richter and adopted by Zwierlein, Chaumartin, and Billerbeck. Viansino
(1965 and 1993), Giardina (1966), and Caviglia avoid the lacuna by jettison-
ing *sero* and keeping *uetera*. In the present text the final *o* of *sero* would be
short, as at *Ag.* 993: see on 109–12.

una...quotiens/How often...one: Seneca has a predilection for verbal
play with *unus*: see e.g. 487, 500, 508, 557, 776, 1114, 1266, 1268; *Ag.* 6, 24,
646, 838; *Med.* 94, 235, 354, 421, 474, 654, 746; *Tro.* 489, 686–7; *Pha.* 665,
1215; *Oed.* 55, 282, 937; *Thy.* 31, 472; *Pho.* 136. Such verbal play was popular
with Roman poets of all periods: see e.g. Enn. *Ann.* frag. 363 Skutsch; Cat.
5.6; Virg. *Aen.* 5.815, 6.846; Luc. 6.141; Stat. *Theb.* 11.578. Seneca's play with
'one' is not confined to the tragedies: see *Marc.* 14.2, *Ira* 3.19.2, etc.

dira ac fera/Dire, savage: many reasons may be offered for Juno's choice
of these epithets for the Theban land. They are evidently fitting, since the
great poet of Thebes uses each of them of his written city (Stat. *Theb.* 9.294,
10.334, 12.200). For *dirus*, see 56 and n. *ad loc.*

Thebana tellus/land of Thebes: Juno signals the scene of the play's action
in accordance with the practice of Senecan prologues: see *Oed.* 29 (Thebes),
Pha. 2 (Athens), *Ag.* 6 (Argos/Mycenae), *Tro.* 4 (Troy), *Med.* 35 (Corinth),
Thy. 119 (Argos/Mycenae), *Pho.* 13 (Thebes). Seneca is fond of denoting a
country through a periphrastic phrase including the word, *tellus*, 'land': e.g.
Spartana tellus (662), *Assyria...tellure* (*Pha.* 87–8), *Graia tellus* (*Pha.* 906),
Argiua tellus (*Tro.* 277), *Pelasga tellus* (*Med.* 240), *Argolica tellus* (*Thy.* 185),
Hyrcana tellus (*Thy.* 631). The mannerism is Virgilian and frequent in Ovid:
see Coffey and Mayer *ad Pha.* 87–8.

matribus sparsa impiis/strewn with impious Mothers: like Zwierlein,
Chaumartin, and the later Fitch (2002*a* and 2018), I accept Axelson's conjecture, *matribus*, for the unmetrical *nuribus*. 'Impious' Theban mothers
include (in addition to Alcmena) Semele, Antiope, Agave, Niobe, Jocasta, of
which only Semele, mother of Bacchus, and Antiope, mother of Amphion
and Zethus, made Juno a *nouerca*. Juno's complaint is echoed (more politely)
by Amphitryon at 264–5. Although a trisyllabic cretic word (*impios*) concludes line 20, the line is not in breach of 'Porson's law', since the fifth-foot
caesura disappears through synaloephe (elision): see also e.g. lines 35, 41,

50, 62, 606, 966, 1180, and Raven (1965: 54). Seneca clearly saw 'elision as a device for unifying the elements of the last dipody' of the iambic trimeter: Fantham (1982: 106). For actual breaches of 'Porson's law' and the latter's applicability to Senecan metrics, see on 249–58 (line 255).

nouercam/stepdame: the contrast with *matribus* of the preceding line seems to index *nouerca* as 'false mother', another of Juno's *falsa nomina* (see on 1–5). The acerbic reference is to a cultural and political concept much more potent in the ancient Roman world than in our own. Divorce and maternal mortality were common among the Roman elite, and stepmothers were plentiful in Roman aristocratic households, where legally the children of a marriage were the property of the father. The 'evil/angry stepmother' paradigm is to be found in the Greco-Roman tradition from archaic Greek poetry onwards (see e.g. Hesiod *WD* 825) and is famously deployed in Virgil's *malae nouercae* allusion at *Geo.* 3.282. The *nouerca* figure appeared often in the exercises of the schools of declamation (Sen. Rhet. *Con.* 4.6, 9.5); the word almost peppers this play (21, 112, 908, 1018, 1201, 1236). Jerome (*Ep.* 54.15) would declare: 'Every comedy, mime-writer and rhetorical commonplace will declaim against the most savage stepmother (*in nouercam saeuissimam*).' The figure is used in relation to Juno by several Roman poets before Seneca (see e.g. Virg. *Aen.* 8.288, Prop. 4.9.43, Ov. *Met.* 9.15, 135, 181). But Seneca's Roman audience and readers would also have been acutely aware of the role of the *nouerca* in Julio-Claudian dynastic history, in which two stepmothers, Livia (stepmother to Augustus' adopted sons/former grandsons, Gaius, Lucius, and Agrippa Postumus) and the younger Agrippina (stepmother to Octavia and Britannicus) wielded considerable, (some would say) injurious power. Notably Tacitus' account of the early principate uses the stepmother figure liberally as a negative frame for the actions of these two empresses (*Ann.* 1.3, 6, 10, 33; 12.2, 26, 41, 65). Quintilian associates the *nouerca* with tragic drama (*Inst.* 2.10.4), as does the later Apuleius (*Met.* 10.2). But, though Seneca and his dramatic successors regularly refer in their dramas to *nouercae* (see e.g. *Oed.* 418, 487; *Ag.* 118, 809; *Pha.* 1200; *Oct.* 21, 151, 171; *HO* 271) and Seneca even has Hippolytus proclaim the stereotype with clarity and dramatic force (*taceo nouercas: mitius nil est feris*, 'Stepmothers—I am silent: beasts are more gentle', *Pha.* 558), in the world inhabited by Seneca's audience *nouercae* were a historical reality, not a fiction. See further on 109–12 and Watson (1994). For Roman referentiality in *Hercules*, see on 46–52.

escendat licet…locum/Though Alcmene…triumphant: there is no Greek or Roman tradition of Alcmene/Alcmena undergoing catasterism.

According to Antonius Liberalis and Pherecydes, Alcmena after her death was taken by Hermes/Mercury to the Isles of the Blessed, where she was married to Rhadamanthus: Gantz (1993: 1.259). Apollodorus (2.4.11) and Plutarch (*Lys.* 28.5) have Alcmena marrying Rhadamanthus while both are alive. Seneca is clearly expanding (at least in Juno's mind) the list of Jupiter's catasterized *paelices* to include Alcmena. I join Fitch, Zwierlein, and others in preferring *escendat* (E^{ac}), to *ascendat* ($E^{pc}A$); the former, as well as being the *lectio difficilior*, has an appropriately critical meaning of 'rising out of' her appropriate station or *locus* (see Kingery *ad loc.*). *Licet* with the subjunctive without *ut* (Woodcock §124 n.iii) is a common construction in Senecan tragedy: the clause is often (but not always: see 121–2, 1172–3) concessive: 873, 1010, 1172–3, 1326–7 below. Note Seneca's use of *Alcmene*, the Greek form of the name of Alcmena, wife of Amphitryon and mother by Jupiter of Hercules (see Introd. 60). It is Seneca's only use of this form, which enables the dramatic poet to have a long final vowel. The author of *Hercules Oetaeus* uses the form often. In the ablative case Seneca uses the Latin form, *Alcmena* (527, 773, *Pha.* 317).

meumque uictrix teneat Alcmene locum/Alcmene…and take my place triumphant: note the *locus* motif (see on 1–5); for *locus* in the sense of position in the family structure, cf. Hippolytus' blithe remark to his stepmother: *tibi parentis ipse supplebo locum*, 'I shall fulfil for you my father's place' (*Pha.* 633). Observe in the Latin a chiastic version (abCBA) of the 'Golden Line', often praised in the hexameter verse of Virgil, Ovid, and others: 'two substantives and two adjectives, with a verb betwixt them to keep the peace' (Dryden). Cf. 367, *Pha.* 626, *Tro.* 184, *Ag.* 711, *Thy.* 44, 113, Virg. *Geo.* 2.540. This chiastic version (abCBA: where lower case letters represent adjectives and upper case their corresponding nouns, except for C, which figures the verb) is sometimes termed the 'Silver Line': Wilkinson (1963: 216). For Seneca's predilection for adjectives and nouns ending in -*x*, see also (in Juno's prologue) *minax* (12), *atrox* (32), *ferox* (57, 90, 97), *ceruix* (73); for his use of -*trix* words, see on 900–8. Presumably the predilection was based on sonal properties. See further Fitch (1987*a*), 470.

natus/son: first direct reference to Hercules in the play, who is not named until line 41.

astra promissa/promised stars: i.e. heaven and immortality, promised by Zeus/Jupiter after the completion of Hercules' labours (Diod. Sic. 2.9.5). Cf. Pind. *Nem.* 1.69ff., Theoc. 24.79ff., where Teiresias prophesies Heracles' immortality. For Hercules' apotheosis as a reward for his benefactions to humankind, see on 955–63. As Fitch notes *ad loc.*, there may also be an allusion here to the constellation of *Engonasin*, the 'Kneeler', sometimes equated with Heracles/Hercules ([Eratosth.] *Catast.* 4, Hyg. *Astr.* 2.6). The 'promised stars' return at 959.

in cuius ortus mundus impendit diem/**For whose rising the world disbursed a day**: Juno puns on *ortus*, 'rising', used of Hercules' birth but often used, of course, of the sun, whose own rising is here delayed, i.e. 'disbursed'. For the long night of Hercules' conception, see 1158–9, *Ag.* 814–26, *Breu. Vit.* 16.5, Prop. 2.22.25–6, Ov. *Am.* 1.13.45–6, Stat. *Silu.* 4.6.17, Hyg. *Fab.* 29, *HO* 147–50, 1697–8, 1865–6. Another version, going back to Pherecydes, has Jupiter tripling the length of night, his motive being, as in *Breu. Vit.*, to spend longer making love to Alcmena: see Diod. Sic. 4.9.2, Stat. *Theb.* 6.289, 12.300–1. For the 'long night' in order to enjoy Alcmena, see also Plaut. *Amph.*112–14, Ov. *Am.* 1.13.45–6. Note the financial metaphor (*impendit*) as at *Tro.* 299, *Med.* 487, 663. For financial metaphors in Seneca, see e.g. 462; *Med.* 234, 487, 603–6, 626–9; *Pha.* 1153; *Tro.* 358; *Thy.* 427, 1052; *Pho.* 664; *Ben.* 3.19.3; *Clem.* 1.17.3.

tardus…Phoebus…iussus/Phoebus…late…Ordered: similar language to *Ag.* 816–17, where again Phoebus is acting 'under orders' at the time of Hercules' conception (cf. Lucian *Dial. Gods* 10). Phoebus, 'Bright One', is the name regularly used by Seneca for Apollo, son of Jupiter and Latona/Leto, brother of Diana, and god of the sun, music, healing, archery, and prophecy. The name, which occurs frequently in this play (see 136, 454–5, 595, 607, 844, 905–6, 940), is obviously most appropriate to him *qua* sun-god.

Eoo/Eastern: note the short initial *e*, which seems to be long elsewhere in Senecan tragedy.

retinere…Oceano iubar/keep his light…in Ocean: *Oceanus*, 'Ocean', was a Titan (son of Gaea and Uranus, husband and brother of the sea-goddess Tethys), identified with the great sea (sometimes = the Atlantic) which was thought to encompass the known land-masses *uelut uinculum*, 'like a chain' (Sen. *Suas.*1.4); see Cat. 64.30: *Oceanusque, mari totum qui amplectitur orbem*, 'And Oceanus, who enfolds the whole world with sea'. It is a frequent referent in Senecan tragedy, perhaps an index of a preoccupation with imperial space and global boundaries: see e.g. 234, 238, 1141, *Tro.* 383–4, *Pha.* 931, *Oed.* 504, *Med.* 376. Significantly, 'Ocean' figured largely in the political rhetoric of the emperor Claudius, who claimed 'the glory of extending the empire beyond Oceanus', *gloriae prolati imperi ultra Oceanum* (*CIL* 13.1668). See also *CIL* 6.920, a fragmentary inscription which (in its restored form) praises Claudius for being 'the first' (*primus*) to reduce to the sovereignty of the Roman people the conquered kings and barbaric tribes of Britain 'across Oceanus' (*trans Oceanum*). Suetonius records the 'naval crown' (*naualis corona*) which Claudius placed on the gable of the palace to indicate that he 'had crossed and as it were tamed Oceanus' (*traiecti et quasi domiti Oceani, Claud.* 17.3). See also Sen. *Apoc.* 12.3.17–18 and *Oct.* 26–8. *Iubar*, used in the fragments of early Roman tragedy and epic of the morning star (e.g. Enn. *Ann.* frag. 571 Skutsch, *Aiax* frag. 13 Jocelyn), is most often used (cf. e.g. *Med.* 100, *Oed.* 2, Ov. *Met.* 15.187) of the morning light of the sun, though Seneca extends its use elsewhere (e.g. *Ag.* 463) to the light of the setting sun and even of the moon (*Med.* 6): see Tarrant *ad Ag.* 463. For Seneca's 'noun style', manifest throughout 26–9, see on 11–18. For Roman referentiality in *Hercules*, see on 46–52. Unlike Zwierlein, I have not followed Axelson's insertion of a question-mark after *iubar* (for arguments against which, see Fitch 2004*b*: 6).

non sic abibunt odia/**My hate will not just stop**: cf. the use of *sic* at 1186. Viansino (1993) *ad loc.* calls this use a 'colloquialismo', citing *Pha.* 262, 477, Ter. *Andr.* 475.

uiuaces aget uiolentus iras animus/**My violent mind Will enact undying wrath**: the first occurrence of *ira*, 'anger/wrath', a defining psychological constituent of Rome's literary Juno, whose anger was 'unforgetting' (*memor*, Virg. *Aen.* 1.4), and a cardinal motif of this play's prologue (see also 34 and 75)—an important concept, too, in the odes and acts which follow (174, 405, 788, 820, 932, 946, 1137, 1167, 1202, 1220, 1277). Both Cicero and Seneca define *ira* as an emotion directly related to vengeance. Thus Cicero: *ulciscendi libido*, 'a lust for revenge' (*Tusc.* 3.11); for Seneca: (i) *ira est…cupiditas ulciscendae iniuriae*, 'Anger…is the desire to avenge a wrong' (definition lost from *De Ira* 1, recovered from Lactantius *De Ira Dei* 17.13); (ii) *concitatio animi ad ultionem uoluntate et iudicio pergentis*, 'a disturbance of the mind as it proceeds to revenge through will and judgement' (*Ira* 2.3.5). Braden (1985) describes *ira* as the emotion which drives Seneca's characters to assert their 'autarkic selfhood'. Thus Atreus enters *Thyestes* describing himself as *iratus Atreus* (*Thy.* 180), while rejecting such *ira* as insufficient; Medea foreshadows the destruction she will wreak by proclaiming that 'I have as yet committed no crime—in anger (*irata*)' (*Med.* 135–6); Juno defines herself as one whose anger is 'undying' (*uiuaces…iras*). Indeed it is characteristic of Senecan tragic figures to acknowledge their 'wrath', as Juno does here and at 34 and 75: so Atreus (above), Clytemnestra (*Ag.* 142, 261, 970), Medea (*Med.* 51, 203, 414, 556, 902, 916, 927, 938, 943–4, 953, 989), and Oedipus (*Oed.* 519, *Pho.* 352). Even Deianira in *HO* (275) self-consciously proclaims her *ira*.

In the prose works *ira* is often, as in the tragedies, an index of the tyrant (*Ira* 3.18–19: Catiline, Caligula, Cambyses, Cyrus). In the non-Senecan *Octavia* it is Nero's *ira* which is most often mentioned. In the tragedies (see especially *Agamemnon*, *Medea*, and *Thyestes*) *ira* can be other-destructive rather than self-destructive. Out of seventy instances of the word *ira* in Senecan drama, half occur in the revenge tragedies, *Medea* (22) and *Thyestes* (13). In *Hercules ira* or its related adjective (*iratus*) or verb (*irasci*) occur some fourteen times (see above), mostly in reference to Hercules. Note the metatheatrical force of *aget*, translated as 'will enact' to bring out the meaning of *agere* as 'play a theatrical part' (see Trinacty: 131), and the juxtaposition of *uiolentus* and *iras*. *Violentus* is applied to Hercules later in this speech at 43 (see n. *ad loc.*), but elsewhere in the play the adjective is used only of natural forces (932, 1324). For Seneca's interest in the pathology of anger, see *De Ira* and Boyle (2019: lvii–lxiv). For the ontologization of *ira*, see on 75–6; for *ira* and Virgil's Juno, see next n. For the plural *iras*, note that in Senecan tragedy *ira* is 'normally plural in the accusative…as in Vergil' (Fitch *ad loc.*). For metatheatrical language in *Hercules*, see 109–12.

saeuus dolor/savage pain: note the first occurrence of *dolor* ('pain', 'resentment', 'grief') in the play, used here in combination with *ira* (as elsewhere sometimes with *furor* or with both) to describe profound psychological disturbance (see e.g. 98–9, *Med.* 893–944, *Thy.* 253–9). In this Seneca seems influenced perhaps by Virgil's complex portrait of Aeneas (beset by *dolor, furor*, and *ira*) in the final moments of the *Aeneid* (*Aen.* 12.945–7: see Putnam 1995). *Saeuus dolor* itself has a Virgilian ring, since it is precisely *ira/irae* and *saeui dolores* that are the defining emotions of Juno at the opening of the *Aeneid* (1.4, 25). For the ontologization of the emotions here and in Senecan tragedy at large, see on 75–6.

aeterna bella…geret/wage eternal wars: more Virgilian intertextuality as Seneca picks up Juno's words from *Aen.* 1.48 (*bella gero*) and the eternity of her wound (*aeternum, Aen.* 1.36). Military language and imagery are obviously pervasive in this play: see esp. 30–3, 44–54, 75–85, 101–2, 116–23, 125–36, 222, 240, 278, 293, 294, 299, 362–9, 397–413, 526–68, 544, 610–17, 634–8, 797–802, 812–21, 828, 833, 895–7, 923, 1112, 1151, 1154, 1186, 1315 and nn. *ad locc.* See also on 63–8 (*uincere/uictor*).

30–46 Failure of Juno's war with Hercules: his *uirtus* and labours have brought him glory.

30–5 *Quae bella*/What wars: a surprising, even startling question, given Juno's martial character and experience in Greek and Roman epic. It is an interrogative of a kind used elsewhere by Seneca to enliven his prologues (*Oed.* 6, *Med.* 26, *Tro.* 41–2, *Thy.* 3–4) and/or to effect a rhetorical transition (see e.g. *Pha.* 112, *Thy.* 890). For 'transitional interrogatives' in *Hercules*, see e.g. 226, 241, 249, 258, 386, 459.

quidquid...tellus creat...quidquid/Every...earth Creates, every: for the phrase *quidquid/quod/quodcumque tellus creat*, see *Med.* 691, 714, and, for variations, *Oed.* 591–2, *Med.* 681–2, and *HO* 28. Note the double anaphora of *quidquid*, as at *Oed.* 983–4, *Pha.* 1161–2; for triple anaphora of *quidquid*, see *Tro.* 382–4, 333–5 below.

tellus...pontus...aer/earth...sea...air: Juno expatiates on the global nature of Hercules' victories, though most of the monsters were from or on the earth. The formulation of universality in terms of earth, sea, and air/sky is a common one: see e.g. Lucr. 5.592, Virg. *Aen.* 1.280, Ov. *Met.* 8.830. Note Hercules' cited statement at *HO* 794: *pacata tellus...et caelum et freta,* 'Earth has been pacified...and sky and sea'. For Hercules' labours, see on 213–48.

terribile dirum pestilens atrox ferum/dread, dire, fierce, ferocious, Pestilential: five adjectives in asyndeton, filling out in the Latin an iambic trimeter: cf. *Pha.* 939 and *Pho.* 223, where five and three adjectives respectively fill out the asyndetic line. Asyndetic lists of adjectives, nouns, or verbs are found frequently in both Senecan tragedy (see e.g. 289, 1260; *Ag.* 45, 51, 112, 991; *Tro.* 578, 1056; *Pho.* 34, 223, 264–5, 285; *Med.* 20–1, 45, 123, 208, 390, 395; *Pha.* 923, 939; *Oed.* 13; *Thy.* 52, 176, 216–17) and the early republican tragedians: see e.g. the list of nouns at Acc. *Neopt.* frag. 468 Klotz: *uim ferociam animum atrocitatem iram acrimoniam,* 'violence, ferocity, will, cruelty, wrath, spite'—also Enn. *Alex.* frag. 40 Jocelyn, *Med. Ex.* frag. 9.6 Boyle (2006), Pac. *Atal.* frag. 52 Klotz, *Per.* frag. 301 Klotz, Acc. *Eur.* frag. 349 Klotz. Indeed asyndetic writing is a feature of Roman literature from its inception: Livius *Od.* frag. 27 Blänsdorf: *uestis pulla purpurea ampla,* 'a robe dark, purple, wide'; Naev. *BP* frag. 37 Blänsdorf: *urit uastat populatur, rem hostium concinnat,* 'burns, wastes, ravages, the enemies' affairs disrupts'. For Quintilian on asyndeton, see *Inst. Or.* 9.3.50. For Greek precedents, see Fitch *ad* 32—to which I add Eur. *Hec.* 810–11. The adjective *atrox,* 'fierce' (derived from *ater,* 'black'), is rarely used by Seneca. It occurs only four times in the tragedies, including twice in *Thyestes* (194, 745), where it seems alliteratively suggestive of Atreus, as if *atrox* meant 'Atrean'. Elsewhere it appears only at *Tro.* 289, where, presumably as here, the initial syllable is long. *Terribilis* is a Senecan tragic *hapax*. For *dirus,* see 56 and n. *ad loc.*

domitum/tamed: *domare* corresponds to the Greek δαμάζειν; it is *le mot juste* for the taming and 'mastering' of animals and monsters: see e.g. 444,

Ag. 835, 959, *HO* 752, Ov. *Met.* 9.183. See also *domitor* at 619, 903, 1066, and nn. *ad locc.* For *domare* and Hercules, see 619 and 955.

superat/He triumphs: mark how the subject of this verb, which is Hercules, is unnamed. Neither the name 'Hercules' nor 'Alcides' has yet occurred. Seneca is careful about his use of proper names, and the delay in the introduction of nomenclature for Hercules seems intentional. The hero so dominates Juno's cognitive and emotional life that no name is required. A name will be supplied at lines 41 and 72, followed by naming at 84, 107, 115, 120. For sudden and unannounced changes of grammatical subject elsewhere in *Hercules*, see also 275, 312, 722, 794, 797.

crescit malis/grows by suffering: I have translated so as to reflect Seneca's use of the common idea of 'growing through suffering', which he also uses (in a grotesque parody) at *Med.* 910 (*creuit malis ingenium,* 'my nature grew through suffering'). Ovid pre-empted Seneca when he described Hercules' decapitated hydra as *crescentem...malo,* 'growing by suffering' (*Met.* 9.74). The whole idea is most famously enshrined in the Aeschylean choral doctrine of πάθει μάθος, 'learning through suffering', *Ag.* 177. *Malis* seems syntactically ambiguous: sociative-instrumental ablative (of 'accompaniment' or/and 'means') or/and ablative of source/origin; see Woodcock §§40, 43.

iraque nostra fruitur/And delights in our wrath: a paradox clearly liked by Juvenal, who echoes it at *Sat.* 1.49–50 (of Marius Priscus in exile): *fruitur dis iratis,* 'he delights in the wrath of the gods'. See also Mart. *Epig.* 8.30.3: *poenaque fruitur,* 'and delights in the punishment'. For paradoxical phrases in *Hercules,* see 168, 245, 447, 565, 606, 726–7, 752, 1051–2, 1305, and nn. *ad locc.* For *ira,* see on 19–29.

mea uertit odia/transforms my hate: the ability to transform evil into good is a property of the *beatus,* 'blessed/happy man', according to *Ep. Mor.* 45.9 (*qui mala in bonum uertit*).

35–40 *saeua impero*/cruel commands from me: elision prevents the breach of 'Porson's law' (see 20 and n. *ad loc.*). For *saeuus,* 'cruel', as a defining epithet of the literary Juno, see Virg. *Aen.* 1.4, where the epithet is the first one applied to her in the epic (*saeuae...Iunonis*). It is the defining epithet of stepmothers: *saeuas...nouercas, Pha.* 356–7; *saeuae...nouercae,* Virg. *Geo.* 2.128; *saeuae...nouercae* (of Juno), VF 3.580; Jerome *Ep.* 54.15 (cited on 19–29).

patrem probaui/Have confirmed his father: picked up by the dramatist of *Hercules Oetaeus* (*HO* 9–10). The importance of bloodline and parentage to an elite Roman's identity cannot be overstated. One's status was inextricably tied to membership of a *gens* through one's father. *Pater, gens, maiores* were defining ingredients of social and personal identity. Hence Lycus' later attempt to undermine the standing of Hercules by attacking his divine parentage.

gloriae feci locum/placed his glory: Juno repeats the Ovidian paradox that her attempts to harm an enemy have helped him (*prosum sola nocendo*, 'I alone help by harming', Ov. *Met.* 2.519). But she does so via a translingual pun, as she alludes to the common etymology of the Greek version of Hercules' name, Ἡρακλῆς, which = 'Hera's glory'. Seneca was not shy of translingual etymological puns (accurate or otherwise): see e.g. 'Aethiopians' (38), 'Aetna' (106), 'Alcides' (186), 'Megara' (203, 1009), 'Ocean' (238), *syrma...trahit* (475), 'Lethe' (680-1), 'Cocytus' (686-7); 'Medea' (*Med.* 179-81, 910), 'Jason' (*Med.* 433-4), 'Idmon' (*Med.* 652); 'Oedipus' (*Oed.* 216); 'Atreus' (*Thy.* 180, 486), 'Thyestes' (*Thy.* 259, 783, 901); 'Andromacha' (*Tro.* 671-7), 'Helen' (*Tro.* 861-3, 892)—and in *Agamemnon* a veritable carnival of puns: 'Agamemnon' (39), 'Clytemestra' (125), 'Achilles' (208), 'Helen' (273-4), 'Cyclas' (370•), 'Eurybates' (391), 'Notus' (481), 'Eurus' (482), 'Aiax' (556), 'Haemonia' (640), 'Hister' (679), 'Strophius' (918-19), 'Electra' (924): see Boyle (2011/2014/2017/2019) *ad locc.* See further on 545 ('Amazon'), 662-7 ('Dis *inuisus*'), 1302-13 ('Amphitryon'), 1341-4 ('Theseus'). Nominal etymological punning goes back to Homer (see e.g. *Od.* 1.55, 62) and is found abundantly in Greek and Roman poets. Translingual etymological wordplay, requiring knowledge of Greek, is evident in Roman drama from its inception (Plautus revels in such, and Ennius even makes some of the punning overt: *Androm.*, frag. 99 Jocelyn). One of Seneca's most influential poetic predecessors, Ovid, was a master of the etymological, nominal pun (see Ahl 1985 *passim*); he even devotes a section of his *Fasti* (1.607-16) to playing games with the name 'Augustus'. Stoicism was especially interested in etymology, which figured strongly in the writings of the early Stoic philosophers, Chrysippus and Cleanthes. Notable, too, was the concern with etymology in the works of late republican Roman intellectuals such as Lucius Aelius Stilo and his pupil, Marcus Terentius Varro (on whom see Čulík-Baird 2022: 156-61). For non-translingual etymological puns, see 115, 782, 799, 929, 1093, and nn. *ad locc.* For Seneca's 'noun style', see on 11-18; for Stoic language and ideas in *Hercules*, see on 162-3. For an excellent discussion of nominal punning in Seneca's plays, including the ones cited from *Hercules* above, see Fitch (2016).

qua Sol reducens...diem/Where the Sun restores...the day: for the alliterative phrase (*red...d*), see *Ep. Mor.* 93.9, Virg. *Geo.* 1.249. The global nature of Hercules' fame is underscored in *Hercules Oetaeus*; see e.g. *HO* 38-51, 315-17, 1698-1700. For similar global images, see 443, 871,

1061–2•, 1139–40. Global imagery is common in Senecan tragedy: see e.g. *Pha.* 54–72, 285–90, *Thy.* 369–79 (on which see Boyle 2017 *ad loc.*); it smacks of *imperium Romanum.* Cf. Statius' 'imperial' imagery at *Theb.* 1.156–62. For Roman referentiality in *Hercules*, see on 46–52.

binos propinqua tinguit Aethiopas face/Tinting both Aethiopians with close torch: the idea of two kinds of Aethiopians, one in the east and one in the west, may be found as early as Homer's *Odyssey* (1.22–4): see also Herod. 7.69. The thesis that Ethiopians, Indians, and others of darker complexion derived their skin pigmentation from greater proximity to the sun (αἴθοψ = 'burnt-looking') is a *topos* of ancient literature from 'Aeschylus' (*Prom.* 808–9) onwards; see e.g. Lucr. 6.722, Prop. 2.18.11, Hor. *Odes* 1.22.21–2, Ov. *Met.* 1.778–9, Pliny *HN* 2.189. For other instances in Senecan tragedy, see e.g. *Pha.* 345, *Med.* 484, *Oed.* 122–3, *Thy.* 602; see also *HO* 41, and Serv. *ad Verg. Aen.* 4.481. The *topos* appears, too, in Elizabethan drama: see e.g. Shakespeare, *MV* II.i.1–3. See also *NQ* 4.2.18. The imaging of the sun as a *fax*, 'torch', is found in Roman literature from Ennius' *Medea* onwards (frag. 243 Jocelyn); see also e.g. *Pha.* 379, *Thy.* 835, Lucr. 5.976 (at Lucr. 5.402 it is the *lampas mundi*, 'lamp of the world'). The origin of the image is Greek: see e.g. Eur. *IA* 1506–7, Theodectes frag. 10.1–2.

indomita uirtus colitur/untamed virtue's worshipped: *uirtus* is one of the pre-eminent motifs of this play. The word appears some seventeen times: 39, 115, 201, 252, 325, 340, 343, 434, 435, 476, 634, 647, 1093, 1157, 1271, 1277, 1315. Elsewhere in Senecan tragedy it occurs thirteen times: *Pha.* 846, 985; *Oed.* 88, 781; *Tro.* 210, 751, 757; *Med.* 160, 161, 977; *Thy.* 529; *Pho.* 190, 237. In *HO* it is found fourteen times, in *Oct.* four times. *Virtus* is a wide-ranging moral term, embracing 'courage', 'virtue', 'endurance', 'self-control', 'knowledge', 'justice', and 'manliness', what may be thought by the Roman elite to be the defining properties of manhood, of being an ideal *uir.* To Sallust (*Cat.* 2.7), who democratized the concept, it may be found in a wide range of human activities, including ploughing, sailing, and building. A quintessential value of elite Romans (inscribed on the Augustan shield of 27 BCE; see *RG* 34.2), *uirtus* was also the hallmark of the Stoic *sapiens* or 'sage', whose *uirtus perfecta* (according to Sen. *Ep. Mor.* 120.11) comprised *temperantia, fortitudo, prudentia,* and *iustitia* (for Stoic language and ideas in *Hercules*, see on 162–3). One of the most startling claimants to *uirtus* in Senecan tragedy is Medea, who labels her filicide *uirtus* (*Med.* 977: see epigraph to Introd. §VII). But *uirtus* was not only a complex moral value—and one, like the emotions (see on 75–6), frequently ontologized, even addressed (1157, 1315)—but a deity with a temple in Rome, shared with Honos, dating from the late third century BCE. I have translated *uirtus* as 'virtue' throughout the play, even though the semiotic range of *uirtus* and 'virtue' is different. Translating the word differently on different occasions, as many translators do, obfuscates the play's attempt to investigate this cardinal Roman value. See further Introd. §VII, 102–7.

I have preferred the translation of *colitur* as 'worshipped' (as opposed to simply 'honoured') because of its proximity to *deus* and because of the tradition that Hercules accepted divine honours following his tenth labour (Diod. Sic. 4.24.2) and that the Ara Maxima, set up by Hercules during the completion of that tenth labour, was consecrated to himself (see Livy 1.7.10–12, Ov. *Fas.* 1.581–2). *Colere* is used by Seneca close to this sense in relation to *uirtus* at *Vit. Beat.* 26.7. Fitch *ad loc.* suggests that the adjective *indomitus*, used of Hercules also at 1079, recalls the cult-title of Hercules Invictus associated with the altar.

toto deus narratur orbe/the whole world Stories him a god: forms of *narrare/enarrare* occur only six times in the tragedies, sometimes as here (see also *Med.* 52, *Tro.* 865, 1067) with a strong semantic charge. People's words have turned Hercules into a god. Members of Seneca's audience would have been aware of several others who had been 'storied a god' by the world (Julius Caesar, Augustus, etc.). In the prologue of *Hercules Oetaeus* it is Hercules who bruits his fame: *nulla me tellus silet*, 'No land is silent in my regard' (*HO* 39). *Toto orbe* seems best taken as locatival ablative: Woodcock §51.

40–6 monstra iam desunt mihi/I've no monsters left: Seneca likes the rhetorical force of *desse*: see e.g. 500, 832; also *Med.* 403, 992; *Tro.* 61, 888; *Pha.* 878, 1186; *Oed.* 68, 693–4. For the important *monstrum* motif, see 1280 and n. *ad loc.*

minorque labor est Herculi iussa exequi/And it's less labour for Hercules to follow Orders: note the play on *labor*, implying that Juno's 'labours' are greater than those of Hercules. The contrast between Juno's and Hercules' fatigue is Ovidian (*Met.* 9.198–9; cf. *Ars* 2.217). This is the first use of Hercules' name in the play, even though he has dominated Juno's mind throughout the prologue. The echo of this idea by the Hercules of *HO* (*quidquid est iussum leue est*, 'Whatever is ordered is easy', *HO* 59) lacks the wordplay. Juno's comments here seem to be the basis of the remark given to Thomas Heywood's Hercules in *The Brazen Age* (1613):

> And step-dame, glut thy hatred now,
> That hast been weary to command, when we
> Have not been weary to perform and act.

mihi iubere/for me to give them: the traditional account is that Hercules was ordered to perform his 'labours' by Eurystheus, to whom he became enslaved (see Introd. 61, n. 154). Hera/Juno was generally involved in the labours in a vague capacity of persecution (Eur. *Herac.* 20–1, Virg. *Aen.* 8.292), but Ovid, like Seneca, also has her 'ordering' the labours (*Met.* 9.15). See also on 77–83. Note the verbal polyptoton (*iussa...iubere*): see on 11–18 and 112–18.

laetus imperia excipit/He loves commands: lit. 'he receives commands with joy'. Billerbeck *ad loc.* compares the joy in adversity recommended in Seneca's philosophical works: see e.g. *Prou.* 4.4.

fera tyranni iussa/tyrant's cruel orders: the 'tyrant' is of course Eurystheus. At VF 1.114–15 Juno calls the 'orders' *nostri...Eurystheos... iussa*, 'orders of my Eurystheus'.

uiolento...iuueni/violent man: like stepmother, like stepson. Juno has moved *uiolentus* from her mind (28) to Hercules. Cf. the description of Hercules by the chorus of *Agamemnon* as *uiolentus ille* (*Ag.* 825), euphemistically translated by both Fitch (2004a: 'aggressive hero') and Braund (2017: 'impetuous hero'). Cf. another epithet attached to Hercules in this play four times: *ferox* (see on 57–63). Quintilian (*Inst. Or.* 11.3.73) defines him as *truculentus* ('truculent/ferocious'). *Iuuenis*, 'man', could be applied to 'any adult male up to the age of 45' (*OLD*), i.e. men of military age.

nempe/Indeed: *nempe* (= 'surely', 'clearly', 'indeed', 'of course', 'certainly', etc.) is used in Senecan tragedy to underscore a statement, often marking its irony: see *Pha.* 244, *Ag.* 702, *Oed.* 76, *Thy.* 412, *Tro.* 325, 340, 744; cf. *HO* 437, Cic. *Phil.* 1.18, Hor. *Sat.* 2.7.80, *Epod.* 12.22.

leone et hydra/Lion and Hydra: i.e. with the skin of the Nemean Lion, which he uses as a shield (see 797–9, 1151), and the poisonous blood of the Lernaean Hydra, with which he has smeared his arrows (see 1195). For the respective labours, see on 222–5, 241–8 respectively. Note the use of a climactic half-line, a regular feature of Seneca's dramatic style: see e.g. 63, 112, 213, 258, 294, 341, 369, 408, 447, 480, 489, 604, 679, 727, 747, 827, 908, 924, 926, 939, 944, 952, 963, 973, 991, 995, 1002, 1015, 1028, 1042, 1048, 1159, 1168, 1173, 1186, 1200, 1221, 1226, 1272, 1310, 1317, 1319, 1329, 1341; *Ag.* 167, 188, 293, 394, 778, 791, 951; *Oed.* 81, 957; *Pha.* 671, 684, 880, 1184, 1196, 1242; *Med.* 157, 238, 425, 965, 971, 1008, 1022; *Tro.* 1117, 1148, 1168; *Thy.* 100; *Pho.* 319, 414, 464, 480, 643, 651. The climactic half-line is especially prominent in Acts IV and V of *Hercules* (see above) and in the final act of *Thyestes* (*Thy.* 901, 918, 983, 1004, 1021, 1030, 1068, 1092, 1096, 1102, 1110).

46–63 Hercules' victory in the underworld and capture of Cerberus (for whom see 782–91 and nn. *ad loc.*).

46–52 *Nec satis terrae patent*/**The wide earth does not suffice:** the phrase recurs (with *non* for *nec*) at 605, spoken by Hercules. The general idea is found in association with Alexander the Great: see e.g. Sen. Rhet. *Suas.* 1, Juv. 10.168. There is perhaps a telling echo of a famous Ovidian line (*Met.* 1.241) cited by Seneca (*NQ* 4A *Praef.* 19) in support of the contention that humanity is fundamentally evil: *qua terra patet, fera regnat Erinys,* 'where the earth spreads wide, savage Erinys/Fury reigns'. The idea is reframed by Hercules at 960.

effregit ecce limen inferni Iouis/**See, he smashed infernal Jove's gate:** Juno emphasizes the violence of Hercules' descent into hell, as does Andromache with similar language at *Tro.* 723: *perfracto limine Ditis,* 'having smashed the gate of Dis'. This violent entry is traditional (see Hor. *Odes* 1.3.36). The 'gates of hell' are as old as Homer (*Il.* 5.646, 9.312, 23.71) and occur prominently at the beginning of Virgil's sixth *Aeneid* (*Aen.* 6.106, 127)—and at its end (*Aen.* 6.893–8). *Limen,* 'gate', is literally 'threshold', and a term with moral and religious implications. Dis, regularly referred to as 'infernal' (see e.g. *Ag.* 1 and Boyle *ad loc.*), receives the nomenclature 'infernal/Stygian Jove/Zeus' in Homer (Ζεὺς καταχθόνιος, *Il.* 9.457) and elsewhere (cf. Ζεὺς ἄλλος, 'another Zeus', Aesch. *Supp.* 231), including Virgil (*Aen.* 4.638) and Ovid (*Fas.* 5.448). At 608 below Dis is referred to as 'dire Jove' (*diro…Ioui*); at *HO* 1705 as 'dark Jove' (*nigri…Iouis*). For the delayed position of *ecce* after a main verb, see e.g. 1040, *Ag.* 908 and *Med.* 738; see further on 329–31.

opima/**prime loot:** note the Roman language here. *Opima* is here functioning substantivally (as at Pliny *Paneg.* 17.3, Stat. *Theb.* 10.27) for *spolia opima,* 'prime loot/spoils', which technically referred to spoils taken from a commanding general defeated in personal combat by his opposing commanding general. The first instance of this in Roman myth/history was Romulus' capture of spoils from Acron, king of Caenina (Livy 1.10.4–6), commemorated in the Forum of Augustus in Rome (Ov. *Fas.* 5.565). *Opima* is used substantivally, if loosely, in Accius' *Armorum Iudicium* (frag. 146 Klotz). For Roman language, imagery, and associations elsewhere in the play, see on 1–124 (introd.), 19–29, 35–40, 46–52, 52–6, 57–63, 63–8, 84–5, 109–12, 152–8, 159–61, 162–74, 162–3, 192–6, 249–58, 258–67, 268–75, 283–95, 299–302, 309–13, 332–57, 337–41, 341–8, 384–96, 408–13, 414–21, 489–94, 495–500, 533–46, 542–6, 618–21, 622–5, 658–827, 720–7, 731–47, 731–4, 735–9, 739–45, 745–7, 760–1, 762–8, 827–9, 838–49, 875–81,

882–92, 893–4, 908–12, 918–24, 926–39, 955–63, 1092–9, 1138–42, 1173–7, 1231–6, 1278–82, 1314–17, 1321–41, 1321–9. For Roman legal language, see on 731–4. *Opimus* reappears in a quite different context at 909 and 923.

regis...refert...reuerti: for paronomasia of *re-* words, see 182, 963, 1072–4, 1243–5, 1337–9; cf. e.g. *Thy.* 419–20, 430–3, 438–9, 531–4, 539–42, *Pho.* 31–3.

ad superos refert/lugs To those above: *superi*, lit. 'those above', is a relative term, referring to heaven (from the perspective of earth: e.g. 17, 74, 898, *Ag.* 394, 511, 609, 694, 755) or to earth (from the perspective of hell: e.g. 318, 568, 583, *Oed.* 573, *Tro.* 179, *Pha.* 145, 626, *Thy.* 83, Prop. 2.28.50, Virg. *Aen.* 6.481, 680, Silius 13.607). Sometimes the term seems deliberately ambiguous, as perhaps it is here and at 423. Is Hercules taking these spoils to show them on earth or is he planning to show them to the gods? The answer is perhaps both. According to Juno (51) he aims to 'flaunt' them to his father, Jupiter.

foedus umbrarum perit/hell's covenant is dead: a reference to the 'covenant' separating the underworld from the world of the living, described here (in overtly ironic language) as broken. *Foedus*, 'covenant', is an important concept in Senecan tragedy, used most notably perhaps in *Medea*, where the Chorus represent the voyage of the *Argo* as a violation of the natural order of the world, viz. the separation of sea and land. The violation is described in legal and religious terms as a breach of the 'covenants of a well partitioned world' (*bene dissaepti foedera mundi*, *Med.* 335) and 'the sacrosanct covenants of the world' (*sacro...sancta foedera mundi*, *Med.* 605–6). The notion of 'laws of nature', *leges naturae*, evident in the constitution of things, places, and people, in the regular rhythms of the cosmos and the structure of the universe, in the separation of land, sea, and sky, of the living and the dead, though essentially absent from Greek literature and science (Lehoux 2012: 57), is found in Roman prose and verse from the late republic onwards: e.g. Cic. *Har* 32, *Tusc.* 1.30, Ov. *Met.* 15.1.71, *Tr.* 1.8.5, Manil. 1.671, Pliny *HN* 2.116. In Lucretius this is extended to the notion of a *foedus* or 'covenant' of nature (Lucr. 1.586, 2.302: *foedera naturai*; 5.924, 6.906–7: *foedere naturae*; 5.310: *naturae foedera*). Virgil's *Georgics* are an exploration of the *leges aeternaque foedera*, 'laws and eternal covenants' (*Geo.* 1.60), imposed by 'nature', *natura*, and end on a failed breach of those covenants by the paradigm of poets, Orpheus. Cf. also Ov. *Met.* 10.352–3 (quoted on 603–6), Colum. 1. Pref. 8. At Manil. 2.48 what Seneca here calls *foedus umbrarum*, 'hell's covenant', separating the dead from the living, is termed *naturae foedus*, 'nature's covenant'. Seneca's prose works discuss the *leges naturae* frequently: see e.g. *Prou.* 1.2, *Ira* 2.27.2, *NQ* 3.29.3. See also VF 1.213, Stat. *Ach.* 1.64. The notion of *foedus*, 'covenant' (= roughly 'social contract'), is also central to Seneca's notion of human social order (see e.g. *Ira* 1.5.3). For a 'covenant', *foedus*, between humanity and nature, see *Pha.* 540; for the *foedera* of Pax/Venus see *Med.* 64. See further Lehoux (2012: 47–76) and Gladhill (2016), who underscores the centrality of the concept in Roman culture. For other legal imagery in the play, see on 731–4. I join Zwierlein and others in leaving line 49 in its MS position rather than placing it after line 54 with Leo and Fitch. *Perit* is probably a syncopated perfect (= *periit*), as at *Tro.* 493, 631, *Med.* 994, *Pho.* 210. For *perire* used elsewhere of the 'death' of moral values etc., see *Ag.* 112, *Thy.* 47–8, Stat. *Theb.* 1.154.

uidi ipsa, uidi/I saw, myself saw: so Talthybius at *Tro.* 170: *uidi ipse uidi*; so the Trojan chorus at *Ag.* 656: *uidi, uidi*. The dramatic use of *uidi* at the beginning of a verse-line may be found elsewhere in Senecan tragedy: e.g. *ipse...| uidi* (Creon, *Oed.* 583–4), *uidi* (Hecuba, *Tro.* 44), *uidi* (Nurse, *Med.* 673); cf. *uidi* (Octavia, *Oct.* 16), *uidi, uidi* (Iole, *HO* 207). Duplication of *uidi* conveys rather more than the 'emotional emphasis', suggested by Fitch *ad loc.*: see 254–7 below: *uidi...uidi* (Amphitryon), and n. *ad loc.* For the 'viewing' motif in *Hercules*, see on 249–58. For other emotional duplication separated by a single word, as here, cf. *maius his maius*, *Med.* 674; *maius hoc maius*, *Pha.* 697.

nocte discussa inferum/night below shattered: by the daylight flooding into the underworld from Hercules' incursion. Note Megara's opening command to her husband at 279–80.

Dite domito/Dis tamed: *Dis*, a contraction of *Diues* (= 'the rich one'), is Seneca's favourite name for Pluto/Hades, brother of Jupiter/Zeus and ruler of the underworld. *Dis* is the Roman/Latin equivalent and calque of the Greek god Πλοῦτος (Pluto). 'Pluto' (*Pluton*) is used by Seneca only once (*Pha.* 628); the author of *HO* uses it three times in a single play. Note *domito*, 'tamed', as if Dis were a wild animal (like Cerberus: see on 52–6).

spolia iactantem patri fraterna/flaunting to his father Fraternal spoils: Juno highlights boastfulness at the core of Hercules' character. She will repeat the emphasis at 58, as will Lycus at 436. Note the juxtaposition of *patri fraterna*. Juxtaposition of familial terms and the frequently resulting focus on boundary violation and the inversion of nature are typically Senecan: cf. *Ag.* 35–6; *Thy.* 40–3, 90, 145, 778, 1050, 1090, 1101; *Pha.* 555–7; *Med.* 283, 955–6; *Tro.* 248, 690–1, 1074; *Oed.* 54, 881, 1039; *Pho.* 134–7. Note also the climactic and emphatic position of *fraterna* as the opening word following enjambement and followed itself by a strong pause: see 379–80 and n. *ad loc.* 'Flaunting spoils to Jupiter', which is what Hercules is alleged to be doing, has, like *opima* above, a distinctively Roman triumphal-ist ring. For Hercules' *spolia* elsewhere, see 240, 294, 544, 761, 1151 (also *spoliare*, 833); there are clearly spoils to be had from the 'wealthy' king him-self, Dis (see above and Fitch 2016). For military imagery in *Hercules*, see on 19–29; for triumphal imagery, see on 57–63. For boundary violation, see on 52–6, 57–63, 77–83, 186–91, 205–98, 283–95, 384–96, 547–9, 770–81, 830–7, 1154–63, 1202–18, 1290–4—and, further, Segal (2008).

52–6 Sarcastic question followed by a summary statement of Hercules' boundary violations both existential and religious. For boundary violation, see on 46–52.

uinctum et oppressum trahit...catenis/**drag...Bound and crushed with chains:** i.e. in the manner of Cerberus, whom Hercules 'binds...with adamant chains' (*adamante texto uincit*, 808) and 'drags' (*tractum*, 819, *trac-tus*, *Ag.* 859) from hell.

paria sortitum Ioui/**Jove's equal:** lit. 'one who drew equal lots to Jove'. The allusion is to the tradition that, after the defeat of Cronos/Saturn by his three sons (Zeus/Jupiter, Poseidon/Neptune, and Hades/Dis), the sons drew lots for the kingdoms they would rule, with Zeus receiving the sky, Poseidon the ocean, and Hades the underworld. The tradition goes back to Homer (*Il.* 15.187–93). For Neptune's kingdom as 'the second realm', see 599 and n. *ad loc.*; for Dis as 'the third realm's king', *tertiae regem...sortis*, see 833 (cf. also 609, 1114). For the 'three realms/kingdoms' elsewhere in Senecan tragedy, see e.g. *Pha.* 1212, *Tro.* 345–6.

Erebo/**Erebus:** Erebus was technically the god of darkness, brother/ husband or father of Night; the name is regularly used metonymically for the underworld, as here and at 1224, *Oed.* 160, 394, 521, *Tro.* 179, *HO* 1065.

et retegit Styga/**and unroof the Styx:** the Styx (derived from στυγέω, 'I abhor') was traditionally the chief river of the underworld, often used by metonymy for the underworld itself. The gods swore their 'greatest and most dread oath' by the Styx (Hom. *Il.* 15.37–8, *Od.* 5.185–6): 712; *Ag.* 755; *Pha.* 944; *Tro.* 391; *Thy.* 667; *HO* 1066–7; Hes. *Th.* 400, 793–806; Virg. *Aen.* 6.323–4; Ov. *Met.* 2.46, *Fas.* 5.250; Stat. *Theb.* 1.291. Normally the Styx is the boundary river of the underworld over which only the buried dead may be ferried. In *Hercules* the boundary river is Lethe: see on 679–88. For 'opening up the underworld', cf. *Ag.* 756, *Oed.* 395, Virg. *Aen.* 8.244–5. Along with Giardina (1966 and 2007), Caviglia, Fitch (1987*a* and 2018), and Chaumartin, I have retained the reading of the MSS, *et*, disregarding Baden's unnecessary emendation, *en*, accepted by Viansino (1965 and 1993), Zwierlein, and Billerbeck. For discussion, see Fitch (2004*b*: 8).

patefacta ab imis manibus retro uia est/A way back from the deep shades has opened: so in *Troades* (724) Hercules 'opened a way back', *retro patefecit iter*. See also *Med.* 638. For the 'opening' of a path or gate to the world above, see the famous line placed in the mouth of Scipio Africanus by Ennius and cited by Seneca at *Ep. Mor.* 108.34: *mi soli caeli maxima porta patet*, 'for me alone the greatest gate of heaven opens' (Enn. *Epig.* 3.b.2 Goldberg and Manuwald). *Imis manibus*, 'deep shades', is a Virgilian phrase (*Aen.* 3.565, 4.387, 11.181, 12.884), used elsewhere by Seneca (*Tro.* 146, *Med.* 968).

sacra dirae mortis/dire death's mysteries: or as Lucan (6.514) calls them, *arcana…Ditis operti*, 'the secrets of buried Dis'. See also Stat. *Theb.* 8.2: *orbis…arcana sepulti*, 'secrets of a buried world'. *Dirus*, 'dreadful/dread/dire', is a frequent adjective in Senecan tragedy (it occurs eight times in *Hercules*: 19, 32, 56, 226, 608, 722, 771, 1221). Cicero (*Leg.* 2.21) notes its use in the language of augury, and the word's power seems to come, as Coffey and Mayer (1990) suggest (*ad Pha.* 131), 'from its application above all to evil omens'. It is often used by Seneca of creatures or places in the underworld. For *dirus* as an epithet of death in Senecan tragedy, see *Oed.* 180, *Tro.* 783; cf. *Oct.* 321, *HO* 928.

in aperto iacent/lie exposed: Hercules' exposure of hell is one of the boasts of his opening speech in the play: *uidi et ostendi inferos*, 'I saw and exposed hell' (613). *In aperto*: Seneca's prose as well as his verse displays a predilection for prepositional phrases involving *in* with the ablative singular of an epithet used substantively: e.g. *in extremo* (695); *in tuto* (1302); *in arto…et ancipiti* (1307); *in ancipiti* (*Tranq.* 10.6); *in praecipiti* (*Ag.* 58, *Ep. Mor.* 23.6); *in dubio* (*Ag.* 58, *Pol.* 5.3); *in incerto* (*Pha.* 630, *Thy.* 422, *Breu. Vit.* 9.1, *NQ* 5.18.4); *in ambiguo* (*Oed.* 208); *in occulto* (*Med.* 976, *Clem.* 1.3.5, *NQ* 1.Pref. 7); *in medio* (*Thy.* 203)—see further Fitch *ad* 1307.

57–63 *at ille*/But he: for the use of *at* to index a change of referents, cf. *at ille*, *Ag.* 892, *Tro.* 796, *Thy.* 757, *HO* 808; *at ista*, *Ag.* 1001; *at misera*, 1008, *Tro.* 949.

rupto carcere umbrarum ferox/savage from bursting death's prison: for *carcer*, 'prison', 'dungeon', of the underworld, see 1222 below, *Pha.* 836, *Thy.* 16, Ov. *Met.* 4.453, *Ibis* 80. *Rumpere* is regularly used of 'breaking out of/ into', i.e. 'bursting the bounds of' hell: see e.g. 280, 290, 566; *Oed.* 160, 572; *Thy.* 88, 1008; *Oct.* 593; Stat. *Theb.* 8.190. It is a verb used often in connection with boundary violation (for which see on 516–20): e.g. Hor. *Odes* 1.3.36: *perrupit Acheronta Herculeus labor*, 'Hercules' labour burst through Acheron'. For *ferox*, 'savage/wild/bold/fierce', which, like *ferus* (see on 516–20), associates its referents with *fera*, 'wild beast', applied to other Senecan characters, see e.g. *Pha.* 416, 1064 (Hippolytus); *Tro.* 46 (Pyrrhus), 721

(Hercules), 1098 (Astyanax), 1152 (Polyxena); *Oed.* 960 (Oedipus); *Med.* 186, 442, 854 (Medea); *Thy.* 96 (Fury). It is attached to Hercules again (by Juno, Lycus, and the Chorus) at 90, 471, 1082. The ablative here seems causal (Woodcock §45) and is found again with *ferox* in an interesting context of boundary violation, viz. Livy's account (1.58.5) of Sextus Tarquin's rape of Lucretia, in the aftermath of which the rapist is described as *ferox expugnato decore muliebri*, 'savage from storming womanly honour'.

   de me triumphat/**Triumphs over me:** a sharply Roman image, in which Juno imagines a Roman triumphal procession with Cerberus paraded by Hercules as pre-eminent captive in his victory over the goddess. Cf. the similarly allusive use of the Roman 'triumph' at *Pha.* 79–80, *Ag.* 804, *Tro.* 150, *Pho.* 578. For 'triumphal' imagery elsewhere in *Hercules*, see 196, 240, 292–4, 544, 619, 761, 828, 1151; for Roman referentiality, see on 46–52.

   superbifica manu/**haughteous hand:** a denigration of Hercules' boastfulness again (cf. 51, 436). *Superbus* is regularly a morally pejorative adjective (see 89, 164, 385, 390, *Med.* 205, *Ag.* 83); here Seneca applies to Hercules a unique word, *superbificus* (= lit. 'proud-making'), translated by the rare adjective 'haughteous', used of 'the haughteous masters of the people', by Karl Marx (1966: 153). For critiques of Hercules' boastfulness, see also 51 and 436. For *manus*, see on 118–22. For Seneca's fondness for adjectives ending in *-ficus*, see *terrifici* (82), *luctifica* (102), *sacrificus* (893), *saxifico* (902). Some of the *-ficus* adjectives in Seneca may have been invented by the dramatist himself, including *superbificus*: see also e.g. *castificus* (*Pha.* 169), *letificus* (*Med.* 577), *nidificus* (*Med.* 714), *incestificus* (*Pho.* 223).

   atrum per urbes ducit Argolicas canem/**Leads the black hound through Argive cities:** this elongated triumphal parade seems unique to this play. It is certainly not in Euripides' version, in which Heracles leaves Cerberus in Hermione at the southern extremity of the Argolid (*Herac.* 615). The climax of the parade will be the entrance of Hercules in Act III. Note the chiastic arrangement of adjectives and nouns: aBbA: see on 11–18. For Cerberus' blackness, see Tib. 1.3.71 (*niger…Cerberus*, 'black Cerberus'), Hor. *Odes* 2.13.34–5 (*atras…auris*, 'black ears'), and his 'black manes' (*nigris…iubis*) at *Ag.* 14. *Ater* is Seneca's favourite word for 'black/dark' in the tragedies, often used with overtones of death; it occurs far more frequently than *niger*. *Argolicus*, like the translation 'Argive', may be ambiguous (see on 6–11): here = (i) 'Greek' (where the epithet functions metonymically); and/or (ii) 'pertaining to Argos or the Argolid' (where the epithet is topographically specific). It was Eurystheus, king of Argos, who ordered the final labour: see on 77–83.

labantem... uidi diem pauidumque Solem/At sight...I saw the day wilt
And the Sun fear: appeals for cosmic disruption, often including the sun's
withdrawal, in reaction to human evil are common in Senecan tragedy (see
on 1202–18), as is the motif of the sun's aversion to beholding creatures of
the underworld, whose world lacks light. Hence at *Ag.* 56 it is assumed that
the sun will not rise until the Ghost of Thyestes returns to hell. Here the Sun
is affronted, or even terrified, by the appearance of Cerberus and the breaking of the boundary between the worlds of light and darkness. Hercules
shows his awareness of this issue when he enters with Cerberus at 592–6;
see also 939–44, 1333–4. Note the verbal polyptoton (*uiso... uidi*) and
emphasis thrown on the second object of Juno's sight, *pauidumque Solem*,
by its initial position in the line following enjambement and before a strong
pause. For this latter technique, see e.g. 74 (*et me prementem*), 207 (*finemque
cladi*), 1338 (*uicemque nostris*); further on enjambement, see on 372–83.
For the repetition of the same syllable at the end and beginning of juxtaposed words (*uidi diem*), see 67 and n. *ad loc.* For polyptoton in *Hercules*,
see on 11–18; for verbal polyptoton, see on 112–18.

inuasit tremor/Trembling blasted: the same phrase is used in the same
metrical position of Oedipus' fear at *Oed.* 659; see further 414 and n. *ad loc.*
Inuadere, 'enter/attack/assault', is an infrequent verb in Senecan tragedy (see
also *Med.* 424, *Pha.* 1160, *Oed.* 659), occurring only here in this play. For
Seneca's 'noun style', see on 11–18; For *tremor* as line-ending, see also *Pha.*
1034, *Ag.* 711.

terna monstri colla deuicti/conquered monster's triple neck: the triple-
headed guard-dog of hell (hence *trigemina... colla*, 'three necks', *Ag.* 14; *tri-
ceps*, 'three-headed', *Oed.* 581), Cerberus, whom Hercules drags from the
underworld (783–827). Hell's guard-dog is mentioned but not named in
Homer (*Il.* 8.368, *Od.* 11.623–5). In Hesiod, where the name Cerberus is
first found (*Theog.* 310–12), he is 'fifty-headed' (πεντηκοντακέφαλον) and in
Horace (*Odes* 2.13.34), as in Pindar (frag. 249b), he is 'one hundred-headed'
(*centiceps*). Indeed Seneca quotes Horace's *centiceps* at *Apoc.* 13.3. But
Cerberus' usual number of heads in the Roman poets is, as here, three: also
e.g. at 784, 796, Virg. *Aen.* 6.417, 421, Ov. *Met.* 4.450–1, Stat. *Silu.* 3.3.27. See
further on 782–91. The distributive adjective is again used of Cerberus'
heads, mouths and barking at 784, 796, *Thy.* 676. For the important *monstrum* motif, see 1280 and n. *ad loc.*

timui imperasse/I feared my commands: for climactic half-lines, see on
40–6. Syncopated perfect infinitives in Senecan tragedy are not unusual: see 91,
216, 473, 640 below. For four such infinitives in four lines, see *Med.* 911–14.

63–74 Juno's fear: Hercules' next step will be the conquest of heaven. Juno here anticipates Hercules' heavenly ambitions to be displayed in the 'mad scene' of Act IV, 955ff. In both the present and the later passage there is a contemporary irony: Hercules' aspirations for divinity may be thought to match those of the Stoic sapiens, 'sage', whose aim was to be *par deo*, 'equal to god' (*Ep. Mor.* 31.9, 48.11, 92.29, *Const.* 8.2). For Stoic language and ideas in Hercules, see on 162–3.

63–8 *Leuia sed nimium queror*/**But I complain too lightly:** again the complaint motif to effect a transition: see 19 and n. *ad loc.* Here the move is from a trivialized past to a more dreadful future, as at *Med.* 48: *leuia memoraui nimis*, 'Too trivial/light my list'. Seneca is fond of using *leuis* for rhetorical intensification (*amplificatio*: Quint. *Inst.* 8.4.19). Thus Andromache (*Tro.* 411): *leuia perpessae sumus*, 'Our sufferings were light'; thus Medea (*Med.* 48): *leuia memoraui nimis*, 'my list is too light'. See further Medea at *Med.* 155, 901, 906, Oedipus at *Oed.* 954–5 and *Pho.* 270, Jocasta at *Pho.* 367–9, the Fury at *Thy.* 47. There is also a metaliterary, generic aspect to *leuis*, suggesting that Juno so far has not been *grauis*, 'heavy', i.e. 'tragic', enough, Note the hyperbaton in which *nimium* may be taken with either *leuia* or *queror* or (preferably) both. Postponement of conjunctions and adverbs is common in Senecan drama: see e.g. (for *sed*) 295, 341, 345, 827, *Ag.* 254, *Thy.* 330, 436; for adverbs, see e.g. 295, 1110, 1174. Here the postponement throws the emphasis forward onto *leuia*. For hyperbaton with *nimium*, see also 186, 295; for *nimium* with an adjective, see on 186–91.

qui uicit ima/**victor of depths:** for *uincere/uictor/uictrix* used of Hercules and those he vanquished, see 48, 62, 69, 84, 116, 242, 278, 487, 505, 546, 558, 582, 591, 612, 615, 778, 800, 815, 816, 898, 1271. Such language necessarily has a Roman resonance because of the role of Victor and Invictus as cult titles of Hercules in Rome, where there were three temples to Hercules Victor as well as the 'Supreme Altar of Unconquered/Invincible Hercules', *Ara Maxima Herculis Inuicti*. In Greece a cult title of Heracles was Καλλίνικος, 'Fair Victor'. For Roman referentiality in *Hercules*, see on 46–52.

sceptra praeripiet patri/**He'll snatch his father's sceptre:** the *sceptrum*, 'sceptre', is a metonym for royal status and power and always an important symbol in Senecan tragedy of kingship, patriarchal authority, and political and sexual power (esp. 'male' power). Neptune and Dis, too, rule with sceptres (599, 707). Its frequent occurrence in *Oedipus* (12, 105, 241, 513, 635, 642, 670, 691, 705) is bound up with Seneca's focus in that play on issues of sex, power, and the father, as is its occurrence here. Cf. the use of this symbol at

272, 331, 342, 399, 430, 502, 599, 707; *Pha.* 217, 617, 868; *Ag.* 10, 60, 111, 194, 340•, 930; *Med.* 252, 982; *Thy.* 229, 341, 532, 604, 971; *Pho.* 40–1, 275.

in astra... ueniet/reach the stars: an Ovidian phrase, used twice of Romulus (*Fas.* 2.478, 3.186; cf. *Fas.* 3.808). For Hercules' reaching for the stars, see 958–9.

lenta... Bacchus uia/Bacchus' slow path: Bacchus (see on 11–18), another of Jupiter's Theban bastards (and listed as such by Juno earlier: 16–17), established his divinity gradually on earth. He is regularly paired with Hercules, most famously perhaps in Anchises' comparison of Augustus to Hercules and Bacchus at Virgil *Aeneid* 6.801–5. For *uia* used of apotheosis, see 74: *quaerit ad superos uiam*, 'He seeks a path to the high gods' (of Hercules); *Med.* 1022: *patuit in caelum uia*, 'Heaven's pathway opens' (for Medea): *Oct.* 476: *petitur hac caelum uia*, 'Heaven is sought by this path'; Virg. *Geo.* 4.562: *uiamque adfectat Olympo*, 'and tries the path to Olympus' (of Octavian).

iter ruina quaeret et/He'll seek a route through ruin and: like Julius Caesar, who, at Lucan 1.150, 'joyfully made a route through ruin' (*gaudensque uiam fecisse ruina*). Deianira, too, seems to echo Juno's statement: *nuptas ruinis quaerit*, 'he (Hercules) seeks brides through ruin' (*HO* 421). Note the repetition of the same syllable at the end and beginning of juxtaposed words (*quaeret et*), a phenomenon disliked by Quintilian (*Inst.* 9.4.41). There are many such repetitions in Senecan tragedy. Clearly the dramatist found them unproblematic. See e.g. 60 (*di di*), 102 (*at at*), 255 (*re re*), 283 (*te te*), 293 (*te te*), 393 (*ca ca*), 449 (*is is*), 704 (*et et*), 730 (*is is*), 871 (*et et*), 946 (*et et*), 951 (*et et*), 995 (*re re*), 1123 (*re re*), 1163 (*is is*), 1341 (*te te*). For Senecan tragic *et et* elsewhere see e.g. *Thy.* 28, 278, 479, 500.

uacuo uolet regnare mundo/want to reign In a vacant sky: a phrase of wide-ranging political semiotics, applicable to any emperor intent on destroying rivals to the throne. By 'vacant sky' (*uacuo... mundo*) Juno may simply mean a sky in which the position of ruler is now vacant, i.e. in which there is no rival to the throne, as in Virgil's description of the palace of the bees, where the better contender for the throne is to 'reign in the vacant court' (*uacua... regnet in aula*, *Geo.* 4.90). Fitch *ad loc.* suggests that 'perhaps' Juno means 'empty' in a stronger sense, a sky from which all the gods have been removed. The phrase certainly seems ambiguous: cf. the ambiguity in Lucan's etymologically punning description of the ruling snake at 9.726: *in uacua regnat basiliscus harena*, 'the basilisk reigns in a vacant/empty desert'. For *mundus* here meaning 'sky', see *mundo* at 70.

68–74 *tumet*/swells: this 'swelling' imagery recurs at 171 (*tumidum*), 384 (*tumidus*), 955 (*tumida*), 1090–1 (*tumultus, tumet*), 1219 (*tumultu*); see also

221, 551, 936. For *tumere* in other plays, see e.g. *Tro.* 1096, *Pho.* 352, *Thy.* 268, 737.

didicit ferendo/By bearing...he learnt: an even closer linguistic reformulation of the Aeschylean πάθει μάθος doctrine (see on 30–5). The 'lessons' of experience are a common motif in Senecan tragedy: hence the pointed, often ironic uses of *discere* and *docere*. See e.g. for *discere*: 398, 491; *Pha.* 1200 (*disce a nouerca*, 'learn from the step-mother'); *Tro.* 242, 264, 730; *Pho.* 328–31. And for *docere*: 242, 1264; *Pha.* 594; *Ag.* 932; *Thy.* 310.

subdidit mundo caput/His head upheld the sky: the allusion is to Hercules' holding up the sky in place of Atlas, a deed often associated from Pherecydes onwards with the former's mission to gather the golden apples of the Hesperides (see on 235–40). Such association may be seen, for example, in the metopes on the temple of Zeus at Olympia. See further Gantz (1993: 1.410–13). The sky-bearing, however, is mentioned as a separate task not associated with the Hesperides mission in the choral ode at Eur. *Herac.* 405–7. Seneca refers to this episode again at 425, 528, 1102 below and *Pha.* 328. For *manus*, see on 118–22.

nec flexit umeros molis immensae labor/The vast bulk's task did not bow his shoulders: four nouns in one iambic line provide a good example of Seneca's 'noun style'; see on 11–18. For the play's focus on Hercules' 'shoulders', *umeros*, see on 622–5. The phrase *molis immensae labor* has a Roman resonance about it, potentially triggering memories of the *tantae molis* used of the founding of Rome (Virg. *Aen.* 1.33).

meliusque/But...better: for the adversative use of -*que*, cf. e.g. 961, *Oed.* 196, *Pha.* 110, 366, 1010, *Med.* 407, *Tro.* 319. I join Fitch (1987a and 2018), Chaumartin, Billerbeck, and Giardina (2007) in reading *meliusque* (*E*^acFMN), as against the Zwierlein reading *mediusque* (*E*^pcA), also printed by Viansino (1965 and 1993), Giardina (1966), and Caviglia.

collo...Herculeo/on Hercules' neck: the use of an adjective instead of the genitive of a proper name is a common Senecan tragic practice: for *Herculeus* in this play, see also 225, 274, 351, 523, 631, 826, 882, 991, 1034, 1100, 1152, 1316.

ceruix...caelum tulit/neck...bore...sky: Juno is borrowing (as elsewhere in this prologue) from Hercules' own speech in Ovid: *hac caelum ceruice tuli*, 'on this neck I bore the sky' (*Met.* 9.198).

et me prementem/and me, Pressing down: an interesting, apparently innovative addition to the traditional legend, which (see Billerbeck *ad loc.*) Sidonius seems to have had in mind when he wrote: *Tirynthius heros* |

pondera suscepit caeli simul atque nouercae, 'The Tirynthian hero bore the weight alike of the sky and his stepmother' (*Carm.* 7.581–2).

quaerit ad superos uiam/He seeks a path to those above: there is acerbic verbal play here. In seeking a path to 'those above' (i.e. on earth), Hercules is seeking a path to 'those above' (in heaven). Juno is sneering at Hercules' social climbing, viewing his ambition as Tacitus views the ambition of the social climbing Sejanus in his portrait at *Annals* 4.1.3 (*summa apiscendi libido*, 'lust to reach the top'). For the ambiguity of the relative term, *superi*, see on 46–52. Note the present indicative, *quaerit*, rather than the future *quaeret* (67). What began as fear of a possible future has changed into a statement of fact. For *uia* of apotheosis, see on 63–8.

75–85 Other monsters would be useless: Hercules must war with himself.

75–6 *Perge, ira, perge*/Go, wrath, go: *perge* is regularly used in Senecan tragedy as an exhortation to someone hesitating: see e.g. *Tro.* 630, 1002, *Pha.* 862 (*perge…perge*), *Med.* 566, *Thy.* 23, 490, 892. It is the opening word of the Fury's initial speech in *Thyestes* (23), where, as here, it is used paratactically with *et* (*perge…et…age*, 'Go…and goad'). Its use is sometimes ironic: *Pha.* 173, *Oed.* 880, *Tro.* 898, 1002. *Perge* is also found in the prose works as an injunction against procrastination: *Ep. Mor.* 76.5. For the doubling of an imperative, sometimes as *geminatio*, see on 92–9. The imperatives would perhaps have been accompanied by some reginal gesture.

Note here the ontologization of *ira*, 'wrath'. The ontologization (personification, objectification, reification) of the emotions is common in Senecan tragedy, where they are often treated as entities separate from the self, sometimes addressed in the vocative (as e.g. here, *Med.* 916, 953: *ira*; *Ag.* 649, *Med.* 139, 914, 944, 1016, 1019, *Thy.* 944: *dolor*; *Med.* 930: *furor*; *Thy.* 882: *timor*), sometimes functioning as third-person subjects of their own verbs (as e.g. 1167, *Ag.* 142, *Pho.* 299, *Med.* 927, 938, 943, *Thy.* 40, 504, 552: *ira*; 28, 99, *Ag.* 142, *Pha.* 99, 366, *Tro.* 282, *Med.* 671, *Thy.* 496: *dolor*; 1240, *Ag.* 138, 288, *Pha.* 250, *Pho.* 301, *Thy.* 925: *pudor*; *Ag.* 142: *spes*; *Ag.* 239, *Med.* 938: *amor*; 363, 991, 1049, 1097•, 1134, 1244, *Pha.* 178, 184, 268, 824, *Med.* 406, *Tro.* 283, *Thy.* 27, 339: *furor*; *Thy.* 922: *maeror, pauor*; 382. *Med.* 952, *Pha.* 354, 696: *odium*).

This ontologization of the emotions was not new: e.g. Dido addresses *pudor* at Virg. *Aen.* 4.27; *dolor* makes Medea kill her children at Ov. *Tr.* 2.387–8, *Rem.* 59–60 (cf. also e.g. *Her.* 12.61, *Met.* 7.19–20). Famously Virgil describes Turnus' dilemma in *Aeneid* 12 (666–8) as an onset of ontologized psychological states, emotions and moral values:

aestuat ingens
uno in corde pudor mixtoque insania luctu
et furiis agitatus amor et conscia uirtus.

In a single heart
Surge immense shame and madness mixed with grief
And love goaded by rage and self-conscious valour.

What *was* new in Senecan tragedy is both the frequency and the range of this ontologization of emotions and values. For *ira*, see also on 19–29.

magna meditantem opprime/grind this glory seeker: note the patterned alliteration of the line: *p/p/m/m/p/p*. Juno, despite her passion, maintains her rhetorical control. With *magna meditari*, cf. the Greek μέγα φρονεῖν.

congredere, manibus ipsa dilacera tuis/Fight, tear him apart yourself with your hands: clearly Juno has slid from addressing her anger to addressing herself. *Congredere manibus*: note the unusual metrics, viz. resolutions in the first two feet (dactyl followed by tribrach), 'expressing the urgency and vehemence of the speaker' (Fitch *ad loc*.); cf. 100. For other instances in *Hercules* of the dactyl-tribrach combination at the start of a line, see 100, 221, 229, 240, 337, 501, 732, 769, 947, 1148, 1154, 1224 (line references courtesy of Professor Joseph Smith of SDSU). *Dilacera* is a Senecan *hapax*, picked up at *HO* 826.

77–83 *quid tanta mandas odia*/Why delegate such hate: Juno has perhaps been reading *De Ira*, where it is specifically stated that the *iratus* 'does not delegate her/his vengeance': *nec mandat ultionem suam* (*Ira* 3.3.3). There is clearly some wordplay here. The presence of *manibus* in line 76 brings out the etymological roots of *mandare* (– *manus dare*).

imperando fessus Eurystheus/Eurystheus…tired from his mandates: Eurystheus was the ruler of the Argolid (Mycenae, Argos, Tiryns) and cousin of Hercules, who imposed the twelve labours upon him. See further on 830–7 and Introd. 61. Note that Juno's statement here implies that Eurystheus ordered Hercules' labours (in accordance with the standard accounts); her words at 42 above (see n. *ad loc*.) imply that she ordered them. Clearly this play implies that both were involved. In any case, Seneca has transferred the phrase 'tired from one's own mandates' from Ovid's Juno (*defessa iubendo*, *Met.* 9.198) to his Eurystheus. See Kingery and Fitch *ad loc*.

Titanas ausos/Titans who dared: Juno envisages a new Titanomachy, in which the defeated old gods (the children of Uranus/Caelus/Sky and Gaea/Terra/Earth), who once rebelled against Jupiter's rule and battled the Olympians, rise up to wage war on Hercules. References to a Titanomachy are common in Roman poetry, where Titanomachy and Gigantomachy are often conflated (e.g. famously in Hor. *Odes*. 3.4), as they are here. At Stat. *Theb*. 8.42–4 Dis describes the restlessness of the Giants and Titans in hell. For *ausus* and Seneca's language of boundary violation, see on 547–9; for boundary violation, see on 46–52.

emitte/Release: presumably from Tartarus, where at Hes. *Th*. 713–35 the Titans are incarcerated. For *emittere* of release from the underworld, see 283, *Ag*. 2, *Oed*. 394, *Thy*. 672, Virg. *Geo*. 3.551, Ov. *Met*. 5.321.

Siculi uerticis/Sicily's peak: the volcanic Mt Etna.

tellus Gigante Doris excusso tremens/Doric land convulse as its Giant shakes: the 'Doric land' is Sicily, so-called because its early colonies (Syracuse, Megara Hyblaea, Gela) were established by Dorian Greeks. The Giant is probably Typhoeus/Typhon, a monster with several snake heads (a hundred at Hes. *Th*. 825), fire-blazing eyes, and manifold voices (of gods or animals); the last child of Mother Earth, he tried to dethrone Jupiter. He is placed by Ovid beneath Etna (*Met*. 5.346–58, *Fas*. 1.573, 4.491, *Pont*. 2.10.23–4) and is termed a 'Giant' by the poet (*Met*. 5.346, *Pont*. 2.10.24) and a rebel against heaven (*aetherias ausum sperare Typhoea sedes*, 'Typhoeus who dared hope for a heavenly abode', *Met*. 5.348: note the description of the Titans at 79). Seneca mentions his rebellion against Jupiter at *Med*. 773–4. Amid variant accounts, a standard Gigantomachy has Typhoeus blasted by Jupiter, whose thunderbolt drives him down to Tartarus: see e.g. Hor. *Odes* 3.4.42–80. The thunderbolt, still embedded in Typhoeus, was sometimes represented as responsible for the volcanic eruptions of Mt Etna in Sicily (*Thy*. 809–10, Ov. *Met*. 352–3) or those of the island of Inarime, modern Ischia (*HO* 1155–6). Here the Giant's 'shaking' is associated with earthquakes, as at Ov. *Met*. 5.356 (*tremit tellus*, 'the earth trembles/convulses'); see also Virg. *Aen*. 3.581: *fessum quotiens mutet latus, intremere omnem…Trinacriam*, 'whenever he changes his weary side, all Trinacria/Sicily trembles/convulses', though Virgil's Giant is not Typhoeus but Enceladus. For Hercules and the Gigantomachy, see on 439–47. The epithet *Doris*, 'Doric', is a Senecan *hapax*.

monstri…terrifici/fierce monster's: for Seneca's fondness for adjectives ending in -*ficus*, see on 57–63. For the important *monstrum* motif, see 1280 and n. *ad loc*.

alias Luna concipiat feras/moon conceive still other beasts: the moon was sometimes regarded as the origin of legendary beasts such as the Nemean Lion (see e.g. Hyg. *Fab*. 30.2). There is no contradiction here with line 77, as Fitch *ad loc*. argues, deleting the line after Leo. The *ferae* of 77 refers to the beasts already sent. The subjunctive, like several in this section (*discedant*, 77, *uacet*, 78, *leuet*, 82), is jussive/hortatory. Along with Zwierlein, Billerbeck, and others, I retain the line. The phrase *concipiat feras* is applied to *terra* rather than *Luna* in Hercules' own speech at *HO* 34.

84–5 *uicit ista*/conquered their like: *ista* seems very general, 'such as these/their like', with reference not only to Hercules' defeat of beasts and monsters but to his participation in the defeat of the Giants and Titans (see Eur. *Herac.* 176–80: Giants; Hor. *Odes* 2.12.6–9: Giants and possibly Titans together). See further on 439–45. For *uincere* and Hercules, see on 63–8.

quaeris Alcidae parem/**You seek Alcides' match:** 'Alcides', descendant of Alcaeus, who was the father of Amphitryon, is a name used of Hercules nineteen times in this play, as against seventeen times for 'Hercules' itself. The name seems first to be encountered in Callimachus (*Hymn.* 3.145) and is found frequently in Roman verse from its first attestation at Virg. *Ecl.* 7.61 (see e.g. Hor. *Odes* 1.12.25, Virg. *Aen.* 5.414, Ov. *Am.* 3.8.52). It is a nomenclature which emphasizes Hercules' mortal nature in a play where his divine paternity is an issue, while paradoxically drawing attention to the adulterous context of his bruited divine birth. Notably in the play's penultimate line, Hercules is addressed as *Alcide* (1343: see n. *ad loc.*). Behind its use, too, seems to lie an etymological association with ἀλκή, 'strength' (see 186 and n. *ad loc.*). In *parem*, 'match', there is perhaps a suggestion of gladiatorial language, as if Hercules fighting himself would constitute a gladiatorial *par*, 'pair'. For the gladiatorial semiotics of *par*, see Masters (1992: 44 and n. 2). For the *quaeris* question, see also *Tro.* 407, Cat. 7.1.

nemo est nisi ipse/**There's none but he:** cf. Massinger, *Duke of Milan* 4.3: 'Her goodness doth disdain comparison | And, but herself, admits no parallel.' There is perhaps an imperial resonance in Juno's language. The emperor, of course, was *nonpareil*, as Seneca observes of Nero at *De Clementia* 1.6, written probably shortly after *Hercules*. For Roman referentiality in *Hercules*, see on 46–52.

bella iam secum gerat/**Now he must war with himself:** the idea of using, as the instrument to punish one's enemy, the enemy himself is not restricted to this play: Atreus' strategy to defeat his brother Thyestes is to use the most powerful weapon of all: *ipso Thyeste*, 'Thyestes himself' (*Thy.* 259). Seneca's formulation in *Hercules* and *Thyestes* may owe something to Ovid's conceit of describing Ajax's suicide as a conquest of Ajax by Ajax: *ne quisquam Aiacem possit superare nisi Aiax*, 'None may Ajax overcome save Ajax' (*Met.* 13.390, trans. Golding). Shakespeare's depictions of antique suicide seem a development of this tradition: 'For Brutus only overcame himself' (*JC* V.v.6–7), 'So it should be that none but Antony | Should conquer Antony' (*AC*

IV.xv.17–18). 'Warring with oneself' is a negative development of the Roman *topos* of 'vying with oneself' (*secum certare*): Cic. *Fam.* 9.14.6, Livy 6.6.9, Pliny *Pan.* 13.5. For *bella*, 'wars', or *bellum*, 'war', used of Hercules' deeds, including the famous labours, see 211, 527, 638, 997. A reworking of these lines in the prologue delivered by Junon in Rotrou's *Les Sosies* (1638) is noted by Fitch *ad loc.*:

> D'autres armes manquant à ma fureur extrême,
> Je n'opposerai plus que lui même à lui même;
> Lui même il se vaincra; s'il naît pour vaincre tout,
> De ce dernier ouvrage il viendra bien à bout.

Hercules' self-warring, however, is not restricted to his madness and murder of his family: see on 112–18 (*uicit*) and Introd. §VII.

86–122 Juno summons the Furies (86–8, 100), expresses her intention to call other fiends from hell (92–9), orders the Furies to 'infuriate' Hercules and herself (100–12) and prescripts the main plot of the play (112–22). As Fitch notes *ad loc.*, Seneca here is building on two famous 'Juno and the Furies' scenes: one at Virg. *Aen.* 7.310–40 (involving a single Fury, Allecto), the other at Ov. *Met.* 4.447–511 (involving all the 'sisters', but primarily Tisiphone). Cf. also Valerius' Juno, who 'will stir the Furies and Dis' (*Furias Ditemque mouebo*, *Arg.* 3.520). Juno's prologic function is obviously underscored by the reminiscences of the Virgilian Juno's second prologue in *Aeneid* 7. But something else is happening here. In the early part of this section of her speech Juno is performing (at one level) the metatheatrical function of asking for 'infuriation' (86–8, 100–12), in the sense of inspiration to prescript the plot of *Hercules* itself—which she does when 'infuriated' at 113–22, even ironically intimating a dramatic sequel (121–2). Cf. Medea's invocation of the Furies at *Med.* 13–18, Atreus' request to the Furies at *Thy.* 250–4 (both are requests for the enactment of vengeance/the plotting of a revenge tragedy), and the pre-scripting of *Thyestes* by a Fury at *Thy.* 23–67 and her inauguration of the play's action. Note also the non-'infuriated' prescripting of *Agamemnon* by Thyestes' Ghost at *Ag.* 37–52. Schiesaro (2003: 186) comments astutely: 'she (Juno) embodies the creative power of the author and the plot which she conceives is the tragedy which happens.' For *furor* as poetic inspiration, see on 92–9. See further Introd. §VII, 71–3. For metatheatre, see on 109–12.

86–8 *imo Tartari fundo*/Tartarus' Deepest pit: often used by metonymy for the underworld itself, Tartarus was strictly the bottommost pit of hell, the grimmest region of the underworld, where the wicked received eternal punishment. Virgil's account of Tartarus (*Aen.* 6.548–627) places the Titans there *fundo…in imo* (*Aen.* 6.581; cf. Hom. *Il.* 14.279), but locates the 'iron chambers of the Eumenides' (*ferrei…Eumenidum thalami, Aen.* 6.280) at the underworld's entrance. Statius follows Seneca in placing the *Eumenidum thalami* in 'deepest hell' (*Acheronte sub imo, Theb.* 1.597–8)—a kind of reversion to Aeschylus, whose Eumenides are located in 'Tartarus beneath the earth' (*Eum.* 72).

Eumenides: one of the Greek names for the Furies (= euphemistically 'the Kindly Ones'). This is the only certain occurrence of the name in the entire Senecan *corpus*, although it may occur at 577 (see n. *ad loc.*) and it is picked up by the dramatist of the *HO* (1002). The Furies, sometimes referred to collectively as the Erinyes, were spirits of the underworld, who avenged bloodshed, caused terror, and implemented curses; they sometimes functioned as the curses themselves (hence they were sometimes called Ἀραί or *Dirae*). Ariadne (like Juno here) invokes them as *Eumenides* at Cat. 64.193, Dido as *Dirae ultrices* at Virg. *Aen.* 4.610. Often regarded as the daughters of Night (see esp. Virg. *Aen.* 12.845–52), they were sometimes referred to as the 'sisters', *sorores* (see e.g. 110, *Ag.* 759, *Oed.* 161, Virg. *Aen.* 7.327, 454, Ov. *Met.* 4.451, Stat. *Theb.* 5.201) and were regularly portrayed as three in number—Megaera (102, *Med.* 963, *Thy.* 252, *HO* 1006, 1014), Tisiphone (984, *HO* 1012, Virg. *Geo.* 3.552), and Allecto (Virg. *Aen.* 7.324ff.). Allecto is never named in Seneca. *Agmen*, 'troop' (101: see n. *ad loc.*), suggests a larger group than three on this occasion. Reference to the Furies in Senecan tragedy is not infrequent: e.g. 982–4; *Med.* 13–18, 958–68; *Oed.* 590, 644–5; *Thy.* 23–121, 250–2. Their weapons included blazing torches (100–1, 983–4, *Med.* 15, 962, *Oed.* 161, *Thy.* 251, *HO* 1005, Enn. *Alc.* frag. 27 Jocelyn, Cic. *Leg.* 1.40, Virg. *Aen.* 7.456–7, Ov. *Met.* 4.508, 10.350), snakes and whips (101, *Ag.* 760–1, *Oed.* 645, *Thy.* 96, *HO* 1002, Virg. *Aen.* 7.450–1, VF 7.149), even 'snake-whips' (*uiperea…uerbera* 88, 982, *Med.* 961–2, *Ag.* 760, Virg. *Aen.* 6.571–2, Stat. *Theb.* 1.113). Here, unusually, their hair, often said to be bristling with snakes (see 101, *Med.* 14), is on fire (*flammeae…comae*, 87): I take it (see the stage directions) that 'their hair flames, bristling with snakes'. At 105–6, pleonastically, they are instructed to inflame themselves. One of the original functions of the Furies was the punishment of bloodshed within the family, but here their primary function is to punish Hercules for his violation of the underworld (104) by 'infuriating' him, i.e. driving him mad, filling him with *Furor*/Rage/Madness (107–8). Euripides put Iris and Lyssa/ Madness onstage in the middle of his play to make Heracles mad (*Herac.* 815–73). Seneca restricts his divine figures to the prologue, leaving the audience to ponder the relationship of this scene to the Herculean madness which is later displayed.

uiperea... uerbera/viperous whips: see previous n. Note that *uipereus* is used only once elsewhere by Seneca at *Oed.* 587 (see also *HO* 169). It is used three times in Virgil's *Aeneid* and several times in Ovid's *Metamorphoses*.

Enter a troop of FURIES...: it is debatable whether the Furies, who are addressed by Juno and given twelve and a half lines of instruction (100–11), are intended by Seneca to appear onstage. Fitch *ad loc.* answers tentatively in the affirmative, based on the Virgilian and Ovidian 'source passages' (see on 86–99), in which Juno addresses a Fury/Furies 'in person'. Such an argument is less than compelling. But, given the dramatist's predilection for theatrical spectacle and his later delight in having a Fury onstage in *Thyestes* (see also *Medea* 958–71, where Furies incite Medea to filicide and may well appear onstage), I am inclined to believe not only that a troop of Furies (there seem to be more than the traditional three: see *agmen*, 'troop', 101 and n. *ad loc.*) should appear onstage but that Seneca created this ending to Juno's speech for a theatrical as well as thematic purpose, i.e. (in part) to give Juno a spectacular climax and exit. Juno will not appear in the play again. Certainly a Roman theatre audience would be familiar with the appearance of Furies on the stage: see e.g. Enn. *Eum.* (frag. 284 Jocelyn—also *Alcmeo* features a hallucination of Furies, frags 24–7 Jocelyn), Pac. *Or.*, (possibly) *Penth.*, Cic. *Ros. Am.* 67, *Pis.* 46, Virg. *Aen.* 4.469–73. Seneca's *Thyestes* begins with the guilty Tantalus terrorized by a Fury onstage. Also important to note is Seneca's detailed comparison in *De Ira* (2.35.5) of anger to one of the Furies rising from hell (*inferna monstra*), girt with snakes and breathing fire (*succincta serpentibus et igneo flatu*), bloody (*cruentam*), hissing (*sibilo*), and brandishing weapons in each hand (*tela manu utraque quatientem*). A spectacular entrance of Furies, perhaps from beneath the stage accompanied by smoke and fire and brandishing snake-whips (88) and blazing torches (101), would ensure that the end of Juno's prologue would not be forgotten. Cicero's observations on the use of a stage trapdoor in Pacuvius' *Iliona* (*Sest.* 126), glossed by a scholiast as 'standard dramatic practice' (Schol. Bob.: *secundum consuetudinem scaenicorum*), shows what was possible even in the republican theatre. Blazing torches are important props in the *epithalamium* choral ode and Act IV of *Medea* and in Act V of *Thyestes*.

Their hair flames, bristling with snakes...: see above.

89–91 Juno acerbically addresses Hercules.

I nunc, superbe....pete/Go now, proud man, seek: Juno's ironic imperative is of a typically Senecan kind: cf. *Med.* 197, 650, 1007 (where the same command is repeated: *i nunc, superbe…pete*); *Tro.* 191–3, 898, 901–2, 1165; *Oed.* 880; *Pha.* 173, 929–30. See also *Helu.* 6.8, 10.10, *Breu. Vit.* 12.8, *Ben.* 6.35.5. Sarcastic commands preceded by *i* or *ite* ('Go') are a regular rhetorical ploy (called *permissio*) of Roman writers; cf. e.g. Prop. 2.29.22, Hor. *Ep.* 1.6.17, Virg. *Aen.* 4.381, Ov. *Her.* 3.26, Mart. *Epig.* 9.2.13, Juv. 10.166–7.

humana temne/Scorn humanity: so Cicero advocates (without the irony) *illa humana contemnito* (*Rep.* 6.20; cf. *Off.* 1.67). *Temnere* is a Senecan *hapax.*

ferox/savage: see on 57–63.

fugisse/left: note the omission of the accusative subject of the verb as often in verse. For syncopated perfect infinitives, see 63 and n. *ad loc.*

hic tibi ostendam inferos/Here I'll show you hell: which she will do in the prescripted play which ensues, the final act of which dramatizes Hercules in a veritable hell on earth. Ironically Juno's words are echoed by Hercules in his opening speech: *ostendi inferos*, 'I showed hell' (613). For metatheatre in *Hercules*, see on 109–12.

92–9 Juno lists the fiends whom she will summon from hell to aid her. The list is specifically chosen for her prime objective, Hercules' madness and murder of kin: *Discors Dea* (Discordia: War-With-Self), *Scelus* (Crime), *Impietas* (Impiety/Offence-Against-Kin), *Error* (Delusion/Error), and *Furor* (Rage/Madness). Much of Act V will pivot on a discussion of *scelus, error, furor,* the claims of *pietas* (love/duty to family, see on 1092–9) and the issue of Hercules' guilt: see 1199–1201, 1219–21, 1237–8, 1240–1, 1246–57, 1329.

reuocabo in alta conditam caligine/I shall call, concealed in caverns of mist: the verb embodies the Roman practice of *euocatio*, the summoning of the spirits of the dead (*inferum euocatio*: Pliny *HN* 30.6). Note how the alliteration of *c*s and the rare quadrisyllabic ending give the Latin line potent, oral force. For the 'mist', *caligo*, of the underworld, see 710 below, Ov. *Met.* 4.455, 10.54.

ultra nocentum exilia/Beyond banished sinners: the sinners are presumably Tantalus, Ixion, etc., also located, like the Furies (86), in Tartarus. *Nocentum* is a form of the genitive plural, used often in Latin verse, esp. with substantival participles, in place of -*ium* for metrical convenience; see also *Tro.* 1009 (*dolentum*), *Med.* 740 (*silentum*), *Pha.* 1109 (*dolentum*). For this 'furthest end' of hell, its 'ulterior pit', see 1225 below (*finem ultimum*) and Stat. *Theb.* 8.15 (*ulteriore barathro*).

discordem deam/divine Discord: lit. 'discord's goddess', i.e. Discordia, a violent figure in Ennius' *Annales* (frags 225–6 Skutsch) and listed with the Eumenides and other dire underworld entities (Grief, Disease, Old Age,

Fear, etc.) by Virgil at *Aen.* 6.274–81. She seems also to be identified with the *discors Erinys* of *Thy.* 251 (so Fitch *ad* 92–4). A brilliant description of her closes out Petronius' civil war poem: *Sat.* 124, lines 271–94.

ingens montis oppositi specus/mountain barrier's vast cave: *specus*, 'cave', is part of the language of the underworld in Senecan tragedy, see *Tro.* 430: *Stygis profundae claustra et obscuri specus*, 'the barriers of the deep Styx and its dark caverns'—also *Herc.* 665, 718, *Ag.* 2, *Pha.* 1201, *Thy.* 105 and (possibly) *Thy.* 9, *Tro.* 178, 198, 520; cf. *HO* 262. The association with the underworld is found in the Roman tradition as early as Ennian tragedy (*Hectoris Lytra* frag. 152 Jocelyn: *inferum uastos specus*, 'vast caves of those below'). Zwierlein's emendation of *oppositi* to *oppositu*, printed in later editions of the OCT, has not been followed by recent editors.

extraham/drag: Seneca elsewhere uses *extrahere* of the effort required to bring up the denizens of hell: see *Oed.* 396–7, where the 'population of internal Styx' has to be dragged up (*extrahendus*); *Thy.* 1, where the Ghost of Tantalus is dragged up (*extrahit*). Cf. Luc. 6.636 (*extractus Stygio populus...Auerno*, 'a multitude dragged up from Stygian Avernus'. At the end of *Oedipus* the protagonist 'drags away' with him out of Thebes the hellish figures cited in the next n.

Scelus...Impietas...Error...Furor/Crime...Impiety...Delusion...Rage: for similarly dire abstractions associated with the operation of the Furies, see Ov. *Met.* 4.484–5 (*Luctus, Pauor, Terror, Insania*). Cf. also those which Oedipus takes with him as he leaves Thebes (*Oed.* 1059–61):

> violenta Fata et horridus Morbi tremor
> Maciesque et atra Pestis et rabidus Dolor.
> mecum ite, mecum. ducibus his uti libet.

> Brutal Fates and blasting tremors of Disease
> And Wasting and black Plague and rabid Pain.
> Come with me, with me. These guides are my joy.

See also 689–96 below and *Oed.* 652. Personified abstractions are to be found in early Roman tragedy (see Jocelyn 1967, 195–6, Acc. *Eurysaces*, frag. 349 Klotz, Pac. *Atalanta* frag. 52 Klotz, *Periboea* frag. 301 Klotz), and were a feature of Greek and Roman literature from Homer onwards (e.g. *Il.* 4.440, 11.37). See further *Oct.* 431, Virg. *Aen.* 6.273–81, Petron. *Sat.* 124.257–8, Stat. *Theb.* 7.47–54, Silius 13.579–87, Claud. *Ruf.* 1.28–38.

Scelus/Crime: a negative moral and legal term, often in Senecan tragedy of strong disapprobation; frequently synonymous with *malum*, 'evil/wrong', and *nefas* 'unspeakable act/sin'. It is used to describe the events of Act IV by the Chorus (1134, see n. *ad loc.*) and is a central word and concept in the debate of Act V (see 121 and n. *ad loc.*).

*suumque lambens sanguinem Impietas ferox/*And savage Impiety licking its own blood: the antithesis of *Pietas* (for which see on 1092–9), described here in a striking image—one which perhaps resonated in the mind of the younger Pliny when he described Domitian as *belua...quodam specu inclusa nunc propinquorum sanguinem lamberet,* 'a beast...locked in a cave now licking relatives' blood' (*Pan.* 48.3). The Pliny allusion reminds the modern reader of the political semiotics underlying the surface of Senecan tragedy. *Impietas,* a Senecan tragic *hapax,* occurs at *Oct.* 431, where it is modified by *furens,* 'raging'.

*Error/*Delusion: 'Error' or 'Delusion', an Ovidian abstraction (*Met.* 12.59) found in company with *Furor* (*Am.* 1.2.35). Hercules' own *error* will be caused by the *furor,* 'madness/rage', which comes upon him in Act IV. Both will be commented upon by the Chorus at 1096–7• and will be central concepts in the moral discussion of Act V (1220, 1237–8, 1240, 1244, 1261).

*in se semper armatus Furor/*ever armed against itself, Rage: cf. Amphitryon's later definition of *Furor,* as he describes Hercules (1220–1): *quodque habet proprium furor,* | *in se ipse saeuit,* 'As is the nature of rage, | It savages itself.' *Furor,* described by Cicero as *mentis ad omnia caecitas,* 'complete mental blindness' (*Tusc.* 3.11), is the Roman poets' term for a violent brainstorm and frenzied emotional state, translated in some contexts as 'rage', 'frenzy', 'bloodlust', 'passion', 'fury', or 'madness'. It is an important motor of human action in Seneca's (and Virgil's) tragic world and a major subject of Seneca's dramatic exploration (see e.g. the last line of *Agamemnon*). It is a term used interchangeably sometimes with *insania,* 'madness' (e.g. Hercules' *furor* at 1049, 1098, 1134) or even *ira* (e.g. Oedipus 'rages with anger', *ira furit, Oed.* 957). It is also used (importantly and frequently) to denote prophetic inspiration (as at *Ag.* 720, *Tro.* 34, 977, Cic. *Diu.* 1.66, Virg. *Aen.* 6.100–2), and poetic inspiration (see esp. Cic. *Diu.* 1.80; cf. Plato *Ion* passim, *Apol.* 22a–c, *Men.* 99c–e), so that the *furor* stipulated by Juno at 109 could be interpreted as having a poetic as well as an emotional dimension (see Introd. §VII, 126). In this play the noun *furor* appears eleven times, including seven times in the final act (98, 108, 363, 991, 1049, 1097•, 1134, 1220, 1240, 1244, 1261) and the verb *furere* and the verbal adjective *furens* appear *in toto* also eleven times (106, 109, 120, 758, 815, 820, 968, 1005, 1009, 1053, 1254). For the personification of *furor* elsewhere in Senecan tragedy, see e.g. *Pha.* 178, *Med.* 391, 396, *Oed.* 590, *Thy.* 27. Though this play defines *furor* as essentially self-destructive (here and at 1220–1) and Seneca's nephew Lucan begins his whole epic with such *furor* (*BC* 1.8), in Seneca's tragedies (see e.g. *Medea* and *Thyestes*) the destruction *furor* wreaks is more often on others. Note in Juno's list not only the climactic position of *Furor*, but also the latter's location in the underworld, as at *Oed.* 590. The Furies are traditionally chthonic powers, but Seneca is the first author attested to have located *Furor* itself in the underworld. In Virgil's idealized Rome *Furor impius* is imprisoned in the temple of Janus behind the Gates of War (*Aen.* 1.293–6)—the subject of a painting in the Augustan Forum (see Serv. *ad loc.*). In Euripides' *Heracles*, Lyssa, 'Madness', accompanies Iris, apparently from the heavens. For *semper* qualifying an epithet in *Hercules*, see also 2, 1256.

hoc, hoc ministro noster utatur dolor/This last, this last must be servant to my pain: cf. the Senecan Oedipus' final words printed above (*Oed.* 1061), where he, too, expresses an intention to use (*uti*) abstract entities from hell. Note the duplication (*hoc, hoc*, lit. 'this, this'), a rhetorical device, known as *geminatio*, which is applied in Seneca's tragedies to a wide range of words (often, as here, monosyllabic and in the first foot of a line of verse), and is a regular feature of his poetic style: e.g. *hoc, hoc*, 99, *Thy.* 916; *hic, hic*, 1313, *Pha.* 1268; *hac, hac, Pha.* 9, 83, *Tro.* 625; *has, has, Tro.* 739; *huc, huc, Pha.* 1247, *Med.* 980; *hunc, hunc, Oed.* 1038, *Thy.* 101; *ille, ille, Oed.* 106, *Tro.* 721; *iam, iam, Ag.* 44, 1011, *Oed.* 28, 668, *Tro.* 1141, *Pha.* 926, *Med.* 692, 949, 982; *sic, sic*, 1218, *Med.* 90, *Thy.* 102; *nunc, nunc*, 498, *Med.* 13, *Tro.* 107; *me, me*, 110, *Tro.* 680, *Pha.* 1159; *te, te*, 900, *Oed.* 642, 1042, *Pha.* 663, 888; *tu, tu, Oed.* 249; *ibo, ibo, Pho.* 12, 407; *est, est*, 523; *da, da, Med.* 32; *ite, ite, Med.* 845, *Tro.* 191, 627, 1165; *duc, duc, Tro.* 993; *absit, absit, Tro.* 854; *iuuat, iuuat, Med.* 911; *uidi, uidi, Ag.* 656; *sequor, sequor, Pho.* 40; *trepidant, trepidant, Thy.* 828; *excipiunt, excipiunt, Pha.* 1129; cf. also *Oct.* 23, *HO* 87, 550, 753, 846, 1880. Although *geminatio*, especially of demonstratives, seems suggestive of 'props and people on stage' (Wills 1996: 78), the present *geminatio* expresses the emotion of discovery, as Juno realizes what will be the central ingredient of her plot to overcome Hercules (= the plot of the play). For the ontologization of the emotions, see on 75–6; for *dolor*, see on 19–29.

100–12 Direct address by Juno to the Furies, ordering them to 'infuriate' themselves, Hercules and herself, to make all mad. The 'infuriations' of Juno and Hercules will take a different form: see on 112–22. Note the plethora of plural imperatives (six), though less than half of those uttered (13) by Oedipus to his sons in a passage of similar length (*Pho.* 334–47). Fitch *ad loc.* cites a plurality (six) of plural imperatives from Pacuvius (*Fab. Incert.* frags 350–2 Klotz), arguing for the 'dramatic impact' of the device. Cf. the 'infuriations' of Medea (*Med*. 965–6) before she kills the first child, and of Atreus (*Thy*. 250–4), as he formulates the plot against his brother. For the debts to Virgil *Aen*. 7 and Ovid *Met*. 4, see on 86–122. The latter passages confirm Juno's 'infuriation orders' as a literary *topos*. Juno is a literary figure bringing into existence a literary form, a tragic drama. See further on 109–12.

100–3 *Incipite…pinum*/**Begin…pine:** alliteration of *in*, *c*, *it*, *d*, and *p* etc. make for a forceful set of commands. Note the metrical resolutions in the first two feet of line 100, as at 76, again 'expressing urgency and vehemence' (Fitch *ad* 76). For the metatheatrical dimension of Juno's command, see Introd. §VII, 71–3.

famulae Ditis/**handmaids of Dis:** Juno addresses the Furies in an unusual and complex way: (i) like a mistress addressing slaves, playing the status card in a heavy-handed way and enforcing her own authority (cf. Amphitryon's address to his own *famuli*, 'slaves', at 1053); (ii) like a poet addressing the Muses and asking for inspiration (see Introd. §VII, 72). For Dis, see on 46–52.

ardentem…concutite pinum/**Brandish blazing pine:** i.e. wield it threateningly as a weapon like the Fury at 982–4. Note that fire is the first image of Juno's address, in which, as Fitch observes *ad loc*. 'the literal fire of the Furies' torches becomes the metaphorical fire of *furor*.' Fire imagery is strongly associated with madness/*furor* in the Greek and Roman literary traditions and is exploited perhaps most famously by Virgil in the *Aeneid*, in which (to oversimplify) Juno's blazing heart of Book 1 (29, 50) leads— through Dido's burning *amor*/*furor* of Book 4 (2, 54), Allecto's flaming incursions of Book 7 (456–7)—to Aeneas' burning *furor* of Book 12's ending (946). For fire imagery and madness/*furor*, see further on 944–52, 1022–31. For the Furies' torches, see further on 86–8.

incitae/**violently:** I have adopted the reading, *incitae* ($E^{pc}A$), as against *citae* (E^{ac}), printed by Zwierlein. Fitch (1987a and 2018) and Viansino (1993) favour the former; Viansino (1965), Giardina (1966 and 2007), Caviglia, Chaumartin, and Billerbeck favour the latter.

agmen horrendum anguibus/**snake-bristling troop:** cf. *agmen*/*agmina* of the Furies at *Med*. 960, *Thy*. 78, Virg. *Aen*. 4.469, 6.572, and *cohors* at *Thy*. 250. Such military language (see Fitch *ad* 101) seems to suggest a larger group of Furies than the canonic three; cf. the Chorus of Aeschylus' and (probably) Ennius' *Eumenides*. *Horridum*, 'bristling', is presumably a reference to the Furies' hair, which 'bristles with snakes' (*squalidae serpentibus*) at *Med*. 14. Their hair is also 'flaming' (*flammeae*, 87). See further on 86–8. For military language in *Hercules*, see on 19–29.

Megaera: see on 86–8. At Luc. 1.576–7, Claud. *Ruf.* 1.79–80, she is again the tormentor of Hercules.

ducat atque: note the repetition of the same syllable at the end and beginning of juxtaposed words; see 67 and n. *ad loc.* Clearly Seneca found this repetition unproblematic: see e.g. *Tro.* 434, 1096, *Thy.* 704.

luctifica manu/**baleful hand:**   Seneca clearly liked this sonorous, compound adjective and uses it at *Pha.* 995, *Pho.* 132, and *Oed.* 3.632. It is a 'high-poetic' word, used by the epic poets Lucan (7.2) and Valerius Flaccus (3.292), and also by Virgil, who applies it to the Fury Allecto in *Aeneid* 7 (324). Such compounds have an especially 'tragic feel' because of their association with the early Roman tragedians (see e.g. Boyle 2006: 92–3). For Seneca's fondness for adjectives ending in *-ficus*, see on 57–63. The ablative is instrumental: see Woodcock §43.1.

uastam… trabem/**massive beam:**   *trabs*, 'beam', is sometimes just a synonym for 'torch' (see *Pho.* 548), but here *uastam* and the fact that it is seized from a pyre indicates something much larger, as it does at 514 below. See Fitch *ad loc.*

rogo flagrante/**from a burning pyre:**   for the *topos* of ill-omened brands stolen from funeral pyres, see 983 below and *Med.* 799–800, *Oed.* 550–1, 874–5, Prop. 4.3.13–14. At Ov. *Met.* 6.430 the Furies light the wedding of Tereus and Procne with such ill-omened torches.

104–9 *hoc agite*/**Do your work:**   lit. 'do it', a colloquial phrase often used, as here, with an imperative to galvanize someone or something into action. There is, however, a religious context where the phrase is used as a technical formula, viz. a public sacrifice, where the person about to inflict the sacrificial blow asks '*agone?*', and the priest commands, '*hoc age*' (see Ov. *Fas.* 1.321–2, also Var. *LL* 6.12, Sen. Rhet. *Con.* 2.3.19, Suet. *Gaius* 58.2, *Galba* 20.1, Plut. *Cor.*25.2, *Num.* 14.2). Cf. *Med.* 562, 976, and *Clem.* 1.12.2 (*hoc agamus*), where a sacrificial nuance may be sensed, or, for a more overtly 'sacrificial' context, the dying Hercules' instructions to Philoctetes at *HO* 1717. Sacrificial imagery is strong in this play (see on 918–24) and may also be involved here.

uiolatae Stygis/**violated Styx:**   *uiolare*, lit. 'to violate', is a strong moral and religious term, occurring some nine times in Senecan tragedy, including thrice in this play: see also 447, 1270. For Styx, see on 52–6.

concutite pectus/**Hammer your breasts:**   an echo of the Virgilian Juno's command to the Fury, Allecto: *fecundum concute pectus*, 'hammer your fertile breasts' (*Aen.* 7.338). Cf. *pectus tundite*, *Tro.* 114. Billerbeck *ad loc.* construes the *pectus* as that of Hercules on the model of *Thy.* 85–6, but this makes little sense of what follows, where the focus seems to be on the Furies' own 'infuriation', especially if the consensus reading of the main MSS is retained at 108 (see below).

excoquat...ignis/scorch...with fire: the fire of *furor*, 'fury/madness', is one of its most ubiquitous images, as Virgil's poetry attests: see. *Geo.* 3.244, *Aen.* 4.66–9, 12.946.

caminis...Aetnaeis/Etna's forge: volcano in eastern Sicily, still active today and of considerable philosophical/scientific interest to Seneca (see *Ben.* 3.37.2, 6.36.1, *Ep. Mor.* 79.2, *NQ* 2.30.1). Etna is regularly used in Senecan tragedy to image *ira* or *furor* (as here and at *Med.* 410; cf. *HO* 284–6) or, as more usual in Latin poetry (e.g. Cat. 68.53, Ov. *Her.* 15.12, *Met.* 13.868), sexual desire (as at *Pha.* 102–3). The 'forge' is that of Vulcan and the Cyclopes beneath Etna, described at Virgil's *Aeneid* (8.416–53) and referred to at *Thy.* 583–5, *Pha.* 156, 190. There seems also some translingual etymological play, since Aetna seems derived from αἴθω, 'I burn'.

animum captus Alcides/capture Alcides' mind: lit. 'Alcides captured in respect of his mind'. *Animum* is an accusative of respect with the verbal adjective *captus*. This was originally a Greek construction (adjective plus accusative to denote 'that in respect of which the adjective is applied': Woodcock §19.1), and seems to have been introduced in relation to parts of the body by Virgil (see *Aen.* 5.97, 5.269, and Austin *ad Aen.* 1.320). It is common thereafter in Latin verse, especially where the adjective is a perfect passive participle (e.g. *Oed.* 403–4, 438–9, 443; *Med.* 801; *Ag.* 15; Ov. *Met.* 7.183; Sil. 2.341). The construction is found, too, in Augustan and imperial prose (Livy 21.7.10, Tac. *Germ.* 17). For the name 'Alcides', see on 84–5.

magno furore percitus/spurred to great rage: cf. the *magnus furor* which Atreus requires from Megaera and the Furies at *Thy.* 252–3. For *furor*, see on 92–9.

uobis prius insaniendum est/you must first be mad Yourselves: against most modern editors, including Zwierlein (but not Fitch 1987*a* and 2018, whom here I follow) I have adopted the consensus MS reading, *uobis* (*EPCSV*), rather than *nobis* (*T τ recc.*). Juno seems to be making sure that Seneca's Furies are literary Furies in the strongest sense: the 'Mad Ones'.

109-12 *Iuno cur nondum furit*/Why is Juno not raging yet: the first and only time Juno uses her own name. Self-naming is often used in Senecan tragedy (but not in *Hercules*) for character identification (see on 1–5). But it is also a self-dramatizing device. Note e.g. the following: 'I'll return Hercules to hell' (*inferis reddam Herculem*, 1218); 'Aegisthus: death is no punishment for one so born' (*Aegisthe: non est poena sic nato mori, Ag.* 233); 'This face befits an Oedipus' *(uultus Oedipodam hic decet, Oed.* 1003); 'I Hecuba saw' *(Hecuba uidi, Tro.* 36); 'If you would force Andromache' *(si uis…cogere Andromacham, Tro.* 576); 'Summon Ulysses' *(aduoca…Vlixem, Tro.* 614); 'I'll strip Phaedra of life' *(anima…Phaedram…exuam, Pha.* 1178); 'Do you whine away playing | Atreus the Angry' *(questibus uanis agis | iratus Atreus, Thy.* 179–80); 'Medea is left' *(Medea superest, Med.* 166). Indeed in *Medea* the heroine's self-naming is a conspicuous feature of the play (8, 166, 517, 524, 567, 910, 934) and an index of her growing power—but see also *Oed.* 216, *Tro.* 569, 863. For Hercules' self-naming, see on 631–40.

Self-naming is found in Attic tragedy, where its use, though less pervasive, is always important (see e.g. Aesch. *Sept.* 6, Soph. *OT* 8, 397, 1366). It is found, too, in Seneca's dramatic predecessors in Rome; notably, Accius' Atreus self-names *(Atr.* frag. 198 Klotz, frag. 2 Boyle 2006). Self-naming is found also in Ovid, whose Medea names herself three times in *Heroides* 12 (5, 25, 182). Renaissance dramatists employed the device constantly (see Boyle 1997: 161–2), sometimes in a character's opening speech: 'Cometh Andronicus, bound with laurel boughs' (Shakespeare, *Tit.* I.i.77); 'Settle thy studies, Faustus, and begin' (Marlowe, *Faust.*I.i.1); 'Can *Sylla's* Ghost arise within thy Walls?' (Jonson, *Catiline* I.i.3). Shakespeare's Hamlet seems to over-indulge (seven 'Hamlet's in seven lines at *Ham.* V.ii.229–35). Tacitus borrows Seneca's self-dramatizing technique when he has his 'Seneca' self-name *(libertatem Senecae, Ann.* 15.61.1).

The self-dramatizing use of personal names was also part of Roman life (so Servius Sulpicius Rufus to Cicero: *noli te obliuisci Ciceronem esse,* 'Don't forget that you are Cicero', Cic. *Ad Fam.* 4.5.5: see Tarrant *ad Thy.* 53). But what results in Roman drama, especially in Senecan tragedy, is a character's overt realization of his/her 'mythic self', and an intensification of a play's self-conscious theatricality, manifested in the implicit allusion to a character's literary and dramatic pedigree. Here at *Herc.* 109 the self-dramatizing move is used to express metaliterary paradox. In the *Aeneid, furor* is the quintessential property of Juno and the one she gives to others (Dido, Amata, Turnus, Aeneas); it is also the property propelling the plots of *Aeneid* 1–6 and 7–12. Juno's question amounts to two separate, interrelated questions: (i) Why is Juno not yet the traditional literary construct, *Iuno furens (Aen.* 2.613: *Iuno…furens;* Ov. *Fas* 2.177: *furit Iuno)*? (ii) Why is Juno not yet inspired/'infuriated' with the plot of this tragic drama, known to most, if not all, members of its audience? For *furor* as poetic inspiration, see on 86–122, 92–9. For metatheatrical/metaliterary language, motifs or effects in *Hercules,* see on 19–29, 86–122, 89–91, 112–22, 112–18, 123–4,

178–82, 186–91, 202–4, 249–58, 205–523 (introd.), 268–75, 329–31, 439–47, 495–500, 501–8, 511–15, 572–6, 622–5, 631–40, 631–3, 634–6, 658–61, 727–30, 747–9, 760, 987–91, 1015–17, 1022–31, 1035–8, 1100–14, 1149–55, 1186–93, 1200–1, 1202–18, 1237–9, 1272–7, 1341–4. For *nondum*, 'not yet', as index of impatient revenge, see also *Thy.* 58.

I have preferred the *A* reading *furit* (in Trevet's text but not favoured by modern editors) because it distances (perhaps more than the second person) the speaker from the character being played, underscoring the metadramatic quality of the lemmatized question; cf. Oedipus', Medea's, Phaedra's, Ulysses', Helen's, Tantalus', and Atreus' and Thyestes' use of their own names in the third person at the following: *Oed.* 216; *Med.* 8, 166, 517, 524, 567; *Pha.* 1178; *Tro.* 569, 614, 863; *Thy.* 3, 271, 476, 937—and Hercules' similar use of his name at 957, 960, 991, 1152, 1155, 1163, 1168, 1218, 1295 (see further on 631–40). For Senecan characters' metadramatic play with their own names, see also e.g. the play with 'Ulysses' at *Tro.* 607, 'Aegisthus' at *Ag.* 233, 'Medea' at *Med.* 171, 910, 'Atreus' at *Thy.* 180, and 'Thyestes' at *Ag.* 4.

The final *o* in *Iuno* is short, as at 615 and 1297; cf. the shortening of the final *o* in *Agamemno* at *Ag.* 514. The tendency to shorten long final *o* is a feature of imperial Latin verse. Seneca's practice in this matter accelerates, as Fitch (1981: 303–5) observes, in *Thyestes* and *Phoenissae*, which Fitch regards as the final plays of the Senecan eight. The practice in *Hercules* is on a par with the other five plays: see also *sero* (19), *immo* (314), *nemo* (326, 1261), *sermo* (352), *ergo* (432), *modo* (854, 1283), *harundo* (994, 1195), *regio* (1138), *uiuo* (1278).

***me, me, sorores*/Me, me, sisters:** Juno requests 'infuriation' by the Furies, as Medea and Atreus do in their plays (*Med.* 965–6, *Thy.* 250–4). For the *geminatio* (duplication) see on 92–9. For the emotional duplication of *me* (rare in Senecan tragedy), see also *Pha.* 1159, *Tro.* 680; cf. Virg. *Aen.* 8.144, 9.427, 12.260. For *sorores*, 'sisters', of the Furies, see on 86–8.

***mente deiectam mea*/unhinge:** lit. 'cast from my mind'; for this separative ablative of *mens* in a phrase indexing madness, cf. *mente lapsos*, 'mentally lapsed', *Ep. Mor.* 36.12.

***facere si quicquam apparo*/if I plot some action:** a metatheatrical translation to underscore that what Juno is 'preparing to make/do' is the action of the play. For metatheatre, see above.

***dignum nouerca*/Worthy of a stepmother:** Juno, at her self-dramatizing, metadramatic best, embraces in this climactic half-line (see on 40–6) the literary and cultural stereotype of the *nouerca*, which she bitterly alluded to at line 21 (see n. *ad loc.*). Ironic statements involving *dignus* ('worthy', 'fit', 'merited') are common in Senecan tragedy: see e.g. *Ag.* 34, 165, *Med.* 363, *Oed.* 653, *Thy.* 55, 271. Often, as here, the irony pertains to the speaker: see e.g. *Ag.* 34, *Tro.* 863, *Pho.* 333, *Pha.* 853, *Thy.* 271, *Oed.* 879, 977. See also the ironic echo of this phrase by Hercules himself at 1038 (see n. *ad loc.*). Such irony could have strongly impacted Rome's male elite, to whose value system the concept of *dignitas* (self-worth/social rank/honour) was central. Cicero writes of the 'demands of *dignitas*' (*dignitas poscit*, *Quinct.* 28) and of men led by its splendour (*dignitatis splendore ductos*, *Fin.* 5.64). What one performs and receives must be worthy of oneself (*se dignum*): see e.g. Sall. *Cat.* 51.6, Suet. *Nero* 23.1 (*ut Nerone dignus reuertar*, 'that my return be worthy of Nero'). Cf. the use of *dignus* at 413, 927, 957, 1038, 1295; also *indignus* at 294. See further Introd. 117–19. For Roman referentiality in *Hercules*, see on 46–52.

112–22 Juno's 'infuriation' (for her *furor* as in part poetic: see on 86–122, 109–12) results in a change of plans and the articulation of a revenge 'plot', the dramatic action of this play, which she now 'prays for', commands and prescripts: see Introd. 71–3. (Contrast Hercules' 'infuriation', which will involve *scelus*, *impietas*, *error* as well as *furor*: 96–8). For a similarly metaliterary, programmatic (but much enlarged) series of commands, prescripting the plot to follow, see the speech of the Fury in the later *Thyestes* (23–67). Cf. also the programmatic jussive subjunctives of Statius' Dis (*Theb.* 8.65–74), who seems indebted to both passages, especially the present one. For metatheatrical language in *Hercules*, see on 109–12.

112–18 *Vota mutentur mea*/**Change my prayers:** Juno, 'maddened/inspired' by the Furies, now sees in detail the path to vengeance, viz. the main action of the play. For a similar change in revenge-strategy after 'infuriation', see Atreus at *Thy.* 267–86. Like Juno, Atreus outlines the tragic plot to follow.

  precor/**I pray:** I have printed the consensus MS reading, accepted by almost all modern editors. Zwierlein's emendation (*pater*) seems groundless.

  manu...fortis/**strong of hand:** a phrase Nepos likes to use of his chosen subjects (Datames 1.1; Epaminondas 3.1; Pausanias 1.2), where, however, it has connotations of 'bravery'. Here the focus seems on 'strength'. For *manus*, see on 118–22.

  *inueni diem.../***I've found the day...:** so the Fury of *Thyestes* in a similarly metatheatrical moment, exulting in her murderous plans: *inueni dapes...*, 'I've found the feast...' (*Thy.* 66). Cf. also Oedipus' ironic 'discovery': *inuenta thalamis digna nox tandem meis*, 'At last I've found night fit for my marriage bed' (*Oed.* 977). Juno, however, has found the 'day' (*diem*), not the 'night' (*noctis*), and there may be an additional metatheatric point involved, viz. a reference to the conventional length of tragic action, 'a single revolution of the sun', prescribed by Aristotle (*Poetics* 1449b). For metatheatre in *Hercules*, see on 109–12.

nos...uirtus iuuet/virtue may delight me: the idea of Hercules' *uirtus* 'pleasing' or 'delighting' Juno is of course counter-intuitive. Seneca is fond of using *iuuat*, lit. 'it delights', counter-intuitively, ironically, or in a way which underscores the perversity of the joy, applying it, for example, to the death-wish (see Oedipus at *Pho.* 144, the Thebans at *Oed.* 201), to such ironic accomplishments as 'having lived', *uixisse* (Oedipus at *Pho.* 337, Cassandra: *iuuat...iuuat*, *Ag.* 1011), 'having dismembered' kin, *rapuisse*, *secuisse*, 'having armed' daughters for patricide, *armasse* (Medea: *iuuat*, *iuuat...iuuat...iuuat*, *Med.* 911–14), or to 'being filled', *impleri*, with evil (*Thy.* 253–4). See also 867 below, *Ag.* 435–6, 664–6, 750–1, and *Thy.* 427, 508, 716, 1101. Cf. *libet* at the end of *Oedipus* (1061). Here in *Hercules* there may also be some wordplay, given the ancient hypothesis of the etymology of Iuno from *iuuare* (Cic. *ND* 2.66, Varro *LL* 5.67). For etymological, nominal wordplay, and for *uirtus*, see on 35–40.

me uicit? et se uincat/Did he conquer me? Let him conquer himself: as at 85 Juno is referring to Hercules' conquest of his own reason and subsequent murder of his family, but the play will also display another self-conquest, as Hercules overcomes his death-wish and chooses to live. The idea of self-conquest appealed to Shakespeare, who has Cleopatra say of the dying Antony (*AC* IV.xv.17–18):

> So it should be that none but Antony
> Should conquer Antony, but woe 'tis so.

For question similarly followed by response, cf. *Ag.* 526, *Tro.* 270. For the verbal polyptoton (or *declinatio*: Cic. *De Orat.* 3.207, Quint. *Inst.* 9.3.42), a common Senecan mannerism in this and other tragedies, cf. *iussa...iubere* (lit. 'to order orders', 41–2); *uiso...uidi* ('at sight...I saw', 60); *fecit...faciet* ('Made...Will make', 266–7); *tenet...tenebit*, ('holds...will hold', 274–5); *trahe | trahes* ('drag...you'll drag', 307–8); *potuit...poterit* ('was able...will be able', 590–1); *dabit...dabit...dat...dedit* ('will pay...will pay...is paying...has paid', 643–4); *timet...timetur* ('fears...is feared', 726–7); *luit...luet* ('atoned...will atone', *Tro.* 194); *petebant...petuntur* ('sought...are sought', *Med.* 218–19); *tenuit tenebit* ('bound will bind', *Thy.* 551). See further 726–7 and n. *ad loc.* The figure is found in the elder Seneca's

Controuersiae (e.g. 2.3.17) and in Ovid (e.g. *Am.* 1.4.57, *Met.* 2.781, 3.465, 15.182). For polyptoton in *Hercules*, see on 11–18. For *uincere* and Hercules, see on 63–8.

cupiat mori/**want death:** as will be displayed at 1202–18, 1221–6, 1258–62. For the death-wish in Senecan tragedy, see on 1022–31. For *cupio* in conjunction with *mori*, see *Ag.* 996, *Med.* 170.

118–22 Juno foreshadows Hercules' murder of his sons in an enigmatic, allusive way.

stabo et...librabo manu/**I'll stand and aim With my hand:** perhaps mimed by the actor playing Juno in such a way as to anticipate the later action of Hercules, described by Amphitryon at 989–91. Hence the stage directions. For Juno's firing of the arrow, see Amphitryon's comment at 1297. For deities guiding the weapons of heroes, see most famously Apollo's guidance of Paris' arrow into the body of Achilles: Virg. *Aen.* 6.56–8, Ov. *Met.* 12.604–6, Hom. *Il.* 22.359–60. See also the Fury Allecto's guidance of Ascanius' hand and arrow at Virg. *Aen.* 7.498–9. For *librare*, lit. 'to balance', used of the handling of weapons, see 1024, 1128, *Pha.* 48, *Ag.* 900, *Pho.* 437.

ut certo exeant emissa neruo tela/**so shafts fly sure from his bow:** in fact one arrow is used in the slaughter—to kill the first son (992–5). The other two sons and Megara are killed without archery. *Certus*, 'sure', appears often in connection with archery: see e.g. 1128; *Pha.* 57, 278; *Ag.* 212; Cat. 68.113; Prop. 1.7.15; Ov. *Am.* 1.1.25, 3.10.26.

scelere perfecto/**When the crime's done:** Juno classifies Hercules' actions as *scelus*, 'crime'. The matter is debated in the final act, where the word or a derivative occurs almost a dozen times: 1162, 1193, 1199, 1237, 1238, 1262, 1278, 1300, 1313, 1319, 1336. See esp. 1199 and 1237 and nn. *ad locc.*

licet admittat illas genitor...manus/**father may admit those hands:** an ironic reference to Hercules' future apotheosis, perhaps envisaged as a tragic sequel (i.e. a *Hercules Oetaeus*): see on 86–122. Note the sarcastic force of *licet* (as at *Thy.* 750, Ov. *Met.* 3.193) and the climactic position of *manus*, 'hands', which will function as a permeating motif of this play. 'The story of Hercules as Seneca tells it is, in fact, a story of hands' (Miola 1992: 114). Forms of *manus* occur some fifty-six times, forms of *dextra* some fifteen times: see esp. 58, 114, 122, 279, 331, 371, 400, 442, 519, 528, 566, 614, 625, 882, 895, 914, 919, 969, 989, 1002, 1005, 1011, 1017, 1040, 1044, 1103, 1192–6, 1211, 1236, 1260, 1272, 1281, 1314, 1318, 1319, 1326, 1328, 1342. *Manus* and *dextra* are regularly associated not only with Hercules' proclivity for physical violence (as in Euripides' *Heracles*: see Worman 2020: 85–7, on 'Heracles' Killing

Hands'), but also with his related concept of *uirtus*. In *Phoenissae*, where *manus* is again a prominent word and motif, *manus* is primarily associated with violence but is also linked (in the initial section of the play) with control and restraint: see Frank *ad Pho.* 51. Shakespeare continued the *manus* motif in *Love's Labour's Lost* (V.ii.586: 'Thus did he (Hercules) strangle serpents in his *manus*') and elsewhere, especially in *Macbeth* (on which see Introd. §VIII, 138, and Miola 1992: 114–17). *Genitor*, a 'high register' word for 'father', first found in Ennius (*Ann.* frags 108, 444 Skutsch), absent from Roman comedy, employed by Virgil, who restricts it to the *Aeneid* (apart from its application to a river god at *Geo.* 4.355), appears some thirteen times in this play, and is here intentionally encompassed by *illas manus*. For Seneca's fondness for nouns ending in *-tor*, see on 299–302. For *licet* with the subjunctive in a non-concessive sense, see 1172–3, *Med.* 296, *Ag.* 332, *Pho.* 650. For a similarly clo-sural use of sarcasm, see Megara at 395 below.

123–4 Let the war (and play) begin. Dawn rises. Like other protatic prologue-speakers (the Ghost of Thyestes in *Agamemnon*, the Fury in *Thyestes*), Juno refers to the rising dawn and exits the stage—but not before starting the play already prescripted, standing in for the dramatic poet himself. Note that (following occasional Attic practice: e.g. Soph. *Aj.* 21, *Ant.* 16, *El.* 17–19, Eur. *El.* 102, *IA* 1ff.) Seneca regularly inserts a marker of the play's time (dawn) in his prologue: see *Pha.* 41, *Oed.* 1, and (at the end of the pro-logue, as here) *Ag.* 53–6, *Thy.* 120–1. For other 'exit' or 'closural' lines in Seneca indicating the end of an act, see e.g. *Ag.* 308–9, 802–7; *Oed.* 708, 880–1, 1059–61; *Tro.* 812–13, 1178–9; *Med.* 299–300, 847–8, 1026–7; *Pha.* 81–4; *Thy.* 545, 788. Such final lines often connect strongly, as here, with the choral ode which follows: see e.g. 523, *Pha.* 272–3, 734–5, *Med.* 578, *Thy.* 111–19, 784–8—and esp. 827–9 below, *Oed.* 401–2 and *Ag.* 586–8, which 'cue in' their ensuing choral odes.

Mouenda iam sunt bella/**Let war now begin:** a metatheatrical moment, couched in terms reminiscent of Virgil's commencement of his war poem, *Aeneid* 7–12: *dicam horrida bella...maius opus moueo*, 'I shall relate grim war...a greater work I begin' (*Aen.* 7.41–5). The war is between Juno and Hercules and (more importantly) within Hercules himself (see on 84–5). This is one of four occasions (cf. *Oed.* 108, *Ag.* 56, *Med.* 54) where *iam* is used to end a prologue. Elsewhere other pointers are used, such as *iamdu-dum* (*Tro.* 65), and *en* (*Pha.* 81, *Thy.* 120)—or no pointers at all (*Pho.*). Note how Juno's *iam* will be immediately echoed by the incoming chorus (125). For metatheatrical language in *Hercules*, see on 109–12.

clarescit dies/day starts to glow: as Fitch notes *ad loc.*, *clarescit* is a Senecan tragic *hapax* and the first extant use of the word in Latin literature of 'visual clarity'. It is a striking word which is about to expand into a full-scale choral description of the dawn sky. For *dies* = daylight, see 821, *Pha.* 675, *Tro.* 21.

ortuque Titan lucidus croceo/Bright Titan...from the saffron east: though 'Titan' is technically 'Hyperion', the pre-Olympian Titan father of the sun (Hes. *Th.* 371-4), with whom in the Roman tradition he was also identified (Ov. *Met.* 8.565), the name (from Cicero's *Aratea* onwards) is commonly used in Latin poetry for the sun-god, Apollo (e.g. 133, 443, 1060, 1333 below, Virg. *Aen.* 4.119, Ov. *Met.* 1.10, Luc. 3.40). Seneca *tragicus* uses it as often as *Phoebus* and prefers it to *Sol*. In art the sun-god is generally imaged with rays of light emanating from his head (*radiis frontem uallatus acutis*, 'crowned with a palisade of pointed rays', Ov. *Her.* 4.159; cf. 'Titan radiate', *radiate Titan*, at Sen. *Pha.* 678 and *HO* 1518; also *Oct.* 3). The image appealed to Nero, who in his later years (perhaps from 64 CE onwards—certainly well after the composition of this play) had himself depicted on his coins with radiate crown (Mattingly 1923: 'Nero' 191-5, 197-8, 200-6, 208-10, 213-24, etc., pll. 43 and 44). Notoriously, he had intended to erect a colossal gilded bronze statue of himself as the sun-god, with rays of light spurting from his head, in the vestibule of his Golden House (Pliny *HN* 34.45, Suet. *Nero* 31.1). Notice the interlocking chiastic pattern of nouns and adjectives (ABba: see on 11–18), here used for closural effect. For *croceus*, 'saffron', of dawn/its goddess Aurora, see Virg. *Geo.* 1.447, *Aen.* 4.585, 9.460, Ov. *Am.* 2.4.43, *Ars* 3.179, *Met.* 3.150, *Fas.* 3.403. Cf. Homer's κροκόπεπλος, 'saffron-robed', applied to the goddess in the *Iliad* (e.g. 8.1, 24.695).

Exeunt ALL *into the palace*: Juno is not likely to exit in the direction of heaven or hell (the latter through a trapdoor), and there is no point in having her depart from Thebes (stage right) or go downtown (stage left). The most obvious move is to have her exit into one of the buildings onstage, and, since the palace will be the building in which the raging Hercules will kill his family, that seems the appropriate one. Making the Furies go back to hell would be absurd. There is also the further point that, if Lycus makes his entrance in Act II from the palace (see n. before 329–31), having Juno and the Furies in the place from which he enters would add dramatic and thematic piquancy to Lycus' role in the play and underscore his comparability with Hercules.

First Choral Ode: The 'Dawn Ode' (125–204)

The Chorus of Thebans enter. Juno has already established the stage-set as Thebes, and their casual opening references to Mt Oeta, Cadmus, and the bloody Bacchantes (133–5), supplemented by their displayed awareness of Hercules' descent into the underworld (187), establish their identity as knowing residents of the city. This will later be confirmed by Theseus' identification of them as a festive crowd celebrating Hercules' victory over Lycus (827–9). There is, however, no indication in the text of gender or age, except that they are clearly not fragile, old men, as in Euripides' play, where the Chorus make a plethora of references to their physical infirmity in the opening lyrics (*Herac.* 107–29), nor are they all women (*ipsi*, 873). Either an all-male or male-female chorus (see 878–9) may reasonably be postulated. Like the actors in the play, this Chorus of Thebans would have been masked and their gender made clear.

Self-identification by the chorus, common in the parodos or entrance-song of fifth-century Attic tragedy and also found in the opening odes of both *Octavia* (288–93) and *Hercules Oetaeus* (esp. 119–42), is more rare in Senecan tragedy, where explicit self-identification takes place only in two opening choral lyrics (*Oed.* 124, *Tro.* 67ff.). Senecan choruses sometimes identify themselves (e.g. *Ag.* 310ff.) or are identified by others (e.g. 827ff., *Ag.* 586ff.) later in the plays, or identify themselves implicitly by the content and dramatic function of their opening song (here, *Med.* 56ff., *Thy.* 122ff.). Only the chorus of *Phaedra* neither identify themselves nor are identified by others (but see Boyle 1987: 154). *Oedipus, Medea, Agamemnon,* and *Thyestes* feature a chorus of local subjects, as does *Hercules.* In each of these five plays a central purpose of the chorus is to show the impact of the play's action on the city's people as a whole. The representation of that people and its relationship to its rulers seems modelled (most overtly in *Thyestes*) on the political realities of imperial Rome. In the non-Senecan *Octavia* the local subjects of the main chorus are Roman citizens.

The songs of the chorus in Attic tragedy of the fifth century BCE and in Hellenistic drama were delivered away from the stage-building (the *skene*) in the circular or semi-circular space, the *orchestra*, which lay in front of it (see Bieber 1961: 59–60, figs 238–40). This enabled the chorus to function as a bridge between audience and actors and/or as an overtly 'theatrical' frame for the dramatic action itself. In the Roman theatre from 194 BCE the 'orchestral' area had been given over to senatorial seating (Livy 34.44.5, 54.3–8, Cic. *Har. Resp.* 24, Val. Max. 2.4.3—for Augustan Rome, see

Vitruvius 5.6.2). Confined as they were to the elevated Roman stage (*pulpitum*), the chorus of Roman tragedy occupied for most of their existence the same theatrical space as the actors themselves. They seem generally to have been smaller in number than their classical or Hellenistic predecessors (some suggest a normal figure of between three and seven members: see Introd. §II, 27, n. 65), although a larger chorus representing a crowd of people would certainly have been possible when the play required it. The performance of Accius' *Clytaemestra* in Pompey's Theatre in 55 BCE, attested by Cicero (*Fam.* 7.1.2), reveals the kind of numbers the Roman stage could accommodate (see Introd. §II, 21).

Restriction of the chorus to the *pulpitum* meant that their dancing and movement were reduced in scale from the chorus of the fifth-century Attic theatre. That the Senecan tragic chorus did dance during at least some of their odes seems clear from *Agamemnon*'s second choral ode, the 'Victory Ode' (310–87), and several other odes where dancing or ritual movement seems invited: e.g. the opening *kommos* or 'Dirge Ode' of *Troades* (67–163), the 'Processional/*Epithalamium* Ode' of *Medea* (56–115), the 'Star Ode' of *Thyestes* (789–884), the 'Bacchus Ode' of *Oedipus* (403–508). Though such dancing and movement would have been somewhat restricted in comparison with those of the classical Greek theatre, among the advantages of a more varied, often smaller chorus was increased flexibility—both in the matter of choral entrances and exits and in the number of choruses involved. (Seneca's *Agamemnon* has two choruses, as do *Octavia* and *Hercules Oetaeus*—and, if Chaumartin (2002: 59) is right, Accius' *Brutus*.) Unlike the Attic chorus, the Senecan chorus may exit and reenter during the course of the play. *Phaedra* 599–601 make it clear that the chorus are not onstage, and *Hercules* 827–9 reveal that the chorus are absent at least from the preceding section of that act (see n. before 590–1). Indeed there is no reason to regard the Senecan chorus as onstage in any act in which they neither speak nor are addressed, unless their own lyrics indicate otherwise. In this Seneca was probably following existing Roman (and Hellenistic) tragic conventions.

Advantages of this flexibility are clear. In Seneca the chorus do not have to be sworn to silence every time a plot is hatched or an intrigue conducted (see e.g. *Med.* 568ff., 740ff., *Ag.* 108ff., *Thy.* 176ff.)—they are simply not onstage. Seneca is free, too, to use choral re-entry or exit for theatrical, visual effect. Seneca's chorus serve several dramatic functions, some of which (including their division of the dramatic action generally into five 'acts') were to have a lasting impact on European drama. But they perform only to a limited degree the 'part of an actor' (*actoris partes*, AP 193) recommended by Horace (but see on 1054–1137 introd. below). Choral odes and all other lyric sections of Roman tragedies were sung to the accompaniment of music provided by a flute-player/piper, *tibicen*—see e.g. Cic. *De Orat.* 1.254, *Orat.* 183f., *Ac.* 2.20. The absence of strophic corresponsion in this and the other choral odes in *Hercules* is in line with Senecan and probably Roman tragic practice.

This play's first ode, as in *Agamemnon* and *Phaedra*, is one of meditation and reflection, and, as in those two plays, generates clear tonal contrast with the surrounding and emotionally turbulent acts. Its initial subject is taken from the prologue itself: the light of dawn, which Juno had signalled in her concluding lines (*clarescit dies... Titan lucidus*, 'The day starts to glow; Bright Titan', 123–4). After the opening description of the stars withdrawing before the rising sun (125–36), the ode focuses on the rural world: man, animal, bird, awake and filled with life and activity (137–58). A contrast is made between the peace, *quies*, of the rural world and the human vices (hopes, fears, greed, delusion, ambition, corruption) generated by urban life (159–77). Moral imperatives follow: grasp the fleeing moment, for death is inevitable and fixed (178–91); live unobserved, humbly and secure: for spirited *uirtus* falls (192–201). Then comes a segue to Act II, in which the Chorus announce the entry of Megara, her sons and Amphitryon (202–4). The closural injunctions, direct and implied, have a direct bearing on the subject matter and action of the play: live in obscurity and grasp the moment; avoid the paradigm of Hercules and *uirtus animosa*, 'spirited virtue'.

These conclusions seem all the more powerful because of the ode's main subtext: the parodos of Euripides' *Phaethon*, which (63–86 Diggle) moves from the dawn sky (stars), land (nightingale, herdsmen, hunters, etc.) and sea (sailors), to an unintentionally ironic celebration of Phaethon's forthcoming marriage (87–108 Diggle). *Phaethon* seems to have been a well-known ancient text (its prologue had been anthologized by the third century BCE: Diggle 1970: 34); and Phaethon is a prominent mythic figure in *Medea* (599–602), *Phaedra* (1090–3), and Ovid's *Metamorphoses* (Books 1 and 2), cited by Seneca (*Prou.* 5.10: see on 197–201). Phaethon seems also to have been used politically in association with the emperor Gaius (Suet. *Gai.* 11), possibly by Seneca himself (*Pol.* 17.3). Any member of Seneca's audience appreciating the allusions to Euripides' *Phaethon* would see the analogy between its hero and Hercules and the proleptic properties of the analogy (see on 197–201). There are other important intertexts, too, most especially poems by Seneca's three great Roman predecessors, Virgil, Horace, and Ovid (see Comm. below), which 'Romanize' the ode's reflections and injunctions, as the ode turns more and more into a mirror of the audience's moral world.

Unlike the parodos of *Phaethon*, Seneca's ode moves not to celebration but to moral injunction, transforming its initial descriptive lyricism (125–58) into a preamble for epigrammatic, sententious diatribe (159–201). Indeed the second half of the ode is punctuated with *sententiae* (aphorisms or maxims trenchantly expressed): 178, 185, 188, 191, 198, 201. The employment of *sententiae* is a conspicuous feature of the declamatory style of early imperial Roman literature and of Senecan tragedy: see e.g. (in Act II) 251–3, 328, 340–1, 344–5, 353, 433, 435, 437, 463–4, 476, 511–13. Quintilian criticized Seneca's *sententiae* (*Inst.* 10.1.130) and cautioned restraint in their use (*Inst.* 8.5.25–34), but understood their power (*Inst.* 12.10.38): 'They strike the mind and with one blow frequently impel it, and by their very brevity cling there the more (*ipsa breuitate magis haerent*) and through pleasure persuade (*delectatione persuadent*).' They are sometimes used climactically by Seneca to end a speech, as at 476, 706 (cf. e.g. *Oed.* 86; *Pha.* 430, 735; *Tro.* 291, 425; *Med.* 55; *Thy.* 470, 529), or to round off a section, scene, or choral ode, as at 201, 328, 340–1, 353, 513, 874 (cf. e.g. *Med.* 109, 176, 431, 559; *Tro.* 162–3; *Pha.* 356–7, 1153; *Oed.* 909–10; *Thy.* 401–3, 454, 489–90, 572, 883–4). They are also regularly used in argument as in the Lycus-Megara-Amphitryon dialogue of Act II (esp. 422–64), even for rebarbative purposes (cf. the verbal duel between Phaedra and Theseus at *Pha.* 872–81, between Pyrrhus and Agamemnon at *Tro.* 327–36, between Medea and the Nurse at *Med.* 157–67, between Atreus and the *Satelles* at *Thy.* 204–19). Seneca was especially taken with the *sententiae* of Publilius Syrus, which were popular with the declaimers (Sen. Rhet. *Con.* 7.2.14, 3.8, 4.8) and which Seneca declared were often more appropriate to tragedy than mime: *quam multa Publilii non excalceatis sed coturnatis dicenda sunt*, 'How many lines of Publilius should be spoken not by comedy/mime actors but by those of tragedy' (*Ep. Mor.* 8.8). Seneca, of course, did not only adapt existing aphorisms but, as here, often created his own *sententiae*. His sententious style was widely imitated by Renaissance dramatists: see Boyle (1997: 162–3).

All Senecan opening choral odes have a strong thematic relationship to the preceding and ensuing acts and thus accord with the Horatian dictum of *proposito conducere* ('contributing to the theme', *AP* 195). But they vary in respect of 'dramatic' motivation (*Tro.* 67ff.: need for joint lamentation; *Oed.* 110ff.: Thebes' plague; *Med.* 56ff.: wedding celebration; *Thy.* 122ff.: communal fear). At *Pha.* 274ff. and *Ag.* 57ff. there seems little 'dramatic' motivation.

The first entrance of the Chorus in *Hercules* has clear 'dramatic' motivation (the heralding of dawn announced by Juno at 123–4), but it has also, like all Senecan opening choral odes, been prepared for thematically. Its major function in this regard is to provide the audience with a critical frame for the prologue's presentation of Hercules' *uirtus* by linking Hercules' ambition and values to the vices of the city and by setting up as a preferable mode of life a quasi-Epicurean ideal of withdrawal, peace, and isolation more in accord with the natural rhythms of the cosmos.

The network of language, theme, and imagery binding this ode to the prologue and the ensuing act is discussed above (Introd. §VII, 73–7). It merits emphasis, because 'philosophical' odes of this kind, which are common in Senecan tragedy (see e.g. *Ag.* 57ff. on *Fortuna*; *Tro.* 371ff. on death; *Oed.* 882–914 on the *media uia*, 980–97 on fate; *Pha.* 959ff. on nature, 1123ff. on *Fortuna*; *Thy.* 336ff. on kingship), are sometimes inappropriately classified as 'interludes'. (Perhaps with more justification Aristotle at *Poetics* 1456a29–30 criticized as 'interludes', ἐμβόλιμα, the choral odes on stock themes in the plays of the late fifth-century Attic tragedian, Agathon.) The strong personal note at the end of the ode (see on 197–201) seems designed not only to signal the Chorus' commitment to the stated ideals but to impress their importance on the minds of Seneca's audience for an evaluation of the tragic action.

The anapaestic metre, first attested in early Spartan marching songs (Page 1962: 856–7) and often used in Attic tragedy for the entrance and exit odes of the chorus, is the favourite metre of Seneca, being employed by him in some form or other in all the seven plays which contain lyric. Part of its semiotics here in *Hercules* is perhaps to index choral entrance, even as its potentially marching rhythm may quicken the ode's initial, military imagery. Anapaests are used for the entrance odes of the chorus in three plays (*Hercules*, *Agamemnon*, and *Troades*) and, partially, in two others (*Oedipus* and *Phaedra*). It is also used for the opening lyric prologue of *Phaedra*. It is noticeable that three of these five plays are often regarded as the earliest (see p. 6). Note that *Hercules* is book-ended, as it were, with anapaestic choral odes. Because of the association of anapaests with lament, which will come to the fore in the play's final ode (see on 1054–1137 introd.), some ominous undercurrent of lamentation may be argued to be proleptically present here. The parodos of neither Euripides' *Phaethon* (choriambic dimeters) nor his *Heracles* (iambics and trochaics) is in anapaests. Discussion of the Senecan chorus may be found in Davis (1993) and Mazzoli (2014).

Worth comparing with Seneca's 'Dawn Ode', and perhaps indebted to it, is Megara's less layered description of the dawn in the opening of the sixth scene of George Cabot Lodge's *Herakles* (1908):

> The golden wings of light beat up the sky;
> The stars are set; the dew-fall and the dawn
> Are everywhere, quiet as benediction;
> The earth's fresh perfumes, like an incense, rise
> Into the windless, universal air;
> And even the old, blank city ways are still
> And flushed like pathways in love's paradise…
> It is morning!

This morning, like that of Seneca's *Hercules*, will prove preface to child-murder. For further discussion of this choral ode and its dramatic and thematic function in the play, see Introd. §VII.

Metre: anapaestic dimeters and monometers. See Introd. §IX. For metrical semiotics, see above.

Enter…from stage left (the city): see 'Scene' above.

They sing, accompanied by the double-piped **tibia:** for the *tibia*, see Introd. §II, 19, n. 35.

125–36 The Chorus observe the stars withdrawing as the sun (Titan) rises. Seneca immediately underscores the dramatic character of his chorus by presenting their awareness of the time just indicated by Juno. This is a chorus integrated into the action of the play, as their continuation of the language of Juno (*iam…bella*, 123) shows. With Seneca's description, cf. that of Ovid at *Met.* 2.112–18:

> Ecce uigil nitido patefecit ab ortu
> purpureas Aurora fores et plena rosarum
> atria. diffugiunt stellae, quarum agmina cogit
> Lucifer et caeli statione nouissimus exit.
> quem petere ut terras mundumque rubescere uidit
> cornuaque extremae uelut euanescere lunae,
> iungere equos Titan uelocibus imperat Horis.

> Look, wakeful Aurora from her bright rising
> Has opened the purple gates and courts glowing
> With roses. The stars flee—Lucifer marshals
> The troops, last to leave his station in the sky.

> When he saw him setting and the world begin
> To blush and the horns of the waning moon fade,
> Titan orders the swift Hours to yoke his horses.

To which Seneca seems indebted for both vocabulary (*nitidus, diffugiunt, stellae, agmina, cogit, rubescere, equos, Titan*) and military imagery (*diffugiunt, agmina cogit, statione, imperat*). Significantly Ovid's description is of the dawn of Phaethon's fatal ride.

125–31 *Iam rara micant sidera*/Now scattered stars…glitter: Seneca begins by echoing the start of the parodos of Euripides' *Phaethon* (63–4 Diggle): ἤδη…Ἀώς ('Now…Dawn'). Initial *iam* will repeat itself (132, 134; note non-initial *iam* at 162), as ἤδη does at *Phaethon* 75 (Diggle). Seneca here uses *iam* to index separate, concurrent (not 'successive', as Viansino 1993 *ad loc.*) perceptual moments (cf. the quintuple use of *iam* at *Ag.* 456–61, the quadruple use at Cat. 46, the triple use at Luc. 2.719–25, the double use at Hor. *Odes* 1.4.3–5, Stat. *Theb.* 7.470–1), and to pick up and develop Juno's use of the word in the penultimate line of the prologue (123). The latter is important, because Seneca often seems keen on securing a verbal connection between act and ode: see e.g. *tuta…tuta*, *Ag.* 105–8; *annis…annis*, *Ag.* 866–7; *immitis…non miti*, *Pha.* 273–4; *flamma…flammae*, *Med.* 578–9; *turbine…turbo*, *Thy.* 622–3. (The dramatist of *Octavia* learnt from this technique: *capta…captus*, *Oct.* 33–4.) Here the act-ode suture is seen, too, in the continuation of words for the light of dawn (*micant…ignes luce…nitidum*, 'glitter…fires…light…gleaming'), which seem also to echo the early part of Juno's speech (*clara…signa…micant*, 'glitter…bright stars', 14). For other verbal connections, see below. *Rara micant* is a Virgilian phrase (*Aen.* 9.189: *lumina rara micant*), used of the night fires in the camp of the Rutulians just before the bloody massacre of Nisus and Euryalus; here it is used of the dawn-sky which heralds the day of Hercules' slaughter of his family. For initial *iam* used to open a new narrative or dialogic section, see e.g. *Ag.* 44, 456, 775; *Med.* 982; *Oed.* 1, 28. *Iam* is the only adverb to begin a Senecan tragedy (*Oedipus*). It also begins *Octavia*.

prono…mundo/In the setting world: an arresting phrase to describe the disappearing night sky, and one which suggests that the Chorus are looking and gesturing west—in the opposite direction to that to which Juno directs her gaze in her final lines just before the Chorus enter. For *mundus* = the firmament or sky, cf. *Oed.* 1028, *Ag.* 827, *Pha.* 333, 961, Hor. *Odes* 1.12.15, Luc. 6.463. The Latin phrase can be construed as locatival ablative, as translated, or ablative absolute—or (preferably, given the syntactic ambiguity) as both. For *pronus*, cf. Luc. 4.28–9: *prono…Olympo in noctem*, 'when the sky was setting toward night'; VF 2.35–6: *prono…aethere*, 'in the setting heavens'.

nox uicta uagos contrahit ignes/vanquished night Rallies stray fires: the military imagery, found elsewhere in dawn descriptions (see e.g. *Tro.* 171, Virg. *Aen.* 3.521, Ov. *Met.* 2.114–15 cited on 125–36, 144, *Oct.* 2), is notable and will continue in this opening section with *cogit…agmen* (128) and *fugit* (136). Such imagery is a development of Juno's language of the prologue (most recently *bella*, 123) and is thematic; it anticipates the military energies and 'victories' of Hercules, in the way that the imagery of the 'banishment' of night in the opening line of *Oedipus* (*nocte…expulsa*, *Oed.* 1) prefigures Oedipus' own expulsion. For further verbal linkage to the prologue, note *uagantes*, 'strayed', 11 (see n. *ad loc.*). With *uagos…ignes*, 'stray fires', cf. also *cursusque uagos…astrorum*, 'and wandering/stray courses of the stars' (*Pha.* 962), *uaga picti sidera mundi*, 'spangled world's vagrant/stray stars' (*Thy.* 834), *uaga…sidera*, 'vagrant/stray stars' (*Oct.* 1), *noctis uaga lumina*, 'the night's wandering/stray lights' (Stat. *Theb.* 3.63). For *contrahere* of 'rallying scattered military troops', see e.g. Livy 33.38.12, Curt. 8.4.9. For military language and imagery in *Hercules*, see on 19–29.

luce renata/as light's reborn: for *renatus* of dawn, see *Tro.* 10: *renatum…diem*, 'the reborn day', repeated at *HO* 861.

cogit nitidum Phosphoros agmen/Phosphoros marshals gleaming troops: military imagery and a Grecism/Senecan *hapax*, Phosphoros, the Greek name (= 'bringer of light') for the morning star, used instead of its Latin equivalent, Lucifer. The Grecism, which might be thought to add local colour to this Theban ode, is found again (perhaps imitated) in Statius (*Silu.* 2.6.79) and Martial (*Epig.* 8.21.1–2). For the phrasing Seneca seems indebted to Ovid (*Met.* 2.114–15, cited on 125–36; cf. *Met.* 11.97–8). The ancients were aware that the morning star and the evening star (Hesperus/Vesper) were the same and to be identified with the planet Venus: see e.g. *Pha.* 749–52, Cic. *ND* 2.53. Both Greek and Roman poets played with the notion of their identity: see e.g. Callim. frag. 291 Pfeiffer, Cinna *Zmyrna* frag. 6 Courtney, Hor. *Odes* 2.9.10–12. Note again the verbal connection to the prologue: *nitidum* not only continues the light imagery of 123–4, but picks up Juno's earlier *nitet* (9).

signum celsi glaciale poli/The high pole's icy sign: an echo of Juno's language at 6: see *ad loc. Signum*, as well as meaning 'star' or 'constellation', also of course can mean 'military standard', and thus continues the military imagery.

septem stellis Arcados Vrsae/the Bear Of Arcas with its seven stars: the 'Great Bear' (see on 6–11, 1138–42), here described as the Bear of Arcas, son of the raped Arcadian nymph, Callisto. When Arcas was unknowingly on the point of killing his mother, who had been changed into a bear, he was transformed into Arctophylax (*Thy.* 874), the constellation of the 'Bear-Watcher', and his mother was transformed into the adjacent constellation of the 'Great Bear' (Ov. *Fas.* 2.179–90, [Eratosth.] *Catast.* 1, Hyg. *Astr.* 2.1). The constellation was also known as the 'Wain' ('Charles' Wain'), Ἅμαξα, *Plaustra* or *Plaustrum* (see *Oed.* 477, 722, *Tro.* 439, *Med.* 315, *Thy.* 873, *Oct.* 233, *HO* 1923, Hyg. *Astr.* 2.2), and by metonymy, as below, *Temo* (lit. 'Pole' of a wain or plough, Stat. *Theb.* 1.371). In that case Arctophylax became Bootes, and was imagined as 'driving' or 'turning' the 'Wain' (Ov. *Met.* 10.447, Manil. 1.316–17). Greeks used the constellation to find north (see 6–7 above and n. *ad loc.*). Seneca here participates in the Hellenistic and Roman tradition of playing on the double identity of this constellation: cf. *Med.* 315, Arat. *Phaen.* 26–7, Luc. 4.523 (*Vrsae temone*), 5.23 (*plaustrum...Vrsae*), *HO* 1524 (*plaustro...Vrsae*). For the seven stars of the constellation, see *Tro.* 439, Acc. *Philocteta* frag. 566 Klotz, Manil. 1.297, 620. *Stellis* functions as instrumental and/or descriptive ablative: Woodcock §43.1 and 6. *Vrsae* is genitive of definition or appositional genitive: see Woodcock §72.5.

lucem uerso temone uocat/turned its wain and summons light: the turning (towards its setting) of this constellation was generally thought of as taking place in the middle of the night (as at *Tro.* 439, Ov. *Met.* 10.446–7) rather than just before dawn. In Euripides' *Phaethon* it is not the turning of the Great Bear/Wain which is associated with dawn but the flight of the Pleiads (*Phaeth.* 66). For *Temo*, 'Wain', and the constellation of the Great Bear, see preceding n. For stars' 'summoning', cf. *Thy.* 795: *nocturna uocat lumina Vesper*, 'Vesper summons the stars of night'—an extension of the notion of stars as 'messengers' (see *nuntius*, *Thy.* 794). For Ovid the star which 'summons' dawn is of course Lucifer (*Met.* 4.629–30).

132-6 *iam caeruleis euectus equis Titan*/Now Titan drawn by cerulean Horses: the chariot of the sun is traditional, although the colour of the horses here is unusual. *Caeruleus*, 'cerulean', is a colour associated with the sky (*caeli caerula templa*, Enn. *Ann.* frag. 48 Skutsch), and is used of the dark horses of Pluto at Ov. *Fas.* 4.446 and of Triton at Ov. *Her.* 7.50. Seneca applies it to the waters of the ocean at *Ag.* 69. Indeed Zwierlein and Billerbeck prefer the reading of *recc.* (*aquis*) to that of E (*equis*), which I have printed here (along with Viansino 1965 and 1993, Giardina 1966 and 2007, Caviglia, Fitch 1987*a* and 2018, and Chaumartin). For discussion, see Fitch (2004*b*),

11-12. For repeated *iam*, see on 125-31, and on 1314-17; for *euehor* of the Sun, see Ov. *Met.* 2.73 (the Phaethon episode); for Titan, see on 123-4.

Oeta: Mt Oeta lies some sixty miles north-west of Thebes, and thus would not feature in a sunrise viewed from that city. Seneca has chosen a site in the vicinity of Thebes but (as often) has not got the topographical relationships right. It has clearly been chosen not simply as a 'local landmark', but because of its ominous semiotics. It will be the site of Hercules' death and deification, and thus foreshadows them. At *HO* 861-2 its reception of the day's first light is mentioned (but by someone in the vicinity of the mountain).

iam Cadmeis inclita Bacchis/Now…famed for Cadmean Bacchantes: though a reference to the biennial Theban Bacchic festival held on Mt Cithaeron (see Virg. *Aen.* 4.302-3) may be intended by the Chorus, the audience would be reminded by the language of line 135 (see next n.) of the death and dismemberment of the Theban king, Pentheus, at the hands of 'Cadmean', i.e. Theban, Bacchantes. Pentheus had opposed the introduction of Bacchus' cult to the city. Among the Bacchantes who tore Pentheus apart was his mother Agave, daughter of Cadmus, founder of Thebes. The subject, famously dramatized in Euripides' *Bacchae*, was also explored by the post-Ennian Roman tragedians, Pacuvius (in his *Pentheus* or *Bacchae*) and Accius (in his *Bacchae*), and by Ovid (*Met.* 3.708-33). Seneca refers to the dismemberment of Pentheus in the other Theban plays: *Oed.* 436-44, 484-5, 615-18, 626-30, 933, 1005-7; *Pho.* 15-18, 256-7, 363-7. The language here serves both to identify the chorus as Thebans and to anticipate the slaughter of kin to follow. Note the earlier references to Bacchus by Juno at 16-17, 66-7, to Agave at 758, and to 'Bacchus' groves' at 1286. For the repeated *iam*, see on 125-31.

aspersa die dumeta rubent/thickets…blush with splashing day: *aspergere*, 'splash', is regularly used of blood in the tragedies: see e.g. 372, *Tro.* 256, *Thy.* 95, *Pho.* 268. For *rubeo*, 'blush', 'redden', of objects red with blood: see *Pha.* 552; Ov. *Met.* 12.71, *Fas.* 2.212; of the light at sunrise: see Lucr. 5.462, and note *rubescere* at Ov. *Met.* 2.116 (see on 125-36). At the back of Seneca's mind may have been Virgil's description of the aftermath of the death of Mettus Fufetius at *Aen.* 8.645: *sparsi rorabant sanguine uepres*, 'the brambles dripped, splashed with blood'. For *spargere* used of *dies*, see Sil. 5.56: *solis equi sparsere diem*, 'the horses of the sun splashed the day/scattered the daylight'.

Phoebique fugit reditura soror/Phoebus' sister flees and will return: Diana, the moon, whose action (*fugit*, 'flees'), suggested perhaps by *diffugiunt* in Ovid's Phaethon episode (*Met.* 2.114: see on 125–36), continues the military imagery. Her promised return (*reditura*), like sunrise itself, points to the order and regularity of the world's cosmic cycle, as perceived by the Theban chorus. *Reditura* clearly marks a difference between the cosmos and the human world: see 177, where the word returns, and n. *ad loc.* Diana and Titan (= Apollo) are the only gods mentioned in this ode other than the Parcae. Both were presented by Juno as Jupiter's bastards (15), symbols of cosmic disorder rather than stability. This section of the ode ends on the first word of Juno's prologue, *soror*, underscoring the network of language binding act and ode.

137-58 The rural world (man, animal, bird) is described as it awakens and begins its diurnal activities. The interconnection of dawn and human labour/activity is a traditional one in Greek and Roman literature from Hesiod onwards (*WD* 578–81) and is emphasized in Euripides' dawn ode (*Phaeth.* 71ff. Diggle) and Callimachus' *Hecale* (frag. 260.63–9 Pfeiffer). A *locus classicus* in the Roman tradition is Ov. *Am.* 1.13; Statius (*Theb.* 6.25) notably attaches to dawn's chariot the epithet, *laborifer*, 'bringer of toil'. Some editors favour transposition here. Zwierlein follows 136 with 146–51, after which he resumes with 137–45. I print the manuscript order, as do Viansino (1965 and 1993), Giardina (1966 and 2007), Billerbeck, and Chaumartin. As, too, did Fitch in his 1987 edition, but in his recent Loeb edition (2018) he follows Zwierlein.

137-40 *Labor exoritur durus*/**Hard toil rises**: this seems far away from the idyllic picture of piping drovers described in Euripides' choral lyric (*Phaeth.* 71–2 Diggle; see Fitch: 159), and closer to the much harder life of Virgil's farmers (*Geo.* 2.412, 4.114) and of Hesiod's rustics, for whom dawn is the beginning of work (*WD* 578–81). But *exoritur*, 'rises' (like Aurora *ab ortu* in Ovid's master text: see on 125–36), depicts it as part of nature's rhythm rather than (as in Virgil) something imposed on man for his betterment (*Geo.* 1.121–46). There seems also an implied contrast between the natural *labor* of the rustic and that of Hercules, whose *labores* will be constantly referred to in this play (see 71, 248, 313, 605, 656, etc.).

aperitque domos/**and opens homes**: the first occurrence in the play of *domus*, 'house/home/palace', a word which occurs some twenty-four times in the play (almost always as here at a line's end), reinforcing the *locus* theme announced in the prologue: for which, see on 1–5 and Introd. 69–71.

pastor...pabula carpit/**shepherd...Plucks pasture**: the phrase, used of animals grazing by Ovid (e.g. *Met.* 1.299), is here used of the *pastor* picking fodder for his animals, underscoring the man-nature harmony already implied by *exoritur*. This 'natural' activity contrasts with the later 'unnatural' *pabulum*, 'fodder', of 227 and the 'unnatural' *pastor*, 'drover/ shepherd', of 232. The shepherd's 'plucking' of pasture (*carpit*, 140) will return in the 'plucking' of life itself (*carpit*, 874). Cf. also Virg. *Geo.* 3.324–5, which may have influenced Seneca here. For the *pastor* image in Senecan tragedy, see also *Med.* 101 (*pastor roscidus*, 'dewy pastor'), *Pha.* 1051–2, *Oed.* 147–8. Caviglia *ad loc.* reflects upon (but does not assert) a possible Senecan influence on the opening of Dante's 24th Canto of the *Inferno* (24.4–15).

gelida cana pruina/cold-grey with frost: lit. 'grey with cold frost'. Seneca is being a little Horatian here: cf. Hor. *Odes* 1.4.4.

141–5 With this picture of animals at peace and play, cf. Lucr. 1.255–61, 3.7; Virg. *Geo.* 2.524–6, Hor. *Odes* 3.18.9.

ludit prato liber aperto/plays free in the open Fields: cf. lines 144 and 146, which, as Fitch notes *ad loc.*, have an identical structure. The three lines begin with a verb, followed by an adjective-noun phrase in the ablative sandwiching an adjective in the nominative. Such initial verbs have 'an enumerative effect' (Fitch, who compares 756–9); i.e. they suggest the plethora of rural activity occurring at dawn. Seneca uses *ludit* of animals also at *Pha.* 49 (*fera*, 'wild beast') and *Ag.* 449 (*Tyrrhenus…piscis*, 'dolphin'). Note also the attractive parallel pattern of *l*s and *p*s in the Latin of 141.

nondum rupta fronte/brow still unhorned: a common description of a young calf; see e.g. *Tro.* 538, Ov. *Am.* 3.13.15, Stat. *Theb.* 6.267.

uacuae…matres/Idling dams: there seems to be deliberate semiotic ambiguity here; *uacuae* = both 'idling' (which contributes to the notion of *tranquilla quies*, 'tranquil peace', 160) and 'empty', the latter clearly activated by the juxtaposed *reparant*, 'refill'. For *uacuus* applied to the body, see 1086 (*dextra*, 'hand'), *Pha.* 391 (*ceruix*, 'neck'), *Thy.* 152 (*gutture*, 'gullet'). For *uacuus* at moments of high drama, see *Pha.* 1268, *Oed.* 1012.

molli petulans…in herba/Friskily in the tender grass: *petulans*, 'frisky', is used by Seneca of the bull which kidnaps Europa (*Pha.* 303). Note the postponed preposition, not uncommon in Senecan tragedy; see e.g. 148, 720, 883.

146–51 *pendet summo…ramo*/Perched upon the highest bough: imitated with slight change by the dramatist of *Octavia* at *Oct.* 921–1•: *tenui ramo pendens*, 'perched on a slender bough'. Bough and nightingale are also conjoined at *Ag.* 671, *Oct.* 921–3, and Virg. *Geo.* 4.514, as here, in ominous contexts (see further below).

stridula/shrill: a startling, onomatopoeic adjective to use of the nightingale, although both Sophocles (*Trach.* 963) and Babrius (12.3, 12.19) use the
Greek epithet ὀξύφωνος, 'shrill voiced', of the bird. Seneca uses the adjective
on two other occasions: of the 'shrill notes' (*stridulos cantus*) of the trumpet
(*lituus*) at *Oed.* 934, and of the 'thin and shrill voice' (*tenuem et stridulam
uocem*) of the hair-plucker (*alipilus*) at *Ep. Mor.* 56.2. This disconcerting epithet creates a sharp contrast with the 'subtle harmony' (λεπτὰν ἀηδὼν
ἁρμονίαν, *Phaeth.* 67–8 Diggle) of Euripides' nightingale. The epithet draws
attention to itself and to the bird, marking the latter (and the myth it here
explicitly embodies: see below) as an ominous signal of the bloodshed to
come. For *stridor* or *stridere* of grieving or ominous bird-sound, see *Marc.*
7.2, Stat. *Theb.* 3.510.

pinnasque nouo tradere soli/spread wings To the new sun: cf. Virg.
Geo. 1.398: *ad solem pennas...pandunt*, 'they spread wings to the sun' (of
halcyons).

querulos inter nidos/Amid plaintive nests: the phrase is Ovidian: *quer-
ulo...uolucrum nido*, 'plaintive nest of birds', *Medic.* 77; cf. *argutis...nidis*,
'shrill nests', *Ep. Mor.* 122.12 (citing Julius Montanus), *nidis...loquacibus*,
'chattering nests', Virg. *Aen.* 12.475. For *querulus/queror* of the sound of
birds, see *aues querulae*, *Pha.* 508; *queruntur aues*, Hor. *Ep.* 2.26, Ov. *Am.*
3.1.4. Note the semiotic position of *inter*, situated 'between' the words it
governs, a Senecan lyric mannerism (see e.g. 883; *Med.* 621, 649, 667; *Oed.*
148, 436; *Pha.* 409, 494; *Ag.* 678–9; *Tro.* 1174; *Thy.* 34—cf. *HO* 1736), found
also in Virgil (e.g. *Ecl.* 9.12, *Geo.* 1.33, 445, *Aen.* 2.632, 4.61, 4.256, 7.679)
and Tacitus (e.g. *Ann.* 4.55, 69).

Thracia paelex/whore of Thrace: the nightingale. Euripides simply
refers to the bird by the relatively rare Greek word ἀηδών (from ἀείδω,
'I sing'), used famously by Aeschylus at *Ag.* 1146 and 1147. Seneca himself
uses the Latin transliteration of that word, *aedon*, at *Ag.* 671, where it is a
Senecan *hapax*. Here he has chosen to have his chorus allude to the legend
behind the nightingale and unknowingly pick up Juno's preoccupation with
Jupiter's *paelices* (4–5), while also (again unknowingly) anticipating the
family slaughter to come. The 'whore of Thrace' is Philomela, the Ovidian
paelex of *Met.* 6 (537, 606) and *Trist.* 2 (389), sister of the Thracian queen,
Procne. The latter's husband, Tereus, had raped and mutilated Philomela; in
revenge the two sisters killed Itys, son of Procne and Tereus, and served him
up for Tereus to eat. All three were turned into birds: Philomela into a
nightingale (or swallow), Procne into a swallow (or nightingale), and Tereus
into a hoopoe: *Thy.* 56–7, 272–7; *HO* 192–3, 199–200, 952–3; *Oct.* 8, 915–23;

Hom. *Od.* 19.518-23; Aesch. *Ag.* 1142-9; Soph. *El.* 147-9, 1077; Cat. 65.13-14; Virg. *Ecl.* 6.78-81, *Geo.* 4.511-15; Prop. 2.20.5-6; Hor. *Odes* 4.12.5-8; Ov. *Her.* 15.153-4, *Am.* 2.6.7-10, *Met.* 6.424-674; [Virg.] *Culex* 251-3; Stat. *Theb.* 12.478-80, *Silu.* 2.4.21, 5.3.84; Mart. *Epig.* 10.51.4, 14.75-6. Among Roman poets, though it is not always clear, Philomela tends to become a nightingale (Virg. *Geo.* 4.15; Ov. *Ars* 2.383-4, *Fas.* 2.853-6, *Tr.* 3.12.9-10) and Procne a swallow (Virg. *Geo.* 4.511, Mart. *Epig.* 14.75). See also Hyginus *Fab.* 45, Apollodorus 3.14.8, Antoninus Liberalis *Met.* 11. The subject had been dramatized by Sophocles and by Livius Andronicus and Accius. Accius' play, *Tereus*, was part of the dramatic repertoire of the late republic. Cf., too, [Ovid], *Consolatio ad Liuiam* (dated to 54 CE by Schoonhaven 1992), which begins its list of mythological paradigms of grief (105-8) with Procne, the *Daulias ales*, 'Daulian bird', and the 'Halcyons'. Notice the negative resonance of *Thracia*, 'Thracian', which points not only to the geographical locale of the gruesome tale but to its 'barbaric' nature: cf. e.g. *Thy.* 56, Stat. *Silu.* 2.4.21. Ovid's canonic account in *Met.* 6 begins with the word *Threicius* (6.424). Those who think that the nightingale is an inappropriate herald of dawn I refer to the excellent discussion of Diggle (1970: 101-2), summarized thus: 'The nightingale...is as much a harbinger of dawn as is the cock or the swallow' (101).

turba...confusa...testata diem/**mingled choir Witness day**: Fitch *ad loc.* aptly compares the final words of Robert Bridges' *Nightingales*: 'the innumerable choir of day | Welcome the dawn'. For a different kind of *confusa turba*, see the noisy wedding attendees of Ov. *Met.* 12.214.

sonat murmure mixto/**with diverse sound**: for *murmur* of bird-sound, see Ov. *Ars* 2.466 (doves), Stat. *Theb.* 8.619 (nightingale and swallow). For the focus on sound, see on 1002-9.

152-8 *carbasa uentis credit*/**trusting Sails to winds**: *credit*, 'trusting', suggests the danger involved; cf. *Med.* 304, *Ag.* 106, and esp. *Ag.* 443, *credita est uento ratis*, 'ships were trusted to the wind', where such trust results in the wreck of the Greek fleet. For *carbasa uentis praebere/dare*, see Ov. *Her.* 7.171, Luc. 5.560.

dubius nauita uitae/**The sailor risks life**: a Senecan and Roman touch not in Eur.'s *Phaethon*. Roman poets regularly underscore the dangers of navigation. For the genitive with *dubius*, cf. Ov. *Met.* 15.448 (*dubioque salutis*), *Am.* 2.13.2 (*in dubio uitae*), and, as here, *Tr.* 3.3.25 (*dubius uitae*). For Roman referentiality in *Hercules*, see on 46-52.

hic exesis pendens scopulis/**A man perched on battered rocks**: fishermen appear in ancient literature from Homer onwards (*Il.* 16.406-8, *Od.* 12.251-4), often, as here, fishing from rocks. A famous image of a fisherman on a rock may be found on the cup of Theoc. *Id.* 1 (39–44). See also Ov. *Met.* 13.922–3: *in mole sedens*, 'sitting on a boulder'; Petron. *Sat.* 3.4: *piscator…morabitur in scopulo*, 'the fisherman…will linger on a rock'. For *exesus*, 'battered/eroded' of weathered rock or stone, see *Tro.* 831, *Thy.* 75–6, *Pho.* 72.

deceptos instruit hamos/Baits cheated hooks: an ironic description. The hooks, meant to deceive, are themselves deceived, cheated of their prey. For *decipere* and fishing, see Ov. *Met.* 3.586–7: *linoque solebat et hamis decipere*, 'and he used to deceive with line and hooks'; also Mart. *Epig.* 5.18.8, 13.68.1.

spectat…praemia/gazes At the prize: an unflattering echo here perhaps of Ovid's description of Tereus' lustful triumphalism, as he gazes upon the woman he will shortly rape: *spectat sua praemia raptor*, 'the rapist gazes at his prize' (*Met.* 6.518).

sentit tremulum linea piscem/His line feels the quivering fish: as Fitch notes *ad loc.*, Seneca has moved the epithet *tremulus* from the line (*tremula…saeta/linea*, Mart. *Epig.* 1.55.9, 3.58.27) or rod (*tremula…harundine*, Ov. *Ars* 2.77, *Met.* 8.217) to the fish—and, one might add, has done so astutely; for the fish activates the 'trembling', and, when caught, does not cease to quiver and tremble.

159–77 A contrast is drawn between the life of rural peace and that of the city: the latter is marked by anxiety, ambition, greed, and delusion. The contrast was at the heart of the doomed Hippolytus' defence of his lifestyle at *Pha.* 483–564. The structure of this section is essentially that of a priamel (see e.g. Horace's first ode): a list of modes of (urban) life to be rejected (162–74: *ille…hic…illum…hic…*) is followed by the *modus uiuendi* to be preferred (175–7). The Chorus also begin with this life (159–61: *haec… quibus…*), which thus frames the morally inferior lifestyles of the city.

159–61 The pivot of the ode: a moral description of the rural life so far described, with which the Chorus will now contrast urban life (162–74). Several conclusions, including personal ones (197–201), will be drawn.

Haec/So live: there is a verbal ellipse (*agunt*, perhaps). *Haec* is the first of a cluster of demonstratives in 159–72: see on 1226–30.

innocuae…uitae tranquilla quies/tranquil peace Of guiltless life: the pleonastic phrase, *tranquilla quies* (also found at *Tro.* 994–5 and borrowed by Lucan at 1.250; cf. *placidam…quietem*, 'restful peace', *Ag.* 60, Virg. *Aen.* 4.5), anticipates *secura quies*, 'carefree peace', at the end of this section (175), where the advantages of the 'peaceful life' are restated. The phrases smack of Epicureanism, especially its goal of ἀταραξία, 'tranquillity', with *secura quies* itself being taken not only from Virgil's idealized description of rural life

(*Geo.* 2.467, which also influenced *innocuae...uitae*: see below) and from Ovid's sarcastic reference to Epicurean divinities (*Ars.* 1.639), but also (ironically) from Lucretius' descriptions of death (3.211, 939). Seneca sometimes speaks negatively of *securitas, quies*, etc.: see e.g. *Ben.* 7.2.2 (*inerti otio*, 'sluggish rest'), *Ep. Mor.* 67.14 (*uita secura*, 'carefree life', is not *tranquillitas*), *Ep. Mor.* 96.5 (*putida quies*, 'rotting peace'). But sometimes he speaks positively, even nominating *securitas et perpetua tranquillitas* as the constituents of the 'happy life' (*Ep. Mor.* 92.3); and the life according to nature, which the first part of this ode has described, is elsewhere prescribed as Stoic (*secundum naturam uiuere, Ep. Mor.* 5.4). *Quies* also became the *mot juste* in Senecan prose (and elsewhere) for retirement from public life: see e.g. *Ot.* 6.5, *Tranq.* 4.7, 6.2, *Breu. Vit.* 4.2. Even the Tacitean Seneca says to Nero: *possumus seniores amici quietem reposcere*, 'We older friends can ask for retirement', Tac. *Ann.* 14.54.5. For Stoic language and ideas in *Hercules*, see on 162-3. Apart from *tranquilla, secura*, and *placida*, epithets attached to *quies* in Senecan tragedy are *tacita* ('silent', *Med.* 158), *sola* ('only', *Med.* 426), *aeterna* (*Oed.* 785, *Ag.* 592), *dulcis* ('sweet', *Thy.* 393), *magna* (*Thy.* 469), *nocturna* ('nocturnal', *Pha.* 100), and *obscura* ('humble/unnoticed', *Pha.* 1126). See also the later description of *Somnus*, 'Sleep', as *requies animi*, 'the mind's peace' (1066•). With the phrase, *innocuae...uitae*, 'guiltless life', used of non-urban existence, cf. *ruris innocui*, 'guiltless land', 930 below, and *innocuus* of the rural life envisaged by Hippolytus (*Pha.* 502). Cf. also Virgil's *nescia fallere uita* ('life ignorant of fraud', *Geo.* 2.467).

   quibus est/those with: lit. 'to whom is/belongs'; the dative is possessive. For the postponement of relatives, see e.g. 412, 426, 427, 469, 599, 645, 723, 835, 1293, 1344.

   laeta suo paruoque domus/homes joyous in their own and little: the ideal of living 'content with a little' (*contentus paruo*) is a commonplace of the Roman moral tradition: see e.g. Cic. *Off.* 1.70 (*contenti...et suo et paruo*, 'content with both their own and a little'), *Att.* 12.19.1; Tib. 1.1.25; Hor. *Odes* 2.10.5-8, 16.13-16. Seneca exhorts Lucilius at *Ep. Mor.* 110.18: *disce paruo esse contentus*, 'Learn to be content with a little'. The ideal is presented as realized in the pre-technological Golden Age described at *Med.* 331ff., when people were 'rich with a little' (*paruo diues, Med.* 333). It is as Roman as the urban vices which follow. For Roman referentiality, see on 46-52. *Laeta*, 'joyous', is picked up at 178 (*laeti*): see n. *ad loc.* For *laetus* applied to *domus*, see *Ag.* 924.

162-74 Urban life, the values and ambitions of which are castigated through four social and moral *exempla*: client, *auarus*, politician, lawyer. The first and third of these are motivated by *ambitio*, the second and fourth by *auaritia*. The depiction is anachronistic and thoroughly Roman. Much of it is indebted to Virgil's denunciation of urban life in *Georgic* 2 (458–540): patron-client (*Geo.* 2.461–2); avarice (*Geo.* 2.462–4); desire for popular favour (*Geo.* 2.508–9); 'insane forum' (*Geo.* 2.502). Cf. also Lucretius' denunciation of urban luxury at 2.22–8, Hippolytus' condemnation at *Pha.* 486–500, and the Chorus' indictment of the pursuit of glory, land, wealth, and power at *HO* 616–39. See also Hor. *Epod.* 2.1–8 and *Odes* 1.1. For Seneca's own indictment of contemporary *auaritia* and *ambitio*, see *Breu. Vit.* 2.1–4. Comparison of urban and rural lifestyles was a regular topic in Roman declamation: Quint. *Inst.* 2.4.24. For Roman referentiality in *Hercules*, see on 46–52

162–3 *iam magnis urbibus*/Now in the great cities: along with Giardina (1966), Caviglia, Viansino (1965 and 1993), I have printed the reading of *E* (*iam magnis*) as against the conjecture of Schmidt (*immanes*), accepted by Zwierlein, Fitch (1987*a* and 2018), Chaumartin, and Billerbeck. Fitch and others have problems with *E*'s *iam*. But it seems clearly a pointer, like *nunc iam* of *Med.* 364 (perhaps even the opening *iam* of *Oedipus*), to Seneca's own era and to the Roman world, as does the ensuing focus on 'cities' (*urbibus*) and urban life. For Roman referentiality in *Hercules*, see on 46–52.

   spes…errant trepidique metus/roam hopes And trembling fears: hope/desire and fear are important in Seneca's Stoicism because they are strictly to be avoided. They are two of the four Stoic πάθη or *adfectus* ('passions'), from which the sage is free. Pleasure and pain are the other two: Arnim *SVF* (1903–24), 3.92.16, 93.12, 94.7, 95.16. Throughout his philosophical writings, Seneca adheres to the standard Stoic belief in the irrationality and thus unacceptability of the passions, which are 'diseased conditions of the vicious soul'. He adheres, too, to the Chrysippan theory of the identity of emotion/the passions and belief or evaluative judgement (see Nussbaum 1997: 226, Strange 2004: 40). Because the passions derive from the assent to false impressions, i.e. impressions of false goods or false evils, and assent is voluntarily given, they constitute to Seneca the voluntary subversion of reason, which by necessity prevents the attainment of the life of *uirtus*, 'virtue', exemplified by the Stoic 'sage' or *sapiens*. Hence 'the happy man (= the sage) can be said to be one who neither desires nor fears through the gift of reason', *potest beatus dici qui nec cupit nec timet beneficio rationis*, *Vit. Beat.* 5.1; the sage 'knows nothing of living in hope or fear', *nescit nec in spem nec in metum uiuere*, *Const.* 9.2. At *Ep. Mor.* 5.7 Seneca cites Hecato: *desines…timere, si sperare desieris*, 'You will cease to fear, if you have ceased to hope'. See also *Breu. Vit.* 7.9, *Const.* 9.2, *Tro.* 399, 425, *Pha.* 492, *Thy.* 388–90, Hor. *Ep.*

1.16.65–6, Stat. *Silu.* 2.2.125. Epicurus, too, 'put a limit on desire and fear' (*finem statuit cuppedinis atque timoris*) according to Lucretius (6.25). In more modern times, note the epitaph for the Greek writer Nikos Kazantzakis (died 1957): Δεν ελπίζω τίποτα, δεν φοβούμαι τίποτα, είμαι λέφτερος, 'I hope for nothing, I fear nothing, I am free'. For Stoic language and ideas in *Hercules*, see on 35–40, 63–74, 159–61, 178–82, 197–201, 359–69, 397–402, 402–8, 426–9, 463–4, 524–32, 604–15, 689–96, 926–31, 952–4, 955–73, 973–5, 987–91, 1022–31, 1054–62•, 1240–5, 1258–62, 1265–72, 1278–82, 1341–4. For *errare*, 'roam', used of emotions, see Luc. 2.21, VF 5.145–6; for the (almost) pleonasm *trepidi metus*, see also *Ag.* 916.

164–74 *ille…hic…illum…hic*/One…One…another…Another: lists of diverse pursuits/professions etc. are common in priamels: see e.g. Hor. *Odes* 1.1 and Nisbet and Hubbard *ad loc.*, who trace the concern with the diversity of human pursuits back to Solon. The influence of Horace seems strong in this section, as well as that of Virgil (see *Geo.* 2.503–10: *alii…hic…alius…hic…hunc*).

superbos aditus regum durasque fores/**proud doorways And hard thresholds of the great:** Seneca is referring to the Roman social practice of *salutatio*, whereby clients would rise early in the morning to be at the house of their patron in time to greet him and perhaps accompany him to the senate, law courts, or some other place of business. The practice was a regular one (Lucr. 1.318, Manil. 5.64–6) and a frequent target of satire: *Tranq.* 12.6, *Breu. Vit.* 2.1, 4.3, *Ep. Mor.* 4.10, Hor. *Epod.* 2.7–8, Virg. *Geo.* 2.461–2, Mart. *Epig.* 1.55.5–6, 4.8.1, and, most notably, Juv. 1.95–126. The vice of the client was primarily ambition: see e.g. Claud. *Laud. Stil.* 2.114–15: *ambitio, quae uestibulis foribusque potentum excubat*, 'ambition, which keeps watch at the vestibules and doorways of the powerful'. *Superbus* is regularly used by Seneca, as here, in a transferred sense: see e.g. *Ag.* 880; *Tro.* 188, 829; *Ep. Mor.* 4.10, 68.10. He follows Augustan (Hor. *Epod.* 2.7–8), especially Virgilian, precedent: Virg. *Geo.* 2.461, *Aen.* 1.639, 8.196, 721, etc. The 'hard thresholds' (*duras fores*), as Fitch and Billerbeck observe *ad loc.*, generate an analogy between the client and the elegiac lover, the *exclusus amator*, barred from the house of his *puella*: see Prop. 1.16.18, Tib. 1.1.56, Ov. *Am.* 2.1.22. For *reges* as 'the great', i.e. powerful patrons, as often in Roman comedy and Horace, see *OLD* 8.

expers somni/**Sleepless:** juxtaposed with *duras fores*, the phrase underscores the analogy with the *exclusus amator* of Roman erotic elegy. There is also the clear suggestion that the ambitious client's actions contravene the day's *natural* rhythms. For the sleep-deprived Roman *cliens*, see also *Breu. Vit.* 14.4, Mart. 10.70.5, Juv. 5.19–23.

beatas componit opes/gathers blessed riches: *beatas*, 'blessed', is ironic, given the context of moral indictment. The *auarus* or miser is a ubiquitous target of Roman satire: see e.g. Virg. *Geo.* 2.507, Hor. *Sat.* 1.1.70-2. For ironic *beatus*, see Hor. *Odes* 1.29.1, *Epod.* 2.1. For *beatas opes*, see also Stat. *Silu.* 1.5.43-4. With *componit opes*, 'gathers riches', cf. Virg. *Aen.* 8.317 (*componere opes*) and *HO* 636 (*ponat opes*).

gazis inhians/gawps at his treasure: the language is Horatian (*Odes* 1.29.2, *Sat.* 1.1.71), but see also, at Sen. Rhet. *Con.* 7.7.11, the description of the *auarus* as *lucro inhiantem*, 'gawping at gain'.

congesto pauper in auro/A pauper amid heaps of gold: semiotic, verbal placing in the Latin line, a veritable *callida iunctura* depicting the 'pauper' strangled by his own gold. Cf. Hor. *Odes* 3.16.28: *magnas inter opes inops*, 'unwealthy amid great wealth', where, however, the visual paradox is missing. See also Hor. *Sat.* 2.3.142. For *congerere* of 'piling up' gold, see Tib. 1.1.1. For a similarly concessive, paradoxical use of *in*, see *in amne medio* ('amid a stream', 752 below), *in undis* ('amid water', *Thy.* 5), and *tanto in metu* ('amid great fear', *Tro.* 323). For paradoxical phrasing in *Hercules*, see on 30-5.

illum populi fauor...fluctuque magis mobile uulgus.../The people's favour...A mob more fickle than the waves...: this vignette of the ambitious politician rewrites Hor. *Odes* 1.1.7-8:

> hunc si mobilium turba Quiritium
> certat tergeminis tollere honoribus.
>
> This man if the fickle Quirite mob
> Strives to lift him with triple honours.

Like Horace, Seneca has the Roman 'mob' very much in mind, and, like Horace, Seneca conveys the politician's dependency on the mob by making him the object of their activity. Cf. the *fragilis fauor* of the *uulgus infidum* ('faithless mob') at *Pha.* 488-9, the *numquam stabilis fauor uulgi praecipitis* ('reckless mob's ever fickle favour') at *Thy.* 351-2, the *funestus multis populi dirusque fauor* ('the people's foul favour, fatal to many') at *Oct.* 877-8, and the *mobile uulgus* ('fickle mob') at Ov. *Tr.* 1.9.13, Stat. *Silu.* 2.2.123—also the *populi fasces* ('the people's honours') and *plausus plebis* ('applause of the plebs') of *Georgic* 2's finale (495, 508-9). Tacitus was later to comment on the 'brief and ill-omened loves of the Roman people', *breuis et infaustos populi Romani amores* (*Ann.* 2.41.3). Seneca's rewriting of Horace here involves the introduction of wave and breeze imagery (*fluctu, aura, tumidum*), reminiscent perhaps of the treacherous seascape that is Horace's Pyrrha (*Odes* 1.5). But, as Fitch *ad loc.* observes, 'the comparison of the common people to the sea for changeability is traditional'. He cites *inter alia* Livy 28.27.11; but see also *Oct.* 878–81—and (for a later possible 'imitation') Norton and Sackville, *Gorboduc* V.i.72–3:

> So giddy are the common people's minds,
> So glad of change, more wavering than the sea.

For the moral perversity of the *populus*, 'the people', see *Pha.* 983–4.

attonitum/**stuns:** the word is Virgilian (*Geo.* 2.508, where it is used of listeners 'stunned' by orators in the forum).

aura tumidum tollit inani/**Lifts and swells him with empty air:** for the wind and breeze imagery, see above; cf. *Ag.* 247–8. For *aura*, 'air/breath', of the people's will or favour (and its vanity), see *Pha.* 488: *aura populi*; Virg. *Aen.* 6.816: *popularibus auris.*

clamosi rabiosa fori iurgia uendens/**sells the raucous forum's Rabid strife:** potent phraseology to depict the proverbial noise, chaos and venality of the Roman law courts. Cf. Virgil's *insanum...forum*, *Geo.* 2.502; Ovid's *uerbosi garrula bella fori*, 'noisy wars of the wordy forum', *Tr.* 3.12.18, and *fortia uerbosi...arma fori*, 'strong arms of the wordy forum', *Tr.* 4.10.18; and Statius' possible echo: *nulla foro rabies aut strictae in iurgia leges*, 'no rabid madness in the forum or laws drawn for strife', *Silu.* 3.5.87. According to *Ira* 1.4.2, *clamosus*, 'raucous', and *rabiosus*, 'rabid', signal 'different kinds of anger', *irarum differentiae*. Kingery *ad loc.* relevantly cites the younger Pliny's vivid description of the noise generated (and paid for) at the Centumviral Court (*Ep.* 2.14). For *clamosus* used of other noisy cultural environments, see Stat. *Silu.* 3.5.16, Mart. *Epig.* 10.53.1. On the venality of the Roman courts, see *Apoc.* 12.3.30: *o causidici, uenale genus*, 'O lawyers, you venal tribe'; Mart. *Epig.* 5.16.6; Tac. *Ann.* 11.5.2. For legal language and imagery in *Hercules*, see on 731–4.

improbus...locat/**Wantonly trading:** cf. *Apoc.* 12.28, where Seneca inveighs against the corruption of advocates, calling them *uenale genus*, 'a venal species'. Ancient lawyers, like their Renaissance and modern counterparts, were regular targets of abuse: see Tac. *Ann.* 11.5.2 on the *aduocatorum perfidia*, 'the perfidy of lawyers'.

iras et uerba/**wrath and words:** an interesting conjunction which reflects on the play itself and its focus on *ira* and *uerba*. For *ira*, 'wrath/anger', see on 19–29; for the related epithets, *clamosus* and *rabiosus*, see above.

175-7 The last and preferred mode of life—one which instantiates the rural ideal of 159–61. It contrasts markedly with the urban activities of the preceding lines, in which the focus was on the future, not the present.

nouit paucos secura quies/Carefree peace knows but few: the *pauci*, 'few', have been variously identified, but it seems clear from the structure of this section and the ode that the Chorus' reference is to the rustics of line 159 and those who have modelled their life upon their exemplary harmony with nature. For the idiom, see Hercules' last words in the play at 1341 and n. *ad loc.* For *secura quies*, see on 159–61.

uelocis memores aeui/mindful of the speeding years: i.e. the years of one's life ('die Lebenszeit': Billerbeck *ad loc.*) rather than 'time' ('die Zeit') in the abstract.

tempora numquam reditura/unreturning time: contrasting with the cyclic time of the cosmos (*reditura*, 136) is the linear time of humanity—a *topos* of Seneca's prose works (see e.g. *Breu. Vit.* 8.5) and of Roman poetry from Catullus 5.4–6 onwards; see also Hor. *Odes* 4.7.13–16, Mosch. *Epit. Bion* 99–106. At *Breu. Vit.* 17.5 Seneca criticizes those who take no account of 'unreturning time' (*numquam amplius redituri temporis*).

178–91 The Chorus draw from their reflections a moral imperative: grasp the fleeting moment, 'while fate allows'; for death is fated and certain. There is little innovation in the Chorus' recommendation (Hor. *Odes* 1.9, 11; 2.3, 11; Prop. 2.15.23–4) or in its statement of mortal certitude, which gain their purchase in both play and ode from the context of Hercules' premature descent to the underworld and their role as critical frame for the evaluation of the hero's conduct. Beneath the statements, however, lies Seneca's concern in the prose works (esp. *De Breuitate Vitae*, 'On the Brevity of Life', and the *Epistulae Morales*) with the relationship between death and time and with the moral imperatives for the utilization of time dictated by death itself. Among the imperatives of the opening sentence of the *Epistulae* are *tempus...collige et serua*, 'Gather and preserve time' (*Ep. Mor.* 1.1), a pair of actions equated with personal liberation. At *Breu. Vit.* 8.1 Seneca even describes time as the 'most precious thing of all' (*re omnia pretiosissima*). See further Edwards (2014). For other choral pronouncements on fate in Seneca, see *Oed.* 980–97, *Thy.* 615–22; cf. *Oct.* 924–8.

178–82 *Dum fata sinunt*/While fate allows: a common phrase; cf. Prop. 2.15.23 (*dum nos fata sinunt*), Tib. 1.1.69 (*dum fata sinunt*), Virg. *Aen.* 4.651 (*dum fata deusque sinebat*). *Fatum* or *fata*, 'fate', is a semiotically loaded word in Senecan tragedy and is used in complex ways. It often = 'fate', which is generally cyclic in Senecan tragedy (see esp. *Tro.*, *Med.*, *Pha.*, *Ag.*, *Thy.*), the unimpedable revolution of human history, sometimes associated, like *fortuna* (*Ag.* 72; also *HO* 703) and *casus* (*Pha.* 1123; also *HO* 715), with the notion of 'spinning/revolving', *rotare*: *sic ordinem fati rerum aeterna series* *rotat*, 'So the eternal chain of events spins the order of fate', *NQ* 2.35.2. Cf. *Thy*. 618: *rotat omne fatum*, '(Clotho) spins every fate'. *Fatum* in this sense is aligned in the prose works with fortune, nature and 'divine reason', *diuina ratio* (*Ben*. 4.8); it is fixed and unchangeable: *fata aliter ius suum peragunt nec ulla commouentur prece…cursum irreuocabilem ingressa ex destinato fluunt*; 'The fates fulfil their own ordinance otherwise and are not moved by any prayer…Having entered on their irrevocable course they flow according to their plan', *NQ* 2.35.2. For the irrevocability of fate, see also 181–2 and 559. For the personified 'Fates' or Parcae/Sisters, spinners of the threads of destiny, see below.

Fatum is important in Stoic ethics. To offer oneself to *fatum*, to 'fate' (*praebere se fato*), is a Stoic ideal (*Prou*. 5.8) and the mark of the Stoic sage; it is also the mark of the true gladiator, with whom the sage is often compared (e.g. *Tranq*. 11.4f., *Ep. Mor*. 30.8, 70.20–7). Living in accord with fate/nature is to live in accord with the providential cosmic plan: *posse laeto animo aduersa tolerare*; *quidquid acciderit, sic ferre quasi tibi uolueris accidere. debuisses enim uelle, si scisses omnia ex decreto dei fieri* ('To be able to endure adversity joyfully; to bear whatever has happened as if you wanted it to happen to you. For you would have been right to want it, had you known that everything happens according to god's decree', *NQ* 3 Pref. 12). In the tragedies *fatum*, 'fate', and 'god' seem less providential. But what is clear, as in the prose works, is the 'truth' of Cicero's aphorism (translated from Cleanthes and quoted by Seneca at *Ep. Mor*. 107.11): *ducunt uolentem fata, nolentem trahunt*, 'Fate leads the willing, drags the reluctant.' Cf. the maxim at [Virg.] *Cat*. 11.3–4: *sua quemque sequuntur | fata*, 'Each one's fate follows them.'

Fatum in Latin also means 'one's fate', i.e. 'death', an ambiguity frequently exploited by Roman poets, including Seneca (see e.g. 184, 867). But it means literally 'what has been said', and is regularly used of decrees of the gods, oracles, prophecies, etc. In Senecan tragedy, too, 'what has been said' seems sometimes to include 'what has been said in the literary tradition'. In such cases the focus on *fatum* in part seems metatheatrical, index of a concern with the determinism of the literary tradition, the imperatives of the myth and its previous dramatic and literary manifestations, as well as with the philosophical concept of fate itself. For *fatum/fata* in this play, see also 184, 396, 497, 566, 612, 867, 1270. For metatheatrical language in the play, see on 109–12.

uiuite laeti/live joyously: again a standard poetic imperative of the *carpe diem* mode (Hor. *Odes* 1.11.8, 2.3.13–16, 2.11.13–17; Ovid *Ars* 3.61–6); cf. Prop. 1.19.25, *quare, dum licet, inter nos laetemur*, 'therefore, while we can, let us be joyous'; Hor. *Sat*. 2.6.96: *dum licet, in rebus secundis uiue beatus*, 'while you can, live happy amid your blessings'. Phaedra's Nurse (vainly to Hippolytus): *aetate fruere*; *mobili cursu fugit*, 'Enjoy the time; with rapid speed it flies' (*Pha*. 446); Phaedra's Chorus (again vainly to Hippolytus): *dum licet, utere* (*forma*), 'while you may, use it (beauty)' (*Pha*. 774). Note how *laeti*, 'joyously', picks up the *laeta domus*, 'joyous home' of line 161. The Chorus align themselves with the rustics of their depicted idyll, as they propose what is essentially an Epicurean ideal, *uoluptas*. Their exhortation to joy will soon be followed by two characters locked in pain.

Apostrophe is common in Senecan choral odes: see below 186–7, 524–5, 547–9, 558–68, 834, 858–60, 870–3, 1057–65, 1066–81, 1092–1114, 1115–18, 1122–37. Sometimes the apostrophe is to people beyond the play (see e.g. *Thy*. 607–12, and, though not in a choral ode, Theseus at 745–7 below: see n. *ad loc.*); sometimes the apostrophe is to *dramatis personae* not onstage (547–9, 558–68 to Hercules, *Oed*. 709–12 to Oedipus, *Pha*. 777–94 to Hippolytus, *Thy*. 339–43 to Atreus and Thyestes); sometimes the apostrophe is to a city (*Ag*. 808–13 to Argos), people (*Oed*. 110 to Thebans) or (frequently) a deity (see on 524–32). The addressees here are left open: Seneca's audience, certainly, but perhaps more generally the human world. For apostrophe without a vocative elsewhere in the choral odes of *Hercules*, see 547–9, 834, 858, 1092, 1122; for 'unidentified' addressees, see on 1122–30. The dramatist of *Octavia* continued the practice of choral apostrophe: see *Oct*. 295–303, 356–8, 806, 887–9.

properat cursu uita citato/**Life rushes with rapid steps:** one of the most frequent commonplaces of the Greco-Roman literary tradition and one especially associated with Horace: e.g. *Odes* 1.4.15, 11.7–8; 2.5.13–14, 14.1–2; 3.30.5; 4.7.7–8. For the *properare*/'rushing' motif, see on 186–91. The ablative *cursu…citato* is of manner: Woodcock §43.5.iv.

uolucrique die rota/**wheel As days fly by:** the 'wheel' of the year is a Euripidean notion (ἐνιαυτοῦ κύκλος, *Or*. 1645, *Phoen*. 477). For time's and/or the year's 'wheel' in Latin literature, see also Virg. *Aen*. 6.748, Stat. *Silu*. 5.1.17, Sil. 6.121. For the day as lit. 'winged/fleeting', see Hor. *Odes* 3.28.6, 4.13.16. Edwards (2014: 328) argues that Seneca's notion of present time is 'often…conceptualized in terms of the individual day'. Life as a series of present times stops on the day of death (190). *Volucri die* seems best taken as an ablative of accompaniment (Woodcock §43.5): lit. 'with flying day'.

durae peragunt pensa sorores/**The brutal sisters spin the wool:** the three Parcae or (personified) Fates (= 'the sisters': see above), who spin the threads of an individual's destiny, figure often in ancient poetry; for the Roman tradition, see e.g. Catullus 64.327, Virg. *Ecl*. 4.46–7, Hor. *Epod*. 13.15–16,

Odes 2.3.15–16, Sil. 1.281 (*duraeque sorores*), and 188, 559 below. For the Fates' distaff (*colus*), see 559 below and *Oed*. 985, *HO* 768; for their 'allotted portions of wool' (*pensa*), see *Apoc*. 4.1.7, 1.11; Petron. *Sat*. 29.6; Mart. *Epig*. 4.73.3. One of the three Parcae (the name might seem ironic, since they do not 'spare', *parcere*, anyone: see 559 and n. *ad loc*.) was named 'Clotho' ('Spinner'). The other two were named 'Lachesis' ('the Disposer of Lots') and 'Atropos' ('the Unchangeable'). The three figure famously in Plato's 'Myth of Er' (*Rep*. 10.617c–e, 620d–e), but are not named in extant Latin literature before Ovid. They are brilliantly represented as solemn, robust, and dismayed figures in the tapestry of Pat Taylor and Fiona Abercrombie based on a Henry Moore drawing (exhibited in *The Fabric of Myth* at Compton Verney, Warwickshire, UK, June–Sept 2008). The spinning of the Fates seems almost triggered by the *rota anni*, since *rotare* is a verb used of their 'spinning' of fate itself (see above). *Pensa* or (singular) *pensum*, 'wool', is literally the portion of wool 'weighed out' for spinning or weaving. With *durae*, 'brutal', cf. *durum...fatum*, 'brutal fate' (867).

   ***nec sua retro fila reuoluunt*/And their thread is not rewound**: cf. 559 below and Stat. *Theb*. 7.774–5: *immites scis nulla reuoluere Parcas | stamina*, 'you know that the unpitying Parcae do not rewind their thread'. For paronomasia of *re-* words, see on 46–52.

183–5 *gens hominum fertur rapidis obuia fatis*/race of men Is swept to meet the grasping fates: the issue of the speed of the human advance to death/fate returns as an issue later in the play (867). Note the focus here, too (through the use of the passive *fertur*, 'is swept'), on the impotent passivity of the human race before death's/fate's power. With *gens hominum*, 'race of men', cf. *humanum genus* at 674 (see n. *ad loc*.), 1075, *mortale genus* (*Oed*. 983, *HO* 1433, and *Oct*. 924), and Cicero's common phrase *hominum genus*. For 'grasping' fate or fates, see Luc. 9.786 (*rapidi...fati*), *Oed*. 125 (*rapiente fato*), *HO* 107 (*fata rapacia*).

   incerta sui/**self-unsure**: cf. *Ep. Mor*. 23.2: *sollicitus est et incertus sui quem spes aliqua proritat*, 'anxious and self-unsure is the man prompted by any hope'.

   Stygias ultro quaerimus undas/**We seek Stygian waves ourselves**: note the change to the first-person plural, as the Chorus both personalize the lyric and present themselves as included in their critique of *gens hominum*. *Stygias...undas*, 'Stygian waves', is not only a common metonym for the underworld (e.g. *Med*. 805; Virg. *Aen*. 3.215, 7.773; Ov. *Met*. 3.272, *Tr*. 1.2.65) but a means of effecting a transition to the underworld conqueror himself, Hercules. Phaedra's Nurse offers an identical proposition in her attempt to persuade Hippolytus of the imperatives of sex: *atram Styga | iam petimus ultro*, 'We seek black Styx ourselves' (*Pha.* 477–8); see also 872–4 below, *Tro.* 390. For Styx, see on 52–6.

186-91 *nimium, Alcide, pectore forti*/**Too strong your heart, Alcides:** a switch to the second-person singular in a return of apostrophe (see on 178–82), as the Chorus directly criticize Hercules for excess, essentially for boundary violation, breaching the *certus ordo* of the Parcae (188–91). In addressing him as 'Alcides' (used earlier at 84, 107) they draw attention both to his strength (note how *forti* brings out the semiotics of the name, *Alcides*) and to his mortal origins: see on 84–5. With *nimium...pectore forti*, cf. *pectus o nimium ferum*, 'O too savage heart', 1226, addressed by Hercules to himself. For *nimium/nimis* qualifying an adjective (something of a mannerism of Seneca *tragicus*), often in a criticism of excess, see e.g. 63 (possibly), 295; *Ag.* 59, 616; *Oed.* 75, 763; *Med.* 48, 301, 326; *Tro.* 264–5; *Thy.* 299, 402, 615. The ablative *pectore forti* is of manner: Woodcock §43.5.iv. For hyperbaton with *nimium*, see also 63. For boundary violation, see on 46–52. For addresses to a character by name, see on 637–40.

properas maestos uisere manes/**Rushing to meet the grim ghosts:** that the Chorus know of Hercules' descent into the underworld underscores their already implied identification as knowing residents of Thebes: see on 125–204 (introd.). The 'rushing'/*properare* motif, begun at 179, continues but is used here and later (589, 867, 873, 938, 1279) with a critical and/or ironic edge. *Maestus* ('sad/mournful/grim'), like *tristis*, is one of the defining epithets of the underworld: *maestos...manes*, 'grim ghosts', again at 648; *maestus finis*, 'grim cessation', 703; *maestus Acheron*, 'grim Acheron', at *Thy.* 17. For an ironic pick-up of *uisere*, see 1137 and n. *ad loc. Visere* is infinitive of purpose after a verb of motion: see Woodcock §28.

certo...citatos/**In fixed...throngs:** four 'lapidary, end-stopped lines' (Mader 1990: 15) appropriate for sharp, authoritative gnomic utterances. The Chorus' authority seems underscored by the legal imagery permeating these lines (*cessare, scriptum diem, proferre diem, citatos, urna*: see Fitch *ad loc.*), even as that imagery draws attention to the existential laws broken by Hercules. For legal imagery and language in *Hercules*, see on 731–4.

certo ueniunt ordine Parcae/**In fixed order the Parcae come:** I join Viansino (1965 and 1993) and Caviglia in preferring *ordine* (E^pcA) to *tempore* (FMNe), favoured by Zwierlein and other modern editors. The former is clearly the *lectio difficilior* and has better MS attestation. For the Parcae, see on 178–82. For their 'order' see *Oed.* 991–1•: *ratus prece non ulla | mobilis ordo*, 'a fixed order immune to prayer'; for that order's 'fixed/certain' nature, see Hor. *Epod.* 13.15: *certo subtemine Parcae*, 'the Parcae with unalterable thread'.

scriptum... diem/day inscribed: legal language which in this context has a marked metaliterary resonance, as Seneca's play reinscribes the day of Hercules' murderous madness, already inscribed in the mythic and literary tradition. For metaliterary language in *Hercules*, see on 109–12.

recipit populos urna citatos/The urn admits its summoned throngs: note the (deliberate) ambiguity of *urna*: cinerary urn (*Tro.* 375) and/or the urn of fate/death (Hor. *Odes* 2.3.26, 3.1.16. Stat. *Silu.* 2.1.219) and/or the legal urn with the names of those to be tried in the underworld by the judges of the dead (Virg. *Aen.* 6.432, Prop. 4.11.19, Stat. *Theb.* 11.571). As Fitch notes *ad loc.*, the plural form of *populus* is used often in *Hercules* to denote the multitudes of the dead: see also at 293, 557, 560, 667, 708, 775.

192–201 The Chorus close with a return to priamel structure (*alium... alius ...me...*: see on 159–77), in which they express a preference for their own humble lives (described in both personal and Epicurean terms) to the life of fame and glory. This advocacy of apolitical quietism, whatever the degree of sympathy it might elicit from a Roman audience, suggests a citizen body not likely to resist a violent takeover of its monarchy.

192–6 *Alium multis...terris tradat*/transport one man to Many lands: though the language is general, specific allusion is being made to Hercules and his global fame, even if the sentiment is not restricted to such.

Gloria...Fama...garrula/Glory...prattling Fame: I have joined Fitch in capitalizing *Gloria* and *Fama*. Fitch cites the excellent note of Pease (1935) on the famous passage in *Aeneid* 4 (173–88), where *Fama* is described as a many-eyed, many-tongued 'monster' (*monstrum*) as she works her destruction on Dido. Pease lists such a massive array of references throughout Greek and Roman literature (and beyond) of the personification of *Fama* (including Ovid's 'House of Fame', *Met.* 12.39–63) that capitalization seems required in a modern text. Billerbeck *ad loc.* notes the satirical undertone here of the epithet *garrula*, 'prattling', which reduces a central value of elite Roman culture to mere prattle. But note also the etymological force of the epithet, which, in creating a pleonasm with *Fama*, unpacks the latter into what it literally means ('being spoken of': *fari* etc.), even as it trivializes it.

caeloque parem tollat et astris/and lift him equal To heaven and stars: an echo of Horace's description of the victorious charioteer in his much-cited priamel (*Odes* 1.1.6), but a description with additional resonance. The phrase is clearly metaphorical as it applies to the regular glory-seeker, but not metaphorical as it applies to the pursuit of *fama* by Hercules, who is clearly one of the implied referents.

alius curru sublimis eat/Let another soar in his chariot: perhaps Horace's charioteer (see previous n.) and/or perhaps an image of a Roman *triumphator* during his triumphal procession, an image already used of Hercules by Juno (58: see n. *ad loc.*) and to be used as a contrast to Hercules' death by the dramatist of *Hercules Oetaeus* (*HO* 1683–4). The openness of the reference allows Seneca's audience to apply the injunction to contemporary figures, political, military and cultural, as well as to Hercules and (the lesser Hercules) Lycus. *Sublimis curru* is a phrase of Livy (28.9.15), applied to a consul in a triumphal procession. For Roman referentiality in *Hercules*, see on 46–52; for triumphal imagery, see on 57–63.

197–201 A personal coda, in which the Chorus employ first-person singular forms (*me mea*) to articulate an ideal of the lowly, obscure life of peace and private contentment. The individual, personal tone is the more striking because the Chorus has only once in the ode referred to themselves in the first person (*quaerimus*, 185: see n. *ad loc.*) and then in the plural and primarily as members of *gens hominum*. The safety and desirability of the life of obscurity, simplicity, inactivity, 'poverty', and rest—especially in contrast to the life of fame, ambition, wealth, and political and military power—is one of the great *topoi* of European literature: see e.g. Virgil's 'Praise of Rustic Life' (*Geo.* 2.458–540); Tibullus' exaltation of *paupertas* (1.1); Horace's 'Ode on *Otium*' (2.16); Pope's 'Ode on Solitude'; or King Henry's soliloquy (Shakespeare, *Henry VI* 3 II.v.21ff.): 'O God! Methinks it were a happy life | To be no better than a homely swain…'. See also Theog. 1375–6; Eur. frag. 793 Nauck; Hor. *Epod.* 2.1–3, *Odes* 2.16.13–16, 3.29.14–16; Mart. *Epig.* 10.47. The *topos* occurs elsewhere in the tragedies (sometimes as emblematic of the Golden Age): see *Pha.* 483–525, 1123–40; *Ag.* 102–7; *Med.* 329–34, 603–6; *Oed.* 882–910; *Thy.* 446–70, esp. 391–403, the end of the 'Kingship Ode', where the contrast between the insecure 'high' and secure 'low' life receives a similarly first-person singular choral articulation (*me…perfruar…mei… moriar*):

> stet quicumque uolet potens
> aulae culmine lubrico.
> me dulcis saturet quies.
> obscuro positus loco
> leni perfruar otio.   395

nullis nota Quiritibus
aetas per tacitum fluat.
sic cum transierint mei
nullo cum strepitu dies,
plebeius moriar senex.   400
illi mors grauis incubat
qui, notus nimis omnibus,
ignotus moritur sibi.

Let those who wish lord it
On a court's giddy peak.
Fill *me* with sweet repose,
Tucked in a place obscure,
Enjoying gentle ease.   395
Let my life flow silent,
Known to no Quirites.
So when my days have passed
Without din, may I die
An old man of the plebs.   400
Death lies heavy on one
Who, known too much to all,
Dies unknown to himself.

See also *Breu. Vit.* 4.1; *Ep. Mor.* 90.40–3, 94.72–4; *Oct.* 377–90, 896–8; *HO*
644–99; *Culex* 68–97—and several epigrams in the *Anthologia Latina* attributed to Seneca, esp. 407, 440, 444 (= 16, 48, 52 Prato). Both the *topos* and its
moral corollary belong to popular wisdom, but are also connected with the
'withdrawal ethics' of Epicureanism (see below).

The use of a singular personal pronoun and adjective at the head of this
section does not necessarily mean that these lines were to be spoken by a
single member of the chorus, e.g. by the Chorus Leader. In Greek tragic
choral lyric singular and plural forms are used interchangeably. In Senecan
tragedy choral plural forms are the norm (see e.g. 864, 872, 873), but singular forms occasionally occur: e.g. *Tro.* 115; *Oed.* 882; *Pha.* 356; *Ag.* 327, 656,
694; *Med.* 90; *Thy.* 393, 395, 398, 400—nor only in Senecan tragedy: *Oct.*
932, 977. Tarrant's suggestion *ad Thy.* 393 that sometimes 'there is an unmis-
takable sense of strong personal feeling' in the use of singular forms seems
applicable to this coda. It associates the Chorus directly with the ideology of
the ode. For the Chorus' personalization of subject matter later in the play,
see on 864–74. For personal codas to choral odes elsewhere in Senecan

tragedy, see *Thy.* 391–403, 875–84; for personal prologues to choral odes, see *Oed.* 881–91.

me mea tellus lare secreto tutoque tegat/Me—let my own land conceal in safe, Secluded home: a strong echo here of the Epicurean injunction, λάθε βιώσας, 'Live unobserved' (frag. 551). At *Kuriae Doxai* 14 Epicurus writes of the 'safety arising from peace/rest and withdrawal from the many' (ἡ ἐκ τῆς ἡσυχίας καὶ ἐκχωρήσεως τῶν πολλῶν ἀσφάλεια). This was sometimes interpreted quite specifically as 'avoid the political life' (μὴ πολιτεύεσθαι: Cicero *ad Att.* 14.20.5). For the theme of the perilous nature of eminence, see 201 below; *Thy.* 391–2 (printed above), 598–622; *Med.* 221–2; *Ag.* 57–107; *Tro.* 1–27, 259–64; *Pha.* 1123–43; *Oed.* 6–11; *HO* 675–99; Horace *Odes* 2.10.9–12, 3.16.18–19. The verbal formulation here impresses: the emphatic *me mea*, followed by a complementary, alliterative pattern of *t*s. The strong initial *me* (also at *Thy.* 393), which gives especial strength to *mea* (*mea tellus* seems almost to have the force of Horace's *propria tellus* at *Serm.* 2.2.129: hence 'my own land'), is reminiscent of such lyric priamels as Hor. *Odes* 1.1 (see line 29) and 7 (see line 10). There is more; for the Chorus' language is ambiguous. *Me mea tellus…tegat*, translated as above, could also mean 'Let/may my own earth cover me', as in the funereal formula, *terra/tellus tegat*, 'may the earth cover'; see Propertius' proclamation to Tullus: *me quoque terra tegat*, 'may the earth also cover me' (1.6.28). The Chorus' words contain within themselves the suggestion that their personal ideal might be a form of human death. For *lar* as a religious metonym for 'home', see on 913–18.

uenit ad pigros cana senectus/Grey old age comes to the inert: *cana senectus* occurs, as Fitch *ad loc.* notes, at Cat. 108.1 and Ov. *Her.* 14.109. But here *senectus* is treated favourably, as it is in Tibullus' *pigra senecta* (1.10.40), which may have influenced Seneca here. Contrast Euripides' *Heracles* (107ff.), where old men enter bemoaning their decrepitude; or the position taken by the Chorus at *HO* 643: *rarum est felix idemque senex*, 'Felicity and old age are rarely conjoined' (cf. Sen. *Ira* 2.33.2). Note the *apparently* positive use of *piger*, 'inert/inactive', as in the Tibullus citation and in the praise of the inhabitants of the Golden/Radiant Age at *Med.* 331. *Piger* is normally pejorative in Latin writers, and Seneca frequently criticizes *pigritia* and the *pigri* in his prose works (*Ira* 3.2.1, 3.24.2; *Ep. Mor.* 66.16, 74.30, 82.2—but not *Ep. Mor.* 77.3). Structurally *pigros* picks up *quies* at 160 and 175, just as *senectus* picks up the focus on new birth and youthfulness in the opening of the ode. *Piger* may have been chosen here because it signals the precise opposite of the life of Hercules, whom Horace famously described as *impiger Hercules* ('active/dynamic/tireless Hercules', *Odes* 4.8.30).

humilique loco/**lowly place:** cf. the 'lowly roof' (*humilis tecti*) of the 'plebeian home' of *Pha*. 1139. For the *locus* motif, see on 1–5.

certa sedet sordida paruae fortuna domus/**The foul fortune of a little home Sits secure:** a pick up of *paruoque domus*, 161 (see n. *ad loc.*). Similar sentiments are expressed by Thyestes about his 'small circumstances/life' (*rebus…paruis*, *Thy*. 469) and by Agamemnon's and Phaedra's chorus in their pronouncements on the 'modest life' (*modicis rebus*, *Ag*. 102) and on 'the plebeian home with lowly roof' (*humilis tecti plebeia domus*, *Pha*. 1139). The sentiment is of course commonplace and Horatian: see on 161 above. *Fortuna* here is 'fortune', not the goddess; see on 524–32. For *sordidus*, 'foul', used descriptively rather than negatively, see Virg. *Ecl.* 2.28: *sordida rura*, 'foul fields'.

alte uirtus animosa cadit/**Spirited virtue falls from the heights:** *cadit*, 'falls', inverts the earlier deluded 'lifting' (*tollit*, 171, *tollat*, 195), in an overt pointer, as Trevet observed *ad loc.*, to Hercules, his choices, values, and his coming 'fall'. Given the Euripidean subtext for this ode, the fate of Phaethon lurks beneath this line. For Phaethon the 'fall from the heights' was both figurative and literal. For similar choral *sententiae*, see e.g. *Ag*. 101 (*quidquid in altum Fortuna tulit* | *ruitura leuat*, 'What Fortune raises high | She lifts to cast down'), *Oed*. 909–10 (*quidquid excessit modum* | *pendet instabili loco*, 'All that exceeds the mean | Stands poised upon the brink'), and *HO* 691 (*male pensantur magna ruinis*, 'Greatness is tragically repaid with a fall'); cf. also Sophocles' famous choral sentiments on ὕβρις at *OT* 873–9. Note that *animosa* is used of Antigone in *Phoenissae* (94), Andromache in *Troades* (588), and later in *Hercules* of Megara (1150). It is also used in *Hercules Oetaeus* of Deianira (977). In the prose works, where *animosus* is used some thirty times, Seneca praises *uirtus animosa*: *Ep. Mor.* 71.18, *uirtutem intellego animosam et excelsam, quam incitat quidquid infestat*, 'I understand virtue as spirited and exalted, aroused by whatever harasses it.' At *Prou.* 5.11 he remarks (in relation to the paradigm of Phaethon): *per alta uirtus it*, 'Virtue soars.' Deeply relevant, too, is Statius' attachment to *animosus*, which he uses ten times in the *Thebaid*, including three times in association with either death or the desire/hope for death (*Theb*. 9.80, 717, 12.456–7). Evidently not only Freudians would interpret Hercules' *uirtus animosa* as a 'spirited death-wish' (*leti animosa uoluntas*, ascribed to Polynices, *Theb*. 9.80). Statius' attribution of *uirtus egressa modum*, 'boundary-violating virtue', to Capaneus at *Theb*. 10.834 is an evident development, even Flavian exegesis, of Seneca's cardinal phrase. Zwierlein (1984), 27, sees *uirtus animosa* 'als stoisches Motto'; but, while Epicurean and Stoic ideals clearly jostle for choral favour or rejection, the conceptual picture is not so simple. Contrasting with the Chorus' sentiment here is the Virgilian Sibyl's claim that there are 'few' (*pauci*, who clearly include Hercules) 'whom blazing virtue has lifted to heaven, sons of gods' (*quos...ardens euexit ad aethera uirtus | dis geniti*, Virg. *Aen*. 6.130–1). For the dangers of eminence, see above; for the dangers of the greatest 'virtues' (*maximis uirtutibus*), see 325–8. For Stoic language and ideas in *Hercules*, see on 162–3. For *uirtus*, see on 35–40. For the phrase *alte cadere*, 'to fall from the heights/on high', see *Ira* 3.23.6, *HO* 406, Cic. *Orat*. 98. For *sententiae* closing an entire choral ode, see 590–1 and n. *ad loc*.; *Pha*. 357, 1153; *Oed*. 992–4; *Tro*. 162–3; *Thy*. 401–3, 883–4. For the closural use of *sententiae* more generally, see on 125–204 (introd.).

Enter MEGARA ...: see next nn.

202–4 The Chorus announce the entrance of Megara, her three sons by Hercules (the youngest of whom seems to be of 'toddler' age, since he will be carried by his mother at 1008 and be described as *infans* at 1022) and Hercules' foster-father and Megara's *de facto* father-in-law, Amphitryon. Cf. Eur. *Herac*. 442, where the Chorus announce (in lyric metre) the entrance of the same characters (albeit later in the play). The use of a character or chorus onstage to identify for the audience a new, entering character is one of the standard techniques of ancient drama, and is common in Senecan tragedy (see on 1–5). In Seneca the announcement either begins with a question (see e.g. *Ag*. 913; *Oed*. 202–5; *Pha*. 829–34, 989–90, 1154–5—cf. *Oct*. 778–9) or, as here, is referential (see e.g. 329–31; *Pha*. 358–9; *Ag*. 388–91, 586–8, 778–81, 947–50; *Oed*. 288–90, 838–40, 911–13; *Tro*. 518; *Med*. 178—cf. *Oct*. 435–6, 844–5; *HO* 1603–6). In each case short descriptive phrases are generally attached. It should be observed that neither *Medea* nor *Troades* use the chorus to announce a character's entrance (although *Tro*. 858–60 seem to gesture in this direction)—a technique which is essentially restricted to *Hercules*, *Phaedra*, *Oedipus*, and *Agamemnon*. *Phoenissae* and *Thyestes* are unusual in that not a single entrance is announced either by a character or chorus (*Pho*., of course, lacks a chorus). Here in *Hercules*, as generally elsewhere in Senecan tragedy, the choral announcement of the entrance of other characters would presumably have been delivered by the Chorus Leader.

Note the unusual way in which the announcement is made: two lines in lyric verse (anapaests), giving way to a final line in iambics. Iambic trimeters are the standard verse form for the Chorus when (generally, it seems, through the Chorus Leader) they act the part of a *dramatis persona* within an act (e.g. 1032–4; *Ag*. 710–19, 775–81; *Pha*. 1244–6; *Oed*. 1004–9; *Tro*. 166–7; *Med*. 881–7; *Thy*. 633, 638–40), or when they provide a link between their ode and the ensuing act: see e.g. *Ag.* 388–91; *Pha.* 358–9, 824–34, 989–90, 1154–5; *Oed.* 202–5. The exceptions to this are the present passage and *Oed.* 911–14 (glyconics). If these latter two passages had been completely in iambics, they would have been placed at the beginning of the ensuing act rather than just before it (for *Oedipus*, see Boyle 2011). They are in any case transitional. Seneca's dramatic successors use lyric metre for the choral announcement of entering characters at *Oct.* 778–9 and *HO* 700–5, 1128–30. For metatheatrical aspects of these lines, see Introd. §VII, 76 and below.

Sed maesta/But…in mourning: *maesta* functions as a key epithet here explaining Megara's behaviour and physical appearance: see next n. For *sed* used to announce the entrance of a new character, see on 329–31.

uenit/comes: the Chorus do not specify where Megara and her family are coming from. Since they are unlikely to be coming from the royal palace or from outside Thebes (stage right), the choice is either from the city (i.e. they enter stage left) or from the temple. I have opted for the latter, since it would balance dramatically the exit of Juno and the Furies into the palace and index the temple as the family's place of refuge. 'Sanctuary temples' were associated by the Romans especially with Greece: see Livy 35.51. Lycus will later order that 'the temple fall blazing on its suppliants' (*templa supplicibus | suis iniecta flagrent*, 506–7).

crine soluto/Hair unbound: a sign of mourning; see *Tro.* 84–5, 99–100; Tib. 1.1.67–8, 1.3.8; Virg. *Aen.* 3.65, 11.35; Ov. *Fas.* 4.854; Petron. *Sat.* 111.2. Megara's dress also signals mourning, esp. her wearing of the hooded shawl known as the *ricinium*, though the hood apparently is not up: see before 332–523, 355–6, 626–7 and nn. *ad locc*. She has much to lament: the deaths of father and brother (even apart from the fact that she thinks that her husband is now in hell).

Megara paruum comitata gregem/Megara…tending her small flock: *grex*, 'flock', is a term regularly used of a group of people (*OLD* 2 and 3), including a troupe of actors (*OLD* 3b). The modifier *paruum*, 'small', brings out both the metatheatrical, subtextual meaning (Megara and her little troupe of players) and the metaphoric, emotive force of the term (cf. *comitatae gregibus paruis*, 'accompanied by their small flocks', *Pha.* 19), here intensified by the Chorus' earlier use of *grex* in its pastoral idyll (140). This almost sentimental metaphor for 'children' will be used again in two lethal contexts (507, 1037), which are here anticipated. Its final metaphoric use will be similarly 'sentimental' (1149). Note the translingual wordplay here, viz. how the juxtaposition of Megara and *paruum*, 'small', brings out the 'greatness' (μέγα) inherent in Megara's name (see also 1008–9). This 'greatness' will be apparent in her rhetoric and fierce repudiation of Lycus. For translingual punning on proper names, see on 35–40. *Comitata* (here transitive, lit. 'having accompanied') seems sometimes used by Seneca with a present participial sense (hence 'tending'); see *Ag.* 84, *Pho.* 506, *Oed.* 432 (and Billerbeck *ad loc.*). The final *a* of *Megara* is here long, as in Greek; so perhaps, too, at 347, 1009. For metatheatrical language and motifs in this play, see on 109–12.

tardusque senio graditur/steps slowed by age: entrance announcements regularly comment on the *gradus, gressus* or *incessus* of an entering character, occasionally, as here, with reference to age: see e.g. 330 (Lycus), 523 (Hercules); *Ag.* 388 (Eurybates), 587 (Cassandra), 781 (Clytemnestra); *Pha.* 431 (Nurse); *Oed.* 289 (Tiresias), 1004 (Jocasta); *Tro.* 522 (Ulysses), 999 (Pyrrhus); *Med.* 382 (Medea). Cf. *HO* 254 (Deianira), 702 (Deianira); *Oct.* 435 (Nero). Romans paid particular attention to a person's gait or mode of walking, which was regularly treated as index of gender, moral character, and/or social status, as well of course of age: see *Tranq.* 17.4; *Ep. Mor.* 52.12, 114.3; *NQ* 7.31.2—and O'Sullivan (2011). Even the gait of gods proves telling: *uera incessu patuit dea*, 'in her step she was revealed a true goddess' (Virg. *Aen.* 1.405). Here, as at *Pha.* 431 (*seniles...gradus*, 'aged steps') and *Oed.* 289 (*tremulo tardus...genu*, 'slowed by trembling knees'), the focus is on the physical fragility of old age. Euripides' chorus also comment on Amphitryon's slow movement, but much later in the play (*Herac.* 1039–40).

Alcidae parens/Alcides' father: again the patronymic used of Hercules, which focuses on his mortal line from Alcaeus, father of Amphitryon: see on 84–5. Euripides' chorus make regular reference to Hercules as 'the son of Zeus' (Διὸς ὁ παῖς, *Herac.* 696; also 798–804, 877, 907, 1020); Seneca's chorus never do, even as they extensively praise Hercules' deeds. Their silence on this matter seems telling. As representative of the Theban people, they seem to index where the city stands on the Herculean paternity issue.

Act II (205–523)

Act II of *Hercules* (319 lines) is perhaps the longest second act in Senecan tragedy. Only if one were to consider lines 358–755 of *Phaedra* to be that play's second act (rather than, as seems probable, its third act) would there be a longer Senecan second act. The two scenes of the act in a sense correspond to (but are very different from) the dialogue and action of the prologue and first two episodes of Euripides' *Heracles*. Scene i (205–328) begins with the entrance of Hercules' family and consecutive appeals for Hercules' return and potent statements of political, moral and/or personal malaise from Amphitryon and Megara (205–308). The rest of the scene (309–28) falls into the common Senecan category of a 'Passion-Restraint' scene (cf. Acts II of *Phaedra, Agamemnon, Troades, Medea, Thyestes*, also Act III of *Troades*), in which Amphitryon attempts to restrain the intense and turbulent emotions of Megara. As in Act II of *Medea* and Act III of *Troades*, the Passion-Restraint scene leads to confrontation with a 'tyrant-figure', Lycus, the usurping ruler of Thebes. Scene ii (332–523), the 'Lycus Scene', is the longer of the two scenes and is discussed below (see on 332–523) and above (Introd. §VII, 78–80).

The second act of *Hercules* is prefaced by a choral link (202–4). Four of the seven act-divided plays begin their second acts without any choral link but with a speech by a protagonist revealing his/her emotional state, followed by a dialogue with a subordinate character (a courtier/*satelles* or a nurse) who advises restraint (*Med.* 116 ff., *Pha.* 85 ff., *Ag.* 108 ff., *Thy.* 176 ff.). Another of the seven starts with a brief exclamation by a messenger (*Tro.* 163–4). Only *Hercules* (202–4) and *Oedipus* (if the allocation by *A* of *Oed.* 202–5 to the Chorus is accepted) preface or begin their second acts with the chorus speaking (in the case of *Hercules*, partly) in iambics and providing an entrance cue for *dramatis personae* or a *dramatis persona*, whom they identify. *Phaedra* joins *Hercules* and *Oedipus* in this, if it is construed as a five-act play. In fact the technique is used throughout *Phaedra*, in which the chorus perform this function after each of the play's choral odes (*Pha.* 358–9, 824–34, 989–90, 1154–5), i.e. before Acts III, IV, V, and VI (if *Phaedra* has six acts: see my edition, p. 134) or before Acts II, III, IV, and V (if the play is of five acts)—again speaking in iambics. The technique is also used at the opening of Act III of *Agamemnon* (*Ag.* 388–91), and in lyric at the end of the penultimate ode of *Hercules* (893–4) and of the final two odes of *Oedipus* (911–13, 995–7). It is not used in *Troades, Medea*, or *Thyestes*. Fitch (1981: 306) regards this as a dramatic technique of the early plays, which was later abandoned.

For further discussion of Act II and its dramatic and thematic function in the play, see Introd. §VII, esp. 76–80.

Metre: iambic trimeters. See Introd. §IX.

The time is early to mid-morning: even though the choral ode segues seamlessly into Act II, whose initial main characters are announced by the Chorus, it is reasonable to assume that the ode has indicated, as often in

Senecan tragedy, some passage of time, and thus that the time is now a little later than the break of dawn. (The view of Shelton (1978: 20), that the dramatic time here precedes that of the prologue, given the continuity of prologue to ode and ode to act, seems mistaken. Amphitryon and Megara are unaware that Hercules has already emerged triumphantly from hell, but the audience are not. They have been privy to Juno's superior knowledge.)

AMPHITYRON, MEGARA, *and her three* SONS *gather around the altar* (*perhaps before statues of* JUPITER *and* CERES): for the possible presence of these statues onstage, see before 1–18.

205–78 Amphitryon's prayer for Hercules' safe return from the underworld—to be followed by Megara's prayer to Hercules (279–308). Cf. the consecutive appeals of Megara and Amphitryon later in Euripides' play (*Herac.* 490–502), the order of which Seneca has reversed, favouring rather the order of Amphitryon's and Megara's speeches in Euripides' prologue. Invocations of, and prayers to, the gods feature prominently in *Hercules* and in Senecan tragedy as a whole with potent dramatic effect and are found in both the main acts and the choral odes: see 277–8, 279ff., 516 ff., 592 ff., 900 ff., 926ff., 1063 ff., 1202 ff.; *Oed.* 248ff., 868ff.; *Med.* 1 ff., 595 ff., 740 ff.; *Tro.* 1005–8; *Pha.* 54 ff., 406 ff., 671 ff., 945 ff., 1159 ff., 1201 ff.; *Ag.* 310 ff., 802 ff.; *Thy.* 122 ff., 1006 ff., 1068 ff. In *Hercules* they also serve a structural purpose, since a prayer opens Acts II, III, and IV and closes Act II itself.

After a brief prayer to Jupiter and statement of Hercules' unceasing toils (205–13), Amphitryon's opening speech is essentially bipartite: a detailed description of Hercules' struggles from birth, including the famous 'labours' (213–48), is followed by an account of the political turmoil and deaths in Thebes caused by the hero's absence (249–78). The latter culminates (275–8) in a direct appeal to Hercules to return to Thebes as 'Saviour', which mirrors the direct appeal to Jupiter in the speech's initial lines (205–7).

205–13 Amphitryon's prayer/appeal to Jupiter.

205–9 *O magne Olympi rector et mundi arbiter*/**O great lord of Olympus and world-judge:** Jupiter. In Greek and Roman literature it is common to address gods by defining descriptions rather than by their names. For Seneca's tragedies, see e.g. 299–300, 516–18, 592–4, 597–8, 559, 903–4; *Ag.* 802–4; *Pha.* 960–3; *Med.* 1–4, 56–70. Often characterized as exemplifying the allusive style of a *poeta doctus*, it is a form of invocation as old as Homer (see e.g. *Il.* 3.278–80). Sometimes Seneca combines defining descriptions with the names of the deities, as e.g. at 592–5, 900–2; *Ag.* 382–5, 805–6; *Pha.* 54–80, 406–23, 960–3; *Oed.* 403–7. *Olympi rector*, 'lord/ruler of Olympus', is an Ovidian title (*Met.* 2.60, 9.499; cf. also Manil. 1.916, Luc. 2.4, 5.620), found again at *Pha.* 960 (for further on *rector*, see on 516–20; for Seneca's fondness for nouns ending in *-tor*, see on 299–302). *Arbiter*, 'judge', is a controversial term. Fitch *ad loc.* dismisses the translation 'judge', preferring 'lord, controller', but, even when the word is used in its sense of 'overseer, controller' (*OLD* 3), it is difficult to suppress entirely its prime sense of 'arbiter/judge' (*Thy.* 14, Prop. 3.19.27, Ov. *Tr.* 5.2.47, Stat. *Theb.* 4.530), clearly evident in Seneca's application of the term to Nero at *Clem.* 1.1.2 and the use of the term again concerning 'Nero' at *Oct.* 488. The dramatist of *Hercules Oetaeus* uses *arbitri* of the judges of the underworld (*HO* 1007). Seneca deploys his legal language with purpose in his tragedies, and of the eleven uses of *arbiter* in his dramas five occur in this play. Of the remaining six, one is used of perhaps the most famous mythological judgement of all, the Judgement of Paris (*Ag.* 731). Here Amphitryon is appealing to Jupiter for help on moral grounds: Hercules has been unjustly treated. The title he accords him, *arbiter mundi* ('world-judge'), is not only singularly appropriate in this context but anticipates the 'arbitration' of the final act, in which Theseus, the final *arbiter* (1336), offers to remove Hercules to Athens. For legal language and imagery in *Hercules*, see on 731–4. For the difference between *arbiter* and *iudex* (the latter being controlled/restricted by the law, the former not), see *Ben.* 3.7.5.

Vocatives in Latin are not normally accompanied by *o*, as in Greek. *O* with the vocative in Latin indicates a formal address (e.g. as in prayers, hymns, and other formal contexts, as here, and at 299, 359, 524, 592, 646, 1066, 1068, 1072 below; *Ag.* 57, 310, 340, 356, 828; *Pha.* 409, 959; *Oed.* 250) or impassioned/pathetic address (as at 309, 622, 1135, 1236, 1334 below; *Ag.* 783, 910, 940; *Thy.* 625). Its frequent use in tragedy and epic is to be attributed among other things to their 'elevated' literary style. *O* may also be used with other cases (e.g. the nominative, as at *Ag.* 928, *Pha.* 991) or with other constructions (as at *Ag.* 610, *Thy.* 449) to express high emotion: see 1226 below. Note that Amphitryon will use the formal *o* later in addressing Megara (309) and Hercules (622). For *magnus* as a standard epithet of Jupiter, see e.g. 1054, *Ag.* 356, *Tro.* 140, *HO* 1863.

tandem grauibus aerumnis modum/at last a limit to the grave toils: cf. Amphitryon's similar request (this time to Hercules himself) at 924–6. Seneca clearly liked the tragic 'feel' of *aerumnae*, a portentous word which appears frequently in republican drama and was considered archaic by Quintilian (*Inst.* 8.3.26). It occurs more often in Seneca's tragedies than in the prose works: see e.g. *Ag.* 305, 491, 661, 790, *Thy.* 305, 426, *Tro.* 421, *Pho.* 78. Its archaic flavour was presumably why Persius included it in his parody of Pacuvius at *Sat.* 1.78. *Modus*, 'moderation/limit/measure', is a cardinal notion of Senecan tragedy, in which it features most especially in relation to the passions but is not restricted to them: see e.g. 403; *Ag.* 150, 691–2; *Med.* 397, 884; *Tro.* 259, 812; *Oed.* 694, 909; *Pha.* 141, 359, 553; *Thy.* 26, 198, 255, 483, 1051–2. It is also a cardinal notion of this play, which, though *modus* itself only appears twice elsewhere in the sense of 'limit' (403, 1141), is, like *Medea* and *Thyestes*, conspicuously concerned with the absence of limit, viz. boundary violation: see on 46–52. For boundary violation in the prose works, see esp. the rejection of *modus* by Seneca's debauchee, Hostius Quadra (*NQ* 1.16.8: cited on 1052–7). *Tandem*, 'at last', will return in the final line of this speech (278), providing circular closure, while reminding the audience of the 'long wait' of Hercules' family.

nulla lux...secura fulsit/No carefree dawn...shone: note the implied reference to the dramatic time, already underscored by the preceding choral ode, and the pick-up of the ode's language: *luce*, 127, *lucem*, 131, *secura*, 175. The *secura* echo is particularly important because of its ideological ramifications. See next n. Cf. Octavia's similar, if lyric, remark at *Oct.* 18: *o lux semper funesta mihi*, 'O dawn ever my doom'.

finis alterius mali gradus est futuri/The end of one evil Is step to the next: for a similar idea, cf. Andromache: *exoritur aliquod maius ex magno malum*, 'From great evil a greater rises up' (*Tro.* 427); or the proverbial, *aliud ex alio malum*, 'One evil arises from another' (Ter. *Eun.* 987). Cf. the erotic formulation at Ov. *Her.* 19.104: *fitque nouus nostri finis amoris amor*, 'and new love our love ends'. Interestingly Heracles' later wife, Deianeira, in Sophocles' *Trachiniae* (28) has a similar, if less epigrammatic, complaint to Amphityron's: 'I ever nourish fear after fear (τιν' ἐκ φόβου φόβον)'. Caviglia *ad loc.* notes an insertion of the Senecan aphorism in Carlo de' Dottori's seventeenth-century tragedy *Aristodemo* I.v.535: 'Il fin d'un mal grado è dell' altro'. It was also cited by the Florentine humanist, Colucio Salutati, in his *De laboribus Herculis* (1406: Ullman 1951: 181). For the unstoppable cycle of evil, see the Fury at *Thy.* 29–32, esp. *semper oriatur nouum*, 'let it (crime/evil) always rise anew'. For the *finis/gradus* opposition, see e.g. *Thy.* 746–7, *Marc.* 20.1, *Helu.* 11.4.

209–13 *reduci*/on his return: as in Juno's prologue (33ff.), Hercules is the implied referent without being named. This is Hercules' drama whether he is named or not. For the intransitive use of *redux*, see *Ag.* 218, 579; *Pha.* 629, 856; *Tro.* 167, *Thy.* 441.

laetam domum/house Of joy: the irony here is complex. Hercules' house is certainly not one of joy, but it would be if Hercules were to return. For the ironic application of *laetus* to *domus* elsewhere in Seneca, see e.g. the non-joyful 'joyful house' of Agamemnon (*laeta in domo*, *Ag.* 924), and Cadmus (*laeta...domus*, *Oed.* 627).

aliud...ad bellum/to another war: *bellum* is regularly used of Hercules' conflicts (see e.g. 527, 638, 997). Fitch (2002 and 2018) translates *bellum* as 'fight', but, given Hercules' status as a global, civilizing figure, the more global 'war' seems appropriate. Statius calls Hercules' labours 'the wars of Eurystheus' (*bella Eurysthea*, *Theb.* 6.311).

nec ulla requies tempus aut ullum uacat/There is no rest, no idle time: the pick-up of the language of the Chorus again (*quies*, 175, *tempora*, 177) is significant. Amphitryon is describing a mode of life antithetical to the one advocated by the Chorus, to which he seems sympathetic: see Introd. §VII, 77. Note the postponement of *aut*, as at 454 and *Pha.* 511. For the postponement of conjunctions, see on 63–8.

nisi dum iubetur/except While he's being ordered: note here a Senecan rhetorical mannerism, viz. the positioning of *nisi* at the beginning of a climactic new half-line after enjambement to secure a pointed effect: see e.g. *Med.* 299, 487; *Thy.* 196, 241, 289, 1098; *Pho.* 84. For climactic half-lines, see on 40–6.

213-48 Hercules' infant exploits and twelve labours. The 'labours' of Heracles/Hercules are referenced in Homer (*Il.* 8.367–8, 19.132–3; *Od.* 11.621–6), but it is not until their depiction on the metopes in the porches of the temple of Zeus at Olympia (*c*.460 BCE)—the earliest extant, clear depiction of the 'twelve' labours—that the number twelve starts to move towards becoming canonic. By the third century BCE canonicity seems 'firmly established' (Stafford 2012, 29): Theoc. 24.82–3, Ap. Rhod. 1.1318, Callim. *Aet.* frag. 23.19 Pfeiff. Seneca has omitted one of the 'twelve', the bringing of Cerberus from the underworld (traditionally the final labour), because Amphitryon is unaware that this has been completed. But in order to reach the number twelve he has included Hercules' creation of the Strait of Gibraltar as a labour. Cf. the catalogue of labours at *Agamemnon* 827–66, where, as here, one of the canonic labours (the cleaning of the Augean Stables) is omitted and another added (the sack of Troy). In the *Agamemnon* catalogue, too, as here, the order of the labours differs substantially from those found in Diodorus Siculus (4.11–26), Hyginus (*Fab.* 30), Apollodorus (2.5), and Quintus of Smyrna (6.208–68). For incomplete, hybrid lists of the labours, see 526–46 below, the opening of Lucr. 5 (22–38), the song of the Salii at Virg. *Aen.* 8.285–302, the epistle of Deianira at Ov. *Her.* 9.84–100, the speeches of Hercules at Ov. *Met.* 9.182–98 and *HO* 16–27, and the choral ode at Eur. *Herac.* 359–435 (to which Seneca seems indebted). See also Eur. *Herac.* 1266–80, where Heracles' account of his labours is prefaced by his slaying of serpents when an infant. Individual or groups of labours feature regularly on Greek vases, Roman sarcophagi and mosaics, and (rarely) on coins (see Stafford 2012: 30). Émile Verhaeren's poem *Hercule* (1910) features a twenty-four-line catalogue of Hercules' labours by Hercule himself even as he burns on Mt Oeta. For this he had good precedent in Thomas Heywood's similarly incendiary Herculean catalogue at the end of *The Brazen Age* (1613). Grandiloquent speeches on the labours are mocked by Robert Greene in his *Groats-worth of Wit* (1592), 'Robertoes Tale', a 'player' speaking: 'The twelue labors of *Hercules* haue I terribly thundred on the Stage'. A modernized version of the labours figures in the new millennium play, *Mister Heracles*, by Simon Armitage (2000), who has his chorus sing twelve songs, one for each labour (pp. 14–17). For catalogues in *Hercules*, see on 6–18. Fitch *ad loc.* notes several stylistic features of the present catalogue, including its arrangement into statement (216–25), *praeteritio* (226–30), statement (231–40), rhetorical question (241–4), and statement (245–8). For the function of this catalogue in the play, see Introd. §VII, 76–7.

213–22 Infant Hercules' slaying of twin/two serpents. For other accounts, see esp. the extensive accounts in Pind. *Nem.* 1 and Theoc. 24; also Plaut. *Amph.* 1107–19, Virg. *Aen.* 8.288–9, Ov. *Ars* 187–8. There is a famous painting of the incident on the walls of the House of the Vettii in Pompeii (Ling 1991: pl. VIIIA); see also Pliny on Zeuxis' painting of the scene: *HN* 35.63. Part of Nero's self-imaging was a 'Herculean' story about being protected while an infant by snakes or a snake: Tac. *Ann.* 11.11.6, Suet. *Nero* 6.4. For possible later influence, see e.g. Dracont. *Rom.* 4.20–5.

Sequitur/hunts: I agree with Fitch *ad loc.* that this is probably not a historic present.

infesta Iuno/Hostile Juno: the adjective, used discriminately by Seneca, is used of Agamemnon's hostile wife at *Thy.* 43. Ovid applies it to Jupiter (*Ibis* 467), Virgil's Juno to herself (*Aen.* 7.299), the elder Seneca to a stepmother (*Con.* 7.5.15). It connotes active hostility and is used of armies 'threatening attack' (*OLD* 3).

numquid: more colloquial than *num* and more common than it in Senecan tragedy and prose: see on 1178–86.

immunis … infantis aetas/infancy … immune: the noun *infantia* is not used by Seneca outside the prose works, where the phrase *infantis aetas* also occurs (*Ep. Mor.* 121.16). For the absolute use of *immunis* ('scilicet a periculo' notes Trevet *ad loc.*), see *NQ* 6.1.13, *Pha.* 24.

monstra superauit/He overpowered monsters: for the important *monstrum* motif, see 1280 and n. *ad loc.* For Hercules as 'monster-slayer', see esp. 241–2, 435, 528, 1029, and Virg. *Aen.* 8.293–302.

nosse/know: for syncopated perfect infinitives, see 63 and n. *ad loc.*

gemina…ora/twin mouths: *geminus* is an epithet Virgil likes to use of serpents (e.g. *Aen.* 2.203–4, 225, 7.450), including those the infant Hercules kills (*Aen.* 8.289); see also Ov. *Her.* 9.21.

cristati caput/Crested: lit. 'crested as to their head'; *caput* is an accusative of respect with the verbal adjective. See 107 and n. *ad loc.* Note that these snakes are 'crested' (as at Plaut. *Amph.* 1108), like the snake into which Cadmus changes at 392 below. As Fitch observes *ad loc.*, 'crests or manes are a traditional feature of supernatural snakes'; see most dramatically the snakes from Tenedos at Virg. *Aen.* 2.206—also e.g. Livy 41.21.13; Ov. *Met.* 3.32, 4.599, 7.150; *HO* 1254.

reptabat/crawled: along with Giardina (1966 and 2007), Chaumartin, and Fitch (1987*a* and 2018), I have preferred the reading of *E*, *reptabat*, which matches the preceding *ferebant* (2017), to that of *A*, *reptauit*, printed by Viansino (1965 and 1993), Caviglia, Zwierlein, and Billerbeck.

igneos serpentium oculos/snakes' fiery Eyes: Euripides' 'snakes' are 'gorgon-eyed' (γοργωποὺς ὄφεις, *Herac.* 1266), but for flaming-eyed serpents, see Hes. *Th.* 826–8, Theoc. 24.18–19 (Heracles' serpents), Nic. *Ther.* 178, Virg. *Geo.* 3.433, *Aen.* 2.210, [Virg.] *Culex* 173, Ov. *Met.* 3.33, Stat. *Theb.* 5.508—and the later Dracontius: *flammea lux oculis*, 'a flaming light in their eyes' (*Rom.* 4.22). Note the standard genitive form, *serpentium*. Seneca uses *serpentum* at *Med.* 705 for metrical reasons.

remisso lumine ac placido/with a relaxed and tranquil look: Zwierlein prefers the reading of *A*, *pectore*, rather than that of *E^{ac}FMN*, *lumine*, printed here. I am joined in this preference by Viansino (1965 and 1993), Giardina (1966 and 2007), Caviglia, Fitch (1987*a* and 2018), Chaumartin, and Billerbeck.

artos serenis uultibus nodos/tightening coils with face serene: perhaps an echo of the Horatian Cleopatra's 'face serene' (*uultu sereno*, *Odes* 1.37.26), as she contemplated fallen kingdom and serpents. Notice the stylistic mannerism here of two epithets and their nouns interlocked in a chiastic pattern (here abBA): see 225 (aBbA), 231 (aBbA), 238 (abBA) below and on 11–18. Note the plural *uultibus*: '*Vultus* probably has a tendency to plurality even when it means "face"' (Frank *ad Pho.* 42–3).

tumida tenera guttura…manu/swollen throats with tender hands: the swelling is presumably a puffing up at the neck, rather than inside the throat; cf. Ov. *Met.* 3.73: *plenis tumuerunt guttura uenis*, 'its throat became swollen with full veins'. Note the careful interlocking of pairs of adjectives and nouns in a parallel pattern, a Senecan mannerism quite frequent in this part of Amphitryon's speech (also at 223, 236, 240, 246, 248): see further on 6–11. For the resolutions at the beginning of this line, see 76 and n. *ad loc.*

prolusit hydrae/**Practised for the Hydra**: the notion of 'practice' appealed to Seneca, who uses this technical term for preliminary military exercise (Prop. 4.4.19) or gladiatorial 'warm-up' practice in the arena (Cic. *Orat.* 2.325) elsewhere in the tragedies: *Pha.* 1061 (for *ira*), *Tro.* 182 (for Troy's fate), *Med.* 907. See also *Ira* 2.2.5, *NQ* 3.28.3, *Ep. Mor.* 102.23, Ov. *Ars* 3.515, Virg. *Geo.* 3.234, *Aen.* 12.106. For military imagery in *Hercules*, see on 19–29.

222–48 Amphitryon lists the twelve labours of Hercules, substituting a non-canonic labour, the opening of the Strait of Gibraltar (235–8), for the canonic retrieval of Cerberus from the underworld—a labour which Amphitryon is unaware has been completed. See on 213–48. Amphitryon lists the labours in the following order, which differs substantially from that found in other authors (see below): Arcadian Hind, Nemean Lion, Horses of Diomedes, Erymanthian/Maenalian Boar, Cretan Bull, Cattle of Geryon, Strait of Gibraltar, Apples of the Hesperides, Lernaean Hydra, Stymphalian Birds, Hippolyte's Belt, Augean Stables. The tone of the list is a complex mixture of complaint and laudation.

222–5 First two labours: Arcadian Hind and Nemean Lion.

Maenali pernix fera/**Maenalus' swift beast**: i.e. the Arcadian hind, Maenalus being a mountain in Arcadia. Often referred to as the Cerynitian hind (Hind of Mt Ceryneia), its capture was Apollodorus' third labour (2.5.3) and the fourth of Diodorus (4.13.1), Hyginus (*Fab.* 30), and Quintus (6.223–6); here it is listed first. The hind had golden horns and was sacred to Diana/Artemis (Pind. *Ol.* 3.26–30, Eur. *Herac.* 375–9), but Hercules managed to capture it and take it alive to Mycenae, where Eurystheus, who had ordered the labours, was king. In some versions (e.g. Virg. *Aen.* 6.802, *HO* 17) Hercules kills the animal. See also *Ag.* 831–2, *HO* 1238–9.

deprensa cursu/**Was run down and caught**: the omission of *est* with a perfect passive participle (or perfect of a deponent) occurs often in Roman verse and in Seneca: see e.g. 233, 855, 955, 1195 below.

maximus Nemeae timor/**Nemea's greatest fear**: for *timor* = object of fear, see Ov. *Met.* 12.612, *Fas.* 1.551. For *metus* as object of fear, see 230 below and n. *ad loc.* For Nemea, see next n.

lacertis...Herculeis leo/Lion...in Hercules'...arms: the Nemean Lion, which terrorized the area around Nemea in the north-east Peloponnese. It was choked to death by Hercules: *pressus lacertis* (cf. *arto pressus lacerto*, 'choked by tightened arms', *Ag.* 829–30; see also Ov. *Her.* 9.61–2, *Met.* 9.197). This was generally considered to be the first labour (*Ag.* 829–30, *HO* 1235–6, Pind. *Isth.* 6.48, Eur. *Herac.* 359–60) and is recognized as such by Hercules himself in the 'mad scene' (*primus en noster labor*, 'Look, my first labour', 944). It is also the first labour in the catalogues of Diodorus Siculus (4.11.3–4), Hyginus (*Fab.* 30), Apollodorus (2.5.1), and Quintus of Smyrna (6.208–11), and was the one most frequently depicted on Greek vases. The lion skin which Hercules habitually wore (45–6, 797–9, 1151–2) is often represented as being from this lion: see e.g. Eur. *Herac.* 359–63. The lion itself, according to some, was catasterized as the constellation Leo (see 944–52, Ov. *Ars* 1.68, Germ. *Arat.* 550, Manil. 2.531, [Eratosth.] *Catast.* 12, Hyg. *Astr.* 2.24.). For the use of the adjective *Herculeus*, see 72 and n. *ad loc.*

226–30 Three more labours: Horses of Diomedes, Erymanthian/Maenalian Boar, Cretan Bull. Fitch *ad loc.* comments on the unusual number of resolutions in line 229, which he posits 'suggests the trembling of the woods'.

quid...memorem/Why recall: *praeteritio* and a common rhetorical device to inject variety into a catalogue. Cf. *quid...loquar*, 'Why mention', 386. The subjunctive is potential: Woodcock §§118–19. For interrogatives used to effect a rhetorical transition, see 30 and n. *ad loc.*

stabula...dira Bistonii gregis/Bistonian herd's dire stables: the stables of the man-eating horses/mares of Diomedes, king of the Bistones in Thrace. After killing Diomedes (*regem*, 'king', 227) and feeding him to his own horses, Hercules, in one version (DS 4.15.3–4, Apollod. 2.5.8, apparently here) took the horses and drove them to Eurystheus in Mycenae; in another version (Ov. *Met.* 9.194–6, Hyg. *Fab.* 30) he killed the horses. Diodorus, Hyginus, and Apollodorus list this as the eighth labour; to Quintus it was the ninth (6.245–8). Here it is listed third. See also 1169–70; *Tro.* 1108–9; *Ag.* 842–7; *HO* 19–20, 1538–40, 1789–90, 1896–8; Eur. *Alc.* 481–505, *Herac.* 380–8; Ov. *Her.* 9.89–90, *Met.* 9.194–6, *Pont.* 1.2.120; Luc. 2.162–3; Claud. *Ruf.* 1.254–5; Boeth. *Cons. Phil.* 4 Metrum 7.20–1; Racine, *Phèdre* III.v.970. For *dirus*, see 56 and n. *ad loc.*

pabulum armentis/as pasture for his horses: Diomedes as 'pasture' sets up an opposition to the natural 'pasture' (*pabula*) gathered by the earlier shepherd (140); as Fitch notes *ad loc.*, the concept was taken up by Boethius and Racine (see prev. n.). The use of *armenta* ('herds', 'cattle') for 'horses' is Virgilian: see *Aen.* 3.540, where an etymological suggestion seems intended between *armenta* and *arma*. See also *Tro.* 818. For the appositional use of *pabulum*, see *Thy.* 12: *recenti pabulum monstro iacet*, 'lies as pasture for a fresh fiend'.

hispidum…Maenalium suem/**bristly Maenalian Boar:** also called the Erymanthian Boar. Capturing alive this boar, associated with Mt Maenalus (here) or Mt Erymanthus (Ov. *Her.* 9.87–8, *Met.* 9.191–2; Virg. *Aen.* 6.802–3) in the Peloponnese and which ravaged Arcadia, was Diodorus' (4.12.1–2) and Hyginus' (*Fab.* 30) third labour, Apollodorus' (2.5.4) and Quintus' (6.220–2) fourth; here, too, it is listed fourth. *Hispidus*, 'bristly', is almost a defining adjective of the boar: see also *Ag.* 832, Phaedr. 5.10.4, Apul. *Met.* 8.4.

Arcadia quatere nemora/**shook Arcadian groves:** 'Arcadian' often has a double resonance: it can denote the mountainous area of the central Peloponnese and/or the ideal pastoral landscape created by Virgil. Ovid's description of the boar as *Arcadiae uastator* ('ravager of Arcadia', *Met.* 9.192), like that of Seneca here and at *Ag.* 832 (*Arcadii populator agri*, 'ravager of Arcadian field'), does both. Note the successive resolutions in the first three feet of this line suggesting the boar's rapid rush and its shaking of the groves; in all there are sixteen syllables in this line. For similar resolutions, cf. *Tro.* 1178.

taurum/**Bull:** the Cretan Bull, which, according to the most common version of the myth, Hercules captured on the island and brought to Mycenae. Diodorus (4.13.4), Apollodorus (2.5.7), Hyginus (*Fab.* 30), and Quintus (6.236–40) list it as Hercules' seventh labour. Here it appears fifth. See also *Ag.* 833–4, *HO* 27. Hercules' fight with the bull was a popular subject in Attic vase-painting. At Virg. *Aen.* 8.294–5 Hercules is said to have killed the bull.

centum…populis/**one hundred towns:** the defining attribute of Crete (*urbibus centum spatiosa Crete*, 'broad Crete of a hundred cities', *Tro.* 820); see also *Pha.* 150, *HO* 1876, Hom. *Il.* 2.649, Ov. *Met.* 7.481.

non leuem…metum/**no slight scare:** for the use of *non* to negate an adjective, see on 489–94. Litotes involving *leuis* is also found at *Ag.* 192, *Pho.* 284, 338, *Oed.* 353, *HO* 547. For *metus* as 'object of fear' again in apposition and with the dative, see *metus agricolis*, 'terror/scare to farmers' (*Pha.* 29), *Cecropiis metus terris*, 'terror/scare to Cecrops' land' (*Thy.* 1049–50); see also *Pho.* 516, *Med.* 516, *Tro.* 62, 243, 742.

231–4 The next labour: Cattle of Geryon.

gentis Hesperiae/**Hesperia's folk:** 'Hesperia' is a relative geographic term, (roughly) = 'the west', used sometimes in reference to Italy, here to Spain.

'Hesperian' is used of Geryon's cattle at *Ag.* 840 (*Hesperium pecus*), and regularly used of the Mediterranean west of Italy to the Atlantic (1140 below, *Med.* 727).

pastor triformis litoris Tartesii/triformed drover of the Tartesian shore: Geryon (named also at 487, 1170), a monster of triple form (τρισώματον, Eur. *Herac.* 423), who lived on the island of Erythia near the Strait of Gibraltar and was usually conceived of as having the bodies of three men fused into one (Aesch. *Ag.* 870, Lucr. 5.28). The stealing of his herd of cattle is the tenth labour in Diodorus (4.17.1), Hyginus (*Fab.* 30), Apollodorus (2.5.10), and Quintus (6.249–55); here it is listed sixth. Hercules' slaying of Geryon is told by Hesiod (*Theog.* 287–94, 981–3); cf. also *Ag.* 837–41, *Apoc.* 7.2.6–8, *HO* 26, 1203–4, 1900. *Pastor* is used of Geryon by Ovid at *Met.* 9.184. Tartes(s)us was an area or town in south-west Spain; the phrase *Tartes(s)ium litus* is also Ovidian (*Met.* 14.416).

peremptus/Was killed: *Ag.* 839 has Hercules clubbing Geryon. The slaying was a frequent subject in Attic vase-painting, but the more usual account in both visual and literary representations (Gantz 1993: 402–3) has Hercules killing Geryon with arrows (as at Eur. *Herac.* 423–4) or a sword. Auxiliary *est* is omitted; see on 222–5. Further on *perimere*, see on 1159–63.

Cithaeron: mountain in Boeotia near Thebes, 'sacred' to Bacchus (*Oed.* 484–5), famous in Greek and Roman literature for Bacchic orgies, Agave's dismemberment of Pentheus, and for the exposure of Oedipus. Called by Seneca's Oedipus *scelerum capax*, 'a breeding-ground for sin' (*Oed.* 930).

Oceano/Ocean: see on 19–29. Here it is primarily a reference to the Atlantic.

235–40 Two more labours: Strait of Gibraltar and Apples of the Hesperides.

solis aestiui plagas/zones of the summer sun: i.e. north Africa/Libya (cf. *arentem plagam*, 'arid zone', 319, *torrente plaga*, 'scorching zone', Luc. 9.861), though technically the phrase refers to places near the Tropic of Cancer. See Cic. *Arat.* 263–5: *Cancer,* | *in quo consistens conuertit curriculum sol* | *aestiuus*, 'Cancer, where the summer sun halts and turns his chariot'.

medius...dies/midday: cf. *sol medium tenens* at 884. *Medius dies* often = 'the south': see Virg. *Geo.* 3.303, Luc. 1.16, 9.606.

montes soluit/split mountains apart: the reference is to the creation of the Pillars of Hercules, mentioned as early as Pindar (*Nem.* 3.22), but that their creation was, as described here, brought about by Hercules splitting a continuous land-mass between Africa and Europe (into Mt Abyla/Jebel Musa/Ximiera on the African side and Mt Calpe/Gibraltar on the European side) is found only in such (relatively) later authors as Diodorus (4.18.5),

Mela (1.27), the elder Pliny (*HN* 3.4), and the dramatist of *Hercules Oetaeus* (1240): see Fitch *ad loc*. This feat was not normally regarded as one of the labours 'ordered' by Eurystheus, though here it is claimed to be exactly that (*iussus*, 235). It has clearly been included to maintain the canonic number of twelve: see on 213–48. In 1634 Francisco de Zurbarán produced a painting of the Herculean event as part of a commission from King Philip IV of Spain.

rupto obice/with the barrier Burst: Seneca's treatment of *obex* as masculine (here and at 999) accords, as Billerbeck notes *ad loc.*, with 'kaiserzeitlichen Gebrauch'.

ruenti…Oceano/Ocean's rush: the rushing waters of the Atlantic. The participle *ruenti* brings out the translingual etymological associations of Oceanus with ὠκύς, 'swift': see Fitch (2016: 330). For Ocean, see on 19–29.

post haec/Next: the implication seems to be that Hercules' 'labour' in the gardens of the Hesperides took place immediately after the creation of the Pillars as culmination of the same journey. If so, as Fitch notes *ad loc.*, this is an unusual version.

nemoris opulenti domos/rich grove's domain: the gardens of the Hesperides, nymphs who inhabited a garden in the far west or north. The garden featured golden apples: hence 'rich grove' (Lucan's 'golden wood' and 'shining grove', *aurea silua…nitidi…luci*, 9.360–2). The apples had been given to Juno/Hera as a wedding gift, and were guarded both by the nymphs and a serpent (in some accounts with a hundred heads). To fetch these golden apples and take them to Eurystheus was Hercules' eleventh labour in Hyginus (*Fab.* 30), Apollodorus (2.5.11), and Quintus (6.256–9); in Diodorus (4.26.2–4) it is Hercules' twelfth/final labour. In Amphitryon's list it is number eight. In some versions Hercules kills the snake (e.g. Soph. *Trach.* 1099–1100, Eur. *Her.* 394–400, Lucr. 5.37, DS 4.16.4, Hyg. *Fab.* 30, *HO* 18), but in *Herc.* (520–2) and at *Ag.* 852–8, *Pho.* 316–17, he appears not to do so. There are also versions (derived from Pherecydes and attested in several works of visual art, including the Hesperides metope at Olympia), in which Atlas acquires the apples on Hercules' behalf and Hercules takes them from him (e.g. Apollod. 2.5.11). At [Eratosthenes] *Catast.* 3–4 the snake guarding the apples is catasterized as the constellation Draco. For the 'golden' nature of the apples, see *Ag.* 852, *HO* 18, Soph. *Trach.* 1099–1100, Eur. *Her.* 396–7, Lucr. 5.32, Mart. *Epig.* 9.101.4. *Domus* (lit. 'house/abode/home') is found with *nemoris* only once elsewhere in the tragedies at *Med.* 766, where again it means 'sheltering enclosure' (Fitch *ad loc.*). For *domus* and the Hesperides, see also Sil. 4.636.

aurifera uigilis spolia serpentis/wakeful serpent's golden spoils: the golden apples, guarded by a wakeful serpent; see previous n. The serpent's vigilance is regularly underscored: 531 below, *Ag.* 856, Ov. *Met.* 9.190. Seneca's fondness for compounds in *-fer* in his tragedies is on display in this play: also *caeliferam*, 528; *pestiferas*, 562; *flammifero*, 593; *luctifer*, 687; *pomiferos*, 700; *anguifera*, 812; *pestiferi*, 976; *flammifera*, 982; *astriferae*, 1068. There are ten instances, too, in *Medea*. The fondness was shared by Ovid, Lucan, and the Flavian epicists: see Billerbeck (1988: 40–1). For *spolia*, see 51 and n. *ad loc.*; for military imagery, see on 19–29. For the dactyl-tribrach combination at the start of the line, see 76 and n. *ad loc.*

241–8 A final four labours: Lernaean Hydra, Stymphalian Birds, Hippolyte's Belt, Augean Stables.

Quid/What: cf. 459 for a similar initial single *quid?* to mark the transition to another point. For interrogatives used to effect a rhetorical transition, see 30 and n. *ad loc.*

saeua Lernae monstra/Lerna's fierce monster: the many-headed hydra/ water-serpent of Lerna, a city and lake in the north-west Peloponnese south of Argos. Each of the hydra's mortal heads was able to regenerate as two heads when chopped off. Hence Seneca (781 and *Ag.* 835), Ovid (*Her.* 9.95), and Martial (*Epig.* 9.101.9) play with the adjective, *fecundus*, 'pregnant/ productive', to describe its regenerative properties (cf. *feracia* at 529). Apollodorus (2.5.2) writes that there were 'nine' heads, eight mortal, one immortal, but the number varies. Virgil refers to its 'crowd of heads' (*turba capitum*, *Aen.* 8.300). Its unsuccessful fight with Hercules goes back to Hesiod (*Theog.* 313–18). Hercules subdued the monster with the assistance of his nephew, Iolaus, who, when a head was removed, (on the advice of Minerva/Athena) cauterized the roots of the heads to prevent new heads from sprouting. It seems to have become a constellation of the same name: see Arat. *Phaen.* 443–9, Cic. *Arat.* 214–18, Manil. 1.612. Listed here in ninth position, the defeat of the Lernaean Hydra features second in the lists of Diodorus (4.11.5–6), Hyginus (*Fab.* 30), Apollodorus (2.5.2), and Quintus (6.212–19). See also 529, 780–1, 1195; *Med.* 701–2; *HO* 19, 918–20, 1192–4, 1534–5, 1813; Virg. *Aen.* 8.299–300. Note the possible witticism in *monstra*, which is presumably a 'poetic plural' and has been accordingly translated as singular, but may also have a plural sense because of the hydra's plurality of heads. For the important *monstrum* motif, see 1280 and n. *ad loc.*

numerosum malum/numerous pest: a wry description of this many-headed monster. For *monstrum* as *malum*, 'pest/thing of evil', see *Pha.* 1032 (of the bull from the sea).

igne/with fire: the now canonic version of the killing of the hydra with the aid of cauterization begins with Euripides (*Herac.* 419–21).

docuit mori/Train it in death: lit. 'taught to die', another wry description, this time of the prolonged process of destroying all the monster's heads. For this rhetorical use of *docere*, see on 68–74. Seneca is similarly witty in his description of this same process at *Ag.* 835–6, where the hydra is 'pregnant with death' (*morte fecundum*) and Hercules 'aborted its dying necks' (*uetu-itque collo pereunte nasci*).

pinnis condere obductis diem/shroud of feathers buried day: *pinna* is 'feather' and by metonymy 'wing'. There seems to be some play here between the metonymic and literal meanings. The Stymphalian Birds were renowned for firing their feathers as arrow-like weapons (Ap. Rhod. 2.1088, Hyg. *Fab.* 30). For the Stymphalians' blocking of daylight, see also *Pho.* 422–3.

petit ab ipsis nubibus Stymphalidas/from the very clouds shoot Stymphalids: the killing of the terrifying Stymphalian Birds, which plagued the Stymphalian Lake in Arcadia in the central Peloponnese, was Hercules' sixth labour in Apollodorus (2.5.6), fifth in Diodorus (4.13.2), Hyginus (*Fab.* 30), and Quintus (6.227–31); here it is listed tenth. One tradition has it that Hercules shot the birds with arrows poisoned with the blood of the Lernaean Hydra. Here it is unclear whether the arrows are poisoned. In Ap. Rhod. (2.1052–7) Hercules drives the birds away with a bronze rattle. See also *Ag.* 850–1 (*sagittis nube percussa*, 'clouds struck by arrows'), *Med.* 783, *Pho.* 422–3, Hyg. *Fab.* 30, Ov. *Met.* 9.187, Mart. *Epig.* 9.101.7–8—and *HO* 17, 1236–7, 1389–90, 1650, 1889–90. Note the polysyllabic ending in a Greek name, as at 246. See on 6–11. *Petit*, the reading of *E*, is contracted perfect, as at 825. For the contracted/syncopated perfect of *petere*, see *Tro.* 348, *Ag.* 358, *Oed.* 803, *Med.* 248, *Ira* 2.34.4, *Oct.* 421, *HO* 1843. Cf. the syncopated *abit* (321, 1151).

caelibis semper tori/ever virgin bed: the mythic Amazons were not of course virgins, but legendary female warriors who did not cohabit with men but had sexual intercourse for reproductive purposes. They inhabited the area around the mouth of the river Thermodon on the south-eastern shore of the Black Sea: see below. According to Pompeius Trogus (Justin's epitome: 2.4.10), Amazons killed their male offspring, keeping only the female. They are mentioned as early as Homer (*Il.* 3.189). Seneca refers to them often: see e.g. 542–6; *Ag.* 217–18, 736, 848–50; *Pha.* 232, 399–403, 909–11; *Oed.* 479; *Tro.* 12–14, 672–3; *Med.* 214–15. *Caelibis…tori* is a genitive of description/quality (Woodcock §72.1.6) and something of an oxymoron, since *torus* is used more regularly of the conjugal bed; cf. Agamemnon's *caelebs torus* at

Ag. 185. Less paradoxical are Catullus' (68.6) and Ovid's (*Her.* 13.107) *lecto...caelibe.* For paradoxical phrasing in *Hercules*, see on 30-5.

regina... uidua/**manless queen:** Hippolyte, queen of the Amazons, possessed a golden war-belt (*aurato...balteo,* 542 below), given to her, according to Apollodorus, by Mars/Ares. Hercules took the belt either by force (as at *Ag.* 848-50 and Hyginus, *Fab.* 30, Apollod. 2.5.9, Quintus 6.240-5) or was given it by Hippolyte herself (543-4 below, Ap. Rhod. 2.966-9, DS 4.16.4). Hercules' capture of the war-belt is the ninth labour in Diodorus, Hyginus, and Apollodorus, the eighth in Quintus. Here it is listed in penultimate position. See also *HO* 21, Ov. *Met.* 9.188-9. Hercules' Amazonomachy (in which the Amazon fighting him is more often named Andromache than Hippolyte) is regularly depicted on Attic vases. See further below on 542-6. For *uidua,* 'manless', applied by Seneca to Amazons, see on 1-5.

gentis... Thermodontiae/**Thermodon race:** the Thermodon was a river (modern Terme River) flowing into the Pontus/Euxine/Black Sea from its southern shore near Themiscyra and traditionally associated with the Amazons (Aesch. *Prom.* 723-5). Ovid addresses it in one of his final poems: *tu, femineae Thermodon cognite turmae,* 'Thou, Thermodon known to the women's army' (*Pont.* 4.10.51). Cf. *Med.* 215, *Oed.* 481. At *Tro.* 12-13, *Pha.* 399-403, Seneca locates the Amazons on the northern side of the Pontus. Note again the polysyllabic ending in a Greek name (see on 244), this time a pentasyllabic word. Pentasyllabic endings to Seneca's iambic trimeter are quite rare (Billerbeck *ad loc.* counts sixteen): see e.g. *Tro.* 861, *Ag.* 660, *Med.* 215, *Thy.* 23.

ad omne clarum facinus audaces manus/**hands bold for all deeds of glory:** there is perhaps an unintentional ambivalence about Amphitryon's claim concerning his son's unrestricted *audacia.*

stabuli...Augei/**Augean stables:** the climactic labour of Amphitryon's list is ironically the one omitted from the Chorus' laudation of Hercules at *Ag.* 29-66: viz. the cleaning of the stables of Augeas, king of Elis in the Peloponnese. This is the most obscure and perhaps least 'heroic' of the labours; it is represented (in rather poor condition) on one of the metopes of the temple of Zeus at Olympia, for the interpretation of which we are dependent on Pausanias' account (5.10.9). There are several versions of what transpired, including Hercules' completion of the task in a single day and his diversion of the Alpheus, the main river of Olympia, to clean the dung from the stables. Hercules was not paid for his services. There may be a reference to the labour at Pind. *Ol.* 10.26-30. Diodorus (4.13.3), Hyginus (*Fab.* 30), and Quintus (6.232-6) list it as the sixth labour, Apollodorus (2.5.5) as the fifth. For *Augei* here as an adjective, 'Augean', see Fitch *ad loc.*

249–78 Amphitryon concludes with a description of the moral and political malaise in Thebes (where *uirtus = scelus*), caused (he implies) by Hercules' absence. In Euripides' *Heracles*, the play begins with such a description (*Herac.* 26–59), but in that speech, also by Amphitryon, attention is given to *stasis*, civil disorder, within the city of Thebes itself (*Herac.* 31–4; also 272–3, 590), which has allowed Lycus' usurpation of the throne. There is no mention of *stasis* by Seneca's Amphitryon, who ends his speech with a direct invocation of Hercules, mirroring the prayer to Jupiter with which he began.

249–58 The moral and political turmoil and royal murders during Hercules' absence in the underworld. The whole passage deals with the recent past; but its focus on the witnessing of the slaughter of children and kin foreshadows the witnessed slaughter to come. Lines 251–3 are constructed from *sententiae* (for which see on 125–204 introd.).

Quid ista prosunt/**What good is served by this:** *quid prodest* is a very Roman question; it is asked of Octavia and Agrippina at *Oct.* 286, 356–7. See also *Ag.* 279, [Ov.] *Cons. Liu.* 41–6, and Prop. 3.18.11–12: *quid genus aut uirtus aut optima profuit illi | mater,* 'What profit to him his lineage or virtue or a paragon of mothers'. For interrogatives used to effect a rhetorical transition, see 30 and n. *ad loc.*

orbe defenso caret/**He lacks the world He saved:** cf. Hercules' own outburst against the ingratitude (*ingrata tellus*) of the world which he saved (*defensus orbis*) at 631–2. Billerbeck *ad loc.* sees here and at 633 an allusion to one of Hercules' cult titles, viz. *defensor*, attested in the epigraphic record.

sensere terrae…abesse terris/**Earth felt…Absent from earth:** for *sentire* in the context of global or area reaction (the 'pathetic fallacy'), see 956; *Ag.* 824, 829; *Oed.* 159, 471; *Tro.* 177; *HO* 2; Ov. *Met.* 13.785, *Fas.* 2.135. Note the repetition of *terrae*; cf. *HO* 1593–4. For analogous repetitions, see *Ag.* 691–2, *Med.* 436–7, *Thy.* 861–2.

pacis auctorem/**author of…peace:** for Hercules as pacifier of the world, see Introd. 66–7, 105, and on 882–8. Note the Roman character of the phrase, which is used by Ovid of Augustus in the opening poem of his Pontic Epistles: *proderit auctorem pacis habere nihil?* 'Will it profit nothing that my poem contains the author of peace?' (*Pont.* 1.1.32). It will be used by 'Seneca' of 'Nero' at *Oct.* 488, and by Statius of King Creon's son, Menoeceus, at *Theb.* 10.684. It was used by Cicero of himself (*Phil.* 7.8, 14.20, *Att.* 9.11a2). Like several other Roman allusions, the phrase links Hercules to the politics and culture of Seneca's audience. Seneca saw the power of this phrase and used it with acrid contextual irony in *Phoenissae*: (Messenger to Oedipus) *auctorque placidae liberis pacis ueni,* 'And come as author of tranquil peace for your children' (*Pho.*

349). For Roman referentiality in the play, see on 46–52. For Seneca's fondness for nouns ending in -*tor*, see on 299–302.

prosperum ac felix scelus uirtus uocatur/Successful crime thrives—It's called 'virtue': cf. *Pha.* 598: *honesta quaedam scelera successus facit*, 'success makes some crime honourable'. Amphitryon embarks on a cultural *topos*, viz. the convolution of language which attends civil strife, aptly described in Thucydides' account of the Corcyraean *stasis* (3.82), as also by Sallust (*Cat.* 52.11), who follows his Greek master in the presentation of civil war as the occasion when the 'true words for things' (*uera uocabula rerum*) disappear (see also Tac. *Hist.* 1.37.4). For transformation in the meaning of *uirtus*, see also Luc. 1.667–8 (*scelerique nefando | nomen erit uirtus*, 'and unspeakable crime will be named virtue'), and the more alliterative but less subtle imitation of the lemmatized line at *HO* 421–2: *uitium impotens uirtus uocatur*, 'Unbridled vice is called "virtue"'. Amphitryon's words became a much-cited *sententia*, as Fitch *ad loc.* notes, in the Renaissance. It appears, too, in William Cornwallis's *Discourses upon Seneca the Tragedian* (1601), and is enshrined in Jacobean verse by Marston (*The Malcontent* IV.iii: 'Mischiefe that prospers men do vertue call') and Jonson (*Catiline* III.iii.504–5: 'Let 'em call it mischiefe; | When it is past, and prosper'd, 'twill be vertue').

sontibus parent boni/The good serve the guilty: the first part of a triple *sententia* which seems to have influenced Silius (2.504–5):

> vis colitur, iurisque locum sibi uindicat ensis,
> e probris cessit uirtus.

> Force is worshipped, the sword replaces justice
> And virtue yielded to vice.

ius est in armis, opprimit leges timor/Justice lies in arms, terror stifles law: Amphitryon's sentiment will be repeated by Lycus at 400–1. Cf. also Hippolytus at *Pha.* 544, and Lucan's famous opening *iusque datum sceleri canimus*, 'And justice bestowed on crime we sing', 1.2; see also Ov. *Tr.* 5.7.47–8. The moral antithesis of *ius*, 'justice', and *arma/ferrum/uis*, 'arms/steel/violence', is evident in Roman literature from Ennius onwards (*Ann.* frag. 252 Skutsch). At *Ira* 3.2.1 Seneca might seem to associate the doctrine of 'might is right' (*quibus iura distinguit modus uirium*, 'those for whom might makes right') with *barbari*, but the doctrine, as was apparent from Marius and Sulla onwards and as Lucan showed, was quintessentially Roman. See 401–2 below, where Lycus articulates the doctrine, and *Clem.* 1.12.4, where Seneca, criticizing the tyrant's use of excessive terror, still advocates to Nero a moderate use of fear (*temperatus timor*). For legal language and imagery in *Hercules*, see on 731–4.

ante ora uidi nostra…uidi/Before my eyes I saw…I saw: this kind of 'eye-witness perfect', used of the painful, impotent gaze, is employed elsewhere by Seneca of terrifying, often bloody sights, in which *uidere* seems close to meaning 'bear the sight of' (Tarrant *ad Ag.* 612): see *uidi, ipsa uidi*, 'I saw, myself saw', 50; *uidi…uidi*, 'I saw…I saw', 606…613; *uidi*, 'I saw', 737; *uidi, ipse uidi*, 'I saw, myself saw', *Tro.* 170; *uidi*, 'I saw', *Oed.* 584, *Tro.* 36, 44, *Thy.* 1064; *uidimus*, 'we saw', *Ag.* 611, 625, 648; *uidi, uidi*, 'I saw, I saw', *Ag.* 656, *Pho.* 552; *uidit*, 'saw', *Ag.* 848, *Oed.* 424, *Thy.* 1047, *Pho.* 543, 545, 551. Cf. *Oct.* 16, 231; Virg. *Ecl.* 1.42, 10.26, *Geo.* 1.472, *Aen.* 2.499–501; Hor. *Odes* 1.2.13; Ov. *Her.* 3.45–9; Luc. 1.255. One of the starting-points in the Roman tradition is Ennius' eye-witness *uidi* in *Andromacha* (frags 92–4 Jocelyn):

> haec omnia uidi inflammari,
> Priamo ui uitam euitari,
> Iouis aram sanguine turpari.

> All this I saw in flames,
> Priam's life unlifed with force,
> Jove's altar blood befouled.

Seneca is writing after Virgil, and Amphitryon's initial *uidi* is rendered more emphatic and emotional not only by its literary forerunners but by the addition of *ante ora* 'before eyes', a phrase used on particular occasions by Virgil (*Geo.* 4.477, *Aen.* 2.531, 663, 6.308, 11.887) to underscore the pathos or horror of an event.

A metatheatrical point seems worth making. A special theatrical charge is always generated by characters who, like Amphitryon here or Juno earlier (50), are the object of the Roman audience's gaze, describing themselves as the subject of the gaze in relation to an off-stage or on-stage spectacle. Such characters set up a model of viewing for the audience themselves. It is not necessarily a model (here one of painful impotence) the audience will choose to accept. See further on 46–52 (*uidi, ipsa uidi*). For metatheatre, see on 109–12.

Worth noting, too, is that Seneca especially likes to draw attention to the 'viewing' of dead loved ones: here and 1159–61 (*cerno*), *Pha.* 1168–9 (*intuor*), *Med.* 1001 (*te uidente*), *Thy.* 1038 (*cerno*)—see esp. *Tro.* 44–50 (*uidi*) and *Ag.* 656 (*uidi, uidi*), where Hecuba/Trojan Captives give an eye-witness account of Priam's death. For 'seeing evil' (*uidere nefas*), see *Oed.*

444, *Pho.* 497–8. In epic the 'viewing moment' features in several lamentations: see e.g. Virg. *Aen.* 9.481 (lamentation of Euryalus' mother), Ov. *Met.* 13.495 (lamentation of Hecuba), Stat. *Theb.* 12.322–4 (lamentation of Argia). For the 'viewing' motif, see also on 46–52, 604–15, 735–9, 1054–62•, 1159–63.

truculenta manu/savage Hands: for *truculentus*, 'maddened/savage/ferocious', used of tyrants, see *Ag.* 950 (Clytemnestra), *Thy.* 547 (Atreus), Val. Max. 5.3.3 (Cinna). At *Pha.* 461 it is hypothetically applied to Hippolytus *qua* primitive, ignorant wild-man.

natos/sons: these brothers of Megara are mentioned also in Euripides (*Herac.* 539) and referred to again at 303, 373, 379, 403.

paterni cadere regni uindices/fall…in defence of their father's kingdom: the death of Creon's sons is taken up later in the exchange between Megara and Lycus (373, 379, 403). Seneca has followed Euripides here in having Creon's sons killed by Lycus (*Herac.* 539–41), whom Euripides almost certainly invented (see on 332–57 and Introd. 63). In Statius' *Thebaid* the two sons (Menoeceus and Haemon) and Creon himself die either during the attack on Thebes by the 'Seven' and or during the subsequent attack by Theseus. In Sophocles' *Antigone* Haemon kills himself after the death of Antigone herself. Note that in Euripides' play (*Herac.* 42–3, 168–9), it is Heracles' children, not Creon's, who are marked out as possible *uindices*, 'avengers/defenders'. Mark the breach of 'Porson's law' in this line. 'Porson's law' prohibits a caesura in a spondaic fifth foot of an iambic trimeter unless a monosyllabic word precedes or follows the caesura: see West (1987), 25. Porson's law is derived, of course, from the Attic tragedians' use of the iambic trimeter—not from its use in Roman drama. As Fantham (1982: 106) comments, 'There is no reason to believe that Seneca was aware of the Greek principle we call Porson's law'. In *Hercules* may be found at least twelve examples of what Raven (1965: 54), misleadingly terms 'extremely rare' Senecan breaches: 255, 397, 495, 641, 652, 657, 698, 715, 992, 998, 1042, 1333. There seem to be ten such breaches in *Medea*, seven in *Phaedra*, six each in *Troades* and *Agamemnon*, five in *Thyestes* and *Phoenissae*, and three in *Oedipus*. There are many cases where such breaches are prevented by synaloephe: see on 19–29. Note also in the words *cadere regni* the repetition of the same syllable at the end and beginning of juxtaposed words; see 67 and n. *ad loc.*

ipsumque/And the king himself: lit. 'and himself'. The reference is to Creon, father of Megara. Although he is sometimes regarded as distinct from the brother of Jocasta, who takes over the Theban throne after the demise of Oedipus, his brother-in-law and nephew, Euripides seems to regard him as that Creon (*Herac.* 8–9). See further Fitch *ad loc.*

Cadmi nobilis stirpem ultimam/**last of noble Cadmus' line**: Cadmus, a Phoenician immigrant, was the founder of Thebes. He founded the city after ploughing the land and sowing it with serpent teeth, from which arose armed men, Spartoi (see on 258–67). Creon was a descendant from Cadmus through his daughter, Agave, and a descendant of the Spartoi through Agave's husband, Echion. Technically the children of Oedipus and Jocasta and those of Hercules and Megara were the last of Cadmus' line. See further on 384–96.

regium capiti decus/**head's royal crown**: the exact phrase recurs in the same position of the line at *Ag.* 8 and *Thy.* 701, where, as here, *capiti* is a possessive dative. *Decus* is a favourite Senecan word for 'beauty', 'splendour', 'glory', etc., often with reference to the splendour of the heavens, the stars, the sun and moon, etc.: see e.g. 592, *Pha.* 410, *Thy.* 791, *Oed.* 250, 405. For this concrete use of *decus* (= 'crown'), see also *paternum…decus*, *Thy.* 528; *capiti regium…decus*, *Clem.* 1.1.2; *regale decus*, Ov. *Met.* 9.690; *capiti decus*, Stat. *Theb.* 11.161. For *decus* with the genitive, see on 592–7.

258–67 Lamentation for the glorious city of Thebes, crushed by a foul yoke.

Quis satis Thebas fleat/**Who could mourn Thebes enough**: for the *topos* of unworthy or inadequate lament/the search for appropriate mourners, see e.g. 1227–8, *Ag.* 667–92, *Tro.* 409–12, *Oct.* 914–15•, *HO* 185–206, Virg. *Aen.* 2.362, [Ov.] *Cons. Liu.* 105–12, Vell. Pat. 2.67.1, Stat. *Silu.* 5.3.80–115. For interrogatives used to effect a rhetorical transition, see 30 and n. *ad loc.*

ferax deorum terra/**god-fruitful land**: the most famous divine son is Bacchus, but the plural *deorum* can be justified by including Ino, Bacchus' aunt and foster-mother, and her son, Melicertes, who became respectively the sea-goddess Leucothea (Roman Mater Matuta) and the sea-god Palaemon (Roman Portunus): see *Oed.* 445–8.

e cuius aruis/**from whose fields**: *cuius* is the first of five relatives following *terra*: *cuius* (260)…*cuius* (262)…*cuius* (264)…*quae* (265)…*quae* (266). The repetition lends the lamentation a formal, even hymnic quality.

eque: lit. 'and out of', a unique combination in Seneca, but found in Lucretius, Virgil and Ovid: see Billerbeck *ad loc.*

iuuentus orta/**Arose warriors**: the Spartoi, 'Sown-Men', who grew fully armed from the land ploughed by Cadmus and sowed with serpent's teeth (on Athena/Minerva's instructions). These warriors, on arising, proceeded to fight and kill each other. The last five made a truce, and with them Cadmus founded the city of Thebes. See *Oed.* 731–50, Eur. *Pho.* 670–5, Ov. *Met.* 3.101–30.

muros/**walls:** Seneca shows a distinct preference for the plural form of *murus* when referring to the wall/walls of a city.

Amphion: son (with Zethus) of Antiope and Jupiter and husband of Niobe; legendary musician, who with Zethus built the walls of Thebes (Hom. *Od.* 11.262–5, Ap. Rhod. 1.735–41). Amphion, who is said to have drawn the stones after him with the music of his lyre (see *Oed.* 611–12, *Pho.* 566–70), is the one usually associated by Roman poets with the Theban walls (e.g. Prop. 1.9.10; Hor. *Odes* 3.11.1–2, *AP* 394–6; Ov. *Met.* 6.178–9, 15.427; Stat. *Theb.* 4.356–60).

canoro saxa modulatu trahens/**Hauling the stones with songful harmonies:** note the onomatopoeic qualities of the rare noun, *modulatus* (found here for the first time in Latin literature), with its pair of short syllables completing a tribrach in the fourth foot (a common metrical phenomenon of Senecan tragedy: there are fifty-two fourth-foot tribrachs in the iambic trimeters of *Hercules* alone, as Professor Smith of SDSU informs me). For a similarly onomatopoeic use of the associated verb, applied to another songster, the nightingale, see *Ag.* 672 (*modulata*). *Canorus*, 'songful/melodious', used here in relation to Amphion, is applied to the Sirens at *Med.* 356 and Ov. *Ars* 3.311, and to Orpheus at Hor. *Odes* 1.12.11 and Virg. *Aen.* 6.120. Amphion is in good, if ambivalent, company.

non semel diuum parens/**the father of gods not just once:** Jupiter's sexual liaisons with young Theban women embrace Antiope, Alcmene, and Semele. *Diuum parens* is an epic-style title for Jupiter, the full display of which is *diuum pater atque hominum rex*, 'father of gods and king of men' (Enn. *Ann.* frag. 203 Skutsch, Virg. *Aen.* 1.65, 10.2; cf. Homer's tag, πατὴρ ἀνδρῶν τε θεῶν τε, and also Enn. *Ann.* frags 591, 592 Skutsch, Livy 8.6.5, Ov. *Met.* 14.807, *Oct.* 204). Amphitryon's euphemistic litotes, *non semel*, 'not just once', contrasts with Juno's irate exclamation at 19–21. The litotes itself (*non semel*) occurs again at *Med.* 474, *Tro.* 825, *Thy.* 410, *Prou.* 2.9, *Ira* 2.29.3. Cf. *HO* 1948. The genitive plural form *diuum* appears infrequently in Senecan tragedy (see also *Pha.* 680, *Oed.* 1028, *Ag.* 651). For Jupiter as *parens*, see on 516–20.

caelo relicto/**Left heaven:** the same phrase is used at 1157–8 of Jupiter and at *Pha.* 294 of the gods, abandoning heaven to pursue earthly amours. The phrase (lit. 'heaven having been left') is a temporal ablative absolute and a variant of a common line-beginning formula: cf. *uulnere relicto*, 'the wound having been left', 995; *Phocide relicta*, 'Phocis having been left', *Ag.* 918; *die relicto*, 'the day having been left', *Med.* 768; *ratibus relictis*, 'the ships having been left', *Tro.* 1078.

caelites recepit/welcomed gods: *caelites* is taken by Billerbeck *ad loc.* as a rhetorical plural. But Amphitryon may be referring not only to the visits of Jupiter noted above but also to the divine guests at the wedding celebrations of Cadmus and Harmonia (Pind. *Pyth.* 3.86–95, Eur. *Pho.* 822–3). The city infamously did not welcome its prime god, Bacchus—to the considerable discomfiture of the then king, Pentheus, as Euripides' *Bacchae* bloodily shows.

fecit et…faciet/made and…Will make: a Roman audience would know all about the 'making' of gods; see *Oct.* 449. For Roman referentiality in *Hercules*, see on 46–52. For the verbal polyptoton, see on 112–18; for polyptoton, see on 11–18.

fas sit loqui/be it right to say: a Virgilian phrase (*Aen.* 6.266), which Ovid made a subtext of his great work, *Fasti* (see *Fas.* 1.25). *Fas* is invoked at 658, as Theseus starts to reveal the secrets of the underworld.

sordido premitur iugo/is pressed by a foul yoke: so, too, the dramatist of *Octavia*, describing not Lycus' Thebes but Nero's world (*orbis*), which the emperor 'presses with a base yoke' (*premit turpi iugo*, *Oct.* 250). *Octavia*'s author seems to have seen in Lycus intimations of Nero.

268–78 A powerful end to this act's opening speech, as Amphitryon moves from the indignity of Herculean Thebes being ruled by the exile, Lycus, to confidence in Hercules' triumphant return. The concluding address to Hercules and prayer for his return balance not only the address to the Theban people (268–70), but the prayer to Jupiter which opens both speech and act (205–7).

268–75 *Cadmea proles atque Ophionium genus*/Seed of Cadmus and Ophion's race: i.e. Thebans. Though Amphitryon's address is directed to the whole Theban city, the Chorus of Thebans who are on stage would presumably react to this outburst. Some members of Seneca's audience may have been reminded of the famous opening of Sophocles' *Oedipus Tyrannos*, Ὦ τέκνα Κάδμου, 'O children of Cadmus' (although the syntax pushes Κάδμου towards the following phrase), and (even more specifically, if Seneca's *Oedipus* predates his *Hercules*) of the Chorus' opening address to the Theban elite at *Oed.* 110: *Cadmi generosa proles*, 'High-born seed of Cadmus' (note the development: *Cadmi generosa proles* > *Cadmea proles…genus*). Cf. also Κάδμου πολῖται, 'Citizens of Cadmus', the initial words of Aeschylus' *Septem*. Ophion is an obscure figure (also at *Oed.* 485); his name may be a variant of Echion (both names mean 'Serpent Man'), one of the five surviving Spartoi, the 'Sown-Men' who arose from the serpent's teeth (see on 258–67). Echion was the husband of Agave, father of Pentheus and, like Cadmus, an ultimate ancestor of Creon, father of Megara (Eur. *Bacch.* 507, 1119, *Pho.* 942–4; Ov. *Met.* 3.126, 513, 526; Stat. *Theb.* 4.569). With *Cadmea proles* (the phrase apparently is a Latin literature *hapax*: Haimson Lushkov 2016: 303), cf. *Cadmeae...genti*, *Oed.* 29–30, *Cadmea progenies*, *Pho.* 392, *Cadmique proles*, *Pho.* 648—and the Ovidian *proles Mauortia*, 'Seed of Mars' (*Met.* 3.531). *Proles*, 'progeny', translated here as 'seed', has an archaic ring; Cicero (*De Orat.* 3.153) classified it as belonging to *uerba prisca*, 'ancient words'; it is found some thirty times in Virgil. It occurs again at 987. For Cadmus, see on 249–58. With *Ophionium genus* (Bentley's widely accepted emendation for *EA*'s *ophionius cinis*), cf. *genus Amazonium*, 'Amazon race', *Pha.* 232.

quo reccidistis/How far you've fallen: the allusion to the first choral ode of Seneca's *Oedipus* continues. Its opening word, addressed to the *Cadmi generosa proles*, is *occidis*, 'you fall' (*Oed.* 110). There may be a metaliterary/ metatheatrical touch in the prefix *re-*, with its possible suggestion of repetition: you fell with Oedipus and the plague; you have fallen again. What Amphitryon could not have seen but members of Seneca's audience could have recognized was that Thebes' 'fallen state' will involve not only Lycus but Hercules, and that, like earlier Theban disasters (those attending the death of Pentheus and the 'fall' of Oedipus), it will involve the failure to recognize kin. For metatheatrical language in *Hercules*, see on 109–12. *Reccidistis* is the contracted and usual second-person plural perfect indicative form of *recido*. Zwierlein prints the lemmatized phrase as a question.

ignarum exulem/obscure exile: for *exul*, 'an exile', as a derogatory term, see 274 (used of Lycus again), *Ag.* 291 and 884 (used of Aegisthus), *Med.* 857 (used of Medea), *Pho.* 652 (used of Polynices). The horror of 'exile' in the ancient world—the personal and social exclusion, the 'homelessness', insecurity, and deprivations—cannot be overestimated. Medea's sentence of exile is a sentence of more than social death. Amphitryon is unconcerned with exile's horror, only with its connotations of social rejection and displacement. Lycus is a man without 'place'. In this he resembles Juno, exiled from heaven (see on 1–5). *Ignarus* is here used in an infrequent passive sense, 'unknown'; see Ov. *Met.* 7.404 (*proles ignara parenti*, 'child unknown to his father': of Theseus), and *OLD* 3. *Ignarum* is the reading of *EPT*ᵃᶜ*CSV*, printed by Viansino (1965 and 1993), Giardina (1966 and 2007), Caviglia, Fitch (1987*a* and 2018), Chaumartin, and myself. Zwierlein and Billerbeck favour the reading of *T*ᵖᶜ*τ*, *ignauum*.

suis carentem finibus, nostris grauem/Lacking his own land, a weight upon ours: For the rhetorical use of antithesis, cf. *Med.* 654: *omnibus uerax,*

sibi falsus uni, 'true to all, false but to himself'; *Ag.* 180: *in nos fidelis augur,
in captas leuis*, 'trusted augur for us, ignored for captive girls.'

qui scelera terra quique persequitur mari/**The man who hunts crime by
land and by sea:** for Hercules as the liberator of the world from crime and
evil, see Introd. 66–7 and on 882–8. *Terra… mari*, 'by land and by sea', has a
Roman ring; the formula, *terra marique* or *terra et mari*, appears regularly
in statements of imperial expansion: see e.g. Aug. *Res Gestae* 3, 4, 13, and
26. For Roman referentiality in *Hercules*, see on 46–52.

saeua…sceptra confringit/**crushes cruel sceptres:** among the 'cruel
sceptres', i.e. tyrants, crushed by Hercules are Busiris (see on 480–9),
Diomedes (see on 226–30), Eryx, king of the Elymians in Sicily, and
Laomedon, king of Troy before Priam. For Hercules as civilizer and saviour
of the world, see on 882–8. Along with Viansino (1965 and 1993), Giardina
(1966 and 2007), Caviglia, Chaumartin, and Billerbeck I have preferred the
present tense, *confringit* (*EP*) to the perfect, *confregit* (*TCSV*), printed by
Zwierlein and Fitch (1987*a* and 2018). For *sceptra*, see on 63–8.

nunc seruit absens/**Now a slave and gone:** Hercules is 'slave' to Eurystheus,
absent from Thebes in hell carrying out the Argive king's orders. With *absens*
Amphitryon reverts to his initial frustration with Hercules' absence (209–13).
It will come to the fore again in the final act at 1256.

fertque quae fieri uetat/**suffers what he forbids:** an interesting transformation of Ovid's description of Jupiter, who 'does himself what he forbids' (*fieri quod uetat ipse facit, Fas.* 6.762).

tenetque Thebas exul Herculeas Lycus/**And the exile Lycus holds
Herculean Thebes:** a neatly structured line with alliterative *t*s at the start
and effective *l* and *c* alliterative pattern at the end together with verbal interlocking (AbaB) and an effective juxtaposition of the names of Hercules and
Lycus. 'Herculean Thebes' (*Herculeae…Thebae*) recurs at *Oed.* 749. For the
use of the adjective *Herculeus*, see 72 and n. *ad loc.*

tenet…non tenebit/**holds…shall not hold:** for the verbal polyptoton,
see on 112–18; for polyptoton, see on 11–18.

exul/**exile:** see above.

275–8 *aderit*/**He'll come:** note the sudden change of subject from the previous sentence without any indication to that effect (cf. *aderit*, 312): see on
30–5. Hence the italics. There is an interesting ambiguity here, since *adesse*,
lit. 'to be present', is used not only of human 'presence', but is regularly used
of the epiphany of a god, as in the repeated invocation to the god Hymen in
Catullus 62: *Hymen ades o Hymenaee.* It is especially frequent in prayer: see
e.g. *adsit*, 646, 903; *ades, Pha.* 54, 412, 423, *Med.* 703, *Oed.* 405, *Ag.* 348,

Ov. *Fas.* 1.67, 69; *adeste, Med.* 13; *adsis,* Virg. *Aen.* 8.78. Cf. also Seneca's use of an 'epiphanic future' at *Apoc.* 13.3: *Claudius...ueniet,* 'Claudius will come'. The quasi-divine invocation of Hercules which follows is here anticipated: see below.

poenas petet/**seek revenge:** such revenge is presumably the killing of Lycus and the destruction of his rule. At Eur. *Herac.* 568-73 Heracles 'plans a revenge of heroic proportions' (Bond *ad loc.*), involving a slaughter of Thebans of sufficient magnitude that it would choke Ismenus with corpses and make Dirce run with blood. There is, however, no suggestion here or later in Seneca's play that this is what Amphitryon intends (or Hercules intended). The view of Heil (2014: 551), that Amphitryon may be making 'a concealed threat to the chorus', is difficult to reconcile with Amphitryon's and the Chorus' later behaviour.

subitusque ad astra emerget/**Rise sudden to the stars:** deliberately ambiguous language on Seneca's part. Amphitryon presumably means 'rise to earth', i.e. to the sight of the stars (cf. Cerberus *tractus ad caelum,* 'dragged to the (sight of the) heavens, i.e. earth', *Ag.* 859), but an audience could not help but see the secondary meaning, 'rise to heaven' and become a god.

inueniet uiam/**He'll find...A path:** picked up by the Hercules of *HO* is his self-aggrandizing prologue: *inueniam uiam,* 'I'll find a path' (*HO* 33). The 'path' Hercules later suggests that he will find will be to death: *mortis inueniam uiam* (1245: see n. *ad loc.*). For the phrase, *inuenire uiam,* see Virg. *Aen.* 3.395, 10.113. For finding a path from hell, see also *Pha.* 224 (re Theseus).

adsis Sospes et remees precor/**I pray you come, Saviour, return:** Amphitryon's final move in this opening speech is a prayer to Hercules, as if he were already a god (verifying Juno's statement of 39-40); cf. his invocation of Hercules at 520. Note *Sospes,* 'Saviour', a title unattested for male divinities and designed apparently to mirror a cult title of Juno (Iuno Sospita: see e.g. Cic. *ND* 1.82, *Diu.* 1.4, Ov. *Fas.* 2.56)—also the jussive subjunctives, and *precor* ('I pray'). *Adsis,* which picks up *aderit* (275), is a metrical variant for the more usual *ades. Ades* and *adeste* (lit. 'be present') are the standard terms in Roman prayer and in Senecan tragedy for the invocation of deities: see e.g. *Oed.* 257 (several gods), 405 (Bacchus); *Pha.* 54, 412, 423 (Diana); *Med.* 13, 16 (Furies); Ov. *Fas.* 1.67, 69 (Janus), 3.2 (Mars). According to Tarrant *ad Ag.* 348, the *ades* formula (equivalent to Greek ἐλθέ, ἱκοῦ, μόλε, or προφάνητε) is 'made necessary by the local character of pagan gods'. *Sospes* seems deliberately ambiguous: 'Saviour', but also (uncapitalized) 'safe and sound'; so, too, at 307. *Precor,* the reading of *E,* rejected by Zwierlein in favour of *A's tuis,* seems confirmed, as Fitch observes *ad loc.,* by the Horatian echo (see next n.). For *precor* at the end of an iambic line, see also e.g. 900; *Oed.* 528, 773, 855, 975, 1021; *Ag.* 754, 755; *Med.* 12, 282, 1014; *Thy.* 995; *Oct.* 754. I am joined in printing *precor* by Viansino (1965 and 1993), Giardina (1966 and 2007), Caviglia, Fitch (1987*a* and 2018), Chaumartin, and Billerbeck. See Fitch *ad loc.*

   tandemque uenias uictor ad uictam domum/**And appear at last—victor to a vanquished house:** more prayer language. Seneca echoes Horace's famous appeal to Apollo at *Odes* 1.2.30: *tandem uenias precamur*, 'Appear at last, we pray'. For *uenire* in prayers, see e.g. *Med.* 750, Cat. 61.9. *Tandem*, 'at last', in initial linear position here, is both emphatic and emotive: see *Ag.* 396, 782, *Pha.* 835, and Hor. *Odes* 1.2.30, cited above. Mark the closural, triple alliteration (cf. *Pha.* 482, *Ag.* 202), and the verbal play with *uictor*/*uictus* (also at 368–9, 409, 815–16; *Tro.* 257, 914; *Ag.* 412–13, 754, 869; *Const.* 6.6; *Ira* 3.43.2; *Clem.* 1.9.8—see also e.g. Virg. *Aen.* 2.367–8, 10.757; Liv. 25.31.15; Ov. *Met.* 3.95, *Fas.* 1.523, 3.101–2). Seneca is fond of paronomasia featuring antitheses: see also *felix...infelix*, 'winners...losers', 364; *piae...impium*, 'pious...impious', *Med.* 261; *somno...insomne*, 'sleep...sleepless', at *Med.* 472–3; *innocens...nocens*, 'guiltless...guilty', *Med.* 503; *piae...impiae*, 'pious...impious', *Med.* 779; *casta...incesta*, 'chaste...unchaste', *Pha.* 1184–5; *castus...incesto*, *Pha.* 1195; *notus...ignotus*, 'known...unknown', *Oed.* 841–2, *Thy.* 402–3; *incertum...certum*, 'uncertain...certain', *Pho.* 632–3. Note the contrast between the 'vanquished house' (*uictam domum*) of Megara and Amphitryon and the 'joyous homes' (*laeta...domus*, 161) praised in the 'Dawn Ode'. For Seneca's fondness for alliterative closure, see also e.g. 123–4, 353, 828–9, 1053, 1344; *Ag.* 36, 202; *Tro.* 290–1; *Med.* 362–3; *Thy.* 470. For alliteration of *u*, cf. e.g. *Tro.* 701, *Med.* 190. For military imagery in *Hercules*, see on 19–29; for *uincere*/*uictor* and Hercules, see on 63–8. *Tandem*, 'at last', returns the audience to the speech's opening prayer: see 206 and n. *ad loc.*

279–308 Megara, who, like Amphitryon, spoke in the prologue of Euripides' *Heracles* (60ff.), has been standing silent throughout Amphitryon's long speech as she did in Euripides' prologue. Her repressed emotion is now released. Her opening speech, triggered by Amphitryon's closing prayer to Hercules, is a passionate appeal to her husband to return from hell. She follows an initial, emotional appeal (279–95) with thoughts of reunion with her husband and with promises to Jupiter and Ceres to be fulfilled on his return (295–305). Of that return, however, she seems to despair by the speech's end (305–8). For prayers in Senecan tragedy, see on 205–78. Cf. also the brief invocation of Heracles by Megara at Eur. *Herac.* 490–4.

279–83 *Emerge, coniunx…*/**Rise, husband…:** Megara continues Amphitryon's invocation and language (*emerget*, 276) and personalizes them, giving
the invocation extra urgency through transforming Amphitryon's future
indicatives and jussive subjunctives into raw imperatives (*emerge*, 'Rise',
abrumpe, 'burst', *redi*, 'return', *emitte*, 'Release'). This joint invocation of
Hercules is turning into a ritualistic evocation of the dead hero. Note how
Megara, already identified by the Chorus (203), re-identifies herself with her
second word.

dispulsas manu abrumpe tenebras/**dispel and burst the darkness With
your hand:** note the violent language which will continue (*diducto*, 'rip',
281, *dirutis*, 'Shattering', 283, *scissa*, 'split', 285) and Megara's immediate
identification of Hercules with his *manus*, 'hand' (see on 118–22). For
rumpere and 'breaking out' of hell, see on 57–63. The imagery returns at 290
(*erumpe*) and will be employed in a transferred sense by Theseus in the final
act (*perfringe*, 1275: see further *ad loc.*).

nulla si retro uia/**If there is no way back:** Megara is still feeding off
Amphitryon's ending (*uiam*, 276). Note also *retro uia* at 55.

redi/**return:** intensifying Amphitryon's less forceful *remees* (277).

emitte tecum/**Release with yourself:** for the repetition of the same syllable at the end and beginning of juxtaposed words, see 67 and n. *ad loc.* For
emittere used of releasing/being released from the underworld, see on
77–83.

283–95 *qualis…talis*/**As…So:** Megara appeals to Hercules in a version of
the common formula for prayer: 'as you helped/acted in the past, so help/act
now'. Cf. Medea's similar (but much shorter) appeal to the Furies at *Med.*
16–17: *adeste…quales stetistis*, 'Come…as (in the past) you stood…'

praeceps citato: juxtaposition of synonyms or near-synonyms is a
Senecan mannerism. See e.g. 397, 536, 680, 683, 744, 763, 822, 950, 1082.

quaerens iter/**to find a…path:** as at *Tro.* 187, contrary to Fitch *ad loc.*

stetisti/**stood:** in the heroic sense, almost = 'took your stand'; cf. *stetit* of
Hercules at 791.

Tempe: the beautiful river valley of the Peneus in Thessaly between Mt
Ossa and Mt Olympus. It is often alluded to by Roman poets: see e.g. *Med.*
457 (*Thessala…Tempe*), Cat. 64.35, Virg. *Geo.* 4.317, Ov. *Met.* 7.222).
Seneca's 'scientific' view was that the two mountains concerned were separated not by Hercules but by an earthquake (*terrarum motu, NQ* 6.25.2). The
myth of Hercules' partition of the mountains is found also in Diodorus
(4.18.6) and in the epic of Seneca's nephew, Lucan (6.347–9), who describes
the 'cascade of sudden waters' of the river Peneus (*subitaeque ruinam…*

aquae) caused by Hercules' action. Lucan opens his eighth book by sardon-
ically naming Tempe the 'gorge/gullet of Hercules', *Herculeas fauces* (8.1).
The construction of waterways was very much a Roman activity. Octavian
and Agrippa had constructed waterways to form the Portus Iulius (Suet.
Aug. 16.1), and the emperor Nero became notorious for his attempt to produce one between Lake Avernus and the Tiber (Stat. *Silu.* 4.3.7–8, Tac. *Ann.*
15.42) and another through the Corinthian Isthmus (Suet. *Nero* 19.2). The
construction of a canal through the Isthmus was also entertained by the
emperor Gaius (Suet. *Gai.* 21). For Roman referentiality in *Hercules*, see
on 46–52.

pectore impulsus tuo...uia/struck by your chest...course: note the use
of a parenthesis to enlarge the simile; cf. *Thy.* 710–11, 734–6.

huc...et illuc/asunder: lit. 'here and there'. For this iambic trimeter line
opening, see 801, 999, *Med.* 222, and with variation *Ag.* 900.

Thessalus torrens/Thessaly's torrent: the river Peneus (modern Pineios),
134 miles in length, originating in the Pindus mountains and passing
through the Tempe valley before emptying into the Aegean. See previous n.

parentes liberos patriam petens/to find parents, children, homeland: two Senecan mannerisms on display, alliteration and asyndeton. For
similarly asyndetic lists involving family, see 379, 388, 630, 1260. The alliteration of *p* will climax through enjambement in *erumpe*, 'Burst' (290). For
asyndeton, see on 30–5.

erumpe rerum terminos/Burst...the bounds of things: the violent language continues (see on 279–83), this time applied to a 'grand' phrase, indicating at the ontological level the nature of Hercules' actions. Cf. the elder
Seneca *Suas.* 1.10 on Alexander the Great: (Fabianus' argument)
Alexandrum rerum naturae terminos supergressum, 'Alexander had trans-
gressed the bounds of the nature of things'. The *termini* of 'reality' in
Hercules, however, are not those of Seneca's father. They are the boundaries
which separate the different spheres of existence: hell, earth, heaven. Seneca
also explores the issue of 'boundary violation' in *Medea*, where the *termini*
are those separating land from ocean, violated by the Argonauts through
their breach of the 'sacrosanct covenants of the world' (*sacro...sancta foedera mundi*, 605–6; cf. 335). As Jason's experience in *Medea* shows, ontological breaches are moral breaches. For *rumpere* and 'breaking out' of hell,
see on 57–63; for boundary violation, see on 46–52.

auida...aetas/lusty time: the greed/lust of death, fate, and time are proverbial: see 555, 782, *Tro.* 400, *Ag.* 752, *Pha.* 1152, *Oed.* 164, 411; Tib. 1.3.4;
Virg. *Geo.* 2.492; Hor. *Odes* 2.18.30; Stat. *Silu.* 2.1.186, *Theb.* 11.410. See also

677: *auidum chaos*. Seneca also applies the epithet *auidus* to *pestis*, 'plague' (*Oed.* 4), and to Dis himself (*Ag.* 752). *Auidus* was, a member of the audience might remember, the epithet of Aeneas as he plucked the golden bough, the talisman for entry to the kingdom of the dead (*auidusque refringit | cunctantem*, 'lustily he breaks if off as it resists', Virg. *Aen.* 6.210–11).

oblitos sui lucisque pauidos ante te populos age/drive before you The self-forgetting throngs fearful of the light: imagery here of a Roman military triumph (cf. Hor. *Odes* 1.12.54: *egerit iusto domitos triumpho*, 'drive the conquered in just triumph'), sharpened by *spolia* to follow. The dead and other denizens of the underworld are regularly represented as afraid of the light: see e.g. 821–7 below; *Oed.* 608–9; *Ag.* 862; Virg. *Aen.* 8.246; Ov. *Met.* 5.358, *Fas.* 4.449–50 and (with respect to hell's king and queen) *Met.* 2.261; Stat. *Theb.* 8.32–3; Sil. 5.618–19. Self-forgetting seems, as Fitch and Billerbeck note *ad loc.*, to allude to the drinking of the river Lethe (mentioned at 680). For the plural *populos*, see on 186–91. For the repetition of the same syllable at the end and beginning of juxtaposed words (*ante te*), see 67 and n. *ad loc.* For military imagery in *Hercules*, see on 19–29.

indigna te sunt spolia/Spoils are not fit for you: again military imagery and again the Roman touch. For Roman referentiality in Hercules, see on 46–52. For *indignus* and *dignus*, see on 109–12. For *spolia*, see 51 and n. *ad loc.*; for triumphal imagery, see on 57–63.

295-308 Megara changes her tone, as she moves into *prosphonetikon* mode, envisaging a reunion with Hercules and loving welcome of her husband, although her final thoughts collapse into despair. Fitch *ad loc.* draws attention to some of the features of the *prosphonetikon* ('welcome-home poem', e.g. Catullus 9) present in this section.

295-8 *Magna sed nimium loquor*/But I speak too mightily: cf. Juno at 63 above, where the phraseology is similar, involving postponement of *sed* and *nimium*, as here: *leuia sed nimium queror*, 'But I complain too lightly'. Cf. also Andromache at *Tro.* 475: *tam magna timeo uota*, 'I fear such mighty prayers'. *Magna loqui* (often = 'to boast', as at Ov. *Tr.* 5.3.29) is a property later attributed to Hercules by Lycus (436). For change in emotion during a speech: cf. *Med.* 137 (Medea), *Tro.* 474 (Andromache). For *nimium* with an adjective, see on 186–91. For the postponement of conjunctions, see on 63–8.

unde illum...diem/How will that day come: there is an ellipse of a verb in this idiom; cf. e.g. Hor. *Serm.* 2.5.102, Luc. 7.28, Stat. *Silu.* 1.2.188–9. Such ellipses perhaps suggest intensity of emotion on the part of the speaker or poet.

te tuamque dexteram amplectar/clasp you and your right hand: exactly how Aeneas attempts to greet his father in the underworld (Virg. *Aen.* 6.697–8). There will be an interesting contrast between how Megara envisages greeting the returning Hercules and what actually happens. Like Aeneas, Megara will fail to embrace. There may also be an echo here of the Ovidian Laodamia's futile hope of embracing Protesilaus (*Her.* 13.115).

reditusque lentos nec mei memores querar/And scold your slow return, forgetting me: Megara is almost playing the elegiac *puella* here, using some of the standard vocabulary (*lentus, memor, queror*) to be found plentifully in Propertius and Ovid. *Nec mei memores*, 'forgetting me', points to a property of more than one archetypal hero: see e.g. Theseus in Catullus 64 (*immemor*: 123, 135, 248); Ulysses at Ov. *Her.* 1.41; Jason at *Med.* 560–2. The forgetfulness of the lover is a *topos* of erotic discourse: see e.g. Prop. 1.11.5, 19.1–6; Ov. *Her.* 2.105.

299–302 *tibi … tibi … tibi*/For thee … For thee … for thee: repetition, especially repetition (often initial) of the second-person pronoun, as here, is a common feature of invocations/prayers/hymns from the Hellenistic period onwards. See e.g. the *epithalamium* ode of *Medea* (71–3); Medea's invocation of Hecate at *Med.* 797ff.; Oedipus' invocation of Jupiter and others at *Oed.* 248ff.; Hecuba's dirge for Hector at *Tro.* 117ff.; the 'Victory Ode' of *Agamemnon* (310–87); the 'Bacchus Ode' of *Oedipus* (412ff.); Hippolytus' invocation of Diana at *Pha.* 60–4. Cf. Lucr. 1.6ff. (to Venus); Cat. 34.13ff. (to Diana); Hor. *Odes* 2.19.17–29 (to Bacchus); Virg. *Aen.* 8.293ff. (to Hercules); Ov. *Met.* 4.17–24 (to Liber). Cf. similar repetition later in the play at 597–9 and 658–9; see also 1231. Zwierlein rejects the consensus MS reading in 299, *tibi o*, accepted by most modern editors, and prints the emendation of Bothe, *tum tibi*.

o deorum ductor/O Leader of Gods: Jupiter, only here apparently receiving the noun *ductor*. *Ductor* has a military ring and seems, as Billerbeck notes *ad loc.*, a variant of the *imperator* title sometimes assigned to Jupiter (see e.g. Plaut. *Amphit.* 1121, *Rud.* 9). Seneca has a predilection for nouns ending in *-tor* (see e.g. *quaesitor*, 731, *Ag.* 24; *domitor*, 619, 903, 1066, *Ag.* 76; *deceptor*, *Thy.* 140; *uictor*, 278, 368, 409, etc.; *ultor*, 385, *Ag.* 205; *ductor*, 299, *Ag.* 236, 1007, *Thy.* 226; *auctor*, 250, 735, 1071, 1166, *Ag.* 294, 295, 385, *Pha.* 907, *Pho.* 349, etc.; *genitor*, 122, 509, 626, etc., *Ag.* 568, 597, *Thy.* 421, etc.; *excubitor*, *Thy.* 458; *rector*, 205, 517, 592, 730, *Ag.* 382, *Thy.* 607, etc.; *dominator*, 1181, *Thy.* 1078; *aestimator*, *Tro.* 546; *contemptor*, *Ag.* 605; *sortitor*, *Tro.* 982; *pastor*, 139, 232, 451, *Ag.* 731; *mactator*, *Tro.* 1002; *populator*,

Ag. 832; *subsessor, Pha.* 52; *stuprator, Pha.* 897; *assensor, Pha.* 1207; *donator, Pha.* 1217; *peremptor, Oed.* 221), some of them probably coined by Seneca, who seems to have been attracted by the sonorous, even portentous, quality of this ending. Many, including *ductor*, have distinctly Roman resonance. For Roman referentiality in *Hercules*, see on 46–52. See further Billerbeck (1988), 35–7. For *o* and the vocative, see on 205–9.

indomiti…tauri/**untamed bulls:** i.e. bulls not yet broken or 'tamed' for the yoke, a regular property of sacrificial victims; see *Oed.* 300, *Med.* 62, *Ag.* 354–5, Ov. *Fas.* 1.83. Only unblemished animals were fit for sacrifice. In this context such 'untamed' sacrificial animals reflect ironically the future 'untamed' sacrificer himself (*indomita uirtus*, 39, *indomitos…artus*, 1079). For sacrificial language in *Hercules*, see on 918–24.

centena…colla/**a hundred necks:** the Romans seem to have taken the heroic 'hecatomb', used in Greek literature of a large sacrifice, literally: see e.g. *Pha.* 500, Cat. 64.389, Hor. *Epod.* 17.39, Ov. *Met.* 8.152, Stat. *Silu.* 2.7.17.

frugum potens/**Queen of Crops:** Ceres, who receives the same title from Ovid (*Am.* 3.10.35). Some versions of Hercules' final labour have him initiated in the Eleusinian Mysteries before going to the underworld (Eur. *Herac.* 613, Diod. Sic. 4.25.1, Apollod. 2.5.12). Hence perhaps the importance of Ceres to Megara, who seems to be casting the goddess in the role of her husband's protector. Ceres, of course, is also an appropriate addressee because she had experience both of losing a loved one (Proserpina) to death and of bringing her back. The objective genitive with *potens* is common in titles of the gods: see *uentorum potens* (Neptune, *Oed.* 254), *tenebrarum potens* (Dis, *Oed.* 868), *potens Cypri* (Venus, Hor. *Odes* 1.3.1), *siluarum potens* (Diana, Hor. *CS* 1), *potens uteri* (Lucina, Ov. *Met.* 9.315).

secreta…sacra/**mystic rites:** the core Eleusinian Mysteries still remain essentially secret, but they seem to have been an intensely sensual experience of light, fire, darkness, voice, sights, sounds, and revelation, perhaps underscored by the imbibing of the *kykeon*, a compound drink regarded by some as psychoactive. The rites, which took place around the time of the autumnal/fall equinox, were essentially, it seems, a celebration of the restoration to life of Demeter/Ceres' daughter Persephone/Proserpina. Features such as the waving of long torches (see next n.), the wearing of myrtle wreaths, and the silence of the initiates (*muta fide*, 'by mute pact', 301) are attested. They are elsewhere in Senecan tragedy called the 'silent rites', *tacita sacra*: *Pha.* 107, *Tro.* 843. Here *tacitus* is applied to Eleusis itself (302). See also 842–7 below.

muta fide/**mute pact:** lit. 'mute loyalty', a property of Eleusinian initiates as of royal attendants and servants (see *Oed*. 799, *Thy*. 335, *HO* 477, 480, 535).

longas Eleusin tacita iactabit faces/**Silent Eleusis will wave the long torches:** Eleusis was a deme of Athens, about a dozen miles north-west of the centre of the city, famous for its sanctuary of Demeter/Ceres and Kore/ Persephone/Proserpina, to which flocked previous and potential initiates from far-flung parts of the Greek world, eager to participate in the 'secret rites'. The rites included the waving of long torches, mentioned in the previous n. and also referred to at *Pha*. 107: *iactare tacitis conscias sacris faces*, 'torch-waving in witness of the silent rites'; see also Stat. *Silu*. 4.8.51–2. Such torches are pictured in the representation of the rites on the Ninnion Tablet (*c*.370 BCE, now in the National Archaeological Museum in Athens). The silence of Eleusis alludes to the silence of the initiates. For the *mutus/tacitus* combination in stark juxtaposition, see 536.

303–5 An interesting and in part very Senecan statement. The idea that great success rewrites the past may be found in the exultations both of Medea, whose triumph over Jason restores (*inter alia*) the brother she dismembered, the realm she abandoned, the virginity she lost and the Golden Fleece (*Med*. 982–4), and of Atreus, whose triumph over his brother restores his adulterous wife's chastity and his sons' biological parentage (*Thy*. 1098–9). Worth noting here is the position of this fantasy of the dead restored to life immediately following the allusions to the Eleusinian Mysteries (see on 299–302): as Ceres brought about the restoration to life of her daughter, Proserpina, so Hercules' return will restore to life (in the mind) a dead brother and father. Beneath the fantasy, too, lies something colder and more real: the heroic *topos* (see Andromache at Hom. *Il*. 6.429–30, Briseis at Ov. *Her*. 3.52) that a husband compensates for the loss of father, mother, brother, etc.

restitutas fratribus…meis animas/**my brothers' lives restored:** like that of Proserpina; see above.

ipsum…patrem/**father himself:** Creon; see on 249–58 (*ipsumque*). Note the lengthening of the initial syllable of *patrem*, as at *Ag*. 537, *Tro*. 691, *Thy*. 41, *Pho*. 121, 617.

305–8 Megara's thoughts shift from potential triumph to despair.

maior…potestas/**mightier power:** i.e. the power of death.

sequimur/**we follow:** similarly Phaedra (*uirum sequamur*, *Pha*. 254) and Andromache (*coniugem sequerer*, *Tro*. 418) suggest 'following' their husbands into death. Interestingly Seneca's Antigone inverts the *topos* by promising to 'precede' her father in dying or 'follow' him in living (*si moreris*, *anticedo*; *si uiuis, sequor, Pho.* 76). Euripides' Megara expects death but seeks to live (*Herac.* 70ff.).

omnes tuo defende reditu, Sospes/return, Saviour, and protect all: for the semiotic ambiguity of *Sospes*, see on 275–8.

omnes trahe. trahes/drag all down. You'll drag all down: as Fitch observes *ad loc.*, Megara's final and despairing line is triggered by her own language: *trahe* begets *trahes* (verbal polyptoton: see on 112–18; and also anadiplosis, i.e. line-ending repeated as line-beginning). Such linguistic determinism is typical of Seneca *tragicus* (see 29–30: *bella* to *bella*) and is especially prominent in stichomythic exchanges (see 422–38, 499–56).

nec ullus eriget fractos deus/No god will lift the broken: a strong protestation of despair, undermining the assumptions of Megara's opening invocations.

309–31 Dialogue between Amphitryon and Megara.

309–13 Amphitryon's first direct speech to Megara.

O socia nostri sanguinis/O partner in our blood: Amphitryon begins his second speech, as he did his first at 205, with the formal *o* (see on 205–9). There he was addressing Jupiter; here he is addressing the sole surviving member of the Theban royal family, his *de facto* daughter-in-law. His grand, formal address contrasts sharply with his first address to Megara in Euripides' play: ὦ θύγατερ ('daughter', *Herac.* 88). When he first greets Hercules in Seneca's drama, he will again use the more formal address (*O nate*, 622). The phrase with which Amphitryon addresses Megara exactly reproduces that used by Cicero in his citation of an address by Prometheus to a chorus of brother-Titans (*Tusc.* 2.23), ascribed by some to an 'Aeschylean' *Prometheus Lyomenos*, by others to Accius' *Prometheus*. Is Amphitryon here playing a version of the bound and tortured Prometheus? Seneca shows a fondness for *socius* with the genitive (900, *Tro.* 677, *Med.* 568, etc.), perhaps derived from Ovid (see *Met.* 1.620, where Juno is *sociae generisque torique*, 'partner in both kin and bed'). Cf. Theseus' opening address to his wife: *O socia thalami*, 'O partner in my bed', *Pha.* 864. For the Romanness of the term, see on 900–8.

casta fide seruans/loyal, chaste custodian: lit. 'preserving with chaste loyalty'. *Casta fides*, the quintessential value of the Roman *matrona*, is what the adulterous Clytemnestra claims to have lost at *Ag.* 110 and which she professes to aim for at *Ag.* 241. Euripides' Heracles attributes this quality to his dead wife at *Herac.* 1372. The ablative in *casta fide* is one of manner, a sociative-instrumental function: see Woodcock §43.5.iv. For *fides*, see on 414–21; for Roman referentiality in *Hercules*, see on 46–52.

magnanimi/great-souled: an epic word (a Latin version of the Homeric μεγάθυμος, used in Virgil's *Aeneid* a dozen times, where it is applied to Aeneas, Jupiter *et al.*), applied by Amphitryon in this play to Hercules (here) and Theseus (647). Applied to Hercules also by Lucan (4.611) and Valerius (1.634), and by Statius to Theseus (*Theb.* 12.795), Achilles (*Ach.* 1.1) and Domitian (*Theb.* 12.814), it is used elsewhere in Senecan tragedy of Theseus (*Pha.* 869) and (with contextual irony) of Oedipus (*Oed.* 294, *Pho.* 182). It is used in the prose works twice. Leconte de Lisle also applies the epithet to the baby Hercules/Heracles—or at least to his future deeds: *tes faits magnanimes* ('L'Enfance d'Hèraklès', 46).

meliora mente concipe.../Be of better thoughts...: Amphitryon is playing the role of 'the advisor of restraint' in an unusual Senecan 'Passion-Restraint Scene'. Normally such scenes begin with a passionate outburst from a socially superior character (Clytemnestra, Phaedra, Medea, Atreus, Oedipus) followed by an attempt to calm that character by a socially inferior character (Nurse, Courtier, Wife, Daughter): see *Ag.* 125ff., *Med.* 150ff., *Oed.* 81ff., *Pho.* 182ff., *Pha.* 129ff., 246ff and *Pho.* 347ff. Cf. also the *Senex*, 'Old Man', at *Tro.* 512ff., Octavia's Nurse at *Oct.* 83ff., Deianira's Nurse at *HO* 275ff. Here in *Hercules* the second speaker is the passionate one and the counsel of restraint comes from her father-in-law. Other Senecan characters advocate restraint: e.g. Amphitryon at 973ff.; as does Seneca himself, who promotes the restraining (*compescere*) of anger as one of his two therapies (*Ira* 2.18.1).

aderit profecto/He will surely come: *adesse* is a favourite verb of Amphitryon (275, 277, 646); for its implications, see on 275-8. Note again, as with *aderit* at 275, an unannounced change of grammatical subject from one in the previous sentence: see on 30-5. *Profecto*, an allegedly 'prosaic' word ('truly/surely'), occurs again at *Ag.* 150, 227 (*adest profecto*); see also *HO* 713.

maior/greater: Amphitryon does not know it, but he is echoing Juno's fear of Hercules becoming greater because of his labours (*crescit malis*, 33).

313-16 Initial exchanges, employing the 'Stichworttechnik' used in *stichomythia*: see on 422-38.

Quod nimis miseri uolunt.../What the wretched want too much...: Megara shows similar scepticism in Euripides' play (*Herac.* 92). Here her criticism of Amphitryon's wishful thinking is in the form of a common *sententia*, found not only in public performance literature (drama and oratory) and in Ovid's erotic instructions (*Ars* 3.674) but even in Caesar's *Gallic War* (3.18.2). Jonson adapted it for his *Sejanus* IV.491-2. A corollary of this is the slowness to believe unfavourable news: *tarde quae credita laedunt credimus*, 'We are slow to believe where belief hurts' (Ov. *Her.* 2.9–10). Alcmena at *HO* 1979 takes a different and simpler tack: *misera mens incredula est*, 'the suffering mind does not believe'. Note the substantival use of *miser*, which is common in Senecan tragedy: see also 513, 1012. In *Troades* (unsurprisingly) this substantival use occurs eight times.

Immo quod metuunt nimis/No, what they fear too much: *quod nimis* is picked up and Megara's verb replaced with an antonym. *Immo* is used paradigmatically here 'to introduce the correction of a preceding statement' (*OLD*): see *Ag.* 6, *Ep. Mor.* 120.17. For the shortening of the final *o* of *immo*, see on 109–12.

prona est timoris semper in peius fides/Fear's conviction ever veers to the worse: *sententia* neatly and alliteratively expressed. Cf. Statius' trenchant description of fear: *pessimus in dubiis augur*, 'In a crisis the worst of prophets' (*Theb.* 3.6). Lucan dwells on the matter more wordily at 1.484–6. For this sententious use of *semper*, see e.g. 462, *Tro.* 1013, *Pha.* 161, 205.

317–24 Demersus ac defossus et... oppressus/sunk, buried, crushed: a trio of participial sibilants, suggesting Megara's contempt for Amphitryon's optimism as well as her umbrage at the suggestion that she is afraid. For a similar, triple set of modifiers, cf. *fessus ac deiectus et fletu grauis*, 'exhausted and downcast and weighted with tears', *Tro.* 449; *fessus...et deuinctus et pessumdatus*, 'exhausted and fettered and overwhelmed', *Ag.* 137. Note the combination, *ac...et*, in the *Tro.* passage, as here; cf. also *Oct.* 631. Euripides' Megara shows similar scepticism about the possibility of Hercules' return in her remarks to Amphitryon at *Herac.* 295–7. For *mergere* and descent into the underworld, see 422 and 674 below.

ad superos/to those above: for the ambiguity in the relative term, *superos*, see on 46–52.

cum per arentem plagam...abit/when he crossed the arid zone: Amphitryon here describes an otherwise unknown Herculean episode in which the hero's ship gets stranded in the Syrtes and Hercules makes his way on foot (*pedes*, 324). With *arentem plagam* cf. *solis aestiui plagas*, 'zones of the summer sun', 235. *Abit* is contracted perfect, as at 1151; cf. *petit* (244) and n. *ad loc.* *Abit* (*E*^pc*A*), also printed by Fitch (1987*a* and 2018) and Viansino (1993), has been preferred to *adit* (*E*^ac), favoured by Zwierlein and most modern editors. For discussion, see Fitch (2004*b*: 17).

bisque...et bis/and the twice...and twice: for the *-que...et* formulation, cf. *Pha.* 545, 1248, *Ag.* 232, *Oed.* 264–5. On the ebbing and returning, see Mela 1.35 cited next n.

deprensus haesit Syrtium breuibus uadis/caught stuck in Syrtes' shoals: the Syrtes were notoriously dangerous sand-banks off the coast of north Africa (Libya), referred to also at *Pha.* 570, *Thy.* 292, *Ag.* 64, 480. The *locus classicus* of their depiction: Luc. 9.303–18; see also Pliny *HN* 5.26–8 and Mela 1.35, who comments on the 'alternating movements of the sea flowing in and out' of the shoals (*alternos motus pelagi affluentis et refluentis*). Seneca elsewhere writes of those 'caught in the waters of Syrtes' (*deprensi mari Syrtico, Beat. Vit.* 14.1). For *breuibus uadis*, see also *Ag.* 572, Virg. *Aen.* 5.221; for *uadum*, see on 679–88.

puppe fixa/with vessel Grounded: for *fixus* of a grounded ship, see (of Agamemnon's fleet) *acutis rupibus fixae rates*, 'ships grounded/impaled on jagged rocks', *Ag.* 571.

325–8 *Iniqua raro maximis uirtutibus Fortuna parcit*/Hostile Fortune rarely spares the greatest Virtues: cf. 524–5 below and the similar remarks concerning 'fate' at *Pol.* 3.2: *o dura fata et nullis aequa uirtutibus*, 'O fate, insensate and kind to no virtues'. The statement is a variation on the *topos* of the dangers of human eminence (see e.g. Hor. *Odes* 2.10), and more specifically of *uirtus animosa*: see 201 and n. *ad loc.*, and on 197–201. For *Fortuna* (initial *f* is not capitalized by Zwierlein), see on 524–32; for 'fate', see on 178–82; for *uirtus*, 'virtue', and its central role in this play, see on 35–40. For *Fortuna* and the dangers of human eminence, see *Pha.* 1123ff., *Ag.* 57–107, *Tro.* 259ff., *Oed.* 8–11, *HO* 675–99, *Oct.* 377–80, 897–8; also *NQ* 3 Pref. 7, *Ep. Mor.* 19.9, 94.72–4. *Iniquus* suggests an attitude of hostility, spite or prejudice rather than injustice: see Servius' comment *ad* Virg. *Aen.* 5.809: *dis iniquis, hoc est aduersis*; cf. *iniqui…Tonantis*, 'hostile Thunderer' (*Ag.* 594–5). See also Nisbet and Hubbard *ad* Hor. *Odes* 1.2.47: 'as applied to the gods it [*iniquus*] is a euphemism for *iratus*'.

nemo…potest/No one…long: 'imitated' by Thomas Hughes, *The Misfortunes of Arthur*, II.iii.39: 'No danger can be thought both safe and oft.' Note the shortening of the final *o*, as e.g. at 1261, *Ag.* 153, 284, *Thy.* 213, 312. Indeed the final *o* in *nemo*, though it can be either short or long in Senecan tragedy (for long, see *Med.* 430, 565), is far more often short. See further on 109–12.

quem saepe transit casus, aliquando inuenit/Whom chance often misses, someday it finds: a ringing *sententia* (see on 125–204 introd.) to close the initial scene of Act II. For the thought, cf. *NQ* 6.1.13: *circumit fatum et, si quid diu praeterit, repetit*, 'Fate circles and, if it has long missed something, it seeks it again'. *Casus* is a wide-ranging term, covering both a literal 'fall' (*Tro.* 1111–12) and that which 'befalls', 'occurrence/accident/chance' (*Oed.*

809, *Tro.* 273). It is often aligned, as here, with *fortuna*: see e.g. *Med.* 519–20 (*casus...fortuna*); *Thy.* 34–6 (*fortuna...casus*); *Pha.* 1123 (where, like *Fortuna* at *Ag.* 72, it is the subject of *rotare*: *quanti casus humana rotant*, 'How chance wheels man about')—cf. *Oct.* 927, *HO* 715. For *casus* in Seneca's prose works, see e.g. *Ep. Mor.* 71.3: *necesse est multum in uita nostra casus possit, quia uiuimus casu*, 'By necessity chance has much power in our lives, because we live by chance'. The present *sententia* is repeated in Hughes, *The Misfortunes of Arthur* II.iii.42: 'Whom chance hath often miss'd, chance hits at length'. *Aliquando* is an ordinary language, so-called 'unpoetic' word, used only five times in Senecan tragedy (including twice in this play: see also 925) and 213 times in his prose works.

Enter LYCUS *from the palace...*'*brandishes*' *the sceptre of Thebes*: it is not stated where Lycus enters from. Scott Smith (2011) *ad loc.* suggests 'from the wings'. He will definitely exit stage left (to the city) to sacrifice to Neptune (515), and it seems preferable not to have him enter from where he will exit and near where Megara and Amphitryon are positioned (by the altar before the temple, stage left: see on 616–17), but from the palace itself, which would reinforce his 'tyrannical' status, as does the sceptre which he brandishes (for which see n. below). If, as seems likely, Juno exited into the palace (see n. after 123–4), Lycus' entrance from the palace would associate him immediately with the anti-Herculean figures of Juno and the Furies. In Euripides' *Heracles* the stage-building represents the house of Heracles, from which the Euripidean Lycus obviously does not enter. He enters from the side (*Herac.* 138–9).

329–31 A transitional passage, announcing the entrance of a new character, Lycus: see on 202–4, where the Chorus announce the entrance of new *dramatis personae* without any evaluation of their 'character', i.e. moral nature. Here Megara interprets facial expression, gait, and carriage as indices of Lycus' inner self: cf. *Tro.* 518, 522–3, *Med.* 178 (where, as here, a Passion-Restraint scene has led to a confrontation with an enemy); *Tro.* 999–1000, *Med.* 380, 394, *Pha.* 431–3, *Oct.* 435–6. See also on 472–6 (*parum forti gradu*).

Sed ecce saeuus...Lycus/But look, the savage...Lycus: almost as if to underscore Megara's pessimism, instead of the arrival of the object of her and Amphitryon's prayers, Hercules, the stage witnesses the appearance of an anti-Hercules, Lycus, the meaning of whose name ('wolf': Greek λύκος) seems triggered by its modifier, *saeuus*, 'savage'. *Sed ecce*, 'But look', is an obvious phrase to introduce a new (or returning) character: see *sed ecce* at *Ag.* 388 (introducing Eurybates), *Ag.* 586 (introducing a new chorus), *Oct.* 435 (introducing Nero). Sometimes *ecce* serves this purpose by itself: *Oed.*

838, *Med.* 738, *Thy.* 918; sometimes *sed*: 202, 827, *Pha.* 583, *Oct.* 844—cf. the use of ἀλλά in Attic tragedy: Aesch. *Pers.* 150, Soph. *Ant.* 155, Eur. *Hipp.* 170. For a different use of *ecce*, see 47, 793, 1040, 1298, 1300, and of *sed ecce*, see 987.

minas uultu gerens/face marked by threats: Seneca in both the tragedies and the prose works gives special attention to the 'gaze/look' (*uultus*) of the powerful and arrogant: e.g. *Tro.* 1000, *Thy.* 609, *Const.* 2.13.3, *Ira* 3.19.1, *Ben.* 1.9.2. For good reason, since *uultus*, 'face' (the looking part of the face, the 'gaze' or even 'eyes', as opposed to *os*, the speaking part, or 'mouth', and *facies*, the physical contours themselves) is for Seneca (as it was for Cicero; *De Orat.* 3.222) the site of emotion and feeling. Thus: *totus in uultu est dolor*, 'the whole pain is in the face' (the Nurse to Clytemnestra at *Ag.* 128, Jason on Medea at *Med.* 446). Similarly: Clytemnestra's 'ferocious face mirrors the crimes' (*uultusque prae se scelera truculenti ferunt*, *Ag.* 950); the feelings of Phaedra (*Pha.* 363) and Octavia (*Oct.* 541–2) are 'betrayed' by their 'face' (*uultu*); the 'face of fear' (*trepidus...uultus*) in the case of Atreus' sons would reveal much (*Thy.* 330–1). See also *HO* 247–8: *in uultus dolor | processit omnis*, 'all the pain went into her face'. Though the idea that thoughts and feelings can be seen in the face is commonplace (see e.g. Cic. *Pis.* 1; Sall. *Cat.* 15.5; Ov. *Ars* 1.574, *Met.* 2.447; Sen. Rhet. *Con.* 2.5.2), it is also grounded in Seneca's theory of the passions, in which he underscores the *signa* or *indicia*, the physical marks of the passions, especially (but not only) of anger: see *Ira* 1.1.7, *neque enim ulla uehementior intrat concitatio quae nihil moueat in uultu*, 'no violent disturbance enters without affecting the face'. Cf. *Ben.* 6.12.1: *uultus tuus loquitur*, 'Your face speaks'; *HO* 705: *uultus loquitur quodcumque tegis*, 'Your face speaks whatever you hide'. See also *Ag.* 237–8, 950. Note that, though the realities of masked performance in both Greek and Roman drama prevented actor's faces from being seen, references to facial expression are still made while the masked character is on stage, as here and at *Med.* 446: see also e.g. Aesch. *Cho.* 731, Soph. *Ant.* 526ff., Eur. *Hipp.* 172, Ter. *Ad.* 643. Indeed, even though actors borrow emotions (*adfectus*) from their masks (Quintilian *Inst.* 11.3.73), it is necessary for any complex visual 'emotionality' (blushes, profound sorrow, etc.)—in Attic as well as Senecan tragedy—to be reported by others. Facial expressions are often described in Senecan tragedy when a character enters, as here: see also e.g. *Ag.* 950; *Tro.* 522–3, 1000; *Pha.* 829, 990.

For *uultus* as the looking part of the face, the 'gaze' or the 'eyes', see Virg. *Aen.* 9.251. It is used often in this sense by Ovid (e.g. *Met.* 1.265, 5.30) and Seneca (e.g. 371, 596, 641, 721, 724, 953, 1022, 1044, 1174, 1334; *Thy.* 265,

331, 422, 506, 609, 635, 719, 899, 936, 950; *Pha.* 363, 433, 692; *Ag.* 49, 128, 238; *Oed.* 326, 509; *Pho.* 43, 178; *Tro.* 933, 966, 1092, 1152). Here *uultu* = the 'face' of the actor wearing the tragic mask (almost = 'mask')—cf. *Thy.* 422, 506, 936; *Oed.* 1003; *Med.* 396, 446; *Pha.* 1168. For metatheatrical language in *Hercules*, see on 109–12.

qualis animo est, talis incessu uenit/Gait matching his spirit: entrance announcements regularly comment on the *incessus*, *gradus*, or *gressus* of an entering character: see e.g. 523; *Ag.* 388 (Eurybates), 587 (Cassandra), 781 (Clytemnestra); *Pha.* 431 (Nurse); *Oed.* 1004 (Jocasta); *Tro.* 522 (Ulysses), 999 (Pyrrhus); *Med.* 382 (Medea)—cf. *HO* 254 (Deianira), 702 (Deianira); *Oct.* 435 (Nero). Romans paid particular attention to a person's gait or mode of walking, which was regularly treated as index of gender, moral character, and/or social status: see *Tranq.* 17.4, *NQ* 7.31.2, *Ep. Mor.* 52.12, 114.3, and O'Sullivan (2011). For depictions of a character's physical behaviour or appearance onstage in Senecan tragedy, see on 991–5.

aliena dextra sceptra concutiens/Brandishing another's sceptre: an unusual detail (and stage direction). Lycus is not just gripping or bearing his sceptre (*sceptrum tenere/gerere*), but wielding it like a weapon, like Hector 'brandishing' (*concutit*) his arms at *Tro.* 683. Cf. the announcement of Phaedra, sword drawn, at *Pha.* 1157–8. For *alienus*, used, as here, for disparagement or mockery, see e.g. *Ag.* 551, *aliena...tela*, 'another's spear'; Ov. *Met.* 9.76, *arma aliena*, 'another's weapons'. For *dextra*, see on 118–22; for *sceptra*, see on 63–8.

Pulls hood of the ricinium *over her head*: clearly the hood is over her head at 355 and apparently not over her head at 202. This seems the apposite moment for Megara's hooding. For the *ricinium*, see on 354–7.

332–523 The 'Lycus Scene'. The 'tyrant', a regular figure in Greek tragedy, was a common figure on the Roman stage from its inception (see e.g. Naevius' *Lycurgus*), and was perhaps most popularly attested in the many plays on the Atreus-Thyestes saga from Ennius to Seneca (see Boyle 2017: lxxiii–lxxviii). The elder Seneca's works display the centrality of the figure in Roman political discourse by relating its importance to the schools of declamation (*Con.* 1.7, 2.5, 3.6, 4.7, 5.8). Seneca himself in his treatise on kingship, *De Clementia* (1.12.3–4), sets up the tyrant as a negative model for the ideal ruler, citing Accius' *Atreus*.

This long scene should be compared to other second act dialogues involving monarchs or 'tyrants': e.g. that between Medea and Creon at *Med.* 177–300, between Pyrrhus and Agamemnon at *Tro.* 250–352, and between Atreus and the Courtier/*Satelles* at *Thy.* 176–335. Cf. also the dialogues between

Oedipus and Creon at *Oed.* 511–29, 668–708, between Andromache and Ulysses at *Tro.* 524–812, Jocasta and Eteocles at *Pho.* 645–64, and between Seneca and Nero at *Oct.* 435–592. Worth noting, too, is the famous dialogue between Seneca and Nero described by Tacitus at *Ann.* 14.53–6, during which Seneca asks to retire from public life and which Tacitus places in 62 CE. One of the functions of such scenes in Senecan tragedy is, as here, to provide a context for theatrical monarchs to display their character, values and attitude to power. Among the more interesting features of this display is Lycus' quintessentially Roman preoccupation with lack of social pedigree (*nouitas*) and individual 'manliness/virtue' (*uirtus*): see below. Another much discussed aspect of the scene is its evident relationship to the famous 'wooing' scene of Shakespeare's *Richard III*: see Introd. §VIII: 135–6. Miola (1992: 82–3), notes other Renaissance 'wooing scenes' which seem indebted: Arée's wooing of Octave in Garnier's *Porcie*, Richard's of Elizabeth in Legge's *Richardus Tertius*, Locrine's of Estrild in *Locrine*, Malevole's of Maria in Marston's *The Malcontent*. For further discussion of the 'Lycus Scene', see Introd. §VII, 78–90.

332–57 In a 'closed soliloquy' (i.e. unheard by anyone onstage) Lycus opens up his mind. Entrance monologue soliloquies ('open' or 'closed') or asides of a 'self-analytical' or 'character-defining' kind are a feature of Senecan tragedy and an index of its concern with psychological interiority: see e.g. *Ag.* 108ff., 226ff.; *Med.* 1ff., 116ff., 179ff., 431ff.; *Tro.* 1ff., 861ff.; *Pha.* 85ff., 835ff.; *Oed.* 1ff.; *Thy.* 176ff., 404ff., 491ff., 885ff.—see also the entrance monody of Octavia at *Oct.* 1ff. and the entrance monologues of Seneca and Nero at *Oct.* 377ff. Seneca seems likely to have been influenced by the entrance monologues of Euripidean tragedy (see e.g. those at *Bacch.* 215ff., *Tro.* 860ff.), which are not, however, 'asides'. Indeed no aside of pure form (involving suspension or freezing of dramatic time) seems to occur in extant fifth-century Attic tragedy (Tarrant 1978: 243–46). The often-cited passage in Euripides' *Hecuba* (*Hec.* 736–51: see e.g. Bain 1977: 13–15) is partially heard self-address, and seems a precursor of the aside-convention rather than an instance of it. The earliest instances of 'pure asides' clearly attested are found in Aristophanes, and asides become a common and accepted convention in later comedy and (probably) in Hellenistic drama as a whole. They may have been a standard feature of Augustan tragedy.

Senecan entrance monologue asides may occur right at the start of an act, like those of Helen (*Tro.* 861ff.), Clytemnestra (*Ag.* 108ff.), Oedipus (*Oed.* 764ff.), and Thyestes (*Thy.* 404–20), or in the middle of an act, like that of Lycus here and those of Aegisthus (*Ag.* 226–33), Atreus (*Thy.* 491–507),

Creon (*Med.* 179-87), and Jason (*Med.* 431-46). Frequently, too, like other 'closed soliloquies' such monologues involve, as here, a suspension of dramatic time. Their psychological nakedness is both evident and potent, often manifesting itself in a fusion of emotional chaos and rational analysis, reminiscent of Ovid's *Heroides* and *Metamorphoses*. Here the tone is one of self-assurance, pride, and practical optimism. Though entrance monologues are often used to establish dramatic authority, Lycus' preoccupation with social status and, at line 348, his own *nouitas* (a Senecan tragic *hapax* and the first use of the word in poetry in the sense of 'lacking pedigree') points to personal insecurity beneath the confidence and power. *Virtus* is not enough. There is something about the situation of Lycus which would have resonated with Seneca, himself a *nouus homo*, who strove to create his distinct position and identity from a preoccupation with *uirtus*. Tacitus captured this well in his portrait of Seneca in *Annals* 14, where he has Seneca speak of his *nouitas* in the midst of *nobiles* with their *longa decora* (14.53). For a Shakespearean entrance monologue dealing with the issue of the speaker's disadvantageous birth, see Edmund's opening soliloquy in *KL* I.ii.1-22.

What Seneca dramatizes is the mind of a tyrant. It is one of several and diverse portraits of power in Seneca's tragedies: see e.g. *Ag.* 981-1000 (Aegisthus), *Med.* 179-87 (Creon), *Tro.* 250-91 (Agamemnon), *Pha.* 903-58 (Theseus), *Oed.* 669-708 (Oedipus), *Pho.* 651-64 (Eteocles), *Thy.* 176-204, 491-507, 885-919 (Atreus); see also *Oct.* 820-43 (Nero). Though the figure of the 'tyrant' loomed large in the declamatory exercises of the rhetorical schools (see on 332-57), no exercise is attested comparable to Seneca's dramatic portraits, of which the presentation of Lycus is an especially nuanced example. Resonating with Seneca's audience, as it did later with Tacitus, would have been the issue of imperial succession: the nature of the transfer of supreme power and the qualities (ideal or otherwise) of the new ruler. Seneca's *De Clementia*, perhaps written shortly after *Hercules*, investigates the latter. Here the focus is on the psychology of a usurper of power, and the portrait produced is far more complex than that of the simple villain of Euripides' play. The Greek dramatist seems to have invented the figure of Lycus (Bond 1981: xxviii); Seneca not only makes of him a foil to Hercules, a quasi-parody of the achievements of *clara uirtus*, but gives him impressive, psychological depth and relevance to imperial Rome: see further on 337-41. For Roman referentiality in *Hercules*, see on 46-52.

332-6 A boastful and detailed description of Lycus' *regnum*, using place-names (Thebes, Phocis, Cithaeron, Isthmos) as markers both of extent and value. Each of the names comes with a history—a pedigree, as it were, to add lustre to a man without one. In a play with such an obsession with *locus* (see on 1–5), this extensive description of 'place' makes Lycus a paradigm of the newly *located* man. There is overt irony in this violator of boundaries listing the boundaries of his new *locus* to project his new identity. Contrast Medea, who at *Med.* 211–16 lists her former Colchic boundaries to describe the *locus* (both geographic and societal) which she has lost. For geographical/topographical catalogues in Senecan tragedy (of which there are many), see e.g. 1163–5, 1323–7 below; *Pha.* 285–9; *Ag.* 315–18•; *Oed.* 424–8; *Tro.* 8–14, 814–57; *Med.* 705–27; *Thy.* 369–79; *Pho.* 124–30. For the Romanizing 'global catalogue', see on 1321–41. For Senecan tragic catalogues generally, see on 6–18. Billerbeck *ad loc.* compares 'die wichtigtuerische, breitspurige Art' of Lycus' speech with that of the anonymous tragic fragment cited by Seneca at *Ep. Mor.* 80.7.

opulenta…loca/rich places: *opulentus* is similarly used of Thebes by Antigone at *Pho.* 54 (*opulenta…regna*, 'rich kingdom(s)').

quidquid uberi…solo…quidquid…quidquid/all that…With fertile soil, all that…All that: Phocis (see below), being predominantly mountainous, has little fertile soil (Billerbeck and Guex *ad loc.* mention 'la vallée du Céphise' and 'la plaine de Krisa'), but Lycus is bragging, and braggarts are not the most accurate of speakers. It is well known, too, that Seneca is not famous for geographical exactitude. There is thus little justification for altering the text to the unattested *uberis…soli* (used of Boeotian fields at *Pho.* 130) with Heinsius, Karsten, Müller, Zwierlein, Fitch (1987*a* and 2018), Viansino (1993), and Giardina (2007). Caviglia, Chaumartin, and Billerbeck join me in printing the attested reading. The ablative is instrumental (see Woodcock §43.1). Of relevance (wrongly dismissed by Fitch *ad loc.*) is Ovid's description of Phocis as *terra ferax*, 'fertile land' (*Met.* 1.314). For the anaphora of *quidquid*, see on 30–5.

obliqua Phocis/sloping Phocis: mountainous region (hence *obliqua*) of central Greece in which Delphi was situated. It lay between Locris and Boeotia, of which Thebes was the major city; it was bounded on the south by the Gulf of Corinth.

Ismenos: a river in Boeotia, which flowed past Thebes, rising to the south of the city and proceeding north into the Theban plain. It is named elsewhere in Senecan tragedy: see e.g. 1163 below, *Ag.* 318• (Boyle), *Oed.* 42, *Pho.* 116—also *HO* 141. Allusion to a place or people by reference to a local river is a common technique of Greek and Roman poets from Homer onwards (*Il.* 2.825–6). See e.g. 1163 below, *Ag.* 316–18•, *Oed.* 427–8, *Med.* 373–4, *Tro.* 8–11, *Pho.* 127.

quidquid Cithaeron…uidet/All that's viewed by…Cithaeron: *uidere* is regularly used with inanimate subjects in Seneca and other authors: in

Senecan tragedy, see e.g. *Ag.* 95 (*nemus*, 'grove'), 409 (*ratis*, 'ship'), 885 (*extremae dapes*, 'last course'); *Tro.* 785 (*muri*, 'walls'); *Med.* 44–5 (Phasis, Pontus, Isthmos), 212 (Pontus); *Pho.* 543–4 (*patria*, 'fatherland'), 613 (*mare*, 'sea'). For Cithaeron, see on 231–4.

   bina findens Isthmos exilis freta/slender Isthmos, splitting the two straits: the Isthmus of Corinth and its double shore or two seas (the Ionian Sea and the Aegean/Myrtoan Sea) are often alluded to in Latin poetry and in Senecan tragedy: see e.g. 1164–5 below; *Ag.* 564–5; *Med.* 35–6; *Oed.* 266–7; *Thy.* 113, 124–5, 181–2, 628–9; *Pho.* 374–5; *HO* 82–4; Hor. *Odes* 1.7.2; Prop. 3.21.22; Ov. *Her.* 12.104, *Met.* 6.419–20, *Fas.* 6.495–6; Luc. 1.101; Stat. *Theb.* 1.120, 7.107. Thinness or narrowness are regular properties of the Isthmus (*artus*, *Ag.* 564, *gracilis*, *Thy.* 113). The city itself, situated in the northern Peloponnese on the southern side of the Isthmus, is regularly described as *bimaris*, 'of two seas': *Oed.* 282, Hor. *Odes* 1.7.2, Ov. *Her.* 12.27, *Met.* 5.407. The line is inappropriately deleted by B. Schmidt, Peiper and Richter, Leo, and Fitch (1987*a* and 2018). The Greek orthography, *Isthmos*, is retained for the Latin text in accordance with the MS reading.

337–41 Seneca has Romanized this Greek figure. He seems to have been introduced into the story by Euripides (see Introd. §VI, 63), who gives him a family connection to the Theban throne (through Lycus an earlier Theban king, husband of Dirce: *Herac.* 26–34) and has him come to power in the midst of civil strife (*Herac.* 34). Seneca's Lycus has no aristocratic pedigree; he is aggressively a *nouus homo*, 'new man', parading his *nouitas* (348) and *uirtus* (340) in opposition to the 'idle' aristocracy with their inherited wealth, nobility and 'titles'. This issue of 'family', *genus* (39, 340, 347), is at the forefront of his mind, as is political marriage (345–8): both will guide his actions. For the *uirtus* versus *genus* debate as a criterion for individual worth, see e.g. Cic. *Verr.* 5.180, Sall. *Iug.* 85 (speech of the *nouus homo*, Marius), Juv. *Sat.* 8, and Acc. *Diomedes* frag. 272 Klotz: *non genus uirum ornat, generis uir fortis loco*: 'It's not the case that birth adorns a man, that a man is brave by the status of his birth'. Seneca himself is equally explicit (*Ep. Mor.* 44.5):

> quis est generosus? ad uirtutem bene a natura compositus...
> non facit nobilem atrium plenum fumosis imaginibus...
> animus facit nobilem.

> Who is well-born? The man well fitted by nature for virtue...
> An atrium filled with grimy busts does not make a nobleman...
> Mind makes a nobleman.

For Roman referentiality in *Hercules*, see on 46–52.

***non uetera patriae*:** again the dactyl-tribrach combination at the start of the line. See 76 and n. *ad loc.*

***ignauus heres*/idle heir:** so Sallust (*Iug.* 85.14) represents Marius, faced with criticism of his own *nouitas*, abusing the aristocracy for their *ignauia*, 'idleness'. Members of Seneca's audience familiar with Virgil's *Georgics* and/ or *Aeneid* may have caught the echo here of *ignauum pecus*, 'idle herd', Virgil's description of the 'drones', *fuci*, of the community of bees (*Geo* 4.168, *Aen.* 1.435).

***nobiles...aui*/noble Forebears:** the *nobiles*, Roman 'nobility', were the members of consular families, i.e. families (patrician and plebeian) who boasted members who had held the highest political office, the consulship. Roman society was constructed from a strict hierarchy of classes, at the top of which were the *nobiles*, who alone had the right to *imagines*, wax portrait masks of distinguished ancestors (*aui*). These *imagines* were displayed in the houses of the *nobiles* and worn by actors at family funerals and other ceremonial occasions.

***altis inclitum titulis genus*/family famed for lofty titles:** such titles would embrace not only those derived from political office, but also names derived from special accomplishments ('Africanus', 'Numantinus', 'Torquatus', 'Coruus', 'Magnus', 'Felix', 'Augustus', 'Pater Patriae', etc.: see Ov. *Fas.* 1.587–616, *Clem.* 1.14.2). These *tituli* would be proudly displayed with the ancestral *imagines* (see previous n.). For *tituli*, see Prop. 4.11.32, Ov. *Fas.* 1.602, Luc. 8.8.73. *Inclitus*, 'famed', which appears three times in *Hercules*, including twice in this speech (also at 347), is a word of some pedigree itself, found in Ennius' *Annales* (*Horatius inclutus*, *Ann.* frag. 123 Skutsch) and tragedies (*Alexander* frag. 48 Jocelyn), but clearly already regarded as 'grand', since it is only found in paratragic contexts in Plautus (see Jocelyn 1967: 220). Lycus uses it (on both occasions) of Megara's *genus* in an almost parodic manner.

***clara uirtus*/renowned virtue:** for this see on 35–40.

***qui genus iactat.../Flaunting one's birth...*:** a neat closural *sententia* to end the section. For the thought, see Seneca's own attack on so-called *nobilitas* at *Ep. Mor.* 44.5: *nemo in nostram gloriam uixit nec quod ante nos fuit nostrum est*, 'No past life was for our glory nor is what preceded us ours'. See also *Ben.* 3.28.2. Cf. Acc. *Diomedes* frag. 272 Klotz (cited above), Ov. *Met.* 13.140–1. For denunciations of pedigree, see Sall. *Iug.* 85 and Juvenal's attack in *Sat.* 8. For *genus iactare*, see Hor. *Odes* 1.14.13, Ov. *Her.* 17.51. For *sententiae*, see on 125–204 (introd.).

341–8 In an avalanche of *sententiae* (for which see on 125–204 introd.), Lycus acknowledges his awareness of the instability of power wrested by force or hated—and its attendant fear. For the latter, see *Oed.* 705–6:

> qui sceptra dura saeuus imperio gerit,
> timet timentis. metus in auctorem redit.

> The savage who kings it with merciless power
> Fears those who fear. Terror recoils on its author.

For violent power's instability, see *Tro.* 258:

> uiolenta nemo imperia continuit diu.

> Violent rule has never lasted long.

Cf. *Med.* 196, *Thy.* 215–17, 258–9, *Pho.* 660, *Ira* 3.16.2, *Clem.* 1.11.4, 1.25.3; cf. also Hor. *Odes* 3.4.65–6, and, related to this, 737–45 below. Lycus' lines here had a literary impact. Cunliffe (1893: 68) saw lines 341–5 as influencing Shakespeare in *King John* (III.iii.135–8):

> A sceptre snatch'd with an unruly hand
> Must be as boisterously maintain'd as gain'd;
> And he that stands upon a slipp'ry place
> Makes nice of no vile hold to stay him up.

Fitch (2018) *ad loc.* cites Voltaire's adaptation of lines 345–8 at *Mérope* 1.4.291–4:

> J'ai besoin d'un hymen utile à ma grandeur
> Qui détourne de moi le nom d'usurpateur,
> Qui fixe enfin les voeux de ce peuple infidèle,
> Qui m'apporte pour dot l'amour qu'on a pour elle.

See also the imitation of 341–2 at Hughes's *The Misfortunes of Arthur*, I.iv.95–6: 'The wrongful sceptre's held with trembling hand. | Whose rule wants right, his safety's in his sword.'

But note that, in contrast to tyrannical figures such as Atreus (*Thy.* 204–18) and Eteocles (*Pho.* 654–9), Lycus adopts a plan designed to change the Theban people's hatred, even if he intends to resort to a typical tyrant's behaviour should that plan fail. The relationship of king to subject, ruler to ruled—an issue at the heart of Rome's autocracy—is a prominent theme of *De Clementia* and a recurrent topic of the tragedies: see e.g. 489, 737–47; *Med.* 195–6, 221–5, 252–7; *Pho.* 653–64; *Tro.* 332–6; *Oed.* 699–706; *Thy.*

205–18. See also *Ira* 2.31.3, *Oct.* 450–61, *HO* 1590–2, Soph. *Ant.* 506–7. For Roman referentiality in *Hercules*, see on 46–52.

Rapta sed trepida manu sceptra/But stolen sceptres…With trembling hand: on the fear experienced by rulers, see also *Oed.* 699–700, 705–6 (also *Oct.* 441), *Ag.* 73, *Thy.* 207–8, 447–9, 599–606, *Clem.* 1.7.3, 13.1–3, 19.5, *Ira* 2.11.3, *Ep. Mor.* 14.10, 105.4; its especial association with kings and tyrant-figures is a major theme of Plato's *Republic* (see e.g. 579d–e) and a commonplace of the Greco-Roman literary tradition: see e.g. Aesch. *PV* 224–5, Enn. *Trag. Inc.* frag. 348 Jocelyn, Pub. Syr. 379: *multos timere debet quem multi timent*, 'He should fear many whom many fear'. For the postponement of *sed*, see on 63–8. For *sceptra*, see on 63–8.

omnis in ferro est salus…strictus tuetur ensis/All safety lies in steel…The drawn sword protects: Lycus' position is unwittingly and ironically cited by 'Nero' as the latter's own policy at *Oct.* 456: *ferrum tuetur principem*, 'steel protects the emperor'. It is, as Billerbeck observes *ad loc.*, 'eine programmatische Variation' of the *oderint dum metuant* apophthegm (discussed below on 348–53). For Nero, as for Lycus, such protective steel proved illusory. Contrast the Senecan thesis that the *certissima salus*, 'surest safety' for the ruler lies in *clementia*, 'clemency' (*Clem.* 1.11.4, 19.6). For the tyrant's use of *arma*, see e.g. *Clem.* 1.12.3.

quod ciuibus tenere te inuitis scias/What you know you hold against the city's will: such generalizing second-person singulars are often used in 'sententious' pronouncements: see e.g. *Thy.* 195–6, 416, *Pha.* 876. The present potential subjunctive is used here, as at 463–4, *Oed.* 26, *Tro.* 254, and commonly in Latin of all periods, for such generalizing statements: Woodcock §119.

alieno in loco haut stabile regnum est/In an alien place Power is unstable: a *sententia* of wide-ranging import, applicable to Hercules, the great transgressor of boundaries who is ever *alieno in loco*, as well as to Lycus. For the thematic importance of *locus* in this play, see on 1–5 and Introd. §VII. For the insecurity of power on quite different grounds, see the remarks of the *Satelles* at *Thy.* 217: *instabile regnum est*; cf. also *Tro.* 258–9, *Med.* 196. Note how Shakespeare's Richard III tries to stabilize his power through royal marriage (*Richard III* IV.ii.60–1):

> I must be married to my brother's daughter
> Or else my kingdom stands on brittle glass.

Some members of Seneca's audience may have thought of the emperor Claudius, who after the attempted coup of Messalina, stabilized his power through marriage in 49 CE to a 'Julian', a great-granddaughter of Augustus, the younger Agrippina, the death of whose brother had paved the way for Claudius' ascension to the throne. For Roman referentiality in *Hercules*, see on 46–52. For *sententiae*, see on 125–204 (introd.); for the use of *sententiae* as grounds for action (a common Senecan strategy, evident here), see e.g. *Med.* 428, *Tro.* 869–71, *Oed.* 834, *Pha.* 598, *Ag.* 307, *Thy.* 319, 330–2, 487. Note the form *haut*, used five times in this play (also at 415, 678, 922, 1305), where there are no instances of *haud* (unless one accepts the reading of *T* at 922).

una sed/But one woman: for the postponement of *sed*, see on 63–8.

fundare uires/secure my might: similarly another tyrant ('Nero') will aim to 'secure his house' (*fundaro domum*) with offspring (*Oct.* 532).

iuncta regali face thalamisque/joined through royal torch And chamber: if *Hercules* is dated to 54 CE, Seneca's Roman audience would have remembered a recent 'joining through royal torch and chamber' of Claudius and his niece Agrippina in 49 CE (see above) and, even more recently, that of Nero and Claudius' daughter, Octavia, in 53 CE. Though neither Claudius nor Nero, of course, were *noui homines*, both had much to gain from these 'royal' marriages. For *face/facibus iungere* = 'to marry', see *Oct.* 142, *HO* 404, Ov. *Met.* 7.49. For *thalamis*, 'chamber', see on 348–53. See also *facibus et thalamis*, *HO* 1491.

Megara: for the quantity of the final *a*, see 203 and n. *ad loc.*

ducet e genere inclito… colorem/will draw Colour from her famed family: the 'colour' is presumably that of *nobilitas* (viz. high social status, tradition, antiquity, even legitimacy), something to erase the blank newness of Lycus' power. For other metaphorical uses of *color*, see *Tranq.* 1.3, *Ep. Mor.* 108.5. For *genus inclitum*, see on 337–41.

nouitas… nostra/My 'newness': *nouitas* is a Roman cultural term and a Senecan tragic *hapax*. According to Fitch *ad loc.* this is 'its first use in poetry…in the technical sense of "lack of ancestry"'. See further on 332–57. For Roman referentiality in *Hercules*, see on 46–52.

348–53 *non equidem reor fore ut…* /Indeed I don't think It'll be that…: this extraordinary periphrasis, which occurs rarely in Latin verse and nowhere else in Senecan tragedy, suggests some unease underlying the surface confidence (cf. *trepida manu*, 'trembling hand', 341), although Lycus has grounds for believing that a proposal of marriage would be successful. Amphitryon had himself slain Alcmena's father (accidentally) and then married her (Eur. *Herac.* 16–17). So slaying the father of a would-be bride, as Lycus has already done, would not appear to be a hindrance. Cf. the confidence of Shakespeare's

Gloucester in the seduction of Anne at *Richard III* I.ii.116: see Introd. §VII, 136. *Equidem*, 'indeed', an emphatic particle, is always used in Senecan tragedy in association with a first-person singular verbal form, as at 415; see also e.g. *Med.* 184, 254, *Pha.* 525, 1119, *Tro.* 276. Sometimes its use is overtly sarcastic, as at *Tro.* 310, *Ag.* 158.

meos...toros/my bed: *torus*, 'bed', 'cushion', 'couch', like *thalamis*, 'chamber' (347), are regular metonyms for marriage or wedding. Lycus will use the word in his explicit proposal at 413. Seneca's imitator, the dramatist of *Octavia*, will use the two words a combination of thirty-six times in his play.

si impotenti pertinax animo/if her wild will stubbornly: for the elision of the long vowel in the monosyllabic *si*, see *Ag.* 199, 552; *Pha.* 121, 1120, 1121, 1185; *Oed.* 699, 1028; *Tro.* 245; *Pho.* 413. For *impotens* used of mental states, see *Med.* 851–2, *Thy.* 350, *Ag.* 126, *Oed.* 865; cf. also *Thy.* 547. *Pertinax* will be used of Megara again at 493.

stat tollere.../I'm resolved to raze...: Lycus' sole goal in Euripides' play, where he seeks to kill Hercules' sons to forestall their vengeance (*Herac.* 168–9). Perhaps this play's main irony is that it will be Hercules who implements Lycus' second plan. This impersonal use of *stat* ('it is my fixed intent') with the infinitive in verse starts with Virgil (*Aen.* 2.750, 12.678); see also Stat. *Theb.* 11.131, Sil. 14.555. For initial *stat*, see 540 and n. *ad loc.*

Herculeam domum/Hercules' house: variation of a standard line-ending: see 631, *Ag.* 223, *Tro.* 871, *Thy.* 22. For the use of the adjective *Herculeus*, see 72 and n. *ad loc.* For destruction of the *domus*, cf. *Ag.* 912, *Med.* 886, *Thy.* 190–1, *Pho.* 345.

inuidia...ac sermo popularis/hatred and the people's voice: a similar question is asked of Atreus by his Courtier at *Thy.* 204–5. The question would have not been lightly dismissed by the play's Roman audience, since it involves *fama*, 'talk', 'report', 'rumour', 'reputation', 'fame' etc., generally considered a cardinal value not only of Rome's political and social elite but of the civilized world, making the inhabitants of that world subject to moral and legal constraints. Creon's criticism of Medea as having 'no thought of reputation' (*nulla famae memoria, Med.* 268) classifies her as barbaric. Notably the ideal king of *De Clementia* (1.8.1) and emperors, *principes* (1.15.5), are most concerned about *fama*; Virgil's Dido is indifferent (*Aen.* 4.170). Lycus, like the *tyranni* Atreus (*Thy.* 205–18) and Eteocles (*Pho.* 654), but unlike the *rex* Creon, places no value on *fama*. In line with Creon's position, rather than that of Lycus, Atreus and Eteocles, is the astute attitude to the political importance of *fama* displayed by Nero at *Oct.* 583–5. Note also the cynical dismissal of *fama* by Phaedra's Nurse at *Pha.* 269–70. Here the question is asked not only to draw attention to Lycus' dismissal of fame, but to enable him to conclude with line 353. For *inuidia*, see next n. Note the shortening of the final *o* of *sermo*: see on 109–12.

ars prima regni est posse et inuidiam pati/Kingship's prime art is the power to cope with hate: for similar 'tyrannical' *sententiae* in Senecan tragedy, see Oedipus at *Oed*. 703–4: *odia qui nimium timet | regnare nescit*, 'Too great a fear of hate shows ignorance of kingship'; and Eteocles at *Pho*. 654: *regnare non uult esse qui inuisus timet*, 'Who fears to be hated does not want to be king'. Kingship, its nature, morality, cares, fragility, etc. are ever-present themes of Senecan tragedy: see e.g. 737–47; *Oed*. 6–11, 82–6, 695–708; *Ag*. 57–76, 995; *Tro*. 1–6, 250–352; *Med*. 192–271, 203–6; *Pho*. 645–64—and most esp. *Thy*. 204–19, 336–403, 442–70. Cf. also the discussion between Seneca and Nero at *Oct*. 440–532. Behind Lycus' statement (and those of Oedipus and Eteocles) lies the great apophthegm of Roman tragedy—*oderint dum metuant*, 'Let them hate, provided they fear' (Acc. *Atreus* frag. 3 Boyle 2006)—and its Ennian predecessor (*Inc*. frag. 348 Jocelyn): *quem metuunt oderunt*, 'Whom they fear, they hate'. Accius' apophthegm echoed throughout the Roman literary and cultural tradition from Cicero (*Off*. 1.97, *Sest*. 102, *Phil*. 1.34) through Tiberius (Suet. *Tib*. 59.2) and Caligula (Suet. *Gai*. 30.1) to Seneca's prose works (*Ira* 1.20.4, *Clem*. 1.12.4, 2.2.2), Lucan's Caesar (3.82–3), and Seneca's own Atreus (*Thy*. 212). The relationship between hate and power continued in Renaissance drama: 'Let them hate me, so they feare mee' (Edwards, *Damon and Pithias* 870); 'Whom hatred frights, Let him not dream on sovereignty' (Jonson *Sejanus* II.174–5).

Inuidia ('hatred/malice/jealousy/envy'), branded as *omnibus his uehementius et importunius malum*, 'a more potent and insistent evil than all these (greed, ambition, desire)' (*Ben*. 2.28.1), appears in three other tragedies: *Ag*. 134, *Pha*. 489, *Tro*. 299, 479 (see also *Oct*. 485–6, *HO* 612–13). For *pati* = 'to cope' (*OLD* 6), see Lucan's advice to Caesar: *disce sine armis | posse pati*, 'Learn the power to cope without arms' (Luc. 5.314), and Cato's to his rebellious army: *nescis sine rege pati*, 'You cannot cope without a king' (Luc. 9.262). Cf. Thyestes' remodelling and inversion of Lycus' *sententia* at *Thy*. 470: *immane regnum est posse sine regno pati*, 'Great kingship is power to cope without kingship'. Seneca has a fondness for *pati* as the ultimate word of a line: see e.g. 398, 486, 541, 656, also *Ag*. 131, *Thy*. 470, *Med*. 189, 545—and for the phrase *posse pati*, lit. 'to be able to endure/cope', in both the prose works and the tragedies: e.g. *Med*. 545, *Ag*. 131, *Thy*. 470, *Ira* 3.13.4, *Clem*. 1.18.1, *NQ* 3 Pref. 6. For the closural use of *sententiae*, see on 125–204 (introd.); for alliterative closure, see on 275–8. On sonic and other grounds,

I join Giardina (1966 and 2007) and Caviglia in preferring Grotius' emendation (*et inuidiam*) of the faulty MSS readings to that of Richter (*in inuidia*), favoured by Zwierlein and several other modern editors.

354-7 Lycus now notices Megara and Amphitryon. So Hercules notices his family at the end of his long entrance monologue (616-17); so the Nurse notices Hippolytus at the end of her monologue/prayer (*Pha.* 424-30); so Jason catches sight of Medea at the end of his entrance monologue (*Med.* 445-6). As Lycus here, Jason and the Nurse end their monologues by seeing a character onstage and expressing an intention to address her/him. Billerbeck *ad loc.* sees this as a technique of post-Attic tragedy.

Temptemus igitur/So, let's try: Lycus begins to bring his soliloquy to a close with a jussive/hortatory subjunctive, as Atreus does in his second entrance monologue (*Thy.* 505). *Igitur* ('so/therefore') is a rare word in Senecan tragedy, occurring only twice elsewhere. Fitch *ad loc.* takes the rarity of connectives meaning 'therefore' (there are only four uses of *ergo*) as an index of tragic Seneca's 'paratactic style'.

Fors dedit nobis locum/Chance has granted us a place: for the personification of *fors*, see *Tro.* 5. Fors Fortuna was worshipped as a goddess with two temples in Rome, one on the right bank of the Tiber allegedly founded by Servius Tullius. There may be something of an analogy here with Julius Caesar, represented by Lucan (1.224) as an adherent of the goddess Fortuna (*te, Fortuna, sequor,* 'I follow thee, Fortune'). With Lycus' statement, cf. that of the Nurse at *Pha.* 425-6: *dedit | tempus locumque casus,* 'Chance has granted time and place', also spoken just before a failed attempt at sexual seduction. Cf. also Circe's failed seduction 'having secured time and a place' (*nacta locum tempusque,* Ov. *Met.* 14.372). Reference to the right time to address someone on stage is a feature of Roman comedy: e.g. Plaut. *Most.* 714, *Pseud.* 958. The initial *f* in *Fors* is not capitalized by Zwierlein.

tristi uestis obtentu caput uelata/head covered with the cloth of mourning: Megara's funereal appearance is referenced also at 202 and 626-7. The *uestis,* 'cloth', here is the *ricinium,* a kind of shawl worn around the shoulders with a hood or cowl for the head, used esp. (so *OLD*) 'by women in mourning'. *Caput* is accusative of respect with the verbal adjective *uelata.* See 107 and n. *ad loc.*

praesides...deos/guardian gods: Lycus seems to be referring to statues of deities on stage. The best candidates are statues of Jupiter and Ceres, to whom Megara has prayed and to the former of whom Amphitryon prayed at the opening of the act. Hence the stage set described at the beginning of Act I. Statues of divinities are probably part of the stage set of other Senecan tragedies (*Agamemnon, Thyestes, Phaedra*); in the case of *Phaedra* a shrine and statue of a divinity (Diana) features prominently in the dramatic action.

laterique adhaeret/**By her side clings:** the phrase occurs only here in Seneca; its tone is clearly contemptuous.

uerus Alcidae sator/**Alcides' true begetter:** Lycus' use of the grand term *sator*, applied only to Jupiter (*Pha.* 157, *Oed.* 1028) and to Sol (*Med.* 28) elsewhere in Senecan tragedy, is heavily ironic. Lycus is giving Amphitryon Jupiter's title while denying Jupiter's Herculean parentage. The irony is underscored by the nomenclature 'Alcides', obviously intended to index Hercules' non-divine origins: see on 84–5. Euripides' Lycus similarly disavows the story of Heracles' divine parentage (*Herac.* 148–9).

358-9 Megara has not spoken since 331 and her questions, which could be delivered as an aside but are more likely (note the demonstrative *iste* and the possessive *nostri*) to be spoken *sotto uoce* to Amphitryon, are a continuation of her earlier speech, the time between having been essentially 'frozen' to allow Lycus' soliloquy to be delivered. If the lines are to be delivered as an aside, there would be two asides in conjunction here as at *Tro.* 623–6.

Quidnam iste...noui parat/**What's he plotting now:** lit. 'What new thing is he plotting?' *Noui* is partitive genitive with a neuter pronoun: see Woodcock §§51, 77. Cf. *Thy.* 254: *Quid noui rabidus struis?* 'What are you madly plotting now?' Billerbeck *ad loc.* views *quidnam*, which occurs three times in Senecan tragedy, as more colloquial and intimate than *quid*; Fitch *ad* 205–523 assigns it to 'the forceful language of drama'. Cf. *quonam* at 1151.

nostri generis exitium ac lues/**holocaust and plague On our family:** Andromache has a similar but asyndetic run of abuse for Helen at *Tro.* 892–3: *pestis exitium lues utriusque populi*, 'blight, holocaust, plague on both nations'. Seneca's presentation of Megara has much in common with that of Andromache, who, like Hercules' wife, resists the tyrannical male (Ulysses in Andromache's case) but fails to protect her offspring. Cf. also Theseus' description of Hippolytus as *generis infandi lues*, 'infection of our foul family' (*Pha.* 905). For other applications of *lues* to persons, see *Tro.* 853 (Helen); *Med.* 183 (Medea). This usage seems first attested in Cicero (*Har.* 24). For *exitium*, 'holocaust', as a term of personal abuse, see *Tro.* 892 (of Helen, above); *Oed.* 876 (Oedipus of himself); *Marc.* 17.5 (of Dionysius, tyrant of Syracuse); Hor. *Odes* 1.15.21 (of Ulysses); Ov. *Met.* 13.500 (of Achilles). It has good tragic precedent: see Enn. *Alexander*, frag. 61 Jocelyn: *exitium Troiae, pestem Pergamo*, 'Troy's holocaust, Pergamum's plague' (of Paris). *Nostri generis* is probably best taken as objective genitive.

359–438 Megara-Lycus confrontation and *agon*: Part I (359–421), speeches of seduction and resistance; Part II (422–38), *stichomythia* and *antilabe* on the topic of Hercules' worth, laced with threats from Lycus.

359–69 Lycus' opening address to Megara here contrasts sharply with his opening address (to Amphitryon) in Euripides' play. The latter (*Herac.* 140–3) is overtly sarcastic; the former reverential, even deferential. It is accompanied by an argument for an end to mutual hatred, articulated in military language (for which in *Hercules*, see on 19–29) but substantially in line with Seneca's advocacy of *clementia* in his seminal work. For Stoic language and ideas in *Hercules*, see on 162–3.

O clarum trahens a stirpe nomen regia/O heir To a renowned name received from royal stock: a most formal and character-revealing address, in which Lycus not only engages in *captatio beneuolentiae* by using deferential language (typical of social inferiors: the Nurse at *Pha.* 129, *Ag.* 125), but reveals the two major properties which he lacks (*clarum nomen* and *stirps regia*) and which draw him towards partnership with Megara. Lycus likes the epithet *clarus*, 'renowned' (340, 359). For *o* with the vocative, see on 205–9.

aure...patienti/patient ear: for the phrase, see Hor. *Ep.* 1.1.40: *patientem commodet aurem*, 'lend a patient ear'.

si...gerant...cedat...teneat...paret...relinquent: for this combination of present subjunctives in the protasis of a conditional sentence and future indicative in the apodosis, cf. 503–5, *Med.* 525–6.

si aeterna semper odia mortales gerant/If mortals ever bear eternal hate: the tension between *mortales*, 'mortals', and *aeterna*, 'eternal', is intensified by the pleonastic *semper*. With the pleonasm, cf. Lucretius' description of Epicurus' 'golden words' (*aurea dicta*): *perpetua semper dignissima uita*, 'ever most worthy of life perpetual' (3.13). With the argument here, cf. Sen. Rhet. *Con.* 1.1.6: *perierat totus orbis nisi iram finiret misericordia*, 'The whole world would have perished if pity did not put an end to anger'. For the elided *si* at the start of an iambic line, cf. *Pha.* 1120, 1185; for the phrase *odia gerere*, see *Thy.* 329.

furor/rage: for the ontologization of the emotions, see on 75–6; for *furor*, see on 92–9.

felix...infelix/winners...losers: Seneca likes to play with antithetical adjectives: see on 275–8.

tum uastis ager squalebit...gentes cinis/Fields will then lie waste... buried nations: Seneca revels in descriptions of devastation; see 1284–94, *Pha.* 469–74, *Oed.* 133–59, *Ag.* 571–6, *Thy.* 827–34•. As does his nephew, even in his preface (Luc. 1.24–9). For *squalere*, see Virg. *Geo.* 1.507.

subdita tectis face/after homes are torched: for *subdere* used of 'applying (a torch/fire etc.) beneath', see e.g. *Tro.* 381, *Thy.* 59, *Ira* 2.14.1.

altus...cinis: note the structure of the line (two epithets and two nouns arranged in chiastic order and separated by a central verb), a so-called 'silver line' (abCBA). See on 19-29. For the phrase, *altus cinis*, 'deep ash', see also *Med.* 147.

pacem...uictori...uicto/peace...for the victor...For the vanquished: another closural *sententia* (see on 125-204 introd.). For a similar sentiment in a 'historian', see Tac. *Hist.* 3.70. The *sententia* appealed to Hughes, *The Misfortunes of Arthur* II.iii.59-60: 'if conquerors ought | To seek for peace, the conquered must perforce.' For the *uictor/uictus* verbal play, see on 275-8.

369-71 Lycus invites Megara to join him in ruling the city. His language is strong on political and moral values (*particeps, sociemur, pignus fidei, continge*) but weak on sexual precision.

Particeps regno ueni/Come, share my rule: the audience know that Lycus is in effect proposing marriage, although his language here and in the following line is so vague that Megara will not understand it as such. *Particeps* normally takes the genitive (but see [Quint.] *Decl.* 3.3: *marito particeps*); the dative here is perhaps 'influenced' (so Fitch *ad loc.*) by the verb of motion, *ueni* (for dative of the 'goal of motion', see Woodcock §57).

sociemur animis/Let's join our hearts: close to marital language, but still imprecise; contrast (i) Virgil's *me uinclo sociare...iugali*, 'to join myself with bonds of matrimony' (*Aen.* 4.16); (ii) the later (413) and blunter phrase, *sociemus toros*, 'let's join our beds'. *Animis* could be construed as instrumental ablative or ablative of respect (or better, both): Woodcock §§43.1, 55.

pignus hoc fidei cape. continge dextram/Accept this pledge of faith. Clasp my hand: a conglomerate of political and moral language that could have been taken from the pages of Livy (25.16.13): *praesentisque contingere dextram et id pignus fidei secum ferre*, 'to clasp the hand of the man before them and to take with them that pledge of faith.' Cf. also Virg. *Aen.* 3.610-11. For the hand as pledge of *fides*, 'faith', see also *fidem...dextrae*, 'good faith of the right hand' (*Med.* 248), and the grisly 'hands given in faith', *datas fidei manus* (*Thy.* 764). Note how *dextra* is given the emphatic final position in Lycus' invitation, undercutting (as Megara sees) the *pignus fidei* which precedes. Further on *fides*, see on 414-21; for *dextra* (and the *manus* motif), see on 118-22.

Quid truci uultu siles/Why the silence and savage look: again, as at 329, the focus is on the face. Such descriptions of facial expression were necessary in a context where the masked actors were unable themselves to mimic such. Indeed *uultus* almost = the tragic mask: see on 329–31. For descriptions elsewhere in the tragedies of the physical signs of emotion, see e.g. *Med.* 382–96 (Medea's *furor*); *Pha.* 360–83 (Phaedra's *amor*); *Ag.* 237–8 (Clytemnestra's *dolor* and *ira*); *Oed.* 921–4 (Oedipus' *furor*). Cf. Deianira's *furor* at *HO* 233–53. *Truci uultu* is applied to the 'savage look' of Polyxena, as she faces the fatal blow at *Tro.* 1152. *Vultu* is descriptive ablative: Woodcock §43.6.

372–96 Megara's response to what she takes to be a plea for reconciliation (*not* a marriage proposal) is disgust, moral outrage, and hate (372–83), focusing on the bloody 'hand' proffered by Lycus and his slaughter of her kin. It culminates in a threat derived from Thebes' tragic past (384–96).

372–83 *Egone ut…contingam*/**Would I clasp:** a 'repudiating', 'indignant' question in the subjunctive, sometimes expressed in English with 'really': 'Would I really clasp?' The idiom—found in republican tragedy (Enn. *Med. Ex.* frag. 226 Jocelyn, 9.2 Boyle 2006; Acc. *Melan.* frag. 427 Klotz) and frequent in Roman comedy and epistles—smacks of ordinary language (see Billerbeck *ad loc.*). It is also employed by Seneca at *Oed.* 671, and at *Med.* 398–9, 893, 929. Cf. also 1187 below. The idiom throws emphasis on *ego*; hence the italicized 'I' in the translation. The strong pause in line 373 after the fifth foot is, as Fitch notes *ad loc.*, 'unusual'; see also 644.

parentis sanguine aspersam manum/**a hand splashed with father's blood:** similar revulsion and horror are expressed by Oedipus toward his own hands: *paterno sanguine erret manus*, 'hands splashed with father's blood' (*Pho.* 268). *Aspergo* is generally associated with blood in Senecan tragedy: see also *Tro.* 256, 1107, *Thy.* 95, and Frank *ad Pho.* 267–8.

prius extinguet ortus…occasus…/**Sooner Will the East quench…the West…:** the listing of impossibilities (*adynata*) is a common device of ancient rhetoric, used in Greek and Latin poetry (but especially the latter), to underline a proposition which has been advanced: see e.g. *Pha.* 568–73; *Thy.* 476–82; *Pho.* 85–7; *Oct.* 222–6; *HO* 335–8, 467–72, 1582–6; Aristoph. *Peace* 1076; Theoc. 1.132–6; Virg. *Ecl.* 1.59–63; Prop. 2.15.31–5; Hor. *Odes.* 1.33.7–9; Ov. *Ibis* 31–40. For its presence in Rome's declamation schools, see Sen. Rhet. *Con.* 1.5.2. The device is often used to express love, gratitude, or, as here, hate. It may be found in Renaissance tragedy: see e.g. Pompeo Torelli's *Merope* (1589), 137ff. (cited by Caviglia *ad loc.*). For the *ortus* and *occasus/obitus* (East/West) combination elsewhere in Senecan tragedy, see e.g. 871, 1061–2, 1330, *Ag.* 824, *Thy.* 814. For this particular *adynaton*, see also e.g. *Pha.* 570–1, *Pho.* 86–7, *HO* 335–6, Ov. *Tr.* 1.8.2.

pax ante fida niuibus et flammis erit/Sooner will snow and fire make trusted peace: a standard *adynaton*, used regularly in such lists: see e.g. *Pha.* 568, *Thy.* 480, *Oct.* 223, *HO* 280, Ov. *Tr.* 1.8.4. At *Med.* 889 this *adynaton* is realized: *alit unda flammas,* 'water feeds the flames'.

Scylla Siculum iunget Ausonio latus/Scylla join Sicily's flank to Ausonia: i.e. sooner will the Strait of Messina between Italy (= Ausonia) and Sicily dry up. (Sicily and Italy were often thought to have originally been a single land-mass: Virg. *Aen.* 3.414-19, Ov. *Met.* 15.290-2, Luc. 2.435-8, Pliny *HN* 2.204.) The notorious sea-monster, Scylla, inhabited the Strait of Messina on the Italian side of the strait opposite the monstrous whirlpool known as Charybdis on the Sicilian side, and preyed on sailors passing through the strait. The sea-monster and the whirlpool are known as early as Homer (*Od.* 12.85-107). From the fifth century BCE onwards Scylla was envisaged as a beautiful young woman in the upper half but girdled with the heads of baying dogs in the lower half. She is later transformed into a rock. Ovid straddles Books 13 and 14 of *Metamorphoses* (13.898-14.74) with an account of her metamorphosis into the sea-monster and rock; see also Lucr. 5.892-3; Virg. *Ecl.* 6.74-7, *Aen.* 3.424-8; Ov. *Am.* 3.12.22, *Her.* 12.123, *Met.* 7.62-5. Scylla provided the model for Spenser's description of 'Errour' (*Faerie Queene* 1.1.14-15) and for the misogynistic Milton's description of Sin, the 'formidable shape' beside the Gates of Hell (*Paradise Lost* 2.650-61). For Senecan allusions to Scylla and/or Charybdis, see *Med.* 408-9, *Thy.* 579-81, *Marc.* 17.2, *NQ* 3.29.7, *Ep. Mor.* 14.8, 31.9, 45.2, 79.1, 92.9.

uicibus alternis/shifting tides: the same phrase occurs at *Pha.* 1028. The ablative is perhaps best taken as of manner modifying *fugax*: Woodcock §§43.5.iv, 48. See also *reuocata uice* at 1212 and n. *ad loc.*

Euripus unda stabit Euboica piger/Euripus…Stand motionless in Euboea's waters: Euboea (modern Evia) is the large island off the west coast of Boeotia in central Greece, separated from the mainland by the narrow Strait of Euripus. The turbulent currents of the strait are a *topos* of Greek and Roman literature from Aeschylus (*Ag.* 190-1) and Plato (*Phaed.* 90c) to Livy (28.6.10), Seneca (*Tro.* 838), *Hercules Oetaeus* (778-81) and beyond. See Pomponius Mela's description (2.108). Euripides' Lycus comes from Euboea (*Herac.* 32).

patrem abstulisti regna germanos larem patriam/You took my father, kingdom, brothers, home, Fatherland: cf. Hercules' analogous list of losses at 1260-1 (see n. *ad loc.*) and those of Oedipus at *Pho.* 237-8. Note how *patriam*, 'fatherland', is given particular emphasis by the enjambement, followed by a pause after the first foot. For this device (enjambement followed by a pause after the first word of the next line) see e.g. 51–2, 401–2, 416–17, 993–4, 1207–8, 1280–1, 1316–17; *Pha.* 978–9; *Oed.* 15–16, 92–3, 336–7, 1031–2, 1034–5; *Med.* 25–6, 217–18, 881–2; *Tro.* 475–6, 936–7; *Thy.* 199–200, 915–16, 1101–2; *Pho.* 491–2, 645–6; Virgil *Aen.* 6.210–11, 12.950–1. For other pauses after a line's initial word, see e.g. 1042, *Med.* 20, *Oed.* 257, 385, *Thy.* 100, 911, *Ag.* 233. For the asyndeton, see on 30–5. Like Viansino (1965 and 1993), Fitch (1987*a* and 2018), and Chaumartin I see no reason to reject the consensus MS reading *patriam* for *patrium*, first printed apparently in the *editio Patauina* of 1748 and adopted by Zwierlein and some other modern editors. Fitch (2004*b*), 18, notes the imitation at *HO* 1492. For asyndeton, see on 30–5 and 283–95. *Lar* is a religious metonym for 'home': see on 913–18.

una res superest/One thing's left: for Seneca's sense of *superest* and its dramatic and thematic possibilities, see *Med.* 166, *Medea superest*, 'Medea is left'; *Oed.* 108, *una iam superest salus*, 'One salvation now is left'; and 891 below, *iam nullus superest timor*, 'Now no fear is left'. For significant and revealing variations of the formula, see e.g. *Med.* 37, 498, *Oed.* 1033, *Tro.* 888, Ov. *Met.* 2.471.

odium tui…commune doleo/Hatred of you…to my pain—I share: again the reification of the emotions; see on 75–6. For other 'communal' emotion, see *communis iste terror*, *Tro.* 435. There is an especial irony here in Megara's inversion of the common idea that shared negative emotions lessen the pain: see the choral ode at *Tro.* 1009–12.

pars quota/What small part: for other occurrences in Senecan tragedy of this rhetorical phrase, see 1191, *Oed.* 67, *Ag.* 22, *Med.* 896. The dramatist of *HO* uses it five times (51, 95, 96, 164, 640). The phrase seems Ovidian (see e.g. *Am.* 2.12.10, *Her.* 12.89, *Met.* 7.522, 9.69, *Pont.* 2.10.31). Mark the hyperbaton caused by postponement of the interrogative/exclamatory adjective *quota*. Postponement of relative and interrogative pronouns, adjectives, and adverbs (see on 159–61, 501–8, 1149–55, 1173–7) occurs often in Senecan tragedy. As with the postponement of conjunctions (see on 63–8), the word/phrase preceding seems emphasized. Zwierlein punctuates as a question rather than an exclamation.

384–96 *Dominare tumidus*/Play the swollen despot: for *tumidus*, 'swollen', applied to the ambitious, proud, or high-handed, see 171, *Ag.* 84. *Tumere*, *tumidus*, *tumor*, etc. are specifically linked by Seneca with the emotions, especially with anger (*Ira* 1.20.1, *Pho.* 352, *Thy.* 519–20) and pride and with the arrogance of power: see e.g. *Ag.* 248 (Agamemnon), *Tro.* 301

(Agamemnon), *Med.* 178 (Creon), *Thy.* 609, 613 (earthly rulers); also *Oct.* 109 (Nero), Stat. *Theb.* 2.346 (Eteocles), 11.756 (Creon). Cf. *regius… tumor*, 'royal swelling/pride', *Pha.* 137. See further 1089–91 (and n. *ad loc.*), *Ira* 1.1.4, 3.11.3. Cf. Shakespeare's 'the swelling act | Of the imperial theme' (*Mac.* I.iii.128–9).

sequitur superbos ultor a tergo deus/A vengeance-god follows behind the proud: probably conceived as a Fury or Erinys: cf. *Ag.* 83: *quaeque superbos urit Erinys*, 'And Erinys, who burns the proud'. For the expectation of, or hope for, the appearance of a revenge-god, cf. Thyestes final (if futile) statement: *uindices aderunt dei*, 'The gods of vengeance will come' (*Thy.* 1110). See also Octavia at *Oct.* 255 and *Clem.* 1.13.2, *Const.* 17.4. See further Boyle *ad Thy.* 1110–12. For the substantival use of *superbi*, see also *Pha.* 519, *Tro.* 6.

Thebana noui regna/I know Thebes' realm: Megara's argument here, viz. that Thebes' tragic past will dictate a tragic future, is repeated by Jocasta in her advice to her son, Polynices, at *Pho.* 645–51. It is summed up at *Pho.* 648–9: *sceptra Thebarum fuit | impune nulli gerere*, 'No one has borne Thebes' sceptre with impunity'. Behind the argument lies the Senecan theme of *semper idem*, the tragic cycle of history, the recycling of the past as the present and the present as the future. It is an especially strong theme in *Phaedra, Agamemnon, Troades, Medea*, and *Thyestes*. See Boyle *ad Ag.* 44–8, and Boyle (1997), 34ff., 58ff. For the Theban past and its repetition (Megara's subject here), see the list of the risen Theban dead at *Oed.* 609–18 and the words of the Ghost of Laius which follow at *Oed.* 626–30; also the words of Oedipus at *Pho.* 276–87, which begin with an echo of Megara's *noui*, 'I know' and her final phrase (396), *regni fata… erret*, 'the fate of our realm':

> optime regni mei
> fatum ipse noui: nemo sine sacro erret
> illud cruore.

> I know well the fate
> Of my realm: no one will bear the sceptre
> Without sacral blood.

With this semiotically loaded use of *noui*, cf. also *Pho.* 83, *Tro.* 341. Statius, for whom Seneca was a major model, famously focuses in detail on the Theban past in the extensive *praeteritio* at the start of his epic: *Theb.* 1.4–16. It is important to note that Seneca's preoccupation with the *semper idem* theme is a function of his tragic concept of fate and, though influenced by, should not be identified with, the transgenerational curse theory evident in the Attic tragedians, especially Aeschylus. Seneca is also likely to have been influenced by the dramatizations of familial calamity in Accius (see Boyle 2006: 112–13) and by the sustained focus on the tragic cycle of history in Virgil's *Aeneid*. Statius' *Thebaid* continues the exploration of this theme.

quid…loquar/Why mention: for this rhetorical move, see 226 and n. *ad loc.*

matres…passas et ausas scelera/mothers Who suffered and dared crimes: there are several candidates: Agave, daughter of Cadmus, who in a fit of Maenadic frenzy dismembered her own son; Autonoe, sister of Agave and fellow-Maenad, mother of the doomed Actaeon; Niobe who offended Latona/Leto, Apollo, and Diana/Artemis and suffered the loss of her four-teen children (see further below); Jocasta who committed and suffered incest; and Ino, mother of Learchus and Melicertes, who was attacked by her husband Athamas and plotted against the lives of Phrixus and Helle. Semele, mother of Dionysus/Bacchus, and Antiope, mother of Amphion and Zethus, might also be included, at least under the category of victims of crime. For the *ausae/passae* combination/antithesis, see also *Pha.* 723–4. For *ausus* and boundary violation, see on 547–9; for boundary violation, see on 46–52.

geminum nefas/twin sin: an allusion to Oedipus' two crimes of patricide and incest (*Pho.* 264–73) and perhaps, as Fitch notes *ad loc.*, to 'the "doub-ling" of relationships' caused by him, as suggested by the next line. *Nefas*, lit. 'the unspeakable', major moral/religious transgression (translated in this play as 'sin', 'horror', or 'evil'), is used in Senecan tragedy of such crimes as patricide and incest (*Ag.* 31, 35, 124; *Oed.* 18, 661; *Med.* 261; *Pha.* 128), frat-ricide (*Pho.* 412, *Med.* 131), and filicide (*Thy.* 56, 1006, *Med.* 931). It is used six times elsewhere in this play (500, 603, 632, 1099, 1159, 1264) of mariti-cide, Cerberus, the slaughter of the Theban royal family, general 'sin', the slain bodies of Hercules' family, the familial slaughter itself. The cognate adjectives, *nefandus* (translated as 'vile' or 'monstrous': 988, 1004) and *infandus* (translated as 'monstrous': 977), occur twice and once respectively. Attention to *nefas* in the play focuses not only on the moral horror of Hercules' deeds but on the drama's defining paradox: the speaking of 'the unspeakable'. Note how *geminum nefas*, 'twin sin', seems to echo the *gemina caede*, 'twin slaughter' of Megara's brothers, as if to confirm that Lycus is already enmeshed in Theban *nefas*.

mixtumque nomen coniugis nati patris/And the name of husband, son, father fused: Oedipus was husband and son of Jocasta, and father and brother of Antigone, Ismene, Eteocles, and Polynices. With the focus on nominal fusion/confusion here, cf. *Oed.* 636–7 (*proles…parens…natus*, 'offspring…father…son'), 1009–12, 1023, 1034–6, and *Pho.* 225 (*parentis nomen aut nati,* 'name of father or son'); also Tiresias' prophecy at Soph. *OT* 457–60. Sidonius focuses on Oedipus' multiple *nomina* at *Carm.* 22.98–9, citing an additional one: *ultricus ipse suus,* 'stepfather to himself'. 'False names' and nominal confusion are important issues in the tragedies: see also Aegisthus' 'ambiguity of name' (*nomen ambiguum,* Ag. 984–5), Phaedra's desire to take on a 'more lowly name' (*humilius nomen,* Pha. 610) as she erotically pursues Hippolytus, Thyestes' denunciation of the 'false names' (*falsis…nominibus,* Thy. 446) accorded to so-called 'greatness', and the Thyestean Ghost's preoccupation with his own nominal confusion (*Ag.* 35–6). Note also Seneca's focus on *falsa nomina* in the prose works, see e.g. *Ben.* 1.5.5, *Ep. Mor.* 110.8, 119.12. For earlier preoccupation with this issue, see Cic. *Cluent.* 199, Ov. *Met.* 10.346–8. For the asyndeton of family terms, see on 30–5 and 283–95.

bina…castra…totidem rogos/two camps…two pyres: those of the warring brothers, Eteocles and Polynices, whose duel, deaths, and funeral pyre(s) are narrativized in Books 11 and 12 of Statius' *Thebaid* and whose conflict is the chief subject matter of Seneca's *Phoenissae.* The 'two pyres' (*totidem rogos*) is an allusion to the splitting of the flames when Polynices' body is placed on the pyre of Eteocles: Luc. 1.549–52, Stat. *Theb.* 12.431–2; also *Oed.* 321–3.

riget superba Tantalis luctu parens/Mother Tantalis stiffens proud in grief: 'Tantalis' is Niobe, queen of Thebes, daughter of Tantalus and wife of Amphion, the man who built the walls of Thebes with his music. By Amphion she had many children (the numbers vary: at *Med.* 955 and Ov. *Met.* 6.182–3 there are seven sons and seven daughters). All the children were killed by Apollo and Diana/Artemis as punishment for Niobe's boast that the number of her children made her superior to Latona/Leto, mother of Apollo and Diana/Artemis. Niobe mourned unceasingly and was transformed into a rock on Mt Sipylus, down which flowed the water of Niobe's eternal tears. The story is told by Achilles to Priam at *Il.* 24.602–17; Aeschylus wrote a tragedy, *Niobe,* which was ridiculed by 'Euripides' in Aristophanes' *Frogs* (911ff.), but only survives in fragments; the main incidents were represented in ivory on one of the doors of the Augustan temple of Apollo on the Palatine in Rome (*funera Tantalidos,* Prop. 2.31.14). Allusions to the myth may be found throughout Greek and Roman literature and beyond: e.g. Soph. *Ant.* 823–32, *El.* 150–2, Cic. *Tusc.* 3.63, Prop. 2.20.7–8, 3.10.8, Ov. *Her.* 20.105–6; Shakespeare, *Hamlet* I.ii.149: 'Like Niobe, all tears'. See especially Ovid's canonic account at *Met.* 6.148–315; also *Ag.* 375–9, *Oed.* 613–15, *Med.* 954, *HO* 185, 1849–51. Phyllis Wheatley's eighteenth-century poem, *Niobe*, proclaims itself as based on Ovid's account and on Richard Wilson's 1768 painting, 'The Destruction of Niobe's Children'. For *Tantalis* (Niobe) and *funera*, see also Stat. *Theb.* 4.575–8. For *rigere*, 'stiffen', cf. Andromache *malis rigens*, 'stiff with affliction' (*Tro.* 417), Thyestes *rigentem tot malis*, 'stiff with so much affliction' (*Thy.* 304). Like most modern editors I have retained the consensus MS reading, *superba*, 'proud', the standard epithet for Niobe (*Oed.* 614, *Med.* 954, Ov. *Her.* 20.105: *superba parens*). Zwierlein and Billerbeck print the emendation of Ascensius: *superbo*.

Phrygio...in Sipylo/**on Phrygia's Sipylus:** Mt Sipylus (modern Spil) is situated near Manisa in western Asia Minor/Anatolia (modern Turkey)— technically ancient Lydia, but 'Phrygia' is often used without geographical precision: *Ag.* 376–7, *HO* 189, Prop. 2.20.8. Niobe was a daughter of Tantalus, ruler of the city of Sipylus; the area was her native home.

quin ipse...Cadmus/**Even Cadmus:** for this rhetorical, climactic use of *quin* (*quin ipse* = 'even'), cf. *Ag.* 410, *Oed.* 57, 62, *Med.* 441, *Thy.* 673, 990, Virg. *Geo.* 4.481. There is argumentative force in Megara's ending her catalogue of Theban disaster with its beginning: the metamorphosis of Thebes' founder (see below).

toruum...crista caput/**savage, crested head:** the Cadmus serpent is similarly crested at Ov. *Met.* 4.599. See further on 213–22 (*cristati caput*). For *toruus* of serpents, see Virg. *Aen.* 6.571–2 (*toruos...anguis*); for *toruus* in Senecan tragedy, see on 720–7.

Illyrica Cadmus regna permensus/**Cadmus...crossed Illyria's realm:** Cadmus, son of King Agenor of the Phoenician city of Tyre, was founder and first king of Thebes. He eventually fled the city and, together with his wife Harmonia, was transformed into a serpent: see Eur. *Bacch.* 1330–2, Ov. *Met.* 4.563–603, Apollod. 3.5.4. His early career is the subject of the third choral ode (709–63) of *Oedipus*. See further on 249–58. Illyria was the western area of the Balkan peninsula, covering parts of modern Albania, Croatia, and Bosnia and Herzegovina. Both Ovid (*Met.* 4.568) and Apollodorus (3.5.4) also place Cadmus' serpent transformation in Illyria. For the syllabic repetition in *Illyrica Cadmus*, see 67 and n. *ad loc.*

longas reliquit corporis tracti notas/**left long marks from his slithering body:** echoes here perhaps of Hippolytus' torn and dragged body in *Phaedra* (1107): *longum cruenta tramitem signat nota*, 'traces a long path with bloody marks'.

haec te manent exempla/**These examples await:** there is an unconscious irony here. These *exempla* also await Megara's husband, Hercules. Note the appeal to a central ingredient of Roman culture. Exemplarity was at the core of Roman history and social practice, in which *mos maiorum*, 'the practice of ancestors', was the guiding principle of action for the Roman elite. Atreus is being thoroughly Roman when he seeks guidance from the *exempla* of his ancestors, Tantalus and Pelops (*Thy*. 242–3). Repetition of the past is a permeating theme of Senecan tragedy (Pasiphae to Phaedra, Iphigenia to Polyxena, Tantalus to Atreus/Thyestes, Agave to Jocasta), as it was a goal of elite Roman culture. For Roman referentiality in *Hercules*, see on 46–52.

dominare ut libet/Play despot as you please: Megara herself plays the skilful orator, picking up the opening phrase of this section, *dominare tumidus* (383), to conclude her speech. Cf. the similarly closural use of sarcasm by Juno at 121–2 above.

solita regni fata … nostri/our kingdom's common fate: Megara returns to the phrase *solita fata* in her final response to Lycus at 497. The words signal not only the determinism of history but its repetitive cycle. Statius has Oedipus himself wish the repetition of Thebes' tragic history on Creon, his successor (*Theb*. 11.701–3). For the use of *soleo* in other plays to underscore the *semper idem* theme, see e.g. *Med*. 1022, *Tro*. 249, 360. See also 1344. For the echo of the lemmatized phrase at *Pho*. 276–7, see above.

397–413 Lycus' proposal of marriage, prefaced by a defence of his military violence. In Euripides' *Heracles*, Lycus questions the hero's paternity but makes no offer of marriage to Megara. Fitch (p. 185) sees a possible precedent for Lycus' proposal to Megara in a proposal of the tyrant Polydectes to Danae in Euripides' lost play, *Dictys*. A more immediate and decidedly Roman precedent was Nero's marriage to Octavia: see on 341–8. With Lycus' self-defence here, cf. those of Helen, Medea, Jason, and Phaedra cited below.

397–402 *Agedum … amoue*/Come … drop: *agedum* with the imperative is a colloquial use. See 1281, Ben. 3.2, *Oed*. 787, 1032.

efferatas rabida uoces amoue/my rabid one, drop these frenzied words: Lycus begins by playing the passion-restraining role often given to a socially inferior figure such as a nurse (in *Medea*, *Agamemnon*, and *Phaedra*) or a courtier (in *Thyestes*). The resistance of the emotions to control and the necessity to bridle them are central to Stoic ethics (e.g. *Ira* 3.1.1) and feature regularly in Seneca's plays: *Med*. 157 (*siste furialem impetum*, 'curb this furious impulse'), 381, 591–2, 866–9; *Ag*. 203; *Tro*. 279–81; *Pha*. 251, 255, 574; *Thy*. 496–505; cf. also *Oct*. 813f. *Rabidus*, 'frenzied/rabid/mad', can be a strongly pejorative term (see e.g. *Thy*. 254, used of Atreus; *Ag*. 708, used of Hecuba), derived from its association with 'rabid' animals: see e.g. *Med*.

351, *Pha.* 1070, *Oed.* 932, Lucr. 5.892, Virg. *Aen.* 6.102, Ov. *Am.* 3.12.22. Here, given the context (a marriage proposal), its use seems intended to suggest that Megara's behaviour is 'over the top'. *Voces amoue,* 'drop…words': Seneca is fond of periphrastic phrases involving *uox/uoces* and a verb; see e.g. *uoces…hauriam,* 'I'll drink your words', *Oed.* 395; *uoces…dedi,* 'I have produced chants', *Med.* 801–1•; *dimoue uocis moras,* 'Set aside delays of speech', *Pha.* 587; *quas…uoces dabo,* 'What words shall I give', *Thy.* 1036. For Seneca's 'noun style', see on 11–18. For the juxtaposition of synonyms, see on 283–95. For Stoic language and ideas in *Hercules,* see on 162–3. Note the breach of 'Porson's law': see on 249–58.

disce regum imperia ab Alcide pati/**Learn from Alcides to cope with kings' commands:** so Creon to another rebellious female (Medea): *regium imperium pati aliquando discat,* 'she needs to learn sometime to cope with a king's command' (*Med.* 189–90—cf. *Oct.* 842, Cic. *Rab. Post.* 29). The reference to Alcides/Hercules is to his 'coping with' the commands of Eurystheus, a topic to which Lycus will return (430–2 and n. *ad loc.*). For *discere,* see on 68–74; for *pati* as the ultimate word of the line, see on 348–53.

rapta quamuis sceptra uictrici geram dextra/**Though my triumphant hand bears a stolen Sceptre:** Lycus' *uictrix dextra,* 'triumphant hand', will be mirrored by Hercules' own (800). For *dextra* (and the *manus* motif), see on 118–22; for *sceptra,* see on 63–8. Deianira at *HO* 874–9 (perhaps with reference to Lycus) remarks that after Hercules' death such kings will go unpunished.

sine legum metu quas arma uincunt/**unafraid of laws Vanquished by my arms:** Lycus articulates his version of the 'might is right' doctrine, which Amphitryon lamented (254) was now operating in Thebes.

pauca pro causa loquar nostra/**I'll briefly defend My case:** legal language, which is often used to frame a weak defence; see e.g. Aeneas, defending himself to Dido: *pro re pauca loquar,* 'I shall briefly defend the matter' (Virg. *Aen.* 4.337). In Senecan tragedy characters regularly mount a defence of their conduct: e.g. Medea at *Med.* 203–51, Jason at *Med.* 431–44, Helen at *Tro.* 903–24, Phaedra at *Pha.* 177–94. Thyestes is unusual in refusing to defend himself (*Thy.* 512–17). For *causa* in the legal sense, as here, see Hercules' *causa* at 1306; Medea's *causa* at *Med.* 202, 242, 262; Helen's *causa* at *Tro.* 905, 923; Creon's and Oedipus' at *Oed.* 695, 697; Phaedra's at *Pha.* 664; Atreus' and Thyestes' at *Thy.* 276, 514, 1087; Polynices' at *Pho.* 378 (cf. *Pho.* 384). For the language of law in *Hercules,* see on 731–4. For enjambement followed by a pause after the first word of the next line, see 379–80 and n. *ad loc.*

402–8 Lycus' self-defence makes use of the rhetorical technique of *praesumptio* or προλημψις: see below. He also engages in the conventional strategy of transferring agency for acts of war to the constituents of war (arms, wrath, swords) or to war itself (cf. the modern blame-removing banality, 'the fog of war'), and dismissing the issue of causation. War's brutality and killing have always been made acceptable by its practitioners through such rhetorical moves, and it has been up to others to show that 'arms and the man' are the same.

cruento…in bello/**in bloody war**: a neat move, to treat the blood spilt by men not as the responsibility of those who do the killing (as Megara indicated in her outraged comment at 372–3) but as a property of war itself.

arma non seruant modum/**Arms observe no bounds**: similarly the war-weary Agamemnon places the responsibility for war's carnage on *furor* and the 'teeming sword' (*gladius felix*) 'maddened with lust by blood's taste' (*cuius infecti semel | uecors libido est, Tro.* 284–5). For *modus* and its transgression in Senecan tragedy, see on 205–9.

nec temperari facile…potest…ira/**wrath…cannot easily Be tempered**: for the resistance of the emotions to control and the necessity to bridal them in Stoic ethics, see on 397–402. For Stoic language and ideas in *Hercules*, see on 162–3.

stricti ensis ira, bella delectat cruor/**The wrath of drawn swords…war's pleasure is blood**: Seneca's 'noun style' (see on 11–18) and reification of emotions (see on 75–6) and human practices operate here in service of a larger point, viz. the depersonalization of war and the transference of responsibility for its horrors to abstract entities outside the sphere of human control or agency or even to the weapons themselves. So Homer at *Od.* 16.294, 19.12: αὐτὸς γὰρ ἐφέλκεται ἄνδρα σίδηρος, 'For iron itself draws a man to it'; so Virgil at *Aen.* 1.150: *furor arma ministrat,* 'Rage furnishes arms'. With *bella delectat cruor,* cf. the final line of *Octavia* (982: *ciuis gaudet Roma cruore,* 'Rome delights in citizen blood') and Seneca's own condemnation of blood-lust (*Clem.* 1.25.1): *ferina ista rabies est sanguine gaudere ac uulneribus et abiecto homine in siluestre animal transire,* 'It is the madness of the beast to revel in blood and wounds and, casting off one's humanity, to change into a wild animal.' See also Sen. *Ira* 2.5.1—and Virg. *Geo.* 2.510, where Romans are also described as 'delighting' (*gaudent*) in civil blood. For the 'wrath of drawn swords', the literary paradigm in the Roman tradition was the closing scene of Virgil's *Aeneid,* when Aeneas 'terrifying in his wrath' (*ira terribilis, Aen.* 12.946–7) slays Turnus. With *ensis ira,* cf. *ira flagelli,* 'the wrath of the lash' (VF 7.149); for *ira,* see on 19–29. *Delectare,* quite common in the prose works, is used only here in the tragedies.

sed ille…/But did he…: in the Latin text there is an ellipse of a verb (*egit*, 'acted', *pugnauit*, 'fought', or *sim.*). What follows is a rhetorical move known as 'anticipation' (*praesumptio* or πρόληψις), in which the speaker articulates an anticipated objection in order to refute it: Quintilian *Inst.* 4.1.49–50, 9.2.16–18. See esp. Helen's self-defence at *Tro.* 903–24. Quintilian complains about the excessive use of this strategy in contemporary declamation (*Inst.* 4.1.50).

improba cupidine/base lust: lust for power, *cupido dominandi* (Tac. *Ann.* 15.53.4). For Cicero's Scipio, being *dominandi cupidus*, 'lustful for power', was the mark of the tyrant: *Rep.* 1.50.

quaeritur belli exitus, non causa/War's outcome, not its cause, Is the issue: a spin on the Ovidian maxim, *exitus acta probat*, 'The end/outcome justifies the deeds' (*Her.* 2.85). The legal language continues. Cf. the words of Armitage's (but not Euripides') Lycus to Amphitryon: 'it's the outcome that counts, not how it looks' (*Mister Heracles*, p. 29). For legal language in *Hercules*, see on 731–4.

408–13 *Sed nunc pereat omnis memoria*/But let all memory now fade: Lycus' own 'noun style' (see on 11–18) continues, as he attempts to obfuscate the horror of what he has done. Note the infrequent dactylic fifth foot, created by the quadrisyllabic *memoria*; cf. *Med.* 268, *Oed.* 847. See also e.g. *Med.* 512, 709, *Tro.* 195, 1080 (reading *cacumine*), *Thy.* 115, *HO* 804, where the lines similarly end in a quadrisyllabic word.

uictor…posuit…uictum…deponere/victors lay down…vanquished…lay down: for *uictor/uictus* verbal play, see on 275–8, 359–69. Linguistically interesting is the *ponere/deponere* verbal play, since *posuit* is here used in its common sense of *deposuit*; see e.g. *Thy.* 348, 519, 601, 609, 921, 1025.

decet/Rightly: lit. 'it is right'. Characters in Senecan tragedy frequently appeal to 'probity', what 'becomes', 'befits', 'suits', or 'is right' (*decet*): see e.g. 510, 990; *Ag.* 52, 124; *Tro.* 256, 261, 332, 336, 619, 1003; *Pha.* 216, 453, 610, 618, 803; *Oed.* 1003; *Med.* 50, 175, 281; *Thy.* 86, 183; cf. *Oct.* 440, 454. Occasionally, as here, the appeal is (ironically) in the context of *scelera*, *nefas*, *sanguis*, or *cruor*: see e.g. *Ag.* 52, 124 (*nefas*), *Med.* 50 (*scelera*), *Tro.* 1003 (*sanguis*). The appeal to *quod decet* is common in Seneca's prose works; see e.g. *Ep. Mor.* 85.26: *cautio illum decet, timor non decet*, 'Caution becomes him, fear not so'. *Decorum*, 'what is right', of course, has both a moral and a literary/aesthetic dimension, the latter promoted famously by Horace in the *Ars Poetica*; frequently in Senecan tragedy both senses are present, as e.g. at 990, *Ag.* 52, *Oed.* 1003, *Med.* 50, *Thy.* 86. For the Stoic concept of *decorum*/τὸ πρέπον, see Cic. *Off.* 1.93–9.

428 COMMENTARY LINES 414-21

inflexo genu/on bent knee: not of course a Roman practice but one associated with the east; see *Thy.* 600: *genu nixae...gentes,* 'kneeling nations'. At
Nero 13.2 Suetonius describes Tiridates' kneeling supplication before Nero.

placet/I like: the word seems to be used here in its sexual sense (*OLD*
1d), 'it attracts me'; cf. Hippolytus' complaint at *Pha.* 684: *placui nouercae,*
'I (sexually) attracted my stepmother'.

animo ruinas...capis magno tuas/embrace your ruin with great
spirit: Billerbeck *ad loc.* points out the irony that greatness of spirit, *mag-
nanimitas,* is precisely what the *sapiens* displays before the tyrant (*Const.*
11.1). With *ruinas capere,* cf. *aduersa capere,* 'embrace adversity', at *Oed.* 83;
fortunam capit...suam, 'embrace his own good fortune', *Oct.* 90.

rege...digna/fit for a king: for *dignus,* see on 109-12.

sociemus toros/let's join our beds: *sociare* is a quintessentially Roman
term for 'to join' politically and/or socially, and is frequently used of marital
union; see e.g. the Chorus' description of Octavia (*Oct.* 284) as *sociata toris,*
'bed-joined' to Nero. One of Nero's criticisms of his wife in *Octavia* is that
her heart is *insociabile* (*Oct.* 541), 'not able to be allied/joined with'. With the
lemmatized phrase, cf. also Ovid's *sociare cubilia* (used of Atalanta's erotic
musings, *Met.* 10.635); also *iuncti...uincla tori,* 'the bonds of wedlock', Ov.
Fas. 4.602; *iunge toros,* 'join beds', Stat. *Silu.* 1.2.182. For Roman referentiality in *Hercules,* see on 46-52.

414-21 Megara fiercely rejects Lycus' proposal. Seneca is clearly drawn to
the theme of female resistance to tyranny/male power, as several scenes in
his tragedies attest: see e.g. Andromache's resistance to Ulysses in *Troades,*
Phaedra to Theseus in *Phaedra,* Medea to Creon and Jason in *Medea,* Electra
and Cassandra to Aegisthus and Clytemnestra (who has usurped
Agamemnon's male power) in *Agamemnon.* Lines 414-18 can be taken as an
aside or normal dialogue. I have chosen the former because of Seneca's interest in the dramatization of the female mind (witness Phaedra, Clytemnestra,
Andromache, Medea) and because of the focus on the self in Megara's words.
The first line seems more redolent of the opening of an aside, as at *Oed.* 659,
than of a reply to Lycus (contrast Megara's earlier reply). See also Schmidt
(2000: 425).

Gelidus per artus uadit exangues tremor/A chill tremor runs through
my bloodless limbs: fairly formulaic description of an emotional reaction—of a kind found in Greek and Roman literature from Homer onwards:
see e.g. 61 above; *Oed.* 585-6, 659; *Pha.* 1034; *Ag.* 711; *Tro.* 168; *Oct.* 735;
HO 706; Hom. *Il.* 10.93-5; *Aen.* 2.120-1, 3.30, 6.54-5, 12.447-8; Ov. *Met.*
1.548, 9.290-1 (*frigidus artus...horror habet,* 'a chill horror possesses my

limbs', says Megara's mother-in-law, Alcmena). For *exanguis and tremor*, cf. *exanguis tremo*, *Pho*. 528. For *membra/artus* and somatic reactions, see also 621; *Ag.* 5, 508; *Tro.* 168, 487, 623; *Oed.* 224; *Med.* 926; *Thy.* 436; *Pho.* 530. For *tremor* as line-ending, see on 57–63.

quod facinus aures pepulit/What crime struck my ears: periphrases involving *aures* are used to express a reaction to onstage or offstage sound from Plautus onwards (*Poen.* 1375–6). Here Seneca uses *aures* with *pellere* to express a shocked response from Megara (to the outrageous offer of marriage from Lycus at 415). Cf. the similar language used of the shocked response of Theseus to the cry from the palace at *Pha.* 850, and that of Medea to the wedding-song for Jason's new marriage at *Med.* 116. See also *Oct.* 72. In respect of *quod facinus*, Fitch *ad loc.* compares the Plautine formula *quod ego facinus audio*, 'What crime do I hear?', found at Plaut. *Aul.* 796, 822.

haut equidem horrui/Yet I didn't shiver: for the form *haut*, see 345 and n. *ad loc.*; for *equidem*, see on 348–53.

muros... circumsonaret/Roared round our walls: for pentasyllabic words in the first half of the trimeter elsewhere in Senecan tragedy, see e.g. 716; *Ag.* 478, 955; *Oed.* 389; *Tro.* 215; *Med.* 264, 557; *Pha.* 109, 690, 940, 950, 1005, 1068; *Thy.* 302, 744; *Pho.* 265. Several of the pentasyllabic words are *hapax legomena* in the Senecan tragic *corpus*. Here the pentasyllabic word gains extra emphasis from the enjambement, the initial position in the line and the strong pause following it (see on 372–83). For *murum circumsonare*, see *Aen.* 8.474; for Seneca's preference for the plural form of *murus*, see 262.

capta nunc uideor mihi/now I seem enslaved: either an echo or an anticipation of Hecuba's remark on hearing that she has been allotted to Ulysses: *nunc uicta, nunc captiua... mihi... uideor*, 'Now I seem conquered, now enslaved...' (*Tro.* 988–9). What both women are alluding to is the enslavement which befell the women of those defeated in war, including, in the case of younger women, sexual enslavement, concubinage (cf. Cassandra, the 'whore of the royal bed', *regii paelex tori*, *Ag.* 1002).

*Grauent catenae.../*Let chains shackle...: an enumeration of the tortures to be expected from the victims of a tyrant. Torture is rarely far from the surface in Senecan tragedy, especially in scenes where information is being sought: e.g. *Ag.* 989–90; *Pha.* 884–5; *Oed.* 518–19, 852–67; *Tro.* 578–81; see also *Thy.* 92, 257. More often the 'tyrant-figure' specifies the tortures: Aegisthus (*Ag.* 988–93), Theseus (*Pha.* 882–5), Oedipus (*Oed.* 707, 862), Ulysses (*Tro.* 578–81). But again a parallel with *Troades* manifests itself: Andromache similarly recounts the possible tortures awaiting her (*Tro.*

582–6). Torture was generally treated in the rhetorical schools as the practice of a tyrant and features extensively in Sen. Rhet. *Con.* (see e.g. *Con.* 2.5 'The Woman Tortured by the Tyrant for her Husband's sake'). For threats of torture in Attic tragedy, see e.g. Aegisthus at Aesch. *Ag.* 1621–3, Oedipus at Soph. *OT* 1152–4. For reference to the 'rack' in early Roman tragedy, see Pac. *Dulorestes*, frag. 159 Klotz (cited on 988–93). In the Roman criminal system torture (to gain evidence/to index the truth-value of purported evidence) was restricted to slaves. *Grauent* and *protrahatur* (420) are jussive subjunctives used in a concessive sense: see Woodcock §112, n. i.

longa fame…protrahatur/long starvation Stretch: an especially Roman punishment and one meted out to the elder Agrippina, who was banished to the island of Pandateria in 29 CE and starved to death in 33 CE: see *Oct.* 940, Tac. *Ann.* 6.25, Suet. *Tib.* 53. Starvation seems threatened against Andromache (*Tro.* 583) and Electra (*Ag.* 991). For *protrahatur*, see previous n.

non…uis ulla/No force: cf. the similar protestation of Antigone (*Pho.* 51–2) and Virgil's Latinus (*Aen.* 12.203–4).

fidem/fidelity: *fides*, 'faith/trust/fidelity/loyalty/faith/promise', is a recurrent motif of Senecan tragedy (it occurs eight times in *Hercules*, the modifier *fidus* occurs twice) and of Roman amatory poetry (e.g. Prop. 1.1.16, 4.16, 12.8, 18.18; Ov. *Am.* 1.3.6, 10.57, 2.15.28, *Ars* 3.544). Its use here to suggest sexual fidelity and the bond between wife and husband (as at *Med.* 145) does not exclude its larger semiotics. To Romans *fides* was both a cardinal value (frequently professed, if less frequently displayed) and a goddess in her own right, *Fides Publica* or *Fides Publica Populi Romani*. A shrine to her was associated with Numa, the second king of Rome (Livy 1.21.3–4, DH 2.75.3), and a temple was dedicated to her in the middle of the third century BCE and restored some two hundred years later. This temple was situated on the Capitol within the Area Capitolina next to the great temple of Iuppiter Optimus Maximus; in its vicinity were placed the texts (on bronze tablets) of various treaties and laws: see Richardson (1992: 151). A shrine of Fides (*Fidei fanum*) features as part of the stage-set for Plautus' *Aulularia* (583ff.). Horace calls Fides *incorrupta*, 'uncorrupted', and the 'sister of Justice' (*Iustitiae soror*), *Odes* 1.24.6–7; to Cicero she is *fundamentum…iustitiae*, the 'bedrock of justice' (*Off.* 1.23). At *De Ira* 2.28.2 Seneca groups the imperatives of *fides* with those of *pietas, humanitas, liberalitas,* and *iustitia.* Further on *fides* (including its relationship to *foedus*), see Gladhill (2016: 20–2).

moriar, Alcide, tua/I'll die, Alcides, yours: a brilliant ending, redolent with social and erotic overtones and tragically ironic ('ein Beispiel

tragischer Ironie', Billerbeck *ad loc.*). Megara will die 'yours'. The erotic overtones are clear: see e.g. Prop. 1.19.11. The social overtones are clear, too:
Megara is subscribing to the old-fashioned, conservative Roman ideal of
uniuiratus, 'single husbandness', according to which women have only one
husband in their lifetime and are honoured for doing so (Livy 10.23.5, Varro
apud Serv. *ad Verg. Aen.* 4.166, Valerius Maximus 2.1.3: see Rudd 1976:
42ff.). But there is, unknown to the speaker, quite a different meaning inherent in *tua*, 'yours', which the play will reveal and which the audience could
here perceive: viz. 'your victim'. For addresses to a character by name, see on
637–40; for Roman referentiality in *Hercules*, see on 46–52.

422–38 Part II of the Megara-Lycus *agon*: Hercules' worth, debated in a
quickfire dialogue of *stichomythia* (422–5, 430–8) and *antilabe* (426–9), fur-
nishing 'an opportunity for real dialectical interchange' (Henry and Walker
1965: 22). Dialogic exchanges using *stichomythia* (single-line utterances) or/
and *antilabe* (division of a line between speakers) are common in Seneca.
Stichomythia occurs in all the tragedies and only *Phoenissae* lacks *antilabe*.
Such exchanges are frequently marked by a use of *sententiae* (see 426, 433,
435, 437, 463–4, and on 125–204 introd.) and the employment of
'Stichworttechnik' (Seidensticker 1969: 44), viz. the repetition of key words
(sometimes via polyptoton), or the use of synonyms, antonyms, and cog-
nates in the construction of the responses: *inferis/inferna* (422–3),
telluris/caelum, pondus/onere, premit/premetur (424–5), *cogere/cogi* (426),
mortem/moriere (428–9), *famulus/famulus* (430–1), *reges/regi* (431–2),
uirtus/uirtutem/uirtutis (433–5). Cf. 449–56, 463–4, 1186–91, 1263–4 below.
For other exchanges involving *stichomythia* and/or *antilabe*, see e.g. *Ag.* 145–
57 (Clytemnestra and the Nurse), 284–94 (Clytemnestra and Aegisthus),
791–9 (Agamemnon and Cassandra), 955–71 (Electra and Clytemnestra);
Tro. 327–48 (Pyrrhus and Agamemnon); *Pha.* 239–45 (Phaedra and the
Nurse), 872–81 (Theseus and Phaedra); *Oed.* 210–46, 511–29, 678–704
(Oedipus and Creon), 776–867 (Oedipus and others); *Med.* 155–76 (Medea
and the Nurse), 192–8, 281–97 (Medea and Creon), 492–530 (Medea and
Jason); *Thy.* 442–5 (Thyestes and Tantalus), 534–41, 1100–3 (Atreus and
Thyestes). See also *Oct.* 185–8, *HO* 436–42, 891–902. In the case of *antilabe*
the exchanges, often ironic, are regularly a sharp rebuttal of the other's state-
ment or a telling completion of an incomplete utterance.

  Stichomythia is both more frequent and more extensive in fifth-century
BCE Attic tragedy than in the Senecan tragic *corpus*. In the latter it is usually
combative, the 'formalized control' augmenting the 'passionate intensity'
of the characters (see Garton 1972: 202). Less combative stichomythic

exchanges, such as that between Medea and her Nurse (*Med.* 159-63) or Clytemnestra and her Nurse (*Ag.* 145-57: the longest passage of stichomythia in Senecan tragedy), fall into the Seidensticker category of *Beratungs-Stichomythie* ('Counsel-Stichomythia'). Elizabethan dramatists (under the influence of the inherited Senecan *corpus*) also exploited stichomythic exchanges (often structured by 'Stichworttechnik'): see e.g. Edwards, *Damon and Pithias* 861-92; Shakespeare, *Henry VI 3* III.ii.31ff., *Richard III* IV.iv.212ff.; Kyd, *Spanish Tragedy* I.iv.77-89. Corneille (e.g. *Le Cid* 215ff., *Cinna* 647ff.), Racine (e.g. *Britannicus* 1051ff.), and Schiller (e.g. *Maria Stuart* II.viii) also employed this technique. The longest passage of *stichomythia* in the Senecan tragic *corpus* (fifteen lines) is the exchange between Seneca and Nero at *Oct.* 440-54. It is worth noting that many stichomythic exchanges and passages of *antilabe* would flounder in recital by a single speaker (see esp. 791-9, 955-71, or *Med.* 170-1). As indicated in the Introduction above (26), there were several modes of performance open to the dramatist. But what such passages show is that the thesis that Senecan tragedy was written only or primarily for recitation (purportedly by a single speaker) is untenable.

422-5 *Animosne mersus inferis coniunx facit…premit/*Such spirit with a husband sunk in hell…crushes: Lycus begins by echoing (unconsciously) Megara's language (*demersus*, 'sunk', *oppressus*, 'crushed', 317-18) and position in her dialogue with Amphitryon. For *mersus*, 'sunk' in hell and not likely to return, see Phaedra on Theseus at *Pha.* 220. With Lycus' sarcastic question (422), cf. Andromache's question to Ulysses regarding Astyanax: *spiritus genitor facit*, 'His father inspire him?' (*Tro.* 743). For criticism of *animi*, 'spirit', see *Tro.* 339.

*Inferna tetigit/*He has touched hell: Megara immediately takes issue with Lycus, rejecting his *mersus*, 'sunk', with *tetigit*, 'touched'.

*posset ut supera assequi…Nullo premetur onere/*to reach the higher realm…No weight will crush: the altercation forces a change of mood, as Megara argues against the position she espoused earlier (308, 313-14, 317-18, 325-8), presenting to the tyrant before her a more optimistic view of her husband's likely emergence from the underworld. For the ambiguity of *supera*, see on 46-52.

*Telluris illum pondus immensae premit/*The weight of the vast earth crushes him: Lycus' statement gains force not only from the iteration of Megara's earlier language (see above) but also from its allusion to the grave-side formula: 'let earth lie gently on him/her'; cf. Theseus' final command in *Phaedra*: *istam terra defossam premat*, 'let earth crush her buried body' (*Pha.* 1279).

qui caelum tulit/**bearer of the sky:** see on 68–74.

426–9 Four lines of *antilabe*: see on 422–38. Note the speaker change before the main caesura in line 426, which is not common in Senecan tragedy, where it generally seems to have been chosen for particular dramatic effects: see e.g. 991, 1295; *Pha.* 880; *Tro.* 680, 926, 978; *Oed.* 337; *Med.* 170–1, 882; *Thy.* 100, 257, 321, 745, 747, 1102.

Cogi qui potest nescit mori/The 'forced' don't know how to die: cf. the Trojan Chorus at *Ag.* 610: *o quam miserum est nescire mori*, 'O pity! not to know how to die!'; and Andromache at *Tro.* 574 (also in response to a threat of being 'forced'): *tuta est perire quae potest debet cupit*, 'She's safe who's able, ought, desires to die'. Behind the *sententiae* lies the notion of the freedom conferred by death (*libera mors*, *Ag.* 591) and the moral acceptability of suicide: see further 1027–8 and n. *ad loc.* Once one understands death's freedom, one can never be 'forced'. Luigi Groto inserted the present *sententia* into a similar dialogic confrontation at Act III.ii.22 of his tragedy, *La Hadriana*: 'Sforzato esse non può chi sa morire'. Lucan's Cato expands Megara's claim at *BC* 9.211: *scire mori sors prima uiris, sed proxima cogi*, 'Man's prime lot is to know how to die, but the next best thing is to be forced'. For Stoic language and ideas in *Hercules*, see on 162–3. For the postponement of the relative, see on 159–61.

Effare/**State:** like *proles* (268, 987), an archaism noted by Cicero (*De Orat.* 3.153).

potius/**rather:** note the late position. Seneca is quite free in his positioning of *potius*: see e.g. *Oed.* 628–9, *Tro.* 689–90, *Thy.* 1021. Billerbeck repositions *potius* after *effare* against the MS testimony.

regale munus/**royal gift:** Lycus veers from the threat of compulsion for a moment to try bribery, apparently believing in the great power of *munera* (Plato *Rep.* 3.390e, Eur. *Med.* 964–5, Ov. *Ars* 653).

Aut tuam mortem aut meam/**Your death or mine:** sarcastic responses are common in Senecan *antilabe*; see e.g. *Pha.* 245, *Tro.* 339, *Med.* 529—and the replies of Cassandra at *Ag.* 791–4.

Moriere demens/**You'll die, mad woman:** Lycus is in good tyrannical company with his blunt death-sentence: thus Clytemnestra (to Electra at *Ag.* 971), *morieris hodie*, 'You'll die today', and (to Cassandra at *Ag.* 1012), *furiosa morere*, 'Rage and die'; thus Creon to Medea at *Med.* 297: *capite supplicium lues*, 'You'll pay with your life'. Cf. also Oedipus at *Oed.* 521–2, Atreus at *Thy.* 188–9, and Nero at *Oct.* 437–8, 861. Ironically, of course, the present death-sentence will be carried out, but not, as the audience know, by Lycus. For *demens*/*amens* used of what the speaker construes as another's irrational behaviour, see e.g. 1021 (of Hercules), 1033 (of Amphitryon);

Med. 174 (of Medea); *Ag.* 244 (of Clytemnestra); *HO* 226 (of Iole), 314 (of Deianira).

Coniugi occurram meo/I'll meet my husband: a strongly ironic response. Megara will meet her husband and will die but not in the order or the way she imagines. The response, however, places her in good Senecan female company. Medea (*Med.* 170), Electra (*Ag.* 971), Cassandra (*Ag.* 1012), Phaedra (*Pha.* 710–12), Andromache (*Tro.* 576–7) respond in similar terms to the idea or threat of imminent death. Cf. also Deianira's response to her nurse at *HO* 332.

430-8 A return to *stichomythia.*

Sceptroque nostro potior est famulus tibi/So you prefer a slave over my sceptre: Lycus describes Hercules as a slave because of the latter's servitude (by command of the Delphic oracle) to Eurystheus, who ordered the 'twelve labours' (see on 77–83, 830–7, and Introd. §VI, 61). I have accepted the *EA* reading *sceptroque* against the normalized reading of *recc., sceptrone*; as Fitch notes *ad loc.,* 'questions expressing skepticism, expostulation, etc. not infrequently begin with *et* or *-que*' (see *Ag.* 961, *Thy.* 320–1). I also accept the word order of *A, potior est famulus,* against that of *E, famulus est potior.* Both of my rejected readings are printed by Viansino (1965 and 1993), Giardina (1966 and 2007), Caviglia, Zwierlein, and Billerbeck. Fitch (1987*a* and 2018) adopts the readings printed here. *Sceptro* is comparative ablative: Woodcock §§78–9. For the semiotics of *sceptrum,* see on 63–8.

Quot...tradidit reges neci/How many kings...sent to death: for kings or tyrants slain by Hercules, see on 268–75. For Senecan periphrases for 'killing', see on 1048–53.

ergo/then: note the shortening of the final *o*; see on 109–12.

regi seruit/serve a king: i.e. Eurystheus; see above.

Imperia dura tolle: quid uirtus erit/Remove harsh commands: what will virtue be: the first of three consecutive *sententiae* (see also 435, 437) used by Megara in this stichomythic battle of wits as a form of personal shield to keep the tyrant at bay. Cf. Phaedra's use of *sententiae* with Theseus at *Pha.* 872–81; Andromache's with Ulysses at *Tro.* 574, 588, 633; Medea's with Creon at *Med.* 196, 199–200. For the thought of 433, see *Prou.* 2.4: *marcet sine aduersario uirtus,* 'Virtue withers without an opponent'; cf. also *Const.* 3.4, *Ep. Mor.* 66.49–53. For the idiom with *tollere,* cf. Ov. *Ars* 3.594: *has artes tolle: senescet amor,* 'Remove these arts: love will grow old.' For *sententiae,* see on 125–204 (introd.).

Obici feris monstrisque/being thrown to beasts and monsters: Euripides' Lycus similarly pours scorn on Heracles' success in fighting beasts (*Herac.*

151–4). Interestingly Seneca himself was somewhat dismissive of this skill of Hercules, which he described as the activity not of the *sapiens* but of 'the hunter and rustic' (*uenatoris agrestisque*, *Const.* 2.2). *Obici*, 'being thrown to', removes Hercules' agency from his labours. It is the *mot juste* for criminals 'being thrown to' wild beasts in the arena: see *Ira* 3.23.1, *Ep. Mor.* 7.4, Sall. *Iug.* 14.15. The first foot of the line is an anapaest; the initial syllable in *obici* is short. For the important *monstrum* motif, see 1280 and n. *ad loc.*

Virtutis est domare/It is 'virtue' to tame: for the construction, *est* plus the possessive genitive plus infinitive, cf. *est regis alti…dare*, 'It's the mark of a high king to give' (*Tro.* 327); *timidi est optare necem*, 'It's the mark of a coward to want death' (Ov. *Met.* 4.115). See Woodcock §72.1.1 n. iii.

loquentem magna/braggart: an Ovidian phrase; see *Met.* 13.222. Lycus is not alone in attacking Hercules' boastfulness; see Juno at 51 and 58. Bentley's emendation (*sequentem*) of the *EA* reading is adopted by Zwierlein and Giardina (2007), but lacks justification. Most modern editors print, as here, the MS reading. For discussion, see Fitch (2004*b*: 19).

Non est ad astra mollis e terris uia/The path from earth to stars is not gentle: Megara's closural line and *sententia*. She (or at least her creator) seems indebted to Virgil's comment on *uirtus* at *Aen.* 9.641 (*sic itur ad astra*, 'this is the path to the stars'), cited by Seneca at *Ep. Mor.* 73.15. Note, too, how Seneca devotes a number of lines of *De Prouidentia* (5.9–11) to the steep path that virtue must climb, culminating with the paradigm of Phaethon and the axiom: *humilis et inertis est tuta sectari; per alta uirtus it*, 'It is the mark of the lowly and inactive to pursue the safe path; virtue climbs through the heights'.

Quo patre genitus/Who's his father: the issue of Heracles' paternity is at the forefront of the Euripidean Lycus' mind in his opening speech (*Herac.* 147–50). It comes to the fore here at the close of this interchange in part to effect a transition to Amphitryon, the character most fitted to discuss this subject.

caelitum sperat domos/hopes to live with gods: cf. Atreus' acrid depiction of Thyestes' ambition: *regna nunc sperat mea*, 'Even now he hopes for my crown' (*Thy.* 289).

AMPHITRYON *intervenes*: the interruption seems brusque and Amphitryon's *sile*, 'silence' (439), somewhat peremptory and indicative of gender hierarchy. Megara does not remain silent for the rest of the play or even the act, but her speech henceforth is restricted to a six-line outburst against Lycus (495–500) and two short exchanges with her murderous husband just before her death (1015–17, 1021). Onstage throughout Act III, when

Hercules enters the play, she says nothing in that act, although in the corresponding Euripidean 'episode' she breaks through the gender hierarchy (*Herac.* 534–7) and takes the lead in informing her husband of the dire situation in Thebes (*Herac.* 539–61).

439–94 The Amphitryon-Lycus confrontation and debate (*agon*). Part I (439–64): Hercules' divine origins. Part II (465–94): Hercules' heroic nature. For remarks elsewhere in Senecan tragedy on the important ancient topic of paternity and parentage, see e.g. *Tro.* 339–48 (Pyrrhus and Agamemnon); *Ag.* 292–301, 983–5 (Aegisthus); *Oed.* 634–40, 1032–9 (Oedipus); *Pha.* 687–93 (Phaedra); *Pho.* 134–7 (Oedipus).

439–47 *Miseranda coniunx Herculis magni*/Hapless wife of great Hercules: the opening modifier displays Amphitryon's empathy as he intervenes in this charged stichomythic debate: note the alliterative *m*s in the Latin framing this formal address. Cf. the reference to Deianira as *Herculea coniunx* at *HO* 241. Deianira is never called by name in *HO*; Megara's name is used four times in *Hercules* (203, 347, 1009, 1016), though her most common designator is *coniunx* (ten times). For *magnus*, 'great', as the quintessential epithet of Hercules, see 646, 829, *Ag.* 813, *Med.* 648, *HO* 771, 1823.

sile/silence: for Amphitryon's imperative and Megara's 'silence', see above.

partes meae sunt/It's my role: note the intriguing fusion here of theatrical (*OLD* 9) and disputatious (*OLD* 15), quasi-legal language. For meta-theatrical and legal language in the play, see (respectively) on 109–12 and 731–4.

reddere Alcidae patrem genusque uerum/to restore to Alcides his father And true descent: in Euripides' *Heracles* Amphitryon leaves the defence of Heracles' divine paternity to Zeus (*Herac.* 170–1).

Post...post...post...post...post/After...after...After...after...after: the fivefold repetition of *post* is matched in Senecan tragedy by the fivefold repetition of *per* at *Med.* 478–81 and of *dum* at *Oed.* 503–7. Note the rhetorical structure: bicolon with increasing colonic length, followed by tricolon with increasing colonic length. For repeated *post*, see e.g. *Med.* 637–8, *Thy.* 178, *HO* 79.

ingentis uiri/mighty hero's: there may be a pun on *gens*, 'family', brought out by the preceding *genus*, 'descent', giving rise to a latent meaning of 'family hero'. For similar, possible puns see e.g. 1238, *Tro.* 357, *Ag.* 810, *Med.* 223, *Thy.* 91, 234, *Oct.* 363, 605 (and further Ginsberg 2011: 357). Seneca may have derived his fondness for this pun from Ovid: see esp. *Met.* 7.426–7, on which see Keith (1991); but the pun is evident, too, in Virgil (see e.g. *Aen.* 1.263).

memoranda facta/famous deeds: the phrase is repeated at 1265.

pacatum manu/his hand pacified: for the *manus* motif, see on 118–22. For Hercules as 'pacifier' of the world, see on 882–8.

quodcumque Titan ortus et labens uidet/All that Titan views, risen and setting: for similar global images, see 37–8 and n. *ad loc.* For Titan, see on 123–4.

post monstra tot perdomita/After many monsters tamed: for Hercules as 'monster-slayer', see Virg. *Aen.* 8.293–300. For the important *monstrum* motif, see 1280 and n. *ad loc.*

post Phlegram impio sparsam cruore/after spattering Phlegra with impious blood: a reference to the battle between the Olympian gods and the monstrous sons of Earth known as Giants, which was fought on the plains of Phlegra (Pallene), the westernmost peninsula of Chalcidice in north-eastern Greece (see e.g. Pindar *Nem.* 1.67–8, Luc. 7.145–50). The gods, assisted by Hercules, proved victorious. Euripides' Amphitryon begins his defence of Heracles' bravery with the latter's participation in this battle (*Herac.* 176–80; see also 1190–2). The most famous representation of the Gigantomachy may be found on the Altar of Zeus at Pergamum (200–150 BCE). See also 81–4, 457–8, 976–81; *Thy.* 805–12•, 1082–4; Pind. *Nem.* 1.67–8; Hor. *Odes* 2.12.6–9; Apollod. 1.6.1–2—and the Titanomachy/Gigantomachy conflation at *Ag.* 334–9, Hor. *Odes* 2.12.6–9, 3.4.42–80. See further on 976–86. The blood of the Giants is designated as 'impious' because they attacked the Olympian gods: similarly at *Odes* 2.19.22 Horace refers to the 'impious band of Giants', *cohors Gigantum…impia*. For *sparsus cruore* at the beginning of a line elsewhere in the tragedies, see *Med.* 709, *Ag.* 448. With the phrase used here of Hercules' deeds, cf. Megara's description of Lycus, whose hand was 'splashed with the blood' (*sanguine aspersam*, 372) of her father.

postque defensos deos/after defending gods: see previous n.

nondum liquet de patre/His father's still unproven: legal language again. *Non liquet* is a judicial formula for a verdict of 'not proven': Cic. *Clu.* 76.

Iunonis odio crede/Trust Juno's hate: for climactic half-lines, see on 40–6.

447–56 One and a half lines, followed by a third bout (eight lines) of *stichomythia* (see on 422–38).

Quid uiolas Iouem/Why blaspheme Jupiter: a shortened version of the phrase *uiolare numen* plus the genitive, 'violate the godhead of' (Lucr.

2.614–15, Tib. 1.2.79). For similar protests against improper citation of the gods, see Andromache's reprimand of Ulysses at *Tro.* 753–4, and Clytemnestra's of Aegisthus at *Ag.* 297: *quid deos probro addimus*, 'Why add gods to sin?' For *uiolare*, see 104 and n. *ad loc.* For the *conuersio*, see on 895–9.

mortale caelo non potest iungi genus/The mortal race cannot be joined to heaven: a pronouncement with strong political and cultural charge in the context of imperial Rome, where several mortals (Romulus, Julius Caesar, Augustus, Livia, Drusilla, Claudius) had been or were about to be apotheosized.

Communis ista: note the repetition of the same syllable at the end and beginning of juxtaposed words; see 67 and n. *ad loc.*

deis/gods: Hyginus (*Fab.* 224) has a list of mortals who became immortal. More notable members of the list are Bacchus/Liber, Castor, Pollux, Perseus, Callisto, Asclepius, Pan, Ganymede, Ino, Melicertes—not to mention the Roman *diui* named in the n. above, esp. Julius Caesar, whose apotheosis is dwelt upon in Ovid's *Metamorphoses*: *Caesar in urbe sua deus est*, 'Caesar is a god in his own city' (*Met.* 15.746).

Famuline fuerant/were they slaves: another allusion to Hercules serving Eurystheus: see on 430–8.

Pastor…Delius/Delian shepherd: Phoebus Apollo (see on 19–29), who served as shepherd or herdsman to Admetus, king of Pherae in Thessaly. At *Pha.* 296–8 Apollo is herding cattle for Admetus. This was often deemed to be a punishment handed to him by Zeus/Jupiter for killing the Cyclopes (Apollo. 3.10.4) or (according to Pherecydes) the sons of the Cyclopes. There are several variants of this myth of Apollo's servitude, including (from the Hellenistic period onwards) one involving Apollo's erotic love for Admetus, as in the cited *Phaedra* passage (cf. e.g. Tib. 2.3.11–28, Ov. *Met.* 2.680–5): see further Gantz (1993; 1.92). Other deities, too, were servants to mortals: e.g. Demeter/Ceres nursed the son of Plemnaeus, king of Sicyon; Poseidon/Neptune (together with Apollo) served the Trojan king, Laomedon, in building his city's walls.

exul/exiled: Lycus unconsciously underscores the analogy between himself and Hercules by using the word chosen by Amphitryon to identify Lycus himself: *exul* (269, 274).

profuga terra mater errante/fugitive mother…on wandering land: Latona/Leto who gave birth to Apollo and Diana/Artemis on the island of Delos; see on 11–18 (*quibusque natis*). For Latona's exile, see Ov. *Met.* 6.189–91. Zwierlein punctuates line 453 as a question.

monstra/**monsters:** for the important *monstrum* motif, see 1280 and n. *ad loc.*

saeuas Phoebus aut/**Phoebus…or savage:** I join Fitch (1987*a* and 2018) in printing the *lectio difficilior* of A. Most modern editors print that of *E*, *saeua*, which, as Fitch observes *ad loc.*, 'appears to be an accommodation of the adjective to the adjacent noun'. For the postponement of *aut* by two words, see Fitch (*ad loc.* and 2004*b*: 19). For the postponement of conjunctions, see on 63–8. For Phoebus, see on 19–29.

Primus…imbuit…draco/**First to stain…snake:** the snake was Python, who guarded the oracle at Delphi and was slain by Phoebus Apollo. The killing was often regarded as occurring when Apollo was a child, even a baby: Eur. *IT* 1245–53, Callim. *Hymn* 2.97–104, Ov. *Met.* 1.438–44, Luc. 5.79–81, Hyg. *Fab.* 140. *Imbuere* sometimes has the sense of 'to wet first', even 'to inaugurate' (*OLD* 3), and so sits playfully here with *primus*, 'first', as at Prop. 4.10.5: see Billerbeck *ad loc.*

grauia paruus…mala/**grave tests…when small:** Lycus is alluding to baby Hercules' confrontation with two serpents, described at length by Amphitryon at 213–22; see nn. *ad loc.* For *grauia mala*, cf. *Thy.* 301. Like most recent editors I have kept the *EA* reading, *paruus*. Zwierlein prints Housman's conjecture, *partus*.

457–62 Amphitryon cites two examples of deities threatened as babies.

fulmine eiectus…fulminanti/**cast by lightning…lightning:** as Fitch notes *ad loc. eicere* is the *vox propria* for 'to miscarry', and is found in this sense in the *Digest* (9.2.27.22). Note the paronomasia of *fulmine/fulminanti*.

puer mox…proximus patri stetit/**The boy…soon stood next to his…father:** to parallel Hercules' childhood troubles Amphitryon first cites Bacchus/Dionysus, 'child of pitiless lightning' (*proles fulminis improbi*, *Med.* 84), son of Cadmus' daughter Semele and Jupiter *qua* lightning-bolt (see on 11–18), referencing Bacchus' participation in the Gigantomachy (see on 439–47): see e.g. Eur. *Ion* 216–18, Hor. *Odes* 2.19.21-4, Diod. Sic. 3.70.6, Apollod. 1.6.2. The alliteration of *ps* joins son to father. For the pairing of Hercules and Bacchus, see on 63–8. For *stare* as 'taking a military stance', see 118 (Juno), 261 (Spartoi), 948 (Leo). *Mox*, 'soon', is a Senecan tragic *hapax*.

quid/**What:** see 241 and n. *ad loc.*

qui gubernat…/**he who directs…:** the supreme god, Jupiter/Zeus (*gubernator poli*, *Pha.* 903), Amphitryon's second example. He was hidden from his father, Saturn/Cronos, as a baby and nursed by nymphs in a cave on Mt Ida or Mt Dicte in Crete.

qui nubes quatit/who shakes clouds: a Latin amplification of the Homeric descriptor of Zeus, νεφεληγερέτα, 'cloud-gatherer' (*Il.* 1.511, etc.). Cf. *Pha.* 300: *ipse qui caelum nebulasque ducit*, 'Even he who controls the sky and clouds'; also *Ag.* 803.

latuit…rupis exesae specu/Hide…in a cave on a crumbling cliff: reused by Seneca at *Pho.* 359 (Oedipus): *latebo rupis exesae cauo*, 'I'll hide in the cave of a crumbling cliff'.

sollicita…deum/Anxiety…god: a   double   *sententia*   rounds   off Amphitryon's six-line speech, underscoring Amphitryon as a man of authority.

sollicita…pretia…semperque magno constitit/Anxiety is the price…It's always costly: note the financial imagery occasionally evident in the tragedies; see 24 and n. *ad loc.* For the financial use of *constare*, see also *Pha.* 1153, *Tro.* 358, *Med.* 603, *Pho.* 664, Ov. *Her.* 7.47 For the sententious use of *semper*, see 316 and n. *ad loc. Magno* is ablative of price, a form of instrumental ablative: see Woodcock §43.2. For *sollicitus*, lit. 'anxious', as a transferred epithet elsewhere, see *Pha.* 518, *Tro.* 406.

463-4 A stichomythic exchange of *sententiae* (see on 125-204 introd.), which effects a transition from the issue of Hercules' divine origins to that of his heroic nature. The two lines are an extreme instance of 'Stichworttechnik' (see on 422-38), as at *Med.* 504-5 and *Thy.* 1111-12. Readers interested in the utilization of antiquity by later socio-political organizations might note that the first *sententia* (463) may be found in the top margin of page 6 of the 1868 Ku Klux Klan pamphlet, 'Revised and Amended Prescript of the Order of the * * *'. The second *sententia* (464) is a version of the Stoic idea that *uirtus* is incompatible with misery: see esp. *Ep. Mor.* 92, including: *ita miser quidem qui uirtutem habet non potest*, 'Thus he who has virtue cannot indeed be wretched' (92.14). Medea's remark at *Med.* 176 is a related quasi-Stoic variant: *fortuna opes auferre, non animum potest*, 'Fortune can remove wealth, not the spirit.' For Stoic language and ideas in *Hercules*, see on 162-9. For rebarbative reuse of an interlocutor's preceding statement, see *Tro.* 323-6, 343-4, *Med.* 504-5, *Ag.* 157-8, *Thy.* 1111-12. *Scias* and *neges* are second-person singular potential subjunctives used in generalizations: see 343 and n. *ad loc.* Such use is common in *sententiae*.

465-94 Part II of the Amphitryon-Lycus debate (*agon*): Hercules' heroic nature.

465-71 Lycus reports some less glorious Herculean deeds to undermine his status as a *uir fortis* or 'hero', in the process giving the audience an unflattering portrait of an effeminate Hercules to add to those given by Amphitryon, Megara, and Juno. The Hercules described here is the lover of Omphale, queen of Lydia, of whom Hercules was enamoured and for whom he served as a slave, wearing effeminate dress and jewellery and performing women's duties. See *Pha.* 317–29, *HO* 371–6, Prop. 4.9.47–50, Stat. *Ach.* 1.260–1, Ov. *Fas.* 2.305–30, but esp. *Her.* 9.55–118, to which the accounts here and in *Phaedra* seem indebted. In Apollodorus (2.6.2–3) Hercules was not in love with the queen, but simply sold as a slave to her as punishment for the killing of Iphitus, son of King Eurytus of Oechalia (for whom see on 477–80).

umeris/shoulders: for the play's focus on Hercules' 'shoulders', see on 622–5.

donum puellae/a girl's gift: note the ambiguity; the 'girl' is (i) Omphale, (ii) Hercules, who is described at Ov. *Her.* 9.65 as *lasciuae more puellae*, 'like a naughty girl', and who describes himself at Prop. 4.9.50 as *apta puella*, 'a likely girl'. Note the rare and elegiac use of *puella* (see 18 above and n. *ad loc.*), moving the tone towards the erotic. For the lion skin and club as fashion accessories for Omphale, as she gazes in the mirror, see Ov. *Her.* 9.111–18; see also *Fas.* 2.325.

fulsitque pictum ueste Sidonia latus/gaudy flank shimmered in Sidon dress: Sidon was a Phoenician port city, here representing not only Phoenicia but eastern effeminacy. Similarly, at Ov. *Her.* 9.101, Hercules' dress is 'Sidonian' (*Sidonio...amictu*), but, at *Fas.* 2.319 and *Pha.* 329, it is 'Tyrian'—Tyre being another maritime Phoenician city, famous for its finely woven fabrics and purple dye. Cf. the ironic recall of this description at *HO* 788, where Hercules is again 'shimmering in a dress' (*ueste...fulgens*), but the dress is a poisoned robe. *Pictum*, 'gaudy' (lit. 'painted'), presumably refers to the purple colour of the dress, as Billerbeck notes *ad loc.*

horrentes comae maduere nardo/bristling hair dripped With nard: cf. the Messenger's description of Thyestes (*fluente madidus unguento comam*, 'his hair drips with scented oils', *Thy.* 780) and Thyestes' description of himself (*pingui madidus crinis amomo*, 'my hair drips sleek with oil', *Thy.* 948), where the focus is similarly on indulgence and emasculation. See also Seneca's portrait of Pleasure, *Voluptas*, 'dripping with wine and oils' (*mero atque unguento madentem*, *Vit. Beat.* 7.3). Nard is an aromatic plant used by the ancients to produce an ointment or, as here, perfume, and, though such unguents were used by male banqueters and lovers (e.g. Prop. 2.4.5, Hor. *Odes* 1.5.2, 2.11.14–17), nard was often treated negatively by Roman poets. For a similar description of Hercules, see *HO* 376: *hirtam Sabaea marcidus myrrha comam*, 'his shaggy hair drooping with Sabaean myrrh'. Shaggy or dishevelled hair suggests 'manliness'; see the description of Hippolytus at *Pha.* 757 and 803–4.

qui/who: for the postponement of the relative, see on 159–61.

non uirilem tympani…sonum/unmanly sound of a timbrel: the timbrel, *tympanum*, is one of the primary musical instruments of the castrated Galli, as described in the only Greek or Latin Galliambic poem to survive: Catullus 63. It is an appropriate instrument for an effeminate Hercules. Cf. Statius' description of Hercules at *Theb.* 10. 646–9. For the use of *non* to negate an adjective, see on 489–94.

mitra ferocem barbara frontem/savage brow…with foreign turban: more connections with the east and with Ovid, who has Hercules 'binding shaggy hair with a turban' (*hirsutos mitra redimire capillos, Her.* 9.63). The *mitra*, an eastern headgear (*Lydia mitra*, 'Lydian turban', Prop. 3.17.30), which in Rome had connotations of effeminacy (Virg. *Aen.* 4.216, Mart. *Epig.* 2.36.3), is associated elsewhere in the tragedies with Bacchus: *Oed.* 413, *Pha.* 756 (cf. also Soph. *OT* 209). It is said to be worn by Hercules also at *HO* 375. Like *syrma* below, it is associated, too, with the stage: Pollux (4.115) includes it in a list of headgear worn by tragic actors. *Barbara* here is 'foreign' in a contemptuous sense (*Pha.* 227, *Ag.* 185), reflective of the prejudices of this newly minted king. Juvenal (3.66) reproduces its contempt with the phrase *picta lupa barbara mitra*, 'foreign prostitute in a gaudy turban'. Not contemptuous is Amphitryon's answering *barbarico* (475). For *ferox*, 'savage', see on 5–63.

472-6 Some of Amphitryon's language seems borrowed from the 'Bacchus Ode' of *Oedipus*, which probably predates this play (see Introd. 6–7): cf. *effusos…sparsisse crines*, 'tossed His streaming hair' (472–3), and *spargere effusos…crines*, 'toss his streaming hair' (*Oed.* 416); *manu molli leuem uibrare thyrsum*, 'shake the light thyrsus With soft hands' (473–4), and *thyrsumque leuem uibrante manu*, 'hands shaking the light thyrsus' (*Oed.* 441); *syrma*, 'Tragic robe' (475), and *syrma*, 'tragic robe' (*Oed.* 423).

Bacchus…tener/Tender Bacchus: again (see on 457–62), as if triggered by the use of *mitra* (see previous n.), Amphitryon compares Hercules with Bacchus (for whom see on 11–18), describing the latter's much bruited effeminacy, represented widely in Greek and Roman literature and art. An effeminate appearance (hence *tener*, 'tender': Tib. 2.3.63, Ov. *Am.* 3.2.53), esp. long hair and soft arms/hands, and the wielding of the thyrsus are standard properties of Bacchus/Dionysus; see e.g. *Hom. Hym.*7.4–5, 26.1; Eur. *Bacch.* 150, 240, 453–9; Acc. *Bacch.* frags 253, 255 Klotz. Bacchus is summoned by Hercules at 903–4.

effusos…sparsisse crines/toss His streaming hair: a practice ascribed to Bacchus from his *Homeric Hymn* (7.4) onwards. For Bacchus' 'streaming hair', see *Oed.* 416 (cited above), *Pha.* 754 (*intonsa coma*, 'unshorn hair'), and Eur. *Bacch.* 150. For syncopated perfect infinitives, see 63 and n. *ad loc.*

leuem uibrare thyrsum/shake the light thyrsus: the thyrsus, mentioned again at 904, was the much-debated Bacchic wand, carried by Bacchus and his followers. It consisted of a giant fennel/artichoke stalk, regularly decorated with ivy (Prop. 3.3.35) or vine-leaves (Ov. *Met.* 3.667), and topped either with the artichoke head or, in the case of fennel, with a cluster of ivy leaves which looks like a pine cone. Sometimes (see 904 below, Cat. 64.256, Ov. *Met.* 3.667), the thyrsus is tipped with a concealed spear-point and functions as a weapon. At *Pho.* 18 Agave's thyrsus is tipped with the head of her son, Pentheus. Countries conquered by Bacchus might be called 'thyrsus-bearing' (*thyrsigera…India, Pha.* 753). *Vibrare* is the quintessential verb for 'shaking' the thyrsus; see also *Oed.* 441 (cited above), 628, and *Pho.* 18.

parum forti gradu/with dainty step: this is not the 'heroic' stride of the *fortis* (464, 465, 468), but an effeminate step, able to be seen as a sign of 'womanly softness', *muliebris mollitia*, according to Seneca (*Tranq.* 17.4, *Ep. Mor.* 114.3). Cf. the description of Hymen, son of Bacchus, as *gradu…ebrio*, 'with drunken step' (*Med.* 69). For Seneca and other elite Romans, gait (*gradus, gressus, incessus*) was an index of character; see on 329–31.

auro decorum syrma barbarico trahit/trails A tragic gown crusted with foreign gold: the *syrma* (σύρμα) was a robe with a long train, worn by tragic actors (Juv. 8.229); it sometimes functioned as a metonym for tragedy (Mart. *Epig.* 4.49.8, 12.94.4). Seneca is the first Latin author in whom this word is attested. It occurs only once elsewhere in his writings, viz. at *Oed.* 423, where it is again associated with Bacchus and seems designed to reinforce the god's association with tragedy. Writers after Seneca use *syrma* only of the tragic actor's gown. *Trahere* is used regularly of 'trailing' long robes (e.g. Hor. *Odes* 2.18.8, *AP* 215), but here its use is enlivened by a clever, translingual, etymological pun: *syrma traho* = σύρμα σύρω: see on 35–40. For *auro…barbarico*, 'foreign gold', see Virg. *Aen.* 2.504 and Austin's n. *ad loc.*

post multa uirtus opera laxari solet/After much work virtue often relaxes: another closural *sententia*, in which Amphitryon keeps the focus on Hercules' *uirtus*. Seneca seems to agree with this proposition at *Tranq.* 17.4, where he offers the *exempla* of Socrates, Cato, and Scipio who found time to 'relax the mind' (*laxabat animum*). See also *Eleg. Maec.* 1.69–86, where Hercules' 'relaxation' in Lydia is presented as acceptable and as

Roman as relaxing after the battle of Actium. For the verb *solere*, 'to be accustomed', in Senecan *sententiae*, see e.g. *Tro.* 581: *necessitas plus posse quam pietas solet*, 'Necessity is often stronger than *pietas*'; *Oed.* 699–700: *dubia pro certis solent* | *timere reges*, 'Kings often take dubious fears for real'; also *Pha.* 735, *Tro.* 515, *Thy.* 474. For the *uirtus* motif, see on 35–40.

477–80 Lycus, quick-witted as ever, responds to Amphitryon's *sententia* by ironically citing, as instances of its 'truth', notorious examples of Hercules' excessive 'relaxation', which he then classifies as Hercules' actual 'work' (*ipsius opera*, 480), picking up Amphitryon's language (476).

   Hoc...fatetur/As witnessed by: neat, sarcastic phrasing.

   Euryti...euersi domus/ruined Eurytus' house: the phrase is enlarged (without transferred epithet) at *HO* 100–1: *Euryti uictos lares* | *stratumque regnum*, 'Eurytus' conquered house and flattened kingdom'. Eurytus was king of Oechalia, apparently located by Sophocles in Euboea (*Trach.* 401). According to Sophocles, Apollodorus (2.7.7), Hyginus (*Fab.* 35), and *Hercules Oetaeus* (207–14), Eurytus and his son(s) were killed and the city sacked by Hercules, enamoured of his daughter, Iole, whom he subsequently brought or sent home. The episode is sometimes criticized for its anachronism, being generally considered one of the last episodes of Hercules' life (see e.g. Soph. *Trachiniae* and *Hercules Oetaeus*), when the hero was living in exile with his final wife, Deianira, at Trachis in southern Thessaly. But the chronology and details of the story vary widely: see Gantz (1993: 1.434–7).

   pecorumque ritu uirginum oppressi greges/flocks of virgins harried like sheep: taken by some as referring to the Thespiades, the fifty daughters of Thespius, king of Thespiae near Thebes in Boeotia. Hercules had sexual intercourse with the fifty daughters to generate grandchildren for their father (see e.g. Ov. *Her.* 9.51–2, *HO* 369–70, Stat. *Silu.* 3.1.42–3). Others (e.g. Fitch *ad loc.*) see a reference to all the women molested by Hercules. *Oppressi greges* and *pecorum ritu*, 'like sheep' (the latter phrase suggests bestial promiscuity: see Livy 3.47.7, *pecudum ferarumque ritu*, and Hor. *Serm.* 1.3.109, *rapientis more ferarum*) suggest to me the first alternative, as does the allusion in Ovid's *Heroides* 9 (Deianira to Hercules), a poem clearly in Seneca's mind during this debate. For *opprimo* in an explicit sexual sense, see *CIL* 4.1879 (cited by Adams 1982: 182). For the phrase *pecorum ritu*, see *Vit. Beat.* 1.3.

   hoc nulla Iuno.../No Juno...: a fine alliterative and assonantal line, echoing a statement made by Sophocles' Heracles in *Trachiniae* (1048–9). For Eurystheus, who ordered the twelve 'labours', see Introd. §VI, 61.

ipsius haec sunt opera/They are his work: an overt echo of Amphitryon's *opera* (476). For climactic half-lines, see on 40–6.

480–9 Amphitryon in turn picks up Lycus' *ipsius…opera*, 'his work' (480), with his own *ipsius opus* (481, repeated in the same position at 485), and produces a mini-catalogue of Herculean feats not ordered by Juno or Eurystheus, although his final example (the killing of Geryon), while strictly not being ordered, occurred during such an order. This catalogue of violence overcome by Hercules is a clear warning to Amphitryon's interlocutor. For catalogues in *Hercules*, see on 6–18.

caestibus fractus suis/smashed by his own gloves: Seneca focuses regularly on the ironies of modes of death. See also the deaths of Busiris, Cycnus, and Geryon.

Eryx…Antaeus Libys/Eryx…Libyan Antaeus: Eryx, son of Boutes and Venus, was king of the Elymoi in western Sicily; he was fatally defeated in a boxing match by Hercules as the latter was returning from the west with the cattle of Geryon. Virgil (*Aen.* 5.410) also has the contest as a boxing-match rather than a wrestling contest (as is presented in Diodorus, Apollodorus, and Pausanias). Antaeus was (in the Roman tradition) a Giant, son of Earth, in Africa, who was fatally defeated in a wrestling bout by Hercules. Hercules (so Ov. *Met.* 9.183–4, Luc. 4.593–653, Stat. *Theb.* 6.893–6) lifted Antaeus in the air away from the earth, from which he derived his strength. Antaeus and Busiris (see below) seem referred to by Hercules later at 1171 and by Amphitryon at 1255.

Eryx et Eryci: note the polyptoton; see on 11–18.

qui/which: for the relative pronoun *qui* in elision, as here, see 593, 604; for *quae*, see 674, *Ag.* 274 and *Thy.* 978; for *quam*, see *Ag.* 131; for *qua*, see *Pho.* 22; for *quo*, see *Pho.* 639.

bibere iustum sanguinem Busiridis/drank the just blood of Busiris: Busiris was an Egyptian king and son of Neptune, who sacrificed to Jupiter all strangers at his altars (Ov. *Ars.* 1.647–52), until he was slain by Hercules at the same altars: see 1254–5 below, *Tro.* 1106–7, *HO* 25–6, Callim. *Aet.* 2. frg. 44 Pf., Virg. *Geo.* 3.5, Ov. *Met.* 9.183, *Tr.* 3.11.39, *Pont.* 3.6.41. For figurative 'drinking' elsewhere, see *Ag.* 700, *Tro.* 1164, *Med.* 778, *Oct.* 521–2, *Clem.* 1.12.2; cf. also Ov. *Met.* 13.409–10 (and Bömer *ad loc.*), Soph. *El.* 785–6. For non-figurative drinking or libations of blood: 636, 920, *Thy.* 917–18. Note the polysyllabic ending in a Greek name: see on 6–11. For *iustus sanguis*, 'just blood' = 'blood justly spilt', see *Pha.* 708–9; for sacrificial language and imagery in *Hercules*, see on 918–24.

uulneri et ferro inuius/impervious to wound And steel: along with Fitch (1987*a* and 2018), Chaumartin, Billerbeck, and Giardina (2007), I have printed the conjecture of N. Heinsius, *inuius* (which seems dictated by *integer Cycnus* in 486: see next n.), instead of the *EA* reading *obuius*, accepted by Zwierlein and others. Cf. the Ovidian description (*Met.* 12.166-7):

> uisum mirabile cunctis
> quod iuueni corpus nullo penetrabile telo
> inuictumque a uulnere erat ferrumque terebat.

> It seemed a marvel to all
> That the youth's body was penetrable by no spear
> And unmastered by wound, and it blunted steel.

Cycnus: Seneca/Amphitryon has conflated two figures: (i) son of Neptune, renowned for his magic and his white hair (*cana nitentem...iuuenem coma*, 'gleaming white-haired youth', *Tro.* 184), who, unable to be harmed by a spearpoint, had to be killed 'intact' (*integer*), and was choked to death by Achilles at Troy, turning into a swan (= *cycnus*) through the agency of his father: see *Tro.* 183-4, *Ag.* 215, Ov. *Met.* 12.72-145; (ii) son of Mars, killed by Hercules' spear in Thessaly (see [Hesiod] *Aspis* 413-23).

pati/to suffer: for *pati* as the ultimate word of the line, see on 348-53.

nec unus una Geryon...manu/un-single Geryon...by one hand: Hercules was ordered to bring back the cattle of Geryon (see on 231-4); he was not ordered to kill him—that was Hercules' own work, *ipsius opus*, 485. For Seneca's verbal play with *unus*, see on 19-29. For adjectival polyptoton elsewhere in Senecan tragedy, see e.g. *Pha.* 237, *Oed.* 829, *Tro.* 791, *Thy.* 31, *Ag.* 62, 607. For Seneca's play with *unus* in connection with Geryon, see also *Ag.* 838. The present verbal play is imitated at *HO* 26. For polyptoton in *Hercules*, see on 11-18.

eris inter istos/You will join them: a trenchant conclusion to Amphitryon's list with a deft use of the pejorative force of *istos*.

stupro/debauched: this is the only occurrence in *Hercules* of *stuprum*, a technical legal term for prohibited sexual activity, heterosexual and homosexual, used more often by tragic Seneca (twelve times) than by any other Latin poet (Ovid uses the word five times, Propertius three, Virgil not at all). *Stuprum* ('shameful/unnatural sexual behaviour', 'lust') had been prohibited by the republican *Lex Scantinia*, first attested in Cicero (*Fam.* 8.12.3, 14.4) and much debated by scholars. In Senecan tragedy *stuprum* is used in reference to rape (as here, *Tro.* 342, and *Pha.* 897, where Hippolytus is labelled a *stuprator*; cf. also *Oct.* 303), incest (*Oed.* 664), and adultery (*Ag.*

1009, *Thy.* 222), which was criminalized by the Augustan legislation of 18 BCE. For further discussion of *stuprum*, see Adams (1982: 200–1), Williams (1999: 96–124).

489–94 Responding to Amphitryon's climactic *thalamos*, 'bed/bedchamber', Lycus draws an ironic parallel between his own situation in respect of Megara and that of Jupiter in respect of Amphitryon's wife, Alcmena.

Quod Ioui hoc regi licet/**What Jove may do, a king may do**: exemplarity was used by Megara to threaten Lycus at 386–96 (see n. *ad loc.*); here Lycus turns the tables to use it as an argument in favour of his marital plans. The issue of 'what is allowed' (*quod licet*) to king, ruler, master, conqueror, etc., is another question (see on 341–8) with pointed relevance to imperial Rome and one debated elsewhere in Seneca in both the tragedies and prose works: e.g. *Tro.* 335–6, *Ag.* 272, *Thy.* 214–18, *Pol.* 6.4–5, 7.2, *Clem.* 1.8.2, 11.2. In the last passage Seneca advances the paradoxical proposition to Nero: *quam multa tibi non licent quae nobis beneficio tuo licent*, 'how many things are not allowed to you, which are allowed to us thanks to you'. The more regular position was the one advocated by Lycus here, which is similar to that attributed to Caligula by Suetonius: *memento omnia mihi et in omnis licere*, 'Remember that I am allowed to do anything to anyone', *Gaius* 29.1. Cf. also *Oct.* 450–1, 574. For the ruler's total license, see Sall. *Iug.* 31.26: *impune quae lubet facere id est regem esse*, 'To do with impunity what one pleases is to be a king'. For the relationship of king to subject, see on 341–8; for Roman referentiality in *Hercules*, see on 46–52. Disquisitions on *quod licet* seem to have been popular with the orators: see Cic. *Rab. Post.* 11–12, *Balb.* 8.

regi dabis/**you'll give one to the king**: under Roman law, since Megara's own father and her brothers are dead, it would fall to Amphitryon, Megara's 'dead' husband's father and effectively *paterfamilias* in the absence of Hercules, to betroth Megara. On Roman betrothal procedure, see Treggiari (1991: 138–45). Like most modern editors I have printed the consensus MS reading, *dabis*. Zwierlein prints Leo's emendation, *dabit*.

te magistro non nouum hoc discet nurus/**teach your daughter a lesson un-new**: 'un-new', *non/haud nouum*, is a provocative Senecan formula for something already experienced once (or twice): cf. *Med.* 447, *Ag.* 302, *Thy.* 62. For Seneca's ironic use of *nouus*, see e.g. *Med.* 743, 894; *Tro.* 900, 1154; *Oed.* 180, 943–4; *Pha.* 170. For the use of *non* to negate an adjective, a form of litotes common in Senecan tragedy, see e.g. 230 (*non leuem*), 470 (*non uirilem*), 525 (*non aequa*), 559 (*non reuocabiles*), 575 (*non solitis*), 945 (*non minima*); *Pha.* 237 (*non casta*), 274 (*non miti*), 994 (*non imparatum*); *Tro.* 67 (*non rude*), 82 (*non indociles*), 404 (*non facili*), 408 (*non nata*); *Oed.* 367

(*non...capax*), 385 (*non timida*), 448 (*non uile*); *Med.* 915 (*non rudem*); *Thy.* 169 (*non leuior*), 490 (*non dubio*), 874 (*non stabilis*), 931 (*non inflexa*). For this ironic use of *discet*, lit. 'will learn', see on 68–74.

copulari pertinax taedis/stubborn...wed: lit. 'stubborn...couple with torches', *taedae*, 'wedding torches', being, as often, metonymic for the wedding itself. The ablative is perhaps best taken as one of accompaniment: see Woodcock §43.5. *Pertinax*, 'stubborn', marks the repetition of Lycus' fear of 350.

nobilem partum/noble offspring: Lycus brings into the open the concern with his own ignoble roots (338–40, 345–8) and his need to rectify them.

495–500 Lycus' threat of rape draws from Megara an immediate response of outrage, as she hurls Oedipal and Danaid precedents at her oppressor, repeating her initial threat (396) of a customary Theban outcome.

Vmbrae Creontis et penates Labdaci/Ghost of Creon and gods of Labdacus: Labdacus was an early king of Thebes: grandson of Cadmus, father of Laius, grandfather of Oedipus. In Greek tragedy the house of the Labdacids is the paradigm of a doomed royal house (see e.g. Soph. *Antig.* 594–5, Eur. *Pho.* 800). See also *Oed.* 710. Here Megara is invoking the *penates Labdaci* to threaten death. *Penates*, 'gods', are the 'household gods', gods of the inner reaches of the Roman house, technically of the storecupboard. They were frequently used by metonymy for the house itself, giving the latter a quasi-religious dimension: see *Pho.* 556, 663; *Ag.* 396, *Oed.* 23; *Med.* 450; *Thy.* 24, 52, 775; *Oct.* 149, 278. Cicero (*ND* 2.68) derived the name either from *penus* ('store') or from the fact that these gods resided *penitus*, i.e. in the recesses of the house. Like *lares* (see on 913–18), with which it is often paired, *penates* is a specifically Roman term. For Roman referentiality in the play, see on 46–52. For Creon, father of Megara, see on 249–58 (*ipsumque*). Note the breach of 'Porson's law': see on 249–58.

nuptiales impii Oedipodae faces/nuptial brands of impious Oedipus: the juxtaposition of *nuptiales* and *impii* gives the *faces*, 'brands/torches', an ominous flavour. The conflation of wedding and funeral is a *topos* of ancient literature and a regular motif in ancient tragedy, figuring strongly in Seneca's *Troades* and in *Octavia*. The conflation often revolves, as here, around the ambiguous image of the wedding/funeral torch: see e.g. Erinna, *AP* 7.712.5–6; Ov. *Her.* 6.41–2, 21.172; Sen. Rhet. *Con.* 6.6: *subiectae rogo felices faces*, 'The celebratory torches were put to the pyre'. For the conflation in Greek tragedy, see Rehm (1994). For other 'impious torches', see that of Medea at *Ag.* 119, and again that of Oedipus at *Oed.* 20–1. The form *Oedipodae*, genitive here, as at Stat. *Theb.* 1.17, may be found as a dative at *Oed.* 216 and *Pho.* 89.

solita…fata/common fate: Megara returns to the theme of the closural line of her initial response to Lycus (*solita…fata*, 'common fate', 396).

nunc, nunc…adeste /Now, now…Come to me: by invoking dire creatures from hell, Megara is echoing Juno's invocation of the Furies in the prologue (86ff.), playing Juno to Lycus' Hercules. A strong metadramatic level also comes to the surface, as Megara reaches out to other texts and other plays for an appropriate response to Lycus: cf. Horace's witch, Canidia, invoking *Nox* ('Night') and Diana (*Epod.* 5.53); Seneca's Medea invoking the Furies in the prologue of her play (*Med.* 13); Seneca's Theseus invoking the 'savage monsters of the deep' (*Pha.* 1204). Later dramatists followed suit: thus Thomas Hughes's Queen Guenevera: 'Come, spiteful fiends, come heaps of furies fell, | Not one by one, but all at once' (*The Misfortunes of Arthur* I.ii.39–40); so, too, Shakespeare's Lady Macbeth 'Come, you Spirits | That tend on mortal thoughts' (*Macbeth* I.v.40–1). Cf. also Atreus' summoning of Procne as his Muse in the later *Thyestes* (275–7). *Adeste* and the singular *ades* (lit. 'be present') are the standard terms in Roman prayer and in Senecan tragedy for the invocation of deities, though of course the Danaids are not deities: see e.g. *Oed.* 257 (several gods), 405 (Bacchus); *Ag.* 340 (Juno); *Pha.* 54, 412, 423 (Diana); *Med.* 13, 16 (Furies); Ov. *Fas.* 1.67, 69 (Janus), 3.2 (Mars). For the *geminatio*, see on 92–9; for the anaphoric use of temporal adverbs, see on 1272–7. For metatheatricality in *Hercules*, see on 109–12.

cruentae regis Aegypti nurus/gory wives of King Aegyptus' sons: the Danaids or daughters of Danaus, founder of Argos, who were fifty in number and were forcibly married to their cousins, the fifty sons of Danaus' brother, Aegyptus, king of Egypt. All but one (Hypermestra)—on the instructions of their father—killed their husbands on their wedding-night. Hypermestra disobeyed and spared her husband (see Hor. *Odes* 3.11, Ov. *Her.* 14); the forty-nine who obeyed were (at least in the Roman tradition) condemned to spend eternity in the underworld filling a leaky jar or carrying water in perforated pitchers (see below at 757, *Med.* 748). Ovid calls them *turba cruenta*, 'a gory mob' (*Ib.* 178). They are also summoned by Medea (*Med.* 748–9). The story of the Danaids is the subject of a trilogy by Aeschylus, of which the first play, *Supplices*, 'Suppliant Women', survives. Statues of the Danaids adorned the Portico of the Augustan temple of Apollo on the Palatine in Rome (see e.g. Ov. *Ars* 1.73–4), and the bloody mariticide itself was engraved on the *balteus* of Virgil's Pallas (*Aen.*

10.495–500, 12.941–6), prompting Aeneas' foundational slaughter. This is an invocation with strong Roman resonance. For Roman referentiality in *Hercules*, see on 46–52.

infectae manus/hands drenched: *manus* is accusative of respect; see 107 and n. *ad loc.* For the *manus* motif, see on 118–22.

dest una numero Danais/One Danaid's missing: Hypermestra; see above. Euripides' Antigone similarly promises to model her marriage-night on that of the Danaids (*Pho.* 1675). Line 500 is closely imitated at *HO* 948 (Deianira speaking). For the Danaid paradigm in Groto's *La Hadriana*, see III.iii.99. For Seneca's concern with 'number', see 832, *Ag.* 811, *Pha.* 1153, *Oed.* 782, *Med.* 1011, *Thy.* 57; for verbal play with *unus*, see on 19–29. *Dest* (= *deest*) is a common syncopated/contracted form of *deesse*, which all modern editors print on metrical grounds instead of the *EA* reading *deest*; see also 832. Despite the testimony of the main MSS, it seems that the dissyllabic forms, *deest, deesse,* etc., frequent in the prose works, do not occur in the tragedies. For the rhetorical use of *desse*, see 40 and n. *ad loc.*

explebo nefas/I'll complete the horror: for *nefas*, see 387 and n. *ad loc.*

501–8 Lycus, clearly reeling from Megara's menacing outburst, finally drops his marriage plan or even his goal of royal children and moves to Plan B (350–1): the destruction of Hercules' whole family. His instructions to burn down the temple seem to smack of the transgression of religious boundaries sometimes associated with tyrants (e.g. [Quint.] *Decl. Min.* 329). Such impiety reaches its most famous Senecan dramatization in the figure of Atreus, who takes pride in offending and terrifying gods (*Thy.* 265–6, 704–5, 885–95). Cf. also the focus on the religious transgressions of Nero in *Octavia* (89, 240–1, 449). Lycus, however, is no straightforward 'impious tyrant'. His final words in the play (515) are ones of religious devotion. With Lycus' instructions for the piling of wood (506–8), cf. those of Euripides' Lycus at *Herac.* 240–6. Ironically Megara's mother-in-law, Alcmena, was similarly threatened with being burnt alive at an altar—by Amphitryon in Euripides' *Alcmene*: see Collard and Crop (2008*a*: 101).

Coniugia quoniam: for the dactyl-tribrach combination at the start of the line (*quoniam* is trisyllabic), see 76 and n. *ad loc.*

sceptra quid possint scies/you'll know a sceptre's power: cf. Oedipus, playing the tyrant-figure with threats against Creon: *quid arma possint regis irati scies*, 'you'll know the armed power of an angry king' (*Oed.* 519). Note the postponed interrogative; see 383 and n. For *sceptra*, see on 63–8.

Complectere aras/Embrace the altar: presumably (hence my stage directions) in response to Megara already putting her hands on the altar, seeking the gods' protection. The altar was an asylum from which it was impious to drag someone away. For the phrase, see Ov. *Met.* 9.772. For Seneca's use of the plural form of *ara*, see on 875–81. For the religious importance of 'touching' an altar, see on 875–81.

eripiet…si…queat: for this combination of future indicative and present subjunctive, see 362–5 and n. *ad loc.*

orbe…remolito/**upheave the world**: note in this ablative absolute the passive use of the deponent verb *remoliri* (lit. 'the world having been upheaved').

ad supera…numina/**to the gods above**: earth or heaven? For the ambiguity of *supera*, see on 46–52. *Numina* is the consensus MS reading; Zwierlein prints the emendation of Heinsius, *lumina*, but of modern editors only Giardina (2007) follows him.

Congerite siluas/**Pile up wood**: for this kind of unadorned imperative addressed to slaves, guards, attendants, or other *personae mutae*, see on 1048–53 (*famuli*).

templa supplicibus suis iniecta flagrent/**Let the temple fall blazing On its suppliants**: In Euripides' *Heracles* (240–6), Lycus threatens to burn the suppliants at the altar; so, too, Labrax at Plaut. *Rud.* 768 and Theopropides at Plaut. *Most.* 1114. Seneca's Lycus wants them all in the temple with the latter burning down on top of them. For 'temples burning down on top of their own gods' (*templa deos super usta suos*), see the Trojan Chorus' description of the fall of Troy at *Ag.* 653. See also *Pho.* 344: *templis deos obruite*, 'crush the gods with their temples'; *Const.* 6.2: *inter fragorem templorum super deos suos cadentium*, 'amid the crash of temples falling on their gods'; cf. also 1288–9, *HO* 173–4. Here, of course, though the temple will fall on its gods, Lycus' intention is to have it fall on Hercules' family.

coniugem et totum gregem consumat unus…locus/**consume Wife and her whole flock in a single place**: cf. Andromache at *Tro.* 686–7: *ruina mater et natum et uirum | prosternis una*, 'Do you, a mother, destroy both son and husband with one collapse'. For the play with *unus*, see on 19–29; note how Lycus here matches in his closural line Megara's play with *unus* in her closural line (500). For the importance of *locus*, 'place', in *Hercules*, see on 1–5 and Introd. §VII. Here the word is given prominence by its final position and conjunction with *unus*, as Lycus seeks to impose on Hercules' family and the great hero's immeasurable and transcendent cosmic career, bruited powerfully at the opening of this act, a single fiery, fatal, and confining 'place'. There are also metadramatic resonances. The *unus locus*, 'single place', where Hercules' wife and sons will be consumed, albeit not through the agency of Lycus, will be the theatre itself in which the tragedy is being performed (or, in the case of readers of the play, the text in their hands). *Gregem*, 'flock', which has an especial, sacrificial resonance in this context of potentially imminent slaughter, also, of course, has a theatrical meaning, deployed perhaps at Megara's entrance in the play: see on 202–4. For meta-drama/metatheatre in *Hercules*, see on 109–12. *Locus*, the *EA* reading, is unjustifiably replaced with *rogus* (from the 1517 edition of Auantius) by Zwierlein and other modern editors. If there were conflicting MS readings, *locus* would be the *lectio difficilior*. As it is, both *E* and *A* agree on *locus*, a thematically crucial word in this play, here given climactic emphasis. Emendation to *rogus* turns this focus into a banality.

509-10 Similarly Euripides' Amphitryon (*Herac.* 321–25) asks Lycus to kill him and Megara before killing the children. For the death-wish in Senecan tragedy, see on 1022–31.

genitor Alcidae/**Alcides' father:** Amphitryon seems somewhat concili-atory in this plea, apparently conceding Lycus' claim concerning Hercules' paternity by referring to Hercules as Alcides and proclaiming himself his 'father'. Billerbeck *ad loc.* calls this proclamation 'sarkastisch', but such a tone would undermine Amphitryon's plea. For Seneca's fondness for nouns ending in -*tor*, see on 299–302.

rogare quod me deceat/**Which it is right I ask:** Euripides' Amphitryon articulates his motive for being the first to die: to avoid witnessing the deaths of his grandchildren. Here the motive claimed is probity, what is right: *quod me deceat*. For the frequent appeals to 'probity' in Senecan tragedy, see on 408–13.

ut primus cadam/**that I die first:** Amphitryon will reiterate a wish for death at 1028–31, 1039–42, and 1300–13; see nn. *ad locc.*

511-15 *Qui… nescit tyrannus esse*/**One who … does not know Tyranny:** the word *tyrannus* elsewhere often denotes an absolute ruler, monarch, etc. with-out negative implications (e.g. Virg. *Aen.* 7.266, 342); but it sometimes also has the pejorative connotations of the English word 'tyrant', as here and at *Ag.* 252, 995, *Tro.* 303, *Clem.* 1.11.4–12.3, and throughout *Octavia*, where it is used of Nero some eight times: *Oct.* 33, 87, 110, 250, 610, 620, 899, 959. Cf. also Cicero's Scipio: *cum rex iniustus esse coepit…est idem ille tyrannus*, 'When a king has begun to be unjust…that same man is a tyrant' (*Rep.* 1.65). It is noteworthy that *Octavia*'s Nero never uses the word of himself—unlike Lycus here or the self-consciously tyrannical Aegisthus (*Ag.* 995, printed below) and Atreus, the latter of whom not only defines himself to the audience as a *tyrannus* (*Thy.* 177, 247) but seems fashioned in part to recall Seneca's own discussion of the *tyrannus* in *De Clementia* (1.12). For the *nescire* idiom, cf. Oedipus' statement: *odia qui nimium timet | regnare nescit*, 'One who fears hate too much | Does not know kingship' (*Oed.* 703–4).

Lycus' teachings/*sententiae* on tyranny inevitably mirror those of his fellow tyrants, especially Aegisthus (*Ag.* 995):

> rudis est tyrannus morte qui poenam exigit.
>
> The untutored tyrant punishes with death.

Cf. Atreus at *Thy.* 247, Oedipus at *Pho.* 98–100 (printed below), Andromache at *Tro.* 576–7—and Nero at *Oct.* 825. As Tarrant observes *ad Ag.* 995, the Julio-Claudian emperors were sometimes accredited with such views: note Suetonius on Tiberius: *mortem…leue supplicium putabat*, 'He thought death was a light punishment' (*Tib.* 61.5). See also Seneca on Gaius (*NQ* 4A Pref. 17), in whose reign death was regarded as 'an act of mercy' (*inter misericordiae opera*); *Tro.* 329 (Pyrrhus); *Thy.* 247–8 (Atreus); Luc. 2.509ff. (Julius Caesar); and *Ira* 1.16.3: *interim optimum misericordiae genus est occidere*, 'sometimes the highest form of pity is to kill'. For 'death = boon under a tyranny' as a declamatory *topos*, see Sen. Rhet. *Suas.* 6.10 (cf. *Con.* 8.4). For earlier variations, see Euripides' Theseus at *Hipp.* 1045–50; for later variations, see Giraldi's Sumone at *Orbecche* III.iii. Mark also the metadramatic implications of Lycus' pronouncement, viz. his awareness of his role as *tyrannus* and pride in that role: this is how well-scripted tyrants act in tragedy. For metatheatricality, see on 109–12. For *sententiae*, see on 125–204.

inroga…ueta…iube/Vary…keep…order: generalizing imperatives.

miserum ueta perire/keep death From the wretched: cf. *Pho.* 98–100:

> qui cogit mori
> nolentem in aequo est quique properantem impedit.
> occidere est uetare cupientem mori.
>
> To force death on the unwilling
> Is the same as to stop those in a rush.
> To keep death from those wanting it is to kill.

See also Sen. Rhet. *Con.* 8.4, Publ. 502 (Duff): *plus est quam poena sinere miserum uiuere*, 'It is more than punishment to let the wretched live'. For death being preferable to a wretched life, another of the great *topoi* of ancient literature, see most especially the ode of the Trojan Chorus in *Agamemnon* (589–610), where it is tied to the concept of death's freedom (*libera mors, Ag.* 591: see Boyle *ad loc.*). For the substantival use of *miser*, see on 313–16.

cremandis trabibus accrescit/**grows with logs for burning:** the ablative is of material or means (Woodcock §§41.3, 43.1)—or, better, both.

sacro regentem maria uotiuo colam/**I'll worship the sea-lord with votive rites:** the sacrifice motif regularly concludes an act in both Greek and Roman tragedy, often manifesting itself in a character exiting the stage to sacrifice: see e.g. Aesch. *Pers.* 521–6, *Ag.* 1055–8; Soph. *El.* 466–71, *OC* 503–9; Sen. *Oed.* 401–2, *Ag.* 583–5, 802–7 (again *colam*, 807), *Med.* 299–300, 577–8, *Thy.* 545—also *Oct.* 756–61, *HO* 579–80 (again *colam*, 580). In Euripides' *Heracles* Lycus exits the stage (after 335) without any clear motivation. Seneca's Lycus exits with articulated motivation and, perhaps reflective of the protagonist of Seneca's *Oedipus* (*Oed.* 707–8), he exits after pronouncing sentence on his enemy/enemies. With *uotiuo colam*, 'I'll worship with votive', cf. *uotiuo…colam*, *Ag.* 806–7. The 'sea-lord', *regentem maria* (note the substantival use of the participle: Woodcock §101), is Neptune, from whom (i.e. Poseidon) the Lycus of Euripides is sometimes said to have been descended (Apollod. 3.10.1, Hygin. *Fab.* 31, 32). Caviglia *ad loc.* argues that Seneca's Lycus is sacrificing 'all' antenato divino'. But this cannot be the case, since he is a self-proclaimed *nouus homo* and can have no genealogical connection to any divinity of which he is aware. Fitch *ad loc.* seems content to assert an inconsistency on Seneca's part due (though he does not clarify this) to his incompetent use of source materials. But scholars, not Seneca, are forcing a genealogical connection between Seneca's Lycus and Neptune. Sacrificing to Neptune may simply be designed to place Lycus in a different theological camp from Hercules despite the latter's brief invocation of that deity in his opening speech (599–600), and/or to index Lycus' desire to shore up some divine support of his monarchy after the failure of his marriage proposal. At the same time, of course, Seneca could be winking metadramatically at those members of his audience familiar with the traditional connection of Lycus with Neptune. Lycus' apparent 'piety' here might be thought to contrast with his 'impiety' in the burning of the temple onstage. But such partial religiosity seems in keeping with Lycus' status as tyrant. For sacrificial language and imagery in *Hercules*, see on 918–24. For metadrama/metatheatre, see on 109–12.

516–23 The last words of this long act, like the first, are given to Amphitryon, who will invoke Jupiter as *rector* once more (205, 517).

AMPHITRYON *prays* (*perhaps turning to* **JUPITER'S** *statue*): for the possible presence of a statue of Jupiter onstage, see before 1–18.

516–20 Amphitryon prays to Jupiter, as he did at the start of the act (205–7), and follows with an invocation of Hercules. In Euripides (*Herac.* 339–47, 498–501) Amphitryon invokes Zeus (with acerbic criticism) after Lycus has left and before Heracles arrives, but does not invoke the latter, as here, where the invocation is done almost impiously (see below). For prayers in *Hercules* and Senecan tragedy, see on 205–78.

Pro…pro…/O…O: the interjection *pro* with the nominative, vocative, or accusative is a common formula for exclamations in Latin: cf. *Pha.* 903 (*pro…pro…*), *Oed.* 19, *Ag.* 35, *Breu. Vit.* 12.2, *Pol.* 17.4, *Oct.* 147, *HO* 219.

numinum uis summa/divine force supreme: clearly the reference is to Jupiter, but the disguised Allecto's *caelestum uis magna*, 'heaven's mighty force' (Virg. *Aen.* 7.342), seems more general, even if Juno lurks beneath.

rector parensque/lord and father: *rector* is often used of Jupiter by Seneca; cf. e.g. *magne Olympi rector,* 'great lord/ruler of Olympus', 205; *pater ac rector,* 'father and ruler', *Ag.* 382; *igniferi rector Olympi,* 'ruler of fiery Olympus', *Pha.* 960; *rector maris atque terrae,* 'ruler of sea and earth', *Thy.* 607; *caeli rector,* 'ruler of the sky', *Thy.* 1077. See also *caelitum rector,* 'ruler of sky-dwellers', *Oct.* 228; *rector poli,* 'ruler of heaven', *HO* 1275. The phrase, *rector parensque,* is a variation of the *pater/rex* formula attached to Jupiter: see e.g. Enn. *Ann.* frag. 203 Skutsch, *diuom pater et hominum rex,* 'father of gods and king of men', repeated (with *atque* for *et*) by Virgil at *Aen.* 2.648, 10.2, 743; cf. also Ov. *Met.* 2.848, *pater rectorque deum,* 'father and lord/ruler of gods', and *Met.* 9.245, 15.860. See also Enn. *Ann.* frag. 591 Skutsch, *diuomque hominumque pater, rex.* Behind all lies the Homeric tag, πατὴρ ἀνδρῶν τε θεῶν τε, 'father of both men and gods', *Il.* 1.544, etc. But specific to the Latin *Iuppiter* is the presence of *pater* in the god's name itself (see e.g. Varro *LL* 5.66). For *parens* of Jupiter, see 264, 598, 1054. For Seneca's predilection for nouns ending in -*tor,* see on 299–302. See further on 205–9.

cuius excussis tremunt humana telis/whose hurled shafts Make mankind tremble: i.e. Jupiter is being invoked in his capacity as *Iuppiter Tonans,* the 'Thunder-god' (line 1), which happens elsewhere in Senecan tragedy, as here, in the context of a great wrong needing to be rectified: see e.g. Hippolytus at *Pha.* 671ff., Medea at *Med.* 531ff., Thyestes at *Thy.* 1077ff. A laudatory reference to the deeds or powers of the invoked divinity (often by means of a descriptive relative clause following a vocative) is a standard feature of ancient prayer: see e.g. 593–4 (re Phoebus); *Ag.* 358-8•, 384-4•; *Oed.* 249–56; *Pha.* 55–9, 406–12; *Med.* 2–7; *Thy.* 790–1, *HO* 1–2; Cat. 61.3–4; Virg. *Geo.* 1.5–23; Hor. *Odes* 1.10. 2–4, *CS* 9–11. For laudatory reference not in a relative clause, see e.g. *Ag.* 343–5, 369–9•, 375–5•.

impiam regis feri compesce dextram/check the impious hand Of this brutal king: note the force of *ferus*, 'brutal', 'savage', 'wild', 'feral', 'bestial', a term which will become a prominent leitmotif in *Thyestes*, and is applied by Hercules to himself at 1226, 1280; see also 1118. That *ferus* still retained its force as a term of condemnation when applied to humans is clear from *Ben.* 7.19.5: *Quid si...non tantum malus sed ferus, sed immanis qualis Apollodorus aut Phalaris*, 'What if...he is not only bad but brutal, but monstrous like Apollodorus or Phalaris'. For *dextra* (and the *manus* motif), see on 118–22.

Quid deos frustra precor/Why invoke the gods in vain: a cynical, even desperate question, intensifying the Euripidean Amphitryon's 'I labour in vain' (μάτην πονῶ, *Herac.* 501; cf. also *Herac.* 339–47) and smacking of impiety, as Amphitryon changes addressee to his 'son'. Cynical attitudes to the gods are found elsewhere in the Senecan *corpus*: see e.g. Electra at *Ag.* 930: *per dubios deos*, 'by doubtful gods'; Theseus at *Pha.* 1242–3: *non mouent diuos preces*; | *at, si rogarem scelera, quam proni forent*, 'My prayers move no gods'; | But if I asked for evil, how ready they would be'; or Thyestes at *Thy.* 407, *si sunt tamen di*, 'If, however, gods exist', and 1021, *fugere superi*, 'The gods have fled'; or Oedipus at *Oed.* 75, *o saeua nimium numina, o fatum graue*, 'O too brutal gods! O crushing fate!'; or Jason in the last line of *Medea* (1027): *testare nullos esse, qua ueheris, deos*, 'Bear witness, where you ride, there are no gods'; or Hecuba's categorization of the gods as *leues*, 'fickle', at *Tro.* 2 (so too the Trojan Chorus at 605 below), the Messenger's description of them as *saeuos*, 'brutal', at *Tro.* 1101, and Octavia's proclamation at *Oct.* 912: *nec sunt superi*, 'No gods exist'. Such criticisms are found in Greek tragedy (especially Euripides) and Roman republican tragedy (see e.g. Enn. *Telam.* frags 265, 270–1 Jocelyn; Acc. *Antig.* frags 142–3 Klotz, *Ter.* frag. 6 Boyle 2006). For contrast with the providential attitude to the gods in Seneca's philosophical works, see e.g. *Ira* 2.27.1.

Sounds are heard by AMPHITRYON: the announcement of noise (520–3) is not unusual in Senecan tragedy. Offstage or onstage sounds are regularly drawn attention to: see e.g. *Med.* 116, 177, 738–9, 785, 971; *Pha.* 81–2, 850–3, 1154; *Oed.* 381–3, 911, 994; *Thy.* 918–19; cf. *Oct.* 72–3, *HO* 254–5.

520–3 Amphitryon's language is that of an epiphany from the underworld: see *Tro.* 171–80 (Achilles' Ghost), *Oed.* 569–83 (Theban Ghosts)—cf. also *Med.* 785, *Thy.* 262, 696–8—in keeping with the implications of the invocation of Hercules. Amphitryon is unaware that Hercules exited the underworld some time ago (46–63) from the hellmouth at Taenarus (813); so his appearance in Thebes might seem like such an epiphany. But the appearance of Hercules is delayed and there is no corroboration of the meaning of these sights and sounds by Megara, by the Chorus, who continue the pleas for Hercules' return (558–68) rather than celebrating it as already accomplished, or by the soldiers, who will continue to guard the temple until Hercules' appearance in Act III. As he is led across the stage under guard, Amphitryon's interpretation of the stage sights and sounds is unconfirmed; and, when he sees Hercules, he seems to express surprise (618–21). I have accordingly printed Amphitryon's final line as two climactic questions, continuing the interrogative mode of 520–1. Cf. *Tro.* 684–5, Virg. *Ecl.* 8.108. All other modern editors (Viansino 1965 and 1993, Giardina 1966 and 2007, Fitch, Zwierlein, Chaumartin, Billerbeck) print them as statements, sometimes as exclamations, presumably assuming with Fitch (1987*a*: 45) that 'Seneca either did not notice, or was not concerned by' the resulting inconsistencies.

mugit solum/**ground rumble:** a regular portent, presaging the rising of the dead; see e.g. *Tro.* 171–2, *Oed.* 173–5, and esp. Ov. *Met.* 7.206: *et mugire solum manesque exire sepulchris*, '(I command) the ground to rumble and the dead to leave their tombs'. Cf. also *mugire solum* at Virg. *Aen.* 6.256. When Atreus conceives his hellish revenge at *Thy.* 262, 'the ground rumbles from its lowest depths': *imo mugit e fundo solum*. There may also be a suggestion of divinity here: at *Theb.* 7.65–6, Statius uses quaking ground and 'bellowing', *mugire*, to mark the arrival of a god. For *mugitus* of the 'bellowing/rumbling' of the earth, see e.g. Cic. *Diu.* 1.35, Sen. *NQ* 6.13.5. It is clear from Statius (*Theb.* 6.28: *gemitu iam regia mugit*, lit. 'now the palace bellows with groaning') that *mugire* was closely allied to *gemere* in meaning.

imo sonuit e fundo fragor/**roar...rises from the lowest depths:** cf. *Thy.* 262 (cited prev. n.). But here *fragor* is used, lit. a 'breaking/splitting' (cf. *frangere*, 'to break'), a strong word to apply to a sound; it is a sound which splits or shatters the air. Seneca uses it of the Delphic oracle at *Oed.* 232 and below (795) of the 'voice' of Cerberus.

audimur? est—est/**We're heard? Is—is it:** for construing these as questions, see above. For *est* as a question without *-ne*, see 430, 119. The imitation at *HO* 1130 (*est est Herculeus sonus*, 'It is/Is it, it is/is it the sound of Hercules') could be either a question or a statement; it is immediately followed by the appearance of Hercules on a litter. With *audimur*, cf. Stat. *Silu.* 3.2.50, *audimur*, 'We're heard', and Tiresias' *audior*, 'I am heard', at *Oed.* 571. For the *geminatio* see on 92–9.

sonitus Herculei gradus/**sound of Hercules' tread:** for the focus on sound, see on 1002–9. Trevet *ad loc.*, who read *en est sonitus* rather than *est est sonitus*, interpreted this 'sound' as that 'Herculis gradientis et ascendentis de inferno'. That is certainly what Amphitryon fervently hopes. Hercules of course entered and exited the underworld at Cape Taenarus in the southern Peloponnese. For the use of the adjective *Herculeus*, see 72 and n. *ad loc.*

AMPHITRYON *is led under guard to the doors of the temple together with* MEGARA *and her* SONS: when Hercules enters, he does not mention seeing anybody at the altar but only refers to the guards at the temple doors (616–17). It thus seems appropriate to have guards move Hercules' family to the temple doors in readiness for the ordered cremation. Guard/slave-action is common in Senecan tragedy, in which guards and/or slaves are regularly used to 'escort' characters from the stage (e.g. Astyanax and Polyxena in *Troades*, Electra in *Agamemnon*, Creon in *Oedipus*). Other actions involving guards/slaves include blocking access to the ruler (*Medea*); grabbing a character in preparation for torture (*Phaedra*); attacking a tomb (*Troades*). Slaves are also used for routine tasks, such as the opening of doors (*Phaedra*, *Thyestes*), attending to characters onstage (*Agamemnon*, *Phaedra*), bringing of characters from offstage (*Oedipus*), taking news offstage (*Phaedra*), the removal, bringing on or carrying of props (*Hercules*, *Thyestes*).

ALL *remain onstage*: it is not unusual for characters to remain onstage during Senecan choral odes. Characters remain onstage in this play between Acts III and IV (Amphitryon, Megara, Theseus) and between Acts IV and V (Amphitryon and Hercules). In other plays Theseus remains onstage between the last two acts of *Phaedra* and Hecuba and Andromache remain on stage between the final two acts of *Troades*.

Second Choral Ode: The 'Hercules Ode' (524–91)

This second choral ode is the closest in Seneca's play to any of the choral lyrics in Euripides' *Heracles*, whose long first stasimon (348–441), a lamentation for the (supposedly) dead Heracles, celebrates the hero's labours (in greater detail than Seneca's ode), as the Chorus themselves await the imminent execution of Amphitryon, Megara, and the children. They include ten 'labours' (μόχθοι/πόνοι/ἆθλοι), several not part of the later canon. Seneca's ode is less comprehensive, a veritable mini-catalogue (for catalogues see on 6–18), restricting itself to four canonic labours amid brief celebration of other deeds. Its tone is quite different, arising from its assumption that Hercules is far from dead. In the new millennium Simon Armitage created twelve songs for the twelve labours to be sung by the chorus in his *Mister Heracles* (2000: 14–17; first performed 2001). A powerful way of staging this ode would have been through the use of pantomime, especially in the final, Orpheus section (see on 569–89).

The choral ode, like the final one at 1054ff. and others in Senecan tragedy (e.g. *Oed.* 110ff., 403ff.; *Pha.* 274ff., 959ff.; *Ag.* 57ff., 808ff.; *Thy.* 122ff., 789ff.), commences with apostrophe. The Chorus take their cue from the end of Act II, where ambiguous signs of Hercules' approach were reported by Amphitryon, and sing a song of protest, celebration, and exhortation. They begin conventionally with a divine address to Fortune (see below), which they turn into a proclamation of Hercules' unjust treatment (524–5) and a protest against the burdens/'wars' (*bella*, 527) imposed upon him: his bearing of the sky, slaying of the Lernaean Hydra, retrieval of the Apples of the Hesperides, wanderings in Scythia, defeat of the Amazon queen and descent into hell (526–57). Indeed, as Fitch observes (p. 253), the landscape of his Scythian wanderings (533–41) mirrors the landscape of the dead, suggesting that even before his descent to the underworld Hercules had been forced to live a life of hell on earth. But the protest gradually merges into celebration, culminating in apostrophe and a fusion of descriptive and jussive, even imperative modes, as the Chorus narrate Hercules' earlier victory over the death-god and plead for the hero's return to the upper world (558–68). Orpheus is introduced as a paradigm of the successful conquest of death and an apparent precursor of the conquest of death through *uires*, through physical force (569–91).

The style of the ode is formal, almost ritualistic, involving repetition, parallel clauses, alliteration, and verbal play. The chosen metre, the lesser asclepiad, makes for balanced lines, each neatly divided at its centre, and for a stately, onward movement. Used in several other Senecan tragedies in a variety of contexts, this verse-form is far from univocal. Most important for this ode, however (as in its appearance in *Phaedra*, *Troades*, and *Medea*), is the meaning derived from its use by Horace. Employed only twice in the first three books of his odes (*Odes* 1.1, III. 30) and used there as book-ends to celebrate Horace's own poetry, esp. its conquest of death, this quasi-ritualistic verse-form seems to lend the ode an evolving triumphalist tone, which reverses the lamentation of Euripides' dirge, transforms protest into celebration and anticipates Hercules' own triumphant arrival on stage. The final couplet, upon the singing of which Hercules enters, is unreservedly triumphalist. However, the Chorus are attempting to do what Orpheus did, and the audience have been reminded by the Chorus themselves of what followed that singer's initial success. As a paradigm of the future, the Thracian bard is a decidedly tragic one. For further discussion of this choral ode and its dramatic and thematic function in the play, see Introd. §VII, 80–1.

Metre: lesser asclepiad. See Introd. §IX. For its semiotics, see above.

524–32 The Chorus criticize Fortune for the unfair treatment of Eurystheus and Hercules. Cf. the Ovidian Hercules' complaints, as he dies in agony (*Met.* 9.182–204). Note how the section is encased by highly alliterative first and final lines (524: *f*/*t*/*u*/*u*/*f*/*t*; 532: *p*/*d*/*t*/*p*/*p*/*d*/*t*). The ode begins with an invocation, a feature common to several Senecan choral odes (see on 524–91 introd.), in which such invocation only occasionally leads to prayer (see e.g. 1054ff.).

O Fortuna uiris inuida fortibus, quam non aequa/O Fortune, envious of heroes, How unjust: the blindness, amorality, deceptiveness, power, and mutability of *Fortuna*/*fortuna* (*nihil stabile ab illa datum esse*, 'Nothing given by her is stable', *NQ* 3 Pref. 7) are regular motifs of Roman tragedy (Enn. *Trag. Inc.* frags 338–40 Jocelyn, Pac. *Inc.* frags 366–76 Klotz, Acc. *Andr.* frags 109–10 Klotz, *Med. s. Arg.* frags 422–3 Klotz, Seneca *passim*: see below) and *topoi* of Roman declamation (see e.g. Sen. Rhet. *Con.* 2.1.1 and 9, *Suas.* 1.9), Roman historiography (Sall. *Cat.* 1.8.1: *sed profecto fortuna in omni re dominatur*, 'But assuredly fortune is mistress in all things'), and (partly as a result of the influence of the Senecan tragic *corpus*) of Elizabethan and Jacobean tragedy: see e.g. Shakespeare, *Richard II* III. ii.156ff., Jonson, *Sejanus* V.878–87. Kyd, *Spanish Tragedy* III.i.1ff., and Chapman, *Bussy D'Ambois* V.ii.46–53, who adapt the *Fortuna* ode of *Agamemnon*. Even Dante has his disquisition on 'la fortuna' (*Inferno* 7.70–96), as does Jodelle ('l'inconstante fortune', Act III Le Choeur, *Cléopâtre Captive*). *Fortuna* is important in Lucan's epic, in which Caesar claims her as his guiding principle (1.226). In more recent times Carl Orff commences his *Carmina Burana* with his famous invocation, *O Fortuna*.

For Fortune's 'amorality' or 'injustice', as here: see 325–6 above, *Pha.* 978–80, Pliny *HN* 2.22 (*indignorum...fautrix*, 'favouring the unworthy'); for her 'wheel' (*Fortunae rota*), see e.g. Cic. *Pis.* 22, Tib. 1.5.70, *Pha.* 1123, *Ag.* 72, *Thy.* 618; for her changeability/revolutionary character, see *Oct.* 452, Enn. *Ann.* frags 312–13 Skutsch, Ov. *Tr.* 5.8.15–16, Pliny *Ep.* 4.11.2, Juv. 7.197–8; for her 'swift wings' (*celeres pinnae*), see Hor. *Odes* 3.29.53–4, cf. *Pha.* 1141–3; for her 'rapacity', see Hor. *Odes* 1.34.14–16; for her cruel 'assault' (*impetus*), see Sen. *Pol.* 3.4, *Helu.* 5.3; for her 'storm', see *procella Fortunae*, *Ag.* 594; for her 'pleasure', see Sen. *NQ* 3 Pref. 7, Men. frag. 630 Körte, and Hor. *Odes* 1.34.16, 3.29.49. A more infrequent property of *Fortuna*, stipulated here, is her envy (*inuida*), an obvious transference of the long-standing ancient notion of the envy of the gods (φθόνος θεῶν); but see also Stat. *Theb.* 10.384–5.

The notion of a capricious Fortune (Greek Τύχη) is found in fifth-century BCE Greek literature (esp. late Euripides) and occurs frequently in Hellenistic and post-Hellenistic literature, art, religion, and thought. In Menander's *Aspis* she appears as a character and proclaims her power (146–8 Arnott). In the Roman world the goddess *Fors* or *Fortuna* (or *Fors Fortuna*) was well established. At Praeneste (modern Palestrina) on a spur of the Apennines just over twenty miles east of Rome was an enormous sanctuary to *Fortuna* built in the early first century BCE by Sulla, her other great centre being at Antium (modern Anzio) on the Latin coast south of Rome. Originally an Italian fertility goddess, *Fortuna* quickly took on the identity of the Greek Τύχη. Rome itself had several monuments to *Fortuna*, some of which were believed to go back to Servius Tullius (sixth century BCE). One such 'Servian' shrine to *Fortuna* was rebuilt by Nero after the Great Fire of 64 CE and incorporated in his *Domus Aurea* (Pliny *HN* 36.163). Imperial coins and gemstones regularly bore an image of the goddess (with cornucopia or rudder or rudder and globe).

At *Ben.* 4.8 Seneca identifies *fortuna, fatum,* 'fate', and *diuina ratio,* 'divine reason', with *natura,* 'nature', and in *Agamemnon* the operations of *Fortuna* seem to be governed by a cosmic logic (see Boyle on *Ag.* 57–107 introd.). But at *Pha.* 959ff. *natura* and *fortuna* are set in opposition, at *Oed.* 825 *ratio* and *fortuna* are presented as alternatives, and here *fortuna,* as in *Phaedra,* is presented as amoral, even morally perverse. Often in the prose works *fortuna* (= the individually variable and adversarial aspect of 'externally imposed circumstances': Asmis 2009) is resisted, fought, conquered and contemned by the *sapiens,* as he aligns himself with fate, nature and god: e.g. *Helu.* 15.4, *Ben.* 5.3.2, *Ep. Mor.* 71.30, 104.22, 107.7–8. Fortune's favour was not something sought by the Stoic sage (see *Ep. Mor.* 72.4). Enjoyed by Julius Caesar (Luc. 1.226, 5.677, 696–7, Plut. *Mor.* 319b–d) and Nero (*Oct.* 451), it was spurned by men like Cato (*Ep. Mor.* 118.4), whose suicide was a defiant victory over *Fortuna* (*Ep. Mor.* 24.7). In *De Clementia* (1.1.2) Nero is Fortune's mouthpiece. For *fatum,* 'fate', see on 178–82. For another apostrophe to *Fortuna,* see *Ag.* 57 (*O...fallax Fortuna,* 'O false Fortune'). For Stoic language and ideas in *Hercules,* see on 162–3.

Disquisitions on Fortune are common in both the tragedies and prose works: see e.g. Megara at 325–8, Thyestes at *Thy.* 446–70, Hecuba at *Tro.* 1ff., Agamemnon at *Tro.* 259–63, Oedipus at *Oed.* 6–11—and *Pol.* 3.4–5, 15.1–2; *Helu.* 5.3–5; *Breu. Vit.* 17.4; *Ep. Mor.* 4.7, 8.3–4, 94.72–74; *NQ* 3 Pref.

7, 4 Pref. 22 (see also the opening lines of the speech of 'Seneca' at *Oct.* 377ff.). Sometimes, as here, the disquisitions are in the form of choral lyric: *Pha.* 959–88, 1123–53; *Ag.* 57–107, *Thy.* 596–622 (cf. *HO* 583–699). I have favoured the capitalization of the initial letter here, as at 326 and *Ag.* 57, to underscore her status as a Roman goddess.

The commencement of a choral ode with divine address occurs often in Senecan tragedy: 1054ff.; *Pha.* 274ff., 959ff.; *Ag.* 57ff., 311ff.; *Oed.* 403ff.; *Thy.* 122ff., 789ff.; *Med.* 56ff. It is a practice with ample Greek precedent: e.g. Aesch. *Cho.* 783ff., Soph. *Oed.* 151ff., Eur. *Hipp.* 525ff. For apostrophe in the choral odes of this play, see on 178–82. For *o* with the vocative, see on 205–9.

non aequa/**unjust:** syntactically ambiguous, modifying either *Fortuna* (cf. *iniqua...Fortuna*, 325) or *praemia* (= *iniqua praemia*, *Tranq.* 16.1), or (better) both. For Fortune's injustice/amorality, see above. For the use of *non* to negate an adjective (*non aequa*), see on 489–94.

Eurystheus facili regnet in otio/**Should Eurystheus reign in ease and peace:** note the dying Hercules' complaint: *at ualet Eurystheus*, 'But Eurystheus thrives', Ov. *Met.* 9.203. For Eurystheus, see on 77–83, 830–7 and Introd. §VI, 61.

regnet... exagitet... resecet... referat/**Should ... reign ... Thrust ... Re-slice...Retrieve:** the subjunctives are deliberative (Woodcock §§109, n. ii, 172–5), here used to express a series of indignant questions. Note the *re-* repetitions.

otio... bella/**peace...wars:** there is a play on the double meaning of *otium*: 'leisure' (opposed to *negotium*, 'business') and 'peace' (opposed to *bellum*, 'war').

Alcmena genitus/**Alcmena's son:** Hercules, whose birth from Alcmena was delayed by Juno/Hera so that Eurystheus might be born first and inherit the Argolid throne (see on 830–7). The contrast between Eurystheus' untroubled life and that of Hercules is made by the Ovidian Hercules as he burns on Mt Oeta (*Met.* 9.203, cited above). *Alcmena* is—in both a literal and syntactical sense—ablative of source. See further on 770–81.

monstris... caeliferam manum/**sky-bearing hands at monsters:** *caelifer* is a defining adjective of Atlas (e.g. Virg. *Aen.* 6.796, Ov. *Fas.* 5.83, Stat. *Silu.* 1.1.60), whom Hercules briefly replaced; see on 68–74. For the important *monstrum* motif, see 1280 and n. *ad loc.*; for the *manus* motif, see on 118–22. For the compound in *-fer*, see on 235–40.

serpentis/**serpent's:** the Lernaean Hydra, the defeat of which was generally considered the second of Hercules' canonic labours; see on 241–8.

resecet/Re-slice: the *re-* prefix underscores the laborious side of the 'labours', while participating in a pattern of alliteration from *regnet* to *referat*.

colla feracia/fertile necks: *feracia* is a later shift from the consensus manuscript reading of *ferocia*, a 'certain Renaissance correction', as Fitch *ad loc.* terms it, because of Seneca's concern elsewhere with the hydra's regenerative properties: cf. *fecunda...capita*, 'fecund heads', 781; see n. *ad loc.* See further on 241–8.

deceptis...sororibus/duped sisters: the Hesperides, nymphs who inhabited a garden in the far west or north. To fetch the golden apples to be found in the garden was more often listed as Hercules' eleventh labour: see on 235–40.

somno dederit peruigiles genas/ceded vigilant eyes to sleep: the snake which guarded the Apples of the Hesperides is (at least in the version evident in Euripides' *Heracles*, 398ff.: see on 235–40) actually slain by Hercules, not simply put to sleep (by Hercules or the Hesperides). Similarly at *Ag.* 855–6 and *Pho.* 316–17 the serpent remains unkilled by Hercules. Perhaps Seneca is conflating this serpent with the one guarding the Golden Fleece in Colchis (*Med.* 472–3). For *genae* = *oculi*, 'eyes', see also 767, *Pha.* 364, *Ag.* 726, *Pho.* 538, *Tro.* 441, 1138.

pomis diuitibus/precious fruit: with this use of *diues*, 'rich' = 'precious', cf. Virgil's 'golden bough' (*diues...ramus*, *Aen.* 6.195–6) and Valerius' 'golden fleece' (*diues...pellis*, *Arg.* 5.203).

533–46 The Chorus describe Hercules' expedition against the Amazons. His capture of the queen's war-belt is generally listed as the eighth or ninth labour: see on 241–8. The description of the frozen Pontus/Black Sea seems to owe much to Ovid's description in his *Tristia* (3.10.25–50), but see also Virg. *Geo.* 3.360–2. At Ov. *Pont.* 4.10.32 winter is said to make the waters of the Pontus 'passable even on foot' (*uel pediti peruia*). See further Fitch *ad loc.* Like Ovid's exile, this labour of Hercules was at the edges of the Roman empire, as references to Scythia and Sarmatians index. One thing Seneca emphasizes (which is not in Virgil or Ovid), as Caviglia notes *ad loc.*, is the silence of these frozen waters (536). This mute wasteland seems prologue to the silence of the underworld (576, 620, 680, 713, 794, 848, 862). For Roman referentiality in *Hercules*, see on 46–52.

533–41 *Scythiae multiuagas domos*/Scythia's nomad homes: the Scythians were famous for their nomadic life: see Hor. *Odes* 3.24.9–10 (*Scythae* | *quorum plaustra uagas rite trahunt domos*, 'Scythians, whose cars duly pull their nomad homes'). They inhabited the area north and east of the Pontus (Black Sea) stretching from Europe to Asia. In Shakespeare's *King Lear* they function as a paradigm of barbarity: 'barbarous Scythian' (*KL* I.i.116; cf. *Tit.* I.i.134). They and their nomadic nature are referred to frequently in Senecan tragedy: see e.g. *Thy.* 631 (*uagi passim Scythae*), *Oed.* 473–4, *Tro.* 12 (*uagos...Scythas*), 1104 (*sedis incertae Scytha*), *Pha.* 168 (*sparsus Scythes*), *Med.* 212. Seneca's description of the Scythians here contrasts with the favourable description of their life-style by Horace (*Odes* 3.24.9–24): Allendorf (2017: 155–7). Association with the Scythians places the Amazons on the north side of the Pontus (see also *Pha.* 399–403, *Tro.* 12–13); they are also frequently located on the south side near the river Thermodon (246, *Oed.* 479–81, *Med.* 214–15, Ov. *Pont.* 4.10.51). According to the Greek historian Herodotus (4.110), the Amazons moved from the south side of the Pontus to Maeotis (Sea of Azov) and Scythia on its north-east side. This is the first attested use in Latin literature of the adjective *multiuagus*.

patriis sedibus hospitas/**estranged in their fatherland:** a strong expression for nomadic tribes.

calcauitque freti terga rigentia/**And trod on the water's stiffened back:** influenced by the Ovidian account in *Tristia* 3.10 (3.10.39: *calcauimus*; 3.10.48: *rigidas...aquas*). At *Thy.* 377 walking on the frozen Danube is expressed as *pedes ingredi*.

mutis tacitum/**muted...silent:** for the juxtaposition of synonyms, see on 283–95. For the *mutus/tacitus* juxtaposition, see Luc. 1.247, for their combination, see 301–2; for the emphasis on 'silence', see on 533–46.

dura carent aequora fluctibus/**hardened sea-plains have no waves:** again Ovidian influence: *durum...aequor*, 'hardened sea-plain', *Tr.* 3.10.39; *fluctus...nullus erit*, 'there will be no wave', *Tr.* 3.10.46

qua plena rates carbasa tenderant/**where ships had spread:** this contrast between navigable waters and frozen waters on which humans might walk and horses and wagons be driven is a *topos* found in Virgil (*Geo.* 3.362) and Ovid (*Pont.* 4.10.32–4), and evident in the *Tristia* passage cited above (3.10.31–4). Along with Viansino (1965), Giardina (1966), Caviglia, and Fitch (1987a and 2018), I have printed the reading of *A* (*TCV*), the (possibly uniquely attested) unreduplicated pluperfect indicative form *tenderant*, rather than that of *E*, *tenderent*, favoured by Zwierlein, Viansino (1993), and Chaumartin. Billerbeck and Giardina (2007) print *panderant*, posited but not printed by Zwierlein. For discussion, see Fitch (2004b: 20).

intonsis teritur semita Sarmatis/**The long-haired Sarmatians tread paths:** brilliant effects of sound, emanating from the alliteration of *ts*, *ss*, *rs*, and *n/ms*, complemented by the surprising wordplay of *semita Sarmatis*. Sarmatia, the western part of Scythia (see above), was a huge area in (from Rome's point of view) north-eastern Europe, stretching on some estimates from the Vistula in Poland to the Don in Russia and even to the Caspian Sea. Their first appearance in extant Latin literature is in the exile poetry of Ovid (see e.g. *Tr.* 1.5.62, *Ibis* 637, *Pont.* 1.2.45, 58, 112). Sarmatians are also mentioned at *Pha.* 71, *Thy.* 375. Being 'long-haired' was to Romans a mark of the savage or at least the uncivilized: Livy 21.32.7 (the Gauls), Virg. *Geo.* 3.366 (Scyths), Ov. *Tr.* 5.7.18 and 50, *Pont.* 4.2.2 (the Getae and Sarmatians). The author of *Hercules Oetaeus* (158) gives the Sarmatian the transferred epithet *frigidus* (see on 127–31).

stat pontus/**The sea stands:** overt verbal play in the Latin on *pontus* = sea and *Pontus* = the Pontus or Euxine/Black Sea. Note Seneca's fondness for *stat* at the start of a line, both iambic (351, 554, 861, 948, 1040; *Ag.* 908; *Thy.* 693) and lyric (540, 554, 861; *Thy.* 152, 391; *Ag.* 376; *Oed.* 131).

nauem nunc facilis…pati/**Ready to bear now ships…:** a neatly alliterative, balanced line closes the lengthy description. Its 'model' seems to be Virgil's equally balanced, though more alliterative line (*Geo.* 3.362): *puppibus illa prius, patulis nunc hospita plaustris*, 'formerly welcoming ships, now wide wagons'. For *pati* as the ultimate word of a line, see on 348–53. For the construction (adjective and epexegetical infinitive) found elsewhere with *facilis*, see e.g. *facilisque regi*, 'ready to be ruled', *Oct.* 813•; *facilis cedere*, 'ready to yield', Prop. 1.11.12; cf. *audax ire*, 548; *inuius renauigari*, 715–16. This use of the infinitive with adjectives is common in Greek and became a mannerism of Augustan poets, who imitated the Greek construction. See further Woodcock §26.

542–6 Hercules' winning of the war-belt of the Amazon queen, Hippolyte. This non-violent 'victory' contrasts with the violent account of *Ag.* 848–50: see below and further on 241–8.

quae uiduis gentibus imperat/**queen-general of manless tribes:** Hippolyte, queen of the Amazons. For *uiduus*, 'manless', applied to the Amazons, see on 1–5.

aurato religans ilia balteo/**Groin bound with a gilded baldric:** this golden war-belt or baldric (ζωστήρ, *aurato…balteo*, 543), the *spolium nobile* ('noble spoil', 544), is clearly bound around the waist/groin; whereas in *Agamemnon* (848–50) it is the one 'worn diagonally across the shoulder for a sword or quiver' (Harrison *ad* Virg. *Aen.* 10.496–7: cf. *Aen.* 5.312–13, 12.941–2). Euripides, too, emphasizes the Amazon queen's golden dress (*Herac.* 41). Ovid anticipates in his final poem of the *Heroides* (21.119), where we find Hippolyte's 'baldric chased with Amazonian gold' (*Amazonio caelatus balteus auro*). Note the alliterative pattern of *ls* in the lemmatized phrase.

detraxit spolium nobile corpori/**Stripped her body of the noble spoil:** an ironic inversion of *Agamemnon*'s more violent account, in which it is Hercules who does the stripping (*Ag.* 848–50):

> vidit Hippolyte ferox
> pectore e medio rapi
> spolium.
>
> Wild Hippolyte saw
> Spoils torn from parted
> Breasts.

Spolium nobile would strike a Roman audience as close to *spolia opima* (see on 46–52). But how 'noble' or 'glorious' is the spoil when the vanquished hands it to the victor? For military imagery in *Hercules*, see on 19–29. *Corpori* is dative of person/thing affected by the action of the verb, common with verbs denoting 'removal' or 'separation' where one might have expected an ablative of separation (with or without a preposition); often (misleadingly) called 'dative of separation'. Cf. 1153. See Woodcock §61.

et peltam et niuei uincula pectoris/**And shield and bands of her snowy breast:** the *pelta* was the light shield carried by Amazons with a semi-circular indentation on one edge, giving it the appearance of a crescent moon; see e.g. *Pha.* 402–3, *Ag.* 218, *Med.* 214, Virg. *Aen.* 1.490, 11.663, Ov. *Pont.* 3.1.96, Sil. 2.80, Arrian 7.13.2, Plut. *Pomp.* 35.5. The 'bands', *uincula*, were presumably straps supporting the Amazon's quiver/bow-case and running diagonally across her chest. (At *Ag.* 848–50 it is the *spolium*, i.e. *balteus*, which serves this purpose: see Boyle *ad loc.*) The phrase *niuei...pectoris*, 'snowy breast', eroticizes the scene (cf. *niueo pectore*, Tib. 1.4.12; *niueum latus*, Prop. 3.14.11; *niueo corpore*, Ov. *Am.* 3.2.42). Virgil's description of the Amazon warrior Penthesilea, *aurea subnectens exsertae cingula mammae* ('binding her golden cincture beneath a thrusting breast', *Aen.* 1.492) is canonic. Etymological play (μαζός = 'breast') seems also evident. Again alliteration, this time chiastic, patterns the line.

posito...genu/**knelt:** the standard position of the suppliant as suggested by Andromache (for her son Astyanax) at *Tro.* 715.

547-57 The Chorus ask for a reason for Hercules' journey to the underworld and describe the latter's desolate nature.

547-9 For apostrophe in the choral odes of this play, see on 178-82. Note, as at 178, the lack of a vocative.

Qua spe…/**What hope…**: Fitch and Viansino *ad loc.* note the republican tragic fragment (*Poet. Inc.* frags 249-50 Klotz):

> quaenam <curae> te adigunt, hospes,
> stagna capacis uisere Auerni?

> What <cares> drive you, stranger, to visit
> The pools of capacious Avernus?

praecipites…ad inferos/**to hell's pit**: a bold application of the modifier, *praeceps* (= 'steep' *OLD* 4), to the inhabitants of the underworld, used here metonymically.

audax ire uias irremeabiles/**to walk Bold the paths of no return**: lit. 'bold to walk…'. For the infinitive with *audax*, see Hor. *Odes* 1.3.25, *audax…perpeti*, lit. 'bold to endure', the first known occurrence of the construction. Note, too, the use of *audaces ire* by Albinovanus Pedo in a passage cited by Seneca's father (*Suas.* 1.15). For the infinitive with adjectives, see 541 above and n. *ad loc. Audax* and *audere* feature largely in Seneca's tragic vocabulary of transgression and 'boundary violation'. See e.g. 79, 387, 772, 834, 1162; *Pha.* 94; *Oed.* 908; *Med.* 301, 318, 599, 607, 700; *Thy.* 20, 193, 284, 377. *Irremeabiles* is a Senecan *hapax*, of perfect syllabic form to fill the second half of a lesser asclepiad and evidently taken from Virgil's hexameters (*Aen.* 5.591, 6.425). The word translates the Greek ἀνόστιμος, used by Euripides in a similar context (*Herac.* 431). The idea of the *uia irremeabilis* of death is one of the most common *topoi* in Greek and Roman literature: see Catullus' simple description of it at 3.12: *unde negant redire quemquam*, 'whence they say no one returns'. For boundary violation, see on 46-52.

uidisti Siculae regna Proserpinae/**see Sicilian Proserpina's empire**: Proserpina was the daughter of Ceres and Jupiter. Pluto/Dis snatched her from Enna, Sicily, in the upper world to be his wife in the world below: see e.g. Ov. *Met.* 5.385-571, *Fas.* 4.419-618, Stat. *Ach.* 1.824-6, VF 5.343-7. In the *Homeric Hymn to Demeter* (17) Persephone/Proserpina is snatched from Nysa, a 'mythical locality, variously located' (West 2003*b*: *ad loc.*). Note the scansion of the first syllable of *Proserpinae* as short against standard poetic practice. Seneca is taking his cue from the use of the phrase *regna Proserpinae* (and similar scansion) by Horace (*Odes* 2.13.21), where it forms the final part of an Alcaic line. The phrase may be found also at Hor. *Epod.* 17.2. For the *uidere* motif, see on 249-58.

550-7 The landscape of the underworld. As Fitch notes *ad loc.*, the scene (no waves, motionless sea) replays aspects of the Scythian episode (537–40).

*nulla...nulla...non/*no...no: Seneca is fond of negative description; see e.g. 698–700 below and n. *ad loc.* Sometimes, especially in moral diatribes, there is a veritable catalogue of negatives: see e.g. *Pha.* 483–500, *Thy.* 455–70. Note the triple and successive alliteration of *n* in 550.

*Noto...Fauonio/*Notus...Favonius: *Notus* (νότος) is the Greek name for the south wind. It is identified with Auster at *NQ* 5.16.6, but distinguished from it at *Ag.* 481–2. It is generally conceived of as a wet wind: see Ov. *Met.* 1.264–9 and *Ag.* 481–2, where Seneca seems to play with the etymology of the name (Gellius 2.22.14: from νοτίς, 'moisture'; Nonius p. 50, 20: νότος = *umor*). It is sometimes depicted as 'stormy', *procellosus* (Ov. *Am.* 2.6.44, *Her.* 2.12), even *uiolentus* (Virg. *Aen.* 6.356). *Fauonius*, a *hapax* in Senecan tragedy, is the balmy west wind, associated with the arrival of spring and the release from the cold of the north wind, Boreas: Ov. *Fas.* 2.147–8. Seneca's (and Ovid's) usual term for the west wind is *Zephyrus* (see 699). Virgil never uses *Fauonius*. Here it completes the asclepiadic line perfectly. The absence of wind in the underworld is noted again at 699.

*consurgunt tumidis fluctibus/*rise with swelling waves: an Ovidian touch. Ovid's sea 'whitens with swelling waves', *tumidis albescere...fluctibus*, at *Met.* 11.480–1. Cf. also *Pha.* 1015.

*geminum Tyndaridae genus/*twin Tyndarids: again appositional phrasing in connection with the Gemini (see on 11–18), this time in a form (noun between a noun and its modifying adjective) to which Seneca was especially drawn: see e.g. *alta muri decora*, *Tro.* 15; *turba captiuae mea*, *Tro.* 63; *maesta Phrygiae turba*, *Tro.* 409; *fida famuli turba*, *Ag.* 800; *funebris famuli manus*, *Pha.* 1105; *fortis armiferi cohors*, *Med.* 980. Sometimes the appositive phrase, instead of enclosing the noun as here, is itself enclosed by noun and modifier (*Pha.* 305), or, as at 14 above, interlocks with them. The mannerism derives from earlier Roman poets, especially Virgil (e.g. *Ecl.* 1.57, 2.3, *Geo.* 2.146–7, 4.168), Propertius (e.g. 1.19.13), and Ovid (e.g. *Ars* 1.125, *Met.* 6.131, 8.226), and seems to have been common in Hellenistic verse.

*succurrunt...sidera/*with their stars Bring succour: lit. 'as stars bring succour', *sidera* being appositional. The reference is to the electrical occurrence known as 'St. Elmo's fire', which manifests itself on the masts and rigging of a storm-tossed ship. The Gemini were thought to be protective of sailors and shipping (see on 11–18), and this 'fire' was seen as evidence of their 'starlike' presence: see Sen. *NQ* 1.1.13, Horace *Odes* 1.3.2 (and Nisbet and Hubbard *ad loc.*).

stat nigro pelagus gurgite languidum/**The sea stands motionless, its pool black:** cf. *stat pontus*, 'The sea stands', 540, of the Scythian landscape, and the Messenger's description of the hell-like inner sanctum of the palace of Atreus at *Thy.* 665–6: *fons stat sub umbra tristis et nigra piger | haeret palude*, 'in the shadows a spring stands grim and motionless, stuck in a black swamp'. Cf. Horace's application of *languidus* to hell's waters at *Odes* 2.14.17. For initial *stat* in Senecan tragedy, see on 533–41.

Mors auidis pallida dentibus/**pale Death with its lusty teeth:** a vivid blend of Horace's *pallida Mors* (*Odes* 1.4.13) and the 'lusty jaws', *auidos oris hiatus*, of black Death at *Oed.* 164; cf. also the 'lusty hands', *auidas…manus*, of black Death at Tib. 1.3.4, and 'pale (*pallidus*) Orcus' at Virg. *Geo.* 1.277. Note, too, the 'pale gods' (*pallentes deos*, *Oed.* 583) seen by Creon in the underworld. For 'death's teeth', see Lucr. 1.852: *leti sub dentibus ipsis*, 'beneath the very teeth of death'. The transferred use of *auidus* is common: see e.g. *Thy.* 2. See further on 283–95. For the personification of *Mors*, 'Death', see e.g. 1069, *Pha.* 1188–90, *Med.* 742, *Tro.* 1171–5, *Oed.* 126, 652.

gentes innumeras/**unnumbered tribes:** a Virgilian phrase for the count-less dead at *Aen.* 6.706, where it is conjoined (as here in the next line) with *populi*. The whole line has an epic tone, recalling the opening of Homer's *Iliad* (see esp. *Il.* 1.3).

uno tot populi remige/**One oarsman…the multitudes:** the oarsman is Charon; see 764–77 and nn. *ad loc.*, and *Oed.* 166–70. For Seneca's verbal play with *unus*, see on 19–29. For *populi*, see previous n. and on 186–91.

558–68 The Chorus directly address Hercules. For apostrophe in the choral odes of this play, see on 178–82.

ferae Stygis/**wild Styx:** the Styx (for which, see on 52–6) is accorded sev-eral other adjectives in Senecan tragedy: see e.g. *sacra* ('sacred', 713), *dira* ('dire', *Ag.* 493, *Thy.* 666), *atra* ('black', *Pha.* 477), *perpetua* ('eternal', *Pha.* 148), *tacita* ('silent', *Pha.* 625), *inferna* ('infernal', *Oed.* 396, *Thy.* 1007), *pro-funda* ('deep', *Oed.* 401, *Tro.* 430), *nota* ('well-known', *Med.* 632), and, of course, *tristis* ('sad/grim', *Ag.* 607).

Parcarumque colos non reuocabiles/**The Parcae's irrevocable distaff:** for the spinning of the Parcae or Fates, see on 178–82. *Reuocabilis* is a Senecan tragic *hapax*, but may be found also at *Ira* 1.6.3. *Non reuocabiles* brings out the irony of the name: the Parcae 'spare' no one. For the use of *non* to negate an adjective, see on 489–94.

hic qui rex/**This king who:** Dis; see on 546–52. For the formula *hic qui…*, see *Pha.* 1144, and its triple use in *Thyestes* (844, 848, 852).

populis pluribus imperat/**rules the most nations:** the idea is that the kingdom of the dead is larger than the kingdoms of the living. Cf. *HO* 560, where Dis is called *turbae ducem maioris*, 'leader of the larger throng'. For *populi* used of the dead, see on 186–91.

bello cum peteres Nestoream Pylon/**When you sought war with Nestor's Pylos:** the allusion is to Hercules' expedition against Pylos in the southwest Peloponnese, in which he slew all the sons of Neleus (except Nestor: Hom. *Il.* 11.690–3, Ov. *Met.* 12.549–76) and fought against several gods, including Dis/Hades, whom he wounded (Hom. *Il.* 5.395–7, Apollod. 2.7.3, Paus. 6.25.2–3, where it is also stated that there was a temple to Hades at nearby Elis and that Hades was worshipped at Pylos).

pestiferas manus/**pestilential hands:** an Ovidian phrase used in the singular of the 'pestilential hand' of the Fury, Tisiphone (*Met.* 4.496). For the compound in -*fer*, see on 235–40.

telum tergemina cuspide praeferens/**Brandishing his spear of triple point:** a trident, more usually attributed to Neptune or other sea-god. It was one of the weapons of the gladiator known as the *retiarius* ('net-man'). For *praeferre* of 'holding/wielding/brandishing' weapons, see *Ag.* 735. *Tergeminus* occurs only twice elsewhere in Seneca: *Thy.* 1083, *Apoc.* 7.2.6. *Tergemina cuspide* is a descriptive ablative: Woodcock §43.6.

mortis dominus pertimuit mori/**The lord of death was afraid to die:** epigrammatically expressed paradox bound together by alliteration of *ms* and *ts* and the wordplay of the initial and final word. For paradoxical phrasing in *Hercules*, see on 30–5. *Pertimere* is a Senecan tragic *hapax*, though it does appear in the prose works.

fatum rumpe manu/**Break fate with your hand:** an echo of Juno's description of Hercules' violence in the underword: *rupto carcere umbrarum*, 'bursting death's prison' (57). Cf. Andromache's command to the dead Hector: *rumpe fatorum moras*, 'Break fate's chains' (*Tro.* 681). For *rumpere* and breaking/bursting fate, see also Lucr. 2.254, Livy 1.42.2, Virg. *Aen.* 6.882; for 'breaking out' of hell, see on 57–63. *Manu* underscores the physical violence of the act: for the importance of this motif, see on 118–22.

tristibus inferis/**grim dead:** almost a tautology, since *tristis* is the quintessential epithet of the underworld (the 'sad' and/or 'grim' realm: *regnum triste*, *Med.* 11, *regna tristia*, Hor. *Odes* 3.4.46; see further e.g. 611, 620; *Med.* 631, 680, 804; *Oed.* 545; *HO* 1065; Virg. *Aen.* 6.534) which (in the sense of 'grim') is almost a pun on *Styx* (558), derived from στυγέω, 'I abhor'.

prospectus pateat lucis/**See the light:** the opening up of the underworld was also a motif of Juno's prologue (55–6) and Megara's opening speech (290–5).

inuius limes det faciles…uias/pathless border Grant easy paths: Augustan verbal play (cf. Virg. *Aen.* 3.383, Ov. *Met.* 14.113) ends the section, together with a teasing inversion of the Virgilian Sibyl's remarks (*Aen.* 6.126–9) that it is the descent to the underworld which is easy (*facilis*), not the way back.

ad superos/to the world above: the world of the living, but there is again (see on 46–52) the ambiguity that Hercules' ultimate path is to the world of the gods.

569–89 The Chorus move to Orpheus as exemplary conqueror of death. Here Seneca has borrowed heavily from the two canonic Latin versions of Orpheus' all but successful recovery of his wife from the kingdom of death: viz. those of Virgil (*Geo.* 4.467–503) and Ovid (*Met.* 10.1–11.66), the latter itself a rewriting of the former: see on 572–6, 577–81, 582–9, 590–1 below. Seneca's account and that of *Hercules Oetaeus* (*HO* 1061–1101) were themselves rewritten by Boethius (*Cons. Phil.* 3 Metrum 12), who bases his speech of Pluto (40–6) on that of Seneca (see Fitch *ad loc.*). One area in which Seneca does not follow Virgil and Ovid's account here is the inclusion of the singer's dismemberment by Thracian women (Virg. *Geo.* 4.520–2, Ov. *Met.* 11.3–43), an event he refers to at *Med.* 630–1. The paradigm of Orpheus, a poet of great, transformative power, who entered and returned from the land of the dead but lost his wife, has obvious ramifications for the rest of this play: like Orpheus, Hercules will send to death what he loves. The Chorus, unbeknown to themselves, are foreshadowing the action to come. An ancient audience would be aware that entering and returning alive from the underworld always involves the loss of someone's life: Theseus/Hippolytus (*Pha.* 1149–53), Odysseus/Elpenor (Hom. *Od.* 11.51–83), Aeneas/Misenus (Virg. *Aen.* 6.149–235). A dramatically powerful way of staging this section would have been to have had the Chorus pantomime what they sing or to have had an actual pantomime enter the stage to dance the failed Orphic rescue described by the Chorus. See Slaney (2013*b*), Boyle (2019) *ad Ag.* 589–658 (introd.). This Orpheus section seems to have impressed Kyd's Seneca-citing Hieronimo, who plans to model himself on the Thracian bard (*Spanish Tragedy* III.xiii.114–23).

569–71 *Immites…umbrarum dominos*/the shades' pitiless Lords: Dis and Proserpina, referred to as *reges*, 'kings/monarchs', at 1137. For *immites*, 'pitiless', see Virg. *Geo.* 4.492: *immitis…tyranni*, 'pitiless tyrant'; 4.470: *nesciaque humanis precibus mansuescere corda*, 'and hearts ignorant of softening to human prayers'; Hor. *Odes* 2.3.24: *nil miserantis Orci*, 'Orcus pitying nothing' (also *Odes* 1.12.17); Stat. *Theb.* 8.23: *nil hominum miserans*, 'Pitying nothing human' (of Dis). See further on 577–81 (*lacrimis difficiles*). The underworld's lack of pity goes back to Homer (*Il.* 9.158). *Vmbrarum dominos*, 'lords of the shades', seems derived from Ovid's Orpheus account (*Met.* 10.16); it is repeated by Boethius (*Cons. Phil.* 3 Metrum 12.28). With *domini = dominus* and *domina*, cf. *uterque...dominus* (805). Notice how the opening line of this section is echoed in the concluding two lines of the ode (590–1).

Orpheus: son of the Muse Calliope (Apollon. 1.23–5, Virg. *Ecl.* 4.57) and one of Jason's Argonauts (attested as early as Pindar: *Pyth.* 4.176–7), he was the famed Thracian singer and musician who had a transformative effect on nature, and, after the death of his wife Eurydice, journeyed to the underworld and almost recovered her. The Ciconian/Thracian women, whom he subsequently spurned, tore him limb from limb (Virg. *Geo.* 4.453–527; Ov. *Met.* 10.1–85, 11.1–66). He was regarded as the founder of the Orphic religion. Orpheus figures prominently also in choral odes of *Medea* (348–60, 625–33) and *Hercules Oetaeus* (1031–1130, with 1061–89 on the loss of Eurydice), and features also at *Med.* 228–9: see C. P. Segal (1983). To Virgil Orpheus was a paradigm both of poetic power and of poetic failure.

***Eurydicen...suam*/his dear Eurydice:** note the climactic and, as in Virgil (*Geo.* 4.490), emotional emphasis on *suam*; hence the additional 'dear'. The Greek form of the accusative, which helps perhaps with the evocation of mythological distance, is reproduced from Virgil and Ovid and repeated at 581.

572–6 The power of Orpheus' poetic art to affect nature. For Orpheus' transformative effect on nature, see also *Medea* 625–29; *HO* 1036–60; Simon. 567; Aesch. *Ag.* 1629–30; Eur. *Bacch.* 561–4; Apollon. 1.26–31; Virg. *Ecl.* 3.46, *Geo.* 4.510; Prop. 3.2.3–4; Hor. *Odes* 1.12.6–12, 3.11.13–24, *AP* 391–3; Ov. *Met.* 10.86–105, 11.1–2; Phaedr. 3. Prol. 57–9.

***quae siluas et aues saxaque traxerat*/which had moved forests and birds And rocks:** powerful, subtly alliterative line with its mixture of *q*s, *ss*, *us*, and *ax*s. Seneca clearly liked *saxa traxerat*; cf. *saxa...traxit* of Amphion at *Oed.* 612.

***ars*/The art:** the focus not on Orpheus but on his art sharpens the metaliterary resonance of this poetic figure. Orphic power is poetic power; and Seneca presents not only an analogue to Hercules but, like Virgil and Ovid, through a glass darkly a metapoetic image of himself. For metatheatre, see on 109–12.

***praebuerat fluminibus moras*/had made rivers delay:** lit. 'had provided delays to rivers'; a good example, as Fitch notes *ad loc.*, of Seneca's 'noun style' (for which see on 11–18). For similar periphrastic uses of *mora*, see 1171; *Med.* 35, 149, 173, 281, 1015; *Tro.* 929; *Thy.* 158, 762, 1022; *Pho.* 246.

ad cuius sonitum/with its sound: for the focus on sound, see on 1002–9.

mulcet non solitis uocibus/Soothes…with unfamiliar notes: for *mulcere*, 'to soothe', used of Orpheus elsewhere, see *Med.* 356, Virg. *Geo.* 4.510, Hor. *Odes* 3.11.24, Boeth. *Cons. Phil.* Metrum 12.17. For the use of *non* to negate an adjective, see on 489–94.

surdis…in locis/in that noiseless place: the inhabitants of the underworld are traditionally represented in Greek and Roman poetry as either silent or squeaking. In Virgil they are the 'silent shades', *umbrae silentes* (*Aen.* 6.264); at *Med.* 740, the 'silent throng', *uulgus silentum*; in Valerius Flaccus, the 'voiceless shades', *sine uocibus umbrae* (7.402); at *Pha.* 221, the underworld is the 'silent house', *silentem…domum*. See further Ov. *Met.* 10.30, Luc. 6.513. In Homer the shades gibber like bats (*Il.* 23.101, *Od.* 24.5–9). The silence of the underworld is further underscored at 620, 713, 794, 848, 862–3. The use of *loca* (lit. 'places') qualified by an evocative epithet is used elsewhere in the play to describe the underworld: see 673, 707, 794, 1221. This is not simply an inheritance from Virgil (e.g. *Aen.* 6.462) and Ovid (e.g. *Met.* 10.29), as Fitch notes *ad loc.*, but an aspect of the *locus* motif permeating this tragedy: see on 1–5.

577–81 The Eumenides, Dis, and Proserpina, and the judges of the dead weep.

deflent Eumenides Threiciam nurum/The Eumenides weep for Thracian Bride: so, too, they are moved or weep in Virgil (*Geo.* 4.481–3), Ovid (*Met.* 10.45–6), and Statius (*Theb.* 8.58–9). Like Zwierlein, Fitch (1987*u* and 2018), and Giardina (2007), I have accepted the emendation of Schmidt (1865). Caviglia, Viansino (1965 and 1993), and Chaumartin print the difficult reading of the MSS: *deflent Eurydicen Threiciae nurus*.

deflent et lacrimis difficiles dei/gods also weep, not prone to tears: the gods are Dis and Proserpina. Dis, normally regarded as *immitis*, 'pitiless' (569: see n. *ad loc.*) or *illacrimabilis*, 'incapable of tears' (Hor. *Odes* 2.14.6), is also described as weeping about Orpheus by Manilius (5.328). Note the anaphoric repetition, appropriate to this section's quasi-hymnic quality. For the dative with *difficilis*, see Hor. *Odes* 3.10.11, Ov. *Pont.* 1.6.47, 2.2.20.

qui fronte nimis crimina tetrica quaerunt/who examine crimes With sternest brow: note the legal sense of the verb, *quaerere*, to describe the activities of *quaesitores*. For legal language in *Hercules*, see on 731–4. For *tetricus* (again with *nimis*), 'stern/gloomy', see *Ep. Mor.* 36.3: *nimis horridi animi…et tetrici*, 'of a very gruff and stern temperament'.

ueteres excutiunt reos/review ancient Guilt: *excutere* is another legal term, used of legal scrutiny or examination; see e.g. Cic. *S. Rosc.* 97, *Har.* 37, and *OLD* 9a.

Claudian prefers to combine *ueteres reos* with the verb preceding the phrase (*quaerunt*) in his Senecanesque description of Rhadamanthus: *ueteresque reos...quaerit* ('and he examines ancient guilt/the accused of old', *Ruf.* 2.495).

flentes Eurydicen iuridici sedent/judges...sit weeping for Eurydice: note the alliterative and assonantal pattern (especially *flentes* picking up *deflent*, 577, *deflent*, 578, and the sonal playfulness of *Eurydicen iuridici*), again appropriate to a quasi-hymnic tone. The *sedent*, 'sit', is in the sense of 'sitting in judgement', as of Dis at 721. *Iuridici* is a Senecan *hapax*, indeed according to Fitch *ad loc.* 'something of a neologism', at least in this sense of 'judges'. For modifiers ending in *-dicus* in Senecan tragedy, see *ueridicus* (*Ag.* 255) and the more common *fatidicus* (*Oed.* 269, 302, 1042; *Tro.* 1100). For the three judges of the underworld, Minos, Rhadamanthus, and Aeacus, see on 731-4.

582-9 The speech of Dis. Again a remodelling of Virgil (*Geo.* 4.485-7) and Ovid (*Met.* 10.50-2), transforming the narrative of those poets into direct speech 152-64. For direct speech cited in tragic lyric, a common Euripidean technique (e.g. *Helen* 1459-64: Galaneia; *Bacch.* 152-64: Dionysus; *IA* 1062-75: Centaurs), see *Tro.* 726-8 (Hercules), 1053-4 (Trojan boys and mothers), *Oct.* 332-44 (Agrippina), 371-2 (Agrippina). Boethius *Cons. Phil.* 3 Metrum 1240-7 was clearly influenced by this passage.

Mortis...arbiter/Death's arbiter: Dis. Cf. *umbrarum arbiter*, 'arbiter of ghosts', *Thy.* 14, although here the genitive seems possessive rather than objective; see also Claud. *Rapt.* 1.56. For the *arbiter* motif, see on 205-9.

euade ad superos/Go to those above: cf. Virg. *Geo.* 4.485-6: *euaserat... superas ueniebat ad auras*, 'had escaped...was approaching the air above'; also *Aen.* 6.128. For the ambiguity of *superos*, see on 46-52.

lege tamen data/but on these terms: cf. Virgil's *hanc...legem*, *Geo.* 4.487, and Ovid's *legem*, *Met.* 10.50.

tu...coniugem/You...your wife: note the anaphora, alliteration, and structural parallelism of these two lines, generating a formal, ritualistic tone.

non...respice/don't look back: *ne* with an imperative is common for prohibitions in Latin verse. Here *non* has replaced *ne* perhaps to emphasize the terms of the prohibition, 'look back on your wife NOT before...'. Fitch *ad loc.* compares Livy's use of *non* with the subjunctive at 9.34.15. Cf. also the use of *non* at 936.

ante...quam cum...: a pleonastic construction, apparently unattested before this.

clara deos...dies/Clear daylight...gods: Dis especially must be adroit at this kind of verbal play. For *deos*, 'gods', as metonymic for 'the world above', see 505, where, as here, there is a covert allusion to Hercules' aim at heaven itself. Note the feminine form of *dies*, used very occasionally by Seneca for metrical convenience to procure a final short syllable in the accompanying epithet (cf. e.g. 875, *Oed.* 689, *Med.* 223, *Pha.* 771). His preference normally is for masculine forms, as at 190, 236, 296–7, 653, etc.

Spartani...ianua Taenari/Spartan Taenarus' gate: Taenarus (modern Cape Matapan or Cape Tainaron) was a promontory in Laconia in the southern Peloponnese, situated at the intersection of the Ionian and Aegean/Myrtoan seas. On the promontory was a cave which supposedly led down to the underworld. Taenarus was often used by metonymy for the underworld itself. Both Virgil (*Geo.* 4.467) and Ovid (*Met.* 10.13) make it Orpheus' entrance point for the underworld (see also Hor. *Odes* 1.34.10). Importantly it is mentioned again at 663 and 813 below as both the entrance and the exit point for Hercules' journey, underscoring the analogy between Orpheus and Hercules. For reference to it in Greek literature, see e.g. Pind. *Pyth.* 4.43–4, Eur. *Herac.* 23 (where it is Heracles' point of entry to the underworld). For its use elsewhere in Senecan tragedy, see *Oed.* 171, *Pha.* 1201, *Tro.* 402. Cf. also Apollod. 2.5.12.

odit uerus amor nec patitur moras/True love hates delay, nor suffers it: Seneca has avoided Virgil's psychological causal analysis (Orpheus' action was caused by *furor*: *Geo.* 4.495) and developed that of Ovid (it was caused by the fear and desire of the 'lover', *amans*: *Met.* 10.56–7). For other Senecan dramatic statements about 'true love', see *Med.* 416 and *Thy.* 551. In the latter the label is applied with contextual irony to the relationship of Atreus and Thyestes. Here there seems no such irony. For the phrases *pati moram/moras* or *patiens/impatiens morae*, see e.g. 773, *Oed.* 99, *Pha.* 583, *Ag.* 131, *Thy.* 158, 769. The phrase is Ovidian: Ov. *Met.* 4.350, *Fas.* 2.722. Cf. *Oed.* 850, where it is 'truth' itself which 'hates delay' (*ueritas odit moras*). Seneca has made the banal oxymoronic: 'true love hates'.

munus dum properat cernere/Rushing to see his gift: Ovid focuses on this more simply with the phrase *auidus uidendi*, 'avid to see' (*Met.* 10.56). For the *properare* motif, which unites Hercules, Orpheus, the Chorus, and humankind, see 187 and n. *ad loc.*

perdidit/lost: the final Latin word of this whole section is taken from the Virgilian Eurydice's plangent cry (*Geo.* 4.494–5):

> illa 'quis et me' inquit 'miseram et te perdidit, Orpheu,
> quis tantus furor?'

> 'What', she asks, 'has destroyed/lost poor me and you, Orpheus,
> What great fury/madness?'

The brilliance of Seneca's rewriting is in the position of the word.

590-1 The Chorus sententiously draw a conclusion from the Orpheus story with linguistically parallel lines, varying the vocabulary (but not the gender or cases) of the first and last words and employing verbal polyptoton at each line's centre. Cf. *Tro.* 510–12, *Pho.* 522–4, and (in choral odes) *Thy.* 388–9, 613–14; also *Ep. Mor.* 10.5. Ovid employs parallel lines at *Met.* 1.325–6, 481–2, but not, as here, for a ringing sententious conclusion. For similarly strong, contextually ironic closure to a choral ode, see 201, 1137; *Oed.* 199–201, 992–4; *Tro.* 162–3, 408; *Pha.* 1153; *Thy.* 401–3, 883–4. For final choral lines, see on 1131–7.

uinci potuit...uinci poterit/**one could conquer...one can conquer:** for the verbal polyptoton, see on 112–18; for polyptoton, see on 11–18. For *uincere* and Hercules, see on 63–8.

cantibus/**with song:** I have chosen the reading of *A*, rejected by Zwierlein and modern commentators, who favour *E*'s *carmine*, because the conventional arguments against it—it picks up the *cantibus* of the opening line (569) of the Orpheus section and is assonantally similar to *uiribus* (591): see Fitch *ad loc.*—seem to me reasons for accepting it. The reading of *A* underscores the parallelism and closural strength of the clauses and increases their dramatic power.

The **chorus** *remain onstage:* the Chorus are absent for most of Act III, since they are described as returning to the stage by Theseus in the final lines of the act (827–9). Davis (1993: 19) has the chorus absent throughout the whole act. However, given the laudation of Hercules and exhortation of him to return in this second ode, it would be odd not to keep them onstage for Hercules' entrance. They could then exit the stage with Hercules at 640, just as they will return with him at 827.

Act III (592–829)

The third acts of four Senecan tragedies dramatize a confrontation between the play's major figures: Andromache and Ulysses in *Troades*, Medea and Jason in *Medea*, Thyestes and Atreus in *Thyestes*, Hippolytus and Phaedra in *Phaedra* (taking *Phaedra* as a six-act play). The other two act-divided plays, *Agamemnon* and *Oedipus*, devote most of their third acts to an extensive narrative of events outside but relevant to the dramatic action, delivered not by an anonymous messenger but by a named character (Eurybates in *Agamemnon*, Creon in *Oedipus*). *Hercules'* third act is thus aligned with those of *Agamemnon* and *Oedipus*, with greater similarity to *Oedipus* in that the named 'messenger' has an important dramatic role elsewhere in the play. There is, however, a major difference between the messenger narrative of *Hercules* and those of the other two plays in that it is discontinuous. It is also very long. Eurybates' messenger speech of *Agamemnon* is the longest unbroken monologue in Senecan tragedy, exceeding one hundred and fifty lines (*Ag.* 421–578), and is longer than many Senecan acts. Theseus' discontinuous messenger narrative (658–96, 698–706, 709–27, 731–47, 750–59, 762–829) exceeds one hundred and seventy lines, and bears comparison with, though it exceeds in length, the discontinuous messenger narrative of Act IV of *Thyestes*, where, as here, the discontinuity arises from interruptions by the interlocutor (in *Thyestes* the Chorus, in *Hercules* Amphitryon). For analysis and discussion of Theseus' narrative, see on 658–827 below, and Introd. §VII, 83–6.

Theseus' messenger-style narrative of Hercules' *catabasis* is not the whole of Act III. It is preceded by the audience's first sight of Hercules, who, almost as if in response to the Chorus' final words, enters victoriously with the captured Cerberus and with Theseus, delivers both a prayer and an entrance soliloquy (592–615), sees Lycus' soldiers by the temple, who rapidly dis‐ appear (616–17), is greeted by Amphitryon, learns from him of recent events in Thebes, briefly addresses him and Megara, and exits to kill Lycus (618–40), taking with him Cerberus and accompanied by the Chorus (so I interpret: see stage directions and Comm. *ad loc.*). After less than fifty lines onstage, Hercules, the figure who has defined every dramatic figure so far and been avidly awaited by Seneca's audience, is gone. Part of the function of what follows (641–827) is to cover the time needed for Hercules to exit the stage, kill Lycus, and return. But there is much more at issue than dramatic time: see below on 658–827.

A final point on the acting/gestural possibilities of the act. The opening prayer of Hercules (592–604) and the concluding part of Theseus' narrative (807–27) would have presented actors with a potent opportunity to utilize through visual gesture the verticality of the Roman theatrical space. See on 1–124 (introd.).

For further discussion of Act III, its treatment of Hercules, and its dramatic and thematic function in the play, see Introd. §VII, 81–6.

Metre: iambic trimeters. See Introd. §IX.

Enter from stage right (outside Thebes) HERCULES, **bearded, wearing a lion skin draped over his left shoulder, and equipped with bow, quiver, arrows, club, and sword:** Hercules enters in his traditional mythic costume and with his traditional weapons. The bow and arrows are found in Homer (*Il.* 5.392–404, *Od.* 8.224–5, 11.601–8); the club, first attested in the archaic poet, Pisander (West 2003: 180), becomes Hercules' most defining weapon in visual art (see esp. the metopes of the temple of Zeus at Olympia) and in literature (see e.g. Theoc. 17.31, Prop. 4.9.17, 39, Ov. *Met.* 9.236, VF 3.162): see 625 and n. ad loc. The sword, less associated with Hercules but certainly in evidence in early representations of the slaying of the Lernaean Hydra (see Gantz 1993: 1.384–5), is mentioned at 1229 and is required in the action of the play (see on 1302–13). The lion skin, featured in early visual representations of Heracles (see Introd. 60) and first textually attested in Pisander's *Heraclea* (frag. 1 West 2003), would have been expected, but sets the hero apart, underscoring his liminal status on the boundary between animal and human, and between human and god, and confirming his status as what Silk (1985: 6) terms, 'an interstitial figure'. Cf. the dress of another son of Jupiter, the god Bacchus, who is often depicted wearing a leopard-skin. All the items with which Hercules is equipped (including the sword: 1312) will be mentioned and used in the dramatic action to follow. For the position of the lion skin, see 797, 1150–1.

They drag a movable platform onto the stage behind them: this of course is only one possible way of staging this spectacular scene, but it seems dramaturgically the simplest and most efficient way of resolving the appearance of Cerberus on stage. The platform could have been the *exostra* or *ecclyclema*, used for interior scenes (see Introd. 18), or a version thereof. For the possible use of the *exostra* or *eccyclema* (or *sim.*) to stage other complex, often similarly spectacular scenes in Senecan tragedy (the final choral ode and Act V of this play, the Strophius scene of Agamemnon at *Ag.* 913–43, the cannibalistic feast of Thyestes at *Thy.* 908–1112, the Theseus interrogation scene at *Pha.* 864–958, Medea's incantations at *Med.* 740–842, and the interior scene of the non-Senecan *Octavia* at *Oct.* 75–272), see before 1054–62• and my editions of the relevant plays *ad locc.*

592–617 Hercules' first speech in this tragedy is in what Shakespeare's Bottom was to call 'Ercles' vein' (*MND* I.ii.40). It displays a high rhetoric befitting his status in the play—a declamatory rhetoric which will be repeated in the acts to come. Here the rhetoric structures an entrance monologue, complex in its development. Contrasting with Lycus' entrance monologue soliloquy (332-57), Hercules' initial words in the play are heard by all on stage, as the hero prays publicly to Apollo, Jupiter, and Neptune to pardon him for bringing Cerberus into the light (592-604). (For prayers, see on 205-78.) The speech mode then seems to shift to 'aside' (see n. *ad loc.*), as Hercules moves into a typical entrance soliloquy, in which he describes his conquest of the underworld in vainglorious fashion and challenges Juno to test him further (604-15). There is a strong contrast, too, with Euripides' Heracles who enters alone (without Theseus or Cerberus) and in secret (*Herac.* 514, 598), and plans bloodthirsty revenge against the Thebans who did not help his family (*Herac.* 568-73). MacLeish in his *Herakles* (1967) uses the Senecan mode for the second-act entrance of his hero, who addresses Apollo immediately (Introd. §VIII, 142). Hercules similarly enters Handel's 1744 opera in 'Ercles' vein' (*Herc.* I.v: libretto by Thomas Broughton):

> Thanks to the pow'rs above, but chief to thee,
> Father of gods, from whose immortal loins
> I drew my birth!

The Senecan Hercules' aside ends with his perception of onstage activity: viz. the guards outside the temple (616-17).

592-7 *O lucis almae rector*/O lord of gentle light: like 'father', like 'son'; cf. the similar opening of Act II with Amphitryon's invocation of Jupiter, *O...rector* (205), with *rector* in the same position of the line. The focus on 'light' will continue (*flammifero, inlustre, Phoebus*) in this invocation of Apollo, effecting a dramatically potent contrast with the dark world of the previous ode. The first words of Euripides' Heracles refer to his returning to 'the light' (φάος, *Herac.* 524) but lack both the magniloquence and the concern with *uenia* of this opening address. *Almus*, 'gentle' (lit. 'nourishing/ fostering' as of a nurse: see Lucr. 5.230), famously modifies Apollo *qua* Sol at Hor. *CS* 9, and also regularly qualifies *dies*, 'day' or its *lux*, 'light' (as here and at *Ag.* 726; *Oct.* 224; Hor. *Odes* 4.7.7; Virg. *Ecl.* 8.17, *Aen.* 1.306, 3.311, 5.64, 8.455; Ov. *Met.* 15.664); but it qualifies *nox* at *Ag.* 74, *Med.* 876, *Tro.* 438. *Rector* is more usually used of Jupiter by Seneca (see on 516-20), but seems here used of Apollo to create the parallelism with the opening of Act II. For *o* and the vocative, see on 205-9. For address to gods through defining descriptions, see on 205-9.

caeli decus/heaven's glory: used of Phoebus and his sister Diana (the moon) at Hor. *CS* 2, and of a similar 'adornment' of the heavens, the goddess Iris (the rainbow) at Virg. *Aen.* 9.18, and by Seneca of Bacchus at *Oed.* 405; cf. *noctis decus*, of Diana at *Pha.* 410. *Decus* with the genitive is something of a descriptive mannerism in Senecan tragedy; see also e.g. 619, 1270–1; *Tro.* 766, 876; *Med.* 130, 226, 571; *Pha.* 900, 1189; *Ag.* 395; *Oed.* 250, 1026; *Thy.* 790–1. Cf. *Oct.* 390, 424, 534. The mannerism is found elsewhere: e.g. Lucr. 3.3: *o Graiae gentis decus,* 'O glory of the Greek race' (Epicurus); Cic. *Phil.* 2.54: *imperii populi Romani decus,* 'glory of the empire of the Roman people' (Pompey); Virg. *Aen.* 11.508: *o decus Italiae uirgo,* 'O virgin, glory of Italy' (Camilla). Further on *decus,* see on 249–58.

qui alterna…spatia/Whose…both spheres: i.e. the two hemispheres, occasionally referred to in ancient texts: see e.g. *Pha.* 411, Virg. *Geo.* 1.249–51, where the possibility of two hemispheres, one of which is in darkness when the other is in light, is suggested; and similarly Manil. 1.242–6, Luc. 8.159–61. For Seneca's use of *spatia,* see on 821–7; for the elision of *qui,* see on 480–9; for relative clauses in prayer and laudatory references to a deity, see on 516–20.

curru…flammifero/chariot of fire: or, in the language of Medea's prologue, *ignifera…iuga, Med.* 34. Seneca's compound adjective not only has greater dramatic power than Horace's description of the Sun's chariot (*curru nitido,* 'shining chariot', *CS* 9), with which it is occasionally compared, but also has tragic pedigree. *Flammifer* has Ennian connections, occurring in his *Alcmeo,* frag. 25 Jocelyn. Silius clearly admired the Senecan phrase: 1.210, 5.55. For compounds in *-fer,* see on 235–40. For the compound in *-fer,* see on 235–40.

inlustre laetis exeris terris caput/And lifts thy shining head above joyous lands: a 'Golden Line' in the Dryden sense: see line 22 and n. *ad loc.* I have preferred (with Zwierlein) *laetis* (A) to *latis* (E), adopted, for example, by Fitch, because *laetis* seems more likely to be corrupted to *latis* than vice versa and the 'joy' of the land seems a patent and potent objective correlative of Hercules' joy at seeing the light. *Laetis…terris* is ablative of separation (Woodcock §41.8.), found with *exero* at *Ag.* 554, *Oed.* 532.

da, Phoebe, ueniam/Grant pardon, Phoebus: *uenia,* 'pardon/forgiveness', is an important motif in the tragedies: see 1266–7, *Oed.* 263, *Pha.* 225, 440, *Ag.* 267–8, *Tro.* 547, and esp. *Med.* 595, where again it is used in prayer as the Corinthian Chorus collectively beg 'forgiveness' (*ueniam precamur*). For the imperative, *ignosce,* see *Tro.* 922, *Oed.* 863, *Med.* 813, *HO* 983. It is an important issue in this play's final act: see on 1265–72, 1314–17; also on 1015–17. *Phoebus,* 'Bright One', is the sun-god, Apollo: see on 19–29.

si quid inlicitum tui uidere uultus/**if thine eyes have seen Things forbidden:** the Sun's initial terror at the sight of Cerberus was described by Juno at 60–1 above (see n. *ad loc.*). Euripides' Heracles does not have the problem of offending the sight of the Sun and the other gods with Cerberus: he has left the dog in Demeter's grove at Hermione (*Herac.* 615). Behind all this is the general idea that the gods may not look upon/are defiled by (*pollui*, 601) scenes of death: see Eur. *Hipp.* 1437–8. Cerberus of course is the dog of death. A corollary of the Sun's aversion to scenes of evil, death, and horror (demonstrated even more famously in *Thyestes*) is the concern to prevent such scenes being accessible to the Sun's view: note Hercules' later desperate desire to hide himself (from among other things, the Sun: 1333–4). See also Eur. *Herac.* 1231. For *uultus* = 'eyes', see on 329–31.

iussus in lucem extuli/**On orders I brought to light:** note the grounds of the appeal for 'pardon', *uenia*, viz. he acted 'on orders'. *Iussus*, lit. 'ordered', makes a telling contrast with *illicitum*, 'forbidden' (595), while repeating the notion of the 'ordered' nature of Hercules' labours, which the play has underscored (35, 41–2, 63, 78, 211, 213, 235, 295) and will continue to underscore (604, 615, 831, 1268). Note especially the ironic iteration of *iussus* by Hercules at 1268, where he uses it to show that he deserves no *uenia*.

arcana mundi/**The world's secrets:** Hercules is referring to his opening up of hell with special reference to his parading of Cerberus. For *arcana* of the 'secrets' of the underworld, see Luc. 6.514; for *arcana mundi* of the 'secrets of the universe', see Luc. 5.198.

597–604 *caelestum arbiter parensque*/**judge and father Of gods:** Jupiter; for whose titles, see on 516–20. For *arbiter*, see on 205–9. For address of gods through defining descriptions, see on 205–9.

uisus fulmine opposito tege/**shield thy sight with a thunderbolt:** perhaps modelled on Ov. *Met.* 4.799–800, where Minerva 'shielded her sight with the aegis' (*aegide uultus…texit*) to prevent her eyes from witnessing Neptune's rape of Medusa in Minerva's own temple.

secundo…qui sceptro/**whose second sceptre:** the sceptre of Neptune is called second, because his realm, the sea, was the second of the three *regna* (heaven, ocean, the underworld) allocated by lot after the defeat of Cronos/Saturn. See on 52–6. For the notion of the second realm, see also *Med.* 598, *Pha.* 904. For the postponed relative, see on 159–61; for *sceptrum*, see on 63–8.

quisquis…/**All who…:** it was a regular practice in prayer to conclude with an *inuocatio generalis*, a general invocation of appropriate deities to ensure that none were omitted (and thus offended): see Hercules again below at 907–8, Virg. *Geo.* 1.21–3, Livy 6.16.2. At *Oed.* 248 Oedipus begins his prayer with such an invocation.

pollui metuens/fear pollution: see on 592–7.

aciem reflectat/Should turn their eyes: *acies* is literally 'field of vision'; it is a favourite Senecan word for eyesight: see 652, 671, 1042, *Ag.* 458, *Tro.* 1079.

hoc nefas cernant/should see this evil: *nefas* is a strong moral and religious term, sometimes translated as 'unholy thing'; see 387 and n. *ad loc.* It is applied by Aeneas to Helen of Troy at Virg. *Aen.* 2.585.

qui aduexit et quae iussit/He who fetched it, she who ordered it: Hercules and Juno. In Seneca's mind (see 42 and 78 and nn. *ad locc.*) both Eurystheus and Juno seem to be involved in giving the orders. *Aduehere*, used with an animal object, is extremely rare, and may be found at *Apocol.* 7.2.11. For climactic half-lines, see on 40–6; for the elision of *qui*, see on 480–9.

604–15 The speech mode seems to change as Hercules moves into a long aside or closed soliloquy. There seems little point in regarding this section as an open soliloquy, since no reference is made to it by other speakers, and the freezing of dramatic time which may accompany a closed soliloquy renders more appropriate Hercules' delay in noticing the guards. The change of speech mode seems triggered by the reference to Juno which precedes (604).

In poenas meas/For my pains: *in* with the accusative here and in the next line suggests purpose, as at *Thy.* 38 (*in scelera*, 'for crime'), Ov. *Her.* 1.72, *Am.* 1.1.22, *Tr.* 4.3.84.

non satis terrae patent/the wide earth does not suffice: Hercules repeats Juno's language at 46.

Iunonis odio/Given the hate of Juno: note the ambiguous genitive. *Iunonis* seems primarily a subjective, possessive genitive (Juno's hatred of me), but beneath it lurks an objective genitive (my hatred of Juno). Hercules will present himself as obsessed with Juno as the latter is with him: see 614–15, 908, 963, 1010–11, 1018–19, 1036–8. The reference to Juno might also have stirred the audience's recollection of Juno's earlier words, referred to above, underscoring the transparent, situational irony here: the audience know what Juno-inspired *poenae* await. *Odio* is a causal ablative: Woodcock §45.

uidi inaccessa omnibus/I saw things banned To all: note the focus on Hercules 'viewing' hell, effecting a contrast with his initial prayer to the sun and light (presumably with his head lifted to the sky). *Vidi* is repeated at 613, and repeated by the later Hercules of *Hercules Oetaeus*: *uidi silentum fata*, 'I saw the fate of the silent' (*HO* 22). For such 'eye-witness' perfects and the repeated Senecan concern with visual witness, see on 249–58. *Inaccessa* is a Senecan tragic *hapax* (used twice by Virgil: *Aen.* 7.11, 8.195), here involved in a rare double elision (cf. *Med.* 199, *HO* 1339), the second one of which prevents a breach of 'Porson's law'; see line 20 and n. *ad loc.*, and on 249–58.

ignota Phoebo/unknown to Phoebus: i.e. to Phoebus *qua* sun-god; cf. *Phoebo non peruia*, 'not penetrable by Phoebus', Luc. 6.645. The underworld is by definition 'sunless', ἀνήλιος: see Eur. *Herac.* 607–8.

deterior polus/baser pole: for *polus* applied to the underworld, see 1105 and n. *ad loc.*

diro…Ioui/dire Jove: Dis; see on 46–52. Cf. 47, where Dis is called 'infernal Jove' (*inferni Iouis*). For the ominous nature of the description of Dis as 'dire Jove', see Introd. §VII, 108. For *dirus*, see 56 and n. *ad loc.*

tertiae sortis loca/places of the third lot: for the 'third lot' see 833 and on 52–6.

regnare potui/I could have reigned: it would have been difficult for a Roman audience not to have construed this claim as hybristic, especially when juxtaposed with the description of Dis as 'dire Jove'. What Hercules' assertion amounts to is a claim of power over death.

noctis aeternae chaos/eternal night's chaos: *chaos*, the Greek loan-word used by Latin poets for a formless mass (or void), is used only once in Seneca's prose works (of the Epicurean void at *Ep. Mor.* 72.9), but quite frequently in the Senecan tragic *corpus*: e.g. 677, 861, 1108; *Tro.* 400; *Pha.* 1238; *Ag.* 487; *Oed.* 572; *Med.* 9 (again *noctis aeternae chaos*), 741; *Thy.* 832, 1009; *Oct.* 391; *HO* 1115, 1134. See also Virg. *Aen.* 4.510–11, 6.265; Ov. *Met.* 2.299, 10.30, *Fas.* 1.103; Luc. 1.74, 5.634. Ovid offers a definition of chaos at *Ars* 2.467—*rerum confusa sine ordine moles*, 'a confused mass of things without order'—and an even longer definition at *Met.* 1.7–9:

> rudis indigestaque moles
> nec quicquam nisi pondus iners congestaque eodem
> non bene iunctarum discordia semina rerum.

> A raw and unstructured mass
> Nor anything but inert bulk and warring seeds
> Of things not well joined heaped into one.

Chaos is a Hesiodic divinity (*Theog.* 116), and is invoked as a divinity in the Greek magical papyri (*PGM* iv. 443, 1459). The term was regularly applied to the underworld, as it is here. For *nox aeterna/perpetua*, 'eternal night', used elsewhere by Seneca of the underworld, see e.g. *Pha.* 221, 835; *Oed.*

393; *Med.* 9. For *nox* of the darkness of the underworld, accompanied by other epithets, see 705, *Thy.* 1072 (*atra*, 'black'), *Ag.* 494 (*inferna*, 'hellish'), *Oed.* 585 (*uera*, 'true/real').

nocte quiddam grauius/something heavier than night: cf. the similarly evocative use of *quiddam* at *Thy.* 270: *grande quiddam*, 'a thing sublime'. See also *HO* 1867: *ipsa quiddam plus luce*, 'something more than light itself'. What Hercules refers to is left deliberately vague. Fitch's suggestion *ad loc.* ('a darkness more impenetrable and oppressive than that of night') seems more persuasive than Billerbeck's ('wohl eine Umschreibung für Cerberus'). The power of the phrase comes from its unspecificity. For *nox* as 'heavy/ oppressive', see *Thy.* 787, *Tro.* 1142, *Ep. Mor.* 82.16, Hor. *Odes* 1.4.16, Virg. *Aen.* 6.827, Ov. *Her.* 10.112.

tristes deos et fata uici/I vanquished…the grim Gods and fates: another vainglorious boast (cf. 610), made ironic by its unconscious echo of the grieving Evander's statement that he had lived too long: *uiuendo uici mea fata*, 'By living I vanquished my fate' (Virg. *Aen.* 11.160). Like Evander, Hercules will live on to see his dead offspring. For a failure to 'conquer fate' (*uincere fata*), see Ov. *Met.* 2.617. *Fata*, 'the fates', here also includes death: see on 178–82. *Tristes deos*, 'grim gods', are the gods of the underworld, the *regna tristia*: see 566 and n. *ad loc.* For *uincere* and Hercules, see on 63–8.

morte contempta/spat on death: Hercules is playing the Stoic. Seneca's writings, both prose and verse, are permeated with the theme of the contempt for death: *contemnite mortem*, 'Spit on/despise death' (*Prou.* 6.6); *mors contemni debet magis quam solet*, 'death should be despised more than it is accustomed to be' (*Ep. Mor.* 82.16). See also e.g. *Ag.* 604–10, *Pho.* 197, *Ep. Mor.* 23.4, 24.6–14, 36.9–12. Note Publilius Syrus' *sententia* (405 Duff): *mortem ubi contemnas uiceris omnes metus*, 'Spit on/despise death and you have conquered every fear'. Correr would later develop this idea in *Progne* (673–4): *quisquis contemnit necem | rex est tyranni*, 'Whoever belittles death, is king over a tyrant'. The dramatist of *Hercules Oetaeus* was mindful of Hercules' death-contempt (*HO* 1161, 1681). For Stoic ideas and language in *Hercules*, see on 162–3.

quid restat aliud/What else is left: the irony needs no demonstration.

uidi et ostendi inferos/I saw and exposed hell: Hercules confirms Juno's description of his opening up of the underworld for viewing from above: see 56 above. There is also an ironic, unconscious echo here of Juno's promise at 91 above: *hic tibi ostendam inferos*, 'Here I'll show you hell'. Hercules may have 'shown' or 'exposed hell', but Juno will later in this play 'show hell' to Hercules. For the 'eye-witness' perfect, *uidi*, see above.

da, si quid ultra est… Iuno/**If there's more, give it, Juno:** note the rich ambiguity of *ultra*, 'more'. The audience know what 'more' is to come. For Hercules' obsession with Juno, see above; for his need for further challenges, cf. 937–9, where again it features as a climax to Hercules' thinking. The final *o* of *Iuno* is short, as at 109 and 1297: see on 109–12.

iam diu/**Now…long:** for a similarly rhetorical (hyperbolic) use of *diu*, see *Tro*. 308.

cessare/**idle:** for Hercules' problem with idleness, see Introd. §VII, 108.

quae uinci iubes/**What conquest do you command:** the question, as Fitch observes *ad loc.*, is immediately answered by the situation on stage. Note the final emphasis on *iubes*, 'command/order', which triggers memories of Juno's frustrations with her and Eurystheus' commands in the prologue (35, 41–2, 63, 78), and the ease with which Hercules carried them out. Equally important is the related focus on *uinci*, 'conquest'. The audience know that another conquest is to come, inspired specifically by Juno: Hercules' 'conquest of himself' (*se uincat*, 116). What the audience do not know is how that self-conquest will itself mutate. Cf. the similar irony at 937–9.

616–17 It is standard Senecan dramaturgy to have a character enter, utter a number of lines, before seeing or visually attending to another character onstage. See the speeches of Agamemnon (*Ag*. 782–9), Strophius (*Ag*. 918–24), Jason (*Med*. 431–46), and Helen (*Tro*. 861–87) before they attend respectively to Cassandra, Electra, Medea, and Polyxena. The actual width of the Roman stage (*c*.95 metres in the case of the Theatre of Pompey) meant that it was not straining credulity to have one character not noticing (or being unable/slow to identify: 618–25, *Pha*. 829–34, *Oed*. 202–5) another character on the stage itself. In the case of Hercules the delay in the recognition of his family is mitigated both by the freezing of dramatic time during the second part of his monologue (605–15), but also by the probable position of the temple stage left, i.e. as far away as possible from Hercules' entrance point from the opposite side of the wide Roman stage. There is a strong contrast here with Euripides' Heracles, who notices the situation on stage (*Herac*. 525) after two lines of joy on returning home (*Herac*. 523–4).

terror armorum obsidet/**armed terror besiege:** powerful combination of abstract subject and concrete verb. The genitive is subjective.

Exeunt GUARDS (*alarmed*) *stage left* (*to the city*): a necessary stage-direction, given the evident absence of these guards during the rest of this act and play. It is possible to have the guards exit after Amphitryon's identification of his son (621), but the spectacle of the captured Cerberus onstage

and the sight of Hercules advancing towards them seem dramatically sufficient to drive the guards from the stage. They leave in the direction of the
city and of Lycus.

618-25 Amphitryon's response to Hercules' appearance comes in two
stages: surprise, uncertainty, and joy (618-21); direct address, gradual belief,
and recognition (622-5). In Euripides' play it is Megara who takes the lead
in recognizing Heracles, whose children rush to embrace him (*Herac.* 514-
22). The emotionality of Amphitryon's greeting of Hercules will be repeated
in his later attempts to dissuade Hercules from suicide: see 1256-7.

618-21 Note Amphitryon's surprise to see Hercules (as in Euripides: *Herac.*
515, 531-2). It attests to his uncertainty at the end of Act II concerning
Hercules' imminent appearance (see on 520-3).

Vtrumne...an: this construction is infrequently used in Latin verse (but
not prose) for alternative direct questions (where *-ne...an* or simply *an*
between the alternatives is normal), but is more common in drama than in
other verse forms. For the construction or its variant, *utrum...an*, in
Senecan tragedy, see *Oed.* 309-12, 345-6, 1036-7; *Tro.* 928-9; *Ag.* 579; *Thy.*
1032-3; also *HO* 1254-5.

uisus uota decipiunt meos/**prayers trick my eyes:** similarly later
(1042-4) Amphitryon will draw attention to his failing eyesight. For
uncertainty in identifying a character onstage, see the Chorus at *Oed.*
203-4.

ille domitor orbis et Graium decus/**the tamer Of the world and the glory
of Greece:** a potent combination of an especially 'Roman' phrase and a
Greek tag. Amphitryon initially addresses Hercules as a triumphant Roman
general with a title (*domitor orbis*) both political (cf. Manil. 1.793, applied to
Pompey; Val. Max. 6.7.1, applied to Scipio Africanus Maior; Luc. 8.553,
9.1014, where *domitor mundi* and *terrarum domitor* are applied respectively
to Pompey and Caesar) and befitting his role as 'tamer' of beasts (see *domitum*, 33, *domitor magne ferarum, HO* 1989). Cf. Leconte de Lisle's title for
the baby Heracles: 'dompteur des anciens crimes' ('L'Enfance d'Hèraklès',
45). Here *domitor* is coupled with an epicizing, Latinized version of a
Homeric tag (*Graium decus* is probably modelled on Homer's κῦδος Ἀχαιῶν,
'Glory of Achaeans', *Il.* 9.673, of Odysseus, 14.42, of Nestor). Cf. Eurybates'
description of Agamemnon as *telluris...Argolicae decus,* 'glory of the Argive
land', *Ag.* 395. Notably, Hercules' status as Amphitryon's 'son', *natus*, mentioned two lines later, is not prioritized. For Seneca's fondness for nouns
ending in *-tor*, see on 299-302. *Graium* is genitive plural. For *decus* with the

genitive, see on 592–7. For *domare* and Hercules elsewhere in the play, see 33 and 955; for Roman referentiality in the play, see on 46–52; for triumphal language and imagery, see on 57–63.

tristi silentem nubilo...domum/silent house and its melancholy gloom: *tristi...nubilo* is a sociative-instrumental ablative functioning almost as an ablative of description; cf. *silentem nocte perpetua domum*, 'silent house of perpetual night' (*Pha.* 221). See Woodcock §§43, 83. For the silence of the underworld, see on 572–6; for *domus* of the underworld, see on 662–7; for *tristis* and the underworld, see 566 and n. *ad loc.* For the 'gloom' or 'mist' (*caligo*) of the underworld, see 92 and 710.

membra laetitia stupent/My limbs are numb with joy: for this kind of somatic description of an emotional reaction, see on 414–21. For the unusual sensation of being 'numb with joy', see also Virgil's Aeneas and Achates at *Aen.* 1.513–14, who are numb (*obstipuit*) with 'both joy and fear' (*laetitiaque metuque*).

622–5 Amphitryon addresses his son in gentle, loving terms, which, however, are not reciprocated by Hercules, who answers him (626–8) in a formal, almost scolding manner.

O nate/O son: Amphitryon's initial address to Hercules as 'son' picks up the *nate* of 520 and will be repeated in the similarly 'strong' dramatic contexts of Act IV (918, 953, 1039). For this formal style of address with *o*, used by Amphitryon also at 205 and 309, see on 205–9.

certa at sera...salus/sure, if late, salvation: lit. 'sure but late salvation'. *At* is the widely accepted conjecture of Gruterus; cf. Sen. Rhet. *Con.* 10. Pref. 6: *lenti quidem sed certi*, 'slow but sure'. With the insertion of an adversative between two adjectives, cf. also *propitios attumen lentos*, 'slow yet propitious', *Ag.* 403; note 974–5 below. *Salus* has a Roman political ring: the 'health/safety/salvation' of the people was one of the prime duties of the emperor, see *Clem.* 1.3.3, 17.2, 26.5. For Roman referentiality, see on 46–52.

teneone/Do I hold: so, too, mother (Jocasta), as she embraces son (Polynices) at *Pho.* 501.

uana fruor deceptus umbra/take false joy In an empty shade: similarly the Chorus at *Oed.* 204 have difficulty in recognizing Creon: *an aeger animus falsa pro ueris uidet?* ('Does my cankered mind see false for true?'). In the recognition scene in Euripides' *Heracles* both Megara and Amphitryon similarly question what they are seeing (*Herac.* 514–18); Megara wonders whether it is a 'dream' (ὄνειρον, *Herac.* 517). Note also the Senecan Amphitryon's uncertainty about his eyesight (618, 1042–4).

agnosco/I recognize: a semiotically rich word, uttered by 'father' recognizing 'son' in an almost legal sense, where 'recognizing' a son is a legal acknowledgement of him (Nepos *Ag.* 1.4, Quintil. *Inst.* 7.1.14). Important, too, are the literary resonances. 'Recognition', Seneca's distinctive redeployment of ἀναγνώρισις, Aristotle's much debated ingredient of complex tragic action (*Poet.* 1452a12ff.), well attested in extant Greek plays, constitutes an important motif in Senecan tragedy and defines some of its most powerful scenes: see 1016 (*agnosce*, 'recognize'), 1196 (*uideo*, 'I see'); *Med.* 785, 923, 1021; *Pha.* 113, 698, 1249, 1260; *Ag.* 923; *Tro.* 95, 504; *Thy.* 1005–6; *Pho.* 332—and *HO* 955, 1946. For Seneca's employment of the motif in his prose works, see e.g. *Ep. Mor.* 5.5, 29.11, 59.11, 108.8, but especially the opening phrase of *Epistle* 31: *agnosco Lucilium meum*, 'I recognize my Lucilius'. Seneca's nephew, too, saw the importance of this motif (Luc. 1.686, 2.193, 7.794), as did Renaissance imitators. Notice how 'recognition' here is entirely physical, restricted to properties of the body or what the body bears (the club). The word, when used in Roman drama, necessarily has a metatheatrical resonance; cf. Hecuba's lyrical outburst to the Chorus of Trojan women: *agnosco Troada turbam*, 'I recognize a Trojan band' (*Tro.* 95). The list of properties 'recognized' similarly have a metatheatrical feel (see below). For metatheatrical language in *Hercules*, see on 109–12. For Seneca and Aristotle, see on 1237–9.

toros umerosque et alto nobilem trunco manum/Muscles, shoulders, hand, known for its tall club: central constituents of Hercules' identity and defining properties of a 'stage-Hercules' (see above). For the weapons as part of Hercules' identity, see 1149–55 and nn. *ad loc.* For the *manus* motif, see on 118–22. Hercules' 'shoulders' are emphasized in the play (see also 71, 465, 1119, 1291), but his 'muscles' (cf. *Pha.* 807, *HO* 751: *Herculeos toros*) are mentioned only here. Mark Seneca's attitude to brute strength as displayed at *Ep. Mor.* 80.2: *cogito mecum...quam imbecilli animo quorum lacertos humerosque miramur*, 'I reflect...how weak-minded are those whose arms and shoulders we admire'; see also *Ep. Mor.* 15.2. Zwierlein rejects the *EA* reading, *nobilem trunco manum*, printed here and by Viansino (1965 and 1993), Giardina (1966 and 2007), Caviglia, Fitch (1987*a* and 2018), Chaumartin, and Billerbeck. He prints instead the bland (and unwarranted) emendation of Axelson: *nobile in trunco caput*. For *truncus* as 'club', see [Virg.] *Culex* 192, Stat. *Theb.* 4.301. *Alto...trunco* seems best taken as ablative of respect: Woodcock §55.

626-8 *genitor*/father: Hercules' initial address to Amphitryon as 'father' will not be repeated (*genitor* or *pater*) until Act V, where it will permeate the dialogue: 1176, 1184, 1189, 1192, 1199, 1202, 1245, 1269, 1314. Note the 'high register' word which he uses here, employed earlier of Jupiter by Juno: see 122 and n. *ad loc.*

squalor/squalor: the quintessential word for unkempt appearance, often applied to figures in hell or returning therefrom, even to death itself; see the description of Charon as *squalidus…senex*, 'foul/squalid old man', at 765; Theseus' *squalor incultus*, 'unkempt squalor', returning from hell at *Pha.* 833; the Ghost of Hector's 'face…hidden by squalid/foul hair', *uultus…squalida obtectus coma*, at *Tro.* 448–50; *squalidae Mortis*, 'foul/squalid Death', *Med.* 742. See also *Oed.* 554, 625; *Ag.* 759; Virg. *Aen.* 6.299. Here, somewhat ironically, *squalor* is attributed by a figure returning from hell to a figure on earth.

lugubribus amicta coniunx/wife dressed For mourning: for Megara's funereal appearance, see also 202, 355–6 and nn. *ad locc.* Euripides' Heracles finds his family dressed for their own funeral (*Herac.* 442–50, 525–7, 548–9). The scene plays with the formula, man-comes-upon-weeping-woman, exemplified by the Theseus-Phaedra meeting at *Pha.* 850ff. and the Strophius-Electra meeting at *Ag.* 922ff. For *lugubria* = 'mourning clothes', see *Helu.* 16.2, Prop. 4.11.97, Ov. *Met.* 11.669, *Tr.* 4.2.73.

tam foedo obsiti paedore nati/sons so foully Smothered in filth: *paedor* is a poetic word of tragic pedigree, attested in Accius (*Andromeda* frag. 111 Klotz); it is employed elsewhere in Senecan tragedy (*Ag.* 991, *Oed.* 625) and by the tragic and epic poets whom it influenced (*HO* 392, Luc. 2.73, Stat. *Theb.* 4.616). Cicero (*Tusc.* 3.62) did not approve of 'filth-saturation' as a style of mourning.

629–30 The play lacks a formal messenger. This act will supply two informal ones. Amphitryon plays the first messenger, giving tragic 'news' in a lapidary, quasi-objective, 'messenger' style of speech with its own rhetorical structure: two lines, three asyndetic, carefully balanced sentences, each with a single main verb and no subordinate clauses, with the longest sentence functioning as the climax. Mark, too, how the alliterative use of *p* binds the three sentences. Cf. official messengers at *Pha.* 997, *Tro.* 1063–4, *Ag.* 395–6, *Med.* 879–80—and *Ag.* 925–7, where another 'non-messenger' (Electra) offers a similar news bulletin. See also Hercules' self-messaging at 1160–1 below. Contrast with Euripides' *Heracles*, where the hero receives a very detailed account of events from Megara (not Amphitryon) at *Herac.* 533–61. For the 'headline news' approach (if not the lapidary style) in Attic tragedy, see e.g. Soph. *El.* 673, *OT* 1234–5, Eur. *Ion* 1111–12. See further 912 and n. *ad loc.* For the asyndeton of family terms, see on 30–5 and 283–95.

leto petit/He intends to kill: lit. 'he seeks for death'; *leto* is dative of purpose; see Kennedy 226, Woodcock §67. For the same construction with *petere*, see *Tro.* 330.

631–40 Hercules' final speech of this act. He expresses his response to the situation in Thebes (631–3), resolves to kill Lycus (634–6), orders Theseus to remain, his father and wife to defer embraces, and exits with a triumphant cry (637–40). Hercules has no need of a strategy to get rid of Lycus as in Euripides' play; he will just use physical violence. Note Hercules' self-naming at 631 (*Herculeae*) and 636 (*Alcidae*), something he did not do in his entire entrance monologue, where the only names are those of Phoebus and Juno. Self-naming will become something of a pattern in Acts 4 and 5, where ten instances of Hercules' self-naming occur (see on 955–63). Self-naming is not only a character-revealing device, suggestive of 'vanity and self-centredness' (Fitch *ad* 631, 635), but (and perhaps more importantly) a metatheatrical device, reminding the audience of the inherited literary/dramatic archetype against which the present instantiation is to be judged. Over Euripides' Heracles hovered the image of 'The famous Heracles', ὁ κλεινὸς Ἡρακλῆς (see Eur. *Herac.* 1414). Seneca's self-naming hero makes sure that the inherited image is never far from a viewer's mind. For self-naming and metatheatre, see further on 109–12.

631–3 *Ingrata tellus*/Ungrateful land: similarly Euripides' Heracles complains about the lack of help on his behalf (*Herac.* 558), but he also promises bloody revenge on the citizens who so betrayed him (*Herac.* 568–73). Seneca's Hercules (at least for the moment) restricts his punishment to Lycus. For a similar Herculean outburst against the 'ungrateful world' (*ingrate orbis*), see *HO* 1332–6.

Herculeae domus/The house of Hercules: first instance of twelve self-namings by Hercules (9x Hercules, 3x Alcides: see on 631–40). The phrase is a variation of a standard line-ending, see 351 and n. *ad loc.* For the use of the adjective *Herculeus*, see 72 and n. *ad loc.*

uidit hoc tantum nefas/Watch such evil: watching/viewing *nefas*, 'evil', and not acting is an issue elsewhere in Senecan tragedy: see e.g. Medea's criticism of the Sun (*Med.* 28–31) and Hippolytus' outburst against Jupiter (*Pha.* 671–81). For the viewing of *nefas*, see also *Oed.* 444, *Tro.* 44, *Thy.* 1047, *Pho.* 497–8, Ov. *Met.* 11.70. For *nefas* itself, see 387 and n. *ad loc.*

defensus orbis/the world I saved: Hercules is conscious of his reputation as protector of the world. Cf. Amphitryon's *orbe defenso*, 'the world he saved' (249). For a possible allusion to a cult title of Hercules as *defensor*, see on 249–58.

COMMENTARY LINES 634-6   491

Cur diem questu tero/Why waste the day whining: repeated by the dramatist of *Hercules Oetaeus* (1774), replacing *cur* with *quid*. Cf. also *Tro.* 758-9, *Pho.* 387-8.

634-6 In *E* this is still part of Hercules' speech. In *A* 634b-6 are assigned to Theseus. As Fitch observes *ad loc.* 'few editors have followed *A*'s arrangement'. For compelling arguments in support of *E*, see Fitch.

mactetur hostis, hanc ferat uirtus notam/An enemy must be slaughtered, virtue marked: the 'mark' (*notam*) is often taken as a 'stain' or 'stigma' (Fitch and Billerbeck *ad loc.*, *OLD* 4), arising from the killing of a lesser opponent (see *HO* 815-16, 1454-5, which seem to imitate the present passage). But *nota*, 'mark', may also connote a 'mark of writing' (*OLD* 6), suggesting a meaning of 'virtue must be marked in writing'. Hercules may intend the first sense, but the second metaliterary sense is fulfilled by Seneca's text, which devotes the end of the third choral ode and the start of Act IV to 'marking' Hercules' *uirtus*. *Mactare* is one of the prime verbs for sacrificial slaying (*OLD* 4): see *Tro.* 196, 248, 361 (Polyxena/Iphigenia), 943, 1063; *Ag.* 219; *Med.* 645, 1005; *Oed.* 872; *Thy.* 244, 713; Livy 21.45.8; Prop. 3.7.24 (Iphigenia); Ov. *Met.* 13.185 (Iphigenia); Sil. 5.653. The verb will recur in two important contexts (923, 1042), where it will underline Hercules' perversion of animal sacrifice. Intimations of that perversion begin here. For sacrificial imagery and language in *Hercules*, see on 918-24. For the *uirtus* motif, see on 35-40. For metaliterary language and motifs, see on 109-12.

fiatque summus hostis Alcidae Lycus/And Alcides' last foe must be Lycus: note again Hercules' self-naming, i.e. his reference to himself in the third person (see on 631-40), and the potent juxtaposition of *Alcidae Lycus*, which could underscore difference and/or similarity. The dramatist of *Hercules Oetaeus* substitutes *labor* for *hostis* in his imitation of this line (*HO* 816, 1455)

ad hauriendum sanguinem inimicum/to drink his hated blood: bloodthirsty language reflecting a bloodthirsty 'drive'. For the strength of the language, cf. Livy 26.13.13: *tanta auiditas supplicii expetendi, tanta sanguinis nostri hauriendi est sitis*, 'Such is their lust for exacting punishment, such their thirst for drinking our blood'; *Oct.* 521-2: *hausit cruorem incesta Romani ducis | Aegyptus iterum*, 'Again incestuous Egypt drank a Roman leader's blood'. Seneca may have been influenced by the Euripidean *Heracles'* bloodthirsty language when describing the vengeance he planned on the Theban citizens who had betrayed him (*Herac.* 568-73). For 'drinking blood', see on 480-9.

637–40 *Theseu*/Theseus: Theseus is addressed by name more than any other character in the play: also at 654, 914, 1177 (*bis*), 1242, 1318, 1335. Hercules is addressed by name three times, always through the vocative, *Alcide*: 186 (by the Chorus), 421 (by Megara), 1343 (by Theseus). For vocatives at the beginning of a Senecan iambic line, see 639, 914, 1245, 1318; *Ag.* 49, 125, 203, 260, 660, 749, 914, 917, 924, 952, 953, 978–9, 981, 986, 1012 (?); *Tro.* 501, 925; *Pha.* 115, 358, 954, 1244; *Oed.* 353, 824; *Thy.* 73, 442.

me bella poscunt/I'm called to war: after which, as Juno has indicated (85), he will 'war' with himself. For a similarly grandiose use of *poscere*, cf. Aeneas' *ego poscor Olympo*, 'I'm called by heaven', Virg. *Aen.* 8.533.

Differ...differ/Defer...defer: Hercules will repeat this command at 1175. Note the epanadiplosis/epanalepsis (use of the same word at the start and end of a line, clause or sentence). For epanadiplosis elsewhere in Senecan tragedy: see e.g. 907–8, 1156, 1167–8, 1230; *Thy.* 202, 326, 335, 494–5, 836, 847, 907; *Med.* 218–19, 922–3, 947–8, 954–6•, 984; *Tro.* 94–5, 465–6; *Oed.* 980; *Ag.* 526, 967–8, 1012. *Medea* even employs a kind of macro-epanadiplosis by beginning and ending with the same word.

coniunxque differ/Wife, defer: the only words addressed by the sane Hercules to his wife. Contrast Euripides' treatment (*Herac.* 514–82), where Megara and the children embrace Hercules and Megara has a long verbal exchange with her husband. For vocatives at the beginning of an iambic line, see above.

nuntiet/take...a message: there is obvious, metatheatrical irony here. Lycus is to play the messenger in a play without one. For the dying or newly dead as messengers to the underworld, see *Ag.* 1005–6 (Cassandra to the Trojan dead) and *Tro.* 801–2 (Astyanax to Hector). Closer to the tone of the present passage is Virg. *Aen.* 2.547–8, where the murderous Pyrrhus makes his victim Priam an underworld 'messenger' (*nuntius*). For other such messengers, cf. e.g. Eur. *Hec.* 422 (Polyxena to Hector and Priam), Stat. *Silu.* 3.3.205–7 (Etruscus' father to Etrusca), Sil. 1.398–400 (Ladmus to Hamilcar), Suet. *Tib.* 57.2 (a *scurra* to the dead Augustus).

me iam redisse/I have now returned: a trenchant message, befitting the climax of Hercules' words in this act, appropriately self-aggrandizing and brilliantly ambiguous. 'Returned' to where? To the upper world? To Thebes? To hell (which is Thebes/the upper world)? For syncopated perfect infinitives, see 63 and n. *ad loc.*

The platform on which the representation of CERBERUS *stands is wheeled offstage behind* HERCULES, *surrounded and/or followed by the* CHORUS: this is obviously the place to remove the chained Cerberus and the Chorus;

the latter return later at 827 (see above after 590–1). Eliot (1951c: 69), in his several misplaced criticisms of this play's dramaturgy, writes of Cerberus 'evaporating'. It seems preferable simply to have the platform on which his representation stands wheeled offstage with Hercules as he exits.

640–57 Hercules' exit is followed by a short interlude, in which Theseus comforts Megara and predicts/states Hercules' successful revenge (640–4) and Amphitryon requests from Theseus an account of the virtues, *uirtutes* (647), displayed by Hercules in the underworld (645–57). In doing so, Amphitryon enacts the traditional urging of a messenger to speak: see e.g. *Ag.* 404–5, 414, 419; *Tro.* 167, 1065; *Pha.* 996, 999; *Oed.* 211, 215, 510, 914; *Thy.* 633–40. In Euripides' play Amphitryon briefly questions Heracles himself about his *catabasis* (*Herac.* 610–20), which Seneca transforms in this act into one of the great ecphrases of imperial Latin literature.

640–4 *Flebilem ex oculis fuga, regina, uultum*/**Banish from your eyes, Queen, that doleful look:** note the reverential *regina*, 'Queen', only here applied to Megara in the play. It restores Megara to her proper station and reflects (for a brief moment) a confidence that the social and political hierarchy has been restored to Thebes. Though similar to such addresses from social inferiors (e.g. the Nurse to Clytemnestra at *Ag.* 125, the *Satelles*/Courtier to Jocasta at *Pho.* 387), its closest Senecan *comparandum* is Aegisthus' use of the royal title of Clytemnestra at *Ag.* 303. For *uultus*, see on 329–31. For other formal address, see 205, 309, 622 and nn. *ad locc.*

For the breach of 'Porson's law' in 641, see on 249–58.

tuque nato sospite/**and you—your son safe:** interesting use of a causal ablative absolute of attendant circumstances to identify a new addressee.

si noui Herculem/**If I know Hercules:** the phrase 'has the ring of everyday speech' (Fitch *ad loc.*; also Billerbeck *ad loc.*); cf. *Ep. Mor.* 16.7, 18.3, 19.10. It is repeated by the Nurse at *HO* 911 in an analogous attempt to calm Hercules' wife (Deianira).

dabit…'dabit': *dat…dedit*/**will pay…'Will pay'…he pays…he paid:** a terse description of Lycus' death to be matched by a similarly terse description of the same event by Hercules at 895–6. Contrast the emphasis given to the death of Lycus at Eur. *Herac.* 701–814, in which trickery is involved, the dying cries of Lycus are heard from offstage and the chorus are jubilant in their praise of Heracles. Mark the imitation by Jonson at *Catiline* III.iii.174–6: 'He shall die. | "Shall" was too slowly said; he's dying. That | Is yet too slow; he's dead'. Fitch *ad loc.* also cites Molière's *L'Avare* IV.vii: 'Je meurs, je suis mort, je suis enterré.' For verbal 'correction', see Jocasta at *Pho*. 367-9, Phaedra at *Pha*. 611-12, Atreus at *Thy*. 257. The tone here might be regarded as slightly comic. In the hands of Euripides Attic tragedy admitted comic touches: see e.g. *Tro*. 1050, *El*. 487ff., *Bacch*. 170ff. The rhetorical technique (*correctio*: *Rhet. Her*. 4.36) is exemplified by Seneca's father (*Con*. 10.5.1): *parum... parum...satis*, 'too little...too little...enough'. The second '*dabit*' is a quoted word: cf. Cat. 86.3: '*formosa*'; Prop. 1.18.31: '*Cynthia*'; Ov. *Met*. 15.96: '*aurea*'. For the *conuersio*, see on 895-9. For the verbal polyptoton, see on 112-18; for polyptoton, see on 11-18.

MEGARA, *who sits down with her* **SONS** *by the altar*: this is not a necessary stage direction. But given that Megara will not speak during Theseus' long narrative and that she and her sons (played by child-actors) remain onstage throughout it, it seems a good direction to have them sit down during the rest of the act and to rise when the Chorus arrive at its conclusion (see stage directions at 827-8). This also has the advantage of making the Amphitryon-Theseus dialogue a more intimate series of exchanges. In the final act of *Agamemnon* Seneca has Cassandra, who begins and ends the act, sit down at the stage altar during the middle of the act, when she neither speaks nor takes part in the action.

645-9 *rebusque lassis adsit*/aid troubled times: as at *Thy*. 658, *Polyb*. 16.6, *Ben*. 6.25.4. The *EA* reading is sound. For *adesse* (used here in prayer), see on 275-8; *adsit* is jussive subjunctive (Woodcock §109).

O magni comes magnanime nati/O great-souled comrade Of great son: rhetorical flourish based on the alliteration of *m* and *n* and the word-play of simple and compound adjective. For *o* with the vocative, see on 205-9; for *magnanimus*, here used of Theseus, as it is at *Pha*. 839, see 310 (and n. *ad loc*.), where Amphitryon used it of Hercules. The *magnanimus* Theseus becomes a stand-in for the absent *magnus/magnanimus* Hercules, who in Euripides' play is himself questioned by his 'father' (*Herac*. 610-21). For *magnus* as the quintessential epithet of Hercules, see on 439-47.

pande uirtutum ordinem/disclose his virtues in order: for other requests for narrative sequence (*series*) or 'order' (*ordo*), see Andromache at *Tro*. 1065 and Theseus at *Pha*. 999. The messenger of *Troades* even attests to the narrative sequence: *hic ordo sacri*, 'This the order of the ritual' (*Tro*. 1162). *Pande* is one of the standard imperatives used to elicit information from a Senecan tragic messenger: it is used twice by Clytemnestra, followed up by two more imperatives, *effare*, 'tell', and *exprome*, 'speak out' (*Ag*. 404-20), as the queen overcomes the messenger's traditional reluctance. Amphitryon similarly will use four imperatives (*pande...peruince...neue frauda...fare*, 'disclose...conquer...don't deprive...tell', 647–57), and follow these later with a fifth (*ede*, 'present', 760). Oedipus expends two imperatives (plus threats) in a similar situation (*exprome...fare...*, 'speak out...tell', *Oed.* 510–18), Theseus three (*ne metue...proloquere...effare*, 'fear not... proclaim...tell', *Pha.* 993–9), Andromache also uses four (*expone... persequere...ede...enarra*, 'Recount...describe...present...narrate', *Tro.* 1065–7); the Chorus of *Thyestes* use five (*effare...pande...ede...indica... effare*, 'tell...disclose...present...show...tell', *Thy.* 633–40). For *pande* as a command to speak, see also 1301. For the *uirtus* motif, see on 35–40. *Virtutum* here is not simply 'abstract for concrete' (i.e. = 'heroic deeds', as Fitch 2018 translates, or even just 'deeds' as Konstan 2017 offers). Amphitryon is requesting an exposition of a plurality of *uirtutes*, 'virtues', displayed by Hercules; he is asking for an aretalogy.

maestos...manes/grim ghosts: see 187 and n. *ad loc.*

650–3 Theseus seems reluctant to play the 'messenger-from-hell' and displays the tragic messenger's traditional reluctance to deliver his appalling 'news': see e.g. *Oed.* 223–4, 511–29; *Tro.* 168, 1056–8; Aesch. *Pers.* 249ff.; Soph. *OT* 1146ff., *Phil.* 329–30. Seneca's messengers sometimes even recoil from the horrors they are about to disclose: *Pha.* 991–5, *Thy.* 623–38, *Ag.* 416–18. Cf. also the 'non-messengers' here and at *Med.* 670 (Nurse). Seneca, too, seems to have been influenced by Virgil's Aeneas, 'bidden' to tell his 'untellable sorrow' (*Aen.* 2.3–13: see below). Behind Aeneas lies Odysseus (Hom. *Od.* 9.12–13). For an amusing parody of the *topos*, see Mozart (librettist: da Ponte), *Così Fan Tutte* Act 1.iii and iv.

securae...menti/mind of one now safe: *securus* seems to have a double sense here: (i) 'free from anxiety' (*OLD* 1); (ii) 'free from danger' (*OLD* 5). See Billerbeck *ad loc.*

horrenda/dreadful: *horrendus*, *horridus*, and *horreo* pepper Theseus' account: 657, 689, 705, 764, 786, 795.

uix...uix/scarce...scarce: for the anaphora of *uix*, see *Thy.* 496; it was a mannerism of Ovid (see e.g. *Met.* 2.863, 4.350, 8.35, *Fas.* 1.508).

fides uitalis aurae/trust the vital air: cf. the Ovidian Deucalion's lack of *uitae...fiducia nostrae*, 'trust in our life' (*Met.* 1.356), where again *fides* takes the objective genitive; cf. also Luc. 9.204–5: *uera fides...libertatis*, 'real belief in liberty'. *Vitalis aura* is a Lucretian phrase (3.405, 577, 5.857, 6.1227), used again evocatively at *Oed.* 651.

torpet acies luminum hebetesque uisus/my eyesight's dazed, My dull vision: cf. Hercules' self-description at 1042–3. Note the breach of 'Porson's law' in the fifth foot of line 652: see on 249–58. For *acies*, see 602 and n. *ad loc.*

hebetesque uisus uix diem insuetum ferunt/My dull vision scarce endures the strange daylight: Theseus is almost repeating his words from *Phaedra* (837): *et uix cupitum sufferunt oculi diem*, 'My eyes scarce endure the daylight they longed for', if, as seems likely, *Phaedra* predates this play. Cf. also Ov. *Fas.* 4.449–50, which has clearly influenced both passages. For fear of the daylight, see also 293 (denizens of hell), 821–8 (Cerberus), *Ag.* 861 (Cerberus).

654–7 *Peruince, Theseu*/Conquer, Theseus: this is the second address to Theseus by name; see on 637–40.

neue te fructu optimo frauda laborum/Don't be robbed of labour's Greatest joy: Amphitryon clearly likes the relationship between *labor* and *fructus* (a Virgilian 'georgic' ideal), since he repeats the phrase *fructus laborum* at 1253 with reference to his own failure to receive 'joy' from Hercules' 'labours'. For similar statements involving *fructus*, see *Med.* 563–4, *Tro.* 422, *Thy.* 906.

quae fuit durum pati meminisse dulce est/What was hard to bear is sweet To remember: a piece of worldly wisdom dating at least from Homer (*Od.* 12.212, 15.400–1) and memorialized in the shipwrecked Aeneas' consolatory utterance: *forsan et haec olim meminisse iuuabit* ('Perhaps one day it will bring joy to remember even this', Virg. *Aen.* 1.203), cited by Seneca at *Ep. Mor.* 78.15. Note *meminisse* in both Virgil and Seneca. Cf. *Ep. Mor.* 78.14: *quod acerbum fuit ferre tulisse iucundum est*, 'What was painful to bear is pleasurable to have borne' (accepting the emendation of Bartsch). See also Cic. *Fin.* 2.105. For *sententiae* addressed to messengers in an attempt to elicit speech, see also *Oed.* 515–29, *Tro.* 1066–7, *Ag.* 419–20. For *pati* as the ultimate word of a line (656), see on 348–53.

fare casus horridos/Tell the fearful story: for *fare*, see on 645–9. For the breach of 'Porson's law', see on 249–58.

658–827 Theseus' narrative of Hercules' final labour is in essence a discontinuous messenger-speech, structured in a way similar to the messenger-speech of Seneca's late masterwork, *Thyestes* (641–788). The messenger speech/scene is a regular constituent of ancient tragedy, which is handled with considerable variety by Seneca. The long, unbroken messenger speech is restricted to the (probably) early plays: *Pha.* (Act V.1000–1114), *Oed.* (Act III.530–658, Act V.915–79), *Ag.* (Act III.421–578); it may also be found in the non-Senecan *Hercules Oetaeus* (Act III.775–841). In the (probably) middle Senecan tragedies there is no long continuous messenger speech. In *Troades* there are two messengers, as in *Oedipus*; one offers a short speech

(Act II.168–202), the other two separate speeches (Act V.1068–1110, 1117–64). In *Medea* (Act V.879ff.), as in Creon's first messenger narrative in *Oedipus* (Act II, 223–32) and the non-Senecan *Octavia* (Act IV.780–805), the messenger's report is extremely brief, and in the case of *Medea* and *Octavia* interleaved with exchanges with the Chorus. In *Hercules* a brief messenger-style report is given by Amphitryon in Act III (629–30, see n. *ad loc.*), but the main 'messenger-speech' is Theseus' long, discontinuous account of Hercules' expedition to the underworld, in which Amphitryon acts like a chorus, asking questions or making a comment (658–827). In the later *Thyestes* (Act IV.641–788) a messenger again provides a discontinuous account broken up by questions/comments, this time articulated by the Chorus. In *Phoenissae*, perhaps Seneca's final play, there are short 'messenger-speeches' from both a Messenger (*Nuntius*: 320–7) and a Courtier (*Satelles*: 387–402). In *Hercules Oetaeus* the final messenger-speech is bipartite (1618–90, 1693–1757). Though there is no messenger in the last act of the three six act plays of the Senecan *corpus*, since there is a messenger in the final acts of *Medea* and *Troades*, it is apparent that the messenger may appear in any act other than the first. Three messengers are named by Seneca: Talthybius in *Tro.* Act II, Creon in *Oed.* Acts II and III, and Eurybates in *Ag.* Act III. As noted above, the messenger-style narrative of *Hercules* Act III is also spoken by a named character. The messengers in *Hercules Oetaeus* are also named characters (Hyllus and Philoctetes). But elsewhere, as generally in Greek tragedy, the messenger is anonymous.

   Fitch *ad loc.* treats Theseus' whole narrative in *Hercules* as essentially bipartite: (i) 'the physical setting of the underworld' (662–759); (ii) 'Hercules' capture of Cerberus' (762–827). I favour a more dramatic structure with six segments or narrative 'acts', following a formal invocation (658–61), and separated by five 'choral interventions' by Amphitryon (697, 707–8, 727–30, 747–9, 760–1): (i) Prologue: entrance to and riverscape of the underworld (662–96); (ii) Hell as barren wasteland/Death as the negation of life (698–706); (iii) Palace of Dis and Dis himself (709–27); (iv) Justice of the afterlife (731–47); (v) Punishment of sinners (750–9); (vi) Hercules' conquest of death (762–827). Theseus' discourse closes in an announcement of the Chorus' re-entry (827–9). Notice how two long sections (i and vi) frame four short sections (ii–v). The final and climactic episode, Hercules' capture and removal of Cerberus, is by far the longest. All sections of the speech contain or are even constituted by extensive descriptions (*ekphraseis*, see on 709–27). For an analogously discontinuous 'messenger' account, given by an anonymous messenger, prone to *ekphrasis* and interleafed with questions (this time by the play's actual chorus), see Act IV of *Thyestes* (641–788). Such widespread employment of ecphrastic technique may well have been part of the dramatic tradition which Seneca inherited.

Important to note, too, is the dramatist's indebtedness to the two great epics of Augustan Rome, Virgil's *Aeneid* and Ovid's *Metamorphoses*, the utilization of which, together with the use of similes (671–2, 676, 683–5), underscores the discourse's epic quality. Hercules was a model for Aeneas in Virgil's epic; here Aeneas becomes a measuring rod, a canon, from Hercules' future and Rome's past for the evaluation of the hero's *catabasis*. For Virgilian and Ovidian engagement, the former most especially, see Comm. below *passim*. The 'afterlife' of Theseus' description of hell is substantial. It influenced writers from Statius, Silius, and Claudian to Bernat Metge (*Lo somni*, c.1399), Thomas Kyd, and Edmund Spenser.

For discussion of Theseus' narrative as 'pausa al mezzo', psychological critique and thematic keystone of the play, its focus on the similarity/difference between the world of the dead and the living, its rhetorical and emotional appeal, its status as recitation drama within an acted drama, see Introd. §VII, 83–6.

658–61 Almost as if in imitation of Hercules' opening words in this act and the play, Theseus begins with prayer. The deities addressed, however, are not the Olympians, but Dis (see on 46–52) and Proserpina, rulers of the underworld, whom he asks for permission to reveal with impunity (*impune*) the underworld's secrets. There is overt allusion to Virgil's similar prayer in *Aeneid* 6 (264–7):

> di, quibus imperium est animarum, umbraeque silentes
> et Chaos et Phlegethon, loca nocte tacentia late,
> sit mihi fas audita loqui, sit numine uestro
> pandere res alta terra et caligine mersas.

> Divine lords of souls, and voiceless ghosts, and Chaos
> And Phlegethon, places wide-silent in the night,
> May I rightly speak things heard, rightly with your leave
> Disclose things buried in deep earth and mist.

The allusion has a metaliterary resonance. Theseus' recall of Virgil's poetic invocation brings to the surface Seneca's own dramatic voice permeating the character's words. For metatheatre in *Hercules*, see on 109–12; for the structural role of prayer in the play, see Introd. 78, n. 210.

Fas omne mundi/**the world's whole Sanctity:** an enlargement of Virgil's use of *fas* at *Aen.* 6.266, which Seneca clearly admired since he re-orders the Virgilian phrase *sit fas loqui* in his own line 266 above (see also the double use of *fas* by Sinon at Virg. *Aen.* 2.157–8). In a sense Seneca has split *sit fas loqui* into a direct invocation of *Fas* followed by *eloqui* three lines later. This is the only direct invocation of *Fas*, 'Right/Sanctity', in Senecan tragedy. For indirect invocation, see *Oed.* 1023: *per omne nostri nominis fas ac nefas*, 'by all the sanctity and sin of our names', where *fas* is again found with a dependent genitive. For the emotive use of *omne* with *fas*, see also *Med.* 900, *Thy.* 179, *Oct.* 164, Virg. *Aen.* 3.55, Sen. Rhet. *Con.* 1.2.8. For the personification of *Fas* in prayer, see also Livy 1.32.6, 8.5.8, VF 1.792.

regno capaci/**endless realm:** lit. 'capacious realm'. The infinite capacity of the underworld to receive the dead is a *topos* of Latin verse; see esp. Ovid *Met.* 4.439–42, where again *capax* is used, as at Hor. *Odes* 3.1.16. By underworld logic, *capax* is also used of Charon's boat: see 775.

teque quam tota inrita quaesiuit Aetna mater/**and thee whom thy mother Sought vainly round all Etna:** *te*, 'thee', is Proserpina, daughter of Ceres, whose failed attempt to find her daughter after she had been snatched away by Dis from her home in Enna, Sicily, is told by Ovid in two separate versions (*Met.* 5 and *Fas.* 4). Proserpina became the bride of Dis and queen of the underworld, but was allowed to live with her mother Ceres for a part of each year (half, according to Ov. *Fas.* 4.613–14 and *Met.* 5.564–7, two-thirds according to the Homeric *Hymn to Demeter* 445–7). See further 549 and n. *ad loc.* For Mt Etna, the great volcanic mountain of eastern Sicily, see on 104–9. For the Senecan mannerism of attaching *totus* to place-names: see e.g. 1328; *Ag.* 506, 742–3; *Med.* 239–40; *Pha.* 717, 1276; *Thy.* 184, 1016. The *EA* reading, *tota…Aetna* (*ethna*), is not printed by Zwierlein, who favours the emendation of Schmidt, *toto…orbe*. No recent editor apart from Giardina (2007) seems to have followed him.

iura/**laws:** cf. *temerata ponti iura*, 'ocean's violated laws' (*Med.* 614–15). For *iura* of the underworld, see Ov. *Met.* 14.118. For the language of law in *Hercules*, see on 731–4.

abdita et operta terris/**hidden and buried in the earth:** cf. Virg. *Aen.* 6.267, printed above.

liceat impune eloqui/**let me safely Tell:** the phrase has a ritualistic ring: cf. Virgil's *sit mihi fas loqui* (*Aen.* 6.266); Ovid's *si licet et fas est* (*Fas.* 1.25). For *loqui* = 'tell' in this sense of 'reveal', see *Tro.* 578.

662–96 Prologue: entrance to and riverscape of the underworld. This extended *ekphrasis* (see on 709–27) is in two parts: (i) The entrance to the underworld at Taenarus and the path downwards (662–79); (ii) The rivers Lethe and Cocytus and allegorical figures nearby (679–96). Notice how Theseus clothes his description of the entrance to the underworld (664–6) with a kind of animal imagery (*ora soluit*, 'opens its mouth', *hiat*, 'gapes', *faucibus uastis patet*, 'yawns with its vast throat'), in anticipation of the later appearance of the hell-hound itself.

662-7 *Spartana tellus*/**Spartan land:** for Seneca's predilection for denoting a country in this way, see on 19–29.

aequor...premit/**presses the sea:** Taenarus is at the intersection of the Ionian and Myrtoan/Aegean seas. For *premit* of dominating, oppressive features of a landscape, see *Thy.* 643, *Pho.* 22, Stat. *Theb.* 5.154.

Taenarus: see on 582–9. See further on 813–21.

ora soluit/**opens its mouth:** for the animal imagery, see on 662–96.

Ditis inuisi domus/**house of hated Dis:** for *Ditis domus*, see *Med.* 741, Virg. *Aen.* 5.731-2, 6.269; the phrase is modelled on the Homeric 'house of Hades' (δόμον Ἄιδος, *Il.* 3.322, etc.). *Inuisi* seems to translate Homer's στυγερός, applied to Hades (*Il.* 8.368), but may have been chosen to generate a translingual pun: 'unseen Dis' = Ἄιδης, as Fitch *ad loc.* tentatively suggests. For *inuisus* of the underworld, see Hor. *Odes* 1.34.10, Virg. *Aen.* 8.245. For translingual puns, see on 35–40.

hiatque rupes alta.../**A high cliff gapes wide...:** echoes of Virg. *Aen.* 6.237. For the animal imagery, see on 662–96.

immenso specu ingens uorago.../**huge abyss Of an immense cave...:** strong echo here of Virg. *Aen.* 7.569-70; see also Virg. *Aen.* 6.237 and *immenso sinu* of the chasm leading to hell at *Oed.* 582. For the 'throat' or 'jaws' (*fauces*) of Taenarus, see Virg. *Geo.* 4.467; for 'Taenarian caves' (*Taenarii specus*), see *Pha.* 1201. For *specus* and the underworld, see on 92–9.

faucibus uastis patet/**yawns with its vast throat:** for the animal imagery, see on 662–96.

omnibus populis iter/**highway for all nations:** for the immeasurable size of the pathway to hell (*nec ulli exiguus populo*, 'not too small for any nation'), see Ov. *Met.* 4.439–42. For the plural, *populis*, see on 186–91.

668-72 The complexities of the increasing loss of light as one descends are dwelt upon. Note how the words for 'light', *lucis, nitor, fulgor, solis, lumen, dies*, are nuanced by attendant adjectives or phrase to suggest the shifting quality of the light itself. There will again be a focus on light when Hercules (with Theseus and Cerberus) exits the underworld: 813–27.

fulgor...dubius/dubious glimmer: *dubius* is used of light (the 'dim/ doubtful' light of sunset or dawn) by Seneca at *Pha*. 42, *Tro*. 1142, and in the opening line of *Oedipus*: *iam nocte Titan dubius expulsa redit*, 'Now is the night banished; doubtful Titan returns'. Seneca also likes to use *dubius/dubitare* psychologically to index *dubitatio* or 'hesitation', see *Ag*. 50, 908, *Thy*. 120, and on 1283-4. In *Oedipus* the dubiety of the light seems to reflect the anxiety of the protagonist, as here in *Hercules* it seems to index the anxiety and *dubitatio* of humans themselves. For an earlier application of *dubius* to light, see Ov. *Met*. 11.596.

ludit aciem/tricks the eye: for *acies*, see 602 and n. *ad loc*.

nocte sic mixta.../just as the day's start...: Theseus' first simile indexes his leisurely, intensely descriptive narrative and triggers another analogy with Virgil, who inserts one of his most famous similes to describe the nature of the light accompanying Aeneas and the Sibyl's entry into the underworld (*Aen*. 6.270-2). For similes, see further on 679-88.

673-9 The focus on the downward pull of hell is unVirgilian (though written in Virgilian language) but fits well with, even foreshadows, the procession to death in the following ode.

uacuis...laxantur locis/open up with empty places: *uacuis* seems suggested by Virg. *Aen*. 6.269. For the *locus* motif and the use of *loca* with an evocative adjective of the underworld, see on 572-6.

in quae omne mersum pergat humanum genus/Into which plunge the whole human race: Ovid makes the same claim slightly differently, *omnes animas locus accipit ille nec ulli | exiguus populo*, 'the place receives all souls and is not too small for any nation' (*Met*. 4.441-2). For *mersus*, 'plunge', of the descent into the underworld, see 422 (also *demersus*, 317), *Tro*. 198, *Pha*. 220. *Humanum genus* is a regular phrase for the 'human race': see e.g. 1075, *Ira* 3.26.3, *Pol*. 16.6, *Ben*. 7.3.2, Lucr. 2.699, Virg. *Aen*. 1.743, Livy 21.30.7, *Oct*. 399, 568, *HO* 323; cf. *gens hominum* at 183. For the elision of *quae*, see on 480-9. Peiper's conjecture *pergat* for the MSS *pereat* seems clearly right.

nec ire labor est/To go is no labour: again a famous Virgilian text is recalled, as Theseus here plays the Sibyl: *facilis descensus Auerno...sed reuocare gradum...hoc opus, hic labor est*, 'The descent to hell is easy...but to retrace your steps...this is the work, this the labour' (*Aen*. 6.126-9). See also *Apoc*. 13.3: *omnia procliuia sunt: facile descenditur*, 'Everything slopes down: the descent is easy.'

ut saepe.../As currents...: Theseus' second simile seems a terse variation of Virgil's simile at *Geo*. 1.201-3, built around the same potent verb, *rapit.* The simile is rewritten in fuller form at *Pha.* 181-3; see also *Thy.* 438-9 and *Ag.* 139-40. The Virgilian simile was still in Seneca's mind in his final prose works: see: *Ep. Mor.* 122.19. For similes, see further on 679-88.

pronus aer/down-draught: hell itself is windless (550, 699, 704), but a down-draught helps the descent itself. *Pronus* is one of the telling epithets in the Virgilian *Georgics* simile: *prono…amni,* 'down stream' (*Geo.* 1.203).

auidum chaos/lusty chaos: a phrase echoing or echoed by the 'Death Ode' of *Troades: tempus nos auidum deuorat et chaos,* 'time's lust and chaos devour us' (*Tro.* 400). For *auidus,* see on 283-95. For chaos, see on 604-15.

gradum…retro flectere/Retrace your steps: cf. Virgil's *reuocare gradum* (above). *Retro flectere* is Ovidian: *Met.* 3.187-8, 10.51 (of Orpheus); for the phrase, see also 825, *Ag.* 239, *Pho.* 541-2, *HO* 1347.

umbrae tenaces/grasping ghosts: a disturbing image closes the first part of this section of Theseus' narrative. What is suggested seems to index the *umbrae* themselves, the 'ghosts', as instruments of the tenacity of the underworld *qua regnum tenax,* 'grasping kingdom' (*Pha.* 625). *Vmbrae tenaces* do not feature in Aeneas' *catabasis.*

679-88 *immenso sinu*/in a vast chasm: *E's* descriptive genitive, *immensi sinus,* printed by Giardina (1966 and 2007), Caviglia, Fitch (1987*a*), and Chaumartin, is rejected in favour of *A's* locatival ablative, *immenso sinu,* printed by Viansino (1965 and 1993), Zwierlein, Billerbeck, and Fitch (2002 and 2018). The ablatival phrase is also used of the underworld at *Oed.* 582 in the same metrical position. For discussion of the competing MS readings, see Fitch (2004*b*: 22).

placido quieta labitur Lethe uado/Silent Lethe glides with its placid stream: cf. the silence of the Styx at 713 and *Pha.* 625. Lethe, though not in Homer, was traditionally the river of 'oblivion' (Greek λήθη) in the underworld, for which it sometimes functions as a metonym. Here unusually it is used as the boundary river of the underworld, across which Charon ferries the newly dead (777) and which prevents hell's new entrants from returning. Seneca would have been aware that this is unVirgilian, but he may perhaps have chosen Lethe because of the river's erosion of memory, i.e. individual identity: see Virg. *Aen.* 6.703-15, 748-51. Hence the description of the dead at 292-3 as *oblitos sui…populos,* 'self-forgetting throngs'. See Fitch *ad loc.* Line 680 is a 'Golden Line' in the Dryden sense: see line 22 and n. *ad loc.* Cf. *Apoc.* 7.2.16: *tacitus quietis adfluit ripas uadis,* 'silently washes the banks with mute waters', also a 'Golden Line'. For the juxtaposition of synonyms (*placido quieta*), see on 283-95. *Vadum* (sometimes used in reference to 'shallows', as at 323) is also applied to the waters of a river without indication of depth: see 716, 762, 889; *Pha.* 183, 507. *Placido…uado* seems ablative of manner or respect: see Woodcock §§43.5.iv, 55.

demitque curas/**And removes care**: the Senecan Theseus plays on the meaning of the river's name. Cf. Ovid, who calls the river *secura Lethe* (*Pont.* 2.4.23), and Virgil, who terms its waters *securos* (*Aen.* 6.715). At *HO* 936 the river is simply *immemor Lethe*, 'unremembering Lethe'.

flexibus multis/**In many loops**: for *flexibus* of a river or stream, see Virgil's description of his Mincius at *Geo.* 3.14–15.

qualis incerta uagus Maeander unda ludit…/**just as wandering Maeander Plays with shifting waters…**: Theseus' third simile and his most 'epic', occupying two and a half lines. Seneca's use of the so-called 'epic simile' has been much criticized, but, as Tarrant *ad Thy.* 497–503, observes, 'none is without dramatic point, and the most successful are well adapted to the character who delivers them'. Similes are a regular feature of Senecan dialogue: see e.g. 671–2, 676, 1047–8; *Med.* 382ff., 940–2; *Ag.* 139–40, 776–7, 892–4, 898–9; *Tro.* 537ff., 672ff., 794ff., 1093ff., 1140ff.; *Oed.* 8ff., 315ff., 598ff.; *Pha.* 181–3, 382–3, 399ff., 580ff.; *Thy.* 497ff., 707ff., 732ff. Messenger narratives are particularly prone to feature them: see esp. the animal similes of the messenger speech of *Thyestes* (707–11, 732–6). Fitch *ad loc.* claims seven similes for the messenger's speech of *Phaedra*. They also occur in Senecan lyric: see e.g. 838–47, 1089–91, *Pha.* 764–72, *Ag.* 64–70, *Thy.* 577–95. It should also be noted that Giraldi (*passim*), Marlowe (*1 Tam.* III. ii.76ff.), and Shakespeare (*RII* III.ii.106ff.) were not averse to 'epic similes'. For short similes, see 1047–8 and n. *ad loc*; for two-word similes, see 712, 1009 and nn. *ad locc*. *Vagus* is a conventional epithet of rivers, but here its application has especial point.

The Maeander or Meander (modern, Büyük Menderes) was a famously winding river in Ionia (south-west Turkey); it entered the Aegean near the city of Miletus: see Strabo 12.8.15. Seneca at *Ep. Mor.* 104.15 calls it *poetarum omnium exercitatio et ludus*, 'every poet's *topos* and plaything': see e.g. Prop. 2.34.35–6; Ov. *Met.* 2.246, 8.162–6, *Her.* 9.55–8; Silius 7.139–40—and Seneca again at *Pho.* 605–6. There is a particular debt to Ov. *Met.* 8.162–6. Note, too, the wordplay with *ludit*, 'plays'. *Ludere* is used both of the 'play' or movement of water (e.g. Ov. *Met.* 8.163) and of 'beguiling', 'tricking', 'mocking' (671, *Ag.* 17, *Med.* 748). There is a similar wordplay at *Ag.* 770 and *Pha.* 1232. For the juxtaposition of synonyms (*incerta uagus*), see on 283–95. For *qualis* used with or, as here, without its correlative *talis* (or *sic*, *non aliter*, etc.) to introduce a simile, cf. *Pha.* 102, 399, 749, 1029; *Med.* 382; *Thy.* 707, 732; Virg. *Geo.* 4.511; Stat. *Theb.* 9.532. For the phrase *incerta unda*, 'shifting/uncertain water', cf. its use in the simile at *Ag.* 139–40. The reading of *A* printed here is not favoured by Zwierlein and several modern editors, who adopt *incertis* (*E*)...*undis* (*E*ᵖᶜ). Along with Fitch (1987*a* and 2018), I favour the 'more stylish' (so Fitch *ad loc.*) *A* reading.

dubius litus an fontem petat/**Undecided to head for shore or source:** cf. (concerning the river Arar/Saône) *dubitans quo suos cursus agat*, 'Undecided to where to drive its course' (*Apoc.* 7.2.12). Seneca frequently uses *dubius* or *incertus* (or, as here, both) to index *dubitatio* (for which see on 1283–4), and is wide-ranging in his ascriptions, applying them to rivers (*Apoc.* 7.2.12: *dubitans*), seas (*Ag.* 140), palaces (*Thy.* 697), corpses (*Thy.* 724), the sun (*Oed.* 1), fortune (*Ag.* 146, *Thy.* 33–4), buildings (*NQ* 6.1.2), and cities (*Tro.* 206) as well as to human and divine agents (*Thy.* 714–15, 1087). A similar catholicity of ascription is evident in Seneca's nephew: see Luc. 3.589, 5.602.

palus inertis foeda Cocyti/**The foul marsh of listless Cocytus:** Cocytus, a transliteration of the Greek word, κωκυτός, 'wailing', was one of the regular rivers of the underworld. Its 'black slime', *limus niger*, 'unlovely marsh', *palus inamabilis*, and 'sluggish waters', *tarda unda*, are described by Virgil (*Geo.* 4.478–9); it figures prominently in *Aeneid* 6 (132, 297, 323). For hell's 'marsh/swamp', *palus*, see *Ag.* 768, *Thy.* 665–7, *Aen.* 6.414–16 (*paludem...informi limo*, 'marsh...ugly slime'); cf. the *limosa palus* of the setting of Tiresias' necromancy at *Oed.* 547.

hinc...illinc/**Here...there:** I follow Billerbeck *ad loc.* in printing the emendation of the MS reading by E. J. Kenney, which was received 'brieflich', i.e. *per litteras*. Cf. *Pha.* 508 and *Thy.* 668, where the reading of *E*, *hinc*, is clearly preferable to that of *A*, *hic*, and seems to show Seneca's desire to indicate the *source* of the noise concerned.

uultur...bubo...strigis/**vulture...owl...screech-owl:** three birds of ill omen (for the three together again, see Ov. *Am.* 1.12.19–20, Stat. *Theb.* 3.508–12, Sil. 13.597–8) are appropriately found by the 'Wailing River'. The *bubo* is the eagle-owl and was associated by the Romans with death; see e.g. Virg. *Aen.* 4.462–3; Ov. *Met.* 10.453, 15.791; Pliny *HN* 10.34; Stat. *Theb.* 3.511. The *strix* is difficult to identify precisely (see Pliny *HN* 11.232), but seems to cover a wide variety of owls; it featured regularly in (literary) witches' brews: Hor. *Epod.* 5.20 (Canidia), Prop. 3.6.29, Ov. *Met.* 7.269 (Medea), and *Med.* 732–4 (where both the *bubo* and the *strix* form part of Medea's concoction). At *Fas.* 6.131–68 Ovid describes the *strix* as a kind of vampire which feeds on children. In the same passage he mentions the belief that *anus* ('old women', i.e. witches) were thought to change into *striges*. In Apuleius' *Metamorphoses* (3.21) the witch Pamphile turns into a *bubo.* In later literature the association between owls, death and witches is strong: see e.g. Chaucer, *Parlement of Foules* 343, Spenser, *Fairie Queene* 2.12.36, Shakespeare, *Macbeth* II.ii.3–4, IV.i.17.

luctifer bubo gemit/wails…baneful owl: Pliny (*HN* 10.34) describes the sound uttered by the *bubo* as *gemitus*, 'a groan/moan'. *Gemit* is here translated as 'wails' to unite the sounds of vulture and owl and to bring out the implied semiotics of Cocytus (see above), termed appropriately *gementis…Cocyti*, 'wailing Cocytus', at *HO* 1963. See Fitch (2016: 329). Epithets for the *bubo* include *maestus* ('mournful', *Med.* 733), *funereus* ('funereal', Ov. *Met.* 10.453), *funebris* ('funereal', Pliny *HN* 10.34). For the compound in *-fer*, see on 235–40.

omen…triste resonat infaustae strigis/curséd screech-owl's grim omen echoes: in Senecan tragedy omens are regularly negative: see *Pha.* 408, 624; *Tro.* 488; *Oed.* 359, 855—also *Oct.* 80. Even *Ag.* 939, though interpreted by Tarrant *ad loc.* as positive, which is certainly what the character using the word intends, would have been taken as negative by many in Seneca's audience. For *infaustus*, 'curséd', see 1135 and n. *ad loc.* For the focus on sound, see on 1002–9.

689–96 Theseus concludes the prologue to his account with a list of personified abstractions located by the Cocytus at the beginning of hell. Several of these abstractions will be concretized, i.e. experienced, in the later parts of the play, as if Hercules' breach of the boundaries between life and death brings them to the upper world. Personified abstractions are a literary device as old as Homer and Hesiod (see e.g. *Il.* 4.440, 11.37, *Theog.* 226–32) and may be found in Senecan tragedy earlier in this play (96–8) and in *Oedipus*: see the figures in Tiresias' necromancy (*Oed.* 589–94) and those which Oedipus takes with him into exile (*Oed.* 652, 1059–60). Note also those encountered in the *catabasis* of Virgil's Aeneas (*Aen.* 6.273–84) and of Ovid's Juno (*Met.* 4.484–5), which have clearly influenced Seneca here. As Fitch notes *ad loc.*, possibly eight of Seneca's eleven abstractions (allowing Seneca's *Funus*, 'Death', to replace Virgil's *Letum*, 'Death') come from the Virgilian list; *Pauor, Pudor,* and *Dolor* are non-Virgilian. Statius' House of Mars (*Theb.* 7.47–54), Silius' 'Virgilian/Senecan' hell (13.579–87) and Claudian's (*Ruf.* 1.28–38) continue the long tradition of personified abstractions. Cf. also Petron. *Sat.* 124.257–8.

opaca fronde nigrantes comae/Black foliage…with shady leaves: note the constellation of adjectives and nouns connoting 'darkness' in Theseus' descriptive narrative and Amphitryon's interjection: *opaca…nigrantes* ('Black…shady', 689), *ater* ('black'. 694), *nox atra* ('black night', 705), *opaca* ('dark', 707), *obscurus* ('gloomy', 709), *umbris...caligo* ('mist...shadows', 710), *umbrante* ('shady', 718). *Opaca* here seems picked up from Virgil's elm (*Aen.* 6.283): see next n.

taxo....segnis Sopor/yew...dull Sleep: a rewriting of Virgil's elm of 'empty dreams' (*Somnia...uana*) at *Aen.* 6.282–4, though the ultimate source of the image of Sleep and tree is Homeric (*Il.* 14.286–91). *Sopor* is 'deep or overpowering sleep' (Keulen *ad Tro.* 436), as is clearly evident when it recurs at 1050, 1079; see also *Pha.* 100, *Tro.* 436, *Oed.* 788. The association between the yew and death (*mortifera...taxus*, 'the deathly yew', *Oed.* 555) seems to begin with Ovid (*Met.* 4.432): see Fitch *ad loc.* It is common thereafter: see e.g. Luc. 6.645, Val. Fl. 1.777, Stat. *Silu.* 5.3.8, Sil. 1.83, 13.595–6. The berries of the tree were regarded as poisonous.

Fames...tabido rictu/Hunger...with rotting jaws: the personification of hunger starts with Hesiod (*Theog.* 227), appears in Virgil (*Aen.* 6.276), and climaxes in the Roman tradition with the withering and lengthy portrait of Ovid, where the scabrous, putrid nature of Hunger's appearance is emphasized (*Met.* 8.799–808). See also Claud. *Ruf.* 1.31, Prudent. *Psych.* 464.

Pudorque serus conscios uultus tegit/And tardy Shame veils its guilty face: *pudor*, a disposition to feel shame or the feeling of shame itself, is an important moral concept in Senecan tragedy, as it was in Roman life and thought. Expressive of moral conscience, self-respect and regard for community standards of propriety, *pudor* is both a disposition to avoid being seen by others 'in discreditable terms' (Kaster's phrase) and the feeling consequent upon the awareness of being so seen. It is used frequently in relation to (esp. female) sexual chastity and fidelity (see Clytemnestra at *Ag.* 113, 138, 288), but is not restricted to them. Phaedra's essential struggle is between *pudor* and *amor* (see e.g. *Pha.* 250ff.): see also Oedipus at *Oed.* 19, 1010, Diana at *Oed.* 763, Jocasta at *Oed.* 1008, Hecuba at *Tro.* 91, Medea at *Med.* 238, 488, 900; cf. 1240 below, *Pho.* 301. For a taxonomy of *pudor*, see Kaster (2005: 28–65). It is unclear how *pudor* is to be evaluated here. At Ovid *Fas.* 5.29 it is treated (along with *Metus*) as a positive abstraction, accompanying *Maiestas*, 'Majesty', but Seneca in his prose works adheres to the standard Stoic belief in the irrationality and thus unacceptability of the passions (πάθη, *affectus*), which are 'diseased conditions of the vicious soul' (Strange 2004: 34). For Stoic language and ideas in *Hercules*, see on 162–3. *Pudor* will appear later in the actions of the major characters, especially in Act V (1147, 1178, 1180, 1240). For *serus pudor*, 'tardy shame', see *Pha.* 595. There were two republican shrines in Rome, not to *pudor*, but to its allied value, *pudicitia* (Pudicitia Patricia and Pudicitia Plebeia: see Richardson 1992: 322). *Pudor*, as noted above, is absent from the Virgilian list.

Metus Pauorque/Fear and Panic: Deimos and Phobos, sons of Ares/ Mars (Homer *Il*. 4.440). They are conjoined again at Claud. *Stil. Cons*. 2.373: *Metus cum fratre Pauore. Metus* is in the Virgilian list, but *Pauor* is absent.

Funus/Death: though of course 'Death', i.e. *Mors*, is regularly personi-fied, *Funus* (= *Letum* in the Virgilian list) rarely is. Billerbeck cites Dracont. *Rom*. 10.571 (*Funera* alongside *Mors*).

frendens Dolor/grinding Pain: this is not in Virgil's list. Hesiod personi-fied 'Pain' (Ἄλγεα, *Theog*. 227), like Seneca, in conjunction with 'Hunger' (Λιμός). Seneca seems to have been the first in the Roman tradition to per-sonify *Dolor*, as occurs here and also at *Oed*. 652, 1060.

Luctus…Morbus tremens/Grief…trembling Disease: both in the Virgilian list (*Aen*. 6.274–5) and at *Oed*. 592–3. *Morbus* is also in Oedipus' list at *Oed*. 1059 (*Morbi tremor*).

cincta ferro Bella/War, iron-girt: personified at least from Ennius onwards, where the Gates of War adorning the temple of Janus are first mentioned (*Ann*. frag. 226 Skutsch). War, *Bellum*, is in the Virgilian list, and the Gates of War, *dirae ferro*, 'grim with iron', are mentioned at *Aen*. 1.293–4 (also at 7.607–22).

in extremo/at the end: for *in* with the ablative singular of an epithet used substantivally, see on 52–6.

iners Senectus/Listless Old Age: cf. *grauis Senectus sibimet*, 'self-wilting Old Age' (*Oed*. 594) in Creon's necromancy speech, and *tarda…senecta*, 'slow old age', at 849. Ironically the character to whom Theseus is speaking here will disprove the epithet *iners* by taking control of the suicide problem of the final act. In Euripides the latter issue is resolved by Theseus. *Senectus* is in the Virgilian list (*Aen*. 6.275), where it is somewhat blandly labelled *tristis*, 'sad/grim', and in the post-Senecan lists of Silius (13.583, where the epithet is *queribunda*, 'querulous') and Claudian (*Ruf*. 1.31).

adiuuat baculo gradum/helps its step with a stick: assuming, as seems probable, the earlier dating of *Oedipus* (see Introd. 6–7), the audience might have thought of that play's eponymous hero 'feeling his grim path with an old man's stick' (*baculo senili triste praetemptans iter, Oed*. 657). For old age and the *baculum*, see also Calp. Sic. *Ecl*. 5.13.

697–706 Amphitryon intervenes, like a chorus (see on 707–8), with a question on the agricultural and viticultural properties of the underworld and Theseus follows a statement of the absence of earth's fertility (697–9) with a blistering description of the sterility of hell (absent from Virgil's underworld), influenced perhaps by Ovid's negative descriptions of his exilic environment (see *Tr.* 3.10.70-6, *Pont.* 1.3.51-2) and articulated through a potent amalgam of abstract and concrete diction. Seneca is a master of the negative landscape, *locus horridus*, a landscape so described as to stir an audience's negative emotions, 'anxiety, fear, terror, and especially dread' (Felton and Gilhuly 2018: 2); see e.g. *Oed.* 530-47, *Thy.* 650-82. For analogously blighted landscapes in Senecan tragedy, cf. plague-ridden Thebes (*Oed.* 154-9) and thirsting Argos (*Thy.* 107-21), both caused by visitors from hell. Note the strong alliteration of *m*s in 703-6, one of Seneca's favourite letters for alliteration: see e.g. 75-7, 110, 205, 241-2, 428-9, 565-6, 806-7, 996-8, 1047-50, 1063-5, 1214-15, 1243-5, 1327-8; *Ag.* 359-60; *Pha.* 113, 170; *Med.* 362; *Tro.* 694, 736, 869.

tellus Cereris aut Bacchi ferax/**land rich in Ceres or Bacchus**: has Amphitryon been reading Ovid? There are echoes of Ovid's well-known description of his native Sulmo as *terra ferax Cereris multoque feracior uuis*, 'a land rich in Ceres and richer still in grapes' (*Am.* 2.16.7). For *ferax* with the genitive, as here and in the first half of the Ovidian line, see Hor. *Epod.* 5.22, Ov. *Met.* 7.470. 'Ceres' and 'Bacchus', as often in Roman verse, are metonyms for 'grain/wheat/corn' and for 'wine' (see e.g. *Oed.* 49, 566; *Pha.* 373, 445, 970; *Ag.* 886; *Thy.* 65, 467; *Pho.* 219, 371). But a god's name can never simply be a metonym. Ceres is the mother of Proserpina, queen of the dead, and Bacchus has strong associations with Thebes. Translations of their names as 'wheat' and 'wine' lose those associations. Hence the retention of the name of the god.

Non...nec...non/**No...No...No**: anaphora of *non/nec* was a common rhetorical device, much used by Seneca in his tragedies; see e.g. *Ag.* 178-81, 208-17; *Oed.* 37-8, 154-7; *Med.* 309-17; *Pha.* 100-8, 483-500, 530-3; *Tro.* 774-5; *Thy.* 345-64, 455-68; cf. also *Oct.* 400-1, *HO* 1202-5. Cf. Ovid's triple anaphoric *non* in his description of the sterility of the frozen north at *Pont.* 1.3.51-2. Line 698 is in breach of 'Porson's law': see on 249-58.

germinant/**flower**: first attested by Horace in his antithetical, idealizing image of the fertile Islands of the Blessed, *Epod.* 16.45. The word is a Senecan *hapax*.

nec adulta...seges/**No grown crops...**: so Tibullus describes the world of black Death: *non seges est infra, non uinea culta*, 'No crops are below, no cultivated vineyard' (1.10.35). For *adulta seges*, see *Pho.* 561.

leni...Zephyro/**gentle Zephyr**: Zephyr is the balmy west wind, associated with the arrival of spring (see *Pha.* 11-12) and the release from the cold of Boreas, the north wind: Ov. *Fas.* 2.147-8. At 550-1 above the absence of wind in the underworld is similarly observed.

pomiferos/laden with fruit: for the compound in *-fer*, see on 235–40.

sterilis…uastitas squalet/barren vastness encrusts: note not only Seneca's 'noun style' (see on 11–18), but the power of his abstract poetic language juxtaposed with the concrete *squalet*, 'encrusts' (lit. 'is encrusted'), underscored by the alliteration of *s* and *t*, which continues into the next line. *Vastitas* is a Senecan tragic *hapax*.

et foeda tellus torpet aeterno situ/The foul earth stiffens with eternal mould: a sonally brilliant line with its finely paced alliteration of *t*s. *Situs*, 'mould/decay', is a regular constituent of infernal descriptions: *longinquo situ*, 'long-standing mould', *Ag.* 767; *senta situ*, 'rough with mould', Virg. *Aen.* 6.462; and is used by Ovid of the living hell of Tomis: *rigido…situ*, 'stiff mould', *Trist.* 3.10.70. Statius seems to echo *foeda* and *torpet* in his own description of the underworld at *Theb.* 2.3–5: *torpidus…aer…foeda…aura*, 'torpid air…foul breath'.

rerumque maestus finis et mundi ultima/The grim cessation of things, the world's end: Seneca seems to be echoing a line from the Germanicus fragment of Albinovanus Pedo, a younger contemporary and friend of Ovid, known personally to Seneca (*Ep. Mor.* 122.15): *ad rerum metas extremaque litora mundi*, 'To the ends of things and the world's furthest shores' (line 4 Courtney 1993). Note *-que…et* for 'both…and', as at *Oed.* 264–5, Virg. *Aen.* 8.731, Ov. *Met.* 4.739, 10.482. *Mundi ultima* is an inverted Ovidian phrase (*Tr.* 4.4.83). The line has been much questioned, but for persuasive defences of it see Fitch and Billerbeck *ad loc.*

immotus aer haeret et/The air clings motionless and: cf. Lucan's phrase *aer…iners*, for dead, windless air (6.648–9) and Statius' *torpidus…aer* (*Theb.* 2.3). Note with *haeret et* the repetition of the same syllable at the end and beginning of juxtaposed words; see 67 and n. *ad loc.*

pigro sedet nox atra mundo/black night sits On a languid world: for *nox* and the underworld, see on 604–15. For words connoting 'darkness' in this section, see on 689–96.

ipsaque morte peior est mortis locus/The place of death is worse than death itself: Seneca seems fond of this kind of polyptoton involving an ablative of comparison: *peior est bello timor ipse belli*, 'Worse than war is fear of war itself', *Thy.* 572; *noui facies leti | grauior leto*, 'form of novel death | Graver than death', *Oed.* 180–1 (see also *Oed.* 175). Cf. (without polyptoton) *Tro.* 783: *o morte dira tristius leti genus*, 'O form of death more grim than dire death'—also Martial's imitation (with polyptoton) at *Epig.* 11.91.5: *tristius est leto leti genus*, 'The form of death is more grim than death'. See, too, Pliny *Ep.* 5.16.6: *o morte ipsa mortis tempus indignius*, 'O time of death more cruel than death itself'. For the closural use of *sententiae*, see on 125–204 introd. Note how the whole of this section (in the Latin text) ends on the seminal notion of place: see on 1–5, 572–6.

707–8 Another 'choral' question from Amphitryon: cf. the Chorus at *Thy.* 690, 716, 719, 730–1, 745–8.

Quid ille opaca qui regit sceptro loca/**What about the dark places' sceptred king:** for the elliptical idiom, see *OLD* s.v. *quis* 12b—also 1194; *Pha.* 149, 154–5; *Ag.* 701. Cf. *quid cum*, *Med.* 350, 355; Hor. *Ep.* 1.1.97; Ov. *Ars* 1.429, 431. The preoccupation with *locus/loca* continues: see on 1–5. For the 'sceptre', *sceptro*, see on 63–8. *Opaca*, 'dark/shadowy/gloomy', is one of the defining modifiers of the underworld (see also 809, 857); it is the opening word of Seneca's *Agamemnon*. For words connoting 'darkness' in this section, see on 689–96.

populos leues/**weightless throngs:** the phrase is Ovidian (*Met.* 10.14), but for 'weightless', *leuis*, of the spirits of the underworld, see *Oed.* 562, *Ag.* 757, *Oct.* 522, Hor. *Odes* 1.10.18. For the plural, *populos*, see on 186–91.

709–27 Description of the palace of Dis (709–20) and of Dis himself (720–7). This passage is essentially a double *ekphrasis* within the larger *ekphrasis* of hell: see below.

709–20 *Est in recessu Tartari obscuro locus*/**There is a place, in a gloomy recess Of Tartarus:** initial *est*, 'there is', or *erat*, 'there was', is a standard index of an *ekphrasis* or extended descriptive passage (*descriptio*), often picked up by a demonstrative word (here three demonstratives: *hic… hoc…haec*, 718–20); see e.g. *Tro.* 1068, 1075; *Ag.* 558, 567; *Oed.* 530, 548; *Thy.* 225, 234, 641, 682; Virg. *Aen.* 1.159, 170, 5.124, 129, 8.597, 606; Luc. 3.399, 426; VF 3.398, 406. Many *ekphraseis*, like this one, are primarily topographical, but not all are: see also e.g. Virg. *Aen.* 1.441ff., 6.20–33, 8.626–728. Nor are all *ekphraseis* marked by initial *est* or *erat*: see e.g. *Thy.* 641. Extensive, topographical *ekphraseis* are a regular feature (especially) of epic (see e.g. Hom. *Il.* 2.811ff., *Od.* 3.293ff., 4.844ff.; Virg. *Aen.* 1.159ff., 5.124ff., 7.563ff.; Ov. *Met.* 11.592ff.; Silius 1.81ff.); smaller ones are found in extant Attic tragedy (see e.g. Aesch. *Pers.* 447–9), and also in Seneca (*Pha.* 1057–8, *Tro.* 483–6). Senecan *ekphrasis*, which is not restricted to messenger speeches (see e.g. *Thy.* 225–35, *Oed.* 276–85), probably owes much to the deployment of *ekphrasis* in Roman declamation (see e.g. Sen. Rhet. *Con.* 1.4.8–9), and is a constitutive aspect of Seneca's 'declamatory style'. A Senecan messenger's topographical *ekphrasis* usually occurs at the start of his speech, as it does in *Hercules* (662ff.; cf. *Oed.* 530–47, *Tro.* 1068–87, *Thy.* 641–82);

but at *Ag.* 558–67 it is found towards the end. The present *ekphrasis* with its regular markers has the distinction of being an *ekphrasis* within an *ekphrasis*. For this rhetorical move to a secondary *ekphrasis* within an initial one, see also *Pha.* 1057ff., *Thy.* 650ff. For *ekphrasis*, see Putnam (1998), Elsner (2004). For Tartarus, see on 86–8. For *locus*, see on 1–5. For words connoting 'darkness' in this section, see on 689–96.

*spissa caligo/*dense mist: for the 'mist', *caligo*, of the underworld, see 92.

*discors…latex/*discordant streams: cf. *Med.* 941: *fluctus…discordes*, 'discordant waves'.

*quieto similis/*like a thing at rest: the Styx is regularly portrayed as almost motionless, often described as a 'marsh', *palus* (Virg. *Geo.* 4.479, *Aen.* 6.323, Ov. *Met.* 1.737). For the two-word simile, cf. *furenti similis*, 'like a mad woman', 1009 (of Megara), *Pho.* 427 (of Jocasta), *HO* 240 (of Deianira); *uicto similis*, 'like one vanquished', *Ag.* 412 (of Agamemnon); *fluctuanti similis*, 'like a thing wavering', *Thy.* 698 (the royal palace).

hunc iurant dei…sacram…Styga/(gods swear by it)…the sacred Styx: *sacer*, 'sacred', is regularly used of rivers, fountains, etc. (see e.g. *Med.* 81, *Thy.* 116), which Romans thought of as inhabited by deities, but here the epithet seems to reflect the river's connection with the oaths of the gods: see Fitch *ad loc. Sacer*, of course, sometimes means 'execrable/accursed', and there may be something of that meaning in its use here. For other adjectives assigned to the Styx in Senecan tragedy, see on 558–68. For the simple accusative with *iurare*, cf. *Med.* 7–8. For Styx, see on 52–6.

*tacente…fluuio/*with silent flow: for the silence of the underworld, see on 572–6; for the silence of the Styx, see *Pha.* 625: *tacitae Stygis. Fluuius* is a Senecan tragic *hapax*.

*saxa…uoluit Acheron/*Acheron…rolling rocks: Seneca has been reading Virgil's description of Phlegethon in the underworld, which 'rolls thundering rocks' (*torquet…sonantia saxa, Aen.* 6.551), but he has switched rivers, opting for Acheron, 'the river of woe' (= *sine gaudio*, acc. to Servius *ad Verg. Aen.* 6.107), as opposed to Phlegethon, 'the river of fire'. Acheron, Pyriphlegethon, Cocytus, and Styx are all interrelated in Homer's hell (*Od.* 10.513–14). For the breach of 'Porson's law' in 715, see on 249–58.

*inuius renauigari/*None may recross: *renauigari* forms a weighty pentasyllabic opening to 716, emphasized by enjambement and the stop which follows; cf. *circumsonaret* at 417 and see n. *ad loc.* This prosaic verb appears only here in Seneca. In Virgil the Styx is the river which none may recross: *inremeabilis undae* (*Aen.* 6.425). Note the rarely attested use of an epexegetical infinitive (see 541 and n. *ad loc.*) with *inuius*.

cingitur duplici uado/Ringed by this double moat: cf. Virgil's description of the castle of Rhadamanthus at *Aen.* 6.549: *triplici circumdata muro*, 'surrounded by a triple wall'. For *uadum*, see on 679–88.

aduersa Ditis regia/The palace of Dis looms: for the 'palace' of Dis, see Hor. *Odes* 2.18.30–1: *aula*; Ov. *Met.* 4.438: *regia Ditis*; Stat. *Theb.* 8.80: *regia tristis*.

uasto specu/vast cave: for *specus* and the underworld, see on 92–9. I have translated the ablative here as locatival rather than separative.

tyranni limina/tyrant's doors: the use of *tyrannus* connects Dis to Lycus (512, 897); Hercules' defeat of one foreshadows his defeat of the other (see also 43, 937). For Dis as *tyrannus* see *Pha.* 1153, Virg. *Geo.* 4.492. For the semiotics of *tyrannus*, see on 511–15.

720–7 Dis described. Cf. Claudian's description at *Rapt.* 1.79–84, which seems to have been influenced by these lines.

campus hanc circa iacet/Round it lies a field: *campi*, 'fields/plains', are regular constituents of the landscape of the underworld; cf. Virgil's *Lugentes Campi*, 'Mourning Fields'(*Aen.* 6.441), and *Campi Nitentes*, 'Shining Fields' (*Aen.* 6.667). For the postponement of prepositions, see also 145, 148, 883.

superbo digerit uultu sedens animas recentes/sits with prideful mien and sorts The new souls: the subject of *digerit* is not stated but is clear (see on 30–5). Dis is not regularly associated with the judgement of souls in the underworld, as implied here. Presumably the 'sorting' is of souls requiring trial and those not. But Dis or Pluto as judge goes back to Aeschylus (*Suppl.* 230–1), and may be found, too, in Flavian epic (Stat. *Theb.* 8.21–31, Sil. 13.601–12), following Seneca's lead. Its presence here may be influenced by the contemporary political and legal reality of the emperor's role as judge. Seneca's Claudius in the *Apocolocyntosis*, written perhaps soon after the composition of this play (see Introd. 7), even brags to Hercules about his judicial imperial role (*Apoc.* 7.4–5); see also *Apoc.* 12.3.19–31, Suet. *Claud.* 14, Dio 60.4.3. For Roman referentiality in *Hercules*, see on 46–52. *Superbo uultu* is ablative of manner: Woodcock §43.5.iv. For *recens* of recently arrived spirits, cf. Ovid's *umbrae recentes* (*Met.* 4.434) and Virgil's *recens...Dido, Aen.* 6.450. For *uultus*, see on 329–31. For *sedere*, 'sitting', in the technical, legal sense, see 731 and n. *ad loc.*

dira maiestas deo/Fearsome the god's majesty: for *dirus*, see 56 and n. *ad loc.* Cf. Claudian's powerful imitation of 721–2 at *Rapt.* 1.79–80:

> ipse rudi fultus solio nigraque uerendus
> maiestate sedet.

> He sits propped on a primitive throne, fearsome
> In his dark majesty.

frons torua/Fierce his brow: *toruus* is used in Senecan tragedy of animals (*Pha.* 117, 303, 1063), Furies (*Oed.* 590), savage waters (*Pho.* 116), human beings associated with animals (Hippolytus and his mother, Antiope: *Pha.* 416, 658, 798; Oedipus, *Oed.* 921; Hercules, 1080 below; Atreus, *Thy.* 706), warriors at their fiercest (Achilles, *Ag.* 209; Hector, *Tro.* 467; Pyrrhus, *Tro.* 1000), Cadmus turned into a snake (392 above), and (here) Dis. A *torua facies* ('fierce/savage/ferocious/animalistic expression') is, according to Seneca (*Ira* 1.1.3), one of the sure signs of *furor.*

fratrum quae tamen specimen gerat/yet bearing signs of both brothers: *specimen*, 'signs' or 'proof' as at *Med.* 389 (*omnis specimen affectus*, 'proof/signs of every passion'), rather than 'token' as at *Thy.* 223 (*specimen antiquum imperi*, 'ancient token of power'). The *specimen* in the case of Dis is family resemblance. For the postponed relative, see on 159–61. *Gerat* is in the strongest sense a generic subjunctive in a relative clause of characteristic. See Woodcock §155.

uultus est illi Iouis/His face is that of Jove: for Dis as 'infernal Jove', see on 46–52. For *uultus*, see on 329–31.

sed fulminantis/But of Jove when he thunders: so Claudian makes sure that his Dis also 'thunders' (*tonat, Rapt.* 1.84). Billerbeck *ad loc.* suggests that *fulminans* = *iratus*, 'angry' (see e.g. 1202). For the qualifying use of *sed*, see 1177; *Ag.* 31; *Tro.* 343; *Med.* 576, 965; *Pho.* 106, 110; *Oed.* 951—and (the famous double *exemplum*) *Thy.* 1067–8: *sed nesciens | sed nescientes*.

magna pars regni/large part Of the realm: for the conceit, see *Pho.* 55–6, where Antigone's 'chief part of her father's great kingdom' (*pars summa magno patris e regno*) is her father, Oedipus, himself. The *magna pars* with the genitive formula is one which Seneca likes: see *Ep. Mor.* 34.3, 71.36, 90.43, 94.69, 123.3.

timet quidquid timetur/the feared fear: both the thought and the wordplay are traditional, used often in relation to rulers/tyrants. See Publ. 379: *multos timere debet quem multi timent*, 'The man feared by many ought to fear many'—see the almost identical *sententia* of Laberius, quoted by Seneca at *Ira* 2.11.3: *necesse est multos timeat quem multi timent*, 'It is necessary that the man feared by many fear many'. Cf. also *Oed.* 706: *timet timentis*, 'he fears those who fear him'; *Ep. Mor.* 105.4, *qui timetur timet*, 'The man feared fears'; and the paradox of kings (*reges*) at *Ag.* 73, *metui cupiunt metuique timent*, 'They desire to be feared and dread to be feared'. Mussato redeploys the *topos* at *Ecerinis*, 257, of the eponymous tyrant: *timet et timetur*, 'he fears and is feared'; cf. also Marston's 'Yet feared fears', *Antonio and Mellida*, III. ii. 54. For the wordplay on active and passive verbal forms (*uincam…uincar*), a kind of verbal polyptoton or *declinatio* (see on 112–18): cf. e.g. *colis…coleris* ('love…are loved', *Pha.* 406–7); *spectat…spectatur* ('view…is viewed', *Med.* 28–9); *petebant…petuntur* ('sought…are sought', *Med.* 218–19); *flet…fletur* ('weeps…is wept', *Tro.* 1099–1100); *uincam…uincar* ('surpass…be surpassed', *Ag.* 25–6); *non uideo…uideor* ('not see…seen', *Pho.* 9–10); *premo premorque* ('crush and am crushed', *Thy.* 1050–1). For climactic half-lines, see on 40–6. For paradoxical phrasing in *Hercules*, see on 30–5.

727–30 Amphitryon turns Theseus towards moral and legal issues.

***Verane est fama*/Is the rumour true:** a classic instance of what Ross (1975a: 78) terms an 'Alexandrian footnote', viz. an overtly metaliterary marker by the poet that he is operating in a self-consciously allusive mode. Here Seneca is pointing to the Virgilian Sibyl's account of Tartarus and its punishments at *Aen.* 6.562–627. Cf. *utque fert fama*, 'as rumour says', 748, *fama* (*est*) at *Oed.* 172, *Thy.* 669, also 'Alexandrian footnotes', with similarly Virgilian referents (see Boyle *ad locc.*). Note Lucan in the Massilian grove passage of Book 3 (417): *fama ferebat*, 'rumour told'. Sometimes metaliterary markers are simply adverbial: see *semper* at 1336 and n. *ad loc.* For metaliterary and metatheatrical language in *Hercules*, see on 109–12.

***iam sera reddi iura*/now get justice late:** cf. 1202–4, where Hercules demands 'late' (*serus*) punishment. Along with Fitch (1987a and 2018) and Billerbeck I have accepted the emendation of Ageno, *iam*, in place of EA's reading *tam*, printed by Zwierlein and most other modern editors. *Tam*, as Fitch *ad loc.* points out, seems tonally inappropriate. The confusion of *iam* and *tam* may be found at 614 and elsewhere in the tragic *corpus*. For the legal phrase, *iura reddere*, 'render justice', see Ov. *Met.* 13.25–6.

***oblitos sui sceleris*/for crimes they forgot:** lit. 'having forgotten their crime'. These crimes are in the distant past, hence they have been forgotten. There is no suggestion, as Billerbeck observes *ad loc.*, that this forgetting is caused by the river Lethe.

***quis iste ueri rector atque aequi arbiter*/Who is the lord of truth and judge of justice:** Amphitryon utilizes titles (*rector, arbiter*) which he bestowed on Jupiter in his opening speech: 205. *Arbiter aequi* is used/reused by Boethius (*Cons. Phil.* 4 Metrum 6.37). Note the repetition of the same syllable at the end and beginning of juxtaposed words; see 67 and n. *ad loc.* For legal language and imagery in *Hercules*, see on 731–4.

731–47 Theseus expatiates on the justice meted out in the underworld. The relationship of ruler to subject is the major theme of *De Clementia* and a regular issue in Senecan tragedy: see on 489–94. The Roman referentiality of this section is overt: see further on 46–52. Lines 737–40 and 745–7 were reused by Fray Martin de Córdoba, *Jardín de nobles donzellas* (1468): see Romero (2016: 117).

731–4 The three magistrates of the underworld, sitting in judgement. Although this trio of judges may be found together in Plato (*Gorg.* 523e–4a, *Apol.* 41a, the latter with Triptolemus), the Roman legal resonance is strong. For Roman legal language and imagery elsewhere in *Hercules*, see on 46–52, 164–74, 186–91, 205–9, 249–58, 397–402, 402–8, 439–47, 577–81, 658–61, 720–7, 727–30, 735–9, 745–7, 802–6, 807–12, 1237–9, 1265–72, 1295–1301, 1302–13, 1334–41, 1341–4.

alta sede quaesitor sedens/**magistrate sitting aloft:** note the Roman legal language, *alta sedes*, *sedere*, and *quaesitor*. For *sedere* of a judge, see e.g. *Ag.* 730, *Pha.* 628, *HO* 1007, Cat. 52.2, Cic. *Mur.* 69, *De Orat.* 2.196, Livy 3.46.9, Prop. 3.19.27 (Minos), 4.11.19 (Aeacus), Ov. *Pont.* 3.5.23, Tac. *Ann.* 11.11. The Roman technical term, *quaesitor*, denotes a Roman magistrate with the authority to conduct a *quaestio*. It is used by Virgil (*Aen.* 6.432) and Claudian (*Ruf.* 2.476–7) of Minos, as it is by Seneca at *Ag.* 24, where Minos is called the *quaesitor…Cnosius*, 'Cnosian magistrate'; see also *quaerunt* (580 above). Here it is applied to each of the three judges of the dead. With the etymological play (*figura etymologica*), *sede…sedens* (lit. 'sitting on a seat'), cf. *tegmine…tegit* ('shields with shielding', 799), *uirtusque uiro* ('manliness to the man', 1093); *carmen…canit* ('sings a song', *Thy.* 692), *gemitu…gemit* ('groans with a groan', *Thy.* 1001); *partu…peperit* ('bore with a bearing', *Pho.* 136), *indomitum domas* ('tame the untamed', *Pho.* 307). For Seneca's fondness for nouns ending in *-tor*, see on 299–302.

iudicia trepidis sera sortitur reis/**allots Trembling prisoners their tardy judgements:** more Roman legal language. *Sortitur*, 'allots', implies an urn (see *Ag.* 24); the resulting *iudicia*, 'judgements', could be either 'trials' or 'verdicts/sentences'. Perhaps the latter seems more likely, given the 'trembling' of the prisoners. For the dactyl-tribrach combination at the start of the line, see 76 and n. *ad loc.*

aditur illo Cnosius Minos foro/**Cnossian Minos controls one court:** Minos, a legendary king of Crete and a son of Zeus/Jupiter, figures from Homer onwards (*Od.* 11.568–71) as one of the three judges of the dead in the underworld (the others being Rhadamanthus and Aeacus); see also *Ag.* 24, *Thy.* 23, Virg. *Aen.* 6.430–3, Prop. 3.19.27. For the spelling *Cnosius* (adopted by Leo) rather than Zwierlein's *Gnosius*, see Housman (1928). Minos is called 'Cnossian' after the great palace at Cnossos in north central Crete, which was the capital of Minoan civilization. For *Cnosius* elsewhere in the tragedies, see *Pha.* 649, *Ag.* 24, *Oed.* 892. Both *aditur* and *foro* have overtly Roman legal resonance.

Rhadamanthus... Thetidis... audit socer/Rhadamanthus..., Thetis' in-law presides: the former, son of Zeus/Jupiter and Europa, and the latter, Aeacus, son of Zeus/Jupiter and the nymph Aegina, father of Peleus (husband of the sea-nymph Thetis) and grandfather of Achilles, were the other two traditional judges of the dead. For Rhadamanthus, see Virg. *Aen.* 6.566–9. *Audire* is regularly used of a legal 'hearing' (*OLD* 7b); hence the translation of *audit* as 'presides'.

735–9 Crime and punishment with the focus on tyrants. This section clearly has a bearing on what's happening offstage: the punishment of Lycus. Cf. Silius' similar focus on 'kings', *reges*, and 'tyrants', *tyranni*, in his underworld punishment description at *Pun.* 13.602–12. For kingship in Senecan tragedy, see on 348–53. For legal language in *Hercules*, see on 731–4.

quod quisque fecit, patitur/All suffer their own deeds: the so-called *lex talionis* or 'an eye for an eye' version of justice, seen again in Seneca's treatment of the emperor Claudius at *Apoc.* 14.2, and mentioned, too, in the *Epistles* (*quod quae fecere patiuntur*, 'that they suffer their deeds', *Ep. Mor.* 39.5). This 'simple requital' theory of justice was attacked by Aristotle, who associated it with Rhadamanthus (*Nic. Eth.* 1132b). It can, however, be seen more broadly as an aspect of a theory of accountability/responsibility; and, though modelled on Virgil's famously elusive *quisque suos patimur manes*, 'We each suffer our own ghosts' (*Aen.* 6.743), offers a clarity of meaning similar to that of Jupiter's concluding declaration in the Council of Gods in *Aeneid* 10 (111–12): *sua cuique exorsa laborem | fortunamque ferent*, 'To each will his own endeavours bring suffering and success'. In *De Clementia*, of course, Seneca offers a more nuanced approach to the issue of crime and punishment. For *facere* and *pati* in conjunction elsewhere in Senecan tragedy, see *Tro.* 257, *Oed.* 983–4.

auctorem scelus repetit/Crime seeks its author: for similar sentiments see *Tro.* 870–1, *Oed.* 706, *Thy.* 311, *Clem.* 1.26.1, *Ep. Mor.* 7.5, 81.19. Cf. the 'Bloody instructions, which, being taught, return | To plague the inventor', Shakespeare, *Mac.* I.vii.9–10; see also Hes. *WD* 265–6. Variations of the *sententia* form a *topos* in Roman elegy: see e.g. Tib. 1.6.10, Ov. *Am.* 1.4.46, *Ars* 1.655–6. See further on 341–8.

uidi cruentos carcere includi duces/I saw blood-drenched leaders locked in a jail: ironic foreshadowing; Theseus will shortly see another *cruentus dux*, 'blood-drenched leader', viz. Hercules, as he enters Act IV only to become more 'blood-drenched' by the end of the act. *Dux* and *carcer* have an especially (but not exclusively) Roman resonance: the former is used regularly of the emperors Augustus and Tiberius by Ovid throughout the *Fasti* and by the dramatist of *Octavia* of Nero (see Boyle *ad Oct.* 235–7); the latter (*Carcer*, 'The Jail') is the name of the Roman prison at the foot of the Capitoline, where criminals and especially non-citizens were shortly detained prior to execution (see Richardson 1992: 71). *Vidi* is another 'eye-witness perfect' (see on 249–58). Note in the Latin text the alliterative *ds* and *cs*.

impotentis terga...tyranni/backs of raving tyrants: for the punishment of tyrants in the underworld (including being flayed), see Plato *Rep.* 10.615c–616a. For *impotens*, 'raving', 'unbridled', of the tyrant/ruler, see 1180 (Eurystheus), *Med.* 143 (Creon), *Tro.* 266 (Agamemnon), [Quint.] *Decl.* 13.4.

plebeia manu/plebeian hands: *plebeius*, 'plebeian' (as opposed to 'patrician'), is an expressly Roman term for the lower social orders, used also at *Pha.* 1139, *Thy.* 400, and (in the substantival form, *plebs*) at *Tro.* 1077. The *plebs* constitute the vast majority of Roman citizens. In this context and often in the works of Roman moralists (see Tarrant *ad Thy.* 400) it lacks the negative connotations of the English 'plebeian', but approximates more to the idea of the 'common (Roman) man'. Cf. Seneca's use of *Quirites* (lit. 'descendants of Quirinus/Romulus') for 'citizens' at *Thy.* 396. For Roman referentiality in *Hercules*, see on 46–52.

739–45 Underworld rewards with the exclusive focus on the ideal monarch. Theseus' ideal here is that of *De Clementia* (see e.g. *Clem.* 1.5.4–5, 13.4–5, 17.3), which is dated to early 56 CE (see Braund 2009: 16) and was probably written shortly after the composition of *Hercules*. Cf. Medea, lecturing Creon on the responsibilities of kingship (*Med.* 222–5), Antigone, counselling a vengeful Oedipus (*Pho.* 290–3), and 'Seneca' advising 'Nero' (*Oct.* 472–5). Theseus' ideal sits ill with the play's presentation of Hercules (see Introd. §VII). For the Senecan cardinal themes of the relationship of king to subject and the interdependence of stable political power and moral values, see on 341–8. For Roman referentiality in *Hercules*, see on 46–52.

quisquis est placide potens/The gentle monarch: cf. Seneca's comments at *Clem.* 1.13 on the 'gentle and tranquil king' (*placido tranquilloque regi*), who wields his power 'gently and for his citizens' well-being' (*placide ac salutariter*). Note the advice of 'Seneca' to Nero at *Oct.* 578: *obsequere...ciuibus placidus tuis*, 'Gently defer to your citizens'. See also *Tro.* 694, *Oed.* 528, *Clem.* 1.5.4, *Ben.* 2.13.2.

dominusque uitae/And life's master: abbreviation of *dominus uitae necisque*. The 'power over life and death' (*uitae necisque potestas*) belonged to every *paterfamilias* over his children until he died (see Crook 1967: 107–8), and was still referred to in the Theodosian Code (429–438 CE). Here it is applied to a ruler, where it seems normally to have had negative associations (Westbrook 1999, 204: 'for Cicero it is the essence of tyranny', *Rep.* 3.23). Here there seems no negativity. Cf. Seneca's description of Nero as *uitae necisque gentibus arbiter* ('Arbiter of life and death for nations') in *De Clementia* (1.1.2), in which the power to 'give and remove life' (*dandi auferendique uitam*, 1.21.2) is presented as a 'gift of the gods' (*munere deorum*). See also Seneca on Mark Antony at *Polyb.* 16.2; also *Thy.* 608, *Pho.* 103. At 4.549 Manilius associates the power *uitaeque necisque* with the emperor. Livy (2.35.2) associates it with the *plebs* and their judicial power over Coriolanus.

incruentum mitis imperium regit/**rules an empire mildly without blood**: cf. *Clem.* 1.13.4: *qui potentiam suam placide…exercet*, 'who exercises his power gently'; 1.17.3: *si uim suam continet*, 'if he restrains his power'; 1.19.9: '*qui…beneficus ac largus et in melius potens*, 'who…kind and generous wields power for the better'. On bloodlessness, see *Clem.* 1.11.3: *praestitisti, Caesar, ciuitatem incruentam*, 'You have provided, Caesar, a state without bloodshed'. For the ideal of the mild and compassionate ruler, see also *Clem.* 1.9.1 (where *mitis* is used of Augustus), *Med.* 222–5, *Oct.* 472–5, Ov. *Pont.* 2.9.11. I have translated *imperium* as 'empire', as at Ov. *Tr.* 2.166, *Pont.* 3.3.61. Fitch *ad loc.* prefers to take *imperium* 'as an internal object of *regit*'; cf. Virg. *Aen.* 1.340. In either case *imperium* retains its Roman resonance: see on 1314–17 and 46–52.

animaeque parcit/**Sparing life**: an obvious echo of Anchises' famous *parcere subiectis*, 'spare the conquered' (Virg. *Aen.* 6.853), at the climax of his enunciation of Rome's imperial mission. Cf. a similar Virgilian echo in the speech of 'Seneca' at *Oct.* 473 (*parcere afflictis*). For Roman referentiality in *Hercules*, see on 46–52. Giardina (1966), Zwierlein, Viansino (1993), and Billerbeck replace the consensus *EA* reading, *animaeque*, with *animo*, found in *recc.* And Trevet's text. Caviglia, Fitch (1987a and 2018), and Chaumartin also print *animaeque*. For *anima* = 'life' in general, see Fitch *ad loc.*

longa permensus diu…spatia/**measures for years long tracks**: the duration of this happy rule is underscored by pleonasm: *longa*, 'long', *diu* = 'long/for a long time/for years'. For the great age reached by just monarchs (*reges*) and the brevity of the power of tyrants (*tyranni*), see *Clem.* 1.11.4; on the brevity of violent or unjust rule, see *Tro.* 258, *Med.* 196.

felicis aeui/**happy age**: some interpret this phrase as happy 'life' (*Leben*, Billerbeck), which would seem otiose, given the *felix* to follow (hence

Bentley's unnecessary, pleonastic emendation, *uiuacis aeui*, printed by Fitch 1987*a* and 2018). It seems better to take the lemmatized phrase in the socio-political sense of a 'happy/golden age', what Seneca calls a *felix saeculum* (of the new emperor Nero) at *Apoc.* 1.1, 4.1.23–4.

caelum petit/**heads for heaven:** this is the reward for just statesmen at Cic. *Rep.* 6.13; cf. also *Oct.* 476.

laeta felix nemoris Elysii loca/**the Elysian grove's joyous places happy:** the 'Elysian Fields', as the paradise of the afterlife reserved for the blessed, dates from Homer (*Od.* 4.563–8). There among sunlit plains and shady groves the *fortunati* lived paradisiacal afterlives patterned after their earthly ones. See Virg. *Aen.* 6.637ff.; also *Tro.* 158 (*Elysii nemoris*), 944 (*campo…Elysio*). For the juxtaposition of synonyms (*laeta felix*), see on 283–95. For the *locus* motif, see on 1–5.

iudex futurus/**A judge-to-be:** to join Minos, Aeacus, and Rhadamanthus (for whom see on 731–4). Minos and Rhadamanthus are praised for their earthly justice in the opening of Plato's *Laws* (624b–625a). A similar earthly apprenticeship is here envisioned for the gentle monarch.

745–7 The direct address of people outside the dramatic framework (a breaking of the 'fourth wall') is infrequent in Senecan tragedy, and occurs elsewhere only in the choral odes: 178 below (*uiuite laeti*, 'live joyously'); *Tro.* 407 (*quaeris quo iaceas?* 'you ask where you lie?'), 1018ff. (*tollite felices*, 'remove the happy'); possibly *Thy.* 339–41, but most especially *Thy.* 607–14:

> uos quibus rector maris atque terrae
> ius dedit magnum necis atque uitae
> ponite inflatos tumidosque uultus.
> quidquid a uobis minor expauescit,
> maior hoc uobis dominus minatur.
> omne sub regno grauiore regnum est.
> quem dies uidit ueniens superbum,
> hunc dies uidit fugiens iacentem.

> You to whom lord of sea and earth
> Gave great power of death and life
> Doff those proud, tumescent looks.
> What an underling fears from you
> You're threatened by mightier lord.
> All thrones lie 'neath a greater throne.
> The dawning day sees a man proud;
> The fleeing day sees him laid flat.

Cf. *HO* 604–15, 1560–3. For apostrophe in Senecan choral odes, see on 178–82.

sanguine humano abstine quicumque regnas/**Abstain from human blood, All you who rule:** as Fitch *ad loc.* indicates, the lesson Theseus is drawing from underworld punishments and rewards is, like the apostrophe of the choral ode of *Thyestes* cited above, politically more specific and incisive than the banal instruction yielded by Virgil's Tartaraean punishments: *discite iustitiam moniti et non temnere diuos*, 'Be warned to learn justice and not to slight the gods' (Virg. *Aen.* 6.620). Theseus' injunction stands in stark contrast with Hercules' desire 'to drink his (Lycus') hostile blood' (*ad hauriendum sanguinem inimicum*, 636). For 'political' criticism of the 'drinking of human blood', see *Clem.* 1.12.2; see also 'Seneca' at *Oct.* 473–4. Theseus' *abstine* imperative is not only potent but richly charged with intertextual irony, since one of the climactic prisoners in Virgil's Tartarus, doomed never to escape, is Theseus himself (*infelix Theseus*, *Aen.* 6.618). With the phrase, *quicumque regnas*, cf. *tu quicumque es qui sceptra tenes*, 'You, whoever you are, who hold a sceptre', of the choral apostrophe at *HO* 604.

scelera...uestra/**Your crimes:** notice *uestra*, despite the preceding singular imperative and indicative. This use of *uester* for *tuus* is rare. Cf. *Med.* 265, where, as here, it seems dictated by the metre. See Housman (1972: 790–4).

taxantur modo maiore/**Greater punishments await:** lit. 'are assessed in/with greater measure'. *Modo* is ablative of manner: Woodcock §43.5.iv. For *taxare* elsewhere in Seneca with the meaning of 'to assess' in penal, legal contexts, see *Thy.* 92, *Clem.* 2.7.3. For the language of law in *Hercules*, see on 731–4.

747–9 More chorus-style questions from Amphitryon.

Certus...locus/**fixed place:** cf. the *plaga decreta*, 'district decreed' (1222–3), for the guilty. Again the focus on *locus*: see on 1–5, 572–6.

inclusos tenet...nocentes/**imprison The guilty:** Theseus has already mentioned the jailing of *cruentos...duces*, 'blood-drenched leaders' (737), though his language was topographically vague. For a more precise topography of the imprisonment of *nocentes*, 'the guilty', again given by Theseus, see *Pha.* 1226–7, where the fiery river Phlegethon is said to imprison them.

utque fert fama/**as rumour says:** another metaliterary pointer (see also 727 and n. *ad loc.*) to the most important poetic account of the underworld, that of Virgil's sixth *Aeneid*. A clue seems provided by the focus on *uinclis*, 'chains', in the next line. *Stridor ferri tractaeque catenae*, 'The clank of iron and dragging of chains' (*Aen.* 6.558) are what draw Aeneas' attention to

Tartarus. For metaliterary/metatheatrical language in *Hercules*, see on 109–12.

750–9 Punishment of sinners. A catalogue of sinners punished in the underworld, beginning with the famous quartet of Ixion (750), Sisyphus (751), Tantalus (752–5), and Tityos (756). The four form a canon of sinners in descriptions of/references to the underworld: e.g. *Pha.* 1229ff., *Thy.* 4ff., *Ag.* 15–21, and also *Oct.* 621–3, *HO* 1068ff. See also *Apoc.* 14.3, *Ep. Mor.* 24.18. The list sometimes includes the Danaids, as here (757): see also *Med.* 744–9; *HO* 942–8; Lucr. 3.978–1010; Tib. 1.3.73–80; Ov. *Met.* 4.457–61,10.41–4, *Ibis* 169–94. The canon without Ixion can be found in Homer (*Od.* 11.576ff.), and some or all of the torments without the sinners' names in various authors, including Virgil (*Geo.* 3.39, *Aen.* 6.616–17), Propertius (3.5.42), and Claudian (*Rufin.* 2.506–11). Juvenal (1.9–10) complains about having to listen to lists of *umbrae* tortured in the underworld. The canon was taken up in the Renaissance: 'The hellish prince adjudge my damned ghost | To Tantale's thirst, or proud Ixion's wheel, | Or cruel gripe to gnaw my growing heart', Norton and Sackville, *Gorboduc* 478–80; see also Correr, *Progne* 12–14, 102–6; Kyd, *The Spanish Tragedy* IV.v.31–44. Here Seneca extends the list of the canonic four to include not only the Danaids (757), but the Cadmeids (758) and Phineus (759). But, even with the extension, Seneca's catalogue does not embrace the range of sinners evident in Virgil's Tartarus (*Aen.* 6.608–24). The list is structured for the emphasis to fall on Tantalus, who receives four lines (752–5) in a ten-line passage, in which each of the remaining six sinners is allotted a single line. The passage is strongly alliterative. For Senecan tragic 'catalogues', see on 6–18.

Rapitur uolucri tortus Ixion rota/Ixion is racked and spun on speeding wheel: Ixion was a legendary king of Thessaly and the first 'parricide' (his victim was perhaps his father-in-law); he was purified by Jupiter, who, however, later punished him for attempting to rape Juno. His punishment was to be 'racked' on an eternally spinning wheel; see also *Pha.* 1235–7, *Med.* 744, *Ag.* 15–16, *Thy.* 8, *Oct.* 623, *HO* 945–6, 1011, Ov. *Met.* 4.61, Hyg. *Fab.* 62. Mentioned by Pherecydes (*FGH* 3 F 51a–b), Ixion also features in Pindar (*Pyth.* 2.21ff.) and the Attic tragedians (e.g. Soph. *Phil.* 676–9), but the location of his punishment in the underworld (*pace* Lloyd-Jones's imaginative supplement to the text of *Philoctetes*) is first attested at Ap. Rhod. 3.61–2. For an ancient representation of Ixion on the wheel contemporary with Seneca (63–79 CE), see the celebrated painting in the Ixion Room of the House of the Vettii in Pompeii: Andreae (1978), pl. 74. *Volucer/rapidus/celer* etc. are regular modifiers of Ixion's wheel: *Ag.* 15., *Thy.* 8, Tib. 1.3.74, Ov. *Ibis* 176, 192. For the canon of sinners, see above.

ceruice…Sisyphia/**on Sisyphus' neck:** Sisyphus was the legendary founder and first king of Corinth and an infamous trickster who overcame death. He was the son of Aeolus and one of the most notorious 'sinners' in Hades, punished for 'impiety' (*impietas*) by being forever made to roll uphill a stone that rolled back again. See Hyg. *Fab.* 60. Such is the usual myth (Hom. *Od.* 11.593–600, Virg. *Aen.* 6.616). But here and at *Pha.* 1229–31, *Thy.* 6–7, *Apoc.* 14.3, 15.1.8, *Ep. Mor.* 24.18, Seneca employs a variant in which Sisyphus carries the rock uphill on his shoulders or neck only to have it slip and roll back down the hill. At *Ag.* 16–17 it is unclear whether the usual myth or the variant is applicable. For the variant, see also Prop. 2.20.32, Mart. *Epig.* 10.5.15 and *HO* 942–3. For the canon of sinners, see above.

in amne medio faucibus siccis/**Amid a stream with dry throat:** note the concessive, even paradoxical, use of *in*, as at 168 above (see n. *ad loc.*). Cf. the concessive use of *inter* at *Ag.* 19 (*inter undas*, 'amid a stream/waves'). The ablative seems one of accompaniment/attendant circumstances or an ablative absolute: see Woodcock §43.5.i–iii. For paradoxical phrasing in *Hercules*, see on 30–5.

senex/**old man:** Tantalus (also referred to as *senex* at *Ag.* 22, 769, *HO* 1075; cf. ὁ γέρων, Hom. *Od.* 11.585, 591; cf. Eur. *Or.* 986), a celebrated figure of the Greek literary tradition from Homer onwards. A son of Jupiter/Zeus and one of the first generation of mortals, Tantalus was king of Sipylus in Phrygia. He became famous for his wealth and even more famous for his great sin against the gods and subsequent punishment in the underworld. There are different accounts of what Tantalus' sin was (see e.g. Apollod. *Epit.* 2.1, Hyg. *Fab.* 82). Tantalus had been granted the honour of dining with the gods, but he seems to have abused this privilege by disclosing the gods' secrets or by stealing ambrosia and nectar to share with humans or (the most common version and the one followed in *Thyestes*) by killing and cooking his own son, Pelops, and offering Pelops' flesh to the gods for their consumption (see *Thy.* 144–8, *Ag.* 21). Only Ceres/Demeter, overcome by grief for the loss of her daughter Proserpina/Persephone, partook of the 'meal'. Tantalus' punishment was to be placed in a pool of water which receded when he tried to drink and beneath a tree whose fruit-laden boughs pulled away when he tried to eat (Hom. *Od.* 11.582–92, Sen. *Ag.* 769–72, and *Thy.* 4–6, 149–75, the latter being the most detailed account of Tantalus' punishment in extant ancient literature). Apollodorus and Hyginus add (though Seneca does not—but see e.g. Pind. *Ol.* 1.55ff., Eur. *Or.* 5–7, Lucr.

3.980–1) that Tantalus was positioned beneath a rock which threatened to crush him. Pelops was subsequently restored to life, but required an ivory shoulder to replace the part of his body consumed by Ceres (Ov. *Met.* 6.403–11, Hyg. *Fab.* 83). Tantalus was the father of the tragic mother Niobe, the grandfather of Atreus and Thyestes, and the great-grandfather of Agamemnon. References to Tantalus are common in all periods of Greek and Roman literature before Seneca himself dramatized two generations of the saga in *Agamemnon* and *Thyestes*. Such references are prominent in Ovid (*Am.* 2.2.43–4, 3.7.51–2, *Ars.* 2.605–6, *Her.* 16.211–12, 18.181–2, *Met.* 4.458–9, 10.41–2, *Ib.* 179–80, 193). There are also allusions to Tantalus in Senecan tragedy outside the Tantalid plays (see e.g. here and at *Med.* 745, *Pha.* 1232; cf. also *HO* 943–4, *Oct.* 621).

saepe decepto/so often tricked: *deceptus* is almost a defining modifier for Tantalus; see *Ag.* 20, *Thy.* 159.

praebet uolucri Tityos aeternas dapes/Tityos feeds the bird an eternal feast: Tityos (also Tityus) was a Giant, whose punishment for attempting (on Juno's orders) to rape Latona was to have his liver eaten out each day by a vulture (or vultures). The liver grew back overnight, ready to be eaten once more: *semperque renascens | non perit ut possit saepe perire*, 'always being reborn | It does not die in order that it can die often' (Ov. *Pont.* 1.2.39–40); hence the liver is termed 'fecund' (*fecundum iecur, Ag.* 18) and the feast 'eternal' (*aeternas*, 756). Regularly, as here, a single bird/vulture seems to do the eating: see *Ag.* 18, *Pha.* 1233, *Oct.* 622, *HO* 947, Hor. *Odes* 3.4.78, Virg. *Aen.* 6.595–600, Ov. *Ibis* 182. In Homer (*Od.* 11.576–9) and generally in the Greek tradition two or an unspecified plurality of birds seem involved. At *Thy.* 10 a plurality of birds is mentioned, as it is at Lucr. 3.984, Prop. 2.20.31, and Ov. *Met.* 10.43, *Ibis* 194. For the formulation here, cf. esp. Ov. *Ibis* 182: *uisceraque assiduae debita praebet aui*, 'he feeds the assiduous bird the forfeited guts'. For the canon of sinners, see above. For Tityos and the Giants, see 976–8, *Thy.* 805–8, Luc. 4.593–7.

Danaides/Danaids: see on 495–500.

impiae Cadmeides/impious Cadmeids: daughters of Cadmus, Agave and Autonoe, who, as frenzied Bacchantes, tore apart the son of Agave, Pentheus, king of Thebes. Agave, the Bacchantes, and Pentheus appear in the underworld scene of *Oedipus* (615–18), but no mention is made of their punishment. Here the daughters of Cadmus are envisioned as suffering in the underworld itself the *furor* which blinded them in their dismemberment of kin. A third daughter of Cadmus, Ino, should not be included, since, although in Euripides' *Bacchae* she participated in the dismemberment

(*Bacch.* 1228), she was the foster-mother of Bacchus and became the goddess Leucothea/Mater Matuta (Sen. *Oed.* 445–6, Ov. *Fas.* 6.483–550). For Agave, see further on 132–6. For polysyllabic Greek names closing the trimeter, see on 6–11.

auida…auis/ravening bird: Seneca likes this epithet for birds; see 1207 below, *Ag.* 18; cf. *HO* 1378. On earth the 'birds' who spoiled Phineus' food were Harpies.

Phineas/Phineus': a legendary Thracian prophet and king (in some versions the brother or nephew of Cadmus), who was blind either through choice (in preference to a shorter life with vision) and/or because of a punishment from the gods. He was certainly punished on earth by the gods in respect of his eating habits, by having his food constantly snatched away and defiled by Harpies. Apollonius (2.178ff.) has the Argonauts encounter Phineus and the Harpies on their outward voyage (see also *Pho.* 425). Accounts of his offence vary. According to Apollonius he revealed the 'sacred will' (ἱερὸν νόον) of Zeus/Jupiter. Ovid accuses him of having blinded his own sons (*Ars* 1.339–40). Phineus is punished with hunger in the underworld at Prop. 3.5.41, and grouped with Tantalus at Lucian *Tim.* 18.

760–1 Amphitryon's final choral intervention.

ede/present: not only a move by Seneca to vary Amphitryon's imperatives (see on 645–9), but metatheatrical language inviting the audience to 'view' the narrative as a theatrical spectacle. Though the uses of *edere* are wide, the word is connected with *editor*, the producer of a Roman spectacle (*CIL* 9.2237, 10.539), and Seneca sometimes uses the word as an invitation to someone to speak, who then 'presents/produces' a spectacular verbal account; see e.g. *Oed.* 222, 914, *Tro.* 1067, *Thy.* 639. See also Hercules' use of *ede* at 1177. For metatheatrical language in *Hercules*, see on 109–12.

patrui uolentis munus an spolium/willing uncle's gift—or spoils: Euripides' Amphitryon asks virtually the same question of Heracles with one telling difference: the gift would have been that of Persephone/Proserpina (*Herac.* 612). Seneca's Amphitryon replaces the goddess with the 'uncle', *patruus*, which in late Claudian/early Neronian Rome could have been distinctly political in its reference. Dis was the uncle of Jupiter's son, Hercules, but the imperial 'uncle' (of Caligula and Agrippina and the great-uncle of Nero) was Claudius. Note the emphatically Roman terms, *munus* and *spolium*, used here by Amphitryon. The answer to Amphitryon's question, as Theseus' narrative makes clear, is (despite the terrified consent of Dis, 804–5) *spolium*, 'spoils' (see also Fitch *ad loc.*). Juno was right (51). For *spolia*, see 51 and n. *ad loc.*; for military imagery, see on 19–29; for triumphal imagery, see on 57–63. For Roman referentiality in *Hercules*, see on 46–52.

762–827 Theseus' climactic narrative of Hercules' capture and removal of Cerberus deals with an event referred to from Homer onwards (*Il.* 8.362–9, *Od.* 11.623–6). Yet, as Fitch remarks *ad loc.*, the present passage constitutes 'the fullest extant treatment' of this final labour. It falls into three sections: (i) Encounter with Charon and crossing of Lethe (762–81); (ii) Defeat of Cerberus (782–806); (iii) Taking of Cerberus to the upper world (807–27). Cf. the account of Apollodorus (2.5.12), where Heracles is initiated into the Eleusinian Mysteries before descending into the underworld. There he asks Pluto for the hound and agrees to defeat Cerberus without weapons. Here Hercules utilizes the skin and head of the Nemean Lion and his great club. Theseus' account, which ignores any help received by Hercules from deities (Homer mentions Athena and Hermes), is indebted primarily to Virgil and Ovid (see below). The counterpoint with Virgil is particularly important, since Hercules, whose violent removal of Cerberus is commented upon in *Aeneid* 6 (392–7), here confirms that description, repeating the contrast with the Virgilian Aeneas' peaceful behaviour in the underworld, conspicuous for its *pietas* (filial piety) rather than its *uis* (violence): *Aen.* 6, 398–407. Kyd's Hieronimo, well versed in Seneca's tragedies from which he quotes, models himself quite pointedly on Hercules' *catabasis* (*Spanish Tragedy* III.xiii.108–13):

> Though on this earth justice will not be found,
> I'll down to hell, and in this passion
> Knock at the dismal gates of Pluto's court,
> Getting by force, as once Alcides did,
> A troop of Furies and tormenting hags
> To torture Don Lorenzo and the rest.

762–8 Theseus introduces Charon. Neither Charon nor the crossing of Lethe or Styx feature in Apollodorus' narrative (2.5.12). Seneca's description, like that at *Oed.* 166–70 (see Boyle *ad loc.*), is clearly indebted to Virgil (*Aen.* 6.295–304):

> hinc uia Tartarei quae fert Acherontis ad undas.
> turbidus hic caeno uastaque uoragine gurges
> aestuat atque omnem Cocyto eructat harenam.
> portitor has horrendus aquas et flumina seruat
> terribili squalore Charon, cui plurima mento
> canities inculta iacet, stant lumina flamma,
> sordidus ex umeris nodo dependet amictus.

ipse ratem conto subigit uelisque ministrat
et ferruginea subuectat corpora cumba,
iam senior, sed cruda deo uiridisque senectus.

Hence a road leads to Tartarean Acheron's waters.
Here a whirlpool seethes, riotous with its mud
And vast eddy, belching all its sand in Cocytus.
A grim ferryman guards these waters and rivers,
Dreadful in his squalor, Charon, on whose chin lies
A tangled mass of white hair; his eyes freeze in flame;
A filthy cloak hangs by a knot from his shoulders.
He propels his boat with a pole, tends to the sails,
And ferries bodies on his ferruginous bark,
Now old, but a god's old age is fresh and green.

Ferale...fretum/A deathly...stagnates: a two-line atmospheric mini-*ekphrasis* of oppressive landscape begins the finale. Seneca has avoided the topographical specificity of Virgil's description of Charon's location at the confluence of the rivers Acheron and Cocytus (*Aen.* 6.295-7, see above). Instead he has chosen keynote words to suggest both the torpid nature of the landscape and by transposition the deathly nature of Hercules, for whom the *ferale saxum*, 'deathly crag', seems an overt 'objective correlative' (to use T. S. Eliot's term). It is with some point that Theseus begins his account of Hercules' 'heroic fight' (*nobilem pugnam*, 761) with *ferale*, 'deathly'. The use of synonyms in line 763, including juxtaposed synonyms, is not untypical: see on 283-95.

imminet/overhangs: for Seneca's use of this word elsewhere in descriptions of threatening landscape, see 690 above, *Ag.* 562; for its sense of 'threatening', see also *Pha.* 952, *Thy.* 42.

uadis/waters: see on 679-88.

hunc seruat amnem cultu et aspectu horridus/vile in his dress and looks, Guards the stream: the language is clearly indebted to the Virgilian passage printed above and to Seneca's (probably) earlier description of Charon at *Oed.* 166•-7: *flumina seruat | durus senio nauita crudo*, 'the ferryman, tough in his vigorous old age, guards the river.' For *horridus* with the ablative of respect, see 1004, *Oed.* 223.

pauidosque manes...gestat/and ferries the frightened ghosts: Seneca is correcting Virgil's *subuectat corpora*, 'ferries bodies', though Virgil seems to mean 'even bodies', referring to the likes of Hercules and Theseus and now Aeneas.

squalidus...senex/A foul old man: Charon; note how, unlike Virgil, Seneca delays Charon's name until the description is complete (771). For *squalidus/squalor*, see on 626–8.

impexa...ratem/A tangled...pole: a dogged rewriting of aspects of the Virgilian passage printed above, with repetition or near repetition of vocabulary, including *impexa/inculta* ('tangled'), *pendet/dependet* ('hangs'), *deformem/sordidus* ('ugly', 'filthy'), *sinum/amictus* ('cloak'), *nodus/nodo* ('knot'), *lucent/flamma* ('blaze', 'in flame'), *genae/lumina* ('eyes'), *regit/subigit* ('directs', 'propels'), *portitor/portitor* ('ferryman'), *conto/conto* ('pole'), *ratem/ratem* ('boat'). For *genae = oculi*, 'eyes', see 531 and n. *ad loc.*

nodus/knot: like other aspects of the unkempt Charon, the lack of a *fibula*, 'pin', to fasten his cloak indexes a quintessentially non-Roman, i.e. 'uncivilized', figure.

concauae...genae/sunken eyes: not normally a sign of good health. 'Sunken eyes', *cauati oculi*, according to Lucretius (6.1194), were a sign of the Athenian plague; *oculi concavi* (Celsus 2.6.1) suggest the final stage of severe disease. This is an interesting variation of the Virgilian *stant lumina flamma* (*Aen.* 6.300: printed above)—one which further emphasizes decay as the defining property of hell. There might even be a nod here to a physical characteristic of someone in Seneca's early imperial circle, viz. the emperor Caligula, to whom Suetonius attributes 'sunken eyes and temples' (*oculis et temporibus concauis, Gai.* 50.1). Cf. Seneca's own description of the young emperor at *Const.* 18.1. For *genae* = 'eyes', see 531 and n. *ad loc.*

portitor/ferryman: a word of strong Roman resonance = originally, 'harbour-officer' (from *portus*, 'harbour'), but applied to Charon by Virgil (*Geo.* 4.502, *Aen.* 6.298, 326), Propertius (4.11.7), and Ovid (*Met.* 10.73), and regularly used thereafter to mean simply 'ferryman' (e.g. *Ben.* 6.18.1), as if from *portare*. For Roman referentiality in *Hercules*, see on 46–52.

769–81 **Hic onere uacuam**/He...without its load: *uacuam* (*E*) competes with *uacuus* (*A*), favoured by Zwierlein. Most modern editors print the reading of *E*. In either case *onere* is separative ablative: Woodcock §§40–1. For the dactyl-tribrach combination at the start of the line, see 76 and n. *ad loc.*

dirus exclamat Charon/Dread Charon exclaims: similarly in the Virgilian encounter Charon is the first to speak (*Aen.* 6.387). For *dirus*, see 56 and n. *ad loc.*

quo pergis, audax.../Where do you go, bold one...: Charon's opening line rewrites his second line in Virgil (*Aen.* 6.389): *fare age quid uenias, iam istinc, et comprime gressum*, 'Come tell me why you come, even from there, and check your step.' For *audax* and boundary violation, see on 547–9. For boundary violation, see on 46–52.

non passus ullas…moras/**brooks no delay:** for the phrase in Senecan tragedy, see on 582–9. Note especially the link here between Orpheus (588) and Hercules.

natus Alcmena/Alcmena's son: the same nomenclature at *Pha.* 317. Cf. *Alcmena genitus* at 527. The ablative is of source. For Alcmena, the mother of Hercules, see on Dramatis Personae (Amphitryon and Hercules), and on 524–32.

cumba…bibit/The skiff…both sides: these two and a half lines rewrite the effect of the living and large (*ingens*) Aeneas (and the Sibyl) embarking at Virg. *Aen.* 6.413–14:

> gemuit sub pondere cumba
> sutilis et multam accepit rimosa paludem.

> The sewn skiff groaned beneath
> The weight and received much marsh through its gaps.

Cumbae were small boats, such as pleasure or fishing boats, found on lakes (Ov. *Tr.* 2.330) and at leisure resorts such as Baiae on the Bay of Naples, where, according to Seneca (writing with disapproval), there were *tot genera cumbarum uariis coloribus picta*, 'so many kinds of boats painted in diverse colours' (*Ep. Mor.* 51.12). For other Senecan vignettes involving the *cumba*: see e.g. *Med.* 368, *Thy.* 592. Seneca uses *cumba*, too, of the boat of Charon in the underworld at *Oed.* 166, as does Virgil at *Aen.* 6.303. The word is regularly used metaphorically for poetic composition: Prop. 3.3.22, Ov. *Tr.* 1.1.85, 2.330, *Pont.* 2.6.12.

cumba populorum capax succubuit uni/The skiff with room for nations Sank beneath one man: Seneca is engaging in one of his favourite games here, the play between one and many, focusing on *unus*: see on 19–29. With *cumba…capax*, cf. *Oed.* 166, where the same phrase is used of Charon's vessel. For *capax* of the underworld, see 659. For Seneca's fondness for the plural of *populus*, see on 186–91.

sedit et grauior ratis/The boat sat heavier: Hercules/Heracles had the same effect on the *Argo* according to Apollonius (1.532–3), who seems to have influenced Virgil. In a sense Seneca is returning this motif to its rightful owner. See also Stat. *Theb.* 5.400–2. *Sedit*, the consensus reading of the MSS, is replaced by Zwierlein and Billerbeck with the emendation of Gronouius, *sidit*. Viansino (1965 and 1993), Giardina (1966), Caviglia, Fitch

(1987*a* and 2018), and Chaumartin, like myself, see no reason to alter the *EA* tradition.

Lethen/**Lethe:** in Virgil the river across which Charon ferries the buried dead is the Styx. But Seneca has made Lethe the boundary river, and is sticking to it. See on 679–88.

latere titubanti bibit/**As it rocks, it gulps:** *titubare* is used regularly by Seneca, especially in his prose works, in a psychological sense, 'waver', as also at *Med.* 937. For its physical connotation, as here, cf. *nido...titubante*, 'in rocking nest', *Ag.* 685•, and *HO* 1599. For the figurative use of *bibere*, see Ov. *Am.* 2.11.6 (re the *Argo*), and 484 above and n. *ad loc.*

tum.../**Then...:** Hercules' enemies human and non-human cower before him, just as dead Greek soldiers tremble before Aeneas at Virg. *Aen.* 6.489–93. I have chosen *tum* (*E*) rather than *tunc* (*A*), favoured by Zwierlein, not only because there is a preference for *tum* among Roman poets, but also because in Seneca tragedy *tum* is statistically more likely before a consonant than *tunc*: see Fitch (2004*b*: 24).

tum uicta trepidant monstra/**Then conquered monsters cower:** Virgil's Aeneas encounters *monstra*, including Centaurs and the Lernaean Hydra, at the entrance to the underworld before meeting Charon (*Aen.* 6.285–8). It is, however, Aeneas' former military enemies, the dead Greek warriors, who cower before him (*ingenti trepidare metu*, 'cower in mighty fear': *Aen.* 6.491). See also *HO* 1925–8, which has been influenced by the present passage. For several of the *monstra*, including the Lyrnaean Hydra (780–1), see on 222–48. For the important *monstrum* motif, see 1280 and n. *ad loc.*

Centauri truces/**brutal Centaurs:** an allusion to Hercules' successful and lethal fight against the Centaurs, traditionally located on Mt Pholoe in the Peloponnese. Centaurs were wild, savage creatures, half-human and half-horse, who lived in Arcadia in the Peloponnese and in northern Greece, especially in the vicinity of Mt Pelion. With their uncontrolled violence and lust they represented the antithesis of Greek (male/elite) civilized life. They attacked Hercules when he was staying with another and somewhat exceptional Centaur, Pholus: see Apollod. 2.5.4; Diod. Sic. 4.12.3–7. Billerbeck *ad loc.* notes that Virgil seems to have been the first to place the Centaurs in the underworld. Statius (*Theb.* 4.534, *Silu.* 5.3.280) and Silius (13.590) followed suit. *Trux*, 'brutal/savage/wild', is a strong word, originally used of animals (Plaut. *Bacch.* 1148, Pac. *Ant.* frag. 3 Klotz) and applied by tragic Seneca to 'monsters' (*monstris, Ag.* 337), Amazons (*Oed.* 479), Achilles (*Tro.* 252), Hercules (*Tro.* 720), the passions (*adfectus, Ag.* 224), the *animus* (*Ag.* 250)—and in *Hercules* to 'looks' (*uultu,* 371), the underworld (725), Centaurs (778), Zethus (916), chariots (1169) and tyrants/kings (936, 1255).

Lapithaeque multo in bella succensi mero/And Lapiths, made hot for war by much wine: the Lapiths were a Thessalian clan against whom Hercules fought, allied to their enemy, Aegimius, king of the Dorians. In the fight Hercules killed many, including the Lapith king, Coronus: Apollod. 2.7.7; Diod. Sic. 4.37.3. The descriptive phrase attached to the Lapiths may seem a little odd, since in the famous battle between the Lapiths and the Centaurs, sculpted on the metopes of the Parthenon and narrated vigorously and bloodily by Ovid (*Met.* 12.210-535), Centaurs were the ones drunk. There seem insufficient grounds for excising the line, as Fitch *ad loc.* proposes.

Stygiae paludis/Stygian Swamp: from earthly swamp (Lerna) to infernal swamp (Styx) seems a fitting move for the hydra. In this play's underworld the Styx is not the boundary river of the underworld. It joins with Acheron to form a double moat around the palace of Dis (711-17). See further on 52-6. For *Stygiae paludis*, see *Pha.* 1151; the phrase is Virglian: *Aen.* 6.323, 369.

fecunda mergit capita Lernaeus labor/The labour of Lerna...sinks its fecund heads: the reference is to the Lernaean Hydra and its bi-reproductive heads; see on 241-8. The sinking of the heads may serve a dual purpose: to hide from Hercules, and to cool the hydra's cauterized necks. With the hydra's *fecunda capita*, cf. its *colla feracia*, 'fertile necks', at 529, and its status as *numerosum malum*, 'a numerous pest', at 241. See also *Ag.* 835, *HO* 258, Ov. *Her.* 9.95. For this metonymic use of *labor*, see 944, Prop. 4.9.17.

782-806 Hercules' victorious fight with Cerberus. The narrative here and at 807-27 proceeds through a series of vividly realized scenes 'like consecutive photographic stills or video clips' (Zanobi 2008: 250).

782-91 The location and description of Cerberus, offspring of Echidna and Typhon/Typhoeus (according to Hesiod, *Th.* 311, and Quintus of Smyrna, 6.261), and the named guard-dog of the underworld from Hesiod onwards (*Th.* 769-74). The guard-dog in Homer is unnamed (see on 57-63). Ovid calls him the 'Echidnean dog' (*Echidnaeae...canis*, *Met.* 7.408-9). In Virgil (*Aen.* 6.417-25) and apparently at *Ag.* 13-21, Cerberus guards the far side of the Styx; here he protects the palace of Dis. Elsewhere in Seneca (see *Tro.* 403-4, *Thy.* 16) he guards the gates of Tartarus. At *Oed.* 171-3 he is reported to have broken out of hell and to be scouring Thebes. Though he has fifty heads in Hesiod (*Theog.* 312), the canonic number, as evident in Seneca, is three: see on 57–63. The number is three also in Spenser's *The Fairie Queene* 1.5.34:

> Before the threshold dreadfull Cerberus
> His three deformed heads did lay along,
> Curled with thousand adders venemous,
> And lilled forth his bloudie flaming tong:
> At them he gan to reare his bristles strong,
> And felly gnarre, until Dayes enemy
> Did him appease; then downe his taile he hong
> And suffred them to passen quietly:
> For she in hell and heaven had power equally.

auari Ditis/greedy Dis: for the proverbial greed/lust of death, see on 283–95. There is also some etymological wordplay here: Dis, a contraction of *Diues* ('Rich'), is necessarily *auarus*, 'avaricious/greedy'. Cf. *auidi…Ditis*, *Ag.* 752. Billerbeck *ad loc.* oddly calls the lemmatized phrase 'ein pointiertes Oxymoron'. See further on 35–40.

umbras territat Stygius canis/hell-hound terrifies shades: the hell-hound (lit. 'Stygian dog', as at *Pha.* 223) is of course Cerberus. For the dog's terrifying of the shades, see Virg. *Aen.* 6.401, cited by Seneca at *Ep. Mor.* 82.16. For Styx, see on 52–6.

trina uasto capita concutiens sono/Shaking its triple heads with mighty roar: Cerberus' triple-throated bark, which terrified shades, was famous: see Virg. *Aen.* 6.400–1, 417–18, Prop. 3.18.23, Ov. *Met.* 4.450–1, [Virg.] *Culex* 220, Stat. *Silu.* 2.1.184, Sil. 13.594—and 793 below. Hence sometimes the focus is on the heroic achievement of silencing the dog: see *Ag.* 860–60•. *Trina*, 'triple', is used only twice elsewhere in Seneca: *Thy.* 676, *Ep. Mor.* 86.14. For the focus on sound, see on 1002–9.

regnum tuetur/guards the kingdom: for Cerberus as guard-dog for the palace of Dis, see e.g. Horace (*Odes* 3.11.16) and Virgil (*Aen.* 8.296), who refer to him/it as *ianitor aulae* and *ianitor Orci* ('gatekeeper of the court', 'gatekeeper of hell') respectively. See also Virg. *Aen.* 6.400, Eur. *Herac.* 1277. A frequent term for Cerberus is *custos*, 'guard/guardian': 809 below and n. *ad loc.*

sordidum tabo caput/its heads Foul with gore: for the plural translation, see *trina…capita* (784). The phrase *sordidum tabo* is non-Virgilian; it increases the sensational horror of the portrait. The words are applied by the author of *HO* (786) to Hercules' lion skin. Statius applies them to Oedipus: *sordida tabo…canities*, 'white hair foul with gore' (*Theb.* 11.582–3).

colubrae,   uiperis…draco…angue/Serpents…vipers…snake…snakes: Cerberus' snaky appearance is represented in archaic Greek art and elsewhere, and is frequently referenced in Roman literature: e.g. Tib. 1.3.71–2, Hor. *Odes* 3.11.17–18, Virg. *Aen.* 6.419, Lygd. 4.87, Ov. *Am.* 3.12.26, *Met.* 10.21–2 (where snaky Cerberus is called a 'Medusan monster', *Medusaei…monstri*), [Virg.] *Culex* 221.

uiperis horrent iubae/manes bristle with vipers: similarly in Virgil Cerberus' 'necks bristle with snakes', *horrere…colla colubris* (*Aen.* 6.419).

torta sibilat cauda/hisses in the twisted tail: so, too, the Fury Megaera's snake 'hisses twisted in the cracked whip', *excusso sonat | tortus flagello* (*Med.* 961–2). Seneca's verbal imaging embraces sound, sight, and movement.

par ira formae/Its anger matches its looks: Cerberus' *ira* is also emphasized at *Oed.* 580: *ira furens*, 'raging with anger'. For *ira*, see on 19–29.

791–802 The fight.

propior stetit Ioue natus antro/Jove's son Stood nearer the cave: Theseus is decidedly on one side of the Hercules' parentage controversy. Cerberus' cave is Virgilian (*Aen.* 6.418). With *stetit*, 'stood', cf. *stetisti* at 285 and see n. *ad loc.* I join Zwierlein, Chaumartin, Giardina (2007), and Fitch (2018) in placing a comma after *antro*, allowing it to function as dative with *propior*. Giardina (1966), Fitch (1987*a*), Viansino (1993), and Billerbeck place the comma after *natus*.

et uterque timuit/And both felt fear: I have retained the EA reading, *et uterque*, as do Viansino (1965 and 1993), Giardina (1966), Caviglia, Fitch (1987*a* and 2018), and Chaumartin. Zwierlein and Billerbeck, not wanting Hercules to show fear, favour Madvig's unnecessary emendation, *leuiterque*. Note that not only does Hercules show fear at 1147, he admits it.

ecce latratu graui/Look! With deep bark: note the immediacy of Theseus' account; Cerberus seems to be in front of him. For a similar use of *ecce* to enliven a 'messenger-narrative', see e.g. Eurybates at *Ag.* 528, or Virgil's Aeneas at *Aen.* 2.203; see also on 329–31. For Cerberus' bark, see on 782–91.

loca muta terret/it scares The silent places: an unindicated change of grammatical subject, as here, is not rare in tragic Seneca: see 797 and on 30–5. With *loca muta*, cf. Virgil's infernal *loca…tacentia, Aen.* 6.265. For the *locus* motif, see on 1–5, 572–6; for the silence of the underworld, see on 572–6.

uocis horrendae fragor/A monstrous voice roars: for *fragor* of sound, see on 520–3.

soluit/He frees: another unindicated change of grammatical subject, which could be made clear in dramatic performance through an actor's gestures.

feros…rictus…Cleonaeum caput/fierce jaws…Cleonaean Head: the jaws and head of the Cleonaean or Nemean Lion, which Hercules killed by choking as his first labour: see on 222–5. He wears the lion's skin and head draped over his left shoulder (*a laeua*, 797; cf. Ov. *Her.* 9.62) and will use it as both shield and bedding (see 1151–2). Apollodorus 2.5.12 also states that Hercules used the lion skin as shield during his fight with Cerberus. Hercules is often depicted wearing the lion's head as a helmet. For *feros rictus*, see also *Thy.* 77–8. The adjective *Cleonaeus*, a Senecan *hapax*, is used here of the Nemean Lion for the first time in Latin literature (notice the etymological pun within the word), but is used in such a way also by Lucan (4.612) and the Flavian poets: see e.g. Mart. *Epig.* 5.71.3, Silius 3.34, and esp. Valerius, who seems influenced by this passage (1.34: *Cleonaeo…hiatu*, 'Cleonaean jaws': see further Zissos 2008 *ad loc.*). Cleone was a neighbouring town on the eastern side of Nemea in the northern Argolid.

tegmine…tegit/shields…shielding: for similar, etymological wordplay (*figura etymologica*), see on 731–4. See further on 35–40. For *tegmen* again of the lion skin, see 1151 below, Virg. *Aen.* 7.666, Ov. *Her.* 9.62, Stat. *Silu.* 4.6.68. Along with Fitch (1987*a* and 2018) and Chaumartin I have printed *E*'s *tegit* rather than *A*'s *clepit*, favoured by Viansino (1965 and 1993), Giardina (1966), Caviglia, Zwierlein, and Billerbeck. The etymological play itself inclines one towards the acceptance of *E*, even apart from the inappropriate connotations of theft generated by *A*'s reading (see Fitch *ad loc.* and 2004b: 25).

uictrice magnum dextera robur gerens/Wielding the great club in triumphant hand: Quintus of Smyrna (6.265) also has Hercules use his club in the fight. Note how Hercules' *uictrix dextra*, 'triumphant hand', mirrors that of Lycus at 399.

huc…et illuc/Here and there: for this iambic trimeter line opening, see 287 and n. *ad loc.*

ingeminat ictus/doubles the strikes: *ingeminare* is a Senecan *hapax*; the phrase is Virgilian (*Aen.* 5.457).

802–6 The aftermath.

infregit minas/broke off Its threats: for *minas infringere*, cf. Silius 7.125.

antroque toto cessit/And left the entire cave: a wry Virgilian allusion. Virgil had made the point that Cerberus was so large as to fill 'the entire cave' (*toto…antro*, *Aen.* 6.423), when stretched out. For the ablative of starting point (Woodcock §41.1) with *cedere*, see also e.g. *Med.* 299, *Ag.* 304–5, *Oct.* 671.

extimuit…uterque…dominus/Both rulers quaked: fear expressed by the god of the underworld in the underworld goes back to Homer: *Il.* 20.61–2. For *dominus* = *dominus* and *domina*, see on 569–71.

duci iubet/ordered it led away: no such permission is given in the account of this incident by Virgil's Charon at *Aen.* 6.395–6. Note the legal language. *Duci* = to be led away into the possession of another/for punishment, enslavement etc.: see *OLD* 4. Cerberus now legally belongs to Hercules, his new master (*erum*, 811). For legal language in the play, see on 731–4. It continues in the next line.

me quoque petenti munus Alcidae dedit/At Alcides' petition they gifted me, too: Theseus' rescue from the underworld is added almost as an afterthought, as at *Pha.* 845, which also begins with the casual *me quoque*, 'me, too'. Here Seneca has expressed the matter more legally—the 'obligatory gift', *munus*, is in response to Hercules' 'petition' (*petere* often has a legal sense: *OLD* 11). Note that at the end of *Phaedra* Theseus regrets being a 'gift': *tuum Diti remitte munus*, 'Return your gift to Dis' (*Pha.* 1217–18). For the rescue (which in these versions also involved Pirithous), see also Diod. Sic. 4.26.1, Hyg. *Fab.* 79. Like Virgil, Apollodorus (2.5.12) preserves a version in which Hercules took Theseus without the permission of Dis.

807–27 Removal of Cerberus in chains to the upper world. Note how Cerberus' movement to the upper world is focalized through the hellhound itself, whose alienation and accompanying darkness are precursors of Hercules' madness. Cf. the Chorus' brief account of Cerberus' ascent at *Ag.* 859–61 and that of Ovid at *Met.* 7.410–15. Billerbeck *ad loc.* notes the resemblance of Cerberus' initial behaviour (807–12) to that of Odysseus' old dog Argos on seeing his master's return (Hom. *Od.* 17.301–2: wagging of tail, drooping of ears). For Seneca's 'visual' narrative here, see on 782–806.

807–12 *monstri*/monster's: for the important *monstrum* motif, see 1280 and n. *ad loc.*

adamante texto uincit/binds them with adamant chains: cf. Juno's sarcastic remark at 52–3 about extending this chaining to Dis himself. The material of the chains is Ovidian (*Met.* 7.412). The ablative is instrumental: see Woodcock §43.1.

custos opaci peruigil regni canis/the dark realm's unsleeping guard-dog: for Cerberus as *custos*, 'guard', see also *Thy.* 16, *Tro.* 404, *Ag.* 13, Virg. *Aen.* 6.395, 424, Stat. *Theb.* 7.783, *Silu.* 3.3.27. At Hor. *Odes* 3.11.16 Cerberus is *ianitor*. Note Seneca's clever verbal placement, with the guard-dog encompassing the realm he guards and wide-awake in the middle of it. For *opacus*, see 707 and n. *ad loc.* For *peruigil* or *uigil* 'unsleeping', as a defining modifier of other monstrous guardians, see 240 and 531 (Hesperidean serpent), 531, and *Med.* 703 (Colchian serpent).

componit aures timidus/Timidly droops its ears: the tradition of Cerberus' timid, even fawning behaviour after capture, seems to go back at least to Sophocles: see his *Phaedra* frag. 687 (Lloyd-Jones 1996). With the description here, cf. Horace's depiction of Cerberus' meek behaviour in respect of Bacchus at *Odes* 2.19.29–32.

erumque fassus/Accepts its master: again the legal language, for which in *Hercules* see on 731–4. For *erus* as 'master' of an animal, see Stat. *Theb.* 4.272–3.

utrumque cauda pulsat anguifera latus/thumping each flank with its snake-tail: Theseus is adding almost a comic touch, climaxing his description with Cerberus' 'snake-tail wagging', clearly portrayed as a sign of affectionate excitement towards its new master (cf. Argos' behaviour noted on 807–27). *Anguifer* is a Senecan *hapax* used previously by Ovid (*Met.* 4.741). For Seneca's fondness for compounds in *-fer*, see on 235–40.

813–21 *Taenari*/Taenarus: see on 582–9 and 662–7. Seneca is consistent throughout *Hercules* in making Taenarus the point of entry to and exit from the underworld. Several variants for Hercules' exit point exist, as Fitch observes *ad loc.*, but both Pausanias (3.25.4–5) and Strabo (8.5.1) agree with Seneca on Taenarus.

nitor...lucis ignotae nouus/strange light's novel glow: cf. *Ag.* 862, where Cerberus is described by the Chorus as *lucis ignotae metuens colorem*, 'dreading the strange light's hue'; also Ov. *Met.* 7.411–12. For the *topos* of underworld figures having difficulty with unaccustomed daylight, see 293 and n. *ad loc.* Like Chaumartin, Billerbeck, and Fitch (2018), I favour *nouus*, the conjecture of Bücheler, to the *nouos* of Ageno and Rutgers, favoured by Viansino (1965 and 1993), Zwierlein (1986), and Fitch (1987a and 2002). *EA*'s *bono* cannot stand. Zwierlein (1986) also inappropriately introduces a sense-pause by punctuating after *ignotae*, which he removes in later editions when he prints *nouus* as here.

resumit animos uictus/gains strength from defeat: a not uncommon phenomenon; see e.g. Virg. *Aen.* 2.367, Tac. *Agr.* 37.3. For the *uictor*/*uictus* wordplay, see on 275–8.

uastas furens quassat catenas/shakes the huge Chains in rage: similarly Ovid's Cerberus, reacting to the light, is *rabida...concitus ira*, 'stirred with raging anger' (*Met.* 7.413).

mouit gradu/**pulled him from his post:** military imagery; for *gradus* of a military position or stance, see *Ag.* 549: *me...pepulerunt gradu*, 'drove me from my post'; *Const.* 19.3: *ne motus quidem gradu*, 'not even moved from his post'; Livy 6.32.8, 7.8.3. See Fitch *ad loc.* For military imagery in *Hercules*, see on 19–29.

meas respexit...manus/**looked to my hands:** in Euripides (*Herac.* 1386–7) Heracles at the end of the play asks for Theseus' help in taking Cerberus to Argos. He does not mention any help from Theseus in dragging Cerberus from the underworld, nor does Theseus himself in his account of the same incident in *Phaedra* (843–5).

geminis uterque uiribus/**With twice the strength both of us:** with this pleonasm, cf. *Ag.* 563, *Oed.* 267, *Thy.* 181–2. For a similar pleonasm with *uterque*, see Virg. *Geo.* 3.33.

ira furentem/**Raging with anger:** cf. Ov. *Met.* 7.413, cited above. For *ira*, 'anger', see on 19–29.

821–7 Cerberus' adverse reaction to daylight. Cf. Cerberus' reaction at *Ag.* 860–1, Ov. *Met.* 7.411–15.

clarum diem/**Clear day:** for *dies* = 'daylight', see on 123–4.

pura nitidi spatia...poli/**bright heaven's lucent spaces:** *spatia* is not used by Ovid and is used by Virgil only sparsely, but it occurs some eighteen times in Senecan tragedy at the service of his 'noun style' (see on 11–18), sometimes in the most 'dramatic' contexts: see *Med.* 30, 1026. The word appears again of the heavens at 593 and 958. For the juxtaposition of synonyms (*pura nitidi*, 'bright...lucent'), see on 283–95; the juxtaposition intensifies the looming contrast with *nox*, 'darkness', in the next line.

oborta...dedit/**Darkness...ground:** this line is deleted by Bothe, Peiper-Richter, Zwierlein, and Fitch (1987*a* and 2018), but not by Viansino (1965 and 1993), Giardina (1966 and 2007), Caviglia, Chaumartin, Billerbeck, and myself. For discussion, see Billerbeck *ad loc.*

aciemque retro flexit/**Turned away its gaze:** cf. Ovid's treatment at *Met.* 7.411–12: *contraque diem radiosque micantes | obliquantem oculos*, 'turning away its eyes from the day and its gleaming rays'. For the phrase, *retro flectere*, see 678 and n. *ad loc.*

petit/**lowered:** contracted perfect, as at 244: see n. *ad loc.*

sub Herculeas caput...umbras/**its heads In Hercules' shade:** Theseus' narrative of Hercules' heroic exploits in the underworld ends, like Virgil's *Aeneid* (12.952), with the word *umbras*. For the use of the adjective *Herculeus*, see 72 and n. *ad loc.* For *caput* = 'heads', as at 785; see n. *ad loc.*

MEGARA *and her* SONS *rise from their seated position at the altar:* see after 640-4.

827-9 Lines not only indicating the end of the act (see on 123-4), but also announcing the entrance of the chorus (as at *Ag.* 586-8, *Oed.* 401-2, *Tro.* 63-6, *HO* 581-2) and initiating a change of atmosphere from grim, individual narrative to joyous, collective celebration. Announcements of choral entry are found in Euripides (*Pho.* 196) and Greek New Comedy (Men. *Aspis* 246-8, *Dysc.* 230-2, *Epitr.* 169-71, *Peric.* 261-2ff.), though the Greek examples attested all occur before the parodos (first entrance of the chorus). Also in the announcements of Seneca's *Agamemnon* and *Oedipus* the lines are also exit-lines. Not so here. Theseus will remain onstage for the choral ode and the early part of Act IV; Amphitryon will remain onstage until the end of the play. Theseus also provides a pointer to the subject of the ensuing choral ode, as does Tiresias at *Oed.* 402.

The Chorus of Thebans who enter are clearly the vanguard of Hercules' triumphal procession, just as the Chorus of Trojan Women, whose entry is announced at *Ag.* 586-8, are the vanguard of Agamemnon's triumphal procession. There is no need, however, to posit a second chorus, as in *Agamemnon* (which Sutton 1984 and 1986: 41-2, argues), since the chorus of *Heracles* could have exited after their last choral ode or (more likely) could have exited with Hercules at 640 (see n. after 590-1). The Theban chorus wear laurel wreaths on their heads and are singing, as Theseus proclaims, 'great Hercules' merited praises' (*meritas Herculis laudes canit,* 829). For the Roman semiotics of this, see below. Physical descriptions of the chorus are not common in Senecan tragedy: cf. *Ag.* 311-14•, 586-7, and, most remarkably, *Tro.* 83-116; see also *HO* 119-20. For alliterative closure (828-9), see on 275-8. For Roman referentiality in *Hercules*, see on 46-52.

*sed/*But: for *sed* used to introduce a new or returning character (or characters), see on 329-31. For the postponement of conjunctions, including *sed*, see on 63-8.

frontibus laurum gerens/brows wreathed with laurel: a Roman touch. Laurels had an especial association in Rome with military victory. The victorious Roman general, the *triumphator*, riding in his chariot, wore (or had held above his head by an accompanying slave) a laurel crown. The triumphal procession would culminate in his placing of the laurels adorning the general's *fasces* 'in the lap of Jupiter' (*in gremio Iouis optimi maximique:* Pliny *HN* 15.134; cf. Stat. *Silu.* 4.1.41), i.e. on the lap of the cult image of Jupiter in his great temple on the Capitol. Laurels also adorned victorious military dispatches (*litterae laureatae*, Livy 5.28.13, 45.1.6, Tac. *Agr.* 18.6), and sometimes wreathed, as emblem of victory, the points of military spears (*hastae laureatae*: see *Ag.* 390 and Boyle *ad loc.*). The victorious Roman soldiers, too, wore laurel wreaths (*laureati*), even as they paraded through the city 'singing their own and their general's praises' (*suasque et imperatoris laudes canentes*, Livy 45.38.12). The Salii who sing Hercules' praises in Virgil's eighth *Aeneid* are crowned with poplar (*Aen.* 8.286). For Roman referentiality in *Hercules*, see on 46–52; for military imagery, see on 19–29; for triumphal imagery, see on 57–63.

magnique meritas Herculis laudes/great Hercules' merited praises: this is the Chorus' initial (830–7) and concluding (875–92) theme. But the main theme will be something else: see below. Though the triumphal laurel is here worn rather than the Herculean poplar (see on 893–4), both the triumphal imagery and Hercules' own worship in Rome (the Ara Maxima was perhaps the oldest cult centre in the city: see further Introd. §VI) make the Roman semiotics of this scene evident. Romans in Seneca's audience would perhaps have drawn an analogy between Hercules' slaying of Lycus and his killing of the Palatine monster, Cacus, described by Virgil at *Aen.* 8.225–67, where it is followed with an account of a choral band of Salii singing *laudes Herculeas* (*Aen.* 8.287–8). The phrase *meritae laudes* is a Roman formula: see Tib. 3.7.3, Livy 7.7.3, 7.36.9. For *magnus* as the quintessential epithet of Hercules, see on 439–47. For *laudes* as 'encomium/praises' to be sung by a chorus, see *Oed.* 402, where as here the word functions almost as a stage-direction to the play's chorus. See also *Tro.* 293.

ALL *remain onstage*: both Amphitryon and Theseus are onstage at the beginning of Act IV. It is obviously more appropriate to have them remain onstage during the inter-act ode, sung by a chorus who represent the vanguard of Hercules' triumphal procession, than to have them exit here and return after the ode has finished. For characters onstage during a choral ode in Senecan tragedy, see before 524–91.

Third Choral Ode: The 'Celebration Ode' (830–94)

Regularly in Senecan tragedy (see *Oed.* 709ff., *Pha.* 736ff., *Ag.* 589ff., *Med.* 579ff, *Thy.* 546ff.) the choral ode following the third act takes its impetus directly from the dramatic action. In only one other play (*Agamemnon*, 586–8), however, are the singers of the third choral ode announced in advance, as they are here, at the end of Act III (cf. *Oed.* 401–2, where a choral ode is announced at the end of Act II). The pre-announced theme of this ode in *Hercules* is the hero's 'merited praises' (*meritas Herculis laudes*, 829). But though the ode is enclosed by this theme (830–7, 875–92), the substance of the ode is concerned with another, not unrelated matter, to which much recent narrative has already been devoted: death. Many have observed the contrast between this choral ode and the celebratory stasimon sung with sustained joy and praises after the killing of Lycus in Euripides' *Heracles* (763–814). Fitch *ad loc.* remarks: 'The Euripidean Chorus maintains its joyful confidence throughout the stasimon, asserting that the hero's victory proves divine concern for justice (772ff., 813f.). But in Seneca the thought of Hercules' last labour leads the Chorus into a meditation on the world and condition of death, filled with powerful images and sombre echoes of the Virgilian *catabasis* in *Aeneid* 6.' The expected triumphalism is suspended for a joyless song of death.

What this sung meditation leads to is not what Seneca himself concludes when 'thinking on death' in *Epistle* 26, where he equates death with *libertas*, 'freedom' (*meditari mortem = meditari libertatem, Ep. Mor.* 26.10). For the Chorus, as noted in the Introduction, the world of death is foul, lightless, empty, and mute (861–3), quite lacking apparently in any of the positive properties assigned to it in Seneca's prose works. The Chorus indeed underscore this, when their reflections lead to an articulation of their own existential position (872–4)—an articulation, however, immediately followed by an exuberant lyric ending to the ode (875–92), in which the metre is changed from sapphics to glyconics to make the ode's celebratory purpose clear (see below). The lyric ends as it began, with praises of Hercules but with the laudation, too, of something absent from the corresponding Euripidean ode: the *Pax Herculea*, universal peace.

The structure of the ode is straightforward: (i) Hercules' praises: victory in the underworld (830–7); (ii) great number and diversity of the dead, and the darkness, lethargy, and silence of death (838–63); (iii) personal coda: we should not rush to death; death is universal and with us at birth (864–74); (iv) Hercules' praises: bringing peace to earth and hell (875–92). Two lines of lyric instruction to the entering Hercules follow (893–4). Note how the apostrophe to Hercules (without a vocative) in the opening section (830–7) leads to apostrophe to death (without and with a vocative) in the middle section (870–3), thence to apostrophe to Hercules (without a vocative) at the close (893–4).

The double change of tone in the ode is remarkable and is discussed in the Introduction (§VII, 88). One could label the closural laudatory tone as contextually 'ironic', and Senecan tragedy features other ironic celebratory odes: the '*Pietas* Ode' of *Thyestes*, esp. 546-95; the 'Victory Ode' of *Agamemnon* 310-87; the 'Bacchus Ode' of *Oedipus* 403-508; the 'Processional Ode' of *Medea* 56-115. Ironic celebratory odes are found, too, in Greek tragedy; there are several, for example, in Sophocles (*Ajax* 693-717, *Trach.* 633-62, *Ant.* 1115-54, *OT* 1086-1109) which express momentary optimism before disaster strikes. The celebratory stasimon in Euripides' *Heracles* (763-814) is also contextually ironic. But what results here in *Hercules* is more complex than Sophoclean or Euripidean irony and inherently problematic.

Also problematic is the main metre of the ode, the lesser sapphic. Seneca adopts his usual practice of continuous, i.e. non-stanzaic, sapphics, unalleviated here by a single adonius: see e.g. (without adonii) *Pha.* 274-324, and (with adonii) *Tro.* 814-60, 1009-55; *Oed.* 110-53; *Pha.* 736-52; *Thy.* 546-622. For stanzaic sapphics, see *Med.* 579-669. The semiotic resonances of the sapphic metre are complex and diverse (see Morgan 2010: ch. 3). Sappho was renowned for (among other things) kletic verse, and, as one might expect in kletic sapphics, Seneca's verse here begins with apostrophe, an apostrophe to Hercules (830-7) in accordance with Theseus' announcement (829). But the apostrophe to Hercules transforms itself into an apostrophe to death (870-3), before the ode completely shifts both metre and theme. There is another layer of semiotics here, too. Horace had used sapphics for kletic poems such as *Odes* 1.2 and *Carmen Saeculare* which were prominently political, indeed politically laudatory, and in the process had established the 'political' as a sphere for sapphic lyric in the Roman context. *Odes* 3.14, for example, is a sapphic lyric poem which is not kletic, erotic, or hymeneal (Sappho's three main poetic areas) but political: its goal is to praise Augustus and in those praises, as it happens, the poem compares him to Hercules, as Virgil had done (*Aen.* 6.801-3). Seneca's audience are primed by both Theseus' announcement and the sapphic metrical form for a kletic, laudatory ode on Hercules. The ode, however, goes awry in both its meditations and invocations and has to reorient itself dramatically, metrically, and thematically to fulfil its original goal of singing 'Hercules merited praises' (*meritas Herculis laudes*, 829). For the celebratory semiotics of the closural glyconics (influenced perhaps by Euripides), see on 875-92. For political semiotics and the sapphic metre elsewhere in Senecan tragedy, see *Thy.* 546-622 and Boyle *ad loc.*

For further discussion of this choral ode and its dramatic and thematic function in the play, see Introd. §VII, 86-8.

Metre: lesser sapphics (830–74); glyconics (875–94). See Introd. §IX. For metrical semiotics, see above.

830–7 Hercules' praises: the despoliation of Dis.

Natus Eurystheus properante partu/**Eurystheus, born with quickened birth:** Eurystheus' early birth (after seven months gestation) before the 'delayed birth' of Hercules was engineered by Juno to ensure the Argolid throne and regal authority for Eurystheus. Jupiter had promised the throne to one of his blood born on the relevant day (Eurystheus was a grandson of Perseus, son of Jupiter). The story and Juno/Hera's trickery are told by Agamemnon in Homer's *Iliad* (19.95–133). The whole episode had a special coherence for a Roman audience, for whom Juno, *qua* Juno Lucina, was the goddess of childbirth. With the phrase *properante partu*, cf. *partu remorante*, 'with delayed birth', used of the birth of Paris at Ov. *Her.* 16.43. See further on 77–83 and Introd. §VI, 61.

derat hoc solum numero laborum/**Number of labours lacked but this:** Hercules' capture of Cerberus in the underworld was traditionally the final labour. For the twelve labours, see on 213–48; for Seneca's interest in 'number', see on 495–500. *Derat hoc solum* is a variation of a standard Senecan formula, often used sarcastically: see *Tro.* 888, *Pho.* 369–70, *Pha.* 1186–7, *Med.* 992. Note the syncopated form *derat*, printed by modern editors instead of the unmetrical *deerat* of the MSS; see 500 and n. *ad loc.* For its rhetorical use, see 40 and n. *ad loc.*

tertiae regem spoliare sortis/**Taking spoils from the third realm's king:** lit. 'the third lot's king'. For the three kingdoms and the drawing of lots, see on 52–6. For the 'third lot', see 609. Cf. also Tib. 3.5.22: *sortiti tertia regna dei*, 'gods who obtained by lot the third kingdom'. Note again the military language/imagery (see on 19–29) and the possibly implied play on the name, Dis (see 51 and n. *ad loc.*).

ausus es/**You dared:** apostrophe without a vocative; see on 178–82. The *ausus es* of E (adopted by most modern editors) is preferable to the *ausus est* of A, because, as Fitch remarks *ad loc.*, such apostrophe is not only 'common in Senecan choral odes' but is 'especially appropriate here in a song of praise'. For *ausus* and boundary violation, see on 547–9; for boundary violation, see on 46–52.

qua/**Where:** for the postponement of relatives, see 159 and n.

nigra metuenda silua/**dismal with its dark woods:** for the plethora of epithets denoting darkness applied to the underworld, see on 689–96; see further 857 (*opaca*).

magna comitante turba/with great, attending throng: an adaptation, as Fitch notes *ad loc.*, of a repeated Virgilian phrase, *magna comitante caterua*, 'with great, attending crowd' (*Aen.* 2.40, 370, 5.76). The 'throng' is presumably that of the recent dead, attending or accompanying Hercules on the descent. Theseus has just described the Chorus as a 'dense throng' (*densa... turba*, 827–8). The Chorus extend that language to the dead and, in so doing, project themselves to the audience as an image of the thronging dead. That image will be sustained by what follows. Note that the dramatist of *Octavia* also applies the phrase, *comitante turba*, to the dead (*Oct.* 729).

838–63 Death: number and diversity of the dead; death's darkness, lethargy and silence.

838–49 The great number of the dead compared (via three similes) to: (i) crowds moving to the theatre (838–9); (ii) spectators at the Olympic Games (840–1); (iii) crowds of initiates and others at the Eleusinian Mysteries (842–7). Each *comparandum* is of course anachronistic. But each has Herculean relevance. The references to the Olympic Games and the Eleusinian Mysteries are perhaps most obvious in that regard, since there is a tradition that Hercules founded the former (Pind. *Ol.* 10.23–5, 43–59, Diod. Sic. 4.14.1–2) and was initiated in the latter before his *catabasis* (Diod. Sic. 4.25.1, Apollod. 2.5.12). More interesting and essentially self-reflective is the Herculean allusivity of the opening simile, since Hercules/Heracles was not only a major theatrical figure of Attic drama and Roman pantomime, even if perhaps a minor one of earlier Roman tragedy (see Introd. 65–6), he is the major theatrical figure of this play. What each *comparandum* also has in common is cultural relevance: Seneca has avoided the traditional comparison of the numbers of the dead to natural phenomena (leaves, flowers, waves, birds: see *Oed.* 600–7, printed below), and chosen *comparanda* from the cultural life of his contemporary urban world. For Roman referentiality in *Hercules*, see on 46–52. For similarly anachronistic reference to the Olympic Games, see *Tro.* 849–50, *Ag.* 918–39, *Thy.* 123, Ov. *Her.* 18.166, *Met.* 14.324–5. Compare the procession to death in the (almost certainly) earlier *Ad Marciam* (11.2), which seems to lie behind Seneca's famous lines and where again Seneca's cultural eye is evident:

> hoc omnis ista quae in foro litigat, spectat in theatris, in templis precatur turba dispari gradu uadit.

> Hither (to death) process at different pace the whole crowd who litigate in the forum, watch in the theatres, pray in the temples.

There is an interesting progression in the *Hercules*' similes from 'joi de vivre' activities (theatre, games) to those at the boundary of life and death (Eleusinian Mysteries), before the ode crosses to the main subject: the numbers of the dead. Many (including Fitch *ad loc.*) compare these Senecan lines to T. S. Eliot's *The Wasteland*, 'The Burial of the Dead', 61–3:

> Under the brown fog of a winter dawn
> A crowd flowed over London Bridge, so many,
> I had not thought death had undone so many.

Worth comparing, too, is the description of the numbers of dead raised by Tiresias in *Oedipus* (600–7):

> non tot caducas educat frondes Eryx
> nec uere flores Hybla tot medio creat,
> cum examen alto nectitur densum globo,
> fluctusque non tot frangit Ionium mare,
> nec tanta gelidi Strymonis fugiens minas
> permutat hiemes ales et caelum secans
> tepente Nilo pensat Arctoas niues,
> quot ille populos uatis eduxit sonus.

> More than all the falling leaves on Mount Eryx,
> All the flowers budding in Hybla's mid-spring
> When the dense swarms cluster in soaring balls,
> More than all the breakers of Ionia's sea,
> All the birds fleeing icy Strymon's threats,
> Quitting winter and slicing through heaven
> To swap Arctic snows for the balmy Nile,
> Was the number raised by the seer's voice.

Or the description in Virgil's sixth *Aeneid* (309–12) of the number of ghosts rushing to the banks of the Acheron/Styx:

> quam multa in siluis autumni frigore primo
> lapsa cadunt folia, aut ad terram gurgite ab alto
> quam multae glomerantur aues ubi frigidus annus
> trans pontum fugat et terris immittit apricis.

> As many as the forest leaves which drop and fall
> At autumn's first chill, or the birds which flock landward
> From the swirling deep when the chill year drives them
> Over the ocean and sends them to sunny lands.

See also Virg. *Geo.* 4.473–4, and Dante *Inf.* 3.55–7, which Eliot (above) remodels.

Quantus incedit populus…/As great a crowd move…: note the stately, ritualistic, initial sonal repetitions (*Quantus…quantus…quinta…quanta*) setting up a hymnic quality to this part of the ode, as it adopts a highly alliterative mode. *Incedere* sometimes = stately, even self-consciously stately, walking, as at *Const.* 13.2: *omnis hos qui togati purpurati incedunt,* 'all those who strut about in togas and purple'; see also *Oct.* 705. Cf. also the procession (*pompa*) moving towards death at *Oed.* 126–8. For *populus* = 'crowd/multitude', see *Oed.* 396, *Vit. Beat.* 2.4.

ad noui ludos auidus theatri/Avid for a new theatre's shows: although no new stone theatre was built in Rome during Seneca's lifetime, the Theatre of Pompey was rededicated under Claudius in 41 CE (Suet. *Claud.* 21.1, Dio 60.6.8–9), and a new wooden amphitheatre was constructed under Nero in 57 CE (Calp. Sic. 7.23ff., Tac. *Ann.* 13.31.1, Suet. Nero 12.1). A temporary wooden theatre is also a possible referent as are new theatres constructed in the provinces. *Noui* may simply be a transferred epithet (so Caviglia *ad loc.* interprets). The centrality of the theatre in late republican and early imperial culture is reflected in the allusions to it in Roman poetry: see e.g. Lucr. 4.75ff., 6.109ff.; Virg. *Aen.* 5.286ff.; Ov. *Met.* 3.111ff.; [Virg.] *Aetna* 297ff.; Luc. 7.9ff.; Calp. Sic. 7.23ff. The analogy of the theatre is also used at *Tro.* 1125. References to the theatre in dramatic texts are necessarily self-reflective. Fitch *ad loc.* notes the irony of *auidus*, 'avid', 'lusty', an epithet elsewhere associated with death: 555, *Ag.* 752, *Oed.* 164, 411. Billerbeck *ad loc.* takes *ad* with *incedit* (838) rather than *auidus*; but it is clearly syntactically ambiguous and may be taken with either or (better) both.

Eleum…Tonantem/Elis' Thunderer: the temple of Zeus/Jupiter at Olympia, a metonym for the Olympic Games, which traditionally began in 776 BCE. This metonym is especially appropriate because the temple's metopes featured what became the canonic twelve labours of Hercules, including his *catabasis* (see Introd. 61). Olympia was situated in Elis, a region of the western Peloponnese (as well as the name of the major city within it). For *Eleus* = 'Olympic', see *Ag.* 918, Prop. 3.2.20.

ruit/rush: the verb anticipates *properant*, 'rush' (846); both anticipate the 'rush' to death (*properare*, 867; *properamus*, 873).

quinta…reuocauit aestas/five summers revive: the Olympic Games were held every four years or (counting inclusively, as here) every fifth year. For *reuocare* = 'to revive', see *Tro.* 781, *Pha.* 292, *Thy.* 576.

longae ... nocti crescere/**night grows long:** lit. 'for the night to grow long'; *longae* seems protreptic. The time referred to is the period following the autumnal/fall equinox (see next n.). In this context *longae nocti* has a clear resonance of death. For the 'long night', *longa nox*, = 'death', see 1076, Hor. *Odes* 4.9.27–8, Prop. 2.15.24. To Catullus (5.6) death was *nox perpetua*; to Ovid (*Her.* 10.112) it was *nox aeterna*. *Crescere* is an infinitive of purpose after a verb of motion: see Woodcock §28.

Libra: the Balance or Scales, the seventh sign of the zodiac, traversed by the sun September to October. Originally seen as the Claws (*Chelae*) of Scorpio and represented as such in Aratus (*Phaen.* 89, 232, etc.), the constellation was only viewed as the pans of a balance from the first century BCE onwards: Hyg. *Astr.* 2.26, Ov. *Fas.* 4.386. Even in Virgil's *Georgics* the name is still *Chelae* (*Geo.* 1.33). The time indicated is the autumnal/fall equinox, in the vicinity of which (in the month of Boedromion) the Mysteries were celebrated. For personification of Libra, see e.g. *Pha.* 839, Virg. *Geo.* 1.208, Lucan 8.467.

turba secretam Cererem frequentat/**mass pack mystic Ceres:** the sanctuary of Demeter/Ceres at Eleusis, which attracted large crowds every year for the celebration of the Eleusinian Mysteries and the introduction of new initiates: see on 299–302. The great hall (Telesterion) in the sanctuary had a capacity of about three thousand people. The general procession from Athens to Eleusis, some fifteen miles away, would have been much larger. With the phrase *secretam Cererem*, cf. the synonymous *Cereris...arcanae* of Horace (*Odes* 3.2.26–7); with the whole lemmatized phrase, cf. *arua... secreta frequentant*, 'pack fields set apart', a Virgilian phrase used at *Aen.* 6.477–8 of dead military heroes. *Turba* is used, as here, of devotees of a particular deity (Juno) by Seneca at *Ag.* 341–2 (*tua...turba*, 'thy throng/mass'), and by Ovid (re devotees of Bacchus) at *Ars* 1.542.

*et citi.../*and Attic...: the syntactical awkwardness of this second main clause is noted by Fitch *ad loc.*, who compares *Oed.* 332–3, *Pha.* 335–7, *Med.* 821–3. Poetry, esp. dramatic poetry, revels in pushing syntactic boundaries. This is a line of considerable sonal power.

properant/**rush:** see on *ruit* (above) and on *properare* (867).

Attici...mystae/**Attic Initiates:** Athenian initiates. Another Greek loanword (μύσται), used of the same initiates by Ovid (*Fas.* 4.536) and Statius (*Silu.* 4.8.51), and at *HO* 599. See further on 1122–30. Seneca uses *mystae* again of followers of Bacchus (*Oed.* 431).

per campos agitur silentes/**is herded through Mute fields:** the verb suggests being driven like cattle or goats; see Virg. *Ecl.* 1.13. For the silence of the underworld, see on 572–6.

849–57 The diversity of the dead. A well-known passage of Virgil (*Aen.* 6.305–8) is rewritten:

> huc omnis turba ad ripas effusa ruebat:
> matres atque uiri, defunctaque corpora uita
> magnanimum heroum, pueri innuptaeque puellae
> impositique rogis iuuenes ante ora parentum.

> Here poured all the crowd, rushing to the banks:
> Mothers and men, and lifeless bodies of great-souled
> Heroes, boys and unmarried girls and young men
> Placed upon pyres before the eyes of parents.

Lines 306–8 are a repetition of Virgil, *Geo.* 4.475–7, which themselves rewrite Homer (*Od.* 11.36–43). Notably in Seneca's procession there are no great-souled heroes, just non-heroic, ordinary humans, displaying their mortality.

pars…uita/Some…life: the alliterative mode continues, esp. of *t*s and *s*s from the previous line. Note the initial alliterations in lines 848–50: *tanta…turba…tristis*.

tarda…senecta/slow old age: Seneca employs reverse temporality in his listing, beginning with the old and ending with infants (854–6), increasing the pathos as he does so. *Tardus*, 'slow', is one of old age's regular modifiers; see Enn. *Thy.* frag. 300 Jocelyn, Virg. *Aen.* 9.610, Tib. 2.2.19, Ov. *Tr.* 4.8.23, *Oct.* 74.

tristis/Grim: another regular modifier of old age; cf. *frons decet tristis senem*, 'a grim brow befits the aged', *Pha.* 453; see also *Pha.* 799, 917.

longa satiata uita/surfeited with long life: it is regarded by Seneca at *Ep. Mor.* 30.12 as a great blessing to be 'led to man's necessary rest surfeited' (*satiatus ad requiem homini necessariam…perductus est*); see also *Ep. Mor.* 24.26, *Breu. Vit.* 7.9.

pars…melioris aeui/Others of better years: the 'better years' = 'in their prime'; see Ov. *Ib.* 441. The genitive is of description or quality; see Woodcock §72.6.

comis nondum positis ephebi/Ephebes with tresses not yet shorn: *ephebus* is a Greek loan-word (ἔφηβος) for boys who have attained puberty, when the long hair of childhood was cut; here its modifying descriptive phrase directs its reference to boys on the cusp of puberty and ephebic status. The word continues the Greek flavour of this ode (Olympia, Eleusis), which is sung by Theban Greeks. See further on 1122–30. A Roman audience would interpret these unshorn *ephebi* as *pueri*, 'boys', just before they took on the *toga uirilis* (generally between the ages of fourteen and seventeen).

modo doctus infans/Infants just taught: the climactic focus of Seneca's list and a category to which he devotes three lines. *Infans* is collective. Note the shortening of final *o* in *modo*; see on 109–12. The only confirmed instance of adverbial *modo* with a long final *o* in the Senecan tragic corpus is at *Oct.* 273.

his datum solis/These alone…May: for the omission of auxiliary *est*, see on 222–5.

igne praelato releuare noctem/ease the dark with carried flame: the focus on darkness continues with a detail which displays both 'touching charm' ('the souls of children are allowed to carry torches in the Underworld because they are afraid of the dark': Trinacty 2015: 38) and cultural irony. Seneca's audience would have sensed the latter, since in Rome children were buried at night by torchlight: *Tranq.* 11.7, *Breu. Vit.* 20.5.

ceteri uadunt per opaca tristes/The rest go grimly through the gloom: though the only common word is the preposition *per*, the line clearly echoes Virgil's famous *ibant obscuri sola sub nocte per umbram*, 'Dimly they went under the lone night through the darkness' (*Aen.* 6.268). For *opacus*, see 707 and n. *ad loc.*

858–63 Apostrophe to the dead, followed by a focus on death's darkness, lethargy, and silence. For apostrophe in the choral odes of *Hercules*, see on 178–82.

qualis est uobis animus/How do you feel: cf. the chorus' question at *Tro.* 1047: *quis status mentis miseris*, 'what will we wretches feel'. Here, however, *uobis* indexes apostrophe, again without a vocative: see on 178–82 and 1122–30.

obrutum tota caput esse terra/The whole earth crushing their head: an obvious inversion of the conventional funerary formula: *sit tibi terra leuis*, 'may earth lie lightly on you'. Seneca's Theseus also inverts the formula in *Phaedra*'s final line (1280). Cf. also Lucr. 3.893.

stat chaos densum…/Dense chaos yawns…: this phrase, with its oxymoronic juxtaposition of 'density' and 'void' (for *chaos* = 'void', see *inane chaos*, *Thy.* 1009, *Epicureum illud chaos*, *Ep. Mor.* 72.9), introduces a powerful, polysyndetic description of the empty darkness of the underworld. Some of the sense of chaos as formless mass may also be present, as Fitch suggests *ad loc.*: see on 604–15. For initial *stat*, see on 533–41.

tenebrae…noctis/darkness…night: again attention to infernal darkness.

silentis otium mundi/mute World's lethargy: for the silence of the underworld, see on 572-6; for its lethargy, see 554, 698-706. For *otium* as an 'unhealthy torpidity' here, see Fitch *ad loc.*

uacuaeque nubes/and empty clouds: for the 'emptiness' of the underworld, see *uacuis locis*, 'empty places', 673, and, more famously, Virgil's chiastic phrase, *domos Ditis uacuas et inania regna*, 'empty halls of Dis and the insubstantial realm', *Aen.* 6.269.

864-74 Personal coda: we should not rush to death, for which we are all doomed at birth. Lines 870-4 were 'imitated' ('paraphrased' is Fitch's term *ad loc.*) by Hughes, *The Misfortunes of Arthur* I.iv.12-16:

> Thine (death) is all that east and west can see:
> For thee we live, our coming is not long:
> Spare us but whiles we may prepare our graves.
> Though thou wert slow, we hasten of ourselves.
> The hour that gave did also take our lives.

See, too, Hughes's 'imitation' of 865-7 at *The Misfortunes of Arthur* I.iii.37-40. Fitch (2018) *ad loc.* also compares Edward Young's eighteenth-century *Night Thoughts* 5.719-20:

> Our life is nothing but our death begun;
> As tapers waste, that instant they take fire.

Some more recent variations are noted below. But Seneca had his own debts. Cf. the Ovidian Orpheus' song to Dis and Proserpina (*Met.* 10.32-5):

> omnia debemur uobis, paulumque morati
> serius aut citius sedem properamus ad unam.
> tendimus huc omnes, haec est domus ultima, uosque
> humani generis longissima regna tenetis.

> In all things we're owed to you; we delay awhile,
> But sooner or later we rush to one abode.
> Hither we all move; this is our final home.
> You hold the longest sway over humankind.

nos illo referat/carry us there: note the immediate move to the personal. The first choral ode ended with a personal coda, where, however, first-person singular forms were used: see on 197-201. This personal coda does not end the ode, but it does end its focus on death. *Illo* for *illuc* is rare in Senecan tragedy: see also *Thy.* 637, 710.

ad id: literally 'to that', i.e. 'there'; only here in the Senecan tragic *corpus*, but found in Seneca's prose works at *Marc.* 18.8, *Ep. Mor.* 18.11, 24.12, and elsewhere.

unde numquam cum semel uenit potuit reuerti/**from where, Once come, he can never return:** an echo here of a Catullan line (3.12) cited elsewhere by Seneca (*Apoc.* 11): *illuc, unde negant redire quemquam*, 'there, from where they say no one returns'. *Semel*, 'once', is widely used in these funereal pronouncements: see e.g. *Pha.* 219–21, Hor. *Odes* 4.7.21–4, Prop. 4.11.3–4. *Potuit*, 'can', is a gnomic perfect, used instead of the present to articulate a universal truth (it states what has been true in the past and can be taken as a general rule). 'Gnomic' perfects are so-called because they are common in proverbs (γνῶμαι) and *sententiae*. They are used frequently in the prose works. The 'gnomic' past is found in English: 'A May flood never did good'; 'A wild goose never laid a tame egg.' See also 1187, 1238.

quid iuuat durum properare fatum/**What joy lies in rushing harsh fate:** this 'rush' (*properare*) to death, anticipated at 840 (*ruit*) and 846 (*properant*) and to be repeated in 873 (*properamus*), was an important motif of earlier odes: see 187 (*properas*), 589 (*properat*). See further on 186–91. For death's 'savage rush' (*properas saeua*), see *Tro.* 1173; for the human 'rush' to death, see *Marc.* 11.2, Ov. *Met.* 10.31 (*properata…fata*, of Eurydice's death). For *iuuat* and perverse desires, see on 112–18. The punctuation of this line by Zwierlein, following Axelson—*quid iuuat, durum, properare, fatum*—has not been followed by recent editors: for discussion see Billerbeck *ad loc.*

facietque inerti uela Cocyto/**and sail listless Cocytus:** for this river of the underworld, see on 679–88. Horace uses the river in a similar context of the inevitability of death: *uisendus ater flumine languido | Cocytos errans*, 'We must view the black Cocytus, wandering with its languid stream' (*Odes* 2.14.17–18). Seneca is being deliberately paradoxical: 'sailing' the 'listless Cocytus' will be difficult: as *inerti* implies (see also 686), there is no wind in the underworld. Note the striking juxtaposition of *inerti uela*.

tibi crescit omne/**For thee grows all:** as Nisbet and Hubbard comment *ad* Hor. *Odes* 2.8.17: '*tibi crescit* may be a phrase applied to sacrificial victims'; if so, it is singularly appropriate, as well as darkly ironic. Note again apostrophe without a vocative (supplied at 872). For apostrophe in choral odes, see on 178–82.

quod occasus uidet et quod ortus/**that The sun sees, set and rising:** cf. Ovid *Met.* 1.354: *terrarum quascumque uident occasus et ortus*, 'of whatever lands the sun sees, set and rising'. For similar global images, see 37–8 and n. *ad loc.* For the *occasus/obitus* and *ortus* combination, see on 372–83.

With *uidet et,* note the repetition of the same syllable at the end and begin-ning of juxtaposed words; see 67 and n. *ad loc.*

parce uenturis/spare The doomed: cf. Ovid's plea to the gods 'to spare one doomed/about to die' (*morituro parcere*) at *Tr.* 3.3.31. For *parcere* in Senecan tragedy, see on 1015–17.

tibi, Mors, paramur…properamus ipsi/For thee, Death, we are groomed…ourselves we rush: apostrophe to Death, as by Phaedra at *Pha.* 1188–90 and by Hecuba at *Tro.* 1171–5; it is found, too, in the Attic trage-dians (e.g. Soph. *Phil.* 797–8). Note the hymnic repetition and alliteration, and the articulation of a regular Senecan proposition; cf. *NQ* 2.59.6: *omnes reseruamur ad mortem,* 'We are all reserved for death'. It is also an Ovidian proposition: see *Met.* 10.32–5 (cited above). Cf. also Megara's comment in MacLeish's *Herakles* (1967), Act II: 'Destiny waits for us. We go ourselves'. Mark the first-person plural forms, in line with *nos* (864) and as at 185, where a similar statement is made: *Stygias ultro quaerimus undas,* 'We seek Stygian waves ourselves'. Contrast the use of singular forms in the personal coda of the first choral ode: see on 197–201. For the *properare* motif, see above.

sis licet segnis/Though thou be slow: for *licet* with the subjunctive, see 21–2 and n. *ad loc.*

prima quae uitam dedit hora carpit/Life's first hour begins its end: cf. *Prou.* 5.7, *Marc.* 10.5, 21.6, esp. *Oed.* 988 (*primusque dies dedit extremum,* 'The first day has fixed the last') and *Ep. Mor.* 24.19–20 (*cotidie morimur. cotidie enim demitur aliqua pars uitae,* 'We die each day. For each day a part of life is taken from us'); also *Ep. Mor.* 1.2, 58.23, 120.18. Cf. the famous inscription (= Manil. 4.16), *nascentes morimur finisque ab origine pendet* ('As we are born, we are dying, and our end hangs from our beginning', *CIL* II.4426). The idea that one's death begins at birth goes back to Homer (*Il.* 20.127–8, 23.78–9); it reappears in early modern and Renaissance drama: see e.g. *prima dies ultima nouit,* 'the first day knows the last' (Loschi, *Achilles* 936); 'the first day leads the last' (Hughes, *The Misfortunes of Arthur* II.iii.128); and displays itself in twenty-first-century media: see e.g. Walter White's remark in the award-winning television series, *Breaking Bad* (Season 4, Episode 8, 2011, written by Sam Catlin and George Mastras, AMC): 'Every life comes with a death sentence' (which seems to combine the lemmatized aphorism with *Ep. Mor.* 71.15: *omne humanum genus, quodque est quodque erit, morte damnatum est,* 'The whole human race, both what is and what will be, has a death sentence'). Note also Orlando Jackson's tart comment in the more recent Canadian television series, also award-winning, *Sensitive Skin* (Season 1, Episode 2, 2014, written by Bob Martin, HBO Canada): 'We start dying as soon as we're born'. The beginning of the third millennium CE is a Senecan age. For Seneca on death and time, see on 178–91. For *carpere* = 'erode', 'wear away', see *Ep. Mor.* 26.4, 120.18; as a euphemism for 'to kill', see *Pha.* 476, *Oed.* 113. Even in its most cited and allegedly most affirmative occurrence (*carpe diem*, Hor. *Odes* 1.11), *carpere* has a melancholic resonance. For the closural use of *sententiae*, see on 125–204.

875–92 The Chorus return to the theme of Hercules' praises, which they abandoned at 837. Their metrical mode switches from sapphics to exuberant glyconics, a terse, octosyllabic Aeolic line (here with a spondaic 'base': see Introd. §IX), used by Seneca (*Med.* 75–92) and Catullus (poem 61) for the festive celebration and joy of a wedding-song or *epithalamium*. Here the celebration is of Hercules' pacification of earth and hell. It is a much stronger presentation of the *Pax Herculea* than the brief reference to Heracles 'making peaceful the life of mortals and destroying fearsome beasts' (*Herac.* 698–700) at the end of Euripides' second stasimon. That stasimon employs Aeolic metres, including glyconics. Cf. also the glyconics sung by Euripides' chorus in the third stasimon's triumphalist celebration of Heracles' slaying of Lycus at *Herac.* 781ff. It is difficult not to think that Euripides prompted Seneca to adopt the present metre.

875–81 Address to the Theban people (including farmers outside the city) and to each other to begin the celebratory supplications and sacrifices. Again there are no vocatives: see on 178–82. Commands of this kind (some addressed to persons not in Thebes) obviously specify the range of appropriate activities for the festal day rather than instruct forms of immediate onstage action. Cf. the choral commands issued during the *epithalamium* ode of *Medea*. For mixed dancing, involving members of the chorus and others, see *Ag.* 315–18•. For sacrificial language and imagery in *Hercules*, see on 918–24.

Thebis laeta dies adest/Thebes' joyous day is here: the Chorus in Euripides' *Heracles* similarly celebrate after the killing of Lycus (*Herac.* 763–4), but their celebration and their praises of Hercules are more sustained (763–814). Note *laeta/laetus dies* (rather than *festus dies*, 'festal day': *Thy.* 942–3, 970): see Cic. *Phil.* 1.30, 10.8; Livy 22.30.6; Hor. *Odes* 4.2.41; Ov. *Fas.* 1.87. For the feminine form of *dies*, see 586 and n. *ad loc.*

aras tangite supplices/Touch altars in prayer: a ritual of thanksgiving supplication (*supplicatio*) is being requested. For touching the altar as part of Roman religious ritual (supplicatory/sacrificial/juratory etc.), see e.g. Plaut. *Rud.* 694–5, 1333; Hor. *Odes* 3.23.17; Virg. *Aen.* 4.219, 12.201; Ov. *Met.* 5.103–4. See also 503 above. Only plural forms of *ara* (see also 503, 899, 911, 922, 1040, 1255; *Oed.* 303, *Tro.* 1106, *Med.* 808, *Thy.* 706) occur in Seneca's tragedies. But *aras* here seems a genuine plural. Virgil, too, shows a preference for the plural form of this word.

pingues caedite uictimas/Slay the fattest victims: *caedere* is used especially of 'slaughtering' sacrificial animals: 899, 1037, *Tro.* 296, Virg. *Geo.* 2.537, 3.23, 4.547. It is used of the 'sacrificial' killing of Priam at *Tro.* 141, and the slaughter of Pelias at *Med.* 259 and of Thyestes' children at *Thy.* 1058.

permixtae maribus nurus/young women join with Husbands: this seems rather different from the double choruses of girls and boys familiar from Horace's *Odes* (1.21) and *Carmen Saeculare*, and from Catullus 34 and 62. Older representatives of the sexes seem involved.

cessent deposito iugo/Put down their yoke and rest: the cessation of work on a 'feast day', *dies festus* or *dies nefastus*, was standard in Roman religion: Plut. *Quaest. Rom.* 25, Serv. *ad Verg. Geo.* 1.268, although certain minor agricultural work was allowed: Virg. *Geo.* 1.268–75, Colum. 2.21.3. For the specific image here, see Tib. 2.1.5–7, Ov. *Fas.* 1.665. For Roman referentiality in *Hercules*, see on 46–52.

arui fertilis incolae/tillers of rich fields: for Boeotia's rich fields, see *Pho.* 129–30: *Boeotios…agros uberis…soli*, 'Boeotian fields of rich soil'. See also Lycus' bragging monologue at 332–4. The verbal context here gives *incolae* a more precise meaning than 'dwellers' (*Pha.* 922), bringing out some of the force of *colere* = 'to till/cultivate' (*OLD* 3); hence 'tillers' (also chosen by Fitch 2018).

882–8 The Chorus describe Herculean Peace as global in a manner reminiscent of the imperial *Pax Romana*: east and west (883), south (884–5), the whole world (886–7). For Roman referentiality in *Hercules*, see on 46–52. For Euripides' praise of Heracles as pacifier, see *Herac.* 698–700 (cited on 875–92).

Pax est Herculea manu/Peace from Hercules' hand Reigns: for Hercules as pacifier, civilizer, and saviour, see 249–51 (esp. *pacis auctorem*, 'author of peace'), 271–2, 442–3, 890, 929, *Med.* 637, and *Ben.* 1.13.3, where he is described as *malorum hostis, bonorum uindex, terrarum marisque pacator*, 'the enemy of evil, defender of good, pacifier of land and sea' (1.13.3). In the prologue to *Hercules Oetaeus* Hercules prays to Jupiter: *protuli pacem tibi*, 'I have brought forth peace for thee' (*HO* 3). Cf. Eur. *Herac.* 20, Prop.

3.11.19, 4.9.73, Ov. *Her*. 9.13–14 (cited below), Epictetus 3.24.13, 3.26.2, and Introd. 66. For 'Hercules' hand' and the mastery of others, see Hor. *Odes* 2.12.6, where again the phrase *Herculea manu* (instrumental ablative, as here) is used. For the *manus* motif in *Hercules*, see on 118–22; for the use of the adjective *Herculeus*, see 72 and n. *ad loc.*

Auroram inter et Hesperum/**from Dawn to Hesperus:** Aurora (Greek Eos) was goddess of the dawn, sometimes identified as daughter of the Titan Pallas (Ov. *Fas*. 4.373, *Met*. 9.421) or the Titan Hyperion (Ov. *Fas*. 5.159). Hesperus (or Vesper) was the evening star (son of Aurora and Astraeus, Atlas or the mortal Cephalus—traditions vary), correctly identified by the ancients with the planet Venus and the morning star: see e.g. *Pha*. 749–52, *Ag*. 819–21, Cic. *ND* 2.53. The lemmatized phrase has both a temporal and a geographical meaning: between sunrise and sunset, from east to west (*Hesperia* being a standard term for 'the west'). Note the postponement of the preposition: see 145 and n.; for *inter*, see 148 and n.

qua Sol medium tenens umbras corporibus negat/**where the midday Sun Gives bodies no shadows:** the tropics, the south, described in an unconsciously ironic way to invert the situation in hell, where shades, *umbrae*, are denied bodies. For no (or almost no) shadows being cast in Egypt: see Strabo 17.1.48; Luc. 2.587, 9.528–30; Pliny *HN* 2.183. With *medium tenens* one may supply *diem, iter, cursum,* or *sim.* (= 'at midday' or 'at mid-journey'), or treat *medium* as a substantival use of the adjective (cf. *Med*. 768). Unlike most modern editors, I have chosen to capitalize the *s* of *Sol* (as at 37 and 61) in the midst of this collection of names. Zwierlein prints a lower-case *s*.

alluitur/**is lapped:** for *alluere* used to mark geographical location, see also *Oed*. 475, *Tro*. 227, *Apoc*. 7.2.13, *Helu*. 7.2, Virg. *Geo*. 2.158, *Aen*. 8.149.

longo Tethyos ambitu/**Tethys' long circuit:** a reference to the great sea encompassing the world known as 'Oceanus', for whom Tethys deputizes here: see on 19–29. Cf. the Ovidian Deianira's description of Hercules' global pacification (*Her*. 9.13–14):

> respice uindicibus pacatum uiribus orbem,
> qua latam Nereus caerulus ambit humum.
>
> Look at the world pacified by your vengeful strength,
> Where blue Nereus circles the broad earth.

Tethyos is a Greek genitive singular form.

Alcidae domuit labor/**Alcides' toil has tamed:** the climactic use of *labor* here illustrates not only Seneca's 'noun style' (see on 11–18), but shows the style's dramatic and thematic potential. On the imperial implications of *domuit*, 'tamed', note Seneca's description of Augustus' pacification of the Alpine regions as 'taming' (*perdomat*, *Breu. Vit.* 4.5).

889-92 *uada Tartari*/**Tartarus' streams:** for Tartarus, see on 86-8; for *uada*, see on 679-88.

pacatis...inferis/**Pacified hell:** of course Hercules did no such thing. But the ideological thrust is clear: Hercules is the great pacifier of hell and earth. For Hercules as *pacator*, see on 882-8.

iam nullus superest timor/**Now no fear is left:** for the ironic analogy with Epicurus, see Introd. §VII, 87-8. Banishment of the fear of death was a prime Epicurean goal.

nil ultra iacet inferos/**Nothing lies beyond hell:** for final choral lines, see on 1131-7.

Enter **HERCULES** *from stage left (the city), dressed as before but drenched with blood. He is accompanied by* **SLAVES** *and* **ATTENDANTS** *leading animals (or carrying sculpted heads of the same) for the planned sacrifice:* the animals, attendants, and paraphernalia of sacrifice will remain onstage throughout Act IV, drawing attention to the perversion of sacrifice exhibited by Hercules' slaughter of kin rather than kine. In terms of staging, live animals could certainly have been used in this scene (they were used, for example, for the staging of Agamemnon's entrance in the performance of Accius' *Clytaemestra* at Pompey's Theatre in 55 BCE: Cic. *Fam.* 7.1.2), but it seems perhaps—for obvious reasons—less likely that they would have been used for a sacrificial scene. I favour, as in my editions of *Oedipus* (before 288), *Medea* (before 56), and *Agamemnon* (778), the use of props (sculpted heads) instead of the animals themselves. On the whole issue of live animals versus props, see Boyle (2011) on the extispicy scene in *Oedipus* (*ad Oed.* 291-402).

893-4 The Chorus address the entering Hercules, in effect announcing his arrival on stage and binding ode to act. For this (occasional) function of the Senecan chorus, see on 205-523 (introd.). The switch to the second-person singular (*tege*, 894) marks a return to the second-person address to Hercules with which they began (*ausus es*, 834).

sacrificus/**For sacrifice:** the Chorus see that Hercules is about to sacrifice and they give appropriate instructions, which he will follow (912). In so doing they strike a thematic note. For the ensuing act will feature a conflation of sacrifice and bloody murder: see e.g. 1035-42. For the language and imagery of sacrifice in *Hercules*, see on 918-24. For Seneca's fondness for adjectives ending in *-ficus*, see on 57-63. *Sacrificus*, which occurs also at *Ag.*

166, 584, *Med.* 38, perhaps originated with Ovid (see e.g. *Met.* 12.249); it is here used predicatively.

Stantes...comas dilecta tege populo/crown rough Hair with cherished poplar: poplar was esp. associated with Hercules (Virg. *Ecl.* 7.61: *populus Alcidae gratissima*, 'Poplar is most pleasing to Alcides'; see also Theoc. 2.121, Ov. *Her.* 9.64, Virg. *Geo.* 2.66, *Aen.* 8.276). Poplar wreaths were worn by Evander and the Salii as they sacrificed at the Ara Maxima in *Aeneid* 8 (276–7, 286); and the wearing of them continued in republican and imperial Rome for sacrifices at the Ara Maxima. The normal Roman practice when sacrificing was to cover the head with one's toga, but an exception was made in sacrifices at the Herculean Ara Maxima, which were done in the Greek manner 'with uncovered head' (*operto capite*, Macr. 3.6.17), i.e. with head wreathed rather than covered. The Chorus make reference here to a Greek custom, but it is one practised in imperial Rome. Hercules repeats the poplar wreath requirement at 912. See also *HO* 578, 789, where again not only the poplar wreath but also Hercules' 'stiff' (*rigentem...comam*) or 'rough' (*horrentem comam*) hair is mentioned. For Roman referentiality in *Hercules*, see on 46–52.

Act IV (895–1053)

The fourth acts of Seneca's plays vary considerably. That of *Hercules* is closest to the fourth act of *Oedipus* (764–881), in that it presents what Aristotle terms a situational 'reversal', περιπέτεια (*Poet.* 1452a22–9), in respect of the protagonist, who in Seneca's *Oedipus* moves from anxiety to knowledge and in *Hercules* from vainglorious exultation to lethal madness. Act IV of *Hercules* rivals two very different fourth acts, those of *Agamemnon* (659–807) and *Medea* (670–848), in terms of spectacle, with its initial, crowded scene of prayer and sacrifice dissolving into a prolonged, multi-delusional attack of madness, involving darkening skies, blazing constellations, a Titanomachy and Gigantomachy, and the onset and vision of the Furies themselves, followed by the bloody murders of sons and wife—murders realized essentially offstage but described gruesomely by a powerless Amphitryon, who offers himself as Hercules' final victim, even as the great killer collapses before him.

The act has three parts, each of which in performance would have made potent use of the Roman theatrical space (see on 1–124 introd.). The action takes place on a crowded stage, filled with people celebrating Hercules' killing of Lycus and awaiting or preparing the thanksgiving sacrifice. Present are Theseus, Amphitryon, Megara, and Hercules' sons, the Theban Chorus, who just sang celebratory glyconics, Hercules and several slaves and attendants, who entered with him and lead animals for the sacrifice (or carry sculpted heads of the same). The act's first part (i. 895–939), which precedes the madness, consists of Hercules' victory speech, instructions for sacrifice to attendants and to Theseus (who exits), and his 'Golden Age speech', which is broken off as madness and hallucinations come upon him. The second part of the act (ii. 939–86) embraces Hercules' chaotic hallucinations, ranging from darkness at midday to fiery threats in the heavens, battles between Olympians and either Titans or Giants, thence to the Furies with whip, torches, and snakes. The final part (iii. 987–1053) is the slaughter of family which ensues, the attempt of Amphitryon to join the slaughtered, and the collapse of Hercules onstage. For the language of sacrifice, see on 918–24; for perverted sacrifice as the master metaphor of Act IV, see Introd. §VII, 88–93.

Hercules' madness and collapse were so well known in the Renaissance that epilepsy was often called *morbus Herculeus/Herculanus*, 'the Hercules disease' (see Soellner 1958: 314, Riley 2008: 99), as it is still sometimes today. The idea goes back at least to the Hippocratic corpus (*Diseases of Women* 1.7) and to the *Problems* assigned to Aristotle, in which it is claimed that epilepsy's nomenclature as the 'sacred disease' derives from Heracles, whose disorder was attributable to black bile (*Problems* 30.953a10–19). Black bile (*atra bilis*) is at the centre of Thomas Farnaby's seventeenth-century explanation of Hercules' madness: its excretions cause the sensation of darkness, delusions, wild delirium, and melancholy, followed by sleep in which the 'black humour' (*ater humor*) is exhaled (*ad Herc.* 954, 1082). More modern diagnoses of Hercules' sudden outburst of violence against his family have likened the hero's mental condition to post-traumatic stress disorder or combat trauma (see Bernstein 2017: 111–12). The extraordinary movements of the *dramatis personae* in this act and the complexity and rapidly changing nature of the dramatic action have required more stage directions than are usual. Several of these stage directions (see esp. 987–1053) are, as Fitch notes *ad loc.*, 'written into the text'.

For further discussion of Act IV and its dramatic and thematic function in the play, see Introd. §VII.

Metre: iambic trimeter. See Introd. §IX.

The time is now midday: see *medium diem* at 939.

895–918 Hercules' opening speech embraces: (i) Statement of victory and intention to offer a thanksgiving sacrifice (895–99); (ii) Invocation of several deities (900–8); (iii) General instructions for the sacrifice (908–12); (iv) Instructions to Theseus (913–18).

895–9 Conspicuous military language: see on 19–29. MacLeish in *Herakles* (1967) creates similarly vainglorious sentiments for his entering hero: see Introd. §VIII, 142.

Vltrice dextra…ore/**My avenging hand…bit the earth:** second terse description of Lycus' death following Theseus' first and witty depiction earlier (643–4). Notice how Seneca has Hercules pick up Lycus's *uictrici dextra* (399–400) and pointedly change it (if one accepts the reading of *A* rather than the *uictrice* of *E*). *Vltrice*, read also by Trevet and Farnaby, seems clearly preferable because of the *poenae* of 897 and what would otherwise be a redundant *uictor* of 898 (see Fitch *ad loc.*). Zwierlein, Chaumartin, and Billerbeck also print *ultrice*. For *dextra* (and the *manus* motif), see on 118–22.

fusus/**sprawl:** the word will later be used by the Chorus of the post-madness Hercules (1082).

aduerso…terram cecidit ore/**He crashed and bit the earth:** the Latin constitutes 'eine epische Phrase', according to Billerbeck *ad loc.*, citing Homer *Il.* 2.418, *Od.* 22.94. The description seems index of a decisive, rather than 'ignominious' (Fitch *ad loc.*) defeat: see Virg. *Aen.* 10.489 (death of Pallas), 11.418 (death of the ideal warrior); Sil. 15.380 (death of Marcellus). Cf. also *Oed.* 480. *Ore* is an instrumental ablative: see Woodcock §43.1.

quisquis comes…et poenae comes/**each comrade…comrade, too, in death:** Hercules (unknowingly) competes with Theseus (643–4) for the wittier description of Lycus' death. His ironic verbal play reveals, as one might expect and as did the description of Theseus, a complete lack of empathy for the victims of the vengeance. *Quisquis*, 'each' (lit. 'any'), shows the completeness of the revenge, which is still less than the bloody massacre of all disloyal Thebans envisaged by Euripides' Heracles (*Herac.* 568–73). For this darkly ironic use of *comes* (*poenae comes* = lit. 'comrade in punishment/death-sentence'), see *Ag.* 926: *comes paternae…neci*, 'father's comrade in death'; and *Oed.* 780: *regio fato comes*, 'the king's comrade in death'. Cf. also Val. Max. 5.5.4: *comes fraternae neci*, 'brother's comrade in death'; Virg. *Aen.* 2.294: *fatorum comites*, 'comrades in your fate'; Ov. *Met.* 4.151–2: *leti…comes*, 'comrade in death', *Ibis* 630: *comites…necis*, 'comrades in death'. Note the rhetorical device (*conuersio* or *epistrophe*) employed at 896–7 of ending successive verses with the same word: see also e.g. 446–7,

643–4, 1229–30, 1242–3; *Tro.* 335–6, 967–8, 1006–7, 1039–40; *Oed.* 685–6; *Ag.* 111–12, 691–2, 754–5; *Thy.* 207–8, 515–16, 596–7.

nunc sacra patri uictor et superis/Now victor, I'll sacrifice to father and gods: a rich line bringing together the motifs of conquest and sacrifice which feature largely in this play. The latter will become the master image of Act IV (see on 918–24). For the contrast with Heracles' post-Lycus sacrifice of purification in Euripides' play, see below and Introd. §VII, 89. The divergent potential referents of *patri* (Jupiter or Amphitryon) wraps Hercules' discourse in ambiguity. For *uincere*/*uictor* and Hercules, see on 63–8.

caesisque meritas uictimis aras colam/Honouring due altars with slain victims: Seneca revels in the ambiguity of *uictima*, the technical term for a sacrificial 'victim'. He has both Medea and Atreus deliberately conflate animal and human 'victim' as the word's referent (*Med.* 39, *Thy.* 545). Hercules is perhaps less cognizant here of the ambiguity than Medea and Atreus, but he will quickly graduate to full knowledge at 922, when he explicitly includes Lycus in the word's compass. The audience of course appreciate the ambiguity from the start; for they know Hercules' 'victims' will be his family. For Seneca's use of the plural form of *ara* (here perhaps a genuine plural), see on 875–81. For *caedere* = 'sacrificially slay', see on 875–81; for sacrificial imagery in the play, see on 918–24.

900–8 Hercules invokes, as preface to his prayer, four deities: Pallas (Athena/Minerva), Bacchus, Phoebus Apollo, Diana, all, as children of Jupiter, half-brothers or half-sisters of Hercules. The hero's religious behaviour here contrasts with that of the Euripidean Heracles, who engages in a ritual purification of the palace from the blood spilt in the slaying of Lycus (*Herac.* 922–7). Note that Seneca's Hercules not only invokes four deities, but does so in respect of their successful infliction of violence. For prayers in *Hercules* and Senecan tragedy, see on 205–78.

Te, te/To thee, thee: for the *geminatio* (duplication) of *te*, see on 92–9; for similar *geminatio* in a prayer, see *Oed.* 249, 1042, *Pha.* 663, 888.

laborum socia et adiutrix/partner, helpmate of my toils: Homer mentions both Athena and Hermes (*Il.* 8.362–9, *Od.* 11.623–6) as guides and helpers of Hercules; Hesiod mentions Athena (*Theog.* 316–18). *Socius*, 'partner/ally', is a quintessentially Roman term, used elsewhere by Seneca to indicate a shared enterprise: *laborum socia*, 'partner in my labours', 900; *furoris socius*, 'ally in passion', *Pha.* 96; *callidi socios doli*, 'partners in a devious plot', *Oed.* 668; *socia...scelerum*, 'partner in crime', *Oed.* 1024; *socia maeroris mei*, 'partner of my grief', *Med.* 568; *pericli socia*, 'partner in peril', *Ag.* 234. For *socius* with the genitive, see on 309–13. *Adiutrix*, used by Ovid's

Medea in an invocation of Hecate (*Met.* 7.195), is a Senecan *hapax*; for *-trix* nouns/adjectives (some of which are perhaps Senecan coinages), see *uictrix* (22), *dominatrix* (*Pha.* 85), *miratrix* (*Pha.* 742), *domitrix* (*Tro.* 816), *machinatrix* (*Med.* 266), *exprobratrix* (*Ben.* 7.22.2), *contemptrix* (*Ben.* 4.2.4, *Ep. Mor.* 88.29). As with nouns ending in *-tor* (see on 299–302), Seneca clearly liked the theatrical, portentous sound of such words.

belligera Pallas/Soldier Pallas: from Homer onwards Pallas Athena/ Minerva was represented as a war-goddess and almost ubiquitously imaged as such in art, often wearing the aegis (see next n.): to Horace she is 'bold in battle' (*proeliis audax*, *Odes* 1.12.21); to the dramatist of *Octavia*, she is 'the goddess ferocious in arms' (*ferox armis dea*, *Oct.* 546); in *Agamemnon* she is depicted as 'lunging at Dardan towers with a spear' (*Dardanias saepe petisti cuspide turres*, *Ag.* 358–8•). For *belligera* again of Pallas/Minerva, see Mart. *Epig.* 7.1.1. The epithet does not appear in Seneca's prose works, but is used of a deity again at *Pha.* 188, 808, in both cases of Mars. To the Romans this daughter of Jupiter/Zeus was a most important goddess, being part of the Capitoline triad in the great temple of Iuppiter Optimus Maximus.

Aegis: in Greek and Roman literature the 'aegis' seems to come in two forms: (i) as a weapon to be shaken (*Il.* 4.167ff., Virg. *Aen.* 8.353–4), associated with Zeus/Jupiter, sometimes lent to Apollo; (ii) as a weapon to be worn, associated with Pallas Athena/Minerva, a kind of breastplate (Hom. *Il.* 2.447–9, *Il.* 5.738–42, Virg. *Aen.* 8.435–8, Ov. *Met.* 2.754–5), or, as here (see also Hor. *Odes* 3.4.57), a shield over the left arm, burnished with the scales of serpents and featuring at its centre the Gorgoneion, i.e. the head of Medusa, encompassed by wreathed snakes. The Gorgoneion, which is referred to here—note the focus on the 'petrifying face', *ore saxifico* (of Medusa, see also *Ag.* 530)—was frequently represented in art and was most famously to be seen on Phidias' great statue of Athena in the Parthenon (reproduced on the replica of that statue in the Parthenon, Nashville, Tennessee, sculpted by Alan LeQuire, unveiled in 1990). For a canonic, literary description of the aegis, see Virg. *Aen.* 8.435–8.

ore saxifico/petrifying face: of the head of Medusa, the Gorgoneion; see previous n. *Saxificus* is a Senecan *hapax*, derived from Ovid's own description of Medusa and her face: *Met.* 5.217, *Ibis* 553; Lucan (9.670) and Silius (10.177) also use it of Medusa. For Seneca's fondness for adjectives ending in *-ficus*, see on 57–63.

adsit Lycurgi domitor et Rubri Maris/Come, tamer of Lycurgus and the Red Sea: invocation of Bacchus (Greek Dionysus), patron god of Thebes and son of Jupiter and Cadmus' daughter, Semele; see on 11–18. Lycurgus, whom

Bacchus is said here to have 'tamed', was a Thracian or Hellespontine king, who opposed Bacchus and his followers, as they travelled from Asia into Europe. Lycurgus captured or killed some Bacchantes and was punished horrifically by Bacchus for this. The story was dramatized by Aeschylus and Naevius, and is alluded to at *Oed.* 471, Hor. *Odes* 2.19.16, Prop. 3.17.23, Ov. *Met.* 4.22–3, *Tr.* 5.3.39, and Stat. *Theb.* 4.385–6. Homer recounted a different version, in which Lycurgus was punished by Zeus (*Il.* 6.130–40). The *Mare Rubrum* or *Pelagus Rubens* ('Red Sea', 'Red Ocean') were terms which the Romans used to designate not only the modern Red Sea but all the seas surrounding Arabia, including those of the Arabian and Persian Gulf: see Pliny *HN* 6.107–8, Strabo 16.4.20ff.—and *Oed.* 120, *Thy.* 371–3, *HO* 660. The reference is to Bacchus' triumphs in the east, especially his legendary conquest of India (see e.g. *Oed.* 113–23, 424–8; Ov. *Met.* 4.20–1; Stat. *Theb.* 4.387–9). Fitch *ad loc.* and Nisbet and Hubbard *ad* Hor. *Odes* 2.19.17 suggest that a specific Moses-like incident is being referred to here, as in the Horace passage. For *adesse* of the epiphany of a god, see on 275–8. Note Hercules' use of *domitor*, 'tamer': see on 618–21. For Seneca's fondness for nouns ending in *-tor*, see on 299–302.

uirenti...thyrso/green thyrsus: the Bacchic wand, see on 472–6. I have printed A's *uirenti*; Zwierlein favours E's *uirente*. Given the frequency of both ablatival forms in the MSS either is possible. I have chosen *uirenti* because, as Fitch (2004b: 25) observes, spondees are much more likely in the third foot of a Senecan iambic trimeter. The ablative seems best taken as instrumental.

geminumque numen/twin gods: also at *Ag.* 381 (*numen geminum*) and *Med.* 700 (*gemina numina*), applied to Phoebus and Diana/Trivia.

Phoebus et Phoebi soror/Phoebus and Phoebus' sister: Phoebus Apollo and his sister, Diana, here invoked through a kind of polyptoton used elsewhere by Seneca (*Tro.* 38, *Pho.* 647–8). Initially the deities seem to be invoked *qua* sun-god and moon-goddess, as at 15, 132–6 (see nn. *ad locc.*), but then Hercules specifies and emphasizes Diana's skill with the bow (see next n.). Diana is, of course, a most complicated divinity, who manifests herself sometimes as Hecate or Trivia, sometimes as Luna/the Moon, sometimes as Juno Lucina, goddess of childbirth, and sometimes (so here, Hercules suggests) as paradigmatic huntress: see Boyle *ad Med.* 1–4, 5–7. For Phoebus, see on 19–29.

soror sagittis aptior, Phoebus lyrae/Sister skilled in arrows, Phoebus in the lyre: an example of the rhetorical figure, *regressio* or ἐπάνοδος, 'returning' (repetition and differentiation: Quint. *Inst.* 9.3.35); cf. *Med.* 697, Prop. 3.14.18. It is employed here to include laudatory material on the two deities, in keeping with the form of invocatory prayer or kletic hymn. Far from being, as Fitch comments *ad loc.*, 'empty' wordplay, it is an ironic precursor of what is to come. Hercules pauses to signal the skill which will begin his downfall and the prop (arrow) around which the final act will conduct its moral debate. With the phrase, *sagittis aptior*, lit. 'rather fit for arrows', cf. *caestibus aptior*, lit. 'rather fit for boxing-gloves', applied to Pollux at *Med.* 89. Along with Billerbeck *ad loc.* I do not take *aptior* as a genuine comparative. Rather, it connotes here a considerable degree of skill rather than 'more' skill (than that to be attributed to Phoebus, which would be singularly inappropriate in a prayer, as well as unpersuasive).

fraterque quisquis…frater/And all…stepmother: note the epanadiplosis/epanalepsis in the Latin text and the emphasis given to the second occurrence by its pointed qualification. For the *generalis inuocatio* (*quisquis…*), see 600–3 and n. For epanadiplosis/epanalepsis, see on 637–40.

non ex nouerca frater/not brothers From my stepmother: these include those already listed (Bacchus, Phoebus) plus Perseus, Orion, and the Tyndarids, all mentioned in Juno's prologue. The dramatist of *Hercules Oetaeus* clearly borrowed from this phrase, when he has Hercules declare of Mars: *est frater quidem—| sed ex nouerca*, 'He indeed is my brother—but from my stepmother' (*HO* 1313–14). For *nouerca*, 'stepmother', see on 19–29; for Hercules' obsession with Juno, see on 604–15. For climactic half-lines, see on 40–6.

908–12 Hercules issues instructions for the sacrifice to his attendants and slaves. In the geographical references to the materials of sacrifice (909–10), which suggest the boundaries of empire, he speaks like an imperial Roman. For Roman referentiality in *Hercules*, see on 46–52.

Huc appellite greges opimos/Drive here the prime flocks: the same verb is used of driving cattle to the altar for sacrifice at *Oed.* 299, where again an unadorned imperative is addressed to slaves, guards, attendants, or other *personae mutae*; see on 1048–53 (*famuli*). *Opimus* is regularly used of prime sacrificial victims: see 923; *Tro.* 296; *Oed.* 303, 844; Varr. *RR* 2.1.20. It is also used of 'prime' spoils: see 48 and n. *ad loc.* For a conflation of the two meanings, see 923 and n. *ad loc.*

quidquid Indorum est seges/Whatever crop the Indians yield: the 'crop' concerned is presumably either frankincense (*tus*) or nard (*costum*): see Ov. *Fas.* 1.341, 3.720. I have accepted Düring's 1914 emendation of the EA reading despite Fitch's criticisms of it *ad loc.* I favour neither the radical conjecture of Schmidt (*quidquid Indi aruis secant*), accepted by Fitch, nor the lacuna after 909 printed by Leo, Zwierlein, and Billerbeck.

Arabesque odoris quidquid arboribus legunt/**Whatever Arabs pluck from perfumed trees:** the reference perhaps, as Fitch suggests *ad loc.*, is to cinnamon (see *Oed.* 117), which, however, as he observes, was not grown in Arabia but imported to Rome via Arabia from Indonesia. Arabia (the southern part of which was known as Arabia Felix or Arabia Beata) was known especially for its export of spices and precious stones. Other possibilities here are frankincense or myrrh or both; see the elder Pliny *HN* 6.154, 12.51: *principalia ergo in illa* (*Arabia*) *tus atque murra*, 'the chief products of Arabia are frankincense and myrrh', *HN* 6.154. Seneca may even be tapping into Ovid's description of the mythological formation of myrrh (*Ars* 1.287) as the 'tears which she (Myrrha) sheds from the perfumed tree' (*lacrimis quas arbore fundit odora*). For Arabia and frankincense (*tus*), see Virg. *Geo.* 1.57, 2.117, *Aen.* 1.416–17; VF 6.138; *HO* 792–3. Note that *tus* is ordered to be thrown onto the flames at 918. See also Agamemnon on the verge of sacrifice at *Ag.* 807 (*Arabumque donis*, 'and with Arabian gifts'). I have not construed *odoris* as a partitive genitive governed by the neuter relative pronoun *quidquid* (as at *Thy.* 21, 509; *Tro.* 33, etc.), but (along with Fitch *ad loc.*) as an epithet modifying *arboribus* in line with Ovid's depiction of Myrrha's tears.

aras/**altar:** the single stage altar is meant. Only plural forms of *ara* are found in Senecan tragedy: see on 875–81.

populea … arbor/**poplar tree:** for its importance in Herculean rituals, see on 893–4.

Puts poplar wreath … on his head: Hercules will be wearing the poplar wreath when he begins the sacrificial prayer at 926. See further on 893–4.

913–17 Hercules gives Theseus particular instructions to conduct appropriate religious rites at several sacred sites in Thebes. As both Fitch and Billerbeck *ad loc.* note, this is clearly a device on Seneca's part to get Theseus offstage for the 'madness and slaughter' scene. Scholars who think that Theseus returns later in this act (or stays onstage throughout the act: see below) miss the dramatic point of these instructions.

ramus oleae fronde gentili/**an olive bough's native leaves:** the olive tree was sacred to Athena/Minerva and it was her gift of the olive tree that enabled her to win the contest for Attica carved on the west pediment of the Parthenon. As king of Athens, it behoves Theseus to wear an olive wreath. *Gentili*, 'native', has strong force here: native to the city of Athens and to the Athenian *gens*. The ablative seems best taken as instrumental.

Theseu/**Theseus:** for vocatives at the beginning of an iambic line and addresses to a character by name, see on 637–40.

Tonantem nostra adorabit manus/My hand will worship the Thunder-god: Hercules unknowingly cites Jupiter by the name with which Juno sarcastically began this play. For the *manus* motif, see on 118–22.

conditores urbis/city founders: Cadmus (and presumably also the surviving Spartoi), and the so-called second 'founders', Amphion and Zethus: see on 249–58, 258–67.

siluestria trucis antra Zethi/woodland Cave of wild Zethus: the cave at Eleutherae near Mt Cithaeron in Boeotia where Amphion and Zethus were born and abandoned by their mother, Antiope, after delivering them. They were reared by herdsmen. See Paus. 1.38.9, Apollod. 3.5.5. While Amphion became the famed musician, Zethus became a herdsman and a hunter; hence the epithet *trux*, 'wild/brutal/savage': see on 769–81. For Zethus, mentioned also at *Oed*. 609–11 and *Pho*. 20, see on 19–29, 258–67. Note that the final *a* of *antra* is short despite being followed by *z*; cf. *Oed*. 421, 541; *Ag*. 433; *Thy*. 845. See Fitch *ad loc*.

nobilis Dircen aquae/Dirce's famous spring: a sacred spring near Thebes (*sacra…Dirce, Pho*. 126), named after an early queen of Thebes, who was tied to the horns of a bull and killed by Amphion and Zethus for mistreating their mother, Antiope. One of the city's seven gates was named after it. The genitive is descriptive: see Woodcock §72.I.6.

laremque regis aduenae Tyrium/And the immigrant king's Tyrian god: the 'immigrant king' is Cadmus from Phoenicia (see on 249–58), sent by his father, King Agenor, to find Europa, Cadmus' sister, who had recently been abducted (by Jupiter, though they did not know this). *Larem…Tyrium*, 'Tyrian god', refers to Cadmus' house-god brought from Phoenicia. Tyre and Sidon were the chief cities of Phoenicia, the former famous for finely woven fabrics of silk or linen and for a purple dye. 'Tyrian' and 'Sidonian' are often used interchangeably for 'Phoenician'. At Eur. *Pho*. 639 Cadmus is from Tyre, as he is here. At *Oed*. 712 he is called *Sidonio…hospite*, 'Sidonian alien/guest'. At *Pho*. 124–5 he is the 'Assyrian king' (*Assyrio…regi*). *Lar* was a Roman domestic tutelary deity, but was also often used as a metonym for 'house', 'home', or 'hearth', as e.g. at 197, 379, *Oed*. 258. Here, as at *Ag*. 392, 782, *Thy*. 264 and *Pho*. 344, its primary referent is the household god or gods, often greeted and venerated by a returning warrior (Eurybates at *Ag*. 392–4, Agamemnon at *Ag*. 782), as here prospectively by Theseus, deputizing for the returning warrior Hercules. Pausanias (9.12.3) reports on Cadmus' palace as a tourist attraction in the second century CE.

coles/You'll revere: the future indicative used as a 'courteous Imperative' (Kennedy 1911: §350).

THESEUS ...*exits stage left* (*to the city*): Theseus does not return until the beginning of Act V. I cannot agree with those scholars (e.g. Glinski 2017: 221, n. 46) who have Theseus onstage and completely silent and non-reactive during the 'mad scene'.

918-24 Hercules' brief instructions to his attendants are followed by an exchange with Amphitryon on sacrificial purity.

Date tura flammis/**Put incense on the flames:** incense was a religious offering to the gods, regularly featured in sacrificial ritual but not restricted to it: see *Oed.* 305-6, *Ag.* 807, *Thy.* 687. The burning of incense, the pouring of libations of wine and the utterance of prayer were among the preliminary rituals of sacrifice before the slaughter of the animals themselves: see e.g. Ov. *Met.* 6.164, 9.159-60, 13.636-7. Most scholars would regard the uses of incense in the cited plays as anachronistic, since the importation of myrrh, frankincense, and spices from southern Arabia to Greece seems not to have occurred before the eighth century BCE. For an early literary attestation of incense on Greek altars, see Sappho frag. 2.3-4. For an unadorned imperative addressed to slaves, guards, attendants, or other *personae mutae*, see on 1048-53 (*famuli*).

manantes...manus cruenta caede/**hands, dripping with...bloody slaughter:** the need to purify before prayer, sacrifice, or other religious rituals is a constant imperative of the heroic world: see Hom. *Il.* 6.266-8, Hes. *WD* 724-6, Virg. *Aen.* 2.718-20. Euripides' Heracles is well aware of this, and is in the process of purifying the palace when madness hits him (*Herac.* 922-30). Pre-sacrificial purification remained an obligatory practice in republican and imperial Rome (Scheid 2003: 80). In the case of Hercules, covered with the blood of the slain Lycus and his supporters, the purification imperative is patent. The religious issue could not have been more clear to Seneca's Roman audience. For Roman referentiality in *Hercules*, see on 46-52.

Manantes, 'dripping' (given special emphasis through the alliterative wordplay with *manus*), probably reflects actual (probably animal) blood being used for theatrical effect (see Introd. §II, 40). Thus the hands of Seneca's Clytemnestra 'even now are dripping with blood' (*sanguine etiamnunc madent, Ag.* 949); his Medea's 'blood drips on the altar' (*manet....sanguis ad aras, Med.* 808). Relevant, too, is Accius' alliterative description of (presumably) Orestes' 'hand stained with the spray of maternal blood', *cui manus materno sordet sparsa sanguine* (*Aeg.* frag. 23 Klotz). The focus on bloody details is typical of the treatment of violence in Roman tragedy and especially by Seneca; see e.g. the bloody murders of Agamemnon (*Ag.*

897–905) and Polyxena (*Tro.* 1148–64); Atreus' preparation of the cannibalistic feast (*Thy.* 755–75); the dismemberment of Hippolytus (*Pha.* 1093–1114, 1246–72) and Astyanax (*Tro.* 1110–17); the self-blinding of Oedipus (*Oed.* 957–79); the suicides of Jocasta (*Oed.* 1040–1) and Phaedra (*Pha.* 1197–8); and (probably) the stabbing of Cassandra (*Ag.* 1012: see Boyle *ad loc.*). In the madness scene to follow Hercules' killing of his own family will be bloody and not lacking in detailed description, even though the deaths take place offstage (see esp. 991–1026). Other imperial Roman authors, especially Ovid, Lucan, and Statius, show the same predilection for the graphic representation of violence. Greek tragedy on the whole avoids corporeal explicitness, although bloody disfigurement (if moderate: Eur. *Or.* 960–4) and bleeding (Soph. *Phil.* 824–5) occur on stage and graphic descriptions of violent death are attested, as in Sophocles' description of Oedipus' blinding (see esp. *OT* 1275–9; cf. Soph. *Trach.* 780–2, Eur. *Med.* 1183–1221).

Vtinam.../**Would**...: Hercules' fantasy here of sacrificing Lycus to Jove conflates human slaughter and divine sacrifice in a disturbing manner. The elder Pliny drew attention to occurrences of human sacrifice even in his own age (*HN* 28.12). But such remained exceptional, and a senatorial decree of 97 BCE specifically prohibited the practice in Rome (*HN* 30.12). Cicero roundly criticized Gallic peoples for their practice of human sacrifice (*Pro Fonteio* 31), and Livy opined that human sacrifice was 'not at all a Roman ritual' (*minime Romano sacro*, 22.57.6). Many members of a Roman audience would have had problems with Hercules' current outburst. In a sense what Hercules is doing is envisioning a repetition of his treatment of Busiris, described by Amphitryon himself at 483–4, in respect of Lycus—exchanging the altar (*aras*) for the hearths (*foci*). What Hercules did to Busiris was what Busiris did to others; Hercules is becoming the monsters he slays. His speech is filled with sacrificial language and imagery: for such language elsewhere in the play, see 104, 299–302, 483–4, 515, 634, 875–7, 895–1053 (introd.), 893–4, 898–9, 908–19, 1035–8, 1039–42 and nn. *ad locc.* For the conflation of sacrifice and murder, see e.g. *Ag.* 162–70, 219; *Pha.* 708–9; *Tro.* 195–6, 287–90, 361, 1148–64; *Med.* 38–9, 969–71; *Thy.* 682ff.; and esp. *Pho.* 174–5 (Oedipus speaking about his self-blinding): *timida tunc paruo caput* | *libauit haustu*, 'Small was the libation it (my hand) timidly poured from my head'. See further on 1035–8 and below.

cruorem...*libare*/**pour blood**: instead of the customary libation of unmixed wine, Hercules envisages a libation of Lycus' blood. For *libare* elsewhere in the tragedies, see e.g. *Oed.* 324, 563, 565; *Ag.* 366; *Thy.* 700, 984–5

Pho. 175. For *libare* used of pouring blood from a human head, see previous n. and Apul. *Met.* 8.12. I join Viansino (1965 and 1993) and Fitch (1987*a* and 2018) in reading *cruorem* (*A*) rather than *cruore* (*E*), printed by Zwierlein and several modern editors. The normal construction with *libare*, as Fitch notes *ad loc.*, is an accusative of the liquid offered.

capitis inuisi/hated head: Seneca is regularly drawn to the synecdochic use of *caput* ('head' = 'person/man/woman/girl' etc.), as at 1334 below (see n. *ad loc.*), but here, despite Fitch's comments *ad loc.*, *caput* may actually mean 'head'. Cf. *inuisum caput*, 'hated head', at *Thy.* 188.

uictima…amplior…magisque opima/choicer victim Or more prime: cf. Hippolytus' outcry to Diana at her altar, as he prepares to slay/sacrifice his stepmother, Phaedra (*Pha.* 708–9):

> iustior numquam focis
> datus tuis est sanguis, arquitenens dea.
>
> Your altars never
> Received juster blood, goddess of the bow.

Hercules' echo of Hippolytus' position and words (assuming *Phaedra* to be the earlier play) seems to signal the tragic mayhem to come. The great Latinist and poet John Milton was to cite Hercules' sentiment in 1649 after the beheading of his own king (*The Tenure of Kings and Magistrates*, 20), and translate it thus:

> There can be slaine
> No sacrifice to God more acceptable
> Than an unjust and wicked king.

To Milton Hercules was 'the grand suppressor of Tyrants', not the imminent familicide.

For *uictima* of human sacrificial 'victim' elsewhere in Senecan tragedy, see 1038; *Tro.* 140 (Priam), 306 (Polyxena); *Med.* 970 (Medea's son); *Thy.* 146 (Pelops)—and, with animal–human ambiguity (see on 895–9), 899, *Med.* 39, *Thy.* 545, 688. Cf. also *Oct.* 146, 664, 957; *HO* 348. Note the religiously and morally disturbing effect of *amplior* ('choicer', 'fatter'), a word regularly used of physical size and, like *opima* ('prime'), especially appropriate to animal sacrifice, used here of the human 'victim'. The use of *opima* has another resonance. Applied already not only to the animal victims about to be sacrificed (909) but to the 'prime spoils' (*spolia opima*) of the Roman military tradition (48), the adjective gives the discourse an uncomfortable military edge, in which the glories of military slaughter are momentarily conflated with perverted religious sacrifice. For Roman referentiality in *Hercules*, see on 46–52; for military imagery, see on 19–29.

mactari/**slaughtered**: see on 634–6.

rex iniquus/**unjust king**: Hercules' reputation as a tyrannicide is touched upon elsewhere in this play (see 227, 272, 431, 895–7, 936–7), but the tyrannicidal claim seems here to be given unusual emphasis. There are many ways to describe Lycus. Seneca, author of a 'kingship' treatise (*De Clementia*), written perhaps quite close to *Hercules*, has put into Hercules' mouth a climactic phrase with strong contemporary relevance. Whether the referent could be taken to be Claudius, whom Seneca critiques and lampoons in *Apocolocyntosis*, depends on the present play's dating (see Introd. 6) and is a matter for speculation.

924–39 Amphitryon's request for a prayer from Hercules for *otium* and *quies* is followed by his 'Golden Age' supplication.

924–6 *genitor tuus*/**your father**: an ordinary phrase given great power because of the importance of the paternity issue in the play, because it is spoken to Hercules by Hercules' other 'father', and because it is unaccompanied by an appositional *Iuppiter* or *sim*. So accompanied, the phrase's impact would have been much softer. *Genitor* is used of Jupiter at 122; see n. *ad loc*.

aliquando otium quiesque/**At last peace and rest**: with Amphitryon's request here, cf. his opening prayer to Jupiter (205–13). Amphitryon's values again seem to accord with those of the opening choral ode: see on 209–13 and Introd. §VII, 77. For *aliquando*, see on 325–8.

926–39 This prayer of Hercules for a return of the Golden Age is his last speech before the onset of madness. Following what seems a self-evidently hybristic statement (926–7), Hercules prays for a world of cosmic stability and global peace (927–31), marked by the end of nature's violence (931–4) and the absence of destructive evil in nature or society (935–7). If any monsters remain, they will be his (937–9). The whole prayer develops the previous ode's culminating theme of the *Pax Herculea*, adorning it with cosmic and Roman imagery strongly suggestive of the imperialism of Senecan Rome. The irony of the final lines leads directly into the 'reversal', περιπέτεια (Aristot. *Poet*. 1452a22–9) which follows.

There is no speech resembling this in Euripides' play, where Heracles' pacification of the world, far from being paraded as an advisory model for Athens, is simply part of the labours imposed on the hero to enable him to regain Argive citizenship for Amphitryon (*Herac.* 17–21). For discussion of the political semiotics of this speech and for its role as the psychological tipping-point into madness, see Introd. §VII, 121–2. The Herculean/ Heraclean figure, Professor Hoadley, of MacLeish's *Herakles* (1967: Act I, p. 22), 'the famed scientist, fresh from his beneficent discoveries' similarly wants an ideal, impossible world:

> To want the world without suffering is all
> There is on earth to want and man's
> Rebellious labor…ultimate pride.

As does Martin Crimp's General, who justifies his anti-terrorist violence by claiming, 'I have purified the world for you' (*Cruel and Tender*, 2004, p. 57). For Roman referentiality in *Hercules*, see on 46–52. The author of *Hercules Oetaeus* was clearly impressed by this speech, since he has his Hercules pray to Jupiter, stressing his own role in pacifying the world, before succumbing to the poisoned robe (*HO* 790–6).

926–31 *concipiam preces Ioue meque dignas*/**I'll form prayers worthy Of Jove and myself:** it may seem not a little hybristic for Hercules to set himself up as comparable to Jove in response to a request for a prayer to the latter (*genitor*, 924). What Hercules prays for is an elaborate version of the *otium quiesque* which Amphitryon has just asked for. *Dignas* is of course ambiguous, and generous readings are possible: Nicholas Trevet *ad loc.* would have *Ioue dignas* = 'worthy for Jove to receive' and *me dignas* = 'worthy for me to make'. Less flattering interpretations seem perhaps more likely, given Hercules' already displayed psychology, Seneca's fondness for the ironic use of *dignus* (see 112 and n. *ad loc.*), and his severe condemnation in the prose works of *superbia*, 'pride' (see e.g. *Ep. Mor.* 106.6, *Ben.* 2.13.1: *o superbia, magnae fortunae stultissimum malum*, 'O pride, great fortune's most stupid evil'). *Concipere* is a technical term for uttering ritualistic, religious, or legal formulae (*OLD* 12) from Cato onwards (*Agr.* 169). See e.g. *Tro.* 1101, *Pha.* 943, *Marc.* 13.1, Ov. *Met.* 10.290, *Fas.* 1.182, Tac. *Hist.* 4.31. With *concipere preces Ioue…dignas*, cf. Ov. *Met.* 1.166 (of Jove himself) *dignas Ioue concipit iras*, 'he forms wrath worthy of Jove'. For the use of *dignus* in imperial rescripts and the political semiotics of its use in *Hercules*, see Introd. §VII, 118–19. For prayers in *Hercules* and Senecan tragedy, see on 205–78.

stet suo caelum loco tellusque et aequor/**Let sky, earth, and sea Stand in their place:** as opposed to the situation described at *Marc.* 26.6: *nihil quo stat loco stabit*, 'nothing will stand in the place in which it stands'. Fear of a universal cataclysm is brilliantly expressed in the 'Star Ode' of *Thyestes*.

Contemporary philosophy supported the belief that the universe would collapse. The Stoics proposed the theory of a cosmic cycle in which the universe periodically collapses and is consumed in a great fire (*ekpyrosis*) prior to its rebirth and a new procession of ages. See Sandbach (1975: 78–9), Long and Sedley (1987: 1.274–9, 308–13); also *Pol.* 1, *Marc.* 26.6–7, *Ben.* 6.22, *Anth. Lat.* 232, Luc. 1.72–80, *Oct.* 391–6, *HO* 1102–27. Seneca at *NQ* 3.27–30 offers a version of this theory in which the universe is destroyed by water as well as fire. I join Fitch (1987*a* and 2018), Chaumartin, Billerbeck, and Giardina (2007) in accepting the emendation of Heinsius (*aequor*) for the *EA* reading *aether* (accepted by Zwierlein), which is clearly inappropriate in this context: see Fitch *ad loc.* For Stoic language and ideas in *Hercules*, see on 162–3.

astra inoffensos agant aeterna cursus/**Let eternal stars drive Unhindered orbits:** contrast Hercules' description of the *astra* at 1332–3. For the 'unhindered speed' (*inoffensam uelocitatem*) of the heavens, see *Prou.* 1.2.

alta pax gentes alat/**deep peace nourish nations:** peace and the absence of weapons, characteristic of the Golden and Silver Races of Hesiod (*WD* 109–42), are constitutive of the Golden Age framed by Aratus and others: see e.g. Arat. *Phaen.* 108–10; Virg. *Ecl.* 4.37–45, *Geo.* 2.536–40, *Aen.* 8.324–7; Tib. 1.3.47–8; Ov. *Met.* 1.98–100; Calp. *Ecl.* 1.46–68; *Oct.* 397–406—and *Pha.* 533–9. *Alat* may have a meaning beyond the metaphor: viz. that peace is necessary for agricultural productivity, which 'nourishes'. For a sustained laudation of *pax*, including its 'nourishment' of agriculture, see Tib. 1.10.45–52 (*pax aluit uites*, 'peace nourished the vines', 47); cf. *Med.* 62–6. Note the *alta/alat* wordplay. For the phrase *alta pax*, see also *Tro.* 324, 326; *Ag.* 596; *Thy.* 576; Luc. 1.249; Stat. *Theb.* 8.625, *Ach.* 1.807–8. For Hercules as peace-maker, see on 882–8.

*ferrum omne…/***All iron…:** the commonplace contrast between the peaceful iron instruments of agriculture and the iron instruments of war: see e.g. Virg. *Geo.* 1.493–7, Tib. 1.10.49–50, Ov. *Fas.* 4.928–31, Juv. 3.309–11, 15.165–8. Kingery *ad loc.* cites the *Hebrew Bible*, 'Isaiah' 2.4: 'They shall beat their swords into ploughshares, and their spears into pruning hooks'.

ruris innocui/**guiltless land:** see 159 and n. *ad loc.*

931–4 *nulla…nullus…nullus*/**no…no…No:** a temperate climate, always implied in articulations of the Golden Age, is specified by Ovid (*Met.* 1.107–9), who describes the Golden Age as a time of 'eternal spring' (*uer aeternum*). Hercules is developing his rhetoric: note the tricolon with initial anaphora and the negative mode of depiction. For descriptions of a golden age or *locus amoenus* through negative formulations, see Virg. *Ecl.* 4.38–42,

Geo. 2.151–4; Hor. *Epod.* 16.51–62; Ov. *Met.* 1.89–100. See also Thyestes' notorious description of his own alleged *locus amoenus* through negative formulations at *Thy.* 455–70.

nullus irato Ioue exiliat ignis/no flame burst from angry Jove: at *HO* 796 Hercules puts his prayer more bluntly: *depone fulmen*, 'lay down the thunderbolt'. For *exilire* of Jove's thunderbolt, see *HO* 829. For Jove's 'bolts of wrath' (*iracunda...fulmina*), see Hor. *Odes* 1.3.40. For *ira*, see on 19–29.

935–9 uenena cessent, nulla nocituro grauis suco...herba/Let poisons cease, no plant...heavy With noxious juice: the negative formulation continues via an obvious allusion to Virg. *Ecl.* 4.24–5: *fallax herba ueneni | occidet*, 'the treacherous poison-plant will perish.' For such poisonous plants, see those gathered by Medea at *Med.* 717–19. *Nociturus* occurs only once elsewhere in Senecan tragedy: *Med.* 658.

non saeui ac truces regnent tyranni/no cruel and brutal Tyrants rule: again the indictment of tyrants; see 737–47, 924. For the negative *non* rather than *ne* with the jussive subjunctive (for a more emphatic negation), see *Pha.* 946, *Oed.* 258–9, *Thy.* 48. For *saeuus*, 'cruel/savage', and the *tyrannus* or *rex*, see 272, 1255; *Ag.* 844–6; *Oct.* 87, 303; *HO* 6. For *trux*, see 778 and n. *ad loc.*

properet/let her rush: the phraseology here is echoed by the dramatist of *Hercules Oetaeus* in his own Hercules' speech at *HO* 34–5. For the *properare*/'rushing' motif, see 187 and n. *ad loc.*

monstrum, meum sit/A monster, let it be mine: the ironic last words uttered before the onset of madness. They are words of self-fulfilment: the *monstrum* will be himself, as Hercules will acknowledge at 1280 (see n. *ad loc.*). Cf. 614–15, the climax of Hercules' opening speech, where the hero's obsessive need for further challenges, displayed here and described earlier from Amphitryon's perspective at 207–13, is evident.

939–86 Hercules hallucinates: he 'sees' the midday sky grow dark (939–44) and the constellation Leo blazing and threatening in the firmament (944–52); he himself threatens a Titanomachy against Jupiter (965–73), and witnesses a Gigantomachy (976–81) and the Furies themselves (982–6). This is madness performed onstage before an audience, not relegated to reports from other characters, as in Euripides (*Herac.* 867–70: Lyssa; *Herac.* 922–1015: Messenger). The Euripidean messenger's account of Heracles' madness, as if taking the cue from Lyssa's focus on physical symptoms (head-shaking, eye-rolling, irregular breathing: 867–70), initially develops that focus (931–4: bloody, agitated eyes, foaming at the mouth) before moving to Heracles' imagined attack on Mycenae (936–49) and his mistaking of his own children for those of Eurystheus (967–1000). The Senecan Hercules' madness will later incorporate the attack on Mycenae (996–8) and a mistaking of his own children for those of his enemy (Lycus: 987–9). But the Senecan hero's manifestation of the madness is both less physical and more wide-ranging and chaotic in its hallucinations, which involve the blackening of day, fighting among the constellations, rebellions against Jupiter, upheavals in heaven, on earth and in hell. What unites the diverse visions is their display of Hercules' mind: see Introd. §VII, 111–12. What Seneca's account lacks is both a coherent narrative (for his aim is to show Hercules' psychological instability) and Euripides' onstage external agent of the madness, Lyssa, though the agents instructed by Juno in the prologue are shown to be embedded in Hercules' mind (see on 982–6). Mark how the hallucinations follow immediately Hercules' express wish for a *monstrum* (938–9). Cf. 616, where Hercules' sight of Lycus' guards follows his request for a new conquest in 615. For hallucinations elsewhere in Senecan tragedy, see *Tro.* 682–5 (Andromache), *Pho.* 39–44 (Oedipus), possibly *Med.* 958–71 (Medea). Note the prophetic 'visions' of Cassandra at *Ag.* 726–74, 875–909. See also *HO* 1001–24 (Deianira).

939–44 Hercules sees the midday sky darken. For disturbances in the heavens perceived by Senecan *dramatis personae*, see 1333–4; *Med.* 768–9; *Ag.* 53–5, 726–7, 908–9; *Thy.* 636–8, 776–88, 789–884, 990–5.

Sed quid hoc/**But what's this:** for this expression of surprise, see 976, 1042, 1193; *Ag.* 868; *Thy.* 421, 985, 992; *Pha.* 705; *Oed.* 353—cf. *HO* 307, 1015, 1432, 1441. At *Oed.* 911 it is used to preface the entry of a new character. Note too: Cassandra's prophetic trance and vision (*Ag.* 726–7) begin with a disoriented question (*ubi sum?* 'Where am I?') and the onset of *tenebrae*, 'darkness' (see next n.); Thyestes' physical disturbance and perception of unnatural darkness are marked by a repetition of *quid hoc* (*Thy.* 985, 992). La Taille's *Saül Le Furieux* (1572) opens with an 'imitation' of these lines, including an echo of Hercules' cry: *Las, mon Dieu, qu'est-ce cy?*

medium diem cinxere tenebrae/**Darkness has besieged midday:** cf. the initial onset of darkness in Cassandra's prophetic *furor* at *Ag.* 726–7. Not all visions/hallucinations are preceded by such darkness: see Medea at *Med.* 958–71 (possible hallucination), Andromache at *Tro.* 683–5. The disorder in the heavens is not only the opposite of what Hercules prayed for (927–9) but an obvious extension of the disorder in his mind, which he projects onto the cosmos. Fitch *ad loc.* cites Hippocrates (*On Diet* 4.89), who saw disorder in the heavens as suggestive of disease and stars chasing stars as an index of 'imminent madness'. *Medium diem*, 'midday', is the first mention of the time of day since the dawn ode.

obscuro…sine nube uultu/**Cloudless…with shrouded face:** lit. 'with face obscured without cloud'. For the rhetorical figure '*x* without *y*', cf. *ardent sine igne*, 'blaze without fire'. *Thy.* 675.

quis diem retro fugat/**Who makes day flee back:** cf. again Cassandra's *furor* at the beginning of which 'the gentle light flees', *fugit lux alma* (*Ag.* 726). The reverse flight of the sun is an index in Seneca's later masterwork, *Thyestes* (776–88), of unspeakable human evil, and generates the famous 'Star Ode' on the imminent collapse of the cosmos. Indeed Medea, granddaughter of the sun, demands such a reverse flight from her ancestor (*Med.* 31) to reflect what she regards as the great evil of her desertion by Jason. It is hard not to see some proleptic 'truth' here in Hercules' madness, as he imagines in the heavens a reflection of great evil.

agitque in ortus/**And drives it to its dawn:** cf. *Med.* 31, *Thy.* 1035–6.

unde nox atrum caput ignota profert/**Why does strange night Rear its black head:** note the juxtaposition of *nox* and *atrum* underscoring the 'blackness' of Hercules' night. Though stars are mentioned in the next question, it is the blackness of night that seems emphasized. Contrast the 'starry head' (*caput…sidereum*) raised by Ovid's 'night' at *Met.* 15.31.

944-52 Hercules 'sees' in the dark sky the constellation Leo blazing with threats. Since Hercules is wearing the skin of the Nemean Lion, draped over his left shoulder (797, 1150–1), some of what he imagines in the firmament (e.g. Leo's attack on Taurus) again reflects upon himself. Fire imagery, which is strongly associated with 'madness' and *furor* (see on 100–3), permeates the passage.

Primus en noster labor/**Look, my first labour:** Hercules' killing of the Nemean Lion was generally regarded as Hercules' first labour: see on 222–5. This whole speech (note the stage directions implied by *en*) shows a dramatically powerful use of the verticality of the Roman theatrical space: see on 1–124 (introd.). *En* is a synonym of *ecce*, with which it is sometimes combined, as at *Pho.* 42, *Oed.* 1004. This is the first of seven uses in the final third of the play. For the postponed use of *en* with a nominative word or phrase, see *Pha.* 91, *Oed.* 1013, *Thy.* 1050, *Oct.* 72, 682. With Hercules' *en*, 'Look', cf. Cassandra's visionary *sed ecce*, 'But look', at *Ag.* 728. For the metonymic use of *labor*, see also 781.

non minima/**no small:** for the use of *non* to negate an adjective, see on 489–94.

Leo: the constellation resulting from the catasterization of the Nemean Lion. It is called *Leo Herculeus* in the 'Star Ode' of *Thyestes* (855–6), as also by Ovid (*Ars* 1.68). Traversed by the sun July to August, it was the zodiacal constellation especially associated with the summer (see next n.). For its connection with the Nemean Lion, see also e.g. Manil. 2.531, 5.206; [Eratosth.] *Catast.* 12; Hyg. *Astr.* 2.24; Mart. *Epig.* 4.60.2, 5.71.3; Stat. *Silu.* 4.4.28.

iraque totus feruet/**Burns hot, consumed with wrath**: similarly at *Thy.* 855 Leo is described as *flammiferis aestibus ardens*, 'flaming with fiery heat', a hyperbolic tautology clearly designed to suggest the oppressive heat of late July to August in ancient Rome, when the sun traverses Leo. Hence Horace's 'raging Leo' (*uesani Leonis*, *Odes* 3.29.19, *furibundus*, *Ep.* 1.10.17); see also *Pha.* 969–70. The 'blazing' (Virg. *Aen.* 10.273) and 'rabid' (Hor. *Ep.* 1.10.16) Dog-Star, Sirius, rose under Leo in late July. For *ira*, see on 19–29. 'Angry' lions are, of course, a commonplace: *Oed.* 150, Lucr. 3.296–8, Virg. *Aen.* 7.15, Luc. 6.487.

feruet et: note the repetition of the same syllable at the end and beginning of juxtaposed words; see 951 below and 67 with n. *ad loc.*

iam rapiet aliquod/**Now it'll seize some**: dactyl followed by tribrach, perhaps conveying 'a sense of urgency and alarm' (Fitch *ad loc.*). See 76 and n. *ad loc.*

ignes efflat et rutilat/**vomits fire and glows red**: for the summer heat and Leo, see above. Here Seneca's language not only suggests the vivid imaginings of Hercules' disturbed mind but seems to liken the constellation to such fire-breathing Virgilian monsters as the Chimaera or Cacus (*Aen.* 7.785–6, 8.198–9) or the fire-breathing bulls of Ovid's Colchis (Ov. *Met.* 7.104–10). The picture clearly impressed Lucan: *incensa Leonis | ora*, 'the inflamed mouth of Leo' (10.233–4). I join Viansino (1965 and 1993) and Fitch (1987*a* and 2018) in keeping the consensus *EA* reading *rutilat*, as opposed to *E*'s reading after correction, *rutilam*, printed by Zwierlein, Chaumartin, and Billerbeck. For discussion, see Fitch *ad loc.*

iubam ceruice iactans/**Tossing mane on neck**: so, too, of Leo at *HO* 70: *iactans feruidam collo iubam*, 'tossing fiery mane on its neck'.

quidquid autumnus grauis…refert/**All that sick autumn…zone**: a large distance, since eight zodiacal zones (Virgo, Libra, Scorpio, Sagittarius/ Chiron, Capricorn, Aquarius, Pisces, and Aries) lie between Leo and Taurus. *Grauis*, 'deadly/sickly' (*OLD* 6b), is almost a defining modifier of autumn, the quintessentially unhealthy season: see Caes. *BC* 3.2.3, Hor. *Serm.* 2.6.19. It was the time of the harmful Sirocco (Hor. *Odes* 2.14.15–16) and the onset of malaria. Juvenal (4.56–7) is quite specific: *leti-foro…autumno*, 'death-bringing autumn'. It is difficult, as Billerbeck observes *ad loc.*, to interpret *grauis* as 'heavy' (i.e. 'laden with fruit') without a clarifying ablative.

gelido frigida/chill...frozen: for the juxtaposition of synonyms, see on 283–95.

frangetque Tauri colla/and crush The neck of...Taurus: Taurus, the Bull, is the zodiacal constellation traversed by the sun April to May; it was connected earlier in the play (8–9) with 'balmy spring' (*tepenti uere*) and with Jupiter. The mythological origins of the constellation were associated with the bull (alias Jupiter) which raped Europa or with the cow into which Io was transformed: Ov. *Fas.* 5.603–20, Hyg. *Astr.* 2.21, Ampel 2.2, [Eratosth.] *Catast.* 14. Fights between lion and bull are a *topos* of ancient epic and art: see e.g. Hom. *Il.* 16.487–9, 17.542; Virg. *Aen.* 10.454–6. But here the fight clearly reflects Hercules' manic ambitions. Since the association of Taurus with Jupiter has already been marked in the play (8–9), the attack of Leo on Taurus seems presented as a cosmic foreshadowing of an attack by Hercules (= Leo, see above) on Jupiter himself. It signals an intended attack on heaven. For *frangere*, 'crush/break', of the action of a lion, see *Tro.* 798; Mart. *Epig.* 1.51.4 (*frangere colla*), 104.19; Stat. *Theb.* 11.28.

952–4 Amphitryon reacts with astonishment and anxiety. The focus here on the physical manifestation of emotions in Hercules' face is in line with the Stoic view of the corporeality of emotions (*Ep. Mor.* 106.5–6): see most especially Seneca's classic description of the *iratus*, 'angry man', at *De Ira* 1.1.3–6. For Stoic ideas in *Hercules*, see on 162–3.

Quod subitum hoc malum est/What's this sudden ill: note the double elision at the end of the line. Cf. *Tro.* 909, 911; *Pha.* 358, 435; *Ag.* 924; *Oed.* 834, 865; *Med.* 25; *Thy.* 718; *Pho.* 629 (also *HO* 882, 940)—where, as here, the second elision is prodelision.

quo, nate, uultus huc et huc acres refers/Son, why turn your gaze fiercely this way and that: *nate*, 'son', uttered with affection and concern, will be implicitly hurled back at Amphitryon by Hercules' focus on his divine *pater*, Jupiter. Cf. Amphitryon's question to the raging Heracles, as reported by Euripides' messenger, at *Herac.* 965–6. The phrase, *uultus referre*, is repeated by Jocasta in her address to her son, Polynices, at *Pho.* 473: *quo uultus refers?* 'Why turn your gaze?' Cf. also the almost identical language used to describe Astyanax just before his death: *uultus huc et huc acres tulit*, 'he turned his gaze fiercely this way and that' (*Tro.* 1092). The actor's mask and the eyes behind it were capable of being used to index a variety of emotions (see Introd. 38). Cicero reports how the eyes of an actor seemed 'to burn from the mask' (*ex persona...ardere*, *De Orat.* 2.193). For *uultus* as the site of character and feeling, see on 329–31. *Huc et huc*: for this variation of *huc et illuc*, see also *Oed.* 343, *Tro.* 970, *Med.* 385. For *quo = cur*, see *Pho.* 473 (and Frank *ad loc.*).

acie...turbida/**with turbulent eyes:** cf. the *incerta...lumina* ('roaming gaze') of the raging Cassandra at *Ag.* 714.

955–73 Hercules responds to Amphitryon's question with a statement of his existing conquests and his need to expand to the heavens promised by his father, Jupiter. If heaven is not unlocked, he will release Saturn and lead the Titans in a new war on Jupiter and heaven. What Hercules threatens is akin to parricide, one of Oedipus' unknowing crimes, and one especially heinous in Roman culture, meriting extraordinary punishment. Cf. the Titanomachy described by the chorus of *Agamemnon* at *Ag.* 334–9. As noted above on 944–52, Seneca's language gives the actor playing Hercules an opportunity to utilize the verticality of the Roman theatrical space. For the Stoic resonances of Hercules' aspirations for divinity, see on 63–74. For Stoic ideas in *Hercules*, see on 162–3.

955–63 An important passage in which Hercules' achievement of peace on earth and in hell (955–6), the *Pax Herculea* celebrated in the recent choral ode (882–92), is presented as a preface to his celestial ambitions, already underscored by Juno in the prologue (74). For Hercules' apotheosis as a reward for his benefactions to humankind, see e.g. *Ag.* 812–13, *HO* 97–8, Cic. *Off.* 3.25, Ov. *Ars* 2.217–18, Sen. Rhet. *Suas.* 1.1, 2.5, Stat. *Silu.* 3.1.25–6. The political ramifications of the present speech for the *Pax Romana* and for Rome itself seem evident; see Introd. §VII, 121–2. For Roman referentiality in *Hercules*, see on 46–52.

Perdomita tellus/**Earth is tamed:** this restatement of the *Pax Herculea* is articulated in language implying that the earth is a wild animal or even monster needing to be 'tamed'. The other use of *perdomita* in the play is precisely in reference to the taming of monsters: *monstra tot perdomita* (444). For Hercules as *domitor orbis*, 'tamer of the world', see 619 (also 33); for omission of auxiliary *est*, see on 222–5.

tumida cesserunt freta/**the swelling seas have yielded:** a general description of the *Pax Herculea* rather than an allusion (as Fitch argues *ad loc.*) to the incident, mentioned by Pherecydes (Athen. 11.471d), in which Hercules cowed Oceanus 'by the threat of his archery'.

dignus Alcide labor/**labour worthy of Alcides:** again the *dignus* motif and the mannerism of imperial rescripts: cf. the use of *dignus* at 112, 927, 1295 and nn. *ad locc.*, and Introd. §VII, 118–19. Note the aggrandizing self-naming, the first of ten instances of self-naming in this and the final act: see also 960, 991, 1152, 1155, 1163, 1168, 1218, 1295, 1314. See further on 631–40. For the self-exemplifying use of *labor*, see 1316 and n. *ad loc.*

in alta mundi spatia sublimis ferar/I **must soar to the high regions of the world:** an interesting amalgam of the standard poetic language of apotheosis (see e.g. the prophecy of Aeneas' deification at Virg. *Aen.* 1.259) and the famous penultimate line of *Medea* (1026): *per alta uade spatia sublimi aetheris*, 'journey through the high regions of the soaring air'—the latter perhaps either an echo or an anticipation of Hercules' apotheotic language here. See also the vainglorious final act entrance pronouncement of Atreus: *aequalis astris gradior...| altum superbo uertice attingens polum*, 'Equal to the stars I stride...| My prideful head hits heaven's height' (*Thy.* 885-6). In the early fourteenth century Mussato gave his Ecerinus Herculean celestial ambitions: *uindicabo forsitan caelum potens*, 'perhaps I'll claim potent heaven', *Ecerinis* 298. In the mid sixteenth century (1544) it was the turn of Muret's Caesar: *caelum petendum est; terra iam uilet mihi*, 'Heaven must be sought; the earth is now cheap to me', *Iulius Caesar* 26. For Seneca's fondness for *spatium*, see on 821-7. Note also how Hercules' language echoes that of the opening choral ode (192-6), where the Chorus criticized the pursuit of 'prattling Fame' (*Fama garrula*).

petatur aether: astra promittit pater/**Aim for the aether: stars are father's promise:** a taut, chiastically alliterative line, permeated by *ps, ts, as*, and *rs*. Again the audience are returned to Juno's prologue (23), where the promised stars were mentioned. Juno's words are proving veridical.

quid si negaret/**If he renege:** lit. 'what if...'. For *quid si...*, see also *Ag.* 552: *quid si ipse mittat*; *Oed.* 699: *quid si innocens sum*. Seneca's language and ideas here are echoed in Hercules' question at *HO* 13: *quid astra, genitor, quid negas*, 'Why, father, why renege on the stars?'

non capit terra Herculem/**Earth cannot contain Hercules:** a continuation of the idea first formulated by Juno at 46, and echoed by Hercules in his opening speech in the play at 605. For analogous use of *capere* concerning another world-conqueror, Alexander, cf. Sen. Rhet. *Suas.* 1.5: *orbis illum suus non capit*, 'his own world does not hold him.' Alexander was the paradigm of the insatiable conqueror (*Alexandro orbis angustus est*, 'For Alexander the world is cramped': *Suas.* 1.3), standing here as a model for Hercules' insatiety and the latter as a model for that of Rome. Hercules' language clearly impressed Marlowe who modelled his Tamburlaine upon aspects of Seneca's creation (*2 Tam.*, IV.i.118-20, cited also by Fitch 2018 *ad loc.*):

> I might move the turning Spheres of heaven,
> For earth and all this airy region
> Cannot contain the state of Tamburlaine.

Cf. Muret's Caesar, cited above. For Hercules' self-naming, see above. For Roman referentiality in *Hercules*, see on 46–52.

tandemque/But…at last: for the adversative use of *-que*, see 72 and n. *ad loc.*

en/Look: see on 944–52.

omnis deorum coetus/whole mass Of gods: Hercules in this self-epicizing fantasy imagines a council of the gods voting on his apotheosis. Seneca's parody of such a council in *Apocolocyntosis* (8–11) seems close in date to the composition of this play.

laxat fores/opens the gates: in the Roman tradition the notion of the 'gates of heaven' begins with Ennius (*caeli maxima porta*, Vahlen *Var*. 24), who is imitated by Virgil (*porta…caeli, Geo*. 3.261), both of whom are cited by Seneca himself at *Ep. Mor*. 108.34. See also Ov. *Met*. 2.113 and *ianuam mundi* below (964). The concept goes back to Homer (πύλαι οὐρανοῦ, *Il*. 5.749, 8.393).

una uetante/one veto: that of Juno (*una*), who votes against the rest of the council. For Hercules' obsession with Juno, see on 604–15. For climactic half-lines, see on 40–6.

963–73 *To* JUPITER, *perhaps turning to his statue*: for the possible presence of a statue of Jupiter onstage, see before 1–18.

Recipis et reseras polum/Do you unlock the sky in welcome: although Juno has just been referred to at 963, the addressee here is clearly Jupiter. Hercules' essential issue is whether Jupiter has reneged on his promises (959–60); and a failure to answer the present question in the affirmative immediately results in an intended assault on Hercules' 'impious father' (*patris impii*) at 965ff. This is the first in a series of short questions characteristic of *sermo praeruptus*: see on 1149–55. For *polus* as the 'heavens/sky', see *Tro*. 354, *Thy*. 49, *Oed*. 249. For *reserare* with *polus*, see *Tro*. 354, *Ag*. 756. For paronomasia of *re-* words, see on 46–52.

ianuam mundi traho/tear down…heaven's doorway: note the indicative instead of a deliberative subjunctive, found especially in the first-person singular. It is most common in early Latin, but occurs in verse elsewhere: e.g. Cat. 1.1, Virg. *Aen*. 4.534, VF 5.285; see also *Med*. 53, *Pho*. 450. For *ianuam*, 'doorway', see previous n. on *laxat fores*.

dubitatur etiam/Hesitation—still: the use of *etiam* (often translated as 'really', 'still', or 'now') to indicate surprise or shock in a question goes back to Livius Andronicus (*etiam minitas?* 'Are you really threatening me?', *Danae* frag. 19 Klotz) and is common in republican comedy (e.g. Plaut. *Aul*. 633). It may be found in Virgil (*Aen*. 3.247, 4.305) and elsewhere in Senecan tragedy, e.g. 1189, *Tro*. 246, *Ag*. 983, *Oed*. 678, *Pha*. 705.

Saturno exuam/I'll strip Saturn: Saturn was an early Roman god of agriculture, who became identified with Cronos, father of Zeus and dethroned ruler of the gods and Titans. According to one tradition going back to Homer (*Il.* 14.203–4), he was imprisoned in the underworld after his dethronement. See Ov. *Met.* 1.113: *Saturno tenebrosa in Tartara misso* ('After Saturn had been sent to dark Tartarus'). *Saturno* is dative of advantage/disadvantage, often used with 'certain verbs of "depriving"': Woodcock §61.

patris impii regnum impotens/impious Father's unbridled rule: powerful, alliterative phrasing with complex semiotics. *Impii*, 'impious', does double duty here, meaning both 'unfilial' (for overthrowing his father, Saturn) and 'unpaternal' (for refusing heaven to his son, Hercules). For the former sense, see e.g. *Pho.* 260, *Med.* 134, *Oed.* 935; for the latter, see e.g. *Med.* 779, *Pha.* 557, *Oed.* 437•. For *pietas*, see on 1092–9. *Impotens* quite often occurs at the end of the verse line in the tragedies, preceded by an elided word, as here: see e.g. 1180; *Med.* 143, 958; *Pha.* 186; *Tro.* 215, 266; *Ag.* 126; *Thy.* 350. As at 1180 and elsewhere (see line 20 and n. *ad loc.*), the elision prevents the breach of 'Porson's law' (for which see on 249–58).

Again Marlowe was impressed, modelling his Tamburlaine's theomachic ambitions on those of Hercules (*1 Tam.* IV.iv.79–80):

> Zenocrate, were Egypt Jove's own land
> Yet would I with my sword make Jove to stoop.

Or again (*1 Tam.* V.ii.389–90):

> Jove viewing me in arms looks pale and wan,
> Fearing my power should pull him from his throne.

Marlowe's Tamburlaine, like Hercules, becomes a filicide, killing his own son, Calyphas, not, however, in a fit of madness.

Titanes/Titans: the pre-Olympian gods, ruled by Cronos/Saturn, who had dethroned his own father, Uranus/Caelus. In the battle of the Olympian gods and the Titans (the 'Titanomachy') the latter were defeated and the supremacy of the Olympian gods, ruled by Zeus/Jupiter, followed.

Centauris/Centaurs: mythical creatures, half-human, half-horse, often regarded as the antithesis of civilized humans, bestial, driven by sexual lust and greed, and prone to drunkenness. There are exceptions, including Chiron: see below.

limitem ad superos agam/I'll drive a path to gods: as Hercules has indicated, this would be a violent process, as it was in the case of Aeneas, of whom *limitem agere* is used when he 'drives a path with his sword' (*limitem agit ferro*, Virg. *Aen*. 10.514) through the ranks of enemy soldiers, looking for Turnus and mowing down all in front of him.

uideat sub Ossa Pelion Chiron suum/Let Chiron view his Pelion beneath Ossa: Chiron, the centaur-tutor of Jason, Hercules, Achilles, and Aesculapius, famous for his knowledge of music, plants, medicine, divination, and archery, had his home on Mt Pelion: see e.g. *Tro*. 829–35, Ov. *Fas*. 5.381–4, Stat. *Ach*. 1.106–58. Associated by Ovid (*Fas*. 5.379–414) and Manilius (5.348–56) with the constellation of the Centaur, Chiron at *Thy*. 860–2 represents the zodiacal constellation Sagittarius, as he does at Lucan 9.536. See further Nigidius Figulus, frag. lxxxxvii Swoboda. Chiron *qua* constellation can view Hercules' climbing to the gods. Both Mt Pelion and Mt Ossa were and are located in Thessaly. Behind Hercules' present hallucination lies the story of the Aloidae, Otus and Ephialtes, who threatened the Olympian gods with war and tried to reach the sky by piling on top of each other the mountains Pelion, Ossa, and Olympus, home of the gods. The order of their attempted structure varied: in Homer (*Od*. 11.315–16) Ossa is piled on Olympus and Pelion is piled on Ossa; in Virgil (*Geo*. 1.281–2) Ossa is piled on Pelion and Olympus is piled on Ossa. Ovid follows the Homeric structure in several places (e.g. *Am*. 2.1.11–12, *Fas*. 1.307–8), as do Propertius (2.1.19–20) and Statius (*Silu*. 3.2.64–6), but at *Met*. 1.154–5 Olympus is piled on Pelion and Pelion on Ossa. Horace (*Odes* 3.4.51–2) condenses the Homeric structure to Pelion piled on Olympus. Seneca's own version here in *Hercules* seems a variant of the Virgilian order (see also *Ag*. 335–9, *Thy*. 812–12•); Martial (*Epig*. 8.36.6) reverts to Homer in piling 'Thessaly's Pelion' (*Thessalicum…Pelion*) on Ossa, as does Seneca himself at *Tro*. 829–30. The *topos* is found in the outburst of Shakespeare's Laertes in Ophelia's grave: *Ham*. V.i.244–7.

Olympus tertio positus gradu/Olympus…as the third step: mountain in Thessaly and home of the 'Olympian' gods ruled by Zeus/Jupiter. For its role in an assault on the gods, see previous n. At *Tro*. 830 it is Pelion which is the 'third step to heaven' (*tertius caelo gradus*). Cf. also *Ag*. 337, where Seneca writes again of these mountains as 'steps' (*gradus*) to heaven. *Tertio…gradu* seems best taken as dative of 'End Aimed At' or 'Result Achieved': Woodcock §67.

973–5 Amphitryon tries to restrain Hercules, playing the role of the Nurse or the *Senex* in the 'Passion-Restraint' scenes of *Phaedra, Agamemnon, Medea*, and *Troades*.

Infandos…sensus/monstrous thoughts: for *sensus* = 'thoughts/senses', see *Pha*. 733 (*recipe iam sensus*, 'recover your senses now'), *Ag*. 789 (*suscita sensus tuos*, 'collect your senses'). Cf. Shakespeare's 'horrible imaginings' (*Mac.* I.iii.138).

pectoris sani parum, magni tamen/heart barely sane, if great: for the idiom, cf. *certa at sera*, 'sure, if late' at 622; see n. *ad loc.* The phrase *pectoris sani parum* is repeated by Deianira's Nurse, attempting to restrain her mistress, at *HO* 275.

compesce dementem impetum/Restrain the demented Impulse: *impetus*, 'impulse', is a translation of the Greek ὁρμή and an important term in the Stoic account of the emotions, in which it figures as what follows the mind's assent to a psychological impression and generates action (Sen. *Ira* 2.1.3–5, 3.4–5). Cf. *Ep. Mor.* 37.5; *Pha.* 255; *Pho.* 347; *Ag.* 127, 203; *Med.* 157, 381, 895; *Thy.* 136—and *Tro.* 250, where Agamemnon addresses the impetuous Pyrrhus: *iuuenile uitium est regere non posse impetum* ('Ungoverned impulse is a fault of youth'). Although *impetus* = 'impulse' is used by the non-Stoic Ovid (e.g. *Fas.* 5.541), it is difficult not to attribute its frequent use in the tragedies to Seneca's Stoic background. For *compescere* of emotional (and verbal) restraint, see *Pha.* 165, *Med.* 174, *Tro.* 349, *Helu.* 1.2. See also *Ira* 2.18.1 for Seneca's advocacy of 'restraint' (*compescere*) as one of anger's two therapies. For Stoic language and ideas in *Hercules*, see on 162–3.

976–86 Hercules imagines that he sees a new Gigantomachy (976–81), then an assault by a Fury (982–4) and finally Tisiphone in hell (984–6). For the battle between the Olympian gods and the Giants, see on 439–47. The whole subject was traditionally associated with the epic genre ('the most epic of epic themes': Williams 1994: 191). The named Giants in Hercules' speech, Tityos (977) and Mimans (981), are included in perhaps the most famous Roman version of the myth, Horace's Gigantomachy at *Odes* 3.4.49–80. Horace's version was a metaphor for the power struggle between the 'brothers', Octavian and Antony (see also Ov. *Tr.*2.333–6), just as Lucan's Gigantomachy at *BC* 7.145–50 figures the civil war between Caesar and Pompey. Seneca is clearly using this paradigmatic myth of boundary violation to underscore and give epic elevation to Hercules' own manic violations. Cf. the Gigantomachy of the chorus of *Thyestes* at *Thy.* 805–12• and the Titanomachy/Gigantomachy at *Ag.* 334–9.

976–81 *Quid hoc*/What's this: for this expression of surprise, see on 939–44.

Gigantes arma pestiferi mouent/Death-bearing Giants brandish arms: Hercules envisions a new battle of the Olympian gods and the Giants (Gigantomachy): see above and on 439–47. For the compound in *-fer*, see on 235–40.

Tityos: for this famous Giant and sinner, see on 750–9.

lacerum gerens et inane pectus/**with torn and gaping chest:** his punishment in the underworld was to have his liver eaten out each day by a vulture or vultures. See on 750–9. With *inane pectus*, cf. the 'gaping trunk', *inane…corpus*, of the sacrificial animal at *Oed.* 379; for *gerere pectus*, see *Pha.* 994, *Tro.* 303–4, *Pho.* 582–3.

quam prope a caelo stetit/**How near he stands To the heavens:** *stetit* is perfect with present meaning, as at *Oed.* 303, *Thy.* 110, and *Pha.* 1100, and often in Latin verse. For *prope a*, see *Tro.* 1177: *quam prope a Priamo steti*, 'How near I stood to Priam'; *Ep. Mor.* 41.1: *prope est a te deus*, 'Near to you is god'. The line is echoed at *HO* 1443 (*tam prope a caelo fui*, 'So near I was to heaven'), spoken by Hercules.

labat…tremit marcentque/**totters…trembles…withers:** a version of the 'pathetic fallacy', here the reaction of nature to the presence of evil in the landscape. Cf. the reaction of the Argive landscape to the presence of the Ghost of Tantalus at *Thy.* 107–19. Along with Fitch (1987*a* and 2018) I have printed the reading of *A*, *marcentque*, as against the reading of *E*, *Macetumque*, favoured by Zwierlein and most recent editors. For arguments, see Fitch *ad loc.* and 2004*b*: 26.

Cithaeron…Pallene…Tempe: for Cithaeron, a mountain near Thebes, see on 231–4; for Pallene, the site of the original Gigantomachy, see on 439–47; for Tempe, a valley in Thessaly, see on 285–95.

Pindi iuga/**Pindus' ridge:** the Pindus mountain range was on the Thessaly-Macedonia border, though it is sometimes (erroneously) located in Thrace, as at 1285, *Oed.* 435. It was an area famous for its Maenads and the worship of Bacchus. For its 'ridge' (*iuga*), see Virg. *Ecl.* 10.11.

Octa: for Mt Oeta, see on 132–6. Because it was the site of Hercules' agonizing death and apotheosis, references to it always have an extra semantic charge, especially if the reference is made by Hercules.

saeuit horrendum Mimans/**Mimans rages terror:** Mimans or Mimas was a Giant with serpent legs who rebelled against Jupiter. At Claud. *Gigant.* (85–91) he rips up the island of Lemnos to hurl at the Olympians (see also Sidon. *Carm.* 15.25–6), but is killed by Mars (see also Apollon. 3.1226–7). Apollodorus (1.6.2) has him killed by Hephaistos (Vulcan). He features in the Gigantomachy/Titanomachy of Horace *Odes* 3.4.53: *ualidus Mimas*, 'mighty Mimas'. *Horrendum* is an adverbial accusative.

982–6 The climax of Hercules' hallucinations before he begins his murderous spree consists of two visions of the Furies (for whom, see on 86–8), with whip, serpents, and torches. He details an assault by one Fury, and then imagines himself seeing in the underworld itself another Fury, Tisiphone, guarding the gate of hell. Encounters with Furies, imagined or real, seem a regular feature of the literary and, especially, the dramatic representation of madness from Aeschylus' *Eumenides* onwards, where the appearance of Furies onstage was probably reproduced in Ennius' *Eumenides*. Sometimes Furies are simply imagined, as here or in the hallucinations of Alcmeo in Ennius' play of the same name (frags 24–7 Jocelyn), recalled by Cicero at *Acad.* 2.88:

> fer mi auxilium, pestem abige a me
> flammiferam hanc uim quae me excruciat.
> caeruleae incinctae igni incedunt,
> circumstant cum ardentibus taedis.
>
> Help me, protect me from the plague,
> This fiery force tormenting me.
> Dark things come wreathed with fire,
> They girdle me with blazing brands.

Sometimes, as at *Med.* 958–71, it is unclear whether the Furies are present onstage or imagined. For Furies, madness and epic, see esp. the operations of Allecto in Virgil's seventh *Aeneid* (323–571). Even 'historians' play with Furies and madness/guilt: note Suetonius' conceit of Nero being hounded by his murdered mother's ghost and Furies at *Nero* 34.4. For seeing directly into the underworld, see Cassandra's vision at *Ag.* 741–74, which also includes seeing the Furies (*Ag.* 759–64). It should not go unnoticed that Hercules' climactic hallucination of the Furies signals the fulfilment of Juno's instructions to them in the prologue (100–9). The Furies may not be onstage as Lyssa is in Euripides, but, somehow or other, they have become lodged in Hercules' mind. Note, too, Lucan's inclusion of a Fury, *Erinys* (1.572), in his description of the prodigies attending the reaction in Rome to the outbreak of civil war; he explicitly compares the Fury to the one which terrified Hercules (1.576–7)

Flammifera Erinys/A flaming Erinys: 'Erinys' is another name for a Fury or Fury-like goddess (*Oed.* 590, 644, *Med.* 953, etc.). The Furies are sometimes referred to collectively as the Erinyes. *Flammifera* may have been chosen because of Ennius' use of it in the *Alcmeo* passage printed above. For Seneca's fondness for compounds ending in *-fer*, see on 235–40.

uerbere excusso sonat rogisque adustas...sudes...serpentibus...face/ has cracked her whip...pyre-charred stake...serpents...torch: for whip, flame, and serpent as the major instruments of the Furies, see on 86–8. For the sound of the Furies' whips, see *Oed.* 645, *Med.* 961–2 (*excusso sonat…flagello*), *HO* 1002. For the *topos* of brands from funeral pyres, see on 100–3; for the focus on sound, see on 1002–9.

in ora tendit/Thrusts…To my face: the face seems to be a regular target of the Furies' fiery brands. Ovid's Myrrha even defines the Furies as 'targeting eyes and face with their cruel torches', *facibus saeuis oculos et ora petentes, Met.* 10.350. See also *Med.* 965.

Tisiphone, caput serpentibus uallata/Tisiphone, head fenced With serpents: one of the three Furies; see on 86–99, 86–8. Virgil presents her as the Fury who guards the entrance to Tartarus (*Aen.* 6.555–6). With Tisiphone's palisade of serpents, cf. Lucretius' description of the Lernaean Hydra, *uenenatis…uallata colubris*, 'fenced with poisonous serpents' (5.27). Cf. also Ovid, who presents Allecto *breuibus torquata colubris*, 'collared with little serpents' (*Her.* 2.119). For *caput* as accusative of respect, see 107 and n. *ad loc.*

post raptum canem/since the dog was snatched: for the construction here (*post* with noun and p.p.p./adjective), see *Oed.* 442, *Ag.* 190, *Tro.* 138, Ov. *Met.* 12.422.

987–1026 The Killings. Fitch *ad loc.* draws attention to the differences between Euripides and Seneca in the modes of slaughter: in Euripides and Seneca the first son is shot with an arrow (Eur.: in the liver, Sen.: through the neck); in both dramatists the second son supplicates, but is killed with the club in Euripides and smashed against the walls in Seneca; in Euripides the third son and Megara are shot with one arrow, but in Seneca the third son dies of fright and Megara is gruesomely clubbed to death. Different versions of the deaths may be found in Pherecydes, Pindar, Diodorus Siculus, Hyginus, Apollodorus, Philostratus, and others. For some of the details of the madness and the murders, Seneca seems also indebted to Ovid (esp. *Met.* 4.512–24, 9.211–18). This moment in the myth of Hercules' madness seems to have been given especially lively treatment in Augustan pantomime. Macrobius reports the story that, when 'Mad Hercules' (*Hercules Furens*) was danced by the pantomime Pylades, the latter sometimes shot an arrow/arrows into his audience (*Sat.* 2.7.16–17).

987–91 Still hallucinating, Hercules mistakes his own children for those of Lycus (in Euripides' play he thinks they are the children of Eurystheus: *Herac.* 970–1, 982–3), and prepares his bow. Note that the first lethal 'mad' act performed by Hercules is a development of his immediately preceding 'sane' action, the killing of Lycus, and that Juno had prescripted this scene in the prologue (118–21). It is not accidental that Hercules' prescripted behaviour follows his hallucinated encounter with the prologue's Furies (982–6). This is the prologue realized as dramatic action.

Sed ecce proles...latet/But look, skulking here...spawn: I cannot agree with Billerbeck *ad loc.* that *proles...latet* refers to the first child to be killed ('der erste Knabe'), who is hiding onstage and then killed onstage. *Vos* clearly signals a plurality, and thus that *proles* and *semen* are being used collectively. Trevet *ad loc.* recognizes this: 'hoc dicit uidens filios proprios, putans eos esse filios Lici'; similarly Farnaby *ad loc.* For *proles*, see 268 and n. *ad loc.* The children are most likely 'skulking' or 'hiding' behind their mother or in her dress. They will quickly make a dash for the palace with her. It is an open question whether the first child to be killed has made it to the palace or not: see below.

haec dextra/This hand: for *dextra* (and the *manus* motif), see on 118–22.

leues...sagittas/light shafts: *leuis*, 'light', is almost a defining modifier of the arrow: see e.g. 1127, *Oed.* 482, *Ag.* 324, *Apoc.* 12.3.8, *HO* 545, Virg. *Aen.* 5.68, 9.178, Luc. 6.196.

sic mitti decet/Such targets befit: lit. 'thus should (weapons of Hercules) be sent'. I do not agree with those who take *sic* as = 'with accuracy' ('treffsicher': Billerbeck *ad loc.*). Rather it = 'against such as these': see Fitch *ad loc.* The force of *sic* is to display Hercules' inhumanity, as in this context it is applied to children (of Lycus in his imagination, of himself in reality). Note the complex incongruity of the appeal to 'what is befitting/right', *decet*, in what is in essence a perversion of the Stoic concept of *decorum* or τὸ πρέπον (Cic. *Off.* 1.93–9), and yet at the same time a correct application of the term in a metaliterary sense. For the appeal to *decet*, see on 408–13. For Stoic ideas in *Hercules*, see on 162–3; for metaliterary/metatheatrical language in *Hercules*, see on 109–12.

Herculea/Of Hercules: more self-naming by Hercules, this time left to the end for particular emphasis. See on 631–40, 955–63. For climactic half-lines, see on 40–6. For the use of the adjective *Herculeus*, see 72 and n. *ad loc.*

As AMPHITRYON *speaks,* HERCULES *strings his bow and fires into the palace through its open door*: dramaturgically there is a choice here between having the first boy killed onstage (enacted through a combination perhaps of mime and blood-bags) and having it take place both onstage (the shooting of the arrow) and offstage (the boy shot just inside the palace) simultaneously. Clearly Megara and the other two sons are in the palace by line 995. Because blood-bags would most certainly have been used if the killing were onstage, the absence of any reference to blood in the description inclines me to favour the second possibility. It is to be noted, too, that all the other deaths take place in the palace, even those of Megara and the baby, who exit the palace at 1008 and then return to the palace at 1020 for their slaying.

991–5 Amphitryon describes the killing of the first child. Extensive depictions of a character's physical behaviour or appearance have sometimes been seen as evidence of a play's unsuitability for performance (see e.g. Zwierlein 1966: 61–2, Costa *ad Med.* 382ff.). But such descriptions are common in Plautus (see e.g. *MG* 200–15) and plentiful in Shakespeare: 'The king is angry; see, he gnaws his lip' (*Richard III* IV.ii.27); 'She embraces him', 'She hangs about his neck' (*The Winter's Tale* V.iii.111–12); 'Do you note | How much her grace is altered on the sudden? | How long her face is drawn? How pale she looks? | And of an earthy cold? Mark her eyes' (*Henry VIII* IV.ii.96–9). Seneca's own imitators had no problem with such descriptions (see e.g. Correr, *Progne* 678–80, Glover, *Med.* II.i, IV.iii). Cf. Amphitryon's account here with the Trojan Chorus' description of Cassandra's prophetic trance in *Agamemnon* (710–19), the Nurse's description of Medea's frantic behaviour in *Medea* (382–96), and the Chorus' description of the suicide of Jocasta in *Oedipus* (1040–1). See also the descriptions of the behaviour of Hercules (1042–8 below), Phaedra (*Pha.* 360–86), Andromache (*Tro.* 615–18), Polyxena (*Tro.* 945–8), and the description by one of Seneca's successors of Deianira's frantic behaviour (*HO* 233–53). Such descriptions sometimes (especially where facial expression is concerned) compensate for the restrictions of masked performance. Several scholars have detected here the influence of pantomime, in which a chorus or solo singer described the behaviour and emotions represented by a mute dancer: see Introd. §II, 22, Zanobi (2008: 233), (2014: 103–5); Bernstein (2017: 101–2).

The focus on blood and violence both here and in the rest of the killings (1002–7, 1022 8) is similar to that evident in the graphic narratives of Seneca's tragic messengers (see esp. those of *Phaedra, Oedipus, Troades, Thyestes*). Cf. also Cassandra's similarly 'real time' description of off-stage violence in *Agamemnon* (*Ag.* 867–909). Like Cassandra, Amphitryon is emotionally involved in the description, though the emotions he displays are utterly different.

Quo se caecus impegit furor/**Where has blind madness struck:** for the phrase *se impingere*, lit. 'to thrust/hurl itself', used of the violent onset of emotions/desire, see *Ira* 2.9.1: *quocumque uisum est libido se impingit*, 'lust thrusts itself/strikes wherever it likes'; see also VF 7.400–1. *Caecus*, 'blind', is used elsewhere in Senecan tragedy (*Oed.* 590, *Thy.* 27) to define *furor*. The phrase *caecus furor* is Horatian: *Epod.* 7.13. See also Val. Max. 9.2.ext.5. For *furor*, see on 92–9. For the ontologization of the emotions, see on 75–6. For speaker changes before the main caesura, see on 426–9.

uastum coactis flexit arcum cornibus/**His huge bow is bent, tips drawn together:** cf. the figurative bow of Shakespeare's raging Lear, fixed in his determination to (socially) slay his daughter: 'The bow is bent and drawn' (*KL* I.i.144). Hercules' bow has a famous future ahead of it: it will be required to take Troy (see Sophocles' *Philoctetes*). Note the breach of 'Porson's law'; see on 249–58. For *cornua* = 'tips', see Ov. *Met.* 1.455, 2.603, *HO* 549, Sil. 2.126 (*OLD* 7c).

harundo/**arrow:** note the emphasis placed on the word because of the preceding enjambement and the pause after the word; see 379–80 and n. *ad loc*. This arrow will be the most important stage prop for the rest of the play. For the shortening of the final *o* in *harundo* (also at 1195), see on 109–12.

medio … collo/**mid-neck:** the arrow of Euripides' Heracles lands in the liver (ἧπαρ, *Herac.* 979).

uulnere relicto/**leaves the wound:** a variant of a common line-beginning formula; see 265 and n. *ad loc*. Note the repetition of the same syllable at the end and beginning of juxtaposed words, here *re re*, as at 1123; see 67 and n. *ad loc*.

995–1002 Hercules attacks the palace.

eruam/**root out:** the verb operates in a different sense with its two objects, constituting a zeugma.

quid moror/**Why delay:** for this self-question, see also *Med.* 988, *Pho.* 30, *Oct.* 960. On delay or hesitation (*dubitatio*) in Senecan tragedy, see on 1283–4.

maius … bellum Mycenis/**Greater war … in Mycenae:** the allusion is to Eurystheus, king of Mycenae/Argos in the north-eastern Peloponnese (the two cities are often conflated in Senecan tragedy), who set Hercules the task of the twelve labours (see Introd. §VI, 61). Clearly Hercules is here contemplating some kind of revenge on Eurystheus. In Euripides' play (*Herac.* 943–6) Heracles thinks that he is attacking Mycenae.

Cyclopia … saxa/**Cyclopian rocks:** the walls of Mycenae were made of huge blocks of stone, which according to legend were the work of Cyclopes: see *Thy.* 407, Eur. *Herac.* 944, 998 (where they feature in Heracles' imagined assault on Mycenae). The Cyclopes, sons of Gaea and Uranus (Hes. *Th.* 139–46), were mighty one-eyed giants who worked as smiths for Hephaestus/Vulcan at his forge under Mt Etna in Sicily: see Virg. *Aen.* 8.416–53. The adjective *Cyclopia* might also have triggered for some members of Seneca's audience the famous Cyclops of Homer's *Odyssey*, who dashed the heads of Odysseus' crew against the earth (*Od.* 9.288–90), just as Hercules will shortly dash the head of his second son against the stone of the palace (1005–7).

manibus...nostris/**with my own hands:** an important instance of the *manus* motif and its association with physical violence. In Euripides' play the raging Heracles imagines uprooting the Cyclopian walls with 'crowbars and pick-axes' (μοχλούς δικέλλας θ', *Herac*. 944). Seneca's Hercules will use his bare hands. See Billerbeck *ad loc*. For the *manus* motif, see on 118–22.

nostris concidant: another breach of 'Porson's law'; see on 249–58.

Huc...et illuc/**all about:** lit. 'here and there'. For this iambic trimeter opening, see 287 and n. *ad loc*.

disiecto obice/**smash the bolt:** for the treatment of *obex* as masculine, see 237 and n. *ad loc*.

rumpatque postes/**Burst the posts:** Littlewood (2017: 163) suggests an ironic analogy here with Epicurus 'shattering the bars of nature's gates', *effringere...naturae...portarum claustra* (Lucr. 1.70–1).

perlucet omnis regia/**The whole palace lights up:** Hercules' remark clarifies (for the modern reader/scholar: no clarification would have been required in performance) which stage-building is under attack, viz. which is the one where his family have sought refuge. Seneca is rewriting the scene in Euripides' *Heracles*, where Megara and the third, youngest child seek refuge in the house of Heracles, which Heracles himself breaks into and where he kills his wife and son (*Herac*. 996–1000).

natum scelesti patris/**An evil father's son:** self-reflective irony, since it is his own son whom he is about to kill.

1002–9 Amphitryon describes the second killing, followed by Megara's rush from the palace. Again (see on 991–5) the description of offstage action seems indebted to pantomime, as well as to the typically graphic narratives of the Senecan messenger. Fitch *ad loc*. suggests the influence here of Ovid's account of the mad Athamas' slaying of his son Learchus at *Met* 4.516–19. Note that Ovid's Athamas had been maddened by the Fury, Tisiphone, sent by Juno. Cf. also Hercules' killing of Lichas at Ov. *Met*. 9.216–18 again by 'rotation': see below. For Seneca's 'gory' violence, see also on 1022–31 and Introd. §IV.

Looking into the palace: both here and at 1022 Amphitryon is clearly looking into the palace and describing what he sees there. Tarrant is in error when he claims (*ad Ag*. 867ff.) that 'there seems to be no valid example of looking through the door of the stage-building in Greek or Senecan tragedy'.

En blandas manus ad genua/**Look...pleading hands to knees:** ancient acts of supplication regularly involved touching the knees of the one supplicated. It is a practice as old as Homer (*Il*. 24.478, *Od*. 3.92, 6.142), and one often dramatized in Senecan tragedy: see *Pha.* 667, 703 (Phaedra before Hippolytus); *Tro.* 691 (Andromache before Ulysses); *Med.* 247 (Medea before Creon); *Thy.* 521-2 (Thyestes before Atreus); *Pho.* 306-7 (Antigone before Oedipus). Cf. also Eur. *Herac.* 986-9, where Heracles' son thrusts his hand at his father's chin and neck and speaks two lines of supplication. Seneca similarly dwells on the pathos of a child about to be killed at *Tro.* 715-17 (Astyanax, supplicating) and *Thy.* 145 (Pelops, running for a kiss) and 720-1 (young Tantalus, not supplicating). So, too, does Ovid (*Met.* 6.639-42: Itys). Note the focus here on 'hands' which prove ineffective. For the *manus* motif, see on 118-22. For *en*, see on 944-52.

scelus nefandum...aspectu horridum/Evil crime...a horror to behold: Amphitryon picks up Hercules' ironic phrase, *scelesti patris*, 'evil father', and applies its language to Hercules' own actions. He will later withdraw the term *scelus*: see 1237. For *horridus* with the ablative of the supine, see 764 and n. *ad loc.*

bis ter rotatum/whirled him round...twice, three times: similarly Ovid's Athamas 'whirls (Learchus) twice and three times', *bis terque...rotat* (*Met.* 4.517-18). Ovid increases the rotations in Hercules' killing of Lichas: *terque quaterque rotatum*, 'whirled him around three times and four times' (*Met.* 9.217). For asyndetic *bis ter*, as here, see *Thy.* 769.

ast/Then: this archaic conjunction, chosen here apparently because of its sonal properties, appears also at *Thy.* 721, where it is also followed by *illi* as a (self-evidently) dative of disadvantage: see Woodcock §64. *Ast illi* is found, too, at *HO* 1752, but *ast* does not occur in Seneca's prose works.

illi caput sonuit/his head cracked: Seneca pays attention to sound, focusing on it regularly, especially at dramatic moments: see e.g. 150, 522-3, 574-6, 688, 784, 790, 982, 1100, 1108, 1114, 1204; *Tro.* 65, 108, 115; *Thy.* 1045; *Pho.* 161. Here the moment is both dramatic and grisly.

cerebro tecta disperso madent/The house drips spattered brains: cf. the similar detail in the matter of Astyanax's death at *Tro.* 1116: *cerebro...expresso*, 'brains squeezed out'. Such grisly detail is found, too, in the battle-descriptions of Virgil (see *Aen.* 10.416, 11.698). Slightly less grisly is the account of the death of the first child in Euripides (*Herac.* 979-80). See further on 1022-31 (*corpori trunco*).

At misera/But poor: for the use of *at* to index a change of referents, see on 57-63.

Megara furenti similis/Megara...like a mad woman: so, too, Jocasta in *Phoenissae* rushes 'like a mad woman', *furenti similis* (*Pho.* 427), as similarly at *Oed.* 1004-7. The gender ideology behind such descriptions seems patent.

Euripides' Megara snatches up the child and takes him inside the palace, barring the door (*Herac.* 996–7). The final *a* of *Megara* is probably long, as at 203, so that the opening foot is anapaestic. Note also, as at 203 (see n. *ad loc.*), the wordplay between Megara and *paruum* (1008). For translingual punning on proper names, see on 35–40. For the two-word simile, see 712 and n. *ad loc.*

1010–11 *Licet…profuga condaris*/**Though you take refuge:** for *licet* with the subjunctive, see 21–2 and n. *ad loc.*

Tonantis…sinu/**in the Thunderer's bosom:** in the bosom of the Thunder-god, Iuppiter Tonans; see on 1–5. Clearly Hercules is addressing Megara, but already mistaking her for Juno (see 1018–19), with Amphitryon perhaps functioning as Jupiter.

temet haec dextra/**This hand…you:** forms of the personal pronouns with the suffix *-met* are not infrequent in Senecan tragedy and imperial verse for emphasis and/or metrical convenience. There is another occurrence of *temet* at 1252. See also *Med.* 899; *Pha.* 257, 588; *Oed.* 809; *Ag.* 51, 203. For *dextra* (and the *manus* motif), see on 118–22.

1012–15 Amphitryon addresses Megara.

Quo misera pergis/**Run where, poor wretch:** for the phrase, see also *Pha.* 142, *HO* 909. For the substantival use of *miser*, see on 313–16.

latebram/**hideout:** the singular *latebram* (*E*) is preferred to the 'particularly awkward' (Fitch *ad loc.*) plural *latebras* (*PT^{pc}CSV*), printed by Caviglia, Zwierlein, and Billerbeck. Viansino (1965 and 1993), Giardina (1966 and 2007), and Chaumartin also print *latebram*.

nullus salutis…est locus/**No place is safe:** note the continuing *locus*-motif, which will loom large at the end of Act V.

amplectere ipsum potius/**Embrace him instead:** some irony here, since this is precisely what Amphitryon and Megara attempted to do in Act III (628–40), when Hercules was 'sane'. The imperative with *potius* is a Senecan mannerism: see e.g. 1265–6, *Ag.* 308, *Oed.* 629, *Med.* 506, *Thy.* 1021.

blanda prece lenire tempta/**try to soften him With gentle prayer:** Amphitryon is echoing Ovid's own plea to Sextus Pompey: *tempta lenire precando | numina*, 'Try to soften the gods with prayer' (*Pont.* 4.15.23–4). Ovid, like Amphitryon, has human deities in mind.

1015–17 *Parce iam…precor*/**Now spare me…I beg:** appeals for 'sparing/ pardon' occur elsewhere in Senecan tragedy (generally) at moments of dramatic crisis: e.g. Hercules at 595 and 1314 (see also 1267); Amphitryon at 1249; the Chorus at *Med.* 595, 669; Jason at *Med.* 1004; Oedipus (cited by the

Messenger) at *Oed.* 975; Thyestes at *Thy.* 995–6; Oedipus at *Pho.* 40—cf. also the Chorus at 872 above, Hyllus at *HO* 982. Several of the above include, as here, the use of the alliterative formula, *parce...precor*, common in such prayers: see e.g. Hor. *Odes* 4.1.2, Tib. 1.8.51, Ov. *Met.* 2.361–2. For *iam* with *parce*, see also 1314, *Med.* 1004, *Pho.* 40, *HO* 982. Like similar appeals for compassion (see Boyle on *Med.* 478–82), appeals for mercy in Seneca's plays are generally fruitless. Oedipus' remark to Creon—*non erit ueniae locus*, lit. 'there will be no place for forgiveness/mercy' (*Oed.* 263)—could function as a definition of Senecan tragedy (excluding the final scene of this play). For the Roman semiotics of such appeals, see on 1314–17. See also on 592–7, 1265–72.

agnosce Megaram/Recognize Megara: at the level of dramatic action Megara sees a delusional husband but cannot correct his vision. At the metatheatrical level, Megara is requesting a tragic recognition scene along the lines of the Amphitryon-Hercules one in Act III (618–25). She fails to receive it. The final recognition scene will come later (1196)—after her off-stage death. For 'recognition' in Senecan tragedy, see on 622–5. For metatheatrical language and motifs in *Hercules*, see on 109–12.

natus hic uultus tuos habitusque reddit/Your son here mirrors Your looks and bearing: for the physical resemblance of father and son elsewhere in Senecan tragedy, see *Tro.* 466, 1113, 1117 (Hector and Astyanax), *Pha.* 655–60 (Theseus and Hippolytus). *Vultus*, 'looks', and *habitus*, 'bearing' are often combined: *Tro.* 464–6, *Ben.* 2.13.2, Stat. *Theb.* 2.230.

cernis ut tendat manus/See how he extends his hands: a brilliant use of the *manus* motif, in which 'hands' are not emblems of violence or power but of the need for compassion. For the motif, see on 118–22.

1018–20 Hercules looks into the face of Megara and sees Juno. This delusion, which is not in Euripides' play, will not last long. At 1035–8 the family he slaughters is again that of Lycus, and he offers his victims sarcastically to Juno. For Hercules' obsession with Juno, see on 604–15.

Teneo nouercam/I hold my stepmother: an ironic pick-up of Amphitryon's utterance of joy: *teneone in auras editum*, 'Do I hold a breathing man?' For *nouerca*, see on 19–29.

sequere/Come with me: a common command in Roman comedy to facilitate an exit from the stage (e.g. Plaut. *Aul.* 349, *Mil.* 78, Ter. *And.* 978); here a command by Hercules to Megara (= 'Juno') to exit the stage with him. Hence the stage direction after 1020. Fitch (351) cites Orestes' similar instruction to Clytemnestra at Aesch. *Cho.* 904 (ἕπου).

iugo/yoke: the yoke of marriage and alleged subservience to Juno.

ante matrem/before its mother: the ambiguity seems patent: (i) (primary sense) before its mother is killed; (ii) (secondary sense) in front of its mother.

paruulum hoc monstrum/this tiny monster: though diminutives with their emotional resonance are rare in Senecan tragedy, this highly suggestive epithet, famously used by Catullus in his first marriage-song (61.209) and used once by Virgil (indeed it is the only diminutive used by Virgil and he uses it of Dido's frustrated hope for a 'tiny Aeneas', *paruulus...Aeneas*, *Aen*. 4.328–9), is deployed to heighten pathos some six times in Senecan tragedy and with one exception always of a very young, male child: see also *Oed*. 806, *Tro*. 456, 1089, *Thy*. 144 (in the last two passages a 'small child', *paruulus*, is about to be killed). At *Oed*. 463 the adjective is applied to *manus*, 'hand'. Here an aspect of its intellectual and emotional power is its oxymoronic and ironic combination with *monstrum*, a term Hercules will eventually use of himself (see 1280 and n. *ad loc*.). *Paruulus* is the only diminutive epithet to appear in Senecan tragedy apart from a single use of *quantulus* (*Pho*. 8: see Frank *ad loc*.). Correr resurrects the adjective for Progne's son Ythis (*Prog*. 891).

1021 I join Zwierlein, Billerbeck, and most modern editors in accepting *A*'s assignment of this line to Megara (*MN* assign it to Amphitryon as the opening line of his speech; E assigns 1021–31 to Hercules). The line rewrites the Euripidean Megara's similar cry, as reported by the Messenger: Ὦ τεκών, τί δρᾷς; τέκνα κτείνεις; 'O father (of our children), what are you doing? Are you killing your/our children?' (*Herac*. 975–6). Fitch and Viansino (1993) print the assignment of *MN* to Amphitryon. It is possible to have Megara's line spoken offstage, but, since Seneca elsewhere never uses offstage speech (there are offstage screams/cries in *Phaedra*), and Megara's line seems to respond to Hercules' previous words, it seems preferable to have the words spoken onstage.

Quo tendis amens/Where with this madness: for *amens*, see on 426–9.

1022–31 Amphitryon describes the deaths of Megara and her baby son (1022–6), reacts emotionally to the sight (1026–8), and demands that Hercules kill him, too (1028–31). This is the second time Amphitryon offers himself to death (see 509–10); he will repeat his wish at 1039–42, and make a final death-offer (in different circumstances) at 1300–13. For the debt to pantomime and tragic messenger narratives, see on 991–5.

Looking into the palace: see on 1002–9.

Pauefactus infans...perit/infant, scared...Dies: similarly (and again alliteratively) in *Hercules Oetaeus*, Lichas, pursued by the raging Hercules, 'spent his death in fear', *mortem metu consumpsit* (*HO* 811). Megara's and Hercules' youngest child seems to be of 'toddler' age, able to rush into the temple with the others but also young enough to be picked up for protection and to be called *infans*.

igneo uultu/fiery gaze: cf. Seneca on the 'brief madness' (*breuis insania*) which is *ira*, 'anger' (*Ira* 1.1.4): *flagrant ac micant oculi, multus ore toto rubor exaestuante ab imis praecordiis sanguine*, 'the eyes blaze and sparkle, the whole face is deep-red with the blood surging from the bottom of the heart'; on *ira* again (*Ira* 2.35.5): *talem nobis iram figuremus, flamma lumina ardentia*, 'Let us figure anger as such, eyes blazing with flame'; see also *Ira* 3.13.2. Here there is an additional contextual/textual irony: in Act II Amphitryon drew attention to the 'fiery eyes' (*igneos...oculos*, 218–19) of the serpents which the infant Hercules killed; Hercules is now the serpent in his own home killing the infant. For fire imagery and madness/*furor*, see on 100–3; for *uultus*, 'gaze', see on 329–31.

timor/terror: for arguments in favour of *timor* (*E*) in preference to *pauor* (*T*ᵖᶜτ *recc.*), printed by Zwierlein and Billerbeck, see Fitch *ad loc.* Most modern editors prefer *timor*.

claua libratur/club's...levelled: the Euripidean Megara is killed in a less gruesome way, with an arrow which slays mother and son (*Herac.* 1000). For *librare*, see 119 and n. *ad loc.*

corpori trunco/truncated body: a very Roman image not in Euripides' play. Cf. Priam's headless body at *Aen.* 2.557–8, Manil. 4.64, *Tro.* 140–1, and Pompey's at Lucan 1.685–6, 8.667ff.—or the plethora of severed heads of Sulla's opponents at Lucan 2.160–73. The lemmatized phrase was used by Catullus (*truncum...corpus*) of Polyxena at Cat. 64.370. In Senecan tragedy note also the *caput amputatum* of Agamemnon (*Ag.* 902), and the severed heads, hands, and feet of the sons of Thyestes (*Thy.* 1004–5). For Seneca's focus on the 'trunk', *truncus*, of a human corpse, see *Pha.* 1098, *Ag.* 902, *Tro.* 141, *Thy.* 728, 761. This 'love of gruesome detail' (Keulen *ad Tro.* 1115–17), which may be found elsewhere in Senecan tragedy (see e.g. 1006–7, *Tro.* 1110–17, *Pha.* 1093ff., 1246ff., *Ag.* 901ff., *Oed.* 961ff., *Thy.* 749ff.), had many Roman precedents from Ennius through to Ovid, and may be found in abundance throughout the epic of Seneca's nephew and that of his Flavian successor Statius. See further Introd. §IV.

nec usquam est/it's nowhere: another darkly ironic phrase; here 'nowhere' (*nec usquam*) = 'everywhere'. The phrase is also used in the 'Death Ode' of *Troades* (390–2) of a person who has died and no longer exists. See Plaut. *Cist.* 686: *neque ego sum usquam*, 'and I am nowhere' = 'and I do not exist'; also Hor. *Serm.* 2.5.102, Ov. *Met.* 1.587.

cernere hoc audes/Can you view this: a powerful metatheatrical moment; Amphitryon's question is addressed to himself but has patent ramifications for the audience. For metatheatre in *Hercules*, see on 109–12, and Introd. §VII, *passim*.

nimis uiuax senectus/Life-clinging age: *uiuax senectus*, lit. 'living/flourishing old age', 'vigorous senility', is an overt oxymoron. Note the ontologization of *senectus* to turn it into Amphitryon's addressee: see Hecuba's similar address at *Tro.* 42 (*uiuax senectus*) and at Ov. *Met.* 13.517 (*annosa senectus*). Cf. the ontologization of the emotions (see on 75–6) and of *uirtus* (see on 1156–9). For the avoidance of the *anime* formula, see also 1157 and n. *ad loc*. The phrase seems inspired by Ovid (*Met.* 13.517–19).

habes mortem paratam/Death stands by: having 'death ready and waiting/standing by' is an existential position of Seneca the philosopher, for whom death 'stands by/is ready in all places and at all times' (*parata omnibus locis omnibusque momentis, Ep. Mor.* 30.16), and of Senecan tragic figures (*mors tam parata, Oed.* 77), many of whom see in death a freedom from pain, dishonour, grief, or other unbearable circumstances (*libera mors, Ag.* 591). This is the second occasion in the play that Amphitryon has expressed a death-wish (see 509–10); there will be a third (1311–13). Acceptance of suicide as a morally appropriate exit from intolerable conditions of life is ancient, and is found in Greek and Roman literature from Homer onwards (see e.g. *Il.* 18.88ff., *Od.* 10.49ff.). It became prominent in Cynicism and in Stoic philosophy. See discussion in Introd. §V, 47–50, where the core Senecan notion of *libera mors* (= 'death's freedom' and 'death freely chosen') and the death-wish exhibited by Senecan characters are also examined.

To HERCULES *In the palace*: Hercules has not left the palace yet; see below after 1032–4.

Pectori tela indue/In my breast sink your arrows: I join Fitch (2018) in printing the emendation of Axelson, *pectori tela* (Zwierlein 1986*b*: 66), to replace the obviously corrupt reading of *EA, pectus in tela*. The emendation accords with Seneca's practice with *induere* at *Pho.* 180 and *Oed.* 341 (see also 1312 below). Zwierlein and most modern editors print the emendation of M. Müller: *pectus en telo*. For discussion, see Fitch (2004*b*: 27–9).

stipitem istum caede monstrorum inlitum/that club smeared with the blood Of monsters: there seems intentional ambivalence here. The club has been smeared with the blood of monsters, but the blood most recently smeared on the club is that of Hercules' wife, Megara (1024–6), perhaps thought of by the deranged Hercules, like the third son (1020), as a monster. For the important *monstrum* motif, see 1280 and n. *ad loc*.

istum/that: the reading of *EA*. Zwierlein prefers Axelson's conjecture *istum huc*, which is also printed by Billerback but not by Fitch (1987a and 2018), Viansino (1993), Chaumartin, or Giardina (2007). This time Axelson's conjecture is neither necessary nor persuasive.

falsum ac nomini turpem tuo...parentem/false father Staining your name: a powerful mixture of sarcasm and personal bitterness.

1032-4 Assigned to Theseus in *EA*, these lines evidently belong to the Chorus, who are required to ask this question of Amphitryon because he is, apart from the Chorus, alone onstage. Theseus left the stage earlier in the act (917) and cannot reasonably be thought to have entered during the slaughters without making some comment upon them. The chorus are given the role of describing the irrational behaviour of another character also at *Oed.* 1004-9 (on Jocasta), *Pha.* 824-8 (on Phaedra), *Ag.* 710-19, 775-8 (on Cassandra). The assignment to the Chorus is recorded in the Ambrosian MS in Milan (*M*), and is printed here, as well as by Zwierlein, Fitch (1987a and 2018), Viansino (1993), Chaumartin, and Billerbeck. Viansino (1965), Giardina (1966 and 2007), and Caviglia reproduce the *EA* assignment.

senior/old man: not likely to be the address chosen by Theseus (see above). It is, however, the address used by Euripides' chorus in addressing Amphitryon at *Herac.* 1045: πρέσβυ.

quo pergis amens/What is this madness: cf. 1021. For *amens*, see on 426-9.

obtectus late/conceal, lie hid: in Euripides this is what Amphitryon says that he will do, as Heracles begins to wake (*Herac.* 1070); in Seneca the advice comes from the Chorus during the mad scene and is ignored by Amphitryon.

unumque manibus aufer Herculeis scelus/And remove one crime from Hercules' hands: Euripides' Amphitryon expresses the same desire to limit Heracles' blood-crimes by removing himself as possible victim (*Herac.* 1075ff.). For the *manus* motif, see on 118-22. For the use of the adjective *Herculeus*, see 72 and n. *ad loc.*

HERCULES *enters from the palace*: it is clear that Hercules enters here, since he seems not to have heard Amphitryon's address at 1028-31. His initial words, too, echo those of Oedipus as he enters his play's final act: see below.

1035-8 Hercules' important first words after the bloody slaughter of his family. They are filled with the most extreme tragic irony, as Hercules proclaims (without, of course, realizing it) that he has fulfilled Juno's plans articulated in the prologue.

Bene habet/**All is well:** the same words begin Act V of *Oedipus* (998) with both similar and different irony. The difference is Hercules' unconscious, metatheatrical echo of Oedipus' statement (if, as seems most probable, *Oedipus* is the earlier play: see Introd. 6–7), which underscores Hercules' affinity to Oedipus, signalled earlier (see on 268–75), in the failure to recognize kin. Hercules' phraseology is resonant of the arena (see Virg. *Aen.* 12.296 and Tarrant 2012 *ad loc.*); cf. Cassandra's description of Clytemnestra's slaying of Agamemnon: *habet, peractum est*, 'he is hit, it is done' (*Ag.* 901), where *habet* = 'he has the wound'. The formula is repeated at *HO* 1457, 1472. Cf. also Medea after killing her second son: *bene est, peractum est*, 'Good, it is done' (*Med.* 1019)—and *Ag.* 870, *Thy.* 889, where Seneca's predilection for the (semiotically loaded) use of *bene* in the final part of a play is similarly evident. (For *bene est* earlier in a play, see *Tro.* 630, *Med.* 550, *Thy.* 279). Here Hercules' approbation not only likens him to Oedipus and to Clytemnestra (*dramatis personae* of probably earlier plays), but also (perhaps prospectively) to the avengers Medea and Atreus—all four being killers of kin. For perhaps the most dramatically pointed use of *bene* in Senecan tragedy, see its employment as the final word of *Phoenissae* (664): *imperia pretio quolibet constant bene*, 'Power is purchased at any price well'. The 'price' in question is fratricide. For *bene habet* used in the prose works, note the double use of it at *Ep. Mor.* 24.9–10 concerning the recently self-killed Scipio after the Battle of Thapsus. Mark the rare elision in a first-foot anapaest of a Senecan iambic line: cf. *Oed.* 998 (*bene habet*), *Thy.* 324, *Pho.* 449, 489, *HO* 1821. For metatheatrical language in *Hercules*, see on 109–12.

pudendi regis/**shameful king:** 'scilicet Lici', Trevet notes. *Pudendus* is a rare modifier in the Senecan prose and verse *corpus*. It is used only once in the prose works and then substantively (*Marc.* 2.3), and four times in the tragedies (also at 1180, *Oed.* 260, *Thy.* 626).

tibi hunc dicatum...gregem cecidi/**For thee...I have slain This consecrated flock:** this whole speech of Hercules is redolent with sacrificial language, making of his family slaughter a perversion of that ritual. The sacrificial killing of children is a prominent part of the action of three other Senecan tragedies: Medea's slaying of the first child at *Med.* 969–71 (onstage), the Greeks' slaying of Astyanax and Polyxena at *Tro.* 1068–1164, and Atreus' slaying of Thyestes' sons at *Thy.* 682–743 (offstage, described in a messenger-scene). Hercules' use of *grex* here for 'flock/children' was foreshadowed by the Chorus, when they announced the entry of Megara and her *paruus grex* (203) at the start of Act II: see n. *ad loc.* For *caedere* =

'sacrificially slay', see on 875–81; for sacrificial language and imagery in *Hercules*, see on 918–24. Euripides' Heracles slays the third child 'sacrificially' (*Herac.* 995). Lodge's Herakles similarly slays his children in sacrificial style in his *Herakles* (1908: Tenth Scene); so, too, Tamburlaine slays his son, Calyphas (*2 Tam.* IV.i.110–19).

maximi coniunx Iouis/**wife of greatest Jove:** a title Juno rejected in the opening of this play (1–5), ironically restored to her by Hercules, who recently excluded her from the sacrificial invocations of 900–8 and the prayer of 926ff., and whom he recently thought he had captured and was threatening (1018–19). For Hercules' obsession with Juno, see on 604–15.

uota persolui libens/**I've gladly paid vows:** more ritualistic language; indeed a version of the religious votive formulae, *V.S.L.* (*uotum soluit libens*, 'gladly pays his vow'), *V.L.S.* (*uotum libens soluit*). Cf. *Ag.* 806–7: *pecore uotiuo libens…colam*, 'I shall gladly worship with votive flock'. For *libens* in prayer, see also Livius Andronicus' *Aegistus* (frag. 9 Ribbeck, text uncertain): *sollemnitusque deo litat laudem et lubens*, 'And he solemnly and gladly praises the god'—which may refer to the returned Agamemnon. See also Lycus' ritual language at 515 above. Notably, too, the Euripidean slaughter is presented as a perversion of the sacrifice begun at *Herac.* 922–30. For sacrificial language and imagery, see on 918–24.

te digna/**Worthy of thee:** a particular irony permeating Hercules' sarcastic statement is that his words are true in a way which he does not mean or see. Another aspect of the irony is that Hercules is echoing Juno's words from the prologue: he has just performed something *dignum nouerca*, 'worthy of his stepmother' (112). For *dignus*, see on 109–12.

Argos uictimas alias dabit/**Argos will give other victims:** a reference to a potential killing of Eurystheus, king of Argos, main city of the Argolid in the north-eastern Peloponnese. Though Seneca prefers the Greek form, *Argos* (as here, see *Tro.* 855, *Thy.* 122, 411, 627), the Latin plural form *Argi* is also used at *Ag.* 304, *Tro.* 245, and *Thy.* 119. In Senecan tragedy Argos and Mycenae, though separate cities in the Argolid, are regularly conflated, as they were in Sophocles and Euripides (see Tarrant 1976: 160–1). Juno was the patronness of Argos; hence the use of Argos here has special resonance. For *uictima* of human sacrificial victim, see on 918–24.

1039–42 Amphitryon applies Hercules' sacrificial language to his own death, asking him to complete the sacrifice by slaying him. This is the third time that Amphitryon has offered himself for death (see also 509–10, 1029–31); it will not be the last (see 1300–13). For sacrificial language and imagery in *Hercules*, see on 918–24.

Nondum litasti/The sacrifice isn't done: lit. 'you have not yet made an acceptable sacrifice' (*OLD* 2a). *Litare/litatio* connoted not simply (normally animal) sacrifice, but a successful sacrifice of appeasement or atonement, involving the 'acceptance of the victim by the gods' (Beard et al. 1998: 36). *Litare* occurs again at similarly cardinal moments in *Agamemnon* (577) and *Medea* (1020), and again the word involves human sacrificial victims. See also *Oct.* 980, Virg. *Aen.* 2.118, used of human victims.

Walks to the altar: see below.

Stat ecce ad aras hostia/Look, a victim stands at the altar: it is possible to take 'stands at the altar' as continuing the metaphor of sacrificial 'victim'. Given the presence of an altar onstage, the phrase could misfire if Amphitryon were not actually at the stage altar. Hence the stage directions preceding. This is the only occurrence of *hostia* in the play (*hostia* at 634 in some editions is an unpersuasive emendation by Leo). Seneca uses the word also at *Med.* 66 and thrice in *Thyestes* (718, 759, 915). For initial *stat*, see on 533–41; for Seneca's use of the plural form of *ara*, see on 875–81.

expectat manum/Waiting for your hand: cf. Electra offering herself as sacrificial victim to Clytemnestra at *Ag.* 975: *intenta ceruix uulnus expectat tuum*, 'My neck is bent to await your blow'. See also Deianira at *HO* 977: *dexteram expecto tuam*, 'I await your right hand'. For the *manus* motif, see on 118–22.

praebeo occurro insequor/I offer, present, insist: for first-person verbs in asyndeton, used, as here, to suggest passionate resolve, see *Tro.* 653 (Andromache): *potero perpetiar feram*, 'I can, I'll suffer, I'll bear it'; *Pha.* 566 (Hippolytus): *horreo fugio execror*, 'I dread, I shun, I curse them [women]'; *Med.* 507 (Medea): *abdico eiuro abnuo*, 'I disown, disavow, disclaim them'.

macta/Strike: lit. '(sacrificially) slay'; see on 634–6.

1042–53 Amphitryon sees and describes Hercules' collapse onstage (1042–8), checks that he is now asleep and orders the removal of his weapons. The act ends. Hercules' collapse/fainting follows his delusions/visions, just as the collapses/faintings of Cassandra (*Ag.* 775–7), Lucan's *matrona* (1.695) and Phemenoe (5.222–4), and Statius' Calchas (*Ach.* 1.536–7) follow their respective visions (see Roche *ad* Luc. 1.695). But what Seneca's audience witness here, viz. violent madness followed by restorative sleep and confused awakening, was to become something of a convention ('the *Hercules Furens* convention': Soellner 1958) in English Renaissance drama: see e.g. Anon., *The Rare Triumphs of Love and Fortune* (1582), Greene's *Orlando Furioso* (1591), and Marston's *Antonio and Mellida* (1599), and *Antonio's Revenge* (1600).

1042-8 *Quid hoc est*/**What's this:** for this expression of surprise, see on 939-44.

errat acies luminum/**Does my eyesight fail:** again Amphitryon draws attention to his failing eyes; see 618 and n. *ad loc.* Note the breach of 'Porson's law', as at 652; see on 249-58. For *acies*, see 602 and n. *ad loc.*

uisus...hebetat/**Dull my vision:** the phrase is Virgilian (*Aen.* 2.605). For the dulling of the senses through suffering or grief, see Thyestes at *Thy.* 920: *pectora longis hebetata malis*, 'Heart dulled by lasting pain'; Boeth. *Cons.* 1. Prosa 4.28. For sickness altering vision, see *Oed.* 204.

an uideo/**Or do I see:** for the use of *an* to introduce a 'shocking suggestion', see Frank *ad Pho.* 577, who cites *Ag.* 195; *Tro.* 890, 973; *Thy.* 745; *Pho.* 498, 577; *HO* 1954.

uultus...moles/**His face...the sea:** this extensive depiction of Hercules' collapse onstage, like other Senecan descriptions of a character's physical behaviour or appearance, seems to show the influence of pantomime (see on 991-5). It also shows the influence of contemporary rhetoric. Descriptions of fainting-spells etc. figure in the elder Seneca's account of declamation and seem to have been especially associated with the elder Seneca's friend, Porcius Latro (*Con.* 1.1.16, 4.7; 7.1.6, 1.20). For descriptions of onstage collapses in Senecan tragedy, see also those of Phaedra (*Pha.* 585), Cassandra (*Ag.* 775-7), Hecuba (*Tro.* 949), and Amphitryon (*Herc.* 1317)—note, too, the undescribed onstage collapses caused by suicide (Phaedra, Jocasta) or a fatal blow (Cassandra). Descriptions of faintings/collapses may be found, too, in the Greek tragedians: see e.g. Eur. *Hec.* 438-43, *Tro.* 462-5. In Euripides Heracles collapses after being felled by a rock hurled at his chest by Athena (*Herac.* 1001-8). Seneca avoids the divine intervention favoured by the Greek dramatist. For *uultus*, 'face', see on 329-31.

ad terram ruit/**crashes to earth:** Heracles crashes to earth in Euripides' play (*Herac.* 1006), but there his fall is caused by Athena's rock.

ut caesa...moles/**Like an ash felled...the sea:** a short double simile. With the first (the simile of the felled tree, common in epic), cf. the brief simile at Hom. *Il.* 5.560 or the more elaborate similes at Hom. *Il.* 4.482-7, Apollon. 4.1682-6, Virg. *Aen.* 2.626-31; with the second, cf. the simile at *Aen.* 9.710-16 (also Silius 4.295-9). Cf. also the similarly short simile used in the collapse of Cassandra at *Ag.* 776-7. For other brief similes, as opposed to the (often criticized) extended similes, see e.g. 1089-91, *Pha.* 102-3, *Med.* 863-5, *Thy.* 87-9 (also a double simile), 438-9, 870. For similes in Senecan tragedy, including 'epic similes', see on 679-88. For two-word similes, see 712, 1009, and nn. *ad locc.*

1048–53 *leto dedit...misit ad mortem*/did...kill...killed: periphrastic phrases for killing are common in Senecan tragedy in keeping with the dramatist's 'noun style' (see on 11–18). See e.g. 431, 1175; *Pha.* 695; *Oed.* 521; *Ag.* 523, 887; *Tro.* 651; *Med.* 17–18, 473, 1005; *Pho.* 234, 579; cf. also *Oct.* 509.

furor/rage: for the ontologization of *furor* and the emotions, see on 75–6. For *furor* see on 92–9.

sopor est/It is sleep: for *sopor* as 'deep, overpowering sleep', see on 689–96.

reciprocos spiritus motus agit/His breathing is regular: similarly Euripides' Amphitryon takes note of Hercules' breathing after his collapse and pronounces it to be sleep: *Herac.* 1060–1. *Reciprocus* is a rare word in Roman verse (Acc. *Philoc.* frag. 545 Klotz) and almost a Senecan *hapax*. It occurs also at *Ag.* 449 of the regular, arcing movement of the dolphin. The word's first attested instance in non-dramatic verse is at VF 8.331.

detur quieti tempus/Give him time to rest: cf. Dido's request for 'rest and space for her madness', *requiem spatiumque furori* (Virg. *Aen.* 4.433). Again Amphitryon is the advocate for *quies*. See Introd. §VII, 77.

somno graui...leuet/heavy sleep...lighten: paradoxical wordplay introduces what will be a main theme of the ensuing choral ode: sleep's ability to cure. *Graui* (*E*) is preferred to *grauis* (*A*), favoured by Zwierlein. The reading of *E* is printed by most modern editors. For paradoxical phrasing in *Hercules*, see on 30–5.

Remouete, famuli, tela/Slaves, Move the weapons: Seneca's Amphitryon is more moderate in his treatment of the sleeping Hercules; his Euripidean counterpart and his slaves/attendants bind Heracles to a broken pillar of the collapsed house (*Herac.* 1009–11). Slaves, of course, sometimes appear in Greek and Roman tragedy as *dramatis personae* (see e.g. Phorbas and the Messenger in *Oedipus*, the *Senex* in *Troades*, the Nurse in *Agamemnon*, *Phaedra*, and *Medea*). They also appear frequently as *personae mutae*, 'silent characters', and perform a variety of stage tasks (see after 520–3). Sometimes explicitly addressed as *famuli* or with an equivalent phrase (*Oed.* 824, *Pha.* 725, *Med.* 188, *Thy.* 901, *Ag.* 787, 800, 997), they are at other times (so, too, other *personae mutae*: guards/soldiers/huntsmen etc.) the recipients of an unadorned imperative (e.g. 506, 908, 918 above, *Pha.* 863, 1275–9) or are commanded periphrastically through *aliquis* and an implied or actual jussive subjunctive (*Oed.* 862, possibly *Med.* 996). See Tarrant *ad Ag.* 787. *Famulus* is the standard term for domestic slave/servant/attendant in Senecan tragedy, in which a form of *seruus* appears only once (*seruam, Pha.* 622). Neither *famulus* nor *famula*, however, occur in Senecan prose. Note the use of an imperative to close the act. Imperatives regularly form the conclusion to a Senecan act, often addressed, as here, to guards/attendants etc. on the stage or to other *dramatis personae*: e.g. *Tro.* 813, 1178; *Oed.* 707; *Pha.* 1275–9; *Ag.* 306, 1010; *Med.* 847–8, 1026–7; *Thy.* 544. See also the self-addressed closural imperatives at *Med.* 54, *Oed.* 880–1, and the one addressed to the *uitia terrarum* which closes *Oedipus* (1061).

ne repetat furens/**lest he want them again—in rage:** as Billerbeck *ad loc.* observes, Amphitryon is tapping into proverbial wisdom ('Volksweisheit'). See Publ. 184 (Duff): *eripere telum, non dare irato decet*, 'It is right to remove a weapon from an angry man, not to give him one'; cf. *Ira* 1.19.8: *male irato ferrum committitur*, 'It's a bad idea to hand a sword to an angry man'. For Seneca and Publilius Syrus, see on 125–204 (introd.). Note the powerful final word of the act, which not only pairs well with the opening word of Act IV (*ultrice*), but encapsulates its major theme. For the alliterative closural line (1053), see on 275–8.

SLAVES *take the weapons (including the lion skin) into the palace*: for the lion skin's removal, see 1150–2.

ATTENDANTS *take the sacrificial paraphernalia and animals (or sculpted heads) offstage left*: this seems the best place to remove the sacrificial animals/sculpted heads and sacrificial equipment etc. from the stage to make room for the dead bodies of Hercules' family, upon which much of the dramatic focus of the following ode and the final act will fall.

ALL *others remain*: it is not unusual to have *dramatis personae* of Act IV remain onstage during the final choral ode and into the final act. This happens also in *Phaedra* (Theseus, Messenger) and *Troades* (Hecuba, Andromache).

Fourth Choral Ode: The 'Lamentation Ode' (1054–1137)

Final choral odes in Senecan tragedy vary in theme and tone. Two are odes of fear: *Medea* 849–78, which is directed to Medea's *furor* and *ira*, and *Thyestes* 789–884, which is concerned with cosmic collapse. In *Phaedra* (1123–53) and *Oedipus* (980–97) the Chorus calmly offer an objective 'philosophical' frame for the terrible events of the action. The final ode of *Troades* is one of bitterness (in the face of imminent separation) and that of *Agamemnon* is a laudation of Hercules, listing and celebrating, though modifying, his 'twelve' labours. *Phoenissae* has no choral odes. An obvious contrast is effected by the present ode with the final ode of *Agamemnon* (probably the earlier drama), which praises rather than decries Herculean violence, and with the second and third choral odes of this play, which are also laudations of Herculean force. More interesting is this ode's relationship to the first ode of the play, the 'Dawn Ode'. There is an obvious contrast of tone between the two odes but also a sense of 'ring-composition': those early themes of the dangers of *uirtus animosa*, 'spirited virtue' (201) and the desirability of *quies*, 'peace' and rest' (160, 175), seem to have come full circle. They find their home in the apostrophe to and *laudatio* of an apotheosized Sleep (1066–81), sung in the same anapaestic metre in which the Chorus had announced their lyric presence in the play.

The 'Lamentation Ode', like the earlier odes of the play and indeed most choral odes of Senecan tragedy (see e.g. *Pha.* 736ff., *Med.* 849ff., *Thy.* 546ff.), responds to the immediate dramatic situation, in this case Hercules' slaying of his family and his bodily collapse. It is, however, the only final choral ode of Senecan tragedy which is a dirge (*nenia*, κομμός, θρῆνος) and (since stage business is conducted by others during the course of the singing) the only Senecan choral ode which responds to and actively uses a changing situation onstage. Probably of all Senecan choral odes it is the one which, through its interaction with characters onstage, living (Hercules, tossing in his sleep) and dead (the sons and Megara, brought from the palace to the stage), and with stage props (the arrow), comes closest to the Horatian ideal (*AP* 194–6):

> actoris partis chorus officiumque uirile
> defendat neu quid medios intercinat actus
> quod non proposito conducat et haereat apte.

> Let the chorus sustain the part and manly duty
> Of an actor and not sing anything between acts
> Not conducive to and aptly fitting the theme.

Much of the ode's energy comes from a pervasive use of apostrophe, its ritualistic alliteration, repetition, and phrasing and the global reach of its referents (1054–62•, 1100–14). Such referents (heaven, earth, ocean, hell) could again have allowed actors (in this case those constituting the Chorus) in their gestures to make potent use of the verticality of the Roman theatrical space: see on 1–124 (introd.). Cf. the shared dirge of Hecuba and the Chorus at *Tro.* 67–163, the 'Trojan Ode' at *Ag.* 589–658, the parodic *nenia* for Claudius at *Apoc.* 12.3, with each of which the present dirge has much in common, and the great *nenia* of Alcmena at the end of *Hercules Oetaeus*,

1863–1939. With the exception of *Ag.* 589–636, all of these passages are, like the present ode, in anapaestic dimeters and monometers: see further below.

The ode, however, is no simple dirge. Its structure is essentially bipartite, with three sections of apostrophe preceding (1054–81) and following (1092–1137) a central, descriptive section (1082–91): (i) apostrophe to the firmament and the sun (Titan), who are asked to weep (1054–62•); (ii) apostrophe to the heavenly gods, who are asked to release Hercules from his madness (1063–5); (iii) apostrophe to Sleep, who is asked to soothe Hercules and restore him to sanity (1066–81); (iv) central, descriptive interlude: Hercules tossing in his sleep (1082–91); (v) apostrophe to Hercules, who is asked to expel his madness or remain insane, and to groan and lament so that the whole cosmos hears (1092–1114); (vi) apostrophe to the fatal arrow and other weapons, which are asked to inflict blows upon Hercules (1115–21); (vii) apostrophe to the dead sons, who are praised and sent with pathos on their way to the land of the dead (1122–37). Though the ode's focus shifts considerably, its beginning and end are strongly threnetic: see Introd. §VII, 94. For apostrophe in Senecan choral odes, see on 178–82.

The Chorus sing in anapaests. The anapaestic metre—in addition to its processional uses, for marching songs and, in Greek drama, for the entrance and exit of the chorus (see on 125–204 introd.)—is also regularly used for lamentation in both Attic tragedy (e.g. Eur. *Tro.* 98–229) and Seneca (*Tro.* 67–163, *Ag.* 637–58, 664–92, *Apoc.* 12), and also perhaps to convey an 'elegiac' tone (cf. *Oed.* 154–201). It is used in *Thyestes* for the great 'Star Ode' (*Thy.* 789–884), which proclaims its terror of cosmic collapse, and, most interestingly, for Thyestes' emotional *canticum* (*Thy.* 920–69), which begins in joy and ends in lamentation and fear. Here it gives form to Theban lamentation over the murder of the innocent and adds an elegiac tone to their moving farewell to the dead sons, even as it contrasts with the more joyous anapaests with which they had opened the main action of the play (125ff.).

For further discussion of this choral ode and its dramatic and thematic function in the play, see Introd. §VII.

Metre: anapaestic dimeters and monometers. See Introd. §IX. For metrical semiotics, see above.

During the ode the bodies of HERCULES' SONS *and the remains of* MEGARA *(and the arrow which killed the first* SON*) are brought from the palace (on stretchers borne by* SLAVES *or on a movable platform) and placed (probably) centre-stage*: this could have been done in many and various ways, including the use of symbolic props, which would have caused no difficulty on the Roman stage: see e.g. the representation of Agave holding a theatrical mask (= the head of Pentheus) on a stucco relief in first-century CE Rome (possibly a scene from pantomime: Péché and Vendries 2001: 49, Hall 2008: 22). As before 592–617 (see n. *ad loc.*), the movable platform could have been a version of the exostra or eccyclema, used for interior scenes. Note that the fatal arrow is addressed at 1115–18, the dead sons at 1122–37, the sons and Megara in Act V (see on 1231–6); the bodies are seen by Hercules when awaking in Act V at 1143–4.

1054–62. The Chorus commence their dirge for Hercules' slaughtered family, asking for the firmament (heaven, earth, ocean, Jupiter, and the Sun) to weep, i.e. for a global response to a global figure. Juno in the prologue had underscored Hercules' global status through allusion to the three areas of the world tamed by him (earth, sea, and air: 30–3); the Chorus here repeat those allusions but cast them in the form of a collective imperative or even moral expectation. For their call for universal tears implies an interconnection between the world of nature and the world of human agency and suffering. This seems to go beyond the literary conceit of the 'pathetic fallacy' or inherited ancient beliefs in the reactive or reflective capacity of nature to imply something like the Stoic doctrine of cosmic 'sympathy' (ἡ τοῦ παντὸς συμπάθεια, 'the sympathy of the whole', the interconnectedness of all things attributed to Chrysippus: Arnim *SVF* 1903–24: 2.473, 475, 532, 912)—in particular the interrelation of cosmology and ethics. The universe is to weep at the injustice of these deaths; for the universe itself is a moral being. Cf. Thyestes' plangent invocation of seas, gods, hell, earth, and night to observe his suffering (*Thy.* 1068–76) or the Chorus' invocation of 'ocean and sky' (*pontus et aether*) in their dirge for Hector (*Tro.* 113). For the opening of a choral ode with an invocation (here leading to prayer), see on 524–32. For Stoic language and ideas in *Hercules*, see on 162–3.

Lugeat aether magnusque parens aetheris alti/**Let sky weep and the soaring sky's Great father:** immediate hymnic repetition (*aetheris... aether*) and alliteration begin the ode. Note the description of Jupiter, which, Fitch argues *ad loc.*, seems to combine his role as 'father of the gods' (see *diuum parens*, 264, *caelestum...parens*, 597–8) with the notion of a creator god (see *Prou.* 5.8; cf. also *Pha.* 466: *maximus mundi parens*, 'the world's great father'). However, there is no need to construe *aetheris alti* as an objective genitive. The phrase may mean no more than the phrase, *pater aetherius*, 'heavenly father', put into the mouth of Hercules by Statius (*Silu.* 3.1.108). For *magnus* as an epithet of Jupiter, see 205 and n. *ad loc.*

uaga ponti mobilis unda/shifting sea's vagrant waves: a potent, chiastic, pleonastic phrase. *Mobilis*, 'shifting/fickle/fleeting', is applied by Seneca to a range of referents, including *fauor* (*Vit. Beat.* 1.5), *hora* (*Pha.* 1141-2), and *casus* (*Thy.* 605-6)—and to the 'flow' of fortune's gifts (*NQ* 3 Pref. 7).

tuque ante omnes...feruide Titan/And thou above all...Blazing Titan: the focus on the sun, its light and its banishment of darkness seems a desperate appeal for something to offset the tragedy the Chorus have witnessed and perhaps to provide illumination and understanding. As the 'Dawn Ode' showed, with its similar, initial focus on light and on Titan (125-36: for the interplay with this ode, see Introd. §VII, 93), Seneca likes to use his choral odes for tonal contrast—a tonal contrast which becomes thematic. This apostrophe is the first of many in this ode. For apostrophe in the choral odes of this play, see on 178-82. For Titan as the sun-god, Apollo, see on 123-4. The phrase, *tuque ante omnes*, lit. 'and thou before all', is also applied to Jupiter in the choral invocation of *Ag.* 382 (see Boyle *ad loc.*, where Jupiter is, like Titan here, not only not the first in the list, but the last. *Feruide Titan* is replaced with *clare Titan*, 'bright Titan', in Hercules' apostrophe at *HO* 42; cf. also *radiate Titan* (*Pha.* 678, *HO* 1518).

terras tractusque maris/lands and ocean's tracts: a slight adaptation of an alliterative Virgilian phrase (*terrasque tractusque maris*), used twice in famous contexts (*Ecl.* 4.51, *Geo.* 4.222). In the latter Virgil is describing the penetration of the whole universe by a *deus*.

obitus...ortus/The west and the east: for similar global images, see 37-8 and n. *ad loc.* For the *occasus/obitus* and *ortus* combination, see on 372-83.

pariter tecum Alcides uidit/Like thee, Alcides has viewed: the Chorus emphasize Hercules' global status to show the appropriateness of a global dirge. For the 'viewing' motif, see on 249-58.

tuas utrasque domos/Thy two abodes: one in the west, one in the east. For *utraque domus* of the Sun's two 'homes', see Ov. *Her.* 9.16; for the plural form as here, cf. *utraeque...domus, HO* 2.

1063-5 The Chorus turn from the Sun to address all the heavenly gods. For prayers, see on 205-78.

Soluite...soluite, superi/Free...Free him, high gods: the reading of *A* (*E* has *soluite o superi* in 1064), and the only instance in Seneca's tragic anapaests of a dactyl-anapaest combination (*soluite, superi*). Leo and Fitch (1987*a*) rearrange 1063-4 to avoid the unique run of four short syllables, favouring *E*'s *o superi* in the process. *A*'s reading at 1064, however, seems to be imitated at *HO* 185•: *fingite superi*, 'Make me, high gods'. The dactyl-anapaest combination occurs twice in *Octavia* (646, 905) and three times in

Hercules Oetaeus (185•, 196, 1883). It is also found (if rarely) in Greek tragedy. Note the hymnic repetition and alliteration appropriate to a dirge.

tantis…monstris/**from these great monsters:** the Chorus, with their second use of *monstrum* in the play (see also 528), place the 'monsters' in Hercules' mind. With the use of *monstra* here (= 'monsters/monstrosities/ horrors'), cf. *Thy.* 253–4: *impleri iuuat | maiore monstro*, 'My joy is to be filled with greater horror'; also Luc. 10.337. For the important *monstrum* motif, see 1280 and n. *ad loc.*

rectam in melius flectite mentem/**Restore his straightened wits:** further hymnic alliteration and assonance. A mind once 'straightened' never changes, according to *Beat. Vit.* 7.4: *numquam enim recta mens uertitur.*

1066–81 Apostrophe to Sleep, in which the Chorus offer a dozen lines of litany parading the properties of Sleep, before articulating their request. Apostrophes to Sleep are among the great *topoi* of Greek and Latin literature. Fitch *ad loc.* lists the following: Hom. *Il.* 14.233ff., Eur. *Or.* 211ff., Soph. *Phil.* 827ff., *Hymn. Orph.* 85, Ov. *Met.* 11.623ff., VF 8.70ff., Sil. 10.343ff., Stat. *Silu.* 5.4, *Theb.* 10.126ff. As commentators regularly observe, Seneca seems influenced by the address to sleep at Ov. *Met.* 11.623–9. Worth noting are some famous apostrophes to Sleep in English literature: Philip Sidney, 'Sonnet 39'; Samuel Daniel, *Delia* 45; Shakespeare, *Henry IV 2* III.i.5–31 (see also *Mac.* II.2.35–9); Robert Johnson, 'Care-charming Sleep' (used in Webster's *Valentinian* V.ii); Keats, 'Sleep and Poetry' and 'To Sleep'. The song of the lutenist Robert Johnson, who was responsible for many of Shakespeare's songs, though taking its opening phrase from the sonnet of Samuel Daniel, seems clearly indebted to Seneca. Johnson's song may be heard in performance on YouTube:

> Care-charming Sleep, thou easer of all woes,
> Brother to Death, sweetly thyself dispose
> On this afflicted prince, fall like a cloud
> In gentle showers, give nothing that is loud
> Or painful to his slumbers; easy, sweet,
> And as a purling stream, thou son of Night,
> Pass by his troubled senses; sing his pain
> Like hollow murmuring wind, or silver rain:
> Into this prince gently, oh gently slide,
> And kiss him into slumbers like a bride.

Tuque, o domitor Somne malorum/**And thou, O Sleep, tamer of woes:** the metaphor of sleep as 'tamer' is Homeric (*Il.* 24.5), but in Roman literature occurs first in Seneca, here and at *Ag.* 75–6 (*curarum somnus domitor*, 'sleep, tamer of cares'). The title in the present context seems especially ironic, since Sleep is being called upon to 'tame' the 'tamer of the world' (*domitor orbis*, 619). For Seneca's fondness for nouns ending in -*tor*, see on 299–302; for *o* and the vocative, see on 205–9. For hyperbaton involving *o*, see also 1068, 1072, 1226; for *tuque o*, see *Oed.* 250.

requies animi/The mind's peace: note the pick-up of the theme of 'rest' and 'peace', *quies* (160, 175), from the opening choral ode. Cf. Ovid's *quies rerum* ('rest of things') and *pax animi* ('the mind's peace') as properties of Somnus (*Met.* 11.623–4); and Shakespeare's 'balm of hurt minds' (*Mac.* II.ii.38).

uolucre o matris genus astraeae/O winged child of starry mother: for Sleep as 'winged', see Callim. *Hym. Del.* 234, Prop. 1.3.45 (*iucundis…alis*, 'with soothing wings'), Tib. 2.1.89 (*furuis circumdatus alis*, 'equipped with dusky wings'), and Claudian *Ruf.* 2.325, where the wings are 'black' (*nigras…alas*). Sleep and Death are famously painted as winged on the Euphronios crater of *c.*515 BCE depicting the death of Sarpedon, previously in the New York Metropolitan Museum, now returned to Italy (Archaeological Museum of Cerveteri). The 'starry mother' is Night, the traditional mother of Sleep from Hesiod's *Theogony* onwards (211–12, 758–9). I have kept the reading of the MSS, and have joined Traina (1967: 171–2) and Billerbeck/Guex in interpreting *astraeae* as a Grecizing adjective (from ἀστραῖος). Fitch (1987*a* and 2018) emends to *astriferae*, Zwierlein (followed by Chaumartin) to *asteriae*, after Bentley's conjecture, *Asteriae*. One thing all agree upon: Sleep is not the child of the virgin goddess Astraea. For *genus* = 'child', see *Med.* 179, 845, *Ag.* 125.

frater…languide Mortis/Languid brother of…Death: see Hesiod above, but also Homer (*Il.* 14.231, 16.672, 682). In Virgil Death and 'Death's brother, Sleep' (*consanguineus Leti Sopor*) are found by the entrance to hell (*Aen.* 6.277–8). In Theseus' account earlier, Sleep (*Sopor*, 690) and Death (*Funus*, 693) are positioned within the underworld. With 'languid' Sleep, cf. *Somni…ignaui*, 'sluggish Sleep', Ov. *Met.* 11.593; *inersque Somnus*, 'and dull Sleep', Stat. *Silu.* 1.6.91; and Shakespeare's *Henry IV 2* III.i.15: 'O thou dull god'. For the personification of *Mors*, 'Death', see 555 and n. *ad loc.*

ueris miscens falsa/Mixing false with true: an interesting development of Virgil's description of the enigmatic Cumaean Sibyl (*obscuris uera inuoluens*, 'wrapping truth with darkness', *Aen.* 6.100) and the Gates of Sleep (*Aen.* 6.893–8), which leads nicely into Sleep's ambiguous authority as a prophet. There is also Ovidian indebtedness: *somnia quae ueras aequant imitamine formas,* 'dreams which imitate and match true shapes' (*Met.* 11.626). Statius continued the tradition (*Theb.* 10.113).

certus…auctor/Sure author: cf. Virgil's 'surest author', *certissimus auctor* (*Geo.* 1.432). For Seneca's fondness for nouns ending in *-tor*, see on 299–302.

pater o rerum/O father of the world: this consensus reading of the MSS has been much questioned, but Valerius Flaccus has Medea address 'father Sleep' (*Somnus pater*, 8.70), and Ovid terms Somnus the *quies rerum*, 'peace of things/the world' (*Met.* 11.623). The term *pater*, as Fitch *ad loc.* notes, is affixed to many deities by Roman poets, from Aether by Pacuvius in *Chryses* (frag. 92 Klotz) to Oceanus by Virgil in the *Georgics* (*Geo.* 4.382), where the same phrase, *pater rerum*, is used. Zwierlein, Fitch (1987*a* and 2018), Chaumartin, and Billerbeck follow Wilamowitz in reading *pax*, not *pater*. But to call Sleep the 'father of things/the world' (the *EA* reading)—perhaps because of its essential role in refreshing and nourishing humankind prior to each day of human activity—is bold but not absurd. And to expand *pater rerum* further: an avid Roman reader of the end of Virgil's sixth *Aeneid* might have thought that Sleep, through whose gates Aeneas passes, was the father of *res Romanae*. Emendation from *pater* to *pax* adds nothing to what has already been said. Viansino (1965 and 1993), Giardina (1966 and 2007), and Caviglia accept the *EA* reading. Trevet, whose text read *o rerum pater*, had no problem with the concept. For *o* and the vocative, see on 205–9.

rerum…requies…regi: for paronomasia of *re*-words, see on 46–52.

portus uitae/port of life: generally the attribute of its brother, Death; see 1131 below and n. *ad loc.*

par regi famuloque uenis/dost visit king and slave Alike: the impartiality of death is one of the great *topoi* of ancient literature, from Homer (see e.g. *Il.* 9.320) to Horace (in whose *Odes* the theme is especially prominent, see e.g. 1.4.13–14, 2.18.32–4, 3.1.14–16) and beyond. It is necessarily implied in the 'Celebration Ode' of this play (838–74) and the 'Death Ode' of *Troades* (371–408). It is made explicit by Andromache at *Tro.* 434 (*certe aequa mors est,* 'Death is absolutely impartial'), and by Seneca himself at *Ira* 3.43.1 (*uenit ecce mors quae uos pares faciat,* 'Look, here comes death to make you equal').

genus humanum/Humankind: for the phrase, see on 674.

longam discere noctem/to learn the long night: the 'long night' is death. See *Pha.* 221: *silentem nocte perpetua domum,* 'the silent house of perpetual night'; Cat. 5.6: *nox…perpetua una,* 'one perpetual night'; Prop. 2.15.23: *nox…longa,* 'long night'. The Chorus give a philosophical purpose to Sleep, viz. learning about death. *Mortem condiscite*, 'learn about death' (*Prou.* 6.8), is something Seneca vigorously advocates in his prose works: see e.g. *Breu. Vit.* 7.3, *Ep. Mor.* 26.9. It is, of course, a development of the Platonic/Socratic idea of philosophy as a 'training for death' (μελέτη θανάτου, Plato *Phaedo* 81a). For knowledge/ignorance of how to die as a regular motif of Senecan tragedy, see on 426-9.

placidus fessum lenisque foue, preme/Calm and gentle, soothe his weariness, Hold: at last the request, couched in Ovidian terms (see *Met.* 11.623, 625), although *placidus* and *lenis* are defining markers of sleep from Ennius' inspirational nap onwards (*Ann.* frag. 2 Skutsch, cited below). Along with Fitch (1987*a* and 2018), Chaumartin, Billerbeck, and others I have followed *E* in placing line 1077 where it is here. *A* places the line before 1075, which is favoured by Zwierlein, who changes the *EA* reading *foue* to *fouens*, following Scaliger. No modern editor seems to have followed. For discussion, see Fitch *ad loc.*

deuinctum torpore/fast in...torpor: a variation of *deuinctus sopore*, 'bound in sleep', as at Cat. 64.122, Lucr. 4.1027; cf. also again *somno leni placidoque reuinctus*, 'bound fast in gentle and calm sleep' (Enn. *Ann.* frag. 2 Skutsch).

sopor indomitos alliget artus/Let sleep chain those untamed limbs: the audience might have remembered here with some irony the 'untamed virtue' (*indomita uirtus*, 39), ascribed to Hercules by Juno. For the phrase *alligare artus* used of *sopor, languor,* or *torpor*, see *Oed.* 182, Lucr. 4.290, VF 1.48. For *sopor* as 'deep, overpowering sleep', see on 689-96.

torua...pectora/savage breast: for *toruus*, see on 720-7.

mens...pristina/former mind: the phrase occurs also at *Ag.* 288 and is Ovidian (*Met.* 3.203).

1082-91 The Chorus describe Hercules tossing and turning in his sleep. For such extensive descriptions of a character's behaviour in Senecan tragedy and the possible influence of pantomime, see on 991-5. There is a brief mention of Heracles turning in his sleep at Eur. *Herac.* 1068-9.

1082-7 *En fusus humi*/Look how he sprawls on the ground: note *fusus humi* of Cerberus at Virg. *Aen.* 6.423 and *fusus* of Lycus at 895, making the Chorus' description doubly ironic. The phrase is also used of the father of Meleager at Ov. *Met.* 8.530. For *en*, see on 944-52.

saeua feroci corde uolutat somnia/Whirling wild dreams in savage heart: for dreams replaying the actions of waking life, which the Chorus are implying here, see Herod. 7.16, Ter. *Andr.* 971-2, Acc. *Brutus* frags 29-31 Klotz, Lucr. 4.962-1036, Petron. frag. xxx Pellegrino, *Oct.* 740-2 (see

Boyle *ad loc.*). The thought is common in Renaissance drama. For frenzied dreams following a day of slaughter, see Luc. 7.764ff. *Corde uolutare* is Virgilian: *Aen.* 1.50, 4.533, 6.185, where it is used respectively of Juno, Dido, and Aeneas at moments of crisis. For the juxtaposition of synonyms, see on 283–95. For *ferox*, 'savage', see on 57–63.

nondum est/Not yet is: for prodelision or aphaeresis at the end of an anapaestic dimeter, see *Ag.* 102, *Pha.* 41, 353; also *Oct.* 9, 297, 300, 944.

clauaeque graui/heavy club: used also as a pillow at Ov. *Met.* 9.236.

uacua…dextra/With empty hand: for *uacuus* applied to parts of the body, see 143 and n. *ad loc.* The ablative is instrumental: Woodcock §43.1.

1088–91 A sea-storm metaphor (*aestus*) leads to a three-line sea-storm simile, the language of which continues metaphorically in 1092–5. Seneca here seems indebted to Ovid's simile at *Fas.* 2.775–6, where again not only swirling but disastrous emotions (of Lucretia's imminent rapist) are the subject. In turn Seneca's simile seems to be the model for that at *HO* 710–11. For similes in Senecan tragedy, see on 679–88, 1042–8; for sea-storm similes, see *Ag.* 138–43, *Med.* 940–2. Caviglia *ad loc.* cites de' Dottori's tragedy *Aristodemo* I.i.63ff., where the influence of Seneca's simile is patent. For sea-storm imagery in the prose works, see e.g. *Tranq.* 2.1, *Beat. Vit.* 2.3.

omnes…aestus/all the storm: Seneca likes to use *aestus* (in the sense of 'tide', 'surge', 'swell', 'storm', etc.) for the imagistic depiction of human emotions: see e.g. *Ag.* 139 (of Clytemnestra), *Med.* 939 (of Medea), *Thy.* 439 (of Thyestes). Cf. *HO* 710–12 (of Deianira). The usage is Virgilian (e.g. *Aen.* 4.532, 564) and Ovidian (*Met.* 8.471).

Noto/Notus: the Greek name (νότος) for the south wind; see on 550–7.

seruat longos unda tumultus…tumet/wave…prolongs its turmoil… swells: a replay of the Ovidian simile describing the passion of Sextus Tarquinius at *Fas.* 2.775–6, but here it is not a question of erotics; the simile returns to a more erotic context at *HO* 710–11. *Tumultus, tumidus, tumere* are almost technical psychological terms for Seneca (see on 384–96), used here concretely of a sea-storm figuring the psychological turbulence in Hercules' mind. 'Tumidity' is a minor leitmotif of the play, evident in descriptions of the psychologies both of Lycus (*tumidus*, 384) and Hercules (*tumultus/tumet*, 1090–1). For *tumultus*, see also 714, 1219; for *tumere* /*tumescere*, see also 68, 936; for *tumidus*, see 171, 221, 384, 551, 955. For *tumultus/tumere/tumidus/tumor* in other Senecan tragedies, see e.g. *Oed.* 329, *Pho.* 352, 585, *Ag.* 127, *Med.* 178, *Pha.* 137, *Tro.* 301—and especially the most 'tumid' tragedy of all, *Thyestes*: 260, 268, 291, 362, 519, 560, 577, 609, 737, 960, 961, 999. See further on 384–96.

uento cessante/though the wind drops: for 'windless' swelling, see *Med.* 765-6, *Thy.* 960. The ablative absolute is concessive in force: see Woodcock §50.

1092-1114 The Chorus now address the sleeping Hercules. As often, there is no vocative, but Hercules (not *Somnus*, 'Sleep') must be the subject of *pelle* ('expel', 1092), as he was the subject of *expulit* ('expelled', 1088). The address is highly alliterative and assonantal.

1092-9 *Pelle insanos fluctus*/Expel the mad billows: the Chorus continue their sea-storm imagery as they address Hercules; see above. Cf. the 'cloud' imagery used by Thyestes as he instructs himself: *sed iam saeui nubila fati | pelle*, 'But now expel the clouds of savage fate', *Thy.* 934-4•. For the application (through metaphor or simile) of 'wave/billow' to emotion, see *Med.* 392 (*fluctus*), 939-43 (*fluctus*); *Pha.* 181-3; *Ag.* 138-41 (*fluctibus*); *Thy.* 438-9; *Tran.* 2.10 (*fluctus*); Aesch. *Cho.* 183-4, *Eum.* 832; Lucr. 3.298 (*fluctus*), 6.74 (*fluctus*); Virg. *Aen.* 4.532 (*fluctuat*), 12.831 (*fluctus*); Luc. 5.118 (*fluctu*).

redeat pietas uirtusque uiro/Let piety and virile virtue Return: which they do in Act V; see Introd. §VII, 106. The Roman value of *pietas*—love/ duty to family and parents and piety/duty to gods—is a cardinal concept of Roman literature at least from Ennius' *Annales* onwards (*o pietas animi*, frag. 4 Skutsch). It was a professed value of the Roman elite and was famously inscribed on the golden shield presented to Augustus in 27 BCE; see *RG* 34.2. It is both a motif of this play (esp. its final act: 1248, 1269, 1319), and a recurrent motif of Senecan tragedy, where it often appears in contexts of flagrant transgression: e.g. at *Med.* 261, 905, *Oed.* 19, *Pha.* 903, *Thy.* 549, 717. It is frequently used in the plays ironically. The conceptual complexity of *pietas* makes it a difficult word to translate, but its thematic importance is such that I translate *pietas* here and at 1269 (its only other occurrence) as 'piety', even if this strains the conventional English meaning. I am encouraged in this by Shakespeare's use of 'piety', 'impiety', 'impious', etc. in *Titus Andronicus*—a drama in which 'family piety' constitutes a cardinal theme ('O cruel irreligious piety!' *Tit.* I.i.147). *Virtus* is similarly difficult to translate: see on 35-40. Here there is overt etymological wordplay (*figura etymologica*), on the derivation of *uirtus*, 'virtue/manliness', from *uir*, 'man'; hence the punning translation, 'virile virtue'. The issue of what constitutes 'virile virtue' is at the core of Act V. Virgil has similar etymological play: *uirtutesque uirosque* (*Aen.* 1.566), *uiri uirtus* (*Aen.* 4.3), *uirtusque uirum* (*Aen.* 8.500). For etymological wordplay in Senecan tragedy, see on 731-4. For Roman referentiality in *Hercules*, see on 46-52.

uel…potius/or, better: for the rhetorical technique of *correctio*, see on 640-4.

sit…mens uesano concita motu/**Your mind seethe with madness:** similarly in *King Lear* (IV.vi.276–9) Shakespeare's Gloucester wishes madness
upon himself with the same aim, viz. to generate ignorance of what has
happened:

> Better were I distract:
> So should my thoughts be severed from my griefs,
> And woes by wrong imaginations lose
> The knowledge of themselves.

error…furor/**error…Rage:** psychological conditions which are also
entities, summoned earlier by Juno from hell; see 98 and nn. *ad loc.* Both
will be central concepts in the moral discourse of Act V (1220, 1237–8,
1240, 1244, 1261). For the ontologization of the emotions, see on 75–6.

qua coepit eat/**surge as it began:** lit. 'go on as it began'; for the phrase, see
Med. 206, *qua coepit ire,* 'go on as he began'.

solus te…furor insontem/**Rage alone…You innocent:** Hercules' *furor*
will ensure that initially he will not realize what he has done. The *furor* will
dissipate—temporarily (1259–61).

puris…manibus/**pure hands:** Horace uses the phrase at *Serm.* 1.4.68,
where he talks about 'living *puris manibus*'. Here the cleanliness involved is
'being unstained by blood', as at Aesch. *Eum.* 313 (καθαρὰς χεῖρας). As the
audience know, Hercules has never had 'pure' hands since the killing of
Lycus; see 918–24. For the *manus* motif, see on 118–22.

nescire nefas/**Ignorance of sin:** a monometer closes this section with
potent alliteration and a clever inversion of Horace's famous *scire nefas* in the
opening line of the *carpe diem* ode (*Odes* 1.11.1). For the ancient commonplace that ignorance of evil is a benefit, see the *sententiae* (probably falsely)
attributed to Publilius Syrus: (i) *felix uidetur qui mala ignorat sua,* 'He seems
happy who does not know his sorrows' (Publ. *Sent. Fals.* Woelfflin 135); (ii)
*suauissima haec est uita, si sapias nihil; nam sapere nil doloris expers est
malum,* 'The sweetest life is one of ignorance. For ignorance is a painless evil'
(Publ. *Sent. Fals.* Woelfflin 355). For comparable situations to that of Hercules,
cf. that of Thyestes, who consumed his own sons, to whom the Messenger,
like the Chorus here, offers the consolation of ignorance of his own *mala*
(*Thy.* 783); that of Euripides' Agave, who dismembered her own son (*Bacch.*
1259–62); and that of Sophocles' Ajax, who utters what seems to be the source
of *sententia* (ii) above (*Ajax* 554). Cf. also Shakespeare's Gloucester cited
above and the filicidal father of [Quint.] *Decl.* 256, who, like Hercules at 1261
below, regrets the loss of his *furor.* For *nefas,* see 387 and n. *ad loc.*

1100–14 In the second part of their address to Hercules the Chorus resume their dirge. They call on Hercules himself to join the mourning and, returning to the dirge's opening theme of cosmic lamentation, invoke all of existence to hear and echo the hero's cries. As Fitch notes *ad loc.*, the focus on breast-beating, groans (*gemitus*), and on the whole world hearing and echoing those groans link this section to parts of the κομμός or *nenia* of *Troades* (esp. *Tro.* 106–15). Such physically expressive lamentation was assigned at a Roman aristocrat's funeral to professional mourners, as was the *nenia* or dirge itself. Here the Chorus play the role of such mourners with the difference that, as Theban citizens, they are personally invested in the fate of Hercules and the Theban royal house. See Introd. §VII, 95.

Herculeis percussa sonent pectora palmis/**let Hercules' breast resound With pounding fists:** strong alliteration in the Latin text; cf. Hecuba's instruction to the Chorus at *Tro.* 64: *ferite palmis pectora et planctus date*, 'strike breasts with fists and shriek your lamentations'; the Chorus' instruction to their own hands at *Tro.* 114: *pulsu pectus tundite uasto*, 'Bruise breast with savage blows'; and the son-consuming Thyestes' similar instruction to himself at *Thy.* 1045–6: *pectora inliso sonent contusa planctu*, 'Let this battered breast Resound with crashing blows'. For *sonare* and lamentation, see also 1114 and n. *ad loc. Pectora palmis* seems a common alliterative phrase in contexts of lamentation: *Apoc.* 12.3.27, Cat. 64.351, *Aen.* 1.481, Ov. *Met.* 2.341. To increase the alliterative effect, the phrase is sometimes combined with a form of *percutere*, as here and at Ov. *Met.* 2.341, 5.473, 10.723. For the use of the adjective *Herculeus*, see 72 and n. *ad loc*; for the focus on sound, see on 1002–9.

mundum solitos ferre lacertos/**arms, often props of the world:** lit. 'arms accustomed to bearing the world'. *Solitos*, 'accustomed to', in a sense rhetorically exaggerates, since Hercules held up the 'world' on only one occasion: see on 68–74. But in a metatheatrical sense there is no exaggeration, for countless narratives and dramas have represented Hercules in such a role. Cf. the use of *solere* at the end of this play (1344) and (most famously) at *Med.* 1022: *sic fugere soleo*, 'I often/always flee like this'. See also e.g. *Pha.* 781, *Med.* 449, *Tro.* 249, 360, *Pho.* 163. For metatheatrical language in *Hercules*, see on 109–12.

lacertos uerbera pulsent/**blows…Strike arms:** cf. again the language of the *Troades* dirge (Hecuba speaking): *tibi nostra ferit dextra lacertos*, 'for you my hand strikes my arms' (*Tro.* 117).

uictrice manu/**triumphant hand:** I retain with Viansino (1965 and 1993), Giardina (1966 and 2007), Caviglia, and Billerbeck the transmitted

EA reading, *uictrice*, against the Heinsius emendation, *ultrice*, accepted by Zwierlein, Fitch (1987*a* and 2018), and Chaumartin. *Victrice* in this context is of course ironic. For the *manus* motif, see on 118–22.

gemitus uastos audiat aether/Let heaven hear your mighty groans: cf. the Chorus at *Tro.* 112: (*gemitus*) *audiat omnis pontus et aether*, 'Let all ocean and heaven hear (the groans)'; and (less closely) Virg. *Aen.* 4.668 (the reaction to Dido's suicide): *resonat magnis plangoribus aether*, 'heaven echoes with mighty wailing'. See also *HO* 1902.

atri regina poli/queen of the dark pole: Proserpina. For the underworld as the 'black/dark pole', see also *Ag.* 756 (*nigrantis poli*), *Pha.* 836 (*umbrantem polum*), *HO* 559 (*nigri…poli*), 938 (*nigrantis poli*). The opposite 'pole' is *siderei poli* ('starry pole', *Pha.* 663, *HO* 1940). See also *deterior polus*, 'baser pole', at 607, *peiorem polum*, 'worse pole' (*HO* 772).

colla…uincta catenis/Necks bound by…chains: note the beginning of a series of harsh *c*s (1106–8).

imo latitans Cerberus antro/Cerberus…Cringing in the lowest cave: Cerberus (see on 782–91) seems to have been returned to the underworld; he still wears (1106) the chains inflicted on him by Hercules (see 807–8, 815–16: Billerbeck *ad loc.* is mistaken in construing the chains as those of a 'Wachhund'). According to the traditional narrative, Hercules takes Cerberus to Eurystheus and then returns him to the underworld (Apollod. 2.5.12). In this play, however, there is no mention of showing Cerberus to Eurystheus, as there is in Euripides' play (*Herac.* 1386–8). For Cerberus' *antrum*, 'cave', see Virg. *Aen.* 6.418, 423.

resonet…chaos latique patens unda profundi et…aer/Let chaos echo…And the vast deep's open waters…And air: the 'three kingdoms' of the world (hell, earth, sky: see on 52–6) to be referred to at 1114. *Chaos* is regularly used of the underworld; see 861 and n. *ad loc.* For the cosmic echoing of cries and grief, see Acc. *Aeneadae siue Decius* (frag. 2 Klotz, frag. 8 Boyle 2006): *clamore et gemitu templum resonit caelitum*, 'With cries and groans the sky-gods' precinct echoes'; Virg. *Aen.* 4.668, 5.228; Ov. *Ars* 3.375. Cf. also the Chorus at *Tro.* 108–12. Note, too, the mock-*nenia* performed for the dead Claudius at *Apoc.* 12.3.2: *resonet tristi clamore forum*, 'Let the forum echo the mournful cries'.

melius tua tela tamen senserat/had felt your weapons More happily: the allusion is to the shooting down of the Stymphalian Birds; see on 241–8. *Melius* (*A*) is to be preferred to *medius* (*E*), favoured by Zwierlein and most modern editors, not only because it introduces a telling comparison but because *medius* would inhibit *aer* from standing for *caelum*, one of the *regna*, 'realms', of 1114 (see Fitch *ad loc.*). Note the postponement of *tamen*, as at *Tro.* 737, *Pho.* 542. For the postponement of adverbs, see on 63–8.

tantis obsessa malis/besieged by massive ills: the military metaphor, *obsessa*, 'besieged', occurs also at *Ag.* 136, *Tro.* 989; see also *Med.* 560. For military imagery in *Hercules*, see on 19–29.

uno planctu tria regna sonent/Three realms should sound one dirge: cf. the chorus of *Troades*: *sonent litora planctu*, 'Let the shores resound with blows' (*Tro.* 108). Of the ten occurrences of *planctus* ('beatings of the breast', 'lamentation', 'dirge') in Senecan tragedy, seven occur in *Troades*. The word seems not to be attested before Seneca and the Neronians: see Petr. *Sat.* 81.2, Luc. 2.57. The Flavian poets also found the word appealing. For the 'three realms' (1104–11: heaven, ocean, hell), see on 52–6. For Seneca's verbal play with *unus*, see on 19–29. Note the identical *uno-tria* play at *Ag.* 838. For *sonare* and lamentation, see also 1100; for the focus on sound, see on 1002–9.

1115–21 The Chorus now turn to Hercules' weapons in their mourning as if they are extensions of himself. All but the fatal arrows have been removed. They address the arrow directly with a vocative and an imperative (which also includes the quiver), leaving more indirect jussive subjunctives for the other weapons not onstage. This apostrophe to *arma*, 'weapons', is unique in Senecan tragedy (Hippolytus almost addresses his sword at *Pha.* 713–14) and not common in Roman literature: see Turnus' address to his *hasta*, 'spear', at Virg. *Aen.* 12.95–100.

decus ac telum/glory And shaft: hendiadys = (almost) *decorum telum*. For weapons considered as 'glorious', even 'beautiful', enhancing the glamour of the weapon-wearer, see e.g. Hor. *CS* 61–2: *fulgente decorus arcu* | *Phoebus*, 'Phoebus, glorious with shining bow'; Ov. *Met.* 2.773: *deam...formaque armisque decoram*, 'the goddess glorious both in beauty and in arms'.

fortis harundo/strong arrow: not, as Fitch *ad loc.* suggests, singular for plural. Rather it is a particular arrow—the one which killed the first son (993–5) and has been brought onstage together with the family's bodies during this choral ode. See stage directions before 1054. The arrow will feature prominently in the final act as the potential instrument of Hercules' threatened suicide.

pharetraeque graues/And the grave quiver: lit. 'heavy' with arrows; see the paradoxical verbal play at *Ag.* 324–5: *graues leuibus telis* |...*pharetras*, 'quiver heavy with light shafts'. The translation attempts a verbal play with the archaic sense of 'grave' (= 'heavy') and its non-archaic senses. For other 'poetic' plural *pharetrae*, see e.g. *Ag.* 217, *Pha.* 317, *HO* 1605, Ov. *Met.* 1.559, Stat. *Theb.* 4.259.

fero ... tergo/**brutal back:** for *ferus*, see on 516–20.

umeros/**shoulders:** for the play's focus on Hercules' 'shoulders', see on 622–5.

robora/**oakwood:** the 'oakwood' of Hercules' club, a metonym for the club itself (= *claua*, Farnaby *ad loc.*), as at 800.

stipesque potens/**potent club:** another alliteration of *ps* (see 1100–1) begins here. Fitch *ad loc.* argues for a touch of personification through the use of *potens*, a modifier normally of persons. Cf. *hasta potens*, 'potent spear', Dracon. *Rom.* 9.185.

oneret pectora/**Tax his breast:** for this sense of *onerare* (a colloquialism, 'Umgangssprache', according to Billerbeck *ad loc.*), see Plaut. *Amph.* 328: *onerandus est pugnis probe*, 'He must be properly taxed/loaded/beaten with fists'.

nodis/**knots:** for Hercules' 'tri-knotted club', *claua trinodis*, see Ov. *Fas.* 575.

plangant/**mourn:** a neat pick-up of *planctu* (1114).

1122–37 The Chorus conclude their dirge with a moving apostrophe to the dead sons. Again there is no vocative, at least in the initial part of this section (1122–30), where, however, the referent of *uos* (1122), obscure in recitation or reading, would be comprehensible instantly in performance.

1122–30 An address to the dead sons, focusing both on what their premature deaths have prevented them from doing and on what they 'dared' to achieve. This seems to have been a standard part of an aristocratic funeral eulogy for the prematurely dead: see Men. Rhet. 2.15 Race. Cf. Andromache's address to the doomed Astyanax at *Tro.* 771–82 and Hecuba's speech over the dead Astyanax at Eur. *Tro.* 1209–11. Perhaps the most famous statement of unrealized potential in this regard (and thus the model for all future Roman iterations) is Virgil's passage on the premature death of Marcellus (*Aen.* 6.870–83). Seneca himself had addressed the issue of the premature death of a son (not his own) in *Consolatio ad Marciam*, written before the dramatist-philosopher's exile and probably well before this play.

Non uos patriae laudis comites/**You were not comrades of your father's Fame:** the referent is immediately clear in performance: Hercules' dead sons. Vocatives are introduced at 1131ff. Cf. the mock-dirge for Claudius at *Apoc.* 12.3 (which Fitch 1987a: 52 contends echo lines 1127–30), where vocatives are introduced in the final four lines. For similarly unidentified plural addressees (also clear in performance), see 178, 858. Note the allusive irony in the phrase *patriae laudis comites*, 'comrades in your father's fame', which Hercules' sons were not. Each of them, however, like the followers of Lycus, was a 'comrade in death' (*poenae comes*).

ulti saeuos uulnere reges/**striking down savage kings:** among the 'savage kings' struck down by Hercules were Diomedes (see on 226–30), Busiris (see on 480–9), Eyrx (see on 268–75), Laomedon (see on 268–75), and, most recently, Lycus. Note the rare omission of the second person of the verb *esse* (*estis*), as at *Oed.* 709 (where *es* is omitted), and the repetition of the same syllable at the end and beginning of juxtaposed words, here *re re*, as at 995 (see 67 and n. *ad loc.*).

Argiua...palaestra/**schools Of Argos:** I prefer to construe *Argiua* here as meaning 'Argive', 'of Argos' (as it clearly means in its other occurrence at 1180), rather than 'Greek', as Fitch and Billerbeck *ad loc.* contend. Argos/Mycenae (for the regular conflation, see on 1035–8) was the native city of Hercules' parents, Alcmena and Amphitryon, now ruled by Hercules' rival Eurystheus. In Euripides' play Heracles' ultimate plan, as understood by Amphitryon, was to move his family to Argos/Mycenae and to reinstate the exiled Amphitryon among its citizens (*Herac.* 13–21). Though this intention is never mentioned in Seneca's play, the Chorus' words here may be an allusion to it, to known plans that now could never be realized. *Palaestra* is another transliterated Greek term (παλαίστρα, cf. *mystae*, 847, *ephebi*, 853), adding what Fitch *ad loc.* terms 'local color'.

fortesque manu/**Strength with hands:** probably in the pancration or a wrestling contest; see *Ben.* 5.3.1, *Ep. Mor.* 88.19.

*iam tamen ausi.../***Yet you dared...:** praise of the 'daring' achievements of the deceased is typical of both the *nenia* and *laudatio funebris* (funeral laudation): see Fitch *ad* 1054–1137.

telum Scythicis leue corytis/**light shaft from Scythian Quivers:** I join Zwierlein and Billerbeck in preferring the spelling *corytis* (*E*; *P* has *goryti*, *S gorriti*) for the Greek loan-word (from γωρυτός), as at *Ov. Tr.* 5.7.15. It continues the alliteration of *cs*. For the Scythians, see on 533–41; for their fame as archers, see Hor. *Odes* 3.8.23–4, Ov. *Met.* 10.588. For *leuis*, see on 987–91.

missum certa librare manu/**Fire...with a sure hand:** an ironic pick-up of Juno's proposed plan at 118–19. For *certa manu*, 'sure hand', of firing arrows, see *Apoc.* 12.3.9, Ov. *Am.* 3.10.26; for *certus* and archery, see on 118–22. For the *manus* motif, see on 118–22. For *librare*, see 119 and n. *ad loc. Missum* is proleptic.

nondum...iubatae/**yet unmaned:** for *nondum* with an epithet of young animals/humans, see 142 (*nondum rupta fronte*), 852 (*nondum...iugatae*), 853 (*comis nondum positis*).

1131–7 The ode's closure has been much admired. In it the ritualistic aspect of the dirge comes to the fore with hymnic simplicity and insistent repetition:

Ite...ite...ite...ite...uisite. Cf. Andromache's farewell to her doomed son: *i, uade liber*, 'Go, walk in freedom' (*Tro*. 791). For ritual repetition, see the dirge of *Troades* (107, 117–20, 125–8, 132–7, 143–52, 156–61). Eliot (1951c: 104) lauds this closure as 'a lovely passage', citing it together with Heywood's translation, which he deems to be 'perfect':

> Goe hurtles soules, whom mischiefe hath opprest
> Even in fyrst porch of life but lately had,
> And fathers fury goe vnhappy kind
> O little children, by the way ful sad
> Of iourney knowen,
> Goe see the angry kynges.

Stygios...portus/**Stygian harbours:** as Fitch notes *ad loc.*, the literal and metaphoric uses of *portus* combine. For death as itself a 'harbour', see *Ag.* 592, *Ep. Mor.* 70.3, *Pol.* 9.7, *HO* 1021, Soph. *Ant.* 1284, Cic. *Tusc.* 1.118, 5.117, Virg. *Aen.* 7.598–9. For *portus* used of death's brother, sleep, see 1072 and n. *ad loc.* For the river Styx, see on 52–6.

in primo limine uitae/**on life's first threshold:** for the metaphor, see Lucr. 3.681, where *uitae limen* is introduced to Roman poetry (cf. *leti limen*, 'death's threshold' at Lucr. 2.960, 6.1208), Luc. 2.106, Stat. *Theb.* 5.535, *Silu.* 2.1.38; cf. also Virg. *Aen.* 6.427–8.

scelus oppressit/**Crime has crushed:** the Chorus conclude on another of Juno's summoned entities (96) and one which will have a major role in the dialogue to come (1162, 1193, 1199, 1237–8, 1262, 1278, 1300, 1313).

patriusque furor/**and father's rage:** for the ontologization of the emotions, see on 75–6. For *furor* see on 92–9.

ite, infaustum genus, o pueri/**Go, boys, O cursèd brood:** an anticipation or an echo of Medea's farewell to her sons as they take Creusa the fatal bridal gifts: *ite, ite, nati, matris infaustae genus*, 'Go, go, sons, brood of a cursèd mother' (*Med.* 845). Relative dates are uncertain, but it seems more likely that *Hercules* is the earlier play. *Infaustus* is a powerful modifier, redolent of fated evil (see 688, 1235; *Oed.* 80, 637; *Med.* 706; *Thy.* 533; *Pho.* 3).

noti per iter triste laboris/**Along that famed labour's grim path:** the Chorus press the irony of Hercules' sons travelling the same road as their father but with different consequences. There is, of course, behind their words the ancient tradition that, for heroes to travel to the underworld and return without dying, someone must die in their stead, so that the 'number tallies for hell's king' (*constat inferno numerus tyranno, Pha.* 1153). Hence the deaths associated with the underworld visits of Odysseus (Hom. *Od.* 10.552ff.), Aeneas (Virg. *Aen.* 6.149ff.)—and Theseus (*Pha.* 1153).

ite, iratos uisite reges/Go, meet the angry monarchs: Dis and Proserpina, the 'shades' pitiless Lords' (*immites…umbrarum dominos*, 569–70), who are angry with the children's father, Hercules, for many things: the theft of Cerberus, the breach of the underworld, the return (together with Theseus) from hell, the alleged conquest of death. Seneca revels in dramatically potent closures to his choral odes: see e.g. 201, 590–1, 892; *Oed.* 201, 993–4; *Pha.* 1153; *Ag.* 386–7, 658, 865–6; *Tro.* 162–3, 408; *Med.* 669; *Thy.* 403, 883–4. This is an especially powerful and beautiful final line with an alliterative pattern of *is*, *ts*, *es*, *rs*, and *ss* and profound, latent ironies. There is a recall here of the Chorus' own criticism of the boys' father for rushing 'to meet the gloomy ghosts' (*maestos uisere manes*, 187): like father, like sons—but also not so. For *uisite* suggests a 'visit' or temporary 'meeting', which applies to the father, not the sons. There seems an echo, too (if, as seems likely, *Phaedra* predates *Hercules*), of Theseus' curse on his son, Hippolytus, whom Theseus prays will meet the 'ghosts angry with his father' (*manes…iratos patri*, *Pha.* 947). That curse and Theseus' tragic, filicidal loss are (within the mythological time-frame) yet to come: like Hercules, like Theseus. For ironic closural choral lines, see on 590–1. For *ira*, see on 19–29.

Act V (1138–1344)

Seneca is a master of the dramatic finale, in which he exhibits considerable diversity of construction. In the final acts of *Agamemnon*, *Medea*, and *Thyestes* the audience witness a plurality of scenes, murders graphically narrated and/or performed, violence threatened and/or committed, great monologues, and even paedophagy. The final acts of *Phaedra* and *Oedipus* are each a single scene filled with passionate speeches of guilt, accusation, and reflection and with the bloody loss of life. The scene of Theseus attempting to piece together the dismembered body of Hippolytus is a metapoetic meditation on Seneca's tragic craft. *Troades* and *Hercules* are alike in that their finales involve no onstage blood, which in *Troades* is relegated to the distancing narrative of the Messenger's report. Both are almost meditative acts, although, unlike that of *Troades*, the final act of *Hercules*, the second longest in Seneca's seven act-divided plays, frames itself between two passionate speeches of the protagonist and is structured around confrontation.

Indeed, with the exception of *Troades*, the final acts of the seven plays are devoted at least in part to confrontation—and a confrontation between major dramatic figures. In *Phaedra*, *Oedipus*, and *Medea* the confrontation is between male (husband) and female (wife); in *Thyestes* the conflict is between brothers (in *Phoenissae*, too, the conflict is between brothers and between brothers and parent, but it is unclear whether the relevant scene is the play's final one); in *Hercules*, *Agamemnon* and *Oedipus* the primary conflict is between 'parent' and child. But such conflicts are never just conflicts; they generate dialogue which reflects, morally, intellectually, even religiously (see *Medea* 1027), on the dramatic action itself. There is a great deal of such reflection in the final acts of all the above plays, but those of *Hercules*, *Oedipus*, and *Medea* are intensely focused on their titular characters.

Act V of *Hercules* moves through five main phases: (i) (1138–86) the awaking of Hercules, who views the bloody corpses onstage, identifies (if not immediately) his dead family, and in deep distress asks Theseus and Amphitryon for information; (ii) (1186–1236) Hercules' recognition of his responsibility for the slaughter, followed by a 'Schreirede' and lamentation; (iii) (1237–95) Hercules' suicide resolution and Amphitryon's and Theseus' resistance; (iv) (1296–1321) return of Hercules' weapons, his threat of suicide with the poisoned, fatal arrow, Amphitryon's own threat of suicide, Hercules' decision to live; (v) (1321–44) Hercules' final speech of dislocation, pain, and despair, followed by Theseus' offer of purification in Athens. Hercules, though he begins the act and dominates it, does not end it. That role is given to Theseus, the 'Placer' (see on 1341–4).

For further discussion of Act V and its dramatic and thematic function in the play, see Introd. §VII, 95–102, and on 1341–4. Miola (1992: 165–8, 203–5) argues that Shakespeare's presentation of Lear in *King Lear* IV.vii and of Posthumus in *Cymbeline* V.i draw on Seneca's dramatization of Hercules in this final act. Richard Glover, too, in his *Medea* is also clearly indebted and not only to this final act. His Medea kills her children in a fit of madness, falls unconscious, and, after regaining her senses, asks for punishment along Senecan/Herculean lines.

Metre: iambic trimeter. See Introd. §IX.

Enter THESEUS, *wearing an olive wreath, stage left*: this seems an apposite place for Theseus, who is referred to at 1173 and speaks later in the act, to re-enter the stage. He exited early in Act IV (917: see n. *ad loc.*) and cannot reasonably be thought to have entered during that act's ensuing bloodbath without responding to it. He is probably still wearing an olive wreath, as instructed by Hercules at 913.

HERCULES...*now semi-naked (i.e. without his lion skin, removed at the end of Act IV)*: for the removal of the lion skin, see 1150–2. For the semiotics of Hercules' 'nudity', see Introd. §VII, 96–7.

1138–86 Hercules awakes and delivers a long, emotional speech, part open soliloquy, part aside, part direct address. The speech ranges from initial confusion about location (1138–42), his awareness of corpses, the absence of family, the loss of weapons, and chaos around him, even of apparent defeat at the hands of another (1143–59), through recognition of his dead children, an appeal for help, a desire for revenge, a challenge to his assumed conqueror (1159–73), to an address (accompanied by asides) to Amphitryon and Theseus for information on the murderers of his family (1173–86). Cf. the analogous speech of Euripides' Heracles at *Herac.* 1089–1108.

1138–42 Following his initial global question Hercules specifies parts of the world already visited by him in his 'labours' and ancillary exploits (in the east, north, far west), as he searches for his present *locus*.

  Quis hic locus, quae regio, quae mundi plaga/**What place is this, what region, what stretch of world:** Act V's initial line brings to the fore the preoccupation with place, *locus*, which has pervaded the play (see on 1–5) and dominates Act V (see Introd. §VII, 122–4); it is both the first and the last noun to be uttered by Hercules in this final act (1138, 1340). The present line was reused by T. S. Eliot as the epigraph to his poem, *Marina* (1930), the first five lines of which develop this opening utterance of Hercules. The epigraph is contextually ironic. Eliot exploits the contrast between Hercules, who has killed his children, and Pericles, who has found his daughter. Seneca here may also be exploiting an ironic contrast through an echo of Aeneas' famous cry before the frescoes of Dido's temple: '*quis iam locus*'. inquit, '*Achate,* | *quae regio in terris nostri non plena laboris*'. 'What place now', he says, 'Achates, | What region on earth is not filled with our labour' (Virg. *Aen.* 1.459–60). Hercules may be playing Aeneas, who has also filled the world with his *labor*, but his situation contrasts markedly with that of the ultimate ancestor of the Roman people. The brief half-line of Euripides' Heracles (ποῦ ποτ᾽ ὢν ἀμηχανῶ; 'Where am I in my helplessness?' *Herac.* 1105), and the line of the waking Homeric Odysseus (*Od.* 13.200) have been transformed rhetorically, allusively, globally, befitting a hero who straddles three worlds. Cf. also the anxiety-filled questions of Andromache (*quis te locus, quae regio...tuto reponet*, 'What place, what region will keep you

(Astyanax) safe?' *Tro.* 498–9), of the Messenger of *Thyestes* (*quaenam ista regio est?* 'What region is this?' *Thy.* 627), and of Statius' young Achilles, waking from sleep and seeing Scyros (*quae loca, qui fluctus, ubi Pelion?* 'What place is this, what waves? Where is Pelion?' Stat. *Ach.* 1.249). Hercules' mother repeats her son's line (replacing *hic* with *me*) at *HO* 1797 (cf. also *HO* 95). The line is shouted by Pasquill *furens* in Act III of Marston's *Jack Drum's Entertainment*. Note, too, the waking Lear at Shakespeare, *KL* IV.vii.52: 'Where have I been? Where am I?'; the post-frenzied Saul in La Taille's *Saül Le Furieux* II.263–9; the confused Henry Tudor in Legge's *Richardus Tertius*, Part III, V.iii.14–15; the distraught Hala in Fulke Greville's *Alaham*, V.iii.99–102 (discussed by Miola 1992: 165–6). The whole sequence (insanity, curative sleep, confused awakening) was termed 'the *Hercules Furens* convention' by Soellner: see on 1042–53. For questions and *sermo praeruptus*, see on 1149–55. *Locus* is often coupled with *regio*: see e.g. *Tro.* 498; *HO* 1797; Plaut. *Pseud.* 594–5, *Rud.* 227; Lucilius 192 Krenkel; Lucr. 2.534, 4.786; Virg. *Aen.* 6.670. Note the adjectival *quis*, common in Latin verse: see e.g. 1161, 1323 (*ter*); *Pha.* 1169–70; *Tro.* 983–4, 1104; *Oed.* 999; *Thy.* 339, 561, 1048–9; *Pho.* 420–1, 557; Virg. *Aen.* 10.9; Stat. *Theb.* 9.70. The final syllable of *regio* is short, as elsewhere in Senecan tragedy: e.g. *Oed.* 369, 772; *Tro.* 498, 558; *Thy.* 650. See further on 109–12. For Roman referentiality in *Hercules*, see on 46–52.

   sub ortu solis, an sub cardine glacialis Vrsae/Beneath rising sun or pole Of icy Bear: the 'pole' is the north pole, the 'turning point' (*cardo*) for the Great Bear (see on 125–31), which was mentioned earlier: by Juno as the apotheosis of a whore (6–7), and by the Chorus in the 'Dawn Ode' (129–30). The echo of Juno's vision of the heavens seems telling. For *glacialis Vrsa*, see also *Pha.* 288. *Cardo*, a 'turning-point', 'hinge', or 'axis' (*Pha.* 963, *Thy.* 877), is used regularly of the world's northern and southern poles. Jonson resurrects the idea in his own Senecan English: 'Shake off the loosened globe from her long hinge, | Roll all the world in darkness' (*Sejanus* V.394–5). For similar global imagery, see 37–8 and n. *ad loc.* Exploits of Hercules in the east and north include the sack of Troy, participation in the Argonautic expedition, servitude to Queen Omphale of Lydia, and the taking of Hippolyte's belt (see on 241–8).

   numquid: more colloquial than *num* and more common in Senecan tragedy and prose: see on 1178–86.

   Hesperii maris extrema tellus/Hesperian Sea's furthest land: Gibraltar, the strait of which Hercules had created through breaking apart the mountain joining Africa and Europe and constructing the 'Pillars of Hercules':

see 237–8 and n. *ad loc.* For 'Hesperian Sea', *Hesperium mare*, see *Med.* 727, *Apoc.* 7.2.7–8; for 'Hesperian', see on 231–4. Other Herculean exploits in the west include the taking of the golden apples of the Hesperides (see on 235–40), the stealing of the cattle of Geryon (see on 231–4), and the holding up of the sky in place of Atlas (see on 68–74).

dat Oceano modum/**curbing Oceanus:** for Oceanus, the great sea encompassing the world, see on 19–29.

quas trahimus auras/**What air do I breathe:** *auras* is not usually governed by *trahere*, though Oedipus uses it of himself at *Pho.* 220, Creon of the throngs of the dead at *Oed.* 599, and the Nurse of the dying Hercules at *HO* 893. Ovid uses it of Phaethon at *Met.* 2.229–30. The analogies tempt.

1143–8 Hercules sees the devastated palace and the corpses onstage. In Euripides, Heracles wakes up to see the corpses and his weapons (*Herac.* 1094–1105); the latter (contrary to what has happened in Seneca's play) have not been removed. In both cases Hercules does not yet identify the corpses.

Certe redimus/**I'm back, surely:** deliberate ambiguity here—'back home' or 'back in hell'? Hercules seems to imply the former, but what he sees seems to suggest the latter. Euripides' Heracles similarly worries whether he has returned to hell (*Herac.* 1101). See further below.

prostrata domo/**palace in ruin:** thus the consensus MS reading. Viansino (1965), Zwierlein, and Billerbeck print the unnecessary conjecture of Schmidt, *ad domum*, in place of *domo*. Giardina (1966), Caviglia, Fitch (1987*a* and 2018), Viansino (1993), and Chaumartin favour the *EA* reading. The ablative is absolute.

simulacra…inferna/**images of hell:** cf. Theseus' remarks on returning 'home' in *Phaedra*: *hospitia digna prorsus inferno hospite*, 'Fit welcome indeed for a guest from hell' (*Pha.* 853). *Simulacra* is a Lucretian term for images which strike/are received by the mind when one is asleep or awake: Lucr. 4.758–9. But, as Fitch *ad loc.* observes, *simulacrum* can also mean 'ghost' (see e.g. *Oed.* 175, *Thy.* 676, Lucr. 1.123, Ov. *Met.* 4.435, and Virg. *Aen.* 2.772, where it is used of the ghost of Creusa), a secondary meaning which enriches its use here in this context of dead bodies.

turba feralis/**horde Of ghosts:** a striking expression (misconstrued by Trevet: 'id est mortifera turba'), in which the phrase is made to mean 'a crowd of the dead' ('mortuorum' Farnaby) rather than the expected 'funerary crowd' (*feralis pompa* = 'funeral/funereal procession' at Calp. Sic. 1.60, Luc. 8.733).

pudet fateri: paueo/**I'm ashamed to say it: I fear:** not the first time Hercules has displayed fear in the play; see 793.

nescioquod mihi, nescioquod animus grande praesagit malum/There's something, Some consummate evil my mind forebodes: similar phrases are used by Thyestes (*Thy.* 958: *mens ante sui praesaga mali*, 'my mind foreboding its ills to come') and Oedipus (*Pho.* 278–9: *praesagit mala…animus*, 'my mind forebodes ills'). Seneca seems to have been impressed by Virgil's *praesaga mali mens*, 'his mind forboding ill' (*Aen.* 10.843), applied to a father, Mezentius, rightly divining the death of his son, Lausus. A parodic version of this tragic/epic *topos* is found in comedy: see e.g. Plaut. *Bacch.* 679, Ter. *Heaut.* 236 (*nescioquid profecto mi animus praesagit mihi*). *Nescioquod* shows the speaker struggling for precise formulation: cf. Pac. *Periboea* (frag. 294 Klotz): *sed nescio quid nunc est: animi horresco*, 'But now there's something: I shudder in my mind'. See also the use of *nescioquid* plus epithet at *Med.* 917 (*ferox*), *Thy.* 267 (*maius*), Prop. 2.34.66 (*maius*). The polysyllabic repetition increases the pathos. Line 1148 is repeated exactly at *HO* 745 (spoken by Deianira: cf. also Deianira's earlier foreboding: *nescioquid animus timuit*, 'There was something my mind feared', *HO* 718). For the dactyl-tribrach combination at the beginning of 1148, see 76 and n. *ad loc.*

1149–55 A veritable plethora of short questions indexes Hercules' confusion and distress. His speech comes in short bursts, exemplifying the *sermo praeruptus*, 'halting speech', which Seneca elsewhere (*Ira* 1.1.4) associates with anger. Cf. Oedipus' speech patterns at *Oed.* 936–57, Medea's at *Med.* 929–39, Cassandra's at *Ag.* 720–5, Hercules' at 963–5 above. Here, of course, Hercules' emotion is more complex than anger but borders on it, and moves towards anger as the questions increase.

Note the disparity between the attention Hercules gives to his family (one and a half lines) and that he gives to his weapons (five and a half lines). What defines Hercules is made clear. Cf. Wyles (2013: 194): 'Seneca makes use of the idea that Heracles' iconic pieces of costume embody his identity'. The focus here on Hercules' costume also has a metatheatrical effect, drawing attention to Hercules' normal status as fictive, costumed character. What happens when the costume is removed? See Introd. §VII, 96–7. For metatheatre in *Hercules*, see on 109–12.

ubi est parens/Where's my father: I have joined Zwierlein, Billerbeck, and others in printing the third person of the *A* reading (*est*) rather than Fitch, who prefers the second person (*es*) of *E*; *est* is in line with the subsequent third-person forms. For another occasion where *E* reads a second-person form and *A* a third person, see 109 above, where again I favour *A*. *Parens* is deliberately ambiguous: the primary referent, as becomes clear from the second question, is Amphitryon; but Jupiter lurks beneath.

natorum grege animosa coniunx/spirited wife With her flock of sons: *animosa* in part has the sense of 'proud' with *grege* functioning as ablative of respect, as at Ov. *Met.* 6.206 (*uobis animosa creatis*, 'proud of your birth'), but it obviously picks up *uirtus animosa*, 'spirited *virtue*', from 201 (the only other occasion where the word appears in the play), and clearly accords with the description of Andromache at *Tro.* 588 (*animosa mater*, 'spirited mother') and of Antigone at *Pho.* 94 (*animosa uirgo*, 'spirited girl'). See further on 197–201. *Grege* has analogous intratextual resonance, picking up with acerbic irony Hercules' perverse use of *gregem* at 1037. For *grex* of Hercules' sons, see on 202–4.

spolio leonis/lion spoils: the skin of the Nemean Lion; see 46, 224–5, 465–6, 797–9. The lion skin was clearly removed together with Hercules' weapons at the end of Act IV (after 1053). Seneca's phrase is Ovidian (e.g. *Her.* 9.113, *Met.* 9.113, *Fas.* 2.325), and is used by the dramatist also at *Pha.* 318; cf. *HO* 786. Note the military imagery, a constitutive feature of Hercules' world view: see on 19–29. For *spolia*, see 51 and n. *ad loc.*

quonam abit tegimen meum...torus/Where is it—my shield...bedding: the lion skin functions as shield (as at 797–9), bedding (as at Ov. *Fas.* 2.339–40, Stat. *Silu.* 4.2.51), and clothing. *Abit*, lit. 'has gone', is a contracted perfect, as at *Oed.* 320, *Tro.* 460. Cf. *petit* (244) and n. *ad loc.* For the suffix *nam* in *quonam*, cf. *quidnam* at 358 and see n. *ad loc.*

somno...Herculeo/Hercules' sleep: the beginning of a litany of self-naming: see also 1155, 1163, 1168, 1218. For the use of the adjective *Herculeus*, see 72 and n. *ad loc.*

ubi tela.../ Where are my arrows...: in the following lines Hercules expresses anxiety over the loss of his weapons, which are such an integral constituent of his identity that their loss is an index of defeat.

quis uiuo mihi...quis...quis.../ Who...from me alive? Who...who: three postponed interrogatives; see on 372–83. *Mihi* is so-called 'dative of separation', see on 542–6.

detrahere potuit/could Have torn: for the dactyl-tribrach combination at the start of the line, see 76 and n. *ad loc.*

1156–9 Statements of resolution followed by more questions.

libet...libet/I want, I want: the epanadiplosis/epanalepis (see on 638–9) in the Latin text (simple repetition in the translation) gives dramatic force to Hercules' resolution. Cf. the triple use of *libet* at *Thy.* 954–6, and the double use of *placet* at *Tro.* 94. Seneca regularly uses the semiotically similar *iuuat*, 'It delights', in repetition (see Boyle *ad Ag.* 435–41), even displaying a quadruple use at *Med.* 911–13.

meum…uictorem/my conqueror: which is, of course, himself, in fulfil-ment of Juno's cry at 116: *se uincat*, 'let him conquer himself'. For the same irony, see 1168.

exurge, uirtus/Rise, virtue: a signal moment, in which the central moral concept of the play (see on 35–40) is ontologized and addressed by the play's protagonist. Cf. the ontologization of *senectus* at 1027. Note that in both places Seneca has avoided using the standard *anime* formula for self-address; e.g. *anime, consurge*, 'Rise, my soul' (*Ag.* 868); *en incipe, anime*, 'On, begin, my soul' (*Pha.* 599). The *anime* formula, common in Senecan tragedy to index a soliloquy or an aside (e.g. *Med.* 895, *Pha.* 592, *Ag.* 108, *Thy.* 423), including statements of psychological resolve, is not used in *Hercules*. Seneca clearly wants *uirtus* centre-stage, as it were, and avoids the morally unspecific *anime*. Hercules will address *uirtus* once more at 1315; see n. *ad loc*. *Virtus* is the generally accepted reading of *E*. *A*, Trevet, and Farnaby read *uictor*, which 'has intruded from 1156' (Fitch *ad loc.*).

Stands up: Hercules clearly stands up at some moment in the early part of this act, since he claims to be 'standing' at 1172. This might seem an apposite moment (*exurge*, 1157, serving as an implied stage direction). Hercules' new vantage point would explain the sudden recognition of his family.

cuius in fetus/For whose conception: Fitch's recent (2018) emendation of the *E* reading improves the syntax. The *E* reading, *in fetu*, is printed by Zwierlein and other modern editors, including Fitch 1987*a* and 2002.

nox longior quam nostra/night…longer than for us: see on 19–29.

1159–63 Questions and statements mingle chiastically.

Quod cerno nefas/What horror do I see: like Theseus, like Hercules; cf. Theseus' reaction to identifying the sword which in turn (so he thinks) identifies the rapist of his wife: *quod facinus…cerno?* 'What crime do I see?' (*Pha.* 898). For Seneca's focus on the 'viewing' (*cerno*) of dead loved ones, see on 249–58. For *nefas*, see 387 and n. *ad loc*.

nati…/My sons…: Hercules here reproduces the 'headline news' mode of message-delivery found often in Senecan tragedy; see on 629–30.

perempta coniunx/My wife slain: *perimere* is the most common and perhaps least emotive word in Senecan tragedy for 'to kill' (ctr. *caesus* at 932). The phrase, *peremptus iacet*, is used (*mutatis mutandis*) of Hector and Memnon (*Tro.* 238–9), Priam (*Tro.* 312), Jocasta (*Oed.* 1040), Agamemnon (*Ag.* 925), Deianira (*HO* 1458)—and here (for *iacet* is understood from 1160) of Megara.

quis Lycus regnum obtinet/What Lycus holds the realm: given the evolving analogy between Hercules and Lycus, the contextual irony is overt. For adjectival *quis*, see on 1138-42.

quis...ausus est/Who dared: for *ausus* and boundary transgression, see on 547-9. For boundary violation, see on 46-52.

scelera/crimes: see 121 and n. *ad loc.*

1163-8 Hercules' cry for help (cf. Heracles' more succinct appeal to his friends at Eur. *Herac.* 1106-7) and desire for vengeance. For appeals for a response from particular localities, see (more famously) 1323-9 below and n. *ad loc.*, and the cries of Hippolytus at *Pha.* 715-18 and of Theseus at *Pha.* 1201-3. Here the topographical references seem to pick up Lycus' description of his newly acquired kingdom at 332-6, furthering the important analogy between Hercules and Lycus. For geographical catalogues in Senecan tragedy, see on 332-6; for catalogues generally in Senecan tragedy, see on 6-18.

quisquis...succurre/All who...help me: for the structure (*quisquis/quicumque* introducing a list with second-person verbs, followed by an imperative), cf. *Thy.* 74-81, *Pho.* 124-31.

Ismeni/Ismenos: see on 332-6. Note in *quisquis Ismeni* the repetition of the same syllable at the end and beginning of juxtaposed words; see 67 and n. *ad loc.*

Actaea...arua/Attic fields: for Seneca's use of *Actaeus* instead of *Atticus* (847), see *Pha.* 900, 1149.

gemino mari/twin seas: the Ionian and the Myrtoan/Aegean Sea; see on 332-6.

Pelopis regna Dardanii/realms Of Dardan Pelops: the northern Peloponnese. Pelops is called 'Dardan' (i.e. 'Trojan') because of his father Tantalus' origin in western Asia Minor/Anatolia, where Tantalus was king of Sipylus. Pelops' eastern origin resulted in his being called both 'Lydian' (e.g. Pind. *Ol.* 1.24, 9.9, Paus. 5.1.6) and (most esp. by Roman poets) 'Phrygian' (Prop. 1.2.19, Ov. *Her.* 16.266, *Tr.* 2.386). Strabo (12.8.3) also calls him 'Phrygian'. Such focus on the 'orientalism' of Pelops contrasts with Virgil's focus on the 'Italianism' of Latinus' ancestors (Italus, Sabinus, Saturn, Janus, and 'Laurentian' Picus, who holds an augural staff of Quirinus, *Quirinali lituo*: *Aen.* 7.170-91). The Romans themselves and most especially their Julian rulers prided themselves on their Phrygian origins. For similar modes of reference to the Peloponnese, cf. *Pelopis...oras*, 'shores of Pelops', *Ag.* 563; *sede Pelopea*, 'seat of Pelops', *Med.* 891 (= Πέλοπος...ἕδραι, Eur. *Tro.* 1099).

succurre/help me: a quintessential word for 'help' in dramatic appeals; see Hor. *AP* 459, Ov. *Fas.* 6.517.

ruat ira in omnes/Let my wrath fall on all: this cardinally destructive emotion in Seneca's philosophical works is central to the dramatization of Hercules in this final act (see e.g. 1220, 1277), as it was of Juno in the prologue (28, 34, 77). It will also be central to Hercules' construction of Jupiter, to whose wrath he will appeal (1202). Hercules is clearly acting not only destructively, but in a self-consciously Jovian manner. The tendency of *ira* towards universal destruction is described (again using *ruere*) at *Ira* 2.35.5 as *terras maria caelum ruere cupientem*, 'desiring that lands, seas, sky fall'. Cf. Hercules' impulse at 1284–94. For *ira*, see on 19–29; for the ontologization of the emotions, see on 75–6. *Ira* continues as a defining aspect of Hercules in *Hercules Oetaeus*.

hostis...hostem/Foes...foe: again epanadiplosis/epanalepsis (see on 638–9), this time with polyptoton, as at *Oed.* 980, *Thy.* 202, 907. For polyptoton in *Hercules*, see on 11–18.

1168–73 Hercules addresses his presumed conqueror.

Victor Alcidae/Alcides' conqueror: the self-naming continues (see on 1149–55), as does the 'conqueror' irony: see 1156 and n. *ad loc.*

procede/Come forth: the translation is intended to reflect the 'elevated tone' (Keulen *ad Tro.* 705) of the word, used also at *Tro.* 705, *Pho.* 419.

currus truces Thracis cruenti/bloody Thracian's brutal chariot: 'chariot' here is metonymic for horses, as at *Pha.* 1063, *Thy.* 797, 819. For the flesh-eating horses of the Thracian king, Diomedes, see on 226–30.

Geryonae pecus/Geryon's Herd: for the cattle of Geryon, see on 231–4. For this form of the genitive of Geryon, see Lucr. 5.28 (where it is pentasyllabic), Virg. *Aen.* 8.202.

Libyaeue dominos/Libya's lords: probably a reference to Busiris and Antaeus, as Fitch *ad loc.* suggests. For Busiris, king of Egypt, and Antaeus, a giant in Africa, see on 480–9. 'Libya' is here used in its regular meaning of 'Africa'.

en nudus asto/Look, I stand naked: *nudus*, 'naked', means not only 'weaponless/unarmed', as Hercules goes on to clarify (cf. *Pho.* 154, *Ep. Mor.* 24.8, and *HO* 57), but also literally 'naked', since his upper body is without its main form of clothing, the lion skin (1150–2). For the semiotics of Hercules' nudity, see Introd. §VII, 96–7. Cf. the semiotics of the nudity of the Chorus in the opening ode of *Troades*. *Asto* is important: clearly by this line Hercules is standing: see on 1156–9. For *en*, see on 944–52.

uel meis armis licet petas inermem/With my arms attack Me unarmed: for the *arma/inermis* wordplay, see also *Tro.* 671. For *licet* with the subjunctive in a non-concessive clause, see on 118–22.

1173-86 Hercules notices Theseus' and Amphitryon's avoidance of his gaze and implores them for information.

1173-7 *Cur meos...fugit...uultus*/**Why...shun my gaze:** Hercules describes in an aside the behaviour of Theseus and Amphitryon, and follows the description with a direct address to them (1175-7). This oscillation between third-person description (aside) and second-person address will continue until line 1200, when Hercules finally recognizes what he has done. What Seneca is delivering to his audience with this technique is not simply a recognition scene but its psychology. Cf. the distressed recognition of La Taille's Saul, imitative of this passage: 'Qu'ay je fait, qu'on prend pour moy la fuite?' (*Saül Le Furieux* 266). For other non-entrance asides in Senecan drama, see e.g. 1178-80, 1193, 1200; *Tro.* 607-18, 623-6, 643-62, 686-91; *Oed.* 103-5, 206-9, 659-68, 860, 1024-32, 1034-6; *Pha.* 136-9, 424-30, 580-8, 592-9, 634-5; *Med.* 49-50. For descriptive asides followed by second-person address, see e.g. 1178-86, *Oed.* 659-70, *Pha.* 580-8, *Med.* 179-91, *Thy.* 491-511, *Tro.* 607-22, 625-31. For the averted gaze joined with tears elsewhere in Senecan tragedy, see *Pha.* 886-7, *Med.* 1020. At *Oed.* 1011-12 Oedipus even averts his 'empty eyes' (*uacuos...uultus*). For *uultus*, see on 329-31. Further 'shunning' is to follow at 1193 (*refugit*).

ora cur condunt sua/**Why do they hide their faces:** at Eur. *Herac.* 1111 Amphitryon is asked a similar question by Heracles. What such averted/hidden faces might suggest is certainly shame (1178-80), but also grief (Eur. *Supp.* 110-11, Ov. *Met.* 2.329), and fear of contamination from the polluted party (here Hercules), which will extend to a refusal to touch his blood-spattered hands (1193). Note the postponement of *cur* as at 1208, *Oed.* 1024, *Pha.* 174. See further on 372-83. For *condere* of 'hiding' one's face, see Ov. *Met.* 2.330, VF 7.390.

Differte fletus/**Defer your tears:** Hercules still has problems with the emotions of others, even when, as here, he is himself filled with emotion. Cf. his earlier 'deferring' instruction (to Amphitryon and Megara) at 638-9 and the identical instruction of another self-isolating figure, Shakespeare's Coriolanus, addressing his family in the opening words of Act IV: 'Come, leave your tears' (*Cor.* IV.i.1). Theseus' and Amphitryon's tears are mentioned again at 1273-4. Tears never fall from a Stoic *sapiens*. For the movement to an open second-person address after third-person 'aside' description in 1173-4, see previous n.

dederit neci/**killed:** for Senecan periphrases for killing, see on 1048-53.

profare/**Say:** an elevated word in the Latin with an 'archaic' feel, used also at *Pha.* 358 and *Thy.* 244. It is first attested in Livius Andronicus'

Odyssey and found almost entirely in epic or tragedy: see Enn. *Ann.* frag. 576 Skutsch, Pac. *Dulorestes* frag. 145 Klotz, Virg. *Aen.* 1.561.

genitor/father: see on 1202–18.

at tu ede, Theseu/Then you, Theseus, deliver: for the elision of the long vowel in the monosyllabic *tu*, see *Ag.* 303, *Pho.* 290, 309, 488, 638. For addresses to a character by name, see on 637–40. With *ede*, 'deliver', Hercules may be asking for a detailed exegesis, perhaps even a messenger-style performance, as Amphitryon requests from him earlier: see on 760–1.

sed tua, Theseu, fide/but, Theseus, by your faith: Theseus does not reply after *ede*; hence the emphatic and morally forceful second appeal. A similar use of a double vocative occurs at *Tro.* 969. Billerbeck *ad loc.* classifies *tua...fide* as 'ein Ausdruck der Umgangssprache', citing Petron. 133.1 (*tua fide*) and Plaut. *Men.* 894 (*mea...fide*), Pliny *Ep.* 1.14.10 (*fide mea*). For the importance of *fides* in Senecan tragedy and Roman culture, see on 414–21. The value seems especially associated in *Hercules* with Megara (see 420–1) and Theseus (see 1334). For members of the audience familiar with Seneca's (probably earlier) *Phaedra* (see *Pha.* 92) and/or with the Roman poetic tradition from Catullus (see esp. Cat. 64.132ff.) through Propertius (1.3.1–2, 2.24.42–4) to Ovid (*Her.* 4.59–66, 10 *passim*), the issue of Theseus' *fides* may have seemed problematic. Though *Thesea fides*, 'Thesean faith/loyalty' to Pirithous, features as an ideal in Propertius (2.1.37–8) and Ovid's *Tristia* (1.3.66, 5.19–20, 9.31–2), *fides* to a would-be rapist of Proserpina is not without its moral difficulties, and *perfidus Theseus* is hard to erase. Certainly the view of Billerbeck *ad* 1334–41 that Theseus' *fides* marks him as a paradigm of 'Athenian humanism' ('verkörpert er das athenische Humanitätsideal') is not easy to accept. For the qualifying use of *sed*, see 725 and n. *ad loc.* For Roman referentiality in *Hercules*, see on 46–52.

1178–86 Again an aside followed by a second-person address. The features underscored in the descriptive aside (silence, face veiled in shame, tears) are those of Ovid's Lucretia (*Fas.* 2.819–20).

ora pudibunda obtegit/veil faces filled with shame: *ora pudibunda* is an Ovidian phrase; see e.g. *Met.* 6.604–5, *Fas.* 2.819–20. *Pudibundus* is used only once elsewhere by Seneca (*Oed.* 619) and again of men, when he applies it to the *pudibundum...caput* of Oedipus' dead father, Laius. Ovid, on the other hand, uses the adjective seven times but only of women. For *pudor*, see on 689–96; see esp. 692, where *Pudor* itself is face-veiling.

furtimque lacrimas fundit/And shed secret tears: similarly in Euripides' play Amphitryon weeps and veils his eyes: *Herac.* 1111. *Lacrimas* or *fletus fundere* is the quintessentially Senecan phrase for the shedding of tears: see e.g. *Ag.* 378, *Tro.* 131, *Thy.* 966–7, *Apoc.* 12.3, *Marc.* 1.2.

quid est pudendum/**What need for shame**: as Billerbeck notes *ad loc.* Hercules is appealing to proverbial wisdom ('Volksweisheit'): see e.g. αἰδὼς γὰρ ἐν κακοῖσιν οὐδὲν ὠφελεῖ, 'For shame is no help amid evil', Soph. frag. 928 Lloyd-Jones; *rebus semper pudor absit in artis*, 'Shame should never have a place in dire straits', VF 5.324. For shame and evil/distress, see also *Oed.* 65, 1008. The rare *pudendus* is used also at 1035; see n. *ad loc.*

Numquid…numquid: a colloquial form of the interrogative particle, *num*, occurring in Roman comedy and satire and in Seneca's prose works, and used more frequently in Senecan tragedy than *num*. Of its thirteen uses in Seneca's plays six are in *Thyestes* and four in *Hercules*, always in a series of rhetorical questions: see also 214, 1140. The author of *HO* (11 *bis*, 1256) also found *numquid* useful.

Argiuae impotens dominator urbis/**raving master Of Argos city**: Eurystheus, king of Mycenae, which is here conflated with Argos (see on 1035–8); see Dramatis Personae (Juno) above. *Dominator*, an uncommon word in Latin, first attested in Cicero (*dominatorem rerum*, 'master of the world', *ND* 2.4, applied to Jupiter) appears five times in the tragedies (also at *Pha.* 1039, 1159, *Med.* 4, *Thy.* 1078) and once in the prose works (*Ep. Mor.* 107.11). Seneca presumably liked its portentous quality. For Seneca's fondness for nouns ending in *-tor*, see on 299–302. For *impotens* as the final word of an iambic line, regularly preceded by an elision, see 966 and n. *ad loc.* For *impotens* and tyrants, see 738 and n. *ad loc.*

infestum Lyci pereuntis agmen/**dying Lycus' Violent troops**: Hercules expressed concern about such a violent attack earlier (637).

per te meorum facinorum laudem precor, genitor/**I beseech you by the fame of my deeds, Father**: note the position of the personal pronoun, *te*, after *per*, separated from its governing verb. For *te* in this position, see also *Ag.* 929, Ter. *Andr.* 538, Tib. 1.5.7; for *ego* in this position, see *Med.* 285, Plaut. *Men.* 990, Enn. *Ach.* frag. 3 Jocelyn, Ter. *Andr.* 289, 834, Virg. *Aen.* 4.314–16, 12.56–7, Ov. *Fas.* 2.841–2, Stat. *Theb.* 10.694. For *genitor*, 'father', see on 1202–18.

tuique nominis semper mihi numen secundum/**and the ever propitious divinity Of your name**: the 'name' is that of 'father', *genitor* (1184), a title of constant controversy in this play. Note the wordplay here: (i) the punning on *nomen* and *numen*; (ii) *secundum* suggests both 'propitious' and 'second': the divinity of Amphitryon's title of 'father' is 'second' to that of Jupiter (contrast Eur. *Herac.* 1265, where Heracles proclaims Amphitryon his father instead of Zeus). For similar puns to *nomen/numen*, see *tumide/timide* (*Tro.* 301–2), *animo/animam* (*Pho.* 141–3), *nomen/omen* (Plaut. *Pers.* 625).

quis fudit domum/Who made our house sprawl: the answer is Hercules, who similarly 'made Lycus sprawl' (*fusus*, 895) and himself 'sprawls on the ground' (*fusus humi*, 1082). *Domum*, 'house', here means 'household' (see 1250).

cui praeda iacui/Who made me fallen prey: lit. 'to whom have I fallen prey?' Hercules is using *praeda* to mean Lucretian 'prey' (5.875), but the effect in this context is particularly strong. Applied to human captives in a military context (as here), the word's effect is to 'dehumanize' (see Frank *ad Pho.* 578). It is used twice of Hecuba in *Troades* (58, 980); see also *Tro.* 150, *Pho.* 578. Cf. the lament of Euryalus' mother, who mourns that her dead son 'is fallen prey' (*praeda...iaces*, Virg. *Aen.* 9.485–6) to dogs and birds. For military imagery in *Hercules*, see on 19–29.

1186–93 A brief exchange between 'father' and son, involving *stichomythia* and *antilabe*, followed by an aside. Such sections of truncated dialogue, involving *antilabe*, are common in Senecan tragedy: see on 422–38.

Tacita sic abeant mala/Let these ills pass in silence: a similar injunction is given to Euripides' Heracles by Amphitryon (*Herac.* 1125). *Tacita* functions predicatively. For the use of *sic*, see 27 above.

Vt inultus ego sim/Would I be unrevenged: the only occurrence of the quintessentially self-dramatizing epithet, *inultus*, 'unrevenged', in the play. Hercules' words touch on a major issue in Senecan tragedy. Being 'unrevenged', *inultus*, is a major motor of tragic action in the great revenge tragedies, *Medea* (*Med.* 399) and *Thyestes* (*Thy.* 178). See also Nero at *Oct.* 463. Oedipus, too, is aware of the force of this state; though blinded and in exile, he still needs to avenge his father, whom he regards as 'unrevenged' (*inultum, Pho.* 90–1). See also the Ghost of Laius' self-description as a *pater inultus*, 'unrevenged father' (*Oed.* 643), and the complaint of Agrippina's Ghost at *Oct.* 599–600 that her 'soul is unrevenged' (*manibus nostris...inultis*). See also *HO* 282, 345 (Deianira). The importance of revenge for the maintenance of personal and social identity is articulated early in Roman literature; see Peniculus at Plaut. *Men.* 471–2:

> non hercle is sum qui sum, ni hanc iniuriam
> meque ultus pulchre fuero.

> I'm not—by Hercules—who I am, unless I avenge
> This injustice and myself beautifully.

Seneca, however, in *De Clementia* (1.20–21) argues against a *princeps* ('emperor') simply avenging himself, suggesting either mild vengeance or (preferably) none at all, proclaiming that there is 'nothing more glorious than a wronged *princeps* not taking revenge' (*nec quicquam esse gloriosius principe impune laeso*, *Clem.* 1.20.3). The *ego* in the lemmatized phrase seems emphatic, as at 372, 1215, 1298. Hence the italics in the translation. For *ego ut* and the subjunctive in 'repudiating/indignant' questions, see on 372–83.

Saepe uindicta obfuit/**Vengeance often harms**: a proposition Seneca advocates (though he would substitute *semper*, 'always', for *saepe*, 'often') throughout *De Ira*, in which he sees anger as a desire for revenge: *concitatio animi ad ultionem uoluntate et iudicio pergentis*, 'a disturbance of the mind proceeding to revenge by choice and judgement' (*Ira* 2.3.5). On the self-injurious nature of vengeance, see *Ira* 3.27.1: *multum temporis ultio absumit; multis se iniuriis obicit*, 'Vengeance consumes much time; it exposes itself to much harm'; cf. *Ira* 2.33.2, *Ben.* 6.32.2. *Obfuit*, 'harms', is a gnomic perfect; see on 864–74. *Saepe* is regularly used in *sententiae*: see e.g. 1238, *Tro.* 329, *Oed.* 827, *Ag.* 130, *Thy.* 311.

Quisquamne segnis/**Has anyone…without action**: the tone is that of disbelief, as is that of Oedipus at *Oed.* 6: *quisquamne regno gaudet*, 'Does anyone find joy in kingship?' For *segnis* as anathema in the context of revenge, cf. *Med.* 399, *Tro.* 805. Cf. the anxiety of Atreus (*Thy.* 176) and Oedipus (*Pho.* 91) about seeming/being *iners*, 'inactive/spineless'.

etiam, pater/**Really, father**: for this use of *etiam* to signal surprise or shock in a question, see on 963–73.

quicquam timeri maius aut grauius potest/**Can something be feared worse or graver than this**: cf. the similar and (contextually) equally ironic question asked of Creon by Oedipus at *Oed.* 828: *malum timeri maius his aliquid potest*, 'Can some evil be feared worse than this?' *Maius* is often a keyword in Senecan tragedy underscoring the motif of the enlargement or intensification of evil (*maius malum/nefas/scelus*); see e.g. *Pha.* 142–3, 688, 697; *Ag.* 29; *Tro.* 45, 427; *Med.* 50, 674; *Thy.* 259, 745; *Pho.* 286, 457, 531.

Cladis tuae pars ista…quota/**How small a part of your tragedy**: at one level perhaps a metatheatrical moment (hence the translation of *cladis* as 'tragedy'), underscored by *miserere* in the next line. For metatheatrical language and motifs in this play, see on 109–12. For *quota pars* and postponed *quota*, see 383 and n. *ad loc.*

Miserere, genitor/**Have pity, father**: the vain appeal for compassion is an important motif in Senecan tragedy, esp. in *Phaedra* (623, 636, 671), *Troades* (694, 703, 762, 792), and *Medea* (482, 1018). Here and elsewhere (*Tro.* 1148) it is paraded as one of the tragic Aristotelian emotions (*Poet.* 1449b27–8).

Orthodox Stoicism, however, classified *misericordia*, 'compassion', as a milder *vitium*, 'fault' (along with *amor*, 'love', and *uerecundia*, 'modesty': *Ira* 2.15.3). For *genitor*, 'father', see on 1202-18. For Seneca and Aristotle, see on 1237-9.

supplices tendo manus/I stretch suppliant hands: Seneca regularly includes scenes which feature characters in acts of supplication (generally kneeling, perhaps sometimes even prostrate): see *Pha.* 666 (*supplex*: Phaedra), *Tro.* 709 (*supplice dextra*: Astyanax), *Oed.* 71 (*supplices...manus*: Oedipus), *Ag.* 394 (*supplex*: Eurybates), *Med.* 282 (*supplex*: Medea), *Thy.* 517 (*supplicem*: Thyestes). It is unclear whether Hercules kneels. Note the *manus* motif (see on 118-22), which climaxes in this act, as the hands which implemented Hercules' violence become the instruments of the recognition of his crime. The word occurs some eleven times between 1192 and the end of the play.

Quid hoc/What's this: for this expression of surprise, see on 939-44.

manus refugit/shuns my hands: again the 'shunning', as at 1173 (*fugit*). See 1318-19, where the present situation is inverted, as Amphitryon 'clasps' the hand of Hercules. Hercules' hands, of course, as he now sees, are covered in blood. Shakespeare's Macbeth is similarly obsessed with his (*Mac.* II.ii.27) 'hangman's hands': 'What hands are here? Ha! they pluck out mine eyes' (*Mac.* II.ii.58).

hic errat scelus/Crime hovers here: for the expression, which involves a 'wandering' metaphor, cf. *Thy.* 473: *errat his aliquis dolus*, 'Treachery hovers here'. For other metaphorical uses of *errare*, see 162 and 1281 (and n. *ad loc*). For *scelus* in this final act, see 121, 1199, 1237 and nn. *ad locc*.

1194-1200 The recognition. Hercules works out from the evidence before him—the blood on his hands and arrow—that he is the slayer of his own family. Seneca revelled in the dramatization of a character working out onstage what is happening (Ulysses at *Tro.* 607-18, Andromache at *Tro.* 926-37, Oedipus at *Oed.* 661-70, Medea at *Med.* 549-50). Theseus' attempt to piece together the body of his son at the end of *Phaedra* (1247-74) is a physical extension of this. There is nothing resembling this moment in Euripides, whose Heracles is simply told by Amphitryon what happened (*Herac.* 1131-9). Lines 1194-8 show Hercules' mind in operation and could be delivered as a continuation of the aside of 1193 (i.e. as a closed soliloquy) or as an open soliloquy. Cf. the awaking/recognition scene in La Taille's *Saül Le Furieux* II.263-7, and the recognition of Cuchulain in Yeats's *On Baile's Strand* (1907), 31-3. Note, too, the implications of this tragic ἀναγνώρισις: *uitia sua confiteri sanitatis indicium est*, 'To confess one's faults is a mark of sanity' (*Ep. Mor.* 28.10). For recognition in Senecan tragedy, see on 622-5.

quid illa...harundo/What of that arrow: note the shortening of final *o* in *harundo* (also at 994); see on 109–12.

puerili madens...leto/Wet with a boy's death: i.e. with the dead boy's blood. Cf. *madere caede*, found at Ov. *Met.* 1.149, Luc. 2.103–4.

tincta Lernaea nece/Stained with Lerna's poison: from the Lernaean Hydra; see on 241–8. This information that the arrow which killed Hercules' son is poisoned is important for Hercules' later use of the arrow to threaten suicide. According to Ovid's *Fasti*, 5.397–414, even accidental piercing from a dropped Lernaean arrow was incurably fatal. The Lernaean reference here is also an omen of the future: a robe 'stained with Lerna's poison' will bring about Hercules' death (see *Med.* 641, *HO* and Ov. *Met.* 9.158). *Tincta* initially qualifies *harundo*, but can also be taken subsequently as qualifying *tela*. One can supply *est* (for the omission of auxiliary *est* see 224 and n. *ad loc.*) or simply regard the phrase as deliberately truncated. There is no need to join Leo and Fitch *ad loc.* in adding *est* before *nece*. Indeed, if *est* is added, the striking ambiguity mentioned above, which I would prefer to retain and have translated accordingly, disappears.

iam tela uideo nostra/Now I see my shafts: the 'recognition' moment (see on 622–5). It is accompanied by a standard recognition 'test' which began in Homer's *Odyssey* (Book 21): only Hercules could have fired this arrow, since only he could have drawn the bow.

sinuare neruum/drawn the string: *sinuare* is a Senecan tragic *hapax*. Ovid uses the verb of 'curving', i.e. bending, the bow: *Met.* 8.30, 381.

genitor, hoc nostrum est scelus/Father, is this crime mine: the issue of *scelus* (see 121 with n. *ad loc.*, and 1237 with n. *ad loc.*) comes to the fore, and figures strongly in the moral debate which follows and its aftermath: 1237, 1238, 1262, 1278, 1300, 1313, 1319, 1336. *Genitor* is used again to refer to a different father of Hercules at 1202; see n. *ad loc.* Contrary to Fitch *ad loc.* there should be strong punctuation before *genitor*, which needs to be taken with the question which follows.

tacuere. nostrum est/They're silent. It's mine: the third person indicates that this is spoken as an aside. Euripides' Heracles speaks openly (*Herac.* 1126), reprimanding Amphitryon (Theseus has not yet entered) for his silence. For climactic half-lines, see on 40–6. The present half-line picks up the famous *meum sit* of 939.

1200–1 A short but thematically important response from Amphitryon.

Luctus...istic/The grief: *istic*, as Fitch observes *ad loc.*, in this adjectival function is rare outside Roman drama. Its sonal as well as metrical properties make it a good choice here.

crimen nouercae. casus hic culpa caret/the crime Your stepmother's. What happened leaves you blameless: Amphitryon acts metatheatrically here, directing the audience to the play's prologue. His 'authoritative' quasi-judicial account parallels analogous 'late' pronouncements by another tragic parent (Jocasta) in *Oedipus* (1019: *fati ista culpa est. nemo fit fato nocens*, 'Fate is to blame. No guilt stems from fate') and *Phoenissae* (451–3: *error inuitos adhuc | fecit nocentes. omne Fortunae fuit | peccantis in nos crimen*, 'Previously an error made us guilty against our wills. The whole crime was Fortune's, sinning against us'. Cf. Antigone at *Pho.* 203–5, Hyllus at *HO* 983)—and also Phaedra's Nurse, as she attempts to absolve her mistress: *mens impudicam facere, non casus solet*, 'The mind makes one unchaste, not circumstance' (*Pha.* 735). For *crimen* and *culpa*, see also *Med.* 935, *Thy.* 321. Amphitryon will later substitute *error* for *casus* (1237), and reiterate Juno's responsibility (1297). There is a strong contrast here with Euripides' *Heracles*, in which Amphitryon assigns blame to Heracles alone (*Herac.* 1139) and it is Heracles who blames Hera (*Herac.* 1303ff.)—to the agreement of the Chorus (*Herac.* 1311–12). Armitage raises the issue of individual responsibility early in *Mister Heracles* (2000), p. 5: (Megara speaking) 'Does chance, fate or choice make us what we are?' For *nouerca*, see on 19–29; for metatheatre in *Hercules*, see on 109–12.

1202–18 Hercules asks for punishment: (i) as a substitute Prometheus having his liver eaten (1205–10); (ii) crushed between the Clashing Rocks (1210–15); (iii) burnt alive on a massive pyre (1216–17). Thence to hell (1218). The speech is not without its ironies (see 1207–8, 1216–17 and nn. *ad locc.*). Diverse forms of death are regularly proposed, canvassed, and/or debated by (actual and potential) tragic suicides or *morituri* in Senecan tragedy: see e.g. Oedipus at *Oed.* 868–78, 927–34; Jocasta at *Oed.* 1036–9; Phaedra at *Pha.* 258–60; Theseus at *Pha.* 1223–42; Antigone and Oedipus at *Pho.* 67–73, 147–9; Electra at *Ag.* 971–7. What Hercules gives vent to here is a 'theatrical scream' or 'Schreirede', an appeal not simply for punishment but for cosmic punishment, for a reaction and disruption of the cosmos itself, as the universe marshals its power to punish the great sinner. 'Schreireden' may be found in several Senecan tragedies: *Oed.* 868–81; *Pha.* 671–84, 954–8, 1199–1242; *Med.* 531–7; *Thy.* 1006–21, 1077–96. See also 1221–6, *Oct.* 245–51, *HO* 847–55, 934–63. Note the 'Schreirede' of Theseus in *Phaedra* (1199–1242), also a plea for cosmic death from one who has recently returned from hell and killed his offspring. Especially in its more cosmic versions (Hercules, Medea, Hippolytus, Theseus, Thyestes), the influence on Renaissance English tragedy is evident. Witness e.g.

Northumberland reacting to the news of his son Hotspur's death at Shakespeare, *Henry IV 2* I.i.153–4:

> Let heaven kiss earth! Now let not Nature's hand
> Keep the wild flood confin'd! Let order die!

For a 'Schreirede' indebted to Hercules' outburst here, see that of Glover's *Medea* (*Med.* V.ii), beginning 'Hear, Neptune'. See further Boyle (1997: 163–4). Here in *Hercules* the 'Schreirede' features a varied list of punishments. Cf. Euripides' *Heracles*, who similarly, if less cosmically, displays an impulse to suicide and lists a variety of modes of death (*Herac.* 1146–52). Behind the Senecan idea that cosmic disruption is an appropriate response to experienced evil seems to lie something like the Stoic doctrine of cosmic 'sympathy' (συμπάθεια): see on 1054–62•. The whole of this speech and its aftermath (1221–6, 1258–62) realize Juno's prayer in the prologue (116–17). For prayers in *Hercules* and Senecan tragedy, see on 205–78; for the death-wish, see on 1022–31.

genitor/**father**: Jupiter, not the *genitor* Amphitryon of 1199. Hercules' ambiguous/dual parentage is thrust to the fore, permeating every instance in Act V of *genitor* (nine occurrences), *pater* (seven), and *parens* (four), even when their referent is solely Amphitryon. Such juggling with 'fatherhood' lays bare one of the essential problems of Hercules, viz. is he man or god?; and it puts pressure on Amphitryon in this final act to prove himself a true 'father'. The final four uses of *pater*, three of *parens*, and three of *genitor* refer only to Amphitryon: see Introd. §VII, 99, n. 273.

iratus tona/**rage and thunder**: similarly (in their 'Schreireden') Medea at *Med.* 531 (*tona*), Thyestes at *Thy.* 1080 (*intona*), and Hippolytus at *Pha.* 682 (*tona*). Cf. also the cry of Shakespeare's Herculean Othello upon recognition of Iago's treachery and his own unjustified killing of his wife (*Oth.* V.ii.232–3):

> Are there no stones in heaven
> But what serves for the thunder?

Or the raging Lear upon the heath (*KL* III.ii.1, 6–7):

> Blow, winds, and crack your cheeks! Rage, blow!
> ...And thou, all-shaking thunder,
> Strike flat the thick rotundity o' th' world.

Or Marston's Malevole, addressing 'heaven': 'If now thy brows are clear, when will they thunder?' (*The Malcontent* III.iii.123). For Hercules and *ira*, see on 1163–8; for Jove's thunder and *ira*, see 932–3, *Ag.* 528; for *ira*, see on 19–29.

oblite nostri/**Thou didst forget me:** the participle is probably concessive in function.

uindica sera manu/**let thy late hand avenge:** *uindicare* is an important term in Senecan tragedy, esp. in *Phaedra* (352), *Medea* (668), and *Thyestes* (1085), where it unites the macrocosmic and microcosmic action of the plays. *Vindicare* embraces the notion of making a legal claim to something (e.g. property) and of exacting legal/moral redress—or vengeance. If this kind of vengeance were exacted (see Thyestes at *Thy.* 1110–11), both the physical and the moral nature of the universe would be stabilized. *Sera manu*, 'with thy late hand', is Hercules' only criticism of Jupiter (cf. Hippolytus' reproach of Jupiter at *Pha.* 671–4). Euripides' Heracles is more critical of Zeus: *Herac.* 1263–5. For the *manus* motif, see on 118–22.

saltem/**At least:** appears elsewhere in Senecan tragedy only at *Ag.* 492, *Med.* 1015. Fitch *ad loc.* Detects 'a note of pathos' when it is used. The dramatist of *HO* uses it some seven times.

stelliger mundus sonet/**starry firmament Roar:** *stelliger* is a Senecan hapax. It is used by Cicero in his *Aratea* (483). Statius liked the word: *Theb.* 12.565, *Silu.* 3.3.77. For the focus on sound, see on 1002–9.

hic et ille…polus/**from pole to pole:** lit. 'this pole and that', i.e. the firmament, as at *Ag.* 384–4• (*extremi…poli*, 'distant poles') or Ov. *Fas.* 2.489–90 (*uterque…polus*, 'both poles').

rupes…Caspiae…atque ales auida/**Caspian Crags and ravening bird:** allusion to the place and torture of Prometheus; see next n. Cf. 759 (*auida…auis*) and *Ag.* 18 (*ales auida*), where a 'ravening bird' is frightening the table of Phineus or eating the liver of the Giant, Tityus.

cur Promethei uacant scopuli/**Why are the Promethean Rocks empty:** Prometheus (mentioned elsewhere in Senecan tragedy only at *Med.* 709 and 824, but alluded to at *Pho.* 318) was the Titan who stole fire from the gods and gave it to humankind, for which he received from Jupiter the punishment of having his liver eaten by an eagle, while he lay chained to a rock on the Caucasus mountains between the Black Sea and the Caspian Sea. The punishment was meant to be eternal (the liver grew back overnight to be eaten again by the eagle), but Prometheus was later released from his chains by Hercules and the bird killed (Hes. *Theog.* 521–31, VF 5.154–76). Hercules' question here is contextually ironic: the 'emptier of the rocks' asks why they are empty. Prometheus was often celebrated as a culture hero, the originator of technology; in *Prometheus Bound*, attributed to Aeschylus, it is claimed that all human skills (τέχναι) derive from him (506). But he also defied the gods. His crime is an obvious and famous example of boundary

violation and is often associated with such paradigmatic boundary violations as the Argonautic expedition: see Apollon. 2.1246–61, Virg. *Ecl.* 6.42–
4, Hor. *Odes* 1.3.17–33. The reference to the Symplegades in the following
lines continues the association. Hercules' reference to Prometheus not only
underscores the former's boundary transgressions (penetration of hell,
attempted assault on heaven, murder of kin) and the irony that the man
who freed Prometheus now wishes to take his place, but also the more disturbing irony (for both Prometheus and Hercules were heralded as bene-
factors of humankind) that helping humankind comes at the most severe
cost. Apparently indebted to this passage is the 'Schreirede' of Glover's
Medea, who specifically requests 'Promethean torture' as punishment for
her filicide (*Med.* V.ii). For the 'emptiness' trope, see the Nurse to Phaedra:
aula cur fratris uacat, 'Why is your brother's palace empty? (*Pha.* 174); the
Fury: *dextra cur patrui uacat*, 'Why is the uncle's hand empty' (*Thy.* 57); and
Oedipus to Antigone: *dira ne sedes uacet*, 'lest that dire abode (of the
Sphinx) be empty' (*Pho.* 121). For the enjambement in 1207–8, followed by
a pause after the first word of the next line, see 379–80 and n. *ad loc.* For
boundary violation, see on 46–52.

   uertice immenso feras uolucresque pascens/feeding beasts and birds On
its measureless peak: Hercules is envisaging himself as such food in place
of Prometheus. For *pascere* of 'feeding' wild beasts and birds, see also *Tro.*
567, *Thy.* 10, 750–1, 1033, *Oct.* 515. 'Birds' as consumers of human flesh are
regularly paired with 'dogs' in Greek texts: see e.g. Hom. *Il.* 1.4, Soph. *Ant.*
205. At Cat. 64.152 this shifts to 'beasts', *feris*, as here and at *Tro.* 566–7, *Thy.*
750–1, 1032–3, and *Pho.* 255–6. Cf. also *Oct.* 515. *Vertice immenso* is perhaps better taken as locatival ablative (Woodcock §51) than (with Kingery
ad loc.) as ablative of quality with *latus*.

   Caucasi/Caucasus: this formidable mountain-range between the Black
Sea and the Caspian Sea was renowned for its wild terrain (Virg. *Aen.*
4.366–7, Serv. *ad* Virg. *Geo.* 2.440), and received the epithet *inhospitalis*
from both Horace (*Epod.* 1.12, *Odes* 1.22.6) and Seneca (*Med.* 43, *Thy.*
1048).

   Pontum Scythen/Scythian Pontus: the Black Sea or Pontus, termed
Pontus Scythicus at *Med.* 212, and by Ovid at *Tr.* 3.4.46, 4.1.45. For Scythia,
see on 533–41. Zwierlein does not capitalize the initial *p* in *Pontus*.

   Symplegas/Symplegades: the Symplegades or 'Clashing Rocks', here
referred to unusually by the singular *Symplegas* (as at Luc. 2.718, VF 4.221,
5.299), were located at the Bosporus and the entrance to the Black Sea or
Pontus. Legend had it that they clashed together, preventing access to the

Black Sea until the *Argo* sailed between them. Thenceforth they were fixed. See Pind. *Pyth*. 4.207–12, Apollon. 2.549–606, Apollod. 1.9.22, VF 4.561–710. The rocks were sometimes identified (according to the elder Pliny: *HN* 4.92) with the Insulae Cyaneae just north of the Bosporus. The Symplegades were often confused by ancient writers with the Planctae or 'Wandering Rocks', which were sometimes located in the Strait of Messina. This reference to the Symplegades is an implied reference to the Argonautic expedition (in which Hercules took part) and its own boundary violations; it is as if Hercules were asking for punishment as an Argonaut. Cf. the imitation of this passage at *HO* 1380–2.

hinc et hinc uinctas manus/My hands, bound to each side: for *hinc et hinc*, cf. *Thy*. 591, 735, 1013; *Pho*. 529. For the *manus* motif, see on 118–22.

distendat alto/stretch…across the deep: *alto* is a locatival ablative (lit. 'on the deep'); see Woodcock §§51–2.

reuocata uice/in turn: a development of the line-ending phrase *alterna uice*, see also *Thy*. 25, *Pha*. 411, *Ag*. 561; cf. also *uicibus alternis* of the 'shifting tides' of the Euripus at 377.

saxaque/rocks: Zwierlein, Billerbeck, and Giardina (2007) replace this *EA* reading with Bentley's otiose emendation, *saxa et.*

medium mare/sea…imprisoned: lit. 'sea between'; cf. *mare deprensum*, 'sea trapped', of the same phenomenon at *Med*. 345•.

ego…iaceam mora/Let *me* lie and block: note the emphasis on *ego*; hence the italics in the translation. *Mora* is the culmination of a fine alliterative pattern of *m*s in 1213–15. *Mora* is used of persons by Seneca at *Tro*. 124 (Hector), 813 (Astyanax), *Ag*. 211 (Hector), *Pho*. 458 (Jocasta). See also Virg. *Aen*. 10.428 (Abas), Luc. 1.99–100 (Crassus). See also Sen. Rhet. *Suas*. 2.19–20 (of Hector). Cf. Homer's use of ἕρκος, 'defence' (*Il*. 1.284, 4.299).

aceruans…aggerem/build a pyre: for *agger* of a funeral pyre, see *Pho*. 110, Luc. 2.300, Ov. *Met*. 9.234 (in lines which seem to have influenced Seneca here).

cruore corpus impio sparsum cremo/Burn my body drenched with impious blood: there is obvious irony in Hercules' unknowingly wishing for what will be his mode of death. He repeats this self-cremation fantasy at 1285–7. Notice the conscious self-castigation in *impio*, 'impious', an adjective and self-castigation (for Hercules' killings violate the core Roman familial value of *pietas*: see on 1092–9) which will repeat themselves at 1241, 1280, and 1329.

sic, sic agendum est/Thus, thus I must act: spoken also by Deianira, as she contemplates suicide in *Hercules Oetaeus* (846). *Agere* often has an additional metatheatrical sense (*agere partes* = 'play a part/act/perform a role'), serving to underscore a play as play, as enactment of tragic theatre. Hence *peractum est* (= 'It is done/It has been performed/acted') is found in the final acts of *Agamemnon* (901), *Oedipus* (998), *Troades* (1168), and *Medea* (1019), uttered respectively by Cassandra, Oedipus, Hecuba, and Medea. Here the *agere* statement is uttered by Hercules, also in the final act. It will be echoed by Theseus at 1277. For metatheatrical language in *Hercules*, see on 109–12. For *geminatio*, see on 92–9. For *sic, sic* qualifying a command, see also *Med.* 90–2, *Thy.* 102–3, and *HO* 846, where the present phrase is repeated.

inferis reddam Herculem/I'll return Hercules to hell: Hercules fulfils Juno's desire of the prologue (*cupiat mori ab inferis reuersus*, 'Let him…want death on return from hell', 116–17), even as he behaves like one already dead. The Ghosts of Thyestes and of Tantalus express precisely the same wish for themselves (*Ag.* 12, *Thy.* 68–83), as does Euripides' Heracles (*Herac.* 1247). Hercules' comrade-from-hell, Theseus, expressed the same desire in *Phaedra*, after confronting the deaths of son and wife (*Pha.* 1217–19). Hercules will continue in this vein in a resumption of the 'Schreirede' at 1221–6, and his final speech in the play will end with the wish for a return to hell (1338–41)—but with qualifications. For the self-dramatizing use of a proper name, see on 109–12.

1219–21 Amphitryon focuses on Hercules' continuing *ira* and *furor*. His depiction of Hercules' psychological state is an abbreviated version of the kind of third-person description offered by the Nurse figure in other plays: see e.g. *Med.* 382–96, *Pha.* 360–83. It was 'imitated' in Hughes's *The Misfortunes of Arthur* I.iii.7–10 (the character described is Guenevera):

> Her breast, not yet appeas'd from former rage,
> Hath chang'd her wrath which, wanting means to work
> Another's woe (for such is fury's wont),
> Seeks out his own, and raves upon itself.

Nondum tumultu pectus attonito carens/His heart's not yet free of frenzied turmoil: strong, alliterative language for psychological upheaval, similar to that used of Oedipus at *Oed.* 329 (*inter tumultus mentis attonitae uagus*, 'wandering amid the turmoil of a frenzied mind') and of Atreus at *Thy.* 260 (*tumultus…attonitus*, 'frenzied turmoil'). Note the hypallage (transferred epithet) here and at *Thy.* 260 in the phrase cited; so, too, *Luc.*7.779. For *attonitus* elsewhere in hypallage, see e.g. *Med.* 675; *Oct.* 436, 759, 778, 785; *Luc.* 7.779 (*attonitos…tumultus*); *Stat. Theb.* 4.382. For *tumultus*, see also *Thy.* 85–6 (*insano…tumultu*), and on 1088–91.

mutauit iras/**The anger shifts:** lit. 'he has shifted his anger' from against all (*omnes*, 1167), or at least against potential enemies, to himself. For *ira*, see on 19–29.

quodque habet proprium furor/**As is the nature of rage:** Amphitryon here fuses *furor* and *ira*, as does Seneca in *De Ira* (1.2), where he supports the idea that *ira* is *breuis insania*, 'brief madness'. For the use here of *proprius* (= 'specific to', 'defining'), see *Thy.* 938: *proprium hoc miseros sequitur uitium*, 'this special fault follows the wretched'; Varro *Men.* 73: *unam uirtutem propriam mortalibus fecit*, 'he made one virtue specific/special to mortals'.

in se ipse saeuit/**It savages itself:** Amphitryon is repeating Juno's definition of *Furor*, 'Rage', at 98 above: *in se semper armatus*, 'ever armed against itself'. Cf. also Seneca's description of *ira* at *Ira* 3.1.5: *ubi aduersarium fortuna subduxit, in se ipsa morsus suos uertit*, 'When fortune has removed its enemy, it turns its teeth on itself'. The Hercules of *Hercules Oetaeus* appears to have seen or read this play; his final words before rending his own flesh: *in me iuuat saeuire*, 'I want to savage myself' (*HO* 825). For *furor*, see on 92–9; for climactic half-lines, see on 40–6.

1221–36 Hercules' 'Schreirede' (see on 1202–18) continues in 1221–6, but then collapses into an address to his dead sons and a promise to destroy his weapons for them and (it seems) for Megara (1226–36).

1221–6 *Dira Furiarum loca*/**Dire haunts of Furies:** a particularly germane description of hell, recalling the Furies summoned by Juno (100–12) to make Hercules mad. The adjective *dirus* is a regular modifier of the Furies themselves, who are also known as the *Dirae*: see on 86–8. Cf. *dira Furiarum agmina*, 'dire ranks of Furies', *Thy.* 78; *dira Furiarum cohors*, 'dire horde of Furies', *Thy.* 250. For *dirus*, see 56 and n. *ad loc.*; for *loca*, 'haunts/places', see on 1–5, 572–6; for the Furies, see on 86–8.

inferorum carcer/**dungeon of hell:** for *carcer* of the underworld, see on 57–63.

sonti plaga decreta turbae/**district decreed For the guilty throng:** the 'district' is Tartarus: see on 86–8. Note that Hercules' address is incomplete. He breaks off to change his addressee to *Tellus*, 'Earth'.

latet ulterius Erebo/**hides Beyond Erebus:** for this desire to be hidden beyond the furthest reaches of hell, see also Thyestes at *Thy.* 1013–19, Oedipus at *Pho.* 145, Hyllus at *HO* 742–4. The idea was not new: see Ov. *Pont.* 4.14.11–12. For Erebus, see on 52–6. *Erebo* is comparative ablative: see Woodcock §78–9. For the dactyl-tribrach combination at the start of 1224, see 76 and n. *ad loc.* Zwierlein replaces the consensus MS reading, *latet*, with his own emendation, *patet*. No editor to my knowledge has yet followed him.

Cerbero/Cerberus: see on 782–91.

hoc me abde, Tellus/Hide me there, Earth: a variant of the standard invocation of Tellus, *dehisce Tellus*, 'Gape Earth', used by Oedipus at *Oed.* 868, Andromache at *Tro.* 519, and Theseus at *Pha.* 1238—and Ovid's Daphne at *Met.* 1.544; cf. *Thy.* 1006–9, *Oct.* 135–6, Petron. *Sat.* 81. See also Virgil's Dido at *Aen.* 4.24. The appeal to Earth to 'gape' is as old as Homer (*Il.* 4.182), prevalent in Greek tragedy and much imitated by modern 'Senecans', influenced especially by Seneca's *Oedipus*: see e.g. Marlowe (*1 Tam.* V.ii.178), Dryden and Lee (*Oed.* IV.i.579, V.i.248), Voltaire (*Oed.* V.v.181), Gide (*Oed.* Acte III). Ovid's Hypsipyle treats it sarcastically as an epic commonplace (*Her.* 6.144). *Hoc* is either the adverbial form, as at *Ag.* 143, *Thy.* 710, 1014 (so Fitch *ad loc.*), or a local ablative (so Billerbeck *ad loc.*, comparing Seneca's use elsewhere of *abdere*).

Tartari ad finem ultimum/to Tartarus' furthest End: cf. *si quid ultra Tartarum*, 'if there's anything beyond Tartarus' (Oedipus at *Pho.* 145); *si quid infra Tartara est*, 'if there's anything beneath Tartarus', Thyestes at *Thy.* 1013. For Tartarus, see on 86–8.

mansurus ibo/I'll go…to remain: a bitter and ironic use of the '*manere*' topos of consolatory literature; cf. e.g. Tacitus' obituary for his father-in-law: *quidquid ex Agricola amauimus…manet mansurumque est in animis hominum* ('Whatever we loved in Agricola…remains and shall remain in the minds of men', *Agr.* 46.4). See further Whitton (2013) *ad* Pliny *Ep.* 2.1.11. Note the climactic position of *mansurus*: cf. *non rediturus*, 'not to return', *Med.* 633 (Orpheus); *non exiturum*, 'not to leave', *Pha.* 1242 (Theseus); *periturum diem*, 'the day to die', *Thy.* 121—also *mansurus* again at *HO* 1939 (Alcmena referring to Hercules). The use of the future participle to express purpose is common, according to Woodcock §92.d, 'from the time of Livy onwards'.

1226–37 Hercules turns to the bodies of his dead sons and laments, offering to destroy his weapons for them.

1226–30 Self-criticism: he cannot weep; his own brutality stops his tears. Contrast Euripides' Heracles (*Herac.* 1355–6), who weeps for the first time in his life. Shakespeare's Macbeth, however, receives the news of his wife's death in Herculean mode with neither tears nor emotion (*Mac.* V.v.17). For more ferocious self-criticism, see 1279–81 and n. *ad loc.*

Pectus o nimium ferum/O too brutal heart: Hercules applies to himself perhaps the defining epithet of the 'Wolf-Man', Lycus, *ferus*, 'brutal/savage' (see 518 and n. *ad loc.*); see also 1118, 1286. For *nimium* with an adjective in Senecan tragedy, see on 186–91; for hyperbaton involving *o*, see 1066, 1068, 1072.

per omnem...sparsos domum/Spattered through all the palace: this, of course, does not mean that the children are still in the palace, as Zwierlein (1966: 43) argues. Their bodies have been brought out and are visible on stage: see stage directions before 1154 and n. *ad loc.* The phrase refers to the fact that the palace is soaked in their blood. For *sparsus* as 'spattered' in this gruesome sense, cf. the description of Orpheus as *sparsus...per agros*, 'spattered through the fields' (*Med.* 630) and Iole's description of her father as *tota...sparsus in aula*, 'spattered throughout all the hall' (*HO* 209). See also *Med.* 133.

deflere digne/shed fitting tears: for the *topos* of inadequate lament, see on 258–67.

lacrimare uultus nescit/This face...cannot weep: interestingly Euripides' Heracles, who had not wept before, weeps at the end of his play (*Herac.* 1353-7)—so much that Theseus needs to check his tears (*Herac.* 1394). Weeping would have been a moral failure to a Stoic, for whom ἀπάθεια, freedom from passion/emotion, was a constituent of virtue. But even the massively flawed Senecan Hercules does not weep. The image of unweeping affliction clearly appealed to Seneca: see Andromache at *Tro.* 416–17, Astyanax at *Tro.* 1099–1100, Cassandra at *Ag.* 695–709. The Hercules of *Hercules Oetaeus* does weep (*HO* 1265–78), but is surprised by his own tears. There is, of course, no problem about tears in a masked performance: 'They (masked actors) do not need to weep inside the mask in order to make the mask weep' (Walton 2015: 43).

huc ensem date, date huc...huc...date/Bring here my sword, Bring here...bring it here: cf. Thyestes' request of Atreus for the latter's sword in order to commit suicide with it: *da, frater, ensem* (*Thy.* 1043). Note the complex rhetorical patterning here: a fusion of anadiplosis, epanalepsis/epanadiplosis (see on 638–9), *conuersio* (see on 895–9), and chiastic repetition. Seneca is fond of clusters of demonstratives. See e.g. 159–72, 718–20, 1193–4. Along with Giardina (1966) and Viansino (1993), I have printed the consensus *EA* reading *ensem*, which was rejected in favour of Bentley's emendation, *arcum*, by Zwierlein, Fitch (1987a and 2018), and Chaumartin. Not only are the MS tradition, Trevet and Farnaby in agreement on the reading but the bringing onstage of Hercules' sword is dramatically necessary to account for Amphitryon's attempted suicide (see on 1295–1301). It is worth noting, as Viansino (1993) observes *ad loc.*, that a sword is often the first thing requested by potential suicides: see *Oed.* 1034 (Jocasta), *Thy.* 1043 (Thyestes), *Pho.* 106 (Oedipus). The sword (φάσγανον) is also initially mentioned by Euripides' Heracles as a potential instrument of his suicide (*Herac.* 1149).

1231–6 Hercules addresses his dead sons and probably the dead Megara (*Tibi …tibi…tuis…tuos*, 'you…you…your…your') in ritualistic, repetitive manner. In Euripides' play (*Herac.* 1377–85) Heracles decides to keep with him the weapons which slew his family. Seneca's protagonist here aims to destroy them. In promising to destroy his weapons, since they were instruments not only of familial death but also of his triumphant labours and are major constituents of his identity, Hercules is offering to destroy himself. Fitch *ad* Act V (1138–1344) compares Prospero's words in Shakespeare's *The Tempest*, V.i.54–7:

> I'll break my staff,
> Bury it certain fathoms in the earth,
> And deeper than ever plummet sound
> I'll drown my book.

See further Introd. §VII, 114.

tela frangam nostra/**I'll break my arrows**: the *frangam* will be picked up by Theseus' *perfringe* (1275: see n. *ad loc.*), as he asks Hercules to transfer his physical strength to his mind.

at tuis stipes grauis…umbris/**But the heavy club…For *your* spirit**: addressed presumably to Megara, who was killed by the 'heavy club' (*claua…grauis*, 1024). I have italicized *your* in the translation to underscore the change of focus indicated by *at*, 'But'.

Lernaeis…telis/**Lernaean shafts**: note the focus on poisoned arrows again; see on 1194–1200.

uos quoque…cremabo…manus/**You, too, I shall burn…hands**: Roman audiences would inevitably have thought of the great *exemplum* of Mucius Scaevola, who thrust his right hand into the fire to punish it for its failure to assassinate Lars Porsenna and to show his indifference to torture (Val. Max. 3.3.1). Seneca himself uses Scaevola's burning of the hand as an exemplary act of a 'great man', *magnus uir* (*Prou.* 3.4–5). Note the shortening of the final *o* of *cremabo*; cf. *compello* (*Oed.* 1043), *accipio* (*Thy.* 542): see further on 109–12. For Roman referentiality, see on 46–52.

infaustas meis…telis/**Curse of my weapons**: for *infaustus*, see 1135 and n. *ad loc.*

o nouercales manus/**O stepmother hands**: apostrophe of the hand (*manus* or *dextra*) occurs elsewhere in Senecan tragedy, generally at moments of high drama: see 1281, *Oed*. 1038, *Pha*. 1262, *Tro*. 113, *Med*. 809, *Pho*. 91, 155. But here the audience are presented with a powerful and ambiguous expression. Nowhere else in this final act does Hercules imply that Juno is to blame. The lemmatized phrase indexes his recognition that he has been fulfilling her will, even if he still regards himself as the responsible agent. One could propose with Shelton (1978: 80) that Hercules here 'tries to divorce himself from his hands and make them belong to Juno', but, if so, he fails. For he never removes the guilt from himself. His anger at the hands, which he threatens to burn, is clearly an attempt to distance himself from them, but it does not nullify or even qualify the sense of his own agency. Cf. the 'distancing' attempt of Shakespeare's Macbeth, who immediately after the murder of Duncan refers to his 'hangman's hands' (*Mac*. II.ii.27), and follows up with: 'What hands are here? Ha! They pluck out mine eyes' (*Mac*. II.ii.58). Seneca was not the only master of the *manus* motif. *Nouercalis* is not found in Roman literature before the Senecas (Sen. Rhet. *Con*. 4.6). For *nouercales manus*, see also *Ag*. 118. For *o*, see on 205–9; but note its rare position after the main caesura (cf. *Tro*. 766, 956, *Thy*. 625—also *HO* 756, 1264, 1778). For *nouerca*, see on 19–29; for the important *manus* motif, see on 118–22.

1237-1317 The suicide drama. Prompted by Hercules' last phrase, Amphitryon tries to absolve Hercules of responsibility for the killings, but Hercules determines to kill himself. Amphitryon vainly tries to reason with him, threatens his own suicide and stops him. Cf. the suicide drama of the opening of *Phoenissae*, where Antigone vainly tries to reason with Oedipus, but throws herself at his feet in tears and stops him (*Pho*. 306–19). Note also the suicide dramas of *Phaedra* (250–73) and *Hercules Oetaeus* (842–1030), the latter of which fails to prevent the suicide. See further on 1237–9, 1240–5, 1246–52, 1258–62, 1314–21.

1237-9 Discussion of criminal responsibilty. For legal language and imagery in *Hercules*, see on 731–4.

   nomen...sceleris errori/error the name of crime: for discussion of *scelus/crimen* v. *error*, cf. *Pho*. 451–3 (cited at 1200–1 above), 535–40, 553–5; *HO* 884–90, 898–902, 982ff.; Luc. 7.58–9; Cic. *Marc*. 13. The distinction is also Ovidian, used to exonerate both Actaeon (*Met*. 3.142) and Ovid himself: *Tr*. 3.6.25–6, 11.33–4, 4.10.89–90, *Pont*. 3.3.73–6 (though at *Tr*. 2.207 one of Ovid's *crimina* was an *error*). One might cite several *sententiae* to underscore Amphitryon's position that intention matters: *uoluntas impudicum, non corpus facit*, 'The will, not the body, makes one impure' (Publ. 710 Duff); *mentem peccare, non corpus*, 'the mind sins, not the body' (Livy

1.58.9); *mens impudicam facere, non casus solet*, 'The mind makes one impure, not circumstance' (*Pha.* 735), spoken by Phaedra's Nurse. Even Seneca's successor, the author of *Hercules Oetaeus*, has Hercules' wife declare: *innocens animus mihi, scelesta manus*, 'My mind is innocent, my hand guilty' (*HO* 964-5). Note that Amphitryon had initially described Hercules' filicide as *scelus nefandum*, 'monstrous crime', 1004. With Amphitryon's attempt to absolve Hercules, cf. that of Jocasta in respect of Oedipus at *Oed.* 1019: *nemo fit fato nocens*, 'No one is made guilty by fate'. Like that of Jocasta, Amphitryon's attempt fails. Indeed Hercules will maintain his guilt to the end of the play despite the attempts to dissuade him. *Error*/Delusion, it should be noted, is one of four agents (*Scelus, Impietas, Error, Furor*) to be summoned by Juno from the underworld at 96-8. See also the Chorus at 1096. For *scelus*, see also 121 and n. *ad loc.*, and 1199 and n. *ad loc.*

   Saepe error ingens sceleris obtinuit locum/Great error is often the site of crime: 'imitated' by Hughes, *The Misfortunes of Arthur* I.iii.67: 'A mighty error oft hath seem'd a sin'. Deianira goes further: *scelera quae quisque ausus est | hic uincet error*, 'This error will surpass crimes which anyone has dared' (*HO* 939-40). There is a metatheatrical dimension to the discussion here, viz. an implicit engagement with Aristotle's theory of tragic ἁμαρτία or 'error' (*Poetics* 1453a7-17), which (from the perspective of this play) affects neither the heinousness of the action nor the guilt of its perpetrator. For metatheatre in *Hercules*, see on 109-12. For Seneca's engagement with Aristotelian tragic theory, see also e.g. 624, 1192 and nn. *ad locc.*, and *Tro.* 1147-8 (with Boyle 1994 *ad loc.*). Note again a possible pun on *ingens*, which might suggest that the error is in the area of the *gens* or 'family', which would be especially appropriate in this context. See on 439-47. *Obtinuit* is 'gnomic' perfect (see on 864-74), as one might expect in this *sententia*. Note the *locus* motif again: see on 1-5. For *saepe* in *sententiae*, see 1187 and n. *ad loc.*

   Nunc Hercule opus est/Now there's need of Hercules: the name, Hercules, is used much in this final act (nine times: also 'Alcides' twice), often by Hercules himself as he attempts to instantiate the mythic *persona* which the name signals. Amphitryon brings into the open the metadramatic use of the name in a short sentence which means: now is the time to live up to the mythic reputation embodied in your name. Cf. *Tro.* 613-14: *nunc aduoca...nunc totum Vlixem*, 'Now summon...Now all Ulysses'; *Tro.* 863: *est auspice Helena dignus*, 'it merits Helen's blessing'; *Med.* 910: *Medea nunc sum*, 'Now I am Medea'; *Oed.* 1003: *uultus Oedipodam hic decet*, 'This face befits an Oedipus'; *Thy.* 53: *imple Tantalo totam domum*, 'fill the whole palace with

Tantalus'. Cf. also the Euripidean Theseus' use of the phrase 'the famous Heracles' (ὁ κλεινὸς Ἡρακλῆς, *Herac*. 1414) to contrast Heracles' present state with his paradigmatic one. What Amphitryon means by 'Hercules' is precisely ὁ κλεινὸς Ἡρακλῆς. Cf. also Theseus' paraenetic use of Heracles' name at Eur. *Herac*. 1250. With Amphitryon's moral imperative, contrast Atreus' black parody: *sobrio…opus est Thyeste*, 'There's need of a sober Thyestes' (*Thy*. 900–1). There will be two more appeals to the name, 'Hercules', by others before the end of the play (1277, 1313) and one to 'Alcides' (1343). Shakespeare often uses names in a similarly metadramatic fashion (see e.g. 'Othello' at *Oth*. V.ii.281ff., 'Antony' at *AC* III.xiii.98 and 192).

Behind Amphitryon's exhortation is the assumption that to continue to live in the midst of great misfortune takes more courage than to die. This is what Antigone urges of her father, as he contemplates suicide, at *Pho*. 79: *resiste*; *tantis in malis uinci mori est*, 'Fight back; in such great tragedy dying is defeat'. Cf. also *Pho*. 188–92.

molem mali/weight of woe: an alliterative phrase already part of Roman literary language: see e.g. Lucr. 3.1056 (where the poet apologizes for the figurative use of *moles*), Livy 5.37.1, Ov. *Met*. 11.494.

1240–5   Shame drives Hercules to suicide.

Non sic furore cessit extinctus pudor/Shame is not gone, nor so quenched by rage: this is the fourth and final time Hercules mentions *pudor* in Act V (see also 1147, 1178, 1180) and the second time of himself (also 1147). It is a moral emotion felt by Euripides' Heracles (*Herac*. 1160, 1200–1) and by Seneca's Hercules, in whom it mingles with guilt, anger, and rage. In Seneca's scene, however, it is never mentioned by Hercules' interlocutors. Before Act V reference is made by Theseus to the figure of *Pudor* in the underworld (692) and (with unconscious irony) by Hercules to the *pudendus* Lycus (1035). For similar, if problematic, statements about *pudor*, cf. Phaedra (*non omnis animo cessit ingenuo pudor*, 'All shame has not gone from this noble heart', *Pha*. 250) and Clytemnestra (*surgit residuus pristinae mentis pudor*, 'My former self's residual shame rises', *Ag*. 288); both statements preface, as here, suicide threats, the former by the speaker, the latter by the addressee; both statements articulate, as here, a struggle between *pudor* and other emotions. The great revenge figures, Medea and Atreus, explicitly reject *pudor* (*Med*. 900, *Thy*. 891), though Medea has more trouble doing so. For the ontologization of the emotions (see also *furor*, 1244), see on 75–6; for *furor*, see on 92–9; for *pudor*, see on 689–96.

populos…omnes/all nations: Hercules never loses sight of himself as a global, even cosmic figure.

impio aspectu/impious face: for *impius*, see 1217 and n. *ad loc.*

arma, arma, Theseu/Arms, arms, Theseus: the repetition of *arma* is a common literary mannerism: see e.g. Virg. *Aen.* 2.668; Ov. *Met.* 11.377–8, 12.241; Stat. *Theb.* 7.135. Here, however, Hercules is not rushing into battle against an external foe, but demanding his arms, the defining indices of his identity, for self-slaughter. For addresses to a character by name, see on 637–40.

mihi…mihi/me…I: for the *conuersio*, see on 895–9.

reddi…referte…remanet…recede/return…Restore…remains…stand back: for paronomasia of *re*-words, see on 46–52.

si…si…/If…if…: this kind of debate between alternatives is a rhetorical figure known as *complexio* or dilemma (Cic. *Inu.* 1.45), used elsewhere by Seneca in the tragedies; see e.g. 1278 below, *Tro.* 510–12, *Pha.* 1184–5, *Med.* 194, *Pho.* 76, 455–7, 522–4—and cf. *HO* 1027–9, Sen. Rhet. *Con.* 1.7.8.

sana si mens est mihi/If I am sound of mind: it is a big 'if'. Cicero makes it clear that it would be criminal (*peccatum*) to return a sword to a madman, and one's duty (*officium*) not to (*Off.* 3.95). Similarly Seneca declares at *Ira* 1.19.8: *male irato ferrum committitur*, 'It's a bad idea to hand a sword to an angry man'.

pater, recede/Father, stand back: for vocatives at the beginning of an iambic line, see on 637–40.

mortis inueniam uiam/I'll find the path of death: a semiotically resonant phrase. It is: (i) an iteration of the death-drive articulated in 1218; (ii) a fulfilment of Juno's jussive wish at 116; (iii) an ironic allusion to his recently completed final labour; (iv) an echo of Amphitryon's earlier claim that Hercules will 'find a path' (*inueniet uiam*, 276) back from death; (v) an inversion of several preceding references to Hercules' 'path to the stars or gods' (*ad superos/astra uia*: 66, 74, 276, 318, 437, 568); (vi) an articulation of a Stoic ideal: *ille uir magnus est qui mortem sibi non tantum imperauit sed inuenit*, 'That man is great who not only ordered death for himself but found it' (*Ep. Mor.* 70.25). For 'path of death', see Jocasta at *Oed.* 1031–2: *mortis uia quaeratur*, 'I must seek the path of death'; and Oedipus at *Pho.* 304: *leti quaero maturi uiam*, 'I seek the path of early death'. For *inueniam uiam*, see Oedipus at *Pho.* 5, and Hercules again at *HO* 33 (cited on 276). For Stoic ideas and language in *Hercules*, see on 162–3.

1246–52 Amphitryon appeals to Hercules not to kill himself. Cf. the appeals of Phaedra's and Deianira's nurses to prevent the suicides of their mistresses (*Pha.* 246–8, *HO* 925–8). Also note Amphitryon's appeal to Heracles at Eur. *Herac.* 1203–13.

Per...per...per/By...by...by: the entreaty, prayer, vow, or oath, accompanied by (often triple) repetition of *per*, 'by...', known as the *figura iuris iurandi*, was common in Roman declamation (see e.g. Sen. Rhet. *Con.* 9.4.4, 10.1.7, *Suas.* 7.9) and features widely in Senecan tragedy: cf. *Pho.* 535–42; *Pha.* 868–71; *Ag.* 929–30; *Oed.* 264–6, 1021–3; *Med.* 285–90, 478–82, 1002–4. See also Virg. *Aen.* 4.314–19, Stat. *Theb.*10. 694–6.

Per sancta generis sacra/By the sacred laws of family: for swearing by the *genus*, 'family', see Ov. *Her.* 8.117, 12.78.

siue...altorem...seu...parentem/whether...'guardian' Or 'father': Amphitryon is not raising the issue of Hercules' paternity, which he has already argued to be settled (439–47). He is simply drawing attention to the fact that he is technically an *altor*, but also receives the honorific title of *genitor* from his 'son'. His language, however, continues to place the focus on the question of Hercules' origin and on the whole issue of 'What is it to be a father?' *Altor*, 'guardian', is literally 'one who nourishes/rears'; it is sometimes translated 'foster-father' (e.g. by Fitch).

per...canos/by my white hair: cf. Phaedra's Nurse: *per has senectae splendidas...comas*, 'By these bright hairs of old age' (*Pha.* 246).

senectae...desertae...annisque fessis//lone old age...And weary years: a common transference of epithets; cf. *Pha.* 267 (*annis...fessis*), Hor. *Ep.* 2.2.118 (*deserta uetustas*), Luc. 2.128 (*fessa senectus*). For the appeal to one's old age, see Phaedra's Nurse at *Pha.* 246, cited in previous n., and Deianira's Nurse at *HO* 925–6.

parce...precor/spare...I beg: for this alliterative prayer formula and appeals for 'sparing/pardon', see on 1015.

unicum lapsae domus firmamen/Sole pillar of a fallen House: cf. Hecuba's eulogy of Hector as the *columen patriae*, 'pillar of a nation', *praesidium*, 'shield', and *murus*, 'wall', *Tro.* 124–6. *Firmamen* is a Senecan *hapax*, found elsewhere in classical Latin, as Fitch *ad loc.* observes, only at Ov. *Met.* 10.491. The construction of *unicus*, however, with an abstract noun, esp. one ending in *-men*, used with reference to a person, is a regular Senecan mannerism: so Medea of her children (*unicum afflictae domus solamen*, 'sole comfort of a house afflicted', *Med.* 945–6); Electra of her brother, Orestes (*auxilium unicum*, 'sole help', *Ag.* 910); Andromache of her son, Astyanax (*spes...unica*, 'sole hope', *Tro.* 462, *unicum...solamen*, 'sole solace' *Tro.* 703–4); Phaedra's Nurse of her mistress (*solamen...unicum*, 'sole solace', *Pha.* 267); Oedipus of Antigone (*unicum...leuamen*, 'sole solace', *Pho.* 1–2). The mannerism is picked up by Correr: *unicum afflictae domus leuamen*, *Progne* 736–7. With the lemmatized phrase, cf. also Andromache's address to Astyanax (again parent to child): *o decus lapsae domus*, 'O glory of a fallen house' (*Tro.* 766).

unum lumen/**the one light:** for the metaphor, see the analogous address to Heracles (either by Megara or Amphitryon; the speaker is disputed) at Eur. *Herac.* 531: ὦ φάος, 'O light'. For *unus* = 'one and only', cf. *spes una* (*Tro.* 462, *Oct.* 68). For the *unicus…unus* conjunction, see *Tro.* 462, Cat. 73.6,

temet reserua/**Keep yourself alive:** Amphitryon's injunction is tonally the precise opposite of Theseus' sarcastic question to the absent Hippolytus: *mihi te reseruas*, 'Do you keep yourself for me?' (*Pha.* 924). Cf. also *Oed.* 31. For *temet*, see on 1010–11.

1252–7 Amphitryon complains about Hercules' continuous absences, picking up and developing the focus in his first speech of the play (207–13) on Hercules' unending labours. The emphasis here, however, is not on Hercules' suffering but on the emotional consequences of Hercules' heroism for his kin. Complaints about the absence of loved ones would be familiar to Seneca's audience from many sources, esp. Augustan love elegy and Ovid's *Heroides*: note the complaints of Hercules' wife Deianira at *Her.* 9.33–8, themselves a rewriting of her Greek predecessor's complaints at Soph. *Trach.* 27–35. See also the complaints of Phaedra about the absent Theseus at *Pha.* 91–8.

fructus laborum/**joy From…labours:** see on 654–7.

dubium mare aut monstra/**fickle seas Or monsters:** examples of Hercules' perils at sea include the shipwreck alluded to above at 319–24 and the storm mentioned by Homer (*Il.* 14.253–6, 15.24–8). 'Monsters' include the Nemean Lion, the Lernaean Hydra, the Stymphalian Birds, the Cretan Bull, Geryon, Cerberus. For the important *monstrum* motif, see 1280 and n. *ad loc. Dubium mare* (also at *Ag.* 407) is Ovidian (*Pont.* 4.10.10). Cf. *dubium…fretum*, *Thy.* 292; *dubium…pelagus*, *Med.* 942.

rex saeuus…manibus aut aris nocens/**cruel king…with guilty hands or altars:** 'altars' allude to Busiris, already mentioned by Amphitryon (483–4); 'hands' could apply to many of Hercules' opponents, including the boxer Eryx and the giant and wrestler Antaeus, also cited earlier by Amphitryon (481–3). See nn. *ad locc.* For *saeuus*, 'cruel/savage', of kings/tyrants, see 272, 936–7.

semper absentis…peto/**I seek…of you:** mark in the Latin the supple, alliterative pattern of *p*s and *t*s. For *semper* qualifying an epithet in *Hercules*, see 2, 98.

1258–62 Hercules maintains his resolve to kill himself, arguing for his loss of all things of value, i.e. the loss of identity, of self, and overtly rejecting Amphitryon's appeal that he live for the latter's sake. Seneca, as is well known, writes that, when a young man, he decided against suicide precisely because of the suffering it would have caused his father (*Ep. Mor.* 78.2: see Introd. §V, 55), and categorizes the failure to stay alive for the sake of a loved one as an act of self-indulgence (*delicatus, Ep. Mor.* 104.3). Chapman was clearly impressed by this passage, which, as Fitch observes *ad loc.*, he rewrote in *Byron's Tragedy* V.iv.69–72:

> Why should I keep my soul in this dark light
> Whose black beams lighted me to lose myself,
> When I have lost my arms, my fame, my mind,
> Friends, brother, hopes, fortunes, and even my fury?

Chapman's figure is more aporetic (along the lines of Euripides' Heracles: *Herac.* 1301–2) than Seneca's Hercules, who offers not questions, but resolute pronouncements. Then there is Shakespeare's creative 'imitation', cited and discussed in Introd. §VIII, 138. Oedipus' meditation on suicide at *Pho.* 233–40 and Fulke Greville's *Alaham* (V.iii.106–7) offer further parallels or 'imitation'.

Cur animam … detineam/cause for me to live: cf. Oedipus at *Pho.* 234–5, contemplating suicide: *quid hic | manes meos detineo?* 'Why do I detain this ghost of mine here?' Virgil's Evander similarly raises this issue in the aftermath of his son's death (*Aen.* 11.177). See also Euripides' Heracles at *Herac.* 1301–2.

morerque/and linger: Billerbeck *ad loc.* construes *morer* as transitive (with *animam*), comparing Virg. *Aen.* 11.177 and Hor. *Odes* 2.17.6.

cuncta iam amisi bona/I have now lost all things Of value: Hercules seems to be performing the kind of examination of self and the quality of a life (*qualis uita, non quanta sit*, 'the quality, not the quantity of life') which Seneca recommends prior to an appropriate suicide (*Ep. Mor.* 70.5). Such a decision needs to be a rational act implemented without haste (*Ep. Mor.* 24.24). Nothing in the list of *bona*, lit. 'good' things, which Hercules provides would have been regarded as a *bonum*, 'good', in Stoic philosophy; most would have been classified as preferred 'indifferents' (*indifferentia, Ep. Mor.* 82.14). Contrast the position of the philosopher Stilbo in Seneca's ninth epistle (*Ep. Mor.* 9.18–19), who, despite the loss of homeland, children, and wife, declares 'all my things of value are with me' (*omnia … bona mea mecum sunt*), alluding to 'justice, virtue, prudence' (*iustitia, uirtus, prudentia*). For Stoic language and ideas in *Hercules*, see on 162–3.

mentem arma famam coniugem natos manus/mind, weapons, glory, wife, sons, Hands: powerful, extended asyndeton, as Hercules lists the defining constituents of his lost identity. It is as if he had said 'Hercules I nothing am' after the model of Shakespeare's famous half-line 'Edgar I nothing am' (*KL* II.iii.21). Cf. Megara's similar list of losses at 379–80, Medea's at *Med.* 488, and those of Oedipus at *Phoenissae* 237–9:

> regnum, parentes, liberi, uirtus quoque
> et ingeni sollertis eximium decus
> periere.
>
> My realm, parents, children, even virtue
> And the high glory of my brilliant mind
> Are lost.

Seneca revels in the rhetorical force of asyndeton: see on 30–5 (and for asyndeton of family terms, see on 283–95). For more conventional lists of *bona*, see Plaut. *Amphit.* 648–53 (virtue, liberty, security, life, property, family, and *patria*); Ter. *Haut.* 194 (*patria*, family, friends, and wealth). *Mentem*, 'mind', seems deliberately wide-ranging. Billerbeck's attempt *ad loc.* to restrict its meaning to 'Verstand' seems misguided. For *manus*, see on 118–22. Note Hughes's asyndetic 'imitation', *The Misfortunes of Arthur* I.iii.18–19:

> All hope of prosperous hap is gone. My fame,
> My faith, my spouse—no good is left unlost!

***etiam furorem*/even rage:** a surprise, even paradoxical climax, given that Hercules' 'rage', 'fury', or 'madness' would not normally qualify even to the non-Stoic as a thing 'of value', a *bonum*. Hercules (with bitter irony) seems to be classifying his madness as a thing of value because it kept him from the reality of his slaughter of kin: see 1098–9 and n. *ad loc.* For other paradoxical climaxes, see e.g. *Med.* 20, *Thy.* 294, *Pho.* 319. For *furor*, see on 92–9; for climactic half-lines, see on 40–6.

    ***nemo*/no one:** for the shortening of final *o*, see on 109–12.

    ***polluto…animo*/mind diseased:** like *impius* (1217, 1241, 1280, 1329), *polluto* is a marker of Hercules' consciousness of his guilt.

    ***morte sanandum est scelus*/Death must cure the crime:** a *sententia*-like, alliterative, moral imperative articulating the *topos* of death as cure for human ills. See Phaedra at *Pha.* 711: *sanas furentem*, 'You cure my madness'; and Deianira at *HO* 890: *mors innocentes sola deceptos facit*, 'Death alone makes the deceived innocent'. Cf. the reformulation (and rationalization) at 1277. For *scelus*, see 121, 1199, 1237 and nn. *ad locc.* Again Hughes's 'imitation' merits attention: *The Misfortunes of Arthur* I.iii.22–3:

1263-4 A more rapid exchange involving two lines of alliterative *antilabe* and no *stichomythia*. For *antilabe*, see on 422-38; for *antilabe* only (i.e. without *stichomythia*) in other plays, see e.g. *Ag.* 791-99, *Pha.* 239-45, *Med.* 168-73, *Thy.* 1100-3. See also *Oct.* 185-8, *HO* 436-42, 891-902.

Perimes parentem/**Will you kill your father:** along with Caviglia and Zwierlein, I print this as a question; cf. *perimes maritum*, 'will you kill your husband' (*HO* 436). Viansino (1965 and 1993), Giardina (1966 and 2007), Fitch (1987*a* and 2018), and Chaumartin print it as a statement.

Facere ne possim, occidam/**I'll die so I can't:** clearly Hercules thinks Amphitryon means that Hercules will kill him with lethal blows, not that Hercules will kill him if he commits suicide.

Genitore coram/**Before your father:** *coram*, used quite frequently in the prose works, occurs only here in the Senecan tragic *corpus*. Priam similarly complains about being forced to watch the death of his son *coram me*, 'before myself', at Virg. *Aen.* 2.538. For *genitor*, see on 1202-18.

Cernere hunc docui nefas/**I've trained him to watch evil:** for this rhetorical use of *docere* (here darkly ironic), see on 68-74. For *nefas*, see 387 and n. *ad loc.*

1265-72 Amphitryon's appeal to Hercules to pardon himself is met with the latter's request for help with his suicide. For legal language and imagery in *Hercules*, see on 731-4.

Memoranda...facta/**deeds, famous:** see 442, where the same phrase is used by Amphitryon.

unius...criminis/**the one crime:** though Amphitryon will continue to blame Juno (1297), here he slips into accepting for a moment Hercules' own perspective, as he continues to plead for Hercules to forgive himself: see Introd. §VII, 114. For the verbal play with *unus* (here opposed to *omnibus*, 'all', 1265), see on 19-29.

Veniam dabit sibi ipse/**Will he pardon himself:** *uenia*, 'pardon/forgiveness', is an important motif in Senecan drama (see on 592-7), though conspicuous for its absence from most Senecan tragic action. In the prose works the treatment of *uenia* is complex. In *De Ira* Seneca regularly advocates the practice of 'pardoning/forgiving', *uenia/ignoscere* (e.g. 1.14.2, 2.34.2-4, 3.26.3), and he inveighs against those who seek *uenia* after having refused it to others. Horace had put the matter quite simply (*Sat.* 1.3.74-5): *aequum est | peccatis ueniam poscentem reddere rursus*, 'It is right that one who demands pardon for their sins should grant it in return'—an axiom which Seneca reduces to three words at *Ben.* 7.28.3 (*ut absoluaris, ignosce*, 'To be pardoned, pardon') and which he dramatizes in Clytemnestra's self-descriptive *sententia*: *det ille ueniam facile cui uenia est opus*, 'Who needs a pardon should readily pardon' (*Ag.* 267). In *De Clementia* (2.7), however, he tries to distinguish between *clementia* and *uenia/ignoscere*, disapproving of the latter, making it clear that the *sapiens* does not remit a punishment which he should exact. For Seneca's advocacy of a humane attitude to wrong-doing, see *Ira* 1.14.3, cited on 1334–41. See further on 1015–17, 1314–17.

laudanda feci iussus/**My lauded deeds were ordered**: note the ironic recall of *iussus* of 596, where it is used to exculpate; here it is used for the opposite purpose.

hoc unum meum est/**this one deed's mine**: even as he echoes the *nostrum est* of 1200, Hercules picks up the *unius* of Amphitryon's argument (1266) and turns it against him, arguing that this 'one deed' is a constituent now of his identity. See Braden (1993: 253). Contrast Euripides' Heracles who proclaims his innocence and explicitly blames Hera (*Herac.* 1308–10).

Kneels: for this stage-direction, see below on *surge* (1274).

Succurre, genitor/**Help me, father**: Hercules repeats his cry from 1166 with the important addition of *genitor*, 'father'. *Epistle* 52 focuses on the need for help from others: *nemo per se satis ualet ut emergat; oportet manum aliquis porrigat, aliquis educat*, 'No one by himself has enough strength to come out on top; he needs someone to offer a hand, someone to help him out' (*Ep. Mor.* 52.2). For *genitor*, see on 1202–18.

siue te pietas mouet/**Whether moved by pious love**: cf. Deianira's appeal to her son Hyllus at *HO* 984. For *pietas*, see on 1092–9; for the phrase, see also *Thy*. 248.

triste fatum/**Grim fate**: for *fatum*, fate, see on 178–82. *Fatum* is the reading of *A*, printed by Viansino (1965), Giardina (1966), Caviglia, Fitch (1987*a* and 2018), and Billerbeck. Zwierlein, Viansino (1993), and Chaumartin prefer *E*'s *factum*. As an ingredient in Hercules' present argument, *fatum* seems more appropriate than *factum*. See Fitch *ad loc*.

uiolatum decus uirtutis/**virtue's violated Glory**: for *uirtus*, see on 39. For *uiolare*, see 104 and n. *ad loc*.; for *decus* with the genitive, see on 592–7.

uincatur mea Fortuna dextra/**Let my hand Conquer Fortune**: Hercules is playing the Stoic. The conquest of Fortune was a goal of the Stoic *sapiens*, who presented himself as superior to *fortuna*: *Ep. Mor.* 71.30: *sapiens quidem uincit uirtute fortunam*, 'The sage conquers fortune through virtue'; *Vit. Beat.* 5.3: *quid enim supra eum potest esse qui supra fortunam est?* 'What can be superior to him who is superior to fortune?' See also *Ep. Mor.* 68.11, 78.16, 84.13; *Const.* 15.3; *Ben.* 7.3.2; Cic. *Rep.* 1.28, *Tusc.* 3.15. It is also a goal shared by Hercules and Medea. For the latter *Fortuna semper omnis* *infra me stetit*, 'Fortune has stood beneath me—all and always', *Med.* 520. Cf. also Oedipus, who, after his *anagnorisis*, envisages being snatched by death from the clutches of Fortune (*Oed.* 934). *Agamemnon's* opening choral ode on *Fortuna* underscores precisely what the goddess has achieved in this play (*Ag.* 101–101•):

> quidquid in altum Fortuna tulit,
> ruitura leuat.
>
> Whatever Fortune raises high,
> She lifts to cast down.

I have printed *Fortuna* (for whom see on 534–42) with a capital *f*; Zwierlein does not. For climactic half-lines, see on 40–6. For the *dextra* and *manus* motifs, see on 118–22. For *uincere* and Hercules, see on 63–8; for military language and imagery, see on 19–29. For Stoic language and ideas in *Hercules*, see on 162–3.

1272-7 At last Theseus, who in Euripides' *Heracles* is the one who persuades Heracles against suicide, speaks, and (more forcefully than in the Greek play: *Herac.* 1246ff.) advises the ending of Hercules' *ira*. For similar pleas for restraint, see Antigone at *Pho.* 182–3 and the various Nurses at *Med.* 157–8, 381, 425–6; *Pha.* 255–6; *Ag.* 203–4, 224–5—and at *HO* 927–8.

patriae preces/**A father's prayers**: a highly charged phrase in a play in which paternity is such a central issue. With a similarly charged phrase Jocasta proclaims her *preces…maternas*, 'mother's prayers', to Polynices at *Pho.* 500.

satis efficaces/**Suffice**: lit. 'sufficiently effective'. *Efficax* is a Senecan tragic *hapax*.

nostro…fletu/**by our tears**: Hercules drew attention to the tears of Theseus and Amphitryon earlier in the act (1175–9).

surge et…perfringe/**Rise up and break through**: Theseus uses muscular language to try to persuade Hercules to display mental strength matching his physical power. This kind of physical imagery was used earlier by Megara (*abrumpe*, 280, *erumpe*, 290), the Chorus (*rumpe*, 566) and Hercules himself (*rumpat*, 1000, *rumpemus*, 1232, *frangam*, 1231), but in a non-transferred sense. *Surge*, 'Rise up', is not necessarily an implied stage direction, but very much seems one. Hence the preceding '*Kneels*' at 1269 and '*HERCULES rises*' before 1278.

impetu…solito/**With customary force**: another metadramatic touch. The audience are fully aware of the narratives of Hercules' violence. The ablative is of manner: Woodcock §43.5.iv.

***nunc ... nunc*/Now ... now:** anaphora of *nunc* is a favourite stylistic man-
nerism of Seneca, who uses it to unite two clauses as here and *Thy.* 1096-7,
or to bind a tricolon, as at *Tro.* 613-14, *Pha.* 966-9, *Oed.* 433-6, *Ag.* 716-18,
or even a tetracolon, as at *Med.* 321-5. For the anaphoric use of temporal
adverbs in Senecan tragedy, see also e.g. 132-4 (*iam*), 497-8 (*nunc*), *Ag.* 47
(*iam*), *Med.* 309-16 (*nondum*), 321-5 (*nunc*), *Thy.* 573-5 (*iam*).

***tuum ... animum ... resume*/recover Your spirit:** cf. the similar appeal to
a former self by Antigone, addressing Oedipus: *pectus antiquum aduoca*,
'summon your heart of old' (*Pho.* 77).

***nunc magna tibi uirtute agendum est*/now you Must act with great vir-
tue:** Theseus echoes Hercules' earlier statement of resolve (1218), even as
he appeals to another mode of *uirtus*, viz. *temperantia*, 'self-control', one of
the four aspects of *uirtus perfecta* itemized by Seneca in one of his final epistles (*Ep. Mor.* 120.11). Cf. Antigone's appeal to *uirtus* in her attempt to dissuade her father from suicide (*Pho.* 190-2):

> non est, ut putas, uirtus, pater,
> timere uitam, sed malis ingentibus
> obstare nec se uertere ac retro dare.

> Virtue lies not, as you think, father,
> In fearing life, but in fighting vast evil
> And not turning away and retreating.

For the metatheatrical resonances of *agendum est*, see 1218, where the
phrase also occurs, and n. *ad loc.* For metatheatrical language in *Hercules*,
see on 109-12.

***Herculem irasci ueta*/Stop Hercules' wrath:** note the intense, climactic
focus on Hercules' *ira*, and the effect (theatrical and metatheatrical) of the
use here of the proper name which is also the title of the tragedy. Theseus in
a sense is asking Hercules to stop, i.e. end, the play. In Euripides' drama it is
Amphitryon who instructs Heracles to check his θυμός (*Herac.* 1210-11).
For *ira*, see on 19-29.

HERCULES *rises*: for this stage-direction, see above on *surge* (1274).

1278-94 Hercules, eager to kill the monster which he has always been
(1278-82), threatens the destruction of Thebes (1284-90) and even the
firmament (1290-4), if his arms are not returned.

1278-82 *Si uiuo, feci scelera; si morior, tuli*/If I live, I did the crimes—
dead, I suffered them:** to a Roman audience Hercules would seem to be
summoning the precedent of Livy's Lucretia (1.58). For the rehearsing of

alternatives (*complexio*), see 1243–5 and n. *ad loc*. For *scelus*, see 121, 1199, 1237 and *nn. ad locc*. For Roman referentiality in *Hercules*, see on 46–52.

purgare terras propero/**I rush to cleanse the earth:** a strong verb (cf. *Med*. 269), indexing the self-revulsion Hercules now feels. His phraseology recalls his role as civilization hero (see on 882–8), the cleanser of the earth through the removal of its monsters. Note Hercules' claim to have cleansed the earth' at *HO* 65 (*purgata tellus*), and Propertius' even more potent statement that Hercules 'had cleansed and sanctified the world with his hands' (*manibus purgatum sanxerat orbem*, 4.9.73). The phrase points the way to his own self-description as *monstrum*. For the *properare*/'rushing' motif, see 187 and n. *ad loc*.

iamdudum/**For a long time:** a heavy, prosaic, important word, used only here in *Hercules* and only three times in the remaining tragedies (*Oed*. 80, *Tro*. 65, *Med*. 191). Hercules reflects on his life and sees himself as a *monstrum* throughout his labours. Fitch *ad loc*. unpersuasively dismisses the adverb as 'rhetorical exaggeration'.

monstrum impium saeuumque et immite ac ferum/**A monster, impious, savage, pitiless, Brutal:** Hercules savages himself verbally. The *monstrum*, 'monster', motif has permeated the play from Juno's prologue onwards, emphasizing Hercules' status as the slayer/conqueror of monsters: 40, 62, 82, 215, 241, 434, 444, 454, 528, 778, 807, 939, 1020, 1029, 1254. At 1063 the Chorus seemed to observe 'monsters' in Hercules' mind. The present reference presents *anagnorisis* on Hercules' part, as the great monster-slayer sees himself as the monster to be slain. It is an ironic fulfilment of his wish at 937–9 for an evil and a monster (*monstrum*) to be slain by him. So Shakespeare's Othello at his suicide represents himself as a typical enemy, 'a malignant and a turbanned Turke' (*Oth*. V.ii.351). As such a monster Hercules is a fitting climax to the monsters slain or captured in the twelve labours (1281–2). Cf. the application of *monstrum* to Medea (*Med*. 191), Electra (*Ag*. 997), and Oedipus (*Oed*. 641, *Pho*. 122), each of whom is perceived as a boundary-violator. Oedipus is especially interesting because he becomes a 'more entangled monster' (*magis…monstrum…perplexum*, *Oed*. 641) than the monster he killed, the Sphinx, just as Hercules becomes the very thing which in abundance he has slain. See also *HO* 55–6, where Hercules says of himself: *Hercules monstri loco* | *iam coepit esse*, 'Hercules has now begun to take the place of a monster'. Cf. Heredia's description of Hercules as 'un monstrueux héros' (*Némée*, 14). Behind all these uses lies the famous Horatian precedent (Hor. *Odes* 1.37.21), where *monstrum* is applied to the notable boundary-violator of late republican Rome,

Cleopatra. For *ferus*, 'brutal', see on 516-20; for *impius*, 'impious', see 1217 and n. *ad loc*.

oberrat/ranges before me: a fusion of the literal and the figurative. The 'ranging' of Hercules was literal, like that of the bull from the sea at *Pha*. 1079 (*oberrat*); and before Hercules' mind has 'ranged' the image of himself *qua* monster. Cf. Atreus at *Thy*. 281-2: *ante oculos meos | imago caedis errat*, 'the image of carnage ranges before my eyes'; Ovid at *Tr*. 3.4.57: *ante oculos errant domus urbsque*, 'before my eyes range my house and the city'. For other metaphorical uses of *errare*, see 1193 and n. *ad loc*. Note the pause after the initial *oberrat*, preceded by enjambement (see 380 and n. *ad loc*.), giving the verb and the psychological interiority which it signals climactic emphasis.

agedum, dextra, conare/Come, hand, try: apostrophe of the hand (for which see on 1231-6) here underscores the irony of Hercules using the instrument of his violence to inflict violence upon himself. For *agedum* with the imperative, see 397 and n. ad loc. For the *dextra* and *manus* motifs, see on 118-22.

agedum...conare aggredi ingens opus/Come...try A mighty task: Hercules' phrasing places him in good Stoic company: see Seneca's 'Cato' at *Prou*. 2.10: *aggredere, anime, diu meditatum opus*, 'Attempt, soul, a task long planned'. For *agedum* with the imperative, see 397 and n. *ad loc*.

labore bis seno amplius/grander than twelve labours: here suicide is proclaimed a thirteenth labour, greater than the canonic twelve. At 1316-17 that honour goes to the labour of 'living'. *Bis seno* and related poetic periphrases for 'twelve', such as *bis sex, ter quattuor*, seem to have begun with Ennius' *Annales* (frags 88, 311 Skutsch), where they were necessitated by the inability of *duodecim* to fit into dactylic metre: see e.g. Virg. *Ecl*. 1.43, *Aen*. 1.393, Ov. *Pont*. 4.9.4. Cf. *bis seno...labore, Ag*. 812, *bis sena, Oed*. 251, *Tro*. 386. *Labore* is a comparative ablative.

1283-94 After an initial self-reproach (printed here as an aside: see below), Hercules threatens the destruction of Thebes, its gods, and the firmament along with himself, if his weapons are not restored. For the desire to drag down the whole universe as you die, see *Med*. 428, *Tro*. 161-3, *Thy*. 883-4, *Prou*. 5.8, *NQ* 6.2.9—cf. Luc. 7.654-5, Pliny *Ep*. 6.20.17. Suetonius records a Greek tragic version of this thought (ἐμοῦ θανόντος γαῖα μειχθήτω πυρί, 'at my death let earth be convulsed with fire'), which was cited in Neronian Rome and occasioned a response from Nero himself (*Nero* 38.1). Seneca translates the verse concerned at *Clem*. 2.2.2; the later Dio (58.23.4) has Tiberius frequently uttering it. The idea has impressive tragic progeny and may be found in such Renaissance figures as Tamburlaine: 'That, if I perish, heaven and earth may fade' (Marlowe, *2 Tam.* V.iii.60). For the desire for universal destruction as a characteristic of *ira*, see *Ira* 2.35.5, cited on 1163–8.

1283-4 *Ignaue, cessas*/**Do you cringe, coward:** delay or hesitation, *dubitatio*, often sudden, and the questioning of it are common behaviour for Senecan tragic figures on the verge of taking action. See Hercules at 996 above; Clytemnestra at *Ag.* 108–9, 193–8; Aegisthus at *Ag.* 228–9; Andromache at *Tro.* 657; Helen at *Tro.* 870; Oedipus at *Oed.* 926, 952, *Pho.* 30; Jocasta at *Oed.* 1024; the Nurse at *Pha.* 425; Atreus at *Thy.* 283–4; Thyestes at *Thy.* 423—and Medea at *Med.* 895, 937, 943, and 988. Cf. the Nurse at *Oct.* 73–4, Octavia at *Oct.* 960, Deianira at *HO* 307–11, 842. Self-questioning of delay may also be found in republican tragedy (e.g. Acc. *Epig.* frag. 302 Klotz), and in Seneca's prose works, where it is a feature of the *meditatio* of the Stoic *proficiens*: *quid cessas?* ('Why delay?'), *Ep. Mor.* 31.8, *dubitamus?* ('Do we hesitate?'), *Ep. Mor.* 123.10 (cf. 988 below). As Tarrant observes *ad Thy.* 283–4, 'sudden losses of nerve' accord with Stoic theory on the passions: *affectus cito cadit, aequalis est ratio*, 'Passion subsides quickly, reason is consistent' (*Ira* 1.17.5). They also stem from the Stoic theory of voluntary action: see above. Sometimes the questioning of delay concerns the delay of another: the Ghost questioning Aegisthus (*Ag.* 50–2), Clytemnestra also questioning Aegisthus (*Ag.* 986), Hecuba questioning Pyrrhus (*Tro.* 1000). For *dubitatio*, see further on 679–88. For *ignaue*, 'coward', note Atreus' use of this vocative in self-address as the first word of his opening monologue at *Thy.* 176. The sudden shift to self-address is not uncommon in Senecan tragic speeches: see e.g. *Med.* 40–3, *Ag.* 192–202, *Oed.* 77–81, *Pha.* 112, *Thy.* 961–4. I have indexed the present self-address as an aside, but it could be (less likely in my view) open self-address. Certainly what follows is decidedly not an aside. For Stoic language and ideas in *Hercules*, see on 162–3.

fortis in pueros modo/**brave only with boys:** for similarly sarcastic Senecan uses of *fortis*, see *Tro.* 755, *Pha.* 93, *Ag.* 236, *Pho.* 45. The final *o* in adverbial *modo* is short, as at 854; see n. *ad loc.*

pauidasque matres/**And frightened mothers:** the reading of *A*, and a rhetorical plural, dictated in part by *pueros* and evidently changed in *E* to the literally accurate singular, *pauidamque matrem*. Rhetorical plurals are common in Seneca and other Roman poets, esp. in the context of acerbic criticism: see e.g. *soceris* (*Med.* 106), *coniuges* (*Med.* 279), *uirginum...matres* (*Med.* 1007–8), *uirginum* (*Pha.* 304), *Phrygiae...nurus* (*Ag.* 194), *senum* (*Tro.* 1002), *fratrum exempla* (*Pho.* 479). Examples may be found in the Attic tragedians (Eur. *Herac.* 455, 1309).

1284-90 Initially the destruction threatened is of Thebes.

Arma nisi dantur/**If I'm not given arms:** the use of the present indicative in the protasis of a 'more vivid' future conditional sentence is often construed as denoting the immediate future: see e.g. Virg. *Aen.* 3.606. For its use in threats elsewhere in Senecan tragedy, see e.g. *Med.* 299, *Tro.* 307, *Thy.* 541.

aut...aut/**either...or:** the first *aut* is the *EA* reading, replaced by Zwierlein with Axelson's emendation, *altum*. The second *aut* is missing in *EA*. It is found, however, in *τ* and *recc.* after *cremabo* in line 1287 and accepted by modern editors (other than Zwierlein), who prefer to print *aut...aut* rather than adopt Axelson's emendation.

Pindi Thracis/**Thracian Pindus:** see on 976-81.

Bacchique lucos et Cithaeronis iuga/**Bacchus' groves and Cithaeron's ridge:** Mt Cithaeron near Thebes was represented in Greek and Roman literature as a haunt of Theban Bacchantes. See on 11-18, 132-6, 231-4. I have taken *lucos* as object of *cremabo* (1287) and the groves themselves as on Mt Cithaeron. Billerbeck *ad loc.* construes *lucos* as object of *excidam* (1285) and the groves as Thracian.

mecum cremabo/**burn...Along with myself:** an unconsciously ironic allusion to his own fiery death, dramatized in *Hercules Oetaeus.*

aut tota cum domibus suis dominisque tecta/**The whole city with its homes and masters:** similarly Thyestes wants the 'whole city', *tota...tecta* (*Thy.* 1010), wrenched from its base.

cum deis templa omnibus Thebana/**Theban temples with all their gods:** like Lycus, like Hercules, who here promises the kind of religious impiety ordered earlier by Lycus: 506-8.

urbe uersa condar/**be buried By the ruined town:** but, unlike Priam buried by Troy (*Tro.* 30, *Ag.* 742-3), Hercules would be the agent of his own burial.

1290-4 The threat expands to include the destruction of the firmament. Hercules again (see 1167) exemplifies Seneca's analyis in *De Ira* of the tendency of anger to move towards universal devastation: see on 1163-8. What Hercules is suggesting is a complete inversion of the cosmic order he prayed for at the beginning of Act IV (926-39). It is, however, to be aligned with his imagined assault upon the heavens in the mad scene of the previous act (963-73).

umeris/**shoulders:** for the play's focus on Hercules' 'shoulders', see on 622-5.

septemque...portis/**And seven gates:** the reference is to the famous seven gates of Thebes. Pausanias (9.8.4-5) names the seven gates: Electran, Proetidian, Neistan, Crenaean, Hypsistan, Ogygian, Homoloid. Archaeological evidence has, however, revealed only three or four gates in the remains of the ancient city: see Berman (2015: ch. 5).

onus omne media parte quod mundi sedet/the mid-firmament's Entire mass: which he has himself supported, as Juno bitterly observed in the prologue (see 69–74; cf. 425, 528, 1102). Gronovius and Billerbeck *ad loc.* wrongly take this line as referring to the earth (for a criticism of this, see Fitch 2004b: 31). For the postponement of the relative, see on 159–61.

dirimitque superos/the boundary of gods: Hercules reminds his Roman audience of the violation of boundaries, which defines much of his career, by threatening to draw down the heavens, 'the boundary of gods'. Juno in the prologue had focused on Hercules' boundary violations, and his wife's first speech in the play had commanded him specifically to 'Burst...the bounds of things' (*erumpe rerum terminos*, 290). Hercules' assault on heaven in the mad scene was in one sense no aberration; boundary violation (for which, see on 46–52) is Hercules' *modus laborandi*.

1295–1313 Two suicides threatened. Amphitryon restores Hercules' weapons only to have Hercules threaten suicide, to which Amphitryon responds with his own suicide threat.

1295–1301 *Reddo arma*/I return the arms: a cardinal moment expressed in two simple words, uttered at the beginning of a new verse line in a manner typical of so-called 'bombastic' Seneca at his dramatic best; cf. Thyestes' *agnosco fratrem* ('I recognize a brother', *Thy.* 1006); Phaedra's *quod uiuo* ('That I live', *Pha.* 880); Oedipus' and Hercules' *bene habet* ('All's well', *Oed.* 998, *Herc.* 1035); Clytemnestra's *furiosa morere* ('Die raging', *Ag.* 1012); Astyanax's *miserere, mater* ('Pity me, mother', *Tro.* 792); Medea's *Medea superest* ('Medea is left', *Med.* 166). See further 1317 and n. *ad loc.*

Vox est digna genitore Herculis/Words worthy of Hercules' Father: Hercules' statement pushes the paternity issue to the fore, which will reach its climax at 1314–18. On *dignus*, cf. its use at 112, 927, 957, and see on 109–12. For Hercules' self-naming, see on 109–12, 631–40; for *genitor*, 'father', see on 1202–18. For the speaker change before the main caesura, see on 426–9. There may also be contextual irony here. Is Hercules suggesting that his father's action is appropriate because it will lead to the death of his son, as Hercules' actions had led to the death of his sons?

Hoc en...spiculo/This shaft, look: an implied stage direction. Hercules has picked up the fatal arrow, which has been onstage since the fourth choral ode. Presumably the restored arms have been placed near it: see stage directions at 1295 and below. This is the first of three initial *hocs*, as theatrical focus is placed on this stage prop. For *en*, see on 944–52. Cf. the phraseology of Hercules' 'tragic' statement to Claudius at *Apoc.* 7.2.2: *hoc ne peremptus stipite ad terram accidas*, 'lest this club fell you to earth and kill you'.

Hoc Iuno telum manibus emisit tuis/**Juno fired this arrow with your hands:** the Prologue returns, as Amphitryon confirms Juno's promise of 118–21. Note the climactic focus on *tuis*, 'your', as Amphitryon again shifts the blame to Juno (see 1201). This contrasts with Euripides' play, where it is Heracles who presents himself as a victim of Hera (*Herac.* 1303–10) and Amphitryon explicitly states to him (*Herac.* 1139): μιᾶς ἅπαντα χειρὸς ἔργα σῆς τάδε, 'All these deeds belong to your single hand'—where there is a similar focus on the hands. Here Hercules' hands are represented as the instruments of Juno's action: *manibus* is a pointedly 'instrumental' ablative (Woodcock §43.1). For the *manus* motif in *Hercules*, see on 118–22. For the shortening of final *o* in *Iuno*, see on 109–12.

Hoc nunc ego utar/**Now I will use it:** note the emphasis on *ego*, reflected in the italics of the translation; see 1187 and n. *ad loc.*

miserum metu cor palpitat…/**poor heart Quivers with fear…:** descriptions of the physical effects/symptoms of emotions are common in Senecan tragedy (see on 414–21), but the phrasing here is not common: *palpitat* is a Senecan tragic *hapax*. For *cor palpitans*, see *Ira* 3.14.3; for *cor palpitat/palpitet/palpitans*, see Pliny *HN* 11.181, 28.97, 30.19. Note also *cor…salit*, 'heart leaps/beats', *Thy.* 756, *HO* 708.

HERCULES *places the poisoned arrow close to his body (perhaps his breast or neck):* see below.

Aptata harundo est/**The arrow is poised:** or, as Caviglia translates, 'la freccia è preparata', but not 'fitted' (Konstan), 'notched' (Fitch 2002 and 2018) or '"aufgelegt" auf die Bogensehne' (Billerbeck *ad loc.*), which generate the self-inflicted difficulties of 'the physical awkwardness, if not impossibility, of drawing a bow against oneself' (Fitch: 47). There has been no mention of a bow or bowstring since Hercules' weapons were returned, but attention was given earlier to the poison on this arrow which killed his son (1194–5) and to the other poisoned arrows in Hercules' quiver (1233–4). Poison from the hydra was especially powerful and incurably fatal (Ov. *Fas.* 5.397–414). Earlier references to the poison make *dramatic* sense as forerunner of the arrow's use here, placed by Hercules near his neck, breast, or other vulnerable part of his body (as indicated in the stage directions). Seneca knew well how to achieve spectacular moments with props—ones which would work dramatically: see e.g. the use of Hippolytus' sword in Act

III, IV, and VI of *Phaedra*, the bridal clothes in Act IV of *Troades*, the paraphernalia for magic in Act IV of *Medea* and for sacrifice in Act II of *Oedipus*, Oedipus' sword in Act VI of *Oedipus*, the crown and sceptre in Act III and the severed heads and hands in Act V of *Thyestes*. Seneca is fully aware of props as 'vibrant presences that, through their materiality, emotionally and even physically affect human agents' (Telò 2014: 1). Any modern director (and almost certainly ancient, too) would utilize the dramatic potential of the fatal arrow in the final part of this play: instrument of Hercules' first filicide (993–5), brought on stage with the slain bodies during the fourth choral ode (after 1054, before 1115), addressed by the Chorus at 1116, commented on by Hercules at 1194–5 and picked up by him at 1296, it realizes here its major dramatic function as the potential instrument of Hercules' suicide.

AMPHITRYON *takes* **HERCULES'** *sword from the pile of weapons and points it at himself*: it is possible to delay the taking of the sword until 1312, when Amphitryon mentions the 'deadly steel', *letale ferrum*. But this moment seems more likely, given what seems an implied stage direction in *ecce* at 1300 and Hercules' words at 1301. Amphitryon has been onstage since Act II, when he was clearly unarmed. The most obvious source of weaponry for him is the pile of Hercules' *arma*. There is also an additional point: by threatening to kill himself with Hercules' sword Amphitryon shows that it is Hercules who is killing him. A similar use of pre-owned swords in actual suicides is made by Phaedra (sword of Hippolytus) and Jocasta (sword of Oedipus) in the final acts of their respective plays. The great precedent was Dido, suiciding with Aeneas' sword at the end of Virgil's fourth *Aeneid*. For the death-wish in Senecan tragedy, see on 1022–31.

Ecce iam facies scelus uolens sciensque/**Look! Now your crime will be Willing and knowing**: for the legal phrase *uolens sciensque*, see also *Ira* 2.28.5, *Ep. Mor.* 114.21. Cf. also Jocasta's statement to her sons: *hoc primum nefas | inter scientes geritur*, 'this is the first crime committed between knowing persons' (*Pho.* 453–4); or the Nurse's to Phaedra: *si quis...uolens*, 'If someone willingly...' (*Pha.* 441). The 'crime' referred to by Amphitryon is not suicide but causing Amphitryon's death; cf. *scelus*, 'crime', at 1313. For legal language and imagery in *Hercules*, see on 731–4. For *scelus*, see 121, 1199, 1237 and nn. *ad locc.*

Pande, quid fieri iubes/**Speak, what do you order done**: Amphitryon's action and focus on *scelus uolens sciensque* make Hercules waver in his resolve. Hercules does so in a contextually ironic fashion by returning to his previous behavioural pattern: acting under orders (41, 211, 235, 596, 604,

831, 1268). Cf. how Oedipus yields to his daughter Antigone's arguments against his suicide by handing himself over to her orders: *iubente te*, 'at your command/on your orders', occurs three times in five and a half lines (*Pho.* 314–19) and closes the act: *iubente te uel uiuet*, 'on your orders he (Oedipus) will even live'. Changes of mind are common in Senecan drama (see on 1314–21): that of Hercules receives an elaborate dramatization, occupying seventeen lines (1301–17) and involving another threatened suicide. For *pande*, see on 645–9. The lemmatized half-line is assigned (implausibly) to Amphitryon in *EA*, but is assigned to Hercules in *O* and was assigned to Hercules by Rutgers (1618: 495). Recent editors (except for Caviglia) have followed the Rutgers assignment printed here.

1302–13 In this speech Amphitryon lives up to the etymology of his name ('distressing both sides': ἀμφί τρύων). He harassed Lycus in the second scene of Act II; now he turns on Hercules, and threatens suicide. Cf. the offers of suicide by Aegisthus (*Ag.* 303–5), Phaedra (*Pha.* 250–66), and Antigone (*Pho.* 66–76), which have the same effect on the addressee. This is the final time in the play that Amphitryon offers himself for death (see also 509–10, 1029–31, 1039–42). This seems to be an old man not only unafraid of death but almost (at least in part) desiring it. For translingual, etymological, nominal puns in Senecan tragedy, see on 35–40.

Nihil rogamus/We ask nothing: Amphitryon will not allow Hercules to play the role of the 'ordered one'. It is Hercules who must decide.

noster in tuto est dolor/My pain has found safety: i.e. it will not be affected by your dying, since I will also be dead. For *in tuto* used of the freedom from pain etc. conferred by death, see *Tro.* 656. The phrase is also found at *Oed.* 24, *Ep. Mor.* 82.1. To have one's life *in tuto*, when something may be added but nothing removed, was a Stoic goal: *Breu. Vit.* 7.9. For *in* with the ablative singular of an adjective used substantively, see on 52–6. For Stoic language and ideas in *Hercules*, see on 162–3.

natum potes…/You alone…: Hercules can save himself for Amphitryon; for, if he does, Amphitryon will still be alive. But he cannot remove himself from Amphitryon; for, if he does so, Amphitryon will be dead. Seneca offers here a variation of a famous Ovidian line: *tu seruare potes, tu perdere solus amantem*, 'You alone can save, you destroy your lover' (*Met.* 9.547)

miserum haut potes me facere, felicem potes/You can't give me pain, you can give me joy: the verbal antithesis structuring this paradoxical *sententia* clearly appealed to Seneca. See e.g. Antigone: *perire sine me non potes, mecum potes*, 'You cannot die without me, you can with me', *Pho.* 66; Atreus on Thyestes: *flecti non potest—frangi potest*, 'He cannot bend—he can break',

Thy. 200. Medea deliberately unites the antithesis into a paradoxical statement of power: *quidquid potest Medea, quidquid non potest,* 'All Medea can
do, all she cannot', *Med.* 567. The antithesis structures *sententiae* in the prose
works, too: *potest enim miser dici, non potest esse,* 'for he (the good man) can
be called wretched, he cannot be so', (*Prou.* 3.1); see also *Ira* 3.26.1. For
paradoxical phrasing in *Hercules*, see on 30–5. For the form *haut*, see 345
and n. *ad loc.*

   causam tuam/Your case: for *causa* in its legal sense, see on 397–402. For
legal language and imagery in *Hercules*, see on 731–4.

   in arto stare et ancipiti/are in perilous straits: for *in* with the ablative
singular of an adjective used substantivally, see on 52–6.

   aut uiuis aut occidis/Your choice is life or murder: a terse formulation
with pointed wordplay. The second syllable of *occidis* is long (= 'you kill'); if
it were short, it would signal the opposite (= 'you die': the usual alternative
to 'you live'). For similar life and death alternatives, epigrammatically
expressed with *aut…aut*, see *Thy.* 203 (Atreus): *aut perdet aut peribit,* 'He'll
kill or be killed'; *Pho.* 406 (Antigone): *aut solue bellum, mater, aut prima
excipe,* 'either stop the war, mother, or be its first victim'; *HO* 340 (Deianira):
aut pereat aut me perimat, 'He must either die or kill me'.

   hanc animam leuem…in ore primo teneo/My very lips Hold back this frail
breath: cf. the 'frail thread' from which Hecuba's 'slight breath' hangs: *quam
tenuis anima uinculo pendet leui* (*Tro.* 952). See also *Ep. Mor.* 30.14, 104.3.

   fessam…fessam/wearied…Wearied: for *fessus* in Senecan tragic appeals,
see also *Pha.* 247.

   Tam tarde patri uitam dat aliquis/Can one so slowly Grant his father
life: for the connection between slowness of action and unwillingness, see
Ben. 1.1.8: *qui tarde fecit diu noluit,* 'Who acted slowly was for a long time
unwilling'; 2.5.4: *tarde uelle nolentis est,* 'Slow willingness is a mark of the
unwilling'. Cf. the description by the *Satelles* of the behaviour of Eteocles
and Polynices towards their mother: *negare matri, qui diu dubitat, potest,*
'One who hesitates long can deny a mother' (*Pho.* 442).

   letale…induam/I'll sink…breast: I have accepted the reading *ferrum
pectori* (*recc.*, Delrius, Fitch 1987*a* and 2018) in place of *EA*'s *ferro pectus.*
This makes the construction with *induere* identical to that printed at 1028
above (see n. *ad loc.*). Zwierlein (following Viansino 1965 and followed in
turn by Billerbeck) prints Withof's conjecture, *senile,* for the *EA* reading
letale, and retains the *ferro pectus* of *EA.* For a list of almost a dozen
emendations/readings of this difficult line, see Billerbeck and Somazzi
(2009), 55–6.

hic, hic iacebit Herculis sani scelus/Here, here shall lie the crime of
Hercules sane: Amphitryon's *scelus* picks up his earlier use (1300); it's the
same 'crime', viz. the killing of Amphitryon, and one done willingly and
knowingly (*uolens sciensque*, 1301). Note the possible echo by Lucan,
attacking Julius Caesar at Pharsalus (7.551): *hic furor, hic rabies, hic sunt tua
crimina, Caesar*, 'Here is your madness, here your rage, here your crimes,
Caesar'. For *scelus*, see 121, 1199, 1237 and nn. *ad locc*. For the *geminatio*,
see on 92-9.

1314-21 Hercules yields and decides to live; he asks Theseus to lift up the
collapsed Amphitryon. With Hercules' decision/change of mind, cf. that of
Oedipus in *Phoenissae*, who, though drawn to suicide, decides to live for the
sake of his daughter, Antigone (see on 1295-1301). For other changes of
mind dramatized onstage by Seneca, see those of Phaedra (*Pha.* 250-66),
Creon (*Medea* 285-95), Clytemnestra (*Ag.* 306-9), Ulysses (*Tro.* 605-18),
and Thyestes (*Thy.* 512-43). The focus on Amphitryon as 'father' in Hercules'
speech (*genitor*, 1314, *patris*, 1315, *parentis*, 1318—these are the final uses of
these words in the play) makes Hercules' decision a dramatized 'proof' of
Amphitryon's paternal relationship, even as the paternity issue remains
strictly unresolved (see further on 1202-18). As Juno 'proved' (*probaui*, 36)
Hercules' filial relationship to Jove by setting him the twelve labours, Hercules
'proves' his filial relationship to Amphitryon by living for the latter's sake. As
noted above (see esp. Introd. §V, 55), Seneca, too, eschewed suicide for the
same reason: *Ep. Mor.* 78.2. Contrast Euripides' Heracles, who, though he
claims to regard Amphitryon, not Zeus, as his father (*Herac.* 1265), rejects
suicide not for his father's sake but to avoid the stigma of cowardice (*Herac.*
1347-50): see further below. Hercules' self-mastery here realizes Juno's prediction (116) in a manner the goddess did not intend: see below.

1314-17 *Iam parce, genitor, parce*/Now spare, father, spare yourself: Hercules words pick up Amphitryon's request of 1249 and, more
importantly, Megara's request of 1015, and, like all *parce* requests in Senecan
tragedy (for which see on 1015-17), point to one of Rome's cardinal, defining virtues—stipulated by Virgil's Anchises (*Aeneid* 6.853), inscribed on
Augustus' shield (*RG* 34.2), and accorded a treatise by Seneca—*clementia*,
'clemency'. In effect, of course, what the audience here witness is Hercules
sparing Amphitryon, giving him back his life. Note the repetition of *parce* as
in Oedipus' appeal to his mother at *Oed.* 1020; cf. also Virg. *Aen.* 3.41-2, Ov.
Met. 2.361-2. See further on 592-7, 1015-17, 1265-72. For *genitor*, see on
1314-21; for Roman referentiality in *Hercules*, see on 46-52.

iam reuoca manum/now—pull back Your hand: for the *manus* motif, see on 118–22. Notice the repetition of *iam*. For the anaphoric use of temporal adverbs in Senecan tragedy, see on 1272–7. For *reuocare* in the sense of drawing/pulling back, see *Ag.* 296, *Oed.* 417, *Thy.* 685. Cf. Manil. 5.148.

succumbe, uirtus/Yield, virtue: another direct address to *uirtus* (for which see on 35–40), as at 1157. What does Hercules mean here by *uirtus*? At 1157 *uirtus* seems to have denoted heroic valour, *fortitudo*. To Seneca (*Ep. Mor.* 120.11) *perfecta uirtus* comprised *temperantia* ('self-restraint'), *fortitudo* ('valour'), *prudentia* ('prudence'), and *iustitia* ('justice'). Is Hercules asking his *fortitudo* to yield and *uirtus* to realize itself in its aspect of *temperantia*? What the audience witness is Hercules conquering himself in a different sense than Juno intended (116), manifesting perhaps the kind of *uirtus* which Seneca has in mind when he writes: *sapiens quidem uincit uirtute Fortunam*, 'The sage indeed conquers Fortune through virtue' (*Ep. Mor.* 71.30). Seneca's Hercules here acts in a way more complex (morally and psychologically) than Euripides' hero, who decides that it is cowardice to die and accepts Theseus' abundant offer (*Herac.* 1347–52). Note the military language here and in the next phrase; it is how Hercules sees the world: see further on 19–29.

perfer imperium patris/bear a father's rule: highly alliterative self-instruction, picking up Amphitryon's earlier command (*perfer*, 'bear' 1239), but rephrasing it in a highly 'Roman' manner through the use of *imperium*, the quintessential term for Roman military power. Again Anchises' instructions are relevant (*Aen.* 6.851). Cf. the echo of this line in Polynices' words to Jocasta at *Pho.* 591: *iubes abire: matris imperio obsequor*, 'You order me to leave: I follow a mother's rule'. For *perferre* and *uirtus*, see *Ep. Mor.* 67.4, where it is *uirtus* that enables 'hardships' (*incommoda*) to be borne (*perferuntur*). There may also be some pick-up of Euripides' ἐγκαρτερήσω βίοτον (*Herac.* 151), if that is the correct reading or at least the reading encountered by Seneca: see below. For Roman language and referentiality, see on 46–52. For *patris*, see on 1314–21.

eat ad labores hic quoque Herculeos labor/To Hercules' labours add this labour, too: Hercules sees more clearly than at 1281–2 (see n. *ad loc.*) the pattern of his life. Living will be his thirteenth labour; he will still be acting under orders (1301, 1315), but the orders of his father and himself. Exemplarity was a central constituent of the mindset of elite Romans, who paraded as exemplary the conduct of their ancestors. Here Hercules, of course, is self-exemplifying (see Bexley 2022: 160–5), using, as Seneca's Medea does, a past self as the model or *exemplum* for the present (cf. his use of *labor* at 957). The power of the hero's statement comes from the nature of his new labour (to live) and the new kind of *uirtus* displayed (see above). Contrast the comparison of Heracles' present labour with the canonic 'labours' at Eur. *Herac.* 1279-80, where the new labour is the filicide; see also Eur. *Herac.* 1410-11. For the rare phrase *eat ad* in the sense of 'let be added to', cf. Ov. *Medic.* 66, Luc. 10.343. The idea of adding to the 'Herculean labours' (*Herculeos...labores*) is voiced by Deianira at *HO* 341-2, where she proposes herself as another labour, and by Philoctetes, who adds the conquest of fire to Hercules' labours (*HO* 1614-16). For the use of the adjective *Herculeus*, see 72 and n. *ad loc.*; for exemplarity in Roman culture, see Langlands (2018).

uiuamus/**Let us live:** Seneca's predilection for the dramatic use of a single word or short phrase at the beginning of a line (sometimes after enjambement) is noteworthy: see e.g. *Ag.* 1012; *Oed.* 16, 81; *Med.* 166, 882, 910, 1008; *Pha.* 880; *Tro.* 476, 937, 1117; *Thy.* 100, 314, 330, 1102; *Pho.* 319, 646. See also on 1295-1301. Here the dramatist has chosen perhaps the most famous jussive subjunctive in Roman literature from the opening of Catullus 5 onwards, found in both Senecas (see also Sen. Rhet. *Con.* 2.6.3) and resurrected in Ausonius (*Epig.* 40.1). It is repeated several times in the prose works and again in the tragedies (*Tro.* 476: *uiuamus*). Cf. the resolution of Euripides' Heracles in his response to Theseus: ἐγκαρτερήσω βίοτον (tentatively accepting with Bond 1981 Wecklein's emendation of βίοτον for L's θάνατον), 'I shall endure life' (*Herac.* 1351). Note (here and at *Tro.* 476) the heavy emphasis given to *uiuamus* by its initial position, followed by a strong pause well before the caesura; cf. e.g. *fraterna*, 52; *perimatur*, *Oed.* 16; *speculare*, *Pha.* 679; *peperi*, *Med.* 26; *spectemus*, *Ag.* 875; *gaudere*, *Tro.* 889; *indocile*, *Thy.* 200. For other dramatic uses of *uiuere*, see Phaedra at *Pha.* 880 (*quod uiuo*, 'That I live'), Medea at *Med.* 20 (*uiuat*, 'let him live', of Jason), and Oedipus at *Pho.* 319 (*uel uiuet*, 'he will even live'). Note, too, Seneca's own decision to live for the sake of his father, as stated at *Ep. Mor.* 78.2: *itaque imperaui mihi ut uiuerem*, 'Therefore I commanded myself to live' (see also *Ep. Mor.* 104.3-4, where suicide is to be resisted *in honorem suorum*, 'for the sake of kin'). The *Epistulae Morales* are undoubtedly later than this play. Is Seneca replaying Hercules? For climactic half-lines, see on 40-6.

AMPHITRYON *collapses:* unlike Hercules' earlier collapse (1042-8; see n. *ad loc.*), that of Amphitryon is not described. It clearly takes place, since Amphitryon has to be lifted up. For onstage collapses in Senecan tragedy, see on 1042-8.

1317–21 *Artus alleua afflictos solo…parentis*/Lift my father's crushed body…from the ground: note the triple alliteration. For the phrase *artus alleuare*, 'lift the body/limbs', see Ov. *Met.* 7.343; for *parentis*, see on 1314–21. Zwierlein prints the reading of *recc.* and Pontanus in Scriuerius 1621*b*, *afflicti*, rather than that of *EA*, *afflictos*, printed here. Viansino (1965 and 1993), Giardina (1966 and 2007), Caviglia, Fitch (1987*a* and 2018), Chaumartin, and Billerbeck print the *EA* reading. *Solo* is separative ablative: Woodcock §41.1.

Theseu/Theseus: for vocatives at the beginning of an iambic line and addresses to a character by name, see on 637–40.

dextra contactus pios scelerata refugit/My criminal hand Shuns contact with the good: similarly Euripides' Heracles is concerned not to 'contaminate' Theseus and even tells him to escape the 'pollution' (μίασμα) which contact with him would bring (*Herac.* 1161–2, 1233). Note how *refugit*, 'shuns', picks up the *refugit* of 1193 but inverts the situation. There Hercules' hands are 'shunned'; here they 'shun', as Hercules admits the *scelus* (for which see 121, 1199, 1237 and nn. *ad locc.*). See also *refugit* at 1332. For *dextra* (and the *manus* motif), see on 118–22. With *contactos pios…refugit*, cf. *refugit…uiriles contactus*, 'shuns contact with men/her husband' (Ov. *Met.* 7.239–40).

Hanc manum amplector libens/I gladly clasp this hand: these words begin Amphitryon's final speech in the play, articulating an important, even climactic moment for a 'father', who revels in the touch of his 'son' (622–5, 1257). Contrast earlier where Amphitryon 'shrinks from his hands' (*manus refugit*, 1193). For the emotive (positive and negative) use of *haec* with *manus* (= 'this hand of yours'), cf. Antigone to Oedipus (*manum hanc, Pho.* 61) and Electra to Clytemnestra (*hac…manu, Ag.* 971). For the *manus* motif, see on 118–22.

1321–41 Hercules' last speech in the play is, like his opening one, 'in Ercles' vein' (see on 592–617). But, unlike that initial invocation of gods, this is a speech of dislocation and pain. The great civilizer of the world and tamer of earthly and infernal monsters, driven by guilt and shame, finds in the wide world and even in hell itself no place to hide, because he has destroyed all place. The allusions are global, cosmic, and infernal, and the focus on the self pervasive (*me* is used six times). The catalogue of rivers, rather than simply airing the playwright's knowledge at the expense of dramatic effect (a common criticism of Seneca's 'catalogues'), seems at home in the rhetoric of this superhuman global figure, as he searches for escape from a monstrous burden of guilt. The psychological dimension of this longing for escape seems reflected in the exotic, distancing effect of the place-names themselves, as 'Hercules, even in defeat, still strains the limits of the known world' (Braden 1985: 50). There are similarities to, but also profound differences from, the catalogue of Medea (*Med.* 451–9), who, like Hercules but for different reasons, is faced with the same problem of having no place of exile. Cf. also Eur. *Med.* 502–5, and the Euripidean Heracles' own concern with a place of exile (*Herac.* 1285–98). For the *topos* of rivers failing to wash away moral pollution or guilt, see also Soph. *OT* 1227–8, Aesch. *Cho.* 71–4. For more recent examples, see below.

Seneca's Roman audience would have been familiar with the category of speech delivered here by Hercules. The 'Where can I flee' speech is attested in Roman literature (both verse and prose) from Ennius' *Medea Exul* onwards (frags 217–18 Jocelyn, frag. 10 Boyle 2006), delivered by some of Roman rhetoric and poetry's most famous figures: Gaius Gracchus (Cic. *De Orat.* 3.214), Cicero (*Muren.* 88–9), Catullus' Ariadne (64.177–91), Virgil's Dido (*Aen.* 4.534–52), Ovid's Scylla (*Met.* 8.113–21). See also Sallust *Iug.* 17. Hercules' question is echoed by his mother at *HO* 1796 (she then follows it with an echo of this act's opening line). It will be reborn in the Renaissance, articulated by such tragic figures as Shakespeare's Othello: 'Where should Othello go?' (*Oth.* V.ii.269). Note how this final speech further 'Romanizes' Hercules; the catalogue is a verbal map of the Roman empire (see below). For the Romanizing 'global catalogue' elsewhere in Senecan tragedy, see e.g. *Oed.* 113–23, 467–87, *Pha.* 54–72, *Med.* 705–27, *Thy.* 344–87. For catalogues in *Hercules*, see on 332–6 and 6–18. For Roman referentiality in *Hercules*, see on 46–52.

The speech is regularly grouped with Hippolytus' shorter request for purification (by Tanais, Maeotis, and Oceanus) at *Pha.* 715–18, of which it may be viewed as a development. It constitutes one of the most memorable speeches of ancient tragedy. Together with its Hippolytan predecessor it became the model for later tragic figures similarly racked by guilt and shame. See e.g. Shakespeare's Macbeth at *Mac.* II.ii.59–62 (cited Introd. §VII, 137); also Marston, *The Insatiate Countess*, V.i.40–4:

> What Tanais, Nilus, or what Tigris swift,
> What Rhenus ferier than the cataract,—
> Although Neptolis cold, the waves of all the Northern Sea,
> Should flow for ever, through these guilty hands,
> Yet the sanguinolent stain would extant be!

And Tristan L'Hermite's *Hérode* (*Marianne* V.ii.1563–4):

> Quel fleuve ou quel mer sera jamais capable
> D'effacer la noirceur de ce crime execrable?

And Glover's Medea (*Med.* V.ii):

> Not the disburthen'd sluices of the skies,
> The wat'ry nereids with the ocean's store,
> Nor all the tears, which misery hath shed,
> Can from the mother wash the children's blood.

And Lodge (*Herakles* sc. xi): 'There are no lustral waters in this world | Can cleanse me of their blood or take away | The stigma of their murder'. Racine's Thésée avoids the watery cleansing but insists on self-removal (*Phd.* V.vii.1608): 'De l'univers entier je voudrais me bannir'.

1321-9 In his search for a place of exile Hercules questions whether any of the great rivers of the world or Tethys herself could cleanse him of his guilt. The *locus* motif (see on 1-5) and exile theme which dominate the opening of the play now dominate its close. The word occurs at the beginning of the speech (1321), at its centre (1131), and at its end (1140).

Quem locum profugus petam/**What place of exile shall I seek:** for the 'Where can I flee?' quandary, see on 1321-41. Note how Hercules' alliterative *ps* continue those of Amphitryon in 1320-1.

quaue tellure obruar/**in what land be erased:** I join Fitch (2018) in taking *obruere* here as 'to bury in oblivion' (*OLD* 9a) rather than (with Konstan and Billerbeck) literally 'to bury'. Hercules in this final speech seems primarily concerned with hiding (*recondam*, 1322, *latebram*, 1335) than with a future burial.

quis Tanais/**What Tanais:** the river to the west of Scythia, now called the Don. It emptied into Lake Maeotis (the Sea of Azov), which adjoined the Black Sea: see 1326-7. It is mentioned also at *Ag.* 680, *Tro.* 9, *Pha.* 401, 715; see also *HO* 86. For the inability of great rivers to cleanse guilt, see the Sophoclean Second Messenger at *OT* 1227-8 (citing the Ister and Phasis). Note adjectival *quis*, used three times in line 1323: see on 1138-42.

quis Nilus/**what Nile:** chief, and by far the largest, river of Egypt; to Romans it often symbolized oriental decadence and the exotic. It is mentioned also at *Oed.* 606, *Oct.* 519. The warmth of this river (*Oed.* 606: *tepente Nilo*) implicitly contrasts with the cold of Tanais (*Tro.* 8: *frigidum*).

quis Persica uiolentus unda Tigris/**what violent Tigris with Persian flood:** one of the major rivers of Mesopotamia in south-western Asia; it rises in the Taurus mountains (Lake Hazar) and flows south, emptying into the Persian Gulf. It is mentioned again at *Tro.* 13, *Med.* 723. *Violentus* is almost an etymological adjective in that the Romans seem to have regarded 'Tigris' as a name derived from the river's *celeritas*, 'swiftness': Varro *LL* 5.100, Pliny *HN* 6.127, Isid. *Orig.* 13.21.9. A regular epithet for the river was *rapidus*: Hor. *Odes* 4.14.46, Luc. 3.256.

Rhenus ferox/frenzied Rhine: the great river of Germania and a main imperial frontier, separating Germania from Gaul. It is mentioned also at *Med.* 374.

Tagus ... turbidus gaza fluens/turbid Tagus awash with ... gold: the Tagus (Spanish Tajo, Portuguese Tejo) is the longest river of the Iberian peninsula. Its source is in eastern Spain and its mouth in Portugal, where it empties into the Atlantic by Lisbon. It was famous for its gold deposits (its defining adjective: *aurifer*, 'gold-bearing')—an association which became a *topos* in Roman poetry: see *Thy.* 354–5; Cat. 29.19; Ov. *Am.* 1.15.34, *Met.* 2.251; *Catalep.* 9.52; Luc. 7.755; *HO* 626–7; Mart. *Epig.* 7.88.7, 10.17.4, 96.3, 12.2.3 (Shackleton Bailey); Juv. 3.54–5, 14.298–9. Spain was the chief source of gold for Rome.

abluere dextram poterit/Can cleanse this hand: for *dextra* (and the *manus* motif), see on 118–22.

Arctoum licet ... transfundat mare/Though ... Pour its Arctic sea: the adjective *Arctous* is first found in Senecan tragedy, where it occurs four times, and is liked by Seneca's imitator, the dramatist of *Hercules Oetaeus*, who uses it three times in the one play. For *licet* with the subjunctive, see 21–2 and n. *ad loc.*

Maeotis ... gelida/icy Maeotis: modern Sea of Azov at the top of the Black Sea between Ukraine and Russia, whose freezing waters are mentioned at *Oed.* 474–5 and *Pha.* 401, 715–16. The catalogue has come full circle: the Tanais (1323) emptied into 'Lake Maeotis'.

The above five rivers and Lake Maeotis are geopolitical markers of the world of Rome, marking boundaries respectively in the north-east, the south, the east, the north-west, the west, and finally the north-east again. Military operations were always likely to break out in those areas, and specific military campaigns were launched in Germany and Armenia during the principates of Claudius and Nero. For Roman referentiality, see on 46–52.

tota Tethys/Tethys ... with all her waters: lit. 'all Tethys', like *toto ... Oceano*, 'all Oceanus' at *Pha.* 717. For the Senecan mannerism of attaching *totus* to place-names, see on 658–61. Tethys was wife and sister of Oceanus, the great sea which encompassed the world; the frequent references to it (and to Oceanus) in Senecan tragedy seem index of a preoccupation with imperial space and global boundaries. See on 19–29.

manus/hands: for the *manus* motif, see on 118–22.

haerebit altum facinus/The crime will stick deep: for an analogous, tragic use of *haerere*, see Enn. *Thy.* (frag. 295 Jocelyn, frag. 2 Boyle 2006): *tanta uis sceleris in corpore haeret*, 'Such force of sin sticks in my body'. The Ennian line was probably delivered by the cannibalistic Thyestes, eater of his own children. Hercules seems to see his own pollution in similar terms. Hence the immediate focus on his own 'impiety' (*impius*, 1329).

1329–34 Hercules addresses himself. Interestingly he seems to play both *Phaedra's* Theseus and *Phaedra's* Hippolytus in his rage. For this oscillation of person (from first to second and even to third, etc.) in respect of the speaker himself/herself, see e.g. *Med.* 129–36, 560–7, 895–957 (Medea); *Tro.* 605–18 (Ulysses); *Thy.* 176–96 (Atreus).

impius/impious man: for *impius*, see 1217 and n. *ad loc.*

ortum an occasum petes/Will you head east or west: for the *ortus/occasus* combination, see on 372–83.

ubique notus perdidi exilio locum/Known everywhere, I've destroyed a place for exile: the *locus* motif again (see 1321 and on 1–5), as the play's thematic circle closes. Hercules finds himself worse off than the prologue's *nouerca*, whose traditional 'place' had been usurped by whores. Juno had to find a new place, earth (1–5). Hercules has no place for himself. He has destroyed all place; yet his pollution requires him to leave the present place for another. Cf. Oedipus whose pollution has contaminated the heavens themselves (*Oed.* 36); Hercules' mother Alcmena/Alcmene, who, like Hercules, is 'known everywhere' (*ubique…nota*, *HO* 1799); and *Phaedra's* Theseus, who, like Hercules, wishes to return to hell but finds no place for his own punishment (*Pha.* 1211–12):

> sidera et manes et undas scelere compleui meo:
> amplius sors nulla restat; regna me norunt tria.

> Stars, shades and ocean I have sated with my sins.
> No region now remains; all three kingdoms know me.

Beneath Hercules' agonized sense of unlocation is the paradox of his global identity. In a completely different context (*Ep. Mor.* 2.2), Seneca writes: *nusquam est qui ubique est*, 'He who is everywhere is nowhere'. For *perdere* and the loss of *locus*, see *Med.* 154.

me refugit orbis…/The world shuns me…: the cosmic disruption Hercules has caused contrasts with the cosmic stability for which he prayed at 928–9. Notice the continuation of the 'shunning' motif: see 1193, 1319.

astra transuersos agunt obliqua cursus/Slanting stars run transverse Courses: not what Hercules prayed for at 928-9. The world's shunning of Hercules manifests itself in cosmic upheaval similar to that witnessed in the final acts and choral ode of *Thyestes* and which Hippolytus prayed for in his moral rage against his stepmother (*Pha*. 676-7):

> uersa retro sidera obliquos agant
> retorta cursus.
>
> Let the stars reverse and, twisted back, run
> Slanting courses.

Titan Cerberum/Titan...Cerberus: for the former, see on 123-4; for the latter, see on 782-91. This overt identification with Cerberus confirms Hercules' self-image as a 'monster', which he articulated at 1279-81 (see n. *ad loc.*) and anticipated at 938-9, immediately before the onset of madness. For the fearful reaction of the Sun/Titan to Cerberus, see 61 (also 595-6). Note the breach of 'Porson's law' in 1333: see on 249-58.

   meliore uultu/more friendly gaze: for *uultus*, see on 329-31. The ablative is of manner. Woodcock §§43.5.iv, 48.

1334-41 Hercules' final words in the play are to Theseus, whom he asks to return him to hell.

   O fidum caput, Theseu/O faithful friend, Theseus: a common synecdochic use of *caput* ('head' = 'person/man/woman/girl' etc.), which in Senecan tragedy is more usually accompanied by a negative epithet: see e.g. *Ag*. 163, 231, 953; *Med*. 465, 1005; *Oed*. 521, 871; *Thy*. 244; *Pho*. 7. Here we encounter a rare instance of a positive, even affectionate use of *caput*; see also *Oed*. 291. Cf. also Hor. *Odes* 1.24.2 (positive use), Virg. *Aen*. 4.613 (negative use). In both its positive and negative senses the term is 'strongly emotional' (Fitch *ad* 920). *Fidus* is almost a defining adjective of a *comes* (646): see e.g. *Tro*. 83, *HO* 601. But its attachment to *caput* joins with the earlier focus on Theseus' *fides* (1177) to project the Athenian king as a paradigm of loyalty. As the Strophius scene of *Agamemnon* shows, Seneca did not treat the value of *fides* lightly, but, given Theseus' mythical and literary history, this emphasis here, like the earlier focus, is clearly problematic: see 1177 and n. *ad loc.* As for the choice between the adjectives, *fidus* and *fidelis*, Seneca clearly preferred the former in his tragedies, perhaps partly because of metrical convenience (so Fitch *ad loc.*). Jocelyn *ad* Enn. *Iph.* frag. 194 suggests that it 'conveyed much more emotion than *fidelis*'. Note again the vocative at the beginning of an iambic line and the address to a character by name: see on 637–40. Here for the only time in the play, the address by name will receive another address by name in reply (1343).

semper sceleris alieni arbiter/whenever you judge another's crime: Seneca is fond of a rhetorical use of *semper* (= 'always'); see e.g. *Tro.* 164; *Pha.* 128, 1164, 1167, 1207; *Oed.* 627; *Ag.* 810; *Pho.* 34. Here it seems designed to function, in 'Alexandrian footnote' mode (see on 727–30), to trigger allusions to Theseus' literary history (see next n.). For *scelus*, see 121, 1199, 1237 and *nn. ad locc.*; for the legal term, *arbiter*, see on 205–9. For legal language in *Hercules*, see on 731–4.

amas nocentes/You love the guilty: a reference to Theseus' support of Pirithous in the latter's attempt to rape Proserpina (see *Pha.* 93–8), of Oedipus, who sought sanctuary in Athens (see Sophocles *Oedipus at Colonus*), and of the suppliant, Argive widows of the 'Seven', who sought funerary rites for their dead husbands (see Euripides' *Supplices* and Statius' *Thebaid* 12). A 'more humane' treatment of wrong-doing is advocated by Seneca at *Ira* 1.14.3: *quanto humanius mitem et patrium animum praestare peccantibus et illos non persequi sed reuocare,* 'How much more humane/human to display a gentle and fatherly mind to wrong-doers and not to hunt them but to call them back.'

gratiam... refer uicemque/thank and repay: 'repayment' and *gratia* were important practices in a patronal society such as Rome. The lack of this is one of the central issues in Medea's grievance with Jason: *Med.* 482: *miserere, redde supplici felix uicem,* 'Have pity, repay this suppliant, man of fortune.' See also Ov. *Am.* 1.6.23: *redde uicem meritis,* 'Repay my deserts.'

refer... redde... reductum... restitue/repay... Recall, return... restore: for paronomasia of *re-* words, see 48–9 and n. *ad loc.*

redde me infernis... umbris/Recall... me... to the shades of hell: Hercules' death-wish abides: see Introd. §VII, 116. Hercules expressed this desire to return to hell earlier (1218). But here he is made to express it in an inter-textually ironic way—through an inversion of the despairing Theseus' request in *Phaedra* (1217–19) to Hercules himself:

> donator atrae lucis, Alcides, tuum
> Diti remitte munus; ereptos mihi
> restitue manes.

> Alcides, giver of black light, return
> Your gift to Dis; restore to me the dead
> I lost.

Cf. also Oedipus' desire to be restored to the place of his near-death on Cithaeron (*Pho.* 31–3). For the desire to be taken to the underworld (a *topos* of Senecan tragedy) see e.g. *Ag.* 589–610, *Oed.* 868–70, *Pha.* 1201–6, *Thy.* 68–73, 1006–19. Shakespeare's Othello, on recognizing his deluded killing of his wife, similarly and imaginatively prays for hell (*Oth.* V.ii. 275–8):

> Whip me, ye devils,
> From the possession of this heavenly sight!
> Blow me about in winds, roast me in sulphur,
> Wash me in steep-down gulfs of liquid fire!

For *Othello* and *Hercules*, see Introd. §VIII, 136–7.

ille...locus/That place: the final use of this seminal noun, the last to be uttered by Hercules in the final act, as it was the first (1138). It was also the first noun to be uttered in this final speech (1321). For the *locus* motif, see on 1–5.

sed et ille nouit/But it, too, knows me: a similar dilemma (and idiom) to that of Theseus in *Phaedra*: *amplius sors nulla restat; regna me norunt tria*, 'No region now remains; all three kingdoms know me' (*Pha.* 1212).

1341–4 As always in Senecan tragedy, the last words of the play are iambic dialogue delivered by one of the main characters. There is a marked contrast here with extant fifth-century Attic tragedy, which ends more frequently than not (it becomes the rule in Euripides) with a short ode or utterance from the chorus. It should be observed that both the 'non-Senecan' plays of the Senecan tragic corpus, *Hercules Oetaeus* and *Octavia*, conclude with a short choral ode, which may well have been standard Roman practice. Complete avoidance of a lyric or choral ending is perhaps Senecan innovation.

As always, too, Senecan final lines provoke. Theseus ends the play with an invitation to a particular 'place', Athens, where even the hands of gods have been cleansed of murder. If the derivation of the name 'Theseus' from τίθημι, 'I place', and θέσις, 'a placing', obtains, Theseus is acting in accordance with the imperatives of his name (for translingual etymological puns, see on 35–40), as he does at the end of *Phaedra* when he places together the fragments of his son's dismembered body. His action to help the distressed Hercules also accords with that of a Stoic *sapiens* (*Clem.* 2.6); but his preceding tears (1273–4) have shown him to be no Stoic, as any reader of Stoic texts would have recognized.

What the audience would perhaps have been most interested in are the ironies and issues which this ending generates and the obvious contrasts with Euripides' play. An evident irony is the role-reversal of Hercules and Theseus: the latter, whom Hercules rescued from hell, now acts as saviour to

Hercules. Obvious, too, would have been the brevity of Theseus' invitation in comparison with the lengthy one in Euripides' play (*Herac.* 1322–39), where Heracles is promised not only ritual purification, but a home, wealth, land, and cultic status. Furthermore, Seneca's Theseus, unlike that of Euripides, who has come from Athens to liberate Thebes (*Herac.* 1163–71), has not yet returned home after his imprisonment in the underworld. The audience know what catastrophe awaits him: exactly what Hercules has suffered, the death of his family, caused by himself.

Most importantly, Euripides' Heracles accepts Theseus' offer (*Herac.* 1351–2) and spends the last seventy lines or so of the play preparing for his departure from Thebes: giving instructions for the burial of his family, speaking eulogies over the bodies, mourning, deliberating whether to get rid of his weapons, embracing Amphitryon and promising to bury him. Seneca's play has none of this; it ends, or rather stops (see on *Curtain* below), without a reply from Hercules. Billerbeck (2014: 426) misdescribes when she writes: 'he (Hercules) follows his faithful friend Theseus to Athens'; similarly Trinacty (2014: 138): 'Hercules…makes his way to Athens for absolution'; or Star (2017: 94): 'Hercules will be purified'. There is nothing *in the text* to support this, as there is in the Euripidean text, which Seneca here rewrites. Neither Juno's prescripting of the play in the prologue nor any language emanating from any character testifies to Hercules' acceptance of Theseus' offer, on which the play ends. Any member of Seneca's audience, including those familiar with Euripides' play and the mythic tradition, could have doubted whether the Senecan Hercules, who has just declared that he has 'lost all place for exile' (*perdidi exilio locum*, 1331), would accept. The audience might also have contemplated the irony that what Amphitryon's actions and Hercules' yielding to them have achieved is the implementation of the penal theory advocated by Lycus: *miserum ueta perire*, 'Forbid the wretched to die' (513). Left in abeyance, as the audience contemplate Hercules' psychological chaos and Theseus' offer, is a question never explicitly addressed in either Euripides' or Seneca's play: how is Thebes now to be ruled? For Stoic language and ideas in *Hercules*, see on 162–3.

Nostra te tellus manet/**Our land awaits you**: Theseus invites Hercules to Athens for purification, as in Euripides (*Herac.* 1322–5). In Euripides' play 'Athens' is directly or indirectly named (1323, 133). As Braden (1993: 252–3) observes, Athens here is not named; *nostra tellus* prevents a Thebes/Athens polarity rising to the surface. Indeed different locations for/versions of Hercules' purification are attested in *Hercules Oetaeus* (Libya: 907–8), Apollodorus (Boeotia: 2.4.12), and others: see Fitch *ad loc.* Note, too, the echo here of Horace's thirteenth *Epode*, where Chiron sends Achilles off to his death at Troy with the phrase, *te manet Assaraci tellus* (*Epod.* 13.13). Is this a contrast or similarity? Certainly Hercules is longing for death. See Trinacty (2017: 182–4), and Introd. §VII, 116. For the repetition of the same syllable at the end and beginning of juxtaposed words (*te tellus*), see 67 and n. *ad loc.*

solutam caede Gradiuus manum/Gradivus cleansed his hands of murder: Gradivus ('the Marcher') is a title of Mars, found again at *Pha.* 188, *HO* 1312. The incident referred to is Mars' acquittal of the murder of Halirrhothius, a son of Neptune, in a trial before a court of the gods, assembled on the Areopagus in Athens (Eur. *El.* 1258–62, Apollod. 3.14.2). Halirrhothius had sexually assaulted Mars' daughter, Alcippe. Even bloody 'hands' can be made clean in Athens. This is the final occurrence of the *manus* motif; see on 118–22.

illa te, Alcide, uocat... terra/This land, Alcides, Calls you: the third and final time Hercules is addressed in the play by name (see also 186, 421). It picks up the nominal address to Theseus at 1335, confirming a strong sense of intimacy between the two 'heroes', and, because the name is 'Alcides', underscoring Hercules' mortal origins. For addresses to characters by name in the play, see on 637–40.

facere innocentes... quae superos solet/It often makes innocents of gods: Seneca is well known for the resonance of his final lines. Each of the other Senecan tragic endings may be compared fruitfully with that of this play: but cf. especially Theseus' closural comment on Phaedra (*Pha.* 1280), Atreus' prediction of Thyestes' continued punishment (*Thy.* 1112), Oedipus' joy in his retinue of fate, disease, wasting, plague, and pain (*Oed.* 1061), and Cassandra's prediction of approaching *furor* (*Ag.* 1012). Note also *Pho.* 664, which may or may not have been the intended final line of that play. All Seneca's tragedies, too, end, like *Hercules*, with a theatrically resonant final phrase: *Oed.* 1061 (*uti libet*), *Pha.* 1280 (*impio capiti incubet*), *Ag.* 1012 (*ueniet et uobis furor*), *Med.* 1027 (*qua ueheris deos*), *Tro.* 1179 (*classis mouet*), *Thy.* 1112 (*liberis trado tuis*); cf. *Pho.* 664 (*constant bene*), the last phrase of the play as we have it. Again the dramatist of *Octavia* learnt from Seneca (*Roma cruore, Oct.* 982). For Seneca's interest in good endings (*bonae clausulae*) in literature and life, see *Ep. Mor.* 77.20. Here the resonance arises both from the assumption apparently underlying *facere innocentes*, 'makes innocents' (viz. that Hercules is at present guilty: see Davis 1993: 136), and from the plurality and ambiguous denotation of *superos*. Only one god was acquitted in Athens. Is *superos* a rhetorical plural or is

Hercules himself to be included in the word's reference with Theseus using the word proleptically? There is a stark contrast here with Euripides' play, in which Theseus is quite clear in proclaiming Hercules' mortality (*Herac.* 1331). But even a proleptic assignment of Hercules to the category of *superi* only underscores that Hercules is not yet a god. Is there a suggestion that Hercules, at present not one of the *superi*, cannot be made *innocens*? The use of *solet*, 'often' (lit. 'is accustomed'), is itself overtly rhetorical (see 1102 and n. *ad loc.*), and its rhetoric seems to infect the preceding noun, which seems to suggest a pattern where none exists. There is also, as at 1102, a metatheatrical dimension to *solet*, viz. a direction of the audience's attention to the customary ending of Hercules' madness in the hero's redemption, most famously in Euripides' play. The absence of any response to Theseus' final speech creates a forceful tension between that 'customary ending' and the conclusion of Seneca's play. For metatheatricality in *Hercules*, see on 109–12. For the phrase *facere innocentes/innocentem*, see *Thy.* 20, *HO* 890; for legal language in *Hercules*, see on 731–4. For the alliterative closural line, see on 275–8. For the postponed relative, see on 159–61. Caviglia *ad loc.* cites a reversal of the play's final line in de' Dottori's *Aristodemo* I.iv.413–14: 'ma far nocenti osaro | gli dèi con empia colpa'.

   Curtain: as often in Senecan tragedy, the play stops rather than ends, in a sense freezing the characters in their final action: see the endings of *Agamemnon*, *Medea*, *Thyestes*. Hence I would replace Scott Smith's stage direction, 'All leave' (2011: 51), with the present one, which leaves open the question of whether Hercules accepts Theseus' offer. The curtain would either have been raised from its slot in front of the stage (the republican *aulaeum* or 'curtain': see Sear 2006: 90) or lowered (Beare's view of the imperial curtain: Beare 1964: 271–4; see also Kragelund 2016: 156) to conceal the stage and its amalgam of living and dead *dramatis personae*.

Select Bibliography

1. Latin Texts: Editions, Translations, and Commentaries

Ageno, F. (1925), *L'Ercole Furioso*. Padua.

Ahl, F. (1986), *Seneca: Medea, Phaedra, Trojan Women*. Ithaca, NY.

Anderson, W. S. (1972), *Ovid's Metamorphoses: Books 6–10*. Norman, OK.

Ascensius, I. B. (1514), *Lucii Annaei Senecae Tragoediae*. Paris.

Astbury, R. (1985), *M. Terentii Varronis Saturarum Menippearum Fragmenta*. Leipzig.

Auantius, H. (1517), *Senecae Tragoediae* (Aldine Edition). Venice.

Austin, R. G. (1955), *P. Vergili Maronis Aeneidos Liber Quartus*. Oxford.

Austin, R. G. (1964), *P. Vergili Maronis Aeneidos Liber Secundus*. Oxford.

Austin, R. G. (1971), *P. Vergili Maronis Aeneidos Liber Primus*. Oxford.

Austin, R. G. (1977), *P. Vergili Maronis Aeneidos Liber Sextus*. Oxford.

Baden, T. (1821), *Lucii Annaei Senecae Tragoediae*. 2 vols. Leipzig.

Barbera, E. (2000), *Lucio Anneo Seneca. Ottavia*. Lecce.

Barchiesi, A. (1988), *Seneca: Le Fenicie*. Venice.

Barrile, R. (1969), *Accius, Lucius: Frammenti delle tragedie e delle preteste*. Bologna.

Bartsch, S. (2017), *Lucius Annaeus Seneca: The Complete Tragedies*. 2 vols. Chicago, IL.

Beckby, H. (1969), *Die Sprüche des Publilius Syrus*. Munich.

Bellfortis, A. (1478), *Senecae Tragoediae*. Ferrara.

Berrigan, J. R. (1975), *Mussato's Ecerinis and Loschi's Achilles*. Munich.

Billerbeck, M. (1999a), *Seneca: Hercules Furens: Einleitung, Text, Übersetzung und Kommentar*. Leiden.

Billerbeck, M., and Guex, S. (2002), *Sénèque: Hercule Furieux*. Berne.

Blänsdorf, J. (1995), *Fragmenta Poetarum Latinorum Epicorum et Lyricorum praeter Ennium et Lucilium*. Stuttgart and Leipzig.

Bömer, F. (1969–86), *P. Ouidius Naso: Metamorphosen*. 7 vols. Heidelberg.

Bonaria, M. (1956), *Mimorum Romanorum Fragmenta*. Genoa.

Bonaria, M. (1965), *Romani Mimi*. Rome.

Borzsák, S. (1992), *Cornelii Taciti: Ab Excessu Diui Augusti Libri I–VI*. Leipzig.

Bothe, F. H. (1819), *Lucii Annaei Senecae Tragoediae*. 3 vols. Leipzig (2nd edn, 1834).

Boyle, A. J. (1976), *The Eclogues of Virgil*. Melbourne.

Boyle, A. J. (1987), *Seneca's Phaedra*. Liverpool (repr. Leeds 1992).

Boyle, A. J. (1994), *Seneca's Troades*. Leeds.

Boyle, A. J. (2008), *Octavia: Attributed to Seneca*. Oxford.

Boyle, A. J. (2011), *Seneca: Oedipus*. Oxford.

Boyle, A. J. (2014), *Seneca: Medea*. Oxford.

Boyle, A. J. (2017), *Seneca: Thyestes*. Oxford.

Boyle, A. J. (2019), *Seneca: Agamemnon*. Oxford.

Bradley, K. R. (1978), *Suetonius' Life of Nero: An Historical Commentary*. Brussels.

Bradshaw, W. (1902), *Ten Tragedies of Seneca*. London.

Braund, S. (1996), *Juvenal: Satires Book I*. Cambridge.

Braund, S. (2009), *Seneca: De Clementia*. Oxford.

Braund, S. (2017), 'Agamemnon', in Bartsch (2017): 2.243–78.

Brink, C. O. (1971), *Horace on Poetry: The 'Ars Poetica'*. Cambridge.

Brink, C. O. (1982), *Horace on Poetry: Epistles Book II*. Cambridge.

Brown, V. (2001), *Giovanni Boccaccio: Famous Women*. Cambridge, MA.

Bücheler, F. (1963), *Petronii Saturae*. 8th edn. Berlin and Zurich.

Buescu, V. (1941), *Cicéron: Les Aratea*. Bucharest.

Bunte, B. (1875), *Hygini Astronomica*. Leipzig.

Casamento, A. (2011), *Seneca: Fedra*. Rome.

Caviglia, F. (1979), *L. Anneo Seneca: Il Furore di Ercole*. Rome.

Caviglia, F. (1981), *L. Anneo Seneca: Le Troiane*. Rome.

Chassignet, M. (1986), *Caton: Les Origines*. Paris.

Chaumartin, F.-R. (1996), *Sénèque: Tragédies*. Tome 1. Paris.

Citti, F., and Neri, C. (2001), *Seneca nel Novecento: Sondaggi sulla fortuna di un 'classico'*. Rome.

Clark, A. C. (1922), *Cicero: Orationes IV*. Oxford.

Coffey, M., and Mayer, R. (1990), *Seneca: Phaedra*. Cambridge.

Colyer, H. (2013), *Agamemnon Freely Adapted from Seneca*. Lulu, NC.

Condos, T. (1997), *Star Myths of the Greeks and Romans: A Sourcebook*. Grand Rapids, MI.

Corrigan, R. W., ed. (1990), *Classical Tragedy Greek and Roman: Eight Plays*. New York.

Costa, C. D. N. (1973), *Seneca: Medea*. Oxford.

Courtney, E. (1980), *A Commentary on the Satires of Juvenal*. London.

Courtney, E. (1993), *The Fragmentary Latin Poets*. Oxford.

Daalder, J. (1982), *'Thyestes', Lucius Annaeus Seneca, translated by Jasper Heywood*. London.

Dangel, J. (1995), *Accius: Oeuvres (fragments)*. Paris.

D'Anna, I. (1967), *M. Pacuvii: Fragmenta*. Rome.

D'Anto, V. (1980), *I frammenti delle tragedie di L. Accio*. Lecce.

Daviault, A. (1981), *Comoedia Togata Fragments*. Paris.

Davis, P. J. (2020), *Valerius Flaccus: Argonautica Book 7*. Oxford.

Degiovanni, L. (2017), *L. Annaei Senecae Hercules Oetaeus: Atti I–III (vv. 1–1030)*. Florence.

Delrius, M. A. (1576), *In Lucii Annaei Senecae tragoedias amplissima aduersaria quae loco commentarii esse possunt*. Antwerp.

Delrius, M. A. (1593/4), *Syntagma tragoediae Latinae*. Antwerp.

Dewar, M. (1991), *Statius: Thebaid IX*. Oxford.

Diehl, E. (1911), *Poetarum Romanorum Veterum Reliquiae*. Bonn.

Duff, J. W. and A. M. (1934), *Minor Latin Poets*. Cambridge, MA, and London.

Eden, P. T. (1984), *Seneca: Apocolocyntosis*. Cambridge.

Editio Patauina (1748). Padua.

Elder, J. (1982), *Seneca: Thyestes*. Ashington and Manchester.

Fantham, E. (1982), *Seneca's Troades: A Literary Commentary*. Princeton, NJ.

Fantham, E. (1998), *Ovid: Fasti IV*. Cambridge.

Fantham, E. (2010), *Seneca: Selected Letters*. Oxford.

Farnaby, T. (1623), *L. & M. Annaei Senecae Tragoediae*. Amsterdam.

Ferri, R. (2003), *Octavia: A Play Attributed to Seneca*. Cambridge.

Fitch, J. G. (1987*a*), *Seneca's Hercules Furens*. Ithaca, NY.

Fitch, J. G. (2002*a*), *Seneca: Tragedies: I*. Cambridge, MA, and London.

Fitch, J. G. (2004*a*), *Seneca: Tragedies: II*. Cambridge, MA, and London.

Fitch, J. G. (2018), *Seneca: Tragedies*. 2 vols. 2nd edn. Cambridge, MA, and London.

Fitch, J. G. (1977), *P. Vergili Maronis Aeneidos Libri VII–VIII*. Oxford.

Fordyce, C. J. (1961), *Catullus*. Oxford.

Franchella, Q. (1968), *Lucii Accii tragoediarum fragmenta*. Bologna.

Frank, M. (1995*a*), *Seneca's Phoenissae: Introduction and Commentary*. Leiden.

Friedrich, O. (1964), *Publilii Syri Mimi Sententiae*. Hildesheim.

Giancotti, F. (1988–9), *Tieste*. 2 vols. Turin.

Giardina, G. C. L. (1966), *L. Annaei Senecae Tragoediae*. Bologna.

Giardina, G. C. L. (2007), *Lucio Anneo Seneca: Tragedie*. I. Pisa and Rome.

Giardina, G. C. L. (2009), *Lucio Anneo Seneca: Tragedie*. II. Pisa and Rome.

Giomini, R. (1955), *Senecae Phaedra*. Rome.

Giomini, R. (1956), *Senecae Agamemnon*. Rome.

Goldberg, S. M., and Manuwald, G. (2018), *Fragmentary Republican Latin*. Vols I–II. Cambridge, MA, and London.

Goodyear, F. R. D. (1965), *Aetna*. Cambridge.

Goodyear, F. R. D. (1972), *The Annals of Tacitus, I: Annals 1.1–54*. Cambridge.

Goodyear, F. R. D. (1981), *The Annals of Tacitus, II: Annals 1.55–81 and Annals 2*. Cambridge.

Goold, G. P., and Showerman, G. (1977), *Ovid: Heroides, Amores*. 2nd edn. Cambridge, MA, and London.

Gowers, E. (2012), *Horace: Satires Book I*. Cambridge.

Grimal, P. (1965), *L. Annaei Senecae Phaedra*. Paris.

Gronovius, J. F. (1661), *Lucii Annaei Senecae Tragoediae*. Leiden (Amsterdam 1661).

Grünbein, D. (2002), *Seneca: Thyestes*. Frankfurt am Main and Leipzig.

Grund, G. R. (2011), *Humanist Tragedies*. Cambridge, MA.

Haase, F. (1852–3), *L. Annaei Senecae Opera Quae Supersunt*. Leipzig.

Hadas, M. (1956), *Seneca: Medea*. Indianapolis and New York.

Hall, J. B. (1995), *P. Ovidi Nasonis Tristia*. Stuttgart and Leipzig.

Hall, J. B., Ritchie, A. L., and Edwards, M. J. (2007), *P. Papinius Statius: Thebaid and Achilleid*. 3 vols. Newcastle upon Tyne.

Harris, E. I. (1899), *Two Tragedies of Seneca: Medea and The Daughters of Troy*. Boston, MA, and New York.

Harris, E. I. (1904), *The Tragedies of Seneca*. London and New York.

Häuptli, B. (1983), *Senecas Oedipus*. Frauenfeld.

Heldmann, K. (1974), *Seneca: Oedipus*. Stuttgart.

Hermann, L. (1924–6), *Sénèque: Tragédies*. 2 vols. Paris.

Heywood, J. (1560), *Thyestes*. London. See Daalder (1982).

Hine, H. M. (2000), *Seneca: Medea*. Warminster.

Hirschberg, T. (1989), *Senecas Phoenissen: Einleitung und Kommentar*. Berlin and New York.

Hollis, A. S. (1977), *Ovid: Ars Amatoria Book I*. Oxford.

Hollis, A. S. (2007), *Fragments of Roman Poetry c. 60 BC–AD 20*. Oxford.

Housman, A. E. (1926), *M. Annaei Lucani Belli Ciuilis Libri Decem*. Oxford.

Jocelyn, H. D. (1967), *The Tragedies of Ennius*. Cambridge.

Kaster, R. A. (1995), *Suetonius: De Grammaticis et Rhetoribus*. New York.

Kaster, R. A., and Nussbaum, M. C. (2010), *Seneca: Anger, Mercy, Revenge*. Chicago, IL.

Kaufmann, H. (2006), *Dracontius: Romul 10 (Medea): Einleitung, Text, Übersetzung und Kommentar*. Heidelberg.

Keil, H. (1857–80), *Grammatici Latini*. 7 vols. Leipzig.

Kenney, E. J. (1996), *Ovid: Heroides XVI–XXI*. Cambridge.

Keulen, A. J. (2001), *L. Annaeus Seneca: Troades. Introduction, Text and Commentary*. Leiden.

Kingery, H. M. (1908), *Three Tragedies of Seneca: Hercules Furens, Troades, Medea*. New York (repr. Norman, OK, 1966).

Klotz, A. (1953), *Scaenicorum Romanorum Fragmenta: I. Tragicorum Fragmenta*, adiuuantibus O. Seel et L. Voit. Munich.

Knox, P. E. (1995), *Ovid Heroides: Select Epistles*. Cambridge.

Koestermann, E. (1963–8), *Cornelius Tacitus: Annalen*. 4 vols. Heidelberg.

Konstan, D. (2017), 'Hercules Mad', in Bartsch (2017): 2.51–103.

Krenkel, W. (1970), *Lucilius: Satiren*. 2 vols. Berlin.

Lamacchia, R. (1981), *Hosidius Geta: Medea: Cento Vergilianus*. Leipzig.

Lanzarone, N. (2008), *L. Annaei Senecae: Dialogorum Liber I De Prouidentia*. Florence.

Leo, F. (1878–9), *L. Annaei Senecae Tragoediae, accedit Octavia praetexta*. 2 vols. Berlin.

Liberman, G. (1998), *Pseudo-Sénèque Octavie*. Paris.

Lyne, R. O. A. M. (1978), *Ciris: A Poem Attributed to Vergil*. Cambridge.

Magno, P. (1977), *Marco Pacuvio: I frammenti*. Milan.

Maguinness, W. S. (1953), *Virgil: Aeneid XII*. London.

Manuwald, G. (2012), *Tragicorum Romanorum Fragmenta*, Vol. II. Göttingen.

Matthiae, A. (1828), *L. Annaei Seneca Medea et Troades, cum Annotationibus I. F. Gronouii*. Leipzig.

Megas, A. Ch. (1969), *Albertini Mussati Argumenta Tragoediarum Senecae: Commentarii in L. A. Senecae Tragoedias Fragmenta Nuper Reperta*. Salonica.

Middendorf, J. F. (1912), *Elegiae in Maecenatem*. Marburg.

Miller, F. J. (1917), *Seneca: Tragedies*. 2 vols. Cambridge, MA, and London.

Moricca, U. (1917–23), *L. Annaei Senecae Tragoediae*. Turin (2nd edn. 1947).

Mottershead, J. (1986), *Suetonius Claudius*. Bristol.

Müller, K. (1975), *T. Lucreti Cari De Rerum Natura Libri Sex*. Zurich.

Myers, K. S. (2009), *Ovid: Metamorphoses: Book XIV*. Cambridge.

Mynors, R. A. B. (1969), *P. Vergili Maronis Opera*. Oxford.

Mynors, R. A. B. (1990), *Virgil: Georgics*. Oxford.

Németi, A. (2003), *Lucio Anneo Seneca: Medea*. Pisa.

Nenci, F. (2002), *Lucio Anneo Seneca: Tieste*. Milan.

Newton, T. (1581), *Seneca: His Tenne Tragedies, Translated into Englysh*. London.

Nisbet, R. G. M., (1961), *Cicero: In L. Calpurnium Pisonem*. Oxford.

Nisbet, R. G. M., and Hubbard, M. (1970), *A Commentary on Horace: Odes, Book I*. Oxford.

Nisbet, R. G. M., and Hubbard, M. (1978), *A Commentary on Horace: Odes, Book II*. Oxford.

Nisbet, R. G. M., and Rudd, N. (2004), *A Commentary on Horace Odes Book III*. Oxford.

Orelli, J. K. von, and Giles, J. A. (1838), *Germanici Caesaris Reliquiae Quae Extant Omnes*. London.

Paduano, G. (1993), *Edipo*. Milan.

Panayotakis, C. (2010), *Decimus Laberius: The Fragments*. Cambridge.

Paratore, E. (2006), *Seneca: Tutte le tragedie*. Rome.

Pease, A. S. (1935), *Publi Vergili Maronis Aeneidos Liber Quartus*. Cambridge, MA.

Peiper, R., and Richter, G. (1867), *L. Annaei Senecae Tragoediae*. Leipzig. (2nd edn. Leipzig, 1902).

Pellegrino, C. (1975), *Petronii Arbitri Satyricon*. Rome.

Perutelli, A., and Paduano, G. (1995), *Lucio Anneo Seneca: Agamennone*. Milan.

Prato, C. (1964), *Gli Epigrammi attribuiti a L. Anneo Seneca*. Rome.

Reynolds, L. D. (1965), *L. Annaei Senecae Ad Lucilium Epistulae Morales*. 2 vols. Oxford.

Reynolds, L. D. (1977), *L. Annaei Senecae Dialogorum Libri Duodecim*. Oxford.

Ribbeck, O. (1897/8), *Scaenicae Romanorum Poesis Fragmenta*. 3rd edn. 2 vols. Leipzig.

Robinson, M. (2011), *A Commentary on Ovid's Fasti, Book 2*. Oxford.

Roche, P. (2009), *Lucan: De Bello Ciuili: Book I*. Oxford.

Roche, P. (2019), *Lucan: De Bello Ciuili: Book VII*. Cambridge.

Romano, V. (1951), *Giovanni Boccaccio: De Genealogia Deorum Gentilium Libri*. 2 vols. Bari.

Rossi, E. (1999), *La follia di Ercole*. Milan.

Rucker, N. (2016), *Tragicorum Romanorum Fragmenta*, Vol. III. Göttingen.

Rudd, N. (1989), *Horace: Epistles Book II and Epistle to the Pisones*. Cambridge.

Saint-Ravy, J. (1555), *Agamemnon*. Basle.

Schauer, M. (2012), *Tragicorum Romanorum Fragmenta*, Vol. I. Göttingen.

Scheid, J. (1998), *Commentarii Fratrum Arualium Qui Supersunt*. Rome.

Schenkl, C. (1867), *Orestis Tragoedia: Carmen Epicum*. Prague.

Schmeling, G. (2011), *A Commentary on the Satyrica of Petronius*. Oxford.

Schmidt, M. (1872), *Hygini Fabulae*. Jena.

Schoonhaven, H. (1992), *The Pseudo-Ovidian Ad Liviam De Morte Drusi*. Groningen.

Scott Smith, R. (2011), *Seneca: Phaedra and Other Plays*. London.

Scott Smith, R., and Trzaskoma, S. M. (2007), *Apollodorus' Library and Hyginus' Fabulae*. Indianapolis and Cambridge, MA.

Scriuerius, P. (1621*a*), *Collectanea Veterum Tragicorum*. Leiden.

Scriuerius, P. (1621*b*), *L. Annaeus Seneca Tragicus, Cum Variorum Notis*. Leiden.

Sedgwick, W. B. (1960), *Plautus Amphitruo*. Manchester.

Seel, O. (1972), *M. Iuniani Iustini Epitoma Historiarum Philippicarum Pompei Trogi*. Stuttgart.

Seidensticker, B., and Grünbein, D. (2002), *Seneca: Thyestes*. Frankfurt am Main.

Semi, F. (1965), *M. Terentius Varro: III*. Venice.

Shackleton Bailey, D. R. (1965–7), *Cicero's Letters to Atticus*. 6 vols. Cambridge.

Shackleton Bailey, D. R. (1977), *Cicero: Epistulae ad Familiares*. 2 vols. Cambridge.

Shackleton Bailey, D. R. (1982), *Anthologia Latina* I.1. Stuttgart.

Shackleton Bailey, D. R. (1990), *M. Valerii Martialis Epigrammata*. Stuttgart.

Shackleton Bailey, D. R. (1993), *Martial Epigrams*. 3 vols. Cambridge, MA, and London.

Share, D. (1998), *Seneca in English*. Harmondsworth.

Sherburne, E. (1701), *Tragedies of L. Annaeus Seneca the Philosopher*. London.

Skutsch, O. (1985), *The Annals of Q. Ennius*. Oxford.

Sluiter, Th. H. (1941), *L. Annaei Senecae Oedipus*. Groningen.

Smith, K. F. (1913), *The Elegies of Albius Tibullus*. New York.

Solomon, J. (2011), *Giovanni Boccaccio: Genealogy of the Pagan Gods*, Vol. I: *Books I–V*. Cambridge, MA.

Strzelecki, W. (1964), *Cn. Naevii Belli Punici Carminis Quae Supersunt*. Leipzig.

Summers, W. C. (1910), *Select Letters of Seneca*. London.

Sutton, D. F. (1998), *William Alabaster: Roxana*. Irvine, CA.

Sutton, D. F. (2003), *Thomas Legge: Richardus Tertius*. Irvine, CA.

Swoboda, A. (1889), *P. Nigidii Figuli Operum Reliquiae*. Vienna.

Tarrant, R. J. (1976), *Seneca: Agamemnon*. Cambridge.

Tarrant, R. J. (1985), *Seneca's Thyestes*. Atlanta, GA.

Tarrant, R. J. (2004), *P. Ovidi Nasonis Metamorphoses*. Oxford.

Tarrant, R. J. (2012), *Virgil Aeneid Book XII*. Cambridge.

Thomas, J. A. C. (1975), *The Institutes of Justinian*. Amsterdam and Oxford.

Thomas, R. F. (1988), *Vergil: The Georgics*. 2 vols. Cambridge.

Töchterle, K. (1994), *Lucius Annaeus Seneca: Oedipus*. Heidelberg.

Trevet, N. (1311–17), *Expositio Herculis Furentis*, ed. V. Ussani, Jr. (1959). Rome.

Ullman, B. L., ed. (1951), *Colucii Salutati De Laboribus Herculis*. Zurich.

Vahlen, J. (1928), *Ennianae Poiesis Reliquiae*. 3rd edn. Leipzig.

Viansino, G. (1965), *L. Annaei Senecae Tragoediae*. Turin.

Viansino, G. (1993), *Seneca: Teatro*. 2 vols. Rome.

Vollmer, F. (1913), *Poetae Latini Minores II.3: Homerus Latinus*. Leipzig.

Vottero, D. (1998), *Lucio Anneo Seneca: I frammenti*. Bologna.

Wakefield, G. (1796–7), *T. Lucretii C. De Rerum Natura*. London.

Warmington, B. H. (1977), *Suetonius: Nero*. Bristol.

Warmington, E. H. (1935–8), *Remains of Old Latin*. Vols. 1–3. Cambridge, MA, and London.

Watling, E. F. (1966), *Seneca: Four Tragedies and Octavia*. Harmondsworth.

Wellesley, K. (1986), *Cornelius Tacitus: Annales XI–XVI*. Leipzig.

Wellesley, K. (1989), *Cornelius Tacitus: Historiae*. Leipzig.

Whitton, C. (2013), *Pliny the Younger: Epistles Book II*. Cambridge.

Williams, G. D. (2003), *Seneca: De Otio, De Breuitate Vitae*. Cambridge.

Wilson, E. (2010), *Seneca: Six Tragedies*. Oxford.

Woelfflin, E. (1869), *Publilii Syri Sententiae*. Leipzig.

Zissos, A. (2008), *Valerius Flaccus' Argonautica, Book I: A Commentary*. Oxford.

Zwierlein, O. (1986a), *L. Annaei Senecae Tragoediae*. Oxford.

2. Other Texts and Works of Reference and Criticism

Abel, L. (1963), *Metatheater*. New York.

Adams, J. N. (1982), *The Latin Sexual Vocabulary*. London.

Ahl, F. M. (1984a), 'The Art of Safe Criticism in Greece and Rome', *AJP* 105: 174–208.

Ahl, F. M. (1984*b*), 'The Rider and the Horse', *ANRW* II.32.1: 40–124.
Ahl, F. M. (1985), *Metaformations: Soundplay and Wordplay in Ovid and Other Classical Poets*. Ithaca, NY.
Albrecht, M. von, (2014), 'Seneca's Language and Style', in Damschen and Heil (2014): 699–744.
Alcock, S. E. (1994), 'Nero at Play? The Emperor's Grecian Odyssey', in Elsner and Masters (1994): 98–111.
Aldrete, G. S. (1999), *Gestures and Acclamations in Ancient Rome*. Baltimore, MD, and London.
Algra, K., Barnes, J., Mansfield, J., and Schofield, M. (1999), *The Cambridge History of Hellenistic Philosophy*. Cambridge.
Allen, D. C., ed. (1946), *Essayes by Sir William Cornwallis the Younger*. Baltimore, MD.
Allendorf, T. S. (2013), 'The Poetics of Uncertainty in Senecan Drama', *MD* 71: 103–44.
Allendorf, T. S. (2017), 'Sounds and Space: Seneca's Horatian Lyrics', in Stöckinger et al. (2017): 137–58.
Allison, W. T. (1911), *The Tenure of Kings and Magistrates by John Milton*. New York.
Altman, J. B. (1978), *The Tudor Play of Mind: Rhetorical Inquiry and the Development of Elizabethan Drama*. Berkeley, CA.
Amoroso, F. (1984), *Seneca uomo di teatro? Le Troiane e lo spettacolo*. Palermo.
Amoroso, F., ed. (2006), *Teatralità dei cori senecani*. Palermo.
André, J.-M. (1966), *L'Otium dans la vie morale et intellectuelle romaine des origines à l'époque augustéenne*. Paris.
Andreae, B. (1978), *The Art of Rome*. London.
Anliker, K. (1960), *Prologe und Akteinteilung in Senecas Tragödien*. Berne.
Anliker, K. (1972), Above 98–101, 122–3, in Lefèvre (1972*a*): 450–6.
Annas, J. (1994), *Hellenistic Philosophy of Mind*. Berkeley, CA.
Argenio, R. (1961), 'Retorica e politica nelle tragedie di Accio', *RSC* 9: 198–212.
Aricò, G. (1981), 'Seneca e la tragedia latina arcaica', *Dioniso* 52: 339–56.
Aricò, G., and Rivoltella, eds. (2008), *La riflessione sul teatro nella cultura romana*, Milan.
Armisen-Marchetti, M. (1989), *Sapientiae facies: Étude sur les images de Sénèque*. Paris.
Armitage, S. (2000), *Mister Hercules*. London.
Arnim, H. F. von (1903–24), *Stoicorum Veterum Fragmenta*, 4 vols. Leipzig.
Arnott, W. G. (1979–2000), *Menander*. 3 vols. Cambridge, MA.
Artaud, A. (1956), *Collected Works*, ed. and trans. V. Corti. London.
Artaud, A. (1961), *Oeuvres complètes*. 3 vols. Paris.
Artaud, A. (1969), *The Cenci*. (trans. S. Watson-Taylor). London.
Artaud, A. (1972), *Collected Works*, Vol. III (trans. A. Hamilton). London.
Asmis, E. (2008), 'Lucretius' New World Order: Making a Pact with Nature', *CQ* NS 58: 141–57.
Asmis, E. (2009), 'Seneca on Fortune and the Kingdom of God', in Bartsch and Wray (2009): 115–38.
Axelson, B. (1945), *Unpoetische Wörter*. Lund.
Axelson, B. (1986), 'Emendations and Conjectures', in Zwierlein (1986*a*).

Aygon, J.-P. (2004), *Pictor in fabula: L'Ecphrasis-descriptio dans les tragédies de Sénèque*. Brussels.

Aygon, J.-P., ed. (2014), *Sénèque, un philosophe homme de théâtre? Pallas 95*. Toulouse.

Aygon, J.-P. (2016), *Ut scaena, sic vita: Mise en scène et dévoilement dans les oeuvres philosophiques et dramatiques de Sénèque*. Paris.

Ayres, P. J. (1990), *Ben Jonson: Sejanus His Fall*. Manchester and New York.

Backhaus, M. (2019), *Mord(s)bilder-Aufzählungen von Gewalt bei Seneca und Lucan*. Berlin and Boston, MA.

Baehrens, E. (1878), *Miscellanea critica*. Groningen.

Baertschi, A. M. (2010), 'Drama and Epic Narrative: The Test Case of Messenger Speech in Seneca's *Agamemnon*', in Gildenhard and Rivermann (2010): 243–63.

Baertschi, A. M. (2015), 'Epic Elements in Senecan Tragedy', in Harrison (2015): 171–95.

Bagnall, R. S., and Harris, W. V., eds. (1986), *Studies in Roman Law in Memory of A. Arthur Schiller*. New York.

Bailey, C. (1926), *Epicurus: The Extant Remains*. Oxford.

Bain, D. (1977), *Actors and Audience*. Oxford.

Bannert, H., and Divjak, J., eds. (1977), *Latinität und Alte Kirche: Festschrift für R. Hanslik zum 70. Geburtstag*. Vienna.

Bañuls, J. V., de Martino, F., and Morenilla, C., eds. (2008), *El teatro clásico en el marco de la cultura griega y su pervivencia en la cultura occidental 11*. Bari.

Barchiesi, A. (1993), 'Future Reflexive: Two Modes of Allusion and Ovid's *Heroides*', *HSCP* 95: 333–65.

Barchiesi, A. (2009), 'Exemplarity: Between Practice and Text', in Maes, Papy, and Verbaal (2009): 41–62.

Barlow, S. (1996), *Euripides' Heracles*. Warminster.

Barrett, A. A. (1989), *Caligula: The Corruption of Power*. London.

Barrett, A. A. (1996), *Agrippina: Mother of Nero*. London.

Barton, C. (1993), *The Sorrows of the Ancient Romans*. Princeton, NJ.

Bartsch, S. (1994), *Actors in the Audience: Theatricality and Doublespeak from Nero to Hadrian*. Cambridge, MA.

Bartsch, S. (2006), *The Mirror of the Self: Sexuality, Self-Knowledge and the Gaze in the Early Roman Empire*. Chicago, IL.

Bartsch, S., and Schiesaro, A., eds. (2015), *The Cambridge Companion to Seneca*. Cambridge.

Bartsch, S., and Wray, D., eds. (2009), *Seneca and the Self*. Cambridge.

Bate, J. (1993), *Shakespeare and Ovid*. Oxford.

Bate, J., ed. (1995), *Shakespeare: Titus Andronicus*. London.

Battistella, C. (2017), 'The Ambiguous *Virtus* of Seneca's Medea', *Maia* 69: 268–80.

Bauman, R. A. (1996), *Crime and Punishment in Ancient Rome*. London.

Beacham R. C. (1992), *The Roman Theatre and its Audience*. Cambridge, MA.

Beacham R. C. (1999), *Spectacle Entertainments of Early Imperial Rome*. New Haven, CT.

Beard, M., North, J., and Price, S. (1998), *Religions of Rome*. 2 vols. Cambridge.

Beare, W. (1964), *The Roman Stage*. 3rd rev. edn. London.

Becker, L. (1998), *A New Stoicism*. Princeton, NJ.

Becker, L. (2004), 'Stoic Emotion', in Strange and Jupko (2004): 250–75.

Bentley, R. (1899), 'Adnotationes ad Senecae Tragoedias', in Hedicke (1899): 9ff.

Berman, D. W. (2015), *Myth, Literature, and the Creation of the Topography of Thebes*. Cambridge.

Bernabò-Brea, L. (1998), *Le maschere ellenistiche della tragedia greca*. Naples.

Berno, F. R. (2004), 'Un *truncus*: Molti re: Priamo, Agamennone, Pompeo (Virgilio, Seneca, Lucano)', *Maia* 56: 79–84.

Bernstein, F. (1998), *Ludi Publici: Untersuchungen zur Entstehung und Entwicklung der öffentlichen Spiele im republikanischen Rom*. Stuttgart.

Bernstein, N. (2017), *Seneca: Hercules Furens*. London and New York.

Betteridge, T., and Walker, G., eds. (2012), *The Oxford Handbook of Tudor Drama*. Oxford.

Bettini, M. (1991), *Anthropology and Roman Culture*, tr. J. Van Sickle. Baltimore, MD.

Betts, J. H., Hooker, J. T., and Green, J. R., eds. (1986), *Studies in Honour of T.B.L. Webster*. Bristol.

Bexley, E. (2015), 'What is Dramatic Recitation?', *Mnem.* 68: 1–20.

Bexley, E. (2022), *Seneca's Characters: Fictional Identities and Implied Human Selves*. Cambridge.

Bieber, M. (1961), *The History of the Greek and Roman Theater*. Princeton, NJ.

Bierl, A., and Möllendorf, P. von, eds. (1994), *Orchestra: Drama Mythos Bühne: Festschrift für Hellmut Flashar*. Stuttgart.

Biliński, B. (1957), *Accio ed i Gracchi: Contributo alla storia delle plebe e delle tragedia romana*. Rome.

Billerbeck, M. (1988), *Senecas Tragödien: Sprachliche und stilistiche Untersuchungen*. Leiden.

Billerbeck, M. (1999*b*), 'Apostrophes de rôles muets et changements implicites d'interlocuteur: Deux observations sur l'art dramatique de Sénèque', *Pallas* 49: 101–10.

Billerbeck, M. (2014), 'Hercules Furens', in Damschen and Heil (2014): 425–33.

Billerbeck, M., and Schmidt, E. A. (2004), *Sénèque le Tragique: Entretiens Fondation Hardt* 50. Geneva.

Billerbeck, M., and Somazzi, M. (2009), *Repertorium der Konjecturen in den Seneca-Tragödien*. Leiden.

Billings, J., Budelmann, F., and MacIntosh, F., eds. (2013), *Choruses, Ancient and Modern*. Oxford.

Binns, J. W. (1974), 'Seneca and Neo-Latin Tragedy in England', in Costa (1974*a*): 215–24.

Binns, J. W., ed. (1981), *Renaissance Latin Drama in England*. Hildesheim and New York.

Bishop, J. D. (1964), 'The Choral Odes of Seneca: Theme and Development', Diss. University of Pennsylvia. Philadelphia.

Bishop, J. D. (1966), 'Seneca's *Hercules Furens*: Tragedy from *Modus Vitae*', *C&M* 27: 216–24.

Bishop, J. D. (1968), 'The Meaning of the Choral Meters in Senecan Tragedy', *RhM* 111: 197–219.

Bishop, J. D. (1985), *Seneca's Daggered Stylus*. Königstein.

Blänsdorf, J., ed. (1990), *Theater und Gesellschaft im Imperium Romanum*. Tübingen.

Blänsdorf, J. (2008), 'Accius als Vorläufer Senecas', in Castagna and Riboldi (2008): 177–93.

Blanshard, A. (2005), *Hercules: A Heroic Life*. London.

Blanshard, A. and Stafford, E., eds. (2020), *The Modern Hercules: Images of the Hero from the Nineteenth to the Early Twenty-First Century*. Leiden and Boston, MA.

Bloom, H. (1973), *The Anxiety of Influence: A Theory of Poetry*. Oxford.

Bloomer, W. M. (1997), 'Schooling in *Persona*: Imagination and Subordination in Roman Education', *CA* 16: 57–78.

Boardman, J. (1989), *Athenian Red Figure Vases: The Classical Period*. London.

Boardman, J. et al. (1988), 'Herakles', *LIMC* IV.1: 728–838. Zurich.

Boardman, J. (1990), 'Herakles', *LIMC* V.1: 1–92. Zurich.

Boas, F. S. (1914), *University Drama in the Tudor Age*. Oxford.

Boas, F. S. (1932), 'University Plays', in A. W. Ward and A. R. Walker, eds., *The Cambridge History of English Literature*, VI: 293–327. Cambridge.

Bobonich, C., ed. (2017), *The Cambridge Companion to Ancient Ethics*. Cambridge.

Bobzien, S. (1998), *Determinism and Freedom in Stoic Philosophy*. Oxford.

Bond, G. (1981), *Euripides: Heracles*. Oxford.

Bonelli, G. (1978), 'Il carattere retorico delle tragedie di Seneca', *Latomus* 37: 395–418.

Bonelli, G. (1980), 'Autenticà o retorica nella tragedia di Seneca?', *Latomus* 39: 612–38.

Bonner, S. F. (1949), *Roman Declamation*. Liverpool.

Bonnet, C., and Jourdain-Annequin, C., eds. (1992), *Heraclès: D'une rive à l'autre de la Méditerranée*. Paris.

Booth, S. (1983), *King Lear, Macbeth, Indefinition, and Tragedy*. New Haven, CT.

Bowers, F. B. (1940), *Elizabethan Revenge Tragedy*. Princeton, NJ.

Bowersock, G., Burkert, W., and Putnam, M. C. J., eds. (1979), *Arktouros: Hellenic Studies Presented to B. M. W. Knox*. Berlin and New York.

Bowman, A. K., Garnsey, P., and Rathbone, D., eds. (2000), *Cambridge Ancient History XI: The High Empire AD 70–192*. 2nd edn. Cambridge.

Boyle, A. J., ed. (1983a), *Seneca Tragicus: Ramus Essays on Senecan Drama*. Berwick, Vic.

Boyle, A. J. (1983b), '*Hic Epulis Locus*: The Tragic Worlds of Seneca's *Agamemnon* and *Thyestes*', in Boyle (1983a): 199–228.

Boyle, A. J. (1985), 'In Nature's Bonds: A Study of Seneca's *Phaedra*', *ANRW* II.32.2: 1284–1347.

Boyle, A. J., ed. (1988a), *The Imperial Muse I: To Juvenal Through Ovid*. Berwick, Vic.

Boyle, A. J. (1988b), 'Senecan Tragedy: Twelve Propositions', in Boyle (1988a): 78–101.

Boyle, A. J., ed. (1993), *Roman Epic*. London.

Boyle, A. J. (1997), *Tragic Seneca: An Essay in the Theatrical Tradition*. London.

Boyle, A. J. (1999), '*Aeneid* 8: Images of Rome', in Perkell (1999): 148–61.

Boyle, A. J. (2003a), 'Introduction: Reading Flavian Rome', in Boyle and Dominik (2003): 1–67.

Boyle, A. J. (2003b), *Ovid and the Monuments: A Poet's Rome*. Bendigo, Vic.

Boyle, A. J. (2006), *Roman Tragedy*. London.

Boyle, A. J., and Dominik, W. J., eds. (2003), *Flavian Rome: Culture, Image, Text*. Leiden.

Boyle, A. J., and Sullivan, J. P., eds. (1991), *Roman Poets of the Early Empire*. Harmondsworth.

Braden, G. (1970), 'The Rhetoric and Psychology of Power in the Dramas of Seneca', *Arion* 9: 5–41.

Braden, G. (1984), 'Senecan Tragedy and the Renaissance', *ICS* 9: 277–92.

Braden, G. (1985), *Renaissance Tragedy and the Senecan Tradition: Anger's Privilege*. New Haven, CT.

Braden, G. (1993), 'Heracles and Hercules: Survival in Greek and Roman Tragedy (with a coda on *King Lear*)', in Scodel (1993): 245–64.

Braginton, M. V. (1933), *The Supernatural in Seneca's Tragedies*. Providence, RI.

Brandt, J. (1986), *Argumentative Struktur in Senecas Tragödien: Eine Untersuchung anhand der Phaedra und des Agamemnon*, Hildesheim.

Braun, L. (1982), 'Sind Senecas Tragödien Bühnenstücke oder Rezitationsdramen?', *Res Publica Litterarum* 5: 43–52.

Braund, D., and Gill, C., eds. (2003), *Myth, History and Culture in Republican Rome: Studies in Honour of T. P. Wiseman*. Exeter.

Braund, S. M. (2013), 'Haunted by Horror: The Ghost of Seneca in Renaissance Drama', in Buckley and Dintner (2013): 425–43.

Braund, S. M., and Gill, C., eds. (1997), *The Passions in Roman Thought and Literature*. Cambridge.

Braund, S. M., and Most, G. W., eds. (2003), *Ancient Anger: Perspectives from Homer to Galen*. Cambridge.

Braunmuller, A. R., and Hattaway, M., eds. (1990), *The Cambridge Companion to English Renaissance Drama*. Cambridge.

Bremer, J. M., Radt, S. L., Ruijgh, C. J. (1976), *Miscellanea Tragica in honour of Kamerbeek*. Amsterdam.

Bremmer, J., and Roodenburg, H., eds. (1991), *A Cultural History of Gesture from Antiquity to the Present Day*. Oxford.

Brommer, F. (1972), *Herakles: Die zwölf Taten des Helden in der antiken Kunst und Literatur*. Darmstadt.

Brooks, H. F. (1980), '*Richard III*: Unhistorical Amplifications: The Women's Scenes and Seneca', *MLR* 75: 721–37.

Brooks, L. M., ed. (1995), *Alternative Identities: The Self in Literature, History, Theory*. New York.

Brooks, P. (1976), *The Melodramatic Imagination*. New Haven, CT.

Brooks, R. A. (1981), *Ennius and Roman Tragedy*. New York.

Broughton, T. R. S. (1951–60), *The Magistrates of the Roman Republic*. 3 vols. New York.

Brower, R. A. (1971), *Hero and Saint: Shakespeare and the Graeco-Roman Heroic Tradition*. Oxford.

Brown, J. P. (1964), *John Webster: The Duchess of Malfi*. London.

Brown, P., and Ograjenšek, S., eds. (2010), *Ancient Drama in Music for the Modern Stage*. Oxford.

Brown, P. G. McC. (2002), 'Actors and Actor-Managers at Rome', in Easterling and Hall (2002): 225–37.

Brunschwig, J., and Nussbaum, M., eds. (1993), *Passions and Perceptions: Studies in Hellenistic Philosophy of Mind*. Cambridge.

Bücheler, F. (1915 and 1927), *Kleine Schriften*. 2 vols. Leipzig and Berlin.

Buckley, E. (2014), 'Valerius Flaccus and Seneca's Tragedies', in Heerink and Manuwald (2014): 307–25.

Buckley, E., and Dintner, M., eds. (2013), *A Companion to the Neronian Age*. Chichester.

Bullen, A. H. (1887), *The Works of John Marston*, Vol. 3. London.

Bullough, G. (1957–75), *Narrative and Dramatic Sources of Shakespeare*. 8 vols. London.

Bullough, G. (1964), 'Sénèque, Greville et le jeune Shakespeare', in Jacquot (1964): 189–201.

Burck, E. (1971), *Vom römischen Manierismus*. Darmstadt.

Burke, E. (1998), *A Philosophical Enquiry into the Sublime and the Beautiful*, ed. D. Womersley. London (orig. publ. 1757).

Burkert, W. (1979), *Structure and History in Greek Mythology and Ritual*. Berkeley, CA, and Los Angeles, CA.

Burkert, W. (1983), *Homo Necans: The Anthropology of Ancient Greek Sacrificial Ritual and Myth*. Berkeley, CA, and Los Angeles, CA.

Burkitt, I. (1994), 'The Shifting Concept of the Self', *Hist. Hum. Sci.* 7: 7–28.

Burnett, A. P. (1998), *Revenge in Attic and Later Tragedy*. Berkeley, CA.

Burrow, C. (2013), *Shakespeare and Classical Antiquity*. Oxford.

Burton, R. W. B. (1980), *The Chorus in Sophocles' Tragedies*. Oxford.

Busa, R., and Zampolli, A. (1975), *Concordantiae Senecanae*. Hildesheim.

Bussotti, S. (2000), *Tieste*: see Camerini (2000).

Butler, S. (2015), *The Ancient Phonograph*. New York.

Cairns, D., ed. (2005), *Body Language in the Greek and Roman Worlds*. Swansea.

Cairns, D. (2011), 'Veiling Grief on the Tragic Stage', in Munteanu (2011): 15–33.

Cairns, F., ed. (1990), *Papers of the Leeds International Latin Seminar 6*. Leeds.

Calabrese, E. (2017), *Aspetti dell' identità relazionale nella tragedie di Seneca*. Bologna.

Calder, W. M. (1975), 'The Size of the Chorus in Seneca's *Agamemnon*', *CP* 70: 32–5.

Calder, W. M. (1976/7), 'Seneca, Tragedian of Imperial Rome', *CJ* 72: 1–11.

Calder, W. M. (1983), '*Secreti loquimur*: An Interpretation of Seneca's *Thyestes*', in Boyle (1983a): 184–98.

Camerini, S., ed. (2000), *Tieste di Sylvano Bussotti*. Ancona.

Cameron, K. N., and Frenz, H. (1945), 'The Stage History of Shelley's *The Cenci*', *PMLA* 60: 1080–1105.

Campbell, D. A. (1990–3), *Greek Lyric*. 5 vols. Cambridge, MA, and London.

Canter, H. V. (1925), *The Rhetorical Elements in the Tragedies of Seneca*. Urbana, IL.

Carandini, A. (2008), *La casa di Augusto: Dai 'Lupercalia' al Natale*. Rome and Bari.

Carlsen, J. (2006), *The Rise and Fall of a Roman Noble Family: The Domitii Ahenobarbi 196 BC–AD 68*. Odense.

Carlson, M. (2003), *The Haunted Stage: The Theatre as Memory Machine*. Ann Arbor, MI.

Carlsson, G. (1929), *Zu Senecas Tragödien*. Lund.

Carson, A. (2021), *H of H Playbook*. New York.

Castagna, L., ed. (1996), *Nove studi sui cori tragici di Seneca*. Milan.
Castagna, L., and Riboldi, C., eds. (2008), *Amicitiae templa serena: Studi in onore di G. Aricò*. Milan.
Castagna, L., and Vogt-Spira, G., eds. (2002), *Pervertere: Ästhetik der Verkehrung: Literatur und Kultur neronischer Zeit und ihre Rezeption*. Munich and Leipzig.
Castiglioni, L. (1926), 'La tragedia di Ercole in Euripide ed in Seneca', *RFIC* 54: 176–97, 336–62.
Cattin, A. (1963a), *Les Thèmes lyriques dans les tragédies de Sénèque*. Neuchâtel.
Cattin, A. (1963b), 'La Géographie dans les tragédies de Sénèque', *Latomus* 22: 685–703.
Cauthen, I. B., Jr. (1970), *Sackville and Norton: Gorboduc, or, Ferrex and Porrex*. Lincoln, NE.
Cave, T. (1988), *Recognitions: A Study in Poetics*. Oxford.
Champlin, E. (2003), *Nero*. Cambridge, MA.
Charlton, H. B. (1946), *The Senecan Tradition in Renaissance Tragedy*. Manchester.
Chaudhuri, P. (2014), *The War with God: Theomachy in Roman Imperial Poetry*. Oxford.
Chaumartin, F.-R. (2002), 'Octavie, une oeuvre à la croisée de divers chemins', *SO* 76: 57–60.
Chaumartin, F.-R. (2014), 'Philosophical Tragedy', in Damschen and Heil (2014): 653–69.
Chevallier, R., and Poignault R., eds. (1991), *Présence de Sénèque*. Paris.
Cinthio: see Crocetti (1973).
Citti, F., and Neri, C. (2001), *Seneca nel Novecento: Sondaggi sulla fortuna di un 'classico'*. Rome.
Cizek, E. (1972), *L'Époque de Néron et ses controverses idéologiques*. Leiden.
Claridge, A. (1998), *Rome: An Oxford Archaeological Guide*. Oxford.
Clemen, W. (1961), *English Tragedy before Shakespeare: The Development of Dramatic Speech*, tr. T. S. Dorsch. London.
Coarelli, F. (2007), *Rome and its Environs: An Archaeological Guide*. Berkeley, CA, and Los Angeles, CA.
Coffey, M. (1957), 'Seneca Tragedies: Report for the Years 1922–1955', *Lustrum* 2: 113–86.
Coffey, M. (1960), 'Seneca and his Tragedies', *PACA* 3: 14–20.
Coffey, M. (1986), 'Notes on the History of Augustan and Early Imperial Tragedy', in Betts, Hooker, and Green (1986): 46–52.
Cohen, J. J., ed. (1996a), *Monster Theory: Reading Culture*. Minneapolis, MN.
Cohen, J. J. (1996b), 'Monster Culture (Seven Theses)', in Cohen (1996a): 3–25.
Coleman, K. M. (1990), 'Fatal Charades: Roman Executions Staged as Mythical Enactments', *JRS* 80: 44–73.
Coles, R. A. (1968), 'A New Fragment of Post-Classical Tragedy from Oxyrhynchus', *BICS* 15: 110–18.
Colie, R. (1966), *Paradoxia Epidemica*. Princeton, NJ.
Collard, C., and Cropp, M. (2008a), *Euripides VII: Fragments*. Cambridge, MA and London.
Collard, C., and Cropp, M. (2008b), *Euripides VIII: Fragments*. Cambridge, MA and London.
Conte, G. B. (1994), *Latin Literature: A History*. Baltimore, MD, and London.
Corbeill, A. (2004), *Nature Embodied: Gesture in Ancient Rome*. Princeton, NJ.

Corneille, P. (1980), *Oeuvres complètes* (ed. G. Couton). 3 vols. Paris.

Cornelissen, J. J. (1877), 'Ad Senecae Tragoedias', *Mnem.* 5.2: 175–87.

Cornwallis, Sir William the Younger (1601), *Discourses upon Seneca the Trage-dian*. London.

Correr, G. (1426/7), *Progne*: see Grund (2011).

Costa, C. D. N., ed. (1974*a*), *Seneca*. London.

Costa, C. D. N. (1974*b*), 'The Tragedies', in Costa (1974*a*): 96–115.

Costa, S. (2013), '*Quod olim fuerat*': *La rappresentazione del passato in Seneca prosa-tore*. Hildesheim.

Coulter, C. C. (1940), 'Marcus Junius Brutus and the *Brutus* of Accius', *CJ* 35: 460–70.

Courtney, E. (1985), 'Emendations in Seneca's Tragedies', *RFIC* 113: 297–302.

Courtois, C. (1989), *Le Bâtiment de scène des théâtres d'Italie et de Sicile*. Providence, RI, and Louvain-la-Neuve.

Couton, G. (1987), *Pierre Corneille: Oeuvres completes*, Vol. 3. Paris.

Cova, P. V. (1989), *Il poeta Vario*. Milan.

Cowan, R. (2009), 'Starring Nero as Nero', *Mnem.* 62: 76–89.

Cowan, R. (2017), 'Bloated Buskins: Seneca and the Satiric Idea of Tragedy', in Trin-acty and Sampson (2017*a*): 75–117.

Craik, E. (1988), *Euripides: Phoenician Women*. Warminster.

Crimp, M. (2004), *Cruel and Tender*. London.

Crocetti, C. G. (1973), *Giambattista Cinthio Giraldi: Scritti critici*. Milan.

Croisille, J.-M. (1982), *Poésie et art figuré de Néron aux Flaviens: Recherches sur l'iconographie et la correspondance des arts à l'époque impériale*. Brussels.

Croisille, J.-M., and Perrin, Y., eds. (2002), *Neronia VI: Rome à l'époque néronienne*. Brussels.

Crook, J. A. (1967), *Law and Life of Rome: 90 BC—AD 212*. Ithaca, NY.

Crook, J. A., Lintott, A., and Rawson, E., eds. (1994), *The Cambridge Ancient History: IX. The Last Age of Roman Republic: 146–43 BC* 2nd edn. Cambridge.

Csapo, E. (1999), 'Performance and Iconographic Tradition in the Illustrations of Menander', in Porter et al. (1999): 154–88.

Csapo, E., and Slater, W. J. (1995), *The Context of Ancient Drama*. Ann Arbor, MI.

Čulík-Baird, H. (2022), *Cicero and the Early Latin Poets*. Cambridge.

Cunliffe, J. W. (1893), *The Influence of Seneca on Elizabethan Tragedy*. London (repr. New York 1965).

Cunliffe, J. W. (1912), *Early English Classical Tragedies*. Oxford.

Cunningham, J. S. (1981), *Christopher Marlowe: Tamburlaine the Great*. Manchester and Baltimore, MD.

Curley, D. (2013), *Tragedy in Ovid: Theater, Metatheater, and the Transformation of a Genre*. Cambridge.

Curley, T. F. (1986), *The Nature of Senecan Drama*. Rome.

Currie, H. MacL. (1981), 'Ovid and the Roman Stage', *ANRW* II.31.4: 2701–42.

Curtis, L. (2017), *Imagining the Chorus in Augustan Poetry*. Cambridge.

Curtius, E. R. (1953), *European Literature and the Latin Middle Ages*. New York.

Dalby, A. (1996), *Siren Feasts: A History of Food and Gastronomy in Greece*. London and New York.

Dalfen, J. et al., eds. (1993), *Romana: Festschrift für Walter Pötscher*. Graz.

Damschen, G., and Heil, A., eds. (2014), *Brill's Companion to Seneca: Philosopher and Dramatist*. Leiden.

Damsté, P. H. (1919), 'Ad Senecae Agamemnon', *Mnem.* II 47: 111–15.

Davies, M. (1988), *Epicorum Graecorum Fragmenta*. Göttingen.

Davies, M. (1991), *Poetarum Melicorum Graecorum Fragmenta*. Oxford.

Davis, P. J. (1989), 'The Chorus in Seneca's *Thyestes*', *CQ* NS 39: 421–35.

Davis, P. J. (1993), *Shifting Song: The Chorus in Seneca's Tragedies*. Hildesheim.

Davis, P. J. (2016), 'Senecan Tragedy and the Politics of Flavian Literature', in Dodson-Robinson (2016): 57–74.

Davis, T. C., and Postlewait, T., eds. (2003), *Theatricality*. Cambridge.

Day, H. J. M. (2013), *Lucan and the Sublime: Power, Representation and Aesthetic Experience*. Cambridge.

Defosse, P., ed. (2002), *Hommages à Carl Deroux* I. Brussels.

Degrassi, A. (1963), *Inscriptiones Italiae*. 13.2. Rome.

Dehon, P. (1992), 'Senecana', *AC* 61: 255–9.

Delarue, F. (1985), 'Le *Thyeste* de Varius', in Renard and Laurens (1985): 100–23.

Delz, J. (1989), 'Textkritisches zu den Tragödien Senecas', *MH* 46: 52–62.

Denooz, J. (1980), *Lucius Annaeus Seneca: Tragoediae Index Verborum*. Hildesheim.

Depew, M., and Obbink, D., eds. (2000), *Matrices of Genre: Authors, Canons and Society*. Cambridge.

Deroux, C., ed. (1989), *Studies in Latin Literature and Roman History*. Brussels.

Derrida, J. (1987), *The Post Card: From Socrates to Freud and Beyond*. Chicago, IL.

Descroix, J. (1948–9), 'Les Travaux d'Hercule dan l'*Hercule furieux* de Sénèque', *Humanitas* 2: 299–303.

Dessau, H. (1892–1916), *Inscriptiones Latinae Selectae*. 3 vols. Berlin (repr. 5 vols. Chicago, IL, 1979–80).

Detienne, M. (1972), *Les Jardins d'Adonis*. Paris.

Dickey, E. (1996), *Greek Forms of Address: From Herodotus to Lucian*. Oxford.

Dickey, E. (2002), *Latin Forms of Address: From Plautus to Apuleius*. Oxford.

Diels, H., and Kranz, W. (1952), *Die Fragmente der Vorsokratiker*. 3 vols. 6th edn. Zurich.

Dingel, J. (1974), *Seneca und die Dichtung*. Heidelberg.

Dingel, J. (1985), 'Senecas Tragödien: Vorbilder und poetische Aspekte', *ANRW* II. 32.2: 1052–99.

Dittenberger, W. (1915–24), *Sylloge Inscriptionum Graecarum*. 3rd edn. Leipzig.

Dodds, E. R. (1960), *Euripides: Bacchae*. 2nd edn. Oxford.

Dodson-Robinson, E., ed. (2016), *Brill's Companion to the Reception of Senecan Tragedy: Scholarly, Theatrical and Literary Receptions*. Leiden.

Dollimore, J. (1984), *Radical Tragedy*. Chicago, IL.

Dominik, W. (1997), *Roman Eloquence: Rhetoric in Society and Literature*. London.

Dominik, W., and Hall, J., eds. (2007), *A Companion to Roman Rhetoric*. Malden, MA.

Doran, M. (1954), *Endeavours of Art: A Study of Form in Elizabethan Drama*. Madison, WI.

Dorey, T. A., and Dudley, D. R., eds. (1965), *Roman Drama*. London.

Dowd, J. (1995), 'The Theatrical Self: Aporias of the Self', in Brooks (1995): 245–66.

Duckworth, G. E. (1952), *The Nature of Roman Comedy: A Study in Popular Enter-tainment.* Princeton, NJ.

Ducos, M. (1990), 'La Condition des acteurs à Rome', in Blänsdorf (1990): 19–33.

Dunbabin, K. M. D. (2006), 'A Theatrical Device on the Late Roman Stage: The Relief of Flavius Valerianus', *JRA* 19: 191–212.

Dunn, F. M. (1997), 'Ends and Means in Euripides' *Heracles*', in Roberts et al. (1997): 83–111.

Dupont, F. (1985), *L'Acteur-roi: Le Théâtre dans la Rome antique.* Paris.

Dupont, F. (1988), *Le Théâtre latin.* Paris.

Dupont, F. (1995), *Les Monstres de Sénèque.* Paris.

Dupont, F. et al., eds. (1997), *L'Humain et l'inhumain.* Paris.

Düring, T. (1914), see Hoffa.

Durkheim, E. (1897), *Le Suicide: Étude de sociologie.* Paris.

Düsing, W., ed. (1998), *Aspekte des Geschichtsdramas: Von Aischylos bis Volker Braun.* Tübingen and Basle.

Eagleton, T. (2002), *Sweet Violence: The Idea of the Tragic.* Oxford.

Earl, D. E. (1967), *The Moral and Political Tradition of Rome.* Ithaca, NY.

Easterling, P. E. (1982), *Sophocles: Trachiniae.* Cambridge.

Easterling, P. E. (1993), 'Gods on Stage in Greek Tragedy', in Dalfen et al. (1993): 77–86.

Easterling, P. E., ed. (1997), *The Cambridge Companion to Greek Tragedy.* Cambridge.

Easterling, P. E., and Hall, E., eds. (2002), *Greek and Roman Actors: Aspects of an Ancient Profession.* Cambridge.

Eck, W. (1993), *Agrippina, die Stadtgründerin Kölns: Eine Frau in der frühkaiser-zeitlichen Politik.* Cologne.

Edert. O. (1909), *Über Senecas Herakles und den Herakles auf dem Oeta.* Diss. University of Kiel.

Edmondson, J., and Keith, A., eds. (2008), *Roman Dress and the Fabrics of Roman Culture.* Toronto.

Edwards, C. (1993), *The Politics of Immorality in Ancient Rome.* Cambridge.

Edwards, C. (1994), 'Beware of Imitations: Theatre and the Subversion of Imperial Identity', in Elsner and Masters (1994): 83–97.

Edwards, C. (1997), 'Self-Scrutiny and Self-Transformation in Seneca's Letters', *G&R* NS 44: 22–38.

Edwards, C. (2005), 'Modelling Roman Suicide? The Afterlife of Cato', *Economy and Society* 34: 200–22.

Edwards, C. (2007), *Death in Ancient Rome.* New Haven, CT, and London.

Edwards, C. (2014), 'Ethics V: Death and Time', in Damschen and Heil (2014): 323–41.

Egermann, F. (1972), 'Seneca als Dichterphilosoph', in Lefèvre (1972): 33–57.

Effe, B. (1980), 'Die Funktionswandel des Herakles-Mythos in der griechischen Literatur', *Poetica* 12: 145–66.

Ehrenberg, V. (1973), *Aspects of the Ancient World: Essays and Reviews.* New York.

Eitner, R., ed. (1966), *Die Oper von ihren ersten Anfängen bis zur Mitte des 18. Jahr-hunderts,* Vol. 12. New York.

Eliot, T. S. (1951*a*), *Selected Essays.* 3rd edn. London.

Eliot, T. S. (1951*b*), 'Tradition and the Individual Talent', in Eliot (1951*a*): 13–22.

Eliot, T. S. (1951c), 'Seneca in Elizabethan translation', in Eliot (1951a): 65–105.

Elsner, J., ed. (2004), *The Verbal and the Visual: Cultures of Ekphrasis in Antiquity.* *Ramus* 31. Bendigo, Vic.

Elsner, J., and Masters, J., eds. (1994), *Reflections of Nero: Culture, History and Representation.* London.

Englert, W. (1994), 'Stoics and Epicureans on the Nature of Suicide', *Proc. Boston Area Colloq. Anc. Philosophy* 10: 67–98.

Enk, P. J. (1957), 'Roman Tragedy', *Neophilologus* 41: 282–307.

Erasmo, M. (2004), *Roman Tragedy: Theatre to Theatricality.* Austin, TX.

Erasmo, M. (2008), *Reading Death in Ancient Rome.* Columbus, OH.

Erskine, A. (1990), *The Hellenistic Stoa.* Ithaca, NY.

Esslin, M. (1976), *Artaud.* London.

Evans, E. C. (1950), 'A Stoic Aspect of Senecan Drama: Portraiture', *TAPA* 81: 169–84.

Evenpoel, W. (2004), 'The Philosopher Seneca on Suicide', *Anc. Soc.* 34: 217–43.

Everson, S., ed. (1991), *Companions to Ancient Thought 2: Psychology.* Cambridge.

Ewans, M. (2007), *Opera from the Greek: Studies in the Poetics of Appropriation.* Aldershot and Burlington, VT.

Fagan, G. G. (2011), *The Lure of the Arena: Social Psychology and the Crowd at the Roman Games.* Cambridge.

Fairbanks, A. (1979), *Philostratus Imagines: Callistratus Descriptions.* Cambridge, MA, and London.

Faller, S., and Manuwald, G., eds. (2002), *Accius und seine Zeit.* Würzburg.

Fantham, E. (1975), 'Virgil's Dido and Seneca's Tragic Heroines', *G&R* NS 22: 1–10.

Fantham, E. (1983), '*Nil iam iura naturae ualent*: Incest and Fratricide in Seneca's *Phoenissae*', in Boyle (1983a): 61–76.

Fantham, E. (1989), 'Mime: The Missing Link in Roman Literary History', *CW* 82: 153–63.

Fantham, E. (1996), *Roman Literary Culture.* Baltimore, MD.

Fantham, E. (2002), 'Orator and/et Actor', in Easterling and Hall (2002): 362–76.

Fantham, E. (2003), 'Pacuvius', in Braund and Gill (2003): 98–118.

Fantham, E. (2008), 'Covering the Head at Rome: Ritual and Gender', in Edmondson and Keith (2008): 158–71.

Farnell, L. R. (1921), *Greek Hero Cults and Ideas of Immortality.* Oxford.

Farrell, J. (2001), *Latin Language and Latin Culture.* Cambridge.

Fears, J. R. (1977), *Princeps a Diis Electus.* Rome.

Feldman, P., and Scott-Kilvert, D., eds. (1987), *The Journals of Mary Shelley 1814–1844.* Baltimore, MD.

Felski, R., ed. (2008), *Rethinking Tragedy.* Baltimore, MD.

Felton, D., ed. (2018), *Landscapes of Dread in Classical Antiquity.* London and New York.

Felton, D., and Gilhuly, K. (2018), 'Introduction: Dread and the Landscape', in Felton (2018): 1–11.

Fitch, J. G. (1974), 'Character in Senecan Tragedy'. Diss. Cornell University. Ithaca, NY.

Fitch, J. G. (1979), '*Pectus o nimium ferum*: Act V of Seneca's *Hercules Furens*', *Hermes* 107:240–8.

Fitch, J. G. (1981), 'Sense-Pauses and Relative Dating in Seneca, Sophocles and Shakespeare', *AJP* 102: 289–307.

Fitch, J. G. (1987*b*), *Seneca's Anapaests: Metre, Colometry, Text and Artistry in the Anapaests of Seneca's Tragedies*. Atlanta, GA.

Fitch, J. G. (2000), 'Playing Seneca?', in Harrison (2000): 1–12.

Fitch, J. G. (2002*b*), 'Transpositions and Emendations in Seneca's Tragedies', *Phoenix* 56: 296–314.

Fitch, J. G. (2004*b*), *Annaeana Tragica: Notes on the Text of Seneca's Tragedies*. Leiden.

Fitch, J. G., ed. (2008), *Oxford Readings in Classical Studies: Seneca*. Oxford.

Fitch, J. G. (2016), 'Speaking Names in Senecan Drama', in Mitsis and Ziogas (2016): 313–32.

Fitch, J. G. (2017), 'Late Thoughts on the Text of Seneca's Tragedies', *CCJ* 63: 53–68.

Fitch, J. G., and McElduff, S. (2008), 'Construction of the Self in Senecan Drama', in Fitch (2008): 157–80 (repr. from *Mnem.* [2002] 55: 18–40).

Flores, E. (1974), *Letteratura latina e ideologia del III–II a. C.* Naples.

Florio, J. (1910), *The Essayes of Michael, Lord of Montaigne*. 3 vols. London.

Flower, H. I. (1995), '*Fabulae Praetextae* in Context: When Were Plays on Contemporary Subjects Performed in Rome?', *CQ* NS 45: 170–90.

Flower, H. I. (1996), *Ancestor Masks and Aristocratic Power in Roman Culture*. Oxford.

Flower, H. I. (2002), 'Roman Historical Drama and Nero on the Stage', *SO* 77: 68–72.

Flower, H. I., ed. (2004*a*), *The Cambridge Companion to the Roman Republic*. Cambridge.

Flower, H. I. (2004*b*), 'Spectacle and Political Culture in the Roman Republic', in Flower (2004*a*): 322–43.

Forestier, G. (1999), *Racine: Iphigénie*. Paris.

Foucault, M. (1986), *The Care of the Self*. London.

Foucault, M. (1988), 'Technologies of the Self', in Martin, Gutman, and Hutton (1988): 16–49.

Fowler, W. W. (1899), *The Roman Festivals of the Period of the Roman Republic*. London.

Fraenkel, E. (1950), *Aeschylus: Agamemnon*. 3 vols. Oxford.

Frangoulidis, S. (2020), 'From Victor to Victim: Metadrama and Movement of Plot in Seneca's *Hercules Furens*', *Eugesta* 10: 144–62.

Frangoulidis, S., Harrison, S. J., Manuwald, G., eds. (2016), *Roman Drama and its Contexts*. Berlin and Boston, MA.

Frank, M. (1995*b*), 'The Rhetorical Use of Family Terms in Seneca's *Oedipus* and *Phoenissae*', *Phoenix* 49: 121–30.

Frank, T. (1931), 'The Status of Actors at Rome', *CP* 26: 11–20.

Frank, T. (1937), 'Curiatius Maternus and his Tragedies', *AJP* 58: 225–9.

Frassinetti. P. (1953), *Fabula Atellana: Saggio populare latino*. Pavia.

Frenzel, F. (1914), *Die Prologe des Tragödien Senecas*. Leipzig.

Freud, S. (1900), *The Interpretation of Dreams*, tr. J. Crick (1999). Oxford.

Freud, S. (1905), *Fragment of an Analysis of a Case of Hysteria*, Vol. 7. Strachey (1953–74).

Freud, S. (1913), *Totem and Taboo*, Vol. 13. Strachey (1953–74).

Freud, S. (1930), *Das Unbehagen in der Kultur*. Vienna. Repr. Severus, Hamburg 2013. = *Civilization and its Discontents*.

Freud, S. (1994), *Civilization and its Discontents*, tr. J. Rivière. New York.

Freyburger, G. (1986), *Fides: Étude sémantique et religieuse depuis les origines jusqu'à l'époque augustéenne*. Paris.

Freyburger, G. (1990), 'Griechischer Exotismus und römische religiöse Tradition in Senecas Theater', in Blänsdorf (1990): 123–32.

Frézouls, E. (1983), 'La Construction du *theatrum lapideum* et son contexte politique', in Zehnacker (1983*a*): 193–214.

Frick, W. (1998), *Die mythische Methode*. Tübingen.

Friedrich, W. H. (1933), *Untersuchungen zu Senecas dramatischer Technik*. Borna and Leipzig.

Friedrich, W. H. (1954), 'Sprache und Stil des *Hercules Oetaeus*', *Hermes* 82: 51–84.

Friedrich, W. H. (1972), 'Die Raserei des Hercules', in Lefèvre (1972): 131–48.

Fritz, K. von (1972), 'Tragische Schuld in Senecas Tragödien', in Lefèvre (1972): 67–73.

Früh, R., Fuhrer, T., and Humar, M., eds. (2015), *Irritationen: Rhetorische und poetische Verfahren der Verunsicherung*. Berlin and Boston, MA.

Fulkerson, L. (2005), *The Ovidian Heroine as Author*. Cambridge.

Fusillo, M. (2000), 'Apollonius Rhodius as "Inventor" of the Interior Monologue', in Papanghelis and Rengakos (2000): 127–46.

Futrell, A. (1997), *Blood in the Arena: The Spectacle of Roman Power*. Austin, TX.

Gabba, E. (1969), 'Il *Brutus* di Accio', *Dioniso* 43: 377–83.

Gair, W. R. (1978), *John Marston: Antonio's Revenge*. Baltimore, MD.

Gale, M. R., and Scourfield, J. H. D., eds. (2018*a*), *Texts and Violence in the Roman World*. Cambridge.

Gale, M. R., and Scourfield, J. H. D. (2018*b*), 'Introduction: Reading Roman Violence', Gale and Scourfield (2018*a*): 1–43.

Galinsky, K. (1972), *The Herakles Theme*. Oxford.

Galinsky, K. (1996), *Augustan Culture: An Interpretive Introduction*. Princeton, NJ.

Ganiban, R. T. (2007), *Statius and Virgil: The Thebaid and the Reinterpretation of the Aeneid*. Cambridge.

Gantz, T. (1993), *Early Greek Myth: A Guide to Literary and Artistic Sources*. 2 vols. Baltimore, MD, and London.

Garani, M., Michalopoulos, A. N., and Papaioannou, S., eds. (2020), *Intertextuality in Seneca's Philosophical Writings*. London and New York.

Garelli, M.-H. (1998*a*), *Rome et le tragique*. Toulouse.

Garelli, M.-H. (1998*b*), 'Tradition littéraire et création dramatique dans les tragédies de Sénèque: L'Exemple des récits de messagers', *Latomus* 57: 15–32.

Garelli, M.-H. (2004), 'Néron et la pantomime', in Hugoniot et al. (2004): 353–68.

Garnier, R. (1578), *Marc Antoine*: see Hill and Morrison (1975).

Garrison, E. P. (1995), *Groaning Tears: Ethical and Dramatic Aspects of Suicide in Greek Tragedy*. Leiden.

Garton, C. (1972), *Personal Aspects of the Roman Theater*. Toronto.

Garvie, A. (1986), *Aeschylus Choephori*. Oxford.

Gelzer, M. (1969), *Caesar: Politician and Statesman*. Oxford.

Gentili, B. (1979), *Theatrical Performances in the Ancient World*. Amsterdam.

Gervais, K. (2021), 'Senecan Heroes and Tyrants in Statius, *Thebaid* 2', in Papaioannou and Marinis (2021): 144–68.

Geue, T. (2019), *Author Unknown: The Power of Anonymity in Ancient Rome*. Cambridge, MA.

Giancotti, F. (1952), 'Note alle tragedie di Seneca', *RFIC* 80: 149–72.

Giancotti, F. (1953), *Saggio sulle tragedie di Seneca*. Rome.

Giardina, G. C. (1964), 'Per un inquadramento del teatro di Seneca nella cultura e nella società del suo tempo', *RCCM* 6: 171–80.

Gibbon, E. (1776–89), *The History of the Decline and Fall of the Roman Empire*. 6 vols. London.

Gibbons, B., ed. (2011), *Christopher Marlowe: Four Plays*. London and New York.

Gigon, O. (1938), 'Bemerkungen zu Senecas Thyestes', *Philologus* 93: 176–83.

Gildenhard, I. (2010), 'Buskins and SPQR: Roman Receptions of Greek Tragedy', in Gildenhard and Revermann (2010): 153–85.

Gildenhard, I., and Revermann, M., eds. (2010), *Beyond the Fifth Century: Interactions with Greek Tragedy from the Fourth Century BCE to the Middle Ages*. Berlin and New York.

Gill, C. (1987), 'Two Monologues of Self-Division', in Whitby, Hardie, and Whitby (1987): 25–37.

Gill, C. (1997), 'Passion as Madness in Roman Poetry', in Braund and Gill (1997): 213–41.

Gill, C. (2006), *The Structured Self in Hellenistic and Roman Thought*. Oxford.

Gill, C. (2009), 'Seneca and Selfhood: Integration and Disintegration', in Bartsch and Wray (2009): 65–83.

Gilula, D. (1989), 'Greek Drama in Rome: Some Aspects of Cultural Transposition', in Scolnicov and Holland (1989): 99–109.

Ginsberg, L. D. (2011), '*Ingens* as an Etymological Pun in the *Octavia*', *CP* 106: 357–60.

Ginsberg, L. D. (2017), *Staging Memory, Staging Strife: Empire and Civil War in the Octavia*. Oxford.

Ginsburg, J. (2006), *Representing Agrippina: Constructions of Female Power in the Early Roman Empire*. Oxford.

Gladhill, B. (2016), *Rethinking Roman Alliance: A Study in Poetics and Society*. Cambridge.

Glinski, M. L. von (2017), 'All the World's Offstage: Metaphysical and Metafictional Aspects in Seneca's *Hercules Furens*', *CQ* NS 67: 210–27.

Gloyn, L. (2017), *The Ethics of the Family in Seneca*. Cambridge.

Goebel, A. (1862), 'Quaestiones Horatianae (pars II)', *Zeitschr. f. d. Gymnasialw.* 16: 734–44.

Goldberg, S. (1986), *Understanding Terence*. Princeton, NJ.

Goldberg, S. (1996), 'The Fall and Rise of Roman Tragedy', *TAPA* 126: 265–86.

Goldberg, S. (1998), 'Plautus on the Palatine', *JRS* 88:1–20.

Goldberg, S. (1999), 'Cicero and the Work of Tragedy', in Manuwald (2000): 49–59.

Goldberg, S. (2003), 'Authorizing Octavia', in Wilson (2003): 13–36.

Goldberg, S. (2014), 'Greek and Roman Elements in Senecan Tragedy', in Damschen and Heil (2014): 639–52.

Goldberg, S. (2018), 'Theater without Theaters: Seeing Plays the Roman Way', *TAPA* 148: 139–72.

Goldhill, S. (1986), *Reading Greek Tragedy*. Cambridge.

Goldhill, S. (1997), 'The Language of Tragedy: Rhetoric and Communication', in Easterling (1997): 127–50.

Goldstein, J., ed. (1998), *Why We Watch: The Attractions of Violent Entertainment*. New York.

Gomme, A. W., and Sandbach, F. H., eds. (1973), *Menander: A Commentary*. Oxford.

Gow, A. S. F., and Page, D. L. (1968), *The Greek Anthology: The Garland of Philip*. Cambridge.

Gowers, E. (1993), *The Loaded Table: Representations of Food in Roman Literature*. Oxford.

Gowing, A. M. (2005), *Empire and Memory: The Representation of the Roman Republic in Imperial Culture*. Cambridge.

Graf, F. (1991), 'Gestures and Conventions: The Gestures of Roman Actors and Orators', in Bremmer and Roodenburg (1991): 36–58.

Graf, F. (1997), *Magic in the Ancient World*. Cambridge, MA, and London.

Grant, M. D. (1999), 'Plautus and Seneca: Acting in Nero's Rome', *G&R* 46: 27–33.

Gratwick, A. S. (1982), 'Drama', in Kenney and Clausen (1982): 77–137.

Graver, M. (2007), *Stoicism and Emotion*. Chicago, IL.

Gray, P. (2016), 'Shakespeare vs. Seneca: Competing Visions of Human Dignity', in Dodson-Robinson (2016): 203–30.

Greenblatt, S. (1980), *Renaissance Self-Fashioning: From More to Shakespeare*. Chicago, IL.

Greenblatt, S., ed. (1982), *The Power of Forms in the English Renaissance*. Norman, OK.

Greenblatt, S. (2018), *Tyrant: Shakespeare on Politics*. New York and London.

Greer, G. (1986), *Shakespeare*. Oxford.

Greunen, B. van (1977), 'Seneca's *Hercules Furens*: A Myth Renewed', *AC* 20: 141–8.

Grewe, S. (2001), *Die politische Bedeutung des Senecatragödien und Senecas politisches Denken zur Zeit der Abfassung des Medea*. Würzburg.

Griffin, M. T. 'Imago Vitae Suae', in Costa (1974a): 1–38.

Griffin, M. T. (1976), *Seneca: A Philosopher in Politics*. Oxford.

Griffin, M. T. (1984), *Nero: The End of a Dynasty*. London.

Griffin, M. T. (1986a), 'Philosophy, Cato and Roman Suicide: I', *G&R* 33: 64–77.

Griffin, M. T. (1986b), 'Philosophy, Cato and Roman Suicide: II', *G&R* 33: 192–202.

Griffith, M. (1999), *Sophocles: Antigone*. Cambridge.

Griffiths, E. (2006), *Euripides: Heracles*. London.

Grimal, P. (1963), 'L'Originalité de Sénèque dans la tragédie de *Phèdre*', *REL* 41: 297–314.

Grimal, P. (1964), 'Les Tragédies de Sénèque', in Jacquot (1964): 1–10.

Grimal, P. (1966), *Sénèque*. Paris.

Grimal, P. (1978), *Le Théâtre antique*. Paris.

Grimal, P., ed. (1992a), *La Langue latine, langue de la philosophie*. Rome.

Grimal, P. (1992b), 'Le Vocabulaire de l'intériorité dans l'oeuvre de Sénèque', in Grimal (1992a): 141–59.

Grisé, Y. (1982), *Le Suicide dans la Rome antique*. Montreal and Paris.

Grisoli, P. (1971), 'Per l'interpretazione del primo canto corale dell' *Hercules Furens* di Seneca', *Boll. Com.* 19: 73–99.

Grotius, H. (1661), Emendations in Gronovius (1661).

Groto, L. (1599), *La Hadriana*. Venice.

Gruen, E. S. (1992), *Culture and National Identity in Republican Rome*. Ithaca, NY.

Grumbine, H. C. (1900), *Thomas Hughes and Others: The Misfortunes of Arthur*. London.

Gruter, J. (1621), in Scriuerius (1621).

Gualandri, L., and Mazzoli, G., eds. (2003), *Gli Annei: Una famiglia nella storia e nella cultura di Roma imperiale*. Como.

Guastella, G. (2001), *L'ira e l'onore: Forme della vendetta nel teatro senecano e nella sua tradizione*. Palermo.

Gunderson, E. (2003), 'The Flavian Amphitheatre: All the World as Stage', in Boyle and Dominik (2003): 637–58.

Gunderson, E. (2015), *The Sublime Seneca: Ethics, Literature, Metaphysics*. Cambridge.

Gurr, A. (1992), *The Shakespearean Stage 1574–1642*. 3rd edn. Cambridge.

Habinek, T. N. (1998), *The Politics of Latin Literature*. Princeton, NJ.

Habinek, T. N. (2000), 'Seneca's Renown: *Gloria, Claritudo* and the Replication of the Roman Elite', *CA* 19: 264–303.

Hadas, M. (1939), 'The Roman Stamp of Seneca's Tragedies', *AJP* 60: 220–31.

Hafemann, K. (2003), *Der Kommentar des Iohannes d Segarellis zu Senecas 'Hercules Furens'*. Berlin and New York.

Haimson Lushkov, A. (2016), '*Cadmea Proles*: Identity and Intertext in Seneca's *Hercules Furens*', *CJ* 111: 303–16.

Hainsworth, B. (1993), *The Iliad A Commentary, III: Books 9–12*. Cambridge.

Hall, E. (2008), 'Introduction: Pantomime, A Lost Chord of Ancient Culture', in Hall and Wyles (2008): 1–40.

Hall, E., Macintosh, F., and Wrigley, A., eds. (2004), *Dionysus since 69: Greek Tragedy at the Dawn of the Third Millennium*. Oxford.

Hall, E., and Macintosh, F. (2005), *Greek Tragedy and the British Theatre 1660–1914*. Oxford.

Hall, E., and Wyles, R., eds. (2008), *New Directions in Ancient Pantomime*. Oxford.

Hall, J. B. (1986), Review of Zwierlein (1984*b*), *CQ* NS 36: 317–17.

Hallett, J. P., and Skinner, M. B., eds. (1997), *Roman Sexualities*. Princeton, NJ.

Halperin, D. M., Winkler J. J., and Zeitlin, F. I., eds. (1990), *Before Sexuality*. Princeton, NJ.

Hammer, D. (2014), *Roman Political Thought: From Cicero to Augustine*. Cambridge.

Hammond, M. (1959), *The Antonine Monarchy*. Rome.

Hammond, P. (2009), *The Strangeness of Tragedy*. Oxford.

Hansen, E. H. A. (1934), *Die Stellung der Affektrede in den Tragödien des Seneca*. Berlin.

Hanson, J. A. (1959), *Roman Theater-Temples*. Princeton, NJ.

Hardie, A. (2003), 'Poetry and Politics at the Games of Domitian', in Boyle and Dominik (2003): 125–47.

Hardwick, L. (2009), 'Can (Modern) Poets Do Classical Drama?', in Rees (2009): 39–61.

Harris, W. V. (1986), 'The Roman Father's Power of Life and Death', in Bagnall and Harris (1986): 81–96.

Harris, W. V. (2001), *Restraining Rage: The Ideology of Anger Control in Classical Antiquity*. Cambridge, MA.

Harrison, G. W. M., ed. (2000), *Seneca in Performance*. London.

Harrison, G. W. M. (2014), 'Themes', in Damschen and Heil (2014): 615–38.

Harrison, G. W. M., ed. (2015), *Brill's Companion to Roman Tragedy*. Leiden.

Harrison, G. W. M., and Liapis, V., eds. (2013), *Performance in Greek and Roman Theatre*. Leiden.

Harrison, S., ed. (2005), *A Companion to Latin Literature*. Oxford.

Harrison, S. (2009), 'Some Modern Versions of Senecan Drama', *Trends in Classics* 1: 148–70.

Harrison, S., Frangoulidis, S. A., and Papanghelis, T. D., eds. (2018), *Intratextuality and Latin Literature*. *Trends in Classics*, Supplementary Volumes, Vol. 69. Berlin.

Harrison, T. (1986), *Dramatic Verse: 1973–1985*. Newcastle upon Tyne.

Harst, J. (2016), 'Germany and the Netherlands: Tragic Seneca in Scholarship and on Stage', in Dodson-Robinson (2016): 149–73.

Hartkamp, R. (2002), 'Evander im Atreus: Die Selbstdarstellung des Tragikers L. Accius und der antiexemplarische Gehalt seiner Stücke als Ausdruck von Alterität', in Faller and Manuwald (2002): 161–72.

Haywood, R. M. (1942), 'Note on Seneca's *Hercules Furens*', *CJ* 37: 421–4.

Hedicke, E., ed. (1899), *Studia Bentleiana*, fasc. II. Freienwald.

Heerink, M., and Manuwald, G., eds. (2014), *Brill's Companion to Valerius Flaccus*. Leiden.

Heil, A. (2013), *Die dramatische Zeit in Senecas Tragödien*. Leiden.

Heil, A. (2014), 'Vision, Sound, and Silence in the "Drama of the Word"', in Damschen and Heil (2014): 547–60.

Heinsius, N. (1742), *Aduersariorum libri IV*. Harlingen.

Heldmann, K. (1974), *Untersuchungen zu den Tragödien Senecas*. Wiesbaden.

Henderson, J. (1983), 'Poetic Technique and Rhetorical Amplification: Seneca *Medea* 579–669', in Boyle (1983a): 94–113.

Henderson, J. (1993), 'Form Remade/Statius' *Thebaid*', in Boyle (1993): 162–91.

Henry, D., and E. (1985), *The Mask of Power*. Warminster.

Henry, D., and Walker, B. (1963), 'Tacitus and Seneca', *G&R* NS 10: 98–110.

Henry, D., and Walker, B. (1965), 'The Futility of Action: A Study of Seneca's *Hercules Furens*', *CP* 60: 11–22.

Herington, C. J. (1966), 'Senecan Tragedy', *Arion* 5: 422–71.

Herington, C. J. (1982), 'Senecan Tragedy', in Kenney and Clausen (1982): 519–32.

Herrick, M. T. (1965), *Italian Tragedy in the Renaissance*. Urbana, IL.

Herrmann, L. (1924), *Le Théâtre de Sénèque*. Paris.

Hershkowitz, D. (1998), *The Madness of Epic: Reading Insanity from Homer to Statius*. Oxford.

Herzog, O. (1928), 'Datierung der Tragödien des Seneca', *RhM* 77: 51–104.

Heyworth, S. J., ed. (2007), *Classical Constructions: Papers in Memory of Don Fowler*. Oxford.

Hexter, R., and Selden, D., eds. (1992), *Innovations of Antiquity*. New York and London.

Hill, C. M., and Morrison, M. G., eds. (1975), *Robert Garnier: Two Tragedies, Hippolyte and Marc Antoine*. London.

Hill, D. E. (2000), 'Seneca's Choruses', *Mnem*. 53: 561–87.

Hill, T. (2004), *'Ambitiosa Mors': Suicide and Self in Roman Thought and Literature*. London.

Himpel, D. (2015), 'Rhetorik der Verunsicherung in Senecas Tragoedien', in Früh et al. (2015): 239–58.

Hinds, S. E. (2007), 'Ovid among the Conspiracy Theorists', in Heyworth (2007): 194–220.

Hinds, S. E. (2011), 'Seneca's Ovidian *Loci*', *SIFC* 9: 3–63.

Hine, H. (1981), 'The Structure of Seneca's *Thyestes*', in F. Cairns (ed.), *Papers of the Liverpool Latin Seminar* 3: 259–75. Liverpool.

Hirsch, E. (2014), *A Poet's Glossary*. Boston, MA, and New York.

Hoffa, W., and Düring, T. (1914), *Materialen für eine Neueausgabe von Senecas Tragödien*. Göttingen.

Hollis, A. S. (1990), *Callimachus: Hecale*. Oxford.

Hoof, A. J. L. van (1990), *From Autothanasia to Suicide: Self-Killing in Classical Antiquity*. London.

Hook, B. S. (2000), ' "Nothing within Which Passeth Show": Character and Color in Senecan Tragedy', in Harrison (2000): 53–71.

Hopkins, K. (1983), *Death and Renewal*. Cambridge.

Horne, P. R. (1962), *The Tragedies of Giambattista Giraldi*. Oxford.

Horsfall, N. (1976), 'The *collegium poetarum*', *BICS* 23: 79–95.

Hose, M. (1999), 'Anmerkungen zur Verwendung des Chores in der römischen Tragödie der Republik', in Riemer and Zimmermann (1999): 113–38.

Housman, A. E. (1928), 'Prosody and Method II. The Metrical Properties of *GN*', *CQ* 22: 1–10.

Housman, A. E. (1972), *The Classical Papers of A. E. Housman*, 3 vols, ed. J. Diggle and F. D. R. Goodyear. Cambridge.

Howard, J. E. (1994), *The Stage and Social Struggle in Early Modern England*. London and New York.

Hudson-Williams, A. (1989), 'Notes on Some Passages in Seneca's Tragedies and the *Octavia*', *CQ* NS 39: 186–96.

Hudson-Williams, A. (1991), 'Notes on Some Passages in Seneca's Tragedies: II', *CQ* NS 41: 427–37.

Hughes, T. et al. (1587), *The Misfortunes of Arthur*. London.

Hugoniot, C., Hurlet, F., and Milanezi, S., eds. (2004), *Le Statut de l'acteur dans l'Antiquité grecque et romaine*. Tours.

Hunter, G. K. (1965), *John Marston: Antonio and Mellida*. Lincoln, NE.

Hunter, G. K. (1967), 'Seneca and the Elizabethans: A Case-Study in "Influence" ', *Shakespeare Survey* 20: 17–26.

Hunter, G. K. (1974), 'Seneca and English Tragedy', in Costa (1974a): 166–204.

Hunter, R. L. (1985), *The New Comedy of Greece and Rome*. Cambridge.

Hunter, R. L. (1993), *Apollonius of Rhodes: Jason and the Golden Fleece*. Oxford.

Hutchinson, G. O. (1985), *Aeschylus: Seven Against Thebes*. Oxford.

Hutchinson, G. O. (1993), *Latin Literature from Seneca to Juvenal: A Critical Study*. Oxford.
Huttner, U. (1997), *Die politische Rolle der Heraklesgestalt im griechischen Herrschertum*. Stuttgart.
Inwood, B. (1993), 'Seneca and Psychological Dualism', in Brunschwig and Nussbaum (1993): 150–83.
Inwood, B., ed. (2003), *The Cambridge Companion to the Stoics*. Cambridge.
Inwood, B. (2004), 'Moral Judgement in Seneca', in Strange and Jupko (2004): 76–94.
Inwood, B. (2005), *Reading Seneca: Stoic Philosophy at Rome*. Oxford.
Inwood, B. (2007), *Seneca: Selected Philosophical Letters*. Oxford.
Inwood, B. (2009), 'Self and Self-Assertion', in Bartsch and Wray (2009): 39–64.
Inwood, B. and Domini, P. (1999), 'Stoic Ethics', in Algra et al. (1999): 675–738.
Izenour, G. C. (1992), *Roofed Theaters of Classical Antiquity*. New Haven, CT.
Jackson, M. P., and Neill, M., eds. (1986), *The Selected Plays of John Marston*. Cambridge.
Jacobson, H. (1983), *The Exagoge of Ezechiel*. Cambridge.
Jacquot, J., ed. (1964), *Les tragédies de Sénèque et le théâtre de la Renaissance*. Paris.
Jagu, A. (1979), *Musonius Rufus entretiens et fragments: Introduction, traduction et commentaire*. Hildesheim.
Jakobi, R. (1988), *Der Einfluss Ovids auf den Tragiker Seneca*. Berlin and New York.
James, H. (2007), *Shakespeare's Troy: Drama, Politics and the Translation of Empire*. Cambridge.
Jameson, M. (2005), 'The Family of Herakles in Attica', in Rawlings and Bowden (2005): 15–35.
Jebb, R. C. (1892), *Sophocles: The Trachiniae*. Cambridge.
Jocelyn, H. D. (1972), 'Ennius as a Dramatic Poet', *Fondation Hardt Entretiens* 17: 39–95.
Jocelyn, H. D. (1980), 'The Fate of Varius' *Thyestes*', *CQ* ns 30: 387–400.
Johnston, S. I. (2004), *Religions of the Ancient World: A Guide*. Cambridge, MA.
Jones, C. P. (1991), 'Dinner Theatre', in Slater (1991): 185–98.
Jones, C. P. (1993), 'Greek Drama in the Roman Empire', in Scodel (1993): 39–52.
Jones, E. (1977), *The Origins of Shakespeare*. Oxford.
Jonson, B. (1603), *Sejanus*: see Ayres (1990).
Jorgensen, P. A. (1971), *Our Naked Frailties*. Berkeley, CA.
Jory, E. J. (1970), 'Associations of Actors in Rome', *Hermes* 98: 224–53.
Jory, E. J. (1981), 'The Literary Evidence for the Beginning of Imperial Pantomime', *BICS* 28: 147–61.
Jory, E. J. (1986), 'Continuity and Change in the Roman Theatre', in Betts, Hooker, and Green (1986): 143–52.
Jourdain-Annequin, C. (1989), *Heraclès aux portes du soir*. Paris.
Jump, J. D., ed. (1962), *Christopher Marlowe: Doctor Faustus*. London.
Kamerbeek, J. C. (1966), 'The Unity and Meaning of Euripides' *Heracles*', *Mnem.* 19: 1–16.
Kampen, N. B., ed. (1996), *Sexuality in Ancient Art*. Cambridge.
Kannicht, R. (2004), *Tragicorum Graecorum Fragmenta*. 5 vols. Göttingen.

Kaplan, E. A. (1992), *Motherhood and Representation: The Mother and Popular Culture and Melodrama*. New York.

Kapnukajas, C. A. (1930), *Die Nachahmungstechnik Senecas in den Chorliedern des Hercules furens und der Medea*. Borna-Leipzig.

Karim-Cooper, F., ed. (2019), *Titus Andronicus: The State of Play*. London.

Kaster, R. A. (2005), *Emotion, Restraint and Community in Ancient Rome*. Oxford.

Kaster, R. A. (2010), 'Introduction', in Kaster and Nussbaum (2010): 133–45.

Kaufmann, R. J. (1967), 'The Senecan Perspective and the Shakespearean Poetic', *Comparative Drama* 1: 182–98.

Kelly, H. A. (1979), 'Tragedy and the Performance of Tragedy in Late Roman Antiquity', *Traditio* 35: 21–44.

Kennedy, B. H. (1911), *Revised Latin Primer*. 8th edn. London.

Kennedy, D. F. (2018), 'Dismemberment and its Critics: Seneca's *Phaedra*', in Gale and Scourfield (2018a): 215–45.

Kenney, E., and Clausen, W., eds. (1982), *The Cambridge History of Classical Literature, II: Latin Literature*. Cambridge.

Keppie, L. (1984), *The Making of the Roman Army: From Republic to Empire*. New York.

Ker, J. (2006), 'Seneca, a Man of Many Genres', in Volk and Williams (2006): 19–41.

Ker, J. (2009a), 'Seneca on Self-Examination: Rereading *On Anger* 3.36', in Bartsch and Wray (2009): 160–87.

Ker, J. (2009b), *The Deaths of Seneca*. New York.

Ker, J. (2011), *A Seneca Reader: Selections from Prose and Tragedy*. Mundelein, IL.

Ker, J., and Winston, J. (2012), *Elizabethan Seneca: Three Tragedies*. London.

Kerrigan, J. (1996), *Revenge Tragedy: Aeschylus to Armageddon*. Oxford.

Keseling, P. (1941), 'Horaz in den Tragödien Senecas', *PhW* 61: 190–2.

King, C. M. (1971), 'Seneca's *Hercules Oetaeus*: A Stoic Interpretation of the Greek Myth', *G&R* 18: 215–22.

Kirichenko, A. (2013), *Lehrreiche Trugbilder: Senecas Tragödien und die Rhetorik des Sehens*. Heidelberg.

Kirichenko, A. (2016), 'Der imaginäre Bühnenraum in Senecas *Hercules Furens*', *Philologia Classica* 11: 258–68.

Knoche, U. (1941), 'Senecas Atreus: Ein Beispiel', *Antike* 17: 60–76 (repr. in Lefèvre 1972: 477–89).

Kohn, T. D. (2004–5), 'Seneca's Use of Four Speaking Actors', *CJ* 100: 163–75.

Kohn, T. D. (2013), *The Dramaturgy of Senecan Tragedy*. Ann Arbor MI.

Köhne, W., and Ewigleben, C., eds. (2000), *Gladiators and Caesars: The Power of Spectacle in Ancient Rome*. London.

Kossman, N., ed. (2001), *Gods and Mortals: Modern Poems on Classical Myths*. New York.

Kotlińska-Toma, A. (2015), *Hellenistic Tragedy: Texts, Translations and a Critical Survey*. London.

Kragelund, P. (1982), *Prophecy, Populism, and Propaganda in the 'Octavia'*. Copenhagen.

Kragelund, P. (2002), 'Historical Drama in Ancient Rome: Republican Flourishing and Imperial Decline?', *SO* 76: 5–51.

Kragelund, P. (2016), *Roman Historical Drama: The Octavia in Antiquity and Beyond*. Oxford.

Kraus, C. S., and Gibson, R. K., eds. (2002), *The Classical Commentary: Histories, Practices, Theory*. Leiden.

Kraus, C., Goldhill, S., Foley, H. P., and Elsner, J., eds. (2007), *Visualizing the Tragic: Drama, Myth, and Ritual in Greek Art and Literature*. Oxford.

Kraus, C. S., and Stray, C., eds. (2016), *Classical Commentaries: Explorations in a Scholarly Genre*. Oxford.

Kugelmeier, C. (2007), *Die innere Vergegenwärtigung des Bühnenspiels in Senecas Tragödien*. Munich.

Kyd, T. (1587), *The Spanish Tragedy*: see Mulryne (1970).

La Grange-Chancel (1706), *Cassandre*. Paris.

La Penna, A. (1979), *Fra teatro, poesia e politica romana*. Turin.

Lacan, J. (2006), *Écrits: The First Complete Edition in English*. New York.

Lana, I. (1958–9), 'L'Atreo di Accio e la leggenda di Atreo e Tieste nel teatro tragico romano', *Atti del Accademia delle Scienze di Torino* 39: 293–383.

Langlands, R. (2006), *Sexual Morality in Ancient Rome*. Cambridge.

Langlands, R. (2018), *Exemplary Ethics in Ancient Rome*. Cambridge.

Lanza, D. (1981), 'Lo spettacolo della parola. Riflessioni sulla testualità drammatica di Seneca', *Dioniso* 52: 463–7.

Lapp, J. (1964), 'Racine est-il sénèquien?', in Jacquot (1964): 127–38.

Larmour, D. H. J. (1990), 'Tragic *Contaminatio* in Ovid's *Metamorphoses*: Procne and Medea; Philomela and Iphigenia (6.424-674); Scylla and Phaedra (8.19–51)', *ICS* 15: 131–51.

Larson, V. T. (1994), *The Role of Description in Senecan Tragedy*. Frankfurt am Main.

Lausberg, H. (1960), *Handbuch der literarischen Rhetorik*. Munich.

Lavery, G. (1980), 'Metaphors of War and Travel in Seneca's Prose Works', *G&R* 27: 147–57.

Lavery, J. (2004), 'Some Aeschylean Influences on Seneca's *Agamemnon*', *MD* 53: 183–94.

Lavesa, C. B. (2008), 'Los tiranos de *Hercules furens*', in Bañuls et al. (2008): 73–93.

Lavesa, C. B. (2010), 'Los prólogos de las tragedias de Séneca: *Hercules furens, Agamemnon y Thyestes*: Estructura y función', *Studia Philologia Valentina* 12: 1–29.

Lawall, G. (1979), 'Seneca's *Medea*: The Elusive Triumph of Civilization', in Bowersock, Burkert, and Putnam (1979): 419–26.

Lawall, G. (1983), '*Virtus* and *Pietas* in Seneca's *Hercules Furens*', in Boyle (1983a): 6–26.

Le Guen, B., and Milanezi, S., eds. (2013), *L'Appareil scénique dans les spectacles de l'Antiquité*. Paris.

Leader, Z., and O'Neill, M. (2003), *Percy Bysshe Shelley: The Major Works*. Oxford.

Lebek, W. D. (1985), 'Senecas Agamemnon in Pompeji (*CIL* iv. 6698)', *ZPE* 59.1–6.

Lee, G. (1991), *A Short Introduction to the Ancient Greek Theater*. Chicago, IL, and London.

Lee, K. H. (1982), 'The Lyssa-Iris Scene in Euripides' *Heracles*', *Antichthon* 16: 44–53.

Lefèvre, E., ed (1972a), *Senecas Tragödien*. Darmstadt.

Lefèvre, E. (1972b), 'Schicksal und Selbstverschuldung in Senecas *Agamemnon*', in *id.* (1972a): 457–76 (orig. publ. *Hermes* 94, 1966: 489–96).

Lefèvre, E. (1973), 'Die Schuld des *Agamemnon*. Das Schicksal des Troja-Siegers in stoischer Sicht', *Hermes* 101: 64–91.

Lefèvre, E. (1976), *Der Thyestes des Lucius Varius Rufus: Zehn Überlegungen zu seiner Rekonstruktion*. Mainz.

Lefèvre, E., ed. (1978a), *Der Einfluss Senecas auf das europäische Drama*. Darmstadt.

Lefèvre, E. (1978b), *Das römische Drama*. Darmstadt.

Lefèvre, E. (1981), 'A Cult without God or the Unfreedom of Freedom in Seneca Tragicus', *CJ* 77: 32–6.

Lefèvre, E. (1985), 'Die politische Bedeutung der römischen Tragödie und Senecas "Oedipus"', *ANRW* II.32.2: 1242–62.

Lehmann, C. (2018), 'The End of Augustan Literature: Ovid's *Epistulae Ex Ponto* IV'. Diss. University of Southern California. Los Angeles.

Lehoux, D. (2012), *What Did the Romans Know? An Inquiry into Science and Worldmaking*. Chicago, IL, and London.

Leigh, M. (1996), 'Varius Rufus, Thyestes and the Appetites of Antony', *PCPS* 42: 171–97.

Leigh, M. (2000), 'Primitivism and Power: The Beginnings of Latin Literature', in Taplin (2000): 288–310.

Lemercier, L. (1804), *Agamemnon: Tragédie en cinque actes*. 3rd edn. Paris.

Lennartz, K. (1994), *Non uerba sed uim: Kritisch-exegetische Untersuchungen zu den Fragmenten archaischer römischer Tragiker*. Stuttgart and Leipzig.

Leo, F. (1878), *De Senecae tragoediis obseruationes criticae*, Vol. I. Berlin (repr. 1963).

Leo, F. (1897), 'Die Composition der Chorlieder Senecas', *RhM* 52: 509–18.

Leo, F. (1910), *De Tragoedia Romana*. Göttingen.

Lessing, G. (1970–9), *Werke*, ed. H. G. Göpfert et al. 8 vols. Munich.

Lessing, G. (1754), 'Von den Lateinischen Trauerspielen welche unter dem Namen des Seneca bekannt sind', in Lessing (1970–9): 4.58–141.

Lethem, J. (2011), *The Ecstasy of Influence*. New York.

Levi, M. A. (1995), *Nerone e i suoi tempi*. Milan.

Levick, B. (1990), *Claudius*. London.

Levick, B. (1999a), *Tiberius The Politician*. Rev. edn. London.

Levick, B. (1999b), *Vespasian*. London.

Lévi-Strauss, C. (1958), *Anthropologie structurale*. Paris.

Levitan, W. (1989), 'Seneca in Racine', *YFS* 76: 185–210.

Li Causi, P. (2006), 'Nella rete di Giunone: Cause, forme e finalità della vendetta nell' *Hercules furens* di Seneca', *Dioniso* 5, 118–37.

Li Causi, P. (2008), 'Padri vicini, padri lontani: L'identità di Ercole e il ruolo di Giove e di Anfitrione nell' *Hercules Furens* senecano', *MD* 59: 103–25.

Liebermann, W.-L. (1974), *Studien zu Senecas Tragödien*. Meisenheim am Glan.

Liebermann, W.-L. (2014), 'Context', in Damschen and Heil (2014): 405–21.

Lightfoot, J. L. (2002), 'Nothing to Do with the *Technitai* of Dionysus?', in Easterling and Hall (2002): 209–24.

Lindheim, S. H. (2003), *Mail and Female: Epistolary Narrative and Desire in Ovid's Heroides*. Madison, WI.

Ling, R. (1991), *Roman Painting*. Cambridge.

Littlewood, C. A. J. (2004), *Self-Representation and Illusion in Senecan Tragedy.* Oxford.

Littlewood, C. A. J. (2015), 'Theater and Theatricality in Seneca's World', in Bartsch and Schiesaro (2015): 161–73.

Littlewood, C. A. J. (2017), '*Hercules Furens* and the Senecan Sublime', *Ramus* 46: 153–74.

Lloyd-Jones, H. (1996), *Sophocles III: The Fragments.* Cambridge, MA, and London.

Lohikoski, K. K. (1966), 'Der Parallelismus Mykene-Troja in Senecas *Agamemnon*', *Arctos* NS 4: 63–70.

Long, A. A. (1971), *Problems in Stoicism.* London.

Long, A. A. (1974), *Hellenistic Philosophy.* London (repr. Berkeley, CA, and Los Angeles, CA, 1986).

Long, A. A. (1991), 'Representation and the Self in Stoicism', in Everson (1991): 102–20.

Long, A. A. (2009), 'Seneca on the Self. Why Now?' in Bartsch and Wray (2009): 20–36.

Long, A. A., and Sedley, D. N. (1987), *The Hellenistic Philosophers.* 2 vols. Cambridge.

Long, A. G. (2019), *Death and Immortality in Ancient Philosophy.* Cambridge.

Loraux, N. (1987), *Tragic Ways of Killing a Woman.* Cambridge, MA, and London.

Loraux, N. (1990), 'Herakles: The Super-Male and the Feminine', in Halperin et al. (1990): 21–52.

Lovatt, H. (2013), *The Epic Gaze: Vision, Gender and Narrative in Ancient Epic.* Cambridge.

Lucas, F. L. (1922), *Seneca and Elizabethan Tragedy.* Cambridge.

Luce, A., ed. (1897), *The Countess of Pembroke's Antonie.* Weimar.

Luck, G. (1969), *The Latin Love Elegy.* 2nd edn. London.

Lutz, C. E. (1947), *Musonius Rufus: The Roman Socrates.* New Haven, CT.

McAuley, M. (2016), *Reproducing Rome: Motherhood in Virgil, Ovid, Seneca, and Statius.* Oxford.

MacCallum, M. W. (1910), *Shakespeare's Roman Plays and their Background.* London and Melbourne.

McCrum, M., and Woodhead, A. G. (1961), *Select Documents of the Principates of the Flavian Emperors, Including the Year of Revolution: AD 68–96.* Cambridge.

McDonald, M., and Walton, J. M., eds. (2007), *The Cambridge Companion to the Greek and Roman Theatre.* Cambridge.

McDonnell, M. (2006), *Roman Manliness: Virtus and the Roman Republic.* Cambridge.

MacLeish, A. (1967), *Herakles.* Boston, MA.

MacGregor, A. P. (1978), 'Parisinus 8031: *Codex Optimus* for the A-Mss for Seneca's Tragedies', *Philologus* 122: 88–110.

MacGregor, A. P. (1980), 'Mussato's Commentary on Seneca's Tragedies: New Fragments', *ICS* 5: 149–62.

MacGregor, A. P. (1985), 'The Manuscripts of Seneca's Tragedies: A Handlist', *ANRW* II.32.2: 1134–1241.

MacKay, L. A. (1975), 'The Roman Tragic Spirit', *CSCA* 8: 145–62.

Macintosh, F. (2000), 'Introduction: The Performer in Performance', in Hall, Macintosh, and Taplin (2000): 1–31.

Macintosh, F., Michelakis P., Hall, E., and Taplin, O., eds. (2005), *Agamemnon in Performance: 458 BC to AD 2004*. Oxford.

Mack, S. (1988), *Ovid*. New Haven, CT, and London.

MacLeish, A. (1967), *Herakles*. Boston, MA.

Mader, G. (1982), 'Paradox and Perspective: Two Examples from Seneca's Tragedies (*Thy*. 470; *Ag*. 869)', *AC* 25: 71–83.

Mader, G. (1990), 'Form and Meaning in Seneca's "Dawn Song" (*HF* 125–201)', *AC* 33: 1–32.

Mader, G. (2002), 'Masks and the Man: Atreus, Lycus and Performances of Power in Seneca', in Defosse (2002): 336–47.

Mader, G. (2014), '*Hoc quod volo / me nolle*: Counter-Volition and Identity Management in Senecan tragedy', *Pallas* 95: 125–61.

Madvig, J. N. (1871–84), *Aduersaria critica ad scriptores Graecos et Latinos*. 3 vols. Copenhagen.

Maehler, H. (2004), *Bacchylides: A Selection*. Cambridge.

Maes, Y., Papy, J., and Verbaal W., eds. (2009), *Appropriation of Latin Literature*. Leiden.

Maggiulli, G. (2007), *Per alta nemora: La poesia del mondo vegetale in Seneca tragico*. Pisa/Rome.

Mainz, V., and Stafford, E., eds. (2020), *The Exemplary Hercules from the Renaissance to the Enlightenment and Beyond*. Leiden.

Malaspina, E. (2004), 'Pensiero politico ed esperienza storica nelle tragedie di Seneca', in Billerbeck and Schmidt (2004): 267–320.

Malaspina, E. (2014), '*De Clementia*', in Damschen and Heil (2014): 175–80.

Mantovanelli, P. (1984), *La metafora del Tieste: Il nodo sadomasochistico nella tragedia senecana del potere tirannico*. Verona.

Mantovanelli, P. (1992), 'Il prologo del "Tieste" di Seneca: Strutture spazio-temporali e intertestualità', *QCTC* 10: 201–12.

Manuwald, G., ed. (2000), *Identität und Alterität in der frührömischen Tragödie*. Würzburg.

Manuwald, G. (2001), *Fabulae praetextae: Spuren einer literarischen Gattung der Römer*. Munich.

Manuwald, G. (2003), *Pacuvius: Summus tragicus poeta. Zum dramatischen Profil seiner Tragödien*. Munich and Leipzig.

Manuwald, G. (2004), 'Römische Tragödien und Praetexten republikanischer Zeit: 1964–2002', *Lustrum* 43 (2001): 11–237.

Manuwald, G. (2011), *Roman Republican Theatre*. Cambridge.

Manuwald, G. (2021), '"Herculean tragedy" in Valerius Flaccus' *Argonautica*', in Papaioannou and Marinis (2021): 93–107.

Marchese, R. R. (2013), '*Veniet et vobis furor*: Seneca tragico e la perennità del male', *Dionysus Ex Machina* 4: 146–67.

Marcosignori, A. M. (1960), 'Il concetto di virtus tragica nel teatro di Seneca', *Aevum* 34: 217–33.

Mariotti, I. (1960), *Introduzione a Pacuvio*. Urbino.

Markham, G. and Sampson, W. (1622), *The True Tragedy of Herod and Antipater*. London.

Marlowe, C. (1590), *Tamburlaine the Great*: see Gibbons (2011).

Marlowe, C. (1592), *Doctor Faustus*: see Jump (1962).

Marshall, C. W. (2006), *The Stagecraft and Performance of Roman Comedy*. Cambridge.

Marshall, C. W. (2014), 'The Works of Seneca the Younger and Their Dates', in Damschen and Heil (2014): 33–44.

Marston, J. (1599/1600), *Antonio and Mellida*: see Hunter (1965).

Marston, J. (1600), *Antonio's Revenge*: see Gair (1978).

Marston, J. (1613), *The Insatiate Countess*: see Bullen (1887).

Marti, B. M. (1945), 'Seneca's Tragedies: A New Interpretation', *TAPA* 76: 216–45.

Marti, B. M. (1947), 'The Prototypes of Seneca's Tragedies', *CP* 42: 1–16.

Martin, L. H., Gutman, H., and Hutton, P. H., eds. (1988), *Technologies of the Self: A Seminar with Michel Foucault*. Amherst, MA.

Martindale, C. (2005), *Latin Poetry and the Judgement of Taste: An Essay in Aesthetics*. Oxford.

Martindale, C., and M. (1990), *Shakespeare and the Uses of Antiquity*. London and New York.

Martindale, C., and Taylor, A. B., eds. (2004), *Shakespeare and the Classics*. Cambridge.

Marx, K. (1966), *Civil War in France (First Draft)*. Peking.

Marx, W. (1932), *Funktion und Form der Chorlieder in den Seneca-Tragödien*. Heidelberg.

Maskell, D. (1991), *Racine: A Theatrical Reading*. Oxford.

Masters, J. (1992), *Poetry and Civil War in Lucan's Bellum Civile*. Cambridge.

Mastronarde, D. (1970), 'Seneca's *Oedipus*: The Drama in the Word', *TAPA* 101: 291–315.

Matthews, V. J. (1974), *Panyassis of Halikarnassos: Text and Commentary*. Leiden.

Matthews, V. J. (1996), *Antimachus of Colophon: Text and Commentary*. Leiden.

Mattingly, H. (1923), *Coins of the Roman Empire in the British Museum*, Vol. I. London.

Mattingly, H. (1930), *Coins of the Roman Empire in the British Museum*, Vol. II. London.

Maurach, G. (1983), *Enchiridion Poeticum: Hilfsbuch zur lateinischen Dichtersprache*. Darmstadt.

Maurens, J. (1980), *Pierre Corneille: Théatre II*. Paris.

Mayer, R. (1994), 'Personata Stoa: Neostoicism and Senecan Tragedy', *JWCI* 57: 151–74.

Mazzoli, G. (1970), *Seneca e la poesia*. Milan.

Mazzoli, G. (1996), 'Tipologia e struttura dei cori senecani', in Castagna (1996): 3–16.

Mazzoli, G. (1997), 'Su alcuni loci tragici di Seneca', *Paideia* 52: 225–40.

Mazzoli, G. (2008), 'La riflessione di Seneca sul teatro nello specchio dell' *Hercules furens*', in Aricò and Rivoltella (2008): 193–207.

Mazzoli, G. (2014), 'The Chorus: Seneca as Lyric Poet', in Damschen and Heil (2014): 561–74.

Meillet, A., and Vendryes, J. (1979), *Traité de grammaire comparée des langues classiques*. Paris.

Meineck, P. (2011), 'The Neuroscience of the Tragic Mask', *Arion* 19: 113–58.

Meineck, P. (2018), *Theatrocracy: Greek Drama, Cognition, and the Imperative for Theatre*. London.

Mellor, R. (1993), *Tacitus*. New York and London.

Mendell, C. W. (1941), *Our Seneca*. New Haven, CT.

Mendicino, K., and Wasihun, B., eds. (2013), *Playing False: Representations of Betrayal*. Berne.

Merkelbach, R., and West, M. L. (1967), *Fragmenta Hesiodea*. Oxford.

Mette, H. J. (1959), *Die Fragmente der Tragödien des Aischylos*. Berlin.

Mette, H. J. (1964), 'Die Römische Tragödie und die Neufunde zur Griechischen Tragödie', *Lustrum* 9: 5–211.

Mette, H. J. (1966), 'Die Funktion des Löwengleichnisses in Senecas *Hercules Furens*', *WS* 79: 477–89.

Meucci, R. (1989), 'Roman Military Instruments and the *Lituus*', *Galpin Soc. Journ.* 42: 85–97.

Michelini, A. N. (1987), *Euripides and the Tragic Tradition*. Madison, WI.

Michelon, F. (2015), *La scena dell' inganno: Finzioni tragice nel teatro di Seneca*. Turnhout.

Miller, J. F. (1993), 'Ovidian Allusion and the Vocabulary of Memory', *MD* 30: 153–64.

Miller, J. I. (1969), *The Spice Trade of the Roman Empire*. Oxford.

Miller, S. J. (2004), *Ancient Greek Athletics*. New Haven, CT.

Milton, J. (1649), *The Tenure of Kings and Magistrates*. London. See Allison (1911).

Miola, R. S. (1992), *Shakespeare and Classical Tragedy: The Influence of Seneca*. Oxford.

Miola, R. S. (2000), *Shakespeare's Reading*. Oxford.

Mitsis, P. (1993), 'Seneca on Reason, Rules and Moral Development', in Brunschwig and Nussbaum (1993): 285–312.

Mitsis, P., and Ziogas, I., eds. (2016), *Wordplay and Powerplay in Latin Poetry*. Berlin and Boston, MA.

Montaigne, M. E. de: see Florio (1910).

Montiglio, S. (2005), *Wandering in Ancient Greek Culture*. Chicago, IL, and London.

Montrose, L. (1996), *The Purpose of Playing: Shakespeare and the Cultural Politics of the Elizabethan Theater*. Chicago, IL, and London.

Moore, T. J. (1994), 'Seats and Social Status in the Plautine Theater', *CJ* 90: 113–23.

Moore, T. J. (1998), *The Theater of Plautus: Playing to the Audience*. Austin, TX.

Moore, T. J. (2012), *Music in Roman Comedy*. Cambridge.

Morelli, G. (1974), *Poesia latina in frammenti*. Genoa.

Morgan, L. (2010), *Musa Pedestris: Metre and Meaning in Roman Verse*. Oxford.

Most, G. W. (1992), '*Disiecta membra poetae*: The Rhetoric of Dismemberment in Neronian Poetry', in Hexter and Selden (1992): 391–419.

Most, G. W. (2000), 'Generating Genres: The Idea of the Tragic', in Depew and Obbink (2000): 15–35.

Most, G. W. (2007), *Hesiod*. 2 vols. Cambridge, MA, and London.

Motto, A. L. (1973), *Seneca*. New York.

Motto, A. L. and Clark, J. R. (1981), '*Maxima Virtus* in Seneca's *Hercules Furens*', *CP* 76: 101–17.

Motto, A. L. and Clark, J. R. (1988), *Senecan Tragedy*. Amsterdam.

Motto, A. L. and Clark, J. R. (1994), 'The Monster in Seneca's *Hercules Furens* 926–39', *CP* 89: 269–72.

Mowbray, C. (2012), 'Captive Audience? The Aesthetics of *Nefas* in Senecan Tragedy', in Sluiter and Rosen (2012): 393–420.

Mueller, M. (1980), *Children of Oedipus and Other Essays on the Imitation of Greek Tragedy 1550–1800*. Toronto.

Mugellesi, I. (1973), 'Il senso della natura in Seneca tragico', in *Argentea Aetas. In Memoriam E.V. Marmorale*. Genoa: 29–66.

Muir, K., ed. (1951), *Macbeth*. London.

Muir, K. (1958), 'Shakespeare and the Tragic Pattern', *Proc. Brit. Acad.* 44: 145–62.

Muir, K. (1978), *The Sources of Shakespeare's Plays*. New Haven, CT.

Müller, F. G. J. (1994), *The Wall Paintings from the Oecus of the Villa of Publius Fannius Synistor in Boscoreale*. Amsterdam.

Müller, M. (1898), *In Senecae Tragoedias Quaestiones Criticae*. Berlin.

Müller, M. (1901), 'Ad Senecae Tragoedias', *Philologus* 60: 261–70.

Mulryne, J. R. (1970), *Thomas Kyd: The Spanish Tragedy*. London and New York.

Munteanu, D., ed. (2011), *Emotion, Genre and Gender in Classical Antiquity*. London.

Mussato, A. (1315), *Ecerinis*: see Grund (2011).

Naiden, F. S. (2006), *Ancient Supplication*. Oxford.

Nauck, A. (1926), *Tragicorum Graecorum Fragmenta*. 2nd edn. Leipzig.

Nees, L. (1991), *A Tainted Mantle: Hercules and the Classical Tradition at the Carolingian Court*. Philadelphia.

Newlands, C. E. (1995), *Playing with Time: Ovid and the 'Fasti'*. Ithaca, NY.

Newman, J. K. (1967), *The Concept of 'Vates' in Augustan Poetry*. Brussels.

Niderst, A. (1984–6), *Pierre Corneille: Théâtre complet*. 3 vols. Rouen.

Nisbet, R. G. M. (2008), 'The Dating of Seneca's Tragedies, with Special Reference to *Thyestes*', in Fitch (2008): 348–71. Repr. from Cairns (1990): 95–114.

Niutta, F., and Santucci, C., eds. (1999), *Seneca: Mostra bibliografica e iconografica*. Rome.

Norland, H. (2009), *Neoclassical Tragedy in Elizabethan England*. Newark, DE.

Norton, T., and Sackville, T. (1561–2), *Gorboduc*: in Tydeman (1992).

Nosarti, L. (1999), *Filologia in frammenti: Contributi esegetici e testuali ai frammenti dei poeti latini*. Bologna.

Nussbaum, M. (1993), 'Poetry and the Passions: Two Stoic Views', in Brunschwig and Nussbaum (1993): 97–149.

Nussbaum, M. (1994), *The Therapy of Desire: Theory and Practice in Hellenistic Ethics*. Princeton, NJ.

Ogden, D. (2009), *Magic, Witchcraft and Ghosts in the Greek and Roman Worlds: A Sourcebook*. 2nd edn. New York.

Ogilvie, R. M. (1980), *Roman Literature and Society*. Harmondsworth.

O'Higgins, D. (1988), 'Lucan as *uates*', *Cl. Ant.* 7: 208–26.

O'Kell, E. R. (2005), '*Hercules Furens* and Nero: The Didactic Purpose of Senecan Tragedy', in Rawlings and Bowden (2005): 185–204.

Oldfather, W. A., Pease, A. S., and Canter, H. V. (1918), *Index Verborum Quae in Senecae Fabulis Necnon In Octavia Praetexta Reperiuntur*. Urbana, IL.

Oliensis, E. (1997), 'Return to Sender: The Rhetoric of *Nomina* in Ovid's *Tristia*', *Ramus* 26: 172–93.

Olszewski, E. (2019), 'Dionysus's Enigmatic Thyrsus', *PAPS* 163.2: 153–73.

Opelt, I. (1951), *Der Tyrann als Unmensch in den Tragödien des L. Annaeus Senecas*. Freiburg.

Opelt, I. (1972*a*), 'Senecas Konzeption des Tragischen', in Lefèvre (1972*a*): 92–128.

Opelt, I. (1972*b*), 'Zu Senecas Phoenissen', in Lefèvre (1972*a*): 272–85.

Orgel, S., ed. (1975), *The Renaissance Imagination*. Berkeley, CA, and Los Angeles, CA.

O'Sullivan, T. M. (2011), *Walking in Roman Culture*. Cambridge.

Owen, W. H. (1968), 'Commonplace and Dramatic Symbol in Seneca's Tragedies', *TAPA* 99: 291–313.

Pack, R. A. (1940), 'On Guilt and Error in Senecan Tragedy', *TAPA* 71: 360–71.

Padel, R. (1992), *In and Out of the Mind: Greek Images of the Tragic Self*. Princeton, NJ.

Padel, R. (1995), *Whom the Gods Destroy: Elements of Greek and Tragic Madness*. Princeton, NJ.

Padilla, M. (1998), *The Myths of Herakles in Ancient Greece*. Lanham, MD.

Paduano, G. (1974), *Il mondo religioso della tragedia Romana*. Florence.

Page, D. L. (1938), *Euripides: Medea*. Oxford.

Page, D. L. (1962), *Poetae Melici Graeci*. Oxford.

Panayotakis, C. (2005), 'Comedy, Atellane Farce and Mime', in Harrison (2005): 130–47.

Papadopoulou, T. (2000), 'Studies in Euripides' *Heracles*', PhD thesis, University of Cambridge.

Papadopoulou, T. (2004), 'Herakles and Hercules: The Hero's Ambivalence in Euripides and Seneca', *Mnem.* 57: 257–83.

Papadopoulou, T. (2005), Heracles *and Euripidean Tragedy*. Cambridge.

Papaioannou, S., and Marinis, A., eds. (2021), *Elements of Tragedy in Flavian Epic*. Berlin and Boston, MA.

Papanghelis, T. D., and Rengakos, A., eds. (2000), *A Companion to Apollonius Rhodius*. Leiden.

Paratore, E. (1957*a*), 'Orginalità del teatro di Seneca', *Dioniso* NS 20: 53–74.

Paratore, E. (1957*b*), *Storia del teatro latino*. Milan.

Paratore, E. (1966), *Il prologo dello 'Hercules Furens' di Seneca e l''Eracle' di Euripide*. Rome.

Parker, R. (1983), *Miasma, Pollution and Purification in Early Greek Religion*. Oxford.

Paul, A. (1953), *Untersuchungen zur Eigenart von Senecas Phoenissen*. Bonn.

Paul, H. N. (1950), *The Royal Play of 'Macbeth'*. New York.

Pavlock, B. (2009), *The Image of the Poet in Ovid's Metamorphoses*. Madison, WI.

Péché, V., and Vendries, C., eds. (2001), *Musique et spectacles à Rome et dans l'Occident Romain sous la République et le Haut-empire*. Paris.

Peirano, I. (2013), '*Non subripiendi causa sed palam mutuandi*: Intertextuality and Literary Deviancy between Law, Rhetoric and Literature in Roman Imperial Culture', *AJP* 134: 83–100.

Pembroke, Countess of (1595), *The Tragedie of Antoine*: see Luce (1897).

Perkell, C. G., ed. (1999), *Reading Vergil's Aeneid: An Interpretive Guide*. Norman, OK.

Perry, C. (2015), 'Seneca and the Modernity of Hamlet', *Illinois Classical Studies* 40: 407–29.

Perry, C. (2016), 'Seneca and English Political Culture', in Smuts (2016): 306–321.

Perry, C. (2019), 'Senecan Belatedness and *Titus Andronicus*', in Karim-Cooper (2019): 15–35.

Petrini, A. (1999), 'La tragedia', in Niutta and Santucci (1999): 127–62.

Petrone, G. (1984), *La scrittura tragica dell'irrazionale*. Palermo.

Petrone, G. (1986–7), 'Paesaggio dei morti e paesaggio del male in Seneca tragico', *QCTC* 4–5: 131–43.

Petrone, G. (1988), '*Nomen/omen*: Poetica e funzione dei nomi (Plauto, Seneca, Petronio)', *MD* 20–1: 33–70.

Petrone, G. (2000), 'La *praetexta* repubblicana e il linguaggio delle celebrazione', in Manuwald (2000): 113–21.

Pettine, E. (1974), *Studio dei caratteri e poesia nelle tragedie di Seneca*. Salerno.

Peyré, Y. (2004), ' "Confusion now hath made his masterpiece": Senecan resonances in *Macbeth*', in Martindale and Taylor (2004): 141–55.

Pfeiffer, R. (1949), *Callimachus*. 2 vols. Oxford.

Phillippo, S. (2005), 'Clytemnestra's Ghost: The Aeschylean Legacy in Gluck's Iphigenia Operas', in Macintosh et al. (2005): 77–103.

Picone, G. (1984), (2004), 'La scena doppia: Spazi drammaturgici nel teatro di Seneca', *Dioniso* 3: 134–44.

Pisi, G. (1989), *La peste in Seneca tra scienza e letteratura*. Parma.

Plass, P. (1995), *The Game of Death in Ancient Rome: Arena Sport and Political Suicide*. Madison, WI.

Pociña Pérez, A. (2003), 'La donna secondo Seneca e le donne degli Annei', in Gualandri and Mazzoli (2003): 327–37.

Pollard, T. (2017), *Greek Tragic Women on Shakespearean Stages*. Oxford.

Porter, J., Csapo, E., Marshall, C. W., and Ketterer, R., eds. (1999), *Crossing the Stages: The Production, Performance and Reception of Ancient Theatre. Syllecta Classica* 10. Iowa City.

Potter, D., and Mattingly, D., eds. (1999), *Life, Death, Entertainment in the Roman Empire*. Ann Arbor, MI.

Powell, J. U. (1925), *Collectanea Alexandrina*. Oxford.

Pratt, N. T., Jr. (1939), *Dramatic Suspense in Seneca and his Greek Predecessors*. Princeton, NJ.

Pratt, N. T., Jr. (1948), 'The Stoic Base of Senecan Drama', *TAPA* 79: 1–11.

Pratt, N. T., Jr. (1963), 'Major Systems of Figurative Language in Senecan Melodrama', *TAPA* 94: 199–234.

Pratt, N. T., Jr. (1983), *Seneca's Drama*. Chapel Hill, NC, and London.

Provenza, A. (2013), 'Madness and Bestializaton in Euripides' *Heracles*', *CQ* 63: 68–93.

Pucci, P., ed. (1988), *Language and the Tragic Hero: Essays on Greek Tragedy in Honor of Gordon M. Kirkwood*. Atlanta, GA.

Pugliese Caratelli, G., ed. (1990–9), *Pompei: Pitture e mosaici*. 10 vols. Rome.

Putnam, M. (1995), *Vergil's Aeneid: Interpretation and Influence*. Chapel Hill, NC.

Putnam, M. (1998), *Vergil's Epic Designs: Ekphrasis in the Aeneid*. New Haven, CT.

Pyplacz, J. (2010), *The Aesthetics of Senecan Tragedy*. Cracow.

Quiller-Couch, A. (1919), *The Oxford Book of English Verse 1250–1900*. Oxford.

Race, W. H. (2019), *Menander Rhetor, [Dionysius of Halicarnassus] Ars Rhetorica*. Cambridge, MA, and London.

Racine, J. (1674), *Iphigénie*: see Forestier (1999).

Radt, S. (1977), *Tragicorum Graecorum Fragments*, Vol. IV: *Sophocles*. Göttingen.

Ramage, N. H., and A. R. (1991), *The Cambridge Illustrated History of Roman Art*. Cambridge.

Raven, D. S. (1965), *Latin Metre*. London.

Rawlings, L., and Bowden H., eds. (2005), *Herakles and Hercules: Exploring a Graeco-Roman Divinity*. Swansea.

Rawson, E. (1991), *Roman Culture and Society*. Oxford.

Rebegianni, S. (2018), *The Fragility of Power: Statius, Domitian and the Politics of the Thebaid*. New York.

Rees, B. R. (1969), 'English Seneca: A Preamble', *G&R* NS 16: 119–33.

Rees, R., ed. (2009), *Ted Hughes and the Classics*. Oxford.

Regenbogen, O. (1927–8), 'Schmerz und Tod in den Tragödien des Seneca', *Vorträge der Bibliothek Warburg*: 167–218.

Rehm, R. (1994), *Marriage to Death: The Conflation of Wedding and Funeral Rituals in Greek Tragedy*. Princeton, NJ.

Rehm, R. (2002), *The Play of Space: Spatial Transformation in Greek Tragedy*. Princeton, NJ.

Reich, H. (1974), *Der Mimus*. Leipzig.

Reid, J. D. (1993), *The Oxford Guide to Classical Mythology in the Arts, 1300–1990s*. 2 vols. Oxford.

Renard, A. (1849), *Études littéraires et dramatiques*. Paris.

Renard, M., and Laurens, P., eds. (1985), *Hommages à Henri Bardon*. Brussels.

Revermann, M. (2006), 'The Competence of Theatre Audiences in Fifth- and Fourth-Century Athens', *JHS* 126: 99–124.

Reydams-Schils, G. (2005), *The Roman Stoics: Self, Responsibility, and Affection*. Chicago, IL.

Reynolds, L. D., ed. (1983), *Texts and Transmission: A Survey of the Latin Classics*. Oxford.

Ribbeck, O. (1875), *Die römische Tragödie im Zeitalter der Republik*. Leipzig (repr. Hildesheim 1969).

Richardson, L., Jr. (1992), *A New Topographical Dictionary of Ancient Rome*. Baltimore, MD, and London.

Richlin, A. (1997), 'Gender and Rhetoric: Producing Manhood in the Schools', in Dominik (1997): 74–91.

Richter, G. (1862), *De Seneca tragoediarum auctore commentatio philologica*. Bonn.

Richter, G. (1899), *Kritische Untersuchungen zu Senecas Tragödien*. Jena.

Riemer, P. (1997), 'Zur dramaturgischen Konzeption von Senecas Agamemnon', in Zimmermann (1997): 135–51.

Riemer, P., and Zimmermann, B., eds. (1999), *Der Chor im antiken und modernen Drama*. Stuttgart.

Riley, K. (2004), 'Heracles as Dr Strangelove and GI Joe: Male Heroism Deconstructed', in Hall et al. (2004): 113–42.

Riley, K. (2008), *The Reception and Performance of Euripides' Herakles*. Oxford.

Rimell, V. (2015), *The Closure of Space in Roman Poetics: Empire's Inward Turn*. Cambridge.

Rist, J. M. (1969), *Stoic Philosophy*. Cambridge.

Rist, J. M., ed. (1978), *The Stoics*. Berkeley, CA, and Los Angeles, CA.

Rist, J. M. (1989), 'Seneca and Stoic Orthodoxy', *ANRW* 2.36.3: 1993–2012.

Ritter, S. (1995), *Hercules in der römischen Kunst von den Anfängen bis Augustus*. Heidelberg.

Robbins, E. (1982), 'Heracles, the Hyperboreans, and the Hind: Pindar *Ol.* 3', *Phoenix* 36: 295–305.

Roberts, D. H., Dunn, F. M., and Fowler, D., eds. (1997), *Classical Closure: Reading the End in Greek and Latin Literature*. Princeton, NJ.

Roisman, H. (2005), 'Women in Senecan Tragedy', *Scholia* 14: 72–87.

Roller, M. B. (2001), *Constructing Autocracy: Aristocrats and Emperors in Julio-Claudian Rome*. Princeton, NJ.

Roller, M. B. (2018), *Models from the Past in Roman Culture: A World of Exempla*. Cambridge.

Romero, M. (2016), 'The Reception of Seneca in the Crowns of Aragon and Castile in the Fourteenth and Fifteenth Centuries', in Dodson-Robinson (2016): 101–21.

Romm, J. (2014), *Dying Every Day: Seneca at the Court of Nero*. New York.

Ronan, C. (1995), *'Antike Roman'. Power Symbology and the Roman Play in Early Modern England, 1585–1635*. Athens, GA.

Roots, E. B. (1991), *A Drama in the Word: The Rhetoric of Senecan Tragedy*. New Haven, CT.

Rosati, G. (2006), 'Libido amandi e libido regnandi, ovvero elegia e potere nel teatro senecano', *Dioniso* 5: 94–105.

Rose, A. (1978), 'Studies in Seneca's *Hercules Furens*', Diss. University of Colorado. Boulder, CO.

Rose, A. (1979–80), 'Seneca's *HF*: A Politico-Didactic Reading', *CJ* 75: 135–42.

Rose, A. (1983), 'Seneca and Suicide: The End of the *Hercules Furens*', *CO* 60: 109–11.

Rose, A. (1985), 'Seneca's Dawn Song (*HF* 125–158) and the Imagery of Cosmic Disruption', *Latomus* 44: 101–23.

Rose, C. B. (1997), *Dynastic Commemoration and Imperial Portraiture in the Julio-Claudian Period*. Cambridge.

Rose, W. S. (1858), trans., *The Orlando Furioso of Ludovico Ariosto*. 2 vols. London.

Rosenmeyer, T. G. (1969), *The Green Cabinet: Theocritus and the European Pastoral Lyric*. Berkeley, CA, and Los Angeles, CA.

Rosenmeyer, T. G. (1989), *Senecan Drama and Stoic Cosmology*. Berkeley, CA.

Rosenmeyer, T. G. (1993), 'Seneca's *Oedipus* and Performance: The Manto Scene', in Scodel (1993): 235–44.

Roskam, G. (2007), *'Live unnoticed' (λάθε βιώσας): On the Vicissitudes of an Epicurean Doctrine*. Leiden.

Ross, D. O., Jr. (1975a), *Backgrounds to Augustan Poetry: Gallus, Elegy and Rome*. Cambridge.

Ross, D. O., Jr. (1975b), 'The *Culex* and *Moretum* as Post-Augustan Literary Parodies', *HSCP* 79: 235–63.

Ross, W. D. (1955), *Aristotelis Fragmenta Selecta*. Oxford.

Rousselle, R. J. (1987), 'Liber-Dionysos in Early Roman Drama', *CJ* 82: 193–8.

Rowland, I. D. (1999), *Vitruvius: Ten Books of Architecture*. Cambridge.

Rozelaar, M. (1976), *Seneca: Eine Gesamtdarstellung*. Amsterdam.

Ruck, C. (1976), 'Duality and the Madness of Herakles', *Arethusa* 9: 53–75.

Rudd, N. (1976), *Lines of Enquiry: Studies in Latin Poetry*. Cambridge.

Rudich, V. (1993), *Political Dissidence under Nero: The Price of Dissimulation*. London and New York.

Rudich, V. (1997), *Dissidence and Literature under Nero: The Price of Rhetoricization*. London and New York.

Runchina, G. (1960), 'Tecnica drammatica e retorica nelle tragedie di Seneca', *Annali della Facultà di Lettere, Filosofia e Magistero della Università di Cagliari* 28: 165–324.

Rüpke, J., ed. (2007), *A Companion to Roman Religion*. Oxford.

Russell, D. A. (1979), 'Rhetors at the Wedding', *PCPS* 25: 104–17.

Rutgers, J. (1618), *Variarum Lectionum Libri VI*. Lyons.

Ryle, G. (1949), *The Concept of Mind*. London and New York.

Safty, E. (2006), 'La Question du suicide dans les tragedies du philosophe Seneque', *Cahiers des études anciennes* 43 (http://journals.openedition.org/etudesanciennes).

Sagar, K. (2009), 'Ted Hughes and the Classics', in Rees (2009): 1–24.

Saller, R. P. (1994), *Patriarchy, Property and Death in the Roman Family*. Cambridge.

Samburský, S. (1959), *The Physics of the Stoics*. London.

Sampson, C. M. (2017), 'Unsettling the Senecan First Act', in Trinacty and Sampson (2017a): 16–34.

Sandbach, F. (1975), *The Stoics*. London.

Scaliger, J. J. (1621), Emendations in Scriuerius (1621).

Schefold, K. (1952), *Pompejanische Malerei: Sinn und Ideengeschichte*. Basle.

Scheid, J. (2003), *An Introduction to Roman Religion*. Edinburgh.

Schiesaro, A. (1992), 'Forms of Senecan Intertextuality', *Vergilius* 38: 56–63.

Schiesaro, A. (1994), 'Seneca's *Thyestes* and the Morality of Tragic *Furor*', in Elsner and Masters (1994): 96–210.

Schiesaro, A. (1997), 'Passion, Reason and Knowledge in Seneca's Tragedies', in Braund and Gill (1997): 89–111.

Schiesaro, A. (2003), *The Passions in Play: Thyestes and the Dynamics of Senecan Drama*. Cambridge.

Schiesaro, A. (2009), 'Seneca and the Denial of the Self', in Bartsch and Wray (2009): 221–35.

Schiesaro, A. (2011), '*Ibis redibis*', *MD* 67: 79–150.

Schlegel, A. W. von. (1846), *A Course of Lectures on Dramatic Art and Literature* (trans. J. Black). London.

Schmidt, B. (1865), *Observationes Criticae in L. Annaei Senecae Tragoedias*. Jena.

Schmidt, E. A. (2000), 'Aparte. Das dramatische Verfahren und Senecas Technik', *RhM* 143: 400–29.

Schmidt, E. A. (2001), 'Der dramatische Raum der Tragödien Senecas', *WS* 114: 341–60.

Schmidt, E. A. (2004), 'Zeit und Raum in Senecas Tragödien: Ein Beitrag zu seiner dramatischen Technik', in Billerbeck and Schmidt (2004): 321–68.

Schmidt, E. A. (2014), 'Space and Time in Senecan Drama', in Damschen and Heil (2014): 531–46.

Schmidt, M. (1960), *Der Dareiosmaler und sein Umkreis*. Munich.

Schmitz, C. (1993), *Die kosmische Dimension in den Tragödien Senecas*. Berlin and New York.

Schnurr, C. (1992), 'The *Lex Iulia Theatralis* of Augustus: Some Remarks on Seating Problems in Theatre, Amphitheatre and Circus', *LCM* 17: 147–60.

Schofield, M. (2003), 'Stoic Ethics', in Inwood: 233–56.

Schofield, M. (2015), 'Seneca on Monarchy and the Political Life: *De Clementia, De Tranquillitate Animi, De Otio*', in Bartsch and Schiesaro (2015): 68–81.

Schubert, C. (1998), *Studien zum Nerobild in der lateinischen Dichtung der Antike*. Stuttgart and Leipzig.

Schubert, W. (2004), 'Seneca in der Musik der Neuzeit', *Fondation Hardt Entretiens* 50: 369–412.

Schubert, W. (2014), 'Seneca the Dramatist', in Damschen and Heil (2014): 73–93.

Schwartz, E. (1887), *Scholia in Euripidem: I*. Berlin.

Scodel, R., ed. (1993), *Theatre and Society in the Classical World*. Ann Arbor, MI.

Scolnicov, H., and Holland, P., eds. (1989), *The Play out of Context: Transferring Plays from Culture to Culture*. Cambridge.

Scullard, H. H. (1959), *From the Gracchi to Nero: A History of Rome from 133 BC to AD 68*. London.

Seager, R. (2005), *Tiberius*. 2nd edn. Oxford.

Sear, F. (2006), *Roman Theatres: An Architectural Study*. Oxford.

Segal, C. P. (1977), 'Euripides' *Bacchae*: Conflict and Mediation', *Ramus* 6: 103–20.

Segal, C. P. (1982), '*Nomen Sacrum*: Medea and Other Names in Senecan Tragedy', *Maia* 34: 214–46.

Segal, C. P. (1983), 'Dissonant Sympathy: Song, Orpheus, and the Golden Age in Senecan Tragedy', in Boyle (1983*a*): 229–51.

Segal, C. P. (1986), *Language and Desire in Seneca's Phaedra*. Princeton, NJ.

Segal, C. P. (2008), 'Boundary Violation and the Landscape of the Self in Senecan Tragedy', in Fitch (2008): 136–56, repr. from *A&A* (1983) 29: 172–87.

Segal, E. (1968), *Roman Laughter: The Comedy of Plautus*. Cambridge, MA.

Seidensticker, B. (1969), *Die Gesprächsverdichtung in den Tragödien Senecas*. Heidelberg.

Seidensticker, B. (1985), 'Maius solito: Senecas Thyestes und die tragoedia rhetorica', *Antike und Abendland* 31: 116–36.

Seidensticker, B. (2010), *Das Antike Theater*. Munich.

Seidensticker, B., and Armstrong, D. (1985), 'Seneca Tragicus 1878–1978 (with Addenda 1979ff.)', *ANRW* II.32.2: 916–68.

Seidler, B. (1955), 'Studien zur Wortstellung in den Tragödien Senecas'. Diss. University of Vienna.

Sentieri, A. de Cavazzani (1919), 'Sulla figura dell' ἀδύνατον', *Athenaeum* 7: 179–84.

Setaioli, A. (1997), 'Seneca e l'oltretomba', *Paideia* 52: 321–67.

Setaioli, A. (2000), *Facundus Seneca: Aspetti della lingua e dell' ideologia senecana*. Bologna.

Shakespeare, W. (1589–1614): for the plays, the Arden editions 1951–. London.

Shaw, M. H. (1980), 'Mussato's Use of Seneca and Statius in *Ecerinis*', *RRWL* 2.1: 1–11.

Shelley, P. B. (1819), *The Cenci*: see Leader and O'Neill (2003).

Shelton, J.-A. (1975), 'Problems of Time in Seneca's *Hercules Furens* and *Thyestes*', *CSCA* 8: 257–69.

Shelton, J.-A. (1978), *Seneca's 'Hercules Furens': Theme, Structure and Style.* Göttingen.

Shelton, J.-A. (1979), 'Structural Unity and the Meaning of Euripides' *Herakles'*, *Eranos* 77: 101–10.

Siemers, T. B. B. (1951), *Seneca's 'Hercules Furens' en Euripides' 'Heracles'.* Diss. University of Utrecht.

Sifakis, G. M. (1967), *Studies in the History of Hellenistic Drama.* London.

Silk, M. S. (1985), 'Heracles and Greek Tragedy', *G&R* 32: 1–22.

Simon, E. (1964), 'Die Typen der Medeadarstellung in der antiken Kunst', *Gymn.* 61: 203–27.

Singleton, C. S. (1970), *Dante Alighieri: The Divine Comedy. I. Inferno.* Princeton, NJ.

Sinn, U. (1979), *Die homerischen Becher: Hellenistische ReliefKeramik aus Makedonien.* Berlin.

Skutsch, O. (1968), *Studia Enniana.* London.

Slaney, H. (2013a), 'Language and the Body in the Performance Reception of Senecan Tragedy', DPhil thesis, University of Oxford.

Slaney, H. (2013b), 'Seneca's Chorus of One', in Billings, Budelmann, and MacIntosh (2013): 99–116.

Slaney, H. (2015), 'Schlegel, Shelley and the "Death" of Seneca', in Harrison (2015): 311–29.

Slaney, H. (2016), *The Senecan Aesthetic: A Performance History.* Oxford.

Slaney, H. (2019), *Seneca: Medea.* London and New York.

Slater, N. W. (1985), *Plautus in Performance.* Princeton, NJ.

Slater, N. W. (1996), 'Nero's Masks', *CW* 90: 33–40.

Slater, N. W. (2002), 'Some Accian Women', in Faller and Manuwald (2002): 289–303.

Slater, W. J., ed. (1991), *Dining in a Classical Context.* Ann Arbor, MI.

Slater, W. J., ed. (1996), *Roman Theater and Society.* Ann Arbor, MI.

Sluiter, I., and Rosen, R. M., eds. (2012), *Aesthetic Value in Classical Antiquity.* Leiden.

Smallwood, E. M. (1967), *Documents Illustrating the Principates of Gaius, Claudius and Nero.* Cambridge.

Smereka, J. (1936), 'De Senecae tragici uocabulorum copiae certa quadam lege', in *Munera Philologica L. Cwiklinski*: 253–61. Posnan.

Smith, B. R. (1988), *Ancient Scripts and Modern Experience on the English Stage 1500–1700.* Princeton, NJ.

Smith, G. G. (1904), *Elizabethan Critical Essays.* 2 vols. Oxford.

Smith, J. A. (1997), 'The Translation of Tragedy into Imperial Rome: A Study of Seneca's *Hercules* and *Oedipus'*, Diss. University of Southern California. Los Angeles, CA.

Smolenaars, J. J. L. (1998), 'The Vergilian Background of Seneca's *Thyestes* 641–682', *Vergilius* 44: 51–65.

Smuts, R. M. (2016), *The Oxford Handbook of the Age of Shakespeare.* Oxford.

Snell, B. (1964), *Scenes from Greek Drama.* Berkeley, CA, and Los Angeles, CA.

Snell, B., Kannich R., and Radt, S. (1971–85), *Tragicorum Graecorum Fragmenta.* Berlin.

Soellner, R. (1958), 'The Madness of Hercules and the Elizabethans', *Comp. Lit.* 10: 309–24.

Solimano, G. (1980), 'Il mito di Orfeo-Ippolito in Seneca', *Sandalion* 3: 151–74.

Solodow, J. B. (1988), *The World of Ovid's Metamorphoses.* Chapel Hill, NC.

Sommerstein, A. H. (2008), *Aeschylus*. 3 vols. Cambridge, MA.

Sourvinou-Inwood, C. (1991), '*Reading' Greek Culture*. Oxford.

Spawforth, A. J. S. (2012), *Greece and the Augustan Cultural Revolution*. Cambridge.

Speka, A. (1937), 'Der hohe Stil der Dichtungen Senecas und Lucans'. Diss. University of Königsberg.

Spengel, L., ed. (1856), *Rhetores Graeci*. 3 vols. Leipzig.

Spenser, E. (1595), *Epithalamion*, in Quiller-Couch (1919).

Spinazzola, V. (1953), *Pompei alla luce degli scavi nuovi di via dell' Abbondanza*. Rome.

Springer, F.-K. (1952), *Tyrannus. Untersuchungen zur politischen Ideologie der Römer*. Darmstadt.

Stacey, P. (2015), 'Senecan Political Thought from the Middle Ages to Early Modernity', in Bartsch and Schiesaro (2015): 189–302.

Stachelscheid, A. (1882), 'Bentleys Emendationem zu Senecas Tragödien', *JKP* 28: 481–93.

Stafford, E. (2012), *Herakles*. London and New York.

Staley, G. A. (2010), *Seneca and the Idea of Tragedy*. New York.

Stambler, B. (1986), 'Hercules as Hero for Seneca', in Uhlenbrock (1986): 35–8.

Stamm, R. (1975), *The Mirror-Technique in Seneca and Pre-Shakespearean Tragedy*. Berne.

Star, C. (2006), 'Commanding *Constantia* in Senecan Tragedy', *TAPA* 136: 207–44.

Star, C. (2012), *The Empire of the Self: Self-Command and Political Speech in Seneca and Petronius*. Baltimore, MD.

Star, C. (2017), *Seneca*. London and New York.

Stärk, E., and G. Vogt-Spira, eds. (2000), *Dramatische Wäldchen. Festschrift für Eckard Lefèvre*. Hildesheim.

States, B. O., Jr. (1957), 'The Stage History of Shelley's *The Cenci*', *PMLA* 72: 633–44.

Steane, J. B., ed. (1986), *Christopher Marlowe: The Complete Plays*. London.

Steegman, A. (1965), 'Seneca and Corneille', in Dorey and Dudley (1965): 161–92.

Steele, R. B. (1922), 'Some Roman Elements in the Tragedies of Seneca', *AJP* 43: 1–41.

Steiner, D. (1995), 'Stoning and Sight: A Structural Equivalence in Greek Mythology', *CA* 14: 193–221.

Steiner, G. (2008), '"Tragedy" Reconsidered', in Felski (2008): 29–44.

Stevens, J. A. (1992), *The Chorus in Senecan Tragedy: The Uninformed Informer*. Durham, NC.

Stevens, J. A. (2000), 'Seneca and Horace: Allegorical Technique in Two Odes to Bacchus (Hor. *Carm.* 2.19 and Sen. *Oed.* 403–508)', *Phoenix* 53: 281–307.

Stevens, J. A. (2002), 'Etymology and Plot in Senecan Tragedy', *Syl. Clas.* 13: 126–53.

Stewart, A. (1990), *Greek Sculpture: An Exploration*. 2 vols. New Haven, CT and London.

Stöckinger, M., Winter, K., and Zanker, A. T., eds. (2017), *Horace and Seneca*. Berlin and New York.

Strachey, J. (1953–74), *Standard Edition of the Complete Psychological Works of Sigmund Freud*. 24 vols. London.

Strange, S. K. (2004), 'The Stoics on the Voluntariness of the Passions', in Strange and Zupko (2004): 32–51.

Strange, S. K., and Zupko, J., eds. (2004), *Stoicism: Traditions and Transformations*. Cambridge.

Stroh, W. (2000), ' "Give us your Applause" ': The World of Theatre', in Köhne and Ewigleben (2002): 103–24.

Stroh, W. (2008), 'Staging Seneca: The Production of *Troas* as a Philological Experiment', in Fitch (2008): 195–220.

Stroh, W. and Breitenberger, B. (1994), 'Inszenierung Senecas', in Bierl and von Möllendorf (1994): 248–69.

Stróżyński, M. (2015), 'Heaven, Hell and the Earth: Infanticide in Seneca's *Hercules*', *Eos* 102: 57–94.

Strzelecki, L. (1938), *De Senecae trimetro iambico quaestiones selectae*. Cracow.

Stuart, C. E. (1911), 'Notes and Emendations on the Tragedies of Seneca', *CQ* 5: 32–41.

Sturz, F. G. (1824), *Commentatio de Pherecyde Vtroque Philosophico et Historico*. Leipzig.

Suerbaum, W. (1968), *Untersuchungen zur Selbstdarstellung älterer römischer Dichter: Livius Andronicus, Naevius, Ennius*. Hildesheim.

Sullivan, J. P. (1985), *Literature and Politics in the Age of Nero*. Ithaca, NY and London.

Sutherland, J. M. (1985), 'Shakespeare and Seneca: A Symbolic Language for Tragedy'. Diss. University of Colorado. Boulder, CO.

Sutton, D. F. (1984), 'Seneca's *Hercules Furens*. One Chorus or Two?', *AJP* 105: 301–5.

Sutton, D. F. (1986), *Seneca on the Stage*. Leiden.

Sutton, D. F., ed. (1994), *William Gager: The Complete Works*. 4 vols. London.

Swoboda, A. (1889), *P. Nigidii Figuli Operum Reliquiae*. Vienna.

Syme, R. (1939), *The Roman Revolution*. Oxford.

Syme, R. (1958), *Tacitus*. 2 vols. Oxford.

Szemerényi, O. (1975), 'The Origins of Roman Drama and Greek Tragedy', *Hermes* 103: 300–37.

Tan, J. K. (2016), 'The Ambitions of Scipio Nasica and Destruction of the Stone Theatre', *Antichthon* 50: 70–9.

Tanner, R. G. (1985), 'Stoic Philosophy and Roman Tradition in Senecan Tragedy', *ANRW* II.32.2: 1100–33.

Taplin, O. (1977), *The Stagecraft of Aeschylus: The Dramatic Use of Entrances and Exits in Greek Tragedy*. Oxford.

Taplin, O. (1983), *Greek Tragedy in Action*. London.

Taplin, O., ed. (2000), *Literature in the Greek and Roman Worlds: A New Perspective*. Oxford.

Taplin, O. (2007), *Pots and Plays: Interactions between Tragedy and Greek Vase-Painting of the Fourth Century* BC. Los Angeles, CA.

Tarbell, F. B. (1906), 'The Palm of Victory', *CP* 3: 264–72.

Tarrant, R. J. (1978), 'Senecan Drama and its Antecedents', *HSCP* 82: 213–63.

Tarrant, R. J. (1995), 'Greek and Roman in Seneca's Tragedies', *HSCP* 97: 215–30.

Tarrant, R. J. (2002), 'Chaos in Ovid's *Metamorphoses* and its Neronian Influence', *Arethusa* 35: 349–60.

Tarrant, R. J. (2006), 'Seeing Seneca Whole', in Volk and Williams (2006): 1–17.

Tarrant, R. J. (2017), 'Custode rerum Caesare: Horatian Civic Engagement and the Senecan Tragic Chorus', in Stöckinger et al. (2017): 93–112.

Taylor, C. (1990), Sources of the Self: The Making of Modern Identity. Cambridge, MA.

Taylor, L. R. (1931), The Divinity of the Roman Emperor. Middletown, CT.

Telò, M. (2014), 'Pregnant Props: Birth and Narrative in Three Plautine Plots', unpublished paper delivered at 'Roman Comedy and its Contexts', Aristotle University, Thessaloniki (May-June 2014).

Thalmann, W. G. (2011), Apollonius of Rhodes and the Spaces of Hellenism. New York.

Thomas, R. F. (1978), 'Ovid's Attempt at Tragedy', AJP 99: 447–50.

Thomson, J. (1762), The Works of James Thomson, Vol. III. London.

Thomson, P. (1983), Shakespeare's Theatre. London.

Tietze, V. (1987), 'The Psychology of Uncertainty in Senecan Tragedy', ICS 12: 135–41.

Tietze Larson, V. (1994), The Role of Description in Senecan Tragedy. Frankfurt am Main.

Timpanaro, S. (1981), 'Uno nuovo commento all' Hercules Furens di Seneca nel quadro della critica recente', A&R 26: 113–41.

Tobin, R. W. (1966), 'Tragedy and Catastrophe in Seneca's Theatre', CJ 62: 64–70.

Tobin, R. W. (1967–8), 'A Hero for All Seasons: Hercules in French Classical Drama', Comparative Drama 1: 288–96.

Tobin, R. W. (1971), Racine and Seneca. Chapel Hill, NC.

Tóibín, C. (2017), House of Names. New York and London.

Torrance, I. (2007), Aeschylus: Seven Against Thebes. London.

Trabert, K. (1953), 'Studien zur Darstellung des Pathologischen in den Tragödien Senecas'. Diss. University of Erlangen.

Traina, A. (1967), 'Le litanie del sonno nello Hercules Furens di Seneca', RFIC 95: 169–79.

Traina, A. (1968), 'Ancora sulle litanie del sonno', RFIC 96: 288–9.

Traina, A. (2003), La lyra e la libra (tra poeti e filologi). Bologna.

Treggiari, S. (1991), Roman Marriage: 'Iusti Coniuges' from the Time of Cicero to the Time of Ulpian. Oxford.

Trendall, A. D., and Webster, T. B. L. (1971), Illustrations of Greek Drama. London.

Treves, G. (1847), Agamennone: see Perrone (1847).

Trillitzsch, W. (1978), 'Seneca tragicus', Philologus 122: 120–36.

Trinacty, C. V. (2014), Senecan Tragedy and the Reception of Augustan Poetry. New York.

Trinacty, C. V. (2015), 'Senecan Tragedy', in Bartsch and Schiesaro (2015): 29–40.

Trinacty, C. V. (2016a), 'Imago res mortua est: Senecan Intertextuality', in Dodson-Robinson (2016): 13–33.

Trinacty, C. V. (2016b), 'Catastrophe in Dialogue: Aeneid 2 and Seneca's Agamemnon', Vergilius 62: 99–114.

Trinacty, C. V. (2017), 'Retrospective Reading in Senecan Tragedy', in Trinacty and Sampson (2017a): 175–96.

Trinacty, C. V. (2018), 'Nulla res est quae non eius quo nascitur notas reddat (Nat. 3.31.2): Intertext to Intratext in Senecan Prose and Poetry', in Harrison et al. (2018): 309–24.

Trinacty, C. V., and Sampson, C. M., eds. (2017a), *The Poetics of Senecan Tragedy*: *Ramus* 46. Cambridge.

Trinacty, C. V., and Sampson, C. M. (2017b), '*Verba Aliter Instructa*: Senecan Poetics', in Trinacty and Sampson (2017a): 1–15.

Tsetkhladze, G., ed. (1999), *Ancient Greeks West and East*. Leiden.

Tsitsiridis, S., ed. (2010), *Parachoregema: Studies on Ancient Theatre in Honour of Professor George M. Sifakis*. Heraklion, Crete.

Tupet, A.-M. (1976), *La Magie dans la poésie latine I: Des origines à la fin du règne d'Auguste*. Paris.

Tydeman, W., ed. (1992), *Two Tudor Tragedies*. Harmondsworth.

Uhlenbrock, J. P., ed. (1986), *Herakles: Passage of the Hero Through 1000 Years of Classical Art*. New Rochell, NY.

Valsa, M. (1957), *Marcus Pacuvius, poète tragique*. Paris.

Venini, P. (1965), 'Echi senecani e lucanei nella Tebaide: Tiranni e tirannidi', *RIL* 99: 157–67.

Vernant, J. P., and Vidal-Naquet, P., eds. (1988), *Myth and Tragedy in Ancient Greece*. New York.

Vessey, D. (1973), *Statius and the Thebaid*. Cambridge.

Veyne, P. (1990), *Bread and Circuses*. London.

Veyne, P. (2002), *Seneca: The Life of a Stoic*.

Vickery, J. B., and Sellery, J. M. (1972), *The Scapegoat: Ritual and Literature*. Boston, MA, and New York.

Virmaux, A. (1970), *Antonin Artaud et le théâtre*. Paris.

Vogt, K. M. (2006), 'Anger, Present Injustice, and Future Revenge in Seneca's *De Ira*', in Volk and Williams (2006): 57–74.

Vogt, K. M. (2017), 'The Stoics on Virtue and Happiness', in Bobonich (2017): 183–99.

Volk, K., and Williams, G. D., eds. (2006), *Seeing Seneca Whole: Perspectives on Philosophy, Poetry and Politics*. New York.

Waith, E. M. (1962), *The Herculean Hero in Marlowe, Chapman, Shakespeare and Dryden*. New York and London.

Walker, B. (1969), Review of Zwierlein 1966, *CP* 64: 183–7.

Walsh, L. (2011), 'Seneca's Medea and the Tragic Self'. Diss. University of Southern California. Los Angeles.

Walter, S. (1975), 'Interpretationen zum römischen in Senecas Tragödien'. Diss. University of Zurich.

Walton, J. M. (2015), *The Greek Sense of Theatre: Tragedy and Comedy Reviewed*. 3rd edn. London and New York.

Wanke, Ch. (1964), *Seneca, Lucan, Corneille, Studien zum Manierismus der römischen Kaiserzeit und der französischen Klassik*. Heidelberg.

Warmington, B. H. (1969), *Nero: Reality and Legend*. London.

Warren, J. (2004), *Facing Death: Epicurus and his Critics*. Oxford.

Waszink, J. H. (1948), 'Varro, Livy and Tertullian on the History of the Roman Dramatic Art', *Vigiliae Christianae* 2.4: 224–42.

Watson, P. A. (1985), 'Axelson Revisited: The Selection of Vocabulary in Latin Poetry', *CQ* 35: 430–48.

Watson, P. A. (1994), *Ancient Stepmothers: Myth, Misogyny and Reality*. Leiden.

Watt, W. S. (1989), 'Notes on Seneca, *Tragedies*', *HSCP* 92: 329–47.

Watt, W. S. (1996), 'Notes on Seneca, *Tragedies* and the *Octavia*', *MH* 33: 248–55.

Webster, J. (1612–13), *The Duchess of Malfi*: see Brown, J. R. (1964).

Weil, H. (1897), *Études sur le Drame Antique*. Paris.

Weinreich, O. (1923), *Senecas Apocolocyntosis: Die Satire auf Tod/Himmel- und Höllenfahrt des Kaisers Claudius*. Berlin.

Weinstock, S. (1971), *Divus Iulius*. Oxford.

Wessels, A. (2014), *Ästhetisierung und ästhetische Erfahrung von Gewalt: Eine Untersuchung zu Senecas Tragödien*. Heidelberg.

West, M. L. (1987), *Introduction to Greek Metre*. Oxford.

West, M. L. (1990), *Aeschyli Tragoediae*. Stuttgart.

West, M. L. (2003*a*), *Greek Epic Fragments*. Cambridge, MA.

West, M. L. (2003*b*), *Homeric Hymns, Apocrypha, Lives*. Cambridge, MA.

Westall, R. (1996), 'The Forum Iulium as Representation of Imperator Caesar', *Mitteilungen des Deutschen Archaeologischen Instituts, Römische Abteilung* 103: 83–118.

Westbrook, R. (1999), '*Vitae necisque potestas*', *Historia* 48: 203–23.

Wetmore, K. J., Jr. (2002), *The Athenian Sun in an African Sky*. Jefferson, NC and London.

Whitby, M., Hardie P., and Whitby M., eds. (1987), *Homo Viator: Classical Essays for John Bramble*. Bristol.

Whitman, J. (1987), *Allegory*. Cambridge, MA.

Wilamowitz-Moellendorff, U. von (1878–9), emendations in Leo (1878–9).

Wilamowitz-Moellendorff, U. von (1895), *Euripides: Herakles*. 2 vols. 2nd edn. Berlin. Vol. II repr. Cambridge, 2010.

Wilamowitz-Moellendorff, U. von (1919), *Griechische Tragödie*. Berlin.

Wilcox, A. (2006), 'Exemplary Grief: Gender and Virtue in Seneca's Consolations to Women', *Helios* 34: 73–100.

Wildberger, J. (2014), 'Ethics IV: Wisdom and *Virtus*', in Damschen and Heil (2014): 301–22.

Wilkes, G. A., ed. (1988), *Ben Jonson: Five Plays*. Oxford.

Wilkinson, L. P. (1963), *Golden Latin Artistry*. Cambridge.

Williams, C. A. (1999), *Roman Homosexuality*. New York.

Williams, G. (1978), *Change and Decline: Roman Literature in the Early Empire*. Berkeley, CA, and Los Angeles, CA.

Williams, G. D. (1994), *Banished Voices: Readings in Ovid's Exile Poetry*. Cambridge.

Williams, G. D. (2012), *The Cosmic Viewpoint: A Study of Seneca's Natural Questions*. New York.

Wills, J. (1996), *Repetition in Latin Poetry: Figures of Allusion*. Oxford.

Wilson, E. (2004), *Mocked with Death: Tragic Overliving from Sophocles to Milton*. Baltimore, MD, and London.

Wilson, E. (2014), *The Greatest Empire: A Life of Seneca*. New York.

Wilson, M. (1985), 'Seneca's *Agamemnon* and *Troades*: A Critical Study'. Diss. Monash University. Melbourne.

Wilson, M. (1990), Rev. of Fitch (1987), *Phoenix* 44: 189–94.

Wilson, M., ed. (2003), *The Tragedy of Nero's Wife: Studies on the Octavia Praetexta.* Auckland.

Wimmel, W., ed. (1997), *Forschung en zur romischen Literatur: Festschrift zum 60. Geburtstag von Karl Buchner.* Wiesbaden.

Winter, K. (2014), *Artificia Mali: Das Böse als Kunstwerk in Senecas Rachetragödien.* Heidelberg.

Wiseman, T. P. (1993), *Historiography and Imagination: Eight Essays on Roman Culture.* Exeter.

Wiseman, T. P. (1998), *Roman Drama and History.* Exeter.

Wiseman, T. P. (2002), 'Praetexta, Togata, and Other Unhelpful Categories', *SO* 76: 82–8.

Wiseman, T. P. (2004), *The Myths of Rome.* Exeter.

Withof, J. (1749), *Praemetium crucium criticarum praecipue ex Seneca tragico.* Leiden.

Woodcock, E. C. (1959), *A New Latin Syntax.* London (repr. Bristol 1985).

Woodruff, P. (2008), *The Necessity of Theater: The Art of Watching and Being Watched.* New York.

Worman, N. (1999), 'The Ties That Bind: Transformations of Costume in Euripides' *Heracles*', *Ramus* 28: 89–107.

Worman, N. (2020), *Tragic Bodies: Edges of the Human in Greek Drama.* London.

Wright, F. W. (1931), *Cicero and the Theater.* Northampton, MA.

Wright, J. (1974), *Dancing in Chains: The Stylistic Unity of the Comoedia Palliata.* Rome.

Wurnig, V. (1982), *Gestaltung und Funktion von Gefühlsdarstellungen in den Tragödien Senecas.* Frankfurt am Main.

Wyles, R. (2013), 'Heracles' Costume from Euripides' *Heracles* to Pantomime Performance', in Harrison and Liapis (2013): 181–98.

Xanthakis-Karamanos, G. (1980), *Studies in Fourth-Century Tragedy.* Athens.

Yavetz, Z. (1969), *Plebs and Princeps.* Oxford.

Yeats, W. B. (1907), *On Baile's Strand.* London.

Yoshitake, S. (1994), 'Disgrace, Grief and Other Ills: Heracles' Rejection of Suicide', *JHS* 114: 135–53.

Zanker, P. (1988), *The Power of Images in the Age of Augustus.* Ann Arbor, MI.

Zanobi, A. (2008), 'The Influence of Pantomime on Seneca's Tragedies', in Hall and Wyles (2008): 227–57.

Zanobi, A. (2014), *Seneca's Tragedies and the Aesthetics of Pantomime.* London and New York.

Zehnacker, H., ed. (1983a), *Théatre et spectacles dans l'Antiquité.* Leiden.

Zehnacker, H. (1983b), 'Tragédie prétexte et spectacle romain', in Zehnacker (1983a): 31–48.

Zeitlin, F. I. (1965), 'The Motif of the Corrupted Sacrifice in Aeschylus' *Oresteia*', *TAPA* 96: 463–508.

Zientek, L. (2018), 'Saeua Quies and Lucan's Landscapes of Anxiety', in Felton (2018): 119–44.

Zimmermann, B., ed. (1992), *Antike Dramentheorie und ihre Rezeption.* Stuttgart.

Zimmermann, B., ed. (1997), *Griechisch-römische Komödie e Tragödie II.* Stuttgart.

Zimmermann, B. (2008), 'Seneca and Pantomime', in Hall and Wyles (2008): 218–26.

Zintzen, C. (1972), 'Alte virtus animosa cadit: Gedanken zur Darstellung des Tragischen in Senecas Hercules Furens', in Lefèvre (1972a): 149–209.

Ziolkowski, A. (1992), The Temples of Mid-Republican Rome and their Historical and Topographical Context. Rome.

Žižek, S. (2008), Violence. New York.

Zografou, A. (2010), Chemins d'Hécate: Portes, routes, carrefours et autres figures de l'entre-deux. Kernos Supp. 24. Liège.

Zorzetti, N. (1980), La pretesta e il teatro latino arcaico. Naples.

Zwierlein, O. (1966), Die Rezitationsdramen Senecas. Meisenheim am Glan.

Zwierlein, O. (1976), 'Versinterpolationen und Korruptelen in den Tragödien Senecas', WJA NF 2: 181–217.

Zwierlein, O. (1978), 'Weiteres zum Seneca Tragicus (II)', WJA 4: 143–60.

Zwierlein, O. (1983), 'Der Schluss der Tragödie "Atreus" des Accius', Hermes 111: 121–5.

Zwierlein, O. (1984a), Prolegomena zu einer kritischen Ausgabe der Tragödien Senecas. Mainz.

Zwierlein, O. (1984b), Senecas Hercules im Lichte kaiserzeitlicher und spätantiker Deutung. Mainz.

Zwierlein, O. (1986b), Kritischer Kommentar zu den Tragödien Senecas. Mainz.

Zyl Smit, B. van (2015), 'Seneca Tragicus in the Twentieth Century: Hugo Claus' Adaptations of Thyestes, Oedipus and Phaedra', in Harrison (2015): 330–47.

Indexes

References in regular type are to line numbers preceding sections in the Commentary, in italics to page numbers in the Introduction, in Roman numerals to page numbers in the Preface, and appear in this order.

I. LATIN WORDS

The list is selective of words and references.

II. PASSAGES FROM OTHER PLAYS OF THE SENECAN TRAGIC *CORPUS*

782–3: *109*
782: 275–8, 913–17
783: 205–9
787: 1048–53
789: 973–5
791–9: 422–38, 1263–4, *31*
791: 40–6
796–7: *52*
800: 550–7, 1048–53
802ff.: 205–78
802–7: 123–4, 511–15
802–4: 205–9
803: 457–62
804: 57–63
805–6: 205–9
806–7: 511–15, 1035–8
806: 6–11
807: 908–12, 918–24
808ff.: 524–91 (introd.)
808–66: *59*
808–13: 178–82
809: 19–29
810: 439–47, 1334–41
811: 495–500
812–13: 955–63
812: 1278–82
814–26: 19–29
819–21: 882–8
824: 249–58, 372–83
825: 40–6
827: 125–31
828: 205–9
829–30: 222–5
829: 249–58
831–2: 222–5
832: 226–30
833–4: 226–30
835–6: 241–8
835: 30–5, 241–8, 769–81
837–41: 231–4
838: 19–29, 480–9, 1100–14
840: 231–4
842–7: 226–30
844–6: 935–9
848–50: 241–8, 542–6
848: 249–58
850–1: 241–8
852–8: 235–40
852: 235–40
855–6: 524–32

859–61: 802–27
859: 52–6, 275–8
860–60•: 782–91
861: 650–3
862: 283–95, 813–21
865–6: 1131–7
866–7: 125–31
867–909: 991–5
868: 939–44, 1156–9
869: 275–8
870: 1035–8
875–909: 939–86
875: 1314–17
884: 1–5, 268–75
885: 332–6
887: 1048–53
892–4: 679–88
892: 57–63
897–905: 918–24
898–9: 679–88
900: 118–22, 283–95
901ff.: 1022–31
901: 1035–8, 1202–18
902–7: 6–11
902: 1022–31
908–9: 939–44
908: 46–52, 533–41, 668–72
910: 1–5, 205–9, 1246–52
912: 348–53
913–43: *before* 592–617
913: 202–4
914: 637–40
917: 637–40
918–39: 838–49
918–24: 616–17
918–19: 35–40
918: 1–5, 258–67, 838–49
922ff.: 626–8
923: 622–5
924: 35–40, 159–61, 209–13, 637–40, 952–4
925–7: 629–30
925: 1159–63
926: 895–9
928: 205–9
929–30: 1246–52
929: 1178–86
930: 63–8, 516–20
932: 68–74
940: 205–9
947–50: 202–4

949: 918–24
950: 249–58, 329–31
951: 40–6
952: 637–40
953: 637–40
955–71: 422–38
955: 1–5, 414–21
959: 30–5
967–8: 637–40
970: 19–29
971–94: *46*
971–7: 1200–1
971: 426–9, 1317–21
975: 1039–42
978–9: 637–40
981–1000: 332–57
981: 637–40
983: 963–73
984–5: 384–96
986: 637–40, 1283–4
988–93: 414–21
989–90: 414–21
991: 30–5, 414–21, 626–8
993: 19–29
995: 348–53, 511–15
996: 112–18
997: 1048–53, 1278–82
1001: 57–63
1002: 1–5, 414–21
1004–11: *31, 46*
1005–6: 637–40
1006: 11–18
1009: 480–9
1010: 1048–53
1011: 112–18
1012: 426–9, 637–40, 637–40, 918–24,
    1295–1301, 1314–17, 1341–4

Hercules Oetaeus
1–2: 516–20
2: 249–58, 1054–62•
6: 935–9
9–10: 35–40
11: 1178–86
13: 955–63
17: 241–8
18: 235–40
19–20: 226–30
19: 241–8
21: 241–8

22: 604–15
26: 231–4, 480–9
27: 226–30
28: 30–5
33: 275–8, 1240–5
34–9: 935–9
34: 77–83
38–51: 35–40
41: 35–40
42: 1054–62•
55–6: 1278–82
57: 1168–73
59: 40–6
65: 1278–82
70: 944–52
79: 439–48
82–4: 332–6
86: 1321–9
97–8: 955–63
100–1: 477–80
107: 183–5
119–42: 124–204 (introd.)
119–20: 827–9
141: 332–6
144: 939–44
147–50: 19–29
169: 86–8
173–4: 501–8
185–206: 258–67
185: 394–96
185•: 1063–5
189: 384–96
192–3: 146–7
196: 1063–5
199–200: 146–51
207: 46–52
209: 1226–30
219: 516–20
226: 426–9
233–53: 369–71, 991–5
240: 709–20
247–8: 329–31
254–5: *before* 520–3
254: 202–4, 329–31
257: 1–5
258: 769–81
262: 92–9
271: 19–29
275ff.: 309–13
275: 19–29, 973–5

1797: 1138–42
1799: 1329–34
1813: 241–8
1821: 1035–8
1823: 439–47
1843: 241–8
1849–51: 384–96
1863–1939: 1054–1137 (introd.)
1863: 205–9
1865–6: 19–29
1867: 604–15
1876: 226–30
1883: 1063–5
1889–90: 241–8
1896–8: 226–30
1900: 231–4
1923: 125–31
1925–8: 769–81
1939–40: 1237–9
1939: 1221–6
1940: 1100–14
1946: 622–5
1954: 1042–8
1963: 679–88

Medea
1ff.: 205–78, 332–57
1–4: 205–9, 900–8
1: 1–12: 6–18
2–7: 516–20
4: 11–18, 1178–86
5–7: 900–8
6: 19–29
7–8: 709–20
8: 1–5, 109–12
9: 604–15
12: 275–8
13–18: 86–122, 86–8
13: 92–9, 275–8, 495–500
14: 86–8, 100–3
15: 86–8
16–17: 283–95, 495–500
16: 275–8
17–18: 1048–53
20–1: 30–5
20: 372–83, 1258–62, 1314–17
25–6: 372–83
25: 952–4
26: 19–29, 30–5, 1314–17
28–31: 631–3

28–9: 720–7
28: 354–7
31: 939–44
32: 92–9
35–6: 332–6
35: 19–29, 572–6
37: 372–83
38–9: 918–24
38: 893–4
39: 895–9, 918–24
40–3: 1283–4
43: 1202–18
44–5: 302–6
45: 30–5
48: 63–8, 186–91
49–50: 1173–7
50: 408–13, 1186–93
51: 19–29
52–70: 205–9
52: 35–40
53: 963–73
54: 1048–53
55: 125–204 (introd.)
56ff.: 125–204 (introd.), 524–32
56–115: 125–204 (introd.), 830–94 (introd.)
56–70: 205–9
59: 1–5
62–6: 926–31
62: 299–302
66: 1039–42
69: 472–6
71–3: 299–302
75–92: 875–92
75: 213–22
81: 709–20
84: 11–18, 457–62
89: 900–8
90–2: 1202–18
90: 92–9, 197–201
94: 19–29
96: 6–11
100: 19–29
101: 137–40
106: 1283–4
109: 125–204 (introd.)
116ff.: 205–523 (introd.), 332–57
116: 414–21, *before* 520–3
123: 30–5
129–36: 1329–34
130: 592–7

131: 384–96
133: 1226–30
135–6: 19–29
137: 295–8
139: 75–6
143: 735–9, 963–73
147: 359–69
149: 572–6
150ff.: 309–13
150–67: *31*
155–76: 422–38
155: 63–8
157–67: 125–204 (introd.)
157–8: 1272–7
157: 1–5, 40–6, 397–402, 973–5
158: 159–61
159–63: 422–38
160: 35–40
161: 35–40
166–7: *37*
166: 109–12, 372–83, 1295–1301, 1314–17
168–73: 1263–4
170–1: 422–38, 426–9
170: 112–18, 426–9, *46*
171: 109–12
173: 572–6
174: 426–9, 973–5
175: 408–13
176: 125–204 (introd.), 463–4
177ff.: *27*
177–300: 332–523
177–8: 1–5
177: *before* 520–3
178: 202–4, 329–31, 384–96, 1088–91
179ff.: 332–57
179–91: 1173–7
179–87: 332–57
179–81: 35–40
179: 1066–81
183: 358–9
184: 348–53
186: 57–63
188: 1048–53
189–90: 397–402
190: 275–8
191: 1278–82
192–271: 348–53
192–8: 422–38
195–6: 341–8
196: 341–8, 430–8, 739–45

197: 89–91
199: 604–15
202: 397–402
203–51: 397–402
203–6: 348–53
203: 19–29
205: 57–63
206: 1092–9
208: 30–5
211–16: 332–6
212: 332–6, 533–41, 1202–18
214–15: 241–8, 533–41
214: 542–6
215: 1–5, 241–8
216: 11–18
217–18: 372–83
218–19: 112–18, 637–40, 720–7
221–5: 341–8
221–2: 197–201
222–5: 739–45
222: 283–95
223: 582–9
226: 592–7
228–9: 569–71
234: 19–29
235: 19–29
238: 40–6, 689–96
239–40: 658–61
240: 19–29
242: 397–402
247: 1002–9
248: 241–8, 369–71
252–7: 341–8
252: 63–8
254: 348–53
259: 875–81
261: 275–8, 384–96, 1092–9
262: 397–402
264: 414–21
265: 745–7
266: 900–8
268: 408–13
279: 11–18, 1283–4
281–97: 422–38
281: 408–13, 572–6
282: 275–8, 1186–93
283: 46–52
285–95: 1314–21
285–90: 1246–52
285: 1178–86

424: 592–7
425: 329–31
431: 92–9
435–592: 332–523
435–6: 202–4, 329–31
435: 202–4, 329–31
436: 1219–21
440–532: 348–53
440–54: 422–38
440: 408–13
441: 341–8
449: 258–67, 501–8
450–61: 341–8
450–1: 489–94
451: 524–32
452: 524–32
454: 408–13
463: 1186–93
472–5: 739–45
473–8: 426–9
473–4: 745–7
473: 739–45
476: 63–8, 739–45
503–7: 439–47
509: 1048–53
515: 1202–18
519: 1321–9
521–2: 480–9, 634–6
522: 707–8
532: 341–8
534: 592–7
541–2: 329–31
541: 408–13
546: 900–8
568: 673–9
574: 489–94
578: 739–45
583–5: 348–53
593: 57–63
599–600: 1186–93
605: 439–47
610: 511–15
620: 511–15
621–3: 750–9
621: 750–9
622: 750–9
623: 750–9
631: 317–24
646: 1063–5
658: 1–5
664: 918–24

671: 802–6
682: 944–52
705: 838–49
729: 830–7
735: 414–21
740–2: 1082–7
754: 275–8
756–61: 511–15
759: 1219–21
764–5: 11–18
766–7: 6–11
778–9: 202–4
778: 1219–21
780–805: 658–827
785: 1219–21
806: 178–82
813–14: 397–402
813•: 533–41
820–43: 332–57
825: 511–15
842: 397–402
844–5: 202–4
844: 329–31
861: 426–9
877–8: 164–74
878–81: 164–74
887–9: 178–82
896–8: 197–201
897–8: 325–8
899: 511–15
905: 1063–5
912: 516–20
914–15•: 258–67
915–23: 146–51
921–3: 146–51
921–1•: 146–51
924–8: 178–91
924: 183–5
925: 325–8
932: 197–201
944: 1082–7
957: 918–24
959: 511–15
960: 995–1002, 1283–4
977: 197–201
982: 1341–4

Oedipus
1ff.: 332–57
1–36: *34*
1: 11–18, 123–4, 125–31, 668–72, 679–88

961ff.: 1022–31
975: 275–8, 1015–17
977: 109–12, 112–18
980–97: 125–204 (introd.), 178–91,
  1054–1137 (introd.)
980: 637–40, 1163–8
983–4: 735–9
983: 183–5
985: 178–82
988: 1–5, 864–74
991–1•: 186–91
992–4: 197–201, 590–1
993–4: 1131–7
994: *before* 520–3
995–7: 205–523 (introd.)
998: 1035–8, 1295–1301
999: 1138–42
1003: 104–9, 329–31, 408–13, 1237–9
1004–9: 202–4, 1032–4, *29*
1004–5: 1002–9
1004: 202–4, 329–31, 944–52
1005–7: 132–6
1008: 689–96, 1178–86
1010: 689–96
1011–12: 1173–7
1012: 141–5
1013: 944–52
1019: 1200–1, 1237–9
1020: 1314–17
1021–3: 1246–52
1021: 275–8
1023: 1–5
1024–39: *46*
1024–32: 1173–7
1024: 900–8, 1173–7, 1283–4
1026: 592–7
1028: 125–31, 258–67,
  348–53, 354–7
1031–2: 372–83, 1240–5
1032: 397–402
1033: 372–83
1034–6: 1173–7
1034–5: 372–83
1034: 1226–30
1035: 1–5
1036–9: 1202–18
1036–7: 618–21
1038: 1231–6
1039: 46–52
1040–1: 918–24, 991–5

1040: 1159–68
1042: 577–81, 900–8
1043: 1231–6
1059–61: 92–9, 123–4
1059–60: 689–96
1059: 689–96
1060: 689–96
1061: 1341–4

Phaedra
1–30: 6–18
2: 19–29
9: 92–9
11–12: 697–706
24: 213–22
29: 226–30
41: 123–4, 1082–7
42: 668–72
48: 118–22
49: 141–5
52: 299–302
54ff.: 205–78
54–80: 205–9
54–72: 1321–41
54: 123–4, 275–8, 495–500
55–9: 516–20
57: 118–22
60–4: 299–302
79–86: 57–63
81–4: 123–4
81–2: *before* 520–3
83: 92–9
85ff.: 205–523 (introd.),
  332–57
85: 6–11, 900–8
87–8: 19–29
91–8: 1252–7
91–2: 1–5
91: 944–52
92: 1173–7
93–8: 1334–41
93: 1283–4
94: 547–9
96: 900–8
99: 95–6
100–8: 697–706
100: 159–61, 689–96
102–3: 104–9, 1042–8
102: 679–88
107: 299–302

628: 46–52, 731–4
629: 209–13
630: 52–6
633: 19–29
634–5: 1173–7
636: 1186–93
649: 731–4
655–6: 1015–17
658: 720–7
662–6: 11–18
663: 92–9, 900–8, 1100–14
664: 397–402
665: 19–29
666: 1186–93
667: 1002–9
671ff.: 205–78, 516–20
671–84: 1202–18, *46*
671–81: 631–3
671–9: *34*
671–4: 1202–18
671: 40–6, 1186–93
675: 123–4
676–7: 1329–34
678: 123–4, 1054–62•
679: 1314–17
680: 258–67
682: 1202–18
684: 40–6, 408–13
687–93: 439–94
688: 1186–93
690: 414–21
692: 329–31
695: 1048–53
696: 75–6
697: 46–52, 1186–93
698: 622–5
703: 1002–9
705: 939–44, 963–73
708–9: 480–9, 918–24
710–12: 426–9, *46*
711: 1258–62
713–14: 1115–21
715–18: 1163–8, 1321–41
715–16: 1321–9
715: 1321–9
717: 658–61, 1321–9
723–4: 384–96
725: 1048–53
733: 973–5
734–5: 123–4

735: 125–204 (introd.), 472–6,
   1200–1, 1237–9
736ff.: 830–94 (introd.), 1054–1137 (introd.)
736–52: 830–94 (introd.)
742: 900–8
749–52: 125–31, 882–8
749: 679–88
753: 472–6
754: 472–6
756: 465–71
757: 465–71
760: 11–18
764–72: 679–88
771: 582–9
777–94: 178–82
781: 1100–14
798: 720–7
799: 849–57
803–4: 465–71
803: 408–13
807: 622–5, *58*
808: 900–8
824–34: 1–5, 202–4, 205–523 (introd.)
824–8: 1032–4
824: 75–6
829–34: 202–4, 616–17
829: 329–31
833: 626–8
835ff.: 332–57
835: 275–8, 604–15
836: 1100–14
837: 650–3, 1173–7
839: 645–9
843–5: 813–21
846: 35–40
850ff': 626–8
850–3: *before* 520–3
850: 414–21
853: 109–12, 1143–8
856: 209–13
862: 75–6
863: 1048–53
864–958: *before* 592–617
864: 309–13
868–71: 1246–52
868: 63–8
869: 309–13
872–81: 125–204 (introd.), 422–38,
   430–8, *37*
876: 341–8

1144: 558–68
1149–53: 569–89
1149: 1163–8
1151: 769–81
1152: 283–85
1153: 19–29, 125–204 (introd.), 197–201,
    457–62, 495–500, 590–1, 709–20, 1131–7
1154–5: 202–4, 205–523 (introd.)
1154: *before* 520–3
1157–8: 329–31
1159ff.: 205–78, *46*
1159: 92–9, 109–12, 1178–86
1160: 57–63
1164: 1334–41
1167: 1334–41
1168–9: 249–58
1168: 329–31
1169–70: 1138–42
1178: 109–12
1181–90: *46*
1184–5: 275–8
1184: 40–6
1185: 348–53, 359–69
1186–7: 830–7
1186: 40–6
1188–90: 550–7, 864–74
1189: 592–7
1195: 275–8
1196: 40–6
1197–8: 918–24
1199–1242: 1202–18
1200: 19–29, 68–74
1201ff.: 205–78, *46*
1201–12: *31*
1201–6: 1334–41
1201–3: 1163–8
1201: 92–9, 582–9, 662–7
1204: 495–500
1207: 299–302, 1334–41
1211–12: 1329–34
1212: 52–6, 1334–41
1215: 19–29
1217–19: 1202–18, 1334–41
1217–18: 802–6
1217: 299–302
1223–42: 1202–18
1226–7: 747–9
1229ff.: 750–9
1229–31: 750–9
1232: 679–88, 750–9

1233: 750–9
1235–7: 750–9
1238: 604–15, 1221–6
1242–3: 516–20
1242: 40–6, 1221–6
1244–6: 202–4
1244: 637–40
1246ff.: 1022–31
1246–72: 918–24
1247–74: 1194–1200
1247: 92–4
1248: 317–24
1249: 622–5
1250–1: 11–18
1260: 622–5
1262: 1231–6
1268: 92–9, 141–5
1275–9: 1048–53
1276: 658–61
1279: 422–5
1280: 858–63, 1341–4

Phoenissae
1–2: 1246–52
1: 1–5
3: 1131–7
5: 1240–5
7: 1334–41
8: 1018–20
9–10: 720–7
12–26: 6–18
15–18: 132–6
18: 472–6
20: 913–17
22: 480–9, 662–7
30: 995–1002, 1283–4
31–3: 46–52, 1334–41
34: 30–5, 1334–41
38–9: *46*
39–44: 939–86
40–1: 63–8
40: 1015–17
42: 944–52
43: 329–31
45: 1283–4
51–2: 414–21
54: 332–6
55–6: 720–7
61: 1317–21
66–76: 1302–13

720–1: 1002–9
724: 679–88
728: 1022–31
730–1: 707–8
732ff.: 679–88
732–6: 679–88
732: 679–88
734–6: 283–95
735: 1202–18
736: 414–21
737: 68–74, 1088–91
744: 414–21
745–8: 707–8, 1186–93
745: 30–5, 426–9, 1042–8, 1186–93
746–7: 205–9
747: 426–9
749ff.: 1022–31
750–1: 1202–18
755–75: 918–24
756: 1295–1301
757: 57–63
759: 1039–42
761: 1022–31
762: 572–6
764: 369–71
769: 582–9
775: 495–500
776–88: 939–44
778: 19–29, 46–52
780: 465–71
783: 35–40, 1092–9
784–8: 123–4
787: 604–15
788: 123–4
789ff.: 524–91 (introd.), 524–32
789–884: 125–204 (introd.), 939–44, 1054–1137 (introd.)
790–1: 516–20, 592–7
791: 249–58
794: 125–31
795: 125–31
797: 1168–73
805–8: 750–9
805–12•: 976–86
812–12•: 963–73
814: 372–83
819: 1168–73
827–34•: 359–69
828: 92–9
832: 604–15

834: 6–11, 125–31
835: 35–40
836: 637–40
844: 558–68
845: 913–17
847: 637–40
848: 558–68
852: 558–68
853: 11–18
855–6: 944–52
855: 944–52
861–2: 249–58
870: 1042–8
873: 125–31
874: 125–31, 489–94
875–84: 197–201
875–81: *13*
877: 1138–42
882: 75–6
883–4: 125–204 (introd.), 197–201, 590–1, 1131–7, 1283–94
885ff.: 332–57
885–919: 332–57
885–95: 501–8
885–6: 955–63
889: 1035–8
890: 30–5
891: 11–18, 1240–5
892: 75–6
899: 329–31, 918–24
900–1: 1237–9
901: 35–40, 40–6, 1048–53
903ff.: *27*
906: 654–7
907: 637–40, 1163–8
908–1112: *before* 592–617
911: 372–83
915–16: 372–83
915: 1039–42
916: 92–9
918–19: *before* 520–3
918: 40–6, 329–31
920–69: 1054–1137 (introd.)
920: 1042–8
921: 408–13
922: 75–6
925: 75–6
931: 489–94
934–4•: 1092–9
936: 329–31

937: 109–12
938: 1219–21
942–3: 875–81
944: 75–6
948: 465–71
950: 329–31
954–6: 1156–9
958: 1143–8
960: 1088–91
961–4: 1283–4
961: 1088–91
964: 19–29
966–7: 1178–86
970: 875–81
971: 63–8
978: 480–9
983: 40–6
984–5: 918–24
985: 939–44
990–5: 939–44
990: 384–96
992: 939–44
995: 275–8
999: 1088–91
1001: 731–4
1004–5: 1022–31
1004: 40–6
1005–6: 622–5
1006ff.: 205–78
1006–21: 1202–18, *31*
1006–19: 1334–41
1006–9: 1221–6
1006: 205–78, 384–96, 1295–1301
1007: 558–68
1008: 57–63
1009: 604–15, 858–63
1010: 1284–90
1013–19: 1221–6
1013: 1202–18, 1221–6
1014: 1221–6
1016: 658–61
1021: 40–6, 426–9, 516–20, 1012–15
1022: 572–6
1025: 408–13
1030: 40–6
1032–3: 618–21, 1202–18
1033: 1202–18
1035–51: *31*
1035–6: 939–44
1036: 397–402

1038: 249–58
1039: 11–18
1043: 1226–30
1045: 1002–9
1047: 249–58, 631–3
1048–9: 1138–42
1048: 1202–18
1049–50: 226–30
1050: 46–52, 944–52
1051–2: 205–9
1052: 19–29
1058: 875–81
1064: 249–58
1067–8: 720–7
1068ff.: 205–78
1068–96: *31*
1068–76: 1054–62•
1068: 40–6
1072: 604–15
1077ff.: 516–20
1077–96: 1202–18
1077: 516–20
1078: 299–302, 1178–86
1080: 1202–18
1083: 558–68
1085: 1202–18
1087: 397–402, 679–88
1090: 46–52
1092: 40–6
1096: 40–6
1098–9: 303–5
1098: 209–13
1100–3: 422–38, 1263–4
1101–2: 372–83
1101: 112–18
1102: 40–6, 426–9, 1314–17
1104: 46–52
1110–11: 1202–18
1110: 40–6, 384–96
1111–12: 463–4
1112: 1341–4

Troades
1ff.: 332–57, 524–32
1–27: 197–201
1–6: 348–53
2: 516–20
4: 19–29
5: 354–7
8–14: 332–6

III. GENERAL INDEX

The list is selective of subjects and references. Passim = 20 or more (often many times more) references. Those interested in tracing the very large number of references in the Commentary to, e.g. Euripides, Ovid, or Virgil are directed to the digital version of this book.